S0-AHQ-024

For Reference

Not to be taken from this room

McGraw-Hill Modern Men of Science

McGraw-Hill

McGRAW-HILL BOOK COMPANY

NEW YORK ST. LOUIS SAN FRANCISCO DALLAS TORONTO LONDON

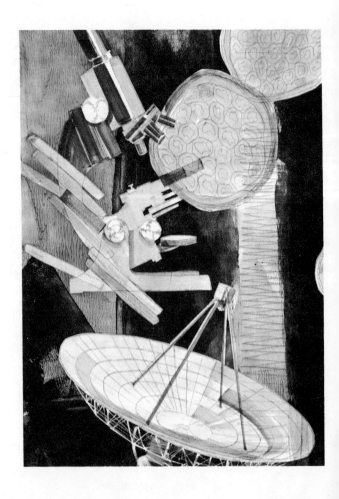

Modern Men of Science

426 LEADING CONTEMPORARY SCIENTISTS

PRESENTED BY THE EDITORS OF THE

McGRAW-HILL ENCYCLOPEDIA OF SCIENCE AND TECHNOLOGY

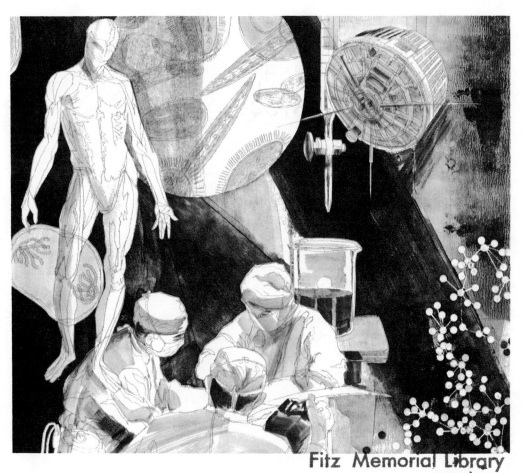

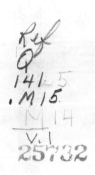
McGRAW-HILL MODERN MEN OF SCIENCE
Copyright © 1966 by McGraw-Hill Inc. Printed in the United States
of America. All rights reserved. This book, or parts thereof, may not be
reproduced in any form without permission of the publishers. Philippines
Copyright, 1966, by McGraw-Hill Inc.

Library of Congress Catalog Card Number: 66–14808

Preface

The *McGraw-Hill Modern Men of Science* was conceived and developed as both a reference book and an educational resource. It thus answers a need keenly felt by teachers, students, and others interested in contemporary science and science education. Although a large and rapidly growing literature deals with every department of modern science, anyone whose interest in science is biographical knows how little material there is on the scientists themselves. Several reference works provide minimal biographical data for many living scientists, and other books offer sketches of a few of the most famous. The *McGraw-Hill Modern Men of Science* seeks to provide, for a substantial number of contemporary scientists, both essential biographical data and extended descriptions of their most significant achievements—what might appropriately be called "science biographies." Its authoritative articles on 426 leading contemporary scientists not only tell what each man did but also describe the background of his work, the problems he faced, and how he solved them. In this way the articles aim to give students a better understanding of modern science and to provide some insight into the workings of the best scientific minds. To the extent that they succeed, this book becomes more than a reference work; it becomes an educational resource of great value to teachers and students in high schools and colleges.

Because science is an international cooperative enterprise, the coverage of the *McGraw-Hill Modern Men of Science* is international. The scientists included in this volume were selected from among the recipients of many of the world's major prizes in science awarded since 1940. We felt that the international scientific community was the best judge of which men and which work have been of the greatest significance in recent decades. Besides the Nobel prizes in physics, chemistry, and physiology or medicine, we were guided by the prizes awarded by U.S.

scientific societies, foundations, and government agencies and by the Royal Societies of London and Canada, many of which are awarded without distinction as to nationality. The reader will find therefore that a significant proportion of this book is devoted to scientists of countries other than the United States, the United Kingdom, and Canada.

The kind of article that we wanted for this book—one that would possess both reference and educational value—proved very difficult to obtain. The work of most contemporary scientists is extremely specialized; often only another specialist is equipped to interpret it correctly for laymen and students. Because we sought to provide articles of unimpeachable authority and accuracy, we invited the scientists themselves to write about their work for us. Nearly 300 very kindly consented to do so; these autobiographical articles are designated in the book by solid stars next to their titles. The remaining articles were written by qualified persons other than the subjects. Wherever possible, these articles were then submitted to the scientists for review and correction; an open star next to an article title indicates that the subject of that article has read and approved it.

The two-part index at the rear of this volume should add greatly to its utility for the general reader and student alike. The first part, an analytical index, will direct the reader to every mention of a person or subject anywhere in the volume. The second part is a classed listing of the biographical articles according to the scientists' fields. There the reader will find a quick guide to all the biochemists, all the meteorologists, all the experimental psychologists, and so forth represented in this volume. Where a scientist has been active in more than one field, his name, of course, appears in more than one class.

The *McGraw-Hill Modern Men of Science* is designed as a supplement to the highly regarded

15-volume *McGraw-Hill Encyclopedia of Science and Technology*, which contains no purely biographical articles. The student will often find it helpful to turn to the *McGraw-Hill Encyclopedia of Science and Technology* for additional background information or fuller discussions of the area or topic dealt with by a particular scientist. Each biographical article in this volume concludes with one or more references to relevant articles in the encyclopedia.

Besides the scientists who so generously participated in the creation of this book, whether as autobiographers or reviewers, we are especially indebted to the following contributors: Professor E. N. da C. Andrade of the Imperial College of Science and Technology, London, for his article on Sir Edward Appleton; Scott E. Forbush of the Carnegie Institution of Washington for his article on Julius Bartels; Professor Frank Press of the Massachusetts Institute of Technology for his article on Hugo Benioff; Dr. Margaret K. Harlow for her article on Harry F. Harlow; Dr. Vincent E. McKelvey of the U.S. Geological Survey for his article on Donnell F. Hewett; Professor I. R. Lehman of Stanford University for his article on Arthur Kornberg; Dr. James E. Mulvaney of the University of Arizona for his article on Carl S. Marvel; Dr. Victor Goertzel for his article on Linus Pauling; Claudio Segrè for his article on Emilio Segrè; Professor Maurice Ewing of the Lamont Geological Observatory of Columbia University for his article on Merle A. Tuve; Dr. Glenn Wiggins of the Royal Ontario Museum for his article on Edmund M. Walker; Professor James B. Hendrickson of Brandeis University for his article on R. B. Woodward; and Professor L. Wilke of the Max-Planck-Institut für Kohlenforschung, Mülheim-Ruhr, for his article on Karl Ziegler.

I am happy to acknowledge also the contributions of: Lt. Col. Cortland P. Auser; Douglas W. Bowden, Jr.; Maj. Ray L. Bowers; Peter Castro; Dr. Charles J. Cazeau; Dr. Charles V. Clemency; Dr. Richard E. Cover; Dr. Leon B. Gortler; Anne Greenberg; Marvin A. Gross; Dr. Hyman Guthwin; Raymond F. Halloran; Dr. Joseph H. Hamilton; Harold G. Kastan; Dr. John S. King; Thomas G. Lawrence; Dr. Norman L. Levin; Alan D. Levy; Moses R. Lipeles; Robert A. Lufburrow; Wallace Manheimer; Herbert A. Nestler; Anne M. Newman; Matthew Notkins; Maj. John H. Scrivner, Jr.; Lavonne O. Tarleton; Dr. Harold Weinstock; Robert Weinberger; Harvey Weiss; Bob D. Wilder; Marvin Yelles; Dr. David D. Zink; and Morris Ziskind.

JAY E. GREENE
Editor-in-Chief

Editorial Advisory Board

A

★★

★ **ADAMS, Leason Heberling**
American geophysicist
Born Jan. 16, 1887, Cherryvale, Kans., U.S.A.

IN THE course of researches on the properties of various materials when exposed to very high pressures, Adams reached the conclusion that precise measurements of the elastic properties of ordinary rocks and rock-forming minerals could be made to yield information, more definite than ever before, on the nature of the Earth's interior. He devised experimental methods for carrying out the necessary measurements and showed how to apply the results to illuminate certain geophysical problems relating to the deeper parts of the Earth. For this achievement, and for other contributions in the field of Earth sciences, he was awarded in 1950 the William Bowie Medal of the American Geophysical Union.

In the late 19th century it was generally believed that the Earth consisted of a relatively thin crust floating on a molten interior. Gradually, however, scientists recognized that this was far too simple a picture of the Earth as a whole. It became evident that with more definite information about the interior, important conclusions could be drawn concerning not only the nature of the interior but the origin and early history of the globe as well. Adams concluded that a key for solving these mysteries would be discovered through a knowledge of the elastic properties of typical rocks under high pressure. The observations of seismologists had given abundant results on wave velocities at various depths below the surface. These wave velocities depended on the elastic constants of the materials, and measurements of elastic properties—especially bulk modulus and rigidity—could be combined with seismological results to furnish a probe to solve some of the mysteries of the Earth's interior. The difficulty was that in those early days no one had ever succeeded in finding a method for making reliable measurements of the elastic constants of common rocks.

In 1919, while engaged in developing techniques for high-pressure measurements at the Geophysical Laboratory of the Carnegie Institution of Washington, Adams turned his attention to elastic constants. The principal difficulty in determining the elasticity of ordinary rocks was their slight but almost universal porosity, which prevented the application of conventional methods. Adams found a practicable method for solving the problem. This consisted of making a cylinder of the rock, enclosing it in a hermetically sealed thin metal jacket, and subjecting it to high pressure while immersed in a mobile liquid within a pressure vessel. The piston displacement required to generate the given pressure provided a measure of the volume change of the rock and hence of its bulk modules. Adams also showed how the bulk modules alone could be used to determine wave velocities with useful precision.

The first important result of these measurements, obtained by applying some well-known mathematical procedures, was the positive conclusion that the high central density necessary to account for the density of the Earth as a whole could not be produced by the compression of ordinary silicate rocks but must be due to an intrinsically heavy material, such as the nickel-iron of metallic meteorites. Even more important was the discovery that, of all the well-known rock types, only two, dunite and eclogite (a garnet-jadeite rock), have elastic properties that can yield the high wave velocities found by the Albanian seismologist A. Mohorovičić to exist at relatively shallow depths. On various grounds, the first of these two choices is generally preferred, and we have the striking conclusion that the whole Earth, except for a nickel-iron core and a thin crust, consists entirely of four chemical elements (iron, magnesium, silicon, and oxygen), the crust being composed of ordinary rock types, with possibly a thin layer of eclogite rock between the crust and the underlying mantle.

These measurements also had a direct bearing on the differentiation of the Earth into a chemically complex crust and a chemically simple mantle. The Earth and other planets are generally believed to have been formed by the compaction of a primeval dust cloud. This, by the effect of the slight, but important, universal radioactive heating, would eventually become molten and then, by well-known crystallization laws, would produce just such a dunite mantle as is indicated by the elasticity measurements. Not all geophysicists agree with this deduction, but there has been no other simple explanation of the formation of the Earth's crust.

A product of the farm belt, Adams spent his early boyhood in central Illinois. He attended a one-room country school, later entering the University of Illinois at 15, and graduating in 1906 with a B.S. in chemical engineering. After serving first as an industrial chemist and then as a physical chemist in the newly formed Technologic Branch of the U.S. Geological Survey, he went in 1910 to the Geophysical Laboratory of the Carnegie Institution of Washington, where he was named director in 1937 and from which he retired in 1952. Thereafter he continued active in research, first as consultant to the director of the National Bureau of Standards and then, from 1958 to 1965, as visiting professor of geophysics (later professor in residence) at the University of California at Los Angeles. He was elected to the National Academy of Sciences in 1943.

During World War I Adams assisted in the production of optical glass, which had not previously been manufactured in the United States. Together with associates, he invented a method of annealing glass that is particularly advantageous for large blocks. The new procedure was successfully applied in the fabrication of the 200-in. mirror for the Mt. Palomar telescope. For this work he was given the Longstroth Medal of the Franklin Institute. In World War II he was chief of Division One (ballistics) of the Office of Scientific Research and Development.

For background information *see* EARTH; GEOPHYSICS in the McGraw-Hill Encyclopedia of Science and Technology.   □

★ **ADAMS, Roger**
American chemist
Born Jan. 2, 1889, Boston, Mass., U.S.A.

WHILE INVESTIGATING hydrogenation of various unsaturated organic compounds, Adams prepared in a very easy way a noble-metal catalyst that enabled reactions to take place more readily at low temperatures and

pressures than had previously been possible with either noble-metal or base-metal catalysts. Now known as Adams's catalyst, this has proved to be of great utility and to be the most satisfactory catalyst for hydrogenation of many types of organic molecules. Not until recently, 40 years after the discovery, have other catalysts been described that are purported to have activities comparable to or superior to those of the Adams catalyst.

In 1816 the British chemist Humphry Davy was the first to note the catalytic action of platinum. During the next decade the German chemist Johann Wolfgang Döbereiner noted that the catalytic effect was enhanced if the platinum was powdered, that is, was made into what is now called platinum sponge. Catalysis is the most satisfactory method for effectively combining hydrogen with an unsaturated compound. Base-metal catalysts, such as nickel or cobalt, were first used for this purpose by the French chemist Paul Sabatier in 1897.

Although scientists had demonstrated that platinum and palladium were the most active catalysts for hydrogenations at low temperatures and pressures, no easy method had been discovered for preparing very active palladium and platinum catalysts and no method was known for preparing with certainty in successive experiments platinum or palladium catalysts of uniform activity. Adams prepared platinum and palladium dioxides by fusing chloroplatinic acid or palladium chloride with sodium nitrate. The resulting metal dioxides were isolated by cooling the melt and digesting with water. When he added a small charge of the brown metal oxide to the solution of the unsaturated compound and treated with hydrogen, the oxide was promptly reduced, and a suspension of the black finely divided metal resulted. The metal then catalyzed the hydrogenation of the organic compound. The convenience in preparation and the great effectiveness of the Adams catalyst under mild conditions has been widely recognized.

Adams made extensive studies on the elucidation of structure of many naturally occurring compounds. In 1925, in collaboration with Ralph L. Shriner at the University of Illinois, he investigated the composition of chaulmoogra oil, a mixture of fatty-acid glycerides once used to treat leprosy. Adams established the structure of hydrocarpic and chaulmoogric acids obtained by saponification of the oil and demonstrated the presence in each of a cyclopentene ring. Following this work he synthesized many analogous acids that, in the form of esters, exhibited physiological action similar to chaulmoogra oil.

Adams determined the structure of gossypol, the toxic yellow pigment of cottonseed, the presence of which restricted for many years the general utilization of cottonseed oil and meal until a cheap and convenient method for its destruction was discovered.

His studies clarifying the structure of the narcotic principle of marijuana demonstrated also that the test commonly used at the time by the Federal Bureau of Narcotics for detection of marijuana was actually indicating merely the presence of an innocuous companion product. Methods for synthesizing analogous substances with similar narcotic properties were developed, and a variety of interesting products was realized.

Researches also were directed to the toxic alkaloids that cause cattle poisoning and that are commonly found in plants on Texas ranches. These compounds occur especially in various species of *Senecio, Crotalaria, Trichodesma,* and *Heliotropium.*

Among Adams's many other investigations were the synthesis of local anesthetics, studies on anthraquinones, organic arsenic compounds, and the synthesis and reactions of a new class of compounds with exceptionally high reactivity, quinone mono- and di-imides. In addition, while serving as a major in the Chemical Warfare Service during World War I, he synthesized phenarsazine chloride, a sternutatory substance, better known as Adamsite.

He also investigated extensively steric hindrance due to restricted rotation about a single bond as found in substituted biphenyls, diphenylbenzenes, phenylpyrrols, bipyrryls, arylolefins, and arylamines. He demonstrated that substitution in the *ortho* positions to the bond between the rings was effective in hindering rotation and that the *ortho* substituents could be arranged in sequence of effectiveness. For example, in the biphenyl series the relative stability of several compounds was studied by measuring the rate of conversion of an optically active form of the substance into its racemic modification. The effectiveness of the groups to slow up the rate of racemization falls into the following order with the bromine atoms showing the greatest effect: $Br > CH_3 > Cl > NO_2 > CO_2H > OCH_3 > F$.

The youngest of four children, Adams was educated at Harvard University, receiving his A.B. in 1909, his A.M. in 1910, and his Ph.D. in chemistry in 1912. In the latter year he went to the University of Berlin and the Kaiser Wilhelm Institute in Dahlem for further study, returning to Harvard in 1913 as an instructor in organic chemistry. In 1916 he became an assistant professor at the University of Illinois; he was appointed professor there in 1919 and chairman of the department of chemistry and chemical engineering in 1926. In 1954 he became a research professor and in 1957 professor emeritus.

Among his many awards were the Davy Medal of the Royal Society of London (1945); the A.

W. Hofmann Medal of the German Chemical Society (1953); the W. H. Nichols (1927), the Willard Gibbs (1936), the T. W. Richards (1944), and the Priestley (1946) medals of the American Chemical Society; the Franklin Medal of the Franklin Institute of the State of Pennsylvania (1960); and the National Medal of Science (1964). He was elected to the National Academy of Sciences in 1929.

His achievements as member of the National Defense Research Committee during 1941–46 resulted in his being awarded the U.S. Medal for Merit and his appointment as Honorary Commander of the British Empire (C.B.E.). He always took an active part in the activities of the American Chemical Society, serving on many committees, as president in 1935, and as chairman of the board of directors from 1944 to 1950. He was president of the American Association for the Advancement of Science in 1950.

Adams was coauthor of *Elementary Laboratory Experiments in Organic Chemistry* (5th ed. 1963), editor-in-chief of *Organic Reactions* for 20 years, and editor of two volumes of *Organic Syntheses.*

For background information *see* FATS AND OILS, NONEDIBLE; ORGANOARSENIC COMPOUNDS; PLATINUM in the McGraw-Hill Encyclopedia of Science and Technology. □

★ **ALBERT, Abraham Adrian**

American mathematician
Born Nov. 9, 1905, Chicago, Ill., U.S.A.

IN 1905 L. E. Dickson defined a class of algebras called *cyclic algebras*. These are a special case of what are now called *crossed product algebras*, and which are defined as follows: Let F be any field and Z be a normal algebraic extension field of degree (that is, dimension) n over F. Then the galois group G of Z over F consists of n distinct automorphisms, $z \rightarrow z^\rho$ of Z, leaving F fixed. Consider a set

$g = \{a_{\rho,\sigma}\}$, of nonzero elements $a_{\rho,\sigma}$ in Z, which are given for every pair ρ, σ of automorphisms in G. Imbed Z in a space A which is the vector space direct sum of n copies Zy_ρ of Z and so has dimension n^2 over F. We make A into an algebra by defining products by the formula

$$(zy_\rho)(wy_\sigma) = [(z \cdot w^\rho) a_{\rho,\sigma}] y_{\rho\sigma}$$

for every z and w of Z and all ρ, σ in G. The condition on g which results from $(y_\rho y_\sigma) y_\tau = y_\rho(y_\sigma y_\tau)$ for all ρ, σ, τ in G, implies that A is associative. In this case A is called a *crossed product* over its center F. When G is a cyclic group and ρ generates G, we can take $y_\sigma = y^i$ for every $\sigma = \rho^i$, and y^n is in F. Then A is a cyclic algebra.

The main problem in the theory of associative algebras is the determination of all division algebras. Every associative division algebra A has dimension n^2 over the field F which is its center. Then n is called the degree of A, and is actually the degree of a maximal subfield of F. All division algebras of degree $n = 1, 2, 3$ have been known to be cyclic since 1921. In his 1928 Ph.D. dissertation, Albert showed that all division algebras of degree four are crossed products. In 1932 he proved the existence of noncyclic division algebras of degree four.

Albert and others developed a theory of direct products of simple associative algebras. As a consequence of these results and some properties of cyclic fields and of associative algebras over a p-adic field, it was shown by Helmut Hasse, Richard Brauer, Emmy Noether, and Albert that every division algebra whose center is an algebraic number field is a cyclic algebra.

The multiplication algebra of a pure Riemann matrix is an associative division algebra over an algebraic number field with certain special properties. Albert determined the precise structure of these algebras in 1934, and also proved the existence of a pure Riemann matrix whose multiplication algebra is any such algebra, and whose elements are all algebraic numbers. He was awarded the Cole prize of the American Mathematical Society for this work in 1939.

In 1941 Albert began his major study of the structure of nonassociative algebras. He produced the general structure theory of Jordan algebras, and later gave a construction of exceptional Jordan division algebras. He also constructed the major classes of finite nonassociative division algebras. This work provided most of the known classes of finite nondesarguesian projective division ring planes.

A merchant's son, Albert majored in mathematics at the University of Chicago, receiving his B.S. in 1926, his M.S. in 1927, and his Ph.D. in 1928. He held a National Research Council Fellowship at Princeton in 1928–29, taught at Columbia from 1929 to 1931, and returned to Chicago in 1931. He became a full professor in 1941, chairman of the department from 1958 to 1962, and dean of the Division of the Physical Sciences in 1962. He was appointed E. H. Moore Distinguished Service Professor in 1960. He was elected to the National Academy of Sciences in 1943.

Albert wrote *Modern Higher Algebra* (1937), *Structure of Algebras* (1939), *Introduction to Algebraic Theories* (1941), *College Algebra* (1946), *Solid Analytic Geometry* (1949), and *Fundamental Concepts of Higher Algebra* (1956).

For background information *see* ALGEBRA in the McGraw-Hill Encyclopedia of Science and Technology.   □

ALDER, Kurt

German chemist
Born July 10, 1902, Königshutte, Germany (now Chorźow, Poland)
Died June 20, 1958, Cologne, Germany

ALDER, ALONG with the German chemist Otto Diels, was responsible for the elucidation and development of the diene synthesis, now more commonly called the Diels-Alder reaction. For this work the two were awarded the Nobel Prize in chemistry in 1950.

The diene synthesis involves condensation of a conjugated olefin, the diene, with an activated double bond, the dienophile, to form a cyclic product. Isolated instances of such condensations were reported as early as 1893, but Diels and Alder were the first to recognize the versatility of the reaction, and in a series of papers beginning in 1928 they demonstrated its remarkably broad scope.

Alder and his coworkers carried out a systematic study of the reactivity of a large number of dienes and dienophiles, many of which they synthesized for the first time. They also established the structure and stereochemistry of all new Diels-Alder adducts. This work provided a firm foundation for all later investigations. Alder was particularly interested in bridged-ring systems, which were formed when cyclic dienes were used. In his early work, Alder determined the structure and the mode of formation of the polymers of cyclopentadiene. Later, he demonstrated the ease with which members of the camphor and norcamphor family, natural products containing bridged-ring systems, could be synthesized.

The Diels-Alder reaction has been invaluable in producing thousands of organic compounds whose syntheses would have been otherwise impossible or at best very difficult. It has been used in the production of insecticides, dyes, drying and lubricating oils, and pharmaceuticals. Its uses are constantly being extended, and its full potential has yet to be realized.

In addition to his work on the diene synthesis, Alder conducted research in problems of autoxidation and polymerization. He also worked on the preparation and composition of synthetic rubber.

Alder studied chemistry at the University of Berlin and then went to the University of Kiel, where he took his doctorate in 1926 under the direction of Diels. In 1930 he was appointed reader, and in 1934 professor of chemistry, at the University of Kiel, remaining there until 1936. He then worked in the research laboratories of I. G. Farben Industrie at Leverkusen until 1940, when he became professor of chemistry and director of the chemistry institute at the University of Cologne. He was named dean of the philosophical faculty at Cologne in 1949.

For background information *see* DIELS-ALDER REACTION in the McGraw-Hill Encyclopedia of Science and Technology.   □

a small glass bulb containing ether. Several groups of physicists started immediately to develop the bubble chamber into a practical tool for use in high-energy physics. The Alvarez group was the first to observe tracks in liquid hydrogen, in 1954. Thereafter they built increasingly larger hydrogen chambers, each of which was in turn the world's largest. (Donald Gow and Paul Hernandez played important roles in this program.) For almost 5 years after its completion in early 1959, the 72-in. chamber was the largest; eventually it was surpassed by the 80-in. Brookhaven chamber.

Concurrently, Alvarez recognized that the measurement techniques then used to analyze cloud chamber pictures were too slow by a factor of 100 to cope with the flood of photographs that would come from his planned large chambers. The basic parameters of the proposed semiautomatic measuring machines were tabulated by Alvarez in 1955; their first embodiment appeared a year later in the "Franckenstein" of Hugh Bradner and Jack Franck. This machine, and others that followed its design philosophy, became the basis for the modern standard measurement technique. As Alvarez suggested in 1955, the final link in the new data reduction technique involved high-speed electronic computer analysis of the "Franckenstein" output data. Many members of his group played important roles in this new project, in particular Frank Solmitz, Lynn Stevenson, and Arthur Rosenfeld.

The computer programs made it possible to observe particles with lifetimes of the order of 10^{-22} seconds; older techniques cut off at lifetimes less than 10^{-12} seconds. In 1960 Alvarez and his collaborators announced the discovery

★ ALVAREZ, Luis Walter

American physicist
Born June 13, 1911, San Francisco, Calif., U.S.A.

IN THE early 1960s, a "population explosion" occurred in the list of elementary particles. This rapid increase from some 30 known particles to more than 100 was primarily the result of the teaming together of the liquid hydrogen bubble chamber and the proton synchrotron. Alvarez was the leader in building a series of ever larger liquid hydrogen bubble chambers, together with the necessary new types of measuring devices and the data analysis systems required to "extract the physics" from the raw bubble-chamber film. For this achievement, he was awarded the new National Medal of Science by President Johnson in 1964.

In 1952 Donald Glaser demonstrated the first bubble chamber, showing cosmic-ray tracks in

of the first three very short-lived strange particles. Members of the Alvarez group have since found about half of the known short-lived particles, or "resonances," as they are commonly called. Almost all the new particles have been found in liquid hydrogen bubble chambers, using Franckensteinlike devices and geometry and kinematics computer programs of the type introduced into physics by the Alvarez group.

Prior to his involvement in bubble-chamber physics, Alvarez had been active in nuclear physics and cosmic-ray research. Either alone or with a single collaborator, he discovered the "east-west effect" in cosmic rays, the radioactivity of tritium, the isotopic stability of He³, K-electron capture, the long-range alpha particles accompanying fission, and several short-lived isotopes. Similarly, he made the first measurement of the magnetic moment of the neutron, the first nonradioactive observation of an artificially created isotope, the spectrum of Hg¹⁹⁸, the first time-of-flight neutron spectrometer, and the first acceleration of heavy ions in a cyclotron. His published suggestion concerning charge-exchange acceleration led directly and quickly to the tandem Van de Graaff generator. From 1945 through 1947, he led a group that built the first proton linear accelerator. In 1956, he and his associates discovered the unexpected phenomenon of fusion catalysis by mu mesons.

Alvarez attended the University of Chicago (B.S., 1932; M.S., 1934; Ph.D., 1936) and in 1938 joined the faculty of the University of California at Berkeley. Active in microwave radar research in World War II, he was the author of a dozen government-owned patents in the radar field. His inventions included ground controlled approach (with Lawrence Johnston), the "eagle system" for blind bombing, microwave beacons, and many linear antenna arrays. At Los Alamos, he suggested the technique used to detonate the implosion weapon. He flew as scientific observer at Alamogordo and Hiroshima. He was elected to the National Academy of Sciences in 1947.

For background information *see* BUBBLE CHAMBER; PARTICLE in the McGraw-Hill Encyclopedia of Science and Technology.   □

☆ AMBARTSUMIAN, Victor Amazaspovich

Soviet (Armenian) astrophysicist
Born Sept. 18, 1908, Tiflis, Georgian Soviet Socialist Republic

WHILE STUDYING stellar associations and stellar evolution, Ambartsumian arrived at a theory of cosmogony based on the process of rarefaction rather than condensation. This theory accounts for a number of celestial phenomena that cannot be adequately explained by any other currently accepted cosmological model.

About 1924 the English astronomer and physicist A. S. Eddington suggested that the enormous densities of white dwarf stars (approaching 60,000 grams per cubic centimeter) were due to the presence of degenerate matter, a gas in which the electrons and ionized nuclei of atoms, under the influence of extreme pressures, are tightly packed to produce very high densities. During the 1930s the Soviet physicist L. D. Landau predicted that immensely dense bodies would be found concealed within the interiors of some of the more massive stars. In 1934 the American astronomers Fritz Zwicky and Walter Baade posited the existence of neutron stars—celestial bodies in which the internal pressure was so great that the atoms were completely stripped of their electrons and the nuclei compressed to densities approximating 5×10^{10} grams per cubic centimeter. The theory of neutron stars was later worked out by the American physicist J. R. Oppenheimer and the Canadian physicist G. M. Volkoff. Thus by World War II the concept of extremely dense celestial bodies was well established.

In the late 1940s, Ambartsumian began to investigate a long-standing question concerning the direction of evolution of cosmic bodies: did such bodies evolve toward condensation or toward rarefaction and disintegration of their substance? In 1947 he showed that our Galaxy contained young stars forming two types of groups: O-associations and T-associations. He showed that these associations were unstable; subsequent observations demonstrated that certain of them were in fact breaking up. Short-term groups of the Trapezium system type were shown to be made up of especially young stars.

From this it followed that stars arise in groups as a result of the disintegrations of very massive bodies, which Ambartsumian called protostars. The disintegration of a protostar

might result in some of its material being changed into diffuse matter. This explained why groups of young stars were densely immersed in gaseous mist. Observation confirmed this process of disintegration. Ambartsumian rejected, however, the idea that the density of a protostar might equal that of a neutron star.

Ambartsumian later turned to the phenomena of radio galaxies. In a series of articles begun in 1955 he showed that the current theory, which held such a galaxy to be the result of the collision of two ordinary galaxies, was incorrect. He considered that radio galaxies arose from ordinary galaxies as a result of enormous explosions in their nuclei.

In the 1950s Ambartsumian was occupied with the consequences of his theory of galactic nuclei, which gained a series of unexpected confirmations after 1960. He concluded that the various characteristics of galaxies resulted from the continued activity of the galactic nuclei over long periods of time. He considered it evident that this activity conditioned the existence of supermassive bodies in galaxies.

Ambartsumian applied the idea of a transition from a dense state to one less dense in the extragalactic province. He maintained that the filaments of cosmic gas connecting many multiple galaxies are the last connections between bodies that were spewed forth by the same protogalaxy. He further contended that the variable dwarf stars found in stellar associations have retained remnants of hypermatter within their cores, since observations have revealed that their irregular fluctuations of brightness are caused by occasional surface emissions.

In addition to his work in cosmogony, Ambartsumian made major contributions to the study of stellar associations, particularly in relation to type O and T stars. He also developed the theory of radial equilibrium of planetary nebulae, demonstrated the role of ultraviolet radiation and the radiation of lines of the Lyman series, and explained the physical composition of the shells of meteorites.

Ambartsumian studied at Leningrad University and Pulkovo Observatory. He became a lecturer and research worker at Leningrad University in 1931, leaving in 1944 to become a professor of astrophysics at Erevan University. In 1945 he became director of the Biurakan Observatory in the Armenian S.S.R. Ambartsumian became a member of the U.S.S.R. Academy of Sciences in 1953. He was awarded the Gold Medal of the Royal Astronomical Society of Great Britain and, in 1960, the Catherine Wolfe Bruce Medal of the Astronomical Society of the Pacific. He was elected a foreign associate of the U.S. National Academy of Sciences in 1959.

Ambartsumian wrote *Theoretical Astrophysics* (1958).

For background information *see* COSMOGONY in the McGraw-Hill Encyclopedia of Science and Technology. ☐

AMMANN, Othmar Hermann

American engineer
Born Mar. 29, 1879, Schaffhausen, Switzerland
Died Sept. 22, 1965, Rye, N.Y., U.S.A.

As ENGINEER and designer, Ammann was responsible for the planning and construction of the George Washington Bridge, the Lincoln Tunnel, the Triborough and Bronx-Whitestone bridges, and the Verrazano-Narrows Bridge, all in New York City. For his engineering achievements he received the National Medal of Science in 1964.

A 1902 graduate in civil engineering of the Swiss Federal Polytechnic Institute, Ammann went to the United States in 1904 and was employed on the construction of steel railway bridges. In 1905 he joined the Pennsylvania Steel Company and worked on the Queensboro Bridge in New York City. From 1912 to 1923 he was chief assistant to the consulting engineer Gustav Lindenthal, helping to design and construct the Hell Gate Bridge in New York City and the Ohio River Bridge at Sciotoville, Ohio.

In 1923 Ammann established his own consulting office and began designing a bridge he proposed to build across the Hudson River, connecting upper Manhattan and New Jersey. The Port of New York Authority in 1924 agreed to undertake and finance this project (later called the George Washington Bridge), and Ammann was made first chief bridge engineer. Completed in 1931, the bridge (spanning 3,500 ft, a record at the time) embodied several departures in design. In so massive a suspension bridge, Ammann believed he could safely omit the customary stiffening trusses at the level of the roadway that serve to minimize sideways vibration, since the bridge's own weight would keep it steady. This economy extended to the design of the towers, whose original plans called for concrete, steel, and stone construction. By substituting an openwork steel design, Ammann also effected an esthetic advance.

From 1930 to 1937 Ammann held the post of chief engineer of the New York Port Authority, and was its director of engineering from 1937 to 1939. In this capacity he directed the planning and construction of the Triborough Bridge, the Bronx-Whitestone Bridge, and the 8,216-ft Lincoln Tunnel under the Hudson River. He also served as a member of the Board of Engineers of the Golden Gate Bridge, which was opened in 1937.

Ammann returned to private consultation in 1939, and for the next several years he designed bridges (including the Yorktown Bridge) and highways in New York and New Jersey. In 1946 he entered into partnership with Charles S. Whitney, an engineer engaged in the design of bridges and specialized structures. The firm of Ammann and Whitney designed and supervised construction of the Throgs Neck Bridge in New York City, the Dulles International Airport in Washington, D.C., and three buildings for New York City's Lincoln Center for the Performing Arts. Ammann drew up plans for the Verrazano-Narrows Bridge, spanning New York harbor from Brooklyn to Staten Island. This bridge, opened in 1965, was the longest and heaviest suspension bridge in the world.

Ammann recognized the importance of esthetics in bridge construction and designed his structures for the optimum combination of simplicity, engineering perfection, and beauty.

For background information *see* BRIDGE in the McGraw-Hill Encyclopedia of Science and Technology.   □

With the genus *Apocynum* he made progeny tests of the rare putative hybrid between two common American species and demonstrated that the chief effect of hybridization in this group is to increase variability in the parental species. This led ultimately to his introduction of the term "introgressive hybridization" to denote the gradual infiltration of the germ plasm of one species into that of another as a consequence of hybridization and repeated backcrossing. In its shortened form, "introgression," this term is now commonly used, and Anderson became most widely known for his short monograph on introgression (1949) and for his studies of the importance of hybridization in evolution.

As a corollary to these studies, Anderson in 1939 analyzed character recombination in the second generation of a semifertile cross between two very dissimilar species of flowering tobacco. He measured the recombinations actually achieved and demonstrated that they were a fraction of those possible without such hindrances as linkage and the multiple effects of single factors. He showed that the total effect of linkage was greater than had been realized and that in such hybrids all the multiple factor characters that went into the cross together tended to be partially associated in the progeny.

This led Anderson to an interest in other wide crosses, and when P. C. Mangelsdorf and R. G. Reeves demonstrated in 1939 that *Zea mays* could be hybridized with *Tripsacum*, he joined H. C. Cutler in studying the latter genus.

He discovered that the prevailing classifications of maize were artificial and that a natural classification might be possible but could only

★ ANDERSON, Edgar Shannon

American botanist
Born Nov. 9, 1897, Forestville, N.Y., U.S.A.

A NDERSON WAS among those who brought the techniques and concepts of cytology and genetics to problems of classification and phylogeny. In 1936 he demonstrated that the semi-isolated local populations of the common blue irises of eastern North America are independent evolutionary units, each differentiating in its own way. From a variety of evidences he established the hypothesis that *Iris versicolor* is a hybrid between two older American species that doubled its chromosome number and is fertile and true-breeding. With cytological and with taxonomic colleagues, he monographed the Tradescantias native to the United States, incidentally discovering *Tradescantia paludosa*, widely useful in cytological and radiation laboratories.

be worked toward as a goal. With his students, he began the study of the total variation pattern of maize, ancient and modern, concentrating on neglected features like the male inflorescence. The innumerable cultivated varieties of *Zea mays* were found to be roughly divisible into natural regional groups (about 200 in the New World). He and his students assisted in the study and monographing of them under a committee set up by the National Academy of Sciences–National Research Council. Through these studies he became interested in the importance of studying cultivated plants and weeds by a fusion of herbarium, cytological, and experimental-plot techniques.

In his attempts to study evolution in natural populations by measuring and analyzing their variation patterns, Anderson worked out a series of semigraphical techniques for dealing with such problems. The most generally adaptable of these techniques, pictorialized scatter diagrams, have been widely used.

The son of a professor of dairy husbandry, Anderson majored in horticulture and botany at Michigan State University, receiving his B.S. in 1918. His graduate training was under E. M. East at the Bussey Institution of Harvard University, where he earned an M.S. in 1920 and an Sc.D. in 1922. From 1931 to 1935 he was arborist to the Arnold Arboretum of Harvard University, and lecturer in botany at Harvard University. From 1922 to 1931, and again after 1935, he held joint appointments in the Henry Shaw School of Botany of Washington University and at the Missouri Botanical Garden, both in St. Louis. He was elected to the National Academy of Sciences in 1954.

Anderson wrote *Introgressive Hybridization* (1949) and *Plants, Man and Life* (1952).

For background information *see* BOTANY; CYTOLOGY; HERBARIUM in the McGraw-Hill Encyclopedia of Science and Technology.   □

line breadths from known molecular interactions. The methods are still being used.

Anderson's attention was next focused on insulating magnetic materials such as ferrites and antiferromagnetic oxides. The problem was to discover what caused the alignment of atomic magnetic moments and spins and the particular arrangements observed. Building on Kramers's old concept of "superexchange," he explored mechanisms for the interactions. Plausible assumptions about the interactions explained the spin patterns and the Curie-Néel points observed. More recently, he tied in this theory (following the work of others) with modern crystal field theory, the theory of the behavior of isolated magnetic ions in insulators, and made a start toward a quantitative as well as qualitative theory of the exchange interactions responsible for this kind of magnetism. Anderson worked, too, on a number of other magnetic problems, notably, the antiferromagnetic ground state and spin waves, where his contribution foreshadowed some of the methodology of modern many-body theory; and the localized state in metals (following Friedel), an idea important in the theory of magnetic alloys and closely related to more general problems of why iron and other transition metals are magnetic.

In the early 1950s, line shapes and breadths in the various fields of magnetic resonance spectroscopy were opening up. Nicolaas Bloembergen, E. M. Purcell, and R. V. Pound had pioneered many fruitful ideas in nuclear resonance, and J. H. Van Vleck had done the same for electronic resonance, but again a quantitative mathematical understanding was needed to help in learning about atomic motions and interac-

★ ANDERSON, Philip Warren

American physicist
Born Dec. 13, 1923, Indianapolis, Ind., U.S.A.

Fᴏʀ ʜɪs contributions to the field of solid-state physics, Anderson received the American Physical Society's O. E. Buckley Prize in 1964.

In the spectroscopy of gases, the line spectra are broadened when the gas density is high. To explain the breadths in terms of intermolecular interactions, or even better to learn about molecular interactions from the breadths, Anderson, building on the simpler theories of H. A. Lorentz, Foley, and others, developed a more general methodology for such problems, useful in the whole range from microwave through infrared and optical spectroscopy, and calculated some of the first quantitative results for

tions from the observed spectrum. Ferromagnetic resonance was even more a closed book from this point of view. Anderson contributed a mathematical methodology for attacking the problems of "exchange narrowing" and "motional narrowing" and relating them to atomic motion and exchange. He also undertook various studies of interactions and mechanisms. In ferromagnetic resonance, collaborative work with Suhl and others pioneered the ideas of imperfection broadening and spin-wave pumping, which clarified the field.

When the first theory explaining the ancient puzzle of superconductivity appeared in 1957 (John Bardeen, L. N. Cooper, and J. R. Schrieffer), basic problems of principle remained. Anderson was among the first to elucidate these questions and generalize the Bardeen-Cooper-Schrieffer methodology.

He contributed to the solutions of a number of problems in the field of superconductivity. For example, the effects of imperfections on superconductivity are puzzlingly small in some cases, large in others. Anderson's "Theory of Dirty Superconductors" and related work introduced concepts and methodology that made this an accessible problem.

Again, the interactions that cause superconductivity are those between electrons and lattice vibrations that are fundamental to many other metallic properties, such as resistance; Bardeen, Cooper, and Schrieffer made no quantitative progress in calculating superconductivity from interactions, or vice versa. A combined theoretical and experimental attack on this problem, involving Anderson and others, led to remarkably detailed confirmation of the basic theory, as well as to ways of obtaining detailed information about metals more easily from superconductivity than from any other source. Essentially, this work led to an entirely new kind of spectroscopy—that of the electron-phonon interaction via tunneling spectroscopy in solids.

The nature of superconductivity is most clearly exhibited when the phenomenon breaks down, that is, when the superconductor shows resistance, or in a weak link such as a "Josephson junction." Anderson worked in this area both theoretically and experimentally with the goal of demonstrating graphically that superconductivity involves coherent matter waves in the way lasers involve coherent light waves. Most recently, with Richards, he observed the analog of the ac Josephson effect in superfluid helium, thus showing the basic similarity of superfluidity and superconductivity and the relationship of both to coherence properties of quantum-mechanical matter waves.

The son and grandson of Middle Western science professors, Anderson majored in electronic physics at Harvard, receiving a B.S. summa cum laude in 1943. After doing antenna engineering at the Naval Research Laboratory in 1943–45, he returned to Harvard to do a thesis on pressure broadening with J. H. Van Vleck

(M.A. 1947; Ph.D. 1949). Thereafter he was associated with the Bell Telephone Laboratories, serving in 1958–60 as chairman of the theoretical physics department there.

Anderson wrote *Concepts in Solids* (1963).

For background information *see* MAGNETISM; SPECTROSCOPY; SUPERCONDUCTIVITY in the McGraw-Hill Encyclopedia of Science and Technology. □

★ APKER, LeRoy

American experimental physicist
Born June 11, 1915, Rochester, N.Y., U.S.A.

STUDIES OF photoelectric emission of electrons from semiconductors by Apker and his colleague, E. A. Taft, led to the discovery of a new process called "exciton-induced photoemission" in potassium iodide crystals. In this phenomenon, energy first was absorbed from a beam of ultraviolet radiation by the ions of the entire crystal. Subsequently, in a secondary process, it was concentrated with surprisingly high efficiency onto a relatively small number of electrons localized in defects called "color centers." For contributions to the understanding of energy transfer in crystals, Apker received the Buckley Prize of the American Physical Society in 1955.

In the early 1930s R. H. Fowler and L. A. DuBridge showed that the quantum theory of electrons in solids substantially explained the previously puzzling behavior of photoemission from metals. E. U. Condon in 1938 pointed out that photoelectrons from semiconductors should behave in a markedly different way. R. A. Millikan had suspected something like this as long ago as 1916, when he was verifying Einstein's photoelectric equation, but theoretical background for further exploration and understanding was lacking at that time.

In 1948, at the General Electric Research Laboratory in Schenectady, Apker, E. A. Taft, and J. E. Dickey completed experiments that clearly showed the effect discussed 10 years before by Condon. They concluded that the fastest photoelectrons from a semiconductor such as germanium or tellurium were much slower than those from a metal like platinum that had the same "work function"—the latter being the quantity that determines the behavior of the thermionic electron emission and the contact potential. Useful conclusions could be drawn about the electronic structure of the semiconductors by making these photoelectric measurements. An important factor here was that process of energy transfer was relatively simple. In a typical case, an electron in the semiconductor first absorbed the entire energy of a photon in the beam of incident ultraviolet radiation. Then it escaped as a photoelectron through the barrier at the semiconductor surface.

At the time that this work was being done, an intriguing group of ionic crystals had been very little explored by photoelectric methods. These were the alkali halides, such as potassium iodide. It is possible for some of the negative iodine ions to be missing in this crystal structure and for the vacant places to be filled with electrons. Such defects, known as "color centers," absorb visible and ultraviolet radiation, coloring the crystal in a range of photon energies for which it is normally quite transparent. It was well known that absorption of visible radiation could set the trapped electrons free inside the crystal, producing photoconductivity. In contrast, there had been very little work on photoemission, and it appeared that this would be an interesting area to examine. It turned out that visible and near-ultraviolet radiation not only produced photoconductivity but also produced photoemission. The latter was similar to that from the more usual metals and semiconductors.

Farther in the ultraviolet, however, a very different kind of photoemission was discovered. In this region of the spectrum, the potassium iodide crystal itself has a very sharp, intense absorption line, which is due to the formation of electrically neutral entities called excitons. These excitons transferred energy with remarkably high efficiency to the electrons in the color centers, the excited electrons being ejected from the crystal as "exciton-induced photoemission." In later work, it became clear that this is a relatively common phenomenon in other ionic crystals, such as barium oxide.

A student of L. A. DuBridge, Apker attended the University of Rochester, receiving an A.B. in 1937 and a Ph.D. in physics in 1941. In that year he joined the staff of the General Electric Research Laboratory in Schenectady, N.Y.

For background information *see* PHOTOEMISSION; SEMICONDUCTOR in the McGraw-Hill Encyclopedia of Science and Technology.   □

APPLETON, Sir Edward (Victor)

English physicist
Born Sept. 6, 1892, Bradford, Yorkshire, England
Died Apr. 21, 1965, Edinburgh, Scotland

APPLETON'S FAME is founded on his demonstration of the existence of the ionosphere and on his detailed investigations of its structure, distribution, and variations. This work had a profound theoretical and practical importance: theoretical, as bearing on the ionization produced by solar photons and particles in the tenuous upper atmosphere and its wide influence on the physics of near space; practical, as concerning the reflection, and so the transmission, of radar waves. For "his work on the physical properties of the upper atmosphere and especially for his discovery of the ionospheric region called the Appleton layer," Appleton received the Nobel Prize in physics in 1947.

An electrified layer in the upper atmosphere had been postulated independently by Oliver Heaviside and A. E. Kennelly in 1902, both of whom pointed out that the reflection of electromagnetic waves by such a layer would account for the transmission of wireless signals from England to Newfoundland effected by Guglielmo Marconi. Such transmission could have taken place only if the waves had followed the curvature of the Earth's surface. There was, however, no other indication of the existence of such a layer, let alone of its nature or height.

During World War I, Appleton, as a temporary officer dealing with radio, became familiar with the use of thermionic valves, then a novelty, with which relatively powerful transmitters and receivers could be built, and was confronted with the problem of fading signals. After the war he conceived the notion of interference between waves reflected from an ionized layer in the upper atmosphere and the direct waves traveling along the Earth's surface. Working with transmitter and receiver about 70 miles apart, he showed, with the assistance of M. A. F. Barnett, that slow frequency modulation in the transmitter produced a series of maxima and minima in the received signal. The number of beats produced by a given change of frequency gave a direct estimate of the height of the reflecting layer above the ground, which came out to be about 90 km. This result was confirmed by determining the angle made by the reflected beam with the horizontal, given by comparing the simultaneous signal variations received with a loop aerial and with a vertical antenna. In this manner the existence of an ionized reflecting layer was first established.

The degree of reflection depends upon the frequency of the waves and the density of ionization. Appleton found that this reflection varied with the time of day, due, as subsequently demonstrated, to the varying intensity of the ionizing solar radiation. In particular, before dawn the reduction of ionization by recombination allowed the Kennelly-Heaviside layer, or E layer as it is now called, to be penetrated by the incident radiation. He established that reflection then took place at an upper layer of intense ionization, which he termed the F layer: it is now generally known as the Appleton layer. The lower boundary of this layer he found to be about 230 km above the Earth.

Appleton then proceeded to investigate in detail the structure and properties of the layers, a task on which he was engaged for the rest of his life. He employed the method of vertical sounding and made extensive use of the pulse method devised by G. Breit and M. A. Tuve in 1925, observing by cathode-ray registration the echo effect from short-duration signals. With the cooperation of G. Builder, he established a new effect of prime importance: the Earth's magnetic field made the ionosphere a doubly refracting medium, which he showed to be theoretically deducible if the effective charged particles were free electrons. This leads to a doubling of the echoes. From a general theory of the propagation of radio waves in an ionized medium under the influence of a magnetic field, he deduced a relation between the electron density and the critical penetration frequency, which enabled him to find the maximum electron density for any layer and to investigate experimentally how this depended upon the time of day, the season of the year, the sunspot cycle, and, in general, any event, including eclipses, that governed the rate of emission of the solar photons producing the ionization. In this way the solar control of the ionosphere was demonstrated in great detail.

Appleton established many details of the structure of the ionosphere, such as a weakly ionized D layer below the E layer and the resolution of the Appleton layer into two strata under certain conditions. He studied the world morphology of the F2 layer, demonstrating the marked geomagnetic control of the ionization and, with his collaborators, showing that lunar tidal oscillations could be detected in the D, E, and F layers. In his last years he devoted much attention to storms in the ionosphere and the perturbations produced by electric currents flowing in it. He took an active part in international investigations of the upper atmosphere, including the Second International Polar Year, 1932–33, and the International Geophysical Year, 1957–58.

At St. John's College, Cambridge, which he entered in 1911, Appleton had a brilliant career, interrupted by his military service in World War I. Upon his return to Cambridge, he began his work on the ionosphere and so distinguished himself that, in 1924, at the age of 32, he was appointed Wheatstone Professor of Physics at the University of London. There he carried out much of his fundamental work. In 1936 he returned to Cambridge as Jacksonian Professor of Natural Philosophy, a distinguished post in which his predecessor had been C. T. R. Wilson. At the outbreak of World War II he was appointed Secretary of the Department of Scientific and Industrial Research, an important administrative post in which he was largely responsible for the government's attitude toward research. In 1949 he was made principal and vice-chancellor of the University of Edinburgh, which offices he held at the time of his death. He was knighted in 1941.

For background information *see* IONOSPHERE in the McGraw-Hill Encyclopedia of Science and Technology.   □

B

★★

(continued)

BAADE, Walter

American astronomer
Born Mar. 24, 1893, Schröttinghausen, West-phalia, Germany
Died June 25, 1960, Göttingen, Westphalia, Germany

WHILE TRYING to resolve the bright stars in the nucleus of the Andromeda Nebula, Baade formulated the concept of stellar populations. He later applied this concept to the results of photometric measurements of classic cepheid variables to increase the distance scale of the universe by a factor of two.

In 1912 the period-luminosity relationship for variable stars in the Small Magellanic Cloud was discovered by Henrietta Swan Leavitt of the Harvard College Observatory. The variable stars were of the short-period RR Lyrae type, but Ejnar Hertzsprung of the Leiden Observatory in the Netherlands showed that these were similar to the long-period classical cepheid variables of the Delta Cephei type, and in 1913 he made the first attempt to correlate the relationship in absolute magnitude. This correlation was successfully achieved by Harlow Shapley of the Mt. Wilson Observatory in 1914, and it served as the basis for his model of the Milky Way galaxy, which was announced 4 years later. During the interim, Shapley noticed that the Hertzsprung-Russell (H-R) diagram for stars in globular clusters differed drastically from the H-R diagram for stars in the neighborhood of the Sun and in galactic clusters. However, this observation was largely disregarded after he announced it in 1915. The period-luminosity relationship, as calibrated by Shapley, was used by Edwin P. Hubble of the Mt. Wilson Observatory to assign a distance of about 900,000 light-years, later reduced to about 750,000 light-years,

to the Andromeda Nebula in 1929. All other extragalactic distances were then based on the distance to the Andromeda Nebula.

Although Hubble had resolved the spiral arms of the Andromeda Nebula into stars in 1923, all subsequent attempts to resolve the nucleus had failed. In 1944, while working at the Mt. Wilson Observatory, Baade decided to use the 100-inch Hooker telescope to try to resolve the nucleus of the Andromeda Nebula into its component stars. He believed that he had an excellent chance to succeed, for the sky was free of artificial light because of the wartime blackout of the nearby cities of Los Angeles and Pasadena. Since the brightest stars in the spiral arms of the nebula are blue supergiants of high surface temperature, Baade chose to use blue-sensitive plates. However, the nucleus remained unresolved. Then, although it was unlikely that a red star could be detected when the far brighter blue stars had failed to appear on earlier plates, he tried a red-sensitive plate. To his amazement, not only did the nucleus of the nebula resolve into individual stars but so did the previously unresolved companion elliptical nebulae M 32 and NGC 205. Baade realized that whereas the brightest stars in the arms of spiral galaxies are blue, the brightest stars in the nuclei of such galaxies and in elliptical galaxies are red. Furthermore, he found that while these red stars are brighter than the red giants observed in the Sun's region of the Milky Way, they are similar to those seen in globular clusters. From these findings, Baade concluded that there must be two distinct classes of stellar populations, which he designated population I and population II. Population I includes younger stars, the brightest of which are the blue-white supergiants associated with interstellar gas and dust; population I stars are found in the arms of spiral galaxies and in galactic clusters. Population II includes older stars, the brightest of which are the red supergiants that are not associated with interstellar gas and dust; population II stars are found in the nuclei of spiral galaxies, in elliptical galaxies, and in globular clusters. Although more recent work has indicated that there are more than two stellar populations and that Baade's conclusions were too general, his contribution has played a significant role in developing the theory of stellar evolution.

The concept of stellar populations led Baade to revise the scale of extragalactic distances. When the 200-inch Hale telescope at the Mt. Palomar Observatory became operational in 1948, Baade used it to continue his investigations. Since the telescope could photograph objects down to an apparent magnitude of 22.4 in a 30-minute exposure, Baade expected plates of the nucleus of the Andromeda Nebula to show RR Lyrae variables, which at maximum brightness should have had an apparent magnitude of 22.4. However, only the brightest population II stars appeared on the plate. Baade realized that since the absolute magnitude of the RR Lyrae stars produced the wrong apparent magnitude when substituted into the equation relating absolute magnitude, distance, and apparent magnitude, the distance assumed for the Andromeda Nebula must be incorrect. He finally obtained satisfactory agreement between distance and magnitude by assuming that there are two period-luminosity curves for variable stars instead of one. One curve gave the relationship for the type-I variables, such as RR Lyrae, of population I, and the other the relationship for the type-II variables, such as Delta Cephei, of population II. The absolute magnitude of the population I variables, Baade found, is 1.5 magnitudes less than that of the population II variables of the same period. Thus, in 1952, Baade announced that, based on the fact that a decrease in magnitude of 1.5 is equivalent to an increase in distance by a factor of two, the Andromeda Nebula was 1.5×10^6 light-years distant. Since all other extragalactic distances were based on the calculated distance of the Andromeda Nebula, this had the effect of doubling the distance to all extragalactic objects. Baade's work has not only been confirmed by a number of observers, but more recent evidence has shown that the correction factor is probably closer to three than to two. By doubling the size of the universe, Baade helped to reconcile a number of contradictions resulting from the previous scale—such as the time interval required to account for the velocity of the external galaxies and the radioactive determination of the Earth's age—to the evolutionary model of the universe.

Among Baade's many other accomplishments was the discovery of two unique asteroids. In 1924 he located Hidalgo, whose aphelion is farther from the Sun than that of any other asteroid, and in 1949 he discovered Icarus, whose perihelion is closer to the Sun than that of any other asteroid. He also identified a distorted galaxy in Cygnus, called Cygnus A, which was the first discrete radio source to be discovered, in 1953.

Baade attended the universities of Münster and Göttingen, receiving his Ph.D. from the latter in 1919. In that year he became an assistant at the Hamburg Observatory, and in 1927 he was appointed an astronomer there. Beginning in 1920, he served simultaneously as a Privatdozent at the University of Hamburg. In 1931 Baade left both posts to join the Mt. Wilson Observatory as an astronomer, and in 1948 he also became an astronomer at the Mt. Palo-

mar Observatory. He retired from these positions in 1958. He returned to the University of Göttingen in 1959 as Gauss Professor, serving in that capacity until his death. Baade was awarded the Gold Medal of the Royal Astronomical Society of Great Britain and the Bruce Medal of the Astronomical Society of the Pacific.

For background information *see* COSMOGONY; GALAXY, THE in the McGraw-Hill Encyclopedia of Science and Technology.   □

★ **BAILAR, John Christian, Jr.**

American chemist
Born May 27, 1904, Golden, Colo., U.S.A.

IN 1933 Bailar conceived the idea that optically active inorganic complex ions might undergo reactions accompanied by optical inversions. With his students, he discovered several reactions of this type and elucidated their mechanism. He also studied the phenomenon of stereospecificity in inorganic complexes and, with E. J. Corey, explained the cause of this phenomenon.

In a long series of papers (1893–1916), Alfred Werner demonstrated that properly substituted octahedral metal ammines can exist in geometrically and optically isomeric forms. He also showed that geometrical isomers can be transformed into each other. Paul Walden observed, in 1895, that certain organic reactions proceed, under some conditions, with retention of configuration but, under other conditions, with inversion—that is, that one optical isomer can be converted into the other. Trained in both organic and inorganic chemistry, Bailar believed that both branches of the science were subject to the same laws and that phenomena exhibited by organic substances might well be observed in the behavior of inorganic substances as well. Subsequent studies showed that the relationship between organic and inorganic structures was not as simple as he had originally supposed, but his guiding principle was sound and led him to search for a "Walden inversion" in the reactions of cobalt complexes. His original goal of using the reactions of inorganic compounds to elucidate the behavior of the simpler organic compounds was not achieved because the mechanism of the reactions of tetrahedral organic structures and octahedral inorganic complexes are not sufficiently similar for direct comparison. But his discovery of optical inversion in the inorganic reactions stimulated research that has opened up the field of inorganic reaction mechanisms.

Stereospecificity in inorganic complexes has been known since the early part of this century, but no adequate explanation for it was offered until Corey and Bailar postulated that most five-membered chelate rings are puckered rather than flat and that such a ring, if it bears a substituent group, achieves the greatest stability (with respect to the remainder of the molecule) when the substituent group occupies an "equatorial" position on the ring. This theory is in accord with the quantitative measurements that have been made, and has been generally accepted. Bailar's work on stereospecificity has led to the discovery of partial asymmetric synthesis of octahedral complexes and to methods of determining the relative configurations of organic molecules.

Bailar's father was a professor of chemistry and began his son's education in chemistry at an early age. The younger Bailar majored in chemistry at the University of Colorado, where he received his B.A. in 1924 and M.A. (specializing in inorganic chemistry) in 1925. The University of Michigan awarded him a Ph.D. in organic chemistry in 1928. During the years at Michigan, he became interested in the phenomena of isomerism and molecular rearrangements. This interest persisted after he assumed a position as instructor in inorganic chemistry at the University of Illinois in 1928, and he soon found that his organic training and interests could be easily transferred to inorganic chemistry. He became professor of chemistry at Illinois in 1943. During World War II he served as an official investigator for the National Defense Research Committee and did research on smoke screens and poisonous gases. In 1964 he was awarded the Priestley Medal of the American Chemical Society.

Bailar coauthored textbooks of general chemistry with B. S. Hopkins and with Therald Moeller and Jacob Kleinberg (1965).

For background information *see* OPTICAL ACTIVITY; STEREOCHEMISTRY in the McGraw-Hill Encyclopedia of Science and Technology. □

★ **BARDEEN, John**
American physicist
Born May 23, 1908, Madison, Wis., U.S.A.

For MANY years after its discovery by Kammerlingh Onnes in 1911, superconductivity was one of the outstanding puzzles of physics. It was not until 1957, nearly 50 years later, that an adequate explanation was given by Bardeen and his associates L. N. Cooper and J. R. Schrieffer. The theory that they proposed, together with its subsequent developments, has not only accounted successfully for the major aspects of superconductivity but has been used to predict new phenomena and has thus given a great stimulus to the field.

Prior to the development of the Bardeen-Cooper-Schrieffer theory, a great deal had been learned about the properties of superconductors, and the general lines along which an explanation might be found on the basis of quantum theory was fairly well established. At very low temperatures, a few degrees above the absolute zero, many metals and alloys become superconducting, losing all trace of resistance to flow of electricity. In 1933, W. Meissner discovered another property that is perhaps even more basic: a magnetic field is excluded from the interior of a superconducting body. The state with the magnetic flux excluded is the unique and stable state in the presence of a magnetic field; the currents that flow near the surface to shield the interior from the magnetic field have no tendency to decay. Shortly thereafter, F. and H. London proposed a phenomenological theory to account for both vanishing resistance and the Meissner effect. Fritz London suggested that an explanation might follow from quantum theory, normally applied only on the atomic scale. He suggested that a superconductor behaves as a single large quantum system and that "the long-range order of the average momentum is to be considered one of the fundamental properties of the superconducting state." He predicted that the magnetic flux threading a superconducting ring or cylinder is quantized to integral multiples of a basic unit, and this has since been observed.

Bardeen first became interested in superconductivity in the mid-1930s and was strongly influenced by London's ideas. A little later he made an unsuccessful attempt to develop a theory. This work was interrupted in 1941, when he went into military work. After the war he took a position at the Bell Telephone Laboratories and became interested in semiconductors. Work done there led to the invention of the transistor, for which he was awarded the Nobel Prize in physics in 1956, jointly with William Shockley and W. H. Brattain. It was not until 1950 that he resumed work on superconductivity, following the experimental discovery of the isotope effect by a group at Rutgers University and by E. Maxwell. They found that the critical temperature below which the metal becomes superconducting depends on isotopic mass.

If mass is important, the motion of the atoms or ions that make up the metal must be involved, and this suggested that superconductivity depended somehow on the interaction between the electrons and the vibrational motion of atoms. Independently of knowledge of the isotope effect, H. Fröhlich also attempted to develop a theory of superconductivity on this basis. These early attempts (about 1950–51) ran into difficulties that were not overcome until 1957.

Bardeen and his associates found that the key to understanding superconductivity is a pairing interaction between the electrons resulting from an effective attraction induced by the interaction between electrons and atomic vibrations. The superconducting ground state is made up of configurations in which the states of the individual electrons are occupied in pairs of opposite spin and momentum, such that if in any configuration one of the states is occupied, the other is also. If there is current flow, the total momentum of each pair is different from zero but is exactly the same for all pairs. It is this that gives the long-range order of the momentum distribution suggested by London. Random scattering of individual electrons does not change the common momentum of the pairs, so that a current once started will persist indefinitely unless subjected to a force, such as an electric field, which acts on all or a large fraction of the pairs at the same time.

The theory has been developed to account quantitatively for many properties of superconductors in terms of a few measurable parameters. Experiments have been done by a number of people that demonstrate the quantum aspects of superconductors in striking ways, in most cases following theoretical predictions.

A similar pairing interaction occurs between the particles (neutrons and protons) in nuclei. Mathematical methods developed to explain superconductivity in metals have been applied successfully to account for various features of nuclear structure. The methods have also been used in the theory of elementary particles.

Bardeen received B.S. and M.S. degrees in electrical engineering from the University of Wisconsin in 1928 and 1929, respectively, and a Ph.D. in mathematical physics from Princeton University in 1936. Prior to his graduate studies at Princeton, he worked for several years with the Gulf Research and Development Corp. as a geophysicist. Subsequently, he was a postdoctoral fellow at Harvard University, assistant professor of physics at the University of Minnesota, a physicist at the U.S. Naval Ordnance Laboratory during World War II, and later research physicist at the Bell Telephone Laboratories. In 1951 he became professor of physics and electrical engineering at the University of Illinois. Bardeen's main research interests were in the theory of solid-state and low-temperature physics, with emphasis on semiconductors and superconductivity. He was elected to the National Academy of Sciences in 1954.

For background information *see* SUPERCONDUCTIVITY in the McGraw-Hill Encyclopedia of Science and Technology.   □

★ BARR, Murray Llewellyn

Canadian anatomist
Born June 20, 1908, Belmont, Ont., Canada

WHILE STUDYING the effects of prolonged activity on the structure of nerve cells, Barr and a graduate student, Ewart G. Bertram, noticed in 1949 that the nuclei of nerve cells of females contained a mass of chromatin that was lacking in the male. Further studies showed that this sex difference in nuclei of resting cells occurred in cells of most representatives of the mammalian class. The sex chromatin (Barr body) of the female is now known to be one of the two X chromosomes of the female, more condensed than other chromosomes in the nuclei of resting cells. Use of the sex chromatin in clinical investigation led to the demonstration of errors of the sex chromosome complex. These errors are responsible for certain forms of developmental defect, including mental retardation.

Prior to this work, the nature of the sex chromosome complex (XX female or XY male) could only be detected at the cellular level by direct examination of chromosomes in dividing cells. Until very recently, the technics for examining chromosomes in man were so unreliable as to lead to only scanty and often erroneous results. The relatively simple and reliable method of establishing whether or not sex chromatin was present in cell nuclei offered a much needed investigative and diagnostic procedure for patients with developmental anomalies of the reproductive system. The sex chromatin test, combined with recently developed methods for direct chromosome analysis, are the basic technics of human cytogenetics.

After establishing that sexual dimorphism of resting nuclei was a mammalian characteristic, Barr and his colleagues developed tests that could be used in the study of patients with defects of the reproductive system. Sections prepared from a small skin biopsy specimen were used in the first instance. This was subsequently replaced by the simple procedure of examining cells obtained by rubbing the lining of the mouth. The buccal smear test is now a standard diagnostic procedure and is used extensively in surveys of newborns, mental retardates, and other populations. The skin biopsy and buccal smear tests have proved useful in differential diagnosis of the several kinds of hermaphroditism, which as a group are characterized by an intersexual anatomy of the external genitalia. The tests have also pointed to an abnormality of the sex chromosome complex in certain diseases that include sterility. For example, the tests were negative for sex chromatin in females with Turner's syndrome and positive for sex chromatin in males with Klinefelter's syndrome.

The examination of human chromosomes became possible with improvements in cell culture methods and other technical advances. J. H. Tjio and A. Levan were able to show (1954) that the correct chromosome number for man was 46, rather than 48 as had been believed for many years. Errors of the sex chromosome complex were then shown to exist in Turner's syndrome (C. E. Ford and colleagues, 1959) and in Klinefelter's syndrome (P. A. Jacobs and J. A. Strong, 1959).

The studies of S. Ohno (1959) and others showed that, whether the sex chromosome complex is normal or abnormal, only one X chromosome is attenuated and genetically active in the resting cell. Such other X chromosomes as may be present are strongly condensed, genetically inactive, and visible as sex chromatin. The number of sex chromatin masses is therefore one less than the number of X chromosomes. This reliable rule has made the simple buccal smear test invaluable in selecting patients who are very likely to have an error of the sex chromosome complex and who merit a full chromosome analysis. Studies of this kind have revealed several sex chromosome anomalies. In females, the XO (X-nothing) error leads to Turner's syndrome, in which shortness of stature and sterility are the main features. Other females have an excess of X chromosomes (3, 4, or 5). They seldom have important physical defects, but there is a high risk of mental retardation. In addition to numerical errors in the sex chromosome complex, structural defects of the X chromosome have been demonstrated. The sex chromatin is smaller than usual when part of an X chromosome has been lost, and larger than usual when an X chromosome is excessively long. Various intersexual sex chromosome complexes have been demonstrated in males with pathological testes, sterility, and a 25 per cent risk of mental retardation, commonly known as the Klinefelter syndrome. The complex is usually XXY; in other males with the syndrome it may be XXYY, XXXY, or even XXXXY.

A farmer's son of Ulster extraction, Barr attended the University of Western Ontario, where he received the B.A. (1930), M.D. (1933), and M.Sc. (1938). Aside from an interruption during World War II, when he served as a medical officer (wing commander) with the R.C.A.F., Barr spent almost his entire career at the University of Western Ontario, where he became head of the department of anatomy in the Health Sciences Center. Barr received numerous awards in recognition of his research, including the Flavelle Medal of the Royal Society of Canada in 1959, an award by the Joseph P. Kennedy, Jr., Foundation in 1962, and the Gairdner Foundation Award of Merit in 1963.

For background information *see* CHROMOSOME; MENTAL DEFICIENCY in the McGraw-Hill Encyclopedia of Science and Technology.   □

BARTELS, Julius

German geophysicist
Born Aug. 17, 1899, Magdeburg, Germany
Died Mar. 6, 1964, Göttingen, Germany

EARLY IN his career Bartels recognized that adequate description and interpretation of the causes of temporal variations in geophysical phenomena required the application of sound statistical analysis. He was the first to discern clearly that statistical tests of significance for apparently systematic variations would be seriously modified unless procedures were devised to take account of the autocorrection present in the deviations from average variations in most geophysical variables. Thus he developed rigorous statistical procedures especially suited to the needs of geophysics. Not only did he describe these techniques in publications for the use of other investigators, he also applied them fruitfully to many problems in geomagnetism and aeronomy.

His investigations led to a clear discrimination between the geomagnetic variations arising from wave and particle radiation from the Sun. He developed measures for the solar-wave radiation, based on the diurnal variations of the horizontal component of the geomagnetic field at the Equator; these have the highest correlations yet found between any geophysical variable and sunspots. He also derived indices for the effects of solar-particle radiation on geomagnetic variations. One of them provided, from geomagnetic data, a sensitive measure for the influx of solar particles into the auroral region. The widely used planetary indices, K_p, were prepared through his efforts for each 3-hour interval since 1932.

Bartels applied his statistical methods to provide a sound description and understanding of the periodic effects of the Moon's gravitational influence on atmospheric tides and the conse-

quent influence on geomagnetic and ionospheric variations. His techniques provided the means of clearly discriminating among random, periodic, and quasi-periodic variations that had often been confused previously. These variations he used to investigate the 27-day variations in geomagnetic activity associated with the solar period of rotation. He found that the phases of the waves from consecutive groups of several 27-day intervals were unrelated, which indicated the decay of particle radiation from one group of sunspots and the subsequent emission from another active group of sunspots appearing elsewhere on the Sun. These waves were designated as quasi-persistent.

Bartels even found 27-day variations in magnetic activity for some intervals with no visible spots on the Sun. From this effect he postulated the existence of active M regions capable of emitting particle radiation. The M regions were later shown by astronomers at Mt. Wilson Observatory to be the same regions where sunspots subsequently developed. From a sequence of 10,000 daily values of geomagnetic activity, he showed that there was not a single 27-day interval having all its days either magnetically quiet or magnetically disturbed. This demonstrated that the solar surface was never everywhere active or everywhere quiet.

Bartels received his Ph.D. from the University of Göttingen in 1923. For the next four years he worked with the famous geomagnetician Adolph Schmidt, at the same time lecturing in geophysics at the University of Berlin. From 1927 to 1941 he was professor of meteorology and physics and head of the Meteorological Institute at the Forstliche Hochschule in Eberswalde, and from 1941 to 1945 professor of geophysics at the University of Berlin. In 1945 he became professor of geophysics and director of the Geophysical Institute at Göttingen. He was also, from 1956, director of the Max Planck Institute for Aeronomy at Lindau. In 1964 he was awarded the Bowie Medal of the American Geophysical Union.

Bartels wrote *Geomagnetism*, with Sydney Chapman (2 vols., 1940).

For background information *see* GEOMAGNETISM in the McGraw-Hill Encyclopedia of Science and Technology.   □

★ BARTLETT, Paul Doughty

American chemist
Born Aug. 14, 1907, Ann Arbor, Mich., U.S.A.

OF THE stages in which organic chemistry developed, the early 19th century saw the development of the art of isolating and analyzing pure organic compounds; in the latter part

of the 19th century molecular structures and arrangements in space were deduced. By the 1930s it was possible to establish electronic fine structures and the molecular mechanisms involved in chemical change. Throughout his career Bartlett sought the principles and particulars of many kinds of mechanisms involved in the reactions of organic compounds. For his achievements in this field he received the American Chemical Society's Roger Adams Award and Willard Gibbs Medal, both in 1963.

As a first result of general applicability Bartlett showed experimentally, with D. S. Tarbell in 1936, that halogenation of the double bond is a two-step process. In the same period he showed that the kinetics of the Wagner-Meerwein rearrangement was consistent only with catalyzed ionization as the rate-controlling step. He was the first to show (in 1939 with L. H. Knox) the value, for the study of reaction mechanisms, of the unreactive "bridgehead halides" (Formula I), which can neither react with the usual umbrellalike inversion nor yield normal

Formula I

Formula II

coplanar carbonium ions like that of tertiary butyl (Formula II). Triptycene was first synthesized as part of this program (M. J. Ryan and S. G. Cohen). With R. Wistar he proved

that, contrary to the textbooks of the time, diazonium ions (which are electron seeking) and not diazohydroxides are the species responsible for coupling to azo dyes, acting on the electron-rich amines or phenoxide ions.

With A. Schneider he synthesized tri-tertiary-butyl carbinol, the most crowded simple molecule yet made at the time, and began a long-term study of the peculiar properties of highly branched molecules, including "steric acceleration" of the ionization process.

In 1943 Bartlett's group at Harvard University began to publish on polymerization. The fate of initiating fragments in polystyrene was traced (S. G. Cohen) for the first time, the peculiar kinetics of the polymerization of allyl esters was accounted for (R. Altschul), induced decomposition of benzoyl peroxide was provided with its now accepted explanation (K. Nozaki), some absolute rate constants in the rapid polymerization of vinyl acetate were accurately measured (C. G. Swain and H. Kwart), and the nature of the action of some one-, two-, and three-stage polymerization inhibitors was worked out (H. Kwart, G. S. Hammond, and D. Trifan). Bartlett's interest in free radicals continued in later studies of the general process of concerted decomposition of peresters and azo compounds into three fragments and of the thermal generation of free radicals by styrene alone (R. R. Hiatt) or with molecular iodine (D. Trifan and A. Factor). Some useful new initiators of chain reactions resulted from the perester studies.

In 1944 Bartlett, F. E. Condon, and A. Schneider discovered the extremely rapid interconversion between carbonium ions and branched paraffins by hydride transfer and showed that this reaction was the missing link in understanding the industrial reaction of paraffin alkylation as an ionic sequence. In 1956 Bartlett and J. D. McCollum showed that the long-lived triphenylcarbonium ion will capture hydride ions from secondary alcohols, as ketones were known to do from alkoxide ions.

Research for the National Defense Research Committee during World War II led to recognition of the roles of the sulfur and nitrogen atoms of "mustard-gaslike" compounds as neighboring groups in displacement reactions in the sense elucidated by S. Winstein for halogen atoms (C. G. Swain and S. D. Ross). In an excursion outside the realm of mechanism, Bartlett's group made 725 compounds for testing as tropical-insect repellents during this period.

Interest in bicyclic compounds led to an explanation of the endo-exo rearrangement in dicyclopentadiene derivatives (A. Schneider) and to the first long-lived carbonium ion demonstrably intermediate in molecular rearrangements by direct physical methods of observation (E. R. Webster, C. E. Dills, and H. G. Richey, Jr.).

Bartlett and his coworkers were the first to treat the interconversion of the molecular forms of elemental sulfur as a problem in reaction mechanisms of ring compounds (G. Meguerian, E. F. Cox, and R. E. Davis). They showed that the less stable S_6 undergoes polymerization by traces of sulfide or sulfite ions to linear polysulfur, which in turn depolymerizes to the stable rings of S_8 (Formula III) (G. Lohaus, C. Weis, and R. E. Davis).

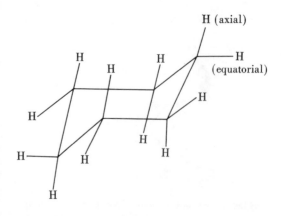

Formula III

In recent years much interest has centered upon those cases in which a carbon-carbon double bond can directly displace a negative ion on carbon, usually with ring closure and often by way of a bridged cation. Bartlett's group undertook a systematic study of these reactions and found evidence that π bonding is involved.

With L. K. Montgomery in 1964 an unusually specific demonstration was provided of the two-step mechanism of cycloaddition of fluorinated ethylenes to dienes by way of biradicals; this work led in turn to a broader comparative study of the mechanisms of different kinds of cycloaddition.

Bartlett attended the Indianapolis public schools and Amherst College. He received his Ph.D. from Harvard in 1931. He was a National Research fellow at the Rockefeller Institute in 1931–32 and instructor at the University of Minnesota in 1932–34 before joining the Harvard faculty. In 1948 he became Erving Professor of Chemistry at Harvard. He was elected to the National Academy of Sciences in 1947.

Besides some 150 papers in the chemical journals, Bartlett wrote *Nonclassical Ions* (1965).

For background information *see* ORGANIC CHEMISTRY in the McGraw-Hill Encyclopedia of Science and Technology.   □

☆ BARTON, Derek Harold Richard

British chemist
Born Sept. 8, 1918, Gravesend, Kent, England

NOTING THE difference in the rates of reaction of steroid and triterpenoid isomers in which the functional group was placed in similar environments, Barton in 1949 conceived the explanation that different spatial orientations of these functional groups were involved. This explanation was proved to be correct and led to the opening of the field in organic chemistry known as conformational analysis. For pioneering this work he received the first Roger Adams Award of the American Chemical Society in 1959 and the Davy Medal of the Royal Society of London in 1961.

By 1947 O. Hassel in Norway had demonstrated

Fig. 1. Structure of the chair-shaped cyclohexane molecule.

Fig. 2. The reaction of two free radical quinones to form "Pummerer's ketone." A is the structure originally proposed, and B is the structure found by Barton.

by electron diffraction studies that cyclohexane (Fig. 1) and its derivatives exist mainly as chair-shaped molecules. The attached hydrogen atoms, or functional groups, can adopt either an equatorial position pointing away from the center or a shielded position parallel to the axis of the ring. Barton realized that in complex systems where the conformation was fixed, the reactivity of a group would depend on whether it was attached in an axial or equatorial position.

To confirm his ideas Barton made extensive studies in the steroid and terpene fields. He found important correlations between chemical reactivity and preferred conformation, thus enabling much stereochemical information to be interpreted rationally.

By 1956 Barton had extended his studies to a wide variety of natural products, including some phenolic materials. At this time he made a further important observation. The structure of "Pummerer's ketone" had been proposed as (A) in Fig. 2. This was disputed on mechanistic grounds, the coupling of radicals from the p-cresol precursor being expected, instead, to give the pattern (B) in Fig. 2. The latter proved to be correct. Barton quickly realized the biosynthetic importance of such oxidative coupling of phenols. On surveying naturally occurring compounds, he concluded that the structures of many phenols and alkaloids could be explained and predicted. He employed two methods of verification to test his hypothesis. In the first, the synthesis of natural products, such as usnic acid and galanthamine from simple precursors, was accomplished in the laboratory. In the second, plants were fed with the postulated intermediates that were radioactively labeled. The theory is of particular value in understanding the biosynthesis of many complex alkaloids.

An interest in radical reactions having been aroused, Barton turned his attention, concurrently with the study of oxidative coupling, to the development of new radical reactions, initially with the object of preparing oxy radicals. Possible photochemical routes were studied. During some related work he noticed that systems containing dienones were rapidly isomerized. He then made a detailed study on

various natural products containing the dienone moiety in which the complex transformations undergone by santonin during photolysis were unraveled.

On conformational grounds, Barton predicted that if a hydrogen atom in the same molecule was spatially oriented in the vicinity of the generated oxy radical, abstraction of that hydrogen atom intramolecularly would be preferred. This prediction was substantiated and culminated in 1959 in the synthesis, by a simple route, of the naturally occurring hormone aldosterone. The work was carried out at the Research Institute for Medicine and Chemistry, Cambridge, Mass.

Besides the discoveries mentioned above, Barton made important contributions to the pyrolysis of organic chlorides (1945–52) and the development and applications of carbanion autoxidations (after 1960), both processes being important industrially. He also determined the constitutions and stereochemistry of many complicated natural products, especially in the terpenoid field, and carried out pioneering work on the relationship of molecular rotation to structure in complex organic molecules.

Barton received his B.Sc. at Imperial College, London, in 1940 and his Ph.D. there in 1942. After a few years in government and industrial research, he returned to Imperial College in 1945, first as an assistant lecturer and then as an I.C.I. Research Fellow (1946–49). For the year 1949–50 he was a visiting lecturer at Harvard University, during which time the concept of conformational analysis was born. Returning to England, he obtained the position of reader at Birkbeck College, London, being elected to a chair in chemistry in 1953. In 1955 he was appointed Regius Professor of Chemistry at Glasgow University. In 1957 he returned to his alma mater as professor of organic chemistry. He gained his D.Sc. (London) in 1949 and was elected to the Fellowship of the Royal Society in 1954. After 1949 Barton had close connections with American chemistry and spent a portion of each year in the United States.

For background information *see* Conformational analysis in the McGraw-Hill Encyclopedia of Science and Technology.   □

BASOV, Nicolai Gennediyevich
Russian physicist
Born 1922

WHILE STUDYING the interactions between in-cident electromagnetic waves and matter, Basov conceived of a method for amplifying the original waves by having atoms or molecules release identical waves, in phase, at a multiplying rate. This method led to the invention by C. H. Townes of the maser, a device for microwave amplification by the stimulated emission of radiation. Subsequently, amplification of visible radiation, the laser, was achieved. The new field known as quantum electronics—electronics with quantum mechanics having a key role—quickly grew out of these achievements. For his fundamental studies in this area, Basov received the 1964 Nobel Prize in physics, which he shared with his coworker A. M. Prochorov and with C. H. Townes of the United States.

In 1917 Einstein conducted a thermodynamic study of the nature of the interaction between electromagnetic radiation and atoms or molecules. Previously, similar analyses had indicated that amplification could never be produced by such interactions without violating the second law of thermodynamics. This law states that a process in which the entropy, the degree of disorder, of an isolated system decreases could not occur. However, Einstein followed thermodynamic reasoning further and derived a relationship governing the rate of change of electromagnetic radiation confined in a region where it interacts with a group of molecules. The first two terms of his equation represented the known processes of absorption and spontaneous energy release. Einstein discovered that the third and last term represented an unknown type of emission from an upper energy state produced by the mere presence of the radiation intensity. This was called stimulated emission.

For equilibrium at any positive temperature, T, Boltzman's law

$$N_B = N_A e^{-\frac{(E_B - E_A)}{kT}}$$

relates the probabilities, N_A and N_B, of electrons in the quantum states A and B. Here $E_B - E_A$ is the energy difference between the states under consideration, and the state B is a higher energy state than A; k is Boltzman's constant; and T is the absolute temperature. This law requires $N_B < N_A$ at any positive absolute temperature. Einstein's discovery showed that if $N_B > N_A$, the rate of change of radiation in the system would always be positive. Thus the incident radiation would become amplified. The condition $N_B > N_A$ was termed population inversion and became known as a condition of negative temperature, since in Boltzman's law it may be obtained by assuming a negative absolute temperature.

Basov reasoned that population inversion was a practical means for amplification of electromagnetic radiation. He realized that, in order to make an assembly of molecules or atoms amplify, the equilibrium of the electrons within the energy levels must be disturbed. The probability of finding electrons in higher energy levels must be greater than that of finding them in the lower levels. He further reasoned that the crucial requirement was to produce positive feedback of the incoming waves to force the electrons to the higher level by some type of resonant circuit. It was also necessary to insure that the gain in energy by the stimulated transition from the higher to the lower level was greater than the circuit losses. If these conditions were satisfied, Basov indicated, then a mass of a certain type could be assembled that would be sensitive to incoming waves. Electrons within the mass would be excited into a higher energy level, producing a population inversion, or the so-called condition of negative temperature. The electrons would simultaneously fall back into the original levels, releasing waves identical to those that first entered.

A successful device was first produced in 1954 at Columbia University by C. H. Townes, who found a way to assemble ammonia molecules in a resonant chamber, such that when a radio wave at 24,000 megacycles, in the radar or microwave region, encountered the chamber, additional waves of that frequency were produced by the ammonia molecules. This produced a cascade effect in the chamber, resulting in an enormous amplification of the original wave and a confirmation of Basov's predictions. In July, 1960, T. H. Maiman announced the construction of a device employing the maser principle for light waves. It consisted of a long crystal of synthetic ruby enclosed in a spiral flashtube of xenon. Flashes of light from the xenon excited the electrons in the crystal and produced a population inversion. When these electrons dropped back to their ground state they emitted a form of visible radiation never seen before. The light wavelengths, all of the same frequency, were precisely in step—a condition known as temporal and spatial coherency. The extraordinary properties of coherent light were quickly put to a wide variety of tasks, including delicate surgical operations where burning is needed, measurements, and precise signaling. In practice the maser and laser stimulated emission may be obtained from the lowest radio frequencies to the ultraviolet region.

Basov joined the Lebedev Institute, Moscow, in 1948, as a laboratory assistant. This was two years before he was graduated from the Moscow Engineering and Physics Institute. In 1958 he became deputy director of the Lebedev Institute. He became a member of the Communist Party in 1951 and received the Lenin Prize in 1959 for the work described above. The degree of Doctor of Physical-mathematical Sciences, more advanced than the American Ph.D., was earned in 1957. He was elected a corresponding member of the Soviet Academy of Sciences in 1962, one step lower than academician.

For background information *see* ELECTROMAGNETIC RADIATION; MASER in the McGraw-Hill Encyclopedia of Science and Technology.   □

central nervous system. Systematic studies of various species of rodents demonstrated a clearcut sexual dimorphism with respect to the involvement of the cerebral cortex and hormones from the sex glands. The mating activities of females appeared to be relatively independent of higher nervous centers and fairly directly controlled by ovarian secretions, whereas analogous behavior in males was powerfully influenced by the cortex and to a limited degree independent of testicular hormone.

Extension of these investigations to include more highly evolved species of mammals resulted in formulation of a working hypothesis describing the possible course of evolutionary changes in the physiological mechanisms controlling sexual life. Beach theorized that in the course of evolution of higher mammals (culminating in the Primates, including man) there occurred a progressive increase in the extent to which mechanisms within the neocortex shaped and directed sexual activities, and a concomitant decrease in the importance of ovarian and testicular chemical products.

This hypothesis helped to explain a number of differences between the characteristics of sexual behavior as it was manifested at different levels in the mammalian scale. For example, the fact that individual learning and experience seem to make a much more pronounced contribution to the sexual psychology of Primates than

★ BEACH, Frank Ambrose

American psychobiologist
Born Apr. 13, 1911, Emporia, Kans., U.S.A.

As a graduate student in experimental psychology, Beach was profoundly influenced by Karl S. Lashley and was led to concentrate in the area of physiological psychology. His doctoral research concerned brain function and instinctive behavior in mammals. Contemporary theory held that learning depended upon the cerebral cortex, whereas instinctive (unlearned) behavior was mediated by lower brain centers. Beach's initial experiments showed that the innately organized pattern of maternal behavior in primiparous rats was disorganized following removal of large amounts of the neocortex. Courtship and mating in males of the same species were reduced or abolished by this type of brain injury. Apparently, those parts of the central nervous system already known to mediate learning were also involved in unlearned behavior patterns.

Investigations of brain mechanisms and sexual behavior led Beach next to questions concerning the role of gonadal hormones—their involvement in mating activities and their relationship to the

to that of rodents and carnivores was tentatively related to the proportionately greater dependence of Primates upon cortical mechanisms. This same evolutionary shift in balance accounted for the apparent reduction in the degree to which Primate sexual expression depends upon gonadal hormones.

Continuation of the experimental program involved studies of more and more vertebrate species in an attempt to elucidate the importance of three major groups of factors affecting sexual activity. These were the central nervous system, the endocrine system, and the individual's previous experience and learning. Beach aimed to develop a broadly comparative theory that would take into account species' differences as reflections of past evolutionary change, and at the same time illuminate general laws or principles applicable to the vertebrate class.

Beach majored in education at Kansas State Teachers College at Emporia, where he received his B.S. in 1933 and his M.S. in psychology in 1934. He took his Ph.D. in psychology at the University of Chicago in 1940. From 1936 to 1942 he was assistant curator in the department of experimental biology at the American Museum of Natural History, New York, then, from 1942 to 1946, curator and chairman of the department of animal behavior. He was professor (1946–52) and Sterling Professor (1952–58) of psychology at Yale University. In 1958 he became professor of psychology at the University of California at Berkeley. Beach received the Warren Medal of the Society of Experimental Psychologists in 1951 and the Distinguished Scientific Contribution Award of the American Psychological Association in 1958. He was elected to the National Academy of Sciences in 1949.

For background information see PSYCHOLOGY, PHYSIOLOGICAL AND EXPERIMENTAL in the McGraw-Hill Encyclopedia of Science and Technology.   □

☆ BEADLE, George Wells

American geneticist
Born Oct. 22, 1903, Wahoo, Nebr., U.S.A.

WORKING WITH the biochemist E. L. Tatum, Beadle demonstrated that in hereditary transmission a single gene was responsible for the development of a single enzyme and that the smallest details of the species' biochemical reactions were governed by particular genes. By putting modern genetics on a chemical basis, he was in part responsible for the development of the new field of biochemical genetics. For their work in proving that genes affect heredity by controlling cell chemistry, Beadle and Tatum were jointly awarded the 1958 Nobel Prize in medicine or physiology. Joshua Lederberg, a former student of Tatum's, shared this Nobel Prize for his related work on the genetic mechanism of bacteria.

Long before the experiments in which Beadle participated, it was known that hereditary characters are transmitted from parents to offspring by means of special elements in the ovum and spermatozoon, called genes. The resulting organism receives from each parent certain characteristics that are determined by this genetic

material. The cells that together constitute the organism will each contain a full set of gene characteristics of the species.

The characteristics transmitted from generation to generation by the genes represent a bewildering multiplicity of variation in function and structure. Until the efforts of Beadle and Tatum, who demonstrated the possibility of chemical analysis of such structures, it was impossible to trace straightforward lines that could serve as a background for an experimental study.

In the early 1900s Thomas Hunt Morgan studied mutant characters in *Drosophila melanogaster* and confirmed the theory of linkage in genetics—the tendency for genes close together on a chromosome to be transmitted together. Later, Calvin B. Bridges supported this linkage theory by demonstrating that the aberrant behavior of sex-linked genes in *Drosophila* is paralleled by the same aberrant behavior of the chromosomes that determine sex.

Up to this time, researchers had been concerned mostly with the mechanisms by which genes and chromosomes are transmitted. Sir Archibald Garrod, however, was one of the earliest to investigate the nature of the genes. He studied congenital diseases, which he called "inborn errors of metabolism," and in particular the disease of alkaptonuria, characterized by the excretion of homogentisic acid in urine, which

makes the urine turn dark on exposure to air. Garrod theorized that this heritable disorder was the result of the lack of a "ferment" (now called enzyme) which catalyzes the normal action and that the lack is caused by a defect in a single recessive gene. In 1923 he wrote: "We may further conceive that the splitting of the benzene ring of homogentisic acid in normal metabolism is the work of a special enzyme, that in congenital alkaptonuria this enzyme is wanting." Although Garrod's theory made little impression on scientists at the time, it was the unrecognized beginning of biochemical genetics.

Beadle, working with the biologist Boris Ephrussi in 1935, advanced a hypothesis like that of Garrod, namely, that genes concerned with eye-pigment formation in *Drosophila* were in immediate control of chemical reactions via specific enzymes. These investigations led directly to Beadle's subsequent research with Tatum.

At that time there were approximately 26 separate eye-color genes known in *Drosophila*. Making a series of transplants of mutant eyes into wild-type hosts, Beadle tried to discover the influence of "diffusible substances," in the host, on transplanted eyes. Specifically, would cinnabar eyes (a bright red eye color like vermilion but differentiated by a second chromosome recessive gene) and vermilion eyes when transplanted into wild-type larvae become wild-type or maintain their initial characters? The result was that the transplanted eyes were wild-type. In a similar experiment these researchers discovered that the vermilion mutant gene blocks one reaction and the cinnabar mutant gene interrupts a second. A vermilion eye in a cinnabar host makes pigment because it can, in its own tissues, convert the vermilion substance into cinnabar substance and pigment. In it, the second type of reaction is not blocked. This scheme involves the following concepts: (1) a sequence of two gene-regulated chemical reactions, one gene identified with each; (2) the accumulation of intermediates prior to blocked reactions; and (3) the ability of the mutant blocked in the first reaction to make use of an intermediate accumulated as a result of a genetic interruption of the second reaction. Beadle, in his Nobel Prize acceptance speech, stated: "What was later called the one-gene–one-enzyme concept was clearly in our minds at this time, although, as I remember, we did not so designate it."

The traditional tools of the geneticists had been corn and fruit flies. However, seeking a simple organism for his work with Tatum, Beadle remembered a lecture he had heard by B. O. Dodge on the red bread mold, *Neurospora crassa*. This simple organism has many advantages for the scientist over either corn or *Drosophila*. It has a shorter generation time and produces many more progeny. It is grown easily in a culture medium containing sugar, salts, and the vitamin biotin. For their experiments, it was decided to produce mutations using x-rays, since Beadle believed that the best way to study the mystery of the chromosomes was to find some mutation that affected the chemical behavior of an organism. By producing a large number of such mutations and by means of an analysis of the material, Beadle and Tatum succeeded in demonstrating that the body substances are synthesized in the individual cell step by step in long chains of chemical reactions, and that

genes control these processes by individually regulating definite steps in the chains.

Neurospora mates and reproduces sexually and can also grow asexually; thus, large quantities can be produced from a single spore. Asexual spores were irradiated, crossed with a strain of the opposite mating type, and the spores thus formed by sexual reproduction were laid out on a sheet of agar jelly containing the minimum nutrients. From this batch some sprouted and grew normally, showing no effect of the x-rays; some had received too much radiation and were dead; and a few sprouted but failed to grow. In an attempt to determine what was lacking in this latter batch, 1,000 spore cultures were fed special diets containing vitamins, amino acids, and other growth-stimulating chemicals.

The 299th culture showed that the addition of vitamin B_6, pyridoxine, was sufficient to restore the ailing strain to proper growth. When that strain was mated with the parental strain, the defect was transmitted to the next nonirradiated generation in the expected mendelian manner: four mutant and four nonmutant spores in each spore sac, proving the involvement of a single mutated gene. Beadle and Tatum pointed out that radiation had damaged a specific gene that had been responsible for producing an enzyme essential for the production of vitamin B_6 out of the simple nutrients. Later trials with other affected genes produced strains requiring other dietary supplements for proper growth. Beadle compared this need on the part of *Neurospora* to the diabetic's need for insulin when it is not manufactured by the body.

Following their initial success, Beadle and Tatum continued their studies and traced the defects they had created in the *Neurospora* to interference with intermediate metabolism in the formation of amino acids and vitamins. Their work was credited with solving some of the basic riddles of heredity and opening new vistas in cancer research. Their methods were utilized during World War II in the manufacture of penicillin, also a mold product, resulting in a fourfold increase in production at a critical period. Beadle's work has also had great value in recent years as scientists have sought to control genetic diseases by chemical treatment. For example phenylketonuria (PKU), a heritable nervous ailment that results in feeble-mindedness, is caused by inability to convert phenylalanine into the amino acid tyrosine. When detected soon after birth, PKU can be controlled by reducing the amount of phenylalanine in the diet.

Beadle received his B.Sc. and M.Sc. at the College of Agriculture of the University of Nebraska in 1926 and his Ph.D. in genetics at Cornell University in 1931. He was a National Research Council fellow and then instructor at the California Institute of Technology from 1931 to 1935. After a year in Paris he was an assistant professor of genetics at Harvard (1936–37), professor of biology at Stanford (1937–46), and professor of biology and chairman of the Division of Biology at the California Institute of Technology (1946–61). In 1961 he became president of the University of Chicago. He was elected to the National Academy of Sciences in 1944.

Beadle wrote *An Introduction to Genetics*, with A. H. Sturtevant (1939), and *Genetics and Modern Biology* (1963).

For background information *see* GENETICS in the McGraw-Hill Encyclopedia of Science and Technology. □

☆ **BÉKÉSY, Georg von**

American physicist
Born June 3, 1889, Budapest, Hungary

WHILE PERFORMING research in physiological acoustics, Békésy determined the physical events that occur in all strategically important points within the transmission system of the ear. His discoveries resulted in the development of refined diagnostic procedures and treatments for diseases of the ear. In recognition of his achievements in the study of the hearing processes, particularly for his discoveries concerning the mechanics of the inner ear, Békésy was awarded the 1961 Nobel Prize for physiology or medicine, the first physicist to receive this honor.

The first study of the hearing processes was made by the German physicist and physiologist Hermann Ludwig Ferdinand von Helmholtz, who in 1857 proposed the resonance theory of hearing. According to this theory, the transverse fibers of the basilar membrane in the cochlea of the inner ear acted as tuned resonators. Each of these fibers was tuned to a particular frequency, and when a sound of a given frequency reached the ear it caused a particular fiber to vibrate. Subsequent theories of hearing differed

in the manner in which the basilar membrane vibrated when a sound wave struck the eardrum. One variation relied on the generation of standing waves and another on traveling waves. A third variation, called the telephone theory, was proposed by the English physiologist William Rutherford in 1886. This theory assumed that the entire cochlear partition moved as a whole.

In 1923, while working at the Research Laboratory of the Hungarian Telephone System, Békésy began his researches in physiological acoustics. His initial studies concerned themselves with the eardrum. He was subsequently led to the intuitive conclusion that the basilar membrane would exhibit traveling waves when one section of it was put into motion by an alternating pressure. Focusing his attention on the elasticity and friction of the basilar membrane, for the next two decades he measured and mapped vibration amplitudes and phases for sinusoidal forces applied to the stapes footplate and determined the physical constants responsible for the vibration patterns. When he had completed these observations and made measurements of such variables of elasticity as the volume elasticity of the cochlear partition, he constructed a mechanical model of the cochlea. The model, whose vibratory behavior was identical to that of the cochlear partition, was made of a rubber membrane stretched over a metal frame. By varying the thickness of the membrane, and thus its volume elasticity, and pressing a pointed object into it, Békésy found he could produce deformation patterns that corresponded to those predicted by the four theories proposed for the vibration of the basilar membrane. He then realized that he could decide which of the theories represented the function of the inner ear by further measurements of the volume elasticity of the cochlear partition. These measurements confirmed that vibrations of the eardrum transmitted to the fluid of the cochlea set up traveling waves in the basilar membrane.

Békésy then proceeded to build an enlarged model of the cochlea. This consisted of a water-filled plastic tube and a membrane 30 centimeters long. This device, which exhibited traveling waves of the same type as those seen in the human ear, had a usable frequency range of two octaves. After some experimentation with this apparatus, Békésy decided to add a nerve supply. The use of a frog skin for this purpose had earlier proved to be impractical. However, he found that by placing his forearm against the model he could sense the vibrations as they traveled along the membrane. He discovered in this way that although the waves traveled the length of the 30-centimeter membrane with almost unchanged amplitude, his arm sensed the vibration in only a 2- to 3-centimeter-long section of the membrane. He further found that when the frequency of the stimulus was increased, the section of sensed vibration moved toward the end of the model that represented the stapes footplate, while the section moved in the opposite direction when the frequency was decreased. Hence, he realized, the cochlea acts as a neuromechanical frequency analyzer.

In addition to his theoretical studies of the hearing processes. Békésy also developed a new type of audiometer. Announced in 1946, the patient-operated instrument has applications other than the testing of the hearing function. For example, it can be used to detect the change in the light sensitivity of the eye during adaptation to darkness.

The son of a diplomat, Békésy studied chemistry at the University of Berne in Switzerland. He then attended the University of Budapest in Hungary, receiving his Ph.D. in physics in 1923. In that year he joined the Research Laboratory of the Hungarian Telephone System, which was operated by the post office.. He remained there until 1946. During that period he spent 1 year, during 1926 and 1927, at the Central Laboratory of the Siemens and Halske A. G. in Berlin, Germany. He was a professor of experimental physics at the University of Budapest from 1939 to 1946. In the latter year he went to Sweden, where he became associated with the Karolinska Institute in Stockholm. Although he emigrated to the United States in 1947, Békésy continued his association with the Institute until 1952. He became a research assistant at the Psychoacoustic Laboratory of Harvard University in 1947, and in 1949 he was appointed senior research fellow in psychophysics there. He was elected to the National Academy of Sciences in 1956.

Békésy wrote *Experiments in Hearing* (English translation, 1960).

For background information *see* EAR; HEARING in the McGraw-Hill Encyclopedia of Science and Technology.   □

★ BENEDICT, Manson

American engineer
Born Oct. 9, 1907, Lake Linden, Mich., U.S.A.

BENEDICT'S PRINCIPAL contributions were to the design of industrial plants for the continuous processing of materials.

His first major assignment was given him by the M. W. Kellogg Co., which engaged him to devise a reliable method for predicting the behavior of hydrocarbons in high-pressure distillation.

Use of distillation to separate individual hydrocarbons from mixtures is important in processing natural gas and in producing feed stocks for petroleum refining processes making high-octane gasoline. Originally, distillation was carried out at pressures close to atmospheric, at which the distribution of each hydrocarbon between liquid and vapor was relatively independent of the amount of other hydrocarbons present. In the late 1930s it became clear that substantial cost savings could be realized by carrying out distillation at pressures of 50 atmospheres or more, because smaller equipment could be used and the costs of compressing separated hydrocarbons for subsequent operations would be reduced. At these high pressures the distribution of each hydrocarbon between liquid and vapor becomes strongly dependent on the nature and amount of other hydrocarbons present. To represent the thermodynamic properties of gases and liquids under these extreme conditions, Benedict developed the first equation of state that was capable of representing accurately the properties of mixtures of hydrocarbons in the vapor state, in the liquid state, and in the critical transition region between them. This equation is now used extensively to predict the distribution of hydrocarbons between vapor and liquid in high-pressure distillation processes.

During World War II it was necessary to extract from refinery streams large amounts of butadiene to make synthetic rubber and toluene for explosives. The M. W. Kellogg Co. proposed to use modified distillation processes, termed extractive or azeotropic distillation, to separate butadiene or toluene. In these distillation processes a nonhydrocarbon solvent such as acetone, methanol, or phenol is added to the mixture to increase the difference in volatility between the desired hydrocarbon and its unwanted and normally hard-to-separate companions. Benedict's second major assignment was to work out the

principles of extractive and azeotropic distillation and to obtain experimental data to implement the design of these processes. For the scientific papers describing this work Benedict and

L. C. Rubin received the William H. Walker Award of the American Institute of Chemical Engineers.

In late 1941 the U.S. government requested P. C. Keith of the M. W. Kellogg Co. to undertake the large-scale engineering development of the gaseous-diffusion process to separate uranium-235 from natural uranium for use in the atomic bomb. Benedict was assigned to this project because of previous work he had done on the related, but dissimilar, mass-diffusion process for separation of hydrogen from refinery gases. In the gaseous-diffusion process, uranium hexafluoride (a gaseous compound of uranium) is pumped through a porous diffusion barrier containing holes whose diameters are smaller than the mean free path of the gas molecules. Under these conditions, the gas passing through the barrier is slightly enriched in the lighter uranium isotope. By recompressing the gas after passage through the barrier and repeating the process thousands of times, the uranium hexafluoride should, in principle, be enriched to any degree desired in U^{235}.

In practice, the gaseous-diffusion process presented many difficulties. For every pound of U^{235} produced, 50,000,000 pounds or more of uranium hexafluoride had to be recirculated and recompressed. A novel, fine-grained diffusion barrier was required, with holes of a controlled size a few millionths of an inch in diameter, made of a material that would not react with uranium hexafluoride or be plugged by its corrosion products. The entire plant, containing hundreds of miles of piping, had to be so vacuum-tight that practically none of the uranium hexafluoride would be lost. Benedict worked out the overall characteristics of the plant, specified the properties the barrier should have to make the process feasible, and determined the optimum size and number of stages for a plant of minimum cost.

As this diffusion plant appeared to be a practical way of separating U^{235}, the U.S. government authorized construction of a plant at Oak Ridge, Tenn. The M. W. Kellogg Co. formed a subsidiary, the Kellex Corporation, to engineer this process, and Benedict was placed in charge of the group of engineers who completed development of the process and worked out the detailed process design of this complex plant. A diffusion barrier with the requisite properties was developed by groups at Columbia under Hugh Taylor and at Kellex under Clarence Johnson. The K-25 Gaseous Diffusion Plant started partial operation early in 1945 and separated some of the uranium used in the first atomic bomb. Completed late in 1945, the K-25 plant surpassed in its performance the prediction of its designers. For his contributions to this and other isotope separation projects Benedict received the Industrial and Engineer-

ing Chemistry Award of the American Chemical Society in 1963.

By 1951 it was apparent that additional production capacity for fissionable material would be required to maintain U.S. superiority in nuclear armament, and that this would involve expenditures of billions of dollars. The Atomic Energy Commission requested Benedict to set up an Operations Analysis Staff to determine the cost of producing U^{235} and plutonium in existing plants and to plan the new facilities needed for increased production. This group, under Benedict, specified the optimum combination of new gaseous-diffusion plants and new plutonium production reactors that should be built to produce the maximum number of nuclear weapons for a given number of dollars. The capacity of the gaseous-diffusion plants at Paducah and Portsmouth and the number of the newest plutonium reactors at Hanford and Savannah River were determined in this way. With decreasing need for additional nuclear weapons, these gaseous-diffusion plants became available to produce enriched fuel for nuclear power stations.

Benedict majored in chemistry at Cornell University and the Massachusetts Institute of Technology, receiving a Ph.D. from the latter school in 1935. He did experimental research in high-pressure thermodynamics at Harvard until 1937. He was with the M. W. Kellogg Co. and Kellex Corp. from 1938 to 1946. From 1946 to 1951 he was director of process development for Hydrocarbon Research, Inc. He was in charge of operations analysis for the AEC in 1951. In 1951 he became professor of nuclear engineering at the Massachusetts Institute of Technology and in 1958 head of the nuclear engineering department. He was appointed to the General Advisory Committee of the AEC by President Eisenhower in 1958, and was its chairman from 1962 to 1964. He was elected to the National Academy of Sciences in 1956.

Benedict was coauthor of *Nuclear Chemical Engineering* (1957).

For background information *see* URANIUM in the McGraw-Hill Encyclopedia of Science and Technology.   □

☆ **BENIOFF, Hugo**
American geophysicist
Born Sept. 14, 1899, Los Angeles, Calif., U.S.A.

FOR HIS contributions to the study of earthquakes, and particularly to instrumental seismology, Benioff received the Arthur L. Day Medal of the Geological Society of America in 1957 and the William Bowie Medal of the American Geophysical Union in 1965.

Benioff developed a family of seismological

instruments of novel mechanical and electronic design. In the 1930s he built a variable reluctance seismograph that, with minor modifications, was selected for use in the world-wide standard seismograph network. It formed the basis of the detection system recommended by the Geneva Conference of Experts for the detection of nuclear tests. It has made possible the precise determination of travel-time curves, the extension of the magnitude scale to teleseismic events, and the world-wide availability of first motion data to recover source mechanism. Benioff's strain seismograph, also developed in the 1930s, can monitor propagating mantle surface waves, free oscillations of the Earth, and secular strain variations. His recently developed version of the mercury tiltmeter will probably be the basis for long-period horizontal seismographs in the next decade. Besides seismographs, Benioff developed sensitive microbarographs, magneto-variagraphs, electronic pianos and string instruments, underwater sound transducers, oscillographs, and galvanometers.

In the area of geophysical theory, Benioff was the first to suggest that the response spectrum was the important parameter to consider in antiseismic design. He demonstrated that the geographic distribution of aftershocks was related to the dimension of the primary fault. He proposed that the distribution of epicenters could be used as evidence for the fault origin of oceanic deeps. His method of using the magnitude-energy relationship to deduce the seismic release of strain has been widely adopted. Using this procedure, he was able to show that rate earthquakes reveal a global pattern of strain accumulation and release. He also showed that the strain rebound characteristics derived from sequences of earthquakes could be used to separate the crust and upper mantle into zones having different mechanical properties. With these data and the geographical and depth distribution of earthquake foci, Benioff was able to

characterize tectonic activity of continental margins and deep-sea trenches in a novel, yet mechanically significant, way.

Intrigued by the source mechanism of earthquakes, Benioff tried to deduce source dimensions from strain-energy considerations. He applied laboratory results on the form of creep strain to explain the source of aftershock energy. He showed how the direction of fault progression should lead to an asymmetrical radiation pattern of seismic waves. He proposed that, although shallow earthquakes can be explained satisfactorily by the elastic rebound theory, certain deep earthquakes appear to involve volume collapse.

Long mantle waves were first analyzed and properly interpreted on records provided by Benioff. It is the standing wave interference pattern of these world-circling waves that gives rise to the free oscillations of the Earth. Benioff's suggestion that instrumental developments made it feasible to detect free oscillations stimulated theorists at the Weizmann Institute to find methods of predicting the periods of free oscillations for real Earth models. Experimental teams at the California Institute of Technology, Columbia University, and the University of California at Los Angeles subsequently found oscillations in one of the most elegant experiments in geophysics.

Benioff was educated at Pomona College (B.A., 1921) and the California Institute of Technology (Ph.D., 1935). He worked as an assistant at the Mt. Wilson Observatory summers from 1917 to 1921, then served as assistant physicist with the Seismological Laboratory of the Carnegie Institution of Washington in Pasadena from 1924 to 1937. In 1937 he joined the faculty at the California Institute of Technology, where he was professor of seismology from 1950 to 1964. He was elected to the National Academy of Sciences in 1953.

For background information *see* SEISMOGRAPH; SEISMOLOGY in the McGraw-Hill Encyclopedia of Science and Technology. ☐

★ BERS, Lipman

American mathematician
Born May 22, 1914, Riga, Latvia

M OST OF Bers's mathematical work concerned the interrelations between two fields of mathematical analysis—complex function theory and elliptic partial differential equations.

The simplest elliptic equation is the classical Laplace equation

$$u_{xx} + u_{yy} = 0$$

Its theory is identical with the theory of analytic functions of a complex variable

$$z = x + \sqrt{-1}\,y$$

that is, of functions representable by power series $\sum_0^\infty a_n(z - z_0)^n$. The theory of a general linear second order partial differential equation in the plane can be reduced to the study of so-called pseudoanalytic functions. The theory of these functions (developed by Bers and, along somewhat different lines, by I. N. Vekua) parallels many essential features of classical function theory.

A typical result reads as follows: For every equation of the type considered, there exist two sequences of particular solutions $\varphi_0, \varphi_2, \ldots$, $\psi_0, \psi_1, \ldots$, analogous to the real and imaginary parts of z^n, such that every solution $\Phi(x, y)$ defined near $z = 0$ may be written as a series $\sum_0^\infty (\alpha_n \varphi_n + \beta_n \psi_n)$ which is both convergent and asymptotic. The latter statement means that the difference between Φ and the sum of the first N terms of the series is of the order $|z|^{N+1}$. Similar particular solutions exist for any other point z_0; they are linear combinations of the functions φ_j, ψ_j.

Pseudoanalytic functions are also used in studying nonlinear elliptic equations, in particular the equation describing the two-dimensional flow of a gas at subsonic speeds. These applications provided the original motivation for the theory. In studying the equation of a gas flow and similar nonlinear equations, one also uses another, much older, generalization of analytic functions—quasiconformal mappings. These are solutions of a certain elliptic equation (Beltrami's equation), which may be described as the Laplace equation on a curved surface.

Recently, quasiconformal mappings have been applied to classical function theory. This approach was pioneered by O. Teichmüller and developed by L. V. Ahlfors, Bers, and others. Here is an example of such an application:

An algebraic curve is the set of pairs of complex numbers (z,w) satisfying an irreducible polynomial equation $P(z,w) = 0$. To every algebraic curve there belongs a nonnegative integer g, the genus of the curve. If $g = 0$, the curve can be represented parametrically by rational functions. For instance, the circle

$$z^2 + w^2 = 1$$

admits the parametric representation

$$z = (1 - t^2)/(1 + t^2),$$
$$w = 2t/(1 + t^2)$$

If $g = 1$, the curve can be parametrized by elliptic functions. The construction of a parametric representation by single-valued meromorphic functions for curves of any genus was one of the major achievements of 19th-century mathematics. Using quasiconformal mappings, Bers proved that it is possible to uniformize simultaneously all algebraic curves of genus $g > 1$. More precisely, there exist, for every fixed $g > 1$, $5g - 5$ analytic functions $\varphi_1(s_1, \ldots, s_{3g-3}, t), \ldots, \varphi_{5g-5}(s_1, \ldots, s_{3g-3}, t)$ of $3g - 2$ complex variables with the following properties: If C is an algebraic curve of genus g, then there exist $3g - 3$ numbers $s_1, \ldots, s_{3g-3}$ and two rational functions p_1, p_2 of $5g - 5$ variables such that

$$z = p_1\,[\varphi_1\,(s_1, \ldots, s_{3g-3}, t), \ldots, \varphi_{5g-5} \\ (s_1, \ldots, s_{3g-3}, t)\,]$$
$$w = p_2\,[\varphi_1\,(s_1, \ldots, s_{3g-3}, t), \ldots, \varphi_{5g-5} \\ (s_1, \ldots, s_{3g-3}, t)\,]$$

is a parametric representation of C. Here $s_1, \ldots, s_{3g-3}$ are fixed and t varies over a certain domain. Conversely, if $s_1, \ldots, s_{5g-5}$ are chosen arbitrarily within a certain domain, and p_1, p_2 are any two rational functions, the above formulas define an alegbraic curve of genus at most g. This result belongs to the theory of moduli, a field which is now under active investigation by many mathematicians.

Bers received his Dr. Rer. Nat. at the University of Prague, Czechoslovakia, in 1938. He went to the United States in 1940 and participated in the wartime research and training program in applied mathematics at Brown University. After teaching at Syracuse University and spending two years at the Institute for Advanced Study, he went to New York University where he taught for 14 years. In 1964 he became professor of mathematics at Columbia University and was elected to the National Academy of Sciences.

For background information *see* DIFFEREN-
TIAL EQUATION in the McGraw-Hill Encyclopedia
of Science and Technology.   □

★ **BESICOVITCH, Abram Samoilovitch**

British mathematician
Born Jan. 24, 1891, Berdiansk, Russia

BESICOVITCH STARTED work in probabilities.
In a sequence of trials, each trial results in
appearance or nonappearance of the same event,
with probabilities p_n and $q_n = (1 - p)$ at the
nth trial. Instead of the usual integral expressing the limit of the probability for the number
of appearance to be included in a large interval,
he gave an asymptotic expression for each particular value of the number.

In early work on the Riemann integrability of
functions, a plane set of segments of length
greater than 1, of all directions, of Jordan outer
plane measure zero was constructed. The existence of such a set being a fundamental point
of set theory led also to a solution of the Kakeya
problem, which attracted great interest among
mathematicians for a decade around 1920. The
problem is on the lower bound of the area of a
domain that is swept over by a segment of length
1 that turns continuously through 360°. The
answer is that the lower bound is 0.

Among problems on integrability, Besicovitch
was concerned with the existence of the integral

$$\int_0^\pi \frac{f(x + t) - f(x - t)}{t}\, dt$$

in the Cauchy Lebesgue sense, for $f(x) \, \epsilon \, L$ for
almost all x. Its existence marks a deep structural property of real functions and in particular
of linear point sets. The existence had been
proved by complicated methods, and a direct
proof by methods of sets of points was desirable.

He gave it first for functions of the class L^2 and
then generalized to the class L.

In the early days of the development of the
theory of almost periodic functions created by
H. Bohr, Besicovitch worked on various generalizations of almost periodicity and on their extent. He showed that none of the generalizations
was wide enough for the Riesc-Fisher theorem
to hold, a theorem without which no natural correspondence between almost periodic functions
and the general trigonometric series existed. By
introducing B^p almost periodic functions ($p \geqslant$
1) this gap was filled up. Later, in a joint paper
with H. Bohr, the study of almost periodicity in
terms of "functional spaces" was carried out.
The basic space A is one of trigonometric polynomials in $-\infty < x < +\infty$. Various distances
between points of the space (functions) are
introduced:

$$D_u\{f, g\} = u.b|f(x) - g(x)|$$
$$D_{S^p}\{f, g\} = u.b\{|\textstyle\int_x^{x+1}|f(t) - g(t)|^p dt\}^{\frac{1}{p}}$$
$$D_{B^p}\{f, g\} = \overline{M}\{|f(x) - g(x)|^p\}^{\frac{1}{p}}$$

Convergence in the sense of each distance is defined naturally and the closure of A in the sense
of each of the distances is defined as the set of
all limit points of A in the sense of each distance. The main results are that for various distances the corresponding closures represent
various classes of almost periodicity, introduced
before, and there is a general result that for
each class an approximating sequence can be
given by Fejer-Bochner polynomials.

For almost periodic functions of a complex
variable Besicovitch gave conditions for the
Parseval theorem to hold beyond the strip of
boundedness of the function. He also carried out
a study under which the Parseval theorem holds
for functions representable by a convergent
Dirichlet series. Other work on complex variables included a study of conditions for a function to be analytic, their behavior in the neighborhood of nonisolated singularities, and conditions for the existence of mean values of analytic
functions in a strip. For integral functions of
order < 1, he gave densities of r for which
Littlewood-Wiman inequalities hold.

The problem on the forms of equilibrium of
a uniform fluid mass had previously been reduced to the existence of the maximum of the
Newton potential. The existence of the absolute
maximum had been known, and Besicovitch
proved that a relative maximum does not exist.

In the general theory of functions of a real
variable Besicovitch's work on differentiation included the first construction of a continuous
function that does not admit either a two-sided
derivative or a one-sided one at any point, which

thus completed the Weierstrass problem. He also solved a number of general problems on differentiation of functions of one or more variables and also differentiation of additive functions and in particular of integrals, with the development of appropriate general covering principles.

Study of general point sets on the background of the measure formed a considerable part of Besicovitch's work on real variables. Two general classes of sets, regular sets and irregular ones, are defined. The two classes are totally distinct. The regular ones have at almost all points the density equal to 1. Also at almost all points they have a tangent, and they differ from a finite set of rectifiable arcs only by a subset of arbitrarily small measure. The irregular sets have no tangent, the lower density is different from the upper one and is $\leq 3/4$ (a strong conjecture is that it is $\leq 1/2$), and the projection on almost all directions is 0. The result obtained is that the most general set consists of a regular component and an irregular one, which really completes the subject.

Similarly Besicovitch studied linearly measurable sets of lines. A fundamental result is that the plane measure of a regular set is always infinite and of an irregular one is 0. The importance of this result is seen if one remembers difficulties connected with the construction of the set wanted for the Kakeya problem, a very particular case of an irregular set. For simple curves of h-dimensional measure, he established the distribution of one-sided densities along the curve.

Besicovitch's study of surfaces started with the definition of area. The dominant definition of the area of a skew surface (Lebesgue-Frechet definition) was shown by him to be inadequate (a finite area having a positive three-dimensional measure, the existence of a solid, which is a topological sphere, with volume as large as desired and area of surface as small as desired). The problems solved with this definition had to be redone, and defining the area as the Hausdorff two-dimensional measure, he proved the existence of the minimum area subtending a given contour.

In the theory of numbers Besicovitch studied some sequences of integers. He proved that the sequence of squares is normal and also that under some restrictions the theorem known by the name of the "$\alpha + \beta$ theorem" was true.

Besicovitch received his first degree from the University of St. Petersburg in 1912. He taught at the universities of Perm and St. Petersburg from 1914 until 1925, when he emigrated from Russia. In England he taught at the University of Liverpool. From 1927 to 1950 he was Cayley Lecturer in Mathematics at Cambridge University; from 1950 until his retirement in 1958

he was Rouse Ball Professor of Mathematics there. He was awarded the Royal Society's Sylvester Medal in 1952.

Besicovitch wrote *Almost Periodic Functions* (1932).

For background information *see* DIFFERENTIATION; INTEGRATION; PARTIAL DIFFERENTIATION; PROBABILITY in the McGraw-Hill Encyclopedia of Science and Technology.   □

★ BEST, Charles Herbert

Canadian physiologist and medical researcher
Born Feb. 27, 1899, West Pembroke, Maine, U.S.A.

AT 22, Best joined F. G. Banting in a partnership that soon resulted in the discovery of insulin. It has been estimated that between 20 and 30 million diabetics would not be alive today had it not been for their discovery. Besides its clinical importance, insulin has proved to be one of the greatest tools ever provided for medical investigators. It has opened doors in many branches of the biological sciences.

Both Banting and Best were interested in diabetes for personal reasons. Before receiving his B.A. in 1921 at the University of Toronto, Best had already decided to take his M.A. and extend the work on sugars that had engaged his attention as a fellow in physiology during his final undergraduate year. About the same time, Banting, while practicing medicine in London, Ontario, had formulated a hypothesis that was vital to the initiation of the work. He approached J. J. R. Macleod, head of the department of physiology at the University of Toronto, to obtain permission to explore his idea at his alma mater. Macleod, extremely skeptical, felt Banting needed to work with someone trained in essential physiological and biochemical methods if any advance in knowledge was to be achieved. Knowing that Best had such training, Macleod finally gave permission for them to work in his department during the summer while he was abroad and the rest of the staff were on holiday. There was no question of remuneration.

The two enthusiasts began their collaboration on May 17, 1921. During the hot summer months they worked day and night in the deserted department. They first prepared a neutral or faintly acid extract of the degenerated pancreas glands of laboratory dogs. This was accomplished by ligation of the pancreatic ducts for 10 weeks, when the degenerated glands were removed and extracted with ice-cold Ringer's solution. The extract, kept at a low temperature, was then injected intravenously or subcutaneously into the moribund depancreatized dogs. The invariable result was marked reduction of the percentage of sugar in the blood and of the amount of sugar excreted in the urine. Banting and Best found that rectal injections were not effective; that the extent and duration of the reduction of sugar varied directly with the amount of extract injected; that pancreatic juice destroyed the active principle of the extract; that the reducing action was not a dilution phenomenon, since (1) hemoglobin estimations before and after administration of the extract were identical, (2) injections of large quantities of saline did not affect blood sugar, and (3) similar quantities of extracts of other tissues did not cause reduction of blood sugar; that extract made by 0.1% acid was effectual in lowering the blood sugar; that the presence of extract enabled a diabetic animal to retain a much greater percentage of injected sugar than it would otherwise; and that extract prepared in neutral saline and kept in cold storage retained its potency for at least 7 days. Boiled extract had no effect on the reduction of blood sugar.

On Nov. 14, 1921, Banting and Best presented their findings for the first time before the members of the medical faculty at a meeting of the University of Toronto Physiological Society. Later they presented their findings to the Academy of Medicine of Toronto. The first insulin was administered to a diabetic patient in the Toronto General Hospital on Jan. 11, 1922, and during the next 6 weeks seven patients were treated and observed. The observations furnished material for the initial clinical publication, which appeared in the Canadian Medical Association Journal in March 1922, and which verified that the findings in diabetic dogs were completely confirmed in human diabetics.

In addition to achieving many important advances in the study of insulin and diabetes, Best introduced the first anticoagulant for the prevention of thrombosis; discovered a new enzyme, histaminase, which destroys histamine; found a new vitamin, choline, which prevents damage to the liver; initiated in 1939 the Canadian Serum Project to provide human serum for military use during World War II; and, as director of the Royal Canadian Navy's Medical Research Division, collaborated with colleagues in making many practical contributions to the war effort.

A doctor's son, Best entered the University of Toronto in 1916. He soon enlisted in the field artillery, returning to the university at the end of World War I. He received his B.A. in 1921, M.A. in 1922, M.B. in 1925, and M.D. in 1932. He was with Connaught Laboratories as director of the insulin division from 1922 to 1925, assistant director of the laboratories from 1925 to 1931, associate director from 1931 to 1941, and honorary consultant after 1941. When the Ontario legislature established the Banting and Best Department of Medical Research at the University of Toronto, Best served there as research associate from 1923 to 1941 and as director following Banting's death in 1941. He was also assistant professor of physiological hygiene in the University of Toronto from 1926 to 1928; in 1929 he became professor of physiology and head of the department. The recipient of numerous honorary degrees and scientific prizes, he was elected a foreign associate of the U.S. National Academy of Sciences in 1950.

With Norman B. Taylor, Best wrote three physiology texts: *The Physiological Basis of Medical Practice* (7th ed. 1961); *The Human Body* (4th ed. 1963); and *The Living Body* (4th ed. 1958). *The Selected Papers of Charles H. Best* was published by the University of Toronto Press in 1963.

For background information *see* INSULIN in the McGraw-Hill Encyclopedia of Science and Technology.   □

★ BETHE, Hans Albrecht

American physicist
Born July 2, 1906, Strasbourg, France (then Germany)

BETHE'S BEST-KNOWN achievement was his theory of energy production in the stars. Published in 1938, this propounded a theoretical description of deuteron fusion and the carbon cycle as mechanisms to explain how the rate of energy production in the interior of the Sun is sufficient to offset energy losses from its surface. While he was mainly known for this theory, he was almost unique among contemporary physicists for the breadth of his contributions to physics, which ranged from the fundamental particles of nuclear physics to ballistic missiles. Among many honors, he received the Draper Medal of the National Academy of Sciences in

1947 and the Eddington Medal of the Royal Astronomical Society in 1963, both for his work on the stars; the U.S. Medal of Merit in 1946 for his work on the atomic bomb; and the Enrico Fermi Award of the U.S. Atomic Energy Commission in 1961 for his general work in nuclear physics and atomic energy.

His principal work was in nuclear physics. In 1935–37, he and two collaborators wrote a comprehensive treatise on this subject, which was then in its infancy. This work remained the standard text for young nuclear physicists for at least 15 years. In it, Bethe clarified the theory of nuclear forces, the structure of nuclei, and the theory of nuclear reactions. During World War II he applied this knowledge as leader of the Theoretical Division of the Los Alamos Scientific Laboratory, which designed the first atomic bomb. After the war he continued to work on nuclear weapons and on the application of nuclear energy for the peaceful production of power. On the more fundamental side, he explored the particles that are responsible for nuclear forces. In recent years he was mainly interested in the connection between the nuclear forces and the structure of actual nuclei.

Bethe worked extensively on the collision of charged particles with atoms. He developed the quantum theory of this process, which he used to predict the distance a fast particle can penetrate through matter. This is important for the design of experiments in nuclear physics and of shields to protect persons from harmful nuclear radiations. He also calculated the radiation emitted from fast electrons.

Unlike most physicists who work on nuclear or atomic problems, Bethe was also interested in classical physics. During the war he worked on the theory of shock waves, and this work was very useful to him in his work on the atom bomb and later on the effects of atomic weapons. He also made contributions to the design of the heat shield for ballistic missiles when they reenter the atmosphere.

When Bethe developed his theory of energy production in the stars in 1938, A. S. Eddington and others had made extensive contributions to an understanding of the probable physical conditions in the interiors of stars. From a knowledge of the mass, radius, and luminosity (amount of energy emitted per second) of a star, detailed information about temperature variations and pressure gradients, as well as a good deal of information about its internal physics, was formulated. Because of the enormous temperature postulated for the Sun's interior, it was considered likely that nuclear energy must be the source that sustained solar radiation. Physicists were at a loss, however, to explain the system of nuclear reactions that would account for the rate of energy production by the Sun consistent with astrophysical observations.

Accepting the astronomers' calculation of $2 \times 10^{7\circ}$ C for the central temperature of the Sun, Bethe found a series of thermonuclear reactions that could proceed with sufficient intensity to support solar radiation. Because of the high temperature in the interior of the Sun, the reactant nuclei possess the high kinetic energy necessary to penetrate each other, each reaction requiring only the collision of two bodies. He carefully examined all possible nuclear reactions, both those observed in experiments performed with the cyclotron and others that were merely postulated theoretically, and divided these into two groups. In one were the reactions in which only protons were consumed, and in the other those in which other light nuclei were also consumed. Astrophysical evidence had shown that protons are enormously more abundant in stars than other nuclei. Some elements, like Li, Be, and B, are extremely rare in stars. Bethe therefore argued that reactions consuming these rare nuclei should be excluded because they could not supply the energy for billions of years as required. Only protons (and perhaps helium nuclei) are abundant enough to supply energy throughout the long life of a star, and among these only protons can penetrate sufficiently easily into other nuclei to develop energy at a sufficient rate. He found only two nuclear reactions that fulfilled all requirements: deuteron fusion and the carbon cycle. Of these, only the carbon cycle will produce energy fast enough to explain the energy production in the more brilliant stars like Sirius.

Bethe found that the nucleus C^{12} is unique. Not only does it react with protons at a sufficient rate to explain the energy production in the Sun and other stars, but also it undergoes a cycle of reactions that terminates in the final stage with the formation of a new C^{12}. The carbon nucleus thus serves as a catalytic agent that is regenerated in the cycle. In fact, the final result of the cycle is equivalent to the fusion of four protons into a nucleus of helium and the release of energy, in terms of the mass energy equivalence law, resulting in a 1 per cent difference of mass.

In the carbon cycle, the first transformation occurs when a proton enters the nucleus of a C^{12}. Under the conditions prevailing in the Sun, this happens on the average of about once in 40,000 years. The product is radioactive N^{13} and the simultaneous emission of a gamma photon. This radiation reaches the surface, Bethe reasoned, not by a straight route but by a complicated zigzag path during which it is constantly being absorbed by other atoms and reemitted in new directions and ultimately at a much lower frequency. It is this slow escape of radiation, which Bethe estimated to require 10^6 years, that maintains the high interior temperature of the Sun and that in turn maintains the thermonuclear reactions. About 10 minutes after it is formed, the N^{13} spontaneously decays with the emission of a positron and becomes the stable isotope C^{13}. Approximately 7,000 years later, the second thermonuclear reaction occurs; the carbon nucleus captures a proton and becomes stable N^{14}, which emits a gamma ray. The next stage, about a 10^6 years later, is a thermonuclear reaction with the penetration of a third proton into N^{14} to produce the isotope O^{15}; this is unstable and decays to N^{15} with the emission of a positron. The final stage, about 20 years later, is still another thermonuclear reaction, in which a fourth proton is captured by N^{15} and the product splits into two parts, He^4 and C^{12}.

Bethe's synthesis of a helium nucleus by the carbon cycle was simultaneously and independently suggested by C. F. von Weizsacker in Germany, but he did not investigate whether this process had the correct rate for the Sun and other stars. At the same time, Bethe and C. L. Critchfield accomplished the calculations for a proton-proton sequence that involved the direct building of the helium nucleus from hydrogen and that fitted the observed facts equally well. The rate at which the competitive cycles proceed is extremely sensitive to temperature, so that the selection of a mechanism depends upon the internal temperature of the star. For stars with interior temperatures greater than the Sun's, the carbon cycle appears to predominate; for cooler bodies with interior temperatures in the region of 10^7 degrees, deuteron fusion is the more important synthesis. Both cycles have the widest possible acceptance among astrophysicists for explaining the relation between solar energy and its lifetime of radiation.

The son of a university professor, Bethe studied at the University of Frankfurt and took his doctorate at the University of Munich under A. J. W. Sommerfeld in 1928. He taught theoretical physics at various German universities until 1933, and for the next 2 years at the universities of Manchester and Bristol. In 1935 he joined the faculty of Cornell University. He was elected to the National Academy of Sciences in 1944.

Bethe wrote *Elementary Nuclear Theory* (1947; 2d ed., with P. Morrison, 1956), *Quantum Mechanics of One- and Two-electron Atoms*, with E. E. Salpeter (1957), *Splitting of Terms in Crystals* (1958), and *Intermediate Quantum Mechanics* (1964).

For background information *see* CARBON-NITROGEN CYCLE; SOLAR ENERGY in the McGraw-Hill Encyclopedia of Science and Technology. □

★ **BIGELEISEN, Jacob**
American chemist
Born May 2, 1919, Paterson, N.J., U.S.A.

BIGELEISEN FOUNDED the modern school of isotope chemistry. His researches, both experimental and theoretical, established the fundamental bases for the differences in the chemical behavior of isotopes. As a result, scientists have been able to predict and develop new processes for the separation of isotopes. For this work he received the U.S. Atomic Energy Commission's E. O. Lawrence Award in 1964. The utilization of the differences in chemical behavior of isotopes has opened up new areas in chemical physics, geochemistry, molecular biology, and chemical kinetics. For his work on isotope effects in chemical kinetics, Bigeleisen received the American Chemical Society's Award for Nuclear Application in Chemistry in 1958.

Isotopes were discovered early in the 20th century by the study of natural radioactive decay of heavy elements. For a long time it was assumed that isotopes were truly indistinguishable chemically. A major change came when Harold Urey discovered deuterium, and large differences were found between the chemical properties of protium and deuterium. Small but definite differences were found for the heavy elements.

Early in World War II Bigeleisen became associated with Urey on problems connected with isotope separation. Late in 1943 he began to ponder two questions: (1) How large could the differences in chemical properties of the isotopes of a given element be? (2) How did these isotope effects depend on the chemical properties and structure of a molecule? Early in 1944 he and Maria Goeppert Mayer found a very simple solution to this question for gases at equilibrium. They found that it was possible to explain all the differences in chemical properties of isotopes in gases at equilibrium by considering the vibrations of atoms in a molecule. According to Heisenberg's uncertainty principle, it is impossible to specify simultaneously the exact position and velocity of a particle. This makes it impossible to confine an atom to a precise position in a molecule. As a result of this motion, an atom in a molecule possesses vibrational energy even at absolute zero. Since the vibrational energy is proportional to the frequency of motion, and since light atoms oscillate with higher frequencies than heavy atoms, it is easier to dissociate a molecule containing a light isotope than a heavy isotope of an element. From this principle, the heavy isotope of an element favors the chemical species in which it is most strongly bound chemically. The differences in chemical properties of isotopes of an element, from one compound to another, are a direct measure of the change in chemical bonding of this element from compound to compound. The answer to Bigeleisen's question—how large can these isotopic differences be—was established on a quantitative scale. At the bottom of the scale, with no difference, was the free atom; at the top were those chemical compounds for which the bonding is strongest. For instance, for isotopes of hydrogen, the largest effects were found in water, and no effects occurred in hydrogen atoms. Generally, the differences decreased with temperature. This is the basis of the oxygen isotope paleothermometer.

The ability of an isotope to measure changes in chemical bonding makes it a valuable tool for the study of molecular forces, the changes in molecular forces as molecules react, and the study of interactions of various types of bonding with one another. With this approach Bigeleisen was able to develop the theory of how isotopes differ in their rates of chemical reaction. From measured differences in rates of isotopic reactions it is now possible for scientists to learn about the paths that molecules follow when they react and to learn about the associated energy changes. Such investigations by the isotopic and other methods are now at the forefront of chemical research.

Later Bigeleisen extended the theory of isotopic behavior to the liquid and solid states. Guided by the theory he had developed for isotopic behavior in liquids, he investigated experimentally the question of how the properties of a liquid depend on the mass distribution in a molecule. At Los Alamos, in 1955, Bigeleisen and E. C. Kerr showed that HT behaved differently from an isotopic molecule with the same total mass, D_2. Subsequent experiments at Brookhaven demonstrated differences between two types of nitrous oxide with N^{15}; in another investigation, the various deuterated ethylenes were studied. The investigation of the effect of molecular mass distribution on the properties of a liquid revealed that the motion of a molecule is different in a liquid or solid from that in a gas, where the translation and rotation of the molecule are independent of one another. Both are independent of the vibrations of the atoms within the molecule. In the liquid or solid, all of these motions become coupled with one another. The experiments confirmed the theory. A new field for investigation had been opened.

The son of immigrant parents, Bigeleisen majored in chemistry at New York University (B.A., 1939). After graduation he started research with Otto Redlich at the State College of Washington (M.S., 1941). He went on to work with Gilbert N. Lewis, the dean of American physical chemists, at the University of California, Berkeley (Ph.D., 1943). During World War II he worked on isotope separation for the Manhattan District at Columbia University. After the war he was a fellow at the Enrico Fermi Institute, University of Chicago. In 1948 he joined the newly formed Brookhaven National Laboratory.

For background information *see* ISOTOPE in the McGraw-Hill Encyclopedia of Science and Technology.   ☐

★ BJERKNES, Jacob Aall Bonnevie

American meteorologist
Born Nov. 2, 1897, Stockholm, Sweden

WHILE WORKING in the storm-warning service in Bergen, Norway, in 1918, Bjerknes noticed that new, growing cyclones (centers of low pressure) frequently originated from a wave on a preexisting atmospheric front over the Atlantic, the nascent cyclone center being formed at the apex of a warm tongue of air intruding into cold air territory. From this initial

finding the typical life cycle of cyclones was formulated and used in weather forecasting in all middle- and high-latitude locations.

The concept of atmospheric fronts was known before 1918, particularly as the "cold front" forming the forward edge of invading cold air. But the frontal wave with a "warm front" ahead of the apex and a "cold front" following it became a new feature on well-analyzed weather maps. As a consequence, young cyclones analyzed to have frontal-wave structure and great contrast in temperature between the air masses on either side of the front could be predicted to intensify; as a corollary, less intensification and eventual loss of kinetic energy could be expected in older cyclones within which the wave shape had been replaced by a vortex structure with cold core.

Intensification of cyclones is due to formation of new kinetic energy or advective concentration of existing kinetic energy into the volume occupied by the cyclone, or both. The latter process could not be investigated until recently, when systematic upper-air observations became available, but the former process was, in 1918, assumed by Bjerknes to convert potential energy into kinetic in the young wave cyclones at a rate sufficient to explain their early growth. J. Holmboe and others later confirmed this qualitative theory through a treatment of hydrodynamical models that simulated atmospheric fronts on the rotating Earth. Such models actually fostered unstable, growing waves whose wavelengths were of the order 1,000 to 3,000 km observed in the atmosphere.

The theoretical picture of the mechanism of growing cyclones was largely developed through the study of weather maps at the bottom of the atmosphere before the three-dimensional picture of the same phenomena could be analyzed with data from networks of radiosonde balloons. Once the daily mapping of the upper

troposphere and the lower stratosphere started during World War II, waves aloft were seen to be coupled with the moving frontal waves below, but also longer waves were discovered that move very slowly or even remain stationary for long periods. Important theoretical innovations followed this break-through in observation technique. Bjerknes's contribution, made in collaboration with Holmboe, was to define the concept of the "level of nondivergence." That level is located roughly at the altitude where atmospheric pressure is half that at the ground. At that level, the absolute vorticity of air parcels is quasi-conservative, and the field of that quantity can be predicted approximately from initial conditions by advective methods. From that idea John von Neumann and C.-G. A. Rossby developed the scheme of day-by-day prediction by electronic computers of the flow at the level of nondivergence that has become the basis of modern weather forecasting.

Bjerknes thereafter confined his research to the phenomena that could not be very well handled by electronic computers, such as the isentropic up and down gliding of the air next to atmospheric fronts, the effect of sharp anticyclonic curvature of upper-air currents leading to deepening of the downwind trough, and so forth, all of which belong in the thinking of the forecaster who is to translate the electronic output into real weather predictions. Increasingly he turned his attention also to the processes of large-scale ocean-atmosphere interaction, which are important for their influence on the long trends of weather changes.

Grandson of mathematics professor C. A. Bjerknes (1825–1903) and son of physics professor V. F. K. Bjerknes (1862–1951), Jacob Bjerknes received his university training in Oslo, Norway, leading to a Ph.D. in 1924. The father's work, in hydrodynamics applied to the atmosphere, inspired the son to seek a meteorological career. He entered the weather forecasting service in Bergen, Norway, in 1918, and became professor of meteorology in Bergen in 1931. He served upon invitation 1 year at the Swiss, and twice for half a year at the British meteorological offices. Unable to return to Norway after a lecture trip in the United States in 1940, he was appointed to the first professorship in meteorology at the University of California at Los Angeles. He became a U.S. citizen in 1946. Elected to the National Academy of Sciences in 1947, Bjerknes was awarded the Bowie Medal of the American Geophysical Union in 1945 and the Rossby Medal of the American Meteorological Society in 1960.

For background information *see* CYCLONE; METEOROLOGY in the McGraw-Hill Encyclopedia of Science and Technology. □

★ BLACK, Harold Stephen

American electrical engineer
Born Apr. 14, 1898, Leominster, Mass., U.S.A.

BLACK WAS 29 when he invented the negative feedback amplifier, which some consider the Bell Telephone Laboratories' greatest electronic contribution during its first 35 momentous years. In 1958 Mervin J. Kelly, then president of Bell Telephone Laboratories, wrote, "Although many of Black's inventions have made great impact, that of the negative feedback amplifier is indeed the most outstanding. It easily ranks coordinate with De Forest's invention of the audion as one of the two inventions of broadest scope and significance in electronics and communications of the past 50 years." For this achievement and for his successful development of the negative feedback principle, Black received many honors, including the 1952 Research Corporation Award.

Early in his career Black was assigned the task of reducing amplifier distortion so that a large number of multichannel amplifiers could be hooked up in tandem to carry telephone calls over longer distances. The job required an amplifier vastly superior to any then existing. Many other researchers before Black were aware of this need. Their only approach, however, and indeed Black's first approach, was to try to improve the tube characteristic. Electron tube research groups vigorously pursued this course in an attempt to provide an adequately linear input-output characteristic, but all to no avail.

In the course of his work, Black attended a talk by Charles P. Steinmetz and came away impressed with the Steinmetz method of getting down to fundamentals. He applied the same method to his own problem and came up with a restatement of his goal: to remove distortion from the amplifier output. Before that he had attempted to obtain amplification without distortion by specifying unrealistically superior vacuum tubes and other amplifier parts. He now turned to an acceptance of imperfect amplifier parts; regarded the output as composed of what was wanted plus what was not wanted; looked upon anything not wanted as distortion; and asked himself how to isolate and then annihilate this distortion.

He immediately observed that by reducing the output to the same amplitude as the input and subtracting one from the other he would be left with distortion only, which could then be amplified in a separate tube and used to cancel out distortion in the original amplifier output. This feedback-feedforward system was set up in 1923 to demonstrate that unwanted output distortion could be either reduced or suppressed. While this demonstration circuit did not use negative feedback, it did prove that a complete and better solution was theoretically possible.

For more than three years Black struggled with his problem, using approaches too complex for satisfactory application. He was searching for an innovation that would simplify the circuit and perfect its operation. Finally, a mathematical analysis convinced him that, merely by utilizing negative feedback to insert a part of the output signal into the input in negative phase, he could obtain virtually any desired reduction in distortion products at the expense of a sacrifice in amplification.

This final mathematical analysis was conceived in a flash as he was crossing the Hudson River on the Lackawanna ferryboat en route from home to the Laboratories. He wrote the equations that led to the solution on the back of his newspaper. Despite immediate recognition of its importance and prompt experimental verification, years of additional work were required before his application of negative feedback found widespread commercial use.

The application of Black's principle of negative feedback was not limited to telecommunications. Many industrial and military applications of amplifiers would not be possible without its use. Many new weapon systems, such as radar-directed bombing and radar-controlled missiles, depend on negative feedback for their success. The entire field of industrial control mechanisms and the development of servomechanisms theory and its applications are extensions of Black's principle of feedback and are generally recognized as such. In psychology and physiology this principle also sheds light on the nature of the mechanisms that control the operations of animals, including humans—that is, on how the brain and senses operate.

Upon completion of his training in electrical engineering at Worcester Polytechnic Institute, Black, in 1921, joined the research organization of the Bell System, where he remained until

1963. In 1963 he became a principal research scientist with General Precision Inc., working as a consultant on advanced communications and guidance feedback techniques pertaining to aerospace interests.

Black wrote *Modulation Theory* (1953).

For background information *see* AMPLITUDE MODULATION; FREQUENCY MODULATION; PULSE MODULATION in the McGraw-Hill Encyclopedia of Science and Technology.   □

☆ BLACKETT, Patrick Maynard Stuart

British physicist
Born Nov. 18, 1897, London, England

AT THE suggestion of Ernest Rutherford, Blackett built an improved version of the Wilson cloud chamber. Utilizing this and subsequent instruments, he was able to photograph the tracks of a nuclear disintegration and the tracks of a cosmic-ray shower for the first time. For these achievements he was awarded the Nobel Prize in physics in 1948.

The cloud-chamber method for tracking atomic and subatomic particles was first developed by C. T. R. Wilson in 1911. Wilson was able to produce a sudden expansion in a chamber containing air saturated with water vapor. When this occurred, the air became supersaturated and the vapor condensed out on any small ionized particles in the chamber. This condensation mechanism is identical to that which gives rise to cloud formation in the atmosphere. As an ionizing particle moved through the chamber, it left a track of condensed vapor affording visible evidence of its path. Photographs taken at random were used to record the tracks. These sometimes showed branching of a particular track, which often

proved to be an indication of a nuclear collision.

Early works by Rutherford on the dynamics of single collisions of subatomic particles using scintillation methods had failed to produce quantitative results, although he believed he had changed nitrogen into oxygen by the bombardment of nitrogen with alpha particles. In fact, he could not determine what actually happened during the collision between an alpha particle and a nitrogen nucleus, although fast protons were observed being emitted. There were two distinct possibilities. One was that the alpha particle could have left the nucleus as a free particle after the collision. In this case a cloud chamber would show a forked track, the three emergent tracks being due to the alpha particle, the ejected proton, and the recoil nucleus. The other possibility was that the alpha particle might be captured. Such a process would be indicated by the observation of only two emergent tracks, those of the emitted proton and of the recoil nucleus.

In 1925 Blackett used an improved cloud chamber capable of taking a photograph every 15 seconds to study the forked tracks due to collisions of alpha particles with nitrogen atoms. The photographs of these collisions showed only two emergent particles. By applying the principles of conservation of charge and mass, Blackett deduced that, in addition to the proton, the other emergent particle must be a heavy isotope of oxygen (O_{17}^{8}). This work gave the first photographic representation and detailed knowledge of a typical nuclear transformation process.

Later, in collaboration with G. P. S. Occhialini, Blackett began to study the energetic particles found in cosmic rays. The major problem in observing tracks of these particles had been that cloud-chamber photographs were taken in a completely random fashion, and only 2 to 5 per cent of these photographs showed cosmic-ray tracks. Blackett and Occhialini devised a method by which cosmic rays could take their own picture. They placed Geiger counters both above and below a vertical cloud chamber so that any ray passing through the two counters would also pass through the chamber. A coincidence circuit, that is, one that emits a pulse only when a particle passes through both counters within a very short time interval, was used to actuate the expansion of the chamber. The expansion was made so rapid that the ions produced by a ray had not had time to diffuse much before the expansion was complete. This method of a Geiger counter–controlled chamber yielded a set of cosmic-ray tracks on 80 per cent of the photographs taken.

By the latter part of 1932, Blackett and his coworker had accumulated 700 photographs of cosmic rays. Many of these photographs showed groups of associated rays. This phenomenon of groups of associated particles was named a cosmic-ray shower. It was determined that about half the particles in a shower were positively charged, while the remaining particles were found to be negatively charged. In addition, the mass of each positive particle was approximately that of the positron, the elementary particle discovered earlier that year by C. D. Anderson. The rough equality of numbers of positive and negative particles, along with the knowledge that positrons do not occur naturally on Earth, led Blackett and Occhialini to the conclusion that the positrons and electrons were created together in collision processes initiated by high-energy cosmic rays. Still later, while working with Occhialini and James Chadwick, Blackett found that electron-positron pairs were also produced when high-energy gamma rays were absorbed by heavy atoms. The creation of an electron-positron pair, as a result of the disintegration of an energetic but massless gamma ray, was found to be in agreement with Einstein's mass-energy conversion relation.

In recent years Blackett engaged in studies of rock magnetism. His aim was to trace back to the beginning of geological time both the history of the Earth's magnetic field and the motion of the continental land masses relative to each other and to the geographical poles. For his work in paleomagnetism, as well as for his earlier studies of cosmic-ray showers and heavy mesons, he was awarded the Royal Society's Copley Medal in 1956.

From 1914 to 1919 Blackett served as an officer in the Royal Navy. After World War I he entered Magdalene College of Cambridge University, receiving his B.A. in 1921 and his M.A. in 1923. As a fellow of King's College he continued his research at the Cavendish Laboratory until 1933, when he was appointed professor of physics at Birkbeck College, University of London. From 1937 to 1953 he was Langworthy Professor of Physics at the University of Manchester. During World War II Blackett headed an operations research group engaged in radar and anti-U-boat work. In 1953 he became head of the physics department at the Imperial College of Science and Technology, London. He retired in 1963 but continued as professor of physics there. In 1965 he was elected president of the Royal Society of London.

Blackett wrote *Rayons Cosmiques* (1934), *Military and Political Consequences of Atomic Energy* (1948), *Lectures on Rock Magnetism* (1956), *Atomic Weapons and East-West Relations* (1956), and *Studies of War* (1962).

For background information *see* CLOUD CHAMBER; COSMIC RAYS; NUCLEAR REACTION; POSITRON in the McGraw-Hill Encyclopedia of Science and Technology.   ☐

BLALOCK, Alfred
American physician
Born Apr. 5, 1899, Culloden, Ga., U.S.A.
Died Sept. 15, 1964, Baltimore, Md., U.S.A.

IN 1944, Blalock, together with Helen Taussig, developed and performed an operation to relieve the circulatory distress of a "blue baby." Although this first patient died within a year, later patients survived, and the operative procedure became accepted. For his contribution to the "blue baby" operation, and to other aspects of pediatric surgery, Blalock received the 1948 Passano Foundation Award and the 1954 Lasker Award of the American Public Health Association.

Blalock's work, which eventually led to the blue baby operation, began in a quite unrelated manner: he was seeking to determine whether any relationship existed between high blood pressure and hardening of the arteries. In order to investigate this, he performed operations on dogs, diverting systemic blood vessels into their lungs in order to increase their pulmonary blood pressure. These operations were inconclusive with respect to Blalock's main investigation, but he did note that the dogs who had been operated on were in exceptionally fine health.

In 1941, Blalock was at Johns Hopkins, where he encountered Helen Taussig. The latter had seen many blue babies and had developed a theory that, due to a congenital vascular malformation, the pulmonary circulation of affected infants was unable to provide sufficient oxygenated blood to their bodies, hence the blue color. Taussig had heard of Blalock's dog operations and felt that a similar procedure might be successfully employed in blue babies.

Eventually, in 1944, Blalock and Taussig performed their first blue baby operation: the patient, a female infant, was born with a defect in the large artery supplying blood to her lungs. So little blood was able to pass to her lungs that her oxygen intake was dangerously curtailed. When Blalock operated, he severed one of the arteries carrying blood to the body from the lungs. One end of this artery he pulled around and fastened to a slit in the opposite lung artery. One of the patient's lungs was then deliberately collapsed, blood thus being forced into the opposite pulmonary artery. With this shunt from the general circulation to that of one lung, enough oxygen was gathered to supply the entire body. This first patient died nine months later, but other patients survived the procedure and went on to lead normal lives—which would otherwise have been impossible.

In addition to his development of the blue baby operation, Blalock is known for his extensive contributions to knowledge of surgical shock. He demonstrated that loss of blood was responsible for shock and instituted the use of plasma or whole-blood transfusions to compensate for the loss.

Blalock received his B.A. from the University of Georgia in 1918 and his M.D. at the Johns Hopkins University in 1922. After an internship and residency at the Johns Hopkins Hospital, he joined the faculty of the Vanderbilt University School of Medicine, becoming professor of surgery there in 1938. In 1941 he returned to Johns Hopkins as professor of surgery and director of the department of surgery at the Medical School and as surgeon-in-chief of the Johns Hopkins Hospital. He retired from these posts in 1964, shortly before his death. Blalock was elected to the National Academy of Sciences in 1945.

For background information *see* CARDIOVASCULAR SYSTEM in the McGraw-Hill Encyclopedia of Science and Technology.   □

★ BLOCH, Felix

American physicist
Born Oct. 23, 1905, Zurich, Switzerland

THROUGH THE combination of electromagnetic and nuclear phenomena, Bloch discovered a method of studying the magnetism of atomic nuclei in normal matter. It permitted measurements of very high precision and became a valuable tool for research in physics and chemistry. Independently and simultaneously the same discovery was made by E. M. Purcell, with whom Bloch shared the Nobel Prize for physics in 1952.

Bloch's interest in nuclear magnetism derived from Otto Stern's 1933 experiments on molecular beams, which showed that the magnetic moment of the proton was almost three times as large as expected and indicated that the neutron that was attached to it in the deuteron also possessed a magnetic moment. In 1936 Bloch pointed out that this property could be used to

produce polarized neutron beams by passing them through magnetized iron. The verification of this effect, and the use of a radio technique previously applied to atomic beams, led him in 1939 to the first accurate measurement of the magnetic properties of the neutron.

Following his work on radar during World War II, Bloch realized in 1945 that the use of radio techniques was not restricted to beams of particles but could be developed into a purely electromagnetic method applicable to normal substances. Under suitably chosen conditions, it proved possible to reorient the magnetic moments of the nuclei in such a way that their resultant moment underwent a precessional variation around the direction of the constant magnetic field to which they were exposed. Bloch achieved this with a radio transmitter in resonance with the precession frequency characteristic of the nucleus under investigation, so that he dealt with nuclear magnetic resonance. The novelty of his method lay in the fact that the variation of the resultant moment produced (according to Faraday's principle of electromagnetic induction) a voltage in a coil surrounding the sample. This nuclear induction was detected in a radio receiver. The signals, thus recorded, conveyed a great variety of information.

In the first place, they revealed the magnetic moment of individual nuclei as well as their angular momentum, both of which were significant for the knowledge of nuclear structure. In the second place, the frequency of the signal from a given nucleus—for example, that of hydrogen in water—depended on the external magnetic field strength and thus led to the con-

struction of reliable and very sensitive magnetometers, used in geophysical studies, among others. A third important property of the signals arose from the fact that they were often markedly influenced by the environment in which the observed nuclei were located, so that they supplied new data about the constitution of solids, liquids, and gases. In many cases, such data were established to be intimately connected with the chemical constitution of molecules and so resulted in a powerful new method of analytical chemistry. Besides several other interesting features that appeared under various circumstances, it was found that the precession frequencies observed from chemically indistinguishable isotopes—that is, from nuclei with different structure of the same element—were widely separated from each other and hence furnished a convenient indicator for isotope analysis.

Planning originally to become an engineer, Bloch entered the Swiss Federal Institute of Technology in Zurich. After 1 year, he switched to physics and, later, went to the University of Leipzig, where he received his Ph.D. in 1928 with a thesis on metallic conduction. After postdoctoral work in several European countries, he held a teaching position in Leipzig but left Germany upon Hitler's ascent to power in 1933. In the following year he joined Stanford University, later becoming Max H. Stein Professor of Physics. He became a U.S. citizen in 1939. During World War II he worked for the Manhattan District and at the Radio Research Laboratory of Harvard University. In 1954 and 1955 he served as the first director general of CERN, the European laboratory for nuclear research in Geneva. He was elected to the National Academy of Sciences in 1948.

For background information *see* NUCLEAR MOMENTS in the McGraw-Hill Encyclopedia of Science and Technology.   ☐

★ BLOCH, Konrad Emil

American biochemist
Born Jan. 21, 1912, Neisse, Germany

IN THE course of metabolic studies with isotopic tracers beginning in 1941, Bloch, in collaboration with D. Rittenberg, demonstrated that acetic acid is a major precursor of cholesterol in animal tissues. This observation permitted him to trace the numerous transformations of fat and carbohydrate metabolites to cholesterol. For this contribution he was awarded the Nobel Prize in physiology or medicine in 1964, sharing it with Feodor Lynen.

In 1932 Harold Urey of Columbia University had discovered heavy hydrogen (deuterium) and devised methods for producing the isotope in large quantities. Soon thereafter the heavy isotopes of carbon (C^{13}), nitrogen (N^{15}), and oxygen (O^{18}) also became available. R. Schoenheimer and D. Rittenberg at Columbia recognized the unique usefulness of isotopic tracers for metabolic studies and developed a methodology that laid the basis for the many achievements of modern biochemistry, including the elucidation of cholesterol biosynthesis.

Cholesterol, a waxlike substance with the elementary composition $C_{27}H_{46}O$, is found in all animal cells. It contains a fused tetracyclic (perhydrophenanthreme) ring system to which an eight-carbon aliphatic side chain is attached. After it had been shown that the two-carbon compound acetic acid contributes to the biological synthesis of cholesterol, Bloch set out to determine in what manner acetic acid molecules combine to form first medium-sized units and then the larger precursor molecules of cholesterol. Animals were given isotopic acetic acid, and the isotopic tracer was located in the various portions of the cholesterol molecules found in the tissues. From the pattern in which isotopic hydrogen and carbon were distributed in cholesterol, Bloch made the following predictions: (1) In the first stages, three molecules of acetic acid combine to form a branched five-carbon or isopentenyl intermediate. (2) Six of the isopentenyl units are linked together to form the acyclic thirty-carbon compound squalene. (3) Squalene cyclizes and undergoes various molecular rearrangements to form lanosterol, a tetracyclic substance closely related to cholesterol. Between 1946 and 1958, Bloch's laboratory, F. Lynen and his collaborators in Munich, and J. W. Cornforth and G. Popják in England provided the experimental basis for the postulated sequence: acetic acid ⟶ isopentenyl unit ⟶ squalene ⟶ lanosterol ⟶ cholesterol. The hypothetical isopentenyl unit

was identified as isopentenylpyrophosphate, and it proved to be a key intermediate in the biosynthesis not only of cholesterol but also of numerous other natural products, including the terpenes, carotenes, and rubber. According to Bloch's estimates, the overall conversion of acetic acid to cholesterol requires 30 to 35 steps. Only about half of the enzymes of the cholesterol pathway have so far been characterized.

Cholesterol is vital for the functioning of animal cells. One of its functions is to supply the chemically related bile acids, compounds that aid in fat absorption. Cholesterol is also the parent substance for the various vertebrate steroid hormones (cortisone and the sex hormones). Some of these relationships were demonstrated by Bloch in 1942 and 1945. Cholesterol also seems to serve in all animal cells in the additional and more general role of stabilizing the various membrane structures which envelop the cell plasma.

In recent years the biological origin of unsaturated fatty acids was one of Bloch's main interests. In animal tissues and in many microorganisms, long-chain fatty acids are synthesized by the repeated addition of malonyl CoA units to acetyl CoA. This process leads to the formation of the saturated compounds palmitic and stearic acids. As Bloch showed, enzyme systems from animal tissues and from yeast then introduce double bonds into the saturated acids to form the corresponding olefins (oleic and palmitoleic acids). These reactions require molecular oxygen and therefore do not occur in anaerobic organisms. The so-called essential fatty acids, that is, those containing two or more double bonds per molecule, are formed by similar oxygen-requiring reactions.

Bloch studied chemistry at the Technische Hochschule, Munich, between 1930 and 1934. After a brief stay in a Swiss research institute he emigrated to the United States in 1936 and entered Columbia University as a graduate student. He received his Ph.D. in 1938 and remained at Columbia until 1946. He then became a member of the biochemistry department of the University of Chicago and in 1954 joined Harvard University as Higgins Professor of Biochemistry. He was elected to the National Academy of Sciences in 1956.

For background information *see* CHOLESTEROL; METABOLISM in the McGraw-Hill Encyclopedia of Science and Technology.   □

★ BLOEMBERGEN, Nicolaas

American physicist
Born Mar. 11, 1920, Dordrecht, Netherlands

W HILE STUDYING the effects of magnetic resonance in crystals at low temperature, Bloembergen conceived the method of three-level and multilevel pumping to energize masers. Solid-state multilevel masers are used as extremely sensitive low-noise receivers in radio telescopes, in radar tracking stations, and in the ground-based receivers of the Telstar satellite communication system, which provides a microwave link between continents. Optical masers or lasers are also energized by multilevel pumping

and have found widespread use as highly directional, highly monochromatic, powerful sources of light. For his discovery Bloembergen was awarded the American Physical Society's Buckley Prize in 1958. He also shared with C. H. Townes the Morris Liebman Award of the Institute of Radio Engineers in 1959.

The practical importance of achieving a medium with an inverted population that could serve as an amplifier and/or oscillator for electromagnetic radiation was realized independently by C. H. Townes at Columbia University and N. G. Basov and A. M. Prochorov at the Academy of Sciences in Moscow. They separated a beam of ammonia molecules. The molecules in the upper state of a pair of energy levels, called an "inversion doublet," were focused in a microwave cavity. Stimulated emission of radiation produced a coherent microwave oscillator or atomic clock with a frequency determined by the separation of the inversion doublet. For this achievement they were awarded the 1964 Nobel Prize in physics. Townes aptly called the new device a maser, an acronym for Microwave Amplification by Stimulated Emission of Radiation.

While the beam device was useful as a frequency standard, its power level was extremely low due to the relatively small number of molecules available in a beam in high vacuum. It also lacked the characteristics of tunability and broad-band amplification desirable in a low-noise amplifier. Bloembergen looked for ways to upset the thermal population of energy levels in a solid on a continuous basis. He reasoned that if the thermal equilibrium of the spin levels of paramagnetic ions in a crystal at low temperature could be inverted, the magnetic resonance absorption could be changed into a

powerful emission. Furthermore, the magnetic resonances are rather broad and can be tuned by the application of an external magnetic field. Populations of spin levels could be changed on a continuous basis by the application of powerful pump fields. This had been demonstrated by Bloembergen in his thesis experiments on nuclear magnetic relaxation carried out in 1947 at Harvard University with E. M. Purcell and R. V. Pound. A powerful pump field at the frequency ν would tend to equalize the population of a pair of energy levels separated by hν. The absorption and stimulated emission at this frequency would be balanced.

Bloembergen then considered the case that this pair of energy levels was not adjacent, but that an intermediate level C existed between the levels whose populations had been equalized by the pump. If C has the same population as the two levels connected by the pump, nothing useful will result. If level C has a higher population, then inversion will occur between C and the lowest level. If C has a lower population, inversion occurs between the highest level and C. Therefore negative absorption or stimulated emission may generally be expected to occur at one smaller frequency or another, if sufficiently strong pumping power is applied between nonadjacent energy levels. This principle proved to be correct. In essence it is similar to that of a heat engine. The pump serves as a hot thermal reservoir; the crystal lattice serves as a cold reservoir. Just as in a thermodynamic Carnot cycle, useful energy can be extracted in the form of stimulated electromagnetic radiation. A coherent oscillator or amplifier results.

In 1956 Bloembergen published directions for the construction of a continuously operating solid-state maser. A crystal containing certain magnetic ions of the iron group and the rare-earth group of the periodic system would be placed in a microwave circuit in a helium dewar between the poles of an external magnet. The magnitude and orientation of this field would be so adjusted that the spacing between two nonadjacent levels would correspond to a pump field supplied by an external source. A weak signal at a lower frequency, such as might be received by a radiotelescope, would also be fed into the microwave cavity containing the crystal. If the stimulated emission were larger than the small eddy-current losses in the walls of the microwave circuit, a low-noise microwave amplifier would result. Bloembergen and coworkers achieved maser operation in 1957 at 21 cm wavelength, which is of interest in radio astronomy because it corresponds to the radiation from galactic and extragalactic atomic hydrogen.

In the meantime the correctness of his reasoning was proved by various other groups working at different wavelengths. Because of its importance for long-range microwave communication via artificial satellites, H. E. D. Scovil at the Bell Telephone Laboratories built in 1956 the first multilevel maser, using gadolinium ethyl sulfate, one of the salts proposed by Bloembergen. Technical improvements have subsequently been made by many people. Broad-band traveling-wave masers have been developed. Ruby, which is a crystal of Al_2O_3 (sapphire) containing chromium ions as an impurity, has proved to be an excellent maser crystal.

Bloembergen received his education at the University of Utrecht in his native country, Netherlands. He obtained the B.A. and M.A. in physics in 1941 and 1943 respectively. The German occupation forces closed the University in 1943, and Bloembergen taught himself quantum mechanics by reading H. A. Kramers's book on this subject by the light of an oil lamp when the electricity was cut off during the "hunger winter" of 1944. In 1946 he went to Harvard University, where he did research for his thesis with Purcell. He obtained a Ph.D. degree in physics in 1948 at the University of Leiden, where he was a research associate. From 1949 to 1951 he was a junior fellow in the Society of Fellows at Harvard. In 1951 he became an associate professor and, in 1957, Gordon McKay Professor of Applied Physics at Harvard University. He was elected to the National Academy of Sciences in 1960.

Bloembergen wrote *Nuclear Magnetic Relaxations* (1948; 2d ed. 1961) and *Nonlinear Optics* (1965).

For background information *see* MASER in the McGraw-Hill Encyclopedia of Science and Technology.   □

★ BOCHNER, Salomon

American mathematician
Born Aug. 20, 1899, Cracow, Poland (then Austria-Hungary)

B OCHNER'S ACHIEVEMENTS were mainly in the field of harmonic or Fourier analysis, that is, in the theory of representation of general functions by trigonometric series, trigonometric integrals, and more comprehensive expansions. But he was also active in the theory of functions of several complex variables, especially on Cauchy formulas, and on functions in tubular domains, which latter topic has applications to hyperbolic differential equations and to problems in quantum field theory. In differential geometry he introduced a general topic that goes under the name "curvature and Betti numbers."

In physics and technology many phenomena

are viewed as "waves" (which subsumes "vibrations" or "oscillations"); there are waves in acoustics, hydrodynamics, electrodynamics, optics, and quantum mechanics, among others. Invariably, a "general" wave is an additive, finite or infinite, superposition of "simple" waves, a simple wave being one with which a specific single "frequency" is associable; also invariably, in each context there is a certain "typical" case, in which all occurring frequencies are integer-valued multiples of a single one, which is then the smallest one. This skeletal "sameness" within physical contexts of different provenance, especially the sameness of the "typical" case, is brought about by the fact that, in each case, a certain function $f(x)$, the wave function (say on an interval of length 2π), is represented as a series, with constant coefficients, of the "simple" functions {sin nx, cos nx} or, in the complex version, of the "simple" functions {e^{imx}}. This mathematical expansion is of course independent of the physical interpretation in which the function $f(x)$ may be involved.

Another "typical" case arises if, as J. B. Fourier did in the early 19th century, we vary the interval over which $f(x)$ is defined, and then let the length of the interval tend to infinity. This replaces the trigonometric series by a trigonometric integral, that is, the Fourier coefficients by a certain function, say $\varphi(\alpha)$, which is called the Fourier transform of $f(x)$. Now the relation between $f(x)$ and its transform $\varphi(\alpha)$ is a "dual" or "reciprocal" one, meaning that $f(x)$ can be reobtained from $\varphi(\alpha)$ in more or less the same manner as $\varphi(\alpha)$ was obtained from $f(x)$. After lying dormant for the better part of a century, this duality began to be studied in earnest at the beginning of the 20th century. The principle underlying it is so general and comprehensive that the awareness and presence of it was felt in ever wider and ever

more numerous areas of mathematics and physics. For instance, if formulated in a suitably comprehensive version, this duality subsumes the de Broglie duality between waves and corpuscles.

A new event occurred in the early 1920s when the mathematician Harold Bohr (younger brother of the physicist Niels Bohr) introduced, on $-\infty < x < \infty$, so-called almost periodic functions (which had been foreshadowed as far back as in the mechanics of Lagrange), each of which has a "discrete" Fourier expansion, in which however the "frequencies" λ, which occur in the "simple" functions {$e^{i\lambda x}$}, can be arbitrary real numbers, with no requirement at all of commensurateness between any two of them.

Bochner soon introduced an algorithmic summability process, the so-called Bochner-Fejer process, which makes it just as easy to handle the Fourier expansion of almost periodic functions—for any type of almost periodicity, however general—as the customary case of periodic functions. Furthermore, Bochner gave an entirely different characterization of the class of almost periodic function on the line, namely, by a certain topological property of compactness. It was this alternate definition that afterwards enabled John von Neumann to extend almost periodicity from the euclidean line to other group spaces.

In the field of Fourier integrals, Bochner found a much applied criterion for a continuous complex-valued function $\varphi(\alpha)$ to be representable as a Fourier-Stieltjes integral

$$\varphi(\alpha) = \int_{-\infty}^{\infty} e^{i\alpha x}dF(x)$$

in which $dF \geqq 0$. For this to be possible it is not only necessary but also sufficient that $\varphi(\alpha)$ be positive-definite, meaning that for any finitely many points $\alpha_1, \ldots, \alpha_n$, and complex constants $c_1, \ldots, c_n$, there is:

$$\sum_{p, q = 1}^{n} c_p \bar{c}_q \varphi(\alpha_p - \alpha_q) \geqq 0$$

This criterion has several applications in the theory of probability; it is also usable for the derivation of the spectral representation of a self-adjoint operator in Hilbert space; and it has been generalized and applied to functions on topological group spaces.

Bochner was also a precursor in the theory of the so-called Schwartz distributions in that he introduced generalized Fourier transforms for functions that do not grow faster at infinity than a power of x.

After attending high school in Berlin, Bochner

studied mathematics at the University of Berlin, terminating with a Ph.D. in 1921. In 1924–26 he studied, partly as a fellow of the International Education Board, with Harold Bohr in Copenhagen, and with G. H. Hardy and J. E. Littlewood in Oxford and Cambridge. In 1926–33 he was lecturer at the University of Munich, where he wrote his first book on Fourier integrals. In 1933 he joined the mathematics department of Princeton University and in 1951 became Henry Burchardt Fine Professor there. He was elected to the National Academy of Sciences in 1950.

Bochner wrote *Several Complex Variables* (1948), *Fourier Transforms* (1949), *Curvature and Betti Numbers* (1953), *Harmonic Analysis and the Theory of Probability* (1955), *Fourier Integrals* (1959), and *The Role of Mathematics in the Rise of Science* (1966).

For background information *see* ANALYSIS OF VARIANCE; FOURIER SERIES AND INTEGRALS; INTEGRAL TRANSFORM in the McGraw-Hill Encyclopedia of Science and Technology.   □

BOHR, Niels Henrik David
Danish physicist
Born Oct. 7, 1885, Copenhagen, Denmark
Died Nov. 18, 1962, Copenhagen, Denmark

WHILE STUDYING atomic structure and radiation, Bohr applied quantum theory to the Rutherford atomic model and developed in 1913 the first consistent theory to explain the arrangement and motion of the electrons in the outer atom. Using his theory, Bohr was able to account quantitatively for the spectrum and atomic structure of hydrogen. The theory was also able to account for variations in properties of the elements and for the main features of the x-ray and optical spectra shown by all the elements. For his achievements in the study of structure and radiations of atoms, Bohr was awarded the Nobel Prize in physics in 1922.

By the beginning of the 20th century, the classical theory of electrodynamics, which assumed continuous emission and adsorption of energy, was found inadequate to explain many phenomena, particularly those connected with electromagnetic radiation. In an attempt to overcome this inadequacy, the German physicist Max Planck, while studying black body radiation in 1900, made the fundamental assumption that a system of oscillating electrical particles emits and absorbs energy discontinuously, in quanta, such that the energy of the quantum, E, was proportional to the frequency of the radiation, ν:

$$E = h\nu$$

where h is Planck's constant. This new theory was used by Albert Einstein in 1905 in the field of specific heats to explain the deviations from the law of Dulong and Petit. Einstein also recognized how physical phenomena like the photoelectric effect may depend directly on individual quantum effects; he concluded that any radiation process involves the emission or absorption of individual light quanta, or photons, which have energy and momentum.

The failure of the theories of classical physics to account for atomic phenomena was emphasized by developments in knowledge of the structure of atoms. The scattering of alpha rays in passing through thin metal sheets led the British physicist Ernest Rutherford in 1911 to propose a theory for the structure of the atom in which electrons revolve in closed orbit around a positively charged nucleus. But the Rutherford atomic model contained inherent defects according to classical physics. Since the orbital electrons are charged bodies moving in the electrostatic field of the nucleus, they should continuously emit radiation. The electrons would thus lose kinetic energy and gradually spiral into the nucleus. In addition, the hydrogen spectrum should have been a broad band from the red end of the spectrum to the violet. Experimental evidence showed, however, that the hydrogen atom is stable and has a line spectrum.

In 1913 Bohr reasoned that Rutherford's atomic model could be saved by applying the new quantum theory. Since it was the assumption from classical physics of the continuous emission of radiation that was causing the difficulties, Bohr assumed that, if radiation were emitted discontinuously in quanta, it was reasonable to suppose that there were certain stable orbits in which electrons could move without loss of energy and that radiation would be emitted only when an electron moved from one such stable orbit into another. He formalized his reasoning into two revolutionary assumptions. One of these was that an atomic system is stable (that is, exists without radiating energy) only when in a definite series of allowed energy states. Further, every change in the energy of the atom is associated with a process in which the atom passes completely from one allowed state to another. The other assumption was that when such a transition between stationary states occurs with the emission or absorption of electromagnetic light waves, the amount of energy emitted or absorbed each time shall equal $h\nu$. Denoting the energy of the atom before and after the emission of radiation by E_1 and E_2,

$$h\nu = E_1 - E_2 \text{ or } \nu = \frac{E_1}{h} - \frac{E_2}{h}$$

Thus, the radiation is of a single frequency; that is, it is monochromatic.

With these assumptions, it was possible to account for the fact that the spectra of the elements consist of sharp lines rather than continuous bands. Since radiation is emitted only in quanta and only when an electron jumps from one allowed state to another, the frequency of the radiation emitted would depend only upon the difference in kinetic energies of the electron in the two states. Since the allowed states are fixed, so too are the kinetic energies in those states. Thus each line in the atomic spectra of the elements corresponds to an electronic transition between two such states. In this way Bohr was able to account quantitatively for the atomic spectrum of hydrogen, giving a quantum number N, which had the values 1, 2, 3, and so on, to the allowed states and showing that the jump of an electron from the second to the first state would give one particular spectral line, the jump from the third to the second another unique spectral line, and so on. During the 1920s the apparent contradiction invoked by the behavior of the electrons in Bohr's atomic model was resolved by two discoveries. The French physicist Louis Victor de Broglie showed that the electron was not only a particle but also a wave form. He then showed (1924) how consideration of a standing wave form for an electron in a Bohr atom would explain the mysterious quantization rule for the electron and permit it to circle the nucleus without radiating. A year later the Austrian physicist Erwin Schrödinger developed his famous mathematical formulation of de Broglie's hypothesis, and the theory of the standing waves was seen to be verified.

Bohr did not abandon classical mechanics in his theory; in fact, he assumed that the motion in the allowed states could be described by its use. Quantum theory was essential to describe the transitions between these states. Moreover, while radiation could not be described on the basis of classical electrodynamics, Bohr felt that there was a far-reaching correspondence between transitions from one stationary state to another and the various harmonic components of motion. He felt that this correspondence was of such a nature that his theory of spectra was a rational generalization of the classical theory of radiation. This reasoning led to a secondary but great contribution by Bohr—his "correspondence principle," in which he states that at sufficiently low frequencies the laws of quantum theory converge toward and become identical with the laws of classical electrodynamics.

Thus Bohr was able to correlate four different theories of radiation and atomic structure: classical electrodynamics; empirical knowledge of the spectra based on the work of J. J. Balmer, W. Ritz, and J. R. Rydberg; Rutherford's atomic model; and Planck's quantum theory of heat radiation. By 1916, other theorists, starting with the German physicist Arnold Sommerfeld, began to associate themselves with the Bohr theory, and the further development of nuclear physics was shaped by the Bohr atom. Although Bohr originally conceived of the atom as having a shell-like structure in which the electrons moved in circular paths about the nucleus, this was later modified into the Bohr-Sommerfeld model of the atom in which the electrons travel in elliptical orbits.

Bohr received his doctorate at the University of Copenhagen in 1911. He then studied at Cambridge under J. J. Thomson and spent a year teaching at the University of Manchester, where he worked with Rutherford on atomic structure. Returning to the University of Copenhagen, Bohr published in 1913 his remarkable series of papers on the spectrum and atomic structure of hydrogen. The Copenhagen Institute of Theoretical Physics was established through his influence in 1920 and became one of the leading intellectual centers of Europe. Bohr served as its director and also as president of the Royal Danish Academy of Science. In 1939 Bohr laid the broad foundations of a "liquid droplet" theory of nuclear phenomena, showing an analogy in the fission of uranium between an unstable atomic nucleus and a rupturing water drop. Again, a bold theory of Bohr's led to much fruitful research toward an understanding of the atom. During World War II he fled from Denmark to England and then to the United States, where he worked on the Manhattan Project. It was Bohr who predicted that uranium-235 was the isotope that would undergo fission and be suitable for the atomic weapon. He was an advocate of international atomic control and won the first Atoms for Peace Award in 1957.

Bohr wrote *The Theory of Spectra and Atomic Constitution* (1922).

For background information *see* ATOMIC STRUCTURE AND SPECTRA in the McGraw-Hill Encyclopedia of Science and Technology.   □

☆ BOLTON, Elmer Keiser

American chemist and research director
Born June 23, 1886, Philadelphia, Pa., U.S.A.

DURING A long association with the chemistry and manufacture of organic compounds, Bolton contributed in leadership and direction to three historic undertakings: the establishment of a domestic synthetic dyestuff industry; the research that led to the first general-purpose synthetic rubber to be developed either in the United States or abroad; and the phase of the program of fundamental studies in polymerization phenomena that led to the discovery of nylon and other long-chain molecular structures of major importance. He was director of what is now the Central Research Department of E. I. du Pont de Nemours and Company from 1930 until his retirement in 1951.

Bolton began his career in industrial organic research in 1915, about the time the Du Pont Company decided to undertake the manufacture of synthetic dyes, for which America was largely dependent upon Germany, and had established the Organic Chemicals Department. The following year, with the supply situation becoming more critical, Bolton was placed in charge of a group of chemists learning, in the laboratory, the complex dye-manufacturing processes that had been developed abroad. Beginning with a small group making intermediates from benzol—with which Du Pont had experience in explosives—the new project grew swiftly into a large unit of several hundred research workers. By 1926, sufficient progress had been made in developing the new industry to enable Du Pont to plan an extension of activities in new areas of organic chemistry.

Bolton proposed that work be undertaken on synthetic rubber. Many years of research by European chemists had failed to produce a satisfactory substitute for the natural latex, but Bolton's management was ready to accept the "long chance" for success offered by his proposal. Recognizing in J. A. Nieuwland's process for making divinylacetylene from three molecules of acetylene a possible path to the ultimate goal, Bolton suggested a modification that produced monovinylacetylene—a compound made by the union of two molecules of acetylene. Treatment of the monovinylacetylene with hydrochloric acid resulted in a previously unknown material, which was called chloroprene. Research chemists assigned to the rubber problem soon determined that chloroprene could be converted into a rubberlike material superior to natural rubber in certain respects.

Beginning in 1928, Bolton was charged with the responsibility of selecting and directing research on promising developments stemming from the fundamental studies carried out by a group of organic chemists under the supervision of Wallace H. Carothers. The efforts of the Carothers group were directed to the condensation of aliphatic amino acids and of aliphatic dibasic acids and aliphatic diamines under conditions that favored long-chain molecules. After establishing a broad knowledge of this class of long-chain molecules, Carothers was encouraged by Bolton to initiate a project aiming at the synthesis of molecules that might have interest as a new textile fiber. The polyamide eventually born of this effort was nylon.

Bolton majored in chemistry at Bucknell University, where he received his A.B. degree in 1908. At Harvard he received his M.A. and Ph.D. degrees and in 1913 was awarded its Sheldon Fellowship, with a reappointment in 1914, under which he engaged in postdoctoral research at the Kaiser Wilhelm Institut für Chemie in Berlin-Dahlem. There, in the laboratory of Professor Richard Willstätter, he isolated and established the chemical constitution of the pigments of geraniums, scarlet sage, and dark-red chrysanthemums. In 1941 Bolton received the Chemical Industry Medal, awarded annually by the American Section of The Society of Chemical Industry; in 1945, its Perkin Medal; and in 1954, the Willard Gibbs Medal, awarded by the Chicago Section of the American Chemical Society. He was elected to the National Academy of Sciences in 1946.

For background information *see* POLYMERIZATION in the McGraw-Hill Encyclopedia of Science and Technology.   □

★ **BONNER, James Frederick**

American biologist
Born Sept. 1, 1910, Ansley, Nebr., U.S.A.

Bonner's work was concerned with the mechanism by means of which a single cell, the fertilized egg, gives rise to an adult creature made up of many different kinds of cells. This process is known as development. All cells contain the directions for cell life written in the DNA of their chromosomes. These directions include specification of how to make the many kinds of protein enzyme molecules by means of which the cell converts available building blocks into substances suitable for making more cells. To make enzyme molecules, the DNA prints off RNA copies of itself—messenger RNA molecules; these messenger RNA molecules are decoded by ribosomes, also made by the DNA; as it decodes the messenger RNA molecule, the ribosome uses the information to assemble a specific kind of enzyme molecule.

This picture of cell life provided by molecular biology applies to all cells of all creatures. But the bodies of higher creatures, such as people or pea plants, possess different kinds of cells. Some cells make hemoglobin, others do not, and so on. The new approach to differentiation is based upon the fact that all the cells in the body of a higher organism have exactly the same amount and kind of DNA—the same genetic information. When a single cell, the fertilized egg, divides into two cells, each of these receives a complete set of the genetic DNA. In the course of embryonic development, however, the cells of the embryo soon become different from one another. Some produce hemoglobin, some produce muscle enzymes, some liver enzymes, and so on. The genetic information for making hemoglobin, for example, is in all cells, but it is used in only those few cells that are to be the red

blood cells. In all the other cells of the body, the genetic information for making hemoglobin is turned off, repressed. To find out what makes development and differentiation take place it is necessary to find out what it is in the cell that determines which particular units of the genetic information, which particular genes, shall be active and make their characteristic messenger RNA and which shall be repressed or inactive.

Bonner's approach to the study of development was first to find out how to isolate chromosomes and cause them to make their messenger RNA in the test tube. It proved easy to isolate chromosomes, and such purified chromosomes made RNA, provided they were given the RNA building blocks. If ribosomes that had been freed of messenger RNA were added to the system, as well as the 20 amino acids (the building blocks of enzyme molecules), enzyme molecules were made. Bonner and his coworker, Ru-chih Huang, showed that the repressed genes were those complexed with and covered by a histone protein. When the histone was removed from the chromosome, the genes previously repressed were derepressed. Whether histones are the only kind of repressor is not yet known. The logic by which repressor histones, which are made in the nucleolus of the nucleus, discover the proper gene to repress is also a subject of current investigation. It now appears that each histone molecule bears an RNA molecule, and that this RNA molecule may have to do with finding the right DNA sequence, and hence attaching the histone to the right gene.

Bonner accomplished the dissociation of DNA from histone by the use of high concentrations of salt. This worked nicely but not selectively, derepressing all repressed genes. In the living cell derepression is selective; one or a few genes may be turned on or off without influencing others. Bonner and his associates found that certain kinds of small molecules were able to turn off or on the activity of particular genes. These small molecules included the hormones. A hormone on arrival at its target organ turns on an individual or whole set of genes, causing the production of characteristic enzyme molecules not previously produced by those cells. This is dramatically exemplified by the case of arousal from dormancy, studied by Bonner and Dorothy Tuan. The buds of freshly harvested potatoes do not grow; they are said to be dormant. The chromosomes of the cells of the dormant bud are almost completely repressed, and cannot therefore make any messenger RNA. Bonner found that dormancy could be ended at any time by supplying the bud with a particular hormone, gibberellic acid, or a synthetic substitute, ethylenechlorohydrin. Treatment with a minute amount of one of these materials caused the buds to grow. The chemical caused a substantial proportion of the genetic comple- ment to be derepressed and to become active in RNA-making. Many hormones work in this way, and Bonner sought to work out in molecular detail the way in which hormone- and histone- DNA complex interact to cause derepression.

Bonner's recent studies grew out of his earlier interest in the study of ribosomes. In the early 1950s it became apparent that the synthesis of enzyme molecules was due to some kind of entity within the cell, an entity larger than enzyme molecules but smaller than the mito- chondria. Bonner and Paul Ts'o isolated this entity in 1955. They found that the particles involved were what we now know as ribosomes and that they were made of equal amounts of RNA and protein. Bonner next tried to find out where the RNA of ribosomes came from. It turned out that the RNA of ribosomes was made in the nucleus, and this led to the study of how RNA was made. This is turn led logically to the discovery in 1960 of chromosomal RNA syn- thesis, the process now known as DNA-depend- ent RNA synthesis. The ribosomal study was built upon earlier studies by Bonner and his colleagues on how to separate the different kinds of particles inside cells from one another. They had developed methods for the isolation of mitochondria from plant cells, and in 1951 had shown that the mitochondria thus isolated not only carried out all of the respiratory oxidations but also conducted the process, now known as oxidative phosphorylation, by means of which the energy liberated in respiration was con- served and made available to all processes re- quiring energy.

Both Bonner's parents were chemists. Like his five brothers and one sister, Bonner majored in chemistry at the University of Utah, receiv- ing his A.B. in 1931. As an undergraduate he became interested in biology through the in- fluence of Theodosius Dobzhansky. At the Cali- fornia Institute of Technology, where he re- ceived his Ph.D. in biology in 1934, he worked with Thomas Hunt Morgan, Alfred H. Sturte- vant, Kenneth V. Thimann, Herman E. Dolk, and F. W. Went, among others. After study abroad in Holland and Switzerland, he joined the staff of the California Institute of Tech- nology in 1935. He was elected to the National Academy of Sciences in 1950.

Bonner wrote *Plant Biochemistry* (1950), *Principles of Plant Physiology*, with A. W. Gal- ston (1952), *The Next 100 Years*, with Harrison Brown and John Weir (1957), *The Nucleohis- tones*, with Paul Ts'o (1964), and *The Molec- ular Biology of Development* (1965).

For background information *see* CHROMO- SOME THEORY OF HEREDITY; DEOXYRIBONUCLEIC ACID; RIBONUCLEIC ACID in the McGraw-Hill Encyclopedia of Science and Technology.   □

★ **BORN, Max**
British theoretical physicist
Born Dec. 11, 1882, Breslau, Silesia, Prussia

IN THE course of a long scientific career, Born made significant contributions to many branches of theoretical physics. He played a central role in the development of quantum mechanics, which is the basis of modern atomic and nuclear physics. For this work he was awarded the Nobel Prize in physics in 1954.

The discovery of quantum mechanics was made at Göttingen, Germany, where Born was appointed professor of physics in 1921. With his assistants, first Wolfgang Pauli, then Werner Heisenberg, he started on a program to investi- gate how far the quantum theory of the atom by Niels Bohr and Arnold Sommerfeld was valid for more complicated systems; Heisenberg and he showed that it did not account for the line spectrum of the He atom. They endeavored then to develop a new atomic mechanics. The first success was due to Heisenberg, who introduced a perfectly new way of dealing with physical quantities. He gave Born his paper to be sent in for publication. Born saw at once its funda- mental importance and discovered soon that Heisenberg's formalism was identical with the matrix calculus well known to mathematicians. He formulated for the first time the famous matrix relation $qp - pq = ih/2\pi$ between a co- ordinate q of a particle and its conjugate mo- mentum p (h being Planck's constant). As Heisenberg was on holiday, Born enlisted the help of P. Jordan, one of his senior pupils, and developed with him the quantum mechanics of the motion of a particle in one dimension. After his return to Göttingen, Heisenberg joined with Born and Jordan in the generalization of this work to three-dimensional problems. A complete quantitative explanation was obtained for the positions and intensities of atomic spectral lines and for other phenomena that had mystified physicists for 20 years. Starting also from Heisenberg's paper, P. A. M. Dirac in Cambridge, England, developed the theory independently.

Meanwhile, in Zurich, Erwin Schrödinger had followed a quite different trend of thoughts initiated by Louis de Broglie, on wave mechanics, leading to the same results. The essential equivalence of Schrödinger's method and that which had been discovered in Göttingen was, however, soon demonstrated by Schrödinger himself. Born was quick to accept and assimilate Schrödinger's contribution and showed how it could be applied to determine the intensity and angular distribution of a beam of particles that had been scattered by an atomic target. The importance of this application eventually transcended that of the theory of the bound states of atomic systems, on which the explanation of spectral lines was based.

In spite of the success of the mathematical theories in accounting for experimental data, the actual meaning of quantum mechanics was still obscure. Perhaps Born's most striking contribution to the subject was the physical interpretation that he supplied. In the mathematical formalism, the state of an atomic system is represented by an abstract vector with an arbitrary and usually infinite number of components. Born showed that each component can be regarded as an amplitude, the square of which is the probability that an experimental measurement on an atomic system will yield a particular result. This statistical interpretation carried with it the implication that atomic phenomena are not deterministic: The result of an individual experiment cannot be predicted with certainty, though the probability of obtaining a given result can be computed, by the use of Born's prescription. The waves determined by Schrödinger's wave mechanics were proved to have no more than a statistical significance and, even so, only in relation to a particular type of ideal measurement. Schrödinger objected strongly to this interpretation, and so, for different reasons, did Max Planck, Albert Einstein, and Louis de Broglie. But, in spite of the eminence of those few who opposed it, the concept of the indeterministic nature of atomic phenomena has been generally accepted. Niels Bohr, as well as Born, eventually played an important part in gaining acceptance of this revolution in scientific thought. But the most important influence was

undoubtedly the wealth of applications that followed, in which experimental work invariably confirmed Born's interpretation. Born took part in some of these applications himself: His work with J. R. Oppenheimer on the quantum mechanics of molecules and his book with Kun Huang on the quantum mechanics of crystal lattices are well-known examples.

This latter book is the last summarizing of another part of Born's life work, *The Dynamical Theory of Crystal Lattices*. His first book had the same title in German (*Dynamik der Kristallgitter*, 1915) but was still based on classical mechanics. He followed the subject of lattice dynamics through his whole life with many collaborators and pupils. It can be regarded as the theoretical base of the modern theory of the solid state.

Born also worked in other subjects, for example, stability of elastic systems, thermodynamics, and statistical mechanics of condensed gases and liquids. He suggested a new type of symmetry in physical systems, called principle of reciprocity, which has recently been successfully used in the theory of elementary particles.

Born's father was professor of anatomy at the University of Breslau; he did fundamental research in embryology and the theory of evolution, and first recognized the corpus luteum as the organ that produced the sex hormones—a discovery that led to modern research on fertility. Born's mother, who came from a Silesian industrial family, died when he was quite young; his father died during his last year at school. Born attended a gymnasium in Breslau, then studied at the universities of Breslau, Heidelberg, Zurich, and finally Göttingen, where the great mathematicians David Hilbert, Hermann Minkowski, and Felix Klein were his teachers. After graduating Ph.D., he visited Cambridge. In 1908 he returned to Göttingen, first as Minkowski's assistant and then as a lecturer. There, in 1913, he married Hedwig Ehrenberg. In 1915 he was appointed to a professorship in Berlin to relieve Planck in teaching; but war had begun, and Born was soon in military service, fortunately in an artillery research establishment where he had time to spare for continuing work in theoretical physics. He cemented a friendship with Einstein during this period. After the war, he went from Berlin to Frankfurt for 2 years, where he did some experimental work. Then he obtained the professorship in Göttingen, where the foundations of quantum mechanics were developed. Many famous theoretical physicists came to work in Göttingen during this period. Along with many Jewish refugees, Born left Germany when Hitler came to power. After 3 years in Cambridge and a visit to India, he was appointed to the Tait Chair at the University of Edinburgh, where he remained for 17 years until his retirement in 1953. He then settled at Bad Pyrmont, a picturesque spa not far from Göttingen. He consistently condemned the warlike uses of modern scientific knowledge. He was elected a foreign associate of the U.S. National Academy of Sciences in 1955.

Born published many papers and books, of which *Atomic Physics* (1935; 7th ed. 1962) became most popular; his Waynflete Lectures, under the title *Natural Philosophy of Cause and Chance* (1949), give a semipopular account of several of his scientific and philosophical interests. A textbook of optics in German (1933) evolved from one of his lecture courses; a modernized version in English was written in collaboration with E. Wolf (1959). Two volumes of *Selected Papers* were published (1963) by the Academy of Göttingen. During his retirement Born wrote many articles and some books on the problem of the responsibility of scientists arising from the use of nuclear energy in war and peace.

For background information *see* QUANTUM MECHANICS in the McGraw-Hill Encyclopedia of Science and Technology.   ☐

BOTHE, Walter

German physicist
Born Jan. 9, 1891, Oranienburg, Germany
Died Aug. 2, 1957, Heidelberg, Germany

W HILE STUDYING the scattering of light on practically free electrons, Bothe devised a technique for the simultaneous detection of the scattered quantum and the recoil electron. This "coincidence method" became the foundation for subsequent investigations by physicists of nuclear reactions and cosmic radiation. For this

achievement Bothe received, jointly with Max Born, the Nobel Prize for physics in 1954.

In 1924 Niels Bohr, H. A. Kramers, and J. C. Slater published a paper dealing with the wave-particle duality of light. To account for this duality in terms of the then accepted theories of optics, they proposed that the laws of conservation of energy and momentum might not be valid on the atomic level; the laws would be statistically satisfied only on a macroscopic scale, not for a single emission of light. Bothe accepted the challenge of devising an experiment to confirm or deny this hypothesis. The experiment was to be designed to answer the question of whether it was a scatter quantum and a recoil electron that were simultaneously emitted in the recoil process or whether there was a chance relationship between the two. His coworker was Hans Geiger, who had just developed a counter for detecting not only heavy particles but also electrons. This so-called needle counter could respond to light quanta of energies sufficiently high to release electrons within the counter. The experimental arrangement consisted of two needle counters that were bombarded by a beam of x-rays. The recoil process occurred in one counter, and this was recorded. The scattered quanta had to penetrate the other counter, actuating it by scattering, with much lower probability, another electron. At this time the readings of both counters were recorded side by side on a moving paper chart and the occurrence of any temporal coincidences between the pointer readings noted. Such coincidences could only arise from two particles emitted in the same recoil process or from a particle that had passed through both needle counters at a high velocity. Bothe and Geiger found that periodic coincidences were occurring; the strict validity of the law of conservation of energy was therefore upheld even on an atomic scale. When the experiment was repeated with radiothorium as a source of impinging gamma radiation instead of the x-rays, the same results were obtained.

Bothe's coincidence method was quickly applied to the field of cosmic radiation. Coincidences caused by cosmic radiation were seen in unscreened counters and when absorbing layers of variable thickness were applied around the counters. These experiments led in 1929 to the conclusion that cosmic radiation does not consist primarily of powerful gamma rays but of material particles with an energy of at least 10^9 electron volts. Following this, coincidence arrangements were used with increasing numbers of counters combined with cloud chambers, ionization chambers, and scintillation counters. Instead of photographic recording, the method used electronic circuits and mechanical counters.

Another important area in which the coincidence method was applied was that of nuclear reactions. For example, Bothe and others found it was possible to determine whether two or more gamma quanta generated in a nuclear reaction came from the same unstable nucleus. If this were so, they would be given off practically simultaneously; if, however, they were formed during conversion of separate nuclei, they would be emitted alternatively. The solution of this problem was necessary to measure reaction energies and determine nuclear mass. Analogous problems in natural and artificial radioactivity were tackled experimentally in this manner.

Bothe studied physics at the University of Berlin, where he was a student of Max Planck. From 1913 to 1930, except for military service during World War I, he worked at the Physikalisch-Technische Reichanstalt in Berlin. In 1930 he became professor of physics and director of the Institute of Physics at the University of Giessen. He moved to the University of Heidelberg in 1932, becoming in 1934 director of the Institute of Physics at the Max Planck Institute for Medical Research in Heidelberg.

For background information *see* PARTICLE DETECTOR in the McGraw-Hill Encyclopedia of Science and Technology. □

☆ **BOVET, Daniel**

Italian pharmacologist
Born Mar. 23, 1907, Neuchâtel, Switzerland

WHILE CONDUCTING research in therapeutic chemistry, Bovet observed organic compounds that proved effective as muscle relaxants (used to supplement light general anesthesia during surgery) and antihistamines (useful in alleviating the effects of allergies). In recogni-

tion of his discoveries relating to synthetic compounds that inhibit the action of certain body substances, and especially their action on the vascular system and the skeletal muscles, Bovet was awarded the 1957 Nobel Prize for physiology or medicine.

The alkaloid curare has long been used by South American aborigines as a dart poison. While it has no effect on the central nervous system, curare causes complete relaxation of the muscles, and death may ensue as the result of respiratory failure. In the mid-18th century, the French geographer Charles La Condamine brought samples of the poison to Europe. The structure of one of the physiologically active principles of curare, *d*-tubocurarine, was identified in 1935, and seven years later a chemically pure alkaloid was introduced as an adjuvant to anesthesia.

Following the first observations by Griffith and Cullen concerning the muscle relaxant properties of curare in surgery, Bovet worked to develop a synthetic curare. He proceeded to synthesize molecules chemically related to the chosen models and to prepare relatively simple derivatives with analogous properties. In this way, Bovet synthesized more than 400 compounds that simulated the effects of the natural product in varying degrees. One of these compounds, succinylcholine, came closest to duplicating the activity of curare, and clinical tests showed it to be an effective substitute. This made it possible to use succinylcholine as a muscle relaxant whose effective dosages could be determined with precision. By its use, the surgeon is able to produce complete muscle relaxation with only light anesthesia, thus avoiding some detrimental effects of deep anesthesia.

Prior to beginning his work with curare, Bovet had developed the first antihistaminic compound. Histamine, which is found in all body tissues, was believed to be the causative agent in producing allergy symptoms. Every body tissue reacts to histamine in some way, and excessive amounts intensify reactions to the point where discomfort sets in. When introduced by means other than adsorption through the intestines, histamine is extremely toxic, an indication that it is undoubtedly present in the body in a nontoxic combination, probably with a protein.

Bovet realized that relief from allergy symptoms would probably require a mechanism that could interfere with the production of free histamine from this combined form. In collaboration with Miss A. M. Staub, he considered the similarities among histamine, adrenaline, and acetylcholine. He then began to investigate substances that demonstrated a specific antagonism for histamine, comparable to that shown by sympatholitics and parasympatholitics for adrenaline and acetylcholine, respectively. In 1937 he succeeded in producing the first antihistamine, thymoxydiethylamine, which was too toxic to be used clinically. However, thymoxydiethylamine served as the basis for the derivation of almost all subsequent antihistamines. Thus, Bovet's research led to the development in the 1950s of new antihistaminic drugs, which have proved to be of use in relieving the symptoms associated with such allergies as hay fever, hives, and poison oak.

Bovet's earliest work was concerned with the development of the sulfa drugs. Soon after its discovery in 1935, the orange-red dye sulfamyldiamino benzene was found to have chemotherapeutic properties by the German biochemist Gerhard Domagk. Since this dye was found to be effective against streptococci in the human body but ineffective when added to laboratory cultures, Bovet theorized that the complex organic dye was broken down in the body to simpler compounds that worked against the streptococci. He therefore proceeded to reduce it to its component compounds. One of these, sulfanilamide, proved to be effective against streptococci both in the body and in the culture. With this evidence to support his premise, Bovet began to synthesize derivatives of sulfanilamide in an effort to discover even more therapeutic compounds. He found that the majority of the superior derivatives had the common feature of a complex organic group in the place of a hydrogen atom in the sulfonamide group, SO_2NH_2. Although this finding led to the preparation of numerous derivatives, only a few had both the high antibacterial activity and the low toxicity to human beings to permit their use in chemotherapy. Sulfanilamide and its derivatives are of value in combatting many types of bacterial infection. Unfortunately, most of the sulfa drugs are only sparingly soluble in water. For this reason they tend to deposit in the kidneys and interfere with the excretory function. This has been overcome in part, however, by having the patient increase his water intake to aid in the solution of the sulfa drugs and speed their elimination from the kidneys.

In addition to his chemotherapeutic work with the sulfa drugs, Bovet studied the ataraxics, or tranquilizers, and the oxytocii, substances that resemble the hormone oxytocin—which regulates uterine contraction during childbirth—in activity.

The son of a professor of pedagogy, Bovet studied at the University of Geneva, receiving the "license" (a degree intermediate between the baccalaureate and the doctorate) in 1927 and his D.Sc. in zoology and comparative anatomy in 1929. He accepted a position as assistant in the Laboratory of Therapeutic Chemistry at the Pasteur Institute in Paris in that year, and was appointed director in 1936. He left this post in 1947 to become chief of the Laboratory of Therapeutic Chemistry at the Instituto Superiore di Sanità in Rome, and later professor of pharmacology at the University of Sassari.

Bovet was the author or coauthor of several books, among them *Curare and Curarelike Agents* (1959).

For background information *see* ANTIHISTAMINES; PHARMACOGNOSY; SULFA DRUGS in the McGraw-Hill Encyclopedia of Science and Technology.   □

★ **BOWEN, Edmund John**
British chemist
Born Apr. 29, 1898, Worcester, England

BOWEN'S EXPERIMENTAL work ranged over the field of photochemistry, fluorescence, and chemiluminescence. For his work on the elucidation of photochemical reactions, and for his study of fluorescence and phosphorescence in relation to the molecular processes concerned, he was awarded the Davy Medal of the Royal Society of London in 1963.

At the time of World War I (in which Bowen served as a gunner officer) photochemistry was just beginning to assimilate the concepts of the early quantum theory. Bowen's first researches were determinations of quantum yields, particularly of the photodecompositions of the oxides of chlorine. These measurements were extended to certain photochanges in crystals, and to carbonyl compounds in solution. The photochemical oxidations of acetaldehyde in the vapor and solution were shown to be chain reactions depending on the square root of the light intensity, changing to a direct dependence in presence of inhibitors.

Quantum yields of light emission during the oxidation of phosphorus vapor under various conditions were examined.

In 1936 Bowen developed the "fluorescent quantum counter" in which ultraviolet or visible light, as from a fluorescent solution, is collected on a fluorescent screen with filter, and the fluorescence emitted from this measured with a photocell. With the advent of sensitive photo-multipliers, this method has been utilized by a number of investigators in late years for the determination of absolute fluorescence yields of solutions. Bowen used it to obtain values for the fluorescent yields of solutions of aromatic hydro-carbons. These measurements were accompanied by determinations of photooxidation and photo-dimerization in the same systems in order to elucidate the mechanisms of reaction and the relation between the alternatives of reemission, reaction, or energy degradation of electronically excited molecules.

The reversible quenching effect of dissolved oxygen on the fluorescence of a number of solutions was discovered in 1939, and it was later shown that such quenching occurs with almost unit efficiency at every molecular encounter. Collisional concentration quenching was shown to be nearly as efficient; both processes are closely diffusion controlled. Studies were also made of the effect of temperature on fluores-cence yields, and it was found that solvent viscosity affected yields even when collisional quenching was absent. For these measurements apparatus was devised in an attempt to minimize the numerous sources of error associated with determinations of absolute fluorescence yields.

After the hypothesis of singlet-singlet elec-tronic energy transfer between molecules had been put forward by Förster, there was a period when some workers attributed the effect to reab-sorption by the second substance of fluorescence emitted by the first. Bowen gave the first incon-trovertible refutation of this view by quantitative measurements on a system where the first (ab-sorbing) substance had a low fluorescence yield and the second a high one (1953). Transfer of energy via fluorescence could not lead to a final high yield, yet a high yield was in fact found.

Son of a primary school headmaster, Bowen won a scholarship to Balliol College, Oxford, coming into residence in 1915–16, then returning after war service to take the degrees of M.A. in 1922 and D.Sc. in 1947. He was elected a fellow of University College, Oxford, in 1922, and worked in the Balliol and Trinity laboratories, transferring to the newly built Physical Chem-istry Laboratory in 1940 and later becoming Aldrichian Praelector in Chemistry. He was elected to the Royal Society of London in 1935.

Bowen wrote *The Chemical Aspects of Light* (2d ed. 1946) and *The Fluorescence of Solu-tions*, with F. Wokes (1953). He edited *Recent Progress in Photobiology* (1965).

For background information *see* FLUORES-CENCE; PHOTOCHEMISTRY in the McGraw-Hill Encyclopedia of Science and Technology. □

☆ **BOWEN, Ira Sprague**

American astrophysicist
Born Dec. 21, 1898, Seneca Falls, N.Y., U.S.A.

WHILE STUDYING the spectra of planetary nebulae, Bowen identified and explained the strong green emission lines, previously at-tributed to some element not known on the Earth, as emanating from ionized nitrogen and oxygen under the influence of low pressures that could not be reproduced in terrestrial labora-tories. The explanation of these "forbidden" lines (so-called in contrast to the "permitted" lines observed in the laboratory) led to major advances in the spectroscopic study of celestial bodies, particularly the nebulae.

The strongest lines in the spectra of planetary nebulae are certain green lines, which were first observed by the English astronomer Wil-liam Huggins during the 1860s. These long resisted identification and were incorrectly at-tributed either to a hypothetical element, nebuli-um, not known on the Earth or to complicated atomic spectra possessing a large number of lines in the optical region. By the early 20th century, however, knowledge of the periodic table had increased to the point where it became doubtful if an element such as nebulium could exist, and the suspicion grew that the nebular spectral lines might emanate from a gas of ex-ceedingly low density.

By this time, also, the mechanism of the production of spectral lines was well estab-lished. A spectral line arises when an electron in an atom jumps from one energy level to an-other. The jumps, or transitions, that are easy to accomplish and normally result in strong lines are called "permitted," while those that are more difficult to accomplish and normally result in weak lines are called "forbidden." By a spectral analysis it is possible to deduce the energy levels between which the jumps occur.

Bowen suggested that the strong green "nebulium" lines of planetary nebulae might result from "forbidden" transitions from metastable states. An atom in an excited state may return to a lower energy level either by radiating energy or by losing it in a collision with another atom. Bowen reasoned that if the atoms were at a metastable energy level in which they remained in an excited state for an extended period, and if the average time between collisions was short, then practically all of the atoms would lose their energy by the collision process instead of by radiation. He assumed that this was the case in terrestrial laboratories, where the average time between collisions under the most rarefied conditions was about 10^{-3} sec, so that no spectral lines of a wavelength indicative of a jump between the metastable and ground (lowest energy) levels could be observed. However, since the average time between collisions of atoms in planetary nebulae was estimated to be between 10^{-4} and 10^{-5} sec, Bowen reasoned that the radiative process of energy loss might be predominant, giving rise to observable spectral lines.

In 1927, Bowen's calculations revealed that the wavelengths of three of the spectral lines attributed to nebulium coincided with those that would be expected from highly improbable transitions within the lowest energy levels of doubly ionized oxygen, O III. As shown in the accompanying diagram, where B and C repre-

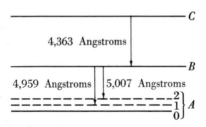

sent metastable energy levels, transitions between B and A_1 and between B and A_2 produce spectral lines with wavelengths of 4,959 and 5,007 A, respectively, which correspond to the wavelengths of a pair of intense, green nebular spectral lines. Also, a transition from C to B produces a spectral line with a wavelength of 4,363 A, the wavelength of another nebular line. By comparing his calculated wavelengths of "forbidden" transitions with observed, but unidentified, wavelengths in nebular spectra, Bowen found that the most conspicuous lines were due to "forbidden" transitions of singly and doubly ionized oxygen, O II and O III, and singly ionized nitrogen, N II. Bowen's discovery led to the identification of other spectral lines, particularly in the solar corona where they had been attributed to another hypothetical element, coronium. This in turn led to advances in the study of the chemical composition, temperature, and density of the Sun and other bodies.

In 1938 Bowen devised the "image slicer," an instrument for increasing the efficiency of a slit spectrograph. In objective prism spectroscopy, a prism is placed in front of the telescope lens to separate the light of different wavelengths. A number of different images are thus formed, each of which is a picture of the celestial body in a particular wavelength of a particular element. However, images of nearly the same color, such as the 4,959- and 5,007-A radiations of O III, overlap to a great extent. The slit spectrograph eliminates this difficulty but has the disadvantage of wasting a large part of the light at the slit. In Bowen's image slicer, the light falls on a system of mirrors before reaching the spectrograph slit. The mirrors slice the original image into a series of strips and align them end to end along the slit. This produces a series of narrow spectra, decreasing the time required to prepare a total spectrogram of a large body. Bowen also contributed to the study of cosmic rays.

Bowen majored in physics at Oberlin College, receiving his A.B. in 1919. He did graduate work at the University of Chicago and at the California Institute of Technology, where he received his Ph.D. in physics in 1926 and remained as a member of the faculty, becoming a full professor in 1931. In 1946 he was appointed director of the Mount Wilson Observatory and in 1948 director of the combined Mount Wilson and Palomar Observatories. He retired from this position in 1964, remaining a distinguished service staff member. Among other awards, Bowen received the Draper Medal of the National Academy of Sciences in 1942, the Rumford Medal of the American Academy of Arts and Sciences in 1948, and the Bruce Medal of the Astronomical Society of the Pacific in 1957. He was elected to the National Academy of Sciences in 1936.

For background information *see* NEBULA, GASEOUS in the McGraw-Hill Encyclopedia of Science and Technology.   ☐

★ BOYD, William Clouser

American immunochemist
Born Mar. 4, 1903, Dearborn, Mo., U.S.A.

IN 1945 Boyd conceived the idea that if some plant proteins could have species specificity for animal erythrocytes, as shown by Karl Landsteiner, then some plants might have individual, or blood-group, specificity. Tested that same day, the idea proved to be correct, and the first plant tested, the common lima bean,

proved to be specific for human blood-group antigen A. His report, followed by a confirmatory report by K. O. Renkonen in Finland, led to the testing in various laboratories of thousands of plant specificities. The name proposed for these substances by Boyd, "lectins," has been incorporated into English and other languages.

This discovery provided a cheap and ready source of substances with various blood-group specificities. Discoveries by Boyd and other workers soon provided reagents for the diagnosis of secretors and nonsecretors and for the separation of persons of blood groups A and AB into the subgroups A_1 and A_2 and A_1B and A_2B. These new methods have become standard.

In addition to its practical application, however, Boyd's discovery had great theoretical significance, for it opened up a practically unlimited source of substances imitating very exactly the specificity and behavior of antibodies. Chemical study of these substances, purified, enables immunochemists to draw conclusions as to the chemical natures of the specifically reactive groups in lectins and ultimately in antibodies. Thus Boyd and S. Matsubara determined the amino acid composition of the portion of the lima bean lectin that combines specifically with the blood-group A antigen. Boyd and H. M. Bhatia determined the number of specifically reactive A sites on a human group A erythrocyte and found a much higher value (over 10,000,000) than previously estimated.

Boyd's techniques were extremely simple. Seeds of various plants were ground in a mill and extracted with saline (0.9% sodium chloride solution). This extract was reacted with suspensions in saline of human red blood cells of various blood groups. The reactions were read in test tubes after centrifuging, without the use of a microscope. In later work he coupled the lectins with radioactive iodine (I^{131}), and determined the amount combining with red cells by radioactive counting. Still later he used lectins

coupled with colored dyes, reading the reaction in the photoelectric colorimeter. By this method he discovered a potent and specific anti-A agglutinin in the expressed body fluids of the land snail *Otala* (*Helix*) *lactea*.

Boyd's discovery has had wide application, and extracts of plants prepared according to his methods are now sold by a number of commercial supply houses. His methods are standard for the determination of subgroups of A and AB and for the diagnosis of secretors. Many investigators have confirmed and extended Boyd's results, and discovered other blood-group specificities in plant extracts. Anti-M and anti-N lectins are now known and are for sale.

Boyd was born and brought up on a farm in Missouri, where he attended high school. He received B.A. and M.A. degrees from Harvard University (1925 and 1926). While a teaching fellow at Boston University Medical School he did research leading to his Ph.D. in 1930. He remained at Boston University, where in 1948 he became professor of immunochemistry.

Besides some 250 papers in various scientific journals, Boyd wrote *Blood Grouping Technic*, with Fritz Schiff (1942), *Fundamentals of Immunology* (1943; 3d ed. 1956), *Genetics and the Races of Man* (1950), *Biochemistry and Human Metabolism*, with B. S. Walker and I. Asimov (1952; 3d ed. 1957), *Races and People*, with I. Asimov (1955), and *Introduction to Immunochemical Specificity* (1962).

For background information *see* BIOLOGICAL SPECIFICITY; SEROLOGY in the McGraw-Hill Encyclopedia of Science and Technology.   □

★ BRAGG, Sir (William) Lawrence
British physicist
Born Mar. 31, 1890, Adelaide, South Australia

IN COLLABORATION with his father, William Henry Bragg, Bragg developed the x-ray analysis of the arrangement of atoms in crystalline structures. This analysis made it possible to study the architecture of matter, to understand the way in which its structure arises from the nature of interatomic forces, and to explain the physical properties of matter in terms of atomic arrangement. For their work they were jointly awarded the Nobel Prize for physics in 1915.

In 1912, M. von Laue in Germany published his famous discovery of the diffraction of x-rays by the regularly arranged atoms in a crystal. At that time W. H. Bragg believed that x-rays were not waves but were neutral particles radiating from the x-ray tube. He was led to this belief by his experiments on the ionization of a gas by x-rays, which he correctly interpreted

as produced by cathode rays excited in individual atoms by the x-ray bombardment. In the summer holiday of 1912 father and son often discussed possible explanations of Laue's results as due to particles shooting down avenues in the crystal. But when the younger Bragg returned to Cambridge, where he was a student, and studied Laue's paper intensively, he was soon convinced on the one hand that his results could only be explained in terms of waves, and on the other hand that certain complex features in the distribution of the diffracted spots were not due to the characteristics of the x-rays, as Laue had supposed, but to the character of the crystalline arrangement. This idea resulted in Bragg's analyzing a few simple crystals, starting with rock salt, and showing that x-rays are specularly reflected from crystal planes.

The elder Bragg based his experimental work on this last discovery, and constructed the x-ray spectrometer and found the spectra of a number of elements. He was at first mainly interested in x-rays, but it soon became evident that the spectrometer was a far more powerful means of analyzing crystals than the Laue photograph. It was at this point that father and son joined forces and together founded the new science of x-ray crystallography.

After the 1914–18 war, W. H. Bragg founded a school of x-ray crystallography at the Royal Institution in London, and W. L. Bragg created one in his physics department in Manchester. These two schools trained almost all the first generation of x-ray crystallographers.

Just after the war W. L. Bragg put forward the idea of "atomic radii." Although in its original form it had a wrong datum line, this conception helped very greatly in analysis. Then with his researchers he developed quantitative methods of measurement, comparing the incident and diffracted beams ("absolute measurements"). This development had a profound influence and made it possible to determine struc-

tures with many uncertain variables or "parameters." They used the silicates as experimental material and were led to a much deeper understanding of minerals in general. He had also a team under A. J. Bradley investigating alloys, and with E. S. Williams and C. Sykes developed the theory of the "order-disorder" phenomenon. Concurrently, his father in London started and developed the analysis of organic bodies.

W. L. Bragg tried consistently to improve x-ray analysis as a tool, and this led to his interest in the analysis of biological molecules containing many thousands of atoms, which was so spectacularly achieved by M. F. Perutz and J. C. Kendrew in the Medical Research Council unit that grew up in the Cavendish Laboratory, and by D. Phillips in Bragg's laboratory in London.

Apart from research, Bragg's main interest was in lecturing and teaching. He was fascinated by the problems of popular lecturing and talks to young people. In the last 10 years he had over 100,000 boys and girls in his audiences.

W. L. Bragg got his first degree in mathematics at Adelaide University, where his father was professor of physics, and then entered Trinity College, Cambridge. In World War I he had the assignment of starting sound ranging (locating enemy guns by sound) for the British Army in France and Belgium. He was professor of physics at Manchester (1919–37), director of the National Physical Laboratory (1937–38), Cavendish Professor at Cambridge (1938–53), and, after 1954, director of the Royal Institution.

Bragg wrote *X-rays and Crystal Structure*, with W. H. Bragg (1915), *The Crystalline State* (1934), *Electricity* (1936), and *Atomic Structure of Minerals* (1937).

For background information *see* X-RAY CRYSTALLOGRAPHY; X-RAY DIFFRACTION in the McGraw-Hill Encyclopedia of Science and Technology   □

★ BRAMBELL, Francis William Rogers

British zoologist
Born Feb. 25, 1901, Sandycove, Co. Dublin, Ireland

STUDYING THE transference of protein molecules in mammals from the circulation of the mother to that of the offspring, Brambell and his associates showed that in the rabbit the transference occurred during gestation by way of the uterine cavity and the fetal yolk sac, not across the placenta as had been supposed. Transmission was shown to be a selective process in that gamma globulins are transmitted more

readily than other serum proteins, irrespective of molecular size, and those of some species more readily than those of others. For this achievement, Brambell in 1964 was awarded a Royal Medal of the Royal Society of London.

In 1892 Paul Ehrlich showed that, in mice, maternal circulating antibodies were transmitted to the young both while they were still in the uterus and after birth by way of the mammary secretions. It was later found that young mammals are equipped with passive immunity transferred to them from their mothers before they develop an active immunity of their own. This occurs before birth in rabbits, guinea pigs, and man, and immediately after birth in domestic ungulates; rats, mice, dogs, and cats acquire it both before and after birth. It was assumed that transmission before birth was by way of the placenta.

In the 1930s Brambell was studying the estrus cycles and reproduction of various mammals in the wild state. This led on to an extensive study of prenatal mortality in wild rabbits, when these animals were of economic importance in World War II. Trying to find the cause of this mortality, he found that maternal serum proteins were present normally in the contents of the embryonic yolk sac. This caused him to suspect that the antibody globulins might be transferred by this route. He and his associates demonstrated that this was so by the use of globulins, labeled by their biological activity, or by radioisotopes, together with experimental surgery of the gravid uterus and fetus. This approach made possible precise comparisons of the rates of transmission of various serum proteins and led to the discovery of the selective nature of the process, those protein molecules that were not transmitted to the fetal circulation being degraded by the fetal cells.

The investigation was extended to transmission in rats and mice, particularly to that which occurs after birth by way of the mother's milk

and the intestine of the young animal. Again the transmission was found to be selective; moreover, some gamma globulins interfered with the transmission of others. To account for these results, Brambell suggested that the globulins were absorbed into the cells by pinocytosis and that the molecules that were to be transmitted to the circulation became attached to specific receptors in the cells, the unattached molecules being degraded. Results from many other laboratories later confirmed the route of transmission in rabbits, the selective nature of the transmission, and, by electron microscopy, the pinocytotic absorption.

Brambell's researches threw light on the method of transmission of large molecules across biological membranes and on the selective attachment of proteins to cells, as well as on the processes by which the young animal acquired its immunity from the mother. They bore not only on problems concerning the resistance of the infant to infections but also on hemolytic diseases of the newborn caused by transmission of maternal antibodies that react with antigens of the young that the mother lacks.

Educated at Trinity College, Dublin, where he graduated B.A. in 1922, and Ph.D. in 1924, Brambell worked subsequently at University College, London, graduating D.Sc. in 1927, and at King's College, London. He was appointed professor of zoology in the University College of North Wales, Bangor, of the University of Wales, in 1930.

Brambell wrote *The Development of Sex in Vertebrates* (1930) and *Antibodies and Embryos*, with W. A. Hemmings and M. Henderson (1951).

For background information *see* BLOOD GROUPS; IMMUNITY in the McGraw-Hill Encyclopedia of Science and Technology.   □

☆ **BRATTAIN, Walter Houser**

American physicist
Born Feb. 10, 1902, Amoy, China

WHILE TRYING to understand the surface properties of semiconductors, Brattain, in cooperation with John Bardeen, demonstrated amplification in a germanium wafer. This experiment led to the invention of the first transistor—the point-contact transistor. For that achievement Brattain received the 1956 Nobel Prize in physics jointly with John Bardeen and William Shockley, his associates at Bell Telephone Laboratories.

The scientific understanding of semiconductors begins with the application of quantum mechanics to the theory of solids in the 1930s.

Particularly important was Sir Alan Wilson's work describing conduction in terms of excess electrons and holes. In semiconductors, electrical current can flow only when imperfections are present in the crystal's electronic structure. These imperfections can be of two types: excess electrons freed from the valence bonds of the crystal or places known as "holes" from which electrons are missing in the bonds. By adding the proper impurities to the semiconductor crystal, one can obtain crystals with either excess electrons ("n-type") or with holes ("p-type").

On the basis of the Mott-Schottky theories of rectification, Shockley believed he could make a semiconductor amplify electrical signals by modulating the flow of electrons inside the material with an external electric field. Failure to get amplification, and other experimental results that were not understood, led Bardeen to suggest that the electric field was prevented from entering the semiconductor by a layer of electrons trapped on its surface.

To test this theory Brattain shone light on n-type silicon and found that this produced a change in potential between the silicon and a metal electrode near its surface (contact potential). The extra holes and electrons produced by the light changed the surface charge and consequently the surface potential of the silicon. Then these experiments were tried with liquids between the metal electrode and the silicon, and R. B. Gibney and Brattain found that if the liquid was an electrolyte the surface potential of the silicon could be changed by the electrical bias between the electrode and the silicon. This was recognized as Shockley's field effect.

Bardeen suggested to Brattain a geometrical arrangement to use the electrolytic field effect to make an amplifier. They first used a block of p-type silicon on which a thin n-type surface layer had been produced by oxidation. A point

contact surrounded by, but insulated from, a drop of electrolyte was made to the layer. A large-area low-resistance contact was made to the base of the block. They found they could control the magnitude of the current from the base to the point by applying a potential to the electrolyte. Current amplification at very low frequencies was then achieved.

The silicon was then replaced with n-type germanium, and power amplification was obtained still only at low frequencies. The lack of any response at higher frequencies, they reasoned, was due to the electrolyte. They tried to replace the electrolyte with a layer of evaporated gold on top of an anodic oxide film formed on the germanium. When this experiment was tried a new effect, now known as "transistor action," was observed. In the process the oxide film had been washed off, and the gold film was in contact with the germanium surface.

They found that current flowing in the forward direction from the gold contact influenced current flowing in the reverse direction in a neighboring point contact in such a way as to produce amplification. This suggested that holes were flowing from the gold contact biased in the forward direction to the other contact biased in the reverse direction with respect to the base contact.

Experiments were continued, and on Dec. 23, 1947, a speech amplifier giving a power amplification of 18 or more, with good quality and good frequency response, was demonstrated. The first transistor was essentially a small wafer of germanium onto one surface of which two gold contacts were made, side by side and very close together. On the opposite surface of the wafer, a third ohmic contact was made. Later the gold contacts were replaced with bronze points cut like a chisel.

A man of a pioneer family, Brattain spent his early life on his parents' cattle ranch in Washington. He majored in physics and mathematics at Whitman College, where he received his B.S. in 1924. Two years later he received his M.A. from the University of Oregon and in 1929 his Ph.D. from the University of Minnesota. Before joining Bell Telephone Laboratories in 1929 as a research physicist, he worked for the radio section of the National Bureau of Standards in Washington. During World War II he was associated with the National Defense Research Committee at Columbia University, where he worked on magnetic detection of submarines. He was elected to the National Academy of Sciences in 1959.

For background information *see* TRANSISTOR in the McGraw-Hill Encyclopedia of Science and Technology.   □

★ **BRAUN, Armin Charles John**

American plant biologist
Born Sept. 5, 1911, Milwaukee, Wis., U.S.A.

USING PLANT tumor cells as an experimental model, Braun defined in physiological and biochemical terms the reason why such cell types grow autonomously and thus fail to respond to the morphogenetic restraints that govern so precisely the growth of all normal cells within an organism. He also determined the nature of the heritable cellular change that leads to the autonomous growth of a plant tumor cell. The significance of this work lies in the fact that the dynamics of these relatively simple plant tumor systems are now rather well understood and may, therefore, serve as useful models for the elucidation of certain principles that underlie tumorous growth generally. For his contributions Braun received the Newcomb Cleveland Award of the American Association for the Advancement of Science in 1949.

The striking similarities that exist between plant and animal tumor cells were recognized early in the present century by Erwin F. Smith of the U.S. Department of Agriculture, and by C. O. Jensen, a Danish pathologist who, because of his pioneering studies in the transplantation of animal tumors, is generally regarded as the father of modern experimental cancer research. It was not, however, until 1941 that Philip R. White, in collaboration with Braun, demonstrated unequivocally, with the use of tissue-culture methods, that the plant tumor cell, like the animal cancer cell, is a persistently altered cell that reproduces true to type and against the growth of which there is no adequate control mechanism in a host. Thus plant tumor cells possess the essential biological characteristics upon which all other diagnostic features of tumorous diseases of animals ultimately depend. Since the tumor problem is, in its very essence, a dynamic problem of abnormal and autonomous cell growth and division, Braun attempted to characterize the cellular changes that result in a capacity for autonomous growth of a plant tumor cell. He found that during the transition from a normal cell to a rapidly growing, fully autonomous tumor cell a series of quite distinct but well-defined biosynthetic systems, which represent the entire area of metabolism concerned with cell growth and division, become progressively and persistently activated. The degree of activation of those biosynthetic systems within a cell determines the rate at which the tumor cell grows. Included among the biosynthetic systems shown to be persistently unblocked in the plant tumor cell are those that produce two hormones, one of which is concerned with cell enlargement, while the other acts synergistically with the first to trigger cell division. In addition, a number of biosynthetic systems, the products of which are required for the production of the nucleic acids, the specialized mitotic proteins, and other substances that are needed specifically for cell growth and division, are functional in the tumor cells. Normal cells do not produce any of those essential growth-promoting substances. Thus, the capacity for autonomous growth of the plant tumor cell finds its explanation in terms of cellular nutrition. The tumor cells have acquired the capacity to produce all of the essential growth substances that their normal counterparts require for cell growth and division but cannot make.

Braun demonstrated further that the essential biosynthetic systems shown to be activated during the transformation of a normal cell to a tumor cell can again be repressed under certain special experimental conditions and thus a complete recovery from the tumorous state can be achieved. The significance of this finding lies in the fact that it demonstrates that the nuclei of the normal and tumor cells are genetically equivalent and thus the tumorous state in the biological system studied depends on a change in the expression rather than on a change in the integrity of the genetic information that is present in a cell.

That results obtained with plant tumor cells may have broader biological implications is suggested by the fact that recently two different but well-documented instances have appeared in the animal tumor literature in which a complete recovery from the cancerous state was achieved experimentally by applying biological principles that had first been successfully used to achieve a recovery of plant tumor cells. This sort of information is of use because it gives insight into the nature of the heritable change that leads to the autonomous growth of a tumor cell.

A teacher's son, Braun majored in plant pathology and microbiology at the University of Wisconsin at Madison, where he received his B.S. in 1934 and his Ph.D. in 1938. Predoctoral study was carried out in several European scientific institutes in 1937. Braun joined the Rockefeller Institute as a Fellow in 1938. Except for the period 1943–46 when he served as captain in the U.S. Army, he remained at the Rockefeller Institute, reaching the rank of professor and member in 1959. He was elected to the National Academy of Sciences in 1960.

For background information *see* TUMOR in the McGraw-Hill Encyclopedia of Science and Technology.   □

★ **BREWER, Leo**

American chemist
Born June 13, 1919, St. Louis, Mo., U.S.A.

WORK WITH the Manhattan District (atom bomb) Project during World War II stimulated Brewer's interest in the chemical behavior of high-temperature systems. Thereafter he engaged in a long series of investigations aiming to establish the general principles of high-temperature behavior and to develop new materials and methods for research in high-temperature systems. For his achievements in this field, Brewer received the U.S. Atomic Energy Commission's E. O. Lawrence Memorial Award in 1961.

In the early 1940s the chemical properties of metallic plutonium were unknown. While engaged on the Manhattan Project at Berkeley, California, Brewer and a group consisting of L. A. Bromley, N. L. Lofgren, and P. W. Gilles were assigned the tasks of predicting the possible range of high-temperature chemical behavior of plutonium metal; of developing refractory materials capable of containing molten plutonium without excessive contamination, even if the worst prediction should be true; and finally

of developing a microanalytical procedure for determination of oxygen.

The first of these tasks led to a fundamental examination of the principles of high-temperature behavior of all of the elements, which resulted in a series of papers describing the high-temperature behavior of metals, oxides, halides, and many other compounds. The second task led to the development of the refractory sulfides of Ce, Th, and U, which were fabricated into forms capable of containing the most electropositive metals. The third task led to a theory of solvents for vacuum-fusion analysis of metals and to the development of a micro method of analysis of electropositive metals using a molten-platinum bath.

The examination of high-temperature data indicated that the commonly accepted values for the enthalpy of C gas and the dissociation energy of N_2 were probably too low. Following the war, Brewer, with Gilles and F. A. Jenkins, undertook the study of the vapor pressure of graphite and demonstrated a much higher enthalpy of C gas. Also a flame study of Brewer, A. G. Gaydon, and N. Thomas demonstrated a high dissociation energy for N_2. These experiments stimulated a large number of confirming experiments that clearly established the high values for both atomic carbon and nitrogen.

The wartime study also uncovered abnormalities in vapor-pressure data that indicated polymerization in high-temperature vapors. With Lofgren, Brewer undertook a study of cuprous chloride and demonstrated that cuprous chloride vapor contained mainly Cu_3Cl_3. This led to a general theory predicting that saturated high-temperature vapors would be complex mixtures of species and that the complexity would increase with increasing temperature. In recent years these predictions have been confirmed by high-temperature workers for many systems. Brewer's interest in halide vapors continued with extensive reviews, together with G. R. Somayajulu, E. Brackett, and M. Shetlar, of the thermodynamics of halide vapors. Interest in the kinetics of high-temperature vaporization processes, initiated by the graphite vapor-pressure work, led to work with K. Moztfeldt on Na_2CO_3 and with J. S. Kane on phosphorus that characterized some features of kinetic barriers to vaporization and resulted in generalizations about the occurrence and consequences of low vaporization and condensation coefficients.

With H. Haraldsen, D. L. Sawyer, D. H. Templeton, C. H. Dauben, and O. H. Krikorian, Brewer continued his work on refractories with pioneering studies of the refractory silicides and borides and consideration of the nature of their chemical bonding. This program was extended to intermetallic compounds through use of the Engel correlation of electronic and crystal structures. As a result, Brewer and his colleagues predicted the structures and compositions of the phases of most of the two-billion multicomponent phase diagrams of the transition metals.

The importance of oxides in high-temperature systems had led Brewer to theoretical and experimental work with A. W. Searcy, D. F. Mastick, R. K. Edwards, F. Greene, P. Zavitsanos, G. R. B. Elliott, J. L. Margrave, R. F. Porter, S. Trajmar, G. M. Rosenblatt, R. M. Walsh, and R. H. Hague that characterized the high-temperature thermodynamics of oxides. The spectroscopic study of gases in equilibrium with graphite, made with L. K. Templeton, J. G. Phillips, O. H. Krikorian, W. T. Hicks, J. L. Engelke, and L. Hagan, was also a substantial effort. With C. G. James, E. R. Worden, R. G. Brewer, F. E. Stafford, R. A. Berg, J. Link, and A. Chutjian, Brewer carried out additional spectroscopic studies designed to fix thermodynamic data of gases by way of radiative-lifetime determinations. Recently the isolation-matrix technique of G. Pimentel was used by B. Meyer, D. Brabson, and Brewer for study of high-temperature species. The thermodynamic applications of these data are well illustrated by the second edition (1961) of Lewis and Randall's *Thermodynamics*, which was revised by Brewer and K. S. Pitzer.

Brewer received his B.S. at the California Institute of Technology in 1940 and his Ph.D. at the University of California, Berkeley, in 1943. After wartime work with the Manhattan District Project at Berkeley, he joined the faculty there in 1946, becoming professor of physical chemistry in 1955 and head of the Inorganic Materials Research Division of the Lawrence Radiation Laboratory in 1961. He was elected to the National Academy of Sciences in 1959.

For background information *see* FLAMES; REFRACTORY; THERMOCHEMISTRY; THERMODYNAMIC PROCESSES in the McGraw-Hill Encyclopedia of Science and Technology.   □

BRIDGMAN, Percy Williams

American physicist
Born Apr. 21, 1882, Cambridge, Mass., U.S.A.
Died Aug. 20, 1961, Randolph, N.H., U.S.A.

A LEAKPROOF seal that Bridgman devised for his high-pressure apparatus enabled him to attain very high pressures and to study their effects on the physical properties of matter. Bridgman's original measurements included many discoveries in the fields of polymorphic transitions of substances, high-pressure effects on both ordinary and heavy water, the viscosity of fluids, and the elastic properties of solid bodies. For his achievements in the design and

construction of high-pressure apparatus and in the formulation of techniques basic to the continued investigation of high-pressure physics, Bridgman was awarded the 1946 Nobel Prize in physics.

The origin of high-pressure physics can be traced to the middle of the 18th century when the English physicist John Canton demonstrated that water was measurably compressible. Although subsequent high-pressure research was limited by the difficulty in preparing suitable apparatus, the French physicists Louis Paul Cailletet and Emile Hilaire Amagat made significant contributions during the second half of the 19th century. Amagat developed a special technique for ensuring an effective seal which permitted him to obtain pressures of 3000 atmospheres. However, the assumption that Amagat's pressure limit of 3000 atmospheres could not be exceeded due to leakages developing in the hydrostatic assembly caused interest in the branch of physics to decline.

In 1905, while working toward his doctorate at Harvard University, Bridgman began to study certain optical phenomena under the influence of pressure. When an explosion damaged part of the equipment, he tried to find a use for the pressure assembly. To this end he developed a sealing device that enabled him to exceed Amagat's limit by ever-increasing factors. The fundamental principle of his apparatus lay in the method by which the piston was packed. The basic hydrostatic equipment is a piston forced into a cylindrical hole in a steel block and made to exert a compressive strength upon a liquid. To prevent the liquid from leaking past the piston, Bridgman designed a packing assembly

consisting of a ring of hardened steel, a cup-shaped washer of soft steel, a packing of soft rubber, and a mushroom-shaped, heat-treated steel device that he inserted between the liquid and the piston. The essential feature of this arrangement was that the stem of the mushroom did not reach entirely through the steel ring but remained unsupported. This method has been described as the principle of the unsupported area. In practice, the entire effort of the piston was transmitted to the mushroom through the packing. Since the total area of the packing was less than the total area of the piston by an amount equal to the area of the stem, the pressure in the packing was greater, by a fixed per cent, than the pressure exerted by the piston in the liquid. The result was a system protected against leakage at any pressure range and effective for any modification of design.

Although greater emphasis had been given to the study of temperature effects on the properties of matter, Bridgman realized that pressure was as important an independent variable as temperature. To demonstrate his assumptions, Bridgman had to develop experimental techniques suited to ascending pressure ranges, to make full and accurate descriptions of the magnitude of these pressures, and to locate transition points in the behavior of substances that could be used as indications of applied pressures. The problem that first presented itself, with regard to technique, was the extension of the range; the second problem was to find what could be done with the new pressures.

Proceeding on the assumption that the limits of a pressure range were set by the strength of the containing vessel, Bridgman made an intensive investigation of materials. His first apparatus was a cylinder of one-piece construction of the best heat-treated alloy steel. At a pressure of 12,000 atmospheres, Bridgman studied nearly all the ordinary physical properties of substances and was able, in some instances, to reach 20,000 atmospheres for brief periods of time.

Bridgman's next step toward a higher pressure range was to combine the best materials with special methods of construction. He equipped the pressure cylinder with an external support and increased the compressive strength of the piston through the use of tungsten carbide or carboloy. With this technique, Bridgman was able to perform routine experiments up to 30,000 atmospheres, to introduce electrically insulated leads into the apparatus, and to repeat practically all the former experiments at this new range. By reducing test volumes, Bridgman was later able to extend the pressure range to 50,000 atmospheres.

A number of techniques now being available to Bridgman, he attempted another extension of the pressure range. By utilizing tungsten carbide construction for the cylinder and immersing the pressure vessel in a fluid, which in turn was subject to a pressure of 30,000 atmospheres, a new pressure range of 100,000 atmospheres was readily sustained. At this range, Bridgman discovered that the pressures were no longer truly hydrostatic, and he had to devise novel departures from his earlier techniques to measure electrical resistance, compressibility, and shearing strength of elements, alloys, and compounds. He was able to extend this range to 425,000 atmospheres in a limited number of cases.

Employing a modification of Bridgman's apparatus to obtain 100,000 atmospheres, in 1955 engineers of the General Electric Company successfully synthesized industrial-grade diamonds from graphite. Among the numerous results that Bridgman achieved were the identification of seven different modifications of ice as well as two new forms of phosphorus: a stable black phosphorus and an unstable form. Bridgman's work is of direct application to geophysics, crystallography, and other branches of science and technology. It is of theoretical importance in the investigation of the effects of high pressure on the outer structure of the atom.

A reporter's son, Bridgman attended Harvard University, receiving his A.B. in 1904, his M.A. in 1905, and his Ph.D. in physics in 1908. He immediately joined the faculty at Harvard, becoming an instructor in 1910, an assistant professor in 1919, and professor of mathematics and natural philosophy in 1926. He retired in 1954.

Bridgman wrote a number of books, among them *The Logic of Modern Physics* (1927), *The Physics of High Pressure* (1931), and *The Nature of Physical Theory* (1936).

For background information *see* HIGH-PRESSURE PHENOMENA; HIGH-PRESSURE PROCESSES in the McGraw-Hill Encyclopedia of Science and Technology.   □

★ **BROUWER, Dirk**

American astronomer
Born Sept. 1, 1902, Rotterdam, Netherlands
Died Jan. 31, 1966, New Haven, Conn., U.S.A.

B ROUWER'S PRINCIPAL scientific contributions were in the field of dynamical astronomy or celestial mechanics, a subject that, according to Laplace, is "a great problem of mechanics, the arbitrary data of which are the elements of the celestial movements. Its solution depends both on the accuracy of observations and on the perfection of analysis." Brouwer's activity was mostly in the direction of perfecting the methods of analysis and adapting them to changing conditions. In addition, his active interest in the observational aspects of celestial mechanics was shown by his contributions to photographic astrometry. For his contributions to celestial mechanics Brouwer received the Gold Medal of the Royal Astronomical Society in 1955.

An important branch of dynamical astronomy is planetary theory. A general planetary theory is a solution of the differential equations of motion of a planet in which the attractions by the Sun and the various principal planets are taken into account. If the planetary attractions were ignored, the body would move in a fixed ellipse in accordance with Kepler's laws. A planetary theory gives expressions as functions of the time for the deviations of the actual motion from the motion in a fixed ellipse. Although the equations of motion are simplest in rectangular coordinates, no satisfactory method for obtaining the perturbations in rectangular coordinates existed until Brouwer (1944) solved the problem and thereby created a new method for constructing general planetary theories.

All conventional forms of planetary theory have the drawback that the time is present in the coefficients of periodic terms. Such a theory may represent the motion of a planet satisfactorily for a number of centuries, but it fails to yield information on the character of the orbital changes over periods of, say, millions of years. The theory of secular variations, first developed by Lagrange, overcomes this drawback at the cost of ignoring the periodic effects. Several such solutions have been made at various times. The most recent and most extensive solution was made by Brouwer and A. J. J. van Woerkom (1950). From such a solution the long-term changes in the orbits of asteroids may be calculated. In this way the Japanese astronomer Hirayama succeeded in establishing the existence of six families of asteroids, the members of which have so nearly identical secular elements that the common origin of the members of a family from a parent body cannot be questioned. Brouwer refined Hirayama's work and showed the existence of additional groups of asteroids that also exhibit similarities in their secular elements. Somewhat related was his earlier study (1947) of the secular variations

of Encke's comet and its relationship with the Taurid group of meteors.

The rapid development of high-speed calculating machines after 1945 benefited the entire field of celestial mechanics. The method of numerical integration was applied with increasing success to the study of orbits. An early major undertaking was that by W. J. Eckert, Brouwer, and G. M. Clemence (1951), which by numerical integration provided accurate orbits of the five outer planets for the years 1653 to 2060.

Other contributions in related fields were a method of orbit correction by W. J. Eckert and Brouwer (1937) that has been generally adopted throughout the world, and a study (1937) of the rounding error affecting numerical integration. The latter yielded the result that the error in the position in the orbit increases statistically as the 3/2 power of the number of integration steps; the errors in the elements that determine the size, shape, and orientation of the orbit increase as the 1/2 power of the number of steps.

Among the most puzzling problems of astronomy was that posed by the gaps in the distribution of the thousands of small planets between the orbits of Mars and Jupiter; Brouwer explained these satisfactorily in 1963. He also showed that the fluctuations in the rate of rotation of the Earth are of a statistical character that would be produced by random disturbances, and he proposed the name *ephemeris time*, which has been adopted throughout the world for the measure of time that is free from such effects. In 1959 he solved the problem of the effect of the oblateness of the Earth on the motions of artificial satellites. This solution, of great practical value as well as theoretical interest, is completely general and immediately applicable to any satellite.

In addition to his contributions to celestial mechanics Brouwer successfully tackled several knotty problems in astrometry, which may be called the accurate mapping of the stars and derivation of their motions. As director of the Yale Observatory after 1941, he gave vigorous support to its traditional activity in this field and devised important new techniques and programs. With the financial assistance of the Ford Foundation he caused to be constructed a double 20-in. astrographic telescope recently installed at the Yale-Columbia Southern Observatory in the province of San Juan, Argentina, which is operated in cooperation with the University of Cuyo, a national university of Argentina. With this telescope the astrometric program initiated at the Lick Observatory for the northern hemisphere will be extended to cover the entire sky.

Son of a civil service employee in the city of Rotterdam, Brouwer studied mathematics and astronomy in the University of Leiden, where he specialized in celestial mechanics under Willem deSitter and received the Ph.D. degree in 1927. In September, 1927, he went to the United States on an International Education Board fellowship for postdoctoral study at the University of California, Berkeley, and Yale University. In 1928 he became research assistant to E. W. Brown at Yale. He remained at Yale, becoming in 1941 a professor, chairman of the department of astronomy, and director of the observatory. In 1944 he was named Munson Professor of Natural Philosophy and Astronomy. He was elected to the National Academy of Sciences in 1951.

Brouwer wrote *Methods of Celestial Mechanics*, with G. M. Clemence (1961).

For background information *see* CELESTIAL MECHANICS in the McGraw-Hill Encyclopedia of Science and Technology.   □

★ BROWN, George Harold

American electrical engineer
Born Oct. 14, 1908, North Milwaukee, Wis., U.S.A.

IN THE course of his thesis work and subsequently in industry, Brown produced a body of theory and analytical deductions, supported by many experimental results, that became the basis for present practices in the design of antennas for radio broadcasting.

In 1934, vertical radiators were just coming into use, and they failed to perform in accordance with the generally accepted theory. In a series of mathematical analyses, measurements on models, and confirming field tests, Brown, an engineer with Radio Corporation of America, demonstrated that the departure from theory was due to nonsinusoidal distribution of current on the antenna and that the error was particularly large for antennas of nonuniform cross section, such as the guyed cantilever type then in vogue. Further field experiments with top loading by means of top hats confirmed this

and led to the now universal use of uniform cross-section towers. The full results of this work were published in April, 1935, in the *Proceedings of the Institute of Radio Engineers* and immediately became, and has remained, the standard reference in this field.

In the January, 1937, issue of the same journal, Brown published his now-famous paper, "Directional Antennas." Explaining the method of calculating directional patterns, and including illustrations of a large number of standard patterns, this paper, along with his earlier papers, found its way into the notebooks of every station engineer and most consultants. A whole generation of broadcast engineers learned about directional arrays from this paper, and most of the directional arrays in use today were probably calculated from it.

In 1936, Brown conceived the Turnstile antenna for FM radio and television broadcasting long before television had become a commercial service. The Turnstile antenna is now the standard unit for commercial television broadcasting.

Continuing his investigations in 1937 and 1938, he derived the now-classic generalized equation that solved a variety of problems such as the flow of heat in materials heated by radio-frequency power, the voltages on guy-wire insulators of transmitting towers, and the performance of wave antennas.

In 1938, Brown turned his attention to television problems and developed the vestigial sideband filter for use with television transmitters. This device doubled the horizontal resolution of television pictures in a given bandwidth. Vestigial sideband filters are now an integral part of the Federal Communications Commission's standards for commercial television broadcasting, and vestigial sideband transmission is used in all other countries where television service has been established.

During World War II, Brown worked on the design and development of radio and radar antennas for the military. At the same time, he established many of the basic principles of radio-frequency heating and applied these principles to produce a rapid method of drying penicillin.

Following the war, he turned to ultrahigh-frequency propagation and color television. He supervised RCA's field test of ultrahigh-frequency television in the Washington area in 1948 and with coworkers published what have become the definitive papers on UHF propagation. After 1948, he was in charge of RCA's color television research and development, and he was one of the leading figures in the lengthy development work that led to the adoption of color television standards in the United States.

Brown majored in electrical engineering at the University of Wisconsin, where he received his B.S. in 1930, his M.S. in 1931, his Ph.D. in 1933, and a professional E.E. degree in 1942. He joined the RCA Manufacturing Company in Camden, N.J., in 1933 as a research engineer and remained there until his transfer to the RCA David Sarnoff Research Center, Princeton, N.J., in 1942. In 1952, he was appointed director of the Systems Research Laboratory of RCA, from which he moved to the position of chief engineer, RCA Commercial Electronic Products Division, in 1957. In 1959, he was appointed vice-president, RCA Engineering, and, in 1961, vice-president, RCA Research & Engineering. In June, 1965, he was elected executive vice-president, RCA Research & Engineering.

Brown wrote *Theory and Application of Radio-frequency Heating* (1947).

For background information *see* ANTENNA (AERIAL) in the McGraw-Hill Encyclopedia of Science and Technology. □

★ **BROWN, Herbert Charles**

American chemist
Born May 22, 1912, London, England

P RIOR TO 1940 the boron hydrides and the organoboranes were laboratory curiosities, not utilized in synthetic work. Together with H. I. Schlesinger of the University of Chicago, Brown developed simple practical methods for the synthesis of diborane and discovered the versatile alkali metal borohydrides, making these materials readily available for organic synthesis. These materials have revolutionized the practice of organic reductions. Moreover, the discovery of the rapid quantitative reaction of unsaturated compounds with diborane has made the organoboranes readily available for synthetic work. Finally, his investigations of the addition compounds of trimethylboron and diborane with amines provided a quantitative basis for steric effects in chemical theory. For his work on steric strains, Brown received the 1959 Nichols Medal of the American Chemical

Society; for his contributions to synthetic organic chemistry he received the 1960 A.C.S. Award for Creative Work in Synthetic Organic Chemistry.

Diborane is a gas, highly reactive to air and moisture. Prior to the discoveries here described, it was prepared only in small quantities, primarily for study of the unusual bonding evident in these derivatives. Brown's and Schlesinger's discovery in 1941 that diborane could readily be synthesized by the reaction of lithium hydride or sodium hydride with boron trihalides made this gas readily available for the first time.

$$6\ LiH + 2\ BF_3 \longrightarrow B_2H_6 + 6\ LiF$$

Diborane readily reacts with lithium hydride to produce the borohydride.

$$2\ LiH + B_2H_6 \longrightarrow 2\ LiBH_4$$

A more direct route to sodium borohydride was then discovered.

$$4\ NaH + B(OCH_3)_3 \xrightarrow{250°} NaBH_4 + 3\ NaOCH_3$$

This reaction is the basis of the present industrial method for the manufacture of sodium borohydride. Both diborane and sodium borohydride are excellent reducing agents for organic substances and, together with lithium aluminum hydride, have revolutionized the methods used to reduce functional groups.

$$RCO_2H \xrightarrow[0°]{B_2H_6} RCH_2OH$$

In 1955 Brown discovered that unsaturated organic compounds can be rapidly and quantitatively converted into organoboranes.

$$6\ RCH{=}CH_2 + B_2H_6 \xrightarrow{R_2O} 2\ (RCH_2CH_2)_3B$$

Exploration of the chemical characteristics of these organoboranes led Brown and his students to the discovery of a number of reactions that cause the organoboranes to be of major utility in synthetic chemistry.

$$(RCH_2CH_2)_3B \xrightarrow{RCO_2H} RCH_2CH_3$$

$$(RCH_2CH_2)_3B \xrightarrow{NaOH,H_2O_2} RCH_2CH_2OH$$

$$(RCH_2CH_2)_3B \xrightarrow{H_2NOSO_3H} RCH_2CH_2NH_2$$

$$(RCH_2CH_2)_3B \xrightarrow{NaOH,AgNO_3} \underset{\underset{RCH_2CH_2}{|}}{RCH_2CH_2}$$

Diborane, boron trifluoride, and trimethylboron react with amines to form molecular addition compounds.

$$(CH_3)_3N + B(CH_3)_3 \longrightarrow (CH_3)_3N{:}B(CH_3)_3$$

The reaction is reversible at higher temperatures. Consequently, study of the dissociation at several temperatures permits calculation of the free energy, the enthalpy, and the entropy of dissociation. By making a systematic study of the stability of the molecular addition compounds as a function of the steric requirements of the boron component and of the amine component, Brown was able to attain a quantitative estimate of the steric strains accompanying the formation of various types of sterically congested structures. He showed that strains of the same order of magnitude were present in related carbon structures. In this way he was led to propose for the first time that steric effects can assist, as well as hinder, the rates of chemical reactions. This led him to explore the role of steric effects in solvolytic reactions, displacement reactions, and elimination reactions. As a result of his work, and that of others, steric effects again have an important and respected place in organic theory.

Born in London, England, Brown was taken to the United States at an early age, and all of his education was in Chicago schools. He attended Wright Junior College (1934–35) and the University of Chicago (B.S., 1936; Ph.D., 1938). Following a year spent as postdoctorate research fellow with M. S. Kharasch, he became research assistant to H. I. Schlesinger. In 1943 he went to Wayne University as assistant professor, and in 1947 went to Purdue as professor. In 1959 he was named R. B. Wetherill Professor, and in 1960 he became the R. B. Wetherill Research Professor. He was elected to the National Academy of Sciences in 1957.

Brown wrote *Hydroboration* (1962) and over 300 scientific papers.

For background information *see* BORANE in the McGraw-Hill Encyclopedia of Science and Technology.   □

★ BRUECKNER, Keith Allen

American physicist
Born Mar. 19, 1924, Minneapolis, Minn., U.S.A.

IN THE late 1940s and early 1950s, experiments carried out with high-energy accelerators made it possible for the first time to determine many details of the interactions between nuclear particles or nucleons (neutrons and protons). The existence and characteristics of the subnuclear particle largely responsible for the nuclear forces, the π-meson, had also been established by this time. In studying the nature of the nuclear forces, Brueckner was led to more general questions concerning the structure of the nu-

cleus, particularly the phenomena of nuclear saturation and the semiempirical model of nuclear motion, the nuclear shell model. He recognized characteristic difficulties in the theories of many-body systems existing at that time and proposed solutions to these problems. His initial steps led to the clarification of several basic problems of nuclear structure and also to the development of the broad-ranging modern theory of "the many-body problem," which now is one of the most important fields of mathematical physics. In addition to the application to nuclear structure, this field covers diverse problems in statistical mechanics, solid-state physics, and the theory of liquids and solids. For this work, Brueckner received the Dannie Heineman Prize of the American Physical Society in 1963.

Before the initial operation in 1947 of the first high-energy accelerator, the Berkeley 184-in. synchrocyclotron, information concerning the forces between two nucleons was derived from the interaction of nucleons at low energy and was insufficient to give details of the interaction. During this period, from the early 1930s until the late 1940s, it was assumed, following a suggestion of W. K. Heisenberg in the absence of information to the contrary, that the saturation of nuclear forces leading to the approximately uniform central densities of all large nuclei was due to strong repulsive exchange forces. These would not affect low-energy phenomena but would become effective at the relatively high energies characteristic of nuclear motion (relative energies as high as 80 Mev). By 1950 the Berkeley experiments had shown that this model

of nuclear forces was invalid. The rapidly increasing experimental knowledge had by the early 1950s also shown that the nuclear interaction appeared to be strongly repulsive at small distances, so that nucleons upon close encounter acted like "hard spheres" with a hard-core repulsion at a range of approximately 30% of the average nucleus spacing in nuclei. These discoveries could not, within the theoretical methods available at that time, be incorporated into a revised theory of nuclear structure.

The problem of utilizing the experimental results and concurrently developing theoretical understanding of the nucleon-nucleon interaction was further complicated by the independent discovery by M. G. Mayer and J. H. D. Jensen of the highly successful nuclear shell model. The most important feature of the shell model was the assumption that the nucleons moved in independent-particle orbits determined by the shell-model potential, which represented the average interaction of the nucleon with the other nuclear particles. For the model to be valid, it appeared to be essential that the very strong short-ranged forces between nucleons not affect their motion. This feature led to several suggestions that, in the dense nuclear medium, the forces were in some way suppressed or averaged out. This view was, however, already contradicted in the early 1950s by high-energy experiments showing marked short-range correlation between nucleons, consistent with the directly measured interactions between nucleon pairs and apparently inconsistent with the shell model.

In the context of these problems, Brueckner, using the techniques of quantum field theory, first examined the possibility of marked modification in the nuclear medium of the nuclear forces measured in two-nucleon experiments. He came to the conclusion that very small alteration was to be expected and that the forces act at very nearly full strength in the nucleus. He then turned to a direct determination of the nuclear properties, assuming the empirically determined two-nucleon forces to be correct for consideration of nuclear properties. To carry out this evaluation, it was necessary to develop an approximation method suitable for dealing with a large number of particles interacting under conditions where quantum effects were important. Brueckner recognized that existing perturbation methods, in which profound convergence difficulties in dealing with this problem had been known (for two decades) to exist, could be readily rearranged into an alternative form. He called this form the "linked-cluster expansion," in which formal difficulties were largely removed and successive approximations to the exact answer to the problem could in principle be calculated. This simplification was based on the intuitive argument that if the energy of a many-body system were expanded in powers of the interaction potential, the contributions from separate groups of particles, interacting within each group but not between groups, should contribute separately to the expansion. This simple feature, obscure in the usual approximation methods, was shown by Brueckner to be derivable in the first few orders of perturbation theory. His conjecture that this feature existed in general was later proven by J. Goldstone.

Within this approximation method, Brueckner further introduced a summation of a sequence of interaction terms between nucleon pairs moving in the external field of the remaining nucleons and, within the constraints of the quantum statistics of the nucleons, a further reordering of the perturbation series he termed the reaction-matrix approximation. The formidable mathematical and computational problems presented by these methods were also first solved by Brueckner and his coworkers, who applied the high-speed electronic computer to the evaluation of the basic equations. The numerical results obtained in 1958 by Brueckner and his collaborator, John L. Gammel, for the energy and density of heavy nuclei, using the best empirically derived nucleon-nucleon interactions of that time, were in excellent agreement with the experimental values. These methods have been further elaborated and improved by many other nuclear theorists and applied in alternative forms to the determination of many detailed properties of nuclei. This work continues actively, the latest information on nuclear forces currently presenting new problems in the quantitative understanding of the nucleus.

Following the initial studies of nuclear properties and of the basic difficulties of the many-body problem, Brueckner proceeded to an examination of the problem of the reconciliation of the nuclear properties as given by the many-body theory and as given by the shell model. He showed that the shell model could be applied literally only for certain low-energy observables of the nuclear motion such as angular momentum, parity, and gross orbital parameters, and that more precise observation of the motion would reveal the more complex correlated motion resulting from the powerful effects of the strong short-range nucleon-nucleon forces, as had already been established by experiment. Further developments of the theory have extended to the study of details of the nuclear shell structure, pairing energies, the surface structure of the nucleus, and the scattering interaction of slow nucleons with the nucleus.

Brueckner also considered other many-body problems, among which his most important contributions were the exact determination of the correlation energy of the dense electron gas (with Murray Gell-Mann), the quantitative prediction of the properties of liquid helium-3 (with John L. Gammel), and contributions to the theory and estimates of the properties of liquid helium-4 (with Katuro Sawada).

The son of a professor, Brueckner entered the University of Minnesota in 1941 where, after an interruption for service in the U.S. Air Force, he received a B.A. in mathematics in 1945. After a year at Minnesota, he entered the University of California, Berkeley, as a graduate student in 1947 and received his Ph.D. in physics in 1950. He spent the following year at the Institute for Advanced Study in Princeton, 1951–55 as assistant and associate professor at Indiana University, 1956 on leave at Brookhaven National Laboratory, and 1956–59 as professor of physics at the University of Pennsylvania. In 1959 he joined the faculty of the new campus of the University of California, San Diego, where he served as chairman of the department of physics, dean of Letters and Science, and dean of Graduate Studies. He also held in 1961 and 1962, while on leave from the University of California, the position of vice-president and director of research of the Institute for Defense Analysis, Washington, D.C.

For background information see NUCLEON in the McGraw-Hill Encyclopedia of Science and Technology.   □

BUCHER, Walter Herman

American geologist
Born Mar. 12, 1889, Akron, Ohio, U.S.A.
Died Feb. 17, 1965, Houston, Tex., U.S.A.

A FTER A lifetime of study on the deformation of the Earth's crust, Bucher set forth a hypothesis to explain the origin and geographic pattern of the great mountain chains on the surface of the Earth. In Bucher's theory, the contraction of the Earth due to cooling and the

Earth's gravitation are the dominant orogenic factors.

It is well known to geologists that the Earth's crust is mobile. Simple proof of this is the occurrence of salt-water (marine) fossils in ancient sedimentary rocks now situated high above sea level miles from the nearest ocean. Rock deformation is nowhere more conspicuous than in the orogenic (mountainous) belts where originally flat-lying sedimentary rock layers have been uplifted thousands of feet, tilted, folded, and smashed.

Bucher realized that these orogenic belts yielded to crustal pressure because within them the crust is weaker. The critical question to Bucher was why the volatiles and water vapor rose in only a few long and narrow belts (the sites of mountain chains). An answer was provided (1939), in part, by Sir Harold Jeffreys, who had studied the occurrence and distribution of deep-seated earthquakes. According to Jeffreys, the depths of these earthquakes are on the same order of magnitude as the most probable depths to which cooling of the Earth can have advanced. In other words, there is a zone between 100 and 700 kilometers within the Earth contracting as cooling takes place, with deep earthquakes being indicative of rock adjustment within that zone.

Bucher, seizing upon the data of Jeffreys and others, reasoned that the contractions due to cooling might be sufficiently intense to produce great fractures reaching upward through the crust. These fractures would be ideal conduits for the transfer of heat, water vapor, and volatiles toward the surface.

Based on these assumptions, Bucher advanced his hypothesis in 1956. Postulating an Earth undergoing shrinkage, he visualized the following sequence of events: (1) development of global fractures due to contraction which affected the Earth as a whole; (2) the rise of excess heat, water vapor, and volatiles from deep within the Earth along the fractures; (3) weakening of the crust along the trend of these fractures as viscosity reduction and other alteration of the rocks took place; (4) buckling of the crust in the weakened zones, causing the rise of welts and furrows; (5) partial collapse of the rocks in the welt zone under the influence of gravity after attaining critical height; and (6) production of recumbent or other folds, thrust sheets, and related structures, with gravity continuing to play a major role.

Bucher found highly suggestive evidence to support the concept of global fractures formed in a shrinking Earth by experimenting with models of the Earth. A model was made consisting of a wooden ball 11.25 cm in diameter and an outer shell of Plexiglas. A concentric space between the wood and the Plexiglas was filled with Castolite, a plastic that shrinks upon hardening, which represented the Earth's crust. The Plexiglas held the Castolite against the wooden ball. Shrinkage of the Castolite produced a fracture pattern that strikingly resembled the distribution pattern of mountain chains on the surface of the Earth. For example, one fracture pattern exhibited the hairpin turn created by the West Indies within the Andes-Rocky Mountain Cordillera in the Western Hemisphere.

In order to explain many of the structural details found in the mountainous belts of the Earth and to complete his overall hypothesis, Bucher assigned a major role to the force of gravity. He noted that it was Jeffreys who first (1931) had stated that rocks, if piled high enough, would flatten out under their own weight. This would lead to the spreading and folding of thick sections of rock that had been uplifted within orogenic belts. Virtually all rock types behave as plastics if they are affected by relatively weak but consistent stresses over a very long period of time. Thus, layers of salt and, according to Bucher, even serpentine will flow like glacial ice under gravitational influence. Bucher demonstrated this added characteristic of "solid" rock by using models in which layers of stitching wax, simulating layered sedimentary rocks, were subjected to compression. He was able to duplicate, in this fashion, many of the structural features found in Alpine mountain areas.

Although born in Ohio, Bucher and his family moved to Germany during his youth. It was there that he received his education, culminating in a Ph.D. in geology from Heidelberg in 1911. He returned to the United States and joined the faculty at the University of Cincinnati in 1913, becoming chairman of the department of geology and geography at that institution in 1937. He went to Columbia University in New York in 1940, served as chairman of the geology department there from 1950 to 1953, and became professor emeritus in 1956. In that year Bucher became associated with the Humble Oil and Refining Company in Houston, Tex., as a consultant in structural geology. It was at that company's research laboratory that many of Bucher's model experiments were conducted with the collaboration of Humble scientists. Bucher was awarded the Bowie Medal of the American Geophysical Union in 1955 and the Penrose Medal of the Geological Society of America in 1960. He was elected to the National Academy of Sciences in 1938.

Bucher wrote *Deformation of the Earth's Crust* (1933; reprinted 1964).

For background information *see* OROGENY in the McGraw-Hill Encyclopedia of Science and Technology. □

★ BUDDINGTON, Arthur Francis

American geologist
Born Nov. 29, 1890, Wilmington, Del., U.S.A.

WHILE STUDYING the base-metal ore deposits in the volcanic rocks of the Cascade Range of Oregon, Buddington found mineral assemblages that included both cherty quartz characteristic of low-temperature formation and tourmaline characteristic of high temperature. Such a combination did not fit into the then current classification for ore deposits. The geologic background of these deposits suggested formation at high temperatures and low pressures, and Buddington proposed (1935) the name "xenothermal" for such mineral assemblages. Many ore deposits were subsequently inferred by others to form under these conditions, and the term "xenothermal" became widely adopted.

As a result of regional geology studies in the Cascade Range of Oregon, the Coast Ranges of Alaska, and the Adirondack Mountains of New York, Buddington became aware that the granitic masses or plutons of these different regions had different habits and that the rocks of the three regions represented exposures at successively deeper levels. Subsequently a study of the literature (1959) showed that this relationship was systematic and that the habits of plutons could be correlated with their depth of emplacement.

Regional geologic mapping and petrologic studies in the northern and northwestern Adirondacks of New York State led Buddington to several new interpretations of general significance.

A very extensive banded complex (Diana complex) of metamorphic rocks was found to vary in composition from pyroxene syenite gneiss with thin feldspathic layers very rich in pyroxene, ilmenite, and magnetite, through pyroxene quartz syenite gneiss to hornblende granite gneiss. Buddington showed (1935) that this complex could be satisfactorily interpreted as a metmorphosed isoclinally overturned folded sheet of differentiated igneous rock. He proposed the term "gravity stratified sheet" to indicate that the variation in composition was the product of fractional crystallization and sorting of crystals in a magma under the influence of gravity.

A study of the great Adirondack anorthosite mass and its bordering rocks led Buddington (1939) to the concept that the rock had formed from a magma intruded into older rocks of sedimentary origin. This was based on the general uniformity of composition, the occurrence of rotated angular inclusions of country rock within the anorthosite, of local garnet and pyroxene aggregates in marble of the wall rock that could be appropriately interpreted as introduced by magmatic solutions, and of sheets of anorthosite isolated within the country rock. At the time the hypothesis of magmatic origin was proposed, the available experimental physicochemical data appeared to preclude a melt of anorthositic composition at any reasonable temperature. Much later (1954, Yoder), however, experimental data showed that H_2O had an exceptionally strong effect in both lowering the melting point of a mixture of diopside and anorthite and in shifting the eutectic ratio toward anorthite. As these two compounds are the major constituents of anorthosite, and the presence of H_2O is reasonable, a probable magmatic origin was supported. Buddington also pointed out that anorthosite in general had two major types of origin, one as crystal accumulates in stratiform sheets and the other Adirondack type, and that the composition of the plagioclase was in general more albitic in the latter as shown by a statistical study of the literature.

The metamorphism of sedimentary rocks is commonly assumed to proceed under conditions such that PH_2O is about equivalent to local pressure at depths of a few miles. Buddington, however, observed (1963) that anhydrous pyroxenic igneous rocks commonly gave rise to equivalent anhydrous pyroxenic gneisses; that hydrous hornblendic igneous rocks commonly yielded hydrous hornblendic gneisses; and that for such orthogneisses, as distinguished from paragneisses, the PH_2O must be considered a variable and not necessarily equal to local pressure.

The use of the compositions of coexistent pairs of titaniferous magnetite and ilmenite as a geologic thermometer stems from the work of Buddington. The history of the idea is interesting as an example of the finding of a significant principle that was completely unanticipated and quite aside from the problem being studied. During World War II, Buddington was engaged in exploration for magnetite ore under the auspices of the U.S. Geological Survey. In 1945 an aeromagnetic map of the northern Adirondacks became available and was used successfully in the search for ore. In 1949 he started a systematic study of the iron-titanium oxide minerals in relation to the normal variations of the magnetic anomalies in general and to certain intense negative magnetic anomalies in particular. He at first thought that the variations in intensity might be due in part to variations in impurities in the magnetite. Magnetite concentrates were made from about 100 different rocks and all analyzed for titanium and some for manganese, magnesium, and vanadium. No effective correlation was found between the composition of the magnetite and the magnetic anomalies. This line of attack proved a blind alley. In the course of the work, Buddington realized that the rocks underlying the most intense magnetic anomalies carried titaniferous hematite as the exclusive iron-titanium oxide mineral. His associate, James R. Balsley, then showed that this mineral had an intense remanent magnetization with the north-seeking pole up instead of the south-seeking pole and was the cause of the negative anomaly. Further mineralogic studies and magnetic measurements showed (1958) that where both magnetite and titaniferous hematite occurred in the same rock the resultant magnetic anomaly could be positive, neutral, or negative depending on the ratio of one to the other, the magnetite tending to give a positive anomaly, the titaniferous hematite a negative anomaly. Granite of similar appearance in the field was reflected in part by positive anomalies and in part by negative anomalies. The facies giving a positive anomaly was found to have magnetite and ilmenite, and that giving a negative anomaly almost only ilmenite. It was thus concluded that in this area titaniferous members of the ilmenite-hematite series of minerals uniformly had a negatively oriented remanent magnetism and were responsible for negative anomalies.

Meanwhile Buddington felt guilty at being responsible for all the work that had gone into analysis of the magnetites, apparently to no good end, and sought to see whether something worthwhile could be salvaged from the data. He explored the possibility that there might be a correlation between the percent of TiO_2 in the magnetite and the temperature at which it formed. To his very great pleasure this hypothesis seemed to have possibilities as a geologic thermometer above 600° C and he published a paper presenting this idea in 1955. He tried to interest several men in doing experimentally the iron-titanium oxide system, but was unsuccessful until Donald H. Lindsley, one of his former students at Princeton, completed a study at the Geophysical Laboratory. This experimental study showed that fantastically small variations in oxygen pressure could cause substantial variations in the amount of TiO_2 dissolved (as Fe_2TiO_4) in magnetite for constant temperature, but did confirm that temperature was a major factor in controlling the percent of titanium compound dissolved in magnetite. The experimental data of Lindsley (1964) showed that the compositions of coexistent magnetite and ilmenite could be used as a thermometer and oxygen barometer between the temperatures of about 550° C and 1100° C. Buddington had available some 35 analyzed pairs of titaniferous magnetites and ilmenites from the same host rock, and the application of the experimental data to them yielded temperatures and oxygen pressures consistent with petrologic considerations. The principle promises to be of great value in the interpretation of the conditions of formation of igneous and metamorphic rocks since the two minerals are present in most such rocks.

A Baptist minister's son, Buddington majored in chemistry and geology at Brown University, where he received the Ph.B. in 1912 and M.Sc. in 1913, and in geology at Princeton, where he received the Ph.D. in 1916. He served successively in the Aviation Section, Signal Corps and as Sergeant 1st Class in the Chemical Warfare Service during 1918. In 1919–20 he worked on the synthesis of the melilite group of minerals at the Geophysical Laboratory in Washington. From 1920 to 1959 he was professor of geology at Princeton. He spent 45 summer seasons in field work, largely under the auspices of the U.S. Geological Survey or the New York State Geological Survey. Buddington received the Penrose Medal of the Geological Society of America in 1950 and the Roebling Medal of the Mineralogical Society of America in 1956. He was elected to the National Academy of Sciences in 1943.

Buddington wrote *Geology and Mineral Deposits of Southeastern Alaska,* with T. Chapin (1929), *Adirondack Igneous Rocks and Their Metamorphism* (1939), and *Regional Geology of the St. Lawrence County Magnetite District,* with B. F. Leonard (1962).

For background information *see* MAGMA; MAGNETITE in the McGraw-Hill Encyclopedia of Science and Technology. ☐

★ **BULLARD, Sir Edward (Crisp)**
British geophysicist
Born Sept. 21, 1907, Norwich, England

FOR HIS contributions to the development, both theoretical and experimental, of the physics of the Earth, Bullard was awarded the Hughes Medal of the Royal Society of London in 1953, the Arthur L. Day Medal of the Geological Society of America in 1959, and the Agassiz Medal of the U.S. National Academy of Sciences in 1965.

Much of Bullard's work dealt with the origin of the Earth's magnetic field. The main facts about the Earth's magnetism have been known for 300 years, but only since World War II have any plausible theories about its source been advanced. Bullard first became interested in the question at the beginning of the war, when he was working on the protection of ships from magnetic mines. He thought about it at intervals for several years and found a suggestion made in 1919 by Sir Joseph Larmor that the Sun's magnetic field might be due to motions of the material in the Sun acting as a dynamo and generating electric currents and a magnetic field. This idea seemed attractive to him until he found that T. G. Cowling had written a paper in 1929 that appeared to show that the process was impossible. Disappointed, Bullard gave up the subject for several years while he worked on other things.

In 1947 P. M. S. Blackett suggested a quite different theory of the field. Although this afterwards proved to be untenable, Bullard at first thought that it might be correct. This brought him back to the subject and started him thinking, not about the source of the field but about the possibility that its variations might be due to motions of the material in the Earth's electrically conducting core: again a type of dynamo. He was getting along very well with this idea when a friend told him that Walter Elsasser had already published some papers about it. When he read Elsasser's papers he found not only that Elsasser had had the same idea about the variations but that he had also revived Larmor's idea about the origin of the field. Elsasser had not, however, shown the process to be possible or done much to meet Cowling's objections.

What was required was a more detailed study of the problem. The essential point was: Do the equations that describe the magnetic field in a moving conductor have solutions in which the field does not fade away to nothing? There were two ways of tackling such a problem: One could use analytical arguments to show that solutions of the required kind did or did not exist, or one could take a particular example and actually hammer out a solution on a computer. Bullard chose the second method because, although it was less elegant, less general, and less convincing than the first, it was much easier. It also had the attraction that the great amount of arithmetic that was needed could be done on the electronic computers that were then just coming into service. Bullard's results were satisfactory and made it almost certain that the process was possible. This was confirmed later by analytical methods by A. Herzenberg and R. H. Backus. Whether the process actually occurs in the Earth is not known, but the hypothesis that the Earth's field is produced by a dynamo in the core is very plausible and is probably the most widely held view today.

Besides his investigations of terrestrial magnetism, Bullard worked on seismology at sea, heat flow on land and at sea, and the hypothesis of continued continental drift.

Son of an English brewer, Bullard majored in physics at Cambridge University, where he received his B.A. in 1929 and his Ph.D. in 1932 for work on the scattering of slow electrons and the measurement of gravity. He stayed at Cambridge until the outbreak of war in 1939. From 1939 to 1945 he worked on the protection of ships from magnetic mines, mine sweeping, and operational analysis, returning to Cambridge after the war. He was professor of physics at the University of Toronto during 1948–49, and for the next 6 years was director of the National Physical Laboratory in England. In 1956 he returned to Cambridge, where in 1964 he was appointed professor of geophysics and head of the department. A fellow of the Royal Society, he was elected a foreign associate of the U.S. National Academy of Sciences in 1959.

For background information *see* GEOMAGNETISM in the McGraw-Hill Encyclopedia of Science and Technology.   □

★ **BULLEN, Keith Edward**
Australian applied mathematician
Born June 29, 1906, Auckland, New Zealand

BULLEN'S PRINCIPAL contributions to scientific knowledge arose in the first instance through his mathematical studies of earthquake waves. As an auxiliary to investigating the effect of the Earth's ellipticity of figure on the travel times of earthquake waves, he derived for the first time (1936) reliable values of the density inside the Earth down to a depth of 5,000 km and set a lower bound of 12.3 g/cm^3 to the central density. He later refined and extended the original calculations and applied the results to many geophysical and planetary problems.

The work on density carried with it correspondingly reliable determinations of the distributions inside the Earth of pressure, of the principal elastic properties (compressibility and rigidity), and of the gravitational intensity. Bullen was able to infer that the Earth's inner core (of radius about 1,200 km) is solid, and he found empirically a connection between compressibility and pressure for materials at pressures of the order of 1,000,000 atmospheres. Relevant parts of the work up to 1950 were incorporated in two Earth models, A and B, which have been much used in geophysics. Bullen also (1940–42) introduced the nomenclature A, B, C, . . . G, which has been widely used for internal layers of the Earth. After 1950, he strengthened the evidence on solidity in the inner core and in 1964 adduced evidence to show that, after an initial change from fluidity to solidity at a certain depth inside the core, there is a likely trend back toward fluidity as the depth further increases. He also applied the results to questions of the internal structures of the inner planets Mars, Venus, and Mercury, and proposed a new mechanism for the origin of the Moon.

In the original density calculations, Bullen combined data from earthquakes with data from geophysical laboratory experiments and other sources. An important innovation, enabling him to set close bounds to the density values, was the application of a moment of inertia criterion to internal spheres of the Earth. The criterion enabled him (among other things) to show conclusively that there are significant departures from uniform chemical composition (or, alternatively, phase changes) inside the Earth's mantle between crust and core. He evolved a direct method of estimating density gradients in chemically inhomogeneous regions of the Earth's deep interior. His assessment of the accuracy of his results on density, pressure, and elasticity as within 5% or less at all depths down to 5,000 km was substantiated when long-period fundamental oscillations of the whole Earth were recorded from the Chilean earthquakes of May 1960.

Other contributions include his early work in collaboration with Sir Harold Jeffreys (who was his teacher and great source of inspiration) on seismic travel-time tables, culminating in the Jeffreys-Bullen tables of 1940, which have been since used in preparing the International Seismological Summary. Bullen was responsible also for the tables that give the corrections due to the Earth's ellipticity. He wrote numerous papers on other aspects of theoretical geophysics, especially on seismic-ray theory, and on local seismological problems, for example, in New Zealand.

Of Irish-English parentage (his father's father having come from Trinity College, Dublin, in the 1870s to be headmaster of a Church of England school in Nelson, New Zealand), Bullen obtained master and doctor degrees from the universities of Auckland, Melbourne, and Cambridge (England). He started work as a secondary-school teacher in Auckland, lectured in mathematics at Auckland, Melbourne, and Hull (England), and in 1946 accepted the chair of applied mathematics in the University of Sydney, Australia. Among other honors, Bullen received the William Bowie Medal of the American Geophysical Union in 1961 and the Arthur L. Day Medal of the Geological Society of America in 1963. He was elected a foreign associate of the U.S. National Academy of Sciences in 1961.

Bullen wrote *Theory of Seismology* (1947; 3d ed. 1963), *Seismology* (1954), and *Theory of Mechanics* (1949; 7th ed. 1965).

For background information *see* EARTH INTERIOR in the McGraw-Hill Encyclopedia of Science and Technology.   □

☆ **BURCH, Cecil Reginald**
British physicist
Born May 12, 1901, Oxford, England

W HILE WORKING in the research department of Metropolitan-Vickers Company, Manchester, in 1927, Burch carried out a single experiment in vacuum distillation that had peculiarly far-reaching consequences. He was asked to try impregnating with transformer oil, in a very much better vacuum than usual, the pressboard used to insulate transformers. It was hoped that the dielectric strength would be improved in this way. Burch doubted whether this would happen—air is soluble in transformer oil—and, in fact, it did not. Then he was asked to steam-jacket the impregnator. This made nonsense of any attempt to get a really good vacuum, for the vapor pressure of oil is high enough to cause visible clouds of mist to form above a testing tank at less than 100°C. A vacuum would not be obtained until all the oil had distilled away down the pump. How much more interesting, he thought, to do some vacuum distillation of organic materials.

Burch set up a vacuum still analogous to the apparatus with which George de Hevesy had separated the isotopes of mercury. An electrically heated copper tray, 2.5 cm × 15 cm, 1 cm deep, filled with distilland to $\frac{1}{2}$-cm depth, was supported inside a sloping water-cooled condensing roof, so that the maximum distance from the liquid surface to condensing roof was about 3 cm. This tube was exhausted by a mercury condensation pump—without a tray to freeze out the 1-μbar (dyne/cm^2) residual vapor pressure of mercury at water-cooling temperature that such a pump cannot remove. The justification for leaving out the cold tray was that the average vapor molecule would have a free path a few cm long in the residual mercury vapor, so that a fraction of the order of $1 - 1/e$—say about ⅔—of the vapor molecules would pass to the condensing surface without let or hindrance from the mercury vapor. Thus, however low the vapor pressure of the distilland might be, distillation would take place at, say, ⅔ of the rate it would go at in a perfect vacuum.

Under these conditions there is no such thing as "the boiling point." Distillation takes place at a rate proportional to the vapor pressure and to the square root of the molecular weight. If vapor molecules do not bounce when they hit the liquid they come from, but are recondensed, vapor is created moving away from the liquid surface with ¼ of mean molecular velocity. A simple calculation shows that, for a molecular weight of a few hundred, Burch's tray would give about 4 drops/minute of distillate for 1-μbar vapor pressure. Translated into other terms—one square yard of evaporating surface would give about 1 ton of distillate per 24 hr at 1-μbar vapor pressure.

If Burch had used a conventional distilling apparatus in which the vapor had to travel, say, 10 cm down a tube 1 cm in diameter to reach the condensing surface, the distillation rate would have been about 400 times smaller than with his still, and temperatures of the order of 100° higher would have been necessary to give distillation at the same rate. So it was reasonable to expect that many organic substances normally regarded as not distillable without decomposition could be distilled unchanged in this still.

He started by distilling the oil used in the rotary pump that produced the 10-μbar or so "backing pressure" for the condensation pump. After part had distilled off, it required 120°C to make it distill at 4 drops/minute; that is, it had at 120° the same vapor pressure as mercury at room temperature. Clearly, if this oil would stand boiling at a pressure high enough—say 100 μbar—one could reasonably expect an oil condensation pump to work and produce vacuums of perhaps 10^{-3} μbar, with water-cooling only.

And this worked. The first oil condensation pump gave 10^{-3} μbar without difficulty, a pressure low enough for high-power triodes. The undistillable residue at 300°C from petrolatum could be expected to be a suitable sealing grease for the ground joints—and this proved to be the case.

Oil condensation pumps were used immediately by T. E. Allibone in the Cavendish Laboratory to evacuate his 350 kv Lenard tube, and the Cockcroft double rectifiers to feed it. With this apparatus J. D. Cockcroft and E. T. S. Walton achieved the first artificial disintegration not involving the use of radioactive material.

Burch's colleagues F. E. Bancroft, G. Burrows, L. H. J. Phillips, J. H. Ludlow, F. Taylor, his brother F. P. Burch, J. M. Dodds, and others made high-power demountable triodes and tetrodes. The latter—developed by Dodds—were used in the early 5-meter radar stations that played a critical part in the Battle of Britain.

Burch measured the ultimate vacuum the pumps would make and got 10^{-4} μbar. Many years later, he communicated to the Royal Society the paper of J. Blears of Metropolitan-Vickers, who showed that he was wrong: 10^{-3} was right. Burch had, in fact, got 10^{-4}, but he had got it by cleanup, and failed to realize this. (10^{-4} is now got by improvements in the oil.)

He found that oils not normally regarded as distillable could be distilled without decomposition—olive oil, arachis oil, and waxes, for example, beeswax. Carr and Jewel, with one of his stills, found that not only vitamin D but also the very much less volatile vitamin A could be distilled without decomposition.

Unknown to Burch, K. C. D. Hickman at Rochester had been led by a different chain of industrial events to the same idea of using organic fluids—dibutyl phthalate, and later butyl benzyl phthalate—in condensation pumps, and to the same general ideas about the distillation of organic compounds. Hickman created a complete new industry—the concentration of vitamins on the large scale.

Meanwhile, E. O. Lawrence used oil condensation pumps to evacuate his cyclotron, and many of the vacuum devices used to produce high-energy particles today are pumped in this way.

Burch received his B.A. and Ph.D. at Cambridge University, where he was a member of Gonville and Caius College. From 1923 to 1933 he was employed as a physicist in the research department of Metropolitan-Vickers Company in Manchester. He held a Leverhulme fellowship in optics at the Imperial College of Science and Technology in 1933–35. Thereafter he was connected with the H. H. Wills Physics Laboratory of Bristol University, as a research associate (1936–44), fellow (1944–48), and Warren Research Fellow in Physics (after 1948). At Bristol he studied the optics of nonspherical surfaces and built the first Schwartzschild–aplanatic-aspheric reflecting microscope. Elected a fellow of the Royal Society in 1944, he was awarded the Society's Rumford Medal in 1954 "in recognition of his distinguished contributions to the technique for the production of high vacua and to the development of the reflecting microscope."

For background information *see* DISTILLATION; VACUUM PUMP in the McGraw-Hill Encyclopedia of Science and Technology.   □

★ BURNET, Sir (Frank) Macfarlane

Australian immunologist
Born Sept 3, 1899, Traralgon, Victoria, Australia

A⊤ A time when his main work was on the growth of influenza virus strains in chick embryos and on their epidemiological and immunological behavior, Burnet developed the concept that the normal components of the body do not provoke antibody or other immune reactions because, during embryonic life, the body develops a tolerance to any potentially antigenic substance then present. He predicted that tolerance could be established experimentally, and this was achieved a year or two later by a group led by P. B. Medawar. For this development, Burnet and Medawar shared the Nobel Prize in physiology and medicine for 1960.

From 1933 onward, Burnet was primarily concerned with the use of the chick embryo in ovo as a means of cultivating and studying viruses. This led to a growing interest in the special character of the embryo by which it seemed to have no power to resist virus infection or to produce antibody against the viruses. Two observations by others brought this interest into definite focus: (1) E. Traub, working at the Rockefeller Institute, had found that a certain virus of mice could infect the young in the uterus without obvious harm. The mice developed normally after birth but carried large amounts of virus in their tissues for the rest of their lives. (2) At the University of Wisconsin, Ray Owen, in 1946, showed that twin calves could interchange blood groups through a common placental circulation in the uterus and that they maintained such a mixture of genetically distinct bloods through life.

In both cases the foreign antigen. Traub's

lymphocytic choriomeningitis (LCM) virus or the red blood cells of the other calf in Owen's work, would have provoked a typical immune response if it had been introduced for the first time in an adult recipient. This seemed to throw light on the old problem of why, although an animal's cells—red blood cells, for instance—will usually provoke antibodies in other species and sometimes even in other individuals of the same species, they never do so in the animal itself. Obviously, an animal must not destroy its own cells, but the means by which it can recognize the difference between what is its own and what is foreign and therefore to be destroyed is by no means obvious. Most of Burnet's work was at the theoretical level and throughout was dominated by the problem of the recognition of "self" from "not-self."

Early attempts in Burnet's own laboratory to use the chick embryo to show that tolerance could be produced artificially against standard antigens failed, for reasons we can now understand. Medawar succeeded by applying the technique of skin transplantation rather than by looking for the presence or absence of antibodies. If, to a newborn mouse of strain A, Medawar gave an adequate number of spleen cells from strain-B mice, he found that a few weeks later the treated A mouse would retain indefinitely a skin graft of B that would otherwise be rapidly rejected.

In the last 10 years there has been a very large output of research on various aspects of immune tolerance. As is the way of biological discoveries, the original concept has been extended and qualified. There are many other ways of imitating nature's method without inoculating the embryo, and in particular the production of tolerance by drugs like 6-mercaptopurine is currently dominating thought and practice in the surgical transplantation of organs like the kidney. Burnet's own theoretical interpretations of the central "self and not-self" problem of immunology led to the development of what he called the clonal selection theory of immunity. This is still controversial but, by general agreement, has stimulated much useful experimental work in a field that is important both for general biology and for practical surgery and medicine.

Burnet was born in a small Australian country town, a son of the local bank manager. He completed his medical course at Melbourne University in 1923 and spent 2 years at the Lister Institute, London, where he gained his Ph.D. in bacteriology. He became assistant director of the Walter and Eliza Hall Institute in 1928 and director in early 1944. He was ex officio professor of experimental medicine at Melbourne University. At the experimental level he became best known for his development of methods for virus propagation in chick embryo and for his early work on bacteriophage. Elected to the Royal Society of London in 1942, Burnet received the Society's Royal Medal in 1947 and Copley Medal in 1959. In 1954 he was elected a foreign associate of the U.S. National Academy of Sciences. He was knighted in 1951.

Burnet wrote extensively, including three semipopular books: *Natural History of Infectious Diseases* (3d ed. 1962), *Viruses and Man* (2d ed. 1955), and *The Integrity of the Body* (1962).

For background information *see* IMMUNITY in the McGraw-Hill Encyclopedia of Science and Technology.   □

C

★★

★ CALVIN, Melvin
American chemist
Born Apr. 8, 1911, St. Paul, Minn., U.S.A.

F OR TRACING the various steps of the path of carbon in photosynthesis, the most fundamental of all biochemical reactions, Calvin received the 1961 Nobel Prize in chemistry.

Long interested in organic molecular structure and behavior, Calvin turned to the problem of photosynthesis when carbon-14 became readily available after 1945. The basic, initial experiment, performed at the Lawrence Radiation Laboratory of the University of California, Berkeley, in 1948, involved the feeding of radioactive carbon dioxide to a photosynthesizing plant for very short periods of time, followed by a search for the earliest compound or compounds into which that radioactive carbon was incorporated. Calvin and his associates had already gone far toward concentrating the radioactive carbon formed in the first few seconds in photosynthetic tissue (algae and leaves as well), and had a bit of information about the chemistry. They knew that the major compound formed in the early phases was very sticky on an anion exchange resin; that is, it was hard to wash out of an anion exchanger whereas simple carboxylic acids, sulfates, and phosphates would wash out relatively easily. This sticky material required strong acid or strong base to displace it from such an anion exchange column. The idea that it was a carboxylic acid of some sort had already been evolved, but no simple carboxylic acid was as tightly held as this material was.

This gave rise to the idea that perhaps it had more than one holding point on it, that is, more than one anionic center. Now if it were a carboxylic acid with more than one anionic center, it would presumably be another carboxylic acid or some other anionic center. It seemed unlikely that it might be a di- or polycarboxylic acid, since sugars and citric acid would wash off the column even ahead of this material. Besides, if the CO_2 was entering in the carboxyl group, and if two carboxyl groups were put in, it complicated the matter. Therefore the other anionic center that would make it sticky should not be a carboxyl group, and the obvious choice for it was a phosphate.

By that time Calvin already had the information that the material contained phosphorus by virtue of the tracer phosphorus combination with tracer carbon experiments. The simplest point at which carbon could enter into a phosphorylated compound would be a reversal of the oxidation of a phosphorylated pyruvic acid to give a three-carbon compound in which the carboxyl group arose from the CO_2 and the phosphorylated two-carbon piece arose from something resembling acetyl phosphate. The only compound of this general type that had the enormous stability of Calvin's unknown was phosphoglyceric acid, and a few tests soon confirmed that this was indeed what he had.

At the same time, it was clear that if this was the way carbon was getting in, there must be some way of making the two-carbon acceptor from phosphoglyceric acid. Calvin conceived a very simple cycle, which turned out to be wrong but which served as his operating hypothesis for a while. The search over the following years for this two-carbon acceptor that had to be made from the phosphoglyceric acid gave rise to the ultimate solution of the problem, but the beginning was in that moment of recognition that the sticky stuff had to be something with two handles and had to be regeneratable.

The son of Russian immigrant parents, Calvin received his B.S. in chemistry at the Michigan College of Mining and Technology in 1931 and his Ph.D. in chemistry at the University of Minnesota in 1935. After spending 1935–37 at the University of Manchester, England, he joined the faculty of the University of California at Berkeley in 1937 as an instructor, becoming a full professor in 1947. In 1946 he was appointed director of the bioorganic chemistry group in the Lawrence Radiation Laboratory. This group became the Laboratory of Chemical Biodynamics in 1960. Calvin was elected to the National Academy of Sciences in 1954.

Calvin wrote *The Theory of Organic Chemistry*, with G. E. K. Branch (1940), *Isotopic Carbon*, with others (1949), *Chemistry of Metal Chelate Compounds*, with Martell (1952), *Path of Carbon in Photosynthesis*, with J. A. Bassham (1957), *Chemical Evolution* (1961), and *Photosynthesis of Carbon Compounds*, with J. A. Bassham (1962).

For background information *see* PHOTOSYN-THESIS in the McGraw-Hill Encyclopedia of Science and Technology. ☐

★ CAMERON, Sir (Gordon) Roy

Anglo-Australian pathologist
Born June 30, 1899, Echuca, Victoria, Australia

CAMERON'S LIFE work was the experimental analysis of structural and functional upset of the liver caused by prolonged disease of the organ. He adapted and improved methods for excluding the blood supply to the liver and preventing bile outflow, as well as for exposing it to a host of toxic agents for the production of its injury and the study of its repair. From these studies came many investigations by his pupils into the precise mechanics and biochemistry of cellular injury, thereby initiating a new discipline of micropathology. For his contributions in the field of cellular pathology, Cameron received a Royal Medal of the Royal Society of London in 1960.

As a young morbid anatomist concerned with autopsy duties at the Melbourne Hospital, Cameron gained an extensive experience of chronic liver disease, especially the varieties now known to be due to viral infections. Under the influence of his teacher in embryology, he applied embryological interpretations as well as existing histochemical methods to the patterns of liver disease. He soon realized the limitations inherent in such techniques, and after a year's postgraduate study in Germany he settled down at University College Hospital Medical School in London to a long experimental analysis of chronic liver damage, using the above-mentioned methods.

Confronted by the regenerative power of the liver, Cameron soon realized its key position in shaping the finished patterns of liver disease and dimly perceived the idea of "poise," a kind of delicate balance between cell destruction and restoration. Later work with chemical and bacterial agents brought out the importance, in chronic liver upsets, of the duration of injury and its phasing as intermittent or continuous. Investigations with carbon tetrachloride given by various routes were especially rewarding and established a reversible and irreversible stage of liver cirrhosis. Cameron thus was able to enunciate the principle that the time-spacing of the noxious agents decided whether recovery or permanent injury, with fibrosis and true cirrhosis, was to be the outcome. These views were confirmed over the next 26 years with many chemical poisons, bacterial infections, and the parasite *Schistosoma mansoni,* as well as with various forms of biliary obstruction and biliary cirrhosis.

Prewar study of various insecticides and industrial chemical agents led to Cameron's investigations of many potential war gases during World War II. He was the first to work out completely the action of lewisite and allied compounds on animals and introduced the first-aid treatment by means of concentrated H_2O_2. He clarified the pathology of intoxication with mustard gas, nitrogen mustard, phosgene, various selenium salts and particulate selenium, and a host of other agents, including phosphorus. With J. H. Gaddum, he defined the role of the nasal cavities in resisting exposure to toxic gases; they were also responsible for much of the earliest work on nerve gases. Cameron carried the burden of toxicological investigation of DDT on human volunteers and laboratory animals that resulted in its adoption as a safe agent against insect pests in the services.

From these years devoted to war problems, Cameron realized the value for pathology, especially of the cell, of modern techniques in following the function of organelles. From 1945 onwards he reorganized his department in London with this clear purpose in mind. His team made many contributions to the understanding of injury to mitochrondria, lysosomes, and endoplasmic reticulum.

From Cameron's interest in war-gas pulmonary edema came one of his most original discoveries, with S. N. De of Calcutta—the production of lung edema by inserting an artificial "blanket" of fibrin or blood over the floor of the fourth ventricle of the brain, with resulting stimulation of the outflow of vagal nerve impulses to the circulatory and respiratory systems. This variety of "neurogenic edema" has close parallels in head injuries and apoplexy.

Cameron's breadth of interest was reflected in his well-known studies of inflammation in earthworms and caterpillars, which contrasted invertebrate coordinated host reaction to non-

specific foreign agents with more specific defense mechanisms and peculiar features of repair. He also gave much time to the detailed
investigation of regeneration in mammalian
tissues such as the alimentary canal lining, the
spleen, adipose tissue, and the skin after
thermal burning. Despite a varying pattern of
research, there was always the underlying challenge of cellular response to abnormal stimulation and downright injury.

An Australian parson's son whose early life
was spent in the bush country, Cameron studied
medicine at the University of Melbourne, graduating M.B., B.S. in 1921 and D.Sc. in 1930.
He was a junior lecturer in pathology at the
University from 1922 to 1925, then deputy
director of the Walter and Eliza Hall Institute
for Medical Research until 1927. After working
with Ludwig Aschoff at Freiburg-i.-Br., Germany, during 1927–28, he settled at University
College Hospital Medical School, London, under
A. E. Boycott, as Graham Scholar in Pathology,
Beit Memorial Fellow, and reader in morbid
anatomy. He succeeded Boycott in 1937 as professor and was director of the Graham Research
Laboratories from 1945 until his retirement in
1964. He was knighted in 1957.

Cameron wrote *Pathology of the Cell* (1952)
and *Biliary Cirrhosis*, with P. C. Hou (1962).

For background information *see* PATHOLOGY
in the McGraw-Hill Encyclopedia of Science
and Technology.   □

★ **CAMERON, Thomas Wright Moir**

Canadian parasitologist
Born Apr. 29, 1894, Glasgow, Scotland

UNTIL ABOUT 50 years ago, parasites were
regarded as a cause of human disease,
mainly in the tropics. They were beginning to
become suspect as a cause of tropical disease in
domestic animals. There was, however, little
knowledge of the almost universal distribution

of the parasitic worms and still less of their
enormous variety. About 40 years ago, after
numerous species had been described by F. P. F.
Ransom from sheep, Cameron found that they
were so common in these animals that it was
unusual to find a single animal free from them,
even when the sheep were clinically healthy. A
little later, he and his colleagues, working
under Leiper at the London Zoological Gardens,
found a similar situation in wild animals that
had died from causes other than parasitic disease. From this date onward, it became obvious
that parasitism was a branch of ecology and
that parasitic disease—of enormous importance
in both human and veterinary medicine—was
essentially due to human interference with the
natural, normal ecology of the parasites. Far
from being confined to the tropics, parasites
were universal in their distribution, occurring
as far north as the islands in the Arctic Ocean.

Since then it has been abundantly established
that no vertebrate species—and few invertebrates—are free from parasitic worms. It has
become equally obvious that most kinds of
parasitic worms are confined to restricted species of hosts and that related species of hosts
tend to have related species of parasites. Moreover, geologically old species of animals, even
if not closely related to each other, often had
parasites that were so related. This suggested
quite definitely that these hosts had become
infected in the distant past, when their internal
environments were more generalized and when
they congregated together so that the ancestors
of the parasites were able to invade the ancestors of the host and evolve parallel with them.
In such hosts—for example, the perissodactyles
(equines, rhinoceroses) and paenungulates (elephants)—numerous closely related variants of
the original stock appeared, testifying to the
appearance of many small morphological mutants during this evolutionary development. This
was particularly the case with certain roundworms and tapeworms. There thus appeared a
form of parallel evolution that could throw considerable light on the evolution and migration of
their hosts. The finding of roundworms in kang-
aroos related to those in horses and elephants,
and in practically no other animals, showed
that all these host groups, even if not related to
each other, must have been in close association
with each other early in their evolution. In the
light of the evidence of other sciences—paleontology, paleomagnetism, and so on—this gave
strong support to the hypothesis of the close
proximity of all the southern continents, including the Antarctic, in the early Tertiary or late
Mesozoic and suggested the Antarctic as a diffusion center for South American and Australian animals.

The occurrence of related groups of parasites

in related hosts has other consequences. For example, it shows quite conclusively that the New World monkeys evolved, in their early days, in association with the Old World monkeys and that the pinworms and malarial parasites of the Primates were inherited from Mesozoic reptiles. It agrees with the hypothesis that the mammals are polyphyletic and may well have originated from therapsid reptiles in more than one part of the world—for example, Africa and Eurasia.

Cameron entered Glasgow University in 1912 intending to become a chemist, but almost immediately he fell under the influence of the professor of zoology, Graham Kerr, whose ability as a teacher and interest in parasites and human disease caused Cameron to enroll as a medical student. After World War I, in which he served in the Highland Light Infantry and as a pilot in the Royal Flying Corps, Cameron included veterinary medicine in his studies. In 1921 he was appointed to the London School of Tropical Medicine and Seamans Hospital, where he worked until 1929. He moved to Edinburgh in 1929 to teach parasitology at both the medical and veterinary schools and to inaugurate a diploma in tropical veterinary medicine. In 1932 he went to Canada to establish the Institute of Parasitology in McGill University, serving as director until 1964. Thereafter he continued at McGill as professor of parasitology in the department of bacteriology and immunology. He received the Flavelle Medal of the Royal Society of Canada in 1957.

Besides some 200 scientific papers, Cameron wrote *Parasites of Domestic Animals* (1934; 2d ed. 1952), *Parasites of Man in Temperate Climates* (1940; 2d ed. 1946), *Parasites and Parasitism* (1956), and *Principles and Practice of Medical Parasitology* (in preparation).

For background information *see* PARASITOLOGY; PARASITOLOGY, MEDICAL in the McGraw-Hill Encyclopedia of Science and Technology. □

★ CARTER, Herbert Edmund

American chemist and biochemist
Born Sept. 25, 1910, Mooresville, Ind., U.S.A.

CARTER'S MAIN research activities involved the chemistry and biochemistry of amino acids; the isolation, structure determination, and biological activity of antibiotics; and the isolation, characterization, and structure determination of complex lipids of animals and of plants.

On receiving his Ph.D. in organic chemistry at the University of Illinois in 1933, Carter accepted a position in biochemistry there and undertook synthetic studies on threonine. In the course of this work he developed a number of methods for the synthesis of threonine and other α-amino-β-hydroxy acids (serine, phenylserine, and so forth).

Studies of the chemical properties of α-amino-β-hydroxy acids led to an extensive investigation of α, β-unsaturated azlactones and the discovery that the latter could be readily converted to α-amino-β-thiol acids. These results were directly applicable to later studies on the structure of penicillin, one of whose degradation products, penicillamine, is an α-amino-β-thiol acid.

The amino-hydroxy acid work brought attention to the long-chain base, sphingosine, an essential component of cerebrosides and other lipids of nervous tissue. Thus was initiated a study of the long-chain base-containing lipids of animals and plants. Initial studies led to the establishment of the structure of sphingosine as D-*erythro*-1,3-dihydroxy-2-amino-*trans*-octadecene-4. Dihydrosphingosine was found also to occur in brain and spinal cord.

World War II interrupted these studies, and for the next five years Carter devoted all his efforts to the antibiotic field, serving as executive secretary for the efforts of a group of Midwestern pharmaceutical firms. In his own laboratories, studies of the detection of new antibiotics and their isolation, characterization structure, and biological properties were pursued. A number of new antibiotics were discovered, including chloramphenicol (simultaneously with the Parke Davis group), endomycin, levomycin, filipin, and others. Extensive contributions were made to the structure of patulin, streptomycin, streptothricin, viomycin, and filipin. In a study of the antifungal properties of filipin, the very interesting discovery was made that this activity was reversibly inhibited by

cholesterol and ergosterol, an observation that has been extended by other workers and provides a tool for study of the biological functions of sterols.

In a study of the antibacterial activity of

streptomycin, Carter found that partial reversal was produced by soybean tryptone. A study of the inositol-containing substances of soybean resulted in the totally unexpected discovery of the presence in plant seed lipids of a long-chain base similar to sphingosine. After 1945, therefore, Carter devoted his chief attention to the sphingolipids of plants as well as of animals. Major contributions included the synthesis of sphingosine, determination of the structure of cerebrosides, characterization of the long-chain base from plants (designated as phytosphingosine) as D-ribo-1,3,4-trihydroxyoctadecane, discovery of dehydrophytosphingosine in plant seeds, discovery of cerebrosides derived from phytosphingosine in plants, and discovery and characterization of a novel type of glycolipid—the mono- and di-galactosyl-diglycerides in wheat flour.

Carter's major contribution in the plant lipid studies, however, was the discovery of a group of related complex glycolipids for which he coined the general term "phytoglycolipid." These materials consist of an acylated long-chain base joined by a phosphate diester group to inositol-containing oligo- and polysaccharides. Carter elucidated the complete structure of one of these substances (in which the oligosaccharide contains glucosamine, glucuronic acid, mannose, and inositol). For this work he received the American Chemical Society's Nichols Medal in 1965.

Carter received his A.B. at DePauw University in 1930 and his Ph.D. in organic chemistry, with Carl S. Marvel, at the University of Illinois in 1933. He moved into the biochemistry division of the chemistry department there, becoming head of the department in 1954. He served as acting dean of the Graduate College from 1963 to 1965. He was elected to the National Academy of Sciences in 1953.

For background information *see* AMINO ACIDS; ANTIBIOTIC; LIPID in the McGraw-Hill Encyclopedia of Science and Technology.   □

☆ CERENKOV, Pavel Alexeyevich

Russian physicist
Born July 28, 1904, Voronezh Region, U.S.S.R.

CERENKOV WAS the first to identify correctly the faint blue light emitted in liquids and solids exposed to a source of fast gamma radiation. His studies, conducted during the 1930s, showed that this phenomenon (later known as the Cerenkov effect) was a new kind of radiation, generated when a particle traveling near the speed of light in vacuo passed through a medium where the speed of light was less than that of the particle. Cerenkov's discovery found

employment in the "Cerenkov counter," a particle detector whose hypersensitivity made it a crucially valuable laboratory tool. For his work Cerenkov was awarded the Nobel Prize for physics in 1958. He shared the prize with I. M. Frank and I. Y. Tamm, two of his colleagues, who developed a mathematical theory of the radiation.

Cerenkov began his investigations of the effect that now bears his name as a graduate student at the Lebedev Institute at Moscow, where he worked under the direction of Academician S. I. Vavilov. The phenomenon had long been known and was assumed to be a luminescence effect such as were often observed in irradiated liquids. To gauge the accuracy of this assumption, Cerenkov realized, an entire sequence of sensitive and (above all) qualitative experiments was needed, in order to determine the effect of varying experimental conditions upon the emission of the radiation.

Such experiments were carried on by him in a darkened room with nothing more than a weak gamma source and a bottle of test solution. Many of the measurements were made by eye, employing a now extinct method of visual photometry in use before the advent of the photomultiplier.

One of the first experiments showed that the emission of the radiation was independent of the composition of the irradiated liquid. By using doubly distilled water as a test solution, Cerenkov disposed of the possibility that the radiation stemmed from the fluorescence of minute impurities.

Cerenkov now examined various characteristics of luminescence phenomena, seeking a line along which to organize further experiments. It was insufficient to establish that the new radia-

tion lacked properties seen only in some luminescences—Cerenkov sought to establish that it failed to exhibit a feature common to *all* luminescent emissions. The feature turned out to be the "quenching" characteristic. All luminescent emissions (which were due to impurities in solution) could be dimmed without being utterly extinguished, and the dying-out period was longer than 10^{-10} sec. It could accordingly be observed.

The next group of experiments were concerned, therefore, with the quenching phenomenon. It was known, for example, that luminescence was quenched by introducing certain substances into the test solution. Painstaking experiments revealed an apparently complete absence of quenching due to additives. The same result was seen when test solutions were heated, another means of quenching luminescence. A variety of additives were used; and, to establish the accuracy of these measurements, Cerenkov conducted a parallel series of experiments, under identical conditions but with solutions known to be luminescent. In those, he observed a definite quenching.

Another important fact emerged from these experiments. Luminescent light, which was known to be polarized, could be altered in the direction of its polarization by heating the solution. In contrast, heating had no effect on the polarization of the new radiation. What was more, the direction of polarization was seen to be parallel to the exciting gamma ray, while luminescent light was always polarized perpendicular to the incoming ray.

Cerenkov suspected that the radiation originated as the incoming gamma radiation, deflected in its passage through the liquid, generated secondary electrons in obedience to the Compton effect. The secondary electrons, he thought, must be the source of the light, rather than the gamma radiation itself. This hypothesis was confirmed in experiments with magnetic poles.

In 1936 Cerenkov performed a series of experiments in which the gamma source was replaced by a source of x-rays. These brought to light the important fact that the radiation was characteristically asymmetrical, being emitted only at a forward angle relative to the direction of the stimulating radiation.

Cerenkov had now determined all the essential properties of the new radiation and proven it to be not a form of luminescence but a new and distinct phenomenon. He lacked, however, any convincing theoretical framework into which to fit the new observations. Such a theory was to appear with the advent of Tamm and Frank, who developed a rigorous mathematical explanation of the radiation and tested their ideas in further experiments conducted in conjunction with Cerenkov. The collaboration led, ultimately, to a complete theoretical model of the phenomenon.

For some years the Cerenkov effect was considered an isolated phenomenon with no practical applications. With the development of sensitive photoelectric devices, however, which were able to measure the very faint light emitted, an important application of the Cerenkov effect came to be known, namely, the Cerenkov counter. This device became extremely important in experimental physics, since its sensitivity was unrivaled among particle detectors. Cerenkov counters played a significant part in the discovery of the antiproton by Owen Chamberlain and Emilio Segrè in 1956.

Born of peasant parents, Cerenkov graduated in 1928 from Voronezh State University's physicomathematical faculty. In 1930 he was appointed a senior scientific officer at the Lebedev Physical Institute at Moscow. He subsequently became section leader and in 1959 assumed control of the photo-meson processes laboratory. In 1940 Cerenkov was awarded the degree of Doctor of Physicomathematical Sciences; he became a professor of experimental physics in 1959, and in 1964 was elected a corresponding fellow of the U.S.S.R. Academy of Sciences.

For background information *see* CERENKOV RADIATION; FLUORESCENCE; PARTICLE in the McGraw-Hill Encyclopedia of Science and Technology.   □

☆ CHADWICK, Sir James

British physicist
Born Oct. 20, 1891, Manchester, England

IN 1932 Chadwick established experimentally the existence of the neutron, a particle whose presence in atomic nuclei he had suspected since 1920. His experiments corroborated the hypothesis that atoms were composed of heavy, uncharged particles as well as of the electrically charged protons and electrons. Chadwick's investigations furnished the first conclusive evidence for such particles, and he was able to give the first determinations of their mass. For this and other contributions to nuclear physics, Chadwick was awarded the 1935 Nobel Prize in physics.

In 1920 the English physicist Ernest Rutherford propounded a neutron theory to help reconcile the numerous contradictions present in the then-current knowledge of atomic behavior. Chadwick, adopting this theory, in the early 1920's (as Rutherford's colleague at the Cavendish Laboratory, Cambridge) initiated a long sequence of experiments to detect such a particle: Rutherford had posited one with zero net charge and mass slightly greater than the proton's. Chadwick worked with a variety of experimental arrangements but at first had no success.

In 1930 the German physicists Walther Bothe and Hans Becker, using a stronger radiation source and better detection equipment than had been available to Chadwick (notably the just-invented Geiger-Muller counter) found that the metal beryllium, under bombardment with fast α-particles, gave off very energetic radiation. This reemitted radiation, while presumed to be some sort of γ-radiation, had several unusual properties. Especially peculiar was the fact that the reemitted radiation from the beryllium was much more penetrating in the same direction as the bombarding particles than it was in the opposite direction. Chadwick noted that this observation would be difficult to explain unless the reemitted radiation consisted of particles of some sort. Moreover, the very penetrating nature of the radiation led him to suspect that it was made up of neutral particles.

Soon after this, the French physicists Frédéric Joliot and Irène Curie reported that paraffin that had been subjected to the radiation from bombarded beryllium emitted high-energy protons, presumably ejected from the hydrogen nuclei in the wax. Learning of this, Chadwick suspected that here, too, was evidence that neutral particles were present in the beryllium emission.

Chadwick set out to duplicate the Joliot-Curie experiments in his own laboratory. Concentrating upon the character of the high-energy beryllium emission, he directed this radiation onto a variety of experimental materials: hydrogen, nitrogen, argon, air, and others. In each of these substances, the beryllium radiation ejected protons from the substances' atomic nuclei. Now, if the beryllium radiation were some form of γ-photons, the energies of these protons could be readily calculated by means of the well-known Compton effect, which described the interactions of γ-radiation and atomic nuclei. Chadwick made the requisite calculations; the results were completely at variance with the proton energies he had measured experimentally in the laboratory. On the basis, therefore, of the observations of these collisions with atoms, Chadwick concluded that the beryllium radiation was composed of neutral particles of about rest mass 1.005 to 1.008 (the proton rest mass being taken as 1.0).

Having tentatively identified the neutron, it now remained for Chadwick to evince conclusive evidence of its existence. For this purpose, he and his associates at the Cavendish Laboratory began in 1932 a new and extensive series of experiments. One crucial experiment made use of an ionization chamber connected to an amplifier, which was in turn attached to an oscilloscope. Ionizing particles entering the chamber would make the oscilloscope trace fluctuate; the trace was recorded continually on photographic paper. A source of radiation was constructed from a disk of metal plated with polonium (a powerful α-emitter) and a disk of pure beryllium, both placed together in an evacuated vessel. With this source stationed at a large distance from the chamber, Chadwick established the rate of oscilloscope deflections as about 7 an hour. When the source was only a few centimeters from the chamber the rate increased to over 200 an hour. (These deflections were due to atoms of air in the chamber set in motion by the radiation.) The interposition of lead sheets between chamber and source had no effect on the deflection rate, which showed the highly penetrating nature of the radiation. Moreover, replacing the lead sheets with sheets of paraffin doubled the deflection rate. Chadwick ascertained that this doubling was caused by the ejection of protons from the wax, just as in the Joliot-Curie experiment.

All this information, taken together, provided Chadwick with the foundation in fact required to gain widespread acceptance for the neutron hypothesis. The concept quickly gained ground and assumed vital importance in subsequent theoretical advances in nuclear physics; it became, in fact, indispensable for any later theoretical approach to the structure of the atom.

Chadwick majored in physics at Manchester University, graduating in 1911. In 1913 he went to Germany to work in the Reichanstalt, Charlottenburg, under H. Geiger; there he discovered the continuous nature of the energy spectrum of the β-emission of radioactive bodies. During World War I he was interned as a civilian prisoner-of-war. After his return to England he was invited by Rutherford to accompany him to the Cavendish Laboratory, Cambridge, where Rutherford was appointed Cavendish Professor in 1919. Chadwick was elected a fellow of Gonville and Caius College in 1921, and was appointed assistant director of research in the Cavendish Laboratory. During this period in Cambridge he worked in very close collaboration with Rutherford in their efforts to open up the new subject of nuclear physics. In 1935 he left Cambridge to become professor of physics in Liverpool University, where he established a new school of nuclear physics. In the winter of

1939–40 he started what was perhaps the earliest work on the atomic bomb. During the latter part of World War II he was head of the British mission cooperating in the Manhattan Project, and for his services in this work he was awarded in 1946 the Medal for Merit by President Truman. In 1948 he returned to Cambridge as Master of Gonville and Caius College, an office that he resigned in 1958. In addition to the Nobel Prize, Chadwick was awarded the Copley Medal of the Royal Society of London in 1950, the Franklin Medal of the Franklin Institute of the State of Pennsylvania in 1951, and numerous other honors. He was elected a fellow of the Royal Society in 1927.

Chadwick wrote *Radiations from Radioactive Substances*, with E. Rutherford and C. D. Ellis (1930), and *Radioactivity and Radioactive Substances* (4th ed. 1953).

For background information *see* NEUTRON; NUCLEAR STRUCTURE in the McGraw-Hill Encyclopedia of Science and Technology. □

★ **CHADWICK, Wallace Lacy**

American engineer
Born Dec. 4, 1897, Loring, Kans., U.S.A.

FOLLOWING KEEN boyhood interest in mountains, water, electricity, and construction, Chadwick made a career of designing, building, and managing large electric-power projects. First was work in development of the hydroelectric resources of the middle Sierra Nevada in California, followed by design and construction of thermal electric plants, design and construction of the transmission systems to serve these, and the planning and preliminary design for the largest nuclear power plant so far under construction. This work occupied him during some 35 years with Southern California Edison Company. It was interrupted for 6 years—from 1931 to 1937—for work on the design, financing, and construction across the eastern California desert of the 243-mile Colorado River Aqueduct of the Metropolitan Water District of Southern California.

The development of water power from the western slope of the central Sierra Nevada Mountains began about 1912. To meet the demand for power in the fast-growing southern California area following World War I, the Southern California Edison Company undertook to divert the South Fork of the San Joaquin River through the 13-mile, 16-foot-diameter Florence Lake Tunnel for use by two existing power plants and one new one. Chadwick went to the project early in 1922. After 2 years in the field headquarters engineering office and in the Los Angeles general office, he was sent to the high-altitude Florence Lake project as division field engineer. There he was responsible for the engineering control of the tunnel. This work was followed by field engineering for Florence Lake Multiple Arch Dam and for location of the diversion works for two other streams, Mono and Bear creeks. He then returned to the headquarters engineering office, where he was in charge of office and field engineering, including, in 1927, construction supervision of the 2,420-foot head, 147-mw Big Creek 2A project.

Returning to Southern California Edison Company in 1937, after his Colorado River Aqueduct experience, Chadwick directed design and construction of four additional developments on the Big Creek–San Joaquin project to achieve a total of 690 mw in eight plants, using the greatest total head in the world—more than 6,200 feet. Included in these works were two large earthfill dams.

Chadwick also became responsible for the Edison Company's engineering and construction, including design and construction of thermal power plants. Before his retirement, Chadwick had directed the design and construction of six large thermal plants totaling 4,000 mw.

For the thermal plants, he directed development of four subaqueous cooling water systems that take water directly from the sea along an exposed seacoast. These systems have operated successfully, even in periods of heavy storm, without sand or fouling interference. Fouling control is unique and is accomplished by periodically reversing the flow in the intake and discharge cooling water conduits. This raises the temperature in the normal intake sufficiently to discourage the growth of fouling organisms.

Chadwick also became interested in control systems that would assist the human operator with his many monitoring functions and reduce the chance of equipment damage from operating errors. This work resulted in the development, jointly with Bechtel Corporation and General Electric Company, of the first digital-computer control system to be used for start-up and control of thermal power plants. Chadwick received the Sprague Award of the Instrument Society of America in 1963 for pioneering in this field.

Other departures from traditional thermal-plant designs were the extensive use of outdoor construction, use of two of the first universal pressure steam generators, and development of several features for minimizing atmospheric pollution.

When peaceful use of nuclear energy was first considered, Southern California Edison Company built the first plant to produce electricity commercially. This was the 7.5-mw turbine-generator plant associated with the AEC-Atomics International sodium graphite reactor at Santa Susana. This installation and its subsequent use by Edison for training of engineers in nuclear-plant operation was directed by Chadwick. He continued his interest in trying to develop nuclear power on a practical commercial scale and, prior to his retirement, had directed enough of the final design for the 450-mw San Onofre reactor plant to facilitate final contracting with Westinghouse and Bechtel Corporation.

A farmer's son, Chadwick received a liberal arts education at the University of Redlands, taking as much engineering as the curriculum allowed. Army service in World War I interfered with graduation, but he continued his education through various extension courses. He was awarded an Honorary D.Eng.S. degree by Redlands in 1965. Chadwick joined the Southern California Edison Company in 1922, becoming vice-president in 1951 and retiring in 1962.

For background information *see* POWER PLANT; WATER SUPPLY ENGINEERING in the McGraw-Hill Encyclopedia of Science and Technology.   □

☆ CHAIN, Ernst Boris

British biochemist
Born June 19, 1906, Berlin, Germany

WITH THE introduction of sulfonamide in 1939, the medical world was alerted to the possibilities of chemotherapy. A great effort was directed toward isolating, purifying, and manufacturing penicillin, a substance discovered in a mold culture in 1928 by Sir Alexander Fleming. The research group that was particularly instrumental in making this valuable antibiotic available for the treatment of human infectious disease was headed by Howard Florey and Ernst Chain. For their achievements in elucidating the

chemical structure of penicillin and performing the first clinical trials with this substance, Chain and Florey, together with Fleming, shared the 1945 Nobel Prize in physiology or medicine.

Fleming's discovery of penicillin was accidental. A culture plate on which pathogenic bacteria were growing became contaminated by mold organisms from the air. Fleming noted that, as the mold grew, it destroyed bacterial growth; he concluded that a substance produced by the mold was responsible for the bacterial destruction. Since the bacteria were of a type infectious to man, he pursued this observation, eventually performing tests on animals that showed penicillin (as he named the substance) to be capable of destroying many pathogenic bacteria in living organisms. Fleming also foresaw the possibility of using penicillin to treat human disease but was unable to perform such trials, largely because he was unable to make a sufficient amount of the substance.

In 1931, three years after Fleming's discovery, another attempt was made to obtain and purify penicillin, but again without success. The group that performed this work, however, did find that during the purifying process penicillin lost its antibacterial properties.

Fortunately, these findings did not discourage investigation completely, for research on penicillin was once more begun at the Pathological Institute of Oxford University. There Chain and Florey, in 1938, started a systematic investigation of antibacterial substances produced by microorganisms. They began their study with a reinvestigation of Fleming's penicillin because its chemical and biological properties seemed interesting and indicated that it belonged to a new class of antibacterial substances.

First, a method was developed whereby the relative strength of a penicillin-containing broth could be determined by comparing its antibacterial effect (as shown on culture plates) with that of a standard penicillin solution, one cubic centimeter of which was said to contain, by definition, one Oxford unit of penicillin.

Work was next directed toward developing a method of purifying penicillin—without destroying its antibacterial effect. The penicillin-producing mold, *Penicillium notatum*, was grown in flasks containing nutritive material and was protected from air-borne bacterial or fungal contamination by filters of cotton wool. Since it had previously been found that after 1 week the penicillin content of the broth reached its optimal value, extraction was begun at this time. In addition, it had been found that free penicillin was an acid, and hence more soluble in certain organic solvents than in water, and that the alkaline salts of penicillin were more soluble in water. By shaking the penicillin broth with acidified ether or amyl acetate (at low temperature to prevent the penicillin from breaking up in water), the Oxford researchers almost completely neutralized its acidity and removed numerous impurities. The purified solution was then evaporated at low temperature, producing a stable, dry form of active substance. Although testing showed that each milligram of this substance contained from 40 to 50 Oxford units of penicillin—and was capable of destroying staphylococci in dilutions of one part per million—the substance was not pure penicillin 1,650 Oxford units).

Through subsequent efforts, Florey and Chain showed (as Fleming had previously done) that penicillin was only slightly toxic and that the presence of blood or pus did not decrease its antibacterial effect. During animal tests they demonstrated 90 per cent recovery rates using penicillin on mice that had been infected with gas gangrene bacteria. All of the control (untreated) mice died.

Chain, working primarily with E. P. Abraham, was able to elucidate the chemical structure of crystalline penicillin, finding, in fact, that there were four different penicillins, each differing slightly in their relative elemental constituents.

The son of a chemist, Chain's interest in chemistry was early stimulated by visits to his father's factory and laboratory. He received his education at Friedrich-Wilhelm University in Berlin, graduating in 1930. He then specialized in enzyme research in the Charite Hospital in Berlin. Emigrating to England in 1933, he spent 2 years in the School of Biochemistry at Cambridge, working on phospholipids under Sir Frederick Gowland Hopkins. In 1935, Chain was invited to Oxford University to the school of pathology. In 1936 he was named demonstrator and lecturer in chemical pathology. After the war, in 1948, Chain was made scientific director of the International Research Center for Chemical Microbiology in Rome, and in 1961 he was appointed professor of biochemistry at the Imperial College, University of London. He was elected a fellow of the Royal Society in 1949.

For background information *see* PENICILLIN in the McGraw-Hill Encyclopedia of Science and Technology.   □

CHAMBERLAIN, Owen
American physicist
Born July 10, 1920, San Francisco, Calif., U.S.A.

FOR MORE than 20 years the demonstration of the existence of the antiproton had eluded experimenters. While many doubted that it existed at all, Owen Chamberlain, using the newly built Bevatron particle accelerator, provided physics with a laboratory demonstration of this particle and a brilliant confirmation of physical theory. For this achievement, Chamberlain and his colleague, Emilio Segrè, received the 1959 Nobel Prize in physics.

In 1930, P. A. M. Dirac published a paper in which he predicted the existence of particles having masses identical to the masses of the electron, proton, and neutron but having opposite electrical charge. These particles came to be known as positrons, antiprotons, and antineutrons, respectively. In 1932, while investigating cosmic ray collisions in the upper atmosphere, C. D. Anderson discovered the existence of the first of these antiparticles, the positron. The production of an antiproton in an analogous manner was estimated to require a considerably higher collision energy, on the order of 6.3×10^9 electron volts, because of the much greater masses of protons and the still hypothetical antiprotons. Such energies were known to occur in cosmic ray events, but close observation failed to provide definite evidence of any antiprotons.

It was not until the completion of the Bevatron particle accelerator at Berkeley, Calif., that the creation of a proton-antiproton pair in the laboratory became a possibility. Working with this new 6-Bev machine in the early 1950s Chamberlain, Segrè, and coworkers were able to bombard stationary neutrons with high-energy protons and thus produce the desired antiparticle. The main problem became one of isolation and identification, since there would be large numbers of auxiliary particles produced, mostly mesons. At first it was estimated that only one particle in a million would be an antiproton, but the frequency of occurrence turned out to be somewhat higher, that is, one in 30,000.

To identify a particle as an antiproton it was necessary to know that it had a negative charge and the mass of a proton. Since positive and negative particles are deflected in different directions by a magnetic field, it was easy to separate out all the negatively charged particles produced in the bombardment. To determine the mass Chamberlain decided to make independent measurements of the velocity and momentum of the negative particles he had separated. Using the fact that the amount of deflection of a negative particle by a given magnetic field is dependent only on the momentum of the particle, he was able to place a shield across the stream of negative particles to select only those in the range of momentum expected for the antiproton. The velocity was then determined by measuring time of flight across a known distance. Thus it was possible to separate the antiprotons from the less massive mesons having the same momentum by virtue of possessing a higher velocity. During the experiment some 20 particles were identified as being antiprotons. The equipment was then exhaustively tested to be sure that there were no failures in the apparatus and that the observed antiparticles were completely real. They were.

Following the experiment described above, Chamberlain and others carried out related experiments using photographic emulsions to produce visual examples of the annihilation of an antiproton and a proton or neutron, in which these particles die simultaneously.

The son of a radiologist, Chamberlain received his B.S. in physics at Dartmouth in 1941. He interrupted his graduate studies to join the Manhattan Project, where he worked from 1942 to 1945. He received his Ph.D. from the University of Chicago in 1949, having worked under Enrico Fermi. In 1948 he joined the faculty of the University of California at Berkeley and became professor of physics there in 1958. He was elected to the National Academy of Sciences in 1960.

For background information *see* ANTIPROTON in the McGraw-Hill Encyclopedia of Science and Technology.   □

★ **CHANCE, Britton**
American biophysicist and physical biochemist
Born July 24, 1913, Wilkes-Barre, Pa., U.S.A.

INTERESTED IN the measurement of rapid reactions in solutions, Chance perfected before World War II new types of flow methods employing oscillographic readout which he termed "stopped flow method" and "accelerated flow method." These sophisticated techniques led to his discovery in 1946–48 of eight of the nine known active or primary enzyme-substrate compounds. Following work on radar-timing and computing circuits at the Radiation Laboratory at the Massachusetts Institute of Technology from 1941 to 1946, Chance developed sensitive dual wavelength spectrophotometric and fluorometric methods in order to extend his studies of the mechanism of enzyme action to living cells and tissues, particularly the enzymatic control of the flow of electrons from cellular metabolites to molecular oxygen. These methods allow the direct recording of the dynamics of intracellular reactions in vivo.

Between 1936 and 1946 Chance invented a number of devices in the general area of automatic control mechanisms, precision-timing circuits, and analog computers. Some of these inventions applied to automatic ship steering, to circuits for manual and automatic distance measuring by radar, and to computers for solving bombing and navigation problems by radar. At the same time he became interested in sensitive optical methods; in 1940 he published one of the first automatic control systems for stabilizing light intensities in precision spectrophotometry, and in 1942 he applied sophisticated electronic circuitry to the measurement of extremely small changes of light absorption.

Following his development of the "stopped flow" and "accelerated flow" methods for measuring rapid reactions in solution, which greatly extended the concentration range of Hartridge and Roughton's flow method and permitted its use for the first time in studying enzyme reactions, Chance turned to the problem of measuring enzymatic reactions in living systems. He approached this first by devising an optical device—the double-beam or dual-wavelength spectrophotometer—suitable for application to living cells and cell particles. This spectrophotometer has been found applicable to the study of a number of reactions in such structured biological systems as the mitochondrion, cell suspensions (particularly yeast and ascites tumor cells), photosynthetic systems, and strips of tissues. However, the study of enzymatic reactions in tissues with intact blood circulation required the devising of as yet another method, namely reflectance fluorometry, which Chance first developed for the study of reduced pyridine nucleotide components of mitochondria. Later he applied it to a variety of organs—brain, liver, kidney, and skeletal muscle—and, most recently, extended it to the study of the flavoprotein component of the tissues.

These sensitive optical techniques were also applied to the study of enzymes in single cells. Chance perfected a microspectrophotometer and a microfluorometer for studying the light absorbency changes in a single large mitochondrion of a spermatid caused by cytochromes or fluorescence changes due to reduced pyridine nucleotide. The sensitivity of these methods was extremely high; roughly 10^6 molecules could be detected.

Finally, Chance developed rapid methods for the study of rapid reactions of living material. A special type of flow apparatus, called the regenerative flow method, permitted the observation of millisecond reactions in cell suspensions and elucidated the sequence of reactions in the cytochrome chain in cells and mitochondria. An extension of these rapid methods to the ultrarapid methods came with the first application of laser techniques to flash photolysis in biological systems. This led to the discovery of chlorophyll-cytochrome reaction times in systems containing chlorophyll a (green plants) and bacterial chlorophyll.

Chance's use of analog and digital computers in studying biological problems began in the 1940s with the first computer solution of the differential equations for enzyme action. Ultimately he applied large digital computers to complex problems in metabolic control involving the interaction of glycolysis and respiration.

Although these many techniques developed by Chance were significant advances, the knowledge yielded by his application of them to important biological problems was an even more important contribution. The first such application was the measurement of the kinetic properties of enzyme substrate compounds, particularly those of the iron-containing compounds

peroxidase and catalase. This was the first kinetic study of intermediates in any enzyme system and led in 1943 to Chance's experimental demonstration of the validity of the 1913 Michaelis-Menton theory of enzyme action. With H. Theorell, he measured the kinetics of intermediates of alcohol dehydrogenase and formulated the current reaction mechanism for this enzyme. His second contribution was the elucidation of the time sequence of reactions in the cytochrome system of cells in intact mitochondria and particles derived therefrom by the rapid-flow method. Chance's third contribution, made with G. R. Williams, was the observation that the oxidation-reduction state of respiratory carriers of mitochondria is controlled not only by the concentration of oxygen but also by the concentration of ADP and phosphate. In 1955 Chance turned to the control of metabolism. In particular, he studied the mitochondria as optical indicators of changes of ADP concentration in ascites tumor cells and in the muscle strips, gaining thereby a better understanding of the role of mitochondria in regulation of glucose utilization. This study was extended by the discovery of oscillating properties of enzymatic systems where sustained oscillations were observed to occur over a period of time in cell-free systems due to feedback properties of the glycolytic system. These studies indicated the role of adenine nucleotide in regulating flux of the glycolytic systems.

Chance applied photometric techniques to biological problems and achieved the in vivo measurement of cell metabolism in various physiological states. With C. M. Connelly, A. M. Weber, and F. Jöbsis, he successfully applied the double-beam spectrophotometer to in vivo material (for example, muscle strips) as long as they were blood-free. The reflectance fluorometer now provides a method for working on a tissue with intact circulation. This achievement helped to lay the groundwork for the direct determination of the mode of action of narcotics, hormones, and poisons and the effects of energy demands on the interworkings of the cell.

The son of an engineer, Chance received his B.S. and M.S. at the University of Pennsylvania in 1936 and a Ph.D. in physical chemistry there in 1940. Before World War II his research centered around the mechanism of enzyme action, but in 1935–39, while a research student at Cambridge University, he applied his talents to the field of electronics, working on devices of his own invention for the automatic steering of ships. From Cambridge he received both a Ph.D. in biology and physiology and a D.Sci. He returned to the University of Pennsylvania in 1941 as assistant professor of biophysics and acting director of the Johnson Foundation. At the Massachusetts Institute of Technology during the war he was leader of the Precision Components Group, associate head of the Receiver Components Division, and one of the younger members of the Steering Committee of the Radiation Laboratory. Resuming his investigations into the nature of enzymes after the war, he studied on a Guggenheim fellowship at the Nobel Institute in Stockholm and at the Molteno Institute in England. He returned to the University of Pennsylvania in 1949 to become professor and chairman of the department of biophysics and physical biochemistry and to assume the directorship of the Johnson Foundation. He was elected to the National Academy of Sciences in 1954.

Chance edited *Energy-linked Functions of Mitochondria* (1963) and was a coeditor of *Waveforms* (1949; 2d ed. 1964), *Electronic Time Measurements* (1949; 2d ed. 1964), *Rapid Mixing and Sampling Techniques in Biochemistry* (1964), and *Control of Energy Metabolism* (1965).

For background information *see* ENZYME in the McGraw-Hill Encyclopedia of Science and Technology.　□

CHANDRASEKHAR, Subrahmanyan
Indian-American astrophysicist
Born Oct. 19, 1910, Lahore, India (now Pakistan)

W HILE ENGAGED in the study of stellar evolution and the internal structure of stars, Chandrasekhar developed a theory of white dwarf stars.

The properties of white dwarf stars were discovered by the American astronomer Walter Sydney Adams about 1915. About 1925 the English physicist Ralph Howard Fowler explained the enormous densities of white dwarfs in terms of degenerate matter, that is, matter in which electrons and ionized nuclei are tightly packed under the influence of extreme pressures. And when the English astronomer Arthur Stanley Eddington suggested in 1926 that the conversion of hydrogen into helium was one of the possible sources of stellar energy, the stage was set for a comprehensive theory of stellar evolution.

Chandrasekhar realized that if a star burned up all of its hydrogen it would not only be unable to maintain its high rate of energy production but would also begin to progressively contract. As it contracted, he assumed, the star would emit progressively less radiation. Chandrasekhar further assumed that during contraction the mass of the star would remain relatively constant and its density would consequently increase. The process, he reasoned, would cease when a sufficiently high internal pressure was reached to produce the collapse of the central atomic structure. The core would then be composed of degenerate matter and the star would have become a white dwarf.

During the period 1930–36, while working at Trinity College, Cambridge, Chandrasekhar evolved his theory of white dwarfs. Among the predictions of this theory are (1) that the greater the mass of a white dwarf, the smaller will be its radius; (2) that no white dwarf can have a mass greater than about 1.44 times that of the Sun; and (3) that a more massive star must undergo some form of mass reduction, probably through violent explosion, before it can collapse into a white dwarf. Although the small number of white dwarfs known makes it difficult to test the theory by observation, the three predictions enumerated above appear to have been substantiated. When mass is plotted against radius for the known white dwarfs and the main sequence stars, the relation for the white dwarfs agrees with Chandrasekhar's theory and is exactly opposite to that for the main sequence stars. No white dwarf has yet been found with a mass greater than 1.44 solar masses. This figure, called Chandrasekhar's limit, is based on the calculation that the dwarf star contains only elements heavier than hydrogen. Since the theory contends that in a white dwarf all of the hydrogen has been burned up, this observation is therefore a dual confirmation of the theory. The third prediction is still more difficult to prove. However, the Crab Nebula, which is the remains of the supernova of A.D. 1054, has been shown to be a gaseous nebulosity surrounding a white dwarf star. The mass of the gases added to that of the white dwarf exceeds Chandrasekhar's limit. Thus, it can be assumed that the supernova resulted from the blowing off of excess mass by a star with a mass greater than 1.44 times that of the Sun before it collapsed into a white dwarf. Chandrasekhar's theory explains the final stages of stellar evolution, thus contributing to cosmological theory. It is also important in understanding stellar structure. Furthermore, it explains why so few supernovae have been observed, for the masses of the great majority of stars do not exceed Chandrasekhar's limit.

In addition to his theory of white dwarfs, Chandrasekhar made other contributions to astrophysics, among them his studies of the radiative transfer of energy in the atmospheres of stars, of convection on the solar surface, and of polarization of the light from early-type stars. More recent studies dealt with the convective motions of fluids with and without magnetic fields.

Chandrasekhar attended Presidency College, Madras University, in India, receiving his B.A. in 1930. He then went to England to pursue graduate work, receiving his Ph.D. at Cambridge University in 1933. From 1933 to 1937 he remained in England as a fellow of Trinity College, leaving to take a position as research associate at the University of Chicago in the United States. He was appointed assistant professor of astrophysics there in 1938, associate professor in 1942, professor in 1943, and Distinguished Service Professor in 1946. In 1952 he was named Morton D. Hull Distinguished Service Professor of Astrophysics in the departments of astronomy and physics and in the Institute for Nuclear Studies. In that year he also became the managing editor of the *Astrophysical Journal*. Chandrasekhar was awarded the Bruce Medal of the Astronomical Society of the Pacific in 1952, the Gold Medal of the Royal Astronomical Society in 1953, the Rumford Medal of the American Academy of Arts and Sciences in 1957, and the Royal Medal of the Royal Society of London in 1962. He was elected to the National Academy of Sciences in 1955.

Chandrasekhar wrote *An Introduction to the Study of Stellar Structure* (1939; reprinted 1957), *Principles of Stellar Dynamics* (1942), *Radiative Transfer* (1950), and *Hydrodynamic and Hydromagnetic Stability* (1961).

For background information see STELLAR EVOLUTION in the McGraw-Hill Encyclopedia of Science and Technology.   □

★ CHANEY, Ralph Works

American paleobotanist
Born Aug. 24, 1890, Chicago, Ill., U.S.A.

IN HIS study of Tertiary forests, Chaney developed a dynamic approach based upon close resemblances between plants of the past and those now living. He considered plant fossils as representatives of the vegetation of their day, in contrast to their study as individual specimens whose structure or phylogeny is the primary concern of many paleobotanists.

Chaney's familiarity with living plants influenced his emphasis on similarities rather than on differences in designating fossil species. But he did not use modern specific names for plants older than Pleistocene, arguing that the incompleteness of their record did not justify assuming that there had been no changes of specific rank since Tertiary time. Firmly believing that taxonomy should be a tool rather than a burden, he set up stratigraphic species where differences in size or other minor characters could be detected in rocks of different ages. In like manner he tended to establish geographic species for similar plants separated by ocean or climatic barriers. Recognition of elements whose fossils had close living equivalents in major areas did much to clarify areal and systematic relationships of fossil plants to each other and to those that have survived in modern forests.

Chaney's collecting procedure required handling of large numbers of specimens, so that variations within designated fossil species could be compared with those of related living plants. A census taken in the field showed which species were abundant near sites of deposition, and perhaps suggested more remote habitats in adjacent uplands for sparsely represented plants.

A standard section was set up in the John Day Basin of eastern Oregon, where abundant and well-preserved fossils occurred in stratigraphic sequence. Successive floras showed differences in composition, and Chaney noted a progressive reduction in size and texture of leaves. This provided a basis for dating the floras of other areas, and for their assignment to the same stage in the Tertiary sequence if they occurred in the same general latitude.

Quantitative appraisal of leaf characters provided a basis for estimating Tertiary climates. Large, thick, camptodrome-veined leaves now characterize the evergreen forests of the tropics,

while trees of higher latitudes are largely deciduous, with smaller, thinner leaves, and craspedodrome venation. The change in leaf characters from Lower to Upper Tertiary shows a response to progressive changes toward the cooler and drier climate of our day.

Chaney pointed out that the temperate Eocene plants of Alaska did not appear in Oregon until Oligocene time, and that subtropical Eocene plants of Oregon have survived only in low latitudes. He suggested the term "geoflora" for groups of plants in mass migration; the Arcto-Tertiary Geoflora has maintained itself with only minor changes in composition since the Eocene, during which time its distribution has been shifted from Alaska southward across the United States. The Neotropical-Tertiary Geoflora has moved from Washington and Oregon into Mexico and Central America. Recognition of a deciduous conifer, *Metasequoia*, as a fossil by S. Miki in 1941, and its almost contemporary discovery as a living tree by T. Wang in central China, has done much to confirm the concept of geofloras. Chaney had previously predicted that a fossil "redwood" might be discovered, with a deciduous habit suited to occurrence at high latitudes. He visited the natural occurrence of *Metasequoia* in 1948 to determine that its associates were members of the Arcto-Tertiary Geoflora, and revised the fossil records of several members of the Taxodiaceae.

Most fossil floras contain plants that lived at low to middle altitudes. Chaney suggested that since the lapse rate corresponds to successively lower temperatures at higher latitudes, an Eocene flora living near sea level in Alaska may have had a counterpart in the mountains of Oregon; its absence or scant representation in the Oregon Eocene was to be expected in view of its remoteness from sites of deposition, but we could reconstruct such a montane flora by studying floras of similar age in deposits to the north. An early elaboration of this concept led to his suggestion that angiosperms may have had their origin at high altitudes during the Jurassic period, although they first appeared in the fossil record in Cretaceous time.

While there has been well-defined latitudinal control of forest distribution during the Tertiary period, Chaney noted significant departures. A given flora lived farther south with increasing distance from the Pacific Coast; it ranged far to the north across ocean basins. Plotting the occurrence of Eocene floras across North America and Eurasia, he showed that lines connecting similar floras (*isoflors*) followed the paths of modern isotherms and of major forest types. He concluded that the Eocene position of continents and oceans in relation to each other and to the axis of rotation was essentially the same as it is today. This placed the burden of proof on advocates of continental drift and polar migrations during later geologic time.

A descendant of pioneer Illinois farmers, Chaney majored successively in zoology, botany,

and geology at the University of Chicago, where he received his B.S. in geology in 1912 and his Ph.D. in paleontology in 1919. Several years of high-school and university teaching (State University of Iowa) preceded his appointment in 1922 as research associate of the Carnegie Institution of Washington; he retired in 1957. From 1930 until 1957, he was also professor of paleontology at the University of California, Berkeley. He carried on field work widely in the Americas and Asia. During World War II he set aside his paleobotanical work to become assistant director of the University's Radiation Laboratory in an administrative capacity. He was elected to the National Academy of Sciences in 1947.

For background information *see* PALEOBOTANY in the McGraw-Hill Encyclopedia of Science and Technology.   □

★ CHAPMAN, Sydney

English mathematician and physicist
Born Jan. 29, 1888, Eccles, Lancashire, England

DURING 1912–17 Chapman generalized the accurate kinetic theory of gases given in 1867 by James Maxwell, removing Maxwell's limitation to molecules that repel as the inverse fifth power of the distance. Thus he independently discovered gaseous thermal diffusion (first deduced by D. Enskog in a special case), and with A. T. Dootson (1916) he confirmed it experimentally. Chapman also studied observationally and theoretically the daily variations of the geomagnetic field (from 1913) and magnetic storms (from 1917). This led inter alia to improved and extended determinations (with A. T. Price) of the electrical conductivity within the Earth. Jointly with V. C. A. Ferraro he inferred in 1930 that streams of solar plasma would confine the geomagnetic field within a space of order 10 Earth radii (verified 30 years afterwards by satellite exploration) and that in this space, the magnetosphere, a ring current would flow (later revealed by J. A. Van Allen's discovery of the radiation belts). With E. H. Vestine he elucidated the electric currents that flow in the polar ionosphere. With S.-I. Akasofu he investigated these currents and those in the magnetosphere and further developed the theory of magnetic storms and the aurora.

Chapman also studied the atmospheres of the Earth and Sun. In 1929 he gave a photochemical theory of atmospheric ozone and inferred that the oxygen in the upper atmosphere, above about 100 km height, would be largely dissociated; this was subsequently confirmed by rocket-borne mass spectrometers. He inferred also that the air glow—the self-luminescence of the atmosphere at night—is mainly energized by the oxygen dissociation energy stored in the atmosphere during the hours of sunlight.

Chapman greatly extended science's knowledge of the lunar tide in the Earth's atmosphere by analysis of long series of meteorological records (barometer, wind, and temperature) and of magnetic data (the latter, to determine the lunisolar daily variations of the magnetic field). He also studied diffusion problems in the lower and upper atmosphere.

While still an undergraduate at Trinity College, Cambridge, Chapman did research in pure mathematics (nonconvergent series and integrals, partly in association with G. H. Hardy) and in gas theory, to which his attention was drawn by J. Larmor. Then he became (co-)chief assistant (with A. S. Eddington) to the Astronomer Royal at Greenwich Observatory (1910–14, 1916–18). There his work included, besides astronomy, the design of a new magnetic observatory to replace the one set up in 1838 by G. B. Airy. This aroused his interest in geomagnetism and its connection with solar phenomena, and led to his analyses of many kinds of geophysical data and to his theoretical researches in these fields. As the solar and lunisolar daily magnetic variations are caused by electric currents in the ionosphere, induced by motions produced thermally and tidally, he investigated the air tides and the ionosphere. Thus he formulated the idealized "Chapman" ionized layer, later much used by radio physicists in studies of radio propagation and other researches. Theoretical work on atmospheric ozone led to his pioneer work on the photochemistry of the upper atmosphere and on the nocturnal emission of light by atoms of oxygen and sodium there.

Thermal diffusion offers a valuable means of studying the fields of force around molecules and provides a method of separating isotopes, made especially convenient after K. Clusius invented the thermal diffusion column. Such isotope separation became nationally and economically important when applied to the separation of the isotopes of uranium, for the development of nuclear energy for bombs and power supply. In 1958 Chapman showed that although thermal diffusion is in general a weak separative agent, it has much greater power in gases that are highly and multiply ionized, as in the solar corona.

Son of a cashier, Chapman took B.Sc. degrees in engineering (1907) and mathematics (1908) at Manchester University, England (M.Sc. 1908, D.Sc. 1912) and the B.A. degree in mathematics (1911) at Cambridge (M.A. 1914). At Greenwich Observatory he worked on astronomy, gas theory, and geophysics. He returned to teach mathematics at Cambridge (1914–16, 1918–19), and later at Manchester (1919–24), Imperial College, London (1924–46), and Queen's College, Oxford (1946–53) as professor of applied mathematics. Visits to the United States as research associate at the department of terrestrial magnetism of the Carnegie Institution of Washington (1935–40), and at the California Institute of Technology (1950–51), led to his long connection with the Geophysical Institute of the University of Alaska (from 1951) and the High Altitude Observatory, Boulder, Colo. (from 1955). He was president (1953–59) of the central organizing committee for the International Geophysical Year, in which he led the planning of the auroral program. For his theoretical contributions to terrestrial and interplanetary magnetism, the ionosphere, and the aurora borealis, Chapman received the Royal Society's Copley Medal in 1964. He was elected a foreign associate of the U.S. National Academy of Sciences in 1946.

Chapman wrote *The Earth's Magnetism* (1936; 2d ed. 1952), *Mathematical Theory of Nonuniform Gases*, with T. G. Cowling (1939; 2d ed. 1952), *Geomagnetism*, with J. Bartels (1940), *IGY: Year of Discovery* (1959), and *Solar Plasma, Geomagnetism and Aurora* (1964).

For background information *see* GEOMAGNETISM in the McGraw-Hill Encyclopedia of Science and Technology.   □

★ CHARNEY, Jule Gregory

American meteorologist
Born Jan. 1, 1917, San Francisco, Calif., U.S.A.

THE LARGE-SCALE weather phenomena in the extratropical zones of the Earth are associated with great migratory waves and vortices (cyclones) traveling in the belt of prevailing westerly winds. Charney developed a mathematical theory of these disturbances, explaining

them as instabilities of a zonal current in which the temperature decreases poleward. His theory led also to a general mathematical characterization of slow motions in a rotating coordinate system, which he applied to a variety of atmospheric and oceanic circulations. In particular, he and his colleagues at the Institute for Advanced Study used it successfully in their pioneering experiments on numerical weather prediction by high-speed computer.

The establishment of an upper-air sounding network in the 1930s permitted for the first time a realistic description of the three-dimensional structure of the atmosphere. The familiar high- and low-pressure areas of the weather map were revealed as but surface manifestations of giant wavelike meanderings of a predominantly zonal flow. These waves were studied by J. Bjerknes, who gave a qualitative explanation for their eastward progression, and by C.-G. Rossby, who derived his well-known formula for their speed of propagation, regarding them as perturbations of a uniform flow of a homogeneous, incompressible atmosphere. Charney was inspired by these works to seek an explanation for the generation of the waves and their three-dimensional structure. He first showed that Bjerknes's treatment could be extended quantitatively to give Rossby's dispersion relationship. He then formulated and solved the problem of wave generation by showing that a zonal flow with a sufficiently strong poleward temperature gradient becomes instable to characteristic perturbation modes having a structure closely resembling the observed wave patterns.

In obtaining this solution, he encountered the difficulty that a compressible, stratified fluid, held gravitationally to the rotating Earth, can support a variety of wave motions, including acoustic and inertio-gravity waves, which are of no meteorological importance but whose existence seriously complicates the solution of the hydrodynamical equations. He found a method

of filtering out these unwanted "noise" motions in the wave problem and later generalized this method to apply to all long-period motions. The generalization was based on the principle that the forces acting on slow motions of a rotating fluid must always be close to equilibrium, that is, must be in a state of quasi-hydrostatic and quasi-geostrophic balance. This principle was incorporated into the hydrodynamical equations by a kind of scale analysis already familiar in the boundary-layer theory of hydrodynamics. The mathematical and physical simplifications thereby introduced have had a far-reaching effect on meteorological theory.

When in 1947 J. von Neumann organized a group at the Institute for Advanced Study to attack the problem of numerical weather prediction by means of high-speed electronic computers, difficulties were immediately encountered which could be traced to the acoustic-gravitational "noise." Charney had found that these difficulties were automatically overcome by the use of the balance equations. In 1948, on accepting an invitation from von Neumann to join the group, he initiated a program to integrate the balance equations for a hierarchy of atmospheric models of increasing complexity, hoping in this way to avoid the difficulties attendant on introducing a great many poorly understood factors all at once. Some degree of success was achieved in 1950 with the first numerical prediction of a two-dimensional model flow approximating the actual flow at a mid-level in the atmosphere, and in 1952–53 he obtained the first prediction of cyclogenesis with a three-dimensional model flow. The latter result had two consequences: it tended to confirm Charney's explanation of cyclogenesis, and it interested the United States government in the possibilities of operational numerical prediction. A joint Weather Bureau–Air Force–Navy numerical weather prediction unit was established in 1954 and began operations in 1955. Since then, similar units have been established in many other countries.

Following the numerical prediction of cyclogenesis, it was natural to study the interactions of the cyclone wave with the zonal flow itself. H. Jeffries, V. Starr, and others had shown that the wave disturbances acted as turbulent eddy elements transferring momentum (against the gradient) to the mean zonal flow. In seeking a mechanism for this phenomenon, Charney proposed the hypothesis that the cyclone waves, in deriving their energy from the unstable zonal flow through release of potential energy associated with the poleward temperature gradient, are also required by the stabilizing effect of horizontal shear to return energy to the flow in kinetic form, and thus maintain it against dissipation by friction. This hypothesis was strikingly confirmed in a numerical experiment carried out at the Institute for Advanced Study by his associate, N. Phillips. Phillips introduced a heating function varying uniformly with latitude and a frictional mechanism into the simplest of the three-dimensional models, in consequence of which a broad westerly current with a uniform poleward temperature gradient was generated. As predicted, this current became unstable and developed wave perturbations which transferred kinetic energy back to the current and caused it to become as narrow and intense as the observed westerlies. For the first time the principal dynamical elements of the general circulation of the atmosphere were assembled in a single mathematical model, and the way was opened to a direct numerical attack on the problems of long-range prediction and the dynamical theory of climate.

In later work Charney showed that the principle of balance is quite generally applicable to large-scale atmospheric and oceanic dynamics, and that where simple (geostrophic) balance is violated, a higher order boundary-layer treatment can often be given. With A. Eliassen he applied these considerations in treating the layer of surface frictional influence as a boundary layer for the large-scale atmospheric and oceanic motions. He also applied them to the explanation of the Gulf Stream as a western inertial boundary layer and the Equatorial Undercurrent as a boundary phenomenon produced by the vanishing of the horizontal Coriolis force at the Equator. In addition, by regarding internal discontinuities (fronts) as boundary layers in an otherwise quasi-geostrophic flow, Charney proved that a necessary condition for their formation was essentially the same as that which he and M. Stern had found for the development of unstable waves in a zonal current of quite general character, namely, that there be temperature variations at the ground.

The tropical cyclone had previously been looked upon as an unbalanced flow with large horizontal and vertical accelerations produced by cumulus convection. Charney and A. Eliassen found that while the individual cumulus cloud is indeed an unbalanced system, the large-scale flow is balanced, and its growth is due to a cooperative, frictionally controlled interaction between it and the cumulus convection. He later applied similar ideas to the study of the general circulation of the tropics.

The son of Russian immigrants, Charney studied at the University of California at Los Angeles, receiving his B.A. in mathematics and physics in 1938, his M.A. in mathematics in 1940, and his Ph.D. in meteorology in 1946. During World War II (1941–45) he assisted in the training of weather officers for the armed services. In 1946 he was awarded a National

Research Fellowship, which he spent at the University of Oslo following a nine-month visit with C.-G. Rossby at the University of Chicago. In 1948 he joined the group in theoretical meteorology at the Institute for Advanced Study in Princeton, N.J., becoming its scientific director and a long-term member of the Institute. In 1956 he became professor of meteorology at the Massachusetts Institute of Technology. He received the Meisinger Award of the American Meteorological Society in 1949, the Losey Award of the Institute of Aeronautical Sciences in 1957, the Symons Memorial Gold Medal of the Royal Meteorological Society in 1961, and the Carl-Gustav Rossby Research Medal of the American Meteorological Society in 1964. He was elected to the National Academy of Sciences in 1964.

For background information *see* CYCLONE; WEATHER (FORECASTING AND PREDICTION) in the McGraw-Hill Encyclopedia of Science and Technology.   □

★ **CHERN, Shiing-shen**
American mathematician
Born Oct. 26, 1911, Kashing, Chekiang, China

CHERN WORKED mainly with problems in "differential geometry in the large." Differential geometry in its origin is the study of geometrical problems by the methods of infinitesimal calculus. Later, the field was widened to a theory of manifolds, finite or infinite dimensional, with geometrical structures defined on them, such as a Riemannian or Lorentzian metric or a complex analytic structure. The main objective of differential geometry in the large is to study the relationship or interplay between local properties (that is, those pertaining to a neighborhood) and properties of the manifold as a whole (for example, its topological properties).

One of the earliest results in differential geometry in the large is the Gauss-Bonnet formula. For a domain D on a surface bounded by a curve C its Euler characteristic $\chi(D)$ can be expressed by

$$2\pi\chi(D) - \sum_i \alpha_i = \iint_D KdA + \int_C k_g ds$$

where K is the Gaussian curvature, k_g the geodesic curvature of C, and α_i the exterior angles at the corners of C. This formula contains as special cases the theorem in elementary geometry that the sum of angles of a triangle is 180° and the theorem that the excess of a spherical triangle is proportional to its area. It also contains the conclusion that the Euler characteristic of a closed orientable surface is $1/2\pi$ times the integral of its Gaussian curvature.

The extension of this result to a high-dimensional space has followed a gradual development, associated with the names of H. Hopf, W. Fenchel, C. Allendoerfer, and A. Weil, among others. After earlier works of Allendoerfer and Weil, Chern gave a proof of the high-dimensional Gauss-Bonnet formula that clarifies in a basic way the concepts involved, namely, the algebraic machinery of curvature and the algebraic topological properties of a fiber space. His work thus opened the way to further results on relations between curvature and the so-called characteristic classes. The latter are the simplest invariants of a fiber space, used to describe its deviation from the special case of a product space.

The characteristic classes so introduced by Chern, later associated with his name, are among the most important invariants of algebraic varieties—that is, loci in an n-dimensional space which are defined by a finite number of polynomial equations. They also constitute an important link between the so-called K-cohomology theory of a general topological space and its ordinary cohomology theory. Recent developments have shown the importance of the "Chern character" to various applications of topology to geometrical problems.

Other areas in which Chern worked, sometimes with others, include (1) decomposition theorem on harmonic forms of Kahlerian G-structures; (2) total curvature of closed submanifolds in euclidean space; (3) uniqueness theorems on submanifolds satisfying geometrical conditions; and (4) kinematic formula in integral geometry.

In Chern's opinion, modern mathematics centers around the theory of high-dimensional manifolds, which are spaces locally indistinguishable from euclidean spaces. It is because of the high-dimensional phenomena that algebra has been playing a vital role. Only recently has analysis entered in an essential way. It is a domain where only the frontiers have been touched.

Chern received his B.S. degree from Nankai University, Tientsin, China, in 1930, and his M.S. degree from Tsing Hua University, Peiping, China, in 1934. He studied in Germany and France and received his D.Sc. degree from the University of Hamburg, Germany, in 1936. From 1937 to 1943 he was professor of mathematics at Tsing Hua University. In 1943 he went to the United States as a member of the Institute for Advanced Study, Princeton, N.J., returning to China in 1946. From 1946 to 1948 he was acting director of the Institute of Mathematics, Academia Sinica, Nanking, China. He became a professor of mathematics at the University of Chicago in 1949, and at the University of California, Berkeley, in 1960. Naturalized a U.S. citizen in 1961, he was elected the same year to the National Academy of Sciences.

For background information *see* GEOMETRY, DIFFERENTIAL in the McGraw-Hill Encyclopedia of Science and Technology.   □

CLARK, William Mansfield
American chemist
Born Aug. 17, 1884, Tivoli, N.Y., U.S.A.
Died Jan. 20, 1964, Baltimore, Md., U.S.A.

WHILE STUDYING the production by bacteria of holes in swiss cheese, Clark became interested in the effect of hydrogen ion concentration on the media used for growing the bacteria. This led him to develop an expanded series of sulfonphthalein indicators for pH determinations on a quantitative basis.

In his doctoral dissertation in 1884, the Swedish chemist Svante August Arrhenius proposed his theory of ionic dissociation. This led to the concept of the concentration of hydrogen ion as a measure of acidity, and in 1909 the Danish chemist Søren Peter Lauritz Sørensen introduced the notation of pH as an expression of this concentration. Although acid-base indicators had long been used to determine acidity, at that time the known indicators, such as litmus and phenolphthalein, did not permit an accurate quantitative determination. For this reason, at the beginning of the 20th century the common practice among bacteriologists was to measure the total titratable acidity when determining the acid environment of their cultural media.

Clark realized that a quantitative determination of the hydrogen ion concentration was of greater importance than the titratable acidity in obtaining the proper environment for the growth of bacteria. However, the lack of proper indicators seemed to be an insurmountable obstacle in the path of this goal. In searching for a way around this obstacle, Clark came upon a description of Sørensen's work. Recognizing the applicability of Sørensen's technique, Clark designed his own hydrogen electrode apparatus with which to study acid-base equilibria.

Shortly after beginning his studies with the hydrogen electrode, while working at the dairy division of the U.S. Department of Agriculture, Clark was joined on the project by Herbert A. Lubs. The two began to extend Sørensen's work, and in the course of doing this they developed a series of buffer solutions containing sulfonphthalein dyes that indicated hydrogen ion concentrations from a pH of 1.2 to a pH of 10 in intervals of 0.2 pH. The results of these studies, published in 1917, proved to be invaluable to bacteriologists and chemists, for the indicators gave reasonably accurate measurements without recourse to the delicate and erratic hydrogen electrode.

In 1920, while working in the Hygienic Laboratory of the U.S. Public Health Service, he continued his interest in the relationship between bacteriological metabolism and environment by studying oxidation-reduction equilibria in dyes and biological systems. Reactions that occur within a cell and release energy to the organism involve the transfer of electrons from one compound to another within the cell, with corresponding oxidation-reduction potentials that may be measured on a relative basis. The potential measured indicates the direction of the reaction. As the potential decreases in a given media the environment changes from one suitable for the growth of aerobic bacteria to one suitable for anaerobic ones. In 1893 the German bacteriologist Paul Ehrlich had arranged different dyes in the order of their ease of reduction by a cell so as to measure the intensity factor in oxidation. However, he had been unable to measure accurately the reducibility of the dyes used. With the improvement of the techniques of physical chemistry, Clark and the German-American chemist Leonor Michaelis did this independently and established a fundamental basis for understanding the reversible oxidation of dyes

and biological systems. Although the basis for measuring oxidation potentials still depends on the hydrogen electrode, the difficulty of using it is so great that the dye systems developed by Clark have been widely used by bacteriologists. This method has been most helpful in the exploration of the living cell to determine the mechanism involved in oxidation-reduction equilibria.

Clark received his B.A. (1907) and M.A. (1908) at Williams College and his Ph.D. (1910) at the Johns Hopkins University. From 1910 to 1920 he was a research chemist in the dairy division of the U.S. Department of Agriculture, and from 1920 to 1927 he was professor of chemistry in the Hygiene Laboratory of the U.S. Public Health Service. In 1927 he was appointed DeLamar Professor of Physiological Chemistry at Johns Hopkins. He became DeLamar Professor emeritus in 1952 but continued at Johns Hopkins as a research professor. Among Clark's numerous scientific honors was the 1957 Passano Foundation Award "for his basic work in the demonstration of the importance of physical methods, particularly in the control of basal metabolism and of oxidation-reduction, to the study of life processes."

Clark wrote *Determination of Hydrogen Ions* (1920; 3d ed. 1928), *Studies on Oxidation-reduction* (1928), *Topics in Physical Chemistry for Medical Students* (1948; 2d ed. 1952), and *Oxidation-reduction Potentials of Organic Systems* (1960).

For background information *see* HYDROGEN ELECTRODE; HYDROGEN ION; pH in the McGraw-Hill Encyclopedia of Science and Technology. □

★ CLAUSEN, Jens Christian

American plant biologist
Born Mar. 11, 1891, N. Eskilstrup, Holbaek County, Denmark

TOGETHER WITH colleagues, Clausen explored the existence of ecological races within species and the hereditary structures that govern the evolution of races, species, and clusters of species within genera. He also clarified the interaction of environment with heredity in the phenotypic expression of the plant. These discoveries have influenced the general thinking about plant breeding, tree breeding, and plant relationships and suggest why certain plant families remain trapped within low, others within high, latitudes.

Charles Darwin in 1859 presented circumstantial evidence that species evolved through natural selection among an immense number of spontaneous variations. In Darwin's time the differences between inherited and noninherited

variation were unknown. By 1920 the relative proportion of the two kinds of variability among wild organisms was still unknown, and notions of what constituted a species were primarily based upon speculation.

In the early 1920s three groups of botanists in different countries, unknown to each other, began experiments designed to answer some of these questions. In Sweden Göte Turesson moved plants of presumably the same species but native to seacoasts, inland localities, high altitudes, and low altitudes to an inland sea-level garden near Lund. He found that races from such diverse climates retained their inherited differences in the uniform garden and he named these races ecotypes.

In California Harvey M. Hall of the Carnegie Institution of Washington went a step further, dividing individuals of perennial plants native to contrasting climates across California and transplanting the divisions to experiment plots at different altitudes. In Hall's experiments the environment varied but the heredity of the divided plant remained the same. He found that generally lowland and high-altitude races of a species were unable to survive in each other's habitats. With E. B. Babcock he also intercrossed races and species of the California hayfield tarweeds and studied their genetic differences in a uniform lowland garden.

In Denmark Clausen studied the wild species of the pansy violets from seacoast and inland habitats, sandy and limestone soils. He found that the uncrossed races and species retained their identity in a uniform environment but that they could exchange elements of their heredities by crossings in the wild and in the experiment garden. Through their early papers the three groups of investigators had by 1922 discovered their common interests and begun exchanging notes and visits.

If the species of large genera were systematically intercrossed, Clausen reasoned, one should expect to find species in all stages of evolutionary separation. This he showed to be the case in his 10-year experimental investigation of pansies. He also showed, for the first time, that the differences between species are controlled by inherited genes as are the differences between varieties or races of one species. The genes are carried by the microscopic chromosomes, and in violets the number of chromosomes varies from species to species.

By 1930 Hall, assisted by D. D. Keck and W. M. Hiesey, had established a series of three altitudinal transplant stations. These were located along the 38th parallel from near sea level at Stanford to 4,600 ft on the west side of Sierra Nevada at Mather, and to 10,000 ft on the east side of Yosemite National Park. The growth season along the 200-mile transect ranged from all year near the coast to only two months at the high station. Clausen joined the California group in 1931; Hall died three months later.

By direct-transplant experiments at the three-station facility, Clausen, Keck, and Hiesey proved that species of many families were composed of as many as 8 to 11 climatic (ecologic) races across the transect, each race adjusted to the periodicities of the climate where it was native and unadjusted to highly different environments.

By combining crossing and transplant experiments in crossing lowland with high-altitude races, and by dividing parents and first- and second-generation progenies for transplantation, they found that each of the differences that adjusted the parental races to their native zones was controlled not by single genes but by small systems of genes, each gene having a minor but cumulative effect. Moreover, the gene system that regulated the expression of a single trait, as for example petal color or time of flowering, was composed of individual genes that might enhance, counteract, complement, or cover each other's effects. The visible expression depended upon the balance of these interactions and could change with the altitude where the hybrid individual was located.

The genes of the gene systems that regulated the distinguishing traits of each race, they found, were stored within the local races, which thereby served as reservoirs for potential variability that could be combined through crossing and released again in later generations, enriching the variability far beyond what occurs naturally. The genes were interlocked into an arrangement among the chromosomes that insured relative reproducibility of the racial characteristics during periods of environmental stability but that mobilized potential variability in times of radical changes in the environment, leading to altered selective pressure and evolution.

In crosses between hundreds of species representing many families and kinds of separation, Clausen and his colleagues discovered that many species do not easily fit into existing classificatory systems. Basic to the initial separation was the adjustment to distinct external environments as observed among the climatic races within a species. The next step was the beginning of an inherited internal separation because the genes of the parental species could not be freely interchanged without damage to the progeny. Finally, species could not be visibly distinguished unless the environmental and genetic separation was accompanied by a morphologically recognizable one, which is the difference the nonexperimenting classifier uses.

It was found that the three modes of evolutionary separation—ecologic, genetic, and morphologic—might proceed simultaneously and gradually through millions of years, or one kind of separation might proceed at a different speed and outrun the others. Groups of species that to a limited extent were able to exchange some of their heredities produced clusters of species (species complexes), such as in oaks or pines, but the experimental work was done with faster-growing herbaceous perennial and annual species.

These new views of the evolutionary processes have changed the prevalent idea that heredity and adjustment to environment are fairly simple; they show that our understanding of the plant kingdom is exceedingly rudimentary. Still largely unexplored are the physiological and biochemical mechanisms that are regulated by the genes and also distinguish races and species.

Son of a farmer and housebuilder, Clausen was taught at home until age 8, then attended the local country school and a private secondary school. At 14 he assumed responsibility for the 15-acre family farm. For some years direct studies in nature guided by master texts substituted for formal schooling. In 1913, at the age of 22, he passed a comprehensive entrance examination for the University of Copenhagen. There he majored in botany with specialties in the systematics of violets under Chresten Raunkiaer and in genetics under Wilhelm Johannsen. In 1921 he received his master's degree in natural sciences and in 1926 his doctorate. From 1921 to 1931 he was research assistant in the new department of genetics at the Royal Agricultural College of Copenhagen headed by Øjvind Winge. In 1931 he joined the staff of the Carnegie Institution of Washington at Stanford, Calif. He became an American citizen in 1943 and was elected to the National Academy of Sciences in 1959.

Clausen wrote *Stages in the Evolution of Plant Species* (1951) and, with Keck and Hiesey, four books on the nature of various kinds of species, published by the Carnegie Institution (1940, 1945, 1948, and 1958).

For background information *see* PLANT EVOLUTION in the McGraw-Hill Encyclopedia of Science and Technology.   □

★ **CLELAND, Ralph Erskine**

American botanist
Born Oct. 20, 1892, Le Claire, Iowa, U.S.A.

MOST OF Cleland's research was devoted to an analysis of the hereditary peculiarities of the evening primrose (*Oenothera*) and the utilization of the facts thus revealed as tools in a study of the evolution of this genus.

Work on *Oenothera* began with Hugo de Vries, who based his mutation theory of evolution largely on this work. *Oenothera* showed, however, certain hereditary anomalies that he was unable to explain. Otto Renner analyzed these peculiarities and found that most Oenotheras behave when inbred as though all their genes lie in one chromosome pair, although they possess 14 chromosomes. When outcrossed, however, these genes behave in many hybrids as though they were scattered among different chromosomes. As a result, *Oenothera* shows many genetical anomalies.

The physical basis for these peculiarities remained obscure until Cleland discovered that the chromosomes of most Oenotheras also behave peculiarly. In other organisms, corresponding chromosomes from father and mother pair at the formation of reproductive cells, and the members of each pair separate into different reproductive cells, it being a matter of chance whether the paternal or the maternal chromosome of a pair goes into a particular germ cell. In most Oenotheras, however, the 14 chromosomes, instead of forming pairs, become associated end to end to form a closed ring, paternal and maternal chromosomes alternating. Adjacent chromosomes then pass into different germ cells—that is, all paternal chromosomes enter one germ cell, all maternal chromosomes enter another. Thus, linking of all chromosomes into one group causes all genes to be linked in inheritance. This type of chromosome behavior had not been observed before, and is still more widespread in *Oenothera* than in any other organism in which it has been observed.

In hybrids, however, chromosomes are not always linked. It is possible to arrange 14 chromosomes in 15 different ways into closed circles and pairs, and all 15 arrangements have been found. Each hybrid has one of the 15 arrangements. When chromosomes form several groups, instead of being linked into a single group, the genes are no longer all linked in inheritance, and a variety of progeny results. Thus, the linking of all genes into a single group in inbred lines, and their separation into different groups in many hybrids, can be explained on the basis of peculiarities of chromosome behavior.

But why do the chromosomes behave so peculiarly? Following a suggestion of John Belling, it was shown that this has resulted from wholesale exchanges of pairing segments that have occurred between noncorresponding chromosomes in the course of evolution. Each set of seven chromosomes in each race has its own arrangement of pairing segments, which is one of 135,- 135 possible arrangements. The two sets of chromosomes in a race with a circle of 14 have quite different arrangements; no chromosome of one set has the same two ends as a chromosome in the other set. Thus, numbering the pairing ends, if one set has the arrangement 1·2 3·4 5·6 7·8 9·10 11·12 13·14 and the other set has 2·3 4·5 6·7 8·9 10·11 12·13 14·1, the pairing of like ends will produce a closed circle of 14 instead of paired chromosomes.

That shuffling of pairing ends through exchange has taken place on an extensive scale is shown by two facts: (1) There are 91 possible associations of two pairing ends—1·2, 1·3, 1·4, etc. All 91 associations have been found in nature. Every end can be and has become associated with every other end. (2) Although only a minute fraction of all Oenotheras have been studied, the more than 380 sets of chromosomes whose end arrangements have been fully analyzed by Cleland and his students have revealed over 160 different arrangements. The total number present in nature must be enormous.

It was early observed by Cleland that when two closely related sets of genes were combined into a hybrid, this hybrid tended to have mostly paired chromosomes. On the other hand, relatively unrelated sets when combined produced hybrids with large circles. In other words,

similarity in the distribution of pairing segments suggests close relationship and vice versa.

Following this lead, it proved possible to trace the evolutionary history of the Oenotheras in a surprisingly detailed manner. Four and probably five different populations of Oenotheras have developed at different periods in geological history. The center of origin has apparently been Central America. Within each population interchanges have occurred as the plants have migrated northward and eastward over the continent. It is possible to trace the migratory pathways in some cases by following the sequence of interchanges as each has occurred in a particular geographical area.

Since, however, the number of possible interchanges is very great, the exchanges that have occurred in one population have usually been quite different from those occurring in another population. For example, when population 1 was invaded by population 2, and crosses occurred, hybrids were occasionally formed in which none of the chromosomes from one population had the same association of ends as any of the chromosomes of the other population. The result was a large circle of chromosomes.

At present, 10 groupings of races may be distinguished, each of which may be considered a species. Six of these have arisen by hybridization between overlapping populations, two are relicts of original populations, one (on the West Coast) has found no population with which it could cross, and one still resides in the center of origin.

In summary, Cleland's work divides itself into three parts: (1) discovery and analysis of the peculiar behavior of the chromosomes in *Oenothera*, and demonstration that this constitutes the physical basis for the unique genetical behavior of the genes; (2) demonstration that circle-formation in *Oenothera* is a result of the extensive shuffling of pairing segments that has been brought about by exchanges of segments between noncorresponding chromosomes; (3) unraveling the story of evolution in *Oenothera* by analyzing the interchanges that have occurred during the migrations of each of a succession of independent populations and showing how these populations have crossed with each other to form the circle-bearing, true-breeding races that now constitute the great bulk of present day *Oenothera*.

Reared in Philadelphia, Cleland received the A.B. from the University of Pennsylvania in 1915, majoring in classics and history. He received the Ph.D. in botany from the same institution in 1919. Following service overseas during World War I he taught at Goucher College from 1919 to 1938, then transferred to Indiana University, where he was chairman of the botany department and later dean of the

Graduate School. In 1963 he became Distinguished Service Professor of Botany Emeritus. He was elected to the National Academy of Sciences in 1942.

For background information *see* CHROMOSOME; PLANT EVOLUTION in the McGraw-Hill Encyclopedia of Science and Technology.   □

★ CLEMENCE, Gerald Maurice

American astronomer
Born Aug. 16, 1908, Smithfield, R.I., U.S.A.

WHILE STUDYING the motions of the Moon and planets, and the fundamental constants of astronomy, Clemence conceived the idea of measuring time by means of the orbital motions of the Moon and Earth instead of by the rotation of the Earth. This new measure of time was adopted throughout the world in 1956. For it and related work he was awarded the Gold Medal of the Royal Astronomical Society, as well as other honors.

It had been suspected for decades, and in 1939 was firmly established, that the Earth's speed of rotation varied in an irregular, unpredictable fashion, such that in the course of a century all the clocks on the Earth would be fast at some times and slow at other times, as compared with uniform time. The size of the error occasionally exceeded thirty seconds, and its statistical behavior indicated that in the course of centuries it would increase to much larger amounts. The cause of the irregularities is not yet fully understood, but is thought to be the interaction between the liquid core of the Earth and the solid mantle.

For many purposes, such irregularities in the measurement of time are of no consequence, so long as all the clocks agree with one another, but in some cases they become important. The values of all physical constants that depend on the time would, in due course, appear to change if the measure of time were not uniform. The velocity of light and the constant of gravitation are important examples.

The motion of the Moon is irregular, like the rotation of the Earth, but with the important difference that the motion of the Moon is precisely calculated by gravitational theory for many centuries in the past and future. The formula giving the position of the Moon at any time may, in principle, be inverted, so as to give the time as a function of the Moon's position; an observation of the Moon's position then yields the time, by substitution in the inverted formula. This was Clemence's basic idea. The Moon, however, is subject to a small acceleration arising from tidal friction between the Moon and the Earth, which is not precisely known; thus it is not suitable as a standard clock for an indefinite period. For this reason Clemence introduced the position of the Earth in its orbit around the Sun as the primary standard. This latter position is observed less accurately than that of the Moon, and hence is not suitable for measuring time day by day, but only century by century. The Moon, then, may be compared with the second hand of a clock, which interpolates and refines the indication of the hour hand corresponding to the Earth's orbital motion.

The new measure of time is named "ephemeris time," and its introduction was accompanied by a new definition of the second. Formerly the second had been defined as the 86,400th part of a day; now it is the fraction 1/31,556,925.9747 of the year.

A farmer's son, Clemence majored in mathematics at Brown University. He went to the U.S. Naval Observatory in Washington in 1930, becoming director of the Nautical Almanac Office in 1945 and scientific director of the Observatory in 1958. Retiring in 1963, he went to Yale University, where he became senior research associate and lecturer in astronomy. He was elected to the National Academy of Sciences in 1952.

With Dirk Brouwer, Clemence wrote *Methods of Celestial Mechanics* (1961).

For background information *see* EARTH (ORBITAL MOTION); TIME in the McGraw-Hill Encyclopedia of Science and Technology.   □

CLOOS, Hans

German structural geologist
Born Nov. 8, 1886, Magdeburg, Germany
Died Sept. 26, 1951, Bonn, Germany

BY CAREFUL measurement of minor structural details, such as the joints, fractures, and orientation of certain minerals in a rock, Cloos showed how it was possible to reconstruct the manner in which large igneous rock masses

moved or flowed into position in the crust of the Earth. He pioneered in the establishment of the branch of geology known as granite tectonics, which is the study of the manner in which rock masses move and the effects of such movement on the components of the rock itself and on surrounding material. Such studies are important in understanding the mode of origin of igneous rocks and related structures and in ascertaining how the crust of the Earth came into its present condition.

Although hundreds of geologists before him had seen these same features in igneous rocks, it remained for Cloos to show how the previously unnoticed details, such as the alignment of platy mica flakes with respect to the contacts of the rocks with surrounding materials, when carefully measured and mapped in detail, could reveal the internal structure of the rock masses. These features are measured in much the same manner as are strike and dip of sedimentary rocks. By examining the maps on which these data have been recorded by means of special symbols, the trained geologist can visualize how the pasty mass of hot magma moved into position in the Earth's crust. Flowing and swirling slowly around and past promontories of hard rock, the viscous magma welled up from some deep-seated source far below the crust of the Earth, pushing aside the rocks previously there and filling crevices created by the great upward pressures exerted on the brittle roof rocks.

Cloos was also one of the first to use true scale models in deciphering the mechanics of faulting. He used soft clays to simulate the behavior of hard rocks undergoing deformation long before the recent development of scale-model theory showed that this was indeed the proper material to use in laboratory models simulating rock behavior. In his later years he extended his investigations from relatively small portions of the crust to the structure and de-

velopment of the continents, and even probed cautiously the origin of the Earth itself.

Cloos received his doctorate in geology from the University of Freiburg im Breisgau in 1907. From 1909 to 1910 he mapped the Erongo Mountains in South-West Africa. For the next 3 years he worked as a petroleum geologist for the Standard Oil Company in Indonesia. After brief service as a military geologist in France in 1914, he was released from the army because of poor health. He became lecturer in geology at the University of Breslau, where he was appointed to the chair of geology in 1919. In 1925 he went to the University of Bonn as professor of geology. After several trips to the United States he wrote a classic paper on the structural characteristics of the North American Cordillera. In 1948 he was awarded the Geological Society of America's Penrose Medal.

Cloos wrote *Conversation with the Earth: A Geologist's Autobiography* (1959).

For background information *see* IGNEOUS ROCKS in the McGraw-Hill Encyclopedia of Science and Technology.   □

★ COCKCROFT, Sir John (Douglas)
British nuclear physicist
Born May 27, 1897, Todmorden, England

WHILE WORKING in the Cavendish Laboratory, Cambridge, whose director was Sir Ernest Rutherford, Cockcroft, together with E. T. S. Walton, conceived the idea of transmuting atomic nuclei of the light elements by using protons accelerated by voltages of up to 500 kilovolts. They were led to this by the theoretical work of George Gamow on the disintegration of elements by α particles. The new wave mechanical theory of penetration of charged particles through nuclear potential barriers showed that protons of comparatively modest energies would have a chance of penetrating these barriers.

Cockcroft and Walton, therefore, built a steady potential generator for 500 kilovolts using a voltage multiplication circuit. They also built a proton source injecting protons into a vacuum tube, where they were accelerated by potentials of up to 500 kev. The high-speed protons emerged from the apparatus and struck targets of lithium, boron, carbon, fluorine, and other elements. Cockcroft and Walton observed that lithium was disintegrated into two α particles and boron into three α particles, and that other reactions, leading to the emission of α particles, took place.

When deuterium became available, Cockcroft and Walton were able to extend their work to the use of deuterons as projectiles, and a wider range of transmutations became possible, particularly those in which protons were emitted.

After the discovery of artificial radioactivity by Frédéric Joliot-Curie, Cockcroft, Walton, and C. W. Gilbert showed that artificial radioactivity could be produced by the bombardment of carbon with protons, leading to the production of nitrogen-13. They compared the energy release in these transmutations in the form of kinetic energy with the mass changes in the transmutations and demonstrated that the Einstein equivalence formula $E = mc^2$ accurately accounted for the observed changes in energy. For their pioneer work on the transmutation of atomic nuclei by artificially accelerated atomic particles, Cockcroft and Walton shared the 1951 Nobel Prize in physics.

The work of Cockcroft and Walton was soon paralleled by the experiments of E. O. Lawrence and his collaborators using the cyclotron as a nuclear accelerator and by the work of R. J. Van de Graaff and collaborators using the Van de Graaff generator as the high-voltage source. As a result, in the period 1932–39, an enormous range of nuclear transmutations was discovered and, in particular, a very large number of radioactive isotopes. A particularly important result of M. L. E. Oliphant and Rutherford was to show that, when deuterons bombard deuterium, neutrons and helium-3, or protons and tritium, are produced in great abundance. This proved to be of great practical importance.

The son of a textile manufacturer, Cockcroft studied mathematics at Manchester University during part of the academic year 1914–15. Returning after the war, he studied electrical engineering at Manchester College of Science and Technology and Metropolitan Vickers Electrical Company. From Manchester he moved to the University of Cambridge in 1922 and studied mathematics for 2 years before joining Rutherford in the Cavendish Laboratory. He worked for a time with P. L. Kapitza on producing magnetic fields of up to 300 kilogauss and in developing a cryogenic laboratory. In the

later 1930s he took charge of the Royal Society Mond Laboratory and became Jacksonian Professor of Natural Philosophy in the Cavendish in 1939. At the outbreak of the 1939–45 war, he became an assistant director of research in the Ministry of Supply and was responsible for erecting emergency radar stations to detect low-flying aircraft approaching Scapa Flow and the east coast ports. After this, he became head of the Air Defence Research and Development Establishment at Christchurch and later at Malvern. In April 1944, he moved to Canada to take charge of the Anglo-Canadian Atomic Energy Project, first at Montreal and then at Chalk River. The laboratory built the first two heavy-water reactors in Canada. He became director of the U.K. Atomic Energy Establishment at Harwell in 1946, and was a member of the U.K. Atomic Energy Authority from its foundation in 1954. In 1964, he became Master of Churchill College, Cambridge.

For background information *see* NUCLEAR REACTION; PARTICLE ACCELERATOR in the McGraw-Hill Encyclopedia of Science and Technology.   □

★ COLLINS, Samuel Cornette

American engineer
Born Sept. 28, 1898, Democrat, Ky., U.S.A.

LONG ACTIVE in means for producing and maintaining very low temperatures, Collins concentrated his efforts during World War II on the improvement of apparatus for the manufacture of oxygen. The resultant heat exchangers, expansion machines, and refrigerative cycles were combined in 1946 to form the highly successful helium cryostat, a machine that was originally intended to provide a cold chamber for low-temperature experiments but is actually chiefly used for liquefying helium for use elsewhere. Its simplicity, reliability, and relatively low cost have made it an indispensable tool for research.

Liquid helium provides the only known approach to temperatures near the absolute zero, and such temperatures are necessary in the study of many of the fundamental properties of matter. Prior to World War II, liquid helium was available in a very few places in the world and there only by the expenditure of much of the investigator's time. There are now about 300 helium cryostats in use in many countries around the globe.

For his invention and further development of the helium cryostat and other cryogenic devices, Collins was awarded the Wetherill Medal of the Franklin Institute in 1951, the Kamerlingh Onnes Gold Medal of the Netherlands Refrigeration Society in 1958, the Rumford Premium of the American Academy of Arts and Sciences in 1965, and the Outstanding Achievement Award of the Cryogenic Engineering Conference in 1965.

Liquid helium exists over a very narrow temperature range, from $-450.3°F$ down to the absolute zero, $-459.7°F$. Liquid hydrogen, the next coldest liquid, freezes at $-434.3°F$. The simplest way to reach very low temperatures is to compel gaseous helium to cool itself by arranging for it to perform external work as it expands against a piston in an engine. This principle of cooling by expansion with the performance of external work was utilized by John Gorrie about 1845 in the making of artificial ice, by Georges Claude in the liquefaction of air about 1900, and by Peter Kapitza in the liquefaction of helium in 1932.

In addition to the engine, a compressor and a counterflow heat exchanger are necessary. The compressor returns the pressure of the expanded helium to its original value. The heat of compression is carried away by water or by air. The function of the heat exchanger is to cool the incoming stream of warm compressed helium by transferring heat to the outgoing stream of cold expanded helium. Because of the action of the heat exchanger the compressed helium arriving at the engine becomes progressively colder until the condensing temperature of helium is attained.

Collins's cycle for helium liquefaction is characterized by the expansion of compressed helium at more than one temperature level. With normal operating pressures the temperature drop across each engine is substantial, and the cold expanded gas provides a thermodynamically ideal coolant for the stream of helium that is to be liquefied. A series of engines spaced at progressively lower temperatures makes possible very high efficiency in the cooling and liquefaction of helium.

Several forms of the expansion engine have proven successful, but the most used one consists of hardened alloy steel cylinders with close-fitting pistons of the same material. There are no piston rings and there is no lubricant other than the helium gas itself. The motion of the piston is controlled by a long piston rod of relatively small diameter operating in tension. The piston rod passes through the expansion chamber and a sheath tube to the stuffing box, which is at room temperature. The slender piston rod gives the piston a high degree of freedom to move without friction along the axis of the cylinder.

Two types of counterflow heat exchangers of extraordinary effectiveness have evolved from Collins's studies of low-temperature systems. One is used in the helium cryostat. It consists of a closely finned tube some hundreds of feet in length coiled in a helix approximately eight inches in diameter and placed in the annulus between two thin-walled stainless steel cylinders. The incoming high-pressure stream flows inside the long tube, the outgoing low-pressure stream flows in the annulus through the fins and across successive turns of the tube.

The second type of heat exchanger was devised for use in the liquefaction of air and the production of oxygen and nitrogen. Two matched channels alternately bear incoming compressed impure air and outgoing waste gas at low pressure. The impurities, mostly water and carbon dioxide, are condensed on the heat-exchange surfaces during one half cycle and are evaporated and carried away by the waste gas during the following half cycle.

A farmer's son, Collins studied agriculture at the University of Tennessee, where he received the B.S. in 1920 and M.S. in 1924. He received his Ph.D. in physical chemistry from the University of North Carolina in 1927. After several teaching positions in Tennessee he joined the faculty of the Massachusetts Institute of Technology in 1930, where he remained until retirement in 1964.

For background information *see* CRYOGENICS; HELIUM, LIQUID in the McGraw-Hill Encyclopedia of Science and Technology.   □

★ COON, Carleton Stevens

American anthropologist
Born June 23, 1904, Wakefield, Mass., U.S.A.

COON WORKED in three fields: cultural anthropology, prehistoric archeology, and physical anthropology. He not only published in all three but also tried to bring them together into a coherent whole. In this sense he was primarily a historian.

His career in cultural anthropology began with field work in Morocco between 1924 and

1928, culminating in the publication of an ethnography of the Riffian tribes. He continued on this line with a similar study of the north Albanian mountaineers. His *Caravan* (1951) is a synthesis of information about Middle Eastern culture that is used as a text by diplomats and others concerned with that part of the world.

Before World War II Coon collaborated with Eliot D. Chapple in writing *Principles of Anthropology* (1942), in which they attempted to analyze human behavior in terms of patterns of interaction and the requirements of institutions of preserve equilibrium, through the operation of the law of least effort. After the war he simplified and elaborated his ideas about these principles in an appendix to his *A Reader in General Anthropology* (1948).

While thinking about these matters overseas during the war, Coon conceived the idea that man converts energy derived from outside his own organism into social structure at a predictable rate of acceleration, culminating in quanta of energy and global institutions such as have since been achieved. He expressed this idea first in lecture courses, then in an exhibit at the University Museum of the University of Pennsylvania, and, finally, in his book *The Story of Man* (1954).

Coon's contribution to archeology consisted mainly of excavation of caves in parts of the world previously unexplored in this sense, and discovery of new cultures. In Morocco he found a succession of Aterian phases under the Neolithic in the High Cave of Tangier. In Iran he found in the cave of Bisitun the first Levalloisio-Mousterian industry reported from that country, and in two neighboring caves on the Caspian shore, Belt and Hotu, a sequence of cultures running from the Epipaleolithic through the Mesolithic and Neolithic to the Iron Age. In these caves he also found the bones of what may have been the earliest domestic animals and

worked out techniques for distinguishing them from those of wild animals of the same species. In the cave of Kara Kamar in Afghanistan he found an Aurignacian culture as old as any in Western Europe, and a Mesolithic over it. In the cave of Jerf Ajla in the Syrian desert he found a transition from Levalloisio-Mousterian to Aurignacian.

Coon's contribution to physical anthropology —for which he was awarded the Viking Fund Medal in 1952—began in the 1920s and early 1930s when he measured large series of Moroccans, Albanians, and Arabs of southern Arabia, particularly in Yemen and Hadhramaut. He discovered remains of Pleistocene fossil man in Morocco in 1939 and 1962 and in Iran in 1949 and 1951. The first two discoveries confirmed the thesis that Bushmen once lived in North Africa. The 1949 discovery was of Neanderthals and the 1951 skeletons were those of modern Caucasoids living near the end of the Pleistocene.

In 1950, in his book *Races*, in which S. M. Garn and J. B. Birdsell also participated, Coon propounded the theory that many of the physical differences between races are results of adaptation to environment. This hypothesis, then received with ridicule, has since been demonstrated many times by physiological research. Coon himself went to southern Chile in 1959 with a team of physiologists who confirmed the superior cold adaptation of the Alakaluf Indians.

In 1962 Coon's *The Origin of Races* appeared, provoking controversy between segregationists and equalitarians although it had nothing to do with race relations in the United States. The publication of that book was the culmination of decades of work in the study of fossil human remains, a task greatly helped by the availability, in the University Museum in Philadelphia, of rubber and plaster molds of many fossil specimens. As a result of these researches Coon came to the conclusion that *Homo sapiens* is divided into five subspecies, and that these same subspecies also existed in his immediate ancestor, *Homo erectus*. The transition from one species to the other involved initial changes in one organ only, the brain. Because each subspecies was physiologically adapted to its environment in other respects, the acquisition of a new gene or genes favoring higher intelligence permitted the existing subspecies to cross the anagentic threshold in concert. Because this mutation probably arose originally in a single subspecies only, and because the human mating pattern retards gene flow, the transmission of this genetic innovation took time, and the subspecies crossed the threshold at different times.

The sequel to *The Origin of Races*, entitled

The Living Races of Man, appeared in 1965. In it Coon reviewed the racial and cultural history of the races of the world up to the present, and in particular amplified his explanation of the roles of climate and culture in racial differentiation.

The son of a Boston importer, Coon attended Phillips Academy at Andover, Mass., and Harvard, where he majored in the classics, English, and, finally, anthropology. He received his B.A. magna cum laude at Harvard in 1925, and his M.A. and Ph.D. in 1928. He did field work for Harvard's Peabody Museum until 1935 and taught at Harvard from 1935 until 1948, except for the war years. During World War II he served in the Office of Strategic Services (OSS) as a combat major. In 1948 he became curator of ethnology at the University Museum of the University of Pennsylvania, devoting himself principally to field work. He retired in 1963 to his home in West Gloucester, Mass. In 1955 Coon was elected to the National Academy of Sciences.

For background information *see* ANTHROPOLOGY, PHYSICAL in the McGraw-Hill Encyclopedia of Science and Technology.   □

★ **COONS, Albert Hewett**
American physician
Born June 28, 1912, Gloversville, N.Y., U.S.A.

COONS ORIGINATED the concept of using fluorescing antibody molecules for the specific microscopic localization of proteins or polysaccharides. For this achievement he received, among other honors, the 1959 Lasker Award of the American Public Health Association and the 1962 Passano Foundation Award.

Coons and his colleagues, Hugh J. Creech and R. Norman Jones, found that a fluorescent compound could be coupled chemically to antibody without interfering in any way with the interaction between the antibody and its specific antigen. This method has since been employed to identify bacteria in infection, to localize individual animal cells infected with a virus, to single out cells producing specific antibody, and to localize cells containing a chosen polysaccharide as a structural constituent. All that is needed is a specific antibody solution; the method of labeling the molecules with a fluorochrome has become routine.

It is perhaps necessary to define "specific" as it is used in connection with immunity. Antibodies have areas on their surfaces resembling perfect castings of part of the surface of the antigen molecule that stimulated the making of the antibodies in the first place. Antibody molecules, therefore, fit their specific antigen. Since large molecules, like proteins and polysaccharides, are each relatively unique in their shape and the arrangement of their surface charges, an antibody specific for an area on one of them reacts little if at all with other kinds of molecules. Hence, a labeled antibody behaves like a stain that stains only one material—say, hen's ovalbumin (a molecular species in egg white)—or one kind of bacterial capsule—say pneumococcus type III.

In 1934 J. R. Marrack produced red antibodies by coupling an antibody solution to a dye-intermediate. The antibodies reacted with bacterial cells of the species against which they had originally been formed and stained them red. This experiment established the principle that antibody molecules could be used as a specific stain. However, the amount of color imparted to a bacterial cell was so faint that it could not be used to localize small amounts of antigen or to identify single bacterial cells. In 1941 Coons, Creech, and Jones labeled an antibody solution with a fluorescent dye, anthracene, which Creech had been coupling to various proteins. Anthracene is a compound that fluoresces brightly in the blue range when bombarded with ultraviolet light. The anthracene antibody (the antibodies used were directed against pneumococci, the bacteria that cause lobar pneumonia) reacted well with its specific bacteria but not with others and, carrying its label with it, made the specific bacteria brightly fluorescent. Single organisms were easily visible under the fluorescence microscope.

The next step was to select the optimal fluorochrome, one with an emission wavelength not usually encountered in biological material and as brilliantly fluorescent as possible. On both counts fluorescein itself seemed to have the necessary characteristics. Its emission wavelength, at 510 mu, was in the yellow-green, an unusual fluorescence color in tissue; and it reemitted 85% of the energy it absorbed—that is, it was almost as brightly fluorescent as possible. In the past it had been used to trace the presence of underground rivers and unsuspected connections between water sources. Its coupling to antibody by the same linkage (carbamido-) that Creech had used for anthracene and other compounds completed the first stage in the development of fluorescent antibodies, the use of which has come to be called immunofluorescence.

Fluorescein-labeled antibodies were first used by Coons and his colleagues in 1942 to trace the fate of pneumococci injected into mice. Later, with the principal collaboration of M. H. Kaplan, he extended its use to the distribution after injection of pneumococcal polysaccharide and foreign plasma proteins, and to the detection of animal cells infected with the intracellular parasites mumps virus and typhus rickettsia.

Since these early studies, which were published in 1950, the use of immunofluorescence has slowly spread through biology. A tool forged from two fields, it gives the specificity of immunological reactions to the microscopist and the resolution of the microscope to the immunologist. It is of use to the student of infectious disease because it makes possible rapid specific diagnosis of an increasing number of diseases; indeed, in principle any infectious disease can be diagnosed by this means. Beyond this, immunofluorescence is of use in the study of some of the basic problems of immunity, such as locating the site of antibody formation and determining the number of cells engaged in the process under various conditions of stimulation. It is also a useful technique for the cytochemist, who can use it to localize various macromolecules such as blood group substances or cell products synthesized for excretion, like enzymes in the cells of the pancreas or albumin and prothrombin in cells of the liver.

In recent years Coons concentrated on the study of the cellular aspects of antibody formation and tried, like many immunologists, to fathom the puzzle of specific antibody synthesis.

Coons received his B.A. from Williams College in 1933 and his M.D. from Harvard Medical School in 1937. After clinical training in medicine at the Massachusetts General Hospital and the Thorndike Memorial Laboratory of the Boston City Hospital, he joined the department of bacteriology and immunology at Harvard Medical School in 1940 as a National Research Council fellow. With the exception of World War II, during which he served in the Army Medical Corps in the Southwest Pacific, he remained a member of that department. He was elected to the National Academy of Sciences in 1962.

For background information *see* ANTIBODY; MICROSCOPE, FLUORESCENCE in the McGraw-Hill Encyclopedia of Science and Technology.   □

☆ CORI, Carl Ferdinand
American biochemist
Born Dec. 5, 1896, Prague, Czechoslovakia

THE ENERGY necessary for the activities of life is supplied through sugar metabolism in the organism. The processes of this metabolism, therefore, are of extreme importance to the study of life itself. The investigations of Carl Cori and his wife Gerty Radnitz Cori in this problem of carbohydrate metabolism resulted in the discovery of the enzymatic mechanism of glucose-glycogen interconversion and the effects of hormones upon this mechanism. For this achievement they were awarded the 1947 Nobel Prize in physiology or medicine.

Over a century ago Claude Bernard discovered a starchlike substance he named glycogen. Glycogen consists of large numbers of glucose molecules bonded together and is found mainly in the liver and muscles and, to a slight extent, in skin and other tissues. The sugar content of the blood is effectively constant since, when sugar intake is high, storage of glycogen in the liver is increased, and when the blood sugar level falls below normal, the glycogen of the liver is converted into glucose, which enters the blood stream. Apparently only the glycogen of the liver can supply blood sugar.

In the early 1930s, then, the Coris faced this challenge: "What are the mechanisms, the chemical reactions, by which glucose is converted into glycogen, and by what means does the reverse process occur?" More than a decade of painstaking effort was needed before an answer was found.

It was known before the Coris began their work that under certain circumstances glucose in living tissues appears to be bound to inorganic phosphate. Closer investigation had demonstrated that the inorganic phosphate was bonded to the sixth carbon atom in the glucose chain, the compound being then designated as glucose-6-phosphate.

After much preliminary work, the Coris were able to show that if ground-up muscle were washed thoroughly with water, the residue could take up free inorganic phosphate, which was found then to be bonded to glucose. In this case, however, the sugar phosphate formed was not glucose-6-phosphate. The new compound, the so-called "Cori ester," was found to have the phosphate bonded to the first carbon atom in the glucose chain; it was glucose-1-phosphate.

The discovery of the Cori ester proved to be the key that opened the door to an understanding of the glucose-glycogen interconversion. The glucose-1-phosphate could be found only in washed muscle, since washing removed an enzyme from the tissue. This enzyme, now known as phosphoglucomutase, catalyzes the migration of inorganic phosphate between the ends of the sugar molecule, between the 1-position and the 6-position. In prior work this enzyme was always present, and thus the Cori ester had all been converted to the 6-ester before it could be detected.

After many years of continuous effort, the Coris were able to show that the glucose-glycogen interconversion was actually a three-step process. The first two of these reactions are readily reversible, and each is catalyzed by its own enzyme. Glycogen reversibly reacts with inorganic phosphate and the enzyme phosphorylase to give glucose-1-phosphate, the Cori ester. The second step consists of transposition of the phosphate group from the 1- to the 6-position. This reaction is catalyzed by the enzyme phosphoglucomutase, which itself must be activated by the presence of magnesium ions. The third reaction is the hydrolysis of glucose-6-phosphate to glucose, the removal of the phosphate group to convert the ester to the sugar. This final reaction, which is not readily reversible, occurs in the presence of the enzyme phosphatase. The glucose formed in this way is released into the blood, which carries it to the tissues. The reverse process, the conversion of blood glucose to glycogen, requires as its first step the presence of the enzyme hexokinase and adenosinetriphosphate (ATP) to form glucose-6-phosphate.

As a demonstration of the validity of their analysis, the Coris succeeded in synthesizing glycogen in vitro from glucose in the presence of hexokinase, adenosinetriphosphate, phosphoglucomutase, and phosphorylase. Further, they were able to show that the hexokinase reaction, the interconversion of glucose and glucose-6-phosphate, is promoted by insulin but checked by another hormone in extracts from the anterior lobe of the pituitary gland, the hypophysis. This discovery is of great importance, since it demonstrates that hormones intervene chemically in sugar metabolism, and thus the relation of endocrine function to glucose utilization becomes clearer.

The son of the director of the Marine Biological Station at Trieste, Carl Cori studied at the gymnasium in Trieste and then at the German University of Prague, where he received his M.D. in 1920. He then spent a year at the University of Vienna and a year as assistant in pharmacology at the University of Graz before accepting in 1922 the position of biochemist at the State Institute for the Study of Malignant Diseases in Buffalo, N.Y. In 1931 he was appointed professor of pharmacology at the Washington University Medical School in St. Louis, where he later became professor of biochemistry. He was elected to the National Academy of Sciences in 1940.

For background information *see* ENDOCRINE MECHANISMS; ENZYME; GLUCOSE; GLYCOGEN in the McGraw-Hill Encyclopedia of Science and Technology.   □

CORI, Gerty Theresa Radnitz

American biochemist
Born Aug. 15, 1896, Prague, Czechoslovakia
Died Oct. 26, 1957, St. Louis, Mo., U.S.A.

FOR THEIR research into the mechanism of carbohydrate metabolism and its relation to certain hormone secretions, Gerty Radnitz Cori and her husband Carl Cori received the 1947 Nobel Prize in physiology or medicine. *See* CORI, CARL FERDINAND.

Gerty Cori also did independent work on hereditable human diseases. Her study of a number of glycogen-storage diseases demonstrated that these diseases were intimately related to defects in the molecular structures of certain enzymes or, in some cases, to their total absence.

Gerty Cori received her M.D. from the medical school of the German University of Prague in 1920, then spent two years at the Carolinen Children's Hospital. She married Carl Cori in 1920 and in 1922 went with him to the United States. From 1922 to 1931 the Coris worked at the State Institute for the Study of Malignant Diseases in Buffalo, N.Y. In 1931 they joined the staff of the Washington University Medical School in St. Louis, Mo. In 1947 Gerty Cori was appointed professor of biochemistry there. □

★ CORNER, George Washington

American medical biologist
Born Dec. 12, 1889, Baltimore, Md., U.S.A.

As a medical student, Corner planned to become a gynecologist, but during his internship he found the problems of human reproduction so fascinating that he devoted himself to laboratory research and medical teaching as anatomist and embryologist.

He became interested in the ovary and especially in the corpus luteum. This is a mass of cells about the size of a cherry that forms for about two weeks in each successive monthly cycle of the human female, filling up the emptied graafian follicle from which the egg cell has been discharged into the oviduct (fallopian tube). In animals there are as many corpora lutea as young in the litter. When the egg cell is fertilized and develops into an embryo, the corpus luteum does not disappear, but lasts throughout the pregnancy.

Corner began his investigation of the corpus luteum by thorough microscopic study of its cell structure and development, and of its cyclic appearance and disappearance. These studies, made principally on the sow, prepared him for observations on human ovaries and subsequent experimental work on laboratory animals.

About 1910 a European surgeon, Ludwig Fraenkel, showed that this transitory structure was somehow necessary for the attachment of the early embryo in the uterus and for its sub-

sequent development. In very early pregnancy in a rabbit, for example, if the experimenter removes the ovaries or the corpora lutea alone, the embryos do not develop. What happens to them was not known. Two European scientists, the embryologist Paul Ancel and the anatomist Paul Bouin, found in 1912 that the corpus luteum produces some sort of internal secretion that changes the lining of the uterus from an inactive state to one seemingly favorable for receiving and nourishing the embryos. The nature of this internal secretion was also unknown.

Corner, whose training included both surgical methods and a knowledge of early embryology, began in 1928 to follow up these earlier findings. By experiments on rabbits he proved that survival and development of the embryos depend upon the change in the uterus induced by the corpora lutea. If the latter are removed, the progestational change does not occur, and the embryos when they arrive in the uterus fail to survive.

These experiments provided a means of identifying the corpus luteum hormone. Corner and one of his medical students, Willard M. Allen, a competent biochemist, made extracts of sows' ovaries collected at the slaughterhouse. They tested the extracts by injection into spayed rabbits to see whether they would produce changes such as would have been produced by the rabbits' own corpora lutea. The two investigators finally obtained partially purified extracts that brought about the progestational change and maintained pregnancy after removal of the ovaries. Allen, by further purification, prepared a crystalline product now known as progesterone. Expert organic chemists elsewhere later worked out its exact chemical composition and made it synthetically.

Corner continued his anatomical studies of the ovarian and uterine cycle, and particularly of the menstrual cycle. Since true menstruation occurs only in Primates (man, apes, and Old World monkeys), Corner organized a small colony of rhesus monkeys, the first in the United States used for long-term study of the physiology of reproduction. In 35 years of continuous research he worked out the anatomical details of the menstrual cycle and also the physiological processes by which the fluctuating levels of the ovarian hormones (estrogen and progesterone) cause the cyclic menstrual hemorrhage. Corner also contributed to knowledge of early human embryology and the causes of embryonic defects and prenatal abnormalities.

Corner was educated at the Boys' Latin School in Baltimore and at the Johns Hopkins University (A.B., 1909). Following a good training in the Latin classics, he developed in later college years a strong interest in biology and proceeded to study medicine at Johns Hopkins (M.D., 1913). After an internship he was assistant professor of anatomy at the University of California, Berkeley (1915–19); associate professor at Johns Hopkins (1919–23); and professor at the University of Rochester, where he organized and directed the department of anatomy (1923–40). From 1940 to 1955 he was director of the department of embryology of the Carnegie Institution of Washington, at its Baltimore laboratory. In 1958 he received the Passano Foundation Award. He was elected to the National Academy of Sciences in 1940.

Corner wrote *The Hormones in Human Reproduction* (1942; 2d ed. 1947) and *Ourselves Unborn* (1944). *Anatomist at Large* (1955) contains an autobiographical sketch and collected essays. Interested since student days in the history of medicine, Corner also wrote extensively on that subject, producing comprehensive histories of the Rockefeller Institute of New York and the University of Pennsylvania School of Medicine.

For background information *see* OVARY in the McGraw-Hill Encyclopedia of Science and Technology.   □

★ **COURNAND, André Frederic**
American physician
Born Sept. 24, 1895, Paris, France

IN A fruitful collaboration with Dickinson W. Richards extending over 35 years, Cournand developed a methodology and a body of knowledge basically related to the understanding of cardiocirculatory and pulmonary functions in both normal and diseased human beings. An essential feature of his work involved the safe use, in clinical investigation, of the technique of cardiac catheterization first applied in man (that is, on himself) by the German surgeon Werner Forssmann in 1929. In 1956 Cournand shared the Nobel Prize in medicine or physiology with

Forssmann and Richards for the many contributions in cardiac and pulmonary physiology and pathophysiology derived from this technique.

In his earliest clinical investigations Cournand studied systematically with new techniques the three main functions of the lungs: ventilation, distribution, and diffusion of respiratory gases. By adding to these techniques catheterization of the right atrium, ventricle, and pulmonary artery in 1941, he made available a complete picture of the transport of respiratory gases between the surrounding atmosphere and the body tissues. With adequate methods and newly devised instrumentation, the output of the heart pump, the blood pressures within its various chambers, and the large vessels issuing from them could be measured accurately.

In the first clinical cardiopulmonary laboratory organized as a result of these developments, Cournand, Richards, and many collaborators trained by them embarked, during World War II, upon a study of the various forms of clinical shock and demonstrated its essential features, namely, a fall in cardiac output, associated with a decreased venous return, and a variable vasomotor response depending on the nature and the extent of circulating fluid lost. More importantly, they proved that in traumatic shock blood replacement is preferable to infusion of plasma. After the war they investigated all forms of cardiac diseases. In congenital heart lesions, by directing the catheter through the abnormal pathways and by multiple samplings of blood and pressure recordings, they greatly improved the accuracy of diagnoses of the anatomic defects, the evaluation of their physiological effects, and the success of surgical correction. In acquired heart diseases, various hemodynamic patterns, including cardiac failure, were defined during their evolution; the role of the heart muscle function in valvular lesions and in constrictive pericarditis was evaluated; and the effects of various drugs, in particular digitalis glycosides, were accurately assessed. Among these contributions in cardiology stands out the analysis of the effects of pulmonary disease upon the cardiac function and the pulmonary circulation, which led to physiological methods of prevention and of treatment of pulmonary heart disease.

Maintaining his early interest in pulmonary physiopathology, Cournand studied the effects of pneumonectomy upon the function of the remaining lung and proposed a physiological classification of chronic obstructive diseases of the lungs. He then investigated the problem of conjunction of air and blood in the lungs in a variety of lung diseases by evaluating the alveolar ventilation-perfusion relationships and the diffusion of respiratory gases across the alveolo-capillary membrane. Thus he was led to an inquiry into the factors controlling the pulmonary circulation, which resulted in the description of the pressure-flow relationships in pulmonary vessels and the demonstration of their vasomotor controls and of the distribution of the perfusion of the lungs by the local concentration of oxygen in the alveoli.

Cournand received his bachelor's degree in 1913 and in 1914 his diploma in physics, chemistry, and biology from the Sorbonne. After serving in the French Army during World War I, he returned to his medical studies, becoming Interne des Hopitaux de Paris in 1925. He was awarded his medical degree in 1930. Cournand then went to the United States and secured a residency on the Tuberculosis Service of the Columbia University Division at Bellevue Hospital in New York, later becoming a visiting physician on this service. From an instructorship, in 1934, at Columbia University College of Physicians and Surgeons, he eventually rose to full professor in 1951. In 1941 Cournand became a naturalized citizen of the United States. He was elected to the National Academy of Sciences in 1958.

For background information *see* CARDIOVASCULAR SYSTEM; HEART in the McGraw-Hill Encyclopedia of Science and Technology.   □

★ **COWAN, George Arthur**

American radiochemist
Born Feb. 15, 1920, Worcester, Mass., U.S.A.

IN 1955, while engaged in design experiments with nuclear explosive devices, Cowan became interested in using the intense neutron fluxes that accompany these explosions to study some fundamental properties of nuclei. The experiments that he initiated were impossible to carry out with the limited numbers of neutrons available from such other sources as accelerators and reactors. In succeeding years, he and other experimentalists demonstrated that nuclear explosives provide a unique scientific tool for investigations in the field of physics known as neutron spectroscopy and that, in addition, they produce neutrons under conditions nearly duplicating processes of element synthesis that have hitherto occurred only in certain rare stars. Cowan's work was recognized by the U.S. Atomic Energy Commission in 1965 when he was selected for an E. O. Lawrence Memorial award.

Since 1932, when James Chadwick first discovered the neutron—a particle with the mass of a proton but zero charge—experiments with neutrons have been responsible for many of the most exciting developments in nuclear science. The neutron reacts with every element except stable helium to make new radioactive species. It produces fission in heavy elements and is responsible for the chain reaction that led to the production of atomic energy and to atomic explosives. Because it has no charge, it can interact at close range with charged particles in nuclear matter and serve as an effective probe of the structure of the nucleus. However, investigations with neutrons have always been hampered by the fact that they are difficult to produce at specific energies in quantities sufficient to permit accurate measurements.

It was apparent to Cowan that a nominal nuclear explosion (20 kilotons) produced as many neutrons in one-millionth of a second as could be produced in the laboratory in many thousands of years. These neutrons occur in a broad distribution in energy. Pulses containing neutrons of mixed energy can provide neutrons of separate energy by "time-of-flight" resolution. If neutrons of different energy, consequently of different velocity, start down a pipe at the same time, the most energetic arrive first and the least energetic last. If measurements are made at the end of the pipe over the entire time interval between pulses, the elapsed time after each pulse to time of arrival identifies the neutron energy. Time-of-flight energy separation is the most generally useful method for production of monoenergetic neutrons at relatively low energies (below 1 Mev). When the pulse is of enormous size, as is the case when it is produced by a nuclear explosion, the accuracy of measurements with neutrons is improved correspondingly.

A second unique phenomenon associated with nuclear explosions is "multiple neutron capture." The probability of a nucleus absorbing a neutron is directly related to the number of neutrons passing through a given target. As the number of neutrons becomes larger, the probability of a single nucleus reacting with two or more neutrons becomes proportionately much larger. Long exposures in high-flux reactors are commonly used to produce multiple neutron capture products. However, in nuclear explosions so many neutrons are made that single nuclei have been struck by and have absorbed up to 19 or more neutrons in a row. If the original target nucleus is at the heavy end of the periodic table, the addition of many more neutrons can produce new elements. It is presently believed that all elements in nature heavier than iron have been produced in neutron-rich environments that result when unstable stars collapse, a phenomenon that terminates in a nuclear explosion on an unimaginably large scale. These stars, called "supernovae," contain a hot neutron gas in their interiors. Similar neutron gases can be made on Earth in nuclear explosions, and subsequent neutron capture phenomena can be duplicated in approximately the same way as they are believed to occur in stars.

The first synthesis of a neutron gas that reproduced the cosmological process came about as the result of the "Mike" nuclear explosion—the historic test of a thermonuclear device at Eniwetok Atoll in 1952. The debris was found to contain 14 new heavy isotopes, including two new elements that were named "einsteinium" and "fermium." Since 1958, efforts have been made to produce even heavier elements in low-yield explosions. In 1964 two experiments at the Nevada Test Site of the Atomic Energy Commission succeeded in producing Fm^{257}, the heaviest isotope chemically identified to date.

To Cowan and his associates, the success of these experiments indicated that new, much heavier atomic species would be made in the near future. Although the heaviest new atoms are quite unstable, they do not appear to be approaching the ultimate limit of stability as fast as had been earlier believed. Scientists are presently predicting that at mass 310 and at element 126 (about 22 elements beyond what is presently known), a new "island" of increased nuclear stability will be found. The present challenge is to find ways to reach this island, if it does indeed exist.

Cowan majored in chemistry at Worcester Polytechnic Institute. Upon graduation in 1941 he went to Princeton University, where he became involved in early cyclotron investigations of possible atomic-reactor designs. In 1942 he joined the Metallurgical Laboratory at the University of Chicago and contributed to the successful development of the first chain-reacting "pile" and the subsequent production of the atomic bomb. In 1946 he participated in Operation Crossroads, the first military tests of nuclear explosives at Bikini Atoll. He completed work for his Sc.D. in chemistry at Carnegie Institute of Technology in 1949 and joined the Los Alamos Scientific Laboratory, where he became group leader in radiochemistry.

For background information *see* NEUTRON in the McGraw-Hill Encyclopedia of Science and Technology.   □

☆ CRICK, Francis Harry Compton
English molecular biologist
Born June 8, 1916, Northampton, England

CRICK AND the American biologist James D. Watson in 1953 proposed a model for the deoxyribonucleic acid (DNA) molecule. This model describes the DNA molecule as consisting of two helical chains, each coiled around the same axis. Their hypothesis was based on data obtained from x-ray diffraction studies done by the English physicist Maurice H. F. Wilkins. All of the previous observations of DNA's structure were accounted for by Crick and Watson's 1953 model.

The Watson-Crick model provided a simple mechanism to explain what had been one of the most baffling problems in biology—the question of how the hereditary material duplicates itself. The model suggested that the two coiled strands that make up the double DNA helix separate, and each then acts as a template to form its complementary DNA strand from nearby molecules. Before very long, the DNA model was also serving as a stimulus for investigations into another related problem—how the genetic material directs the building of enzymes and, through them, the metabolism, growth, and differentiation of the cell.

The determination of the DNA structure has been called the single most important development in biology of the present century. For their work with DNA, Crick, Watson, and Wilkins received the 1962 Nobel Prize in medicine or physiology.

During the 70 years following Friedrich Miescher's discovery of DNA in 1869, its biological role remained vague. Those who sought to discover the chemical basis of heredity focused their attention on protein. However, no one ever brought forth a convincing hypothesis as to how protein could produce copies of itself. By 1925 P. A. Levene and others had learned that DNA molecules are built up of nucleotides, molecules composed of a pentose (a five-carbon sugar), a phosphate group, and a nitrogen base. In DNA, the sugar of the nucleotides was found to be deoxyribose and the nitrogen base either one of two purines, adenine or guanine, or of two pyrimidines, cytosine or thymine. Levene perceived that the deoxyribose was linked to the base and also to the phosphate group, the latter serving as a link to the next nucleotide in the chain. Levene's chemical approach prevented him from perceiving that natural DNA molecules are giants of the molecular world, with thousands of nucleotides arranged in sequence. This fact, however, was learned before Watson and Crick began their work.

The first decisive evidence that DNA, rather than protein, was the actual carrier of genetic "instructions" was the discovery by O. T. Avery, C. M. MacLeod, and M. McCarty in 1944 that DNA from type-III pneumococcus could be incorporated into the genetic make-up of type-II pneumococcus. This incorporation results in the transformation of type-II pneumococcus into type-III pneumococcus. The DNA had brought about a distinct and permanent hereditary change.

The development of paper chromatography in 1944 made it convenient for chemists to separate the components of all sorts of mixtures. Using chromatography, Erwin Chargaff, in the late 1940s, made the provocative discovery that, in DNA, the number of adenine units was approximately equal to the number of guanine units. and the number of cytosine units was approximately equal to the number of guanine units. Another fruitful suggestion came in 1951 from Linus Pauling and R. B. Corey, who formulated the helical structure of polypeptides and calculated the actual dimensions of the helix.

By 1951, it was known that DNA actually transmitted genetic information in at least some instances and that the DNA molecule was an extremely long polymer of nucleotides. At this point, x-ray diffraction photographs clearly indicated that DNA must be a helix. It was a crucial contribution of Crick and Watson to perceive that the DNA helix was a double one, with two strands coiling around each other. Both helices are right-handed, but the sequence of atoms is in opposite directions, "up" in one chain and "down" in the other.

As conceived by Crick and Watson, the two intertwined strands of the DNA molecule are held together by hydrogen bonds between nitrogen bases. The dimensions and structure of the bases require that a purine of a nucleotide in one strand be bonded to a particular pyrimidine in the other strand. Thus adenine is always found opposite thymine, and cytosine is always bonded to guanine. This confirms the observations of Chargaff as to the equal quantities of adenine and thymine and of cytosine and guanine. The pitch of the helix results in a complete turn every 10 base pairs, and the distance from one pair of bases to the pair above them is 3.4 angstroms.

Crick and Watson thought of the double helix unwinding to achieve replication. As the strands unwound, each would serve as a template (or "mold") for the production of a new strand, with new thymine units guided into position opposite the adenines of the old chain and new guanines guided into position opposite the cytosines and vice versa. Within a few years, reports came in from many experimenters, all of which appeared to confirm the Watson-Crick model and their hypothesis of DNA replication.

With fellow workers at Cambridge University, Crick later studied the structure and working of the genetic code—the sequence of the nitrogen bases in DNA that directs the joining of amino acids to build proteins, including enzymes. The term cistron had already been introduced as signifying the functional unit of the old term gene. Crick used the convenient term codon to indicate the set of bases that codes one amino acid. As a result of experiments at Cambridge with L. Barnett, S. Brenner, and R. J. Watts-Tobin, and consideration of the findings of other workers, Crick was able to state general properties of the genetic code, including the following: (1) It is likely that codons consist of three adjacent bases. (2) Adjacent codons probably do not overlap. (3) The message is read in the correct groups of three by starting at some fixed point, probably one end of the gene. (4) In general, more than one triplet codes each amino acid. (5) It is possible that some triplets may code more than one amino acid—that is, they may be ambiguous. (6) The code is probably much the same in all organisms; and in fact, it may be the same in all organisms.

Some of Crick's evidence for triplet codes came from the study, by his group, of mutations in the A and B cistrons of the *r* II locus of *Escherichia coli* bacteriophage T4.

Crick classified all mutations as plus or minus and assumed that a mutation called plus has an extra base added to the genetic message, and a mutation called minus has a base removed. One or two minus mutations or one or two plus mutations render a gene nonfunctional by putting the message out of phase. However, a minus and a plus mutation not too far separated from each other in the gene makes the gene functional. Also, three plus or three minus mutations would put the message in phase again, making the gene functional from that point on. This corroborated his hypothesis that the genetic message is read off in groups of three bases, starting at one end.

Crick was educated at University College, London (B.Sc., 1937) and at Cambridge University (Ph.D., 1953). He contributed to mine development during World War II. In 1949 he joined the staff of the Medical Research Council Laboratory of Molecular Biology at Cambridge. He became a fellow of the Royal Society of London in 1959.

For background information *see* DEOXYRIBONUCLEIC ACID; GENE; MUTATION; NUCLEIC ACID in the McGraw-Hill Encyclopedia of Science and Technology.   □

D-E

★★

★ **DAM, Henrik**

Danish biochemist and nutritionist
Born Feb. 21, 1895, Copenhagen, Denmark

WHILE STUDYING the question of whether chicks can live without dietary cholesterol, Dam noticed that chicks reared on certain artificial diets exhibited a marked bleeding tendency associated with low clotting power of the blood. This condition was not a consequence of the absence of cholesterol from the diet, as the experiments showed that chicks, like many other animals, can synthesize cholesterol. A systematic search for the cause led to the finding of a new fat-soluble vitamin, which in 1935 was termed vitamin K. For this discovery, Dam shared with E. A. Doisy the 1943 Nobel Prize in physiology or medicine.

Dam also took part in the investigation of the role played by vitamin K in hemorrhagic diseases in man. Suitable administration of vitamin K eliminates the risk of fatal bleeding otherwise encountered in surgery on patients with obstructive juandice. This form of bleeding was shown to be due to insufficient absorption of vitamin K from the intestine in the absence of bile. A bleeding tendency sometimes occurring in children during the first week after birth can be prevented by administration of vitamin K to the infant immediately after birth or by administration of an excess of vitamin K to the mother a suitable time before delivery. This type of bleeding tendency is due to limitation of the passage of vitamin K from mother to fetus. Vitamin K was shown to be unrelated to hereditary hemophilia.

In studies with animals raised on artificial diets, Dam and his associates encountered manifestations of dietary imbalances due to the combined effect of more than one factor. In chicks, they observed (1937–38) the "exudative diathesis," a condition in which massive amounts of plasma exude from the capillaries. This condition was traced to the lack of vitamin E. K. Schwarz et al. and E. L. R. Stokstad et al. showed later (1957) that, in addition to the lack of vitamin E, lack of selenium is necessary for the occurrence of exudative diathesis. The "alimentary encephalomalacia" previously described by other investigators and suggested to be caused by lack of vitamin E was shown (1958) by Dam and his associates to be specifically dependent upon dietary fatty acids of the linoleic acid series (as distinguished from the linolenic acid series) concomitantly with absence of vitamin E. A characteristic form of muscular dystrophy in chicks was observed and shown to be caused by lack of vitamin E in combination with low dietary sulfur amino acids.

Other manifestations of vitamin-E deficiency in chicks and rats were investigated with respect to their interrelationship to dietary fat and to the role of vitamin E as an antioxidant. A sign of vitamin-E deficiency in rats, "depigmentation of incisors," described by other investigators, was shown (1945) by Dam and his associates to depend not simply upon deficiency of vitamin E but also upon the presence and type of fat in the diet. Dam and his associates showed that dietary polyunsaturated fatty acids of the type present in fish oils induce autoxidation of body fat in vivo in chicks and rats when vitamin E is lacking. The previously known poor utilization of vitamin A in animals reared on vitamin-E–deficient diets was shown to presuppose dietary highly unsaturated fatty acids capable of inducing autoxidation in vivo.

In hamsters, Dam and his associates found (1952) that rearing on certain artificial diets induces formation of gallstones. Cholesterol gallstones are formed abundantly when the diet is deficient in polyunsaturated fatty acids and carbohydrate is furnished as an easily absorbable sugar. This condition is unrelated to vitamin-E deficiency. Other dietary combinations lead to the formation of amorphous pigmented gallstones. The formation of cholesterol gallstones in hamsters was shown to be associated with low ratios between the concentrations of bile acids and cholesterol and between phospholipids and cholesterol in the bile. These ratios could be raised by giving the carbohydrate in the form of starch and by adding fats rich in polyunsaturated fatty acids to the diet. These investigations led to studies on human bile and to the possibility of changing the composition of the latter, which is usually near the point of saturation with respect to cholesterol.

Dam graduated in chemistry from the Polytechnic Institute of Copenhagen in 1920. From 1923 he was connected with the department of physiology, and from 1928 with the department of biochemistry of the University of Copenhagen. In 1940 he went on a lecture tour to the United States, from where he did not return until 1946. During his stay in the United States, Dam was senior research associate at the University of Rochester (1942–45) and associate member of the Rockefeller Institute for Medical Research in New York (1945–46). In 1941, Dam was appointed professor of biochemistry at the Polytechnic Institute of Copenhagen. From 1956 to 1963 he was also head of the biochemical division of the Danish Fat Research Institute. Dam's work on vitamin K was done primarily in Copenhagen from 1929, the work on vitamin E both in Copenhagen and in the United States from 1937. The gallstone work was done in Copenhagen from 1951.

For background information *see* VITAMIN E; VITAMIN K in the McGraw-Hill Encyclopedia of Science and Technology.   □

★ DANIELS, Farrington

American chemist
Born Mar. 8, 1889, Minneapolis, Minn., U.S.A.

DANIELS'S PRINCIPAL researches lay in the field of basic chemical kinetics, but they led him into several related fields that appeared to have possible significance in human affairs. In recognition of his achievements, the American Chemical Society awarded him its Willard Gibbs Medal (1955) and Priestley Medal (1957).

In 1921 Daniels reported quantitative studies on the decomposition of nitrogen pentoxide, a gas-phase chemical reaction that at room temperature follows the first-order rate law with exactness. These researches led to the abandonment of the then current hypothesis that radiation from the containing vessel was a factor in the activation of chemical reactions. The nitrogen pentoxide studies were followed by investigations on the kinetics and decomposition mech-

anism of all the oxides of nitrogen and other gas reactions. In the thermal decomposition of ethyl bromide, Daniels found that the complete mechanism included the formation of free radicals and wall effects.

The photochemical decomposition of nitrogen pentoxide led to new experimental techniques for the accurate measurements of quantum yields in photochemical reactions. Daniels used these techniques to measure the maximum efficiency of photosynthesis in laboratory algae. A value of about 30 per cent was established corresponding to the requirement of 8 photons of light for each molecule of carbon dioxide reacting with water. In contrast, ordinary agriculture uses only a few tenths of 1 per cent of the annual sunshine in its photosynthesis.

When isotopes became available, Daniels used them as tracers in the elucidation of reaction mechanisms, and in 1937 he calculated the concentration of carbon-13 that might be effected through chemical kinetics. He then carried out experimental measurements of the isotopic concentration in the hydrolysis of urea and other reactions.

In 1940, with N. Gilbert and W. G. Henderson, Daniels applied his knowledge of the chemical kinetics of nitrogen oxides to the fixation of atmospheric nitrogen, using a method proposed by F. G. Cottrell. Air was heated with fuel gas to 2100°C in a pair of pebble bed furnaces of magnesium oxide and then quenched at the rate of 4000°C per second, producing nitric oxide cheaply in concentrations of about 2 per cent. The inflowing air was switched from one furnace to the other every few minutes, thus preheating the air, chilling the products rapidly enough to prevent the decomposition of the nitric oxide, and conserving the heat. Silica gel was used for the catalytic oxidation and recovery of nitric oxide. This Wisconsin process produced 40 tons of nitric acid per day, but it was not quite competitive with nitric acid produced by the oxidation of ammonia synthesized by the Haber process.

During World War II, Daniels was called into the atomic energy program and carried over into this work his experience with high-temperature ceramic furnaces. His design for a peacetime high-temperature, gas-cooled nuclear power reactor was implemented in a large program at Oak Ridge, but after 2 years the program was discontinued because of a change in policy emphasis.

After the war, Daniels extended his kinetic studies from gases and solutions to solids, starting with the phenomenon of thermoluminescence, which had been observed in quartz vessels exposed to radiations in nuclear reactors. With C. A. Boyd, D. F. Saunders, and others, he studied the thermoluminescence glow curves of many hundreds of natural minerals and laboratory crystals. He pointed out that whereas the laboratory crystals must be activated by exposure to x-rays or gamma rays, the natural minerals are sometimes activated by minute traces of radioactive elements that they contain as impurities.

Daniels extended these studies to researches on glow curves as a tool in geological stratigraphy, to possible age determinations of naturally thermoluminescent minerals, to problems in geochemistry, and even to an exploration of a method for recovering uranium from very low-grade ores at the mine. One practical result was the development of thermoluminescence radiation dosimetry. Using small quantities of lithium fluoride, this dosimeter has come to be important in measuring clinical radiation and in monitoring personnel who are exposed to radiation. Other amplifications of the study of solid reactions led to the use of differential thermal analysis in chemical kinetics and rate measurements of chemical reactions between mixtures of different solid particles.

Disappointed in the cancellation of his wartime project for a nuclear power reactor and impressed with the low efficiency of photosynthesis in agriculture, Daniels turned his attention in recent years to the direct use of radiant energy from the Sun. During the 1950s and 1960s, much of his effort was expended in trying to hasten—through lecturing, writing, and research—the direct use of the Sun's energy. In his personal research, he emphasized those investigations that might lead to the early use of the solar energy in rural areas of developing countries. In particular, he worked on the development of small, family-size solar stills for desalting sea water, inexpensive focusing collectors of solar radiation, and fuel cells for obtaining electricity from the direct oxidation by air of waste organic material.

Daniels received his B.S. at the University of Minnesota in 1910 and his Ph.D. at Harvard University in 1914. He taught physical chemistry at Worcester Polytechnic Institute from 1914 to 1917. After 1920 he was connected with the University of Wisconsin. In 1945–46 he was director of the Metallurgical Laboratory in Chicago devoted to research on atomic energy and was a founder and chairman of Argonne National Laboratory. From 1952 until his retirement in 1959 he was chairman of Wisconsin's chemistry department. He was elected to the National Academy of Sciences in 1947.

Daniels was the author or coauthor of over 230 scientific papers and 20 books, including *Physical Chemistry* (6th ed. 1961) and *Experimental Physical Chemistry* (6th ed. 1962). His kinetic researches are described in *Chemical Kinetics* (1937) and *Selected Studies in Chem-*

ical Kinetics (1961). His most recent book was *Direct Use of the Sun's Energy* (1964).

For background information *see* KINETICS, CHEMICAL; SOLAR ENERGY; THERMOLUMINESCENCE in the McGraw-Hill Encyclopedia of Science and Technology. ☐

★ DARLINGTON, Cyril Dean

British biologist
Born Dec. 19, 1903, Chorley, Lancashire, England

DARLINGTON WAS concerned with showing how the mechanisms of heredity, variation, and reproduction work and how they are adaptively connected in evolution, forming what he described as a genetic system.

After a training in agriculture at Wye College, Darlington went to work in November, 1923, under William Bateson at the John Innes Institution. There he was brought face to face with the dilemma of genetics at that time—the choice between the cytoplasm espoused by Bateson and the chromosomes espoused by his cytologist Frank Newton. Both Bateson and Newton died within four years, but not before Newton had given his pupil the idea of using polyploid plants to understand what the chromosomes do at meiosis.

T. H. Morgan, and equally F. A. Janssens, had thought of crossing over between paired chromosomes simply as a matter of recombining their genes. Darlington's first step was to show that it was much more. By way of chiasma formation, it was responsible for association and repulsion, segregation and reduction of the chromosomes—indeed, for the whole succession of events at meiosis. Crossing over was thus the crux of all sexual processes, the prime variable in the character of all sexual populations and species. And, Darlington argued, it had been so from the beginning of evolution (*Recent Advances in Cytology*, 1932; 3d ed. 1965).

This view was long disputed. Its apparent exceptions, however, led to further steps in Darlington's argument. Complex differences, such as occur between the sex chromosomes in animals and plants, arose, he maintained, from the suppression of crossing over between some parts of them. The same was true of the complexes of hybrid species as in *Oenothera*. The size of the gene as a unit of crossing over was thus a function of the similarity of the pairing chromosomes. Hence it depended on the breeding system that brought them together. Again, the absence of crossing over in male flies appeared to him as an adaptation acquired in evolution; it was required to restrict the amount of recombination in species with a short life cycle from one meiosis to the next (*Evolution of Genetic Systems*, 1958).

While using the chromosomes for the study of evolutionary problems, Darlington maintained that they must always be considered adaptively as physiological agents. The special situation of genes of visible action, such as the centromere, he therefore attempted to relate at the same time to the movements, the activities, and the changing linkage relations of chromosomes.

When interpreting the physiological, mechanical, and evolutionary properties of the chromosomes in such genetic terms, Darlington had two aims. The first was to establish a genetic framework for biology. But a second aim was to establish at the center of this framework rules of chromosome behavior that would fit them into a pattern of chemical structure and activity; the basis of this pattern was successively revealed by T. Caspersson and Jean Brachet, J. D. Watson, F. H. C. Crick, and others. Further, the contrast between genetic particles responsible for nuclear and cytoplasmic heredity, which he related to the primary chemical distinction between the two nucleic acids DNA and RNA, was seen by Darlington as overriding the secondary biological distinctions, whether in the higher organisms or in viruses, between heredity, development, and infection (*Elements of Genetics*, 1949; *Genes, Plants, and People*, with K. Mather, 1950).

Darlington began by taking his lead from the recent work of Janssens and Morgan. His ideas, however, led him farther back, first to August Weismann and then to Francis Galton and Charles Darwin. He claimed to have found an even greater connectedness and a more extreme determinism in evolutionary mechanisms than had his predecessors. This he attributed to the role of breeding systems in controlling variation and exploiting its uncertainty as well as its certainty; also to the principle that the heredity of the population provides so much of the environment of the individual.

These new paradoxes suggested to Darlington

that the pitfalls besetting the most difficult of all genetic problems, those of human society, might now be avoided. Hence he was led to investigate the reciprocal relations of technical discovery, religious beliefs, and human breeding systems and to foreshadow genetic interpretations of the origin of agriculture, of the evolution of language and of morals, of the structure of society, and indeed of the processes of history in general (*Genetics and Man*, 1964).

Darlington became director of the John Innes Institution in 1939 and undertook its removal from Merton to Bayfordbury in 1949. In 1953 he was appointed Sherardian Professor of Botany and Keeper of the Botanic Garden at Oxford. He received the Royal Medal of the Royal Society in 1946.

In order to establish the techniques and applications of chromosome study, Darlington wrote *The Handling of Chromosomes*, with L. F. La Cour (4th ed. 1963). *The Chromosome Atlas of Flowering Plants*, with A. P. Wylie (1956), and *Chromosome Botany and the Origins of Cultivated Plants* (1956; 2d ed. 1963). With R. A. Fisher he founded and edited the periodical *Heredity* (1947). Darlington wrote also on the reform of university teaching (*Teaching Genetics*, 1963), on the relations of academies and governments with research, on the Vavilov-Lysenko controversy in Russia (*Conflict of Science and Society*, 1948), and on the history of scientific discovery (*Darwin's Place in History*, 1959).

For background information *see* MEIOSIS in the McGraw-Hill Encyclopedia of Science and Technology.   □

★ DART, Raymond Arthur

South African anatomist
Born Feb. 4, 1893, Toowong, Brisbane, Queensland, Australia

D ART REALIZED that the fossil brain of a man-ape child that he found in 1924 at Taungs, Republic of South Africa, represented an extinct ape group, which he called *Australopithecus africanus*, "South African Ape." With brains no bigger than those of large gorillas, these apes were more advanced intellectually, lived in caves away from tropical forests, had an erect posture, and pursued a hunting life in the most fierce and bitter mammalian environment ever known. At Makapansgat, 400 miles northeast of Taungs, he later identified another site and further specimens of this man-ape and described their predatory behavior and osteodontokeratic (or bone, tooth, and horn) culture by statistical and comparative study of the accompanying faunal re-

mains. For these achievements he received the Viking Medal and Award in Physical Anthropology for 1957.

In *The Descent of Man* (1871), Charles Darwin, who recognized the gorilla and chimpanzee as man's nearest relatives, wrote: "It is somewhat more probable that our early progenitors lived on the African continent than elsewhere." However, E. Dubois's discovery of *Pithecanthropus* in Java—and thus in proximity to the gibbon and orangutan of tropical Asia—concentrated the search for man's ancestors on the Asiatic continent between the First and Second World Wars. Darwin and his followers had also expected that man's progenitors would have developed an appreciably enlarged brain before losing their enlarged canine teeth. The Piltdown *Eoanthropus* discovery of 1912, which was not proved fraudulent until 1953, was officially accepted as supporting this idea. So *Australopithecus* was unacceptable from every current point of view.

The five-year-old infant whose skull Dart found, with its baby teeth still complete and the first adult molars just breaking through, had a brain rivaling that of the largest known gorillas. Furthermore, its face was complete. It differed from chimpanzees and gorillas of similar age in having a vertical forehead instead of eyebrow ridges, a recessed face instead of projecting muzzle and teeth, vertical front teeth and small incisors and canines instead of fangs. It also resembled man in the domelike—not flattened—form of brain, the downward-inclined orbits, and the projection of the forebrain backward over the hindbrain or cerebellum.

The expansion of the brain, due to localized growth between the areas for feeling, hearing, and vision, was measurable through the threefold separation of the parallel and lunate brain furrows. The more forward situation of the foramen magnum in the skull base testified to the ape's erectness. Apart from anatomical features, its divergence from living apes was shown by its geological situation in a travertine believed to be of late Tertiary (Pliocene) age; by its southern geographical situation in the temperate zone on the eastern fringe of the Kalahari desert; and by its troglodytic life in a cave amid the bones of the animals he lived on.

In 1937, R. Broom, who had supported Dart's claims from the outset, found adult man-ape remains at Sterkfontein, 30 miles west of Johannesburg. During the next fifteen years, he made repeated discoveries of adult and infant remains of the australopithecine types he called *Plesianthropus* and *Paranthropus*. His monographs gradually removed all doubts of the australopithecines' anatomical status. Powerful support from Professor (later Sir Wilfred) Le Gros Clark of Oxford and from Sir Arthur Keith turned the tide.

The fifth of nine children of a farmer-storekeeper, Dart majored in biology as a foundation scholar in the University of Queensland. He took his B.Sc. in 1913 and his B.Sc. (hons) examination the following year concurrently with entry upon medical studies in Sydney University. There he graduated M.B., Ch.M. in 1917 while holding the posts of demonstrator in anatomy and acting vice-principal of St. Andrew's College. After serving overseas in England and France as captain in the Australian Army Medical Corps, he became senior demonstrator in anatomy at University College, London (1919–22), and spent a year (1920–21) in America as one of the first two foreign fellows of the Rockefeller Foundation. Shortly after his return to London as senior lecturer in histology and embryology (1922), he was appointed professor of anatomy in the University of the Witwatersrand. He held that post from 1923 to 1958. From 1926 to 1943 he served simultaneously as dean of the Faculty of Medicine.

Dart wrote *Cultural Status of the South African Man-Apes* (1956), *The Osteodontokeratic Culture of Australopithecus promethus* (1957), and, with Denis Craig, *Adventures with the Missing Link* (1959).

For background information *see* FOSSIL MAN in the McGraw-Hill Encyclopedia of Science and Technology.   □

★ DEACON, George Edward Raven

British oceanographer
Born Mar. 21, 1906, Leicester, England

AFTER GRADUATING in chemistry at King's College, London, in 1926, Deacon went to the Antarctic as a member of the scientific staff of the Discovery Investigations, a government project aimed at improving our understanding of the migrations, variations in distribution, and fluctu-

ations in populations of the Antarctic whales. It required detailed study of the breeding and feeding habits of whales and of the factors that influence the distribution of the krill on which the whales feed. His main task was to make a three-dimensional plot of temperature and salinity in the circumpolar Antarctic Ocean; to learn as much as possible about the currents and general circulation of the water; to measure such nutrients as phosphate, nitrate, and silicate that might limit plant growth and general productivity of different areas; and to help in the correlation of the physical and chemical factors with the distribution of whale food and whales.

Deacon wrote a general account of the water masses of the South Atlantic Ocean in 1933, and a similar account of the Southern Ocean—the whole circumpolar ring—in 1937. It is usual in oceanography to regard the water movements as geostrophic, which means that the observed density gradients and computed pressure gradients are balanced by the effect of the Earth's rotation. Deacon felt that his geostrophic map, produced in 1937, underestimated the north and south movements. He retained this view when further observations extended the early picture without altering its character. He maintained that the vertical mixing, which amounts to flow across the density surfaces, and the effect of wind stress were sufficiently large in this region to reduce the value of the geostrophic assumptions. In fact by 1939 he felt that advanced theoretical studies in fluid mechanics and actual measurements of currents at all depths in the Southern Ocean would be needed before much progress could be made. He also believed that a thorough study of the turbulent movements likely to carry the phytoplankton in and out of the near-surface photosynthetic layer would be more interesting than studies of the nutrients, which never seem to be limiting factors in the Antarctic.

During World War II Deacon worked in Navy laboratories on oceanography and underwater acoustics and, toward the end of the war, on sea waves. The team he directed did much to develop wave recorders; they were the first to make a spectrum analysis of sea waves and to show the value of the conception of a wave spectrum. In 1949 the Navy's oceanographic group joined the Discovery Investigations biologists in founding the National Institute of Oceanography, which has done much to advance many aspects of oceanography. It developed methods of measuring deep currents, and Deacon looked forward to the day when these could be used in the Antarctic Ocean.

Deacon was awarded the British Polar Medal in 1942 and the Agassiz Medal of the U.S. National Academy of Sciences in 1962.

For background information see OCEANOGRAPHY in the McGraw-Hill Encyclopedia of Science and Technology.   □

★ DE BEER, Sir Gavin

British biologist
Born Nov. 1, 1899, Malden, near London, England

ORIGINAL RESEARCHES on the segmentation of the head and development of the skull in all groups of vertebrates provided de Beer with abundant material on which to study such general morphological principles as stereometric constancy of topographic relations among blood vessels, nerves, cartilages, bones, etc.; identity of morphological units (two bones in one form homologous with one bone in another); relations of skull to brain; details of evolutionary succession; and bone phylogenetically older than cartilage.

He also investigated afresh the comparative anatomy, development, and histology of the pituitary in all groups of vertebrates, which led to collaboration with L. T. Hogben on the localization of active pituitary principles in different vertebrates. With H. Grüneberg he investigated the action of the gene responsible for dwarfism in mice, which prevents differentiation of eosinophil cells in the anterior pituitary—evidence that these cells secrete growth-promoting hormones, and an example of how genes produce their effects by controlling developmental processes.

Taking up an idea of W. Garstang—that Haeckel's theory of recapitulation was fundamentally unsound—de Beer studied the relations between embryos and ancestors in all groups of animals and some plants, and showed that in many cases adult descendants retained characters of youthful stages of ancestors—the reverse of recapitulation. This principle, paedomorphosis, applies to all cases where a particularly successful and markedly different descendant type evolved from its ancestors (insects, chordates, man). A consequence of this mode of evolution was that in eventually successful groups, the preliminary states of the evolution took place in young stages, unlikely to have been preserved as fossils because of their soft tissues. This de Beer called "clandestine evolution," not revealed in the fossil record, which explains why precursor stages of such groups (insects, chordates) are poorly represented.

Experiments on removal of neural crest from amphibian embryos were known to result in absence of visceral cartilages, thought to be of mesodermal origin, whereas neural crest is ectodermal. This apparent disregard of the germ-layer theory precipitated a crisis in morphology. The orthodox could only accept it on the view that experimental conditions upset the norms of development. It was therefore necessary to establish the developmental fates of the germ layers without experimental manipulation. Taking advantage of the presence of black pigment in ectoderm and yolk in endoderm, de Beer showed that ectoderm (neural crest) did produce visceral cartilages, odontoblasts, and osteoblasts of dermal bones. He also showed that the enamel organ of teeth could be formed either from stomodaeal ectoderm or gut endoderm, whichever was beneath the odontoblasts. This disproved the germ-layer theory and discredited the classification of tumors based on it.

A complete reinvestigation of the fossil *Archaeopteryx* using ultraviolet and x-rays revealed the sternum, which had eluded discovery for a century (it is flat). Some of the features of *Archaeopteryx* are completely reptilian, others completely avian, whence de Beer propounded the theory of mosaic evolution—piece-by-piece complete conversion from one type to the next—which he also showed in transitional forms between fish, amphibia, reptiles, birds, and mammals.

The reptilian structure of the cerebellum in *Archaeopteryx* and its carinate structure in Ratites enabled de Beer to show that the Ratites certainly evolved from former flying birds. Other features showed that *Archaeopteryx* was incapable of flight (it could only glide) and that it was adapted to climbing trees and perching on branches. This provided proof of the arboreal origin of flight.

De Beer's study of Darwin's Notebooks (previously unpublished) showed that Darwin had independently thought out the principle of natural selection before he read Malthus's *Essay on Population*, from which he derived only the inevitably heavy toll of mortality. Close study of Mendel's paper and of his copies of Darwin's books showed that Mendel was not opposed to evolution and that he hoped that his discoveries would fill the gaps in Darwin's theories, which they did.

The possibility of using natural science to solve historical problems was applied by de Beer to prehistoric inhabitants of western Europe (genetics of blood groups and hair color); the origin of the Etruscans (blood groups and skull shape); Hannibal's route across the Alps (physiography, meteorology, glaciology, astronomy, pollen analysis); identification of the "Iktin" of classical authors with St. Michael's Mount, Cornwall (C-14, pollen, mineralogy of neolithic axes); Gibbon's illness (pathology, psychology).

Search for and discovery of manuscripts enabled de Beer and T. Graham Brown to reconstruct in detail the first ascent of Mont Blanc in 1786 by M. G. Paccard and to show the speed of ascent from one identified place to another. Other studies on Voltaire, Rousseau, Gibbon, Byron, Shelley, Mme. Roland, and Mme. de Staël, and on relations between British and French men of science while Great Britain and France were at war, established the background of opinion in the 18th century. He also showed that the tables currently used for converting French Republican Calendar dates to the Gregorian Calendar are wrong.

Son of an English gentleman, de Beer was educated in Paris, at Harrow, and Magdalen College, Oxford. From 1923 to 1938, he was a Fellow of Merton College, Oxford. He was professor of embryology at University College, London, from 1945 until 1950, when he became director of the British Museum (Natural History). Knighted in 1954, he received among other scientific honors the Royal Society's Darwin Medal in 1958 "in recognition of his distinguished contributions to evolutionary biology."

He served in the Grenadier Guards in both World Wars, landing in Normandy in 1944 in charge of psychological warfare.

De Beer published over 300 works, including *Vertebrate Zoology* (1928), *Development of the Vertebrate Skull* (1937), *Embryos and Ancestors* (1940), *Charles Darwin* (1963), and *Atlas of Evolution* (1964).

For background information *see* ARCHAEORNITHES; EVOLUTION, ORGANIC; GERM LAYERS; PITUITARY GLAND in the McGraw-Hill Encyclopedia of Science and Technology.   □

☆ DEBYE, Peter Joseph William

American physical chemist
Born Mar. 24, 1884, Maastricht, Netherlands

FOR HIS work on dipole moments and the diffraction of x-rays in gases, Debye was awarded the 1936 Nobel Prize in chemistry. In addition he collaborated with E. Hückel to formulate a theory of the behavior of strong electrolytes that proved superior to the older theory of dissociation of S. A. Arrhenius.

It was known from earlier work performed by Debye that the noble gases and diatomic molecules consisting of two equal atoms (for example, N_2, O_2) were nonpolar but that when the atoms were different polarity appeared. The dipole moment measuring this polarity could be determined experimentally from the temperature dependence of the dielectric constant. If the atoms were close to each other in the periodic table, this polarity was small; it became great only in molecules such as HCl. The magnitude of the electric dipole moment, however, was nowhere near as great as would be expected of a molecule consisting of an H ion and a Cl ion held at the supposed nuclear distance. In a triatomic molecule, a linear configuration of the atoms produces no moment (for example, CO_2), but a nonlinear arrangement leads to one (for example, H_2O). Debye was able to show that when free molecules are irradiated with x-rays each molecule produces recognizable interferences with its dispersed radiation. He demonstrated how these patterns could be used to compute the interatomic distances, which enabled chemists to draw molecular configurations to scale.

In 1912 Max von Laue suggested that the wavelength of x-rays and the distance between planes of atoms in a crystal might be of the same order of magnitude. If this were true, the crystal plane could serve as a diffraction grating for x-rays. Sir William Bragg, following this suggestion, passed a beam of x-rays through crystals and detected the characteristic reinforcement and interference bands caused by the diffraction of the beam by successive layers of atoms within the crystals. Knowing the angle of incidence of the x-ray beam at a reinforcement band and the wavelength of the x-rays used, he was able to calculate the distance between successive planes in a crystal and to determine the detailed arrangement of atoms (or ions) within the crystal.

However, an obstacle to the use of the Bragg method was its dependence upon a large, well-formed crystal. In 1916 Debye and P. Scherrer resolved this problem by proving that similar results can be obtained from a powder of the crystalline substance. Since the powder consists of innumerable small crystals oriented in random fashion, there will always be a number in correct orientation to give an x-ray diffraction pattern.

In the Debye-Scherrer method the powdered crystalline substance was pressed into the shape of a small rod approximately 2 mm in diameter and 10 mm high. This was positioned upright in the center of a lighttight cylindrical camera. The x-ray beam, sharply defined, was led in a horizontal direction into the camera and impinged on the center of the rod. The diffraction pattern from the rod was photographed on two pieces of film, each of which was bent into a half circle to make a continuous lining of the inside wall of the camera. The diffraction pattern produced on the film provided the information necessary for the determination of the crystal structure by the application of Bragg's method. The components of a solid mixture can be rapidly identified by the Debye-Scherrer powder method, since each crystalline substance has its own characteristic spacings between internal crystal planes.

Another major aspect of Debye's work was his study of electrolytes. Arrhenius had stated that electrolytes in water solution dissociated into positively and negatively charged ions. However, he maintained that this separation is not complete, some of the electrolyte remaining undissociated or in molecular form. About 1923, Debye, working with Ernst Hückel, believed that electrolytes in solution must be completely ionized since x-ray diffraction studies showed that electrolytes in crystal form, such as sodium chloride, were already completely ionized. He suggested that the apparent incomplete dissociation postulated by Arrhenius could be explained by taking into account the electric interaction between the ions according to Coulomb's law.

Debye supposed that each positive ion was surrounded by an ion atmosphere that was, in the main, negatively charged and that each negative ion was surrounded by an ion atmosphere predominantly positive in charge. The application of an external electric field resulted in a movement of the central ions to oppositely charged electrodes, but the surrounding ion atmospheres tended to impede movement, thus causing a decrease in current conduction and making it appear the electrolyte was not completely ionized. Furthermore, when the central ions began to move to oppositely charged electrodes, a frictional drag set in because some of the solvent molecules moved with the ions. Again ion movement was slowed and current conduction was decreased.

The Debye-Hückel theory developed the mathematics for evaluating the magnitude of the factors of ion atmosphere and ion solvation. The theory extended the work of Arrhenius and provided a new approach to the study of properties of solution.

During the 1940s and 1950s, Debye pioneered in the study of polymers. A method of estimating the weight of macromolecules based upon the viscosity of the liquid in which they were dissolved had been worked out by the German chemist Hermann Staudinger. The ultracentrifuge, invented by the Swedish chemist Theodor Svedberg, was also used for weighing macromolecules, but these measurements were not precise for truly giant polymers. Still another method for determing the weight of macromolecules, based on the work of the Dutch chemist Jacobus Henricus Van't Hoff, relied on accurate measurements of osmotic pressures at low concentrations.

In 1944, while working at Cornell University, Debye developed a method, based on the phenomenon that molecules scatter light, for determining these molecular weights with great precision. He found that the increase in turbidity, or light-scattering power, of a solution in which macromolecules had been dissolved is proportional to the number of molecules per cubic centimeter as well as to their molecular weights, whereas in measurements based on the osmotic pressure this dependence on the molecular weight is missing. By combining measurements on the excess turbidity with measurements on the excess refractive index the molecular weight can be determined absolutely. Later he found that the light scattered by polymer solutions has a higher intensity in the forward than in the backward direction. From this angular dissymmetry the sizes of the polymer molecules can be calculated. Debye also applied the light-scattering technique to the study of micellar solutions and contributed to the theory of micelle stability.

Debye graduated from the University of Aachen in 1905 with a degree in electrical engineering. He received his Ph.D. in 1908 from the University of Munich. After teaching in Zurich (1911–12) and Utrecht (1912–14), he worked, while at Göttingen during World War I, with Scherrer in developing the powder method for studying crystal structure. The Debye-Hückel theory was an outgrowth of his work at Zurich during the years 1919–27. In 1928 he taught at the University of Leipzig, leaving in 1935 to go to the University of Berlin, where he built and became director of the Kaiser Wilhelm Institute of Physics, which he named the Max Planck Institut. With the advent of the Nazi regime, politics began to interfere with his work. He left Germany in 1940 to go to the United States, becoming head of the department of chemistry at Cornell University. In 1950 he became professor emeritus. In recent years Debye was honored by the American Chemical Society by the award of its Willard Gibbs Medal (1949), Nichols Award (1961), and Priestley Medal (1963). He was elected a foreign associate of the National Academy of Sciences in 1931 and a member in 1947.

Debye's major papers appear in *Collected Papers of Peter Debye* (1954).

For background information *see* CRYSTAL STRUCTURE; ELECTROLYTIC CONDUCTANCE; SCATTERING (ELECTROMAGNETIC RADIATION) in the McGraw-Hill Encyclopedia of Science and Technology.   □

☆ DELBRÜCK, Max

American biologist
Born Sept. 4, 1906, Berlin, Germany

AT VANDERBILT University in 1946, Delbrück and his coworker, W. T. Bailey, Jr., discovered that bacterial viruses have a sexual mode of reproduction. They were conducting an experiment to learn whether or not different types of bacterial viruses could reproduce in a single bacterial cell. Not only did the subjects of the experiment reproduce, but they also produced offspring reflecting both parental charac-

teristics. Biologists had previously thought that even the one-celled bacterium was asexual and reproduced exclusively by splitting. Nothing was known of the propagation of the virus.

A series of 20th-century investigators (beginning with a Canadian, Felix d'Hérelle, who first discovered bacterial viruses in 1917) studied the organisms in the hope that knowledge about them might have medical application. After d'Hérelle, the Australian microbiologist F. M. Burnet continued the investigation of the organism that d'Hérelle had called the "bacteriophage." Early in the 1930s Burnet discovered the existence of a great variety of mutant bacteriophages and proved d'Hérelle's idea that viruses accumulate within the body of the host bacterium, only to be liberated suddenly when the bacterium is destroyed. The German researcher Martin Schlesinger—before the invention of the electron microscope in 1941 revealed viruses directly—discovered (1933–34) by indirect means the size and mass of the bacteriophage and, more important, that the chemical composition of these organisms resembles that of the substance that carries genetic information, the chromosome. In contrast to these investigators, who were all concerned with the possible medical implications of bacteriophage, another group studied them for any light that they might shed on the mechanism of heredity. This latter group was often from the physical sciences, particularly the new quantum physics. Their work would eventually provide the basis for molecular biology.

Delbrück was a pioneer in this latter group. He was introduced to bacterial viruses in 1937 at the California Institute of Technology by another research fellow, Emory Ellis. Delbrück brought to the study of these viruses his background in theoretical physics at the University of Göttingen and the insights into possible molecular explanations of genetics that he had gathered in discussions with other physicists in Berlin from 1932 to 1937. As Delbrück began

his investigations, very little was known of the mechanics of virus propagation. It was known that these viruses are quiescent outside of a bacterium; their activity begins when they find a bacterium to which they may attach themselves. Penetration of the bacterium follows, and the virus begins active reproduction within its host. This is followed by destruction of the cell walls of the bacterium as the new viruses burst forth. Burnet had previously observed the bacteriophage to produce identifiable mutants, some related and some unrelated. Related mutants were also known to have the ability to reproduce at the same time in a bacterium. In an experiment intended to produce offspring from each of two different types of viruses, the observers were startled to find not only viruses related to the two parent types but two new types representing two different combinations of the characteristics of the two parent viruses.

Delbrück and Bailey realized that this meant that the two parent viruses had exhanged some type of genetic material. Apparently the simple bacterial viruses shared the ability of higher organisms to evolve through mutations and selection in response to hostile environmental conditions and thus avoid extinction. This discovery opened the way for subsequent investigations into the exact biochemical nature of the genetic process by which these organisms transmit their characteristics.

In 1953, working with N. Visconti, Delbrück evolved a theory to explain the genetic processes of the bacteriophages as they mate within the host bacterium. As visualized by this theory, there is not a simple exchange of genetic material but rather a repeated, random mating. While new data have required some modification of the details of this theory, the mathematical relations of the Visconti-Delbrück theory still adequately describe the genetic permutations observed in bacterial viruses.

Delbrück received his Ph.D. in physics at the University of Göttingen in 1930. From 1931 to 1932 he was a Rockefeller Foundation fellow in physics in Copenhagen and Zurich, from 1932 to 1937 an assistant at the Kaiser Wilhelm Institut für Chemie in Berlin, and from 1937 to 1939 a Rockefeller Foundation fellow again, this time in biology at the California Institute of Technology. Thereafter he went to Vanderbilt University as an instructor in physics, remaining until 1947 when he became professor of biology at the California Institute of Technology. Elected to the National Academy of Sciences in 1949, he received the Academy's Kimber Genetics Award in 1965.

For background information see BACTERIAL GENETICS; BACTERIOPHAGE; VIRUS in the McGraw-Hill Encyclopedia of Science and Technology. □

★ DEMEREC, Milislav

American geneticist
Born Jan. 11, 1895, Kostajnica, Yugoslavia
Died Apr. 12, 1966, Laurel Hollow, N.Y., U.S.A.

FROM ITS beginning in 1920, Demerec's research was directed toward a better understanding of the mechanisms of heredity—the nature of genes, their structure and function, and their spontaneous and induced mutability. His earliest work was concerned with the genes responsible for various chlorophyll deficiencies in maize, but he soon turned to investigations of unstable genes in the annual larkspur (*Delphinium ajacis*) and the fruit flies (*Drosophila virilis* and *D. melanogaster*). These studies were developed to include the previously obscure field of biological control of mutability. Demerec discovered that some genes differed in mutation rate at different stages of the life cycle, in different tissues of an organism, or in different genetic lines; that certain regulator genes could modify the mutation rates of unstable genes; and that other genes possessed a high degree of stability. His results provided conclusive evidence that a gene is a unit structure, rather than one made up of two or more components whose assortment could account for the observed reverse mutability of unstable genes (as was proposed by a then current hypothesis).

In Drosophila, a deficiency (absence) of one gene is often lethal to the organism. By means of an intricate technique, Demerec succeeded in showing that such a condition is frequently "cell lethal," so that even a small island of cells within the body of a fly cannot survive if a certain gene is missing. Thus it was demonstrated that genes play a very important role in individual cells of higher organisms.

In 1927, H. J. Muller discovered that ionizing and ultraviolet radiations induced changes in genes and chromosomes; and in 1933, E. Heitz and H. Bauer, as well as T. S. Painter, found that chromosomes of *Drosophila* salivary-gland cells were very large and displayed conspicuous bands that could be correlated with gene loci. Utilizing these disclosures, Demerec extended his studies of induced mutations and of the relation between mutational changes and chromosomal breaks. His experiments showed that lethal events were often due to deletion of chromosomal segments. Moreover, when chromosomes were broken, a portion of one might become attached to a certain region of the same or another chromosome, and the functioning of genes located near the attachment point—sometimes many genes—might be suppressed. This finding further confirmed the view that a gene's function depended not only on its structure but also on its surroundings.

As the research progressed, it became evident that more sensitive methods were necessary to deal with events (such as mutations, deletions, chromosomal rearrangements) that occurred so rarely. Since genetic studies, as a rule, depend on statistical evaluations of frequency of the events being observed, large numbers of individuals are required for significant results. In 1943, therefore, Demerec turned to work with bacteria (*Escherichia coli* and *Salmonella typhimurium*), where experiments involving billions of individuals could easily be carried out. He was among the first of many to utilize bacteria in genetical research. His studies of alleles (different mutant forms of the same gene) revealed recombination between them, thus showing that a gene locus was not an ultimate genetic unit, as had been generally assumed, but comprised a section of chromosome within which mutational changes, occurring at different sublocations, gave rise to different allelic mutants. Other analyses, made with *Salmonella*, showed that its genes were not distributed at random along the chromosome, as might be expected from the results of genetic studies of higher organisms. In this bacterial species, at least, genes affecting related functions were frequently clustered together. Work carried on in several laboratories has since indicated that these clusters form units of operation ("operons").

During World War II, Demerec employed radiation techniques to induce mutations in the mold *Penicillium*, selecting those mutants that were most efficient producers of penicillin. One of the selected strains proved to be such a high yielder of the antibiotic that it immediately replaced those then being used in commercial production. Subsequent adaptations of the principle demonstrated in that work have contributed greatly to the rapid development of the antibiotics industry. A few years later, Demerec proved for the first time that genetic mechanisms were responsible for bacterial resistance to antibiotics, and his research revealed two important principles to be followed in antibiotics therapy. The initial doses of these drugs should be large enough to prevent the occurrence of "second-step" (highly) resistant bacterial mutants; and the drugs should be used in combination rather than singly, since a mutant that is resistant to one antibiotic has a very small chance of being resistant to another one also.

Demerec graduated from the College of Agriculture, Krizevci, Yugoslavia, in 1916 and held a position as adjunct at the Krizevci Experiment Station until 1919, when he went to the United States to study at Cornell University. He received the Ph.D. degree in genetics from Cornell in 1923, working under Professor R. A. Emerson. In 1923 he joined the staff of the department of genetics, Carnegie Institution of Washington, at Cold Spring Harbor, N.Y., as a resident investigator. He was appointed assistant director in 1936, acting director in 1942, and director in 1943. In 1941 he also became director of the neighboring biological laboratory of the Long Island Biological Association. When in 1960 he retired from both these positions, he joined the research staff of Brookhaven National Laboratory, Upton, N.Y., as a senior staff member, continuing his program of research in bacterial genetics. Elected to the National Academy of Sciences in 1946, Demerec received the Academy's Kimber Genetics Award in 1962.

Demerec published some 200 articles in scientific journals, and served as editor of *Advances in Genetics* (9 vols., 1947–58), *Biology of Drosophila* (1950), *Cold Spring Harbor Symposia on Quantitative Biology* (17 vols., 1941–60), and *Drosophila Information Service* (33 vols., 1934–60).

For background information *see* CHROMOSOME; GENE in the McGraw-Hill Encyclopedia of Science and Technology.   □

DIELS, Otto Paul Hermann

German chemist
Born Jan. 23, 1876, Hamburg, Germany
Died Mar. 7, 1954, Kiel, Germany

WHILE STUDYING the reactions of conjugated dienes (organic compounds containing two double bonds separated by one single bond), Diels and his associate Kurt Alder developed a general organic reaction called diene synthesis. Now known as the Diels-Alder reaction, diene synthesis promotes the production of highly stable six-membered ring structures and has made possible great advances in chemical technology. For their achievement, Diels and

Alder shared the Nobel Prize in chemistry in 1950.

It had long been known that molecules containing bonds were exceptionally reactive. In addition, such molecules tend to attach to one another to form long-chain polymers. Diels found that when the temperature of a quantity of a diene, such as butadiene or isoprene, was increased for a period of time, the physical and chemical properties of the compound were altered considerably. On analysis, he discovered that more complex compounds were formed without the need of any outside reagent as a catalyst or participant. His experiments in comparing the activity of a number of dienes with compounds not containing a pair of double bonds showed that the presence of two double bonds was necessary if the rather effortless linking with further chemical components was to take place.

The conditions required for the linkage are so mild, and the basic dienes are so plentiful, that Diels felt a great number of naturally occurring large and complex organic compounds probably are synthesized in this manner. He felt this was especially true within organisms where the necessary temperature regulations can and do take place.

A difficulty in determining what linkages were occurring lay in identifying the orientation of the joining molecules. Early experiments showed cyclopentadiene would polymerize on heating to form a polymer-homologous chain. Thorough analysis of the stereochemical properties of the components of the chain showed that each linkage resulted in another five-membered ring formation. Hence the polymerization must be car-

ried out in all dimensions and cannot occur at each and every double bond but only where another cyclopentane can be formed.

Diels and Alder, who had been working at the University of Kiel, first published reports of their findings in 1928. They showed that the diene synthesis was a union of two unsaturated partners, a diene and a philodiene. The diene is the carrier of a system of conjugated double bonds; the philodiene must carry at least one double bond. The adduct is always a six-membered ring with the reaction taking place in the 1:4 positions, as shown by the general formula

$$\underset{\text{diene}}{\begin{array}{c}X\\Z\end{array}\!C\!=\!C\!\begin{array}{c}X'\\ \\ C\\ \\ C\\ \\ Y\end{array}\!C\!=\!C\!\begin{array}{c}\\Y'\end{array}}\quad+\quad\underset{\text{philodiene}}{\begin{array}{c}R\\ \\ R''\end{array}\!C\!\overset{\displaystyle C}{\underset{\displaystyle C}{\|}}\!\begin{array}{c}R'\\ \\ R'''\end{array}}\quad\rightarrow\quad\underset{\text{adduct}}{\begin{array}{c}X\\Z\end{array}\!C\!\begin{array}{c}X'\\ \\ C\\ \end{array}\!C\!\begin{array}{c}R\\R'\\R''\end{array}}$$

Since the publication of the Diels-Alder reaction, the principles of diene synthesis have enabled scientists to analyze many organic compounds and to artificially reproduce them. Compound synthesis from dienes has resulted in the production of a number of drugs and medicines that had not previously been analyzed. One such compound exhibited properties similar to vitamin K; ensuing research indicates that a number of vitamins and hormones may be produced in living organisms by similar diene synthesis. Butadiene combined with styrene leads to synthetic rubber; plastics and rubberlike materials are produced in similar ways.

Diels was noted also for his research with saturated fats and fatty acids. While performing experiments on cholesterol, he discovered the use of selenium as an agent to remove hydrogen from the saturated organic molecule. This method of dehydrogenation has led to the production of polyunsaturated oils that are commonly marketed. The technique has also contributed to further research in sterol chemistry.

The properties of carbon and oxygen were known, and the ways in which they combine were established, but a synthesis experiment performed by Diels in 1906 produced a carbon oxide composed of three atoms of carbon and two of oxygen. The resultant unique gas, named carbon suboxide, had a penetrating odor and an irritating effect on the eyes. Such variations in "known" properties of elements and compound formation contribute to chemical knowledge even though the product is itself of no great value.

The son of a professor at the University of Berlin, Diels was educated there, receiving his Ph.D. in 1899 under the direction of Emil Fischer. He was immediately appointed an assistant at the university's Institute of Chemistry, becoming a professor in 1906 and head of the department in 1913. Diels became a professor at the University of Berlin in 1915 but left a year

later to become a professor at the University of Kiel and director of the Institute of Chemistry there. Diels retired from those positions in 1945.

For background information *see* DIELS-ALDER REACTION; DIENE in the McGraw-Hill Encyclopedia of Science and Technology.   □

☆ DIRAC, Paul Adrien Maurice

British mathematician
Born Aug. 8, 1902, Bristol, England

IN 1928 Dirac developed an abstract mathematical theory to describe the properties of the electron. Given only the particle's charge and mass, he was able to derive the electron's spin, magnetic moment, and other quantitative aspects of its behavior. This equation was the first to account rigorously for observed properties of the electron. One of its consequences was the prediction of a particle, then unknown, identical to the electron but with positive electric charge. C. D. Anderson's discovery of the positron in 1932 gave experimental confirmation of this consequence of Dirac's theory. For his accomplishment, Dirac shared with Erwin Schrödinger the 1933 Nobel Prize in physics.

In 1925 S. A. Goudsmit and G. E. Uhlenbeck, in attempting to account for anomalies in x-ray spectra, first introduced the hypothesis that an electron spun about its own axis. Although it disposed of the spectroscopic inconsistencies, the new model of the atom introduced difficulties of a theoretical nature, since nothing in current theory required the electron to spin. It thus became necessary to transform the spinning-electron hypothesis from an ad hoc assumption to a theoretically explicable fundamental of quantum theory.

First to make assault on the problem were Wolfgang Pauli and C. G. Darwin. Both their efforts, however, suffered from a multiplicity of assumptions unjustified except for the need to introduce them into an equation describing the electron's spin. It therefore remained for Dirac to propose a new and more satisfactory approach.

In classical relativistic mechanics the energy equation of a particle was written as in Eq. (1),

$$\frac{W^2}{c^2} - p_r^2 - m^2c^2 = 0 \qquad (1)$$

where W represented the particle's kinetic energy; $p_r (r = 1,2,3)$ its momentum; m its mass; and c the speed of light. From this, the quantum-mechanical wave equation was derived by replacing W and p_r by the operators $ih\dfrac{\partial}{\partial t}$ and $-ih\dfrac{\partial}{\partial x_r}$, and causing the left-hand side to operate on a wave function ψ. This gave Eq. (2). This of course gave rise to squared operators $\dfrac{\partial^2}{\partial t^2}$. Dirac's reasoning led him to regard

$$\left[\frac{W^2}{c^2} - p_r^2 - m^2c^2\right]\psi = 0 \qquad (2)$$

this matter as being the crucial difficulty, since, in general, quantum mechanics required energy equations to be linear in $\partial/\partial t$ or W. He therefore sought to replace Eq. (2) with an equivalent one which, however, would be linear in W and thus also would contain only the linear operator $\dfrac{\partial}{\partial t}$.

To do this, Dirac factored the left-hand side of Eq. (2) into two new equations, both linear in W. Either of these, when set equal to 0, became an energy equation of the sort required [see Eq. (3)]. Having shown that the two factors were equivalent, Dirac discarded one and was left with Eq. (3).

$$\left[\frac{W}{c} - \alpha_r p_r - \alpha_0 mc\right]\psi = 0 \qquad (3)$$

Here, the α's were new variables, operating on ψ, which had initially been introduced in order to obtain a wave equation linear in W. Since the α's can be represented by 4-dimensional matrices involving only constants, Dirac concluded that they should refer to some inner property of the electron. He proceeded to demonstrate that the property involved was precisely the electron's spin.

Dirac now modified Eq. (3) so as to represent the energy of an electron in the presence of an electromagnetic field. The resultant equation gave the electron a magnetic moment of one Bohr magneton. It further stated that the orbital angular momentum was not sufficient to uphold the conservation of angular momentum of an electron moving in a central field. Dirac showed

that the conservation of angular momentum was restored by supposing the electron to have an additional spin angular momentum of $\frac{1}{2}\hbar$. He went on to show how his equation accounted for the behavior of the electron in H atoms and the anomalous spectra which had first suggested the idea of a spinning electron. Other experimental verification quickly followed.

Dirac noted that his equation for the electron gave two possible kinds of solution, which seemed to represent a positive or negative kinetic energy for the electron respectively. The solutions yielding a negative kinetic energy seemed impossible to interpret except in terms of a particle identical to the electron in mass but with reversed electric charge and other properties.

To make the interpretation definite, Dirac supposed that in the universe as ordinarily observed, all the negative-energy states of electrons are occupied, with one electron in each. The exclusion principle of Pauli then prevents a second electron from going into one of these states, so that a positive-energy electron cannot jump into a negative-energy state. However, it may happen that a negative-energy state is unoccupied and appears as a hole among the occupied ones. Such a hole is to be interpreted as a positron.

An ordinary or positive-energy electron may jump into the hole and fill it up. Then both the electron and the hole disappear. This is interpreted as the electron and positron annihilating one another. Their energy will be emitted in the form of chargeless photons. Dirac also predicted that the opposite reaction could occur: that two photons could interact to form an electron/positron pair. Both these predictions, little more than speculation at the time they were advanced, were directly confirmed by experiment not long afterward.

In addition to the discovery of the positron, Dirac's theory led eventually to the discovery of the antiproton and the other antiparticles, whose existence was a sign that there were indeed realms of antimatter, which would be highly reactive with ordinary matter, the juxtaposition of the two leading immediately to mutual annihilation. Dirac's theory, then, marked the beginning of the investigation of antimatter that was essential to later developments in particle physics.

Dirac received his B.Sc. from Bristol University in 1921 and his Ph.D. from the University of Cambridge in 1926. He embarked on extensive travel, including stints as visiting lecturer at the University of Wisconsin and University of Michigan (1929) and Princeton University (1931). He then returned to Cambridge where, in 1932, he became Lucasian Professor of Mathematics.

During 1947–48 and again in 1958–59, he was a member of the Institute for Advanced Studies, Princeton, N.J. In 1952 he was awarded the Copley Medal of the Royal Society of London. He was elected a foreign associate of the U.S. National Academy of Sciences in 1949.

Dirac wrote *Principles of Quantum Mechanics* (1930).

For background information *see* ELECTRON; POSITRON; QUANTUM THEORY, RELATIVISTIC in the McGraw-Hill Encyclopedia of Science and Technology.   □

★ **DOBZHANSKY, Theodosius**

American biologist
Born Jan. 25, 1900, Nemirov, Russia

THE WORK of T. H. Morgan and his school on the genetics of vinegar flies, *Drosophila,* elucidated some of the mechanisms of heredity and variation in living beings. Dobzhansky's research in this field added greatly to knowledge of how these mechanisms operate, not only in laboratory experiments but also in natural populations.

The genetic diversity found in *Drosophila* in nature was proved by Dobzhansky to be very great. The idea, entertained by some classical geneticists, that natural populations consisted mostly of genetically similar "normal" or "wild-type" individuals, with a minority of aberrant or mutant specimens, had to be abandoned. It is likely that no two individuals in *Drosophila,* or in man, or in any sexually reproducing and outbreeding species, ever have identical genetic endowments (identical twins excepted). Only a fraction of this genetic diversity is apparent on casual inspection. Most of it is concealed in heterozygous condition.

Dobzhansky used special genetic techniques available in *Drosophila* to show that most apparently normal and healthy individuals are heterozygous for one or more genes, or gene com-

plexes, that are lethal, semilethal, debilitating in various degrees, diminishing the fertility or sterilizing, or causing various kinds of physiological or structural changes in the body. The magnitude of this "genetic load" is not uniform in different species or in different populations of the same species. And contrary to what one might expect, Dobzhansky's experiments with *Drosophila* showed that biologically more successful and versatile species tend to have greater, not smaller, genetic loads than the less successful ones. This is intelligible, because there are several biologically disparate components in the genetic diversity. Some harmful genetic variants arise from time to time by mutation and persist for one or several generations until eliminated by natural selection. Other variants are balanced and are maintained by natural selection. The balancing selection may be due to a hybrid vigor, heterosis, produced in heterozygous condition; it may also be due to diversifying natural selection, when different variants fit different ecological niches, opportunities for living; other forms of balancing selection are also known.

Dobzhansky set up experiments to observe the operation of natural selection in *Drosophila* populations directly. In some of these populations cyclic genetic changes occur at different seasons, year after year. Since 1940, long-range genetic changes have also been observed in a species of *Drosophila* in California and in parts of adjacent states. What causes these latter changes is as yet uncertain; contamination of the natural habitats of the flies by traces of insecticides is a possibility. Some of the seasonal changes have also been reproduced in laboratory experiments, and a rough measure of the magnitude of the natural selection involved has been obtained. This helps to elucidate the origin of genetic differences between local populations and races of certain *Drosophila* species.

The findings made in *Drosophila* by Dobzhansky and others obviously cannot be "extrapolated" to man. Genetic processes in human populations are influenced by cultural factors that have no close analogs in *Drosophila.* Nevertheless, mankind is a biological species, and it is subject to some general biological regularities. Understanding of human evolution, historical and current, is a challenging problem. Here the work of a biologist impinges on matters anthropological, medical, sociological, and philosophical.

Son of a high school teacher, Dobzhansky majored in zoology at the University of Kiev, Russia, graduating in 1921. He taught zoology and genetics as an assistant (lecturer) in Kiev and Leningrad. In 1927 he went as a fellow of the International Education Board (Rockefeller Foundation) to work with T. H. Morgan at

Columbia University and the California Institute of Technology. Returning to Columbia University in 1940, he was a professor there until 1962, when he joined the Rockefeller University. He was a visiting professor in Brazil, Chile, and Australia and did biological research in these and other countries. Dobzhansky received the National Academy of Sciences' Kimber Genetics Award in 1958. In 1964 he was awarded the National Medal of Science.

Dobzhansky wrote *Genetics and the Origin of Species* (1937; 3d ed. 1951), *Heredity, Race, and Society*, with L. C. Dunn (1937; 3d ed. 1952), *Principles of Genetics*, with L. C. Dunn (1950), *Evolution, Genetics, and Man* (1955), *The Biological Basis of Human Freedom* (1956), *Radiation, Genetics, and Man*, with B. Wallace (1959), *Mankind Evolving* (1963), *Heredity and the Nature of Man* (1964), and some 350 papers in various scientific periodicals.

For background information *see* GENETICS in the McGraw-Hill Encyclopedia of Science and Technology.   □

★ **DOISY, Edward Adelbert**
American biochemist
Born Nov. 13, 1893, Hume, Ill., U.S.A.

Doisy's PRINCIPAL scientific contributions were the isolation of pure crystalline compounds of importance to the well-being of man.

In collaboration with a biologist, Edgar Allen, Doisy undertook a study of ovarian factors that regulate the sex cycle of rats and mice. Armed with Allen's method of assay, he continued experiments on the nature of the active principles for 12 years (1922–34), isolating the first crystalline steroidal hormone, estrone, in 1929. Subsequently, he isolated two other related products, estriol and estradiol-17β; about 10 milligrams of the latter was obtained from 4 tons of sow ovaries. Administration of each one of these compounds in microgram quantities to ovari-

ectomized rats or mice caused an estrual response in the animal. These compounds or closely related derivatives have been extensively used in the treatment of diseases of women.

In 1936 Doisy turned to the elucidation of a hemorrhagic condition of chickens that had been discovered in 1929 by Henrik Dam. After 3 years of intensive effort, he and his associates had isolated two pure compounds, vitamin K_1 from a plant source and vitamin K_2 from a mixed culture of microorganisms. With the two compounds at hand the structures were determined. Both contained 2-methyl-1,4-naphthoquinone but differed significantly in the hydrocarbon radical attached at C atom 3. Vitamin K_1 was synthesized, thereby verifying the postulated structure. These compounds have been very effective in restoring the clotting time of blood to normal in patients suffering from obstructive jaundice. For this achievement Doisy and Dam shared the 1943 Nobel Prize for medicine or physiology.

During World War II, Doisy's investigations were diverted to the study of antibiotics. Although a good therapeutic product was not obtained, one of the earliest reports on antibacterial effects (Bouchard 1889) was clarified by the isolation of four active crystalline compounds from *Bacillus pyocyaneous*. Subsequently, one of those engaged in this work completed the study on constitution by synthesizing three of the compounds.

After the introduction of labeling with radioactive carbon, Doisy undertook studies on the metabolism of hormones and bile acids. The most significant aspect of these investigations was the discovery of four new metabolites that were hitherto unknown bile acids. The constitutions of these acids were postulated from the results of degradation and the postulations verified by synthesis.

Doisy was fortunate in being the son of parents, who, although they had little formal education, revered education and encouraged him to attend college. He received his A.B. in 1914 and his M.S. in 1916 from the University of Illinois. He enrolled in the Division of Medical Sciences of Harvard University in 1915, but completion of his education was delayed by 2 years of service in World War I and he did not receive his Ph.D. until 1920. From 1919 until 1923 he served successively as instructor, associate, and associate professor of biochemistry in Washington University School of Medicine, St. Louis, Mo. In 1923 he was appointed to the chair of biochemistry at St. Louis University School of Medicine. He was named Distinguished Service Professor in 1951. He was elected to the National Academy of Sciences in 1938.

For background information *see* BILE ACID; HORMONE; STEROID; VITAMIN in the McGraw-Hill Encyclopedia of Science and Technology. □

★ DOOB, Joseph Leo

American mathematician
Born Feb. 27, 1910, Cincinnati, Ohio, U.S.A.

IN MATHEMATICAL probability theory—that is, in the mathematical model of probability—what corresponds to a real event is a set of points in some space. (For example, in the rather trivial model for tossing a coin once, the mathematical model has two points, say H and T, one identified with heads and the other with tails. The set containing the single point H corresponds to the event that the tossed coin comes up heads.) Events have probabilities. In the model this means that certain subsets of the space are assigned numbers. The function of sets so defined is a measure, and the well-developed theory of measure is now available. Probability concepts in the model are defined as suggested by the background of the real context and the mathematical context. Thus a random variable, empirically a number produced by some probabilistic phenomenon, is defined mathematically as a function on the probability space and its expected value is defined mathematically as the integral of that function with respect to the given probability measure.

This subsuming of the basic concepts of probability theory to those of measure theory had been set up formally by A. N. Kolmogorov in 1933. In accordance with this approach a stochastic process—that is, a process proceeding in accordance with probabilistic laws—has as its counterpart in the mathematical model a family $\{x(t,.),\ t\epsilon T\}$ of random variables. Here for each t in the index set T (usually identified with a set of numbers, as suggested by the idea that t represents time) $x(t,.)$ is a random variable, with value $x(t,\omega)$ at the point ω of the probability space. A complete experiment gives a value to each random variable of the process. Mathematically this means that ω is chosen and t is allowed to vary to obtain the function $x(.,\omega)$

defined on T. This function is called a sample function of the stochastic process (or sometimes a sample sequence if T is countably infinite or finite). In most applications the joint distributions of finite sets of the random variables are given—that is, if $t_1, \ldots, t_n$ are in T, the joint distribution of $x(t_1,.), \ldots, x(t_n,.)$ is given. Natural problems are to find the distributions of other functions and to analyze the properties of the sample functions. Effective work on such problems had been proceeding since the 17th century and it was not clear in the 1930s that the measure-theoretic approach would radically transform the subject. Some mathematicians thought that measure theory would only furnish the necessary but disagreeable rigor and that interesting results would not be inspired by the technical background.

In a series of papers beginning in 1935 Doob investigated various parts of probability theory, ranging from the continuity properties of sample functions to the mathematical version of the concept of a fair game. In each case the point was both to obtain mathematical results and to demonstrate the intrinsically necessary role of measure theory. Of course much other probability research tended in the same direction, but the tendency was somewhat more obvious in Doob's work, at least in the 1930s. Mathematical probability is both duller and more productive as a result of his efforts.

Two examples will give some idea of both aspects of his work. Let the set T above be the real line, and consider the following problem: What are the probabilities that the sample functions of a given stochastic process are everywhere positive, everywhere continuous? Such questions, involving the character of the sample functions at a continuum of points are inevitable, but are also unanswerable in terms of the given distributions of the random variables, as described above. In fact the desired probabilities are not determined by these given distributions using the usual measure-theoretic rules of calculation. It was necessary to modify the allowable procedures to obtain a new context in which such probabilities could be calculated. As a second example, consider the notion of a fair game. One definition of "fair" that seems not unreasonable is that a game is fair to a gambler if his expected fortune after a play is what he had before. This definition can be put into abstract mathematical form to define a certain type of stochastic process, in which the notion of the expected value of a random variable, given the past history of the stochastic process up to a certain time, plays a fundamental role. This kind of process has many applications in pure mathematics (for example, in integration theory and potential theory), and in applied mathematics (for example, in information theory).

Doob majored in mathematics at Harvard

University, where he received his B.A., M.A., and Ph.D. in 1930, 1931, and 1932. He taught at the University of Illinois from 1935. In 1957 he was elected to the National Academy of Sciences.

Doob wrote *Stochastic Processes* (1952).

For background information *see* PROBABILITY; STOCHASTIC PROCESS in the McGraw-Hill Encyclopedia of Science and Technology.   □

☆ DOUGLAS, Donald Wills
American aeronautical engineer
Born Apr. 6, 1892, Brooklyn, N.Y., U.S.A.

IN 1920, when he was not yet 30 and had assets totaling only $600, Douglas started his own airplane manufacturing venture. The small company eventually became one of the giants of the aircraft industry, designing and building transports that played key roles in world air transportation.

Douglas's first contract was to build a plane for a Los Angeles sportsman who wished to fly across the continent nonstop. The plane that Douglas designed and built was a two-place wood and fabric biplane called the *Cloudster*. Although engine trouble forced abandonment of the transcontinental flight in Texas, the *Cloudster* established a major milestone in aircraft design: it was the first airplane ever to airlift a useful load equal to its own weight. Later, the same basic design was utilized to build the U.S. Navy's first torpedo bomber.

World recognition of Douglas's design integrity came with the first flight around the world. U.S. Army pilots, flying Douglas World Cruisers, began their historic journey in March, 1924. They returned six months later to Clover Field, Santa Monica, Calif., where the flight had begun. They had covered 27,553 miles in 15 days, 11 hours, and 7 minutes actual flying time.

Notable in early Douglas history was the development of the DC-3–type transport in 1935. That twin-engine airliner, best known and most widely used in the world, revolutionized passenger air travel by establishing new standards of safety, speed, comfort, and dependability. It is generally credited with having made commercial aviation economically feasible. The basic DC-3 design was adapted for military use during World War II; the adaptation, the C-47 military transport, was used in every theater of war and by all Allied Powers. Nearly 11,000 DC-3–type transports were built.

Another noteworthy Douglas development was the B-19 experimental bomber, until 1948 the largest land-based aircraft built. Conceived as a flying laboratory to prove design details of huge aircraft, the B-19 was first flown on June 27, 1941. Its wingspan was 212 feet and its fuselage length was 132 feet. The B-19 is credited by the U.S. Air Force with paving the way for design and construction of the wartime B-29 and its successor, the B-50 bomber. Until late in 1946 it was used to test new engines, propellers, hydraulic and electrical equipment, and other new devices for large aircraft.

Next in order of development was the DC-4 transport. This four-engined airliner, designed originally for commercial use, was in 1942, before the first aircraft was completed, transformed on the production line into the C-54 military transport. The C-54 proved the practicability of transoceanic service by land-based aircraft by establishing a record of 40,000 Pacific and 30,500 Atlantic crossings in military service.

In 1946 the DC-6 evolved from the DC-4 and established new standards of comfort, speed, and dependability in air travel. In 1951 later versions of the same basic transport were introduced under the designations DC-6A for cargo and DC-6B for deluxe passenger service.

Douglas Aircraft then produced the DC-7, which established itself as the world's fastest piston-powered commercial transport. Retaining the general external configuration of the DC-6 series, the DC-7 had a longer fuselage with increased cabin capacity. It was ultimately expanded through several larger and more powerful versions, ending with the DC-7C.

In 1955 Douglas decided to proceed with manufacture of the DC-8 jet transport. The first flight of the airplane took place May 30, 1958, and it first went into airline service on Sept. 18, 1959.

The short-to-medium-range DC-9 was the next plane in the Douglas line of commercial aircraft. The DC-9 was first flown in 1965 and entered airline service the same year.

Post–World War II military aircraft engineered and produced by Douglas Aircraft include the Navy AD-Skyraider series, the twin-jet F3D Skyknight, the A3D Skywarrior twin-jet attack plane, the A4D Skyhawk, the F4D Skyray, the F5D Skylancer, the RB-66 Destroyer Air

Force bombers, the C-124 Globemaster II, military versions of the DC-6A Liftmaster, and the C-133A and C-133B cargo transports.

Under Douglas's direction his company engaged in development and production of guided missiles for the Army, Navy, and Air Force beginning in 1940. Among these were several models of the Nike ground-to-air missile; the Honest John ground-to-ground missile; and the Sparrow air-to-air series.

Douglas Aircraft was also a leader in the field of space penetration, providing the basic boost that thrust many scientific satellites into orbit. The reliable Douglas Thor, in a variety of modifications, was the first stage in launch vehicles for such satellites as *Explorer I, Pioneer V*, the Discoverer series, *Explorer VI*, Transit, Echo, *Courier IB*, high-altitude nuclear devices, the orbiting solar observatory, Telstar, and the world's first international satellite, the S-51.

Douglas Aircraft also provided leadership in the programs for exploration of lunar areas and outer space. It was assigned development of the S-IV and S-IVB upper stages of the Saturn rocket, booster vehicle in the Apollo programs. In 1965 Douglas was awarded the contract for manufacture of the first Manned Orbiting Laboratory (MOL) by the U.S. Air Force.

The son of a bank official, Douglas attended the U.S. Naval Academy at Annapolis (1909–12) and the Massachusetts Institute of Technology, where he received a B.S. in aeronautical engineering in 1914. He became consultant to the Connecticut Aircraft Company in 1915 and chief engineer for the Glenn L. Martin Company the same year. After serving one year, during World War I, as chief civilian aeronautical engineer for the U.S. Signal Corps, he returned to the Martin Company as chief engineer and designed the first Martin bomber.

For background information *see* AERONAUTICAL ENGINEERING in the McGraw-Hill Encyclopedia of Science and Technology. □

☆ **DRAPER, Charles Stark**

American aeronautical engineer
Born Oct. 2, 1901, Windsor, Mo., U.S.A.

ATTACKING A succession of challenging research and engineering projects, Draper and his associates at the Massachusetts Institute of Technology Instrumentation Laboratory provided the United States with new and advanced weapon technologies. Draper's early studies in aircraft instrumentation led to inquiries into navigational and guidance systems, from which emerged a variety of instruments for sensing, measuring, and controlling physical properties, featuring significant advances in the design and use of gyroscopes. Application of these results helped yield advanced fire-control and gun-director systems during World War II. Subsequently, the MIT group under Draper addressed the problem of inertial navigation and guidance for ships, submarines, aircraft, and missiles. The highly reliable Polaris inertial guidance system, of vast importance to the security posture of the United States, grew from the energies of the Instrumentation Laboratory. Most recently, Draper's group designed the navigational systems for the Apollo manned expedition to the Moon.

Perhaps no weapon more purely bears the Draper hallmark than the Mark 14 gunsight, which, along with the Mark 15 sight, also engineered under Draper, was used to direct the antiaircraft batteries of virtually every U.S. Navy vessel of World War II. The Navy's problem in 1941 was to protect surface vessels from the threat of close-in hostile air attack. One difficulty was smoothing out erratic tracking data to permit computer operation based on human sighting. As late as 1938 it had been held that it was impossible to stabilize effectively such rates for computer prediction. Draper met the problem with "damping"—using rotors immersed in a viscous fluid. His earlier development of rate-measuring gyros of high precision permitted use of these as automatic computers whose output offset the observer's line of sighting an amount corresponding to the correct angle of gun lead. Corrections for range, wind, and ballistics entered the system semiautomatically. The system pointed the way for a host of similar wartime sighting and tracking instruments. Draper defied prevailing methods, vastly simplifying the sight, by using deck coordinates as reference

axes, rejecting the need for gyro-stabilized references. The resulting cross-roll errors proved unimportant.

Vastly more sophisticated was Draper's later work in inertial navigation and guidance systems. Inertial instrument systems are fully self-contained and require no external information such as that from radio signals or celestial bodies. In designing the inertial reference stabilizing system, Draper applied the MIT-developed single-degree-of-freedom gyro of the 1940s, floated in a viscous fluid and equipped with microsyn sensors to measure angular displacements. Accelerometers to measure forces resulting from motions in inertial space became improved with the pendulous gyro accelerometer, where acceleration forces are made to induce measurable precession of a gyro mounted on the stabilized reference. Cumulative displacement of the gyro represents accumulated acceleration, or velocity. This value can then be further integrated by electrical circuits to yield distance, or position. By 1954 the Instrumentation Laboratory had completed the first ship's inertial navigation system (SINS). Thus by the mid-1950s the elements of a ballistic missile inertial guidance system existed. Indeed, the short time of flight of missiles permitted easement in the stringent rate of drift requirements of the earlier ship's navigation system. The 1956 contract of the Draper group with the Navy Special Projects Office for development of the Polaris inertial guidance system was quickly fulfilled, a product of the line of development begun three decades earlier in Draper's investigations of simple flight gyros.

Draper studied at the University of Missouri and at Stanford University, receiving the B.A. degree in psychology from the latter in 1922. His decision to enroll in electrochemistry at the Massachusetts Institute of Technology later that year constituted the principal turning point in his life, leading to a continuing and distinguished association with that institution. A series of fellowships and research appointments furthered his early studies and investigations at MIT. He earned the B.S. degree in electrochemical engineering in 1926, the M.S. in 1928, and the Sc.D. in physics in 1938, all at MIT. He attained the faculty rank of assistant professor in aeronautical engineering in 1935, rising to the rank of full professor in 1939 and becoming chairman of the aeronautical engineering department in 1951. Draper's contributions to the nation's defense posture have been acknowledged by many awards from the U.S. Navy and Air Force; his yet more numerous awards from professional societies include the Holley Medal of the American Society of Mechanical Engineers (1957), the Sylvanus Albert Reed Award (1945) and the Louis W. Hill Space Transportation Award (1962) of the Institute of the Aeronautical Sciences, and the William Proctor Prize of the Scientific Research Society of America (1959). In 1964 Draper was awarded the Na-

tional Medal of Science. He was elected to the National Academy of Sciences in 1957.

Draper wrote *Inertial Guidance*, with Walter Wrigley and John Hovorka (1960) and *Instrument Engineering*, with Walter McKay and Sidney Lees (3 vols., 1952, 1953, 1955).

For background information *see* GUIDED MISSILE; GYROSCOPE; INERTIAL GUIDANCE SYSTEM in the McGraw-Hill Encyclopedia of Science and Technology.   □

★ DUBOS, René Jules

American microbiologist
Born Feb. 20, 1901, Saint Brice, France

ALTHOUGH HIS early training was in agricultural sciences, Dubos devoted most of his professional life to the experimental study of microbial diseases and to analysis of the environmental and social factors that affect the well-being of men.

His Ph.D. thesis (Rutgers University, 1927) dealt with the decomposition of cellulose by soil microorganisms under various physiological conditions. While seemingly unrelated to medicine, this study helped Dubos to develop an awareness of the wide range of potential activities of microbial life and of the profound influence that the environment exerts on biological processes. This awareness was reflected in the different phases of his subsequent career.

In 1930, while associated with the Hospital of the Rockefeller Institute, Dubos isolated from a soil bacterium an enzyme capable of hydrolyzing the capsular polysaccharide of type-III pneumococcus, a cause of lobar pneumonia in man. As the capsular polysaccharide normally protects pneumococci against the defense mechanisms of the host, the enzyme proved to have therapeutic effectiveness against pneumococcal infections in various animal species.

Dubos observed that the bacterial polysaccharidase was highly specific for the pneumococcus polysaccharide and was produced only when the soil bacterium was compelled to use it, or a closely related substance, as source of energy. These findings constituted the first extensive documentation of the phenomenon of induced production of enyzme. Furthermore, it led Dubos to develop techniques for the production of other induced bacterial enzymes specific for creatine and creatinine. By virtue of their specificity, the bacterial enzymes proved useful in the study of the metabolism of these substances.

The demonstration that the bacterial polysaccharidase isolated in 1930 had a therapeutic effect against pneumococcal infection encouraged Dubos to search for other anti-infectious substances in soil microorganisms. In 1939, he reported the isolation from a soil bacterium of a product, "tyrothricin," that proved effective in the treatment of certain bacterial infections in animals and man; he showed later that tyrothricin was a mixture of two complex antibacterial polypeptides: gramicidin and tyrocidine. Although tyrothricin and the two peptides of which it was made proved too toxic for large-scale use, they are of historical interest because they were the first "antibiotics" manufactured commercially and used in the practice of veterinary and human medicine.

After working on problems of war medicine during World War II, Dubos turned his attention to tuberculosis, developing new methods for the cultivation of tubercle bacilli, for the production of experimental tuberculosis in mice, and for the study of BCG vaccination. More importantly, however, the work on tuberculosis gave him the opportunity to investigate the influence of hereditary, nutritional, physiological, and social factors on susceptibility to infection. From then on, most of his investigative work was focused on the study of the environmental agencies that play a role in resistance to disease—not only to tuberculosis, but also to other infectious processes, as well as to various noninfectious stresses.

During recent years, concern with the effects of the environment on growth and health led to the recognition in Dubos's laboratory that the indigenous microbial flora, in particular the flora of the gastrointestinal tract, profoundly influences the rate of growth of the host, its ultimate size, its efficiency in food utilization, and its resistance to many forms of stress.

The studies of the indigenous flora also revealed that, while certain of its microbial species are of course deleterious to the host, others in contrast are absolutely essential for physiological well-being. In fact, it appears that each animal species, including man, requires association with a certain specialized microbial flora in order to achieve normal development and function.

Dubos showed, furthermore, that the microbial environment to which the host is exposed during early life determines to a very large extent the composition of the indigenous flora. Many microbial species acquired at that time persist throughout the life span and condition many important physiological and immunological characteristics. Indeed, many traits—such as body size or resistance to infection—that had been thought to be genetically determined are in reality the expression of very early influences.

It will be apparent from the preceding account that Dubos's scientific research followed an ecological approach; health and disease were analyzed as manifestations of the interplay between the host, the environment, and the microbial pathogens (or other stressful agents). The more bacteriological aspects of this ecological attitude he presented in four books: *The Bacterial Cell* (1945), *Biochemical Determinants of Microbial Diseases* (1954), *The Unseen World* (1962), and *Bacterial and Mycotic Infections of Man* (4th ed. 1965). Concern with the effects of environmental and social forces on human welfare was expressed in a number of other books that deal with subjects ranging from history of science to social philosophy: *Louis Pasteur: Free Lance of Science* (1950), *Pasteur and Modern Science* (1960), *The White Plague: Tuberculosis, Man, and Society* (1952), *Dreams of Reason: Science and Utopias* (1961) and *The Torch of Life: Continuity in Living Experience* (1962).

In his latest book, *Man Adapting* (1965), Dubos analyzed the biological and social mechanisms through which individual human beings and human societies become adapted to different kinds of environments, and he discussed the relevance of this adaptability to the science and practice of medicine.

Dubos was born in a very modest family and received his early education in a small French village. After graduating from the Institut National Agronomique in Paris, he worked for 2 years at the International Institute of Agriculture in Rome (Italy). He emigrated to the United States in 1924 and became an American citizen in 1938. Except for 2 years as professor of comparative pathology and tropical medicine at Harvard University (1942–44), he spent all his professional life at the Rockefeller Institute in New York. Among his many national and international awards were the John Phillips Memorial Award of the American College of Physicians (1940), the Lasker Award of the American Public Health Association (1948), the Trudeau Medal of the National Tuberculosis Association 1951), the Passano Foundation Award (1960), and the American Medical Association's Scientific Achievement Award (1964). He was elected to the National Academy of Sciences in 1941.

For background information *see* BACTERIAL ENZYME; BACTERIOLOGY, MEDICAL in the McGraw-Hill Encyclopedia of Science and Technology.   □

★ DUNBAR, Carl Owen

American geologist
Born Jan. 1, 1891, Hallowell, Kans., U.S.A.

DUNBAR WAS an American pioneer in the study of the Fusulinacea, a prolific group of large Foraminifera that was an important rock maker in late Paleozoic time and is one of the most widely used means of dating and correlating the rock formations of that time.

About 1920, J. W. Beede, who had done extensive field work in the Upper Carboniferous rocks of the Mid-Continent region, ventured the prophecy that when the evolutionary history of the fusulines was known they could be used to identify faunal zones not over 100 feet thick. With this stimulus, Dunbar began a comprehensive study of these fossils, of which only a few species and two genera had at that time been described from America. This proceeded in two stages: the first was to establish their stratigraphic succession, and the second to determine the progressive modifications of shell features that would reveal their evolutionary history. Six summers of field work while serving as paleontologist for the Geological Survey of Nebraska afforded the opportunity to secure large collections of fusulines from every known fossiliferous stratigraphic level in the Pennsylvanian System in Nebraska and adjacent states. With their chronology established, the biologic study was begun.

Because these quite complex shells could be studied only in thin sections, it was necessary, as

the first step, to cut some thousands of carefully oriented slices and grind them to transparent thinness. It was then possible to examine in turn each of the shell structures, measuring their sizes and other characteristics at successive levels in the stratigraphic sequence. Evolutionary trends were thereby established and important changes dated. In 1927 Dunbar and G. E. Condra published the first volume devoted to the study of American fusulines.

The opportunity to extend the study upward into the Permian System came in 1926 when large collections made by Robert E. King in the Permian Basin of West Texas and New Mexico were turned over to Dunbar for study. The stratigraphic succession had been carefully worked out by the brothers Robert and Phillip King. Simultaneously, John W. Skinner of the Humble Petroleum Company was beginning a study of the same faunas. Dunbar and Skinner decided to collaborate, and in 1937 published *The Permian Fusulinidae of Texas.*

From 1925 to 1928 Lloyd G. Henbest was engaged by the Illinois Geological Survey in making systematic collections of the fusulines from every fossiliferous level in the coal measures of that state, and in the fall of 1928 he went to Yale to study with Dunbar. Together they spent part of a summer in the field reviewing the stratigraphy and making additional collections. This project resulted in Bulletin 67 of the Illinois Geological Survey, *Pennsylvanian Fusulinidae of Illinois* (1942), by Dunbar and Henbest.

These three volumes, plus many shorter articles in technical journals, established numerous genera and species and demonstrated progressive evolutionary trends that could be used to date the rocks and correlate equivalent formations in other regions.

Dunbar grew up on a wheat ranch in Kansas, received his undergraduate training at the University of Kansas (A.B., 1913) and graduate training in geology at Yale (Ph.D., 1917). After two years at the University of Minnesota he joined the Yale faculty in 1920 as assistant professor of historical geology and assistant curator of invertebrate paleontology in the Peabody Museum of Natural History. Several years of teaching large undergraduate classes widened his interest in synthesizing the history of the Earth and led to his collaboration with Charles Schuchert on the third and fourth editions (1933, 1941) of the latter's *Textbook of Historical Geology*, and subsequently to two editions of his own *Historical Geology* (1949, 1960). In 1930 Dunbar was promoted to professor of paleontology and stratigraphy. From 1942 until his retirement in 1959 he served also as director of the Peabody Museum of Natural History at Yale. In 1959 Dunbar received the Hayden

Medal of the Philadelphia Academy of Sciences. He was elected to the National Academy of Sciences in 1944.

Besides the books already mentioned, Dunbar wrote *Principles of Stratigraphy*, with John Rodgers (1957). □

★ **DU VIGNEAUD, Vincent**

American biochemist
Born May 18, 1901, Chicago, Ill., U.S.A.

FOR THE first synthesis of a polypeptide hormone, oxytocin, and for his work on other biologically important sulfur compounds, du Vigneaud was awarded the Nobel Prize for chemistry in 1955.

Du Vigneaud approached the study of the posterior pituitary hormones, oxytocin and vasopressin, with a background of knowledge and experience in the area of organic sulfur compounds. He and his associates at Cornell University Medical College first isolated these hormones in highly purified form from the glands. They then proceeded to determine the nature of the hormones and found them to be polypeptides containing eight amino acid residues, the sulfur being present as cystine. On the basis of various degradative studies, they postulated cyclic disulfide octapeptide amide structures for both of these highly active compounds and then tested the correctness of their postulates by synthesizing the compounds so designated and comparing the synthetic compounds with the natural products. The synthesis of oxytocin was accomplished in 1953 by building up the amino acid chain and finally closing the ring through formation of a bond between the two sulfur atoms; the synthetic polypeptide was found to be identical in physical, chemical, and biological properties with the natural hormone. Du Vigneaud and his associates also synthesized both lysine-vasopressin and arginine-vasopressin, the pressor-antidiuretic hormones found respectively in hog and beef posterior pituitary glands.

Synthetic oxytocin was tested in human patients in the Lying-in Hospital of the New York Hospital–Cornell Medical Center through the collaboration of Gordon Douglas, professor of obstetrics and gynecology, and his associates. The synthetic was found to be as effective in the induction of labor as the purified natural oxytocin. When the synthetic compound and natural oxytocin were tested for milk-ejecting activity, they were again found indistinguishable in effectiveness. Thus it was demonstrated that one and the same molecule possesses these two important biological activities.

The synthesis of these posterior pituitary hormones also provided the first opportunity to study the relationship of structure to biological activity of a polypeptide hormone by the total synthesis and biological study of analogs incorporating various structural modifications. Through such studies with oxytocin and the vasopressins insight is being gained as to the structural requirements for the exhibition of the various biological activities of these hormones.

Almost all of du Vigneaud's researches involved sulfur-containing compounds of diverse types—the vitamin biotin; the antibiotic penicillin; the protein hormone insulin; and the sulfur-containing amino acids methionine, homocystine, cystathionine, and cystine. His researches on the posterior pituitary hormones were thus a natural outgrowth of an interest in sulfur compounds dating from 1925, when he showed that the disulfide present in insulin could be accounted for as the amino acid cystine —the same amino acid that du Vigneaud was later to find in the posterior pituitary hormones.

Du Vigneaud received his B.S. in 1923 and his M.S. in 1924 under C. S. Marvel at the University of Illinois. In 1924–25 he was assistant biochemist to W. G. Karr at the Philadelphia General Hospital and was on the staff of the Graduate School of Medicine of the University of Pennsylvania. The University of Rochester conferred the Ph.D. degree upon him in 1927. His thesis work was carried out under John R. Murlin at the School of Medicine. As a National Research Council fellow, du Vigneaud worked with John J. Abel at Johns Hopkins University Medical School, with Max Bergmann at the Kaiser Wilhelm Institute in Dresden, with George Barger at the University of Edinburgh Medical School, and with Charles R. Harington at the University College Hospital Medical School in London. Returning to the United States, he joined the physiological chemistry staff under W. C. Rose at the University of Illinois, and in 1932 became head of the department of biochemistry at George Washington

University School of Medicine. Du Vigneaud was appointed professor and head of the department of biochemistry at Cornell University Medical College in 1938. He was elected to the National Academy of Sciences in 1944.

Du Vigneaud wrote *A Trail of Research in Sulfur Chemistry and Metabolism and Related Fields* (1952).

For background information *see* HORMONE; SULFUR in the McGraw-Hill Encyclopedia of Science and Technology.   □

☆ DYER, Rolla Eugene

American physician
Born Nov. 4, 1886, Delaware County, Ohio, U.S.A.

DYER DISCOVERED the agent of murine typhus in the common rat flea (*Xenopsylla cheopis*) and showed that this flea transmits the disease from rats to man.

Epidemic typhus is a rickettsial disease transmitted in nature only by lice that feed exclusively on human blood. In 1922, K. F. Maxcy began to see evidence of another kind of typhus and to challenge the old notion of "no lice, no typhus." He noted that in the southern United States there had been cases of typhus unassociated with lice and that persons handling foodstuffs risked contracting the disease apparently from an animal reservoir other than man. He suggested the rat and the mouse as the most likely reservoirs and some blood-sucking arthropod that fed both on rodents and man as the most likely vector.

Carrying on where Maxcy left off, Dyer set out to find the reservoir and vector of what had become known as "endemic typhus," to distinguish it from the louse-borne type. His opportunity came when, in 1930, several cases of typhus broke out in rat-infested houses near food-handling firms in Baltimore, Md. Dyer and his associates, L. F. Badger and A. S. Rumreich,

combed rat fleas out of rats they trapped in these houses. Dyer now assumed that the rat was the reservoir of endemic typhus and that the flea was the vector of the disease. He reasoned that he could test the hypothesis only by isolating a strain of typhus rickettsia from the rat flea and comparing it with a strain isolated from a human case.

He and his associates ground up the fleas in saline solution and injected the resulting emulsion into guinea pigs. The pigs got typhus. Dyer and his associates repeated these experiments and achieved the same results with fleas from rats trapped at a house in Savannah, Ga., where there had been two cases of typhus. They also found that the strains of rickettsiae recovered from fleas taken from the Baltimore and Savannah rats were clinically identical with a strain Maxcy isolated from a human case of typhus in Wilmington, N.C., in 1928. Finally, in 1931, Dyer and his associates experimentally transmitted the rickettsiae from rats to rats by fleas. They therefore established that endemic typhus is, in fact, a variety of typhus not transmitted by lice parasitic on man. In 1932, H. Mooser renamed the disease "murine typhus."

Dyer also did pioneer work on scarlet fever, Rocky Mountain spotted fever, and Q fever. In 1928, his studies resulted in a world standard unit for scarlet fever antitoxin. In 1931, he helped determine that Rocky Mountain spotted fever is endemic in the eastern United States. In 1939, he showed that a supposedly new tick-borne disease in the United States was actually the same as Australian Q fever.

Director of the National Institute of Health, U.S. Public Health Service, during World War II, Dyer channeled the resources of the organization into the war effort. Under his leadership, the institute produced a yellow fever vaccine and developed a typhus vaccine for the Armed Forces, carried out fundamental research in blood substitutes and in aviation medicine, conducted toxicological studies on new explosives and synthetic substances, and synthesized and clinically tested antimalarial drugs. After the war, Dyer's efforts led to the recognition of the chronic diseases as a major public health problem. He directed the expansion of the National Institute of Health into one of the world's leading institutions for research in virtually all diseases of man. Under him, it became the National Institutes of Health (NIH) in 1948. He organized the NIH Division of Research Grants and Fellowships. The work of this division in allocating Federal financial assistance to public and private nonprofit scientific institutions greatly expanded the nation's medical research.

The son of a clergyman, Dyer received a B.A. degree from Kenyon College, Gambier, Ohio, in 1907, and an M.D. from the University of Texas in 1915. He completed his internship at Philadelphia General Hospital in 1916, when he was commissioned a medical officer in the U.S. Public Health Service. Until 1920, he engaged in various field activities, including control of bubonic plague and research in pellagra. In 1921, he became a staff member of the Hygienic Laboratory (renamed the National Institute of Health in 1930). He served as assistant director from 1922 to 1942 and concurrently from 1936 to 1942 as chief of the institute's Division of Infectious Diseases (a predecessor of the present National Institute of Allergy and Infectious Diseases). He was director, with the rank of assistant surgeon general, from 1942 to 1950. From 1950 (when he retired from the U.S. Public Health Service) to 1957, he was director of research of the Robert Winship Memorial Clinic of Emory University, Atlanta, Ga. In 1948, Dyer received the Lasker Award of the American Public Health Association for his work on rickettsial diseases and for his service to the nation as director of NIH. His many other awards include the Sedgwick Memorial Medal of the American Public Health Association, the Walter Reed Medal of the American Society of Tropical Medicine, and the James D. Bruce Memorial Medal of the American College of Physicians. In his honor, the R. E. Dyer lectureship, awarded annually to an American who has made an outstanding contribution to knowledge in some field of biomedical research, was established at NIH in 1950.

For background information *see* RICKETTSIOSES in the McGraw-Hill Encyclopedia of Science and Technology.   □

fibers under a wide variety of experimental conditions.

Nerve impulses provide the means of communication within the single units or nerve cells that compose the nervous system. Largely on account of the investigations of the great Spanish histologist Ramón y Cajal it was recognized that nerve cells must communicate with each other not by direct transmission of nerve impulses but by a complex transmission process of another kind that occurs across the regions of intimate contact called "synapses." It was also recognized that this synaptic communication between nerve cells was of two kinds: in one kind, the receiving cell was excited to discharge an impulse or message; in the other, there was depression or inhibition of the actions of excitatory synapses.

In 1952 Eccles and his colleagues at the Australian National University inserted extremely fine glass tubes (about 1/50,000 in. across) filled with conducting salt solutions into nerve cells and so gained a privileged view of the synaptic actions of the other nerve cells upon the one under examination. They were able to show that the excitatory actions were due to removal of electrical charges from the surface of the nerve cell, whereas the inhibitory synapses increased this electrical charge. This latter fact was singled out for mention by the Nobel Committee as a special example of the ionic properties of the surface membrane that Hodgkin and Huxley had done so much to clarify.

Subsequent work enabled Eccles and his colleagues to define with precision the ionic mechanism normally responsible for the increase in

★ ECCLES, Sir John (Carew)

Australian physiologist
Born Jan. 27, 1903, Melbourne, Australia

ECCLES SOLVED the problem of how brief electrical messages or nerve impulses act across the zones of close contact between nerve cells. For this achievement he received the 1963 Nobel Prize in physiology or medicine.

A. L. Hodgkin and A. F. Huxley, who shared this Nobel Prize with Eccles, had shown how the nerve impulse was generated by the movements of ions such as sodium and potassium across the membrane surrounding nerve fibers. Their work was done largely on the giant nerve fibers of the squid, which offer singular advantages for precise quantitative studies of electrical potentials and of ion movements. In this way they were able to elaborate one of the most elegant and satisfying theories in biology and to convert it into mathematical terms. Their theory has had great success in predicting the behavior of nerve

charge on the nerve cell membrane and the consequent inhibition of this cell. The increase in charge, they found, was due to the opening up of very fine pores or holes on the membrane of the order of about 1/10,000 millionth of an in. (about 3A) in diameter. This size allowed the passage of small ions with their surrounding water molecules such as chloride and potassium, but obstructed the movement across the membrane of the larger ions such as sodium with its surround of water molecules. This theory has been tested by a wide variety of ions in many laboratories and has been shown to be an essentially correct account of the mode of operation of this fundamental nerve action. The excitatory synapses differ in that they cause the membrane of the cell to have rather larger pores—in fact, at least twice the size—so that sodium ions go through very readily.

The son of a teacher, Eccles graduated M.B., B.S. at the University of Melbourne in 1925. He was Victorian Rhodes scholar in 1925 and at Oxford studied for the Final Honours School in the Natural Sciences in 1927 and for his D.Phil. in 1929. He was a fellow of Exeter College, Oxford, from 1927 to 1934, and then was a fellow of Magdalen College, Oxford, from 1934 to 1937. In 1937 he returned to Australia and for 7 years directed the Research Institute at Sydney Hospital. From 1944 to 1951 he was professor of physiology at the University of Otago Medical School, Dunedin, New Zealand. In 1951 he was appointed professor of physiology in the Australian National University, Canberra.

Eccles wrote *The Neurophysiological Basis of Mind: The Principles of Neurophysiology* (1953), *The Physiology of Nerve Cells* (1957), and *The Physiology of Synapses* (1964).

For background information *see* SYNAPTIC TRANSMISSION in the McGraw-Hill Encyclopedia of Science and Technology. □

★ EDLUND, Milton Carl

American physicist
Born Dec. 13, 1924, Jamestown, N.Y., U.S.A.

WHILE DESIGNING the Indian Point, N.Y., nuclear reactor, Edlund conceived the spectral shift control principle, an improved method for controlling reactors. For his work in reactor development, he received the U.S. Atomic Energy Commission's E. O. Lawrence Award in 1965.

During work on the first round of pressurized-water reactors, it became clear that their performance could be substantially improved by eliminating the use of neutron-absorbing control rods for the reactivity shim required to offset burnup of fuel and build-up of fission products. Control rods reduced fuel utilization by absorbing neutrons that could otherwise by absorbed in fertile material; they distorted the power distribution in the reactor core, thus limiting the maximum power capability of a given core and primary coolant system.

By using as moderator a mixture of heavy and light water, the proportions of which could be changed as the reactor was operated, Edlund effected a substantial improvement in both neutron economy and power. The reactivity of the close-packed lattices typical of pressurized-water reactor cores can be changed by the addition of heavy water, primarily because heavy water is not as effective a moderator as light water. The slowing-down power of light water is seven times greater than that of heavy water, and thus the resonance neutron flux and resonance absorptions are increased by addition of heavy water. Since the ratio of the effective absorption cross sections of fertile material to fuel is larger in the resonance energy region than at thermal energies, the addition of heavy water to the moderator decreases reactivity. Thus, by shifting the neutron spectrum toward the resonance region by having a high concentration of D_2O at the beginning of operation with a new core, the fertile material acts as a control rod—except that the neutrons that would normally be lost to the fuel cycle are now producing new fuel.

The principle of spectral shift control was confirmed by an extensive series of critical and exponential experiments performed at the Babcock and Wilcox Company's Critical Experiment Laboratory in Lynchburg, Va., under contract to the U.S. Atomic Energy Commission.

Edlund majored in mathematics and physics at the University of Michigan, where he received his B.S. and M.S. in 1948. He did additional graduate work at the University of Tennessee and Princeton University. Starting work at the

Oak Ridge National Laboratory in 1948 as a mathematical physicist, he became deeply interested in neutron diffusion and the design of nuclear fission chain reactors. Within a short time he had collected and organized the major theoretical work done at the various laboratories of the Manhattan Project during World War II. This led to his coauthorship, with Samuel Glasstone, of the first authoritative textbook on nuclear reactor theory, *The Elements of Nuclear Reactor Theory* (1951). During this period he also taught reactor theory at the Oak Ridge School of Reactor Technology and contributed to several reactor development projects, including the aqueous homogeneous reactor and the aircraft nuclear propulsion projects. In 1955 Edlund joined the Babcock and Wilcox Company, where he was successively manager of physics and mathematics, manager of development, and assistant division manager of the company's atomic energy division, and where he was in charge of the nuclear design and development of the Indian Point and the NS *Savannah* reactors.

For background information *see* REACTOR, NUCLEAR in the McGraw-Hill Encyclopedia of Science and Technology. □

☆ ELSASSER, Walter Maurice

American geophysicist
Born Mar. 20, 1904, Mannheim, Germany

ELSASSER'S STUDIES of the make-up and movement of the Earth's core led to his formulation of the "dynamo" theory of the permanent terrestrial magnetic field. According to this model, the presence of a magnetic field, H_1, in the core will result in motion of matter, V_1, perpendicular to the field, which in turn will give rise to a field, H_2, producing motion, V_2, and so on in self-sustaining action. For this and other work, Elsasser was awarded the Bowie Medal of the American Geophysical Union in 1959.

The origin of the Earth's permanent magnetic field has been a prime question in the study of geophysical phenomena. In the past, efforts to account for the presence of the "permanent" field included explanations based on (1) the supposed ferromagnetism of the Earth's interior and (2) circulation of electrical currents in the interior. The second divided again into (2a)

production of electrons by circulating matter impinging on crossed thermal gradients in the magnetic field, and (2b) a "dynamo" hypothesis, such as the one outlined above. Neither theory, however, was elaborated to the point of constituting a plausible model; each suffered from severe internal contradictions.

Elsasser assumed that, if the Earth's metallic core were in convective motion, it might obey the same laws of cosmic magnetohydrodynamics that govern, for example, the ionized gases in the Sun's magnetic field. He first attacked the phenomenon of the "secular variation," reasoning that any theory of the permanent field would also have to explain this slight, cumulative change in the field. Assuming the core to be in thermally induced convection, Elsasser's formulation of the magnetohydrodynamics of a spherical conductor furnished quantitative results in agreement with the observed secular variation. However, it was still necessary to account for the self-sustaining nature of the permanent field.

While Elsasser was conducting these researches, evidence emerged for the concept of the coexistence of toroidal and poloidal modes in the Earth's magnetic field. Using this information, he contributed to the development of a model of the Earth as represented by an assembly of concentric spheres, in mutual electrical contact and rotating relative to each other. In this model, the magnetic field is amplified by the nonuniform rotation as magnetic torques are transmitted outward from the core to the surface.

It still remained to furnish an explanation of the regularity of the permanent field; the "dynamo" model thus far would not necessarily produce a field even partially regular. It appeared that there must be some force that regulated and ordered the amplification effect of the magnetic field, relative to the axis of rotation of the core. Elsasser's theory called for the formation of eddies near the boundary layers of the revolving spheres, very similar to the major perturbations of the atmosphere. His studies of atmospheric circulation prepared him for the conclusion that the same force could be instrumental in ordering both varieties of eddy— namely, the Coriolis effect, the force producing a deflection toward the center of a rotating mass.

Elsasser's "dynamo" model represented the Earth's permanent field as initially quite weak, building up very gradually to its present strength. It provided a full explanation of the permanence of the field and the presence of the secular variation. Moreover, it has led subsequent investigators to an explanation of observed fluctuations in the Earth's rate of rotation. His work has been subsequently independently confirmed and elaborated upon by H. Takeuchi, E. C. Bullard, and others.

After early work in nuclear physics, Elsasser

took up atmospheric studies and devised a graphic method of calculating spontaneous emission of infrared by various gases in the atmosphere. He did research in magnetohydrodynamics and terrestrial magnetism. His book, *The Physical Foundation of Biology* (1958), is an inductive investigation of the relationship between the biological sciences and the quantum-mechanical concepts of theoretical physics.

Elsasser took his Ph.D. in physics in 1927 at Göttingen and subsequently taught at Frankfurt and the Sorbonne. In 1936 he went to the California Institute of Technology, becoming an American citizen in 1940. After taking part in war work and industrial research, he was professor of physics at the University of Pennsylvania from 1947 to 1950 and at the University of Utah from 1950 to 1958. In that year he became professor of theoretical physics at the Scripps Institution of Oceanography and the University of California at La Jolla. In 1962 he was named professor of geophysics at Princeton University. He was elected to the National Academy of Sciences in 1957.

Elsasser wrote *The Physical Foundation of Biology* (1958).

For background information *see* GEOMAGNETISM; MAGNETOHYDRODYNAMICS in the McGraw-Hill Encyclopedia of Science and Technology. ☐

ELVEHJEM, Conrad Arnold

American biochemist
Born May 27, 1901, McFarland, Wis., U.S.A.
Died July 27, 1962, Madison, Wis., U.S.A.

ELVEHJEM IS best known for his identification, in 1937, of nicotinic acid as the factor in the vitamin-B complex necessary in the cure and prevention of canine black tongue. Joseph Goldberger and his associates had previously demonstrated that the factor in liver that cured black tongue in dogs also cured human pellagra, both diseases being characterized by skin, gastrointestinal, and neurologic symptoms. Elvehjem's contribution in identifying this compound was therefore of great importance in the prevention and treatment of human pellagra, a disease that was common in tropical and subtropical countries.

By the 1930s the principal vitamins, A, B, C, and D, had been discovered and their role in nutrition evaluated. Goldberger had proven that pellagra was caused by a vitamin deficiency but had assumed that a deficiency of vitamin B_2 (riboflavin) was the immediate cause. However, this assumption was open to considerable doubt as liver extract in which the B_2 vitamin had been destroyed still displayed excellent therapeutic effects on pellagra. Moreover, by 1933 several German investigators had isolated riboflavin, but it proved ineffective against pellagra.

Elvehjem set out to determine which factor in liver extract was potent against pellagra. Goldberger had developed a special diet for dogs that produced the disease black tongue, a canine pellagra. Using this diet, Elvehjem produced black tongue among his laboratory dogs. He used these dogs to test the efficacy of various liver extracts in curing the condition. By using a variety of organic solvents, adsorbents, and eluting agents, he constantly purified and concentrated his extracts until he produced a white crystalline material that proved to be nicotinic acid. This substance was first prepared in 1867 by C. Huber by the oxidation of the alkaloid nicotine. In 1912, nicotinic acid was isolated from yeast by C. Funk and from rice bran by U. Suzuki during their attempts to find the anti–beri beri factor. They noted that it had no beneficial effect on beri beri but did not suspect that they had actually isolated a vitamin capable of curing a different deficiency disease.

After Elvehjem isolated nicotinic acid, he tried a 30-milligram dose of it on one of the dogs suffering from black tongue. The acid worked almost like magic in its rapid cure of the dog. Within a year Thomas Spies had tried the acid on a human pellagra victim with equal success.

Further study has shown that the human body is able to synthesize some nicotinic acid from tryptophan, an amino acid found in milk and eggs. However, as the quantity of the vitamin produced from this source is insufficient for good health, some nicotinic acid (niacin) must be supplied in the diet. Fortunately, it is widely distributed in foods such as meat, fish, and some cereals. It is now known that pellagra patients do not always recover completely when treated only with nicotinic acid. Other components of the vitamin-B complex must be administered, probably due to the fact that a diet sufficiently deficient in nicotinic acid to cause pellagra would also be deficient in other factors of the vitamin-B complex. This bears out Elvehjem's recommendation that our vitamin needs should be obtained from natural foods if possible. These natural vitamins are generally cheaper, more palatable, and in better balance with other factors when taken in this form. The occurrence of pellagra in the United States has been greatly decreased by enriching white flour with niacin.

A major part of Elvehjem's research work was concerned with studies of metabolism. Beginning in 1928, in collaboration with Hart, Steenbock, and Waddell, he studied anemia produced in rats fed solely on a diet of milk, a food that contains little iron. The addition of soluble iron compounds to their diet had no effect until ashes obtained from the calcining of lettuce, liver, and corn were added. Then the anemia disappeared. The utilization of the iron was found to depend on the slight trace of copper in the ash, without which iron could not be utilized in the rat's metabolism to form the essential hemoglobin. This interest in the effect of traces of elements led to subsequent investigations of manganese, zinc, cobalt, selenium, boron, and cadmium. Like vitamins, these trace elements perform their work as parts of essential enzymes.

Elvehjem attended the University of Wisconsin, where he received his B.S. in 1923, his M.S. in 1924, and his Ph.D. in 1927. He remained at Wisconsin as a member of the faculty, becoming head of the biochemistry department in 1944, dean of the Graduate School in 1946, and president of the university in 1958. Elvehjem received the Willard Gibbs Medal of the American Chemical Society in 1943, the Osborne and Mendel Award of the American Institute of Nutrition in 1950, and the Lasker Award of the American Public Health Association in 1952.

For background information see VITAMIN in the McGraw-Hill Encyclopedia of Science and Technology.   □

the research students were encouraged to develop projects of their own devising. Facilities were rather poor, and all were expected to do their own glass blowing. It was in this setting that Eméleus did his early work on the low-temperature oxidation of phosphorus, arsenic, sulfur, and ether.

In 1927 he spent a year in the laboratory of A. Stock at the Technische Hochschule, Karlsruhe, where he worked with E. Pohland on the chemistry of decaborane. This proved to be a turning point in that it provided an opportunity to learn the preparative techniques that had been developed to a high state of perfection in Stock's laboratory. Eméleus was appointed to the staff at Imperial College in 1931, following a period of two years spent in the laboratory of H. S. Taylor at Princeton as a Commonwealth Fund Fellow. This interlude provided an opportunity to study photochemistry, and the following years at Imperial College were devoted to preparative work linked to some extent with physicochemical studies, particularly on the kinetics of gaseous reactions, and the study of critical explosion limits in, for example, the silicon hydrides.

Eméleus's interest in fluorine chemistry dated from the period 1939–43 when, in association with H. V. A. Briscoe, he directed a small group at Imperial College that was charged with the task of preparing and examining for toxicity a wide range of little-known nonmetallic fluorides. These included chlorine trifluoride, bromine trifluoride, and iodine pentafluoride, work with which was continued when he moved to Cambridge in 1945. Bromine trifluoride and iodine pentafluoride were shown to behave as typical solvent systems and, on the basis of the ionization modes postulated ($2BrF_3 \rightleftarrows BrF_2{}^+ + BrF_4{}^-$; $2IF_5 \rightleftarrows IF_4{}^+ + IF_6{}^-$), it was possible to prepare new series of "acids" and

★ EMELÉUS, Harry Julius

British chemist
Born June 22, 1903, London, England

I N THE period following World War I, it appeared to many that preparative inorganic chemistry had come to a standstill in Britain. Eméleus was one of a small group of researchers who helped to reestablish a flourishing tradition, both by his own research and, in later years, through those who had been associated with him as students.

He received his early training at the Imperial College of Science and Technology in London where, after graduation, he completed his research for the Ph.D. degree under the supervision of H. B. Baker. In Baker's laboratory all

"bases" (for example, BrF_2SbF_6, $KBrF_4$, IF_4SbF_6, KIF_6) containing the cations and anions believed to be associated with the pure solvents. The detailed study of the fluorinating reactions of these interhalogen compounds had a further important consequence when it was shown that reaction between iodine pentafluoride and carbon tetraiodide gave the new compound trifluoroiodomethane, CF_3I. This provided a key to the preparation of a new group of fluoroorganometallic compounds. Reaction with mercury, for example, gave the mercurial CF_3HgI, from which the bis mercurial was readily prepared. Similarly, reaction with phosphorus, arsenic, antimony, sulfur, and selenium led to simple fluoroalkyls of these elements and also, indirectly, or through further reactions of such intermediates as $(CF_3)_2PI$, to a wide range of other compounds. This field has subsequently been greatly extended both by former students from the Cambridge school and in other schools of fluorine chemistry, and remains one of the most active areas of inorganic research. Eméleus and his students extended the work on fluorine chemistry to perfluoroalkyl nitrogen compounds, where inorganic derivatives, such as those of sulfur and selenium, were prepared. There is indeed no indication that this rich field is nearing exhaustion. With the advance of modern spectroscopic techniques, structural studies of many of the new compounds have taken their place alongside the preparative work. The approach adopted throughout has, however, been that of an experimentalist with a highly developed instinct, rather than that of a logical theoretician.

Eméleus was elected a Fellow of the Royal Society in 1946 and was awarded its Davy Medal in 1962. He also received the Lavoisier Medal of the French Chemical Society and the Stock Medal of the Gesellschaft Deutscher Chemiker. A large number of publications by Eméleus and his students and associates appeared in chemical journals. With J. S. Anderson, he wrote *Modern Aspects of Inorganic Chemistry* (1938).

For background information *see* FLUORINE in the McGraw-Hill Encyclopedia of Science and Technology.   □

☆ ENDERS, John Franklin

American microbiologist
Born Feb. 10, 1897, West Hartford, Conn., U.S.A.

FOR THEIR discovery of the capacity of the poliomyelitis virus to grow in test-tube cultures of various tissues, Enders, F. C. Robbins, and T. H. Weller were awarded the 1954 Nobel Prize in physiology or medicine.

In the 1870s the German bacteriologist Robert Koch established the techniques of cultivating bacteria in test tubes. Culture techniques enabled bacteriologists to isolate disease-causing bacteria, study them, and devise effective remedies. Such techniques, however, were not successful for the cultivation of viruses. Viruses could live and develop only in living cells, not in the lifeless culture media of test tubes. For this reason virus research was seriously hampered. With direct experimentation ruled out, virologists had to inoculate living animals with the virus to be studied and then observe the animal's reaction. This inferential procedure was time-consuming and inaccurate, and it was impossible to use on the scale needed to control epidemics.

Early in the 20th century, the French-American biologist Alexis Carrel developed the technique of growing animal tissues in the test tube. The necessity of preventing contamination of the cultures by microorganisms made Carrel's technique extremely complicated. Nevertheless, tissue culture promised to become a valuable tool for virologists. At his laboratory for research in infectious diseases at the Children's Hospital, Boston, Enders, together with Weller and Robbins, took up in 1947 a study of the potentialities of tissue culture for the propagation of viruses. They soon demonstrated that it was possible to grow mumps virus in a simple suspended cell culture consisting of fragments of chick amniotic membrane nourished with a balanced salt solution and ox serum ultrafiltrate.

In 1948 Enders and his coworkers turned to the poliomyelitis virus. It was then generally believed that the poliomyelitis virus could live only in nerve cells; because nerve tissue is the most specialized and difficult to cultivate, prospects for successful experimentation with the polio virus were not bright. Enders, however, along with other scientists, doubted that the

polio virus was strictly neurotropic; if so, how account for the enormous quantities of the virus observed in the feces of polio patients? In their first experiment, Enders, Robbins, and Weller introduced the polio virus in the form of an infected suspension of mouse brain into a culture of human embryonic skin and muscle tissue. These cultures were handled in the same manner as in the experiments with mumps virus. When mice were inoculated with fluid removed from the original cultures it became apparent that the virus had multiplied. When the fluid was introduced into the brains of monkeys, paralysis of the legs typical of polio ensued. These experiments proved that the polio virus was not neurotropic. Enders and his coworkers soon grew the virus in a variety of human embryonic tissues, including intestine, liver, kidney, adrenal, brain, heart, spleen, and lung.

A factor limiting the value of these experiments was that viral multiplication in the culture could be demonstrated only by inoculating experimental animals. However, phenomena indicating viral multiplication were soon discovered in the tissue-culture system itself. Tissues originally infected with the virus strain showed widespread cellular degeneration, while uninoculated tissues in the same culture remained in excellent condition. This direct evidence of viral multiplication was substantiated by indirect evidence: decline in the metabolic rate of tissues infected with virus as expressed by a progressive reduction of acid formation. In investigating these phenomena, Enders and his associates found that the addition of type-specific antiserum to the suspended cell culture before the virus was introduced protected the tissue cells from the destructive effect of the virus. Thus not only had they found a prompt and efficient way of proving viral multiplication, but by demonstrating the inhibitory effect of homologous antiserum they showed that it was possible to determine in vitro the antigenic type of poliomyelitis virus.

Enders, Weller, and Robbins found later that they were not dependent on embryonic tissues for their cultures. Tissues secured from operations on children and adults served just as well. All tissues except bone and cartilage proved suitable. Finally, by successfully isolating the polio virus from various specimens directly in tissue cultures, they established the tissue-culture technique on a par with the bacteria culture.

By means of the tissue culture technique, Enders and T. C. Peebles in 1954 isolated the virus of measles, which previously had not been grown consistently under laboratory conditions. This finding laid the basis for the development by Enders, Samuel Katz, and Milano Milovanovic of an attenuated live measles virus vaccine that is now widely used in the United States either in its original form or after further attenuation, which was accomplished by Anton Schwarz.

A banker's son, Enders served as a pilot in World War I before receiving his B.A. from Yale in 1919. For a time he engaged in the real estate business, then did graduate work in English at Harvard before switching to bacteriology and immunology. He received his Ph.D. from Harvard in 1930, remaining there as a member of the faculty. In 1946 he established a laboratory for research in infectious diseases at the Children's Medical Center in Boston. In 1956 he became Higgins University Professor at Harvard. He was elected to the National Academy of Sciences in 1953.

For background information *see* CULTURE, TISSUE; POLIOMYELITIS in the McGraw-Hill Encyclopedia of Science and Technology.   □

ERLANGER, Joseph

American physician and physiologist
Born Jan. 5, 1874, San Francisco, Calif., U.S.A.
Died Dec. 5, 1965, St. Louis, Mo., U.S.A.

WHILE ENGAGED in neurophysiologic research, Erlanger, in collaboration with Herbert Gasser, adapted the cathode-ray oscillograph for studying the passage of impulses through single nerve fibers. Erlanger and Gasser were able, through their new methods, to demonstrate many significant properties of nerve fibers and the transmission of nerve impulses. For their discoveries, which became the foundation for future work in neurophysiology, Erlanger and Gasser received the 1944 Nobel Prize in physiology or medicine.

The successful collaboration between Erlanger and Gasser began in the early 1900s when Gasser was a student of Erlanger's at the University of Wisconsin. The association that led to their Nobel Prize researches took place at Washington University in St. Louis, where both were on the faculty of the Medical School. There, beginning in 1921, they undertook a systematic study of the transmission of nerve impulses.

By stimulating an isolated nerve fiber, a "picture" of the passage of the electrical impulse through the fiber can be obtained on an oscilloscope. Since the action potential of nervous tissue (the electrical manifestation of the nerve impulse) is of extremely short duration, Erlanger felt that, with the instruments then in use, the details of the nerve impulse configuration had never been accurately recorded. By utilizing a highly sensitive cathode-ray oscillograph, coupled with a special amplifier, he and Gasser were able to record nerve impulses with greater accuracy than had previously been achieved. But it was not until 1932, when an improved amplification device became available, that the fine details of nerve transmission were revealed.

Utilizing nerve fibers from the phalangeal nerve or a spinal root of the frog—and the improved amplification device coupled to the cathode-ray oscillograph—Erlanger demonstrated an instability in the reactivity of the nerve fiber. He attributed this to independent variations in the excitabilities of the individual nerve fibers. To determine the reasons for the variable excitabilities, he exposed the nerve fibers to different conditions that were known to affect their reactivity. Anode and cathode polarization, which respectively decrease and increase nerve excitability, did not have any consistent effect on the variations. Cold, however, which lowers nerve excitability, increased the range of variations by as much as 50 per cent. Strychnine, of all the conditions and agents tested, had the greatest effect: applied to the nerve fibers in a concentration of 1:100,000, it caused a fourfold increase in the range of excitability fluctuations.

Although he made many investigations on variations in nerve fiber excitability, Erlanger was unable to discover the actual mechanism by which they were produced.

Some of Erlanger's most fruitful researches aimed to determine the manner of nerve impulse transmission. One earlier view held that the action potential, as it passes each locus of a nerve fiber, stimulates the next locus, and so on. In effect, the propagation of the excitation acted as an electrical restimulation. (This became known as the local-circuit hypothesis of nerve impulse progation.) An alternate theory proposed that nerve impulse conduction was due to some propagated chemical reaction. Later, it was suggested that a combination of the two theories might account for the phenomenon: a substance called acetycholine is released upon stimulation of a nerve and acts to break down the resistance of the nerve membrane, thereby allowing the impulse to pass to the next nerve locus, where the process is repeated.

Erlanger's experiments elucidated the role of the action potential in nerve impulse propagation. He also performed tests that provided evidence to support the local-circuit hypothesis of nerve impulse propagation.

In addition to his experimental work in neurophysiology, Erlanger made valuable contributions to knowledge of circulatory physiology. He developed a device to record blood pressure, with which he studied the effects of pulse pressure on human kidney secretion.

Erlanger received his B.S. in chemistry at the University of California in 1895 and his M.D. at the Johns Hopkins University in 1899. He remained at Johns Hopkins until 1906, becoming successively an assistant in the department of physiology, instructor, associate, and associate professor. In 1906 he became professor of physiology at the University of Wisconsin Medical School, and in 1910 he was named professor of physiology at the Medical School of Washington University in St. Louis. He retired in 1946. He was elected to the National Academy of Sciences in 1922.

For background information *see* NEUROPHYSIOLOGY in the McGraw-Hill Encyclopedia of Science and Technology.   □

★ ESAKI, Leo
Japanese physicist
Born Mar. 12, 1925, Osaka, Japan

WHILE STUDYING the tunneling effect in semiconductor *p-n* junctions, Esaki discovered a new negative resistance characteristic. This discovery led in 1957 to the tunnel, or Esaki, diode, which is a useful component for communication, computer, and other electronic equipment. For this achievement he received the Morris N. Liebman Memorial Prize of the Institute of Radio Engineers and the Ballantine Award of the Franklin Institute, as well as the Japanese Nishina Memorial Award, Asahi Press Award, Toyo Rayon Foundation Award, and the Japan Academy Award.

The idea of quantum "tunneling" of a particle

through an energy barrier was introduced as early as 1927 in the explanation of field ionization of atoms and the interpretation of field emission of electrons from surfaces. It was also used in the following year to explain alpha-particle emission. According to classical mechanics, a particle arriving at a potential barrier is reflected at the point where its potential energy equals its original kinetic energy. However, in quantum mechanics, electrons and other particles are considered as waves, and these waves may penetrate into the "forbidden" region. In consequence, the particle may travel through the barrier even though it does not have sufficient energy to surmount it. This is called tunneling.

In classical mechanics, the probability of tunneling is zero; in quantum mechanics it decreases exponentially as the length of the forbidden path increases. The first theory of barrier-layer rectification, developed in 1932 independently by A. H. Wilson, L. Nordheim, and J. Frenkel and A. Joffe, was based on the quantum mechanical tunneling effect. This theory was accepted for a number of years until people realized that it predicted rectification in the wrong direction. The ordinary rectifier has a barrier width far greater than 100 A—much too thick for any tunneling current. Tunneling between bands in a dielectric (insulator) was first proposed in 1934 by C. Zener. His idea was applied in 1951 to explain the reverse breakdown of the germanium p-n junction diode, the so-called Zener breakdown, but this interpretation later turned out to be not necessarily correct. Thus, as late as the middle 1950s, no one had yet been able to clearly identify a tunneling current in a p-n junction.

In 1957, while he was a member of a small research group at the Sony Corporation, Tokyo, Esaki decided to look into the tunneling effect in germanium p-n junctions. The major initial requirement was to make the junction extremely narrow so that the probability of tunneling would become large enough to permit a measurable current flow across the junction. This required heavy impurity doping of the semiconductor, since the junction width is inversely proportional to the square root of impurity concentration. The first result of this work was the successful operation of a "backward diode," so-called because it had a polarity opposite to that of the ordinary diode. Esaki was pleased to obtain this situation because of its excellent qualitative agreement with the 1932 quantum-mechanical rectification theory.

One day, while testing one of the more heavily doped diodes, he noticed some fuzziness in the current-voltage characteristic in the forward direction. A measurement at liquid-nitrogen temperatures showed a significant anomaly. Then he realized that because of the energy-band structure of the semiconductor the diode should have a negative resistance region if a large tunneling current was made possible in the forward direction. Esaki quickly proceeded to make still more heavily doped diodes with junctions only 100 A wide and found the expected negative resistance. Thus the tunnel diode was born. Its value as a fast-switching or high-frequency–amplifying electronic device was recognized in 1958, and widespread research was initiated on electron tunneling in junctions. Study of tunneling in semiconductors as well as in superconductors has proved to be a powerful tool in solid-state physics.

After 1961, Esaki spent most of his time working in the semimetals (bismuth, antimony, etc.), a class of materials with characteristics between those of metals and semiconductors. He discovered a strong electron-phonon interaction in bismuth under certain conditions, resulting in a sharply nonlinear current-voltage characteristic. He and his associates also applied a tunneling technique to the band-structure study of semimetals and developed a new experimental field known as tunneling spectroscopy.

An architect's son, Esaki majored in physics at the University of Tokyo, where he received his M.S. in 1947 and his Ph.D. on the tunneling study in 1959. In 1956, he went to work for the Sony Corporation while continuing to work on his thesis at the university. He went to the United States in 1960 to join International Business Machines' T. J. Watson Research Center at Yorktown Heights, N.Y., where he led a group in studies of semimetals and exploratory devices.

For background information *see* ESAKI TUNNEL DIODE; QUANTUM MECHANICS in the McGraw-Hill Encyclopedia of Science and Technology.   □

★ **ESAU, Katherine**
American botanist
Born Apr. 3, 1898, Ekaterinoslav, Russia

E SAU'S INITIAL interest centered on the effects of viruses on plants, particularly at the histological and cytological levels. This work had to be based on a thorough understanding of the development and structure of the normal plant. Esau therefore expanded her developmental studies into a major program of research and became an authority on the structure and ontogeny of the phloem, the food-conducting tissue. Relating normal anatomy to that modified by viruses, she elucidated the relations of viruses to plant tissues with regard to their effects and their distribution in the plant body.

The occurrence of specific relations between viruses and plants became evident soon after research on plant viruses began. Some viruses were found to be more easily transmitted from plant to plant than others, and the differences were reflected in their more or less specific relations to insects serving as vectors in their spread. Concomitantly, variations in the feeding habits of the insects as to the type of tissue selected for obtaining food became known. Viruses exemplifying the more specific relations were frequently those that, to infect the plant, had to be placed into the food-conducting tissue by an insect that required this tissue for successful feeding. Knowledge of the phloem tissue thus became essential to the furtherance of research on plant viruses.

Esau began her work on viruses as a member of the experiment station staff of the Spreckels Sugar Company in the Salinas Valley of California. There she was concerned with developing sugar-beet strains resistant to the virus disease called "curly top." In 1928 this work was transferred to the Davis campus of the University of California, where gradually the histologic aspects of plant virus diseases became dominant in Esau's research; and, since the curly top virus was a distinctly phloem-limited disease agent, the phloem tissue began to receive the major attention in this research.

Esau soon recognized that a complete understanding of plant cells (or plant tissues) had to be based on knowledge of the processes by which these cells assumed their particular forms and structures. Interpretation of the functional specialization of cells and of their responses to injurious agents such as viruses, she realized, presupposed a knowledge of cell ontogeny. The primary symptoms of virus diseases develop in plant parts that are still growing when the virus enters them. If the virus is related to a highly specialized cell, such as for example the food-conducting cell, or sieve element, the developmental history of the cell is doubly important.

Cell specialization is a result of evolution, but evolutionary changes are brought about by changes in ontogeny. Thus, study of development and differentiation was basic to the solution of problems of normal and abnormal anatomy.

In retrospect, Esau's contributions to plant science may be summarized under three topics: (1) In the area of plant virus–plant host relationships, Esau learned to distinguish between primary and secondary symptoms; this distinction provided a means of recognizing whether or not a virus selectively invades a specific tissue. She discovered that a phloem-limited virus may be specifically related to the sieve element in utilizing this food conduit for its movement toward the still-growing parts of the plant where optimal conditions for multiplication prevail. (2) In her attempt to clarify virus-host relations, she carried out a critical analysis of the ontogenetic history of primary vascular tissues, including the meristems involved, and developed dynamic concepts of primary and secondary growth. From these studies came a new appreciation of the fundamental differences in the patterns of initiation of the first xylem and the first phloem elements in the various organs of the plant and a new understanding of the relation between leaf development and vascularization. This work stimulated others to carry out similar studies and served to establish a sound basis for the modern experimental research on differentiation in plants. (3) Her research on the phloem tissue led to clarification of the ontogenetic features of the tissue, especially those of the main conducting cell, the sieve element. This research broadened into comparative studies of both physiological and structural features of the phloem and eventually led to elucidations of the contrast between the specialized sieve element and the less specialized associated parenchyma cells at the ultrastructural level. Esau's research provided an impetus to phloem study in America.

Esau received her initial education, including one year of college, in Russia. In 1919 she and her parents left Russia for Germany, where she continued her college work, completing it in 1922. In the same year the family migrated to the United States. After several years of employment, she entered the University of California as a graduate student and obtained a Ph.D. in botany in 1931. She taught at the University of California, Davis, until 1963, then transferred to the Santa Barbara campus of the same university, where she became professor emeritus in 1965. At Davis, she served also on the staff of the Experiment Station of the College of Agriculture. Most of her research was carried out under the auspices of the Experiment Station. She was elected to the National Academy of Sciences in 1957.

Esau wrote *Plant Anatomy* (1953; 2d ed. 1965), *Anatomy of Seed Plants* (1960), *Plants, Viruses, and Insects* (1961), and *Vascular Differentiation in Plants* (1965).

For background information *see* PLANT ANATOMY; PLANT VIRUS in the McGraw-Hill Encyclopedia of Science and Technology. □

★ EVANS, Griffith Conrad

American mathematician
Born May 11, 1887, Boston, Mass., U.S.A.

E VANS WORKED in the fields of integral and functional equations, harmonic functions, and potential theory.

In second-order partial differential equations, the second-order derivatives often require conditions not essential for the problem. Thus, for example, in 1916 Evans replaced second-order partial differential expressions by integral expressions over variable domains of first-order terms, deriving a corresponding Green's theorem, and so forth.

In 1906, Maxime Bôcher proved that if $u(x,y)$ is of class C^1 and the relation $\int_s (du/dn) ds = 0$ is satisfied for all circles in a bounded domain Ω, then u is of class C^∞ and satisfies Laplace's equation $\nabla^2 u = 0$. A corresponding problem is Poisson's equation $\nabla^2 u = f(x,y)$.

This equation implies a similar generalization, for which Evans in 1919 introduced the concept of mass as a completely (infinitely) additive function of point sets $f(e)$. The statement of the problem and a particular solution become

$$\int_s D_n u \, ds = F(s),$$

$$u_0(M) = \frac{1}{2\pi} \int_\Omega \log \frac{1}{MP} \, df(e_p)$$

valid for closed curves s that intersect a certain set E of two-dimensional measure >0 at most in a one-dimensional set of measure >0; $D_n u$ is the normal component of the vector $D_h u$, defined ex-

cept on E as the limit, when the area $\sigma \to 0$ as in a Lebesgue derivative, of $(1/\sigma) \int_s u \, dh'$, where $\sphericalangle hh' = \pi/2$, and s is the boundary of σ; $F(s)$ is the Volterra function of curves corresponding to $f(e)$. A change in the order of integration of this last relation produces the solution.

With the use of this concept of mass, H. E. Bray and Evans (1923) gave necessary and sufficient conditions for correspondingly generalized forms of the Poisson *integral* for the circle and the sphere. In 1929, Evans and E. R. C. Miles solved Dirichlet and Neumann boundary value problems of new types, on smooth surfaces. Here the functions to be detemined are functions of curves, solutions of Lebesgue-Stieltjes integral equations, with attention to the critical values 1 and -1 in the Poincaré-Robin equations.

The answer to a crucial question about the nature of boundary points, regular for the Dirichlet boundary value problem, is O. D. Kellogg's conjecture of 1926, known as "Kellogg's Lemma": If F is a bounded set of positive capacity, it contains a regular boundary point. Kellogg died before finding a proof of its validity. That Evans succeeded, in 1933, was a result of the use of completely additive set functions. He followed this note with an extensive memoir in 1935 on potentials of positive masses.

In 1936 Evans proved the following theorem: Let F be a bounded closed set in space with exterior domain D, s the interior boundary of D, and $u(M)$ harmonic in D; let M in $D \to Q$, Q in s. Then $u(M) \to +\infty$ for every Q if, and only if, capacity $s = 0$. The necessity part of Evans's theorem he had proved in the above cited memoir. The sufficiency is obtained by examining the energy of the generated potential function in terms of transfinite diameter.

Given a simple closed curve, s, in space, itself of zero capacity—for example, consisting of a finite number of "regular" arcs—Evans proved (1940) that among the surfaces with boundary s there is one, S, of minimum capacity. In fact, the Euler condition is the same as saying that the desired function $V(M)$ can be prolonged across S to form a double-valued function, harmonic in the whole space, with S the unique branch surface and s the branch curve. That the capacity is a strict minimum derives from a comparison of energy integrals. Generalizations of such problems are the subject of publication in 1951 and 1961, the second with consideration of two branch curves, each of order 1, the total space consisting of infinity subspaces. But such problems are not completely solved by any means.

Evans studied mathematics, physics, and philosophy at Harvard University, where he received his B.A. in 1907 and his Ph.D. in 1910. After two years in Europe with V. Volterra, except for a summer with Max Planck, he taught from

1912 to 1934 at the Rice Institute and from 1934 to 1955 at the University of California, Berkeley, becoming emeritus in 1954. With a strong philosophical interest in the relation of mathematics to "reality," he was able to successfully apply his scientific-mathematical knowledge in both world wars. He also wrote extensively in economics, using mostly, but not entirely, elementary mathematics. Beginning in 1924 he and his students initiated theories of dynamical economics, in contrast to those of moving equilibria, by using time derivatives and functionals over time intervals, in economic relations. In *Mathematical Introduction to Economics* (1930), he gave a systematic exposition of this subject, and incidentally showed by examples how small is the change from cycle to crisis. He was elected to the National Academy of Sciences in 1933.

For background information *see* CALCULUS, DIFFERENTIAL AND INTEGRAL; POTENTIALS (MATHEMATICS) in the McGraw-Hill Encyclopedia of Science and Technology.   ☐

☆ EWING, William Maurice

American geophysicist
Born May 12, 1906, Lockney, Texas, U.S.A.

FOR HIS fundamental contributions to general geophysics, including seismology, geodesy, oceanography, and submarine geology, Ewing received the Day Medal of the Geological Society of America (1949), the Agassiz (1955) and Carty (1963) medals of the National Academy of Sciences, the Vetlesen Prize (1960), the Gold Medal of the Royal Astronomical Society (1964), and other medals and awards.

In the late 1920s Ewing spent the summers employed by geophysical prospecting companies. During the early 1930s he engaged in academic research in geophysical exploration. After 1935 his interests extended to applications of all of the major methods of exploration to problems concerning the oceanic crust of the Earth and the transition from continental to oceanic crust at continental margins. This was an environment where little geophysical work had been attempted. Hence methods and instruments had to be devised as needed. Before the end of the decade Ewing had made remarkable progress in his study of the "Emerged and Submerged Atlantic Coastal Plain." The most valuable contribution of this study came from his newly developed seismic method of refraction shooting at sea. He also made gravity measurements with F. A. Vening Meinesz's pendulum method. This work resulted in a series of papers that revealed the great thickness of sedimentary rocks on and near the continental boundary and the great vertical movements that must have been associated with their deposition.

Ewing spent much of World War II working at the Woods Hole Oceanographic Institution on the propagation of sound in the sea and on photography of shipwrecks. Although these investigations were, to a large extent, for defense purposes, this work led to the SOFAR sound transmission system, a utilization of the sound channel in the ocean that formed the basis for subsequent extensive applications. This war work provided bases for Ewing's postwar work at Columbia University's Lamont Geological Observatory, an establishment that he was instrumental in forming and of which he became director at its founding in 1949. Small to begin with, Lamont Geological Observatory is now perhaps the most comprehensive geological and geophysical research unit in the world. The work at Lamont in its early days had three dominant aspects. First, there was the geophysical and geological work at sea: it was in 1949 that Ewing made the first determination of the crustal thickness of the ocean floor, and since that time the Lamont team has established the system of marine geophysical measurement that is used in many other laboratories. Second, there was the development of a powerful group of earthquake seismologists, theoretical and experimental, who built a seismological observatory on the grounds of Lamont and a world-wide network of similar seismograph stations. Third, an active program of radio and isotope geology was established for measuring the ages of marine samples. Ewing's main interest in the field of seismology was the study of surface waves as a method of gaining more information concerning the crustal and mantle rocks of the Earth, particularly the water-covered part. He identified the T-phase from earthquakes as sound waves propagated in the ocean water. His other interests included paleoclimatology, micropaleontology, and radiochemical age determinations.

In marine research, Ewing's name is particularly associated with turbidity currents, abyssal plains, mid-ocean ridges, and crustal thicknesses. This phase of his career began with cruises of the *Atlantis* to the Mid-Atlantic Ridge in 1947 and 1948, during which many of the instruments now widely used were devised. By means of seismic reflections, gravity measurements, photographs, long sediment cores, and dredge hauls from the bottom, Ewing and his fellow Columbia oceanographers showed the ocean floor to be as various a structure as the land surface, with rugged mountains, exposed basaltic rocks, flat-topped plateaus (guyots), pebble-strewn regions, and extremely flat plains; a deep gorge within the Mid-Atlantic Ridge was also found. In 1952 Ewing took sediment cores and soundings that showed that the Hudson Canyon had been carved out by turbulent underseas flows of mud and sediment, which was deposited further seaward to form the abyssal plain. In 1956 he showed that the Mid-Atlantic Ridge followed the known belt of seismic activity and continued around Africa into the Indian Ocean and around Antarctica into the Pacific, forming a world-girdling underseas mountain system. Later, from many crossings, he showed that there was a fault or chasm from 8 to 30 miles wide in the crest of the Mid-Atlantic Ridge, and interpreted this to be evidence that the process that formed the ridge and rift was still active.

Ewing's controversial theory of ice ages stimulated study in the field of paleoclimatology. Periodic ice ages had traditionally been thought to occur at times when, for some obscure reason, the Earth became cooler than normal. During the 1950s Ewing and his group found evidence in deep-sea sediments suggesting that ice ages result from changes in oceanic circulation. He offered the hypothesis that when the Arctic Ocean is free of ice cover it serves as a source of water vapor, which is deposited on Siberia and Canada as snow. As the snow accumulates, it forms a barrier that also increases precipitation from winds from the south. Temperatures drop, glaciers move down from the north, sea level falls, and eventually the Arctic Ocean freezes over. Once that happens, the source of snow is choked off, the glaciers retreat, and temperatures rise until, as now, the glaciers are mostly gone from the lowlands (though still lingering on Antarctica and Greenland) while the Arctic Ocean remains frozen over. If warming continues to the point where the Arctic ice melts, the Arctic Ocean will then contribute water vapor to the polar atmosphere and the cycle will begin again. Beginning in 1960 Ewing organized seven world-wide cruises of the research vessels *Vema* and *Robert D. Conrad* for the primary purpose of systematically mapping stratification and thickness of sediment cover in the world ocean, and sampling the oldest sediments available. An ingenious inventor of instruments, Ewing developed improved echo sounders, magnetometers, bathythermographs, sediment coring apparatus, sediment temperature probes, and an underwater camera that permitted oceanographers for the first time to see what life there was in the ocean depths. Because of the great pressures and the absence of light below a few thousand feet, oceanographers had thought that little marine life existed there. Ewing's photographs proved the presence of marine life, sometimes strikingly different from any known earlier, and gave valuable information about other surface features of the ocean floor, such as burrows, tracks and trails, outcrops, current ripples, and manganese nodules.

Research of this type requires the teamwork of many scientists, and all of these developments were characterized by collaboration with others, usually his former students.

Ewing received his B.A. (1926), M.A. (1927), and Ph.D. (1931) in physics at the Rice Institute in Houston. He was an instructor in physics at the University of Pittsburgh (1929–30) and an instructor and assistant professor of physics at Lehigh University (1930–40). In 1940 he was named associate professor of geology at Lehigh, but he spent much of the next four years on leave of absence at the Woods Hole Oceanographic Institution. In 1944 he was appointed associate professor of geology at Columbia University, becoming a full professor in 1947. In 1949 he was appointed director of Columbia's Lamont Geological Observatory, and in 1959 was named Higgins Professor of Geology. He was elected to the National Academy of Sciences in 1948.

Ewing wrote *Propagation of Sound in the Ocean*, with J. L. Worzel and C. Pekeris (1948), *Elastic Waves in Layered Media*, with Frank Press and W. Jardetsky (1957), and *The Floors of the Oceans: I. The North Atlantic*, with B. C. Heezen and M. Tharp (1959), and a large number of papers and chapters in books.

For background information *see* GEODESY; OCEANOGRAPHY; SEISMOLOGY in the McGraw-Hill Encyclopedia of Science and Technology.

□

★ EYRING, Henry

American chemist
Born Feb. 20, 1901, Colonia Juarez, Chih., Mexico

EYRING PIONEERED in the application of quantum and statistical mechanics to chemistry and developed the Theory of Absolute Reaction Rates and the Significant Structure Theory of Liquids. Absolute reaction rate theory provides a basis for treating all chemical reactions. The theory of liquids provides the basis of

a quantitative formulation of the thermodynamic properties of liquids and, together with rate theory, provides a similar basis for transport properties. Eyring also developed theories of optical activity, mass spectrography, the addition of dipoles and bond lengths in flexible high polymers, and bioluminescence. For his contributions to theoretical chemistry, Eyring was awarded the American Chemical Society's Gilbert Newton Lewis Medal in 1963.

Rate Theory. Quantum mechanics, by providing a theory for calculating the interactions between atoms and molecules, makes it possible to calculate the energy of any configuration of atoms. If this energy is plotted "vertically," and if appropriate interatomic distances are chosen in such a way as to specify the atomic configuration, the resulting multidimensional surface is called the potential surface in configuration space. The low regions of this surface correspond to compounds, and a reaction may be described as the passage of a point from one minimum through the saddle point into a neighboring valley. Fritz London, in 1928, called attention to the possibility of constructing such surfaces and gave approximate formulas for simple three- and four-atom systems.

In 1929 and 1930, Eyring and Michael Polanyi calculated the potential surface for three hydrogen atoms. Subsequently, Eyring with his collaborators extended the quantum-mechanical calculations to many atoms and constructed surfaces for a wide variety of molecular systems. In the meantime, E. P. Wigner and Pelzer, using the Eyring-Polanyi surface, calculated the rate of the reaction

$$H + H_2 \text{ (para)} \longrightarrow H_2 \text{ (ortho)} + H \quad (1)$$

In 1935 Eyring formulated the general rate expression. A system at the saddle point, the activated complex, is like any other molecule in all of its degrees of freedom except for the reaction coordinate, that is, the coordinate normal to the potential barrier. The activated complex is next assumed to be in equilibrium with the reactants. Using the theory of small vibrations to calculate the normal modes, it is possible to arrive at the explicit expression for the specific rate of reaction

$$k' = \varkappa \, \frac{kT}{h} \, e^{-\Delta G^{\ddagger}/RT} \quad (2)$$

Here $\Delta G^{\ddagger}$ is the work required to assemble the activated complex from the reactants. The transmission coefficient $\varkappa$ is ordinarily near unity and is the factor that corrects for quantum mechanical effects and any departure from equilibrium. The symbols k, R, h, and T are the Boltzmann constant, gas constant, Planck's constant, and absolute temperature, respectively.

Theory of Liquids. To remove a molecule from a condensed phase to the vapor state involves breaking all the bonds holding the molecule, whereas to vaporize a molecule only involves breaking half the bonds. It follows that the creation of a vacancy costs the same energy as the vaporization of a molecule. If an isolated vacancy is formed in a solid it is locked in and provides only a positional degeneracy. At the melting point enough vacancies go into a liquid, acting cooperatively, to mobilize the vacancies, giving them gaslike properties.

The result is that the liquid contains a mixture of gaslike and solidlike degrees of freedom. This model leads to an expression for the Helmholtz free energy of the liquid in agreement with experiment. For simple liquids all parameters are calculable from the models. For complicated liquids the appropriate model may be selected by comparing calculated and observed thermodynamic properties much as structure can be determined in x-ray analysis.

Absolute rate theory has been applied successfully to all types of problems. Current developments are concerned with explicit calculations of the transmission coefficient $\varkappa$. Liquid theory, although newer, is also widely applicable and has already had many successes in calculating the properties of ordinary liquids, molten metals, molten salts, and water.

Born in northern Mexico, Eyring rode the range with his father until the Mexican revolution forced the American colonists to leave Mexico in 1912. After a year in El Paso the family moved to Arizona. Eyring attended the University of Arizona, where he obtained a B.S. in mining engineering (1923) and an M.S. in metallurgy (1924). He obtained his Ph.D. in chemistry at the University of California, Berkeley, in 1927; taught two years at the University of Wisconsin, where he collaborated with Farrington Daniels; spent a year at Fritz Haber's laboratory in Berlin working with Polanyi; returned to Berkeley for a year as lecturer; and for fifteen years (1931–46) was on the faculty of Princeton University. In 1946 he became dean of the Graduate School and professor of chemistry and metallurgy at the University of Utah. He was elected to the National Academy of Sciences in 1945.

Eyring published over 375 scientific papers and coauthored five books: *The Theory of Rate Processes* (1941), *Quantum Chemistry* (1944), *The Kinetic Basis of Molecular Biology* (1954), *Modern Chemical Kinetics* (1963), and *Statistical Mechanics and Dynamics* (1964).

For background information *see* QUANTUM MECHANICS in the McGraw-Hill Encyclopedia of Science and Technology.   □

F-G

★ **FELLER, William**

American mathematician
Born July 7, 1906, Zagreb, Yugoslavia

Aₗₜₕₒᵤgₕ ʜᴇ worked in several fields, Feller became best known for his contributions to probability theory starting in 1934. At that time it was not clear whether probability was a mathematical discipline or merely a source of inspiration and problems. Feller tried to develop an appropriate analytical framework for probability and at the same time to build probabilistic models for biological, physical, and statistical phenomena. He showed that the traditional method of considering only expectations (averages) could obscure the dominant effect of chance fluctuations. Widely accepted views concerning the operation of "laws of large numbers" were shown to be without rational foundation. For example, a "fair game" can be grossly unfair in the sense that the accumulated gain may tend (in probability) to infinity. Similarly, it is a myth that prolonged observations on one specimen reflect the typical averages in a large population. Indeed, an individual coin is likely to be "maladjusted" in the sense that for long periods the accumulated number of heads will remain either excessively large or excessively small. The nature of chance fluctuations, Feller concluded, did not agree with preconceived notions, and their analysis required a new framework.

Feller's main work may be summarized under three headings:

Limit Theorems. Feller widened the scope of limit theorems describing chance fluctuations, and clarified the role of infinite expectations. Outstanding was his discovery of the true form of the so-called law of the iterated logarithm, but his early work on the central limit theorem had a greater effect. In modern language this theorem refers to sums $S_n = X_1 + \dots + X_n$ of many independent random variables ("observations"). Viewed on an appropriate scale, such sums are likely to be subject to a normal distribution. This is the law of errors discovered by Abraham Demoivre and Laplace, and elaborated by K. F. Gauss and many later mathematicians. To obtain an appropriate scale these authors considered the reduced variable $(S_n - a_n)/b_n$, where a_n denotes the expectation and b_n^2 the variance of S_n. Feller showed that the problem must be modified by permitting arbitrary scale parameters a_n and b_n and found the most general conditions for the normal limit. The possibility of a purely analytic approach attracted wide attention. Indeed, from a modern point of view a result published simultaneously by P. Lévy is trivially equivalent to one of Feller's theorems, but Lévy's probabilistic conditions were then believed not expressible in analytic terms.

Markov Processes. The probabilistic counterpart to classical mechanics treats chance-dependent processes in which the past history bears no influence on the future development. Basic equations for such processes were derived by A. N. Kolmogorov in 1931, but it was not clear whether they were compatible or whether there existed solutions satisfying the starting conditions. In 1936 Feller found an affirmative answer based on an improved version of the basic model (eliminating the assumption of finite expectations). The highly disturbing discovery of the basic nonuniqueness of solutions led to further research resulting ultimately in a theory of boundaries. Feller introduced the notion of adjoint semigroups and used it for a general theory of Markov processes. He elucidated the nature of various operators associated with such processes and developed a theory of lateral conditions with ramifications outside probability theory. These studies led to a generalized form for differential operators that has many applications. Feller also promoted the use of Markov processes in other fields.

Methodology. Much of Feller's energy was spent on improving and unifying methods. He showed the power of the renewal method and introduced the notion of recurrent events. These endeavors culminated in his book *An Introduction to Probability Theory and Its Applications*, vol. 1 (1950; 2d ed. 1957), which introduced a new style and attitude. Older texts centered on games of chance and combinatorics; the only applications of Markov chains in the mathematical literature were to card shuffling and literary word counts. By contrast, Feller's book contained a huge collection of examples and problems explaining new applications of probability theory. To illustrate probabilistic thinking without the burden of extraneous analytical tools, the first volume was limited to discrete sample spaces. Because of this device the book was accessible to nonspecialists and it became instrumental in establishing probability in college curricula and in several fields of applications. Even specialists had not been aware that so elementary a framework could contain rich material, and the book contributed to the present resurrection of combinatorial methods. The popularity of the book was probably due to the fact that it did not aim at a particular market or audience, but was written for an intelligent uninitiated reader. The second volume was to appear in 1966.

Feller received his M.S. from the University of Zagreb in 1925 and his Ph.D. from Göttingen in 1926. He served at the universities of Göttingen and Kiel (1926–33) and then in Stockholm as consultant to statisticians, biologists, and economists. He went to the United States in 1939 as executive editor of the newly founded *Mathematical Reviews*. From 1945 to 1950 he served as professor of mathematics at Cornell University and then as Eugene Higgins Professor of Mathematics at Princeton University. He was elected to the National Academy of Sciences in 1960.

For background information *see* PROBABILITY in the McGraw-Hill Encyclopedia of Science and Technology.   ☐

FERMI, Enrico
American physicist
Born Sept. 29, 1901, Rome, Italy
Died Nov. 28, 1954, Chicago, Ill., U.S.A.

WHEN FERMI found that neutrons shot into the nucleus of an atom could induce artificial radioactivity, he began a systematic study of the effect of neutron bombardment on each of the elements. His success in producing artificial radioactivity and in analyzing the decay products won for him the 1938 Nobel Prize in physics.

The alpha particle had previously been established as an agent that could induce nuclear transformations. In 1919 Ernest Rutherford had shot an alpha particle directly into a nitrogen nucleus, thus causing the emission of a proton that left behind a stable oxygen isotope. In a similar experiment in 1934 Frédéric and Irène Joliot-Curie shot an alpha particle into an aluminum nucleus, causing the emission of a proton that left behind a phosphorus isotope. Although phosphorus is normally a stable element, the isotope thus produced was radioactive.

When Fermi learned that radioactivity in the light element aluminum could be induced by alpha-particle bombardment, he considered the possibility of inducing artificial radioactivity in the heavier elements. He recognized that the chief obstacle was the fact that the heavier the nucleus the larger its positive charge, and the larger its positive charge the stronger it repels the positively charged alpha particle. As an alternative projectile Fermi thought of the neutron, a particle discovered by James Chadwick only two years before. Since the neutron bore no charge at all, the positive charge of even the heaviest nucleus would provide no protection from such a projectile. With a number of collaborators Fermi set out to test the effect of neutron bombardment on all the elements he could obtain. Within a few months he found that among the 63 elements he had been able to investigate there were 37 that showed easily detectable artificial radioactivity.

Many of these new radioactive elements decayed by emitting beta particles, with the result that the daughter element lay nearer the end of the periodic table than the parent element. This fact led Fermi to bombard uranium, the last element then listed on the periodic table, in the hope of producing a transuranium element. In June 1934 he described the result of this experiment as a "rather complex phenomenon" since the decay curves showed three well-defined half-lives and at least two others. (This complexity arose because he had produced not only the desired transuranium element but also the first atomic fission, a process that was not identified until five years later.) By the following month Fermi and his colleagues had found that if neutrons were first slowed down by collisions with the protons of paraffin, water, or some other hydrogen-rich material, these neutrons might be as much as 100 times more effective in producing radioactivity than a fast neutron. The 1938 Nobel Prize committee cited Fermi "for his discovery of new radioactive elements produced by neutron irradiation, and for the discovery of nuclear reactions brought about by slow neutrons."

Fermi had made his first major contribution to physics in 1926, almost a decade before he began his work with neutrons. S. N. Bose and Albert Einstein, in applying statistical mechanics to a "gas" of photons, had succeeded in deriving Planck's black-body radiation equation by assuming that the individual members of certain sets of photons were indistinguishable. However, photons could pass through one another and in this sense occupy the same space at the same time. The possible locations of electrons are severely restricted, the limitations being set forth in the exclusion principle of Wolfgang Pauli. Fermi recognized the implications of this principle and proposed an alternative statistical mechanics to account for the behavior of a "gas" of electrons. (P. A. M. Dirac independently derived the same theory, which is now called Fermi-Dirac statistical mechanics.) All indistinguishable particles (photons, electrons, neutrons, and others) obey either Bose-Einstein or Fermi-Dirac statistical mechanics.

Fermi's second major contribution was made in 1933, when he solved the beta-decay problem. If an element undergoes alpha decay, all the alpha particles are emitted with the same energy; if an element undergoes beta decay, the beta particles emitted exhibit energies that vary from zero up to a maximum value characteristic of the element. Pauli suggested that this apparent violation of the principles of conservation of energy and conservation of momentum could be explained by assuming that there was emitted with the electron another, up to that time undetected, particle whose properties were exactly those needed to preserve those principles. On the basis of this suggestion Fermi constructed a beta-decay theory analogous to photon-emission theory. He said that just as an atom changes from a high-energy state to a low-energy state by emitting a photon, so a neutron (the high-energy state) changes to a proton (the low-energy state) by emitting both an electron (which is the beta particle) and a neutrino (which is needed to preserve the energy and momentum).

Another major contribution, following his investigations of neutron bombardment, was his work on the design and construction of the first nuclear reactor. Fermi saw in the discovery of nuclear fission, announced in 1939, an important possibility. Since the uranium nucleus is characterized by a neutron-to-proton ratio of about 2.6 while the fission products have a ratio of about 2.5, each fission must produce, in addition to the energy released, a number of free neutrons. If a condition could be achieved in which more than one of the new neutrons struck another uranium nucleus and induced fission, then a chain of reactions would result and a continuous flow of energy would be obtained. To achieve this condition Fermi helped design and construct the first nuclear reactor, a lattice of graphite and uranium built in a squash court under the stands of the unused University of Chicago stadium. A plaque placed near this point reads: "On December 2, 1942, man achieved here the first self-sustaining chain reaction and thereby initiated the controlled release of nuclear energy." This event marked the beginning of the atomic era.

Fermi was awarded a doctor's degree in physics at the University of Pisa in 1922, after which he studied with Max Born at Göttingen and with Ehrenfest at Leiden. While a lecturer at the University of Florence, he published the theoretical papers that first demonstrated his abilities. At the age of 25 he won a position as professor of physics at the University of Rome, where his experimental work was begun (1926–38). In 1930, when he taught in the summer session of the University of Michigan, he began a series of visits to the United States, and after receiving the Nobel Prize he made his home in the United States, becoming an American citizen in 1944. He worked successively at Columbia University, where he began the design of the nuclear reactor; at the University of Chicago, where he completed the construction of this reactor; and at Los Alamos, where he contributed to the design of the first atomic bomb. In 1946 he returned to the University of Chicago as a member of an institute that, in 1955, the year after his death, was renamed the Enrico Fermi Institute for Nuclear Studies. A new element artificially produced that same year, of atomic number 100, was named fermium in his honor.

Fermi wrote *Thermodynamics* (1937), *Nuclear Theory* (rev. ed. 1950), and *Elementary Particles* (1951). A set of lecture outlines in his own handwriting has been reproduced as *Notes on Quantum Mechanics* (1961). Publication of his *Collected Papers* is planned.

For background information *see* Atomic bomb; Fermi-Dirac statistics; Neutrino; Neutron in the McGraw-Hill Encyclopedia of Science and Technology.   □

FEYNMAN, Richard Phillips
American physicist
Born May 11, 1918, New York, N.Y., U.S.A.

I N 1948, Feynman introduced a theory designed to remove certain difficulties that had arisen in the study of the interaction among electrons, positrons, and radiation. This hypothesis proved to be a turning point in the development of modern quantum electrodynamics. For his achievement, Feynman was awarded the 1965 Nobel prize in physics, which he shared with the American physicist Julian S. Schwinger and the Japanese physicist Sin-itiro Tomonaga, both of whom had independently developed theories similar to Feynman's.

Quantum electrodynamics emerged in the late

1920s, in large part out of the fundamental work of the physicists P. A. M. Dirac, Werner Heisenberg, Wolfgang Pauli, and Enrico Fermi. The initial version of the theory was based on the direct application of quantum mechanics to classical electrodynamic theory. It described the interaction of radiation, positrons, and electrons and appeared to give an accurate picture of the processes involved. Problems of a quantitative nature, however, quickly developed. Moreover, measurements of the fine structure of the hydrogen spectrum, obtained shortly after World War II by W. E. Lamb, Jr., and R. E. Retherford, demonstrated clearly that the observed energy levels of the hydrogen atom were not those predicted by the theory of Dirac and others. For these reasons many physicists during the 1930s and 1940s sought a solution to the dilemma in radical departures from the original theory, convinced that the latter must be either fundamentally altered or dispensed with entirely.

During the early and middle 1940s, Feynman worked on this problem at Princeton University. Among the difficulties of the original theory had been the occurrence of "divergent integrals": When measurements involving these terms were pressed beyond first-degree accuracy, infinite and/or meaningless answers resulted. The result of Feynman's mathematical approach was to show that the perplexing infinite terms could be put into a form that would be invariant under the Lorentz transformations. Feynman was able to demonstrate the feasibility of a program of "renormalization" of the electron mass and charge, aimed at eliminating the infinite terms from all actual calculations. In this process the formerly used values were replaced with new ones that would always have immediate significance in measurements of electron charge and mass. These new values made the measurement of electron properties completely finite and unambiguous. Feynman's approach, while not removing the "divergence difficulties," in fact eliminated them from any possible calculation of observable quantities. Part of the value of the new hypothesis was that it did not require the physical basis of the original electrodynamic theory to be abandoned.

An indirect product of Feynman's work on this problem was the "Feynman diagram," a graphical representation of the progress of an electrodynamic interaction that showed intermediate states as well as initial and final ones. This device considerably simplified the analysis of quantum-electrodynamic problems.

Feynman and Schwinger, who had worked independently of one another, announced their results at about the same time. Tomonaga's work, much of which had been completed by 1943, also began to be known in the United States in English translation around 1948. All three had arrived at the same conclusions via different mathematical routes. Their results were immediately subjected to experimental testing, all of which tended to substantiate their claims to provide accurate and unambiguous quantitative calculations.

Acceptance of the Feynman-Schwinger-Tomonaga theory led to a reconstruction of the fundamentals of quantum electrodynamics, which was accompanied by a great advance in the accuracy with which the behavior of the electron could be computed. In one experiment a value was obtained for the magnetic moment of the electron accurate to within one part in 10 million.

Besides his work in quantum electrodynamics, Feynman provided the atomic basis of the theory of liquid helium II that had been developed by the Russian physicist L. D. Landau. Feynman was also jointly responsible, with the American physicist Murray Gell-Mann, for an important and influential theory of β-decay.

Feynman received his B.S. at the Massachusetts Institute of Technology in 1939 and his Ph.D. at Princeton University in 1942. During World War II he worked at Los Alamos on the atomic bomb, returning to academic life in 1945 as an associate professor of theoretical physics at Cornell University. In 1950 he became professor of theoretical physics at the California Institute of Technology. In addition to the Nobel Prize, Feynman in 1954 received the Albert Einstein Award. He was elected to the National Academy of Sciences in 1954.

Feynman wrote *Quantum Electrodynamics* (1961), *Theory of Fundamental Processes* (1961), *Feynman Lectures on Physics* (3 vols., 1963–64), and *Quantum Mechanics and Path Integrals*, with A. R. Hibbs (1966).

For background information *see* QUANTUM ELECTRODYNAMICS; QUANTUM FIELD THEORY; QUANTUM THEORY, RELATIVISTIC; SCATTERING MATRIX in the McGraw-Hill Encyclopedia of Science and Technology.   □

FISHER, Sir Ronald (Aylmer)

English geneticist and statistician
Born Feb. 17, 1890, East Finchley, Middlesex,
England
Died July 29, 1962, Adelaide, Australia

FROM HIS early studies in genetics and evolution Fisher was awakened to the need for precise statistical methods to interpret quantitative data. For his contributions to the theory and application of statistics for making quantitative a vast field of biology, he was awarded the Royal Society's Copley Medal in 1955.

Karl Pearson established the first body of knowledge that could be called statistics and founded the first statistical journal, *Biometrika*. His outstanding achievement was the χ^2 test (chi-square test) in which χ^2 represented the probability of any sample value being obtained from a population with a known mean and variance (distribution about the mean). For a particular sample, χ^2 was found by the formula:

$$\chi^2 = \sum \frac{(O - E)^2}{E}$$

where E is the expected class frequency and O the observed frequency. The corresponding probability was then found in a table of χ^2 values. For example, a low probability could be used as evidence that an experimental treatment was associated with samples differing from the parent population. The test was accurate if large samples were used.

As a rule, limitations of time and funds restricted researchers to small samples in the testing of biological material. The inherent variability of the material thus introduced great uncertainty into their results. Fisher saw that if only the feature of randomization were incorporated into experimental designs, then statistical machinery could provide the needed quantitative

assessments of accuracy. Nonrandom, or systematic, design consisted of distributing individuals receiving different treatments over an experimental area according to a preconceived plan. For example, for three treatments (A,B,C,), a common design was that shown in

A	B	C	A	B	C	A	B	C

the diagram. Though such a design sought to eliminate environmental inhomogeneity, a gradient of environmental condition that existed, let us say, from left to right, would affect treatment A to a greater extent than the others. In agricultural field experiments it had been found that gradients of soil conditions were of universal occurrence and existed over very short distances. Systematic designs were powerless to overcome or measure their effects. Fisher showed that if treatment positions were assigned randomly, the laws of chance would allow statistics to provide unbiased quantitative estimates of the error due both to environmental conditions and to the variability of the material being tested. In addition, a probability statement, in the form of a percentage figure, could be attached to the error estimate. For example, a statement that an error is at the 5% level of significance would mean that the results could be trusted to include the true figure 95 out of 100 times.

One of the most generally applicable of the procedures Fisher supplied for the testing of variance of small samples from a population is the F ratio. This method was found to be important because it utilized the entire population of the experiment. Fisher's analyses first determined the pooled variance (S_p^2) obtained from the entire population. Second, an estimate of the variance of the means for each category of the population (S_M^2) was computed. These two quantities may be tested to see if there is a significant difference between them by forming the F ratio, S_p^2/S_M^2. The hypothesis of equal means is rejected if the F ratio obtained exceeds the critical value of the F table.

Among Fisher's other outstanding contributions to mathematical statistics were his solution for the exact distribution of the correlation coefficient (r), the concepts of consistent, efficient, and sufficient statistics, and the maximum likelihood solution, which was a formula for finding these statistics. Fisher's theoretical work on inductive inference from statistical data and his efforts to popularize the work of others as well as his own laid the foundation for future advances in the realm of statistics.

The other major phase of Fisher's work was in genetics. An important achievement was his demonstration of Mendelian inheritance in certain examples of continuous inheritance that were thought to be non-Mendelian in nature, such as those in human relatives. Also notable is his theory of the evolution of dominance, which has become a cornerstone of the theory that selection and not mutation is the directing force in evolution. It had occurred to Fisher that, if all known mutations were recessive, then selection for advantageous mutations could not be the mechanism of evolution. Mutations were rare events. If they were recessive they would most certainly be eliminated from the population before they had a chance to attain the homozygous state and express themselves phenotypically. Fisher was struck by the claim that crosses between fancy breeds of domestic poultry had shown the mutant and not the wild type to be dominant in a number of cases. He hypothesized that, over the centuries, human selection had resulted in the evolution of dominance. He assumed that mutations had occurred, not wholly recessive, which were deemed desirable by the breeders as curious novelties. These heterozygotes would be selected and bred in favor of the others. In future generations selection would always favor the mutants that showed the greatest amount of influence over the dominant, and the recessive would evolve into a strong but incomplete dominant (that is, its homozygous effect would be distinguishable from its heterozygous effect).

Fisher then proposed that if he were to interbreed the domestic poultry with wild jungle fowl, the mutations would show the history of their development and would be neither recessive nor dominant, but intermediate or semidominant. Fisher believed that crossing the mutants to other domestic breeds would give inconclusive results because they very likely possessed other mutations for the gene in question or for related genes. The recessive was held to have developed its dominance over the dominant gene of the wild ancestors that came out of the forest to cover the domestic hens.

Choosing a single stock for each of seven mutations, Fisher crossed each with wild fowl, backcrossing and inbreeding alternate generations in order to have the mutation contrasted against a great amount of wild germ plasm. After the fifth generation the heterozygotes were interbred in order to obtain homozygotes. With the possible exception of rose comb, none of the factors showed complete dominance. Fisher considered his results good evidence that the raw materials of progressive evolutionary adaptation were recessive mutations that, at first not wholly recessive, were selected for their minute advantages. Once established, selection favored those recessives that showed themselves to be increasingly less recessive or more dominant. This afforded an explanation as to why advantageous genes were dominants. Likewise, harmful mutations, at first not wholly recessive, would be

selected against and would evolve toward a complete recessive condition.

Fisher also played a major part in the genetical clarification of the rhesus system in human blood, which is responsible for erythroblastosis fetalis.

Fisher attended Gonville and Caius College, Cambridge. From 1913 to 1915 he worked as a statistician for the Mercantile and General Investment Company, and from 1915 to 1919 he taught in the public schools. In 1919 he was chosen to work in the statistical department at Rothamsted Experimental Station, Harpenden. He left in 1933 to become Galton Professor of Eugenics at University College, London, leaving only upon his election to the Arthur Balfour Chair of Genetics at Cambridge University. In 1957 he retired, though he remained at Cambridge until his successor was appointed in 1959. For the last years of his life Fisher worked as a researcher for the Commonwealth Scientific and Industrial Research Organization (CSIRO) in Adelaide, Australia. Fisher became a fellow of the Royal Society in 1929. He was knighted in 1952.

Fisher wrote *Statistical Methods for Research Workers* (1925; 13th ed. 1958); *The Genetical Theory of Natural Selection* (1938; 2d ed. 1958); *The Design of Experiments* (1935; 7th ed. 1960); and *Statistical Tables for Biological, Agricultural, and Medical Research*, with F. Yates (1938; 6th ed. 1963).

For background information *see* GENE ACTION; GENETICS; MUTATION; STATISTICS in the McGraw-Hill Encyclopedia of Science and Technology.   □

FLEMING, Sir Alexander
Scottish bacteriologist
Born Aug. 6, 1881, Lochfield, Ayrshire, Scotland
Died Mar. 11, 1955, London, England

IN 1928, while experimenting with bacteria of the staphylococcus group, Fleming noticed on a culture plate, which had been contaminated by mold, a clear, bacteria-free ring around the mold growth. Further experimentation showed that a substance in the mold culture itself prevented the growth of the bacteria. Since the mold organism was of the *Penicillium* group, Fleming named the antibacterial substance it contained "penicillin." For this discovery he received, together with Sir Howard Walter Florey and Ernst Boris Chain, the 1945 Nobel Prize in physiology or medicine.

The observation that one species of microorganism is capable of producing substances that destroy another was first made in 1877 by Louis

Pasteur and Jules François Joubert. They noted that when a culture of anthrax bacilli was exposed to bacteria from the air, the former were destroyed. Although Pasteur realized the significance of this phenomenon in relation to the treatment of infectious diseases, and certain later investigators made similar observations on the antagonistic or inhibitory properties of bacteria, Fleming's work on penicillin marked the beginning of the practical application of these observations.

Fleming himself claimed that although he was well aware of the phenomenon of bacterial antagonisms, and had even discovered another antibacterial substance—lysozome—before penicillin, his discovery of penicillin began as a chance observation. The culture techniques used in his work with lysozome (an antibacterial substance in human tears and saliva), however, were applicable to his later penicillin experimentation.

The age of antibiotics began, in effect, when a culture of staphylococci was accidentally contaminated by exposure to mold organisms in the air. As the mold organisms grew on the culture plate, around each mold colony a translucent area developed, indicating that the staphylococci were being lysed, or destroyed. Because the bacteria undergoing lysis were of a type infectious to man, Fleming decided to pursue this chance occurrence. He isolated the mold organism in pure culture and identified it as *Penicillium notatum*, a mold originally isolated from rotting hyssop (an aromatic plant native to Europe). The pure culture was grown on another plate at room temperature and, after four or five days, was streaked radially with several infectious bacterial cultures. Some of the bacteria grew up to the mold, but others were inhibited from growing in a region several centimeters from the mold colony. Thus the antibacterial substance in the mold destroyed some bacteria but not others. Fleming made compara-

tive studies with mold cultures other than *Penicillium*, but the same bacterial destruction did not occur. *Penicillium notatum* was exceptional.

Next, the *Penicillium* was grown in a fluid medium and the fluid was tested to see whether the antibacterial substance occurred in it. It did, and when a variety of pathogenic bacteria were streaked on an agar culture plate containing a trough of the mold fluid, their growth was strongly inhibited. By noting which bacteria were sensitive to the mold fluid (actually crude penicillin), it became possible to isolate organisms such as the whooping cough and influenza bacteria, which normally occur in the human respiratory tract and are insensitive to penicillin.

Further experiments elucidated more fully the remarkable properties of penicillin. It not only inhibited the growth of human pathogens, it actually destroyed a number of them. When diluted 1,000 times, the culture fluid still retained its antibacterial properties. Unlike earlier antiseptic agents (phenol, for example) with which Fleming had worked, penicillin exerted its inhibitory effect on bacteria without destroying human white blood cells (leucocytes, which are the body's natural defense against pathogenic organisms). Carrying this latter observation further, Fleming injected penicillin into animals and found it to be nontoxic. Although realizing that penicillin had decided therapeutic potential, Fleming was unable to pursue such investigations because of the essentially unstable nature of the substance, which prevented accumulation of an amount sufficient for extensive testing. He also realized that before such work could be undertaken the active antibiotic substance would have to be concentrated and some of the crude culture fluid removed.

Fleming published the results of his penicillin experiments in 1929 and at that time suggested its possible therapeutic applications. His suggestion was largely neglected until about 1939, when the introduction of sulfonamide alerted the medical world to the promise of chemotherapy. Obtaining a sample of Fleming's culture strain of *Penicillium notatum*, Florey and Chain succeeded in concentrating and purifying the active substance, penicillin, and instituted clinical trials that eventually demonstrated its phenomenal antibiotic effect in man.

Sir Alexander Fleming was educated in Scotland and London, qualifying with distinction in 1906 for his medical degree from St. Mary's Medical School, London. He lectured there until 1914, served in the Army Medical Corps during World War I, and returned to St. Mary's in 1918. In 1928 he was elected professor of the School and in 1948 emeritus professor of bacteriology, University of London. In 1943 Fleming was elected a Fellow of the Royal Society; he was knighted in 1944.

For background information *see* ANTIBIOTIC; PENICILLIN in the McGraw-Hill Encyclopedia of Science and Technology.   □

☆ FLOREY OF ADELAIDE, Baron (Howard Walter Florey)

Australian pathologist
Born Sept. 24, 1898, Adelaide, Australia

WHILE WORKING on the properties of antibacterial substances, Florey and his collaborators at Oxford succeeded in extracting and purifying penicillin, an antibacterial of mold origin that had been discovered by Alexander Fleming in 1928. They demonstrated its protective and curative effects in animals, and Florey conducted the first trials in which penicillin was used to treat human infectious disease. For their contributions, Florey and his collaborator Ernst Chain shared, with Fleming, the 1945 Nobel Prize in physiology or medicine.

It might reasonably be thought that advances in medicine would depend on the study of sick people, but this is not necessarily so. The investigation of an invalid at the bedside and in the laboratory may tell us much about his disease and the way it affects him, but it often fails to show what went wrong in the first place so that illness resulted, or why that person was attacked. A different approach is to study the normal body functions and, building on this, to study how such functions may become deranged.

Florey believed that this was a useful, and might be a very profitable, way of investigating disease. When he was first appointed to a chair of pathology, all his research experience had been as a physiologist, and this became the basis for his new work. For example, his interest in the small blood and lymph vessels led naturally to a study of the part played by these structures in inflammation and to other aspects of the inflammatory reaction. He was interested also in the secretions of mucous membranes, and he investigated their role in protecting the stomach and duodenum from ulceration and in helping to prevent bacterial invasion of the respiratory and gastrointestinal tracts. Thus, his attention was drawn to a substance, lysozyme, which was known to be present in human saliva and other bodily secretions and which could dissolve certain bacteria. Following this up with his colleagues, he found that for centuries natural substances had been described as acting against harmful bacteria. These included extracts of plants—of the wallflower, for example—and products of fungi and of bacteria themselves. Working with Chain, Florey chose, in 1939, three such products for investigation; one of them was penicillin, the product of a green mold, or fungus.

The name penicillin had been given by Fleming to a crude broth on which the fungus *Penicillium notatum* had grown. Under Florey, the group of workers at Oxford soon made the first steps toward concentrating and purifying the active substance in the mold broth. Although their first products were crude, they were sufficiently concentrated to make possible certain crucial tests in mice and other laboratory animals. These tests showed that penicillin injected into the body could save the life of an animal that had been given a fatal dose of bacteria some hours before—and without doing the animal any harm. In other words, penicillin had a marked "differential toxicity"; when administered in concentrations that were harmless to the body tissues, penicillin was still capable of destroying harmful bacteria.

With great labor enough penicillin was made in the laboratory to treat a few patients—those with serious infections who had not responded to other treatments. It became clear that in man, as in animals, penicillin could save lives and eliminate certain virulent bacteria from the body. Subsequently, with his colleagues, Florey investigated numerous other antibiotics, contributing substantially to knowledge of these substances and their modes of action.

With the advent of antibiotics, many serious bacterial diseases came under control and Florey turned his attention to another common disease, atherosclerosis, a disease of the blood vessels that gives rise to coronary thrombosis and cerebral "stroke." Since the cause of atherosclerosis was—and still is—obscure, Florey began by studying normal blood vessels, choosing those aspects of their form and function that might throw light on the origins of the disease. Among other contributions, Florey and his colleagues discovered that the domestic pig develops atherosclerosis similar to that of man, thus offering scope for the experimental investigation of the human disease.

Florey qualified in medicine at Adelaide University in 1921. He then went to Oxford as a Rhodes Scholar, where he took a first class degree in physiology in 1924 and began research under Sir Charles Sherrington. He took his Ph.D. at Cambridge in 1927, having studied in the United States on a Rockefeller traveling fellowship during 1925–26. He was appointed professor of pathology at Sheffield in 1931 and at Oxford in 1935. On retiring from his chair in 1962 he became provost of the Queen's College, Oxford. Florey served on the Medical Research Council and other official bodies. He became a fellow of the Royal Society in 1941 and president in 1960. In 1963 he was elected a foreign associate of the U.S. National Academy of Sciences. For his services to medicine he was knighted in 1944 and received a life peerage and the Order of Merit in 1965.

For background information *see* PENICILLIN in the McGraw-Hill Encyclopedia of Science and Technology.   □

★ FOLKERS, Karl August

American chemist
Born Sept. 1, 1906, Decatur, Ill., U.S.A.

FOLKERS'S PRINCIPAL contributions to chemical research were in the field of therapeutic agents, particularly vitamins and antibiotics.

At the research laboratories of Merck and Company, Inc., beginning in 1934, Folkers concentrated on the chemistry of morphine alkaloids, *Erythrina* alkaloids, curare, vitamin B_6, pantothenic acid, biotin, penicillin, streptomycin, vitamin B_{12}, and corticotropin B. Later he studied inhibitors of virus multiplication and participated in the discovery of mevalonic acid, the isolation and structural determination of novobiocin, and the structural determination and synthesis of members of the coenzyme Q group. His research on coenzyme Q was extended to biological studies on sperm motility,

animal nutrition, and an exploration of coenzyme Q in human medicine.

Folkers's studies on the substance that later became known as vitamin B_{12} were begun in 1938. Ten years later he and his research group at the Merck Sharp and Dohme Research Laboratories isolated a red crystalline compound—vitamin B_{12}—that proved to be active in the treatment of patients with pernicious anemia.

In the field of antibiotics, Folkers's research group published nearly 50 papers on the isolation, synthesis, and structural elucidation of antibiotics in the streptomycin series, and on penicillin, neomycin, subtilin, grisein, oxamycin, and novobiocin.

Folkers pioneered in the study of the *Erythrina* alkaloid family. He and his coworkers published many papers on the isolation and characterization of such members of this family as erythroidine, erythramine, erythraline, erythratine, erysodine, erysopine, erysovine, and erysonine.

The discovery of mevalonic acid by Folkers and his coworkers was of major scientific importance. This compound was recognized as a key and fundamental substance in the biosynthesis of a wide range of very important natural products, including steroids, carotenoids, and terpenes.

Folkers received a B.S. in chemistry from the University of Illinois in 1928 and a Ph.D. in organic chemistry, under Homer Adkins, at the University of Wisconsin in 1931. His research concerned the reactions of aldehydes and of esters over oxide catalysts, and later the catalytic hydrogenation of esters to alcohols under elevated temperatures and pressures. From 1931 to 1934 he was a postdoctorate research fellow in organic chemistry with Treat B. Johnson at Yale University. His research at Yale was on the synthesis, mechanism of formation, and reactions of certain pyrimidine derivatives.

In 1934 Folkers joined the Laboratory of Pure Research of Merck and Company, Inc., Rahway, N.J. He became assistant director of research in 1938, director of the organic and biochemical research department in 1945, associate director of the research and development division in 1951, director of organic and biological chemical research in 1953, executive director of fundamental research in 1956, and vice-president for exploratory research in 1962. In 1963 he became president of the Stanford Research Institute, Menlo Park, Calif. Also in 1963 he received courtesy appointments as professor of chemistry at Stanford University and lecturer in vitamin chemistry at the University of California, Berkeley. Among his numerous honors was the 1960 Perkin Medal of the Society of Chemical Industry. He was elected to the National Academy of Sciences in 1948.

Folkers and Arthur F. Wagner wrote *Vitamins and Coenzymes* (1964).

For background information *see* ANTIBIOTIC; COENZYME; VITAMIN in the McGraw-Hill Encyclopedia of Science and Technology.   □

★ **FORD, Edmund Brisco**
British geneticist
Born Apr. 23, 1901, Papcastle, Cumberland, England

FOR HIS contributions to the genetical theory of evolution by natural selection, particularly in natural populations, Ford received in 1954 the Darwin Medal of the Royal Society of London.

From 1923 to 1926 Ford collaborated with Julian Huxley in work on *Gammarus chevreuxi* (Amphipoda), a brackish-water crustacean. They were the first to show that genes control the time of onset and rate of development of processes in the body. That concept, foreshadowed by R. Goldschmidt, is an important one in evolution and physiology.

In 1923 Ford also began collaborating with R. A. Fisher, who in 1927 envisaged the selective modification of the effects of genes in natural conditions. This was followed by the publication of Fisher's *Theory of Dominance* (1928). In view of these developments, Ford expanded the experimental study of adaptation and evolution in wild populations that he had already begun. He did so by identifying certain conditions in which these processes occur rapidly and subjecting them to combined ecological investigations in the field, including the quantitative analysis of populations, and genetic experiments in the laboratory. This technique he named ecological genetics. In 1928 he planned a book on this subject, to be written after about 25 years of research. The work, in fact, took over 30 years, and the volume thus contemplated, *Ecological Genetics*, was published in 1964.

Meanwhile, in 1930, Ford suggested the marking, release, and recapture of specimens as a means of estimating the numbers of animals in wild populations. This proposal, and the paper by F. C. Lincoln initiating that technique, were in press at the same time, but Lincoln's work, which moreover had already undergone a practical test, appeared first. The method, initially crude, was subsequently refined and developed mathematically by R. A. Fisher. Ford and W. H. Dowdeswell then applied it to the Lepidoptera (moths and butterflies) and used it also to estimate survival rates in nature.

In 1939 Ford began work on the moth *Panaxia dominula*. This showed the importance of selection compared with random drift and provided the most extensive quantitative study of an animal population ever carried out in natural conditions. He was also responsible for the early analysis of industrial melanism, which was subsequently investigated by H. B. D. Kettlewell. Ford also further developed Fisher's interpretation of Batesian mimicry, which was later the subject of outstanding researches by C. A. Clarke and P. M. Sheppard, using the techniques of ecological genetics.

Ford was the first to demonstrate experimentally (1940) the evolution of dominance and recessiveness in wild material, working on the moth *Abraxas grossulariata*. He later extended this study to other species, providing a proof that dominance of the same unifactorial character can be built up by dissimilar adjustments of the gene complex in isolated populations.

At this time also he carried out a large-scale investigation of the chemistry of pigments in the Lepidoptera, with reference to classification. By this means he obtained new and independent evidence for the validity of taxonomic groups in that order.

In 1946 Ford and Dowdeswell began an experimental study of evolution using a polygenic character in the butterfly *Maniola jurtina*. In the course of that work, now much extended by others, it proved possible to detect and analyze evolution in progress and to measure selection pressures for advantageous qualities in nature.

In 1940 Ford had provided a precise definition of genetic polymorphism, demonstrating the condition to be a distinct form of variation—one that spreads through a population by favorable selection when "transient" and is maintained by contending advantages and disadvantages in equilibrium when "balanced." He then showed that the human blood groups are balanced polymorphisms (1942) and deduced that they must be associated with liability to specific diseases (1945), a prediction that was fully substantiated in 1953.

Beginning in 1952, the Nuffield Foundation provided grants to assist in maintaining laboratories of ecological genetics at Oxford. Work on that subject showed that selection for advantageous qualities in wild populations is 30 to 40 times more powerful than had previously been supposed—a consideration that affected fundamentally the general concept of evolution.

Ford received the degrees of M.A. and D.Sc. at Oxford. He was the first scientist to be elected a Fellow of All Souls College, Oxford, since the 17th century. Professor of ecological genetics (the subject he himself named) and director of the genetics laboratory at Oxford, he was elected to the Royal Society of London.

Ford wrote *Mendelism and Evolution* (1931; 8th ed. 1965), *Genetics for Medical Students* (1942; 5th ed. 1961), *The Study of Heredity* (1938; 2d ed. 1950), *Butterflies* (1945; 4th ed. 1965), *Moths* (1955), *Ecological Genetics* (1964; 2d ed. 1965), and *Genetic Polymorphism* (1965).

For background information *see* ECOLOGY; EVOLUTION, ORGANIC; GENETICS in the McGraw-Hill Encyclopedia of Science and Technology. □

★ **FORRESTER, Jay Wright**

American electrical engineer and management expert
Born July 14, 1918, Anselmo, Nebr., U.S.A.

THE INVENTION of the random-access magnetic core memory for digital computers and the development of "industrial dynamics" as a way to analyze the behavior of social systems marked the evolution of Forrester's career from electrical engineer to professor of industrial management. His work in computers led to the information-storage method used in nearly all the digital computers in use today. Twelve years later, his book *Industrial Dynamics* (1961) showed a new way to understand the growth and stability of socio-economic systems.

During the late 1940s, when the first digital computers were being developed, each explora-

tory machine reflected the nature and shortcomings of the information-storage system around which it was built. The available storage devices were slow, expensive, or unreliable. Forrester was then director of the Digital Computer Laboratory at the Massachusetts Institute of Technology. His group was developing a digital computer to process air-defense information and to generate instructions to defense weapons. For such computer applications, speed and reliability beyond that of any existing information-storage device were essential. While many techniques would store information, the missing element of a successful system was a low-cost, reliable way to select the stored binary digit of information at speeds of a few microseconds. Previous storage devices had stored information in linear sequence, as along a magnetic wire, where selection was made by moving the wire; or storage was in a two-dimensional array, as on the face of a vacuum tube, where selection was accomplished by scanning with an electron beam.

Forrester undertook to create a reliable storage system with a selection system capable of locating storage cells within a three-dimensional array. To do so would require a storage cell sensitive to a coincidence of signals on each of the coordinate axes. He first devised a selection and storage system using the nonlinear characteristics of a glow discharge in a vacuum, but this was not pursued because of its inherent low reliability. In 1949, still searching for a reliable nonlinear electronic cell, Forrester noticed the extremely rectangular hysteresis loops of magnetic materials that had been developed for magnetic amplifiers. Pressed by the need for a better storage system in the computer he was building, he undertook to use a magnetic cell as both the switching and storage element in a memory system. This led to the coincident-current magnetic memory, in which a memory cell in a three-dimensional array is unaffected by selecting currents on one or two coordinates but does respond to receive or read out information when it experiences proper selecting currents on all three coordinate axes.

In the field of management, Forrester built on his early training in servomechanisms and his later work in digital computers for the control of military operations to develop the "industrial dynamics" approach for analyzing the growth and stability of industrial organizations. The central philosophy of industrial dynamics was based on the ideas of feedback control as first developed by engineers and mathematicians for application to the control of physical systems. His study of decision making during the introduction of computers to military control had shown Forrester the similarity between "policy" in a human organization and the "transfer function" of an engineering device. It thus became possible to formulate mathematical models of the information flows and policy structure of an organization. Such models, however, were far too complex for mathematical solution. Moving away from the mathematical methods then conventional in the social sciences, Forrester emphasized instead the empirical and experimental approaches of engineering by applying computer simulation as a way to determine the implications of the complex models. Industrial dynamics opened the way for designing policies to enhance the desirable characteristics of social organizations. Its methods are already being followed for policy design in a number of industrial organizations and are being taught in some 20 universities.

From his home on a Nebraska cattle ranch, Forrester went to the University of Nebraska to study electrical engineering (B.S., 1939). Graduate study in the same field at the Massachusetts Institute of Technology (M.S., 1945) led to a series of staff and faculty positions there. As a research assistant he was in the group led by Gordon S. Brown, who founded the MIT Servomechanisms Laboratory for the development of feedback-control systems during World War II. From 1945 to 1952 Forrester started and was director of the Digital Computer Laboratory, which built Whirlwind I, one of the first general-purpose digital computers. From 1952 to 1956 he was head of the digital-computer division of the Lincoln Laboratory, where the SAGE (Semiautomatic Ground Environment) system for air defense was designed for installation throughout the continental United States. In 1956 he became professor of management at the Alfred P. Sloan School of Management at MIT.

For background information *see* DIGITAL COMPUTER; STORAGE DEVICES in the McGraw-Hill Encyclopedia of Science and Technology.   □

☆ FORSSMANN, Werner Theodor Otto

German physician
Born Aug. 29, 1904, Berlin, Germany

WHILE ENGAGED in research on the heart, Forssmann developed a method for visualization of the right side of the heart by passing a catheter through a vein into his own right atrium, then photographing the heart by x-ray. This daring experiment made possible many findings in the field of cardiology and paved the way for the use of angiocardiograph. For his pioneering work Forssmann received the 1956 Nobel Prize in physiology or medicine, which he shared with D. W. Richards and A. F. Cournand.

The earliest work on determining blood pressure within the living heart was performed by two French investigators, Auguste Chauveau and Etienne Marey, in 1861. They led manometers from the neck vessels into both compartments of the right heart, and into the left, of an experimental animal and thus recorded pressure changes. In 1912, three German physicians, Unger, Bleichröder, and Loeb, were investigating puerperal sepsis ("childbed fever"). In an attempt to bring a suitable chemotherapeutic agent to the part of the body where it would be most effective, they inserted ureteral catheters into arteries in the leg and pushed them upward to the estimated height of the abdominal aorta, then injected the drug. Although no x-ray verifications of catheter placement were made, these early intra-arterial probings caused no ill effects on the patients.

Forssmann began his work on cardiac catheterization in 1929. To prove that the methods that Chauveau and Marey had employed on animals were applicable to humans, he inserted a narrow catheter into a cubital vein in his own arm, passed it onward into the right atrium, and then had an x-ray examination made to visualize the catheter in his heart. This achievement opened the way to study of pathologic changes in the circulatory system and to x-ray study of the right side of the heart and the pulmonary vessels. Again experimenting on himself, Forssmann twice injected contrast medium directly into his own heart so that x-ray pictures could be made.

During this same period, Forssman conducted his first experiments in angiocardiography. He inserted catheters into the heart of a living dog, then examined them in position with x-ray. He also demonstrated that it was possible, once a catheter had been placed in the right auricle, to pass it diagonally from the upper to the lower vena cava, thus permitting the collection of blood samples from the liver.

Forssmann's work did not bear immediate fruit, in part because of the technical requirements for further investigations; progress in cardiology had to wait, for example, upon the development of modern anaesthetic techniques and antibiotics. Another cause, however, was the extreme criticisms to which Forssman was subjected because of the presumably dangerous nature of his experiments. Deterred from further cardiographic research, he turned to urology, in which field he gained distinction.

Forssmann studied medicine at the University of Berlin, from which he received his degree in 1929. He became chief of the surgical clinic of the City Hospital in Dresden-Friedrichstadt and at Robert Koch Hospital in Berlin. In 1958 he was named chief of the Surgical Division of the Evangelical Hospital in Düsseldorf.

For background information *see* CARDIOVASCULAR SYSTEM; HEART in the McGraw-Hill Encyclopedia of Science and Technology.   □

☆ FOSTER, John Stuart, Jr.

American physicist
Born Sept. 18, 1922, New Haven, Conn., U.S.A.

FOSTER'S MAIN contributions were in the application of nuclear explosives to military and peaceful uses. Although he became best known for a break-through in the development of small, or tactical, nuclear weapons, the long-range potential of his work may be of greatest importance to man in large-scale earthmoving and other nonmilitary engineering projects employing nuclear explosives. For his "unique contributions, demanding unusual imagination and technical skill, to the development of atomic weapons," President Eisenhower bestowed on him the Atomic Energy Commission's E. O. Lawrence Memorial Award in 1960.

Much of Foster's novel applied research was motivated by problems associated with the relative inflexibility and inefficiency of early nuclear explosives. To achieve a nuclear explosion, it is necessary to bring together rapidly two or more fragments of fissionable material to form a mass of critical size. Under these conditions, an explosive chain reaction can take place. The first nuclear weapons had a minimum yield equal in explosive force to about 20,000 tons of TNT. They were relatively large and cumbersome, with consequent limitations on modes of delivery and flexibility of application. The yields were not efficient relative to the amount of fissionable material used. It was militarily desirable to achieve flexibility by obtaining varied yields, both much smaller and larger than the nominal 20 kilotons; by improving the yield relative to fissionable materials used; and by building devices of ligher weight and smaller size.

Foster's break-through in new concepts was facilitated by his development at the Lawrence Radiation Laboratory, Livermore, of the computational and experimental tools necessary to design nuclear explosives in detail. In the course of this research, Foster elaborated upon these and other advanced calculations, and was responsible for significant progress in hydrodynamics, the science of the behavior of matter at very high pressures.

Foster's subsequent leadership in the development of thermonuclear explosives with reduced fission yields (so-called "clean" nuclear explosives) was made possible in part by his earlier work and was motivated by a need for devices for the Plowshare Program. The Plowshare Program, which originated at Livermore, proposed to use the great power of nuclear explosives for projects that were otherwise beyond man's power or were uneconomical by conventional means. Examples are large-scale excavation for canals and other earthmoving projects and new techniques for recovery of natural gas, petroleum, and mineral resources. Plowshare required devices that yielded a minimum fallout of fission fragments and therefore left little residual radiation. Early thermonuclear devices yielded an explosive force generated about half from the igniting fission explosive and half from fusion material. Foster pioneered the development of improved devices, and this line of research resulted in a 100-fold reduction in the amount of fallout from a given explosive yield.

Foster was also a pioneer in the development of Command and Control, a system for retaining central control over a nuclear weapon independent of its location.

In earlier research, Foster developed the first large-scale ion pump for the rapid achievement of improved high vacuums. He applied this device in a Van de Graaf accelerator, in a high-intensity linear accelerator, and in some of the early research in Project Sherwood, the U.S. program of research in controlled thermonuclear reactions. Subsequent advances in ion-pump technology have made the device extremely important in Sherwood machines.

The son of a prominent research physicist, Foster took his B.S. in physics at McGill University in 1948. He received his Ph.D. in 1952 at the University of California, Berkeley. His undergraduate studies were interrupted by World War II, during which he worked at Harvard on the development of radar countermeasures and in the European theater on the implementation of countermeasures to enemy radar. He was in the original cadre of young scientists who formed the staff of the Lawrence Radiation Laboratory at Livermore in 1952. Initially, he was a group leader in research on controlled thermonuclear reactions, entering upon nuclear weapons development in 1953. He became an associate director of the laboratory in 1958, and was appointed director of the Lawrence Radiation Laboratory, Livermore, in 1961. In 1965 he was appointed director, Defense Research and Engineering, U.S. Department of Defense.

For background information *see* NUCLEAR EXPLOSION in the McGraw-Hill Encyclopedia of Science and Technology.   □

★ FRAENKEL-CONRAT, Heinz L.

American biochemist
Born July 29, 1910, Breslau, Germany

FRAENKEL-CONRAT'S research focused on the relationship between chemical structure and biological activity with regard to the macromolecular components of living systems. The achievement for which he is most noted was the disassembly of tobacco mosaic virus into noninfectious protein and almost noninfectious nucleic acid, and the reconstitution of fully infective virus from these components. This led to the discovery of the intrinsic genetic activity of ribonucleic acid and opened up a fruitful field of research. For these contributions, Fraenkel-Conrat was honored by a Lasker Award and the first California Scientist of the Year Award in 1958.

After receiving his Ph.D. in biochemistry at Edinburgh for studies on ergot alkaloids and thiamine under G. Barger and A. R. Todd, Fraenkel-Conrat joined M. Bergmann's group at the Rockefeller Institute for Medical Research in New York. In studying the specificity of proteolytic enzymes, particularly papain, he found, contrary to expectation, that these enzymes were able to form peptide bonds, the equilibrium being shifted toward synthesis by insolubilizing substituents (benzoyl and anilid groups). In a subsequent year at the Instituto Butantan at Sao Paulo, Brazil, he collaborated with his brother-in-law, K. H. Slotta, in the study of the proteinaceous components of snake venoms, separating various enzymatic activities and obtaining a crystalline and physicochemically apparently homogeneous protein that showed both the neurotoxic and the hemolytic activities of rattlesnake venom, crotoxin.

In 1938 Fraenkel-Conrat joined H. M. Evans's Institute of Experimental Biology at the Berkeley campus of the University of California. There he purified several hormones of the anterior pituitary, particularly the follicle-stimulating and thyrotropic hormones. The effect of changes in structure on hormonal activity was studied with the lactogenic and other hormones. He pursued this type of work for over 10 years, in good part at the Western Regional Research Laboratory of the U.S. Department of Agriculture, in collaboration with H. S. Olcott and others. Methods for selective modification of protein groups, such as amino, carboxyl, thiol, disulfide, phenolic, and so forth, were developed and applied to many biologically active proteins, and the effects of these treatments on the ability of these proteins to function were recorded. Several of the methods then developed proved of value when applied a decade later to proteins of known structure.

Methods for protein structure analysis (end groups, amino-acid sequences) were applied by Fraenkel-Conrat to viruses, particularly the plentiful and stable tobacco mosaic virus, since 1952, when he joined the virus laboratory of the University of California, headed by W. M. Stanley. This work, carried out in collaboration with a team of investigators, yielded the complete amino-acid sequence of this protein chain of 158 amino-acid residues, the biggest protein of known structure, in 1958.

The isolation of the viral protein in native form, and the concurrent isolation of native viral ribonucleic acid (RNA) by separate methods, led to experimental attempts to recombine the two to regenerate virus particles. It became clear that the tendency of the two components to combine was a function of the integrity of structure and shape of the above protein subunit. If the RNA chain molecule was also intact, then fully infective virus formed spontaneously under suitable conditions in a process akin to the crystallization of a coordination complex.

Studies of the significance of the reconstitution reaction led to the discovery that viral RNA was per se infective and genetically fully competent. But quantitatively the RNA was very inefficient, largely owing to its susceptibility to nucleases. The coating of the RNA by the protein potentiated its infectivity 1,000-fold. In collaboration with B. Singer (now his wife) and a number of students and colleagues, Fraenkel-Conrat elaborated methods for stabilizing the RNA and for the study of its structure, end groups, nucleotide sequences, and chemical modification. Several of the chemical modifications of RNA produced biologically distinct mutants; the study of the protein of these mutants gave important clues to the nature of the genetic code. A certain type of alteration of the RNA led frequently to certain exchanges of amino acids in the protein, and these data could be correlated with the identification of coding triplets of nucleotides, as elaborated by M. W. Nirenberg and others in cell-free amino acid incorporating systems from *Escherichia coli*.

Fraenkel-Conrat, son of the famed gynecologist Ludwig Fraenkel (discoverer of the function of the corpus luteum), received his preparation for a research career by going through the medical curriculum at Munich, Vienna, Geneva, and Breslau, where he received his M.D. in 1934. He received a Ph.D. in biochemistry at Edinburgh in 1936. In 1958 he became professor of virology and later of molecular biology at the University of California, Berkeley.

Fraenkel-Conrat wrote *Design and Function at the Threshold of Life—The Viruses* (1962).

For background information *see* RIBONUCLEIC ACID in the McGraw-Hill Encyclopedia of Science and Technology. □

★ FRANCIS, Thomas, Jr.

American epidemiologist
Born July 15, 1900, Gas City, Ind., U.S.A.

FRANCIS'S STUDIES centered in problems of infectious disease, especially pneumonia, influenza, and poliomyelitis. For his contributions in these areas he received, among other honors, the 1947 Lasker Award of the American Public Health Association and the 1953 Bruce Medal in Preventive Medicine of the American College of Physicians.

Investigations of the immunologic reactions of pneumonia patients to type-specific polysaccharides of the pneumococcus, carried out in the 1920s by Francis and W. S. Tillett at the Hospital of the Rockefeller Institute, revealed characteristic wheal and erythema cutaneous reactions that subsequently proved to be a valuable guide to serum treatment. It was then demonstrated that these polysaccharides were of themselves able to induce antibodies and immunity in man. This caused a revolution in immunologic theory, which then held that only proteins could function as antigens. Tillett and Francis also described the pneumococcus C reaction, now widely used in clinical medicine as an indicator of pathologic conditions.

In 1934, during a search for a viral precursor of the bacterial invasion of lobar pneumonia, Francis isolated human influenza virus, the first to confirm the 1933 report of W. Smith, C. H. Andrewes, and P. P. Laidlaw in England. This led to establishment of the virus in mice and tissue culture and to the first description, with T. P. Magill, of the extensive serologic variations among strains of the type A virus. In 1940 Francis identified influenza virus, type B, and its earlier epidemic prevalences. In 1950 he and associates established influenza C as an epidemic disease. In 1943 a polyvalent vaccine that Francis had developed was shown by well-controlled studies of the Commission on Influenza of the Army Epidemiology Board, of which he was director, to be highly effective against influenza A in military personnel and, in 1945, against influenza B. Vaccine has been shown by repeated studies since then to be effective.

Despite the demonstrable diversity of influenza viruses, Francis and his colleagues demonstrated that they contain numerous antigens in common. The effort, then, is to compound a

vaccine of multiple strains or antigens that cover the entire range. The different major variants are considered to be rearrangements of antigens, among which previously suppressed ones may reemerge as dominant antigens of apparently new pandemic viruses. When the general population becomes thoroughly immunized by a prevalent variant, the pressure upon the virus for selective variation increases. Thus cyclic recurrences of major antigens were postulated and such was observed in the Asian strains of 1957 *et seq.*, which present the pandemic antigen of the 1890s. This interpretation is based upon the doctrine of original antigenic sin propounded by Francis, F. M. Davenport, and A. V. Hennessy. According to that doctrine, the first childhood infection by influenza virus leaves the imprint of the dominant antigen of that strain on the antibody of the individual; this is enhanced by subsequent experiences with other strains so as to be characteristic of that age group throughout its later life. Hence the history of influenza virus strains is written in the serum antibody pattern of different age groups of the population. Persons first exposed in the 1890 pandemic period had antibodies to the 1957 strain; persons first exposed in the 1918–22 pandemic period have their characteristic antibody to the swine influenza virus described by R. E. Shope. Desirable vaccine would fill the gaps in immunity of the population to potential oncoming strains.

At the University of Michigan, Francis undertook studies in the epidemiology and immunology of poliomyelitis to determine the mode of entrance and spread of that virus in a community. In 1954 he was asked by the National Foundation for Infantile Paralysis to conduct the large-scale evaluation of the inactivated poliomyelitis vaccine developed by Jonas Salk. The test comprised some 1,800,000 children in 44 states. A major component of the study was carried out as a strictly controlled double blind experiment—the largest of its kind. The vaccine was demonstrated to be safe, potent, and effective and has resulted in the remarkable decline of the disease.

In 1955 Francis served as chairman of a visiting committee that drew up the plan adopted by the National Research Council for the studies of the Atomic Bomb Casualty Commission in Japan. In recent years he and his colleagues engaged in a study of a total community in Michigan, seeking to detect the causative factors, genetic or environmental, of arteriosclerotic heart disease and related disorders with the hope of developing preventive measures.

Francis graduated from Allegheny College (B.S., 1921) and Yale Medical School (M.D., 1925), proceeding through a residency in internal medicine and an instructorship at Yale. In 1925 he went to the Hospital of the Rockefeller Institute on the Clinical Pneumonia Service under Rufus Cole and in the laboratory of O. T. Avery. In 1936 he joined the staff of the International Health Division of the Rockefeller Foundation to pursue influenza researches. He went to New York University College of Medicine in 1938 as professor and chairman of the department of bacteriology and attending physician at Bellevue and Willard Parker hospitals. In 1941 he became professor of epidemiology and chairman of the department in the University of Michigan School of Public Health and professor of epidemiology in the University of Michigan Medical School. He was elected to the National Academy of Sciences in 1948.

Francis wrote extensively on basic immunological phenomena, the pathogenesis of infectious disease, immunity to viral infections, and epidemiological studies. He edited *Diagnostic Procedures for Viral and Rickettsial Diseases* (1948; 2d ed. 1956).

For background information *see* EPIDEMIOLOGY; IMMUNOLOGY in the McGraw-Hill Encyclopedia of Science and Technology.   □

FRANK, Ilya Mikhailovich
Russian physicist
Born Oct. 23, 1908, Leningrad, U.S.S.R.

FRANK, TOGETHER with I. Y. Tamm, developed the theoretical interpretation of the so-called Cerenkov radiation. For this achievement he shared with Tamm and Cerenkov the 1958 Nobel Prize for physics. *See* CERENKOV, PAVEL ALEXEYEVICH; TAMM, IGOR YEVGENEVICH.

The son of a professor of mathematics, Frank graduated in 1930 from the Moscow State University, where he studied physics. The next year, he joined the staff of the State Optical Institute in Leningrad. In 1934 he became a scientific officer at the Lebedev Physical Institute of the U.S.S.R. Academy of Sciences. There, in 1941, he took charge of the Atomic Nucleus Laboratory. He also assumed the directorship, in 1957, of the Neutron Laboratory of the Joint Institute of Nuclear Investigations. Frank attained the degree of Doctor of Physicomathematical Sciences in 1935; in 1944, he became a professor on the faculty of the Moscow State University.   □

☆ **FRIEDMAN, Herbert**

American astrophysicist
Born June 21, 1916, New York, N.Y., U.S.A.

BEGINNING IN 1949 with captured German V-2 rockets that had been brought to White Sands, N.Mex., after World War II, Friedman pioneered in the development of rocket and satellite astronomy. Experiments conducted under his direction detected and studied x-ray and ultraviolet radiations from the Sun, produced the first astronomical photographs made in x-ray wavelengths, discovered the hydrogen corona around the Earth, and measured x-ray and ultraviolet radiations from certain stars. For his achievements, Friedman received the U.S. Navy's Distinguished Scientific Achievement Award in 1962, the Presidential Medal for Distinguished Federal Service in 1964, and the Eddington Medal of the Royal Astronomical Society, also in 1964.

The advantages of making observations from space, above the influence of the Earth's atmosphere, were long appreciated by astronomers. The Earth's atmosphere absorbs all radiation with wavelengths shorter than 2,850 angstroms, as well as several other regions of the electromagnetic spectrum. Only in outer space could gamma- and x-radiation, which give evidence of ultrahigh-energy events, be detected; only in outer space could the x-ray and ultraviolet spectra of the Sun and stars be measured.

Friedman and his colleagues at the U.S. Naval Research Laboratory were faced with many problems unknown to ground-based astronomers. The rocket astronomer relies on the same two instruments—the telescope and the spectrograph—but he must design them to function in a vehicle in erratic motion. The instruments must be compact, since the observatory pay load of the rockets is extremely limited; they must be able to withstand accelerations amounting to

several hundred times that of gravity; and the exposed film must be recoverable or the measurements must be radioed to a ground receiver while the rocket is aloft. Early efforts to obtain spectrograms of the Sun met with so many misfortunes that the spectograph was supplemented by sensitive detectors, such as Geiger counters and ionization chambers tuned to narrow bands of wavelengths.

The Sun was the first celestial object to be studied by rocket astronomy. Friedman directed the rocket astronomy program to study the solar x-ray spectrum (below 100 angstroms) and in 1949 obtained the first scientific proof that x-rays emanate from the Sun. Later he directed many studies of the Sun for more than a full sunspot cycle.

Friedman directed the earliest attempts to study solar flares in 1956. A Rockoon, a small solid-propellant rocket carried aloft to 80,000 feet on a Skyhook balloon, was launched each day from a ship in the Pacific Ocean. When a flare was detected optically or was indirectly indicated by a short-wave radio fade-out, the rocket was fired by radio command. In 10 tries, the emission of only one small flare was measured, but this was sufficient to clearly reveal that the energy, radiated as x-rays, represents a major portion of the total energy output of a solar flare and is entirely adequate to explain the accompanying ionospheric disturbances, such as short-wave radio fade-out.

Friedman continued to study the nature and effects of solar flares in 1957 as director of Project Sunflare, the opening event of the International Geophysical Year. By then, two-stage, rail-launched, solid-propellant rockets capable of carrying a 50-lb pay load to about 150 miles had become available. Instrumented rockets were kept in constant readiness and launched by push button when a flare was observed. With this approach, a number of measurements of x-ray and ultraviolet emissions were obtained during solar flares.

During the total solar eclipse of Oct. 12, 1958, Friedman supervised a rocket experiment carried out from the deck of the USS *Point Defiance* near the Danger Islands in the South Pacific. As the Moon crossed the face of the Sun, six solid-propellant rockets were launched in sequence to take turns measuring the x-ray and ultraviolet emission coming from the uneclipsed portions of the Sun. The experiments provided the first proof that x-radiation comes from the Sun's corona, or outer atmosphere, and that ultraviolet radiation comes from its chromosphere, or inner atmosphere.

The first x-ray photograph of the Sun was obtained on Apr. 19, 1960. A simple pinhole camera in an Aerobee-Hi rocket was mounted on a pointing control to aim it continuously at the

Sun. The camera was 6 inches long with a pinhole 0.005 in. in diameter covered with an aluminized plastic film to exclude visible and ultraviolet light. This combination transmitted the x-ray spectrum below 50 angstroms.

The son of an art dealer, Friedman graduated from Brooklyn College in 1936. He received a Ph.D. in physics in 1940 from Johns Hopkins University, where he remained for a year as a physics instructor. He then joined the staff of the Metallurgy Division at the U.S. Naval Research Laboratory. He was named supervisor of the Electron Optics Branch in 1942. In 1958 he was appointed superintendent of the Atmosphere and Astrophysics Division and in 1962 chief scientist at the laboratory's E. O. Hulburt Center for Space Research. His most recent work was in instrumentation of Earth satellites and in studies of x-ray emission from outside the solar system with the possible discovery of neutron stars. He was elected to the National Academy of Sciences in 1960.

For background information *see* ASTROPHYSICS; ROCKET ASTRONOMY in the McGraw-Hill Encyclopedia of Science and Technology. □

★ FRISCH, Karl von

Austrian zoologist
Born Nov. 20, 1886, Vienna, Austria

BY MEANS of the painstaking experiments he carried out with bees, Frisch was able to establish the means by which they determine directions and also the way in which an individual bee can communicate information about the distance and direction of food to the other members of the hive. These studies greatly clarified the behavior of bees and removed a number of misconceptions that had previously been accepted as fact.

At the turn of the century, the prevalent theory was that fish and all invertebrate animals were totally color-blind. To Frisch, however, this seemed inconsistent with the observation that some fish are able to match themselves to their surroundings not only in brightness but also in color. Therefore, his earliest work, conducted about 1910, was concerned with the physiology of the color changes of fish. Through the use of colored foods and similar stimuli, he was able to demonstrate that fish could differentiate between colors of all gradations of quality and brightness, and hence that they had a color sense. When these studies were completed, Frisch decided to attack the same problem with regard to petal-visiting insects. According to the established theory of the biological meaning of the coloration of flowers, the colored petals serve to attract the insects, and in this way pollen is transferred. If, however, the theory of total color-blindness of insects were correct, the coloration of the petals would be negated; hence, the two theories were inconsistent. In a series of experiments with bees, Frisch established that they did have a color sense but that they were blind to light in the red region of the spectrum. It was later shown that bees could see in the ultraviolet region of the spectrum, thus compensating for their partial blindness in the visible region. In 1956 a student of Frisch's, Karl Daumer, showed that, like men, bees have trichromatic vision, differing only in the shift in sensitivity to the short-wavelength end of the spectrum.

Working after World War II in a small private laboratory that he maintained at Brunnwinkl in the Austrian Alps, Frisch conducted his studies of bee communication and direction determination. He constructed special hives, each containing only one honeycomb that could be observed through a glass plate, and marked the bees, individually with numbers and as groups with different colors, to aid his observations. He determined that the bees communicated by means of a rhythmic motion, or dance, which indicated the distance and direction of the food supply, in combination with the odor of nectar pollen, some of which adhered to the body of the insect. Frisch established that there were two types of dances, which he termed "circling dance" and "wagging dance." In the former the bee executed alternate clockwise and counterclockwise circles, while in the latter it moved forward in a straight line while wagging its abdomen from side to side and then circled to retrace its steps. He determined that the type of dance indicated the distance to the food supply. The circling dance showed that the food was within 75 meters of the hive, while the wagging dance showed it to be at a greater distance. The direction to the food was designated by the direction of the straight path of the dance relative to the top of the comb, which represented the position of the Sun. He further found that as the food supply dwindled, the bees visiting it slowed down their dance, stopping completely when the food was completely gone.

Many animals have an accurate time sense, or internal clock, which makes it possible for them to use the Sun as a compass. This ability was discovered and studied simultaneously and independently by Frisch in bees and by G. Kramer in birds. Only bees can determine the solar position, even if the Sun is obscured. In 1949, Frisch established that bees can perceive the direction of the polarized light from the sky and thereby infer the Sun's position. This orientation to the Sun via polarized light has since proved to be common to many forms of life. However, no species other than bees is known for which the sky serves both for the direction orientation of the individual and for the communication of direction to other members of the species.

Among the other studies of bees made by Frisch were that of their sense of odor, which he found similar to that of man in qualitative and quantitative terms; that of their sense of taste, which he found not limited to the quality of sweetness; and the botanical-biological meaning of these senses. Among his other studies of fish was that of their hearing, the results indicating that some fish had an excellent sound-distinguishing ability and an outstanding auditory sharpness, both superior to those of men.

The son of a surgeon, Frisch studied at the universities of Vienna and Munich, receiving his Ph.D., with majors in zoology and comparative anatomy, from the latter in 1910. In 1921 he was appointed director of the Zoological Institute at the University of Rostock, Germany; in 1923 he accepted a similar position at the University of Breslau (Wroclaw), now in Poland. Frisch returned to the University of Munich in 1925, building a new Zoological Institute there (1931–32) with the aid of the Rockefeller Foundation. After the destruction of the Institute during World War II, he accepted a position at the University of Graz in Austria. He returned to the University of Munich in 1950, however, remaining there until his retirement in 1958. Frisch received the Balzan Foundation Award in 1963. In 1951 he was elected a foreign associate of the U.S. National Academy of Sciences and in 1954 a foreign member of the Royal Society of London.

Frisch wrote a number of books, among them *On the Life of the Bee* (7th ed. 1964), *Memories of a Biologist* (2d ed. 1962), and *Dance Language and Orientation of Bees* (1965).

For background information *see* PHONORECEPTION in the McGraw-Hill Encyclopedia of Science and Technology. □

★ GAMOW, George

American physicist
Born Mar. 4, 1904, Odessa, Russia

GAMOW MADE significant theoretical contributions to nuclear physics, astronomy, and biology. He also became well known as a popularizer of science, winning for his achievements in this area the 1956 Kalinga Prize of the United Nations Educational, Scientific, and Cultural Organization.

In his schooldays Gamow became very much interested in astronomy, examining the starry sky through a little telescope that his father gave him on his 13th birthday. He decided then to become a scientist and began his study of mathematics, physics, and astronomy.

After graduation from the University of Leningrad in 1928, Gamow attended summer school in Göttingen and decided to see if the newly formulated quantum theory, so successful in explaining the structure of the atom, could also be applied to the atomic nucleus. Through research he was able to explain the then mysterious phenomenon of natural radioactivity as well as the experiments of Lord Rutherford on the induced transformation of light elements. On the basis of this research Gamow received his Ph.D. from the University of Leningrad in 1928.

Later, in Copenhagen, when he told Niels Bohr of his work, Bohr offered him a year at the Institute of Theoretical Physics on a stipend from the Royal Danish Academy. There Gamow proposed a hypothesis that atomic nuclei can be treated as little droplets of so-called "nuclear fluid." These views led ultimately to the present theory of nuclear fission and fusion.

At this period Gamow also collaborated with F. Houtermans and R. Atkinson in attempts to apply his formula for calculating the rate of induced nuclear transformations to the so-called thermonuclear reaction in the interior of the Sun and other stars. This formula, originally applied only to astronomical topics, is now successfully used for designing H-bombs, as well as for studying the possibility of controlled thermonuclear reactions.

Gamow spent a year working with Lord Rutherford at Cambridge, a second year in Copenhagen, and later became a professor at the University of Leningrad (1931–33). While attending the International Solvay Congress in Brussels, he was invited to lecture at the University of Michigan. He sailed to the United States, eventually obtaining a professorship at the George Washington University, Washington, D.C. (1933–55). During the early years in Washington he collaborated with Edward Teller on the theory of beta decay, and formulated the so-called "Gamow-Teller selection rule for beta emission."

While Gamow was in Washington, he developed the theory of the internal structure of red giant stars. With Mario Schoenberg he developed the theory of the so-called Urca process and, with Ralph Alpher, the theory of the origin of chemical elements by the process of successive neutron capture.

In 1954 Gamow developed an interest in biological phenomena and published papers on the information storage and transfer in a living cell. In these papers he proposed the so-called "genetic code," an idea later completely confirmed by experimental studies in laboratories.

In 1956 Gamow joined the faculty of the University of Colorado. He was elected to the Royal Danish Academy of Sciences in 1950 and the U.S. National Academy of Sciences in 1953. In 1965 he was elected an overseas fellow of Churchill College, University of Cambridge.

Among Gamow's many books are *The Constitution of Atomic Nuclei and Radioactivity* (1931), *Structure of Atomic Nuclei and Nuclear Transformations* (1937), and *Theory of Atomic Nucleus and Nuclear Energy Sources,* with C. Critchfield (1949). Gamow's papers and correspondence are being collected by the Library of Congress.

For background information *see* NUCLEAR STRUCTURE in the McGraw-Hill Encyclopedia of Science and Technology.   □

GASSER, Herbert Spencer

American neurophysiologist and physician
Born July 5, 1888, Platteville, Wis., U.S.A.
Died May 11, 1963, New York, N.Y., U.S.A.

W HILE EXPERIMENTING on the electrophysiology of mammalian nerves, Gasser, in collaboration with Joseph Erlanger, demonstrated that nerve impulses are transmitted at different velocities depending on the thickness of the nerve fibers along which they pass. This work, for which Gasser and Erlanger shared the 1944 Nobel Prize in physiology or medicine, has led to great advances in understanding the mechanism of pain and reflex action.

The first truly significant discovery in neurophysiology was made during the mid-19th century by Emil Du Bois-Reymond, a German physiologist, who demonstrated that the nerve impulse was an electronegative wave propagated along a nerve. Later, the speed of propagation was successfully measured by Herman Helmholtz. Early in the present century an English biologist, Edward Adrian, observed that nerve impulses are discharged by sense organs and neurons (nerve cells) in bursts, like machine-gun fire.

The work that actually paved the way for Gasser and Erlanger was an assumption made in 1907 by Gustaf Göthlin, a Swedish physiologist. Extrapolating from a formula for electrical cable conduction, Göthlin hypothesized that the velocity of nerve impulses is more rapid along thick nerve fibers than along thin ones. His assumption was correlated with the observed fact that the diameters of fibers in a nerve stem differ in cross section. Although indirect supporting evidence for Göthlin's hypothesis was offered by the French physiologist, Louis Lapicque, it remained for Gasser and Erlanger to prove it conclusively.

The early neurophysiologic researches of Gasser and Erlanger (their actual collaboration dates from 1916, when Gasser joined Erlanger at Washington University in St. Louis) were hampered by the insensitivity of existing physical instruments. In 1921, however, an extremely sensitive cathode-ray oscilloscope became available, which, coupled with an improved amplification device, enabled the accurate recording of the electrical manifestations of nerve impulses.

Early in their work on isolated mammalian nerve fibers, Gasser and Erlanger recognized that they would have to simulate, as closely as possible, the natural environment of nerve fibers in the living body. Utilizing an existing technique, the nerves were examined in a 5 per cent carbon dioxide in oxygen atmosphere saturated with water vapor and maintained at normal body temperature. When a comparison was made of the recorded electrical activity of isolated nerve fibers using this technique and nerve fibers in the body, the observed correlation gave assurance that the artificial environment was satisfactory.

In their oscillographic recordings of electrical impulses passing through isolated nerve fibers, the investigators noted the following sequence of events: an initial and rapid negative deviation in electric potential (the spike), a relatively long period of ascending then descending potential (the actual stage of transmission), followed by a sequence of low potential changes (the afterpotential), the latter consisting of first a negative and then a positive deviation. In measuring the potential cycles of different nerve fibers, three distinct patterns seemed to emerge, based on duration of spikes and after-potentials. These constant patterns indicated that there were three main groups of nerve fibers, which were designated A, B, and C. Spike durations in A group fibers were 0.45 msec (milliseconds or one one-thousandths of a second), about 1.2 msec in those of the B group, and 2.0 msec in the C group. After-potentials also varied distinctively in each group as did the velocities of conduction. In the A group conduction velocities ranged from 115 mps (meter per second) to 10 mps; in the B group from 15 to 3 mps; in the C group from slightly over 2 to 0.6 mps. Returning to Göthlin's hypothesis, Gasser and Erlanger concluded that an approximately linear relationship existed between fiber diameter and velocity of nerve-impulse conduction.

As a result of this discovery, it became possible to demonstrate the distribution of the three groups of fibers throughout the nervous system and to elucidate the highly complex problem of nerve-impulse transmission. In addition, Gasser and Erlanger contributed information on the essential differences between sensory and motor nerves and demonstrated how pain is perceived and how muscle is caused to move. Their researches constituted an entirely new synthesis of neurophysiology on which future discoveries would be based.

Gasser received his A.B. (1910) and A.M. (1911) degrees from the University of Wisconsin, where he first encountered Joseph Erlanger. He received an M.D. from Johns Hopkins University in 1915, returned to Wisconsin for a year of research in pharmacology, and in 1916 went to Washington University in St. Louis, there beginning his collaboration with Erlanger. He was named professor of pharmacology in 1921. Gasser next studied in Europe from 1923 to 1925

and then returned to St. Louis until 1931, when he became professor of physiology at Cornell University Medical College in New York City. From 1935 to 1953 Gasser was director of the Rockefeller Institute for Medical Research.

For background information *see* NEUROPHYSIOLOGY in theMcGraw-Hill Encyclopedia of Science and Technology.   □

★ GAYDON, Alfred Gordon

British physicist
Born Sept. 26, 1911, London, England

As an experimental spectroscopist, Gaydon applied molecular spectroscopy to a number of fields, including the determination of dissociation energies, study of flame chemistry and structure, measurement of gas temperature, and interpretation of shock-tube phenomena. In 1960 he was awarded the Rumford Medal of the Royal Society for his work on molecular spectra, and also the Bernard Lewis Gold Medal of the Combustion Institute for his researches on flame spectroscopy.

Sir Norman Lockyer, an early pioneer in spectroscopy and astronomy, had founded an astrophysics department at the Royal College of Science at the end of the last century, and this attracted other distinguished workers, including the 2d Lord Rayleigh and Alfred Fowler, who did valuable work on the excitation and analysis of spectra. Gaydon's early interest in astronomy led him to join this group, under Fowler, in 1932.

Early work on the spectra of afterglows of electric discharges and on the analysis of spectra of diatomic hybrides gave Gaydon an initial training in molecular spectroscopy. One of his early papers, with R. W. B. Pearse, on a wave-mechanical treatment of the intensity distribution of RbH, pioneered the more refined methods of calculating vibrational intensity distributions which are now in use. Other papers described previously unknown types of electronic transitions: $^2\triangle-^2\triangle$ in NiH and $^7\Pi-^7\Sigma$ in MnH. With H. P. Broida, Gaydon was the first to find a laboratory source of the night-sky spectrum of O_2.

Detailed analysis of the spectrum of a molecule gives information about its energy levels and can be used to derive the energy of dissociation to free atoms. In some cases, convergence of vibrational energy levels to the dissociation limit is observed, while in other cases the approximate limit may be determined by a Birge-Sponer extrapolation. Another very accurate way is by observation of a predissociation limit beyond which the spectrum lines become diffuse. Around 1934–37, the dissociation energies of N_2 and CO (the latter especially important because it was related to the heat of sublimation of carbon) were determined from predissociations, and the low values so obtained were widely accepted for a number of years, despite disagreement with the values from Birge-Sponer extrapolations and independent thermochemical observations. Gaydon realized this difficulty and noted that acceptance of the low values involved violation of the rule that the potential energy curves of electronic states of the same symmetry must not cross (noncrossing rule). A critical examination of all data led him to reinterpret the predissociations by assuming a different type of coupling of the angular momenta in the molecule; this led to precise but much higher values of the dissociation energies. After some initial controversy, these higher values were definitely established by further experimental work and received general acceptance. Gaydon then made a systematic study of the dissociation energies of all known diatomic molecules for which spectroscopic data were available.

Gaydon's interest in flame spectroscopy was aroused by early observation of the afterglow of CO_2, the spectrum of which resembled that of a carbon monoxide flame, and direct work on flames has greatly increased knowledge of the chemical and physical processes which occur. His spectroscopic studies included flames at very low pressure; chilled flames; preheated flames; the development of a nitric oxide test to detect atomic oxygen; the effect of adding halogenated inhibitors; flames supported by free atoms from a discharge; flames supported by fluorine; and the use of deuterium as tracer to follow chemical processes. He has also made temperature measurements by spectroscopic methods and showed the occurrence of abnormalities in the reaction zone.

The development of the shock tube as a tool for high-temperature research gave Gaydon a further opportunity to exploit spectroscopic techniques, and he studied pyrolysis, detonation, ignition, and rates of dissociation and of vibrational relaxation of molecules. With colleagues, he developed the spectrum-line reversal method of temperature measurement so that it could be used to follow rapid processes behind shock waves.

Gaydon graduated in physics in 1932 at Imperial College, London, did two years' research with A. Fowler, and then joined the British Cotton Industry Research Association. In 1936, while distilling an ether, he was involved in an explosion that cost him an eye and injured his sight, but in 1937 he returned to Imperial College to resume spectroscopic research. In 1939 he transferred to the chemical technology department with Sir Alfred Egerton. He obtained his London Ph.D. in 1937 and his D.Sc. in 1941. Elected to the Royal Society of London in 1953, in 1961 he became professor of molecular spectroscopy in the University of London.

Gaydon wrote *Identification of Molecular Spectra*, with R. W. B. Pearse (1940; 4th ed. 1965), *Spectroscopy and Combustion Theory* (1942; 2d ed. 1948), *Dissociation Energies* (1947; 2d ed. 1953), *Flames, Their Structure, Radiation, and Temperature*, with H. G. Wolfhard (1953; 2d ed. 1960), *The Spectroscopy of Flames* (1957), and *The Shock Tube in High-temperature Chemical Physics*, with I. R. Hurle (1963).

For background information *see* SPECTROSCOPY OF COMBUSTION in the McGraw-Hill Encyclopedia of Science and Technology.   □

☆ **GELL-MANN, Murray**
American physicist
Born Sept. 15, 1929, New York, N.Y., U.S.A.

IN 1953, Gell-Mann proposed that certain subatomic particles possessed an invariant quality, which he called "strangeness," that was conserved in strong and electromagnetic interactions, but not in "weak" interactions. This "law of conservation of strangeness," first enunciated by him, explained a number of peculiarities in the behavior of the short-lived, heavy, artificially produced "strange" particles. The notion of conservation of strangeness was essential to later symmetry schemes for classification of strongly interacting particles, including the SU(3) symmetry brought forward in 1961 by Gell-Mann himself. In 1959, Gell-Mann received the Dannie Heineman Prize of the American Institute of Physics.

Shortly after 1950, physicists began to notice anomalous tracks in cloud chambers, which were best explained by supposing that an unknown neutral particle had decayed into two charged particles. With further study of these events, it became evident that at least two sorts of neutral particle were being detected. One, about as massive as a nucleon, was called the Λ^0 (lambda-zero); the other, considerably lighter, came to be known as the K^0 (K-zero). Very soon, the list of hitherto unknown particles was extended to include the Σ (sigma) in charged and neutral form; the Ξ^- (xi-minus); and two charged K particles, positive and negative. These particles came to be called, collectively, the "strange" particles, because of several peculiarities that they exhibited. They appeared very frequently in cloud chambers, so that their creation had to be attributed to the rapid "strong process," with a time scale in the order of about 10^{-23} sec. According to theory, therefore, their preferred modes of decay ought to be some variety of strong interaction. However, not only did strange particles not decay in this fashion, but they did not even decay through electromognetic interaction (time scale about 10^{-13} sec); instead, they decayed through the very much slower and less probable weak interactions (time scale about 10^{-9} sec).

To explain the anomalously long lifetimes of the strange particles (ranging from 10^{-8} to 10^{-10} sec), the theory of "associated production" was presently advanced. It stated that the strong forces responsible for the strange particles could only act to create them in batches of two or more at a time. It was shown that, if strange particles thus produced immediately moved apart, their separate decay modes via the strong interactions would always prove to require more energy than had gone into their formation as a pair. This explained how strange particles, forbidden to decay separately by the strong interaction, survived long enough to distintegrate ultimately via the weak processes. The idea of associated production, while helpful in this regard, remained an empirical idea and was not very satisfactory from a theoretical standpoint.

The concept of "isotopic spin" was a mathematical device used to express the fact that protons and neutrons exhibited "charge independence"; all the possible strong interactions between them were equal in force, and they were distinguished only by charge. The isotopic-spin values of $+\frac{1}{2}$ for the proton and $-\frac{1}{2}$ for the neutron were adopted; together they were said to form the "charge doublet" of the nucleon, with two possible charges, $+1$ or 0, and thus a charge "center" at $+\frac{1}{2}$. (The antiproton and antineutron made up another doublet with charge center at $-\frac{1}{2}$, and so on for all the antiparticles.)

The notion of charge multiplets (a general term for doublets, triplets, and so forth) was shown to apply to all particles that conserved isotopic spin in strong interactions. Accordingly, since the pions fitted this description, they were considered a triplet of positive, neutral, and negative states; isotopic spins $+1$, 0, -1; and a charge center at 0.

It seemed natural to apply this terminology to the newly discovered strange particles in the hope of imposing some order on their rather unruly behavior. Since they obeyed the strong interaction and might be hypothesized to exhibit charge independence, the heavy Λ, Σ, and Ξ were tentatively placed in doublets like the nucleon, which they resembled in mass. The lighter K seemed to belong to a triplet like the pion. The rule seemed to be: baryons in doublets, mesons in triplets.

Gell-Mann, contemplating this arrangement, began to suspect that there was no particular reason why this need be the case. In fact, he suspected that if the strange particles could be shown to depart from this scheme of things, the manner of their incongruity would itself be a significant clue to their behavior.

First of all, then, what were the possible varieties of multiplets? Triplets, clearly, could have a charge center at 0; doublets, at either $-\frac{1}{2}$ or $+\frac{1}{2}$; singlets (multiplets with one member only) at 0. Gell-Mann now tabulated the heavy strange particles, assigning each to a tentative multiplet and measuring the charge center of that multiplet according to its displacement from the reference mark $(+\frac{1}{2})$ of the charge center of the nucleon doublet. The Λ^0 he assigned to the possible singlet; and, since its charge center was at 0, it seemed "displaced" by a matter of $-\frac{1}{2}$. Supposing this displacement to be an intrinsic quality of the particles, Gell-Mann began to think of it as a quantum number. (For reasons of arithmetical convenience, strangeness is measured as twice the displacement; thus, the Λ^0 had strangeness -1. Strangeness of antiparticles was measured according to the displacement from the charge center of the antinucleon doublet, which was $-\frac{1}{2}$; thus, the strangeness of the $\overline{\Lambda}^0$, with charge center at 0, was $+\frac{1}{2}$).

Another possibility was a baryon triplet centered at 0, with a displacement of $-\frac{1}{2}$ and thus a strangeness of -1. The Σ might fit here; it did seem to comprise a charge multiplet of positive, negative, and neutral particles. Finally, there was the possibility of a doublet with a charge center at $-\frac{1}{2}$ and therefore a strangeness of -2. Such a pair would contain a neutral and a negative particle. Gell-Mann suggested that the Ξ^- was the required negative particle and that there should exist a Ξ^0 to complete the doublet. (The subsequent experimental detection of this particle formed a striking confirmation of the notion of strangeness.)

Continuing his tabulation, Gell-Mann went on to classify the K particles by placing them in doublets: the K^0 and K^+ in one, with a charge center at $+\frac{1}{2}$; and the $\overline{K}^0$ and K^- in another, with a charge center at $-\frac{1}{2}$. Using the charge center of the pion triplet (0) as a reference mark, Gell-Mann assigned the K doublets strangeness of, respectively, $+1$ and -1.

Gell-Mann was now able to show that strangeness was conserved in all strong interactions; that is, the total strangeness on each side of any strong event must be equal. If this were so, it would immediately provide a theoretical basis for the doctrine of associated production. In an equation with ordinary particles (total strangeness $= 0$) on one side of the reaction, any strange particles on the other side must be produced at least two at a time, so that the resulting strangenesses would add to a net value also of 0.

He was also able to equate strangeness with the isotopic-spin component I_z in explaining how the strange particles avoided decay via the electromagnetic processes, which he also proved must obey conservation of strangeness. The crucial item here was that isolated strange particles were forbidden to decay into ordinary particles, since then the conservation of strangeness would once more be violated. Thus he explained how the strange particles survived long enough to fall into the domain of the weak interaction, for which the conservation of strangeness (like parity) failed.

Using the strangeness formulations (which were proposed independently by the Japanese physicist Kazuhiko Nishijima), Gell-Mann successfully gave detailed predictions of numerous decay events of strange particles, as well as prophesying the existence of the Ξ^0 as mentioned above.

In 1961 Gell-Mann announced a new system of unified classification of strongly interacting particles, which he called the "eightfold way." In this scheme, the varied strange particles, and others, are expressed as "recurrences" of a few ground states. Confirmation was forthcoming almost at once from experiment; the Ω^- (omega-minus) particle, which had been predicted by the eightfold way, was found in 1964.

Gell-Mann received his B.S. at Yale in 1948 and his Ph.D. at the Massachusetts Institute of Technology in 1951. He then became, briefly, a member of the Institute for Advanced Study (1952) and an instructor and later associate professor at the University of Chicago (1952–54). In 1954 he moved to the California Institute of Technology, where he became professor of physics in 1956. He was elected to the National Academy of Sciences in 1960.

For background information *see* STRANGE PARTICLE in the McGraw-Hill Encyclopedia of Science and Technology.   ☐

★ GIAEVER, Ivar

American physicist
Born Apr. 5, 1929, Bergen, Norway

GIAEVER STARTED his career in physics by studying the current flow between two metals separated by an extremely thin insulating film. For sufficiently thin films, almost all the current flow would be due to a quantum mechanical process known as electron tunneling. Giaever realized and showed experimentally that it was possible to get large amounts of information about the electron density of states of superconductors from the current-voltage characteristics obtained in an electron-tunneling experiment. For this discovery he received the 1965 Oliver E. Buckley Prize of the American Physical Society.

According to classical mechanics, when two regions of space are separated by a potential barrier, a particle can pass between them only if it has sufficient energy to surmount the barrier. Almost from the very beginning of quantum mechanics, it was realized that this was not a necessary condition; a particle with insufficient energy to surmount the barrier may pass from one region to another by going through the barrier. This process had been termed tunneling. Early theoretical calculations of electron transport between two metals separated by a thin insulating layer were made by S. Sommerfeld and H. A. Bethe; R. Holm later extended the calculations and furnished the first experimental evidence for the effect.

J. C. Fisher and Giaever made a detailed study of electron tunneling through thin aluminum oxide films separating two layers of aluminum. At that time, a very successful theory of superconductivity by John Bardeen, L. N. Cooper, and J. R. Schrieffer existed. The critical part in this theory is that an energy gap appears in the electron density of states when a metal is taken from its normal into its superconducting state. Giaever guessed that this change in the electron density of states should be reflected in the current-voltage characteristic in an electron-tunneling experiment. This turned out to be true. The current-voltage characteristic for a tunneling experiment between two metals in the normal state is linear at low voltages; between one metal in the normal state and one metal in the superconducting state it is highly nonlinear; and between two metals in the superconducting state even a negative resistance may appear in the current-voltage characteristic.

Hardly more than a week passed between the time in 1960 when Giaever got the idea for his experiment and the time it was shown to be correct. Fortunately, the experiment was a simple one to carry out; the only equipment needed was a vacuum system for evaporating thin films, an ordinary voltmeter, an ammeter, and liquid helium to obtain low temperatures. At the time, Giaever had no background in low-temperature work, but was fortunate to be able to draw upon the experience of many of his colleagues at the General Electric Research Laboratory. The experiment was soon repeated and extended in other laboratories in the United States and abroad. In 1962 B. D. Josephson predicted an interesting new tunneling effect, which was verified shortly afterwards. These experiments have had a large scientific impact and have advanced our knowledge both about superconductors and ordinary metals. Practical devices based upon the effect have been devised but are not yet used, possibly because of the extremely low temperature required to keep a metal in its superconducting state.

Giaever graduated as a mechanical engineer at the Norwegian Institute of Technology (NTH) in Trondheim, Norway. He then served his compulsory year in the Norwegian Army and afterwards worked for a year as a patent examiner in the Norwegian government's patent office. In 1954 he migrated to Canada, where after working a short time as an architect's aide he joined the Canadian General Electric's Test

Program, Peterborough, Ontario. In 1956 he went to the United States, where he attended an advanced engineering program at the General Electric Company, Schenectady, N.Y. In 1958 he became a research staff member in metallurgy and ceramics at the General Electric Research Laboratory. At the same time he started night classes in the physics department at Rensselaer Polytechnic Institute, Troy, N.Y. He received his Ph.D. there in 1964.

For background information *see* SUPERCONDUCTIVITY in the McGraw-Hill Encyclopedia of Science and Technology. ☐

☆ GIAUQUE, William Francis

American chemist
Born May 12, 1895, Niagara Falls, Ontario, Canada

WHILE DOING undergraduate research on the measurement of entropy at low temperatures, under G. E. Gibson, at the University of California at Berkeley, Giauque became interested in what has become known as the third law of thermodynamics. Following graduation, he continued work under Gibson on a Ph.D. thesis which showed experimentally that glycerine glass, which is an example of a system with molecular disorder, retained a large excess of entropy above that of crystalline glycerine at limiting low temperatures. After joining the faculty of the College of Chemistry in 1922, he continued low-temperature research, and his participation in the development of the cryogenic facilities at Berkeley afforded him a means to prove the third law of thermodynamics to be a fundamental law of nature, to determine accurately the entropy at temperatures approximating absolute zero of a large number of substances, and to accurately calculate chemical equilibria. For his work in the field of chemical thermodynamics, particularly on the behavior of substances at extremely low temperatures, Giauque was awarded the 1949 Nobel Prize in chemistry.

In 1906 the German chemist W. H. Nernst announced the Nernst heat theorem, which—after clarification and considerable limitation, such as the exclusion of disordered systems, by Max Planck (1911) and by G. N. Lewis and G. E. Gibson (1920)—was proposed as the third law of thermodynamics. This law associates zero entropy with the perfect crystalline—that is, the perfectly ordered—state at the absolute zero of temperature. Employing what has become known as statistical thermodynamics, Giauque used the actual energy levels of gas molecules, obtainable from the then newly developing work on band spectra of gases, in an attempt to learn and verify the rules of quantum statistics. This was done by comparing the entropies so calculated with experimental entropy values obtained from low-temperature heat capacity measurements on the liquid and solid phases of the condensed gases, and the assumed correctness of the third law of thermodynamics. A large number of repetitions of this procedure, using various gases, with close experimental agreements, served to establish the validity of both statistical thermodynamic calculations and the third law of thermodynamics.

Having provided a sound basis for these closely related methods, Giauque and his students proceeded to use observed molecular data for statistical calculations on gases, and calorimetric observations for third law calculations on condensed phases, to tabulate the free energy and other thermodynamic properties of pure substances from 0° absolute to extremely high temperatures. The general acceptance and use of these methods has created very extensive tabulations, which now provide a major source of chemical thermodynamic data. This work also led to the discovery of a few examples—such as CO, NO, and NNO—where lack of discrimination between the somewhat similar ends of these molecules caused them to crystallize with "frozen in" molecular disorder. Such cases were shown not to approach zero entropy at the absolute zero of temperature by calculable amounts, and they illustrate the requirement that zero entropy applies only to perfect molecular order.

In 1910 the Dutch physicist Heike Kamerlingh-Onnes managed to produce a temperature of 0.8° absolute by evaporative cooling of liquid helium, whose normal boiling point is about 4°, by using a large battery of vacuum pumps. Temperatures of 0.4° absolute have been produced by a similar technique, utilizing the more recently synthetically produced helium-3 isotope, but this appears to be about the limit of this method.

Giauque's work on the magnetic cooling method of producing very low temperatures had

its origin in calculations in which he considered the effect of magnetic fields on various thermodynamic properties, including entropy. Since the heat capacities of substances ordinarily become very small at temperatures in the vicinity of 10° absolute, it had long been assumed that essentially all of the entropy was eliminated from substances at these low temperatures. However, in 1924, on the basis of magnetic susceptibility measurements made on gadolinium sulfate octahydrate at the temperature of liquid helium by Kamerlingh-Onnes, Giauque was able to calculate that a large amount of entropy was removed from the substance when a magnetic field was applied. Giauque reasoned that under normal conditions the atomic magnets within a substance have no regular arrangement, which corresponds to the presence of entropy. He assumed that when a magnetic field of sufficient strength is applied to a paramagnetic substance, such as gadolinium sulfate, the atomic magnets line up with the field and entropy is removed. Since the removal of entropy is accompanied by the evolution of heat, Giauque reasoned that he could use this technique to produce a lowering of temperature. He further reasoned that if he could adiabatically demagnetize the material while causing it to do work, he could lower the temperature still more to a temperature approximating absolute zero. Since no thermometer was calibrated at temperatures below those already achieved, the problem was not only to produce extremely low temperatures by the magnetic cooling method but also to determine the temperature reached.

By 1933 Giauque and his associates had constructed the necessary apparatus. A paramagnetic substance, enclosed in a jacket filled with helium gas to conduct heat, was placed within the coil of a solenoid magnet. The apparatus within the coil was immersed in liquid helium. When an electric current was passed through the coils of the solenoid, the atomic magnets began to orient themselves with the magnetic field. The heat given off as the entropy was removed was conducted by the helium gas to the liquid helium, some of which proceeded to boil off. When the magnetization of the paramagnetic substance was complete, the helium gas was evacuated from the jacket to insulate the material against the flow of heat. The electric current was then turned off, and, as the magnetic field decreased, the paramagnetic material did work at the expense of molecular energy by contributing to the current in the surrounding circuits. In this way the paramagnetic material was further cooled.

To determine the temperature of the material, a measuring coil, immersed in liquid helium, had been placed around the cylindrical sample. As the experiment progressed, it became increasingly difficult for an alternating electric current to pass through the measuring coil as the magnetic susceptibility of the paramagnetic substance increased. This effect made possible the quantitative determination of the magnetic susceptibility of the sample. From early results on several gadolinium compounds, with relatively small magnetic fields, Giauque and his student, D. P. MacDougall, were able to calculate the temperature, which was about 0.1° absolute, since the magnetic susceptibility increases approximately proportionally to the decrease in temperature. However, with the later development of this technique and the availability of high magnetic fields, temperatures of the order of a thousandth of a degree absolute may be attained. Also, by means of appropriate measurements, the temperatures may be calculated by means of rigorous thermodynamic equations. One of the valuable contributions to temperature measurement in this region was Giauque's discovery of the properties of the amorphous carbon resistance thermometer. The extremely large negative temperature coefficient of the electrical resistance of amorphous carbon at very low temperatures enables temperature measurements of great precision in the presence of magnetic fields.

Among Giauque's other significant contributions was his discovery in 1929, with his student, H. L. Johnston, that atmospheric oxygen contains small amounts of isotopes of atomic weights 17 and 18, as well as the more common isotope of atomic weight 16. This not only disclosed that chemists and physicists were unknowingly using different atomic weight scales, it provided a basis for computing the difference between the chemical and physical atomic weight scales (which was not eliminated until the present scale on carbon-12 was adopted in 1961) and also provided scientists with an isotope tracer, oxygen-18, with which respiration and photosynthesis mechanisms could be studied. The isotope work on oxygen also proved experimentally that molecules retain one-half quantum unit of zero point vibrational energy in their lowest energy states, as had been predicted on a somewhat mystical basis by Planck early in the century. Thus a still too common uninformed statement, that motions cease at 0° absolute, is false, as had long been evident in terms of electron motions in atoms that could hardly be expected to cease at any temperature.

Giauque majored in chemistry but included a heavy program of engineering courses at the University of California at Berkeley, where he received his B.S. with highest honors in 1920 and his Ph.D. in chemistry, with a minor in physics, in 1922. He became an instructor in the College of Chemistry of the university in 1922, rising to professor in 1934. From 1939 to 1944 he organized and led a group at Berkeley that worked for the U.S. government on problems of the design and construction of mobile units for the production of liquid oxygen. After 1944 he continued his low-temperature researches with increased emphasis on high field magnet design and magnetothermodynamic measurements. He was elected to the National Academy of Sciences in 1936.

For background information see CRYOGENICS; LOW-TEMPERATURE THERMOMETRY in the McGraw-Hill Encyclopedia of Science and Technology. ☐

☆ GIBBS, William Francis

American naval architect and marine engineer
Born Aug. 24, 1886, Philadelphia, Pa., U.S.A.

DESIGNING SAFER, more efficient, and faster ships for American commercial and naval fleets was Gibbs's purpose throughout his career. His advanced ship design concepts and techniques and his judicious use of materials are especially exemplified in the SS *United States,* which set new speed records in transatlantic passenger service in 1952 that still stand. This record-shattering crossing was made at an average speed for the round voyage of 35.05 knots. Thus 3.71 knots were clipped off the previous record made by the *Queen Mary* 17 years before.

The *United States* incorporated supership design concepts formulated by Gibbs in the previous quarter-century and was built to rigid naval specifications to permit her speedy conversion to a troop transport. Welded construction was employed to reduce weight, and extensive use was made of aluminum alloys as shipbuilding materials. Increased compartmentation was incorporated in the design for maximum practicable safety and survival after collision or war damage. The ship propulsion power plant, well protected from underwater damage, was designed to achieve high efficiency and economy. The ship is capable of long voyages at high speed without refueling. Only fireproof furniture and decorative fabrics have been used, and the only wood on board is in the butchers' chopping blocks and the pianos.

Gibbs's other major contributions include the development of lightweight, compact, high-pressure, high-temperature marine power plants of improved efficiency and economy, advance-designed feed systems and heat balances, and high-speed gearing.

Gibbs devoted more than 40 years to the advocacy of superships. In 1922, at the government's request, he and his brother, Frederic H. Gibbs, organized Gibbs Brothers, Inc., to supervise the reconditioning of the SS *Leviathan*, SS *Republic*, and several American Merchant Line vessels. In 1929, the firm's name became Gibbs and Cox, Inc. In 1924 Gibbs designed and supervised construction of the SS *Malolo*, the fastest liner of its time built in America. She was unique because of extensive watertight compartmentation, which enabled her to survive a severe collision that occurred during her trials. In 1937 he designed the SS *America*, at the time the largest and fastest merchant vessel built in the United States.

Beginning in 1933, in cooperation with the Navy, his firm undertook the design and engineering of destroyers for the U.S. Navy. As a result, there was developed high-pressure, high-temperature steam turbine machinery of exceptional efficiency that was later adopted for the Navy's battleships, aircraft carriers, cruisers, and destroyers. Before the United States's entry into World War II, the firm developed the working drawings for light cruisers, icebreakers, and Army transports. During the war it continued with the preparation of working plans and procurement of materials, apparatus, and equipment for cruisers, aircraft carriers, destroyers, escort vessels, landing craft, and mine sweepers. By the end of the war, the firm had procured materials valued in excess of $2 billion and had directed the preparation of working plans of more than 60 per cent of all ships of major size, except battleships and submarines, constructed in American shipyards and Navy yards during the war. Between 5,000 and 6,000 ships of major size had been built to working plans produced by Gibbs's firm. It was under Gibbs's leadership that the Liberty Ship program and other World War II multiple-shipbuilding programs first became practicable.

During World War II, Gibbs served as controller of shipbuilding, War Production Board, and later as chairman, Combined Shipbuilding Committee (Standardization of Design) of the Combined Chiefs of Staff. He was special assistant to the director, Office of War Mobilization, and representative of the Office of War Mobilization on the Procurement Review Board of the Navy.

After the war, Gibbs and Cox, with the cooperation of the Navy, continued the design and preparation of working plans for various types of naval vessels, including the most modern guided-missile destroyers and frigates. In addition, numerous commercial projects were undertaken by the firm.

Gibbs attended Harvard University from 1906 to 1910; in 1913 he received M.A. and LL.B. degrees from Columbia University. Among the many science awards he received during his career was the 1953 Franklin Medal of the Franklin Institute of the State of Pennsylvania. He was elected to the National Academy of Sciences in 1949 and to the National Academy of Engineering in 1965.

For background information *see* SHIP DESIGN in the McGraw-Hill Encyclopedia of Science and Technology.   □

☆ **GILLULY, James**

American geologist
Born June 24, 1896, Seattle, Wash., U.S.A.

PRIOR TO the mid-20th century, it was widely believed by geologists that mountain-making episodes (orogenies) had occurred at more or less regular intervals throughout the physical history of the Earth. According to this theory, long periods of quiescence, millions of years in duration, were punctuated by relatively short intervals of great crustal mobility, which produced both present and past mountain ranges. In 1949, Gilluly challenged this classic concept. He argued that orogenic activity, while perhaps not continuous, took place little by little rather than as one great "spasm." Further, he doubted that the crustal unrest evident today was any different from that of the past.

Invoking a major premise in geology that "the present is the key to the past," Gilluly cited evidence from California to show that movements of the Earth's crust took place in small "bits." He noted that the northwestern part of the Baldwin Hills in California was rising at the rate of 3 ft per century, as determined by precise leveling, and that the country between San Bernardino and Victorville across the pass in the Mojave Desert was arching upward at a rate of 20 in. per century. He also pointed out that, during the 1933 earthquake at Long Beach, a 4-mile area east of Long Beach was uplifted a full 7 inches. Given the countless centuries of geologic time, Gilluly argued, these apparently trivial rates of rise were quite sufficient to account for any mountains on Earth, and even to make a Mount Everest in only 2×10^6 years.

Gilluly marshaled evidence from the Earth's rock record to support his theory. The record of sediments formed during the Cretaceous Period in the United States (the time of the greatest development of the dinosaurs), he noted, indicated that repeated small uplifts took place rather than one or two major uplifts. At that time, the Nevada-Idaho region was being uplifted, and acted as a source of sediments that were eroded and carried far to the east. Gilluly calculated that nearly 10^6 cubic miles of rock had been eroded away in the Nevado-Idaho region and that this would necessitate a vertical uplift and resulting denudation of about 3 miles in the source area.

If this uplift had taken place all at once, such a great spasm of the Earth's crust should be reflected in the sediments resulting from the erosion of lofty mountains. The sediments would be very coarse, containing boulders and other large pieces in the lower part of the sediment layers. As the source area was worn down, streams and other eastward-flowing currents would transport and deposit finer and finer particles. The Cretaceous sediments, therefore, should show an upward progression of finer and finer sediment, according to the classic theory. On the contrary, Gilluly pointed to the abundant field evidence from the western states showing that the Cretaceous sediments are remarkably uniform in particle size. He concluded that erosion must have kept pace with numerous small uplifts in the Cretaceous source area, thus preventing any marked deviation in sediment character.

Gilluly became well known also for his work on thrust faults and the economic geology of copper deposits.

Gilluly received his B.S. from the University of Washington in 1920 and his Ph.D. from Yale University in 1926. He joined the U.S. Geological Survey in 1921, becoming a senior geologist in 1936, principal geologist in 1943, and chief of the general geology branch in 1954. He later served as chief of the fuels branch. Gilluly

received the Penrose Medal of the Geological Society of America in 1958. He was elected to the National Academy of Sciences in 1947.

Gilluly wrote *Principles of Geology*, with A. C. Waters and A. O. Woodward (1959).

For background information *see* OROGENY in the McGraw-Hill Encyclopedia of Science and Technology.   □

☆ GLASER, Donald Arthur
American physicist
Born Sept. 21, 1926, Cleveland, Ohio, U.S.A.

GLASER INVENTED the "bubble chamber," a device for detecting the paths of high-energy atomic particles. It has yielded much new data unobtainable in other ways and has given precise pictorial information about high-energy particles and phenomena, such as masses, lifetimes, decay modes, and so forth. In 1960 Glaser was awarded the Nobel Prize in physics for his invention.

The "cloud chamber," invented by C. T. R. Wilson in 1927, marked the beginning of precise visual investigation of the interaction of atomic particles. This device contained a supersaturated gas in a state of expansion; ionizing radiation traversing the chamber condensed the gas along its path to form droplets of liquid. It could detect particles with energies ranging up to several million electron volts. However, both it and the nuclear emulsion were severely limited for investigation of the high-energy (several Bev) particles whose production was becoming practicable upon the completion of the giant particle accelerators in the early 1950s.

Glaser, engaged in work on the "strange" particles produced in high-energy cosmic-ray collisions, recognized the need for a high-energy detector. Elaborations of the nuclear emulsion or the Wilson chamber (whose low-density contents permitted relatively few particle collisions), he reasoned, would prove cumbersome and impractical. He sought a high-density, large-volume medium in which to observe the trails of fast particles. Studying the properties of liquids and solids that might be useful, Glaser became intrigued with the instability of superheated liquids. If the surface tension of such a liquid could be drastically reduced, and the vapor pressure simultaneously raised, ionizing radiation passing through the liquid should induce the formation of bubbles along the paths of the particles. Such a reversal of the Wilson-chamber effect—formation of gas bubbles in a liquid, rather than of liquid droplets in a gas—would fulfill the conditions he sought and would also have a conveniently short piston-evacuation cycle. (Large Wilson chambers took up to one-half hour per cycle.)

At the University of Michigan, Glaser began by showing that ionizing radiation would produce boiling in a superheated liquid. In an initial experiment, diethyl ether (chosen for practical reasons) was superheated under pressure to 140°C (normal boiling point 36°C) and exposed to fast gamma radiation. The liquid boiled instantly. Glaser then wished to see if he could make accurate tracks of ionizing particles. He made small glass bubble chambers, in different shapes, each containing a few cubic centimeters of superheated diethyl ether. A hand-operated mechanism simultaneously expanded the chamber (thus lowering the pressure) and operated a high-speed movie camera. The resulting films showed that well-defined bubble tracks were indeed produced by bombardment of fast particles.

Glaser saw indications that other liquids would yield much more accurate data, the most likely theoretically being liquid hydrogen, superheated to about 27°K. In 1953, at the University of Chicago, he constructed the first liquid-hydrogen bubble chamber. For larger chambers and very low temperatures, glass containers had to be abandoned. But he suspected that ordinary structural materials could be used, even though joints and scratches on the inner walls of such a "dirty" chamber would instantly induce boiling. By expanding the chamber extremely rapidly, the liquid in the center of the chamber could be kept superheated long enough to be sensitive to fast particles. This proved to be correct. Construction began immediately on different-sized bubble chambers, equipped with powerful deflecting electromagnets and filled with liquid hydrogen, xenon, propane, and other media.

When used in conjunction with particle accelerators, bubble chambers could be made to react only during the actual emission of particles, thus reducing the problem of background radiation. The short cycling rate and large volume proved to be very convenient, and the use of the bubble chamber quickly spread. Glaser's work, together with independent research by J. K. Wood, L. W. Alvarez, and others, has produced large masses of new data about high-energy reactions and has led to the discovery of several new elementary particles.

Son of a businessman, Glaser received his B.S. in physics and mathematics at the Case Institute of Technology in 1946, and his Ph.D. in the same subjects at the California Institute of Technology in 1950. In 1949 he began teaching physics at the University of Michigan and became a professor of physics there in 1957. In 1959 he took the post of professor of physics at the University of California, Berkeley. He was elected to the National Academy of Sciences in 1962.

For background information *see* BUBBLE CHAMBER; CLOUD CHAMBER in the McGraw-Hill Encyclopedia of Science and Technology.   □

★ GOLDBERGER, Marvin Leonard

American theoretical physicist
Born Oct. 22, 1922, Chicago, Ill., U.S.A.

FOR HIS development of what has come to be called dispersion theory, Goldberger received the American Physical Society's Dannie Heineman Prize in 1961. This theory is concerned with the relation between the real and imaginary parts of scattering amplitudes and is a generalization of much earlier work by H. Kramers and R. Kronig. Goldberger's work in this area began in 1953 in collaboration with Murray Gell-Mann; the fundamental paper on the subject was published with Gell-Mann and W. Thirring. Later Goldberger greatly simplified this work and generalized it from the original electromagnetic case to apply to massive projectiles. The theory played a fundamental role in the analysis of pion-nucleon scattering experiments. The general technique was developed by Goldberger and his collaborators and by many others and was applied to a host of problems involving strong and weak interactions. Indeed, dispersion theory has become a basic part of theoretical physics.

Goldberger began his career in physics on the wartime Manhattan (atom bomb) Project in 1944. While then concerned primarily with problems of reactor design, he also worked with F. Seitz on the theory of neutron diffraction in crystals, a phenomenon now widely employed in the study of the structure of matter. In 1948 he turned to high-energy and elementary-particle physics. Under the supervision of Enrico Fermi, he developed a theory of high-energy nuclear reactions based on the Monte Carlo method of following the trajectory of a particle through a nucleus in detail and predicting the energy and angular distribution of all emerging particles. This work is the basis of almost all theoretical discussions related to shielding of high-energy accelerators as well as to many discussions of high-energy nuclear reactions in heavy nuclei.

In the next few years, in collaboration with G. F. Chew, Goldberger worked on the theory of nucleon-nucleon scattering and on the impulse approximation, a technique for describing the high-energy interactions between nucleons and complex nuclei. In 1952, he and Gell-Mann presented a general theory of collision processes that has been very widely employed.

The work on dispersion theory occupied Goldberger from 1953 to 1961. In 1961, in connection with a study of the theory of complex angular momenta begun by T. Regge, Goldberger and R. Blankenbecler suggested that "elementary" particles such as the nucleon should be regarded as composite, lying on so-called Regge trajectories. This view is now very popular. Goldberger and Gell-Mann pointed out in 1962 that the distinction between conventional field theory and the idea of composite "elementary" particles was not at all clear and that there may well be no difference in the various points of view.

The possibility of utilizing the intensity correlation techniques of R. Hanbury-Brown and R. Twiss in connection with x-rays and particle beams was suggested in 1963 by Goldberger, H. W. Lewis, and K. Watson. They showed that in principle the famous phase problem of x-ray structure analysis could now be solved. This could have great practical consequences, since the structure of complex molecules of interest in biology could be readily determined. Goldberger and Watson explored a number of problems in connection with the quantum theory of measurement pointed up by this work.

Goldberger did his undergraduate work in physics at the Carnegie Institute of Technology, receiving his B.S. in 1943. He received his Ph.D.

at the University of Chicago in 1948. He was a research associate at the University of California and at the Massachusetts Institute of Technology before joining the faculty of the University of Chicago in 1950. In 1957 he was appointed Eugene Higgins Professor of Theoretical Physics at Princeton University. He was elected to the National Academy of Sciences in 1963.

Goldberger wrote *Collision Theory*, with W. W. Watson (1964).

For background information *see* SCATTERING (ELECTROMAGNETIC RADIATION) in the McGraw-Hill Encyclopedia of Science and Technology. □

GOODPASTURE, Ernest William
American pathologist
Born Oct. 17, 1886, Montgomery Co., Tenn., U.S.A.
Died Sept. 20, 1960, Nashville, Tenn., U.S.A.

VIRUSES, UNLIKE bacteria, require living tissues for survival and propagation. This was a great obstacle to scientific study of viruses in laboratories until Goodpasture found, in 1931, that fertile chick eggs offered an inexpensive and sterile environment for the luxuriant growth of the virus of fowlpox. Nearly all the later practical advances in the control of virus diseases of man and animals sprang from this single discovery, since it paved the way for large-scale production of vaccine against diseases such as smallpox, yellow fever, influenza, and typhus. Wartime use of his technique made possible the production of vaccines for use with all troops sent overseas. For his achievement Goodpasture received, among other honors, the Passano Foundation Award in 1946 and the Kovalenko Medal of the National Academy of Sciences in 1958.

In order to produce a vaccine for large-scale use, a virologist must have an abundant source of live viruses. Before the 1930s, there were only two virus vaccines in use: one against smallpox, the other against rabies. Jenner had utilized the cow for the development of the first, and Pasteur had found it possible to grow the viruses causing rabies by infecting rabbits. Though Karl Landsteiner had infected the rhesus monkey with poliomyelitis in 1908 and the Maitlands had cultivated cowpox virus in a flask containing chicken kidney, there was no acceptable method for the mass production of viruses until the work of Woodruff and Goodpasture on the chorioallantoic membrane of the chick embryo.

The membrane had been used by a number of investigators for the study of the growth of various implanted tissues. Rous and Murphy were the first to use this technique for the study of tumors in 1911, and Danchakoff used the method to grow embryonic chick tissues in 1916. Subsequent research using this technique involved experiments with auto- and heteroplastic grafts, as well as auto- and heterogeneous tumors. Only two previous reports of the production of experimental infection using this technique were reported prior to the 1931 report from Vanderbilt University: Rous and Murphy grew virus of Rous sarcoma, and Askanazy reported the production of tuberculous chicks by infection of fertile eggs in 1923.

Goodpasture, professor of pathology at the Vanderbilt University School of Medicine, was interested in pathogenesis, the development of disease, and was, therefore, interested in producing sufficient virus for study. He had been engaged in the study of fowlpox, or sorehead, as it was called by farmers. Though several methods for obtaining sterile virus were known and employed, he found a new method for the propagation of fowlpox virus, free from contaminants, that could provide sufficient quantity for immunological experiments.

To secure sterile fowlpox virus for inoculation of chick embryos, feathers were plucked from the head of a chick 1–2 weeks old, and virus was inoculated at three points, 1 cm apart, to permit the development of separate nodules that could be removed by one stroke of the knife. Since nodules of more than 7 days' development were likely to be invaded by pyogenic bacteria, the chick was sacrificed 6–7 days after inoculation. The head was bathed with a solution 95% alcohol and permitted to dry. A nodule was cut off at a level deep enough to obtain infected cores of most of the follicles. The severed nodule was placed, epithelial surface down, on a sterile glass slide, while the infected cores were forced out of the follicles from the cut surface. The pieces were washed twice with sterile Tyrode's solution and stored at 4°C in a small amount of the same solution. One piece was tested and, if no bac-

terial growth was apparent within 24 hours, the remaining virus was made into a suspension for inoculation by grinding with a few drops of Tyrode's solution.

The technique for opening the eggs, improved upon in later experiments, involved candling the eggs to outline the position of the chorioallantoic membrane in order to insure that the window would be cut directly over it. The surface of the egg shell was coated with a thin layer of melted paraffin over an area somewhat larger than the proposed window to prevent infection from pieces of shell. After the shell was removed, the shell membrane was also coated with paraffin of low melting point so that this membrane might be torn with a sharp-pointed instrument on three sides of the window, exposing the chorioallantoic membrane.

Inoculation was done by pricking the membrane and applying a drop of uncontaminated virus suspension. In order to watch the effects of the virus, a glass cover slip was substituted for the original shell and fixed in position with a petrolatum-paraffin ring. Embryos at various stages of development were used, with those from 10–15 days giving the best results.

Fowlpox infection of the chorioallantoic membrane occurred in every case where the embryo survived for at least 4 days. Three tests were used to prove infection: (1) Tissue, removed with sterile precautions and inoculated into scarified epithelium of adult hens, produced massive fowlpox lesions. (2) Smears of the lesion, stained by Morosow's method, showed Borrel bodies, the etiological agent of the disease, present in large numbers. (3) Histological sections of the tissue showed the typical picture of the fowlpox lesion.

Inoculation, as a method of cultivating virus, gave larger quantities of uncontaminated virus than any other means previously used. The fact that the virus was free of antigens not directly associated with the disease made the technique especially useful in immunological experiments and opened the way for the development of vaccines to protect people from diseases where no protection had previously existed.

The successful infection of the chorioallantoic membrane of chick embryos with fowlpox virus led Goodpasture to investigate the effect of the inoculation of other viruses upon this tissue. He and his coworkers at Vanderbilt were able to show that the viruses of vaccinia and of herpes simplex, which causes cold sores and fever blisters, infect the membrane in spite of the fact that vaccinia is only slightly pathogenic for adult fowls, and that repeated attempts to infect adult and young chickens with the virus of herpes simplex had failed. This emphasized the value of the embryonic cells in virus development and led to the preparation of antismallpox vaccine that could be used for human immunization.

Goodpasture graduated from Vanderbilt University in 1907 and taught for a year before entering medical school at Johns Hopkins University. After graduation in 1912, he stayed on as a research fellow and instructor until 1915. He taught at the Harvard Medical School from 1915 to 1922 and was director of the Singer Memorial Research Laboratory in Pennsylvania from 1922 to 1924. In 1924 he was appointed professor of pathology at Vanderbilt University Medical School, serving as dean from 1945 to 1950 and retiring in 1955.

For background information *see* CULTURE, EMBRYONATED EGG; CULTURE, TISSUE; VIRUS in the McGraw-Hill Encyclopedia of Science and Technology.   ☐

★ GOUDSMIT, Samuel Abraham

American physicist
Born July 11, 1902, The Hague, Netherlands

IN 1925, while a student at the University of Leiden, Goudsmit, together with his fellow student George E. Uhlenbeck, discovered that all electrons spin about an axis. It was soon recognized that spin is a property not only of electrons but also of protons, neutrons, and most other elementary particles, a property as fundamental as mass and charge. For their discovery, Goudsmit and Uhlenbeck received Research Corporation Awards in 1953 and Max Planck Medals in 1964.

Goudsmit had specialized in the structure of atomic spectra and had already published a number of papers on this subject. On Uhlenbeck's return to Leiden in the summer of 1925 after several years in Rome, it was Goudsmit's task to bring his colleague up to date on the advances resulting from Niels Bohr's ideas on atomic structure. In Rome Uhlenbeck had been in contact primarily with older subjects in theoretical physics. Their differences in training and background proved to be extremely fruitful for their discussions, and several useful new ideas resulted, of which the electron spin was the most significant.

Goudsmit and Uhlenbeck were aware that the number of spectral lines observed for any atom was always twice as many as predicted by Bohr's atomic model. The splitting of these lines when the light source was placed in a magnetic field did not agree at all with expectations. Wolfgang Pauli had shown that each electron orbit in an atom had to be characterized by four numbers rather than the three—corresponding to the three dimensions of space—that one would have expected to be sufficient. Assuming that electrons were not merely charged points but were spinning particles, Goudsmit and Uhlenbeck found that these difficulties and many others could be fully explained. A spinning electric charge is also a magnet, and the magnetism of each electron accounted for the unexplained magnetic properties of atoms.

The idea of spin turned out to be far more significant than its original discoverers could have foreseen. It led in 1928 to a fundamental change in the mathematical structure of quantum mechanics by P. A. M. Dirac, who showed that the spin of elementary particles could be considered a relativistic effect. Modern quantum theory, moreover, shows that the picture of an electron as a tiny spinning sphere cannot be taken literally. Abstract mathematical relations now replace the primitive models of atoms and particles, although these models are still very useful in descriptive discussions.

Goudsmit was born in The Hague, where his mother had a millinery shop and his father was a wholesale dealer in bathroom fixtures. He studied theoretical physics at the University of Leiden and did experimental research at the University of Amsterdam. He received his Ph.D. from Leiden in 1927 shortly before going to the University of Michigan, where he taught until 1941. During World War II (1941–45) he worked first on radar at the Massachusetts Institute of Technology and in England and then in 1944 became head of a secret intelligence group that moved with the advancing armies to investigate the German atomic bomb project. In 1948 Goudsmit joined the physics staff of Brookhaven National Laboratory. He was elected to the National Academy of Sciences in 1947.

Goudsmit wrote *The Structure of Line Spectra*, with Linus Pauling (1930), *Atomic Energy States*, with R. F. Bacher (1932), and an account of his war experiences, *Alsos* (1947).

For background information *see* QUANTUM MECHANICS; SPIN (QUANTUM MECHANICS) in the McGraw-Hill Encyclopedia of Science and Technology.   ☐

★ **GRAHAM, Clarence Henry**
American psychophysiologist
Born Jan. 6, 1906, Worcester, Mass., U.S.A.

IN THE course of his studies on vision and visual perception, Graham heard of a young student at Barnard College who seemed to have normal vision in one eye and color-blind vision in the other. Such a subject, referred to as unilaterally color-blind, is very rare. Although about 10 such subjects have been studied effectively in the last 100 years, technical methods and equipment have not been such as to make possible a proper classification of most cases. In addition, the fact that the subjects could not be observed for sufficient periods of time precluded extensive analyses of most cases. Analysis of unilateral cases of color blindness is of great importance to color theory because it is only in the case of the unilaterally color-blind person that we can learn what colors the color-blind person sees. The usual color-blind person, color-blind in both eyes, never sees color in the way a normal person does and hence cannot tell in terms of normal color vision what he views in his color-blind eye (although he early learns to give correct color names to factors other than color—for example, the intensities or relative positions of traffic lights rather than their hues).

Graham decided to study the basic visual discriminations and sensitivities in each eye of the subject. For this purpose, he made the following determinations in each of her eyes: the least energies of lights of pure spectral color that could be seen; the least difference in wavelength that could be seen as a difference in color; the manner in which pure colors of the spectrum entered into a color match involving a reference set of three pure colors—red, green, and blue—called primaries. In addition, other tests were made: the matching of a color seen in the color-blind eye by one seen in the normal eye; and the least rate of alternation of light and dark (flicker) required to give the appearance of steady light for different colors. Observations were also made by the usual screening color-plate and instrument tests for color blindness. The work was done in the psychology laboratory of Columbia University in collaboration with Yun Hsia from 1954 to 1957.

Three major types of color-blind individuals constitute a class called dichromats—that is, persons who confuse pure colors with a mixture of two primaries. Persons in one of the subclasses, protanopes, are mainly insensitive in the red; those in another group, tritanopes, are mainly insensitive in the blue. An important second class, deuteranopes, has been described as showing normal sensitivity in the green linked with a fusion mechanism whereby reds and greens are always seen as yellow. This latter mechanism is not attributed to loss of green receptors but rather to the subject's inability to distinguish red and green.

Graham found, first, that the subject's normal eye functioned in all respects like that of a normal person. However, her color-blind eye showed a number of differences from normal. The so-called luminosity determinations indicated much greater energy requirements for just seeing lights from the violet to the orange than for the normal eye; reds required the same energy as for the normal eye. Thus the subject showed a luminosity loss in the violet-to-orange range. Only two primaries, blue and red, were required to match any pure color of the spectrum. These results were similar to those for the usual deuteranope except for a minor atypical result in the blue. The results on hue discrimination showed that the subject required much greater wavelength changes to see a difference in color than are required by normal subjects. Again the results were similar to those obtained with the usual deuteranope except for a small variation in the blue. On the binocular matching of colors, the results were especially important, for they showed that the subject saw in the color-blind eye all colors in the violet, blue, and blue-green range of the spectrum as corresponding to a single blue of 470 mμ in the normal eye. She saw in the color-blind eye all colors in the green, yellow, orange, and red ranges as a yellow of 570 mμ in the normal eye. Thus her color-blind eye saw two colors, yellow and blue. Finally, the subject required considerably higher energies just to see minimum light in the spectrum over the wavelength range from violet to orange. This luminosity loss was very considerable. The seeing of yellow by deuteranopes has been accounted for by an idea ascribed mainly to A. Fick, according to whom characteristic sensitivities in red and green receptors (hence their absorption properties) become similar but with no change in central brain connections. Thus reds and greens are absorbed indiscriminately by both types of receptors, but their excitations stimulate red and green centers and thus give rise to the yellow mixture of red and green. This conclusion is in accord with the "fusion" idea. However, the fact of luminosity loss in Graham's subject shows that not only does the Fick-fusion type of process take place but some loss of receptors, most likely the green, must also be posited to account for the luminosity deficit seen in this case and probably in deuteranopes generally.

Graham, son of a metalworker, majored in psychology at Clark University, Worcester, Mass., where he received his A.B. in 1927 and his Ph.D. in 1930. He was successively at Temple University, the Johnson Foundation for Medical Physics of the University of Pennsylvania, Clark University, and Brown University until 1945. During World War II he was a member of the Applied Psychology Panel of the National Defense Research Committee. In 1945 he went to Columbia University as professor of psychology. Graham received the Warren Medal of the Society of Experimental Psychologists in 1941 and the Tillyer Award of the Optical Society of America in 1963. He was elected to the National Academy of Sciences in 1946.

Graham edited, and wrote many of the chapters in, *Vision and Visual Perception* (1965).

For background information *see* COLOR VISION in the McGraw-Hill Encyclopedia of Science and Technology. ☐

★ GREENSTEIN, Jesse Leonard

American astronomer
Born Oct. 15, 1909, New York, N.Y., U.S.A.

NEW IDEAS and techniques have shifted emphasis from the classical astronomy of gravitation to the modern astrophysics of atoms and nuclei, stellar evolution, high-energy particles, and magnetic fields. The growth of modern physics has been matched by fundamental advances in our understanding of the nature of the astronomical universe. Greenstein pioneered in opening a variety of such new subjects, combining observational discoveries with theoretical interpretations. Much of his work involved spectroscopic investigation of the atmospheres of stars as connected with theories of the origin of the chemical elements, but he also took part in the discovery of the interstellar magnetic field of our galaxy. He was a leader in the development of radio astronomy in the United States, and in the discovery and interpretation of the quasistellar radio sources.

In the 1930s, the great variety of stellar spectra was recognized to have been caused by differences in the temperatures and pressures in stellar atmospheres. To a first approximation, all stars seemed to have the same composition, even though certain stars were "peculiar." It was therefore logical to suppose that all chemical elements and isotopes had a common origin at the "beginning" of time.

Greenstein made his first spectroscopic investigations of peculiar stars by searching for unusual effects in stellar atmospheres that might explain their anomalous spectra. By 1948, the understanding of nuclear reactions showed how the energy sources of the stars caused nuclear transmutations. Could effects of these fusion reactions be studied as abundance changes at the surfaces of stars? One major source of stellar energy is the successive capture of three additional hydrogen atoms by an initial single proton leading to production of a helium atom. Were there stars rich in helium? In still another process, the carbon-nitrogen cycle, C^{12} captures four successive protons and produces C^{13} and N^{14} as well as He^4. Could stars abnormally rich in C^{13} or N^{14} be found?

In spectroscopic abundance determinations, high resolution is required, and the most interesting stars are often faint. Using the spectrographs at the McDonald Observatory, and later the Mount Wilson and Palomar Observatories, Greenstein developed a method of differential-curve-of-growth analysis permitting comparison of normal stars or the Sun with peculiar stars that by-passed many theoretical difficulties. He

initiated a program of spectroscopic data collection that was closely linked with a parallel growth of new ideas in nuclear astrophysics. This led to the present view that nuclear reactions in stars have produced all the chemical elements from hydrogen. The atoms in our Earth were synthesized in many different, long-dead stars. Peculiar evolutionary histories lead to stars rich in helium or carbon. One star was found in which there was more He^3 than He^4. In the oldest stars, heavy elements are only one per cent as abundant as in our Sun. Greenstein independently suggested the neutron-producing reaction in red giant stars required for the heavier elements.

Beginning with his Ph.D. thesis on interstellar dust in 1937, Greenstein studied the nature of the interstellar medium. With Leverett Davis, he developed the idea that space was pervaded by dominantly regular magnetic fields, near 10^{-5} to 10^{-6} gauss, which aligned nonspherical, rapidly spinning, paramagnetic dust grains and produced interstellar polarization of light. Such magnetic fields became particularly important in his work in radio astronomy. The rapid growth of radio astronomy resulted in his discovery in 1964, with other colleagues, of the quasi-stellar radio sources, the most luminous—and enigmatic—objects in our universe. With Maarten Schmidt, he obtained a detailed physical model for their size, mass, temperature, luminosity, magnetic field, and high-energy particle content.

At one extreme of astronomical size and brightness are the white dwarfs, stars no larger than the Earth but nearly as massive as the Sun. Their significance as the final stage of evolution led Greenstein to a series of discoveries concerning their spectra. In collaboration with Olin Eggen, he greatly multiplied the quantitative information on the size, temperature, motion, and composition of these faint objects. He con-

firmed the Einstein gravitational red shift by velocity measures of members of clusters or binary star systems. Evidences for nuclear evolution were provided by his discovery of white dwarfs containing largely helium and carbon. New evolutionary problems are raised by the apparently great age or rapid cooling of some of these stars.

Greenstein studied at Harvard, receiving his A.B. in 1929 and his Ph.D. in 1937. After two years as National Research Council Fellow, he taught at the University of Chicago, doing research at the Yerkes Observatory, from 1939 to 1948. During World War II, he designed specialized optical instruments, afterwards retaining connections with related defense problems and serving on numerous government advisory committees. In 1948 he joined the faculty of the California Institute of Technology, initiating its Graduate School of Astrophysics. He became executive officer of the Division of Physics, Mathematics, and Astronomy and chairman of the faculty in 1965. In 1948, also, he joined the Mount Wilson and Palomar Observatories. He was elected to the National Academy of Sciences in 1957.

Author of about 250 technical papers, Greenstein edited several books, notably *Stellar Atmospheres* (1960).

For background information *see* ASTROPHYSICS; BINARY STARS in the McGraw-Hill Encyclopedia of Science and Technology.   ☐

H

★★

(continued)

★ **HAFSTAD, Lawrence Randolph**

American physicist
Born June 18, 1904, Minneapolis, Minn., U.S.A.

AFTER THE neutron was discovered in 1932, the various nuclei in the periodic table could be considered as composed of appropriate numbers of neutrons and protons. It was clear that attractive forces, in addition to the well-known repulsive electric forces, must be involved. Theoretical physicists were speculating as to the character and range of these new forces, and experimentalists were seeking approaches that would permit the exploration of these forces with the precision required. With his associates at the Carnegie Institution (G. Breit, M. A. Tuve, O. Dahl, N. P. Heydenburg, and others), with whom he had been working since the late 1920s on high-voltage vacuum tubes for the acceleration of nuclear particles, Hafstad participated in the first precision measurements of the scattering of protons by protons. This involved a study of the distribution of scattered protons produced by the bombardment of hydrogen muclei by high-speed protons. In lay terms this means, in effect, measuring accurately the diameter of a single proton with a dimension of some 10^{-14} centimeter.

The classic experiment of Ernest Rutherford in 1919 in the transmutation of nitrogen by alpha-particle bombardment opened up an exciting vista for the experimental physicist. The alchemists' dreams of transmuting elements, as well as the possibility of releasing the mysterious stored energy of the nucleus, now were moved into the realm of possibility. Three obvious routes for progress were open: first, the use of the very high-energy particles from natural radioactive sources; second, the high-energy accelerator approach, which would give particles of at least as high energy as those from the radioactive sources; and third, after the development of the Schroedinger theory, the use of relatively low-energy particles produced by conventional transformers and condensers, but with large currents to take advantage of the barrier penetration properties within the nucleus, predicted by wave mechanics (George Gamow, R. W. Gurney, A. U. Condon).

Beginning in 1928 the Carnegie group (led by Breit and Tuve and including Hafstad) explored the second route—the high-energy, high-voltage vacuum tube approach—using especially the resonance transformer (Tesla coil) and, finally, the Van de Graaff electrostatic generator as voltage sources. By the early 1930s they had developed techniques sufficiently so that contributions could be made to the rapidly developing field of neutron production, artificial radioactivity, and nuclear spectroscopy.

Because of the uniquely precise voltage control developed by the Carnegie group, their work culminated in a long series of proton-proton scattering experiments that gave the first basis for an evaluation of the magnitude of the specific nuclear attractive forces. In 1939 the same experimental skills and facilities made possible one of the first experimental confirmations in the United States of the nuclear-fission process postulated by Otto Hahn and Fritz Strassmann in Germany, after preliminary work by Lise Meitner and her coworkers. Shortly thereafter the delayed neutron emission from the uranium fission process, which was to prove so important in nuclear reactor control, was discovered by the Carnegie group.

This work was interrupted by war preparations beginning in early 1940, and Hafstad went to work on such ordnance projects as the proximity fuze, ramjet engines, missiles, and missile guidance. After the war his contributions were in the field of nuclear bomb detection, nuclear power for submarines, and developing nuclear reactors for the generation of power.

The son of Norwegian immigrants, Hafstad graduated in 1926 with a B.S. in electrical engineering from the University of Minnesota, did graduate work there in physics, and received his Ph.D. in physics from the Johns Hopkins University in 1933. From 1928 to 1942 he was with the Carnegie Institution. From 1942 to 1947 he was with the Applied Physics Laboratory of Johns Hopkins, serving as its director the last 2 years. During World War II he also served with the government's Office of Scientific Research and Development under Vannevar Bush, and from 1947 to 1949 was executive secretary of the Research and Development Board in the Pentagon under Bush and Karl Compton. In 1949 he became the first director of the Atomic Energy Commission's Reactor Development Division, and until 1951 he was also chairman of the government's Interdepartmental Committee on Scientific Research and Development. In 1955 he went with the Chase Manhattan Bank's atomic energy division, and shortly thereafter he joined General Motors Corp. as vice-president in charge of research. He served additionally as a consultant to the Office of Science and Technology of the White House, to the Department of Defense, and to other government agencies. In 1962 President Kennedy appointed him to the General Advisory Committee to the AEC, and in 1964 he was elected chairman of the GAC. In 1956 the Scientific Research Society of America awarded Hafstad its annual William Proctor Prize.

For background information *see* NEUTRON; PROTON in the McGraw-Hill Encyclopedia of Science and Technology.   ☐

★ HAGIHARA, Yusuke
Japanese astrophysicist
Born Mar. 28, 1897, Osaka, Japan

A SPECIALIST IN celestial mechanics, Hagihara made a number of contributions to the study of the stability of satellite systems, both natural and artificial. These studies opened new avenues of approach to the studies of the orbital behavior of other celestial bodies and of subatomic particles.

While observing Jupiter in 1610, the Italian astronomer and physicist Galileo Galilei discovered the first four satellites—other than Earth's own Moon—known to man. Since his discovery of Io, Europa, Ganymede, and Callisto, 26 other natural satellites have been found. When celestial mechanics evolved from the work of the German astronomer Johannes Kepler and the British natural philosopher Isaac Newton, the orbital data of these satellites became of great importance.

In 1927 Hagihara proved the stability of a satellite system in which two of the satellites have commensurable mean motions and are in-

fluenced by the gravitational attraction of the Sun and of the other satellites in the system. He did this by analyzing the motion of Rhea, one of the Saturnian satellites. Hagihara determined Rhea's apsidal motion and demonstrated the stability of the satellite's orbit by the matrix method of integrating a system of differential equations with periodic coefficients. He extended this method to the study of the rings of Saturn, to libration in general, to secular perturbation of higher orders, and even to the motion of electrons in a magnetron, a thermionic tube used for the generation of very short wavelength oscillations. Hagihara thus showed the matrix method to be advantageous in computing the characteristic exponents of the criterion of stability of motion.

Hagihara studied the motion of artificial satellites while working in the United States at the Smithsonian Astrophysical Observatory during the early 1960s. He applied his general theory of libration to the motion of the satellites at the critical inclination of the orbital plane. He also worked on the rotation of an artificial satellite along its orbit.

Hagihara also contributed to the theory of planetary nebulae. He studied the radiative equilibrium of a planetary nebula and, by solving the equations of radiative transfer, proved the atomic mechanisms involved. In addition, he computed the distribution of electron temperatures in such nebulae and found a deviation in the form of the Maxwellian distribution of electron velocity.

Among his other contributions to astrophysics are studies of the libration phenomena in planetary and satellite motions, based on his extension of the French mathematician Jules Henri Poincaré's treatment of the motion of Hecuba-type asteroids to more general cases, and the proposal of a new proof of the French mathematician Simeon Denis Poisson's theorem on the invariability of the major axes of planetary orbits. Hagihara developed an analytical approach to the trajectories in the Schwarzschild field of general relativity theory, basing his studies on the Hamilton-Jacobi method and on the elliptic functions of the German mathematician Karl W. T. Weierstrass; developed a theory of astronomical refraction; worked on a relativistic explanation of the theory of aberration; and studied the effects of photographic halation and sky scattering in coronal photometry.

The son of a businessman, Hagihara was educated at the University of Tokyo, receiving his D.Sc. in astronomy in 1927. In 1921 he accepted a position as an assistant at the Tokyo Astronomical Observatory. In 1923 he became an assistant professor at the University of Tokyo and was sent abroad as a traveling research fellow of the Japanese government. He spent some two years at Cambridge University in England and also worked at the Sorbonne in France, the University of Göttingen in Germany, and Harvard University in the United States. After returning to Japan, in 1935 he was made a professor of astronomy at the University of Tokyo, and served as director of the Tokyo Astronomical Observatory from 1946 to 1957. In the latter year he accepted a professorship at Tohoku University at Sendai, holding that position until 1960. Hagihara served as president of Utsonomiya University from 1960 to 1964. He was a vice president of the International Astronomical Union and president of its commission on celestial mechanics for 1961–67. During his many visits to the United States, he worked for brief periods at such institutions as the University of Chicago, Yale University, and Arizona University. He received the Watson Medal of the U.S. National Academy of Sciences in 1960.

Hagihara was the author of several books, among them *General Astronomy* (1955) and *Stability in Celestial Mechanics* (1957).

For background information *see* CELESTIAL MECHANICS in the McGraw-Hill Encyclopedia of Science and Technology.   □

★ **HAHN, Otto**

German chemist
Born Mar. 8, 1879, Frankfurt am Main, Germany

B Y IRRADIATING uranium, and later thorium, with neutrons, Hahn and his coworker Fritz Strassmann found that the strong binding forces of the nuclei of these heavy elements could be ruptured to produce elements belonging in the middle of the periodic table. These reactions, which had previously been thought impossible, led to the practical conversion of matter into energy and hence to the atomic age. Hahn was awarded the Nobel Prize in chemistry for 1944 for his discovery of the fission of heavy nuclei.

After the English physicist James Chadwick had discovered the neutron in 1932, the Italian physicist Enrico Fermi recognized the superiority of using this electrically neutral particle instead of the positively charged helium nucleus (alpha particle) or hydrogen nucleus (proton) for atomic transformations. Fermi found that by irradiating the elements of the periodic system up to uranium with slow (low-energy) neutrons he could transform almost all of them into radioactive isotopes of the element of the next higher atomic number. When he irradiated uranium, atomic number 92, with neutrons, a radioactive transformation product was found that Fermi inferred was a "transuranium" element, that is, a hitherto unknown element with an atomic number of 93.

In 1934, working with the Austrian-Swedish physicist Lise Meitner at the Kaiser Wilhelm Institute in Berlin-Dahlem, Hahn decided to repeat Fermi's experiments. They verified the results of Fermi, although they found that the procedure was very complicated. Through the use of the "indicator method," they were able to show that Fermi's transformation product was not an isotope of protactinium, actinium, thorium, or uranium. Thus, they reasoned that the transformation product was a transuranium element with an atomic number of 93. During nearly 4 years of work, in which Hahn and Meitner were joined by Strassmann, a number of other transuranium elements, from atomic number 94 to atomic number 96, were discovered. The results of these experiments were confirmed by other investigators.

In 1938, after Lise Meitner had gone into exile because of Adolf Hitler's regime and had taken up residence in Sweden, Hahn and Strassmann continued their experiments with the production of transuranium elements. One series of irradiations resulted in the production of an alkaline earth isotope whose chemical properties indicated that it was either barium or radium. Since by the prevalent views of nuclear physics at that time the production of barium had to be considered out of the question, the conclusion that radium had been produced was inescapable. They then attempted to separate the suspected artificial radium by fractional crystallization and other chemical techniques, all of which proved unsuccessful. Hahn and Strassmann then turned to indicator tests. Natural radium atoms, in the form of the radium isotopes mesothorium and thorium-X, were mixed with the unknown product, and crystallizations were carried out as bromides, chlorides, and chromates, always with the corresponding barium salt as carrier. When these mixtures were fractionated, the natural radium isotopes could be separated from the barium, but the suspected artificial radium isotopes could not. These results led Hahn and Strassmann to believe that under the action of the neutrons the uranium had split into two pieces, the most accessible of which was the barium.

To substantiate this, a so-called cyclic process was performed. One gram of the unknown substance, a barium salt, was subjected to the following cycle of six crystallizations: barium chloride $\longrightarrow$ barium succinate $\longrightarrow$ barium nitrate $\longrightarrow$ barium carbonate $\longrightarrow$ barium ferriminate $\longrightarrow$ barium chloride. The radioactivity after the cycle was completed was equal to that at the start. One could call the investigations a fivefold indicator experiment. The result of the cyclic process removed all doubts that the nuclei of uranium atoms could be split by slow neutrons. However, soon after the publication of the initial results in January, 1939, but before the publication of the results of the cyclic process in February of that year, Lise Meitner and her nephew Otto Robert Frisch had published an explanation of the fission process. A few weeks after their second publication, Hahn and Strassmann announced the discovery of the second product of the uranium fission, the rare gas krypton. Their discoveries were soon confirmed in the atomic physics institutes of the United States, France, and Great Britain.

Hahn and Strassmann also found that thorium would also fission if it was bombarded with fast neutrons. The hypothesis that they had advanced, that additional neutrons were emitted by the fission of uranium, was proved by the work of Frederic Joliot-Curie and his coworkers. These additional neutrons provided the possibility of a chain reaction and, thereby, the possible uses of the fission process to release the energy of the atomic nucleus. This resulted in the development of the atomic bomb and, more recently, in controlled fission for peaceful uses. Nuclear fission processes promise to replace the natural-energy sources of coal and petroleum, which are gradually becoming depleted, and are used in the production of artificial elements and radioactive isotopes that are needed in small amounts in many areas of chemistry, physics, and biology.

Among Hahn's many other contributions to chemistry were the discovery in 1917 in collaboration with Lise Meitner of the element protactinium (discovered independently by the English chemists Frederick Soddy and John A. Cranston) and the discovery of nuclear isomers, which are atoms with nuclei that differ not in their neutron content but in their energy content and mode of radioactive decay.

The son of a businessman, Hahn studied chemistry at the universities of Marburg and Munich, obtaining his Ph.D. from Marburg in 1901. In 1902 and 1903 he was an assistant in the

Chemistry Institute in Marburg, leaving in 1904 to work with William Ramsay at University College, London. In 1905 Hahn went to Canada to work with Ernest Rutherford at the Physical Institute of McGill University in Montreal. In 1906 he returned to the University of Berlin, joining the Chemical Institute there, and from 1914 to 1918 he had a leave of absence to serve in World War I. In 1928 Hahn became director of the Kaiser Wilhelm Institute for Chemistry, and from 1946 to 1960 he was president of the Kaiser Wilhelm Gesellschaft.

Hahn wrote *Was lehrt uns die Radioaktivität über die Geschichte der Erde?* (1927), *Applied Radiochemistry* (1936), *New Atoms* (1950), and *Vom Radiothor zur Uranspaltung* (1962).

For background information *see* FISSION, NUCLEAR in the McGraw-Hill Encyclopedia of Science and Technology.   □

HALDANE, John Burdon Sanderson
British geneticist
Born Nov. 5, 1892, Oxford, England
Died Dec. 1, 1964, Bhudaneswar, India

A BIOLOGIST OF wide interests, Haldane is probably most noted for the application of mathematical analysis to genetic phenomena and their relation to evolution.

The dominant school of evolutionary thought today derives from Darwin's theory of natural selection. Darwin's "variation," however, is now interpreted according to the gene theory, and statistical techniques are used to analyze the change of gene frequencies within a population. Independently of R. A. Fisher and Sewall Wright, but at the same time, Haldane treated mathematically problems dealing with selection, showing the relation of mendelian genetics to evolution. His investigations included estimates of the rates of change of the frequency of dominant and recessive genes under various types of selection; the possibility of stable equilibria with intermediate gene frequencies when the heterozygote is the fittest of the three genotypes; the effects of selection on a character influenced by many genes; the relative importance of selection and mutation in determining the rate and direction of evolution; and the possibility of estimating spontaneous mutation rates from observations of harmful dominant or sex-linked genes in natural populations.

Haldane's interest in human genetics led him to do much pioneer work in this area. His contributions were based mainly on statistical measurements. Analyzing the pedigrees of hemophiliacs, he calculated the rate of mutation of this sex-linked gene and found it to be between 1 to 5 per 100,000 per generation. While investigating the pedigrees of individuals with both hemophilia and color-blindness, he developed, in collaboration with Julia Bell, methods to measure the linkage of the genes; as a result the map distances between these loci were determined.

In addition to his contributions to genetics, Haldane is well known for his work in the field of enzyme kinetics. He also studied various aspects of human physiology, often acting as his own experimental animal. To prove that sunstroke was caused by an overheating of the brain and spinal cord, he sat in the hot sun for several hours daily, periodically pouring water over his head and back. He did not get sunstroke but did suffer a severe sunburn. During World War II, he investigated methods of alleviating physiological stresses due to rapid decompression of divers surfacing too fast or sailors attempting to escape from submarines. He showed that by controlling the opening and closing of the Eustachian tubes, danger from pressure on the eardrums could be lessened. He determined the safest mixture of gases for breathing, depending on the length of time at various depths, in order to reduce the possibility of the occurrence of the "bends."

Haldane was the son of John Scott Haldane, a professor of physiology at Oxford. He was educated at Eton and received his M.A. from New College, Oxford, where from 1919 to 1922 he was a fellow. In 1922 he became a reader in biochemistry at Cambridge, a post he held until 1932. Between 1930 and 1932 he also served as Fullerian Professor of Physiology at the Royal Institution. In 1932 he was a visiting professor at the University of California. Haldane received an appointment as professor of genetics to London University in 1933, and in 1937 became professor of biometry, a chair he held for 20 years. Leaving London University, he went to India in 1957, where he became head of the Orissa state government's Genetics and Biometry Laboratory. He was elected a fellow of the Royal Society in 1932 and in 1953 "in recognition of

his initiation of the modern phase of study of the evolution of living population," was awarded the society's Darwin Medal. In 1961 he received the Kimber Genetics Award of the U.S. National Academy of Sciences and in 1964 was elected a foreign associate of the Academy.

Haldane wrote many books, both technical and nontechnical. Among the former are: *Enzymes* (1930), *Causes of Evolution* (1932), and *New Paths in Genetics* (1942).

For background information *see* EVOLUTION, ORGANIC; GENETICS in the McGraw-Hill Encyclopedia of Science and Technology. ◻

★ **HALL, Philip**
British mathematician
Born Apr. 11, 1904, London, England

IN 1872 the Norwegian mathematician Sylow made a fundamental discovery: if G is a group of order mn, where m and n are coprime, and if $m = p^k$ where p is a prime, then every subgroup of G whose order divides m is contained in some subgroup of order m; and these subgroups of order m, now known as the Sylow p-subgroups of G, are all conjugate in G.

In 1928 Hall found a theorem that differed from Sylow's in only one respect: instead of assuming m to be a prime power, he supposed the group G to be soluble. The conclusion remained the same.

A subgroup whose order m and index n in a finite group G are coprime is now called a Hall subgroup of G. Particular cases are the Sylow p-subgroups $(m = p^k)$ and the p-complements $(n = p^k)$. Hall proved in 1937 that a finite group G is soluble if, and only if, it contains for each prime p at least one p-complement G_p. By a study of the system normalizer X, which consists of all elements x in G such that $x^{-1}G_px = G_p$ for every p, he developed a general structure theory for finite soluble groups.

In 1956, working in collaboration with Graham Higman, he made a deeper study of the wider class of p-soluble groups. These are the groups G that possess a chain of normal subgroups

$$1 = G_0 < G_1 < \ldots < G_n = G$$

such that each of the factor groups G_i/G_{i-1} is either of p-power order or else of order prime to p. The minimum possible number of factors of p-power order is called the p-length of G. Hall and Higman found bounds for the p-length in terms of certain numerical invariants of the Sylow p-subgroups of G. These bounds proved to be significant for the outstanding achievement in the theory of finite groups, the proof by the American mathematicians John G. Thompson and Walter Feit of the old conjecture that all groups of odd order are soluble.

In the study of prime-power groups, Hall's most interesting contribution—the theory of regular p-groups—was made in 1933. He showed by combinatorial arguments that, in a group G of order p^n with $n \le p$, the elements x such that $x^p = 1$ form a subgroup H and the pth powers of the elements of G form a subgroup K whose index in G is equal to the order of H. None of these statements remains true in the Sylow p-subgroup of the symmetric group of degree p^2. This is the smallest irregular p-group and has order p^{1+p}.

This paper of 1933 also contains the basic laws of the commutator calculus. The lower central series $G = G_1, G_2, G_3, \ldots$ of a group G is defined inductively by $G_{n+1} = [G_n, G]$. Here $[H,K]$ is the subgroup generated by all commutators $h^{-1}k^{-1}hk$ with h in H and k in K. Hall proved that $[G_m, G_n]$ is always contained in G_{m+n}. This law provides one of several links connecting the study of groups with that of Lie rings.

In 1954 Hall began a systematic study of finitely generated soluble groups in relation to various possible finiteness properties that such a group may or may not have. His work brought out a striking contrast between two special classes of finitely generated groups: on the one hand, those for which some term of the lower central series is Abelian; on the other hand, those whose group of inner automorphisms is metabelian. The former class contains only countably many distinct groups, the latter uncountably many. All groups of the former class are residually finite and satisfy the maximal condition for normal subgroups, while groups of the latter need have neither of these properties. As Hall showed, there are several other properties that exhibit the same dichotomy.

To the study of simple groups Hall made two constructive contributions. First, there is his universal countable locally finite group of 1959, defined to within isomorphism by a property of its finite subgroups and universal in the sense that it contains as subgroups uncountably many distinct copies of every countably infinite locally finite group. Secondly, there is his construction for the first time, in 1963, of a class of nonstrictly simple groups. Each of these groups G is the union of an ascending series of subgroups G_n, each G_n being a normal subgroup of G_{n+1}, the next term of the series, although G itself, being a simple group, has no nontrivial normal subgroups of its own.

A notable feature of Hall's later work was his systematic use of closure operations acting on classes of groups. This may sometimes have been merely a way of expressing certain results with greater elegance or conciseness. But it often had the suggestive power of a novel point of view, bringing to light new and interesting problems.

Hall was educated at the Bluecoat School, Christ's Hospital, 1915–22, and at King's College, Cambridge, where he became a fellow in 1927. He was elected to the Royal Society of London in 1942 and received the Society's Sylvester Medal in 1961. In 1953 he became Sadleirian Professor of Pure Mathematics at the University of Cambridge. He received the de Morgan Medal of the London Mathematical Society in 1965.

For background information *see* GROUP THEORY in the McGraw-Hill Encyclopedia of Science and Technology.   □

★ HAMMETT, Louis Plack

American chemist
Born Apr. 7, 1894, Wilmington, Del., U.S.A.

HAMMETT'S CHIEF scientific accomplishment was the recognition that reactions of organic chemical substances can be correlated by quantitative relationships as opposed to the qualitative ones upon which the structure of organic chemistry was founded and by which it existed for some 50 years. One such relationship, involving the effect of certain kinds of change in structure on the reactivity of a wide range of substances, is frequently called the Hammett equation. Another concept, that of the acidity function, enabled chemists to treat quantitatively the reactions of acids and bases in a range of systems far beyond anything that had previously been possible. The American Chemical Society awarded Hammett its Nichols Medal in 1957 and its Priestley and Gibbs medals in 1961.

At the time of Hammett's retirement from active service one of his colleagues at Columbia University wrote: "Professor Hammett's pioneering researches, new concepts, and original texts in physical organic and physical chemistry have had a profound influence on the development of chemistry. His investigations of equilibria and rates of organic reactions by quantitative methods have demonstrated the fruitfulness of this approach to understanding the mechanisms of organic reactions. His famous original concept of Hammett's sigma-rho values has provided the foundation for subsequent physical organic research. It is almost impossible to read an issue of a journal today without encountering an article which uses the Hammett sigma-rho approach as a tool to elucidate the mechanism of a reaction. His textbook, *Physical Organic Chemistry*, is a genuine classic and has proven to be one of the most influential books in contemporary chemistry. By its bold originality, it showed how principles of physical chemistry and quantitative measurements are just as applicable to understanding complex organic reactions as they are to inorganic systems. It played a major role in removing the barriers between the narrow fields of chemistry, and established with a text and a coherent body of theory the field of physical organic chemistry."

Although born in Delaware, Hammett lived during most of his childhood and youth in Portland, Maine. He graduated from Harvard College in 1916, studied with Hermann Straudinger in Zurich for a year, then worked in Pittsburgh in a wartime government laboratory, mostly on materials for airplane construction. He went to Columbia, after a year in industry, in 1920 as a graduate student and instructor in chemistry, obtaining his Ph.D. there in 1923. He remained at Columbia, except for 4 years during World War II when he worked on rocket propellants at the Explosives Research Laboratory at Bruceton, Pa., until he retired in 1961 as Mitchell Professor Emeritus of Chemistry. He was chairman of the Columbia department of chemistry from 1951 to 1957. In 1943 he was elected to the National Academy of Sciences.

Hammett wrote *Solutions of Electrolytes*

(1922), *Physical Organic Chemistry* (1940), and *Introduction to the Study of Physical Chemistry* (1952).

For background information *see* PHYSICAL CHEMISTRY in the McGraw-Hill Encyclopedia of Science and Technology. □

☆ **HARLOW, Harry Frederick**
American psychologist
Born Oct. 31, 1905, Fairfield, Iowa, U.S.A.

IN 35 years of pioneering research on monkeys, Harlow contributed to the areas of learning, neurophysiology, motivation, and love. The love researches had broad import for disciplines outside psychology.

Harlow's research on love began as a demonstration that the complex affectional bonds of Primates could not be explained by the widely accepted theory that love originated in the infant's association of the mother with nursing and then generalized to other family members and to outsiders. Nonsexual relationships, according to this theory, were thus tied to infantile feeding reinforcement. Sexual love was treated separately, being regarded as the outcome of reduction of the sex drive after puberty. Social psychologists further hypothesized that societies originated and persisted because they provided a means for satisfying the sex drive.

Because human infants could not be risked, Harlow studied rhesus monkeys. The monkey is more mature at birth than the human, but both species have similar needs. Moreover, both display the same gamut of emotions, albeit the human's are more subtle.

In his first experiment investigating love for the mother, Harlow took infants at birth and provided half with a nursing wire-dummy mother and a terry-covered nonnursing mother. The remainder had a wire nonnursing mother and a cloth nursing mother. Automatic recording of contact time on the mothers showed that both groups avoided the wire mother and stayed with the cloth mother, suggesting that contact could override feeding reinforcement. When frightened, the infants, regardless of feeding condition, obtained security from the cloth mother. Moreover, the attachment persisted long after separation.

Next Harlow simultaneously investigated the development of love for natural mothers and for playmates and the course of maternal love. One group of mothers and their babies shared a living-play apparatus; other babies shared an identical setup with cloth mothers. Play followed a similar sequence in both groups, but live-mothered infants played earlier and more effectively at first. Infants in each group developed strong affection among themselves as well as for their mothers, and group differences disappeared by one year. Still other monkeys raised without mothers *or* playmates were completely inept socially. These and related studies indicated that while live mothering gave an early advantage, peer experience for the monkeys was even more important for subsequent normality. Mating proved unsuccessful for males and difficult for females raised alone; when achieved in females, they became cruel or indifferent mothers. Harlow concluded that normal sex and maternal behavior depended on development of affectional ties to peers early in life. Monkeys raised by real mothers but delayed in peer contacts were fearful and overly aggressive.

From these researches Harlow formulated a theory of love that in turn inspired more researches. Harlow maintained that Primates have five distinct but interdependent affectional systems, each aroused by its own stimulus conditions and expressed through its own behavior patterns. Each develops in orderly stages supported by different underlying variables and mechanisms. The affectional systems in order of development are: (1) infant-mother, (2) peer, (3) heterosexual, (4) maternal, and (5) paternal. Societies, human and nonhuman, are based not on sex but on the multiplicity of affectional bonds. Contrary to the popular belief that all personal-social abnormalities result from inadequate mothering, Harlow believed that traumatic events in any developing affectional system can be causative, with the peer system being especially vulnerable.

Harlow majored in psychology at Stanford University, receiving his B.A. in 1927 and his Ph.D. in 1930. He immediately joined the University of Wisconsin faculty and established the Psychology Primate Laboratory the following year. Facilities gradually expanded to accommodate ever-widening researches and doubled in 1964 with the addition of the Wisconsin Regional Primate Research Center. Harlow became director of the Center as well as of the Laboratory. He served the Army as chief of the Human Resources Research Branch and worked on numerous government committees and boards. In 1956 Harlow received the Warren Medal of the Society of Experimental Psychology and in 1960 the Distinguished Scientific Contribution Award of the American Psychological Association. He was elected to the National Academy of Sciences in 1951.

For background information *see* PSYCHOLOGY, PHYSIOLOGICAL AND EXPERIMENTAL in the McGraw-Hill Encyclopedia of Science and Technology.   □

★ HARRISON, George Russell

American physicist
Born July 14, 1898, San Diego, Calif., U.S.A.

To FURTHER his studies of complex atomic spectra, aimed at determining the electronic energy levels in atoms, Harrison pioneered in the field of microengineering, inventing several highly precise measuring devices and high-speed analog computers. By developing the first practical ruling engine controlled optically through interferometers and electronic servomechanisms, he was able to produce diffraction gratings of a new order of size and perfection. His development of echelle spectroscopy, made possible by finding how to rule gratings having such coarse but precise groove spacing that they could be used in very high orders in the optical and ultraviolet regions of the spectrum, opened a new era of power in speed and resolution for spectroscopic instruments. His automatic comparator for rapidly measuring spectrum wavelengths to seven-figure accuracy resulted in the compilation of the MIT Wavelength Tables, published in 1938, which he edited. His application of the new Bitter electromagnet to studies of the Zeeman splitting of spectrum lines at field strengths previously unattained led to a long series of analyses of complex atomic spectra in his laboratory.

Physicists and chemists who determine atomic and molecular constants by evaluating the energy levels that give rise to their spectrum lines must often determine with high precision the wavelengths of several thousand lines emitted by a single type of atom or molecule. Methods of speeding up such measurements and the associated computations were especially needed before the introduction of the high-speed digital computer and modern electronic methods of metrology. Harrison anticipated many of these and accelerated the replacement of the older hand-and-eye methods of measurement. With replicas made from gratings ruled on interferometrically controlled engines in the MIT Spectroscopy Laboratory, astrophysicists are now able to study the spectra of faint stars at dispersions previously unattainable. For years following 1955, the MIT engines developed under Harrison's direction provided the world's entire supply of 10-inch master gratings giving high resolution. Spectroscopists everywhere now have available replica gratings with up to 50 square inches of area of high optical quality.

For his development of improved spectroscopic instrumentation, Harrison received eight medals and awards, including the Ives and Mees medals of the Optical Society of America, the Rumford Medal of the American Academy of Arts and Sciences, and the Cresson Medal of the Franklin Institute.

Harrison majored in physics at Stanford University, where he received his A.B. in 1919, his A.M. in 1920, and his Ph.D. in 1922. He taught at Stanford until 1930, when he became a professor of physics at the Massachusetts Institute of Technology. He helped design and became director of the Spectroscopy Laboratory there, which in the years following turned out many graduate students and a large volume of spectroscopic research, particularly in analyses of complex spectra. During World War II Harrison served with the National Defense Research Committee of the Office of Scientific Research and Development as chief of the optics division, and later of the physics division. He also directed an analytical laboratory of the Manhattan District maintained at MIT for routine determination of the purity of uranium samples by spectrographic analysis. In 1943, as assistant chief of the Office of Field Service, he went to General MacArthur's headquarters in Australia and New Guinea to set up a research division for the introduction of new weapons to the field. From 1942 to 1964 Harrison served as dean of the School of Science at MIT while continuing active direction of his research projects.

Harrison wrote *Atoms in Action* (1938), *Practical Spectroscopy*, with R. C. Lord and J. R. Loofbourow (1948), and *What Man May Be* (1956).

For background information *see* SPECTROSCOPY in the McGraw-Hill Encyclopedia of Science and Technology. □

★ HASTINGS, Albert Baird

American biochemist
Born Nov. 20, 1895, Dayton, Ky., U.S.A.

As a graduate student at Columbia University, Hastings engaged in research on the physiology of fatigue, with particular attention to the effects of exercise on the acid-base balance of the blood. Because of his experience in this subject, he became in 1921 first assistant to D. D. Van Slyke at the Rockefeller Institute for Medical Research, where he remained until 1926. While there, his work centered around the blood as a physicochemical system. He applied the Debye-Hückel theory to the behavior of weak electrolytes (for example, carbonic acid and acid-base indicators), to the acidic properties of reduced and oxygenated hemoglobin, and to the solubility of the bone salts.

From 1926 to 1935, Hastings was research professor of biochemistry at the University of Chicago. During this period, he extended his physicochemical interest in the blood to tissues and, with his colleagues, determined the mass and ionic composition of the extra- and intracellular phases of skeletal muscle. Another interest during this period was the role played by oxidation-reduction potentials in the metabolism of lactic acid. He also carried out definitive studies on the acid-base balance of the arterial blood. This work demonstrated that the body's response to pathological amounts of acids and bases is such that it attempts to keep both the CO_2 tension and pH of the blood as close to normal values as possible. The reason for this became the subject of his research activities 35 years later.

Hastings was Hamilton Kuhn Professor and

head of the department of biological chemistry at Harvard Medical School from 1935 to 1959. During this period he continued his study of the intracellular ionic composition of different tissues and began a study of the effect of ions and hormones on intermediary metabolism. In 1940, in company with colleagues, he began the use of the short-lived carbon isotope, ^{11}C, to label substrates that were subsequently metabolized, in vivo, to other substances, such as CO_2 and glycogen. In the course of this work he and his associates made the discovery that CO_2 is incorporated into liver glycogen of the rat. This was a hitherto unsuspected use of carbon dioxide by mammalian organisms. After World War II, when the long-lived carbon isotope ^{14}C became available, this was confirmed by experiments carried out on liver in vitro.

These in vitro experiments were made possible by an event that occurred in his laboratory. When liver slices were incubated in an extracellular type of solution (high in sodium), the liver cells promptly exchanged their high concentration of intracellular potassium for the high concentration of extracellular sodium, thus providing an abnormal intracellular ionic environment. By preparing a solution that mimicked the intracellular fluid with respect to potassium and magnesium, Hastings found that liver slices would synthesize glycogen from glucose, in vitro. This gave him and his associates a useful tissue preparation by which many aspects of carbohydrate metabolism could be studied quantitatively and in detail.

There followed a series of papers in which the quantitative effects of factors such as pH, ions, and hormones on the intermediary metabolic pathways were determined. For this work, ^{14}C-labeled substrates such as glucose, fructose, galactose, glycerol, and pyruvate were used. In the course of their studies on liver from diabetic animals, Hastings and his associates discovered that such livers not only utilize less glucose than do normal livers but also produce more glucose—thus resolving an argument of long standing as to whether diabetes is due to underutilization or overproduction of glucose. Another product of this period was the quantitative evaluation of the extent to which alternate metabolic pathways were affected by factors such as ions and hormones.

In 1959 Hastings retired from Harvard and became a member of the Scripps Clinic and Research Foundation in La Jolla, Calif. This permitted a return to a life of full-time laboratory research. He first undertook to reevaluate the effect of changes in acid-base balance on carbohydrate metabolism. In the course of this he made a discovery that had hitherto been overlooked, namely, that the metabolism of glucose, fructose, and glycerol by liver is quantitatively affected by the concentration of CO_2 present in the environment. This was independent of the influence of CO_2 on the pH of the environment. Subsequently, he and his colleagues extended these studies to lipid metabolism, where they found that the effect of CO_2 concentration was even more striking in promoting fatty-acid synthesis.

From 1941 to 1947 Hastings served on the Committee on Medical Research of the Office of Scientific Research and Development. Subsequently he served on the first Committee on Biology and Medicine of the Atomic Energy Commission (1947–50) and on four advisory councils of the U.S. Public Health Service N.I.H.: Cancer Council (1943–46), Health Council (1947–48), Arthritis and Metabolic Disease Council (1956–60), and Heart Council (1960–64).

Hastings received his B.S. in physical chemistry at the University of Michigan in 1917 and his Ph.D. in physiology at Columbia University in 1921. For his contributions to the knowledge of physiological processes he received, among other honors, the 1962 Banting Medal of the American Diabetes Association, the 1964 American College of Physicians Medal, and the 1965 Modern Medicine Distinguished Achievement Award. He received the President's Medal for Merit in 1948 and in 1964 was cited by the U.S. Public Health Service for 47 years of service. He was elected to the National Academy of Sciences in 1939.

For background information see BACTERIAL METABOLISM in the McGraw-Hill Encyclopedia of Science and Technology.   □

★ HECKMANN, Otto Hermann Leopold

German astronomer
Born June 23, 1901, Opladen, Rhineland, Germany

HECKMANN WORKED in various observational and theoretical fields of astronomy. One of his subjects was astrometry, which aims at the most exact measurements of star positions and, by comparison with earlier observations, leads to the knowledge of proper motions of "fixed" stars. One example of Heckmann's work in this area was his determination, with W. Dieckvoss and H. Kox, of the fainter members of the moving star cluster around α Persei, a cluster that until then had been considered to consist only of brighter stars. Another example was his international organization of the reobservation of 180,000 stars of the so-called AG Catalogs. When completed, this will produce an enormous body of proper motion data obtained through the co-

and assistant professor in 1935. In 1941 he became head of the astronomy department of the University of Hamburg and director of the Hamburg Observatory. In 1962 he was charged with the construction and direction of the European Southern Observatory in Chile, a joint project of Belgium, France, Holland, Sweden, and West Germany. Among other honors, Heckmann received the Watson Medal of the U.S. National Academy of Sciences in 1961 and the Bruce Medal of the Astronomical Society of the Pacific in 1964.

For background information *see* ASTROMETRY; COSMOLOGY in the McGraw-Hill Encyclopedia of Science and Technology. □

operation of observatories in Canada, the United States, Europe, and the Soviet Union.

Another area of Heckmann's research was the photometry of star magnitudes (brightnesses) by photographic methods. This was at its height in the late 1930s, but after World War II photoelectric methods largely replaced photographic. During 1933–37, by refining the methods used until then, Heckmann, together with H. Haffner, succeeded in finding the sharpness of the main sequence in the color-magnitude diagram of the star cluster Praesepe. This object was carefully chosen from others as offering the most favorable chances for the detection. Later photoelectric repetition by others of this photometry confirmed Heckmann's earlier results.

Much of Heckmann's time was devoted to theoretical work in the fields of statistical dynamics and cosmology. In the latter, he proved as early as 1931 that, under the assumption of the homogeneity and isotropy of matter quite commonly made at that time, open hyperbolic and euclidean spaces resulted from general relativity as readily as closed (spherical) ones. He stressed the usefulness of Newtonian mechanics in cosmology. In the 1950s he found, with E. Schücking, the possibility that an expanding universe shows an absolute rotation, which might have considerable influence in evolutionary cosmological models. The relativistic treatment of these anisotropic but still homogeneous models is, however, mathematically so complicated that explicit results have not yet been found.

Heckmann's interest in instrumental problems was manifested in the design of many details of the 80/120/240-cm Schmidt telescope of the Hamburg Observatory.

The son of a notary, Heckmann studied astronomy, mathematics, and physics at the University of Bonn. From 1925 to 1927 he was assistant astronomer at the Bonn Observatory; from 1927 to 1935 he was in a similar position in Göttingen. He became lecturer in astronomy in 1929

☆ HEINEMANN, Edward Henry

American aeronautical engineer
Born Mar. 14, 1908, Saginaw, Mich., U.S.A.

EARLY IN his career, Heinemann recognized the importance of fundamental simplicity in aircraft design. The numerous planes he designed were, consequently, considerably lighter and less complex than competitive aircraft.

Heinemann was responsible for the conception, design, and development of the following aircraft:

The SBD Dauntless dive bomber, used extensively by the U.S. Navy and Marine Corps during World War II in the Pacific theater. This aircraft was credited with having sunk more combatant tonnage than any other weapon during World War II.

The R3D-1 twin-engine transport, commercially known as DC5, was the first transport to employ a nose-wheel landing gear.

The DB-7 Boston attack bomber, developed for the French prior to World War II and operated by the British after France fell.

The A-20 Havoc attack bomber, developed for the U.S. Army Air Force to conduct low-level attack missions against ground objectives. It was used extensively in the European theater during World War II.

The A-24 attack bomber, developed for the U.S. Army Air Force as a dive bomber similar to the SBD Dauntless.

The A-26 Invader twin-engine attack bomber, developed for the U.S. Army Air Force for low-level attack, was the first bomber employed with NASA laminar-flow air foils and double-slotted wing flaps. The A-26 was extensively used in the Pacific theater during World War II in Korea and Vietnam.

The XCG-7 and 8, all-wood troop-carrying gliders developed and demonstrated as a possible way of eliminating metal and using wood structures exclusively. These were never put into production due to changing requirements and the availability of metal.

The SB2D Destroyer bomber, developed for the U.S. Navy.

The TB2D torpedo bomber, developed and tested during the later years of World War II in anticipation of a prolonged naval engagement in the Pacific. This carrier-based torpedo bomber was unique in that it carried four 2,000-lb torpedoes and had performance beyond any other torpedo plane previously developed.

The AD Skyraider attack bomber, developed for the U.S. Navy during World War II and used extensively during the Korean War and in Vietnam in the mid-1960s.

The D558 Skystreak research airplane, developed to prove transonic and supersonic aerodynamic control principles to be incorporated in following combat aircraft.

The D558-2 Skyrocket research airplane, both jet- and rocket-powered, was the first airplane to reach twice the speed of sound. It established an altitude record of 83,000 ft.

The F3D Skynight jet fighter, developed for the U.S. Navy and used extensively by the U.S. Marine Corps in the Korean conflict, was the first jet night fighter equipped with radar and automatic fire-control equipment.

The A3D Skywarrior, the largest jet bomber ever produced for Navy carriers, was developed to carry the largest of the early nuclear weapons developed in the United States. It was capable of taking off from a carrier in the Pacific Ocean and landing on a carrier in the Atlantic Ocean nonstop.

The F4D-1 Navy Skyray, the first Delta-wing fighter developed in the United States, had an extremely high rate of climb.

The F5D-1 Skylancer, an advancement of the Skyray with supersonic capability.

The A4D Skyhawk jet attack bomber, developed after 1952 as a replacement for the AD propeller-driven airplane. The fundamental simplicity of its design made it the lightest, most efficient jet bomber ever developed. It became the standard attack aircraft in the Navy, seeing extensive activity in Vietnam.

Heinemann started his aircraft career as a draftsman for the Douglas Aircraft Company in 1926. In the years immediately following, he also worked for International Aircraft, Morland Aircraft, Lockheed, and Northrop of Burbank. He rejoined the Douglas Company in 1932 at its El Segundo Division, then known as Northrop Aircraft Co. He became, in 1936, chief engineer at Douglas's El Segundo Division and, in 1958, vice-president—engineering for combat aircraft for Douglas. In 1962 he joined the General Dynamics Corporation as vice-president—engineering and program development. Heinemann received the Sylvanus Albert Reed Award in 1952, the Collier Trophy in 1953, and the Paul Tissandier Diploma in 1955. In 1954 he was named Southern California's Aviation Man of the Year. He was elected to the National Academy of Engineering in 1965.

For background information *see* AERONAUTICAL ENGINEERING; AIRPLANE in the McGraw-Hill Encyclopedia of Science and Technology.   □

★ HEISKANEN, Weikko Aleksanteri

Finnish-American geodesist and geophysicist
Born July 23, 1895, Kangaslampi, Finland

HEISKANEN CONCENTRATED mainly on the study of isostasy and gravity. In his Ph.D. dissertation in 1924 he modified the isostatic-floating theory of G. B. Airy, computed needed isostatic reduction tables, and with his students used the modified theory to determine the thickness of the Earth's crust in the Alps, the Caucasus, Norway, the Rocky Mountains, the Ferghana Basin, and the Carpathians. The Airy-Heiskanen isostatic system is one of two theories that seek to explain the forces influencing the shape of the Earth's surface. According to the Pratt-Hayford system, the less their density, the higher mountains rise—like fermenting dough. The Airy-Heiskanen system postulates that the mountains have light roots and that under the oceans are heavy antiroots. The mass surplus of the mountains is isostatically compensated by the light roots, and the deficiency of the oceans by the heavy antiroots. The Airy-Heiskanen system is now much used in geophysics and physical geodesy. The obtained values of the thickness of the Earth's crust are in agreement with the results of other methods.

Better known, perhaps, is Heiskanen's work in physical geodesy and the gravimetric method. The basis of the gravimetric method is this: The visible and invisible mass anomalies Δm, surplus or deficiencies, bring about the gravity anomalies Δg, the undulations N of the geoid, and the deflections of the vertical components ξ and η. The gravity anomalies Δg, which is the difference between the measured gravity g and theoretical gravity γ (or $\Delta g = g - \gamma$), can be observed, and the quantities N, ξ, and η can be computed at the Earth's surface. From the quantities g, γ, Δg, N, ξ, and η we can compute the corresponding quantities at any needed elevations, if a sufficiently large network of gravity stations exists. The better the gravity station network, the more accurately we can compute the undulations of the geodesy and other parameters around the Earth.

Heiskanen's isostatic research resulted in the accumulation in Helsinki of so much gravimetric material, including measurements made at sea, that in 1931 he and his students were able to start on the first gravimetric computation of the size and shape of the geoid. Their first publication on the gravimetric geoid (by R. A. Hirvonen) appeared in 1934; the second geoid (that of L. Tanni), based on a much larger body of material, appeared in 1948. Heiskanen's own "Columbus geoid" was published in 1956.

The ninth son of a Finnish farmer, Heiskanen received his M.S. (1917) and Ph.D. (1924) at the University of Helsinki. He continued his studies in Göttingen and Berlin universities in 1920–21, where his teachers were Hilbert, Landau, Wiechert, Planck, von Laue, and Einstein. From 1929 to 1949 he was professor of geodesy at the Technical University of Finland. After 1950 he divided his time between Helsinki, where he was director of the Finnish Geodetic Institute (1949–61), and Ohio State University, where he became professor of geodesy in 1950 and director of the Institute of Geodesy, Photogrammetry, and Cartography in 1952. In 1956 he was awarded the Bowie Medal of the American Geophysical Union.

Heiskanen wrote *The Earth and Its Gravity Field*, with F. A. Vening Meinesz (1958).

For background information *see* GEODESY; ISOSTASY; TERRESTRIAL GRAVITATION in the McGraw-Hill Encyclopedia of Science and Technology.   □

HENCH, Philip Showalter

American pathologist
Born Feb. 28, 1896, Pittsburgh, Pa., U.S.A.
Died Mar. 30, 1965, Ocho Rios, Jamaica

IN THE course of studies of rheumatoid arthritis made in the 1930s and 1940s, Hench found that under certain conditions the progress of the disease (then thought to be incurable) could be reversed. The condition of sufferers was greatly improved when they contracted jaundice or (in the case of women) became pregnant. This observation convinced Hench that there was a remedy for the disease, and his search resulted, in 1949, in the successful use of ACTH and cortisone, pituitary and adrenal cortex extracts, for this purpose. For this discovery he was awarded the Nobel Prize in physiology or medicine for 1950. He shared the prize with E. C. Kendall and T. Reichstein, who had isolated cortisone, made it available to Hench, and, in the case of Kendall, collaborated extensively with him.

In 1929 Hench, a specialist in rheumatoid arthritis at the Mayo Clinic, noted the improvement in arthritis patients who contracted jaundice, and very similar improvement in pregnant women patients. He began intensive investigations of the exact beneficial effects of jaundice and pregnancy. Hench became convinced that some substance normally found in the human body was responsible for the improvements, in both these cases, of the arthritic condition. Before this conclusion was reached, however, Hench conducted a series of experiments based on the hypothesis that the substance responsible for the improvement was produced by the jaundiced liver. Results were negative. He also briefly entertained the theory that, in the case of the pregnant women, a female sex hormone was causing the improvement. However, both patterns of relief were so similar, and the two above hypotheses so unsuccessful, that by 1938 Hench had concluded that the substance he sought was neither a liver product nor a unisexual hormone, but a bisexual hormone.

In that same year, Hench began his collaboration with E. C. Kendall in searching for "substance X" (as they had named their hypothetical arthritis remedy). Kendall, a biochemist, was engaged in the isolation and synthesis of various substances from the adrenal cortex. Hench had reason to suspect (though the evidence was somewhat ambiguous) that the adrenals played some role in the rheumatic arthritis syndrome. He therefore decided to try some of Kendall's adrenocortical products, which were just then becoming available, as experimental remedies on some of his rheumatism patients. These early efforts were negative: Hench administered Kendall's "cortin" without apparent effect. He was, however, intrigued with a preparation Kendall called compound E, and he wanted to use it in 1941. But at that time insufficient amounts of the substance were available for clinical testing.

Hench continued to experiment with various lines of approach to arthritis, always bearing in mind the hormonal preparations of Kendall. At length, by 1948, Kendall had succeeded in producing a small quantity of compound E. Hench asked him for enough of the material to use upon one patient. A dramatic improvement was seen immediately upon administration: the patient, almost immobilized with the disease, within days was able to walk freely, exercise arthritic limbs, and so on. Swellings and tenderness abated, and all the other manifestations of chronic rheumatoid arthritis were seen to vanish.

Compound E, renamed "cortisone" by Hench, was now given to a series of patients, with uniformly encouraging results. At about the same time, Hench also obtained comparable results in the alleviation of the arthritis syndrome with ACTH (adrenocorticotropic hormone), a preparation from the anterior lobe of the pituitary gland. Several drawbacks of cortisone treatment became apparent: Continuous administration was necessary, or the symptoms of arthritis soon reappeared. There were also some undesirable secondary effects, connected with the substance's hormonal nature, having to do with facial hair, endocrine balance, and so forth. Nevertheless, in 1949 Hench and Kendall could announce the first successful remedy for rheumatoid arthritis, a landmark in medicine.

Hench continued to work on many aspects of cortisone therapy, including synthesis, prepara-

tion, suppression of side effects, long-term action, and biochemical interaction.

Hench received his B.A. from Lafayette College in 1916. Following a brief stint in the Army Medical Corps, he returned to school and in 1920 took his M.D. at the University of Pittsburgh. After a year as an intern at St. Francis Hospital, Pittsburgh, he became a fellow of the Mayo Foundation of the University of Minnesota School of Medicine. There, in 1926, he became head of the department of rheumatic diseases; instructor in 1928; assistant professor in 1932; associate professor in 1935; professor of medicine in 1947; and, in 1958, emeritus professor of medicine. In 1942, Hench became chief of the Army Medical Corps's Medical Service and director of the Army's rheumatism center at the Army and Navy General Hospital. After leaving the Army in 1946 he became an expert civilian consultant to the Surgeon General of the Army.

For background information *see* ADRENAL CORTEX STEROID; ARTHRITIS in the McGraw-Hill Encyclopedia of Science and Technology.   □

★ HENDRICKS, Sterling Brown

American agricultural chemist
Born Apr. 13, 1902, Elysian Fields, Tex., U.S.A.

WHILE STUDYING basic principles in agriculture, Hendricks found many of the underlying causes for the properties of clays and a fundamental controlling factor for the growth and reproduction of plants. The work on clays depended on determinations of the atomic arrangements, that is, the crystal structures, of all the clay minerals and the micas. It related these structures to the properties of clays to absorb water through hydrogen bonding and to hold salts at their surfaces, which is the phenomenon of ionic exchange. A controlling factor for plant growth was found by studying the relationship of flowering to season and light requirements for germination of seed. For the work on clays, Hendricks was awarded the Day Medal of the Geological Society of America in 1952; for the work on flowering, he shared with his coworker H. A. Borthwick the Hoblitzelle National Award of the Texas Research Foundation in 1962 and the Stephen Hales Prize of the American Society of Plant Physiologists, also in 1962.

During the 19th century, agronomists gradually realized that the capacity of soil to hold water depended on the amount and kind of clay present. Fertilizers, when used, were found to be held in the soil against leaching by water. The investigation of these phenomena at the atomic level awaited the discovery of x-ray diffraction by Max von Laue in 1912 and its use in studying the structure of crystals developed by W. H. and W. L. Bragg in England. Hendricks, in 1929, used x-ray diffraction to show that clays in soil were not amorphous materials, as was widely held, but crystalline. During the next 20 years, working in association with C. S. Ross of the U.S. Geological Survey and L. T. Alexander of the U.S. Department of Agriculture, he established the compositions, mineral groupings, crystal structures, ways of identifications, analysis of amounts, and extents of occurrences of clays in soils. In this work, water films were shown to be held in molecular layers by the surface of the clays through hydrogen bonding to oxygen atoms of the layered silicate structures. The surface termination of clay crystals was found to leave an excess negative charge on the crystal lattice that was compensated by external positive charges, cations. The type of soil and its fertility were found to have a basic dependence on these phenomena.

In 1920 W. W. Garner and H. A. Allard of the U.S. Department of Agriculture found that the flowering of plants depended upon the length of the day or night. This was widely recognized as the basic manner of seasonal adaptation of plants and animals. Hendricks joined with H. A. Borthwick in 1945 to seek an explanation for this phenomenon. Their manner of study was to measure the spectral region (color) and radiant energy necessary to counteract the effect of the night on the flowering of the plant. They found that low energies of red radiation were adequate to control flowering and that the effect could be reversed by radiation near the limit of the visible spectrum. This striking reversible effect of light was also shown to control germination of many seeds, lengthening of plant stems, night movement of leaves, and many other growth responses as well as flowering. They discovered that the effect was caused by a blue pigment present in very small amounts in leaves and stems. The pigment, a protein, is changed by red radiation, as shown by physiological methods, to an enzymatically active form that can be changed back

to the inactive form through its enzymatic action or by the light at the red limit of the visible spectrum. Isolated through use of a spectroscopic assay and methods of protein chemistry, the pigment shows all of the spectroscopic properties established by the physiological studies.

A country doctor's son, Hendricks took a chemical engineering degree at the University of Arkansas in 1922, an M.S. at Kansas State University in 1924, and a Ph.D. in physical chemistry at the California Institute of Technology in 1926. He was variously employed in the U.S. Department of Agriculture after 1922, first as a field assistant in chemistry during summers and permanently, after 1928, as a physical chemist working with soils and plants. He was elected to the National Academy of Sciences in 1952.

For background information *see* AGRICULTURAL CHEMISTRY; SOIL in the McGraw-Hill Encyclopedia of Science and Technology. ☐

★ HERRING, William Conyers

American physicist
Born Nov. 15, 1914, Scotia, N.Y., U.S.A.

RECENT DECADES have seen an explosive expansion of science's understanding of why solid matter behaves as it does—an expansion initiated by the discovery of quantum mechanics and nourished by the postwar recognition of the ultimate economic value of such understanding. Herring's career, involving a number of different subareas of theoretical solid-state physics, was typical of the period. For his work on the transport properties of semiconductors, described below, he was awarded the Oliver E. Buckley Prize of the American Physical Society in 1959.

In the 1930s theoretical physicists were just beginning to apply the equations of wave mechanics to the quantitative calculation of the properties of electrons in metals. Herring's early work consisted of clarifying some of the symmetries and topological properties of the energy-momentum relation for such electron waves, and of developing a reasonably simple and practical method, the so-called "orthogonalized-plane-wave" method, for calculating the form of these waves. This method was applied to many substances by various workers in the 1940s and 1950s.

In a quite different area, Herring studied the changes in shape that surface-tension forces are capable of producing in small-scale features of solid bodies, or systems of solid particles, when these are held at high temperatures for long times. The metallurgical process of sintering is an example. Around 1950, he clarified the ways in which surface-tension effects in solids differ from those in fluids and showed how to formulate precisely, when certain conditions are fulfilled, the equations governing the evolution of the shape of a solid system.

Following the discovery of the transistor effect, announced in 1949 by John Bardeen and W. H. Brattain, there was a tremendous increase in research on the behavior of electrons in semiconductors. It was soon evident that for a quantitative understanding of electrical conduction in these materials and its modification by magnetic fields, stresses, temperature gradients, and so forth, it would be necessary to take account of the fact that the electrons of a semiconductor are often anisotropic (they are more easily accelerated in one crystallographic direction than another). Herring developed methods for taking this anisotropy into account in the calculation of electrical properties and showed how it could explain phenomena like the extreme sensitivity of conductivity to an anisotropic stress.

Herring also elucidated the spectacular rise in the thermoelectric power that occurs for many semiconductors as their temperature is lowered. In an inhomogeneously heated crystal, the greater intensity of thermal agitation at the hot end causes a preferential motion of elastic waves from the hot end to the cold. Most of these elastic waves (phonons), though important for thermal conduction, have little effect on the conduction electrons. However, waves with wavelengths comparable to those of conduction electrons—a rather long wavelength in typical cases—can diffract the electrons strongly and push them toward the cold end. This effect, now called "phonon drag," is much larger than earlier workers had supposed, because elastic waves of long wavelength can travel through the crystal with much less interference from the remaining thermal vibrations than can waves of average wavelength, especially at low temperatures. From studies of this phenomenon and its modification by magnetic fields, much has been learned about the interactions of elastic waves with each other and with electrons.

Of interest for theories of magnetism are the forces that cause the moment of a magnetic atom to prefer a direction parallel or antiparallel to that of another magnetic atom nearby. Although the general nature of these forces had been elucidated by the work of W. Heitler, F. London, and W. K. Heisenberg in 1927, there had been no rigorous derivation of their properties, nor any prescription for calculating them accurately. This gap in understanding, due to the difficulty of taking proper account of the correlations between the motions of electrons on the two atoms, was filled by Herring. He also made studies of the magnetic properties of the conduction electrons of metals.

Son of a physician, Herring entered the University of Kansas at 14 and graduated A.B. in astronomy in 1933. He received his Ph.D. in mathematical physics from Princeton University in 1937. During World War II he worked briefly on the physics of underwater explosions and then on operational-research aspects of subsurface warfare. In 1946 he joined the staff of the Bell Telephone Laboratories, Murray Hill, N.J.

For background information *see* MAGNETISM; SEMICONDUCTOR; SINTERING; THERMOELECTRICITY in the McGraw-Hill Encyclopedia of Science and Technology.   □

★ HERSHEY, Alfred Day

American biologist
Born Dec. 4, 1908, Owosso, Mich., U.S.A.

THE PHAGES form a diverse group of viruses that reproduce in bacterial cells and lyse them. The extracellular elements released on lysis, called "phage particles," are composed of about equal amounts of protein and nucleic acid. Because of their small size and simple structure, the phages have stimulated the imagination of biologists ever since their discovery in 1915.

In 1952 Hershey and Martha Chase found that when a phage particle infects a bacterium, only the phage nucleic acid enters the cell, leaving the protein portion of the particle outside. Their experiments confirmed earlier indications that the material basis of heredity resides in nucleic acids, and suggested further that not only individual genetic characters, but the whole program for major aspects of growth, is encoded in nucleic acid structure. Pursuing that thought, Hershey and his colleagues showed that viral growth occurs in two sequential phases: (1) replication of nucleic acid, followed by (2) synthesis of protein and reconstitution of phage particles. For this achievement, Hershey received a Lasker Award, given by the American Public Health Association, in 1958.

R. M. Herriott had shown, in 1951, that phage T2 particles could be emptied of their nucleic acid content, revealing a tadpole-shaped protein shell that was still able to attach specifically to bacterial cells. The attachment itself occurred at the end of the tail of the virus particle, as T. F. Anderson reported in the same year.

F. W. Putnam and L. M. Kozloff in 1950 first infected bacteria with phage particles labeled with radioactive phosphorus and found that some of the phosphorus contained in the parental particles reappeared in the viral offspring. By using different specific labels in this type of experiment, it would be possible to seek to determine which parts of the virus particle were or were not transmitted to the progeny. Such experiments proved technically difficult. In trying to surmount the difficulties, Hershey and Chase began to suspect that only nucleic acid was transmitted, and that parental virus protein persisted in the form of the empty shells described by Herriott, appearing among the phage progeny only as a contaminant.

The facts mentioned suggested that a phage particle might attach to the bacterium by its tail-tip only and function literally as a syringe to inject nucleic acid into the cell. Hershey and Chase reasoned that, if the analogy were valid, it might be possible to break the attachment after injection had occurred and see whether or not nucleic acid alone inside bacterial cells could direct the formation of new virus particles. To test this idea, they infected cells with phage particles labeled either in their nucleic acid with radiophosphorus or in their protein with radiosulfur, and then subjected the suspension of cells to strong shearing forces generated in a high-speed mixer. They found that phage protein could in fact be separated from the cells in this way, leaving phage nucleic acid inside. The treatment did not at all interfere with subsequent phage growth in the cells.

Experiments performed since then with several plant, animal, and bacterial viruses have confirmed the principle more directly, by showing that exposure of cells to the appropriate nucleic acid alone can often induce normal viral growth in them.

Hershey received the B.S. degree in 1930 and the Ph.D. in 1934 at Michigan State College, and taught from 1934 to 1950 at Washington University, St. Louis, where he began studies on genetic recombination in bacteriophage. In 1950 he became a member of the staff of the department of genetics (now Genetics Research Unit) of the Carnegie Institution of Washington at Cold Spring Harbor, N.Y., where he studied nucleic acid structure and served as director of the Unit. He was elected to the National Academy of Sciences in 1958.

For background information *see* NUCLEIC ACID in the McGraw-Hill Encyclopedia of Science and Technology.   □

★ HESS, Walter Rudolf

Swiss physiologist
Born Mar. 17, 1881, Frauenfeld, Switzerland

HAVING DEVELOPED highly specialized techniques in applying electrical stimulation to discrete brain areas, Hess—as early as 1925—systematically began to investigate the effects of stimulation at hundreds of different points in the diencephalon (interbrain) on body function. He was able to map the structures subserving fundamental functions of the organism and to recognize the diencephalon as the control center of the autonomous nervous system. For this achievement Hess shared the 1949 Nobel Prize in physiology or medicine with Egas Moniz.

Prior to Hess's accomplishment, there had been no comparable detailed studies of localization of functions, although much knowledge had been accumulated especially about the peripheral parts of the autonomous nervous system, and important discoveries had been made about its morphological and physiological organization (W. H. Gaskell, J. N. Langley, and others).

Hess started his investigations with the leading idea that each living organism constitutes an unbroken unity. He wanted to determine the physiological bases for the integrative organizaton of the body. One of the difficulties in experimentation was found in the relative inaccessibility of the diencephalon. Another challenge for the critical interpretation of the results was the complexity of the interrelated functions. Anesthesia was used only for the implantation of the fine probe electrodes (insulated except at the tip); weak stimulation was applied to the unrestrained wakeful animal in order to watch the effect the electrical stimulus had on its behavior. By diathermic coagulation he also caused small lesions at the very points the stimulation effects of which had previously been studied, in order to observe the functional deficit.

Weak electrical stimuli within the diencephalon were able to induce autonomous functions such as passing urine, evacuation of the intestines, and changes in respiration and blood pressure. But the animals could also be rendered sleepy so that they would curl up and go to sleep. On the other hand they could be brought to display all signs of rage or utter fear. Such changes of moods and drives were caused by stimulation, especially in the hypothalamus (that is, the deep structures of the diencephalon). Since it was impossible to observe where the end of the probe was exactly located while the experiment was in progress, it was necessary to examine the brain histologically, in serial section, subsequently. The atlases of photomicrographic pictures of these serial sections aided Hess in his topographic analysis of the stimulation areas and enabled him to accurately locate the so-called centers controlling the various body functions.

Other results of the same experiments allowed Hess to recognize the integrative function of the diencephalon on the skeletal muscle system, commanding muscle tone and automatic corrective movements. It could be demonstrated that the upper part of the diencephalon was a mediator of motor functions and that reactions to environmental stimuli were thereby rendered more efficient. His systematic mapping of localizations of diencephalic symptoms ultimately induced successful surgery of certain motor disturbances in man.

The son of a physics teacher, Hess received his M.D. degree in 1906 from the University of Zurich. He specialized in ophthalmology but left his practice in 1912 to become an assistant in physiology, first in Zurich, then in Bonn. In 1917 he was appointed director of the department of physiology at the University of Zurich.

Hess's first publications (monographs in German from 1925 on) covered the physiology of blood circulation, respiration, and related fields

and the organization of the vegetative nervous system. Some of his later works were translated: *The Functional Organization of the Diencephalon* (1948; trans. 1957), *Hypothalamus and Thalamus* (1956), and *The Biology of Mind* (1962; 2d ed. 1964).

For background information *see* AUTONOMIC NERVOUS SYSTEM in the McGraw-Hill Encyclopedia of Science and Technology.   □

★ HEVESY, George de

Hungarian-Swedish chemist
Born Aug. 1, 1885, Budapest, Hungary

HEVESY PIONEERED in the use of radioactive tracers in researches on chemical processes. This technique, which he devised and which has since been greatly refined, has been of inestimable value in physiology and pathology in clarifying metabolic processes of human beings as well as those of plants and animals. For his achievements in this area Hevesy was awarded the Nobel Prize in chemistry in 1943 and the Atoms for Peace Award in 1959.

In 1911, while he was studying in Manchester, England, under Ernest Rutherford, the latter suggested the task of separating radioactive radium D from a compound also containing inactive radium G and lead. For two years, Hevesy sought unsuccessfully to effect this separation by chemical means. It was later discovered that radium D and radium G are both isotopes of lead, and are therefore chemically the same as lead.

Hevesy's efforts were not wasted, however, for he saw the possibility of using radioactive radium D as a tracer to study chemical reactions. In 1913, at the Vienna Institute for Radium Research, he began experimentation with radioactive indicators as tracers. His first application of labeled lead was the determination of the solubility in water of sparingly soluble salts, such as lead chromate. Thorium B, another radioactive isotope of lead, was used as the indicator instead of radium D. Labeled lead chromate was obtained by adding a solution of 100,000 relative units of thorium B to lead nitrate containing 10 mg of lead and converting this nitrate into a chromate. A saturated solution of this compound was evaporated, and the residue was studied with an electroscope. From the number of units of thorium B found in the residue, the amount of lead was computed, one unit corresponding to 10^{-6} grams of lead, and the solubility of lead chromate in moles per liter (2.10^{-7}) was determined.

This was the beginning of Hevesy's clarification of chemical reactions by the use of radioactive tracers. In 1918, continuing his work with radioactive indicators, he dissolved in water 1 mole of labeled lead nitrate and 1 mole of nonradioactive lead chloride. After separating the two compounds he found that radioactivity was equally distributed between $PbCl_2$ and $PbNO_3$.

The first application of radioactive tracers in life sciences took place in the field of botany in 1923. The intake and distribution of lead by bean plants were studied, using as the indicator a radioactive isotope of lead obtained from thorium. By watering plants with a solution containing this radioactive isotope, data concerning their life processes were obtained.

In 1934 Hevesy prepared a radioactive phosphorus isotope by neutron bombardment of carbon disulfide and used this as an indicator in the study of phosphorus metabolism. He found that, during the growth of a plant, a continuous interchange of phosphorus atoms takes place among the different leaves. In another experiment making use of P^{32}, the number of pollen grains was identified in the seeds of the aspen. Female aspen branches were fertilized with labeled pollen of known activity, and the radioactivity of the seeds was determined. One seed was found to contain the amount of P^{32} present in 8.5 pollen grains, giving information on the extent of participation of pollen grains in seed formation.

From reasearch with radioactive tracers on plants, Hevesy proceeded to do research on the life processes of animals. A conversation with H. G. J. Moseley as early as 1919 led Hevesy to consider the possibility of an experiment to determine the path of water molecules present in a cup of tea through his body, using a radioactive indicator. However, it was not until many years later, in 1934, after Harold Urey had discovered heavy water and more was known about radioactivity, that tracer methods were used with living creatures. In an experiment in the 1930s, Hevesy placed a goldfish in a solution of heavy water and was able to demonstrate the rapid exchange between the environmental water and water in the body. He also used radioactive heavy water to make such determinations as the mean time ingested water molecules spend in an organism and the time it takes for intravenously injected heavy water molecules to be evenly distributed in a body.

The discovery of artificial radioactivity by Frédéric and Irène Joliot-Curie in 1934 led Hevesy to apply artificially produced radioactive isotopes as indicators in physiological studies. He sought to determine whether atoms of the mineral constituents of the skeleton interchange during life or not, and he found that $\frac{1}{3}$ of the phosphorus atoms of the mineral constituents of the skeleton of the rat were replaced by phosphorus atoms of the plasma and lymph. Using Ca^{45} as a tracer, he also determined that the calcium atoms of a rat that do not interchange within three months remain stable.

With L. Hahn, Hevesy sought to determine whether molecular components of the brain were renewed during life and discovered that lecithin molecules in fully grown rats were renewed at a remarkable rate. Using a tracing method, Hahn and Hevesy found also that the liver, not the intestine, was the major place of the formation of phosphatides.

Hevesy and collaborators concentrated in 1938 on the intrusion rate of labeled phosphate into muscle cells and on the measurement of the velocity at which ATP and other labile organic phosphorus compounds are renewed in these. The first-mentioned process was found, in collaboration with O. Rebbe, to be a slow, the latter a very rapid, one. In the course of 3 hours, 78 per cent of the creatine P of muscle cells was found to be renewed.

In the 1940s, in Stockholm, Hevesy and collaborators carried out clinical blood volume determinations by using red corpuscles labeled with P^{32}, K^{42}, or ThB. A very stable labeling of erythrocytes was obtained with Fe^{59}, but such labeling could only be obtained in vivo. Therefore Fe^{59}-labeled red corpuscles were not found suitable for clinical experiments but proved most useful in animal studies. In more recent years, Hevesy investigated the formation and life span of red blood corpuscles in patients suffering from cancer.

The most important general finding of Hevesy in his use of tracers with living organisms was his discovery of the dynamic state of the body components. Molecules of body components are constantly being renewed. Not only do molecules taken up as food participate in this ingestion process but atoms and molecules present in one organ will soon be found in another organ or type of molecule.

Another major achievement by Hevesy was his discovery in 1923 of the element hafnium. During 1922, Hevesy was working in Copenhagen under Niels Bohr when he discovered the element of atomic number 72, which Moseley's chart indicated should exist. Prior researchers had sought for the new element in the lanthanide series (elements 58–71), while Bohr suggested the element 72 to be a member of the titanium group. In January, 1923, Hevesy and Dirk Coster, using x-ray spectrochemical analysis of ziroconium ores, discovered the new element, which they called hafnium, the Latin name for Copenhagen. They also succeeded in isolating hafnium from zirconium. Hafnium was obtained by forming an aluminum-hafnium alloy and then distilling off the aluminum. Hevesy made other contributions to isotope separation by physical methods—for example, separation of chlorine and mercury isotopes by diffusion.

Hevesy also discovered that samarium is the only element besides some members of the radioactive series that emits alpha rays. He put forward the principle of lanthanide contraction simultaneously with V. M. Goldschmidt.

Hevesy obtained his Ph.D. in 1908 from the University of Freiberg im Breisgau. He studied with Rutherford in Manchester until 1913. He then worked at the Vienna Institute of Radium Research and the University of Budapest. In 1920, on invitation of Niels Bohr, he went to the University of Copenhagen. He returned to the University of Freiburg as professor physical chemistry in 1926. In 1943 he fled from Copenhagen before the invading Nazi armies and took refuge in Sweden, where he became associated with the University of Stockholm.

Hevesy's books included *Manual of Radioactivity* (1926), *Chemical Analysis by X-rays* (1932), *Radioactive Indicators* (1948), and *Adventures in Radioisotope Research* (2 vols., 1962). His collected papers were published in 1958.

For background information *see* HAFNIUM; TRACER, RADIOACTIVE in the McGraw-Hill Encyclopedia of Science and Technology.   □

☆ HEWETT, Donnel Foster

American geologist
Born June 24, 1881, Irwin, Pa., U.S.A.

BEGINNING IN 1912, Hewett pursued a multifaceted study of manganese ores that culminated during the 1960s in his explication of their origin and interrelations. For this and other achievements, he was awarded the Penrose Medals of the Society of Economic Geologists (1956) and the Geological Society of America (1964).

Neglecting the supergene ores (that is, concentrations of manganese ores formed by the weathering of other kinds of manganiferous rocks or ores), manganese deposits consist mainly of veins that bear a crosscutting relation to enclosing rocks and of stratiform bodies or layers that are generally conformable with enclosing beds. Mineralogically, both kinds of ores are highly diverse, ranging from simple oxides, carbonates, and sulfides to more complex and diverse oxides and silicates. Prior to Hewett's work, most of the oxide veins were considered to be supergene, the manganese in most of the stratiform deposits was considered to be derived from the decay of the lands, and no genetic relation was recognized between them.

On the basis of field, mineralogical, and geochemical studies of numerous deposits throughout the world, Hewett showed that these diverse ores are essentially mineral facies deposited in different environments from a common source fluid—hydrothermal solutions ascending from depth and probably derived from igneous magmas during the late stages of their crystallization. Thus, among the vein deposits those precipitated in deeper and higher temperature zones consist of silicates, carbonates, sulfides, and oxides in which manganese is present in the manganous state. Those deposited in progressively lower temperature zones consist mainly of oxides and oxide-bearing black aragonite in which the manganese is in higher states of oxidation. The vein deposits are frequently associated with deposits of other minerals—base and precious metals in the higher temperature zones, fluorite and barite in the lower temperature zones—and the manganese minerals contain an assemblage of minor elements (W, Pb, Cu, Mo, Tl, As, Sb, Ba, Sr) that are also present in associated deposits.

The ratios of these minor elements differ progressively from deeper to shallower zones, but

manganiferous deposits formed on the aprons of modern hot springs contain notable amounts of W, Pb, Tl, Ba, and other elements of the vein assemblage, and these same elements are also distinctive constituents of most of the stratiform deposits. From this evidence—supported by the facts that throughout the world the stratiform deposits are generally associated with volcanic tuffs and flows, are highly lenticular and discontinuous (unlike most marine or lacustrine precipitates), and are not matched by the far larger quantities of iron that should be present in beds of the same age if both were derived from continental sources—Hewett showed that most of the stratiform deposits are derived from hydrothermal solutions that have reached the surface (marine or lacustrine) environment. The oxides are deposited in shallow water and the carbonates in deeper water; the complex oxides and silicates are largely the result of the metamorphism of the simpler oxides and carbonates.

Hewett's ordering of this complex and diverse assemblage has great economic and scientific significance. Establishing a zonal relationship among the vein deposits and relating them to other hydrothermal deposits provides a prime basis for prospecting for deeply buried and concealed deposits of other minerals. For example, the presence of hypogene manganese oxide, barite, and fluorite deposits points to the presence of precious- and base-metal deposits at depth. The geochemical studies of Hewett and his associates point to a variety of minor elements that may be recovered as coproducts in the refining of manganese ores. Recovery of lead from the Three Kids ore in Nevada is one such result of Hewett's work, but perhaps the most important potentially was Hewett's finding in 1965 that silver is a common and important constituent of the black aragonite characteristic of near-surface veins.

Among Hewett's many other important achievements were his discoveries of the world's largest deposit of vanadium in Peru (1905) and the rare earths in California (1949). His recognition (1928) of the hydrothermal dolomite aureole surrounding base-metal replacement deposits in limestone was the first major contribution to the understanding of dolomitic alteration accompanying the deposition of hydrothermal ore deposits.

Hewett received his B.S. in metallurgical engineering from Lehigh University in 1902 and his Ph.D. in geology from Yale in 1924. His father was a mining engineer, and Hewett's own career began in mine examinations for private concerns. In 1911 he joined the U.S. Geological Survey. He was chief of the Metals Branch from 1935 to 1944 and in that capacity formulated a program of strategic minerals investigations that was an essential part of the defense and war effort. In 1937 Hewett was elected to the National Academy of Sciences.

For background information *see* ORE AND MINERAL DEPOSITS in the McGraw-Hill Encyclopedia of Science and Technology.   □

★ **HEYROVSKÝ, Jaroslav**
Czechoslovakian physical chemist
Born Dec. 20, 1890, Prague, Czechoslovakia
  (then part of Austria-Hungary)

WHILE TRYING to determine the cause of anomalies in the capillarity of mercury, Heyrovský conceived and developed the polarographic method of chemical analysis. This technique, known as polarographic analysis or polarography, can be used to determine the type and concentration of substances in an unknown solution, and has found application in such diverse fields as medicine and metallurgy. For his achievement, Heyrovský received the 1959 Nobel Prize in chemistry.

In 1918, at the suggestion of Bohumil Kučera of the University of Prague, Heyrovský began to study the electrocapillarity of mercury by allowing the metal to flow through a glass capillary into a solution under an externally applied potential and weighing the drops. Because he found this method to be tedious, Heyrovský decided to devise an electrochemical means for performing the measurement. He found that he could measure the electric current produced by a voltage applied between the mercury as it dropped from the capillary and a layer of mercury on the bottom of the solution. He also discovered that the current increased in steps when the applied voltage was steadily increased. The increase, he found, was proportional to the concentration of the ions in the electrolyte into which the drops fell, and the voltage required was a characteristic of each particular ion. Hence, the technique could be applied analytically. Heyrovský also recognized the chief advantage of the dropping mercury electrode: because each mercury drop falls from the mouth of the capillary after a few seconds to be replaced by another, a clean surface is always presented to the electrolyte. Thus, the results obtained are strictly reproducible and can be expressed mathematically with great accuracy.

In 1922, while working at the Charles University in Prague, Heyrovský began to publish his studies of electrolysis using the dropping mercury electrode and to refine the polarographic technique. The solution to be electrolyzed is contained between two electrodes. One of these, the dropping mercury electrode, is polarizable. The other, the pool of mercury at the bottom of the electrolytic vessel that serves as the reference electrode, is of constant potential and unpolarizable. As an external voltage is applied to the electrodes, the current passing through the circuit is measured and a current-voltage curve, called a polarogram, is plotted. By comparing the polarogram with that obtained from a standard solution electrolyzed under identical conditions, the composition and concentration of the electrolyte can be determined. In 1924, with the aid of the Japanese chemist M. Shikata, Heyrovský constructed the first instrument that automatically recorded polarograms. This device, called a polarograph, produced a photographic record on a revolving drum. Since then, many types of pen-recording polarographs have been developed in various countries.

The processes occurring at the dropping mercury electrode were substantiated by an exact mathematical theory, the basis of which were two mathematical formulas. One of these, deduced by the Czechoslovakian physicist D. Ilkovič in 1933, is called the "diffusion current" formula. The other, put forward in 1935, is the equation of the polarographic wave. In addition, the results of polarographic analyses were verified independently by other analytical and physical chemical methods.

Polarographic methods are less accurate than ordinary gravimetric or volumetric analytical techniques. The former are useful, however, for the determination of very small quantities where gravimetric and volumetric techniques are also subject to a large relative error. Both qualitative and quantitative analyses of a multicomponent system can be simultaneously performed. Polarography can also be applied in the determination of electrode reactions, slow and rapid chemical reactions, stability constants, structural parameters, and many other areas of physical and analytical chemistry. In volumetric analysis, for example, polarographic limiting current titrations, called "amperometric" and "polarometric," have been introduced. In medicine, among other polarographic applications the Brdička reaction is used for the detection of cancer.

After 1943 Heyrovský developed alternating current oscillographic polarography, which enables one, in addition to performing rapid analyses, to follow intermediates with very short lifetimes and to detect surface-active substances that are not active in classical polarography.

Other polarographic techniques, such as differential polarography, tensammetry, and chronopotentiometry, have also been developed.

The son of a professor of Roman law, Heyrovský studied mathematics, physics, and chemistry at the Czech University in Prague and at University College, London, receiving his B.S. from the latter in 1913. He received his Ph.D. from the University of Prague in 1918 and his D.Sc. from the University of London in 1921. In 1920 Heyrovský was appointed an assistant at the Institute of Analytical Chemistry of the Charles University in Prague, becoming an associate professor in 1922 and a professor in 1926. He remained at the university until 1954, performing experimental work during the German occupation (1939–45). In 1950 he was appointed director of the newly established Institute of Polarography of the Czechoslovakian Academy of Science, maintaining this position until 1963.

Heyrovský wrote a number of books on polarographic analysis, among them *Application of the Polarographic Method* (1933), *Polarography* (1941; 2d ed. 1944), *Oscillographic Polarography* (1953; 2d ed. 1960), and *Principles of Polarography* (1959; 3d ed. 1965).

For background information *see* POLAROGRAPHIC ANALYSIS in the McGraw-Hill Encyclopedia of Science and Technology.   □

★ HILDEBRAND, Joel Henry

American chemist
Born Nov. 16, 1881, Camden, N.J., U.S.A.

HILDEBRAND STUDIED in depth a variety of problems connected with the solubility of nonelectrolytes. Major results included the following:

1. The construction and testing of a theory for a class of solutions that he designated "regular solutions." These are mixtures of components whose molecules, under the influence of thermal agitation, are in a state of maximum disorder even though they may differ in size and attrac-

tive force. The validity of the theory is illustrated by the solubility of iodine in 18 liquids ranging from 5.58 mole per cent in carbon disulfide to 0.018 mole per cent perfluoroheptane, all of which agree with the predictions of the theory. The iodine in all of these "regular" solutions is violet, as in the vapor, indicating absence of selective, chemical interactions.

2. In certain solvents the colors range through red, brown, and yellow. He and a collaborator, H. A. Benesi, discovered (1948) that such solutions show strong absorption in the ultraviolet, indicating the presence of "electron-donor-acceptor" complexes. This was a discovery of major importance, utilized since by scores of investigators. This kind of interaction has been found to be far more widespread than was formerly suspected. These complexes are the intermediate steps in many reactions.

3. In the theory of regular solutions described in "1," the attraction between the unlike molecules is equated to the geometric mean of the attractions between the like molecules; in the complexes described in "2," it is greater. Systematic studies by Hildebrand and his coworkers revealed other classes of mixtures that also deviate from the simple geometric mean relation. They identified the parts of molecules responsible for these deviations.

4. The Hildebrand group determined the solubility of gases in representative solvents and systematized them in terms of regular solution theory so as to permit predictions of solubility and its change with temperature. An early byproduct of this work was his initiation (1924) of the use of helium-oxygen mixtures in deep diving; this has greatly extended the depth at which divers can work.

Beginning in 1951 Hildebrand brought forward a variety of experimental facts that support the model of maximum disorder in simple liquids and contradict the assumptions made by some theoreticians that there are "liquid lattices," "holes," "cells," "solidlike molecules," and so forth.

He was the first (1913) to show the utility of the hydrogen electrode for following the course precipitation, resolution, and neutralization of weak acids and bases. He was also the first (1916) to give a scientific interpretation of the flotation process for concentrating ores.

Hildebrand graduated in 1903 from the University of Pennsylvania and received his Ph.D. there in 1906. He spent a year at Berlin University with W. H. Nernst, then returned to the University of Pennsylvania as its first instructor in physical chemistry. In 1913 he joined the newly formed group gathered by G. N. Lewis at the University of California, Berkeley. Appointed full professor in 1918, he served briefly as dean of the College of Letters and Science and later of the College of Chemistry. He be-

came professor emeritus in 1952, but continued his active research. He was elected to the National Academy of Sciences in 1929. Among the many honors Hildebrand received were the Nichols Award (1939), Willard Gibbs Medal (1953), and Priestley Medal (1962) of the American Chemical Society, and the William Proctor Prize (1962) of the Scientific Research Society of America.

In addition to over 200 scientific papers by himself and his students and associates, Hildebrand wrote *Principles of Chemistry* (1918; 7th ed., with R. E. Powell, 1964), *Solubility of Nonelectrolytes* (1924; 3d ed., with R. L. Scott, 1950), *Science in the Making* (1957), *Regular Solutions*, with R. L. Scott (1962), and *Introduction to Molecular Kinetic Theory* (1963).

For background information *see* SOLUTION in the McGraw-Hill Encyclopedia of Science and Technology.   □

★ HILGARD, Ernest Ropiequet

American psychologist
Born July 25, 1904, Belleville, Ill., U.S.A.

BEGINNING WITH his doctoral dissertation at Yale University, Hilgard undertook a number of investigations of the conditioned responses of human eyelid reactions, using careful photographic techniques that were adopted by many subsequent workers. This work was recognized by the award of the Warren Medal in Experimental Psychology in 1940, with the citation: "For his analysis of the conditioned response and his demonstration of its integration with the verbal and volitional processes in learning and retention." The interest in the interplay between voluntary and involuntary responses was reflected in his later turning to experimentation on hypnosis, in which problems of control and loss of control come to the fore.

With Donald G. Marquis, a collaborator in a number of his early investigations, he published a summary volume entitled *Conditioning and*

Learning (1940) that introduced the distinction between classical and instrumental conditioning and in other ways differentiated between types of conditioned response and their relationship to the various laboratory studies of learning undertaken by psychologists.

While his experimental work continued, Hilgard became known for his expository writing, as represented not only in the book with Marquis but in his later monographs on *Theories of Learning* (1948; 2d ed. 1956) and *Introduction to Psychology* (1953; 3d ed. 1962). In these he represented the broad functionalism associated with William James, John Dewey, J. R. Angell, and R. S. Woodworth, rather than the more brittle behaviorism of J. B. Watson. The later period of hypnotic studies is represented by his *Hypnotic Susceptibility* (1965). The theme that runs through his writings is that premature systematization may divert attention from important problems; while objectivity and quantification are desirable, so also are breadth and relevance, and these are not to be sacrificed for precision and neatness.

The son of a practicing physician, Hilgard studied chemical engineering at the University of Illinois, where he received his B.S. in 1924. Dissatisfied with chemistry as a career, he remained at the University of Illinois, operating an employment office in the University Y.M.C.A., where he had been the student Y.M.C.A. president, and this diverted him to a year in the Yale Divinity School before he turned to psychology. He received his Ph.D. in psychology at Yale in 1930, remaining there as an instructor in psychology before going to Stanford University in 1933. At Stanford he was executive head of the department of psychology from 1942 to 1951 and dean of the Graduate Division from 1951 to 1955. He was elected to the National Academy of Sciences in 1948.

For background information *see* HYPNOSIS; LEARNING THEORIES in the McGraw-Hill Encyclopedia of Science and Technology.   □

★ HILLE, Einar

American mathematician
Born June 28, 1894, New York, N.Y., U.S.A.

DURING 1934–35 Hille was concerned with the problem of approximation of a function of a real variable by means of various transforms depending upon a parameter. Three of the four transforms finally selected possessed the semigroup property expressed by equation (1). A study of these transforms based upon the

$$T(s+t) = T(s)\,T(t) = T(t)\,T(s),$$
$$0 < s, t < \infty \tag{1}$$

functional equation was published in 1936. For one of the transforms, the Gauss-Weierstrass integral used in heat conduction and the theory of probability, the semigroup property had been observed earlier by F. Tricomi.

The functional equation expressing the semigroup property is that satisfied by the exponential function and one of the fundamental problems of the theory has been to exploit this fact and to carry over as much as possible of the theory of the exponential function to the new situation.

In 1938 Hille considered semigroups of transformations acting in a Hilbert space. Some of the results obtained had been found previously by B. Sz. Nagy.

During 1941–42 Hille returned to the semigroup problem in earnest. This was to occupy him for close to 10 years. The result was the monograph *Functional Analysis and Semigroups* (1948; rev. ed. with R. S. Phillips, 1957). Here the analytical theory of semigroups was developed. This theory has few contacts with the considerably older algebraic theory and the younger topological theory. The main facts of the analytic theory were also discovered in Japan by K. Yosida in 1948 and one of the main results of the theory is known as the Hille-Yosida theorem.

Semigroups arise in the most varied situations in mathematics. They have some properties in common with groups: elements can be combined, and the combining process is associative. On the other hand, they lack two of the basic properties of groups: they need not have a neutral element, nor do elements in general have inverses. A very simple example is furnished by the set of positive numbers that form a semigroup under addition. There is no neutral element and no inverses.

Hille was mainly concerned with families of linear bounded operators depending upon a parameter and having the semigroup property as a function of the parameter. A very simple example is that of a translation. If $f(x)$ is continuous for positive values of x and $T(s)$ operating on f takes $f(x)$ into $f(x + s)$, $s > 0$, then $T(s)$ satisfies (1). Another example is that of fractional integration: the integral of order α of the integral of order β of f is the integral of order $\alpha + \beta$ of f. Heat conduction gives another instance. The temperature at some point of a circular wire after s seconds is a certain function of the original temperature. If we now consider this temperature as the initial one and ask for the temperature after t seconds, we obtain the same result as if we had used the original temperature and asked for the distribution after $s + t$ seconds.

This is a fairly general situation. The principle of determinism, at least in its classical form, asserts that from the state of a physical system at a given time t_0 we may deduce its state at a later instant t. As a consequence, we have the major premise of Huygens's principle: The state of the system at the time t may be deduced from its state at an intermediary time t_1 by first computing the state at the time t_1 and then from the latter the state at the time t, the result being the same as that obtainable by direct computation from the original state. This formulation is due to J. Hadamard (1903), in whose able hands it led to various functional equations for solutions mainly of partial differential equations of hyperbolic type. Here the situation is reversible, and the functional equations brought out the group character of the solutions. In irreversible situations one is led to semigroups rather than to groups. Typical instances are heat conduction, diffusion problems, stochastic processes, and potential theory. In all these theories a profusion of semigroups of transformations is encountered.

If A is a bounded operator acting in a Banach space X (linear vector space with a normed metric under which the space is complete), then the exponential function

$$\exp(sA) = T(s) \tag{2}$$

will have the semigroup property. Actually we are now dealing with a group and s can be any complex number. In the general case, $T(s)$ will not have this simple form. There exists, however, an operator A, known as the infinitesimal generator of $T(s)$, which plays a similar role. There exists a subset D of X, dense in X, such that if $f \in D$ then

$$\lim_{h \to 0} \frac{1}{h} [T(s + h) - T(s)][f] \equiv A[f] \tag{3}$$

exists. Here A is normally unbounded.

The study of $T(s)$ is closely tied up with the study of the resolvent of A, that is, the operator

$$(\lambda I - A)^{-1} = R(\lambda; A) \tag{4}$$

which is defined in a half-plane of the complete λ-plane as the Laplace transform of $T(s)$. Conversely, $T(s)$ can be computed from $R(\lambda; A)$, for example, by the formula

$$T(s)[f] = \lim_{n \to \infty} (I - \frac{s}{n} A)^{-n}[f]$$

$$= \lim_{n \to \infty} \{\frac{n}{s} R(\frac{n}{s}, A)\}^n [f] \tag{5}$$

which is the analog of the classical formula

$$e^{as} = \lim_{n \to \infty} (I - \frac{s}{n} a)^{-n}$$

for the ordinary exponential function. The properties of $T(s)$ are faithfully reflected by those of $R(\lambda; A)$. This makes it possible to decide when a given operator A is the infinitesimal generator of a semigroup. These conditions can be expressed in terms of properties of the resolvent of A. If they are satisfied, we can then define $T(s)$ by (5) or similar formulas.

Educated at the University of Stockholm (Ph.D., 1918), Hille taught there (1915–16, 1919–20) and at Harvard (1921–22) and Princeton (1922–33) before moving to Yale, where he was professor of mathematics from 1933 to 1962. He was elected to the National Academy of Sciences in 1953.

For background information *see* GROUP THEORY in the McGraw-Hill Encyclopedia of Science and Technology. □

☆ **HINSHELWOOD, Sir Cyril (Norman)**
British chemist
Born June 19, 1897, London, England

WHILE ENGAGED in research in chemical kinetics and the mechanism of chemical reactions, Hinshelwood made important contributions to the understanding of the combination of hydrogen and oxygen to form water. His elucidation of chain reactions and chain branching in explaining a wide range of chemical phenomena has led to increased understanding of reactions in general, and explosive reactions in particular. In recognition of these contributions, Hinshelwood and the Russian chemist Nikolai N. Semenov were awarded the 1956 Nobel Prize in chemistry for their independent researches into the mechanism of chemical reactions.

In 1913 the German chemist Max Bodenstein proposed the idea of chain reactions, that is, chemical reactions in which the products of the reaction assist in promoting the reaction itself. Ten years later the Danish and Dutch scientists Christiansen and Kramers initiated the concept of branching chain reactions, which result in the reaction spreading over the entire mixture so that it rapidly culminates in an explosion.

About 1930, while working at Oxford University, Hinshelwood began to study the reaction $2H_2 + O_2 \rightarrow 2H_2O$. Bodenstein had shown that at certain temperatures this combination takes place on the walls of the container. Hinshelwood realized that in the temperature region between that used by Bodenstein and the inflammation temperature, homogeneous processes must come into play. He found that if he placed hydrogen at a pressure of 200 mm and oxygen at a pressure of 100 mm into a 300 cc quartz container at a temperature of 550°C, the rate of reaction was extremely slow. He further found that if he reduced the pressure to 100 mm the rate of reaction became even slower. However, he discovered that when the pressure was reduced to 98 mm an explosion took place. In addition, Hinshelwood found that when the pressure was increased, the reaction rate increased until it became so fast that the mixture exploded.

In order to explain this behavior, Hinshelwood advanced the idea (as Semenov had done a short time earlier for the transition from slow reaction to inflammation of phosphorus vapor) that what was taking place was a branching chain reaction. He proposed that the mechanism of the reaction was:

(a) $H_2 \rightleftharpoons 2H$ [initiation]
(b) $H + O_2 \rightleftharpoons OH + O$
(c) $OH + H_2 \rightleftharpoons H_2O + H$ $\Big]$ propagation
(d) $O + H_2 \rightleftharpoons OH + H$
(e) $H + O_2 \rightarrow HO_2$
(f) $H + wall \rightarrow$ stable species
(g) $OH + wall \rightarrow$ stable species termination
(h) $HO_2 + wall \rightarrow$ stable species

Since the hydroxyl (OH) radical produced in reaction (d) undergoes reaction (c), for every hydrogen atom produced in (a) three others are produced by reactions (b), (c), and (d). The hydrogen atoms and hydroxyl radicals that participate in the propagation of the chain form stable species when they collide with the walls of the container to terminate the chain. If two of the three radicals formed for each hydrogen atom produced in (a) reach the wall, a steady state occurs in which the concentration of radicals is constant. As the pressure increases, however, the number of radicals reaching the walls of the container decreases and there is more than one radical for each hydrogen atom produced in reaction (a). The number of radicals thus increases geometrically until the explosion occurs.

The research that elucidated this mechanism took place over several years. In the beginning a series of observations were made to determine what effect varying the temperature had on the speed of product formation. Previous observations had related generally to the question whether a given reaction was unimolecular, bimolecular, or of some other type. The presence of the postulated radicals was tested by the addition of nitric oxide, which changed the rate of reaction by combining with the free radicals. Through this painstaking procedure, the mechanism given above was eventually evolved.

The combination of hydrogen and oxygen is one of the most fundamental in chemistry, and the understanding of its mechanism has had widespread effect in the understanding of the mechanism of a number of other reactions. A practical derivative of this work was in the elucidation of the mechanism of the hydrocarbon chain reaction, which led to an improvement in the octane rating of gasolines.

After completing his study of the hydrogen-oxygen reaction, Hinshelwood attempted to apply the techniques he had developed in inorganic chemistry to reactions in living organisms. This resulted in the discovery of certain of the kinetic phenomena that occur in the living cell, such as bacterial adaptation.

Hinshelwood was educated at Balliol College, Oxford, receiving his first degree in 1920. He had served as a chemist in the Royal Ordnance Factory in the department of explosives supply during World War I. In 1921 he became a tutor at Trinity College, and in 1937 was appointed professor of chemistry at Oxford University. Elected to the Royal Society in 1929, he served as president from 1955 to 1960. He was knighted in 1948.

Hinshelwood wrote several books, including *Kinetics of Chemical Change in Gaseous Systems* (4th ed. 1946).

For background information *see* CHAIN REACTION, CHEMICAL; KINETICS (CHEMICAL) in the McGraw-Hill Encyclopedia of Science and Technology.   □

★ HINTON OF BANKSIDE, Baron (Christopher Hinton)

British engineer
Born May 12, 1901, Tisbury, Wilts., England

HINTON BECAME best known for his work in designing, building, and operating the industrial establishments needed for the manufacture of fissile materials in the United Kingdom after World War II. This program included the free world's first large nuclear power plant, which was constructed at Calder Hall.

Much of the early scientific work on atomic energy was done in the United Kingdom, but in 1942 it was decided that development of atomic weapons should be the responsibility of the United States, and it was there that the wartime factories were built. Although British scientists played some part in the American program, the industrial techniques were not disclosed, and the United Kingdom started without knowledge of them. Hinton was given the task of designing, building, and operating a factory for the extraction of uranium from ore and for its purification and manufacture into fuel elements; a factory for nuclear reactors and the ancillary chemical separation plants; and a factory for the manufacture of enriched uranium by the diffusion process. He started with no staff and had to build up a department and train men at a time in the immediate postwar period when recruitment was difficult. The task was made more difficult by the fact that the technological problems of the three factories were widely different.

The secrets of Hinton's success lay in the outstandingly good cooperation achieved between scientists and engineers and the policy of seeking the simplest possible engineering solutions to all problems of design. A great strength of the organization lay in the fact that close attention was paid not merely to its technological problems but also to its business organization; programming and progressing of construction work was meticulously done, standardization of engineering and general stores and of specifications was carefully carried out, and there was careful accountancy and cost control. Besides the plants for manufacture of fissile materials for weapons, Hinton was also responsible for the basic design and initial construction of the fast breeder reactor at Dounray and its ancillary chemical plants.

In 1957 Hinton became chairman of the Central Electricity Generating Board, which was then newly formed by the reorganization of the preexisting Central Electricity Authority. Under his charge there was considerable delegation of authority from headquarters to the regional organizations that were responsible for operation of all plants and to project offices responsible for the construction of new plants. The preexisting research organization was greatly expanded and brought up to a standard that had no equal in the electricity supply industry; long-term and short-term planning techniques were greatly improved, as were also the administrative and technical controls of engineering and general stores standardization, programming and progressing, and finance. During the period of his chairmanship there was great progress in design; larger generating sets and power stations were made standard, and supercritical steam conditions were adopted. The problems of electricity transmission were severe where density of use was as great as in England and Wales. To meet these, a new high-voltage network, working at 400 kv, was designed and largely constructed. Hinton showed great sensitivity to the problems of visual amenity that were inseparable from the large program of generation and transmission construction work that the Board had to undertake.

The son of a schoolmaster, Hinton became at 16 an engineering apprentice at the Great Western Railway works at Swindon, where he later became a draftsman; this practical experience in sound mechanical engineering he always considered to be invaluable and to be the basis of his success as an engineer. In 1923 he went to Trinity College, Cambridge, where he took first class honors in mechanical sciences at the end of his second year and did research on vibration of railway bridges in his third year. He then went to Brunner Mond and Co. (manufacturers of heavy alkalis), which became part of I.C.I.; he was made chief engineer at 29. The period immediately following was one of great financial stringency and taught him careful control of cost and economy of design. In 1940 he was seconded by I.C.I. to the Ministry of Supply and later became deputy director general of the Filling Factory Organization, which employed around 100,000 workers. The department was outstandingly successful because good organization and planning enabled a limited number of experienced people to control a large and complex organization.

For background information *see* NUCLEAR POWER in the McGraw-Hill Encyclopedia of Science and Technology.   □

★ **HIRST, Sir Edmund (Langley)**

British organic chemist
Born July 21, 1898, Preston, England

HIRST'S FIRST research was carried out in J. C. (later Sir James) Irvine's laboratory at St. Andrew's University with W. N. (later Sir Norman) Haworth as supervisor. There work on disaccharides and polysaccharides was being resumed after the dislocation caused by World War I. Application of the methylation method to cellobiose led to the isolation of "normal" tetramethyl glucose (then thought to be the 2,3,5,6-derivative) and 2,3,6-trimethyl glucose after hydrolysis of the fully methylated disaccharide. The ring system in the stable, as distinct from the so-called "γ" methyl glycosides, was at that time assumed to be five-membered (now referred to as furanose), but Hirst realized that no firm chemical proof of this had ever been given. Having discovered that controlled oxidation of fully methylated sugars could be effected by strong nitric acid, he saw that this reaction could be used to determine the nature of the ring system present in methyl glycosides. For instance, oxidation of "normal" trimethyl xylose gave a 2,3,4-trimethoxy glutaric acid, proving, contrary to then-accepted views, that the normal α- and β-methyl xylosides—and so by implication xylose itself—possessed a six-membered pyranose ring. Application of the method to other stable methyl glycosides (for example, from rhamnose, arabinose, and glucose) showed that the pyranose structure was common to all. On the other hand the less stable "γ" methyl glycosides were shown to have the five-membered or furanose ring structure.

This work started at St. Andrew's, was continued at Manchester and Armstrong College, Newcastle, where Hirst rejoined Haworth's research school, and there began a close collaboration in carbohydrate research that continued for many years, first in Newcastle and subsequently at Birmingham University. A systematic survey of sugar ring structures by a variety of methods was undertaken, and the fundamental knowledge so obtained was used in structural studies of the oligosaccharides and polysaccharides, with particular reference to cellulose, starch, and glycogen. In the course of this work Haworth and Hirst were approached by Albert Szent-Györgyi with a proposal to investigate the structure of the highly reactive "hexuronic acid" that he had isolated from adrenal cortex, Hungarian paprika, and other sources, and that was subsequently proved to be vitamin C (ascorbic acid). The structure of this substance was established by Hirst and his collaborators in 1933 and, in collaboration with Haworth, its synthesis from L-xylosone followed almost immediately—the first chemical synthesis of a vitamin.

After his move to Bristol in 1936 Hirst continued work on the optical rotatory dispersion of carbohydrates and concentrated his structural studies—with J. K. N. Jones—on the hemicelluloses and plant gums, fields that continued to engage his attention at Manchester and after 1947 at Edinburgh. There he carried out investigations on the fructan group, with special reference to the polysaccharides present in grasses, and in the wide field of algal polysaccharides.

A Baptist minister's son, Hirst was educated at Madras College, St. Andrew's, Scotland, and at the University of St. Andrew's (Ph.D., 1921). He subsequently held teaching posts at the University of Manchester, at Armstrong College, University of Durham, and at the University of Birmingham. In 1936 he became professor of organic chemistry at the University of Bristol, moving to the chair of organic chemistry at Manchester in 1944 and to the newly established chair of organic chemistry in Edinburgh University in 1947. In 1948 he was awarded the Davy Medal of the Royal Society of London. He was knighted in 1964.

For background information *see* POLYSACCHARIDE in the McGraw-Hill Encyclopedia of Science and Technology.   □

★ **HOAR, William Stewart**

Canadian zoologist
Born Aug. 31, 1913, Moncton, N.B., Canada

Hoar's interest in the physiology and behavior of fishes was determined during his Ph.D. studies by his observation of increased thyroid activity in juvenile Atlantic salmon at the time of their migration to the ocean. Through varied studies of fish endocrinology and behavior, this interest broadened and focused on the endocrine mechanisms that coordinate the seasonally changing behavior and physiology of fishes with the cycles of their environment.

Hoar's discovery, in 1937, of thyroid activity in migrant salmon came at a time when the one clearly recognized function of the thyroid gland in lower vertebrates was its triggering action on amphibian metamorphosis. It seemed logical to postulate a causative role for the thyroid in the smolt transformation that precedes the seaward migration of salmon. Hoar's first attempts, in 1939, to test this hypothesis were inconclusive, and his subsequent comparative analysis of thyroid physiology and behavior of juvenile salmonids occupied him for more than 20 years. A second area of research opened in 1953 with his observation of seasonally varying temperature resistance in goldfish and the postulation of a photoperiod control by way of endocrine mechanisms. A third line of investigation commenced in 1958 with a study of the reproductive endocrinology of the male stickleback. The results of these three lines of research were synthesized in a general discussion of the endocrine system as a link between the organism and its environment for a meeting of the Royal Society of Canada in 1965.

The diversity of salmonid species in the coastal waters of the Pacific Northwest provided splendid material for a comparative analysis of the biology of seaward migration. The five species of Pacific salmon range from obligatory seaward migrants to species that are facultative in this part of their life cycle. In addition, several species of trout and char extend the range to some strictly fresh-water varieties. Both the thyroid studies and the behavioral analysis of these many forms paid rich dividends. Although the thyroid hormone does not play a general causative role in downstream migration, Hoar found that the thyroid gland does show heightened activity in those species that undergo a smolt transformation. This, he believed, could probably be interpreted in terms of some fundamental role of the hormone in tissue metabolism; changes in the osmotic and ionic regulatory capacities that occur prior to entrance into sea water are responsible for the thyroid picture. An extension of this analysis of thyroid function to several other genera of euryhaline fish showed that heightening of thyroid activity is a consistent feature during residence in hypertonic environments.

Hoar's failure to associate endocrinology with seaward migration initiated his comparative behavioral analysis of juvenile salmon. These studies were among the pioneer investigations of salmon behavior and the first comparative ethological analysis of the juveniles. They laid the foundations for several subsequent investigations, revealed many details of salmon biology, and provided facts that have become fundamental in the practical problems of conservation and management. In 1958, Hoar summarized his ethological findings in terms of the evolution of seagoing behavior.

Studies of the biochemical changes associated with temperature acclimation in goldfish led to the chance discovery by Hoar that fish acclimated to the same temperature (20°C) and fed a standard diet were relatively more resistant to high temperatures during the summer and relatively more resistant to low temperatures during the winter. Hoar postulated a photoperiodically controlled seasonal cycle of varying temperature resistance. Experiments confirmed the hypothesis and initiated an extended investigation of the endocrine mechanisms responsible for these cycles. Although the action of photoperiod in the regulation of reproductive cycles had been recognized for many years, these studies were the first to demonstrate its action in the control of thermal tolerance.

The endocrinological investigation of the stickleback was a further attempt to describe the hormonal links that coordinate the seasonal changes in the physiology of a fish with those of its environment. The stickleback was used because of its elaborate, well-documented reproductive behavior and its susceptibility to photoperiod. It proved possible to link the presexual behavior with pituitary hormones and to show a gradual transfer of endocrine responsibilities from the hormones of the pituitary to those of the gonad during the process of sexual maturation. Early phases, Hoar found, are pituitary regulated; later phases are entirely under the control of the gonad, while intermediate steps are the joint responsibility of these two organs. Of particular interest was the demonstration that territoriality and presexual aggressive behavior depend on pituitary gonadotropins and not on the gonadal steroids. Since this relationship was first noted in the stickleback, a similar situation has been found in some other lower vertebrates.

Hoar attended the University of New Brunswick as a Beaverbrook Scholar and was graduated with first class honors in biology and geology in 1934. He received his M.A. from the University of Western Ontario in 1936. While working toward his Ph.D. at Boston University during the next 3 years, he demonstrated in the department of anatomy at the Medical School and specialized in the area of medical sciences. On completion of the Ph.D. in 1939 he returned to the University of New Brunswick, where he taught until 1945 except for an absence of 1 year spent on wartime research in the department of physiology of the University of Toronto. During the summer of 1935, he was introduced to field work by A. G. Huntsman and subsequently spent most of his summers for a period of 22 years—first on the Atlantic and then on the Pacific—studying the biology of salmon. In 1945, he joined the University of British Columbia as professor of zoology and fisheries, becoming head of the department of zoology in 1964. He was elected to fellowship in the Royal Society of Canada in 1955 and received the Society's Flavelle Medal in 1965.

Hoar wrote *General and Comparative Physiology* (1966).

For background information *see* ENDOCRINE MECHANISMS; THYROID GLAND in the McGraw-Hill Encyclopedia of Science and Technology. □

★ HODGE, Sir William (Vallance Douglas)

British mathematician
Born June 17, 1903, Edinburgh, Scotland

Hodge's PRINCIPAL mathematical work was concerned with the theory of integrals associated with an algebraic variety defined over the complex field. In 1930, while engaged in trying to generalize to the algebraic double integrals of the first kind on a variety of dimension greater than two the classical properties of simple integrals of the first kind on a variety of dimension greater than one, he realized that the obstacles lay in the fact that some of the basic properties of the simple integrals on which the whole theory depended had not been extended to multiple integrals.

This led him, in the first place, to generalize to nonsingular finite integrals of any multiplicity the classical bilinear equalities and inequalities of Riemann; in doing this, he leaned heavily on a method of obtaining the Riemann relations for curves by a simple topological argument which was due to S. Lefschetz.

In the second place, Hodge came to the conclusion that there were simply not enough algebraic integrals of the first kind on an algebraic variety for it to be possible to extend the methods previously used for simple integrals. Judging that the most hopeful way of overcoming this difficulty was to consider the possibility of extending Riemann's method of establishing the existence of everywhere finite integrals on a Riemann surface, he was led to the concept of a harmonic integral. In the complex plane, with parameter $z = x + iy$, a differential $P\,dx + Q\,dy$ is the real part of an analytic differential $f(z)\,dz$ if it is closed, and if the dual differential $P\,dy - Q\,dx$ is also closed. The relation between the two differentials has the simple geometric interpretation: Using the natural metric $ds^2 = dz\,d\bar{z}$, the value of the differential $P\,dx + Q\,dy$ in the direction $x = \lambda t$, $y = \mu t$ is $(P\lambda + Q\mu)\,dt$ and is equal to the value of the differential $P\,dy - Q\,dx$ in the orthogonal direction $x = -\mu t$, $y = \lambda t$. This idea extends at once to any differentiable manifold of n dimensions with a positive definite Riemannian matrix given by $ds^2 = g_{ij}dx^i dx^j$ for the local coordinate system $(x^1, \ldots, x^n)$. Given a differential form of multiplicity p,

$$P = \sum_{i_1 < \ldots < i_p \leq n} P_{i_1 \ldots i_p}\,dx^{i_1} \ldots dx^{i_p}$$

its dual is defined to be at any point

$$*P = \sum \sqrt{g}\,g^{i_1 j_1} \ldots g^{i_2 j_2}\,P_{j_1 \ldots j_p}\,dx^{i_{p+1}} \ldots dx^{i_n}$$

The value of P on any p-element is the equal to the value of $*P$ on the orthogonal $(n\text{-}p)$-element. P is said to be harmonic if both P and $*P$ are closed. Hodge's main result is that on any closed orientable Riemannian manifold there exists one and only one harmonic p-form whose integral has arbitrarily assigned periods on the cycles of a base for the p-dimensional homology group (real coefficients) of the manifold.

In order to apply this result to algebraic varieties it was necessary to impose a suitable metric onto the existing complex structure. Fortunately, a very convenient metric was already known—the Kähler metric. By its use, the associated harmonic integrals of dimension p are capable of a detailed classification in which one of the classes consists of the p-dimensional algebraic integrals of the first kind. While this classification depends on the metric, it is possible to determine from it many invariants of the variety which depend only on the complex structure. Many unsuspected relations between the algebraic and topological properties of an algebraic variety emerged in this way.

Much of Hodge's later work was devoted to exploiting the foregoing results. By using the theory of sheaves he made other studies of the integrals associated with an algebraic variety, including a detailed study (with M. F. Atiyah) of the algebraic integrals of the second kind on a variety.

The son of a professional man, Hodge received his early schooling in Edinburgh and took his first degree at the University of Edinburgh in 1923. He proceeded to Cambridge (St. John's College), where he took another bachelor's degree and then spent five years as a junior member of the teaching staff of Bristol University. During the next two years he was able, with the support of fellowships, to devote his time entirely to research, and it was during this period that he paid his first visit to the United States (to Princeton). In 1933 he was appointed a university lecturer in Cambridge University, and at the same time joined the teaching staff of Pembroke College in that university, being elected a fellow of the College in 1935. In 1936 he was elected Lowndean Professor of Geometry at Cambridge. He remained in Pembroke as a professorial fellow until 1958, when he became master of the college. He was elected a fellow of the Royal Society in 1938 and a foreign associate of the U.S. National Academy of Sciences in 1959.

Hodge wrote *The Theory of and Applications of Harmonic Integrals* (1941; 2d ed. 1959) and *Methods of Algebraic Geometry*, with D. Pedoe (3 vols., 1947, 1952, 1954).   □

HODGKIN, Alan Lloyd
British biophysicist
Born Feb. 5, 1914, Banbury, Oxfordshire, England

BY EXPERIMENTING with the relatively large nerve fibers of squids, Hodgkin, in collaboration with the British physiologist Andrew Fielding Huxley, was able to devise a system of mathematical equations describing the nerve impulse and to present evidence for the sodium theory of nervous conduction. For these contributions to neurophysiological research, Hodgkin and Huxley shared the 1963 Nobel Prize for medicine or physiology with the Australian physiologist Sir John Carew Eccles, who had extended their work to show what occurred at the synapses during the transmission of the nerve impulse.

The major impetus for the scientific investigation of bioelectricity came from the Italian anatomist Luigi Galvani's late-18th-century demonstrations that ordinary nerve impulses and mechanically produced electricity caused muscles to contract in an identical and unique way. The Italian physiologist Leopoldo Nobili, in the second quarter of the 19th century, was the first to establish, by means of a galvanometer, that ordinary living tissue is a source of electricity. The phenomenon with which he dealt was the electrical relationship of injured tissue to uninjured tissue, called the injury potential. However, it was not until early in the 20th century that J. Bernstein presented a general theory to explain bioelectric currents. He held that a "resting" potential is created across an unstimulated cell membrane because the membrane is permeable to cations but not to their associated anions. When the membrane is broken by injury, the external layer of positive ions flows toward the break, producing the injury current. The electrical change accompanying nerve excitation, called the action potential, was explained as being caused by a temporary breakdown of the membrane, much like that resulting from injury.

Hodgkin assumed that the resting potential was caused by an outward diffusion of potassium ions; the action potential by the membrane's becoming permeable to the externally more concentrated sodium ions. On breakdown, the ratio of permeabilities of these ions would approach their aqueous mobilities and the resulting action potential should approximately equal the resting potential. Hodgkin wanted to compare the two potentials but wished to avoid the variables attendant upon using the nerve with its many fibers, as was the usual practice. He chose, therefore, to use the rather large single nerve fibers from the crab, *Carcinus maenas*. The resting potential was measured between an intact region and one depolarized by injury or isotonic potassium chloride. The results showed that action potentials were greater, often by as much as 40 millivolts, and that a more complex theory was needed to explain this reversal of electromotive force. The key to further progress lay in recording absolute potentials directly across the axon membrane. Hodgkin and Huxley thought this might be possible if one employed the giant nerve fibers of the squid, *Loligo forbesi*, some of which are as much as 0.8 mm in diameter. A microelectrode, a capillary glass 0.1 mm in diameter filled with metal or salt solution, was inserted into the axon core. In order for the test to be made across undamaged membrane, the electrode had to be passed a centimeter or more beyond the entry point without scraping against the axon sheath. As before, the results were incompatible with the Bernstein theory; action potentials were about twice as high as resting potentials and opposite in electrical sign.

In 1951 Hodgkin, in collaboration with Huxley and Bernhard Katz, worked out the sodium theory to account for their findings. The axon at rest is permeable to potassium ions. In responding to the electrical property of the approaching impulse, the axon membrane becomes selectively permeable to sodium ions to a degree greater than it was to potassium. A plasma concentration 10 times that of the axoplasm would result in the reversal of potential, up to $+50$ mv, observed in intact axons. Hodgkin and Katz verified the hypothesis with squid axons that showed reversible reduced-action potentials in sodium-deficient solutions and exaggerated ones in sodium-rich solutions. Subsequent chemical assays showed that there was a net uptake of sodium at the rate of 4×10^{-12} moles/cm^2 per impulse, more than enough to account for the action potential. Even more specialized techniques of electrical measurement were used to obtain independent measures of the potassium

and sodium ion currents corresponding to changes in time and membrane potential. Equations were evolved that proved capable of predicting step-by-step electrical properties of the axon, such as the form, duration, and amplitude of the action potential, impedance changes, and conduction velocity. Scientists now had in their hands the specific information with which to work out the related problems of the metabolic mechanisms supporting conduction and the physical structure of the membrane that complements it.

In the course of his researches, Hodgkin was able more than once to provide classical insight into the nature of nerve activity. The discovery of subthreshold responses by nerves stimulated with currents too feeble to elicit a propagated impulse, and the first experimental proofs that the direct causal agent of impulse propagation was electricity alone, were among his accomplishments.

Hodgkin attended Trinity College, Cambridge, of which he became a fellow in 1936. During World War II he worked on radar for the Air Ministry and the Ministry of Aircraft Production. After the war he was a lecturer and then assistant director of research at the Physiological Laboratory, Cambridge, before being appointed, in 1952, Foulerton Research Professor. Elected to the Royal Society in 1948, he was awarded the Society's Royal Medal in 1958.

Hodgkin wrote *Conduction of the Nervous Impulse* (1963).

For background information *see* BIOELECTRIC MODEL; NEUROPHYSIOLOGY in the McGraw-Hill Encyclopedia of Science and Technology.   ☐

☆ HODGKIN, Dorothy Crowfoot

British chemist
Born 1910, Cairo, Egypt

T HROUGH X-RAY crystallographic analysis, Hodgkin determined the structure of the vitamin B$_{12}$ molecule, one of the most complicated nonprotein molecules so far found in nature. For this achievement she was awarded the 1964 Nobel Prize in chemistry.

Vitamin B$_{12}$ is essential for the building of red blood cells and for the treatment of victims of pernicious anemia. It is found naturally in liver and can be produced synthetically by the same mold that produces streptomycin. Chemists had analyzed the giant molecule and found that it contained cobalt in its center, a nucleotide-like group, and a CN group, which together accounted for $C_{15}H_{18}O_7N_3PCo$ out of a total of approximately $C_{61-64}H_{86-92}O_{14}N_{14}PCo$. There was also chemical evidence for the existence of groups that gave rise to propanolamine upon

hydrolysis and to various simple acids on oxidation. But a major portion of the molecule was largely of unknown character, and the three-dimensional arrangement of these groups was totally unknown.

Hodgkin and her colleagues obtained their first x-ray photographs of vitamin-B_{12} crystals in 1948. During the next 6 years they collected complete three-dimensional diffraction data for four crystals: air-dried vitamin B_{12}, wet vitamin B_{12}, vitamin B_{12}-SeCN (having the CN of B_{12} replaced by SeCN), and a hexacarboxylic acid derived from vitamin B_{12}. By that time electronic computers were sophisticated enough to carry out the necessary calculations much more rapidly than would otherwise have been possible.

To find the three-dimensional arrangements of atoms from the directions in which the electrons that surround them scatter x-rays demands precision, facility in mathematical analysis, imagination, and insight. X-ray photographs record the angular relations and relative intensities only of the scattered x-ray spectra; their phase relations are, in general, lost. A variety of indirect methods have therefore to be used to recombine the scattered waves to show the actual arrangement of known and unknown groupings of atoms within the crystals.

Hodgkin started her analysis of each of the four crystals by finding the positions of the heavy atoms, cobalt or cobalt and selenium, by direct Patterson methods and then calculating three-dimensional Fourier series using observed F values and phases based only on the heavy-atom positions. The resulting distributions gave a crude approximation to the correct electron density series. Through a series of calculations of successive degrees of approximation to the correct electron density distribution, she and her colleagues reached a solution of the crystal structure of the hexacarboxylic acid derived from B_{12}. This provided the solution also to a large part of the chemical structure of vitamin

B_{12}. To carry the refinement of the structure further, more calculations of the electron density distribution were made. The crystal structures of the different B_{12} compounds were completely solved by 1956.

The B_{12} molecule that appeared was very beautifully composed, not far from spherical in form, with all the more chemically reactive groups on its surface. Throughout the molecule, the atomic positions were found to conform with the stereochemical rules established by the study of simpler molecules. The formula of vitamin B_{12}, as determined by crystallographic evidence, was $C_{63}H_{88}O_{14}N_{14}PCo$—within the range determined by other methods of analysis. Later this molecule proved almost certainly not to be the naturally active vitamin, which is still more complicated and easily obtained from it. The structure of the latter, isolated by Barker and his colleagues, was also found by x-ray analysis by P. G. Lenhert and Hodgkin in 1961. It includes a very remarkable feature, a bond between cobalt and a saturated carbon atom.

Born in Cairo while her father was working in the Egyptian education service, Dorothy Crowfoot early became interested in the Near East. Between school and university, she accompanied her father on an archeological expedition to Jerash in Transjordan. She was educated at the Sir John Leman School, Beccles, and Somerville College, Oxford. By her second year at Oxford, in 1929, she was already concentrating on the intricacies of x-ray analysis of large complicated molecules. While studying at Cambridge from 1932 to 1934, she became interested in the sterols and collaborated with J. D. Bernal and I. Fankuchen in a study that was monumental in its scope, even by present-day standards. She returned permanently to Oxford in 1934 to teach and do research. In 1942, she began the structure analysis of penicillin, which she completed in 1946. In 1945 she completed the crystallographic analysis of cholesterol iodide. Later she determined the chemical structure of cephalosporin C, a drug closely related to the penicillin family. She married Thomas L. Hodgkin in 1937.

For background information *see* CRYSTALLOGRAPHY; VITAMIN B_{12} in the McGraw-Hill Encyclopedia of Science and Technology.   ☐

☆ **HOFFMAN, Samuel Kurtz**

American propulsion engineer
Born Apr. 15, 1902, Williamsport, Pa., U.S.A.

HOFFMAN GUIDED the development of a series of early U.S. rocket engines that culminated in power plants for four of the nation's pioneer ballistic missiles and virtually all of its space booster vehicles. For this achievement, he was

cited by the American Rocket Society (1962 Propulsion Award), the American Society of Mechanical Engineers (1962 Spirit of St. Louis Medal), the Institute of Aeronautical Sciences (1960 Louis W. Hill Space Transportation Award), and *Missiles and Rockets Magazine* (1959 Robert H. Goddard Trophy).

In 1949, Hoffman left a position as professor of aeronautical engineering at Pennsylvania State University to join North American Aviation as chief of its Aerophysics Department Propulsion Section. Under development by that group was a rocket engine of approximately 75,000 pounds of thrust to be used to boost the winged Navaho intercontinental missile to flight speed and operating altitude. Immediately recognizing the tremendous potential of the rocket engine, Hoffman led his organization into the early achievement of development and testing goals, including the successful test of a high-thrust rocket engine in March, 1950. Later, a refined version of this engine was to launch America's first satellite, *Explorer I*, and the nation's first manned space flights by astronauts Alan B. Shepherd and Virgil I. Grissom. By 1952, when the first U.S. thermonuclear detonation indicated the military value of the intercontinental ballistic missile, the necessary propulsion technology was already available.

Subsequent missile development schedules were necessarily based on the availability of propulsion systems, and missile designs were evolved from power-plant specifications and estimates of performance. The early on-schedule delivery of production engines for the Atlas ICBM and the Thor and Jupiter IRBM's enabled the United States to proceed swiftly with the testing and operational deployment of these missiles.

The development for these missiles of engines more powerful than any previously built required major engineering advances in the fields of thermodynamics, hydrodynamics, applied mechanics, fuels technology, and controls. These advances permitted for the first time the practical containment and direction of jet gases developing temperatures in excess of 5000°F and energies measured in millions of horsepower. To produce advanced levels of propulsive thrust, North American's Rocketdyne Division, led by Hoffman, devised lightweight pumps developing higher speeds and pressures and operating at lower inlet pressures than any previous turbomachinery of comparable size. They overcame the problem of thrust vector control by developing precise Vernier supplementary power and an effective method of gimballing the thrust chamber of the engine. In reaching new levels of power, they pioneered the use of highly volatile fuels and liquid oxidizers with temperatures lower than −298°F.

The thrust available in such missiles pointed, for the first time, to the imminent feasibility of space travel. This was dramatically realized with the successful orbiting of a Soviet satellite late in 1957, and subsequently by numerous satellite launchings and several space probes, both manned and unmanned, by the United States and the Soviet Union.

Partly in recognition of the extraordinary improvements in thrust, efficiency, and reliability of liquid propellant rocket engines achieved under Hoffman's leadership, the division he headed was assigned responsibility late in 1958 for the development of a cluster of eight rocket engines that would for the first time give U.S. vehicles a launching thrust of more than 10^6 lb. Simultaneously, authorization was given to begin work on a single engine of 1.5×10^6 lb of thrust. These rocket engines, together with a third employing liquid hydrogen as its fuel, were ready for flight in the mid-1960s as the primary propulsion for the multistaged Saturn vehicles intended ultimately to land U.S. astronauts on the Moon.

The son of a metal products manufacturer, Hoffman studied mechanical engineering at Pennsylvania State University, where he received his B.S. in 1925. Employed in design-engineering positions through the early years of his career, he became in 1934 assistant chief engineer and in 1936 chief engineer for the Lycoming Division of Aviation Corporation, serving in the latter capacity through World War II. In 1945 he left industry to return to Pennsylvania State University as professor of aeronautical engineering. He joined North American Aviation in 1949. In 1955, the activities under his direction were designated as the company's Rocketdyne Division, and Hoffman was named its general manager. He was elected a vice-president of the company in 1957 and was appointed president of the Rocketdyne Division in 1960.

For background information *see* PROPULSION; ROCKET ENGINE in the McGraw-Hill Encyclopedia of Science and Technology.   □

★ HOFSTADTER, Robert

American physicist
Born Feb. 5, 1915, New York, N.Y., U.S.A.

HOFSTADTER DISCOVERED that the proton and neutron are bodies of considerable complexity, not pointlike or "elementary" as previously supposed. He measured sizes and distributions of electric charge and magnetic moment in these two particles, which are called nucleons. More precisely, he determined their four electromagnetic "form factors." Each particle has one electric and one magnetic form factor, so that there are four form factors in all. The form factor is a technical quantity that describes how the particle interacts with other particles and fields. Thus its behavior is a more general way of describing size and shape than can be done with a model.

The discovery of the existence and behavior of the form factors of the nucleons led to an apparent anomaly that stimulated theoreticians, notably Y. Nambu, to propose the existence of new types of heavy mesons. These were discovered subsequently and are now known as the rho meson, the omega meson, the phi meson, and so on. These mesons play fundamental roles in the forces and interactions between nucleons.

A related achievement was the clear measurement of the size and shape of many nuclei, and the discovery, from these studies, of the scheme of construction of the fundamental nuclei of atoms. Hofstadter learned how nuclear matter arranges itself in its most stable state. He found that nuclei form around themselves a surface region of constant thickness in which their density gradually falls to zero and that in the centers of nuclei the nuclear density is approximately constant. He found also that the mean

nuclear radius follows accurately a law in which the radius varies as the cube root of the mass number of the nucleus. In making these studies, he determined the sizes and shapes of fundamental nuclei such as the deuteron, hydrogen-3, helium-3, the alpha particle, carbon, oxygen, and calcium.

For his work on the proton and neutron and on atomic nuclei, Hofstadter shared with Rudolph Mössbauer the 1961 Nobel Prize in physics.

When he left Princeton in 1950 to take up a new position at Stanford University, Hofstadter knew that there was a large accelerator under construction there. He thought a great deal about what he could do with this new instrument. The subject that appealed most to him involved the possibility of "seeing" inside nuclei to determine how the protons and neutrons were arranged in their interiors.

Such an investigation seemed possible by analogy with the work done much earlier on atoms and molecules. By using x-rays and electrons in the 50-kev range, G. P. Thomson and others had demonstrated that the diffraction patterns so obtained gave unique determinations of the electronic structure within atoms as well as the positions of the centers of the atoms. Hofstadter felt that similar results could be obtained with nuclei by changing the scales of length by a factor of about 10,000. To do this required using electrons of 100–500 Mev instead of the 50-kev electrons that were suitable for atoms and molecules. The important quantity in this connection is the electron wavelength, $\lambda = \frac{\hbar}{p}$, where $\hbar$ is the reduced value of the Planck constant and p the momentum of the electron. At 100–500 Mev this wavelength is considerably smaller than most nuclei and is just the right length to probe atoms or molecules. A confirmation of these ideas was afforded by some early work at the University of Illinois.

Hofstadter's method was to send an intense beam of monoenergetic electrons at a target containing the nuclei to be investigated, and to detect and count the number of electrons that were scattered at various angles from the original direction of the incident beam. It was necessary to know whether the electrons had interacted elastically—that is, whether they had bounced off without exciting or breaking up a nucleus—or whether some interaction had taken place that did excite or disintegrate a nucleus. This was accomplished with a massive magnetic spectrometer mounted in a precise way on an obsolete U.S. Navy gun mount. With newly developed Cerenkov counters, one could unambiguously detect electrons without background interference. The angular patterns of many nuclei were studied with this apparatus in the years 1953–56.

It was quickly determined that the nuclei had a gradually varying "skin" on their surfaces. The thickness of this skin was determined for a set of nuclei representative of the periodic table. All nuclei were observed to have essentially the same skin thickness $(2.4 \times 10^{-13} \text{cm})$. Furthermore, it was observed that the interior regions of the nuclei exhibited uniform density. This value of density was measured. Another important result was that the distance between the center of the nucleus and the radius at which the density fell to 50% of its central value was a quantity that varied as the cube root of the mass number of the nucleus. From these results, physicists could acquire a precise understanding of the size and shape of the nuclei of the periodic system.

In 1954 Hofstadter realized that his method was powerful enough to study even the proton and the neutron, and he immediately set out with a graduate student, Robert W. McAllister, to look for evidence concerning possible structure in the proton. They were surprised to find that the proton's structure could be seen quite easily at the energy then used ($\sim$188 Mev) and observed that the proton was definitely not pointlike. With McAllister, Hofstadter also determined the exact size of the alpha particle, one of the fundamental particles in the historical development of nuclear physics. The work on the proton encouraged Hofstadter to look for structure in the neutron. With another graduate student, M. R. Yearian, he studied the deuteron and observed clear evidence that the neutron was just as extended in size as the proton. In many ways the neutron's structure was similar to that of the proton. Its magnetic form factor was observed to be the same as that of the proton.

From this point on, Hofstadter's group at Stanford engaged in a long effort to obtain a more precise determination of all four electromagnetic form factors of the proton and the neutron. By repeated trials they determined that the data were reproducible, and their findings were confirmed. In 1960 a group at Cornell University used a similar method of studying the proton but employed a circular accelerator instead of a linear one. The Cornell work completely confirmed the Stanford findings.

The rapid falloff of the magnetic form factor of the proton and neutron dismayed many theoreticians. To explain what was then considered an anomaly, Y. Nambu of the University of Chicago proposed in 1957 that an unknown type of heavy meson might explain this behavior. Four years later there was conclusive evidence that Nambu was correct in his prediction. Since that time the explanation of the structure in the proton and neutron has made great progress but is not yet complete.

Hofstadter attended elementary and high schools in New York City and received his B.S., magna cum laude, from the College of the City of New York in 1935. He received both the M.A. and Ph.D. in physics at Princeton University in 1938. During World War II he worked at the National Bureau of Standards, Washington, D.C., and for Norden Laboratories Corporation. He joined the Princeton faculty in 1946 and in 1950 moved to Stanford University, where in 1954 he became professor of physics. He was elected to the National Academy of Sciences in 1958.

Besides some 125 scientific papers, Hofstadter wrote *High-energy Electron Scattering Tables*, with Robert Herman (1960) and edited *Nuclear and Nucleon Structure* (1963) and *Nucleon Structure*, with L. I. Schiff (1964).

For background information *see* NEUTRON; PROTON in the McGraw-Hill Encyclopedia of Science and Technology. □

★ HOLMES, Arthur

English geologist
Born Jan. 14, 1890, Hebburn, near Newcastle upon Tyne, England
Died Sept. 20, 1965, London, England

As a schoolboy, Holmes was fascinated and puzzled by the date, 4004 B.C., traditionally assigned to the creation of the world as described in the Bible. At school this curiosity about the age of the Earth was intensified by an enlightened teacher who encouraged him to read some of Lord Kelvin's *Addresses* and so introduced him to Kelvin's long controversy with the geologists, who needed a far more generous allowance of time than Kelvin's meager estimates based on the assumption that the Earth had cooled from a molten state. In 1907, having become a student at the newly established Imperial College, London, Holmes soon heard that Kelvin's embarrassing limits no longer had any validity. R. J. Strutt (later the 4th Lord Rayleigh) had discovered that the abundance of radioactive elements in the Earth's crustal rocks was such that the Earth could no longer be assumed to be a simply cooling globe. Following up Ernest Rutherford's suggestion that radioactive minerals might keep a record within themselves of the time elapsed since their crystallization, Strutt, who was then professor of physics at the Imperial College, began his pioneer work on the helium ages of minerals.

Thus it was that Holmes grew up with the earliest applications of radioactivity to geological problems. After graduation, he eagerly grasped an opportunity to work in Strutt's laboratory on the Pb/U ratios of minerals from the Oslo district. This research was interrupted by a long and highly instructive field season of geological exploration in Mozambique, which added petrogenesis and the distribution and correlation of ancient orogenic belts to his major interests. For his subsequent work in these fields, and particularly in the development of "isotope geology," Holmes received many honors, notably including election as foreign associate of the Institut de France (1955), the award of the Penrose Medal of the Geological Society of America (1956), and the award of the Vetlesen Prize of Columbia University "for scientific achievement in a clearer understanding of the Earth, its history or its relation to the universe" (1964).

Holmes made a sustained attempt to construct a Phanerozoic time-scale by plotting radiometric dates, as they became available, against the cumulative maximum thicknesses of the sedimentary systems down to the base of the Cambrian. The value of this method in balancing errors is shown by the remarkable coincidence that his earliest estimate of Phanerozoic time (1913) and his latest (1959) were both about 6 $\times$ 10^8 years, the round figure now in general use.

The oldest known minerals provided only a minimum estimate for the age of the Earth ($>$ 2×10^9 years) until A. O. C. Nier carried out his epoch-making researches on the isotopic constitution of uranium and lead. After the interruption caused by World War II, Holmes showed how Nier's results for galena-leads of known geological age could be used to determine the age of the Earth's crust. The first estimates, about 3.35×10^7 years, were too low, because the ages of some of the lead ores had been underestimated. As the data became more abundant and accurate, the age of the Earth was found to be about 4.55×10^7 years in agreement with C. Patterson's determination of the age of meteorites by the same method.

Inspired by J. J. Sederholm's work in Finland, suggesting that the continents consist of an integration of orogenic belts, Holmes tried to read the African sequence—and later that of India—from the patterns disclosed by geological maps, and to date the closing stages of each orogeny by radiometric methods. In 1948 he summarized his findings in an International Congress address and so inaugurated what has since become a rapidly accelerating application of the methods of geochronology to the inexhaustible task of unraveling the Earth's Precambrian history.

In an early series of papers Holmes tried to reconcile the implications of a cooling and contracting Earth with a model in which radioactivity and heat generation were suitably limited and assumed to decrease exponentially in depth. He found this increasingly difficult after 1926, in which year he had drawn attention to the critical importance of potassium as a source of radiothermal energy. He abandoned the contraction hypothesis because of its failure to account for tectonic phenomena and particularly for continental drift. In 1928 he proposed a subcrustal convective-current mechanism for "engineering" continental drift, with concomitant development of new ocean basins between the separating continents. To overcome the ocean-floor obstruction in front of an advancing continent, Holmes suggested that basaltic rock was transformed into eclogite, which was heavy enough to sink out of the way with the down-turning currents. This material would eventually melt, and then rise with ascending currents to feed continental plateau basalts and form the floors of growing ocean basins.

After describing the volcanic rocks of Mozambique, Holmes made a detailed study of the Arctic basalts, and later, while at Durham, of the Whin Sill and its dyke-suites, which he showed to be of late Carboniferous age and easily distinguishable by helium ages from the Tertiary dyke-swarm of northern England. H. F. Harwood contributed chemical analyses of many of these rocks, and this partnership continued throughout a long investigation of the remarkable potash-rich volcanic rocks of southwestern Uganda. In some of these Holmes discovered the previously unknown mineral kalsilite (a potash equivalent of nepheline). In 1950 he proposed that these unique rocks had been generated by reactions between carbonatite fluids and sialic crustal rocks. This hypothesis received strong support when P. Baertschi determined the isotopic constitutions of oxygen and carbon from travertine still being deposited in one of the craters and found them to correspond with those of known carbonatites and not with those of ordinary limestones. Further corroboration was provided by the discovery of carbonatite lavas in Uganda and by the observed eruption of alkali-rich carbonatite ashes and lavas from a volcano in northern Tanganyika.

Although his father was a cabinetmaker and his mother a schoolteacher, Holmes was descended on both sides from Northumbrian farming stock. From Gateshead Higher Grade School he proceeded to the Imperial College, London, graduating B.Sc. (physics and mathematics) in 1909 and A.R.C.S. (geology) in 1910. For his subsequent work on geochronology and the geology of Mozambique he received his D.Sc. in 1917. He taught geology at the Imperial College from 1912 to 1920, having been found unfit for active service during World War I because of recurrent attacks of malaria contracted in Mozambique; he was, however, attached to Naval Intelligence for compilation of maps and charts as required. After an interval of three years as an oil geologist in Burma, he returned to academic life in 1924 to build up a new department of geology at Durham University, where he remained as professor until 1943. In that year he was appointed Regius Professor of Geology and Mineralogy at Edinburgh. Holmes resigned in 1956.

Holmes wrote *The Age of the Earth* (1913; 3d ed. 1937), *The Nomenclature of Petrology* (1920; 2d ed. 1930), *Petrographic Methods and Calculations* (1921; 2d ed. 1930), and *Principles of Physical Geology* (1944; 2d ed. 1965).

For background information *see* EARTH (AGE OF); PETROLOGY in the McGraw-Hill Encyclopedia of Science and Technology.   □

☆ HOUSSAY, Bernardo Alberto

Argentine physiologist
Born Apr. 10, 1887, Buenos Aires, Argentina

HOUSSAY HAD a long and productive career in biological research and education. His research centered primarily in endocrinology, and particularly on the functions and effects of the hypophysis. From 1923 to 1937, Houssay and his associates intensively investigated the rela-

tionships of this gland to carbohydrate metabolism and its related malfunctions. For this work, Houssay shared the Nobel Prize in physiology or medicine in 1947.

Although his research on the hypophysis had originally begun in 1908, it was greatly intensified after the discovery of insulin by F. G. Banting and J. J. R. Macleod in 1921. It had long been known that lesions of the hypophysis were accompanied by such serious organic disturbances as dwarfism and acromegaly. The frequent occurrence of diabetes in acromegaly was well known, and Borchardt had demonstrated in 1908 that extracts of the posterior lobe of the hypophysis could produce great pharmacological effects, including transient high blood-sugar levels. It was thus commonly accepted that if the hypophysis played a part in carbohydrate metabolism, it would be due to the activity of the posterior lobe. This was the state of affairs when insulin was discovered, and it was natural that such a set of disconnected but related facts should stimulate Houssay to begin a systematic effort to clarify matters.

The techniques used by Houssay and his coworkers were almost exclusively surgical, consisting of the selective removal of various portions of the hypophysis and/or other organs with subsequent observations of blood-sugar level and other physiological characteristics. These experiments were conducted primarily on dogs and large toads of the species *Bufo marinus*, but a number of other animals were used as well. The need to observe the experimental animals for extended periods after surgery introduced some great technical difficulties into their work. Since the hypophysis is a very small organ and is, furthermore, located in the center of the head at the base of the brain, very precise surgical techniques had to be developed to permit survival of the patients.

The following observations resulted from his experiments. Animals that had either the hypophysis or its anterior lobe removed were hypersensitive to insulin and other hypoglycemic agents, but this sensitivity could be corrected by injection of extract from the anterohypophysis. Indeed, such injections could cause diabetes.

When animals had both the pancreas and anterohypophysis removed, the diabetes (which resulted from removal of the pancreas) was attenuated. If such animals were then injected with extract from the anterohypophysis, the usual severity of diabetes was restored or even increased.

Finally, dogs with both pancreas and hypophysis removed were found to show these differences, among others, with respect to dogs with only the pancreas removed: (1) survival was longer, with better healing of wounds and less frequent infection; (2) high blood- and urinary-sugar levels were less marked and sometimes absent; and (3) fasting produced a notable fall in blood and urinary sugar.

The ability of anterohypophyseal extracts to cause diabetes was first demonstrated in animals from which both the hypophysis and pancreas had been removed; it was later found in normal mammals of several species. This effect was shown to be a general one that could be induced by the hypophysis of all vertebrates tested on its own or on other species. The disease so induced is similar in most respects to pancreatic diabetes. It is, however, intimately dependent on the liver and interrelated as well to adrenal function.

The pituitary hormones that have diabetogenic action are somatotropin, adrenocorticotrophin, and prolactin. The actions of the first two hormones are frequently sinergic.

Houssay thus clearly demonstrated the active involvement of the hypophysis in carbohydrate metabolism. Contrary to previous thought, he showed that the anterior lobe and not the posterior portion was active in this complex process. The interrelationships of the various endocrine glands and their hormones in these processes were delineated, and various new causes of diabetes were discovered.

In addition to his work in endocrinology, Houssay worked in many other areas of physiology and pharmacology. He did extensive research in the physiology of circulation and respiration, of the blood and the processes of immunity, of digestion and bile secretion, and of the nervous system. He also investigated in great detail the venoms of snakes, spiders, and scorpions, their physiological effects, and the preparation of antivenom serums.

The son of French immigrants to Argentina, Houssay was a precocious student, obtaining his degree in pharmacy from the University of Buenos Aires in 1904 at the age of 17. In 1911, he received his M.D. from the same university. He was associated with the University of Buenos Aires for most of his adult life, either in the School of Veterinary Medicine or the Medical School. Deprived of his post for political reasons in 1943, he was reinstated in 1955. In the interim he organized the first independent research organization in Argentina, the Institute of Biology and Experimental Medicine. Houssay received honorary degrees from 27 universities and was a member of 38 academies and more than 300 scientific societies in many countries. In 1940 he was elected a foreign associate of the U.S. National Academy of Sciences.

For background information *see* ENDOCRINE MECHANISMS; HYPOPHYSIS in the McGraw-Hill Encyclopedia of Science and Technology.   □

★ HOWELLS, William White

American anthropologist
Born Nov. 27, 1908, New York, N.Y., U.S.A.

WORKING WITH variation in the size and form of the human physique, Howells applied methods of testing the agreement of such variation with predictions of genetic theory. This involved developing new descriptive and comparative methods, using second-order variables or factors derived from measurements.

The early anthropologists, often with the aid of the much-used cephalic index, found that populations or racial groups were relatively constant in their average proportions, although Franz Boas showed in 1911 that these measurements might shift, apparently under environmental stress. From 1905 onward, Mendelian genetics was applied to unit characters in man, especially blood types, with great success; but genetic analysis of quantitative traits made little progress anywhere, and that mostly in animal husbandry. Variation in human form continued to be observed and measured but not otherwise analyzed.

In 1918 R. A. Fisher showed that a multifactorial trait (for example, some measured feature) should, in the absence of disturbing influences, give a correlation between brothers of .50 because of the expectation of their inheriting half their chromosomes in common. Fisher and others later developed different forms of multivariate analysis, handling statistically whole configurations of measurements rather than single ones.

Howells felt (1) that only such methods would allow successful analysis of human form into the significant elements that actually vary from either genetic or environmental causes, since laboratory experiments are nearly impossible with man, and (2) that these methods would be a primary tool in testing various hypotheses of variation, including the traditional anthropological one that a population represents a mixture of ancestral "types" that continue to manifest themselves in succeeding generations. Beginning in 1950, Howells used factor analysis (already applied to some extent by others) to show that the body may be dissected mathematically into regions, or factors, which vary more or less independently of one another. The head, in particular, is less closely related in size or form than other regions to the body as a whole. The method is indeterminate in its results, but by comparing results from skulls and from living heads he found evidence that brain size and skull length are largely independently determined, which is a probable explanation of the well-known variation in head shape.

Applying these methods in family studies, Howells found evidence of distinctly greater heritability in the length of the limbs and the length of the face (although these are not associated) than in other aspects of the body, especially lateral development. Such factors, and certain direct measurements, definitely exceeded the fraternal likeness predicted by Fisher. The excess may be interpreted as being due to the reinforcing influences of a common environmental background and the more similar ethnic origin of brothers compared to the population at large. Perhaps other forces as well are at work, since the effects of common environment and common heredity cannot be separated in such a study. A later study, however, on a long-isolated religious sect, extremely homogenous in both origins and way of life, showed family coefficients not exceeding .50, as Fisher predicted, while maintaining a similar pattern of differences among measurements.

Work by others, such as R. H. Osborne and F. V. De George on twins, and by J. Hiernaux on closely related African tribes, serving to test more specifically the genetic and environmental factors respectively, has produced results in accordance with Howells's findings. Related work by Howells on racial differences by multivariate analysis shows that group distinctions can be defined in the same fashion and gives no sign that populations can be resolved into types; instead, when these special multivariate criteria are used, the individuals are found to be normally distributed in a population. Refinement of such criteria may be expected to bring increasingly better control and definition to studies of genetic and environmental effects in man.

Howells graduated from St. Paul's School, Concord, N.H., and took his B.S. in 1930 and Ph.D. in 1934, both in anthropology, at Harvard. He was on the faculty of the University of Wisconsin from 1939 (serving in the Navy in World War II) until he moved to Harvard in 1954. He was awarded the Viking Fund Medal in Physical Anthropology in 1955.

Howells wrote *Mankind So Far* (1944), *The Heathens* (1948), *Back of History* (1954), and *Mankind in the Making* (1959).

For background information *see* ANTHROPOMETRY in the McGraw-Hill Encyclopedia of Science and Technology.   □

★ HUGGINS, Charles Brenton

American surgeon and cancer researcher
Born Sept. 22, 1901, Halifax, N.S., Canada

DURING A study of the metabolism of the prostate gland of the dog in 1940, Huggins discovered that hormones can directly influence the growth of cancer; this has led to a system of treatment of cancers by endocrinologic methods. From this novel study the basic concept emerged that some sorts of cancer cells differ in a crucial way from ancestral normal cells in their response to modifications of the hormonal environment. Opposite sorts of change of the hormonal status can induce regression and, in some instances, cure of such cancers even when these are in very advanced stages. These hormonal modifications are (1) deprivation of essential hormones or (2) hormone interference with large amounts of critical compounds. Historically, diethylstilbestrol was the first synthetic compound to control cancers. Hence this study was the start of chemotherapy of cancer.

There was an element of luck in Huggins's work, but this is not unusual in the evolution of science. Huggins had found that spermatozoa of man, soon after they are made, live for a time in a fluid devoid of inorganic phosphorus; after the ejaculation of spermatozoa, however, there is a very great increase of acid-soluble phosphorus in their fluid environment. A detailed study of metabolism of phosphorus in man was carried out. When it proved difficult to obtain unmixed secretions from the individual sex glands of man, a simple technique was devised to collect fluids of this sort from dogs—in quantity, at frequent intervals, and for years. It was fortunate that the experiments were carried out on dogs, since this is the only known species, aside from the human, that develops tumors of the prostate; in both man and dog spontaneous tumors, both benign and cancerous, occur very commonly in older individuals. In fact, prostatic cancer is the most frequent neoplasm of men over 50.

At first it was vexatious to encounter a dog with a prostatic tumor during a metabolic study, but soon such creatures were sought, and these are plentiful. Huggins observed that orchiectomy or small doses of phenolic estrogens caused a rapid shrinkage of canine prostatic tumors. As in the dog, orchiectomy or administration of estrogenic substances resulted in regression of cancer of the human prostate, whereas, in untreated clinical cases, testosterone enhanced the rate of growth of the cancer. Measurement of enzymes in blood serum furnished the proof that cancer of the prostate in man is hormone-responsive. Human prostatic cancer that had metastasized to bone was studied at first, and the content of alkaline and acid phosphatases in the blood was studied concurrently at frequent intervals. The level of acid phosphatase indicated activity of the disseminated cancer cells. The titer of alkaline phosphatase revealed the function of osteoblasts as influenced by the presence of prostatic cancers in the bones. By measuring the two enzymes, Huggins obtained a view of overall activity of metastatic cancer and the reaction of normal cells to the presence of that cancer. The great influences of hormones of the host on his cancer cells and upon the osteoblasts that were their near neighbors were demonstrated simply and in mathematical terms.

The first series of cases with prostatic cancer treated by orchiectomy comprised 20 patients with widespread metastases; 4 of these men survived more than 12 years. Obviously there were many failures of hormone therapy, but spectacular regressions occurred. On the whole, life spans were extended, and there was a decrease of man-pain hours. Since then, seven sorts of hormone-responsive cancers of man and animals—cancers of the prostate, breast, thyroid, lymphatic, kidney, endometrium, and seminal vesicle—have been treated by this new system of therapy in clinics throughout the world.

In addition to studies on cancer, Huggins made original contributions to physiology in studies of bone formation, bone marrow, serum enzymes, and protein chemistry.

Huggins received his B.A. from Acadia University in 1920 and his M.D. from Harvard in 1924. The years 1924–27 were spent in graduate training in surgery at the University of Michigan. In 1927, he joined the surgical faculty at the University of Chicago, where in 1951 he became Willaim B. Ogden Distinguished Service Professor and director of the Ben May Laboratory for Cancer Research. Among his many honors was the 1955 Passano Foundation Award. He was elected to the National Academy of Sciences in 1949.

For background information *see* CANCER; HORMONE in the McGraw-Hill Encyclopedia of Science and Technology.   □

★ HUNSAKER, Jerome Clarke

American aeronautical engineer
Born Aug. 26, 1886, Creston, Iowa, U.S.A.

TRAINED AS a naval officer and then as a naval architect, Hunsaker began his 50-year career in aeronautics by measuring the force on a turning destroyer's rudder. This led to estimation of the aerodynamic forces on airplanes by model tests in a wind tunnel. From wind tunnel measurements followed studies of balance, control and stability, propeller action, and structural strength. In 1914 he started a graduate course in aeronautical engineering at the Massachusetts Institute of Technology, the first in the United States.

In 1916, Hunsaker was recalled by the Navy to Washington to organize an Aircraft Division in the Bureau of Construction and Repair. This division was expanded to handle design and production of all naval aircraft during World War I. Hunsaker's responsibilities were mainly administrative, but they included initiation of urgent development projects such as vee-bottom seaplane floats, nonrigid dirigibles, tank-tested flying boats, waterproof laminated wood construction, aluminum alloy of "duralumin" type, and venturi-type air-speed meters. He was charged with two special engineering projects, undertaken as a precaution against the possibility of hostilities continuing for several years. One was a flying boat to cross the Atlantic under its own power; the other was a zeppelin-type airship.

The flying boat was given the name NC because of collaboration with Glenn Curtis. Three giant flying boats, each with four Liberty engines, started from Newfoundland for the Azores in May, 1919. NC4 reached her destination without incident and proceeded to Lisbon and Plymouth. NC1 and NC3 landed at sea some 200 miles short of the Azores because of bad weather. This performance greatly exceeded expectations from the state of the art.

The zeppelin project became the *Shenandoah*, the first such airship to be made in the United States and the first to be inflated with helium rather than hydrogen. Hunsaker had information from wrecked German zeppelins but had to work backward to discover the structural factors of safety or experience used by the German designers. Sample girders, like German girders, made of an alloy corresponding to analysis of the German metal (duralumin), were tested at the Bureau of Standards. Commissioned in 1923, the *Shenandoah* gave two years' service before being lost in a heavy storm. Because it used helium, there was no fire. It then appeared that a better communication of weather information might permit an airship to avoid a dangerous situation.

In 1921, Hunsaker's division was transferred to the new Bureau of Aeronautics, where he served as chief of design. Under his supervision were developed launching catapults and arresting gear for aircraft carriers, air-cooled radial engines (with Charles Lawrance), light shipboard airplanes, and the torpedo plane (with Donald Douglas).

During 1925–26, Hunsaker served as assistant naval attaché at London, Paris, Berlin, and The Hague until he resigned from the regular Navy. He joined the Bell Telephone Laboratories to develop airway wire, radio, and weather services. With support of the American Telephone and Telegraph Company and the Daniel Guggenheim Fund, a model airway was operated between Los Angeles and San Francisco. The combination of communication services, substantially as conceived by Hunsaker, became the operating system for the new airways.

In 1928, Hunsaker joined Goodyear to build the *Akron* and *Macon* and to promote airships for transoceanic transportation. Proposed extension of existing maritime laws to subsidize civil airships failed to interest the Congress. The development of long-range airplanes was even then changing the relative value of airships, which were later found to be not only vulnerable but also unnecessary.

In 1933, Hunsaker returned to MIT as head of the departments of mechanical engineering and aeronautical engineering. He expanded programs at MIT in supersonic aerodynamics, aeroelasticity, vibration and instrumentation, automatic controls, and jet propulsion. There followed a substantial increase of the Graduate School with the completion of a gas turbine laboratory and a supersonic laboratory.

In 1941, on leave from MIT, he was coordinator of research in the office of the Secretary of the Navy, a member of the council of the Office of Scientific Research and Development, and a member of its Guided Missiles Section. He served as an advisor to numerous government agencies. Hunsaker was a member of the National Advisory Committee for Aeronautics, appointed for five-year terms by three Presidents in 1939, 1944, 1949, and 1954. He was chairman from 1941 to 1957. During World War II, he handled the expansion of NACA personnel from 650 to 6,500 people and enlarged research and test facilities at the Langley, Ames, and Lewis laboratories and two flight stations.

Hunsaker grew up in Detroit and Saginaw, Mich., where his father was a newspaper editor and publisher. Graduating first in his class from the U.S. Naval Academy in 1908, he spent a year at sea and then was selected for the Construction Corps of the Navy and sent to the Massachusetts Institute of Technology to study naval architecture. He received his M.S. (1912) and Sc.D. (1916) at MIT. In 1912, the Navy sent him to Europe to investigate the state of aeronautical engineering, preparatory to instituting a graduate course at MIT. He was taken on as an assistant by Eiffel in Paris, Prandtl in Göttingen, and Bairstow in Teddington, thanks to MIT and Smithsonian introductions.

The course at MIT was successful, but Hunsaker was recalled by the Navy in 1916 to apply aeronautical engineering in Washington. He resigned his naval commission in 1926, joining Bell Telephone Laboratories to develop communications for the airways and moving to Goodyear in 1928 to build zeppelins. He returned to the faculty of MIT in 1933, retiring in 1952. He received many honors, among them the 1933 Guggenheim Medal and the 1942 Franklin Medal of the Franklin Institute. He was elected to the National Academy of Sciences in 1935.

Hunsaker wrote *Engineering Applications of Fluid Mechanics*, with B. G. Rightmire (1947) and *Aeronautics at the Mid-century* (1952).

For background information *see* AERONAUTICAL ENGINEERING in the McGraw-Hill Encyclopedia of Science and Technology.   □

★ HUNTSMAN, Archibald Gowanlock

Canadian biologist
Born Nov. 23, 1883, Tintern, Ont., Canada

As DIRECTOR of stations of the Biological (later Fisheries Research) Board of Canada, Huntsman felt the need of trying to solve the problem with which fishermen must deal: What fish will be where, and when? This could typify the general problem of what life there will be at any particular place and time, taking into account all the complexities of the organism and its environment. Such knowledge is basic for handling or managing any kind of organism.

As a university student studying the development of young bass at the Georgian Bay Biological Station, Huntsman observed that black bass, on starting to move from the nests in which they had hatched, behaved like the molecules of a solid in forming a stationary mass above the nest; when confined in a laboratory vessel, the mass expanded or contracted to occupy the available space like a gas. At this station, and later at Pacific and Atlantic stations, he ignored traditional ideas—for example, Aristotle's teleology and Darwin's principle of the survival of the fittest—in studying kinds of plants and animals. The well-known facts that the kinds have more or less peculiar distributions were strikingly in evidence as between water and land and between fresh water and sea water. That the distribution of plants and animals is correlated with physical factors became clear to him when he was associated with Johan Hjort of Norway in the Canadian Fisheries Expedition of 1914–15, an oceanographic survey of a region in which the Gulf Stream from the tropics, the Labrador Current from the Arctic, and the St. Lawrence River from the Great Lakes play prominent roles. It seemed obvious to him that each kind was limited in distribution and abundance by its environment. Fitness of the environment rather than of the individual, Huntsman concluded, was the key factor in ecology.

In 1934 Huntsman began an extended study of the behavior of the salmon (*Salmo salar*). Those of the Margaree River of Cape Breton Island were causing most concern by not entering the river to become available for angling. With a staff of observers, Huntsman soon saw that the fish became large and fat while living near the bottom along the estuarial outflow into the Gulf of St. Lawrence and that they began to cease feeding and to roam to and fro early in June, even crossing the estuary mouth but not entering until there was a heavy freshet. Although there was no appreciable difference between rivers, salmon entered the neighboring Cheticamp River in numbers. The evident difference, Huntsman inferred, was that a bar at the mouth of the Cheticamp estuary gave a rather steady outflow to guide the fish in rheotactically, while the mouth of the Margaree estuary had been kept open to provide a harbor. When the salmon did enter the Margaree, upon subsidence of the freshet, they moved into the Northeast branch and not the Southwest. Here the evident difference was that the Southwest had much of its water stored in a large and shallow lake, which diminished freshet action and let the water warm up as the season advanced. Ignoring the general belief that the salmon ascending the Northeast Margaree against the slackening current were directing their courses homeward despite obstacles, Huntsman inferred that they were being rheotactically directed upstream by the current and that they moved upstream when the current permitted them to do so.

Through the years, Huntsman studied other salmon populations living under varied conditions and verified his inferences as to factors affecting salmon behavior in laboratory and pond experiments. He came to see that entrance of salmon into the Margaree River was dependent upon their being concentrated toward the estuary mouth by the hydrodynamic circulation set up by the mixture there of much freshet water with sea water, and through rheotactic guidance of the fish through the shallow four-mile estuary by such freshet water. Also, he obtained experimental proof in the Moser River for the inference that salmon ascended with the decline of sharp freshets. The chief variables to which they responded were changes in light, temperature, current, salinity, and character of solutes. When thin and less vigorous, when keeping up from the bottom and away from shore, and when not kept too deep by light—that is, particularly when at the surface in midstream just after dark—these fish are carried downstream through failure of rheotaxis. When fat and vigorous, they cease feeding, press into turbulent water near bottom, and move slowly upstream as the current slackens. Only such complex environmental action accounts for where salmon are found to go in migrating, and it should replace the traditional fixed idea (lacking factual support) that they direct their courses first oceanward and later riverward. This elucidation of the role played by environment has broad implications for life in general, including that of man.

Huntsman received a B.A. in 1905 and M.B. in 1907 at the University of Toronto. Appointed lecturer in biology in 1907, he rose to be professor of marine biology in 1927. In 1911 he became curator and in 1919 director of the Atlantic Biological Station. In addition he started from 1924 to 1928 the first of the Biological Board's technological stations for research on fish handling at Halifax, N.S. In 1934 he was made editor and consulting director by the board, retiring from the former position in 1948 and from the latter in 1953. He became a fellow of the Royal Society of Canada in 1917 and its president for 1938. He received the Society's Flavelle Medal in 1952.

Huntsman wrote *Life and the Universe* (1959).

For background information *see* ECOLOGY; SALMON in the McGraw-Hill Encyclopedia of Science and Technology.   □

★ **HURWITZ, Henry, Jr.**

American physicist
Born Dec. 25, 1918, New York, N.Y., U.S.A.

WHEN SERIOUS investigations of nuclear power began at the close of World War II, Hurwitz became interested in reactor physics problems that were to play an important role in this development. He had become familiar with the dramatic progress in atomic energy through his work in Edward Teller's group at the Los Alamos Scientific Laboratory. In 1946 he joined the staff of the Knolls Atomic Power Laboratory, which was being organized by the General Electric Company for the Atomic Energy Commission. This was the first major U.S. laboratory to have as its primary objective the development of practical nuclear power plants.

Although the extensive wartime research had provided much of the fundamental information required for the development of atomic power, Hurwitz and his associates at KAPL found that there were still many basic scientific questions to be answered before atomic power plants could be successfully designed. Not only was it necessary to fill extensive gaps that still existed in nuclear cross-section data, but it was also necessary to extend and refine the methods for using the nuclear data to predict the reactor properties that had to be known before a satisfactory engineering design could be determined. At that time, the available techniques for the direct measurement of nuclear cross sections were still of such limited capability that much of the basic nuclear data had to be deduced from intricate measurements in low-power chain-reacting systems known as critical assemblies.

Of particular interest to the KAPL scientists was the problem of determining how the ability of a reactor to produce more fissile material than it consumes (that is, to breed) depends on its composition and structure. A major obstacle to breeding is the parasitic capture of neutrons by structural material, fission products, and the nuclear fuel itself. It was therefore important to determine how the parasitic neutron capture depends on neutron spectrum and how the neutron spectrum depends on reactor composition. Hurwitz took a leading part in developing and applying theoretical methods suitable both for the interpretation of the neutron-capture experiments performed by the KAPL scientists and for the accurate determination of the neutron spectra characteristic of the various possible reactor designs.

The KAPL investigations demonstrated that in the case of the uranium-plutonium cycle there are stringent limitations on the amount of neutron slowing down that is acceptable in a breeder reactor, but that with proper attention to these limitations it is possible to obtain practical designs of reactors with high power density and good breeding performance. The reactor design methods developed by Hurwitz and his associates were confirmed by the successful operation of a large power-producing liquid-metal-cooled reactor at West Milton, N.Y., in 1955. The experience obtained in the construction and operation of this plant served to clarify some of the nuclear and engineering requirements of the fast neutron power breeder reactor concept that is expected to play a major role in the long-range development of nuclear energy.

Since the West Milton reactor was the first high-power nuclear installation to be located in relatively close proximity to populated areas, it was necessary to give careful attention to the problem of public safety. Hurwitz participated in the studies that established principles for the design of the reactor containment system at West Milton. These have since been applied to nuclear plants throughout the world.

The objective of the West Milton reactor was to serve as a prototype for a naval power plant. After the completion of this project, KAPL continued to work on the development of naval nuclear power, and Hurwitz became leader of this theoretical group investigating advanced naval reactor concepts.

In 1957 Hurwitz was placed in charge of the General Electric Research Laboratory high-temperature plasma physics program. In addition to directing this research, he participated in theoretical investigations relating to fusion power and other potential plasma applications.

Hurwitz's father was an editor and educator, and his mother was a writer. He first became interested in a scientific career through contacts with H. A. Bethe while an undergraduate at Cornell. In 1941 he obtained a Ph.D. at Harvard, where he studied with W. H. Furry and J. H. Van Vleck. In 1961 Hurwitz was a recipient of the AEC's E. O. Lawrence Memorial Award for his contributions in reactor physics.

For background information *see* REACTOR PHYSICS in the McGraw-Hill Encyclopedia of Science and Technology.   ☐

☆ **HUXLEY, Andrew Fielding**
British physiologist
Born Nov. 22, 1917, Hampstead, London, England

WORKING IN collaboration with the British biophysicist Alan Lloyd Hodgkin, Huxley discovered the ionic mechanism involved in excitation in the cell membrane of peripheral nerve. In recognition of this achievement, Hodgkin and Huxley shared the 1963 Nobel Prize for medicine or physiology with Sir John Carew Eccles of the Australian National University who had extended their work to synapses.

Early in the 20th century J. Bernstein proposed the theory that the propagation of a nerve impulse is brought about by the flow of electric current between resting and active regions. During the 1920s, the American physiologists Joseph Erlanger and Herbert Spencer Gasser conducted a series of experiments on nerve potentials that clarified the bioelectric nature of nerve impulses.

In 1939, while in his last year at Trinity College, Cambridge, Huxley began working with Hodgkin on the problem of the transmission of a nerve impulse. By the introduction of a microelectrode into the giant nerve fiber of a squid, they demonstrated that Bernstein's hypothesis was true in all respects but one. As they announced in 1951, the propagation of the nerve impulse coincides with sudden changes in the permeability of the axon membrane. In contrast to the earlier theory, however, it was found that the potential of the axon membrane does not become zero but is reversed, the interior of the cell becoming positive instead of negative. Thus the membrane does not simply "break down" and become equally permeable to all ions. Instead, at excitation the membrane becomes much more permeable to sodium ions, letting them pour into the axon and causing it to become locally more positive. This activity is self-reinforcing in that the flow of some sodium ions through the membrane allows others to follow. The inward movement of sodium continues until the fiber interior has been changed to such a high positive level that the sodium is electrically repelled. The sharp reversal of the internal polarity of the membrane is the nerve impulse, or action potential, which moves like a wave down the length of the axon. The streaming of sodium lasts only a few milliseconds, stopping automatically. The membrane now becomes permeable to potassium ions, which flow through the membrane to restore the original negative charge to the interior of the axon. Thus, within a millisecond or less the cell is ready to transmit another impulse.

In conjunction with several coworkers, Huxley also contributed to the knowledge of muscle contraction. In the late 1940s the British physiologist Archibald Vivian Hill demonstrated that the ordinary diffusion of a chemical substance was too slow to explain the rapidity with which the contraction in the interior of a striated muscle fiber is set off. Using microelectrodes, an interference microscope of his own development, and striated muscle fibers, Huxley showed that action potentials would stimulate the contraction of the cells if the electrodes were applied to certain regions of the striations. If the electrodes were applied to other areas, contraction would not occur. He then hypothesized that the action potential moved into the muscle by means of some structure located in these regions and stimulated the contractile elements of the muscle fiber to shorten.

Grandson of the 19th-century biologist Thomas Henry Huxley, son of the author Leonard Huxley, and half brother of the biologist Julian Sorell Huxley and of the author Aldous Huxley, Andrew Fielding Huxley received his M.A. at Trinity College, Cambridge, where he was later a fellow (1941–60) and director of studies (1952–60). During World War II he did operational research for the Antiaircraft Command and the Admiralty. After the war he was a demonstrator (1946–50), assistant director of research (1951–59), and reader in experimental biophysics (1959–60) in the department of physiology at Cambridge. In 1960 he was named Jodrell Professor of Physiology at University College, London. He was elected to the Royal Society in 1955.

For background information *see* BIOPOTENTIALS AND ELECTROPHYSIOLOGY in the McGraw-Hill Encyclopedia of Science and Technology. □

I-K

★★★

☆ INGOLD, Sir Christopher (Kelk)

British chemist
Born Oct. 28, 1893, London, England

WHILE STUDYING the mechanisms of organic reactions Ingold, with the collaboration of Edward David Hughes, carried out the first detailed kinetic studies of elimination and substitution reactions. These studies resulted in the establishment of four reaction mechanisms, two each for elimination and substitution reactions.

In 1927 Ingold began to study the Hofmann decomposition of quaternary ammonium salts in a basic medium. His technique was to study product composition as a function of structure. By 1930 he had reached the conclusion that there were two types of decomposition. One was a base-promoted bimolecular elimination, similar to the formation of olefins from alkyl halides and bases. The other was a non–base-promoted unimolecular substitution in which an alkyl group was displaced.

From 1930 to 1933, working with Hughes at University College, London, Ingold continued his studies of quaternary ammonium decompositions. By studying product composition as a function of concentration, a third possible reaction mechanism, bimolecular substitution, was established. In order to distinguish between the unimolecular and bimolecular substitution mechanisms, it was necessary to begin kinetic studies of the reactions.

Ingold and Hughes published their results in

1933. The unimolecular substitution mechanism, designated S_N1 (nucleophilic substitution, first-order kinetics), involves a two-step process. The rate-determining step is ionization of the halide to form a carbonium ion. This then combines with an anion as rapidly as it is formed. Equa-

$$R_3C — X \rightleftharpoons R_3C^+ + X^- \quad \text{(slow)}$$

(1)

$$R_3C^+ + AB \longrightarrow R_3C — B + A^+ \quad \text{(fast)}$$

(2)

tions (1) and (2) are the general equations for the S_N1 reaction. The bimolecular substitution mechanism, designated S_N2 (nucleophilic substitution, bimolecular), involves the combination of the two reactants to form a transition state, or intermediate complex. Equation (3) is the

$$B^- + R_3C — X \longrightarrow \begin{bmatrix} R \quad\quad R \\ B\cdots C\cdots X \\ R \end{bmatrix} \longrightarrow B — R_3C + X^-$$

transition state

(3)

general equation for the S_N2 reaction. Similarly, the unimolecular elimination reaction, designated E_1 (elimination, unimolecular), is given in equations (4) and (5), and the bimolecular elimina-

$$CH_3 — \overset{R}{\underset{R'}{C}} — A \longrightarrow CH_3 — \overset{R}{\underset{R'}{C}}{}^+ — R + A \quad \text{(slow)}$$

(4)

$$\overset{H}{\underset{R}{CH_2}} — \overset{+}{C} — R' \longrightarrow H^+ + H_2C = \overset{}{\underset{R'}{C}} — R \quad \text{(fast)}$$

(5)

$$RO^- + CH_3 — CH_2X \longrightarrow \begin{bmatrix} CH_2\cdots CH_2 \\ RO\cdots H \quad X \end{bmatrix} \longrightarrow ROH + CH_2 = CH_2 + X^-$$

transition state

(6)

$$\bar{CH}_2 \!-\! CH \!=\! \overset{+}{X} \qquad \overset{\delta-}{CH}_2 \!=\! CH \!-\! X^{\delta+} \qquad CH_2 \!=\! CH \!-\! \overset{\cdot\cdot}{\underset{\cdot\cdot}{X}}\!:$$

$$(7) \qquad\qquad\qquad (8) \qquad\qquad\qquad (9)$$

tion reaction, designated E_2 (elimination, bimolecular), is given in equation (6). Subsequently, Ingold and Hughes, both in collaboration and independently, built upon this earlier work to develop the theory of reaction mechanisms still further.

In 1926 Ingold introduced the concept of mesomerism to explain the observed physical properties of certain organic compounds. This concept postulates the existence of a resonance state, called the mesomeric state, in which the structure of the molecule is intermediate between those represented by the two bond formulas that are theoretically possible. For example, a molecule of vinyl halide is not represented accurately by the ionic structure (7) or the covalent structure (9); instead, the mesomeric formula (8) is the intermediate that more accurately represents the observed properties of the molecule.

Among Ingold's other contributions to organic chemistry were studies of electrophilic aromatic and aliphatic substitution and the confirmation of the concept of prototropy. He also made a number of contributions to physical chemistry (including the first use of isotopic substitution to identify spectral frequencies) and to inorganic chemistry.

Ingold was educated at University College in Southampton and at the Imperial College of Science and Technology in London, receiving his D.Sc. from the latter in 1922. He became a research chemist at the Cassel Cyanide Company, Ltd., in 1918, leaving 2 years later to become a lecturer in chemistry at the Imperial College. In 1924 he was appointed professor of organic chemistry at the University of Leeds and in 1930 became professor of chemistry at University College, University of London. He remained at this post until 1961, when he became special lecturer in the College and emeritus professor of the University. Among the many awards Ingold received were the Royal Medal of the Royal Society in 1952 and the Faraday Medal of the Chemical Society in 1962. He was knighted in 1958.

Ingold wrote *Structure and Mechanism in Organic Chemistry* (1953) and *Introduction to Structure in Organic Chemistry* (1956).

For background information *see* RESONANCE (MOLECULAR STRUCTURE); SUBSTITUTION REACTION in the McGraw-Hill Encyclopedia of Science and Technology.   □

☆ **JACOB, François**
French biologist
Born 1920, Nancy, France

WHILE STUDYING the mechanisms that regulate the actions of the genes that repress nucleic acid's control of protein synthesis, thus affecting transmission of hereditary characteristics, Jacob discovered a new class of genetic elements, the episomes, and in collaboration with the French biologist Jacques Monod proposed the concepts of messenger ribonucleic acid (RNA) and of the operon. In recognition of his contributions to the study of genetics, Jacob shared the 1965 Nobel Prize for physiology or medicine with Monod and with the French biologist André Lwoff, who had performed pioneering work with lysogenic bacteria.

In 1952 Alfred D. Hershey and Martha Chase of the department of genetics of the Carnegie Institution of Washington clarified the roles played by the deoxyribonucleic acid (DNA) and the protein of a virus during the infective process. They showed that the DNA carried into the infected cell all the information necessary for the replication of complete virus particles. At about the same time André Lwoff of the Pasteur Institute in Paris showed the lysogenic bacteria carried a provirus, that is, a temperate virus that is in a subdued and integrated state.

In 1951, working at the Pasteur Institute in collaboration with Elie L. Wollman, Jacob began to work out the genetic basis of lysogeny, particularly the mechanism of the immunity of the bacterial host from infection by external viruses of the same type as the provirus. By using various biological tests, together with electron microscopy, Jacob and Wollman identified two main groups of viral genes. One group is concerned with the autonomous reproduction of the genetic material of the virus. The second group is involved in the manufacture of the protein molecules that provide the coat and infectious apparatus. In 1961, as a further result of these studies, the concept of the episome was announced. Jacob and Wollman had found that certain nonviral genetic elements of bacteria, such as the fertility, or *F*, factor and the factor that controls the production of colocines in colon bacilli, behave very much like the genetic material of temperate viruses. Such genetic elements were named episomes, meaning "added bodies." Evidence was later found for the existence of episomelike factors in the fruit fly and in maize. The concept of the episome has proved useful in cancer research as well as in cellular genetics. They also proposed that the combination of the provirus and the gene to which it was bound promoted the production of an inhibitor, which they called an immunity substance, that prevented the destruction of the cell by similar viruses.

In 1958 Jacob and Monod began to collaborate in a series of physiologicogenetic studies of the regulation of bacterial enzyme synthesis. Their work, carried out in part with the American biologist Arthur Pardee, resulted in their proposal of the concepts of messenger RNA and of the operon in 1961. The concept of messenger RNA, a nucleic acid that has a base sequence complementary to that of the DNA and that directs the synthesis of specific proteins in the ribosomes, led to the breaking of the genetic code by such experimenters as the American biochemist Marshall W. Nirenberg. The concept of the operon, a unit comprising two related genes and a common gene of regulation called their operator, explained the control of bacterial enzyme synthesis as well as prophage induction.

Another discovery by Jacob, also made in collaboration with Wollman, concerned the sexual conjugation of bacteria, which had been discovered by the American biochemists Edward Lawrie Tatum and Joshua Lederberg in 1946. Jacob and Wollman showed that the transfer of the chromosome of the male bacterium to the female recipient cell proceeds in an orderly fashion and that this transfer can be interrupted by the experimenter at any point to determine the position of specific genes in the chromosome.

Jacob studied medicine at the University of Paris and, after serving with the Free French forces during World War II, received his M.D.

in 1947. He received a D.Sc. from the Sorbonne in 1954. In 1950 he became a staff member in the department of microbic physiology at the Pasteur Institute. He was appointed head of the Pasteur Institute Laboratory in 1956 and head of the department of microbic genetics in 1960. Four years later he was named the first professor of cellular genetics at the Collège de France.

For background information *see* BACTERIA, LYSOGENIC; COLIPHAGE; NUCLEIC ACID in the McGraw-Hill Encyclopedia of Science and Technology. □

★ JEFFREYS, Sir Harold
British astronomer and geophysicist
Born Apr. 22, 1891, Fatfield, Co. Durham, England

WHEN JEFFREYS began his researches before World War I, geophysics could be regarded as a collection of miscellaneous investigations covering a wide range of disciplines. Jeffreys combined the results of these scattered researches, including his own, into a connected whole. For his contributions to geophysics he was awarded the Vetlesen Prize in 1963. His other honors included the Copley and Royal medals of the Royal Society of London, the Gold Medal of the Royal Astronomical Society, and the Bowie Medal of the American Geophysical Union.

Jeffreys's principal scientific achievements were the following:

1. With K. E. Bullen, he was joint author (1940) of the present standard tables of the travel times of earthquake waves.

2. He was the first to state explicitly that the Earth's central core, discovered by R. D. Oldham, is liquid. This was based on the calculation of the theoretical elastic yielding in the bodily tide, for an average value of the rigidity of the shell and various values for the core. Compari-

son with the observed yielding showed that the rigidity of the core must be very low.

3. Jeffreys showed that, on any reasonable view of the initial temperatures of the outer planets, the initial heat has had time to be radiated away and, hence, that the present surface temperatures must be controlled mainly by solar radiation and be of the order of $-120°C$ or less. He inferred from the densities that the principal materials must be of low molecular weight, such as methane and ammonia. This was immediately verified by W. W. Coblentz and D. H. Menzel, contrary to the usual view at that time that these planets were red hot, and led to the revised views of the constitutions by R. Wildt, W. H. Ramsey, and others.

4. He sought for evidence on the strength of the Earth and its imperfections of elasticity at small strains—the former in relation to the support of surface inequalities and departures from isostasy, the latter for an explanation of tidal friction. It appeared that strengths comparable to those of surface igneous rocks must persist to a depth of about a tenth of the radius. G. I. Taylor's result for tidal dissipation in the Irish Sea was extended to other shallow seas, and it seemed probable that turbulence in fast tidal currents could account for the observed secular acceleration of the Moon. It is not, however, available as an explanation of the rotations of the Moon, Mercury, and of those other satellites whose rotations are known, and tidal friction in them must be bodily. Evidence for imperfections of elasticity at strains of the order of 10^{-4} to 10^{-5} was given by C. Lomnitz, indicating a law linear with respect to strain and logarithmic with respect to time. The 14-monthly variation of latitude is the most sensitive phenomenon to such imperfection and has a relaxation time of 10 to 30 years. This, together with the clear transmission of transverse elastic waves, determined the required constants in a modification of Lomnitz's law. The creep after a long time is about as $t^{1/4}$. With S. Crampin, Jeffreys applied this to other data for the Earth, Moon, Mercury, and other satellites and got satisfactory agreement. The elasticoviscous law, which made the creep proportional to t, led to numerous serious contradictions.

5. Lord Rayleigh's theory of the generation of convection in a fluid heated below was adapted by Jeffreys to more usual boundary conditions, first for a sheet of fluid and later for a sphere (with M. E. M. Bland). It seems probable that such convection at a certain stage during solidification is the explanation of the separation of the acidic rocks to form the continents. The modified Lomnitz law, however, does not permit convection at present.

6. Jeffreys's later seismological work showed that there are significant differences between regions; these are at present being investigated more closely.

7. F. Hayn's theory of the Moon's librations has been revised and extended to give improved estimates of the differences between the Moon's moments of inertia.

8. He gave a dynamical explanation of monsoons and sea breezes, and he also discussed the general circulation of the atmosphere, showing that if winds were in the same sense in all latitudes friction would stop the circulation in about 10 days. The only way of making the equation of angular momentum balance is mass transport between different latitudes, on a scale several times greater than ordinary frictional drift across the isobars. The opposite signs of the prevailing winds in low and intermediate latitudes are thus explained; but cyclones have to carry out the transfer and thus are an essential part of the general circulation and not a disturbance superposed on it.

9. With R. O. Vicente, Jeffreys investigated the theory of nutations of the Earth's axis, with allowance for actual mechanical properties of the shell and for a fluid core. He explained why the amplitude of the 19-yearly nutation is somewhat less than the theoretical value calculated for a rigid Earth; agreement for this and other nutations is in fair, but not perfect, agreement with the observational results of E. P. Fedorov.

10. Jeffreys rediscovered the Green-Liouville approximation to solutions of differential equations of the form $y'' + h^2\chi(x)y = 0$, where h is a large parameter, and gave formulas for connecting solutions across a simple zero of χ. Particularly he recommended direct use of Airy functions in this case; this is now generally adopted.

All work in geophysics and astronomy involves extrapolation of laws, based on experiments on a laboratory scale, to distances of the order of 10^8 to 10^{20} cm and times of order 10^9 years. Two views are current among physicists and philosophers of science. One is that the laws are certain for some theoretical reason; the other, that they are guessed. Jeffreys was never able to accept either view, and in particular he pointed out that the second made nonsense of all scientific prediction. (This point was totally neglected by Ernst Mach but put clearly by Karl Pearson.) Jeffreys showed that, with a suitable adaptation of the theory of probability given by T. Bayes, it is possible for any clearly stated law to acquire a high probability given a finite number of observations. Scientific method becomes one of successive approximation to probability distributions.

Jeffreys attended Rutherford and Armstrong colleges, Newcastle (B.Sc. 1910, M.Sc. 1913, D.Sc. 1917) and St. John's College, Cambridge (B.B. 1913, M.A. 1917). He became a fellow of

St. John's in 1914. From 1917 to 1922 he was at the Meteorological Office. He was a university lecturer in mathematics at Cambridge from 1923 to 1932, reader in geophysics from 1932 to 1946, and Plumian Professor of Astronomy from 1946 to 1958. A fellow of the Royal Society of London, he was elected in 1945 a foreign associate of the U.S. National Academy of Sciences.

Jeffreys wrote *The Earth* (1924; 5th ed. 1962), *Operational Methods in Mathematical Physics* (1927; 2d ed. 1931), *Future of the Earth* (1929), *Cartesian Tensors* (1931; 2d ed. 1953), *Scientific Inference* (1931; 3d ed. 1957), *Earthquakes and Mountains* (1935; 2d ed. 1950), *Theory of Probability* (1939; 3d ed. 1962), *Methods of Mathematical Physics*, with B. Jeffreys (1946; 4th ed. 1962), and *Asymptotic Approximations* (1962).

For background information *see* GEOPHYSICS in the McGraw-Hill Encyclopedia of Science and Technology.   □

★ **JENSEN, J. Hans D.**
German physicist
Born June 25, 1907, Hamburg, Germany

WORKING WITH the chemist H. E. Suess and the physicist O. Haxel on the empirical evidence of nuclear shell structure, Jensen in 1949 suggested a nuclear shell model almost identical to that arrived at independently and simultaneously by Maria Goeppert Mayer. The main feature of the model was the strong coupling of the spin and the orbital motion of each nucleon. The hypothesis was corroborated by polarization studies in nucleon-scattering experiments in many laboratories. For their discovery concerning nuclear shell structure, Jensen and Mayer shared the 1963 Nobel Prize in physics. *See* MAYER, MARIA GOEPPERT.

Jensen's other contributions included: his studies (1947), with H. Steinwedel, of the recoil distribution of nuclear radiation in molecules and crystals, the significance of which was emphasized by the discovery of the Mossbauer effect; his interpretation (1950), with M. Danos and Steinwedel, of the "giant resonance" in the nuclear photoeffect; and his suggestion (1955), with B. Stech, prior to the discovery of parity violation, of the so-called γ_5-invariance of the weak interaction.

A gardener's son, Jensen studied physics, mathematics, and philosophy, mainly at Hamburg University, where he received the degree *Doktor der Naturwissenschaften* in 1933. He taught at Hamburg University until 1941, when he was appointed associate professor at the Hanover Institute of Technology. In 1949 he became a full professor at the University of Heidelberg, where in 1954–55 he served as dean of the science faculty. He started his scientific work with quantum mechanical studies of ionic lattices and the behavior of matter under extremely high pressures. Inspired by frequent visits to Niels Bohr's Institute in Copenhagen, he became increasingly interested in the problems of nuclear structure.

For background information *see* NUCLEAR STRUCTURE in the McGraw-Hill Encyclopedia of Science and Technology.   □

★ **JOHNSON, Martin Wiggo**
American biologist
Born Sept. 30, 1893, Chandler, S.Dak., U.S.A.

ALTHOUGH THE bulk of Johnson's work consisted of studies pertaining to the lives of marine organisms in their natural environment, he became widely known to biologists and nonbiologists alike for his solutions to certain acoustical problems important to naval science. For these and other contributions to the field of oceanography he was awarded the Agassiz Gold Medal by the National Academy of Sciences in 1959.

During World War II, the Navy was hampered

in certain operations by a widespread, continuous, high-frequency, underwater, staticlike crackling, with high intensities. The sound could be disabling to listening operations, and it threatened to detonate acoustic mines and torpedos. Several hypotheses, both physical and biological, were advanced to explain the origin of this "static" sound. But upon checking various possibilities, Johnson concluded that none of these hypotheses was correct. He reasoned that the sound must be biological and associated with nonmigrating benthic animals with no marked seasonal change in abundance or reproductive habits. The prevalence of the "static" near heavily fouled wharfs, in harbors with muddy but littered bottoms, and over beds of seaweed or rocky or shaly bottoms led to an array of possible suspects. These diverse habitats had one thing in common, namely, ready space for concealment for small invertebrates. This suggested to Johnson the possibility of certain shrimps known to make a sharp individual snap occasionally when disturbed. However, because of their agility and secretive habits, only rarely could these animals be collected in the area where the sound was heard. The overwhelming crackling seemed to call for an excessively large population, much larger than could be collected and confined in a direct acoustical experiment.

One day, while passing a rifle range where some fifty marines were actively firing, Johnson noticed that the sound simulated the crackling in the sea. It occurred to him that if fifty marines could set up such a crackle, the number of shrimp required to do the same need not be too great. With this further lead, he renewed his efforts and collected about 100 shrimp. In an aquarium these made a fair display of crackle when agitated or flooded with fresh water or weak formalin. The final substantiation, however, had to come from the field. Upon further study and understanding of the restricted living requirements of these animals with respect to concealment, depth of water, type of bottom, life history, and geographic range, Johnson successfully predicted where the crackle would or would not be heard. Accurate prediction of the occurrence and persistence of this ambient noise assisted greatly in formulation of evasion tactics for submarines.

A second puzzle involved the reflection of signals. In 1942, C. F. Eyring, R. J. Christensen, and R. W. Raitt observed that signals were reflected by a widespread, mysterious, "deep-scattering layer" at depths of several hundred meters. No physical cause could be found, but with the possibility that it, too, might be biological, the problem was referred to Johnson. He reasoned that the layer could be made up of sound-reflecting animals vast in numbers and widely distributed, and that the organisms most nearly fitting this definition were members of the zooplankton. Although many zooplankters are so small and so near sea water in density that they might be poor sound reflectors, still they could be a basic element in the layer, serving as prey for larger predators that followed the plankton. Hence, if the layer was associated directly or indirectly with the plankton it should behave biologically by performing vertical, diurnal migrations, a phenomenon not previously recognized for the layer but well known for plankton. A continuous test at sea verified the correctness of Johnson's supposition. This demonstration of the biological nature of the "deep-scattering layer" opened a field of combined acoustical and biological research.

Johnson received his B.S. (1924), M.S. (1930), and Ph.D. (1931) in zoology from the University of Washington, Seattle. He was curator at the University's Friday Harbor Laboratories (1924–29); biologist, Passamaquoddy Bay International Fisheries Commission (1932–33); associate, University of Washington (1933–34). In 1934 he joined the faculty of Scripps Institution of Oceanography.

With H. U. Sverdrup and R. H. Fleming, Johnson wrote *The Oceans* (1942).

For background information *see* SCATTERING LAYER in the McGraw-Hill Encyclopedia of Science and Technology.   □

JONES, Sir Harold (Spencer)

English astronomer
Born Mar. 29, 1890, London, England
Died Nov. 3, 1960, London, England

WHILE PRESIDENT of the Solar Parallax Commission of the International Astronomical Union, Jones directed the redetermination of the value of the astronomical unit, the mean distance between the Sun and the Earth. The value of the astronomical unit is of great importance, since it is the basis for the determination of both the distances of the planets and the distances and dimensions of stars.

The distance between the Sun and the Earth can be estimated by a number of astronomical methods. One of these is by a determination of the solar parallax, the angle subtended by the radius of the Earth at the center of the Sun. Since the radius of the Earth can be established with great precision by geodetic surveys, the value of the astronomical unit can be calculated. A second method is based on the relative dimensions of the planetary orbits, which can be determined with great precision from Johannes Kepler's third law: the square of the period of revolution of a planet about the Sun is proportional to the cube of its mean distance from the Sun. Thus, if any one distance in the solar system can be determined, all of the other dimensions become known. The first of these methods suffers both from the large angular diameter of the Sun in relation to the solar parallax and from the poorly defined quality of its perimeter. For these reasons, it became common practice to attempt to determine the value of the solar parallax by determining the distances to Venus and Mars. However, certain factors, such as the relatively large angular diameters of the two planets when each is nearest to the Earth, make precise position measurements difficult. To overcome these difficulties, the German astronomer Johann Gottfried Galle, in 1872, and the Scottish astronomer Sir David Gill, about 1885, independently suggested that a minor planet, or asteroid, be used instead of Venus or Mars. Such a body, which is seen as a starlike point, would lend itself to precise measurement to a degree impossible with planetary discs. When the minor planet Eros, which approaches closer to the Earth than do Venus and Mars, was discovered by the German astronomer Gustav Witt in 1898, astronomers were presented with the ideal body for their measurements. With data compiled during the opposition of 1900–1901, when Eros came within some 25×10^6 miles of the earth, the English astronomer A. R. Hinks obtained a value of 8.806 seconds of arc for the solar parallax, which corresponds to a value of 92.83×10^6 miles for the astronomical unit.

In 1924, while working at the Cape of Good Hope Observatory in South Africa, Jones derived a value of 8.805 seconds of arc for the solar parallax, based on measurements he had made for the parallactic inequality of the Moon. When the International Astronomical Union met at Leyden, The Netherlands, in 1928, Jones was elected to head its Solar Parallax Commission. The 1930–31 opposition of Eros was to bring it within 16×10^6 miles of the Earth. Since the asteroid was to describe an arc in the sky from north to south, observations could be made in both the northern and southern hemispheres. Thus, in addition to the parallactic displacements derived in right ascension by the usual

methods, displacements in declination could also be obtained. Jones organized a program of international cooperation in which some 40 observatories in all parts of the world made visual and photographic observations during the opposition from October 1930 to May 1931. In 1941, after 10 years of reducing data from 2,847 photographic plates and of innumerable calculations, Jones announced the results of the program. A solar parallax value of 8.7875 ± 0.0009 seconds of arc was found from right ascension observations and a value of 8.7907 ± 0.0011 seconds of arc from declination observations. The mean value was thus found to be 8.790 ± 0.001 seconds of arc, which gave a value of $93,004,000 \pm 11,000$ miles for the astronomical unit. More recent measurements, using radar and other electronic techniques, have shown Jones's value for the solar parallax to have an error of about 0.1 per cent. However, his remains the best value obtained by photographic methods.

Among Jones's other contributions to astronomy was the determination of a value of 81.271 ± 0.021 for the ratio of the mass of the Earth to that of the Moon. He also did research on the motion of the Earth's poles and the irregularity of the Earth's rotation, originated a program at the Cape of Good Hope Observatory to determine the distances and measure the proper motions of stars in the southern hemisphere, and applied observations of Nova Pictoris to the study of stellar evolution. Jones also was responsible for moving the site of the Royal Observatory from Greenwich to Herstmonceux Castle in Sussex.

The eldest son of an accountant, Jones attended Jesus College, Cambridge, receiving his B.A. in 1911. He continued his studies at Cambridge, receiving his M.A. in 1914 and his D.Sc. in 1925. In 1913 Jones was appointed chief assistant at the Royal Observatory in Greenwich, a post he retained until 1923. During World War I he was the assistant director of inspection of optical supplies for the Ministry of Munitions. In 1923 he went to South Africa as astronomer at the Cape of Good Hope, serving in this capacity for 10 years. He returned to the Greenwich Observatory in 1933 as the tenth Astronomer Royal of England, retiring from this position in 1955. Among Jones's many awards are the Gold Medal of the Royal Astronomical Society of Great Britain (1943), the Royal Medal of the Royal Society (1943), and the Bruce Medal of the Astronomical Society of the Pacific (1948). He was knighted in 1943 and created a Knight of the British Empire in 1955.

Jones wrote a number of books, among them *Worlds Without End* (1935) and *A Picture of the Universe* (1947).

For background information *see* EARTH (ORBITAL MOTION) in the McGraw-Hill Encyclopedia of Science and Technology. □

★ JOY, Alfred Harrison

American astronomer
Born Sept. 23, 1882, Greenville, Ill., U.S.A.

THE CONSTRUCTION of the 100-in. telescope at the Mt. Wilson Observatory in California provided an opportunity for Joy to undertake a wide variety of research programs involving the spectra of stars. The most extensive of these concerned stellar distances and radial motions of stars, together with certain physical properties such as intrinsic brightness, temperature, and size.

By direct photography with the 40-in. Yerkes refractor, Frank Schlesinger had obtained the first reasonably accurate values for the distances of stars. As a base line for triangulation he had used the diameter of the Earth's orbit around the Sun. At the Yerkes Observatory in 1914–15, Joy joined in this undertaking and measured the parallax (distance) of a number of stars by this somewhat tedious method.

In 1916 he began spectroscopic observations at Mt. Wilson with the 60-in. reflector and in 1919 continued them with the 100-in. reflector. He was invited to share in the program for obtaining stellar distances by first obtaining their absolute magnitudes (intrinsic brightness) from the intensity of certain sensitive lines of their spectra. The distance resulted from a comparison of the apparent magnitudes with the absolute magnitudes. This powerful spectroscopic method, which had just been developed by W. S. Adams, was applicable to all stars with known apparent magnitudes and suitable spectral lines, whether near or far. The program was carried on intensively by Joy, in collaboration with Adams and M. L. Humason, for more than 20 years and resulted in spectral types, absolute magnitudes, and distances for more than 5,000 stars of many different classes. In this way a large contribution to our knowledge of the location and physical features of the members of our Galaxy was made.

Joy and his colleagues measured thousands of stellar spectrograms for radial velocity determinations from the Doppler displacements of the spectral lines. Many of the stars showed variations of radial velocity and were listed as spectroscopic binaries. For some of them periods and orbits were deduced. When applied to eclipsing binary stars, these observations gave absolute dimensions, masses, and orbital elements.

In 1932 Joy completed an investigation of the dimensions and rotation of the Galaxy based on the radial velocities obtained from the spectra of 130 distant stars of the cepheid class. The distance and direction of the center of the Galaxy were found, and the rotation period for bodies moving in circular orbits at the distance of the Sun was computed.

In the course of an investigation of the spectra of the faintest dwarfs of spectral type M, Joy discovered the presence of hydrogen and calcium emission. In the smallest stars of lowest temperature occasional unexplained flares, lasting only a few minutes, sometimes occur. Two spectra were obtained on such occasions that showed greatly increased excitation in the emission lines and strengthened continuous spectrum at shorter wavelengths.

Joy gave much study to the spectra of variable stars. He found that each class of variables had its characteristic spectrum, so that from a single spectrogram the type of variation could usually be assigned. He observed many novae over considerable portions of their outbursts. At maxima of recurrent novae, the famous highly ionized lines of the solar corona were first observed in stars. At minimum light of Mira Ceti, Joy observed the spectrum of a small hot companion, which was later seen visually. In areas of the Milky Way containing dark absorbing clouds of gas and dust, Joy found irregular T Tauri variable stars of low luminosity with numerous emission lines. These he showed to be members of stellar groups that are at a very early stage in their evolutionary history.

The son of a merchant of New England ancestry, Joy attended Greenville College (Illinois), receiving the degree Ph.B. in 1903. At Oberlin College (Ohio) he was awarded the M.A. in physics in 1904. From 1904 to 1914 he taught in the American University of Beirut (Lebanon), becoming professor of astronomy and director of the observatory. He spent several summers and the year 1914–15 at the Yerkes Observatory as instructor in the University of Chicago. From 1915 to 1948 he was an astronomer on the staff of the Mt. Wilson Observatory of the Carnegie Institution of Washington. He was research associate of the Institution from 1949 to 1952. In 1950 Joy was awarded the Catherine Wolfe Bruce Medal of the Astronomical Society of the Pacific. He was elected to the National Academy of Sciences in 1944.

For background information *see* SPECTROS-COPY in the McGraw-Hill Encyclopedia of Science and Technology.   □

★ **KATZ, Joseph Jacob**
American chemist
Born Apr. 19, 1912, Detroit, Mich., U.S.A.

IN THE course of studying deuterium-isotope effects on living organisms, Katz found that, contrary to earlier conclusions, extensive isotopic replacement of hydrogen by deuterium was not incompatible with life. Numerous organisms could in fact be grown in which substantially all of the hydrogen was replaced by deuterium, thereby opening up a new range of deuterium isotope effects for investigation. For these studies Katz received the American Chemical Society Award for Nuclear Applications to Chemistry in 1961.

The element hydrogen as it exists in nature consists of a mixture of nuclei. The common hydrogen of mass 1 is accompanied by a very small amount of a heavier, stable isotope of mass 2. Isotopes of an element are generally considered to have identical chemical behavior, but in the case of the hydrogen isotopes differences in the chemical behavior of the isotopes are so marked that the heavier hydrogen isotope is given a special name, deuterium.

Deuterium was discovered by H. C. Urey, F. C. Brickwedde, and G. M. Murphy in 1932. It was soon realized that the 100% difference in mass between hydrogen and deuterium would create marked differences in reaction rates. Differences in reaction rate, it was also early recognized, might be particularly important in biological systems, where life can continue only by maintaining very precise balance between the myriad chemical reactions always proceeding in a living cell. Indeed, G. N. Lewis showed in 1935 that deuterium substitution in plants and ani-

mals had dramatic consequences, and the conviction crystallized that extensive substitution of hydrogen by deuterium was always incompatible with life.

In 1957, Katz began an investigation into the possible utility of the deuterium kinetic isotope for the control of cancer growth. The kinetic distortion resulting from replacement of hydrogen by deuterium, he reasoned, would be more severe for a cancer, which is characterized by a very high rate of metabolic activity, than for the host organism. And in fact experiment showed that implanted tumors grew much more slowly in deuterated animals than in controls. The results were not decisive, however, probably because the replacement of more than 25% of the hydrogen in the body fluids of a mouse, rat, or dog rapidly led to severe physiological disturbances and death. A search for the basis of the deleterious effects of deuterium then led to the discovery that microorganisms could be adapted to growth in 99.8% D_2O under suitable conditions.

Katz and his coworkers found many organisms that grew well in fully deuterated form. Many kinds of algae, which normally grow in water with CO_2 and mineral salts as sole nutrients, were induced to grow in 99.8% D_2O by proper control of the adaptation process. Since the hydrogen in the organic compounds made by algae by photosynthesis was derived from water, algae grown in D_2O synthesized organic compounds containing deuterium, and fully deuterated algae thus became the source of a great variety of fully deuterated compounds. The fully deuterated sugars, proteins, and the like in turn could then be used to satisfy the nutritional requirements of more fastidious organisms. It thus proved possible to grow fully deuterated bacteria, yeasts, molds, and protozoa, and to isolate fully deuterated sugars, amino acids, proteins, nucleic acids, and chloroplast pigments from these organisms. These compounds, in turn, could be used to study deuterium-isotope effects previously inaccessible to investigation, and so provided a more substantial basis for the understanding and possible application of deuterium-isotope effects to the control of metabolic processes in living organisms.

Fully deuterated proteins have been used to study the effect of isotopic replacement on coil-helix transitions and side-chain interactions in proteins and on enzyme-substrate interactions. Deuterated organisms, in conjunction with proton magnetic resonance, provide a powerful new tool for following the path of hydrogen in living organisms. By such procedures it has been shown that hydrogen is not transferred from water to chlorophyll during photosynthesis. The combination of deuterated organisms and proton magnetic resonance makes possible the study of the biogenesis of complicated organic compounds, and new insights have been thus achieved into the biosynthetic pathways by which chlorophyll is made in green plants.

Katz received his early education in Detroit, where he received a B.S. in chemistry from Wayne State University in 1932. After several years of industrial experience he returned to graduate school and was awarded a Ph.D. in chemistry from the University of Chicago in 1942. During World War II, he worked in the Metallurgical Laboratory of the University of Chicago and carried out investigations on the chemistry of neptunium and plutonium. In 1948 he became a senior chemist at the Argonne National Laboratory. He did extensive work on actinide-element chemistry, on the chemistry of fluorine, and on nonaqueous solvents.

American editor of the *Journal of Inorganic and Nuclear Chemistry*, Katz was coauthor, with E. Rabinowitch, of *The Chemistry of Uranium* (1951), with G. T. Seaborg of *The Chemistry of the Actinide Elements* (1958), and with A. V. Crewe of *Research, U.S.A.* (1964).

For background information *see* ACTINIDE ELEMENTS; DEUTERIUM in the McGraw-Hill Encyclopedia of Science and Technology.   □

★ KENDALL, Edward Calvin

American biochemist
Born Mar. 8, 1886, South Norwalk, Conn., U.S.A.

THE CHEMICAL investigation of the adrenal cortex during the 1930s and 1940s culminated in the large-scale production of a hormone of the gland. This compound maintained the lives of patients who were deprived of their own adrenal secretion, relieved the symptoms of rheumatoid arthritis, and provided effective treatment of many other inflammatory diseases. Completion of this project was recognized by award of the 1950 Nobel Prize in physiology or medicine to P. S. Hench, Tadeusz Reichstein, and Kendall.

The preparation of an extract that possessed the physiological activity of the adrenal cortex was announced in 1929 by F. A. Hartman and his associates and by W. W. Swingle and J. J. Pfiffner. Shortly thereafter, three separate and independent groups of research workers—Reichstein, Kendall, and O. Wintersteiner with their associates—undertook chemical investigations of the adrenal cortex. At the Mayo Clinic in Rochester, Minn., Kendall employed large amounts of adrenal extract. Between 1934 and 1949, 150 tons of bovine adrenal glands were used. Research on this scale was made possible through utilization of a valuable by-product. The adrenal glands were furnished without cost in exchange for the adrenaline contained in the adrenal medulla. In Kendall's laboratory, the adrenaline was separated in highly purified form and sent without cost to the donor of the glands. The adrenal extract, free of all traces of adrenaline, was the starting material for isolation of the crystalline cortical hormones, experiments on animals, and administration to patients. After 5 years of research, Kendall separated a series of closely related crystalline compounds. Each was designated by a letter—A, B, C, and so forth—in the order of its isolation.

In the absence of the adrenal cortex, the body's control and utilization of minerals—sodium, potassium, and chloride—as well as of sugar are seriously impaired. Kendall's compound E had little effect on sodium, potassium, and chloride, but it was found to restore the formation and utilization of sugar.

The approach of World War II aroused the interest of the National Research Council in the availability of compound E for use by the medical corps of the Army and Navy. In October 1941, concerted effort was organized to make compound E. Kendall was a member of the "adrenal committee," but by June 1944 it was obvious that the preparation of compound E on a large scale could not be attained before conclusion of the war. The adrenal committee was disbanded, but Kendall and his associates at the Mayo Clinic and L. H. Sarett at Merck and Co. continued to carry on attempts to prepare compound E from a source more abundant than the adrenal glands of cattle. They worked independently, and each group made essential contributions. Their efforts were successful. In 1948 a compound present in bile of cattle was converted into compound E.

Between 1930 and 1941, P. S. Hench, head of the rheumatology section at the Mayo Clinic, conferred with Kendall occasionally on the etiology and possible treatment of rheumatoid arthritis. At one such conference in 1941 it was decided to determine the influence of compound

E on the symptoms of rheumatoid arthritis. Neither Kendall nor Hench realized that almost 8 years would pass before compound E could be used. When compound E became available, it was administered to a group of patients with results that established the anti-inflammatory effect of this hormone.

Compound E was designated cortisone. Today cortisone and cortisol—one is converted to the other in the body—are widely used in certain diseases of the eye, skin, kidneys, lungs, heart, blood, blood vessels, gastrointestinal tract, connective tissue, and muscle. In general, the corticosteroids have been found to be effective in suppressing reactions of inflammation and hypersensitivity.

A dentist's son, Kendall received his education at Columbia University, taking his B.S. in chemistry there in 1908 and his Ph.D. in 1910. That same year he joined the research laboratory of Parke Davis and Co. at Detroit, Mich., and was assigned the problem of isolating the hormone of the thyroid gland. He continued investigation of the chemistry of the thyroid gland for 5 months at Parke Davis, then for 3 years at St. Luke's Hospital in New York City, and completed the project with the isolation of thyroxin in December 1914, at the Mayo Clinic, Rochester, Minn. Appointed head of the section of biochemistry, and professor in the Graduate School of the University of Minnesota, Kendall remained at the Mayo Foundation until his retirement in 1951. Thereafter he was visiting professor of chemistry at Princeton University. He was elected to the National Academy of Sciences in 1950.

Kendall published a monograph, *Thyroxine* (1929), and over 200 articles and reviews in scientific journals.

For background information *see* ADRENAL CORTEX STEROID; ADRENAL GLAND in the McGraw-Hill Encyclopedia of Science and Technology. □

★ KENDREW, John Cowdery
British molecular biologist
Born Mar. 24, 1917, Oxford, England

K ENDREW MADE the first successful determination of the structure of a protein, in general outline in 1957 and in atomic detail in 1959. For this achievement he shared with Max F. Perutz the 1962 Nobel Prize in chemistry.

Essential components of all living cells, proteins perform many vital functions. In particular, the enzymes—biological catalysts responsible for controlling almost all the manifold chemical reactions that take place in every cell—are proteins. They are built up of amino acids, which are assembled into long chains called polypeptide chains; the chains generally contain upwards of 100 amino acids. Thus the whole protein molecule is very complicated, containing thousands of atoms. To understand the workings of a living cell it is necessary to know its structure, that is, the relative positions in space of all these thousands of atoms. How can the structure of an object so complex, and on so small a scale, be determined? In the middle 1930s J. D. Bernal, working at Cambridge, realized that use might be made of one particular property of proteins, namely, that many of them form crystals. The structure of crystals can be determined by x-ray diffraction. If a beam of x-rays is allowed to impinge on a crystal, a pattern of spots (the diffraction pattern) is formed on a photographic plate placed behind the crystal. W. L. Bragg had demonstrated during World War I that by studying such patterns it was possible to deduce the structure of the molecule in the crystal.

By the 1930s the structures of many molecules had been determined in this way, but all of them were vastly simpler than those of proteins, generally containing at the most only a few tens of atoms. Although it seemed at the time almost impossible to imagine how crystal structures as complicated as the proteins could be worked out, the problem was so important that Bernal and his group began a study of protein crystal diffraction patterns. By the end of the war most of the members of this group had dispersed, but Bernal's former student, Max F. Perutz, was still in Cambridge, working in the Cavendish Laboratory on the structure of hemoglobin, the red-colored protein in the red blood corpuscles that

carry oxygen from the lungs to the tissues. In 1946 he was joined by Kendrew, who began work on a related protein, myoglobin, which is responsible for the red color of meat and acts as an oxygen store in cells. Kendrew chose this protein because of its close relationship to hemoglobin and because, as proteins go, it is a relatively small molecule, containing only about 2,500 atoms (hemoglobin is four times as big and contains about 10,000 atoms).

Although by 1946 the technique of x-ray crystallography had become more powerful than it was in the 1930s, and although a great many data about hemoglobin and myoglobin crystals were accumulated during the following years, the problem of finding a way to determine the structures of those crystals remained unsolved. A crucial discovery was made by Perutz in 1953, when he showed that as a result of attaching to each hemoglobin molecule in the crystal a single very heavy atom, like mercury or gold, the x-ray pattern of the crystal was slightly altered—some of the spots became a little stronger, others a little weaker. By comparing the two patterns, it was possible not only to deduce where in the molecule the heavy atom must be to produce the observed changes, but also in principle to solve the whole structure. The heavy atom was the key that could unlock the puzzle. This method, called isomorphous replacement, had been used previously to solve simpler structures, but Perutz's use of it in hemoglobin was its first successful application in the field of very complex molecules.

Kendrew and his associates showed that similar techniques could be used in myoglobin, but much remained to be done before the method could actually reveal the structure of the molecule. Many thousands of x-ray spots had to be measured, not only for the protein crystal but for several kinds of crystals of protein plus heavy atom; to solve the structure completely, several different heavy atom compounds must be used. In the event the first successful solution of a protein structure was that of myoglobin by Kendrew and his associates in 1957. The original solution was not at atomic resolution; it was a somewhat blurred picture simply showing the polypeptide chain as a dense rod winding its irregular way around the molecule. By 1959, as a result of measuring many thousands of additional reflections, it was possible to look at the structure at high resolution so that most of the individual atoms were visible. In succeeding years, the structure was refined until the location of almost every atom in the molecule became known. Kendrew's solution demonstrated that the polypeptide chain is for the most part coiled in the spiral arrangement, known as the α-helix, first described by L. C. Pauling, R. B. Corey, and H. R. Branson in 1951; it also revealed the general nature of the forces responsible for holding the component parts of a protein molecule together, and it defined the environment of the iron atom to which oxygen becomes attached in myoglobin.

Since the appearance of the first low-resolution myoglobin model in 1957, the only other protein structures to be determined have been those of hemoglobin, at low resolution, in 1959 and of lysozyme, at high resolution, in 1965. It now appears probable, however, that the field is opening up rapidly and that the structures of a number of other important proteins will be reported from various laboratories during the next few years.

Kendrew graduated at Trinity College, Cambridge, in 1939. During World War II he was engaged in operational research with the Royal Air Force in the United Kingdom, the Middle East, and Southeast Asia. After the war he returned to Cambridge and began his collaboration with Max Perutz. They were the founding members of the Medical Research Council's Unit (later Laboratory) of Molecular Biology, located first in the Cavendish Laboratory under Sir Lawrence Bragg and Sir Neville Mott, and later in its own building. Kendrew became a fellow of the Royal Society in 1960.

For background information *see* PROTEIN in the McGraw-Hill Encyclopedia of Science and Technology.   □

☆ KINZEL, Augustus Braun

American metallurgist
Born July 26, 1900, New York, N.Y., U.S.A.

BY HIS achievements as a metallurgist and his leadership as a research director, Kinzel gave new dimensions to materials research. For these accomplishments, he received many honors, including the 1960 Industrial Research Institute Medal.

When Kinzel joined the Union Carbide Corporation in 1926, industrial metallurgical research was conceived primarily as a means to improve existing materials. Kinzel's training as a mathematician, however, led him to probe more deeply into the very nature of matter and to uncover exciting new properties as greater and greater purity of material was achieved. His personal accomplishments include the development of the first low-alloy engineering steels, major contributions to the theory of stainless steel, a vanadium refining process that made vanadium metal possible, and an exact analysis of pressure design that made possible the elliptical heads of today's pressure vessels. He pioneered the application of metallurgy to welding and oxygen cutting, changing this ancient art to a modern science, and received the basic patent for total surface ingot scarfing. Under his direction, the laboratories of Union Carbide achieved commercial production of titanium, columbium, chromium, calcium, and manganese of previously unattained purity and alloys of tailor-made precision. At the same time the research specialization at Union Carbide resulting from the deepening of materials research was balanced by a corresponding broadening of technological involvement.

The son of a concert pianist and a teacher of mathematics at Hunter College, Kinzel received his B.A. at Columbia in 1919, his B.S. from the Massachusetts Institute of Technology in 1921, and the degrees of D. Met. Ing. (*au titre étranger*) and Sc.D. from the University of Nancy, France, in 1922. He worked for General Electric as a laboratory assistant from 1919 to 1920 and as a metallurgist from 1922 to 1923, and he headed the metallurgical laboratory of Henry Disston and Sons, Inc., from 1923 to 1926. He joined Union Carbide Corporation in 1926, becoming vice-president (research) in 1955. Elected to the National Academy of Sciences in 1960, he was a founder and first president of the National Academy of Engineering.

Kinzel coauthored *Alloys of Iron and Chromium*, vols. I and II (1937; 1940).

For background information *see* METALLURGY in the McGraw-Hill Encyclopedia of Science and Technology.   □

★ KITTEL, Charles
American physicist
Born July 18, 1916, New York, N.Y., U.S.A.

KITTEL CONTRIBUTED to the application of microwave resonance methods to solid-state physics, particularly in ferromagnetic resonance, antiferromagnetic resonance, cyclotron resonance in semiconductors, and studies by resonance methods of color centers in solids, of paramagnetic organic molecules, and of dilute solid solutions of transition metals in nonmagnetic metals. For this work he received the American Physical Society's Buckley Prize in 1957.

The ready availability after World War II of microwave facilities, of liquid helium, of pure crystals, and of methods of analysis derived from atomic beam and nuclear magnetic resonance work made possible the detailed analysis of the electronic properties of solids. Resonance methods became the leading tool for determining "where the electrons were" in solids. Kittel was active in encouraging forefront experiments and in interpreting the results.

He had a wide interest in educational progress, first in solid-state physics in Berkeley, where he helped build up one of the leading university groups in the field of solids, and second in undergraduate physics education. As chairman of an interuniversity group known as the Berkeley Physics Course Committee, he guided one of the major curriculum improvement programs in college physics in the United States. He was also the author of several textbooks on solid-state physics.

The son of a small manufacturer, Kittel majored in physics at the Massachusetts Institute of Technology and at Cambridge, England, receiving his B.A. from Cambridge in 1938. He received his Ph.D. from Wisconsin in 1941. During World War II he worked in operations research in the Navy Department. After a Guggenheim fellowship at MIT in 1946, he went to the Bell Telephone Laboratories for three years. He joined the faculty of the University of California at Berkeley as professor of physics in 1950. He was elected to the National Academy of Sciences in 1957.

Kittel wrote *Introduction to Solid-state Physics* (1953; 3d ed. 1966), *Elementary Statis-*

tical Physics (1958), *Quantum Theory of Solids* (1964), and *Mechanics*, with M. A. Ruderman and W. D. Knight (1965).

For background information *see* MICROWAVE; SOLID-STATE PHYSICS in the McGraw-Hill Encyclopedia of Science and Technology.   □

★ KÖHLER, Wolfgang
American psychologist
Born Jan. 21, 1887, Reval, Estonia

THE DIRECTION of Köhler's work was determined by his interest in natural science and in the characteristics of the experienced, the phenomenal, world.

In 1913 Köhler began to study the behavior of chimpanzees at an anthropoid station in Spanish Africa. Apart from qualitative observations of the apes' behavior in general, he first concentrated on the way in which awareness of essential relations in a situation sometimes allowed the chimpanzees to solve practical problems contained in the situation. Later, he turned to an investigation of the apes' visual perception and demonstrated that they had both brightness- and size-constancy. Through further experiments he proved that when chimpanzees learned to choose one of two visual objects their reactions were often strongly influenced by relationally determined characteristics of the objects. The preference of an ape that had learned to choose, say, the darker of two objects might refer either to the darkness of this object as such or to this object as representing "the dark side" of the given pair. Simple tests in which the dark object of the original experiment was shown together with a still darker partner soon demonstrated that the chimpanzee now chose mainly the latter object, "the dark side" of the new situation. Such relationally determined reactions also occur among animals whose intelligence is far inferior to that of the chimpanzee—for instance, hens.

Findings of this kind reminded Köhler of early statements in Gestalt psychology by Max Wertheimer. But he also saw that the same facts had much in common with the behavior of many inanimate systems as studied in field physics. For instance, in any distribution of electric currents, the flow that occurs in a part of the conducting medium depends not only on the conditions in this part but also on the conditions present in all other parts. This is a consequence of the fact that what happens in a part of the conducting system is largely determined by interactions with the flow in all other parts. Hence, relational determination occurs in physics just as it does in the perception of humans, apes, and hens. At the present time, Gestalt psychologists express this agreement by saying that important characteristics of both physical and perceptual events are consequences of organization.

Further studies soon convinced Köhler that the agreement was not particularly surprising. He reasoned that the principle of evolution, taken in a strict sense, implies that the basic forces, processes, and laws of the inanimate world were not changed while evolution took place. What changed were merely the particular characteristics of the substratum, the tissue, in which these invariant physical factors operated. It seemed natural to him, therefore, to expect that the organization of processes in brains would have much in common with that of physical processes in the inanimate world. And further, if the organizational characteristics of such brain events determine the organizational characteristics of accompanying perceptual facts, agreement between organization in perception and organization in field physics must obviously be expected.

This reasoning, however, was too abstract and formal to satisfy any person accustomed to the ways of empirical science. The number of elementary forces and processes known to the physicist is large, and so far Köhler's reasoning had not indicated what particular physical forces and processes were supposed to determine perceptual organization. He therefore next inspected a list of all forces and processes known to be possible in the neural tissue of animals and men. Quite apart from their organizational tendencies, such forces and processes differ in various respects. For example, the processes responsible for perceptual organization must develop fast, must spread very fast, and must spread across considerable distances in the brain. Among the possibilities available, electric currents alone seemed to fit these conditions. Köhler therefore suggested (1938) that the active brain is pervaded by direct (or quasi-steady) electric currents and that these currents spread in the tissue as a volume conductor. Similar views have, for other reasons, been expressed by several authors.

Do such currents actually flow in the active brain? A few years later Köhler and his collaborators began to register the electric potentials that appear on the heads of human subjects and on the surface of the brains of animals when visual situations are established. They found that many clear records of quasi-steady currents could be taken in such experiments when electrodes were put in the right places. They obtained similar results when they registered the effects of auditory rather than visual stimulation. About the same effects were obtained by other scientists. It now seems clear that nerve impulses that travel in individual fibers of the nervous system are by no means the only functions to be considered in brain theory.

A further development in the same direction occurred when Köhler's physiological findings were used to explain certain newly discovered facts in perception. Currents that pass through neural tissue affect this tissue by the accumulation of ions at cell surfaces and by a reaction of the cells themselves to the flow of such currents through their surface layers. Striking effects of this kind occur where the currents enter the cells. At these places, the flow establishes an obstruction that the physiologist calls "electrotonus." The obstruction weakens the local current and forces it to flow more strongly through less affected regions in the neighborhood. According to the new explanation of perceptual organization, such deflections of brain currents must lead to corresponding changes in the perception of visual objects. When the present theory was not yet known, J. J. Gibson had already demonstrated that under conditions of continued inspection, the shapes of some visual objects are changed. Köhler and H. Wallach later showed that practically all visual objects are affected under such circumstances and that other visual objects afterwards shown in or near the affected region are also displaced or distorted. It seems probable that such "figural aftereffects" are consequences of the changes that electrotonus causes in the currents of the visual tissue. Figural aftereffects in this sense have been discovered not only in vision but also in other modalities.

From 1896 to 1905 Köhler attended the humanistic gymnasium in Wolfenbüttel, Germany. He then studied natural science, mathematics, and psychology at the universities of Tübingen, Bonn, and Berlin. In 1909 he took his Ph.D. at Berlin, then served as assistant at a psychological institute in Frankfurt a.M. from 1910 until 1913, when he went to Africa for his investigation of apes. Soon after his return in 1920, Köhler became head of the psychology department at the University of Berlin. He remained in Berlin until 1935, when the ruthless behavior of Nazi organizations began to disturb his work. Leaving Berlin, he became professor of psychology at Swarthmore College. After 1958 he continued his research at Dartmouth College. In 1947 he was awarded the Warren Medal of the Society of Experimental Psychologists and in 1956 the Distinguished Scientific Achievement Award of the American Psychological Association. He was elected to the National Academy of Sciences in 1947.

Köhler wrote *The Mentality of Apes* (1925), *Gestalt Psychology* (1929), *The Place of Value in a World of Facts* (1938), and *Dynamics of Psychology* (1940).

For background information *see* PERCEPTION; PSYCHOLOGY, PHYSIOLOGICAL AND EXPERIMENTAL in the McGraw-Hill Encyclopedia of Science and Technology.   □

★ KOHN, Walter
American physicist
Born Mar. 9, 1923, Vienna, Austria

KOHN'S PRINCIPAL contributions were in the area of the electronic structure of solids. Because of the very large number of electrons in a solid, all of which are in interaction with each other, physicists today are still far from a full understanding of the electronic structure of solids. For his "extension and elucidation of the foundations of the electron theory of solids," Kohn received the 1961 Oliver C. Buckley Prize of the American Physical Society.

In his work, Kohn attempted to discover and exhibit general features that characterize the motion of electrons in solids. The following example is illustrative: In 1954 observations were reported of electrons trapped in large orbits around point charges in semiconductors. It was found that such electrons gave rise to optical spectra analogous to those of a free hydrogen atom. Stimulated by these experiments, Kohn developed a so-called "effective mass theory" from a many-body viewpoint, in which he showed that, under certain circumstances, in spite of the intimate and strong interaction of the trapped electrons with the electrons in the host material, their behavior was exactly equivalent to that of free electrons except for the replacement of the mass by an effective mass and a reduction of the electrical attraction between charges.

In recent years, Kohn contributed to the theory of the electronic structure of metals. In 1959 he predicted that certain geometrical features of the electronic structure (the so-called "Fermi surface") should lead to characteristic kinks in the dispersion curves of the lattice vibration, and these kinks were subsequently discovered in experiments by B. N. Brockhouse and others. They are believed to be a general property of all metals but in many cases are so small as to have escaped detection so far.

Kohn received a primarily classical high school education in Vienna. In 1939, after the German occupation of Austria, he emigrated to England. In 1940, because of his Austrian nationality, he was interned by the British and sent to Canada. He resumed his studies in 1942 at the University of Toronto. Between 1944 and 1945 he served in the Canadian infantry. He received his B.A. and M.A. in mathematics and physics from the University of Toronto in 1945 and 1946, and his Ph.D. in physics from Harvard in 1948. His dissertation, entitled "Collisions of Light Nuclei," was written under the direction of Julian Schwinger. After spending 2 years as an instructor at Harvard, he joined the Carnegie Institute of Technology as assistant professor in 1950 and the University of California, San Diego, as professor of physics in 1960.

For background information *see* SOLID-STATE PHYSICS in the McGraw-Hill Encyclopedia of Science and Technology.   □

could be applied to interpret, rationalize, improve, and originate methods of analytical chemistry. Inspired by the Danish biochemist S. P. L. Sörensen and the Danish physical chemist Niels Bjerrum, Kolthoff concentrated on the significance of pH in analytical chemistry. His first book (1920) dealt with the colorimetric determination of pH with acid-base indicators and the importance of pH in industry, bacteriology, and analytical chemistry. His *Konduktometrische Titrationen* (1923), *Potentiometric Titrations* (1927), and *Die Maszanalyse* (2 vols., 1927) were instrumental in introducing and developing electroanalytical methods.

After moving to the United States in 1927, Kolthoff worked on properties of precipitates, their formation, crystal forms, and purity. He became known particularly for his work on the "aging" of freshly formed precipitates. By adding a radioactive isotope to the solution after precipitation and then determining the rate of incorporation of the radioactive isotope into the precipitate, he showed that all crystalline precipitates obtained from fairly concentrated solutions are subject to many recrystallizations.

With a student, J. J. Lingane, Kolthoff began in 1935 a study of polarography, a subject initiated by Nobel laureate J. Heyrovsky of Charles University, Prague. This electroanalytical technique, dealing with electrolysis at a dropping mercury electrode, was then hardly known in the United States. Kolthoff and his coworkers did much fundamental work on this subject. The first edition of his *Polarography* was published in 1940.

★ KOLTHOFF, Izaak Maurits

American chemist
Born Feb. 11, 1894, Almelo, Netherlands

For his leadership in the development of analytical chemistry, Kolthoff received numerous honors, among them the American Chemical Society's Nichols Award (1949), Fisher Award (1950), and Willard Gibbs Medal (1964).

Kolthoff received his education at a time when analytical chemistry was empirical in nature. It was practiced as an art but not as a science. In those days, analytical chemists were completely ignorant of the spectacular development of physical chemistry in the last quarter of the 19th century and its fundamental significance to analytical chemistry. Important analytical contributions were made early in this century by outstanding physical- and biochemists. Early in his career Kolthoff began to demonstrate how the new principles of solution physical chemistry

In 1942 Kolthoff was invited by the War Production Board to participate in war research on synthetic rubber. He and his group were first assigned the development of analytical methods to be used in the production of rubber. Relatively soon the program was extended to problems dealing with the kinetics and mechanism of emulsion polymerization. Toward the end of the war the Minnesota group developed a "low-temperature recipe" that yielded superior rubber. Industry was quick to make use of this, and after the war most synthetic rubber was made according to this recipe.

When federally sponsored rubber research was discontinued in 1955, Kolthoff and his group received government grants to continue their research on "induced reactions." In emulsion polymerization, unstable free radicals are formed that initiate polymerization of monomers. Free radicals are usually formed as unstable intermediates in induced reactions. The properties of free radicals are important for all chemists, including industrial chemists.

After 1955 Kolthoff and his group concentrated on acid-base equilibria and titrations in nonaqueous media. Thousands of papers have been written on this subject, but the analytical papers are mainly of an empirical nature. Kolthoff and his coworkers quantitatively interpreted the mechanism of these involved reactions.

Kolthoff received his Ph.D. at the University of Utrecht in 1918. He taught there for 10 years before going to the United States in 1927 to become professor and head of the division of analytical chemistry at the University of Minnesota. He became professor emeritus in 1962. He was elected to the National Academy of Sciences in 1958.

Kolthoff was the author or coauthor of close to 900 publications. Besides the books already mentioned, he wrote, with E. B. Sandell, the widely used *Textbook of Quantitative Inorganic Analysis* (1936; 3d ed. 1952).

For background information *see* ANALYTICAL CHEMISTRY in the McGraw-Hill Encyclopedia of Science and Technology. ☐

McCarty found that highly purified DNA extracted from certain bacteria was capable of transferring some of the properties of one strain to a related strain and that the "transformed" bacteria passed these properties into their progeny. In 1953, A. D. Hershey and H. B. Chase demonstrated that when a bacterial virus infected a bacterium, it was the viral DNA (not its protein) that entered the bacterial cell, and much of the DNA was found in the progeny virus produced in the cell. These two phenomena provided direct evidence that the DNA of the cell was, in fact, the genetic substance. Also in 1953, J. D. Watson and F. H. C. Crick proposed a structure for DNA based on x-ray diffraction patterns obtained by M. F. H. Wilkins and his collaborators. Their model for DNA consisted of two complementary, helical chains wound around a common axis and held together by hydrogen bonds between specific pairs of bases (adenine-thymine; guanine-cytosine). An important feature of this model was that it suggested how DNA might produce an exact copy of itself. The process of replication was visualized as one in which the two complementary chains of a DNA molecule unwound and separated as replication began. Each then built a new complement onto itself, so that when the process was completed, there were two pairs of chains where there had formerly been only one. This was, of course, only a speculative model but was nevertheless a plausible one in the light of the double-helical structure of DNA.

In considering how a polynucleotide of the enormous dimensions of DNA might actually be assembled from its precursors, Kornberg was, to a great extent, guided by his success in elucidating biosynthetic events at the enzymatic level and in particular the mechanism by which the coenzymes diphosphopyridine nucleotide (DPN)

☆ KORNBERG, Arthur

American biochemist
Born Mar. 3, 1918, Brooklyn, N.Y., U.S.A.

K ORNBERG DISCOVERED an enzyme, deoxyribonucleic acid (DNA) polymerase, which in the presence of a DNA template and the appropriate precursors, that is, the deoxyribonucleoside triphosphates of the four bases normally found in DNA (adenine, guanine, cytosine, and uracil), is able to copy the template and produce a new and faithful replica of the original DNA molecule. This enzyme therefore provided for the first time a rational enzymatic mechanism for the replication of the genetic material of the cell. For this discovery, he was awarded the 1959 Nobel Prize in medicine or physiology.

In 1944, O. T. Avery, C. M. MacLeod, and M.

and flavin adenine dinucleotide (FAD) were synthesized from simpler precursors. In each of these cases (and others as well) there was a condensation reaction in which an "activated" nucleoside 5′ monophosphate in the form of a nucleoside 5′ triphosphate participated with the elimination of inorganic pyrophosphate. He reasoned that DNA might be formed by a similar condensation of "activated" nucleotide precursors. In his initial experiments on DNA synthesis in 1955, Kornberg and his collaborators at the Washington University School of Medicine in St. Louis prepared a highly radioactive nucleotide and incubated it with an extract of *Escherichia coli,* a bacterium that reproduces every 20 minutes and might be expected to be a good source of a DNA synthesizing enzyme. ATP was also provided in the expectation that it would serve to "activate" the nucleotide substrate. In these first experiments, only a tiny fraction of the tagged nucleotide was actually converted to DNA; nevertheless, the values were experimentally significant. Relying on a firmly based conviction that enzyme purification was the most powerful tool available for the elucidation of what must be an incredibly complex reaction, Kornberg then turned to the task of extracting from *Escherichia coli* the enzyme or enzyme system that catalyzed the conversion of nucleotide precursors to DNA. This was a formidable task, considering the fact that only a small proportion of the cell's total enzymatic machinery would be devoted to the synthesis of this quantitatively minor, but nevertheless crucial, component of the cell's make-up.

As purification of the enzyme (given the name DNA polymerase) proceeded, many of its remarkable features revealed themselves. For example, it was found that all four of the deoxyribonucleotides present in DNA must be provided as their triphosphates in order for synthesis to proceed; moreover, DNA had to be present to serve as template. Many studies performed subsequently with a highly purified enzyme established conclusively that the requirement for DNA had its basis in a requirement for the specific hydrogen bonding between appropriate base pairs in the DNA template and the deoxyribonucleoside triphosphate precursors. Moreover, the enzymatically synthesized DNA was found to be in most respects an accurate replica of the DNA provided as template. These experiments thus provided a gratifyingly rational enzymatic mechanism by which a molecule of DNA possessing a double-helical structure was able to replicate.

The DNA polymerase that was discovered in the bacterium *Escherichia coli* has since been found in extracts of other bacteria as well as thymus gland and tumor cells. Certain cells infected with viruses synthesize a virus-specific DNA polymerase involved in the syntheses of viral DNA. An analogous enzyme, ribonucleic acid (RNA) polymerase, has been discovered by other investigators. This enzyme catalyzes the synthesis of RNA in an analogous fashion, also under the direction of a DNA template but using the ribonucleoside triphosphates as precursors. It appears to be responsible for synthesis of the so-called messenger RNA that carries the genetic message encoded in the DNA to the protein synthetic machinery of the cell.

Kornberg majored in biology and chemistry at the City College of New York, where he received his B.S. in 1937. He then went to the University of Rochester School of Medicine and was awarded his M.D. in 1941. After an internship at Strong Memorial Hospital, he served as a lieutenant (j.g.) in the U.S. Coast Guard. From 1942 to 1953, he worked at the National Institutes of Health in Bethesda, Md. During this time, he discovered the reactions leading to the synthesis of the coenzymes DPN and FAD and elucidated some of the enzymatic steps leading to the synthesis of phospholipids. He also contributed to an understanding of several of the reactions of the tricarboxylic cycle. From 1953 to 1959, Kornberg was professor and chairman of the department of microbiology at Washington University School of Medicine, where he discovered the enzymatic reactions leading to the synthesis of pyrimidine nucleotides and found a key intermediate in the synthesis of the purine nucleotides. He also discovered the enzyme responsible for the synthesis of large molecular weight polyphosphates in bacteria. At Washington University he initiated his enzymatic studies of DNA synthesis. In all of this work, his wife Sylvy was an active and enthusiastic collaborator. In 1959, he became professor and chairman of the department of biochemistry at Stanford University School of Medicine. He was elected to the National Academy of Sciences in 1957.

Kornberg wrote *Enzymatic Synthesis of DNA* (1961).

For background information *see* DEOXYRIBONUCLEIC ACID; NUCLEIC ACID; RIBONUCLEIC ACID in the McGraw-Hill Encyclopedia of Science and Technology.   □

★ **KOUTS, Herbert John Cecil**
American physicist
Born Dec. 18, 1919, Bisbee, Ariz., U.S.A.

FROM THE time of the discovery of nuclear fission by neutrons, there has been interest in using the energy so liberated to generate electric power. The development of this potential was assigned to the U.S. Atomic Energy Commission as a goal when the Commission was formed. A fundamental obstacle was the lack of understanding of the neutron physics of the

nuclear reactors that would have to be used. The reactors that had been built before about 1950, for purposes of research and the production of material for nuclear weapons, had been designed on a basis of relatively sketchy experimental information on their neutron physics. Their design had been guided by a brilliant intuitional structure of theory developed by Enrico Fermi, Eugene Wigner, J. A. Wheeler, and others. Although these methods had been more than satisfactory for the reactors they were applied to, they were not sufficient for reactors meant for economical electric-power generation.

In 1951, Kouts formed at Brookhaven National Laboratory a small group of physicists to explore experimentally the neutron physics of nuclear reactors with cores of slightly enriched uranium and ordinary water. Over the next few years, this group generated a library of precise experimental data that has been widely used in placing the neutron physics of these and other nuclear reactors on a firm basis. For this research, Kouts received in 1963 the Atomic Energy Commission's E. O. Lawrence Award.

The neutrons emitted after fission have an average kinetic energy of about 2 Mev. Elastic- and inelastic-scattering collisions with the nuclei cause the kinetic energy to be reduced as thermal equilibrium between the neutron gas and the other matter present is approached. The average kinetic energy of neutrons when they produce fissions is therefore lower than the average value that they had when emitted. One useful way of differentiating classes of nuclear reactors is according to the average kinetic energy of the neutrons causing fission. If this average is near the initial maximum value, the reactor is "fast." If most of the neutrons have nearly reached thermal equilibrium with the remainder of the reactor core, the reactor is "thermal." In the broad region between, the reactor is "intermediate."

The nuclear reactors that have been easiest to adapt to power generation have been of the "thermal" variety. In the region of thermal equilibrium, neutron cross sections favor fission of U^{235}, U^{233}, and Pu^{239} compared to neutron capture in these or other nuclei present. It is therefore possible to construct thermal reactors that operate with uranium of natural isotopic composition (in some cases) or with only a little enhancement of the U^{235} content. In such a thermal reactor, a large part of the reactor core consists of moderator, which is a material with a high content of light nuclei that are effective in slowing down the neutrons but not in capturing them.

The moderator now used in most American nuclear-power reactors is light water, and the fissionable material is uranium slightly enriched in U^{235}, as a sintered oxide. The water is either converted to steam in the reactor, or it is passed through a heat exchanger that serves as a steam generator. In either case, the steam drives turbines connected to generators to convert the heat from fission into electricity in a completely conventional way. This choice has permitted a transfer to nuclear power of a great body of technology that has been developed for conventional fossil-fueled electric-power stations. The experiments performed by Kouts and his coworkers anticipated this trend of nuclear-power development and helped to make it possible.

The neutron physics of these nuclear reactors has always been well understood in a way, since the theoretical description of reactor behavior is fully contained in a simplified Boltzmann equation describing the neutron gas. The equation is not really solvable, because the neutron cross sections it contains are not known well, and the structure of the equation is formidable. The approach taken by Kouts and his coworkers was to determine experimentally as many as possible of a set of basic data (such as relative rates of neutron-induced nuclear reactions and the critical reactor size) and use them to refine and test approximate theoretical descriptions that could be solved analytically or with computing machines. These data were measured over a wide range of variables such as size of the uranium element, fraction of moderator, and enrichment in U^{235}. When the experiments were begun, the neutron physics of water-moderated reactors was only poorly understood, and the prior experimental information was contradictory. When the experiments ended, the neutron physics of water-moderated reactors was very well understood.

Kouts received his B.S. in mathematics at Louisiana State University in 1941 and his M.S. in physics at the same university in 1946. He received his Ph.D. in theoretical physics from Princeton University in 1952. During World War II, he was a radar officer in the U.S. Air Force, establishing and directing a school in radar maintenance in England and later supervising air-crew training in radar on the Air Force Special Staff. In 1950 he joined the Brookhaven National Laboratory.

For background information *see* NUCLEAR POWER in the McGraw-Hill Encyclopedia of Science and Technology.   □

☆ **KOUWENHOVEN, William Bennett**
American electrical engineer
Born Jan. 13, 1886, Brooklyn, N.Y., U.S.A.

A N ELECTRICAL engineer who had an outstanding career in the engineering field, Kouwenhoven received the 1962 Edison Medal of the American Institute of Electrical Engineers "for his contributions in the fields of electrical insulation, electrical measurements, and electrical science applied to medicine, and especially for his investigations of the effects of electricity on the human body with the successful development of countershock for the cure of fibrillation of the heart."

His research on the effects of electricity on the human body resulted in the development of three defibrillators for the cure of ventricular fibrillation. The next problem was a search for a means of maintaining a patient's circulation until a defibrillator could be applied, and this was solved by the development of closed chest cardiac massage.

In 1928, Kouwenhoven, who was teaching electrical engineering at the Johns Hopkins University, became engaged in research at the Johns Hopkins Hospital. His experiments with countershock for the cure of ventricular fibrillation resulted in his development of three defibrillators—the open-chest defibrillator, the Hopkins AC Defibrillator, and the Mine Safety Portable Defibrillator. Experiments showed that the cure of ventricular fibrillation was possible only if the countershock could be applied within two minutes of the onset. Since defibrillators are rarely so easily accessible, it was necessary to find some method of circulating oxygenated blood until the defibrillator could be brought to the scene or the patient carried to the defibrillator.

In 1956 Kouwenhoven began his attempts to provide circulation by pressing on the body; anesthetized dogs served as his experimental animals. By 1959 he had developed a method of cardiopulmonary resuscitation that made it possible to circulate sufficient oxygenated blood to maintain a human being's life for an hour or more.

Kouwenhoven's method is to be applied in cases of sudden stoppage of heart or respiration. When the heart stops first, gasping respirations often continue for 20 to 40 seconds. If the respiration stops first, heart stoppage takes place a couple of minutes later. In both cases the supply of oxygenated blood to the brain and body ceases and the pupils dilate. The victim is clinically dead, and in four to six minutes biological death will ensue. Therefore prompt action is essential. When an individual suddenly becomes unconscious and respiration ceases, the first thing a rescuer should do is to place the victim on a firm surface, such as the floor, kneeling beside him. (The patient should not be straddled.) Then: (1) *Diagnosis.* Is the patient breathing? Is there a pulse? (2) *Ventilation.* All foreign matter should be removed from the patient's mouth, and his neck should be extended so as to produce a patent airway. Then the rescuer should apply three or four quick deep breaths mouth-to-mouth, mouth-to-nose, or mouth-to-airway, making sure that the victim's chest rises with each breath. Following this, the pulse should be checked again; if there is no pulse palpable, the rescuer should locate the sternum. (3) *Maintain circulation.* The rescuer should place the heel of one hand on the lower half of the sternum, with fingers extended so that they do not touch the body. The other hand should be placed on top of the first. With arms stiff, pressure should be applied vertically downward at the rate of once per second. After 15 compressions, the rescuer should stop, inflate the patient's lungs with two quick deep breaths, then resume 15 more compressions, and so on. When help has arrived, someone should telephone for a physician and an ambulance. The second rescuer should take over either heart compression or lung ventilation. The person ventilating the lungs should inflate the patient's lungs after every fifth compression, as the hands are being raised. Even if there is a spontaneous recovery, the patient's condition should be checked by a physician. If there has been no recovery, air ventilation and heart compression must be continued until the patient is in medical hands.

Once cardiopulmonary resuscitation had been developed, Kouwenhoven started training seminars in the method. The first classes were given for Hopkins medical staffs, medical students, and nurses. Another group that was instructed in the method was the Baltimore City Fire Department Ambulance Corps; according to a report, this group applied resuscitation techniques to 153 cases of sudden and unexpected death between November, 1961, and March, 1964; 52 of these cases were alive when they reached the hospitals. On behalf of the American Heart Association, during the first six months of 1961 a Hopkins team presented two or more seminars on cardiopulmonary resuscitation at each of 14 Heart Association Centers throughout the United States.

Kouwenhoven received his E.E. and M.E. degrees from the Polytechnic Institute of Brooklyn in 1906 and 1907, and his Diplom. Ing. and Dokter Ing. from the Karlsruhe Technische Hochschule, Baden, Germany, in 1912 and 1913. He joined the Johns Hopkins University in 1914, becoming professor of electrical engineering and dean of the School of Engineering in 1938. He retired in 1954. In 1956 he became a lecturer in surgery in the university's Medical School.

For background information *see* CARDIOVASCULAR SYSTEM; CIRCULATION; HEART in the McGraw-Hill Encyclopedia of Science and Technology.   □

★ KRAMER, Paul Jackson

American plant physiologist
Born May 8, 1904, Brookville, Ind., U.S.A.

BEST KNOWN for his research on plant-water relations, Kramer began by confirming the view of Otto Renner (1915) that two mechanisms were involved in water absorption. He found that the roots of slowly transpiring plants in moist soil behave as osmometers, resulting in root pressure and bleeding from wounds, as in birch and grape in the spring. However, in rapidly transpiring plants tension develops in the water-conducting system, causing water to be pulled in through the roots, which act as passive absorbing surfaces. Kramer then turned to the manner in which low temperature and deficient soil aeration reduce absorption. Both factors, he found, reduce absorption chiefly because they decrease the permeability of roots to water, rather than by direct effects on the absorption mechanism.

In the middle 1950s Kramer realized that many of the contradictory results concerning the relationship between soil moisture and plant growth resulted from the fact that plant-water stress could not be predicted accurately from soil-water stress. The only way to evaluate plant-water stress was by direct measurement, but this was difficult because of lack of suitable methods. Kramer and his students began testing the methods available and contributed to developing the electric psychrometer and the dye methods of measuring plant-water stress.

His interest in water absorption led Kramer to study the absorption of minerals through the root systems of intact plants. He and his co-workers first studied uptake of various radioactive elements by mycorhizal roots of pine trees. They then began to study the absorbing zone of young roots of various species and found that maximum absorption occurs several centimeters behind the root tips, where the xylem is well differentiated, rather than near the apex. Other laboratory research led Kramer to conclude that considerable salt is carried passively into the roots of plants in the transpiration stream, but this conclusion met with opposition from those who claimed that accumulation by the root cells was the first step in salt absorption through roots.

More recently, Kramer's laboratory studied the absorption of water and minerals through suberized roots. Most research had hitherto been done on unsuberized roots, which constitute only a small percentage of the root surface of trees. It appears probable that trees and other woody perennials absorb much of their water and minerals through suberized roots.

Kramer began to study the physiology of woody plants early in his career. His first research was on the relation of dormancy to photoperiod. Later he supervised a series of studies of the physiological differences between pines and hardwoods that aided in explaining why pine seedlings were unable to become established under forest stands where hardwood seedlings thrived. He also carried out some of the early research on thermoperiod as a factor controlling the range of tree species. He helped plan a large environment-controlled laboratory (phytotron) for research on the effect of environmental factors on plant growth.

Kramer was one of the first plant physiologists in the United States to work extensively on woody plants. He and his students did much to point out the necessity of understanding the physiological processes of trees in order to manage forests effectively.

Kramer was born in Indiana and reared on a farm in southwestern Ohio. He majored in botany at Miami University, Oxford, Ohio, and took his Ph.D. at Ohio State University in 1931. He went to Duke University the same year, where he later became James B. Duke Professor of Botany, director of the Sarah P. Duke Gardens, and chairman of the Phytotron Committee. In 1960–61 Kramer was program director in regulatory biology with the National Science Foundation. He was elected to the National Academy of Sciences in 1962.

Kramer wrote *Plant and Soil Water Relationships* (1949) and, with T. T. Kozlowski, *Physiology of Trees* (1960). He published numerous articles in scientific journals.

For background information *see* PLANT PHYSIOLOGY in the McGraw-Hill Encyclopedia of Science and Technology.   □

★ KREBS, Sir Hans (Adolf)

British biochemist
Born Aug. 25, 1900, Hildesheim, Germany

KREBS'S CHIEF contributions concerned the elucidation of metabolic pathways, including the tricarboxylic-acid cycle or "Krebs cycle," which describes some stages of the oxidation of all foodstuffs in living cells. For this achievement he received a share of the 1953 Nobel Prize for physiology and medicine.

In 1932 Krebs made his first major discovery: the "ornithine cycle" of urea synthesis in the mammalian liver. The success of these experiments was due to the fact that he used a new technique. Whereas earlier workers had worked with the intact animal or with the artificially perfused liver, Krebs suspended liver slices in a balanced saline medium, thus making possible the accurate measurement of the rate of a biosynthetic process under controlled conditions. He found that the rate of urea synthesis was catalytically promoted by the amino acid ornithine, and that the related substance citrulline had a similar effect. These two new observations, together with the long-established fact that arginase is abundant at the site of urea synthesis from ammonia, led to the formulation of the three main stages of urea synthesis as shown in

$$CH_2NH_2 \atop CH_2 \atop CH_2 \atop CHNH_2 \atop COOH \text{ (ornithine)} + NH_3 + CO_2 \longrightarrow O=C{\nwarrow NH_2 \atop \searrow CH_2NH} \atop CH_2 \atop CH_2 \atop CHNH_2 \atop COOH \text{ (citrulline)} + NH_3 \longrightarrow$$

$$HN=C{\nwarrow NH_2 \atop \searrow CH_2NH} \atop CH_2 \atop CH_2 \atop CHNH_2 \atop COOH \text{ (arginine)} \longrightarrow CH_2NH_2 \atop CH_2 \atop CH_2 \atop CHNH_2 \atop COOH + CO{\nwarrow NH_2 \atop \searrow NH_2} \text{ (ornithine + urea)}$$

Equation (1)

Equation (1). The overall effect of these reactions is

$$2NH_3 + CO_2 \longrightarrow urea$$

The correctness of this scheme has been fully borne out by later work.

Krebs then turned to the study of the intermediary stages of carbohydrate oxidation in muscle tissue. It was already known at that time that muscle readily oxidizes several di- and tricarboxylic acids—citrate, succinate, fumarate, and malate—but the relation, if any, between these oxidative reactions and the oxidation of carbohydrate, the main fuel of muscle, was ob-scure. In 1936 C. Martius and F. Knoop found that the oxidation of citrate could yield α-keto-glutarate, with *cis*-aconitate and isocitrate as in-termediates. Since α-ketoglutarate was already known to form succinate, which in turn forms fumarate, malate, and oxaloacetate, the discovery of Martius and Knoop established the occurrence of the reaction series leading from citrate to oxaloacetate shown in Equation (2).

$$
\begin{array}{l}
\text{COOH} \\
\underset{|}{\text{C}}\!\!\diagup\!\text{OH} \\
\overset{|}{\underset{\diagdown}{\text{C}}}\text{CH}_2\text{COOH} \\
\text{CH}_2 \\
| \\
\text{COOH}
\end{array}
\longrightarrow
\begin{array}{l}
\text{COOH} \\
| \\
\text{C} \cdot \text{CH}_2 \cdot \text{COOH} \\
\| \\
\text{CH} \\
| \\
\text{COOH}
\end{array}
\longrightarrow
$$

citric acid   *cis*-aconitic acid

$$
\begin{array}{l}
\text{COOH} \\
| \\
\text{CH} \cdot \text{CH}_2 \cdot \text{COOH} \\
| \\
\text{CHOH} \\
| \\
\text{COOH}
\end{array}
\longrightarrow
\begin{array}{l}
\text{CO}_2 + \\
\text{CH}_2 \cdot \text{CH}_2 \cdot \text{COOH} \\
| \\
\text{CO} \\
| \\
\text{COOH}
\end{array}
\longrightarrow
$$

isocitric acid   α-ketoglutaric acid

$$
\begin{array}{l}
\phantom{\text{CO}_2 + }\text{COOH} \\
\phantom{\text{CO}_2 + }| \\
\phantom{\text{CO}_2 + }\text{CH}_2 \\
\phantom{\text{CO}_2 + }| \\
\text{CO}_2 + \text{CH}_2 \\
\phantom{\text{CO}_2 + }| \\
\phantom{\text{CO}_2 + }\text{COOH}
\end{array}
\longrightarrow
\begin{array}{l}
\text{COOH} \\
| \\
\text{CH} \\
\| \\
\text{CH} \\
| \\
\text{COOH}
\end{array}
\longrightarrow
$$

succinic acid   fumaric acid

$$
\begin{array}{l}
\text{COOH} \\
| \\
\text{CHOH} \\
| \\
\text{CH}_2 \\
| \\
\text{COOH}
\end{array}
\longrightarrow
\begin{array}{l}
\text{COOH} \\
| \\
\text{CO} \\
| \\
\text{CH}_2 \\
| \\
\text{COOH}
\end{array}
$$

malic acid   oxaloacetic acid

Equation (2)

Krebs and W. A. Johnson (1937) added one more decisive step, namely, the formation of citrate from oxaloacetate and pyruvate as shown in Equation (3). Since pyruvate was known to be formed from carbohydrate, this reaction established a link between carbohydrate metab-olism and the earlier reaction sequence; more-over, it linked the two ends of that series to a cyclic sequence accounting for the intermediary stages of carbohydrate oxidation. Krebs and Johnson further showed that the rates of the in-

$$
\begin{array}{l}
\text{COOH} \\
| \\
\text{CO} \\
| \\
\text{CH}_2 \\
| \\
\text{COOH}
\end{array}
+
\begin{array}{l}
\text{CH}_3 \\
| \\
\text{CO} \\
| \\
\text{COOH}
\end{array}
\longrightarrow
$$

oxaloacetic acid   pyruvic acid

$$
\begin{array}{l}
\text{COOH} \\
\underset{|}{\text{C}}\!\!\diagup\!\text{OH} \\
\overset{|}{\underset{\diagdown}{\phantom{\text{C}}}}\text{CH}_2 \cdot \text{COOH} + \text{CO}_2 \\
\text{CH}_2 \\
| \\
\text{COOH}
\end{array}
$$

citric acid

Equation (3)

dividual steps were rapid enough to permit the assumption that the whole of the terminal oxida-tion of carbohydrate in muscle passes through this cycle. Later work, notably by F. A. Lip-mann and by F. Lynen, revealed that acetyl co-enzyme A is an intermediate in the formation of citrate from oxaloacetate and pyruvate, and that acetyl coenzyme A is also formed from fatty acids and many amino acids; further, that the reactions of the cycle occur in all metabolically active animal tissues and in plants and micro-organisms.

In 1957 H. L. Kornberg and Krebs discovered a modified tricarboxylic-acid cycle, the "glyoxy-late cycle," in which the reactions between citrate and malate are replaced by two other steps:

isocitrate $\longrightarrow$ glyoxylate + succinate

glyoxylate + acetyl CoA $\longrightarrow$ malate

The glyoxylate cycle thus consists of steps shown in Equation (4). The overall effect of this cycle is the synthesis of succinate from two molecules of acetyl coenzyme A. This cycle plays an important part in the synthesis of cell con-stituents of microorganisms that derive all their carbon atoms from acetate or fatty acids. The glyoxylate cycle also plays a role in the con-version of fat to carbohydrate in seeds that carry a large store of fat (for example, castor bean).

Others of Krebs's discoveries concerned: the presence of a D-amino acid oxidase in mam-malian liver and kidney; the synthesis of gluta-mine in various tissues, including brain cortex and retina; the formation of hypoxanthine as an intermediate in purine synthesis in birds; the occurrence of CO_2 fixation, through the syn-thesis of oxaloacetate from pyruvate and CO_2 in

$$\begin{array}{c}\text{COOH} \\ | \\ \text{CO} \\ | \\ \text{CH}_2 \\ | \\ \text{COOH} \end{array} \quad + \quad \begin{array}{c}\text{CH}_3 \\ | \\ \text{COOH} \end{array} \quad \longrightarrow$$

oxaloacetic acid   acetic acid (reacting as coenzyme A ester)

$$\begin{array}{c}\text{COOH} \\ | \quad \text{OH} \\ \text{C} \\ | \quad \text{CH}_2 \cdot \text{COOH} \\ \text{CH}_2 \\ | \\ \text{COOH} \end{array} \longrightarrow \begin{array}{c}\text{COOH} \\ | \\ \text{C} \cdot \text{CH}_2 \cdot \text{COOH} \\ || \\ \text{CH} \\ | \\ \text{COOH} \end{array} \longrightarrow$$

citric acid   cis-aconitic acid

$$\begin{array}{c}\text{COOH} \\ | \\ \text{CH} \cdot \text{CH}_2 \cdot \text{COOH} \\ | \\ \text{CHOH} \\ | \\ \text{COOH} \end{array} \longrightarrow \begin{array}{c}\text{COOH} \\ | \\ \text{HCO} \\ \text{glyoxylic acid} \\ \\ \text{CH}_2 \cdot \text{COOH} \\ | \\ \text{CH}_2 \cdot \text{COOH} \\ \text{succinic acid} \end{array}$$

isocitric acid

$$\begin{array}{c}\text{COOH} \\ | \\ \text{HCO} \end{array} \quad + \quad \begin{array}{c}\text{CH}_3 \\ | \\ \text{COOH} \end{array} \quad \longrightarrow$$

glyoxylic acid   acetic acid (reacting as coenzyme A ester)

$$\begin{array}{c}\text{COOH} \\ | \\ \text{CHOH} \\ | \\ \text{CH}_2 \\ | \\ \text{COOH} \end{array} \longrightarrow \begin{array}{c}\text{COOH} \\ | \\ \text{CO} \\ | \\ \text{CH}_2 \\ | \\ \text{COOH} \end{array}$$

malic acid   oxaloacetic acid

Equation (4)

animal tissues; and mechanisms playing a role in the regulation of metabolism. Most of these discoveries sprang from the development and use of new methods, especially for the handling of isolated tissue preparations in vitro, and for the quantitative microdetermination of metabolites.

Krebs studied medicine in several German universities from 1919 to 1924. After a further study of chemistry, he joined Professor Otto Warburg's laboratory at Berlin-Dahlem for 4

years. He then returned to clinical medicine and in 1932 became a teacher of internal medicine at the University of Freiburg-im-Breisgau. He left Germany as a refugee in 1933 and joined the Biochemical Laboratory in Cambridge, England. In 1935 he moved to the University of Sheffield, and in 1954 to Oxford where he became professor of biochemistry. He was elected a fellow of the Royal Society of London in 1947 and a foreign associate of the U.S. National Academy of Sciences in 1964. He was knighted in 1958.

For background information *see* KREBS CYCLE in the McGraw-Hill Encyclopedia of Science and Technology.   □

★ **KUENEN, Philip Henry**
Dutch geologist
Born July 22, 1902, Dundee, Scotland

KUENEN'S APPOINTMENT as geologist for the Snellius deep-sea expedition to the Moluccas (1929–30) directed his attention to the sea. He found several arguments in favor of Charles Darwin's theory of atoll formation and concluded that the foundations of atolls were due to subsidence, whereas the upper structures were best explained by R. A. Daly's theory of glacial control. But he emphasized chemical attack above low-water mark instead of mechanical attack as the chief cause of decapitation of the reefs during the low sea levels of the Ice Age.

Kuenen also attempted to interpret the structure of the Moluccas region from the new bathymetric results. He was able to show that the basin shapes had a systematic relation to the gravity field elucidated by F. A. Vening Meinesz.

In 1936 Daly proposed the hypothesis that submarine canyons were formed during the Ice Age by turbidity currents. These currents had been invoked long before by F. A. Forel to explain the channels on the underwater slope of

Swiss lake deltas. Waters charged with clay sediment flowed down the slope in consequence of their density being greater than that of the clear surrounding water. By experiments Kuenen demonstrated the efficacy of the mechanism and some years later showed that sand could also be transported in this manner. He attributed deep-sea sands to transport from shallow areas by turbidity currents. For many years these ideas found very little support, although H. C. Stetson and others granted that the mechanism may have helped in transportation of clay. In 1950 Kuenen joined forces with C. I. Migliorini. They claimed that the emplacement of ancient sandy rocks showing graded bedding could be accounted for by the action of turbidity currents. Again experiments were used as the main source of evidence.

In collaboration with others, Kuenen studied formations that appeared to be composed of an alternation of so-called turbidites and pelagic shales. More than a dozen properties were found to be characteristic. Each of these, such as graded beds of sand, all manner of sole markings, and internal structures, could also be encountered in other types of deposits. But the combination of several in well-developed form was good evidence for turbidites. No less characteristic was the absence of all features indicative of small depth, such as ripple marks, reefs, and temporary emergence. The investigators concluded that turbidites were deposited, almost without exception, in depths exceeding 100 or 200 m, normally 1000 m or more.

The study of turbidites, which date from the oldest geological times up to the recent past, has contributed much to paleogeography, for no other type of deposit gives such pertinent evidence on the direction of transportation and hence of bottom slope and source areas. The important role played by these currents in present oceans in the transportation of materials from the continents to the deep-sea floor has been established by W. M. Ewing, B. C. Heezen, and other oceanographers. Their role in producing submarine canyons is still controversial.

One of the very few experimental geologists, Kuenen was started along these lines by collaborating with his teacher, B. G. Escher, on tectonics of salt domes. Later he treated wind-faceted pebbles, volcanic cones, crustal folds, turbidity currents, various forms of pebble and sand-grain abrasion, lamination, ptygmatic folds, and other tectonic and sedimentary features. Kuenen felt that the value of experiments was (1) to illustrate hypotheses, (2) to suggest new explanations, (3) to produce data, (4) to draw attention to details, (5) to provide better opportunities for observation, and (6) to separate the influence of factors. The main difficulties he acknowledged were in scaling and correct application of results to natural processes.

Kuenen's father was a Dutch physicist; his mother was English. He was educated at Leiden University and held staff positions there and at Gröningen, where in 1946 he became a full professor. He wrote many papers, mostly in English, and a few books in Dutch or English, of which *Marine Geology* (1950) is best known. In 1961 he was awarded the Penrose Medal of the Geological Society of America.

For background information *see* SEDIMENTATION (GEOLOGY) in the McGraw-Hill Encyclopedia of Science and Technology. □

★ KUSCH, Polykarp

American physicist
Born Jan. 26, 1911, Blankenburg, Germany

FOR HIS precision determination of the magnetic moment of the electron, Kusch shared with W. E. Lamb the 1955 Nobel Prize in physics.

One of the great postulates of physics was that of S. A. Goudsmit and G. E. Uhlenbeck in 1925: the electron has an intrinsic angular momentum of $\frac{1}{2}h/2\pi$ and an associated intrinsic magnetic dipole moment of $eh/4\pi mc = \mu_0$, the Bohr magneton. The statement was consistent with all features of atomic behavior observed up to 1947.

The invention by I. I. Rabi in 1937 of the molecular-beam magnetic-resonance method ultimately made possible a much more exacting test of the postulates than had previously been possible. The method is essentially a spectroscopic procedure for measuring the structure of the ground state of an atom or molecule and the further splitting of the structure in a magnetic field. The great beauty of the method lies in the extremely high resolution that may be obtained and the potentially very high precision of the results.

Kusch was associated with Rabi in the exploitation of the method from its first days. The earliest studies, on molecules, yielded a direct measurement of nuclear magnetic dipole moments. Hyperfine structures, a measure of the energy of interaction of the nuclear magnetic dipole moment with the enveloping electron configuration of an atom, were measured for a number of atoms. The determination of the magnetic dipole moment of the proton in terms of the spin magnetic dipole moment of the electron, μ_s, was made. At that time when this was generally believed that $\mu_s = \mu_0$.

In 1947 J. E. Nafe, E. B. Nelson, and Rabi reported a measurement of the hyperfine structure splitting in atomic hydrogen. This can be precisely predicted from a knowledge of the magnetic moment of the proton, the spin magnetic moment of the electron and fundamental constants. A discrepancy, far beyond any uncertainty in the values of the input quantities, was found between the calculated and observed splitting. Gregory Breit suggested that the effect might be due to a departure of the spin moment of the electron from the generally accepted value of μ_0.

Kusch, together with Henry Foley, subjected the suggestion to critical examination. For an atom in a $^2S_{\frac{1}{2}}$ state, the electron has no net orbital angular momentum, and the total electronic magnetic dipole moment, μ_J, is just μ_s. An atom in a ^2P state has an electronic orbital angular momentum of $h/2\pi$ with which is associated an orbital magnetic dipole moment of μ_0. There is also an electronic spin dipole moment of μ_s. For the $^2P_{\frac{1}{2}}$ state, $\mu_J = \frac{2}{3}\mu_0 - \frac{1}{3}\mu_s$ and for the $^2P_{\frac{3}{2}}$ state, $\mu_J = \mu_0 + \mu_s$. The detailed properties of several atoms in $^2S_{\frac{1}{2}}$ states, and of two atoms in $^2P_{\frac{1}{2}}$ and $^2P_{\frac{3}{2}}$ states had already been determined. By observing appropriate transitions between the magnetic levels of an atom, one can calculate the quantity $\mu_J H/h$. If the observation is made for any pair of states, in the same magnetic field, H, the ratio μ_s/μ_0 can be found.

The states may not be as pure as was assumed in calculating μ_J. Nevertheless, essentially the same result was found for all possible combinations of these states, and by using different atoms in the same state. It is inconceivable that all of the states have precisely those perturbations that lead to a consistent result. The net effect is that $\mu_s = 1.00119\,\mu_0$. The experimental result is in excellent agreement with that predicted by Julian Schwinger on the basis of the quantum electrodynamics, $\mu_s = (1 + \alpha/2\pi)\mu_0 = 1.00116\,\mu_0$, where α is the fine structure constant ($\alpha = 1/137.039$).

Subsequently Kusch made a much more precise measurement of the ratio of the spin magnetic dipole moment of the electron to the magnetic dipole moment of the proton. This result, coupled to one that J. H. Gardner and E. M. Purcell and later P. Franken and S. Liebes obtained for the ratio of the orbital electronic dipole moment and the proton moment, at once yields μ_s/μ_0. The result agrees with the theoretical result calculated to the order of α^2.

The son of a Lutheran clergyman, Kusch went from Germany to the United States in 1912. He received his B.S. in physics from the Case Institute of Technology in 1931 and his Ph.D. from the University of Illinois in 1936. His graduate research was in the field of optical molecular spectroscopy. He worked in mass spectroscopy at the University of Minnesota in 1936–37. From 1937 to 1941 and after 1946 he was at Columbia University, where his research centered around an exploitation of the molecular-beam technique in problems of spectroscopy and chemical physics. From 1941 to 1946 he engaged in research and development of very high-frequency generators at the Westinghouse Corporation, a government laboratory at Columbia, and the Bell Telephone Laboratories. He was elected to the National Academy of Sciences in 1956.

For background information *see* DIPOLE MOMENT; MAGNETIC MOMENT; NUCLEAR MOMENTS in the McGraw-Hill Encyclopedia of Science and Technology.   □

L

☆ **LAMB, Willis Eugene, Jr.**
American physicist
Born July 12, 1913, Los Angeles, Calif., U.S.A.

UTILIZING THE microwave techniques acquired during World War II at the Columbia University Radiation Laboratory, Lamb conducted very accurate experiments on the fine structure of levels with $n = 2$ in hydrogen. Lamb used the method of molecular-beam radio frequency resonance to determine precisely the amount of energy required to shift the electron in a hydrogen atom between two very nearly equal energy states, that is, the energy by which the $2^2S_{\frac{1}{2}}$ state lies higher than the $2^2P_{\frac{1}{2}}$ state. The result differed from that predicted by the Dirac theory of the electron. This splitting of energy levels, measured in 1947, is known as the Lamb shift. For his work in precision atomic measurements and its significance in leading to a new understanding in the theory of the interaction of electrons and electromagnetic radiation, Lamb shared the 1955 Nobel Prize in physics.

In 1885, J. J. Balmer found that the lines in the spectrum of hydrogen were spaced in a regular fashion and their wavelengths were described by a simple equation. Using the ideas of the quantum theory founded in 1900 by Max Planck, Niels Bohr in 1913 produced quantization rules for the hydrogen atom that accounted for Balmer's observations and predicted additional lines. However, Bohr's model of the hydrogen atom was not able to explain the fine structure of some of these lines as discovered by A. A. Michelson and E. W. Morley in 1887. An explanation was given by A. J. W. Sommerfeld in 1916 in terms of the relativistic variation of the electron's mass with velocity. In particular, he predicted a doublet separation or energy-level splitting for the $n = 2$ state in hydrogen.

In the early 1920s the newly developed quantum mechanics was applied to the hydrogen atom by Werner Heisenberg, Max Born, and Erwin Schrödinger. Although the Schrödinger wave equation along with the approximate inclusion of relativistic effects gave a new meaning to the Bohr model of the atom, there was only rough agreement with the hydrogen fine structure observations of the time. Theoretical agreement with experimental results came in 1925 when the Goudsmit-Uhlenbeck and Thomas model of a spinning electron with its accompanying magnetic moment was incorporated into the theory. But instead of two levels, three were now predicted—two being degenerate. P. A. M. Dirac in 1928 modified the wave equation so that it would be consistent with the Special Theory of Relativity. This remarkable equation naturally endowed the electron with wave properties, charge, spin, magnetic moment, and a relativistic variation of mass with velocity. By considering an electron with these effects moving in a coulomb field, Dirac was able to compute the fine structure of hydrogen, the calculated energy level separation between the levels $2^2P_{\frac{1}{2}}$ and $2^2P_{\frac{3}{2}}$ being 0.365 cm^{-1}. According to the Dirac theory, this separation arises from spin-orbit coupling. Furthermore, as a result of the coulomb attraction between electron and proton, the theory predicts that the $2^2S_{\frac{1}{2}}$ state exactly coincides in energy with the $2^2P_{\frac{1}{2}}$ state.

For nearly 20 years detailed investigations to examine Dirac's fine structure predictions had been prevented by Doppler effects and the collisions between atoms. There were spectroscopists who found small differences between theoretical and experimental results. But there were also those who found no discrepancies.

During World War II, through his work with radar, Lamb became interested in microwave spectroscopy. In particular, he hoped to make a clear-cut determination of the energy states into which the Dirac theory had split the first excited level of hydrogen. Lamb proposed to make use of the possible metastability of hydrogen. As of then, metastable hydrogen had never been produced or detected. It was previously calculated that the lifetime of the $2^2S_{\frac{1}{2}}$ metastable state of hydrogen in the absence of external perturbations is 0.15 second as compared to a lifetime of 1.6×10^{-9} second for the nonmetastable $2P$ states. The decay mechanism of the $2^2S_{\frac{1}{2}}$ state to the ground state involves the emission of two photons: a straightforward radiative transition is forbidden by the selection rule $\triangle L = \pm 1$.

Lamb proposed to make a stream of metastable hydrogen atoms and apply the resonance method of I. I. Rabi for studying radio-frequency transitions in atomic beams in the presence of a magnetic field. The hydrogen fine structure levels would be subject to Zeeman splitting—that is, the possible transitions would now be a function of magnetic field—but this turned out to be useful since fixed frequency microwave oscillators could be used.

In 1947 Lamb designed an atomic beam apparatus with which Retherford, as part of his Ph.D. thesis requirement, carried out the proposed resonance experiments. They cross-bombarded the hydrogen beam with a 12 ev electron beam. In this process a small fraction of the atoms are raised to the first excited $n = 2$ state. Those atoms in either the $2^2P_{\frac{3}{2}}$ or $2^2P_{\frac{1}{2}}$ states undergo radiative transitions to the ground state almost immediately. However, those in the beam in the $2^2S_{\frac{1}{2}}$ state remain in that state until they reach a detector. This detector is sensitive only to the excited metastable atoms. The metal target emits an electron when a metastable atom collides with it in a "collision of the second kind." The microwave radiation was applied between the exciting and detection regions.

As the magnetic field is varied while the frequency and amplitude of the microwave radiation are held constant, atomic transitions are induced by the radio-frequency radiation of the appropriate frequency. The transitions take place between one of the Zeeman components of the $2^2S_{\frac{1}{2}}$ state and any component of either the $2^2P_{\frac{1}{2}}$ or $2^2P_{\frac{3}{2}}$ states. As a result, a certain fraction of the metastable atoms in the beam are quenched and lose their excitation energy. Since atoms in the ground state do not eject electrons from the detector, a measured reduction in atomic beam intensity is recorded, giving an indication that a resonance condition exists. This resonance effect enables one to know the precise value of the wavelengths corresponding to the energy differences between the $2^2P_{\frac{1}{2}}$ and $2^2S_{\frac{1}{2}}$ states. Thus by analysis the energy difference between these states in a zero magnetic field can be found with great precision. The results indicated that, contrary to the Dirac theory, the $2^2S_{\frac{1}{2}}$ state was not degenerate with the $2^2P_{\frac{1}{2}}$ state, but was higher than the $2^2P_{\frac{1}{2}}$ by about 1000 Mc/sec. Lamb later used this microwave technique to study other fine-structure states, for example, the $n = 3$ state of hydrogen, the $n = 2$ state of deuterium, and the $n = 2$ state of singly ionized helium. This energy-level shift has been explained by H. A. Bethe and other theoretical physicists as resulting from changes in the electron self-energy brought about by its interactions with the electromagnetic and electron-positron fields.

The son of a telephone engineer, Lamb received a B.S. in chemistry at the University of California, Berkeley, in 1934 and a Ph.D. in physics there in 1938. At Columbia University he rose from instructor in physics in 1938 to full

professor in 1948. From 1943 to 1951 he was also associated with the Columbia Radiation Laboratory. In 1951 Lamb was appointed professor of physics at Stanford University. In 1953–54 he was the Morris Loeb Lecturer at Harvard University, and from 1956 to 1962 he was at Oxford as a fellow of New College and Wykeham Professor of Physics. In 1962 he became the Henry Ford II Professor of Physics at Yale University. He was elected to the National Academy of Sciences in 1954.

For background information *see* MICROWAVE SPECTROSCOPY; QUANTUM THEORY, RELATIVISTIC; ZEEMAN EFFECT in the McGraw-Hill Encyclopedia of Science and Technology.   □

★ **LAND, Edwin Herbert**
American scientist and inventor
Born May 7, 1909, Bridgeport, Conn., U.S.A.

LAND'S PRINCIPAL contributions were in the fields of polarized light, photography, and color vision.

In the field of polarized light he was responsible for the first modern polarizers for light, for a sequence of subsequent polarizers, and for the theory and practice of many applications of polarized light.

In the field of photography he conceived the cameras and films that give instantaneous dry pictures directly from the camera, and he carried out the physicochemical investigations that made possible the processes that give neutral-colored, continuous-tone, instantaneous photographs. All this work was the background for instantaneous one-step color photography, for which Land proposed the broad principles and to which he made a number of basic contributions.

In the field of color vision Land showed that it is impossible to describe the color of an object in the world around us in terms of ratios of visible energy, at various wavelengths, coming from the object to the eye. He showed that this deficiency in the elementary theory cannot be corrected by additional terms in an equation nor by description of the color of the surrounding area. These experiments led him to his "retinex" theory of color vision.

Polarized light. Although polarization is a ubiquitous characteristic of light, the eye is not designed to see it. Consequently, it was not until the 17th century that polarization was recognized as the basis of the double image seen through Iceland spar (Huygens); it was not until the early 19th century that the polarization of light reflected from glass plates was described (Malus); and it was not until 1828 that an excellent polarizer for light was produced by William Nicol. The limitations of the Nicol prism are the following: the rhomb must be several times as long as the edge of the entrance window; the "angular aperture" of the device is limited because rays that are too oblique will either be transmitted unpolarized or not transmitted at all; and perfect single crystals with entrance windows an inch square are essentially unavailable and worth thousands of dollars.

About 100 years after the invention of the Nicol prism, Land, as a freshman at Harvard, was deeply impressed by the fact that polarization, although a universal physical characteristic of radiation, was difficult to use in scientific domains and not at all available for applied science or industry. He could see nothing in "the laws of nature" prohibiting the existence of a sheet of glass or plastic as large as a window pane that would resolve incoming light into two components and absorb nearly all of one component while transmitting nearly all of the other. Such a plate of glass cut in half with a glass cutter could have the two halves superposed on each other, and the pair would change from black to transparent as one pane was rotated relative to the other. While he found the concept of such a material an inspiring challenge in itself, Land was moved to action because polarization is involved in the Kerr effect, the Faraday effect, and the Zeeman effect; in the birefringence of all living tissue; in mineralogy, metallurgy, and most high-polymer studies; and in moonlight, nebular starlight, and coronal sunlight. He was also impressed by the fact that a polarizer for light in the form of an extensive synthetic sheet could make possible glare-free headlights, three-dimensional moving pictures, and color television.

He therefore took a leave of absence from his regular courses at Harvard for an intensive study of the background necessary to solve the problem he had set himself. Within a few months he decided to turn from approaches involving large single crystals to his new idea of making the optical equivalent of a large crystal by a homogeneous orientation of submicroscopic polarizing elements suspended in low concentration in a clear sheet of glass or plastic. In 1852 W. B. Herapath had discovered in the microscope the polarizing properties of platelets of iodoquinine sulfate. During the next 100 years Herapath and his successors tried to grow these very thin plates to uniform areas of useful size. Land's approach was to learn to make herapathite in submicroscopic particles and then to learn to mix these into a plastic mass, and finally to learn to orient them within the plastic mass, while forming a finished transparent sheet. The mastery of each of these steps proved extraordinarily difficult, but after about a year and a half of intensive effort Land returned to Harvard, bringing with him the new polarizer. Harvard provided him with a large laboratory where he continued these investigations. At a physics department colloquium he described "A New Polarizer for Light in the Form of an Extensive Synthetic Sheet."

Near the end of his time at Harvard, this whole field of pure and applied science in polarized light had become so promising and demanding that he took a second leave of absence in order to devote himself entirely to this research.

The ensuing years were extraordinarily fruitful. The original polarizer, called Polaroid J-sheet, was followed by an important series of noncrystalline polarizers. "H-sheet" is a stretched sheet of polyvinyl alcohol having a polymeric chain of iodine adsorbed to its long chain molecules. "K-sheet" (coinvented with H. G. Rogers) also starts with oriented polyvinyl alcohol, some of the molecules of which are then dehydrated in the stretched state to form the new molecule, polyvinylene. This extraordinary polarizer, when laminated in glass, is stable over decades exposed on the front of an automobile headlight to ambient irradiation. "L" polarizers employ a series of polarizing dyes that are substituted for iodine. The "D" polarizer is a diffusing polarizer in which uniaxial birefringent needles are embedded in a plastic with an index of refraction matching one of the indices of the needles. Such a polarizer changes from glassy clear to opaque white when analyzed with an ordinary polarizer.

During this period, both the theory and practice of three-dimensional colored movies, automobile headlights, polarizing sunglasses, and polarizing camera filters were fully worked out. Also during this period the nucleus of the Polaroid laboratory was established. The members of this group of enthusiastic young scientists became the center of the ever-growing research laboratory and, along with Land, supplied a continuity of experience that linked together all the fields of investigation.

Land had had the concept of an image in

terms of percentage polarization, that is, a photographic image in which the highlights would not polarize and the shadows would fully polarize. When examined with an ordinary polarizer such an image would vanish, leaving a clear sheet when the polarizing axis was parallel to that of the image. He called such an image a vectograph—an image in terms of vectorial inequality. As the analyzer is rotated, the contrast of the image increases from zero to a maximum, providing the full image.

In 1940 Joseph Mahler joined the group and perceived the analogy between a pair of such images with orthogonal orientation of their polarization direction and the anaglyph using red and green inks for printing with red and green lenses for viewing. (DuHauron had invented the anaglyph for three-dimensional images about 1860.) Land and Mahler undertook a vigorous program to produce first black and white stereoscopic vectographs, and later full-color vectographs. Both programs were successful in the laboratory, and the black and white vectograph was released for extensive use during the war.

With the advent of World War II Land and his group turned their attention to the solution of many military problems. Their research produced infrared polarizers, heat stable filters passing only the infrared, and dark adaptation goggles. A large project was the development of thermal homing-heads, containing miniaturized computers, to be attached to the noses of standard 1000-lb bombs. Land invented the widely used polarizing ring sight, a basal section of uniaxial crystal between circular polarizers. This sight has no optics and no restriction on aperture or exit pupil.

One-step photography. After the war Land turned his full attention to his idea of a handheld camera that would use an apparently dry film and would give a picture instantly. Ordinary photography involves the steps of developing, fixing, washing, and drying; exposing a positive to the negative; then again developing, washing, fixing, washing, and drying. What Land sought was not only a process that could be carried out "dry" in the camera, but one that would replace all the conventional steps by a single step. In 1947 he demonstrated such a camera and process to the Optical Society of America, and at Christmas 1948 the camera and film were made publicly available.

The film employed as a photosensitive element a standard high-speed silver halide emulsion. A rupturable container (pod) located at the edge of the picture area contained a developing reagent. As the assembly was pulled through a pair of rollers in the camera the processing reagents contained in the pod were spread over the picture area between the exposed negative and positive sheet.

Land investigated and described broadly a whole series of procedures that would serve to make a one-step process directly in the camera. In the initial commercial production he chose the method of dissolving unexposed silver in the negative and transferring complexed silver ions to a receiving sheet through the thin layer of viscous developer. At the receiving sheet the silver ions were aggregated into galaxies at the time of reduction.

One of his most important contributions was the concept and structure of this receiving sheet. It was a major contributor in solving the problem of producing from solution a precipitated image that was continuous in tone and uniform in hue. The receiving sheet originally produced for the 1948 film was improved by Land. The present receiving material will accept silver ions from any source and in any concentration to yield in a reducing environment a completely neutral, grainless, silver deposit ranging from clear whites through beautiful grays to deep jet blacks. This silver deposit is essentially a new form of matter, the structure of which is so fine as to be nearly undetectable even in the electron microscope. This receiving sheet solved one of the great problems with continuous tone images. (With line copy, as opposed to continuous tone, it was not necessary for the silver deposit to be particularly neutral for the lines to appear nearly black, nor did line copy present the problem of making many steps in the tone scale the same hue, since line copy requires only two tonal steps.) Given this remarkable receiving sheet, Land was able to produce one-step processes of extremely high photographic speed, equivalent to ASA 3000. This sensitivity made it possible to use long–focal-length lenses of relatively small aperture, opening the way for amateur cameras at modest cost. These cameras, operating at high shutter speeds, provided the ordinary amateur with sharp images of objects in motion, even at very low light levels, and also made possible indoor photography without flash.

Over the years since 1948 a succession of new films came from Land's laboratory—transparencies for continuous tone and, for line copy, 10,000 ASA oscillographic film, films that give a finished negative along with a finished positive, and 10-second x-ray packets.

Concurrent with the research to develop the black and white process, Land also began investigations toward a process for one-step color transfer images. Many concepts of the black and white process were extended to the color film, and its mechanics were made compatible with the one-step black-and-white process and camera. The present form of the color film is due to the development of a new dye-developer principle by H. G. Rogers and to Land's invention of the positive sheet structure that allowed the colors to be stabilized in a hard, clear image layer.

Color vision. Land's work in optics and color led him to experiments that showed inconsistencies in the classical concepts of how color is sensed. He showed in a variety of experiments that color is not dependent upon the relative amounts of red, green, and blue light coming to the eye. To explain the results of these experiments he proposed that there are at least three independent image-forming mechanisms of different spectral sensitivity. The name he suggested for these mechanisms was retinexes. Each retinex is a hypothetical retinal cerebral liaison that contains as much of the retina and cortex as is necessary to form an image in terms of apparent lightnesses. Land proposed that it is the comparison at each point in the image of these independent lightnesses that determines the color we see.

From the inception of Polaroid Corporation, Land was president, chairman of the board, and director of research. The company was so organized that he was able to spend a large part of his time in research. His experience led him to believe that a science-centered industry provides a framework for a rewarding working life for all the members of the company. He was a Visiting Institute Professor at the Massachusetts Institute of Technology from 1956, and was for many years a member of the President's Science Advisory Committee. He received the Presidential Medal of Freedom in 1963. A fellow of the National Academy of Sciences and of the National Academy of Engineering, he was awarded medals by the British Physical Society, Royal Microscopic Society, Royal Photographic Society, Society of Photographic Scientists and Engineers, American Academy of Arts and Sciences, the Franklin Institute, and many other societies.

For background information *see* COLOR; COLOR VISION; PHOTOGRAPHIC MATERIALS; PHOTOGRAPHY; POLARIZED LIGHT; STEREOSCOPY; VECTOGRAPH in the McGraw-Hill Encyclopedia of Science and Technology.   □

LANDAU, Lev Davydovich
Russian physicist
Born Jan. 22, 1908, Baku, Azerbaijan, U.S.S.R.

L ANDAU'S THEORETICAL explanation of the seemingly paradoxical properties of liquid helium and his investigations of condensed matter—that is, matter in the solid and liquid state—won for him the 1962 Nobel Prize in physics. Since earlier attempts at explaining the properties of liquids had met with notable lack of success, Landau's achievement in clarifying the nature of liquid helium is a landmark in this field of physics.

Helium remains a gas until it has been cooled almost to absolute zero. At 4.2°K it liquefies, and if it is cooled still further to 2.2°K or below it begins to exhibit some paradoxical properties. The form of the liquid above this transition temperature is called helium I; below, it is called helium II. Two phenomena serve as illustrations of its behavior. First, helium II will flow freely through a slit so narrow that it holds back helium I almost completely, a fact discovered in 1937 by Peter L. Kapitza, director of the Institute for Physical Problems in Moscow. He found that in these circumstances helium II seemed to have almost no viscosity at all, and he called this quality superfluidity. Yet viscosity was found when measured by the amount of force required to slide one plate over another at a constant speed when the two plates were separated by a layer of helium II.

The second phenomenon was also discovered by Kapitza. If a flask, which had a movable vane mounted in front of its opening, was filled with liquid helium and placed in a bath of liquid helium, the vane was seen to deflect when the flask was heated by shining light on its blackened surface. Even though this deflection showed that fluid flowed from the hole, the flask remained full. The explanation of such paradoxical behavior was not then known, but it was clear what sort of phenomena were being observed. Any substance exhibits two kinds of properties simultaneously: ordinary properties, explainable on the basis of classical mechanics, and quantum properties, describable only by quantum mechanics. At room temperature the quantum properties are masked by the ordinary properties, but as the temperature is lowered the quantum properties begin to dominate. Since all other substances solidify at low temperature,

where they exhibit their quantum properties, helium II was evidently the only known example of a liquid whose properties were the reflection of quantum effects. Such were the experimental observations that Landau sought to explain.

In 1940–41 Landau published his theory to

explain the behavior of helium II. While other theoreticians were directing their attention toward the individual atoms, he considered the liquid as a whole. His theory is necessarily stated in quantum-mechanical language, yet some idea of its implications can be gained through an analogy using a two-fluid model. In this analogy helium II is composed of two components that move through one another completely without drag. The "normal component" is like any ordinary viscous fluid; the "superfluid component" moves as if it were without viscosity. The relative proportions of the two components depend on the temperatures. Above 2.2°K there is only the ordinary component present, at 2.2°K the superfluid component begins to form, and as the helium is cooled the proportion of superfluid increases until at 0°K the entire liquid would be composed of superfluid helium.

The first paradoxical property can then be explained in this way. It is the superfluid component only that flows through the narrow slit while the ordinary component is held behind, being too viscous to flow through. When the sliding plates are used, it is the viscosity of the ordinary component that is measured. The explanation of the second paradoxical property hinges on an unanticipated prediction. The vane is deflected by a stream of the ordinary component flowing from inside the flask. Heating the flask increased the relative amount of this component, which then ran out. The flask remained full because the superfluid component from the bath flowed through the outflow back into the flask to replace what had flowed out. If the superfluid component had the properties of ordinary liquids, no such countercurrent would exist. Landau's theory further stated that the countercurrent should follow the laws of an ideal, irrotational, nonviscous fluid flow. A basic theorem of hydrodynamics then explained why the countercurrent did not exert a force on the vane of the flask that would tend to close it against the outward flow of the ordinary component. Until the discovery of the superfluid component of helium II, no such liquid was known to exist.

In addition to resolving these paradoxical behaviors, Landau's theory made an unusual prediction. It said that helium II should support the propagation of two types of waves: One type was the easily observed sound waves; by analogy the other type was called "second sound." These waves proved impossible to observe experimentally until it was recognized that they were really heat waves. Second sound is now used as a tool to investigate the properties of helium II.

In 1930 Landau published a quantum-theoretical study of the behavior of free electrons in a magnetic field that was internationally recognized as contributing to the understanding of the properties of metals. In 1935 he added to the understanding of ferromagnetism by a mathematical explanation of the behavior of atomic magnets in substances such as iron.

In the 1950s Landau investigated a rare isotope of helium of atomic weight 3 (natural helium has an atomic weight of 4). Study of this isotope has been very difficult because it is formed at extremely low temperatures, that is, less than 1/10 of a degree above absolute zero. From 1956 to 1958 Landau published his theories concerning the properties of this isotope. The most important property that he predicted for it was a new type of wave propagation, called zero sound.

At the age of 14 Landau entered Baku University, from which he transferred to Leningrad University, graduating with his doctorate in 1927 at the age of 19. He studied abroad during 1929–31, visiting Germany, Switzerland, England, and Denmark, where he studied under Niels Bohr. He was head of the theoretical department of the Ukrainian Physicotechnical Institute at Kharkov from 1932 to 1937. In 1937 he became head of the theoretical department of the Institute for Physical Problems of the Academy of Science of the U.S.S.R. in Moscow. He was elected a foreign associate of the U.S. National Academy of Sciences in 1960.

In 1962, in addition to receiving the Nobel Prize, Landau shared with E. M. Lifshitz the Lenin Science Prize for their *Course in Theoretical Physics*. This is being translated, with seven volumes published in 1965. Landau's more important articles were published as *Selected Scientific Papers* (1964).

For background information *see* SUPERFLUIDITY; HELIUM, LIQUID in the McGraw-Hill Encyclopedia of Science and Technology. □

LAWRENCE, Ernest Orlando
American physicist
Born Aug. 8, 1901, Canton, S.Dak., U.S.A.
Died Aug. 27, 1958, Palo Alto, Calif., U.S.A.

LAWRENCE'S INVENTION of the cyclotron gave to science the means to produce streams of highly energetic atomic particles, such as protons, deuterons, and alpha particles. These particle streams were used to obtain nuclear reactions that yielded basic information on the nature of atomic nuclei and resulted in the formation of artificial radioactive elements. For the discovery, development, and use of the cyclotron, Lawrence was awarded the 1939 Nobel Prize in physics.

In the early 1920s Ernest Rutherford had bombarded atomic nuclei with alpha particles,

but these particles were not sufficiently energetic to enter into direct interaction with the nuclei. George Gamow, in 1928, attempted to bombard nuclei with protons, but there were no methods of particle acceleration at that time capable of producing the required energies. Then R. Wideroe, in 1928, reported successful acceleration of sodium and potassium ions to energies of twice an applied voltage of 25,000 volts. His equipment consisted of a rudimentary linear accelerator formed by two in-line tubular electrodes across which an oscillating electric field was applied.

After reading Wideroe's paper, Lawrence conceived the idea of a magnetic field to deflect ionized particles in circular paths so that they would return to the original electrode, thus permitting reuse of the electric field in the gap and building up energy by repeated acceleration in an orbit. He found that the equations of motion predicted a constant period of revolution, independent of energy, so that particles could be accelerated almost indefinitely, in resonance with an oscillatory electric field. This discovery is the basis of the principle of cyclotron resonance.

In the spring of 1930, Lawrence suggested to N. E. Edlefson, a doctoral student of his at the University of California at Berkeley, that he set up an experiment to test his ideas. This initial attempt to produce a magnetic resonance accelerator failed, although Lawrence and Edlefson presented a report in September, 1930, announcing this new principle of particle acceleration, which later proved so successful.

The basic operation of a cyclotron is as follows: Ionized atomic particles are admitted to the central region of a flat horizontal circular metal drum. The circular drum is divided into two semicircular units, or "dees" (so named for their apparent shape), which are separated by a small gap over which a high (radio) frequency electric field may be applied. A fixed magnetic field produced by an electromagnet is introduced in the vertical direction, perpendicular to the plane and over the entire area of the "dees." The ionized particles are accelerated across the gap to one of the "dees" by the electric field. Once beyond the gap, particles acquire no more energy, but the effect of the steady magnetic field causes the particles to move in a circular path concentric with the center of the two "dees." This motion brings the particles to the gap at the opposite side at a time when the electric field has been reversed. The particles are then accelerated across that gap into the other "dee," where they also undergo a circular orbit. This orbit has a larger radius than the previous one, but because the particles now have greater energy and are moving with a greater velocity, they remain in that "dee" for as long as they did in the other one before reaching the gap. Acceleration across the gap occurs once more and the process continues with the particles describing a spiral path over many hundreds of orbits until the outer radius of the "dees" is reached and they are extracted through a porthole.

Another doctoral student of Lawrence's, M. S. Livingston, undertook the problem of achieving resonance acceleration. Using a 4-inch pole diameter electromagnet and a radio-frequency oscillator producing a peak voltage of about 160 volts, Livingston, early in 1931, was able to extract molecular hydrogen ions that had an energy of 13,000 electron volts.

With this initial success, Lawrence supervised the construction of a larger instrument. By the end of 1931, the first cyclotron capable of producing particles energetic enough to cause nuclear disintegration was in operation, yielding protons with 1.2×10^6 electron volts energy. This achievement was most significant because it provided a method for particle acceleration unlimited by the electrical breakdown of dielectrics and gases, thus avoiding a limitation of all previous accelerators. Lawrence continued to enlarge the size of his cyclotrons—a later one employed the use of an 85-ton electromagnet and yielded protons with 11×10^6 electron volts energy—so that higher-energy particles thus produced would be more effective in the study of nuclear reactions and in the production of new artificial radioactive isotopes and elements.

In awarding Lawrence the Nobel Prize in physics, the award committee cited his invention as a research tool of immeasurable importance not only in physics but in chemistry and the biological and medical sciences. In addition, the principle of a magnetic resonance accelerator, involved in the development of the cyclotron, has been used in more recent forms of accelerators producing much higher-energy particles that are being used to unlock still further some of the mysteries of the atomic nucleus.

A son of the superintendent of schools in Canton, S.Dak., Lawrence received a bachelor's degree from the University of South Dakota in 1922 and a Ph.D. from Yale University in 1925. He remained at Yale until 1928, when he went to Berkeley as an associate professor. In 1930, at the age of 29, he was promoted to full professor. Six years later he became director of the Radiation Laboratory at Berkeley, a post he held until his death. The Radiation Laboratory encompassed the cyclotron facilities as well as those of later-model high-energy particle accelerators. He was a key figure in the U.S. scientific effort and in the development of the atomic bomb during World War II, having been a program chief in the Office of Scientific Research and Development. In 1957 Lawrence received the Enrico Fermi Award of the U.S. Atomic Enery Commission. Outside the field of basic science, Lawrence invented and held the basic patent for a color television picture tube.

For background information *see* CYCLOTRON; PARTICLE ACCELERATOR in the McGraw-Hill Encyclopedia of Science and Technology.   □

★ **LAX, Benjamin**
American physicist
Born Dec. 29, 1915, Miskolz, Hungary

ALMOST AT the start of his career as a physicist, Lax became interested in the behavior of matter in magnetic fields. Borrowing techniques he developed in working with microwave gas discharges, Lax pioneered in the important phenomenon of cyclotron resonance in semiconductors. He then extended these techniques to high magnetic fields and to the infrared and opened up a new field of modern magnetooptics in semiconductors and semimetals. For "fundamental contributions to microwave and infrared spectroscopy of semi-

conductors," he received the 1960 Oliver E. Buckley Prize of the American Physical Society.

As a graduate student at the Massachusetts Institute of Technology, Lax was intrigued by an interesting resonance phenomenon of an electron plasma in magnetic fields. Immediately he conceived a thesis project in which he would study the effect of magnetic fields on the microwave breakdown of gases. This proved to be a successful thesis and provided a springboard to postdoctoral study of the behavior of plasmas in magnetic fields at the Air Force Cambridge Research Laboratories in 1950–51. During the course of this research, Lax developed theoretical techniques for gyrotropic media that were later applied to the study of ferrites in wave guides and microwave cavities. Simultaneously, he returned to his first love after reading a proposal by William Shockley for carrying out cyclotron resonance experiments in germanium. He recognized that in order to do the experiments they would have to be modified and would require breakdown techniques at low temperatures very similar to those used in gas discharges. In 1953 he and his colleagues discovered cyclotron resonance by this method and were the first to demonstrate the important anisotropy of the phenomenon as predicted by Shockley. This resulted in a veritable explosion of theoretical and experimental investigations that uncovered the band structure of germanium and silicon and led to the basic understanding of these and other related semiconductors.

Since germanium and silicon were very pure, they succumbed easily to low-temperature microwave techniques. In order to extend cyclotron resonance to metals and other semiconductors, new techniques were necessary. Among these were the nonresonant phenomena that R. N. Dexter and Lax observed in bismuth and the infrared experiments of high field resonance in InSb and InAs. A team at the MIT Lincoln Laboratory under Lax's direction developed pulsed magnetic fields and high-speed–low-temperature detectors in the string and beeswax tradition. The important results of these early experiments were theoretically interpreted in subsequent years and led to a variety of new experiments on oscillatory magnetooptical phenomena, including magnetoabsorption, magnetoreflection, and Faraday rotation techniques, which produced new understanding of the properties of electrons in semiconductors and semimetals.

As early as 1955 Lax realized that the creation of continuous magnetic fields of the order of 250,000 gauss or more would open up a new era of research in basic physics. Togther with his colleagues, he convinced the Air Force to establish a National Magnet Laboratory at MIT for this purpose. In 1960, after the contract was awarded to build this Laboratory, he became its director. A great deal of research using high magnetic fields in a variety of phenomena including optical, magnetic, ultrasonic, and other techniques flourished there. With the advent of superconducting magnets, research with high magnetic fields of the order of 100,000 gauss and under became very fashionable.

Settling in the United States in 1926, Lax in 1941 received a bachelor's degree in mechanical engineering at Cooper Union in New York. In World War II he was a radar officer assigned to the MIT Radiation Laboratory. He received his Ph.D. in physics at MIT in 1949. From 1949 to 1951 he carried on research in microwave gas discharge for the geophysical directorate of the Cambridge Research Center. In 1951 he joined the Solid State Group at the MIT Lincoln Laboratory, becoming head of the group in 1955 and head of the Solid State Division when it was established in 1958. From 1964 to 1965 he was associate director of the MIT Lincoln Laboratory. In 1965 he was appointed professor at MIT, continuing his duties as director of the MIT National Magnet Laboratory.

For background information *see* CYCLOTRON RESONANCE EXPERIMENTS; SEMICONDUCTOR in the McGraw-Hill Encyclopedia of Science and Technology.   □

★ **LEBLOND, Charles Philippe**
Canadian anatomist
Born Feb. 5, 1910, Lille, France

THE DEVELOPMENT and use of radioautography by Leblond and his associates in the study of histology—or microscopic anatomy—helped to change a descriptive science to one that can be described as dynamic. By this method, biological substances prepared in a radioactive form may be traced in and out of cells. It has become possible to follow the secretion of some hormones and the building of some enzymes within cells and thus to open new frontiers of cell biology.

The technique known as radioautography or autoradiography was initiated in 1925 by Lacassagne, when he placed sections of radioactive liver and other tissues in contact with a photographic plate. The developed plate showed a dark shadow corresponding to every radioactive area. But the shadow was hazy, and little use was made of the technique. In 1946, soon after returning to McGill University in Montreal from war service overseas, Leblond, in collaboration with L. F. Bélanger, was able to improve the resolution of the method. Photographic emulsion was melted and poured on the tissue section so as to make a thin coat that hardened as it cooled and acted as a photographic plate to the radioactive parts of the tissue section. After development, a shadow was seen in direct contact with—and over—the radioactive areas; under the high power of the microscope, the shadow proved to consist of tiny photographic grains that could readily be related to cells or parts of cells. Here then was a practical use for radioautography. Over the years, refinements in technique were made (it is now used in the electron microscope) and it became widely utilized in Leblond's and other laboratories as a tool in cell study.

The first element used with the new technique was radioiodine, which was shown to be taken up in the thyroid gland and permitted study of the function of its cells. As other radioactive elements became available, Leblond and his associates were able to reach the cells of many more parts of the body. Thus, investigations carried out with radioactive phosphate emphasized the speed with which ions diffuse through the body, even entering cartilage and bone. Within less than a minute, labeled phosphate was precipitated as bone salt in areas of bone growth. An incidental observation revealed that accretion of bone salt did not occur along the whole outer surface of long bones, contrary to beliefs dating from the 17th century. It could now be demonstrated that in subepiphyseal portions of this surface growth occurred on the inside rather than on the outside, a finding that made it possible to explain why bones can elongate and yet retain harmonious proportions.

More complex radioactive substances, labeled amino acids, were then used to discover where protein synthesis took place and how some of the new proteins migrated. In the cells of the thyroid gland it was found that the label was taken up as protein at the base of the cells, then migrated to the Golgi region, and, finally, was secreted as the so-called colloid. A similar sequence observed in pancreatic cells could be timed. The new protein stayed an average of 6 minutes at the base and 12 minutes in the Golgi region. Within the next 1–3 hours, the molecules were secreted to the outside as pancreatic juice enzymes.

Leblond emphasized not only the speed but also the uniformity in the behavior of substances in cells. In the past, it was assumed that thyroid cells were cyclic; that is, sometimes they secreted colloid and other times they reabsorbed the colloid to release it as thyroid hormone to the circulation. However, when the synthesis of the colloid protein was investigated by radioautography in young animals, all cells were building the precursor into protein; furthermore, counts of photographic grains revealed that they all were doing this at the same rate. Using radioiodine, Leblond found that the rate at which iodine combined with colloid proteins was uniform throughout the gland. These two functions, as well as the release of hormone to the outside, were carried by all cells simultaneously and at the same rate.

Further investigation of protein synthesis throughout the body by radioautography showed that it took place in all cells (with rare exceptions, for example, red blood cells), although the rate varied widely from cell type to cell type. The synthesis of protein in many cells that were believed not to secrete protein suggested that the newly formed proteins have a rapid turnover within these cells. Such renewal of proteins would in fact take place in all live cells. Similarly, when the synthesis of the nucleic acid RNA was examined after injection of its precursor H^3-cytidine, it was again found that all or nearly all cells synthesized RNA continuously. Recent radioautographic investigations of carbohydrate macromolecules seemed to indicate a continuous production of carbohydrate in all cells as well.

These varying syntheses (protein, RNA, carbohydrate, and so forth) take place in different sites within cells: carbohydrate macromolecules are synthesized in the Golgi region (except glycogen), RNA in the nucleus. As for protein, Leblond and collaborators described its synthesis not only in the cytoplasm but also in the nuclei of all cells. Thus renewal of the various types of molecules present in all cells is indicated, even those making up the cell framework. Such a continuous supply of new molecules would be provided to replace any molecule damaged by a nocuous agent.

As DNA precursors became available, such as phosphate-32 around 1946, then C^{14}-adenine, and recently H^3-thymidine, Leblond and associates reported sharp differences among the degrees of DNA synthesis in various cell populations. The cell populations in which radioautography indicated synthesis of new DNA consisted of cells that were renewed at a rapid rate. For example, the group found that the intestinal epithelium is replaced every 2–4 days by migration of the cells to the surface and subsequent loss into the lumen. Similar findings were obtained in all epithelia exposed to digestive enzymes or to the outside air, as well as in blood cells. In contrast, some cells, such as neurons, do not renew themselves. (However, such cells often show a particularly active renewal of their component macromolecules.)

Thus, by means of radioautography, a time dimension has been introduced into histology. Many structures heretofore considered to be static have been shown to be swarming with migrating molecules and cells, and new insight into their function has been gained.

While studying toward the M.D. degree at the University of Paris, Leblond found a method to stain vitamin C in tissues. He taught histology at the University of Paris Medical School for a year, then went to the United States as a Rockefeller fellow, returning to Paris to work with radioiodine provided by Joliot-Curie's group. In 1941, he went to McGill University in Montreal, from which he took leave in 1943 to do personnel selection for the Free French army. After the war, he returned to McGill University to the department of anatomy, which he later headed. He was elected a fellow of the Royal Societies of London and Canada and was awarded the latter's Flavelle Medal in 1961.

For background information *see* AUTORADIOGRAPHY; HISTOLOGY in the McGraw-Hill Encyclopedia of Science and Technology.   ☐

☆ **LEDERBERG, Joshua**
American geneticist
Born May 23, 1925, Montclair, N.J., U.S.A.

For his discoveries concerning genetic recombination and the organization of the genetic material of bacteria, Lederberg received the 1958 Nobel Prize in physiology or medicine, which he shared with E. L. Tatum and G. W. Beadle.

At first with Tatum, and later with other

coworkers, Lederberg pioneered in the field of bacterial genetics. As a graduate student in Yale's department of microbiology in the mid-1940s, he collaborated with Tatum in the discovery that bacterial strains could be crossed to produce an offspring containing a new combination of genetic factors. Prior to this discovery, scientists had known little about the bacterial genetic mechanism, and many had even doubted that bacteria possessed a genetic mechanism similar to that of higher organisms. Because of their simple structure and rapid growth, bacteria now afford geneticists a fruitful field for study.

Later, at the University of Wisconsin, Lederberg showed that bacterial genetic material was exchanged not only by conjugation (when the entire complement of chromosomes is transferred from one bacterial cell to another) but also by transduction (when only fragments are transferred). He did this by introducing bits of genetic material into the bacterial body and found that they became part of the genetic material of the bacterial cell, thereby altering its constitution. This was the first manipulation of any organism's genetic material, and it has opened prospects of far-reaching genetic experimentation.

Lederberg also worked with the breeding and crossbreeding of microbes to produce new strains. One experiment involved the pairing of bacteria resistant to penicillin with others resistant to streptomycin. The new strains that developed proved to be resistant to both antibiotics. He proved, too, that the disease-producing power of bacteria could be increased by genetic processes and that a virulent organism could be made comparatively weak.

Lederberg's technique of replica plating to isolate nutritional mutants of a bacteria species, *Escherichia coli,* has been used by many investigators in the field of bacterial genetics. This technique consists of exposing a suspension of bacteria to some mutant-inducing agent such as ultraviolet radiation. A sample is taken from the suspension and spread with a sterile wire loop over the surface of nutrient agar, which is a complete medium. After incubating the dish of nutrient agar and inoculum, the exact positions of the bacterial colonies on the plate are noted. A sterile piece of velvet is gently pressed to the surface of this plate and then pressed to the surface of a plate of minimal agar medium. (Minimal agar consists of inorganic salts and glucose that permit the growth of the standard *Escherichia coli* strains.) After incubation, the positions of the bacterial colonies that appear on the minimal agar plate are compared with the positions of the colonies on the original plate. The failure of organisms to develop on the minimal agar plate is an indication of nutritional mutants because they were incapable of growing on an inorganic salts-glucose medium, which

they had been able to do before exposure to the ultraviolet radiation.

Lederberg received his B.A. at Columbia College in 1944, then entered Columbia University's College of Physicians and Surgeons. After two years he transferred to Yale, where he received his Ph.D. in microbiology in 1948 under Tatum. From 1947 to 1954 he taught at the University of Wisconsin, becoming a full professor in 1954. In 1958 he was appointed professor of genetics at the Stanford University Medical School. He became director of the Kennedy Laboratories for Molecular Medicine there in 1962. He was elected to the National Academy of Sciences in 1957.

For background information *see* BACTERIAL GENETICS in the McGraw-Hill Encyclopedia of Science and Technology. □

☆ **LEE, Tsung-Dao**

American physicist
Born Nov. 24, 1926, Shanghai, China

IN ADDITION to the work on parity nonconservation with C. N. Yang that earned him the Nobel Prize in physics in 1957 (*see* YANG, CHEN NING), Lee worked in statistical mechanics, astrophysics, nuclear and subnuclear physics, field theory, and other disciplines.

The son of a businessman, Lee received his secondary and undergraduate schooling in China and went to the University of Chicago in 1946 on a Chinese government scholarship. There he worked under Enrico Fermi and in 1950 received his Ph.D. in physics. At Chicago also he met his countryman and future collaborator, C. N. Yang. Following a short period as a research associate in astronomy at Yerkes Observatory, Lee became a research associate and lecturer in physics at the University of California, Berkeley. He was then offered a membership at the Institute for Advanced Study, Princeton, N.J., which he accepted in 1951. In 1953 he became assistant professor of physics at Columbia University; in 1955 he was made associate professor, and in 1956 full professor, the youngest then on the faculty. He returned to the Institute for Advanced Study in 1960 to assume the post of professor of physics there. In 1963 he became professor of physics at Columbia University. He was elected to the National Academy of Sciences in 1964.   □

★ **LEFSCHETZ, Solomon**
American mathematician
Born Sept. 3, 1884, Moscow, Russia

T HE STUDY of the *Traité d'Analyse* of C. E. Picard and *Fonctions algébriques de deux variables* by Picard and G. Smart drew Lefschetz to complex algebraic geometry and the work of the great Italian geometers G. Castelnuovo, F. Enriques, and F. Severi. About a century ago, G. F. B. Riemann had organized the theory of complex algebraic curves $f(x,y) = 0$ around his profound discovery of an associated topological structure, the famous Riemann surface. A similar attempt was made by Picard, with an important aside by J. H. Poincaré, but practically without topology, to extend Riemann's work to surfaces of two or more dimensions. By a vigorous utilization of topology, Lefschetz, between 1913 and 1922, succeeded to a large extent in closing the gap in their work, and in particular establishing a bridge through a brilliant result of Severi, with the parallel geometric results of the Italian school.

From 1923 to 1942 Lefschetz was principally occupied with the development and evident extension of algebraic topology. He was led to this vast operation by the fascinating fixed-point problem. Let a figure F undergo a transformation t into itself. Is there at least one point of F untouched by t? For a very wide class of cases, Lefschetz discovered a magic number $N(t)$ such that if $N(t) \neq 0$ there is at least one fixed point. A simple but very suggestive illustration pro-

vides much insight into what is involved (see figure). Let AB be a line segment in the plane, and $ABCD$ the square based on it. Mark a point

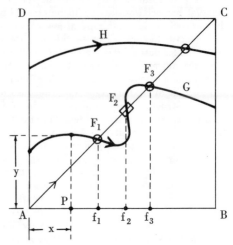

Lefschetz's approach to the fixed point problem.

P of AB by the length $x = AP$. A transformation t assigns to x a value $y = tx$. Erect over P a segment of length y. As x describes AB, y describes a curve G and its intersections F_1, F_2, . . . with the diagonal AC projected back on AB as f_1, f_2, . . . comprises the desired fixed points. The actual number of the points F_1, F_2, . . . does not give the right answer, since, for example, they are not the same for the curves G and H. The right number is obtained as follows: Count the number r of crossings from right to left: 2 for G (marked with a circle on the diagram) and the number l of crossings from left to right for G (marked with a square on the diagram). The appropriate number in this instance is $N(t) = r - l = 1$. The all-important property is that by varying the transformation t so that G becomes H, $N(t)$ is unchanged—still 1 for H. This guarantees that t and all such transformations have at least one fixed point. Examples: sliding a disk on itself yields $N(t) = 1$, sliding a sphere on itself (for example, by a rotation) yields $N(t) = 2$. Hence these slidings always leave some point fixed. This very general result includes a host of previous special cases, notably famous fixed-point theorems due to L. E. J. Brouwer (around 1910). To establish the $N(t)$ property in its full generality Lefschetz had to create a full-fledged intersection theory, which has been at the root of a good part of the modern theory of algebraic topology.

After 1942 Lefschetz was largely occupied with the formation of research groups devoted to the key subject of differential equations, principally with the object of improving the research position of the United States in this topic, and also encouraging the younger generation to follow it.

Brought up in Paris, Lefschetz went to the United States in 1905. He received his Ph.D. in mathematics at Clark University in 1911, then taught at Nebraska (1911–13), Kansas (1913–24), and Princeton (1924–53), from which he retired in 1953 as research professor and chairman of the department of mathematics. Elected to the National Academy of Sciences in 1925, in 1964 he was awarded the National Medal of Science by President Johnson.

Lefschetz wrote *L'Analysis Situs et la Géométrie Algébrique* (1924), *Topology* (1930), *Algebraic Topology* (1942), *Introduction to Topology* (1949), *Algebraic Geometry* (1952), *Differential Equations: Geometric Theory* (1958), *Stability Theory by Liapunov's Direct Method*, with J. P. Lasalle (1961), and *Stability Theory of Nonlinear Control Systems* (1965).

For background information *see* GEOMETRY, RIEMANNIAN; TOPOLOGY in the McGraw-Hill Encyclopedia of Science and Technology.   □

★ LEVINE, Philip
American serologist
Born Aug. 10, 1900, Russia

WHILE STUDYING the cause of hemolytic transfusion reactions in pregnant or recently pregnant mothers, Levine discovered the phenomenon of transplacental isoimmunization as the fundamental process in the pathogenesis of a disease of the fetus and newborn called erythroblastosis fetalis, or hemolytic disease of the newborn. The main feature of the disease was the destruction (hemolysis) of red blood cells of the fetus or the newborn. The blood factor of the red cells involved was later termed Rh. The husband and fetus proved to be Rh positive while the mother was Rh negative. Rh antibodies were responsible for severe intragroup (ABO) compatible transfusion reactions and for the destruction of the red cells of the fetus and newborn. Thus the basis was laid down for prevention of severe transfusion reactions and therapy

of the affected infant by replacement transfusion with Rh-negative blood.

No two human bloods, except those of identical twins, are alike in their antigenic constitutions. In 1901, Karl Landsteiner showed that blood transfusions could be considered safe if recipient and donor belonged to the same blood group—O, A, B, or AB. However, there were exceptions in patients receiving repeated transfusions and in some pregnant women at the very first transfusion. The Rh factor is independent of the four blood groups. In a white population, 85% are Rh positive, while 15% are Rh negative. The latter are susceptible to isoimmunization if they receive Rh-positive blood by intramuscular injection or transfusion, or by the passage of fetal red cells during pregnancy or at delivery. Isoimmunization is manifested by the production of Rh antibodies capable of reacting with Rh-positive blood but not with Rh-negative blood.

Hemolytic transfusion reactions with failure of survival of the transfused red cells was known to occur in patients receiving a series of transfusions. Apparently, the recipient was producing antibodies specific for some blood factor lacking in the recipient but present in the donor(s). When the hemolytic reaction occurred at the first transfusion in recently pregnant women, the antibody production must have been induced as a result of passage of intact fetal red blood cells during the course of one or more normal pregnancies and deliveries. The passage of fetal red cells into the maternal circulation is a physiologic event occurring in all normal pregnancies. Levine assumed that in some Rh-negative women there was sufficient antigenic stimulus for antibody production to occur. In other words, the combined effect of one or more pregnancies and deliveries sufficed to provide enough "foreign" blood in small quantities to induce production of antibodies just as did a transfusion of a much larger quantity.

In 1940 Landsteiner and A. S. Wiener discovered a relationship of human and rhesus cells, and hence the term "Rh" was born. The antibody produced by the pregnant Rh-negative women appeared to reveal the same specificity as the experimental sera of Landsteiner and Wiener.

The maternal anti-Rh was then transported across the placental barrier to react with and destroy fetal red cells in utero, at times causing stillbirths. If the hemolytic process was not so severe, the hemolysis continued into the neonatal period and the infants soon developed anemia and jaundice. The jaundice was the end result of red blood cell destruction with the appearance and accumulation of bilirubin—the end product of blood destruction. Bilirubin has an affinity to certain brain cells, and if the infant is not treated by replacement transfusion, the result is brain damage (kernicterus).

Levine's first studies were carried out in 1937–42 at Beth Israel Hospital, Newark, N.J. Numerous specimens from all over the United States were submitted. When these were tested with human anti-Rh, more than 90% of mothers of erythroblastotic infants were found to be Rh negative, their husbands and affected infants being Rh positive. Many Rh-negative women had anti-Rh antibodies in their sera. Later, other workers found another form of the Rh antibody in the sera of all Rh-negative mothers of affected infants. Confirmation of Levine's findings came from all parts of the world.

Other blood factors were discovered by Levine: s allelic to S, k (Cellano) allelic to K (Kell), and Mi^a (Miltenberger), all capable of inducing transfusion reactions and erythroblastosis. Levine also observed Tj^a, belonging to the P system. Two of the blood factors, s and Mi^a, belong to the MNS system.

Levine graduated from the College of the City of New York in 1919 and from Cornell University Medical College in 1923. During the period from 1923 to 1925 he described the first case of a dangerous universal donor and worked in the field of allergy (atopic reagins). From 1925 to 1932, he was associated with Karl Landsteiner at the Rockefeller Institute and, in joint work, discovered the blood factors M, N, P, and others not identified by name. On the faculty of the University of Wisconsin from 1932 to 1935, Levine studied the specificity of bacteriophage action in the *Salmonella* and *Shigella* group of organisms. From 1934 to 1944 he was bacteriologist and transfusionist at Beth Israel Hospital, Newark, N.J. In 1944 he became director of immunohematology at Ortho Research Foundation, Raritan, N.J. Among other honors, Levine received the Passano Foundation Award in 1951.

For background information *see* BLOOD GROUPS in the McGraw-Hill Encyclopedia of Science and Technology.   □

☆ LIBBY, Willard Frank

American chemist
Born Dec. 17, 1908, Grand Valley, Colo., U.S.A.

WHILE STUDYING the effects of cosmic radiation on the Earth and the Earth's atmosphere, Libby conceived the method of radiocarbon dating that has enabled scientists to determine the absolute ages of such organic materials as wood, charcoal, parchment, shells, and skeletal remains formed within the past 50,000 years. For this achievement he received the 1960 Nobel Prize in chemistry.

In 1939 Serge Korff of New York University discovered that cosmic rays, colliding with air nuclei at the top of the terrestrial atmosphere, generated a shower of secondary neutrons. These neutrons, colliding in turn with the abundant nitrogen isotope N^{14}, form the radioactive carbon isotope C^{14}. Spreading through the atmosphere, the radiocarbon atoms, along with the atoms of ordinary carbon, are absorbed by plants through photosynthesis and are ultimately assimilated by animals as well. Thus all living tissues, and all organic remains, exhibit a measure of radioactivity.

Libby assumed that the average intensity of cosmic radiation had not varied over many thousands of years. He also assumed that the radiocarbon generated by the cosmic radiation spread relatively rapidly and evenly throughout the biosphere. If cosmic rays had been bombarding the atmosphere for a very long time in terms of the lifetime of radiocarbon (radiocarbon has a half-life of 5,730 years), he reasoned, the quantity of radiocarbon on Earth must be steady, the continuous creation of new radiocarbon being balanced by its continuous disintegration. Knowing the rate at which radiocarbon atoms were formed, he calculated the total quantity of radiocarbon, the proportion of radiocarbon to ordinary carbon (about one atom of the former to 10^{12} of the latter), and, finally, the specific radioactivity of living carbon. If his two initial assumptions were correct, it followed that the specific radioactivity of ancient living matter was the same as that of matter living today. Since the assimilation of radiocarbon ceases at death, and since the decay of the already assimilated radiocarbon proceeds at a definite rate, Libby reasoned that the level of radioactivity in any organic material should point clearly to the time

of the organism's death. The problem was to detect and measure the faint beta-ray emission of the decaying radiocarbon.

In 1947 Libby and his associates at the University of Chicago's Institute for Nuclear Studies built an extremely sensitive Geiger counter. To reduce background radiation from terrestrial sources, Libby surrounded the counter with an iron shield 8 in. thick. To eliminate the background from highly penetrating cosmic radiation, he constructed, within the iron shielding and surrounding the sample counter, a permanent layer of Geiger counters in tangential contact with one another. These were wired to turn off the central sample counter during the thousandth of a second that any one of them registered the passage of a cosmic-ray meson. To achieve a maximum count rate, Libby converted the carbon-dating samples into pure carbon (lampblack), with which he lined the sample counter's inner wall. Later it was found that even better results were obtained by converting the samples into a gas (carbon dioxide or acetylene) and using that as the counter's filling gas. With this equipment, and using samples containing up to 5 gr of carbon, Libby measured radioactivity registering from 75 counts per minute for living carbon to 0.07 counts per minute for 57,000-year-old carbon.

Libby first tested the accuracy of the radiocarbon-dating process on objects of known age such as the heartwood of a giant sequoia tree and timbers and wooden artifacts from Egyptian tombs. Passing beyond the historical period, he and others obtained satisfactory results on materials of geology and prehistoric archeology whose ages were known with a high degree of probability. Thus Libby's technique proved reliable for the past 5,000 years and probably for as far back as radiocarbon could be measured—about 50,000 years. A later improvement in the method of measurement increased the potential range to 70,000 years. Radiocarbon dating has produced important new data about world-wide climate changes, recent geologic events, and man's prehistoric development.

A farmer's son, Libby majored in chemistry at the University of California at Berkeley, where he received his B.S. in 1931 and his Ph.D. in 1933. He taught at Berkeley until 1940. During World War II (1941–45), he worked in the War Research Division at Columbia University on the development of the gaseous-diffusion process for separating the isotopes of uranium—an essential step in the production of the atomic bomb. From 1945 to 1954 he was professor of chemistry at the Institute for Nuclear Studies at the University of Chicago. In 1954 President Dwight D. Eisenhower appointed him to the U.S. Atomic Energy Commission, on which he served until 1959. In that year he joined the faculty of the University of California at Los Angeles. He was elected to the National Academy of Sciences in 1950.

Libby wrote *Radiocarbon Dating* (1952; 2d ed. 1955).

For background information *see* RADIOCARBON DATING in the McGraw-Hill Encyclopedia of Science and Technology.   □

★ **LIGHTHILL, Michael James**
British physicist
Born Jan. 23, 1924, Paris, France

LIGHTHILL CONTRIBUTED to the aerodynamics of high-speed aircraft and missiles, to the theory of jet noise, and to the theory of waves in general and particularly of shock waves. He substantially enlarged the range of nonlinear problems for which effective calculations can be conveniently carried out. Such calculations have helped to improve aircraft and missile performance and limit jet engine and supersonic-boom noise.

Before the 1940s physical calculations were perforce confined almost entirely to problems governed by linear equations (for example, linear differential equations). A linear equation is one such that from any collection of simple solutions a huge range of more complicated ones can immediately be written down by adding up those simple solutions in almost arbitrary proportions. Thus, the construction of a solution fulfilling an essential subsidiary condition (for example, on the initial configuration of the system) is made feasible.

Gas motions governed by equations including important nonlinear terms (representing, for example, convection of momentum) were Lighthill's main interest. Although these problems could not be simply "linearized" by ignoring all the nonlinear terms, Lighthill used to the maximum extent "tricks" that transformed the equations into linear equations but retained the essential features of the solutions. Other (usually numerical) methods of calculation had proved inconveniently special, because they obtained only one solution at a time. By transformation, even a rather complicated one, into a linear equation, much more information about solutions in general could be derived.

In certain problems of transonic aerodynamics, a linear equation is obtained if position is regarded as a function of air velocity rather than the other way around (the "hodograph" transformation). Lighthill demonstrated how solutions of these linear equations have to be continued around singular points if solutions representing real flows (for example, through the throat section of a supersonic wind tunnel) are to be obtained.

Shock waves are nonlinear phenomena, namely, pressure discontinuities resulting from the higher-pressure regions in a progressive wave overtaking lower-pressure regions. In the supersonic aerodynamics of straight, sweptback and "delta" wings, and solid and ducted fuselages, Lighthill showed how the forces and shock waves could be calculated in a wide variety of cases. Although the approximations involved in a simple "linearization" break down near a shock wave, or far from the body, or near the fuselage axis, Lighthill used various methods for obtaining approximations that were good everywhere without solving any differential equations but linear ones. The best-known and most general of his techniques for rendering approximations uniformly valid, a method of "straining coordinates," has been widely applied.

Lighthill used different techniques of transformation to linear equations to study diffraction of shock waves around corners and their interaction both with boundary layers (within which solid surfaces cause retardation to adjacent flows) and with turbulence.

The sound radiated into an atmosphere at rest satisfies a certain linear equation, with zero on the right-hand side. To study noise radiated from jets, Lighthill threw the full nonlinear equation satisfied by the jet gases into a form with the same left-hand side but a new nonlinear right-hand side (nonzero in the jet but zero outside it) which he treated as an acoustic source. The turbulent fluctuations in the strength of this source are convected downstream by the jet flow, so that the solutions have the directional characteristics of radiation from a moving source. To a good approximation, the acoustic power radiated varies as the eighth power of the jet speed (Lighthill's Law) up to twice the atmospheric velocity of sound, and thereafter more like the jet speed cubed, in accordance with the theory's indications. This fact encouraged the development of turbofan engines, which for a given thrust minimize jet speed.

Lighthill also studied boundary layers, shear flows, and gas dissociation in hypersonic flows. He gave a general theory of waves in media whose properties depend on the direction of propagation, applying this and his earlier methods to water waves and magnetohydrodynamic disturbances. For his contributions to the knowledge of the flow of compressible gases and of

the mathematical theory of distributions, Lighthill was awarded in 1964 a Royal Medal of the Royal Society of London.

An engineer's son, Lighthill read mathematics at Cambridge, where he graduated in 1943. During World War II he worked at the Aerodynamics Division of the National Physical Laboratory. After a year as fellow of Trinity College, Cambridge, he went to the University of Manchester in 1946 as senior lecturer, becoming Beyer Professor of Applied Mathematics in 1950. From 1959 to 1964 he was director of the Royal Aircraft Establishment, and then became Royal Society Research Professor in the Imperial College, London.

Lighthill wrote *Higher Approximations in Aerodynamic Theory* (1954), *Introduction to Fourier Analysis and Generalised Functions* (1958), and chapters in *Surveys in Mechanics* (1956) and *Laminar Boundary Layers* (1964).

For background information *see* DIFFERENTIAL EQUATION in the McGraw-Hill Encyclopedia of Science and Technology.   □

★ LIPMANN, Fritz Albert
American biochemist
Born June 12, 1899, Königsberg, Germany

LIPMANN'S MAJOR contribution to biochemistry was the formulation of general rules for the biotechnology of energy transmission. In 1941, he proposed a metabolic dynamo with adenosine triphosphate (ATP) as the general link between energy generation and energy utilization. Through coupling mechanisms, energy-rich or high-energy phosphate bonds, ~P, are produced metabolically and fixed as two phosphoryl groups in ATP, AP~P~P. They carry energy to various foci of utilization. Through the analysis of a number of mechanisms by which metabolically derived phosphate bonds are used for biosynthesis, Lipmann furnished examples for the applicability of this rule.

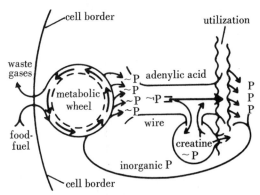

waste gases

cell border

utilization

metabolic wheel

~P adenylic acid

~P

~P   ~P

~P

wire

food-fuel

inorganic P

creatine ~P

cell border

P
P
P
P

The "metabolic wheel" illustrates the biotechnology of energy transmission elucidated by Lipmann.

In the course of studies on the chemical nature of the active acetate, the building block of lipids and an intermediary in carbohydrate oxidation, Lipmann discovered a new coenzyme, the acetyl-carrying coenzyme A (CoA). For this he was awarded a share in the 1953 Nobel Prize for medicine. This discovery was the outcome of initial observations on the oxidation of the 3-carbon compound, pyruvate, a partial reaction in the degradation of 6-carbon sugars. In this study, he used a soluble enzyme extracted from *Lactobacillus delbrueckii*. The oxidation of pyruvate to acetate and CO_2 in this enzyme system proved to be dependent upon the presence of inorganic phosphate. This observation led to the discovery of a novel oxidation product, acetyl phosphate, formed in the following manner:

$$HOPO_3^=$$
$$+$$
$$CH_3 \cdot CO \cdot COOH + O \longrightarrow$$
$$CH_3 \cdot COOPO_3^= + CO_2 + H_2O$$

Pyruvate had been known to yield "active" acetate, and acetyl phosphate appeared to qualify for such a role. It proved to be a precursor that is converted to active acetate by a specifically bacterial enzyme. In animal tissue, however, it proved to be inactive.

Continuing his search, Lipmann used a soluble ATP-dependent enzymatic acetylation of aromatic amines (for example, sulfonamides) as a model reaction for acetate activation, shown in Eq. 1. Isolating such an enzyme from pigeon

liver, he found that it lost its activity on autolysis and dialysis, but activity was restored by the addition of boiled liver extracts. This indicated participation of a heat-stable factor, presumably a coenzyme in the acetyl transfer reaction. The active factor was found in all tissues and seemed to be a general constituent of living organisms. With N. Kaplan, G. D. Novelli, and J. D. Gregory, Lipmann isolated it from pork liver and microbial extracts. The coenzyme turned out to contain the vitamin pantothenic acid. Furthermore, the molecule contained one mole of adenylic acid and two moles of phosphate. It also contained an unidentified SH derivative that turned out to be thioethanolamine (Snell). Analysis and work on biosynthesis yielded the structure for coenzyme A shown in Eq. 2. The SH group carries the acetate in the form of a thioester (Lynen). ATP was found to condense CoA and acetate to acetyl CoA.

Forecasting the role of CoA in fatty acid synthesis, Lipmann and his coworkers observed a condensation of 2-acetyl-CoA to acetoacetyl-CoA and obtained preliminary indications for a synthesis of citric acid from acetyl-CoA and oxalacetate. The discovery of this acetyl-carrying coenzyme promised to open up a large area of metabolic reactions and attracted the attention of many biochemists. Turning to other problems, Lipmann explored the chemical natures of some seemingly unusual phosphate derivatives arising metabolically or through phosphoryl transfer from ATP. Thus, through observations by others on a phosphorolysis of citrulline, he considered the probability of carbamyl phosphate (CMP) representing the metabolically active carbamyl donor:

$$HOPO_3^=$$
$$+$$
$$NH_2CO \cdot NH(CH_2)_3CHNH_2COO^- \longrightarrow$$
$$NH_2COOPO_3^= + NH_2(CH_2)_3CHNH_2COO^-$$

The suspicion proved to be justified. The proof of the metabolic formation and of CMP function, done with Mary Ellen Jones and Leonard Spector, was greatly facilitated by the latter's discovery of an unexpectedly simple method of chemical CMP synthesis through condensation of cyanate and phosphate at room temperature and in excellent yield.

Another unusual phosphate derivative had been indicated through the function of ATP in sulfate activation. Work with Helmut Hilz and Phillips Robbins in this area brought out the

$$CH_3\ COOH + H_2N \overset{ATP}{\longrightarrow} CH_3 \cdot CONH \overline{} + H_2O$$

Equation (1)

$$
\begin{array}{l}
\text{CH}_3 \quad \text{OH} \quad\quad \text{O} \\
\text{CH}_2\text{—C—CH—C—N—CH}_2\text{—CH}_2 \\
\quad\quad | \quad\quad\quad\quad\quad | \quad\quad\quad\quad\quad \text{C—NH—CH}_2\text{—CH}_2\text{—SH} \\
\text{O} \quad \text{CH}_3 \quad\quad \text{H} \quad\quad \text{O} \\
\text{}^-\text{O—P}\rightarrow\text{O} \\
\quad\quad \text{O} \\
\text{}^-\text{O—P}\rightarrow\text{O} \\
\quad\quad \text{O} \\
\text{CH}_2\text{—CH———CH—CH—CH——ADENINE} \\
\quad\quad\quad\quad\quad \text{O} \quad \text{OH} \\
\quad\quad \text{}^-\text{O—P}\rightarrow\text{O} \\
\quad\quad\quad \text{}^-\text{O} \\
\quad\quad\quad\quad \text{O}
\end{array}
$$

Equation 2

existence of a new class of chemical compounds, the mixed anhydrides between phosphate and sulfate; adenosine 5'-phosphosulfate (APS) and 3'-phosphoadenosine-5'-phosphosulfate (PAPS) were identified as "active" sulfates. The latter compound, PAPS, was found in animals and plants to be the common donor in the sulfurylation of mono- or polysaccharides and other sulfate derivatives.

In 1941 Lipmann had proposed that protein synthesis would be driven by energy derived from ATP. This having proven to be true, he returned to the problem of protein synthesis, which he had helped develop and which had remained his major interest.

Lipmann received his medical education in Königsberg. After receiving his medical degree, he turned to the study of chemistry, first in Königsberg and then in Berlin, where he obtained his Ph.D. in the laboratory of Otto Meyerhof. After a year's fellowship in the United States in the laboratory of P. A. Levene at the Rockefeller Institute, New York, he returned to Europe in 1932, where he worked until 1939 in the Biological Institute of the Carlsberg Foundation in Copenhagen, being unable to return to Germany for political reasons. In 1939, just before the start of World War II, he emigrated to the United States and became an American citizen in 1944. From 1939 to 1941 he worked in Vincent du Vigneaud's laboratory at Cornell University Medical College in New York. He moved from there to the Massachusetts General Hospital and Harvard Medical School in Boston until, in 1957, he became a member and professor at the Rockefeller Institute, now the Rockefeller University. He was elected to the National Academy of Sciences in 1950.

For background information see ADENOSINE-TRIPHOSPHATE; COENZYME in the McGraw-Hill Encyclopedia of Science and Technology.   □

★ **LITTLEWOOD, John Edensor**
British mathematician
Born June 9, 1885, Rochester, Kent, England

LITTLEWOOD AND G. H. Hardy were in collaboration—for the most part full time on either side—for the 35 years from 1912 to Hardy's death in 1947. Their work runs to nearly 100 papers. This will be left to the end, and we begin with the rest of Littlewood's work, which also runs to nearly 100 papers, some in collaborations. (He told analyst pupils that they should exercise their mental muscles on a variety of tasks: Ideas from an apparently remote field might prove fruitful.)

His first paper (1907) was on integral functions $f(z)$ of zero order. "The maximum and minimum values $M(r)$ and $m(r)$ of $|f(z)|$ on

$|z| = r$ satisfy $m(r) > M^{1-\epsilon}(r)$ for some arbitrarily large r." The paper shows a predilection, which runs through much of his work, for "elementary" and direct methods.

His most important work before 1914 was his *Converse of Abel's Theorem* (1910). Abel's theorem says that if Σa_n converges to s, then $\Sigma a_n x^n \to s$ as $x \to 1$. Littlewood proves that the converse is true if $n|a_n|$ is bounded, a first result in what has become a large subject called Tauberian theorems. (His further work in this field was all with Hardy.)

A study of the Riemann zeta-function $\zeta(s)$ occupied him at intervals from 1911 to 1927; the results are highly technical. However, in 1914 he published a paper on $\pi(x)$, the number of primes not greater than x [whose theory is bound up with $\zeta(s)$]. The "logarithmic integral" $\mathrm{li}(x)$ is $\int_1^x dt/\log t$, and the difference $\pi(x) - \mathrm{li}(x)$ is positive up to $x = 10^8$. He proves that it must nonetheless change sign sooner or later and, indeed, must do so infinitely often. This created something of a sensation, but he said that he did not consider it one of his best works.

Littlewood wrote on celestial mechanics. A paper (1952) has the "sensational" result that a solar system (idealized) can never "capture" even a grain of dust.

In recent years he wrote on trigonometrical polynomials.

"Most of the functions $\sum_{0}^{n} \pm \cos(m\Theta + \alpha_m)$ have more than An real roots in a period."

"The polynomial $F(\Theta) = \sum_{0}^{n-1} \omega_m e^{m\Theta i}, \omega_m = \exp$

$\{m(m+1)\pi i/n\}$ has the striking property that $|F(\Theta)|$ is asymptotically equal to its mean square $\mu = \sqrt{n}$ except when $|\Theta| < n^{-1/2 + \delta}$."

"No such result can be true for a real polynomial like $\Sigma \cos(m\Theta + \alpha_m)$."

His latest work included five papers in the *Annals of Physics* on adiabatic invariance and a paper settling the long outstanding question of whether all solutions of $\ddot{x} + g(x) = p(t)$ must necessarily be bounded when $p(t)$ is bounded, and $g(x)$ is odd and tends to $+\infty$ as $x \to \infty$, either faster or more slowly than x. The answer in each case is no.

Among Littlewood's collaborations are the following:

1. Important papers with R. E. A. C. Paley are very technical, but it may be mentioned that their "g-function" has a chapter to itself in Zygmund's *Trigonometrical Series*.

2. Papers with A. C. Offord prove that if $\Sigma a_n z^n$ is any integral function of finite nonzero order, then most of the functions $\Sigma \pm a_n z^n$ are exponentially large except in a very uniformly distributed set of exponentially small circles. While the results are clear-cut, the proofs are long and difficult.

3. There are several papers with M. L. Cartwright. One is about van der Pol's equation $\ddot{x} - k(1 - x^2)\dot{x} + x = bk \cos t$ with large k. The proofs are long and difficult, but the results are again clear-cut. For certain values of b there are two sets of periodic stable solutions, of two different periods; there is also an intricate structure of unstable solutions, including a triply infinite set of periodic ones.

As a result of Littlewood's collaboration with Hardy, it has been widely said that there is a special kind of mathematics—"Hardy-Littlewood mathematics," cutting across the usual boundaries of subjects (for example, deducing function-theoretical results from "pure" inequalities—between sums of positive terms—and vice versa).

Their work may be roughly classified under the headings (1) diophantine approximation, (2) Tauberian theorems, (3) Fourier series and associated function theory, (4) the zeta-function, (5) problems of additive number theory, and (6) inequalities.

The first four contain many important, but technical, results.

Their work on problems of additive number theory consists of seven papers (1918–27) about the numbers of representations of integers as sums of (i) kth powers and of (ii) primes. "All large numbers are sums of 19 fourth powers, and almost all are sums of 15." "Assuming a generalized Riemann hypothesis, all large odd numbers are sums of three primes." They produce overwhelming evidence—a mixture of theory and statistics—to show that there will indefinitely recur stretches of a million numbers containing at least 76,501 primes (there are

78,498; 70,433; and 67,885 in the first; second; and third millions).

From their work on inequalities we may single out (a) the theorem $\sum_{r+s+t=0} a_r b_s c_t \leqslant \sum_{r+s+t=0} a^*_r b^*_s c^*_t$, where a, b, c are nonnegative, $a_m = a_{-m}$, etc., and a^*_m is the mth a_r in descending order of magnitude, and so on; and (b) a deduction from a "pure" inequality: If $\int_{-\pi}^{\pi} |f(re^{\theta i})|^\lambda \, d\Theta \leqslant 1$, where $\lambda > 0$, $r < 1$, and if $F(\Theta)$ is the maximum of $|f(z)|$ in a kite-shaped region with vertex at $e^{\theta i}$, then $\int_{-\pi}^{\pi} F^\lambda(\Theta) \, d\Theta < k$. This is very powerful in applications.

Littlewood was educated at St. Paul's School and Trinity College, Cambridge, of which college he was a fellow after 1908 and lecturer from 1910 to 1927, when he became Rouse-Ball Professor in the University, retiring under the age limit in 1950. He was Richardson Lecturer at Manchester University from 1907 to 1910. In the last three years of World War I he was engaged in research in ballistics in the British Army.

For background information *see* FOURIER SERIES AND INTEGRALS; NUMBER THEORY in the McGraw-Hill Encyclopedia of Science and Technology. □

★ **LOCHHEAD, Allan Grant**
Canadian microbiologist
Born June 21, 1890, Galt, Ontario, Canada

IN RECOGNITION of the bearing of many phases of agricultural practice on the activities of microorganisms, the Canada Department of Agriculture in 1923 created a Division of Bacteriology, the first government-sponsored project for general or agricultural bacteriological research in Canada. Lochhead was appointed to head this undertaking. His task was to investigate a wide range of subjects related to dairying, food preservation, soil fertility, apiculture, and others bearing on agricultural production. At the same time he recognized that side by side with applied work should go fundamental research, where the point of application at the outset might be obscure.

Lochhead's earlier research was concerned with soil microbiology and such diverse subjects as the classification, nutrition, and metabolism of osmophilic yeasts, halophilic bacteria, and bacteria causing foul brood diseases of the honeybee. Such work, arising from practical problems, not only contributed to their solution but led to the discovery of new species of yeasts and bacteria.

Lochhead's most significant contributions arose from his soil studies. He recognized that in soil microbiology attention had been concentrated chiefly on processes in which microorganisms were known to participate rather than directed toward a study of the microorganisms themselves. Microorganisms had been studied because of their known functions; little attention had been paid to those whose functions were unknown, although these comprised a large proportion of the micropopulation of soils. Lochhead attempted, therefore, to develop, in place of the functional, a biological approach to the study of soil microorganisms. A program of work was inaugurated falling within the general category of "qualitative" investigations related to microbial ecology, nutrition, the microbiological equilibrium, associations and antagonisms, and particularly the microbe-plant relationship with extensions of this to certain aspects of plant pathology.

The devising of nonselective methods for the isolating and grouping of soil bacteria led to the recognition of the predominant types comprising the indigenous microflora. It was brought out that in soil of a given type a surprisingly uniform balance exists between the morphological and physiological groups comprising the indigenous flora and that the functions of the various components are exercised more fully under conditions of association.

The most significant development of the qualitative studies directed by Lochhead arose from the introduction of methods for classifying soil bacteria according to their nutritional requirements and estimating the relative incidence of different groups. This procedure, based on evaluating the growth response in a series of media of varying complexity, represented a new approach. It proved of value in studying the microbial equilibrium in soil, particularly in relation to plant growth, and was the basis for Lochhead's research into the nature of the microbial growth-promoting properties of soil.

Soil was shown to be a highly important

habitat of vitamin-requiring organisms, approximately 30% of the indigenous bacteria needing one or more for growth. Vitamin B_{12}, requirement for which had been considered to be restricted to a comparatively small group of bacteria, was needed by as many as 4 to 8×10^6 per gram of soil. Other more fastidious bacteria were found to be dependent upon a growth-promoting factor in soil, synthesized by other soil organisms. The factor was found to be a previously unrecognized substance in soil referred to as "terregens factor," first found essential for a species named *Arthrobacter terregens.*

Lochhead and his coworkers extended knowledge of the relationship between soil microorganisms and growing plants. In proximity to the plant (rhizosphere) characteristic changes were found to occur concerning the physiology of the organisms. The most striking features were the pronounced stimulation of bacteria requiring amino acids and the relative suppression of those dependent on more complex nutrients. That liberation of amino acids from the roots was the main factor accounting for their increased availability in the rhizosphere received later confirmation. On the other hand, organisms requiring growth factors were shown to be proportionately much less abundant near the roots, while those synthesizing vitamins were greatly increased. Thus, vitamins in the root zone arise chiefly as products of microbial synthesis and not as components of root excretions, the reverse of the situation respecting amino acids.

In applying such work, shortly before his retirement, to the problem of varietal resistance of certain plants to soil-borne fungal disease, Lochhead and his coworkers found that bacteria, from both the seeds and the roots, that required growth factors were much more abundant with the resistant than with susceptible plants, while the reverse was the case with organisms synthesizing such factors. These findings pointed to a new direction for the application of soil microbiology to certain problems of plant pathology.

The son of a Canadian entomologist, Lochhead studied at McGill University and at the University of Leipzig, completing work for his Ph.D. in 1914. From 1914 to 1918 he was interned at a prisoner-of-war camp near Berlin. Following his return to Canada he served as bacteriologist at Macdonald College, McGill University, as biochemist at the University of Alberta, and from 1923 to 1955 as chief of the Bacteriology Division, Canada Department of Agriculture, Ottawa. Following his retirement from administrative duties in 1955, he remained until 1960 in a purely research capacity. The author or coauthor of some 120 papers, he was awarded the Flavelle Medal of the Royal Society of Canada in 1958.

For background information *see* SOIL MICROBIOLOGY in the McGraw-Hill Encyclopedia of Science and Technology. □

★ **LONSDALE, Dame Kathleen**
British x-ray crystallographer
Born Jan. 28, 1903, Newbridge, Co. Kildare, Ireland

THE MOST fundamental of Kathleen Lonsdale's research work was the proof, by crystal-structure analyses of hexamethylbenzene and of hexachlorobenzene, that the carbon atoms in the benzene nucleus are coplanar and hexagonally arranged and that their distance apart is nearly the same as that of the carbon atoms in graphite. Later, by measuring the diamagnetic susceptibilities in and perpendicular to the planes of a number of aromatic molecules, she was able to show the reality of the concept of molecular orbitals. For this and later work she was awarded the Davy Medal of the Royal Society of London in 1957.

The structure analyses of diamond by W. H. and W. L. Bragg in 1915 and of graphite by O. Hassel, H. Mark, and J. D. Bernal in 1924 had shown that carbon atoms in diamond form puckered hexagons with tetrahedral coordination of all atoms and an interatomic distance of 1.54 A, whereas in graphite there are plane hexagonal networks, in which the C—C distance is 1.42 A, the nets being 3.4 A apart. At first it was supposed that the carbon atoms in aromatic molecules such as naphthalene and anthracene were also composed of puckered hexagons.

In 1929 Lonsdale found that $C_6(CH_3)_6$ formed triclinic crystals with one molecule only in each unit cell. The fact that there were certain sets of planes in the crystal that diffracted x-rays with outstanding intensity indicated that the 12 carbon atoms must lie very close to some of the intersections of these planes. By calculating all the alternatives, Lonsdale showed that the best agreement was obtained for a molecule consisting of a plane hexagon, with the six carbon atoms at about 1.4 A apart, and with a second concentric ring of six carbon atoms having rather more than twice the radius of the first, the $C — CH_3$ bonds being radial. The distances between molecules were of the order of 3.7 A. The structure was thus obtained without any initial assumptions about the shape or size of the molecule, the only fact used being that it contained 12 carbon atoms. Two years later she published the first Fourier analysis of an organic compound, C_6Cl_6, in which again the benzene nucleus and its substituent atoms were shown to be plane (or nearly so).

If measurements of diamagnetic anisotropy combined with absolute measurements of susceptibility are made on crystals of known structure, then the principal diamagnetic susceptibilities of a single molecule can be deduced. This much was already known, but Lonsdale showed that if the classical Lorentz theory, which related diamagnetism to the areas of the electron orbits, were applied to simple aromatic-ring compounds, the results could be quantitatively explained on the basis of atomic orbitals for σ-electrons, but molecular orbitals for π-electrons.

Later she developed a method of making divergent-beam x-ray photographs of single crystals and used it to obtain a simple but very accurate measurement of the $C — C$ distance in individual diamonds (to seven significant figures).

In a series of studies of the "thermal diffuse patterns" from simple substances, which could be obtained by keeping the crystal stationary, using white + characteristic (or monochromatized) x-radiation, and giving intense exposures, she showed: first, that the diffuse scattering of long wavelength was directly related to the elastic constants of the crystal; second, that the diffuse pattern was very dependent upon the crystal structure and could be used to determine molecular orientation; third, that the finer details of the structures of organic compounds could be related to the strengths of the intermolecular bonds; and finally, that some effects were structure- and not temperature-sensitive and must be due to disorder and not to thermal vibration. This particularly applied to the case of diamond, for which she made a careful study of the type-I "extra spots."

For this and her previous work, which was mainly carried out at the Royal Institution, London, of which Sir William Bragg was director, she was elected in 1945 as the first woman Fellow of the Royal Society of London, and became a vice-president in 1960.

More recently she studied intramolecular vibration and thermal expansion by x-ray techniques, and the application of x-ray crystallography to such medical problems as the mode of action of curarelike drugs and the composition of endemic bladder stones.

The tenth and youngest child of an English postmaster, Kathleen Yardley took high honors in physics at Bedford College for Women, University of London, in 1922. She then joined the research team of Sir William Bragg, first at University College and then at the Royal Institution. For two years after her marriage to a fellow-physicist, Thomas Lonsdale, in 1927, she worked at the University of Leeds, but returned with him to London and rejoined the Royal Institution in 1932. In 1946 she became first reader in crystallography and later professor of chemistry at University College, London. She obtained her D.Sc. in 1929 and received a number of honorary degrees. In 1956 she was appointed a Dame of the British Empire (D.B.E.).

Besides several nonscientific books, Lonsdale wrote *Crystals and X-rays* (1948) and edited volumes I, II, and III of the *International Tables for X-ray Crystallography* (1952, 1959, 1962).

For background information *see* CRYSTALLOGRAPHY in the McGraw-Hill Encyclopedia of Science and Technology.   □

★ LOVELL, Sir (Alfred Charles) Bernard
English astronomer
Born Aug. 31, 1913, Oldland Common, Gloucestershire, England

ONE OF the pioneers of radio astronomy, Lovell proved the applicability of radar studies to meteor showers using ex-military radar apparatus immediately after World War II. In 1949 he proposed the construction of the 250-ft diameter steerable radiotelescope at Jodrell Bank. Completed in 1957 under Lovell's supervision, the instrument has an altazimuth mounting with a parabolic surface of sheet steel and is still the largest completely steerable radiotelescope in existence. With this instrument and other smaller ones subsequently constructed, Lovell guided many researches in radio astronomy. His personal researches involved studies of the scintillation effects of the radio sources, the investigation of the low-frequency spectra, and the discovery of the radio emission from flare stars in the galaxy.

The apparatus that Lovell assembled after the war was intended to explore the possibility of detecting radar echoes from large cosmic-ray showers. It was his intention to continue the cosmic-ray researches on which he had been working for several years before 1939. However, Lovell found that the many transient echoes were associated with meteor trails, and this led to the use of radiotelescopes for the study of meteor showers during daylight hours, which is impossible by optical techniques and under overcast weather conditions.

The first radiotelescope observations of meteors were made independently by a number of observers during the Leonid showers of 1931 and 1932, using wavelengths ranging from 47 to 87 meters. Because far too few meteors were optically observed to account for the large number of radio echoes received, doubt was cast on the validity of using radio techniques for such studies. Subsequent radio observations did nothing to remove such doubts. However, in 1945 the English astronomers J. S. Hey and G. S. Stewart, using World War II radar equipment with a wavelength of 4 to 5 meters, made a number of observations that tended to support the theory, advanced earlier by J. A. Pierce, that the echoes were due to broadside reflection from the ionized particles of meteor trails.

Lovell realized that to substantiate the validity of radio astronomical techniques in the study of meteors, a meteor shower with particular characteristics was required. The shower had to be of a relatively short duration, and the hourly number of meteors observed had to build up to an extremely large number at the maximum point. He assumed that the Giacobinid, or Draconid, shower, which emanates from a concentration in a comparatively small space at a point in the Earth's orbit behind the Giacobini-Zinner comet, would be adequate for his purposes. The Giacobinid shower had been observed, with a maximum rate of 17 per hour, in 1926 when the Earth had arrived at the node 70 days before the comet. In 1933 the Earth had arrived at the node 80 days after the comet, and a maximum hourly rate of 4,000 to 6,000 had been observed. In 1939, when the Earth had reached the node 136 days before the comet, no shower had been observed. Since the Earth was to reach the node only 15 days after the comet had passed in 1946, Lovell assumed that the maximum hourly rate would be even greater than it had been in 1933 and hence that this shower would be ideal.

In 1946 Lovell and his associates at the Jodrell Bank Experimental Station, Cheshire, England, constructed a steerable, narrow-beam antenna consisting of 5 yagi aerials mounted on an army-surplus searchlight base. This radiotelescope had a wavelength of about 4 meters. On the evening of Oct. 9, Lovell began to observe the Giacobinid shower. The transient echo rate was found to be about 2 per hour, which agreed with the optical count. About midnight the optical meteor rate and the radio-echo rate began to increase rapidly, reaching a maximum of nearly 12,000 per hour in about 3 hours. The rate then decreased with similar rapidity and by 6:30 A.M. was again only a few per hour. Not only did the increase in the echo rate by a factor of about 5,000 correspond exactly with the Earth's passage through the comet's orbit, but the correspondence between the radar-echo rate and the optical rate was virtually one-to-one. This removed any doubt that all of the echoes observed were of meteoric origin. During 1947 and 1948 Lovell continued his experiments and disclosed meteor streams incident on the daylight side of the Earth that were previously unknown to astronomers. The establishment of the applicability of radio techniques to meteor studies made possible the determination of the orbits and radiants of meteors, and with a number of his colleagues Lovell carried out experiments that demonstrated conclusively that all meteors were members of the solar system and did not have an interstellar origin.

With this same apparatus Lovell investigated the radio-echo returns from the aurora borealis in 1947–48 and used the receiving part of the equipment in studies of the large solar radio outburst of July, 1946.

At this stage the radio emissions from space discovered by K. G. Jansky and further investigated by G. Reber were believed to originate in the ionized interstellar hydrogen gas, but observations that the signals were variable led J. S. Hey to conclude that a variable radio-emitting source of small angular size existed in the constellation of Cygnus. In a communication to *Nature* in 1950 Lovell described spaced receiver experiments that he had carried out initially with a colleague at Jodrell Bank over a base line of a few kilometers and later with Ryle in Cambridge over a base line of 210 km. Over the short base lines the correlation of the fluctuations in the signal at both receivers was complete, but over the long base line there was no correlation whatsoever. This result led to the unambiguous conclusion that the radio source itself emitted with a constant intensity and that the fluctuations were introduced when the radio waves traversed the Earth's ionosphere at a height of several hundred km—in other words, that the phenomenon was analogous to the twinkling of ordinary stars, although in this case the fluctuations are occasioned by the irregularities in the atmosphere at heights of a few km. Subsequently much use was made of this scintillation phenomenon by Lovell's team at Jodrell Bank to study the ionospheric irregularities and drifts.

The variation in strength of the radio sources as a function of wavelength is an important parameter in the study of the physical processes of emission. At long wavelengths the measurements are difficult because of the interfering effects and absorption in the Earth's ionosphere. Between 1955 and 1959 Lovell made measurements down to frequencies of 16 mc/s on the stronger radio sources, in the later series using the 250-ft steerable telescope as part of an interferometer. He showed that the falloff in intensity below 20 mc/s of the radio sources in Cassiopeia and Cygnus was compatible with absorption of the radiation in a typical interstellar ionized hydrogen cloud.

After 1958 Lovell's main researches were concerned with the radio emission from flare stars. Although the Sun is a powerful emitter of radio waves when it is disturbed by solar flares, it was thought that the detection of similar radio emission even from the nearer stars would be impossible because their distance implied that the intensity would be down by 10^{11} times compared with the Sun, and the theories of radio emission from the Milky Way were evolved without the inclusion of a stellar component. Lovell noticed that in the first optical observations of the flare phenomenon on UV Ceti in 1948 W. J. Luyten reported that the energy of the optical flare was much greater than that of the largest optical flares on the Sun. If this difference applied also to the radio emission from the UV Ceti, M-type dwarf stars, then Lovell thought that it might be possible to detect the outbursts of radio emission from a star that was tracked continuously by the Jodrell Bank telescope. After 2 years' work Lovell's results were inconclusive because there were no simultaneous optical observations of the star. He then asked Fred L. Whipple of the Smithsonian Astrophysical Observatory for assistance, and a joint program was arranged for simultaneous radio and optical observations of the flare stars using the Baker Nunn cameras of the Smithsonian's satellite-tracking network. The first positive results relating to observations in 1960 and 1961 were published in *Nature* in April, 1963, and since that time the results of several thousand hours of observation have been analyzed. This work is opening a new avenue for the study of the large-scale processes occurring in stellar atmospheres and has also

shown that the integrated radio emission from the flare stars may account for a few per cent of the overall emission from the Milky Way. These combined optical and radio observations have also led to the establishment of a new value for the constancy of the relative velocity of light and radio waves in space.

Although the programs of the radiotelescope directed by Lovell have been largely concerned with astronomical researches, the telescope was a unique instrument in the early days of the satellite and deep space probe launchings. Lovell and his colleagues succeeded in tracking by radar the carrier rocket of the first Russian Sputnik in October, 1957, and in 1959 he measured, with J. G. Davies, the acceleration in the final stages of descent as the Russian *Lunik II* made impact with the Moon, placing beyond question the reality of the exploit, which was then being extensively questioned in some quarters. For a few years pending the establishment of the American D.S.I.F. network, the Jodrell telescope was a part of the tracking and control system for the American Pioneer series of space probes. The publicity that this work brought to Lovell and Jodrell Bank was concerned with only 2 per cent of the use of the telescope.

Lovell attended the University of Bristol, receiving his B.S. in physics in 1933 and his Ph.D. in 1936 for researches on thin metallic films deposited in high vacua. In 1936 he was appointed assistant lecturer in physics in Manchester, where he carried out research on large cosmic-ray showers with P. M. S. Blackett. On the outbreak of war in 1939 he joined the Air Ministry Research Establishment (later the Telecommunications Research Establishment), where he developed the centimetric airborne radar and was head of the H2S blind bombing and A.S.V. antisubmarine groups. At the end of the European war in 1945 he returned to Manchester as lecturer in physics and at this stage started the development of the experimental station at Jodrell Bank in Cheshire 20 miles south of Manchester. He was appointed senior lecturer in 1947 and a reader in 1949. In 1951 the University created a special chair of radio astronomy for him and the directorship of Jodrell Bank was made an official post at the same time. He was elected a fellow of the Royal Society in 1955, received the Royal Medal of the Society in 1960, and was knighted in 1961.

Lovell wrote a number of books, including *Radio Astronomy* (1952), *Meteor Astronomy* (1954), *The Exploration of Space by Radio* (1957), *The Individual and the Universe* (1959), and *The Exploration of Outer Space* (1961).

For background information *see* METEOR; RADIO ASTRONOMY in the McGraw-Hill Encyclopedia of Science and Technology.   □

★ **LURIA, Salvador Edward**
American biologist
Born Aug. 13, 1912, Turin, Italy

W HILE STUDYING the growth of bacteriophages (bacterial viruses) in their host
cells, Luria became interested in the mechanism
of acquired bacterial resistance to bacteriophage. To decide whether a spontaneous mutation or an adaptive response to infection was
involved, he devised the fluctuation test, which
provided the critical evidence of bacterial mutation and, through its mathematical analysis (by
Max Delbrück), the basis for measurements of
bacterial mutation rates. Extending this work to
viral mutations, Luria showed that phage mutants arise during exponential phage replication
by a similar process of spontaneous mutation.
These experiments formed the starting points for
the genetics of bacteria and viruses and are one
of the foundations of modern molecular biology.

Bacterial variation was recognized from the
earliest years of bacteriology but received significant clarification only in the 1930s with the
work of Macfarlane Burnet, who also discovered
mutations in phage. Burnet's studies provided
evidence for the occurrence of sporadic mutations in these organisms. In 1938, Delbrück
initiated the modern phase of bacteriophage
research by the systematic application of Burnet's methods to the study of phage development. Luria, who had worked on the effect of
radiation of phage and bacteria, started in 1941
to work with Delbrück on the effects of mixed
infection of bacteria with two different phage. In
isolating phage-resistant variants for these
studies, he realized that such variants provided a
material with which he could analyze precisely
bacterial variation and its mechanism. He reasoned that if hereditary resistance developed as
an adaptive response of bacteria to phage attack,
the resistant variants should be a random fraction of the cells in all comparable cultures of a
given bacterium; whereas if resistance developed by spontaneous mutations during bacterial
growth, the resistant mutants would be grouped
into clones of resistant siblings. Such clones
should be recognizable by comparison of the
numbers of resistant cells in samples from separate cultures with the number found in samples
from pooled cultures. More generally, in a series
of cultures the fluctuations of the numbers of
mutants around the mean number would resemble those of the returns provided by a series
of gambling trials in a slot machine. In fact, the
idea of the fluctuation test came to Luria as he
watched a colleague use a gambling machine at
a country club party in Bloomington, Ind., where
he was teaching at Indiana University. The
experimental verification was completed in a few
weeks, and on the basis of the results the
mathematical analysis of bacterial variation was
developed by Delbrück at Vanderbilt University.

This was in 1943. Mutations of bacteriophages
were observed and analyzed by Luria in the
same year. By 1946 microbial genetics was ready
for great new advances: the discoveries of bacterial sexuality by Joshua Lederberg and E. L.
Tatum and of phage sexuality by A. D. Hershey.
It was not until 1951 that Luria completed the
analysis of the spontaneous mutation process in
phage by showing that during phage growth
clones of phage mutants arose by random spontaneous mutations. This provided the basis for
the study of mutagenesis in phage, which underlies the current theories of chemical mutagenesis. Thereafter, Luria and his coworkers were
concerned with studies on the mechanisms of
lysogeny (the attachment of the phage genome
to the bacterial chromosome), of transduction
(the incorporation of bacterial genes into bacteriophages), and of host-controlled properties of
viruses.

Luria studied medicine in Turin, Italy, where
he worked under Giuseppe Levi, the distinguished Italian histologist. After studying
physics and radiology in Rome, he worked at the
Institute of Radium in Paris before going to the
United States in 1940. He was naturalized in
1947. In 1964 he became Sedgwick Professor of
Biology at the Massachusetts Institute of Technology. He was elected to the National Academy
of Sciences in 1960.

Luria wrote *General Virology* (1953), the first
treatment of virus science as a branch of biology.

For background information *see* BACTERIO-
PHAGE; MUTATION in the McGraw-Hill Encyclopedia of Science and Technology.   □

LWOFF, André
French biologist
Born 1902, Allier Dept., France

WHILE STUDYING the action of bacterial viruses on the cells they infect, Lwoff demonstrated the existence of the "latent" bacterial virus and explained the phenomenon of lysogenic bacteria. For his contribution to molecular biology, he shared the 1965 Nobel Prize for medicine or physiology with the French biologists François Jacob and Jacques Monod. Jacob's contribution to molecular biology was his research on the induction and repression of enzymes. Monod was honored for his studies of the genetics of viruses and enzymes.

In 1915, Frederick William Twort, a British bacteriologist, discovered a filterable virus that infected a bacterium and caused it to burst or lyse, thereby releasing the virus contained in it. This phenomenon attracted the attention of bacteriologists, who began investigations to find out how it worked. It also stimulated the interest of medical bacteriologists and physicians, who considered it a possible means of fighting infectious disease. The use of bacteriophage as a specific for various infectious diseases did not prove to be generally effective, and therefore did not gain widespread acceptance.

After World War II, Lwoff returned to the Pasteur Institute and resumed the work on lysogenic bacteria that had been started by the French biologist Eugène Wollman. From the early 1920s on, it had been established that bacteria isolated from nature frequently contained bacteriophages. These bacteria are termed lysogenic because they are capable of producing bacterial lysis. Furthermore, this ability to lyse was transmitted to future generations of the bacterium through cell division. In 1929, F. M. Burnet and M. McKie found that only one in 1,000 of the lysogenic bacteria liberated any

intracellular bacteriophage. To explain why the other 999 cells did not lyse and liberate infective bacteriophage, they hypothesized that the lysogenic bacteria have a noninfective progenitor (anlage) of the phage and that this noninfective entity multiplies and is transmitted to each cell during cell division. Infectious bacteriophage is produced when something activates this anlage.

By 1940, interest of the phage workers had shifted to the T strains of *Escherichia coli*, in which lysogeny did not appear. The previous reports of Burnet and others on lysogeny were ignored, and H. d'Herelle's viewpoint of this phenomenon prevailed. His concept of lysogeny was that any long-term association between host and phage could be regarded as pseudolysogeny. These bacteria can adsorb the phage they carry, but they resist infection by other types of phage. Each cell in a culture of lysogenic bacteria was thought to carry free phage on its surface. D'Herelle accounted for the multiplication of phage during the growth of the culture by infection of the few phage-sensitive bacterial variants that appear in the pseudolysogenic population.

Lwoff first tried to see if the faculty for producing bacteriophages can really be perpetuated without the intervention of exogenous bacteriophage. In collaboration with A. Gutmann, he observed the individual cell of *Bacillus megatherium* in a microdrop and watched its division under the microscope. One of the two daughter cells was taken out of the microdrop immediately after cell division and placed on agar to see whether a colony of lysogenic bacteria could be produced. As soon as the remaining cell in the microdrop had divided, one of the two new cells was withdrawn and placed on agar, to see if a colony of lysogenic bacteria would result. The process of withdrawing one of the daughter cells and placing it on agar went on for 19 cell divisions. During this experiment, samples of culture fluid were also taken from the microdrop and tested for the presence of free phage. Free phage was not found at any time in the culture fluid, and every colony that grew from cells taken from the microdrop was lysogenic. Lwoff showed that lysogeny could persist for at least 19 successive divisions in the absence of free phage.

Lwoff was also able to determine how lysogenic bacteria liberate the phage they produce by watching cells in a microdrop during successive divisions. He and Gutmann noticed that on occasion there appeared to be a spontaneous lysis of a cell in the microdrop. If the culture fluid was tested for free phage after such lysis, several hundred were found to be present. Lwoff concluded that lysogenic bacteria liberated their phage by the lysing of the cell.

The results of these experiments enabled

Lwoff to describe what takes place during lysogeny. The lysogenic bacteria contain a noninfective structure, a prophage, which gives the cell the ability to form infective phage without the help of exogenous phage particles. In a small fraction of the population of growing lysogenic bacteria, the prophage is induced to produce infective phage particles, which are released by lysis of the cell.

There was another aspect of lysogeny that was investigated by Lwoff. He wanted to determine what would induce the prophage to form infective phage particles. He and his pupils, L. Siminovitch and N. Kjeldgaard, were of the opinion that the inducer was something outside the cell. They tried many physical and chemical treatments without success until they irradiated a growing culture of *B. megatherium* with ultraviolet light. Other experiments with hydrogen peroxide showed that it too could induce prophage to form infective phage particles. Other research workers followed Lwoff's lead and determined that nitrogen mustard would also produce this effect in lysogenic bacteria.

During the 1920s, Lwoff studied the morphogenesis of protozoa and discovered extranuclear inheritance in these organisms. In the following decade he studied the nutrition of protozoa, identifying vitamins as microbial growth factors and demonstrating that vitamins function as coenzymes.

Lwoff received a bachelor's degree in natural sciences in 1921, an M.D. in 1927, and a doctorate in natural science in 1932. He joined the staff at the Pasteur Institute upon receiving his bachelor's degree, later becoming the head of the department of microbic physiology there. Starting in 1959, he also served as professor of microbiology at the University of Paris.

For background information *see* BACTERIA, LYSOGENIC; BACTERIOPHAGE in the McGraw-Hill Encyclopedia of Science and Technology.   □

☆ LYNEN, Feodor
German biochemist
Born Apr. 6, 1911, Munich, Germany

L YNEN SHARED the 1964 Nobel Prize in physiology or medicine with Konrad E. Bloch for discoveries concerning the mechanisms and regulation of cholesterol and fatty acid metabolism. Both did their research on the intermediary metabolism of the living cell, seeking to discover how a cell changes simple chemical compounds into the complex molecules of sterols and lipids (fats). Both worked independently along somewhat different lines until publication

of their findings made them aware that they were working on the same problem. The discoveries of the one often complemented the work of the other. Bloch's work was chiefly concerned with sterols, while Lynen paid more attention to fatty acids.

For some time it had been believed that the initial building blocks in forming sterols and lipids were two-carbon molecules. By tagging acetic acid molecules with deuterium atoms, Bloch and Rittenberg in 1942 were able to show that acetic acid was used to form cholesterol in rats. By 1951 Lynen had demonstrated that the acetate radical had to react with coenzyme A to form acetyl thiol ester of coenzyme A (CH_3-COSCoA) for the first step in a chain of reactions that resulted in the biosynthesis of sterols and fatty acids. Long and tedious investigations had to be conducted in order to prove such a reaction. Cell-free preparations were used so as not to confuse the reaction under study with reactions brought about by other enzymes within a cell. Where possible, compounds to be used in the study were prepared synthetically to assure their purity. Besides using standard methods of chemistry such as filtration, precipitation, extraction, and crystallization in obtaining pure samples of the intermediate compounds formed, Lynen and his coworkers purified an intermediate product in one case by means of paper chromatography, used radioactive atoms to follow a reaction, and frequently made spectral studies for assaying enzyme formation. The actual identification of acetyl thiol ester of coenzyme A was done by several different methods. In a biological assay in which a pigeon liver

preparation was used for the acetylation of sulfanilamide in a system containing coenzyme A, acetate, and ATP (adenosinetriphosphate), Lynen's thiol ester was substituted for the above system and the acetylation took place. A color reaction with sodium nitroprusside, the decomposition of the ester with mercury salts, maintenance of acetylation activity after treatment with an iodoacetate—all indicated a SH group protected by an acetate radical. In short, both biological and chemical tests indicated that the assumed composition of the intermediate compound essential to the start of the lipid synthesis was correct.

Carbon dioxide combines with the above intermediate to form malonyl thiol ester of coenzyme A (HO_2C-CH_2-CO-S-CoA). Lynen with his collaborators discovered the role of the vitamin biotin in this and other carboxylations. Biotin is bound in an enzyme system that causes carbon dioxide to react with biotin to form compounds such as 1'-N-carboxybiotin, an essential intermediate for transferring carbon dioxide from solutions to compounds such as acetyl thiol ester of coenzyme A. Biochemists regard this discovery of the role of biotin as fundamental in lipid metabolism and as one of far-reaching implications.

Lynen's group also isolated a multienzyme complex from yeast that catalyzes the formation of long-chain fatty acids. For example, the reaction of acetyl thiol ester of coenzyme A with malonyl thiol ester of coenzyme A results in the production of palmitic acid. Most of the intermediate reactions involved were clarified in Lynen's laboratory. That the complete biosynthesis of a sterol or a lipid requires some 30 consecutive reactions is an indication of the complexity of the investigation.

The biosynthesis of sterols and fatty acids is significant not only for pure chemistry but for the light it sheds on the possible role of cholesterol in heart disease. In choosing the recipients of the prize in physiology or medicine, the Nobel committee pointed out that the great majority of deaths from circulatory diseases are generally accompanied by gravely disturbed lipid metabolisms. Any remedy for this situation will derive from the work done by Bloch and Lynen.

Son of a distinguished professor of engineering in the Technische Hochschule of Munich, Lynen was educated as a chemist at the University of Munich. He studied under Heinrich Wieland, another Nobel laureate, whose daughter Lynen married in 1937. Appointed a lecturer at the University in 1942, he became a professor there in 1947. He was also named director at the Max-Planck Institute for Cell Chemistry in Munich. In 1962 he was elected a foreign associate of the U.S. National Academy of Sciences.

For background information *see* CHOLESTEROL; LIPID; STEROL in the McGraw-Hill Encyclopedia of Science and Technology. □

LYOT, Bernard Ferdinand

French astronomer
Born Feb. 27, 1897, Paris, France
Died Apr. 2, 1952, near Cairo, Egypt

WHILE ENGAGED in studies of the solar corona, Lyot invented the coronagraph and developed monochromatic filters that permit the passage of light from a small portion of the spectrum. The coronagraph made it possible to study the solar corona and prominences at times other than during a total solar eclipse, and when used in conjunction with the monochromatic filters it greatly extended the knowledge of the corona.

The first recorded observation of the solar corona was made by Johannes Kepler during the total solar eclipse of 1605. It was not until the eclipse of 1842, however, that the English astronomer Francis Baily and the French physicist Dominique François Jean Arago independently identified the corona as an appendage of the Sun rather than of the Moon. Although many observations of the corona were made during subsequent eclipses, all attempts to study it outside total eclipse, notably by the American astonomer George Ellery Hale and the French astonomer Henri A. Deslandres, failed.

Lyot assumed that the key to an instrument that could be used to study the corona in full daylight was the elimination of scattered light. Measurements of the brightness of the corona, made during total eclipses, had shown that it gave only about one-millionth as much illumination as sunlight, or about one-half the light of the full Moon. Lyot realized that a single bubble or scratch on the objective lens or the least trace of haze in the Earth's atmosphere would scatter light whose brightness was equal to or greater than that of the corona to obscure the corona from the observer. Thus, Lyot reasoned, there were two requirements for a successful corona-graph. One was that the object lens of the instrument be chosen for the perfect homoge-neity of its glass, carefully ground and polished to avoid scratching, and protected against dust. The other was that the instrument be situated at a considerable altitude above sea level.

During the summer of 1930, working at the Pic du Midi Observatory, which is 9,400 feet above sea level in the French Pyrenees, Lyot constructed his first coronagraph. For the objec-tive, he chose a planoconvex lens that was free of bubbles and scratches and had a diameter of 8 centimeters and a focal length of 2 meters. Behind this a black disk was placed to occult the image of the photosphere, thus in effect producing an artificial solar eclipse. A field lens, located behind the disk, formed an image of the object lens on a small diaphragm which blocked off the light diffracted by the edge of the object lens. A small central screen within the dia-phragm blocked off the light produced by reflec-tion from the surfaces of the object lens. A third lens was used to project the image of the black disk and its surrounding halo onto a photo-graphic plate. Using this apparatus, Lyot ob-tained the first spectrogram of the corona made without the benefit of a total solar eclipse. In July 1931, using an improved coronagraph with an object lens of 20-cm diameter and 4-m focal length, Lyot obtained the first photographs of the inner corona not taken during a total solar eclipse. Spectra of the corona were photo-graphed, and in the infrared region Lyot dis-covered three spectral lines never before ob-served in the corona—a faint line at 8024 ang-stroms, and strong lines at 10,747 and 10,798 angstroms. In 1935 Lyot used the coronagraph to obtain the first cinematographic record of the motions of the solar prominences. The corona-graph has proved to be beneficial in two ways. Although it does not show all of the details that are observable during a total solar eclipse, the coronagraph can be used continually to study the sequence of changes of the corona. In addi-tion, because total solar eclipses are infrequent, last no longer than about 7 minutes, and are observable from only a very small area of the Earth each time, the total time during which the corona can be investigated has been increased by a tremendous factor.

In conjunction with the coronagraph, Lyot developed a monochromatic filter system to iso-late the light of the principal coronal wave-lengths. Called a quartz-polaroid monochroma-tor, or monochromatic polarizing filter, the device consists of a colored filter, a series of polarizing quartz crystals, and polaroid filters. In addition to his studies of the corona, Lyot also investi-gated the polarization of light reflected from the Moon and the planets.

Lyot attended the Electrical High School, Faculty of Sciences, Paris, receiving an engi-neering diploma in 1918. He then became a demonstrator in physics at the Polytechnic Insti-tute, a post he retained until 1929. In 1920 he was appointed an assistant at the Paris Observa-tory at Meudon, becoming an assistant astron-omer in 1928, a joint astronomer in 1930, and an astronomer in 1944. Lyot was awarded the Gold Medal of the Royal Astronomical Society of Great Britain in 1939 and the Bruce Medal of the Astronomical Society of the Pacific in 1946.

For background information *see* CORONA-GRAPH; SUN in the McGraw-Hill Encyclopedia of Science and Technology.   □

M

★★

★ **MacLANE, Saunders**
American mathematician
Born Aug. 4, 1909, Norwich, Conn., U.S.A.

ADVANCES IN mathematical research often depend on the interrelation of different specialities in mathematics, and this has been especially the case in recent years. This may be illustrated by the work of MacLane, which was largely concerned with the elucidation and development of algebraic ideas involved in various aspects of geometry.

The analogy between algebraic number fields on the one hand and algebraic curves on the other led many mathematicians in the 1930s to the study of algebraic curves or of the equivalent algebraic function fields for the case when the ground field of constants is not the classical field of complex numbers but an arbitrary field, even one of prime characteristic. Now algebraic extensions of such fields were known to be manageable only when they are separable (generated by the roots of a polynomial with all roots distinct, that is, separated). For the algebraic function case, one must also consider mixed algebraic and transcendental extensions of such fields of prime characteristic. MacLane's studies here, in a 1939 paper on separating transcendence bases, led to an effective description of a class of transcendental extensions that can be called "separable." One of the basic results on such separable extensions is now known as "MacLane's theorem."

Topology is another field of geometry where algebraic concepts have played a decisive role. In 1941 Samuel Eilenberg and MacLane started a long and effective collaboration on algebraic aspects of topology. The first of their joint papers (1942) dealt with group extensions and homology. If A and B are two abelian groups, an extension E of B by A is another abelian group with B as subgroup and A as the corresponding factor group E/B. In algebra, it had been known that the set E of all these extensions was itself an abelian group, called Ext (A,B). This paper showed how this construction "Ext" could be used to attack the universal coefficient problem in topology: given the homology groups of a topological space, to find the cohomology groups with various coefficient groups. This systematic employment of Ext was one of the first steps in the development of homological algebra. This subject, subsequently developed by many mathematicians, including both Eilenberg and MacLane, has had a widespread effect.

The "connectivity" of a topological space may be measured by two different series of groups: the homotopy groups and the cohomology groups. Stimulated by the work of Heinz Hopf, Eilenberg and MacLane made systematic investigations of the relations between these two types of groups. On the one hand this led to the construction of certain spaces with just one nonvanishing homotopy group; these spaces, under the name of the Eilenberg-MacLane spaces, have turned out to be essential building blocks in the general study of spaces. On the other hand, these investigations led to a new construction: the cohomology groups of a group (the group might in particular be the first homotopy group of a space). This use of cohomology constructions, not just for topological spaces but also for algebraic objects, has been applied to many other types of algebraic systems, as in Hochschild's cohomology of algebras or MacLane's cohomology of rings. Today, rapid progress continues in this field.

Currently, the general notion of a "category" is proving itself an effective tool in organizing many aspects of mathematical knowledge. This notion was first introduced by Eilenberg and MacLane in 1945. Specifically, in topology one considers both topological spaces and continuous maps from one such space to another; in linear algebra one considers both vector spaces and linear transformations from one space to another; in group theory one considers both groups and product-preserving maps from one group to another. Generally, in a category one considers objects of any sort and "maps" from one object to another, with appropriate properties for the composition of maps. The abelian categories (maps can be composed and added) were introduced by MacLane in 1950. Today, this subject is in rapid development; it illustrates how ideas from geometry can penetrate many other parts of mathematics.

MacLane studied at Yale (Ph.B., 1930), the University of Chicago (M.A., 1931), and the University of Göttingen (D.Phil., 1934). He taught at Harvard (1934–36), Cornell (1936–

37), the University of Chicago (1937–38), and again at Harvard (1938–47) before being appointed professor of mathematics at the University of Chicago in 1947. He was elected to the National Academy of Sciences in 1949.

MacLane wrote *Survey of Modern Algebra*, with Garrett Birkhoff (1942) and *Homology* (1963).

For background information *see* GROUP THEORY; TOPOLOGY in the McGraw-Hill Encyclopedia of Science and Technology. □

★ **MANGELSDORF, Paul Christoph**
American botanist
Born July 20, 1899, Atchison, Kans., U.S.A.

VIRTUALLY ALL of Mangelsdorf's research was concerned with the origin, evolution, and improvement of corn, America's principal food plant and the nutritional basis of its prehistoric cultures and civilizations. By combining the primitive characteristics of pod corn, a type with its seeds enclosed in chaff as are those of wild grasses, with the characteristics of popcorn, a type with small hard seeds that explode or "pop" when exposed to heat, he synthesized a genetically reconstructed ancestral form of corn. Later, collaborating with an archeologist, Richard S. MacNeish, he identified prehistoric wild corn from once-inhabited caves in Mexico. This prehistoric corn, dated at 5000 B.C., closely resembled in its principal botanical characteristics the genetically reconstructed ancestral form that he had developed. Separating the components of the genetic locus for pod corn (with W. C. Galinat), he demonstrated that the two components are different in their effects and concluded that there must once have been two kinds of wild corn, which, brought together by the American Indians, hybridized to produce modern corn with its grains not enclosed in chaff.

Corn is a mystery that has puzzled botanists since it was first encountered by Columbus more than 4 centuries ago. It differs from other cereal grasses—rice, wheat, barley, and oats—in having male and female flowers borne in separate flower clusters, the male flowers in a terminal cluster commonly known as the tassel, and the female flowers in a lateral cluster, the well-known ear. Corn differs also from other grasses in having no means of dispersing its seeds. Its grain-bearing structure, the ear, is tightly enclosed in husks. Without man's care, modern corn could not long survive.

Before Mangelsdorf began his research on the problem in 1927, there were three principal theories as to the origin of corn: (1) corn is a direct descendant of a wild pod corn; (2) corn originated from its closest relative, teosinte, by mutation or by the hybridization of teosinte with other grasses now unknown; and (3) corn and its known relatives, teosinte and *Tripsacum*, descended along parallel but independent lines from a remote common ancestor now extinct. Mangelsdorf's studies (with R. G. Reeves) of hybrids of corn with teosinte and *Tripsacum* led (1939) to a tripartite hypothesis: (1) the ancestor of cultivated corn is a form of pod corn; (2) teosinte, the closest relative of corn, is not corn's progenitor but is a hybrid of corn and its more distant relative, *Tripsacum*; and (3) the majority of modern corn varieties are products of the hybridization of corn with teosinte, *Tripsacum*, or both.

Mangelsdorf's research after 1939 was concerned with testing the three parts of this working hypothesis. This involved three related but more or less distinct approaches: (1) experimental research in the genetics and cytology of corn and its relatives; (2) the study and classification of the living races of corn of this hemisphere; and (3) the study and identification of archeological remains of corn. The results tended to support the tripartite hypothesis of 1939, and the discovery of prehistoric wild corn in Mexico and archeological evidence of its subsequent hybridization with teosinte or *Tripsacum* virtually confirmed all parts of the hypothesis. This has important implications for the improvement of modern corn through breeding.

Son of a commercial seedsman and greenhouse owner, Mangelsdorf was exposed from childhood to a great variety of plants. At Kansas State College, where he received the B.S. in 1921, he majored in agronomy and was student assistant to John H. Parker, then in charge of cereal improvement. From 1921 to 1926, while serving at the Connecticut Agricultural Experiment Station as assistant to Donald F. Jones, one of the inventors and developers of hybrid corn, Mangelsdorf also engaged in part-time graduate work at Harvard, receiving his Sc.D. in 1925. From 1927 to 1940 he was agronomist in charge of corn and small-grain improvement at the Texas Agricultural Experiment Station, where he developed hybrid corn for Texas and, with others, produced new varieties of wheat, oats, and barley. In 1940 he joined the faculty of Harvard University as professor of economic botany. He was appointed Fisher Professor of Natural History in 1962. From 1941 to 1962 he served periodically as consultant in agriculture to the Rockefeller Foundation in connection with the Foundation's agricultural programs in Mexico, Colombia, Chile, and India. He was elected to the National Academy of Sciences in 1945.

Mangelsdorf wrote *The Origin of Indian Corn and Its Relatives,* with R. G. Reeves (1939), and was joint author of *Races of Maize of Mexico* (1952), *Races of Maize of Colombia* (1957), *Races of Maize of Central America* (1957), *Races of Maize of Peru* (1961), and *Campaign for Plenty* (1966).

For background information *see* CORN in the McGraw-Hill Encyclopedia of Science and Technology. □

★ MARK, Herman Francis

American chemist
Born May 3, 1895, Vienna, Austria

As a graduate student under W. Schlenk in Vienna, Mark in 1921 achieved the synthesis of several organic free radicals that remained uncombined even in the solid cyrstalline state. His proof of the existence of stable tervalent carbon in the solid state showed that a few aromatic groups (for example, phenyl, biphenyl, naphthyl, and fluorenyl) possess a strong tendency to absorb more of the valence capacity of a carbon atom than normal substituents. Although in 1922 there was no physicochemical concept ready for the explanation of this fact, the exis-

tence of this effect became an important argument in the theory of resonance in organic molecules as it was later developed in a general and fundamental way by Linus Pauling.

After 1922, Mark's x-ray studies of crystals, particularly of organic crystals, led to the first complete structure determination of a few relatively complicated substances such as hexamethylene-tetramine, urea, and pentaerythritol. The ultimate goal of these studies was the establishment of reliable quantitative values for interatomic distances and valence angles in organic molecules. Later, in 1930, electron diffraction on gaseous systems was used to add further data, and at that time a rather complete list of valence distances and valence angles was worked out.

The anomalous dispersion and the polarization of x-rays were quantitatively measured for the first time by Mark around 1927, and the polarization of the Compton radiation was discovered at about the same time. These facts, together with absolute intensity measurements, contributed substantially to the physics of x-rays in terms of a duality between wave and particle character.

His systematic work on natural high polymers began in 1925 with studies of cellulose and rubber and continued until, by 1930, the molecular structures of cellulose, silk, rubber, chitin, and starch had been elucidated in all their essential features. These results stimulated additional efforts in the field of synthetic polymers, which Mark entered at that time. His most important contributions in this field were:

(1) The proof that all natural and synthetic polymers consist of long chains, in which the free, or almost free, rotation about the single bonds of the backbone chain leads to the tendency to assume random conformations, the probability of which depends on the structural details of the chains, on temperature, and on the presence or absence of external forces. This concept explained in a quantitative manner the viscosity of polymer solutions, the phenomenon of rubber elasticity, and the influence of orientation on fiber properties.

(2) The initiation, on the basis of quantitative experiments on the kinetics of polymer reactions, of a general and complete theory of the mechanism of polymerization processes. Its completion by many other contributors led to the present, almost complete, quantitative understanding and a resulting highly developed engineering of most industrial polymerization reactions.

(3) Systematic work on the relationship between structure and properties of macromolecular systems, which provided first general qualitative, and later rather specific quantitative, leads for the designing of new polymers in view

of certain required properties. This capacity of molecular engineering is characteristic of the present successful and self-propelling state of the science and technology of high polymers, has already led to important results, and is the best guarantee for further rapid and useful progress in this field.

Mark spent 45 months on various fronts during World War I. Receiving his doctorate in chemistry at the University of Vienna in 1921, he moved to Berlin-Dahlem in 1922, joined the Fiber Research Institute there, and worked on the physical chemistry and physics of x-rays and crystals. In 1927 he accepted a position in the research laboratories of I. G. Farben in Ludwigshafen on Rhine, where he organized systematic work on macromolecules with a group of physicists, chemists, and chemical engineers. In 1932 he became professor of physical chemistry at the University of Vienna but was dismissed when Hitler took over Austria in 1938. For the next two years Mark worked as research manager for the International Paper Company in Hawkesbury, Canada. In 1940 he joined the staff of the Polytechnic Institute of Brooklyn. In 1946 the Polymer Research Institute was founded and Mark became its first director. In 1961 he was appointed Dean of the Faculty of Polytechnic Institute of Brooklyn. He was elected to the National Academy of Sciences in 1963.

Mark wrote some 400 scientific articles in many languages and authored or coauthored about 20 books. He was also one of the editors of the *Journal of Polymer Science* and the *Journal of Applied Polymer Science*.

For background information *see* PHYSICAL CHEMISTRY; POLYMER in the McGraw-Hill Encyclopedia of Science and Technology.   □

MARTIN, Archer John Porter
English chemist
Born Mar. 1, 1910, London, England

I N 1941 Martin and R. L. M. Synge developed partition chromatography. This quick, inexpensive method of separating the components of complex mixtures has proved useful in a large variety of scientific investigations. In 1952 they were awarded the Nobel Prize in chemistry for this achievement.

Partition chromatography is the fusion of two techniques: absorption chromatography and countercurrent solvent extraction. M. S. Tsvett, a Russian botanist, separated the compounds found in some plant pigments by allowing an extract to trickle down a column packed with sand or some similar material. The separation

depended on differences in the rates at which the components were carried down the column. Eluviation by further additions of solvent separated the material into a series of colored bands, hence the name chromatography.

However, in separating mixtures of similar materials, Tsvett's absorption chromatography is inadequate; a more selective method of separation is needed. Mixtures can often be separated by the distribution or partition of the components between two immiscible solvents, there being a ratio or coefficient of solubility in the two solvents that differs somewhat for each component of the mixture. Countercurrent extraction, wherein the two solvents flow in opposite directions in a series of tubes, produces such a partition of the components between the solvents. Martin built such a machine, large and cantankerous, for his work on the isolation of vitamin E. He and Synge found the application of this method—two liquid phases moving in opposite directions—unsuitable for the separation of acetylated amino acids.

They then got the idea of holding one liquid phase stationary and having the other solvent move by it. The arrangement was thus Tsvett's chromatography combined with partition of materials between solvents, hence partition chromatography. To separate a mixture of acetyl alanine and acetyl leucine, they used silica gel as a packing in a glass tube to hold the water phase and chloroform as the mobile phase with methyl orange as an indicator. Mixtures of amino acids were separated using ninhydrin to record their position.

Experiments were done with a variety of packing materials and solvents. They found cellulose worked well as a packing, and from this they got

the idea of using paper. Strips of paper were found to work as well as packed columns, and paper chromatography was born. Chromatographic analysis could now be done on a minute quantity of material, and so little labor was involved that hundreds of analyses could be done. They then used two-dimensional paper chromatography involving two successive chromatograms, at right angles to each other.

Many modifications of the process have been made. Moore and Stein used columns packed with starch for quantitative analysis of amino acids in a protein hydrolysate. The use of keiselguhr as a column packing allowed work with larger molecules, such as those found in the ribonucleases. Ion-exchange resins have also been used to pack columns.

In 1953 Martin, with A. T. James, developed gas-liquid, or gas, chromatography. Here the mobile phase is a gas, and it is especially useful for the analysis of small quantities of volatile substances. The material is heated and then propelled, by the flow of a gas such as nitrogen or helium, down a long tube packed with celite. Their early work was confined to substances that could be titrated, such as acids and amines. Using heat conductivity of gases as an indicator has greatly broadened the scope of this method. This method can be used with milligrams of material, whereas distillation requires grams.

It is possible to give only a brief selection of the investigations, in addition to the ones mentioned, in which a fundamental role has been played by partition chromatography. Frederick Sanger worked out the order of amino acids in the molecule of the protein insulin. Synge worked out the structure of the antibiotic gramicidin-S. By the methods of partition chromatography it was definitely established that the vast majority of proteins yield, on hydrolysis, only the well-known amino acids and that these account for the entire substance of the protein molecule. This had long been suspected but, until the advent of this method, was almost impossible to prove. It has proved valuable in assessing the purity of antibiotics, diphtheria vaccines, amino acids, peptides, and many other complex chemical products. The method has been successfully applied to the qualitative and quantitative analysis of the hydrolysates of polysaccharides. Use of radioisotopes as tracers permitted the position of a compound on a chromatogram to be readily detected by a counter or radioautograph. This has made possible great advances in studying the intermediate steps in photosynthesis and metabolism.

In short, it would be difficult to find an active area of biochemical research that does not involve the use of partition chromatography. It has also been extended to many areas of inorganic chemistry, such as separation of rare earths.

The son of a physician, Martin became interested in biochemistry through the influence of J. B. S. Haldane. He received his Ph.D. at Cambridge in 1936. He was at the Dunn National Laboratory until 1938. From 1938 to 1946 he was with the Wool Industries Research Association, and from 1946 to 1948 he was head of the biochemistry division of the research department of Boots Pure Drug Company. From 1948 to 1959 he was on the staff of the Medical Research Council, first at the Lister Institute, then at the National Institute of Medical Research. In 1959 he became director of Abbotsbury Laboratories Limited.

For background information *see* CHROMATOGRAPHY in the McGraw-Hill Encyclopedia of Science and Technology. □

☆ **MARVEL, Carl Shipp**
American chemist
Born Sept. 11, 1894, Waynesville, Ill., U.S.A.

TRAINED AS an organic chemist, Marvel worked principally on the structure and synthesis of high polymers, those very large molecules that comprise plastics, elastomers, and fibers. For his achievements in this area he received the American Chemical Society's Nichols Award (1944), Gibbs Medal (1950), and Priestley Medal (1956).

Marvel's first 60 or 70 publications were significant contributions to various topics in organic chemistry, such as amino acid syntheses and procedures for the use of organometallic compounds. His first polymer paper, on the preparation of copolymers of sulfur dioxide and α-olefins, appeared in 1933. Thus began a series that involved structure determinations of other types of sulfur dioxide addition polymers, exploration of initiator systems for these reactions, and a demonstration that the structures of typical polymers obtained by peroxide or ultraviolet light initiation were identical. In 1937 a program was begun that resulted in contributions to the detailed chemical structure of vinyl polymers. This structure work led to a study of the mechanism of vinyl polymerization using optically active monomers and the preparation and polymerization of many new monomers.

During World War II the government launched a large research program aimed at alleviating the critical shortage of natural rubber. Marvel played a major role in this program through studies of synthesis and polymerization of a large number of butadiene derivatives. He contributed to the development of the redox systems that proved so effective in the emulsion polymerization of butadiene and styrene. Of particular note was his study on the effect of structure on the physical properties of butadiene copolymers using free radical initiators as well as alkali metal catalysts. In an effort to develop new types of synthetic rubbers, polysulfides, prepared from diolefins and dimercaptans, were studied intensively by his group, and the experience gained during the war resulted in a large group of new polymers prepared over the next 10 years.

After 1956 a need arose for synthetic materials able to withstand the very high temperatures encountered in space activities. Turning to the syntheses of such materials, Marvel began by elaborating upon the new technique of cyclopolymerization. Later efforts were devoted to making polymers with repeating rigid heterocyclic or benzenoid groups in the main chain. A most significant contribution was the preparation of a polymer having repeating benzimidazole units, a macromolecule of high molecular weight with outstanding high-temperature properties. This work is generally considered to be one of the most significant advances in the chemistry of high-temperature polymers in the past decade.

Marvel was born and grew up on an Illinois farm. He received his A.B. and M.S. degrees from Illinois Wesleyan University in 1915, then moved on to the University of Illinois, where he received his A.M. in 1916 and his Ph.D. in 1920. For the next 41 years Marvel was a member of the University of Illinois faculty, serving as head of the Division of Organic Chemistry from 1926 to 1953, then becoming a research professor and, in 1961, research professor emeritus. In 1961 he moved to the University of Arizona where, with a large research group, he continued his polymer studies, largely in the area of thermally stable materials. He was elected to the National Academy of Sciences in 1938.

Marvel wrote *An Introduction to the Organic Chemistry of High Polymers* (1959).

For background information *see* POLYMER; POLYMERIZATION in the McGraw-Hill Encyclopedia of Science and Technology. □

☆ **MATTHIAS, Bernd Teo**
American physicist
Born June 8, 1919, Frankfurt, Germany

IN 1950, Matthias began a systematic investigation into the phenomenon of superconductivity, seeking to discover an order in the appearance of this behavior in elements and compounds. From his successful experiments with a great many substances he developed empirical rules to predict new superconducting materials. His large-scale investigation and synthesis of superconductors was essential to subsequent developments in theory and applications of superconductivity. For his achievements in this area, and a similar approach to ferroelectricity, Matthias received the 1962 Research Corporation Award.

In 1911, the Dutch physicist H. Kamerlingh Onnes discovered that at temperatures near absolute zero the electrical resistance of some metals, such as mercury, vanished completely. He found that each material he tested had a characteristic "transition temperature" at which it abruptly lost all resistance to a flow of electricity and began to conduct with no discernible energy loss. Further, this superconductivity was destroyed by a sufficiently strong magnetic field, the "critical field" at which this occurred varying with the substance and the temperature, and decreasing to zero at the transition temperature.

Since that time, theories developed to explain the nature of superconductivity offered no means of predicting the occurrence of superconductivity in a given material, or the transition temperature or critical field strength of that material. Matthias and his colleagues at the Bell Telephone Laboratories decided to experiment with large numbers of metals, hoping that a pattern would emerge upon which to base rules for predicting the appearance of superconductivity and some of the physical features associated with the phenomenon.

With an apparatus consisting primarily of a bath of liquid helium into which samples could be lowered, in capsules, and their conductivity and other characteristics measured, Matthias spent several years testing thousands of metals and alloys. It became clear that the decisive factor for a substance to become superconducting was the number of valence electrons in its outermost atomic shell. No substance, he found, was superconductive unless the average number of valence electrons per atom was between 2 and 8. Within this range, materials with 5 and 7 valence electrons became superconducting at higher temperatures.

Matthias also discovered that certain types of crystal structure favored superconductivity, the most favorable being the so-called beta-tungsten structure, a cubical arrangement of eight atoms with a good deal of room between them.

A corollary of the rule concerning the number of valence electrons was that it might be possible to make a superconductor out of other elements, even totally nonsuperconducting ones, provided the average number of valence electrons was favorable for superconductivity. To test this, Matthias proceeded as follows: The rare element technetium, with 7 valence electrons, had the relatively high transition temperature of 11°K. Flanking technetium in the periodic table are molybdenum and ruthenium. Ruthenium has a crystal structure identical to technetium's, the number of their valence electrons being 6 and 8 respectively. Molybdenum is a superconductor with a transition temperature of 0.9°K; ruthenium's transition temperature is 0.5°K. If the two were combined in equal parts, Matthias reasoned, an alloy should result with a net valence electron count of 7. This alloy would tend, he suspected, to resemble technetium in its superconductive behavior. And in fact the molybdenum-ruthenium alloy made by Matthias was superconducting with a transition temperature of 10.6°K, very close to that of technetium.

Using these discoveries Matthias made a niobium-tin compound having a transition temperature of 18°K, high enough to permit its use in the study and development of superconducting magnets (used, among other places, in particle accelerators for producing very strong magnetic fields with less energy expenditure than conventional electromagnets) and in superconducting computer elements, where "cryotron" switches, kept at very low temperature, appreciably raised the upper limits of operating speed.

In addition to his work on superconductivity, Matthias did research in the field of ferroelectrics.

After studying physics at the University of Rome, Matthias went to Switzerland, where, in 1943, he took his Ph.D. at the Federal Institute of Technology in Zurich. He was a scientific collaborator there until 1947, when he went to the United States to join the staff of the Division of Industrial Cooperation, Massachusetts Institute of Technology. After 1948 he was connected with the Bell Telephone Laboratories. In 1949–51 he taught at the University of Chicago, and in 1961 he was appointed a professor of physics at the University of California, San Diego. He was elected to the National Academy of Sciences in 1965.

For background information *see* SUPERCONDUCTIVITY in the McGraw-Hill Encyclopedia of Science and Technology. □

★ **MAYER, Joseph Edward**
American chemical physicist
Born Feb. 5, 1904, New York, N.Y., U.S.A.

MAYER'S PRINCIPAL work was in the field of statistical mechanics and its application to dense gases and to liquids. For his contributions to theoretical chemistry, he received the American Chemical Society's G. N. Lewis Medal in 1958.

Statistical mechanics is concerned with the methods of computing the properties of macroscopic systems (equations of state, heat capacities, and so forth) from the "microscopic" properties of the molecules, utilizing the laws of mechanics. Gerneral methods developed by Willard Gibbs express the relevant thermodynamic potential sought in terms of an integral over all the coordinates and momenta of all molecules in the system. Since the number of degrees of freedom (coordinates) is immense (10^{24}), the integration is completely impractical unless some simplification can be made. Such simplifications are easy for perfect gases and not too difficult for crystals. One of Mayer's early papers, for instance, showed how the coefficients of the expression for the pressure of an imperfect gas in a power series of the density could be calculated. Later work applied the same method to give the deviations from perfect solution of an electrolytic solution.

The methods developed by Mayer depend on the fact that the functions to be integrated [typically the exponentials of minus $(1/kT)$ times the potential energy] are independent of the distances between molecules that are very far apart; if two groups of molecules get far apart, they become products of functions depending only on the relative positions within the two separate groups. In this case the function itself can be developed as a sum of products of "cluster functions," each of small subsets of the total number of molecules and no coordinates of one molecule appearing in two such functions. The total integral sought is then a sum of products of "cluster integrals" of the cluster functions, and the logarithm of the total integral becomes a sum of the cluster integrals multiplied by the powers of the thermodynamic fugacity. The cluster integrals can further be written as sums of products of other simpler integrals, which turn out to be coefficients of a power series of other thermodynamic quantities, in one case of the reciprocal volume per molecule.

Mayer also showed rigorously that the identical methods used for gases at high densities are applicable to treating the properties of solutes in a solvent. In the particular case of an ionic solute, the single cluster integrals are infinite, since the integral of the long-range (reciprocal of the distance) mutual electrostatic potential diverges. By properly summing the alternately positive and negative functions before integration, however, the total sums that have thermodynamic significance can be seen to converge, and a development for the imperfection of the electrolytic solution can be made.

Son of a bridge engineer, Mayer received his B.S. in 1924 from the California Institute of Technology and his Ph.D. in 1927 from the University of California, Berkeley, where he worked under Gilbert N. Lewis. He was postdoctoral assistant to Lewis for 1 year and held a Rockefeller International Education Board fellowship in 1929–30, working with James Franck in Göttingen; there he met and married Maria Goeppert. He was then associate, and later associate professor, at the Johns Hopkins University, Baltimore, until 1939, associate professor at Columbia University from 1939 to 1946, professor at the University of Chicago from 1946 to 1960, and then professor at the University of California, San Diego, at La Jolla. He was elected to the National Academy of Sciences in 1946.

With Maria Goeppert Mayer, he wrote *Statistical Mechanics* (1940). With Smoluchowski and Weyl he edited *Phase Transformations in Solids* (1951).

For background information *see* STATISTICAL MECHANICS in the McGraw-Hill Encyclopedia of Science and Technology. ☐

★ MAYER, Maria Goeppert
American nuclear physicist
Born June 28, 1906, Kattowitz, then Germany

MARIA GOEPPERT Mayer was awarded the 1963 Nobel Prize in physics jointly with J. H. D. Jensen "for their discovery concerning nuclear shell structure."

The work on nuclear shell structure started with the observation, made accidentally in 1947 in connection with other studies, that some nuclei have anomalous properties. They are, for instance, more stable and more abundant in nature than adjacent nuclei. These nuclei are all those that have a special number of neutrons (for example, 50, 82, or 126) and those that have the same special number of protons. Actually, this observation had been made many years earlier by W. M. Elsasser, when, however, the evidence was much scantier. The numbers were dubbed "magic numbers" by disbelievers. These numbers are the shell number of the shell model and are the nuclear counterpart to the closed shells of electrons of the noble gases.

Maria Goeppert Mayer explained these numbers by proposing a nuclear model analogous to the atomic model, one in which the individual nucleons (neutrons and protons) are assumed to move in independent orbits, little influenced by the position of atomic particles. The field of forces is, of course, quite different from that for electrons. The main point of the shell model that is in contrast to atomic structure is the postulate that in the nucleus the intrinsic spin of every nucleon is strongly coupled to the angular momentum of its own orbit. The actual nuclei will be those in which the protons and neutrons are in the level of lowest energy that is permitted by the exclusion principle. One then finds, indeed, that at the shell numbers, one level is completely filled. One more nucleon has to be placed into a level of higher energy and is weakly bound. A host of other nuclear data are also explained by this model. The assumption of a strong "spin-orbit" coupling contradicted common assumptions but has since been corroborated by many experiments.

At the same time, J. H. D. Jensen, with O. Haxel and H. E. Suess in Germany, was following similiar lines of reasoning and arrived completely independently and simultaneously at essentially identical results.

Originally a physical chemist, Maria Goeppert Mayer, in her doctoral thesis (1930), calculated the probability of the simultaneous emission absorption of two phonons. This probability turned out to be so small that the effect was believed to be unobservable. However, by use of the strong light intensity of lasers, it has been found, and found to be in essential agreement with the theory. Her work in physical chemistry included also the calculations of absorption spectra of organic molecules and the separation of isotopes by chemical methods (with J. Bigeleisen).

Descended from six continuous generations of German university professors, Maria Goeppert studied physics, mathematics, and chemistry mainly in Göttingen, Germany, where she received her doctorate in 1930. In the same year she married Joseph E. Mayer, an American physical chemist. They had two children: Maria Ann Wentzel, born in 1933, and Peter Conrad, born in 1938. She went (1931) with her husband to the Johns Hopkins University in Baltimore, and later (1939) to Columbia University, where she worked at the SAM Laboratories on the separation of uranium isotopes. In 1945 she went to the newly finished Institute for Nuclear Studies at the University of Chicago, where, under the influence and guidance of Enrico Fermi, she became interested in nuclear physics. In 1960 she was appointed professor of physics at the University of California, San Diego, at La Jolla. She was elected to the National Academy of Sciences in 1956.

Maria Goeppert Mayer wrote *Statistical Mechanics*, with Joseph E. Mayer (1940) and *Elementary Theory of Nuclear Shell Structure*, with J. H. D. Jensen (1955).

For background information *see* NUCLEAR STRUCTURE in the McGraw-Hill Encyclopedia of Science and Technology. ☐

☆ **McMILLAN, Edwin Mattison**
American physicist
Born Sept. 18, 1907, Redondo Beach, Calif., U.S.A.

M C MILLAN MADE two major contributions to science: the discovery (with P. H. Abelson) of element 93 (neptunium), which led quickly to the creation of the nuclear energy material, plutonium (element 94); and the conception (independently of V. I. Veksler) of the theory of phase stability, which is essential to the operation of high-energy accelerators. For his first contribution he shared with G. T. Seaborg the Nobel Prize in chemistry in 1951. For his second achievement he shared with V. I. Veksler the Atoms for Peace Award in 1963.

Soon after the announcement of nuclear fission in 1939, McMillan, like many other scientists, began to explore details of the process. Using the 60-inch cyclotron in the Lawrence Radiation Laboratory at the University of California, Berkeley, he sought to determine the distance fission products traveled in matter. In one experiment he used a packet of cigarette papers of the "roll-your-own" variety, smearing a target of uranium on one paper and then piling others on top. He exposed the stack of papers to the cyclotron's neutron beam. As expected, the force of fission propelled fission products into the stack of papers, where they could be detected by observing their radioactivity. Thus the distance of penetration could be measured.

McMillan's analysis of the uranium target itself revealed an unexpected radioactivity. All fission products should have been propelled into the "catcher" papers, and the natural conclusion was that the activity that remained in the uranium was not a fission fragment but an isotope of element 93. It was known that uranium-238 nuclei captured neutrons, becoming uranium-239. McMillan interpreted the new activity as the product of the decay of uranium-239 into an isotope of the next element beyond uranium. This reaction had been proposed years earlier by Enrico Fermi, and Fermi and others had believed, erroneously, that they had created transuranium elements by bombarding uranium-238 with neutrons. Doubts about Fermi's results led to the discovery of fission and an explanation of the radioactive species produced in Fermi's bombardments. Now, McMillan believed he had created element 93 at last by the method predicted by Fermi. It took a year, however, to obtain final proof by showing that the new radioactive substance had chemical properties different from those of all other known elements. The definitive experiment was performed by McMillan and P.H. Abelson in the summer of 1940. The line of investigation was taken up by Glenn T. Seaborg and his colleagues, who discovered plutonium early in 1941. Plutonium is an ingredient of nuclear weapons and a future source of nuclear electrical power.

McMillan's second major contribution was a method for overcoming limitations on the energies that could be attained by the cyclotrons of the 1930s. It was known that the mass increase of particles would make them fall out of step with the electrical impulses of fixed frequency that were then used to accelerate particles in cyclotrons. In the spring of 1945, while he was at Los Alamos working on the atomic bomb project, McMillan realized that if the right conditions were created (by varying the magnetic field or the frequency of electrical impulses, or both), particles would automatically lock in step with the accelerating pulses for an indefinite number of revolutions in an accelerator. Subsequent to McMillan's publication of the theory in September 1945, Russian journals which became available to him revealed that the Russian physicist V. I. Veksler had proposed the same concept about a year earlier.

The theory of phase stability is the basis of the high-energy accelerators of the postwar period. McMillan coined the name "synchroton" for accelerators based on the principle. The great proton synchrotrons include the Bevatron at Berkeley and the alternating gradient synchrotrons at Brookhaven National Laboratory and at CERN in Switzerland. With the synchrotrons, antimatter has been discovered, there has been a proliferation of new particles, and a revolution has occurred in man's ideas about the ultimate structure of matter.

The son of a physician, McMillan studied physics at the California Institute of Technology, receiving the B.S. in 1928 and the M.S. in 1929. He took his Ph.D. at Princeton in 1932. He spent 2 years as a National Research Council fellow at the University of California, Berkeley, joining the staff of E. O. Lawrence's Radiation Laboratory and the physics faculty in 1935. In World War II he contributed to the development of radar, sonar, and nuclear weapons. He became a full professor of physics at Berkeley in 1946, associate director of the Radiation Laboratory in 1954, and in 1958 was named director of the Laboratory. He was elected to the National Academy of Sciences in 1947.

For background information *see* NEPTUNIUM; PARTICLE ACCELERATOR in the McGraw-Hill Encyclopedia of Science and Technology.   □

★ McSHANE, Edward James

American mathematician
Born May 10, 1904, New Orleans, La., U.S.A.

THE INTEGRAL devised in 1902 by H. Lebesgue, with its later generalizations, has been a powerful tool in establishing new results in analysis and in unifying known theories. McShane's research was largely guided by an interest in the power and the uses of integration theory.

His first research was in the calculus of variations. A simple problem of the calculus of variations is that of minimizing an integral

$$\int_a^b f(x,y,y')\,dx \qquad (1)$$

in a class of curves satisfying given end conditions. If we wish, we may regard y in (1) as an n-componented vector. We may also seek the minimum when only those curves are considered that satisfy certain differential equations

$$g_i(x,y,y') = 0 \quad (i = 1, \ldots, p < n) \qquad (2)$$

This is the "problem of Lagrange." Another problem is to minimize a double integral

$$\iint f(x,y,z, \partial x/\partial u, \ldots, \partial z/\partial v)\,du\,dv \qquad (3)$$

in the class of surfaces $x = x(u,v)$, and so forth, satisfying certain boundary conditions.

This last yielded at least partially to Tonelli's method. We choose a sequence of surfaces for which the integral (3) tends to the smallest possible limit m; then we must show, first, that a subsequence converges to a limit surface and, second, that the integral over this limit surface is at most m. The latter offers a difficulty; whereas

$$\lim_{n \to \infty} \int_a^b x'_n(t)\, dt = \int_a^b x'_0(t)\, dt$$

if $x_n \longrightarrow x_0$, the corresponding statement for double integrals is false. This is overcome by using only selected pieces of the sequence of surfaces. The convergence proof needed the extra hypothesis that f is independent of x, y, and z. The resulting existence theorem gave a direct solution of Plateau's problem, which however had been solved earlier by Douglas and Radó.

McShane's treatment of the Lagrange problem was by way of a detour. L. C. Young had defined "generalized curves"; a generalized curve can be imprecisely pictured as a curve made up of imperceptibly small zigzags executed so fast as to be simultaneous to our perception. The Lagrange problem can easily be extended to generalized curves and a definition of limit devised according to which a minimizing sequence exists having a limit which also satisfies (2) and gives (1) the limiting value of (1) for the sequence, which is the minimum. But this limit does not solve the original problem, because it is merely a generalized curve. The remaining stages are, first, to extend the classical variational theory to generalized-curve problems; and second, to use the facts thus learned about the minimizing generalized curve to show (under some extra hypotheses) that it is really an ordinary curve.

If y minimizes (1) among all curves satisfying (2) and boundary conditions, it has long been known that there exist "multipliers" λ_0, $\lambda_1(x)$. . . . , $\lambda_p(x)$, not all 0, such that for the function

$$F(x,y,y') = \lambda_0 f(x,y,y') + \Sigma \lambda_i(x) g_i(x,y,y')$$

the Euler equations are satisfied by y. The Weierstrass and Legendre conditions were established only for "normal" problems, in which the multipliers are unique up to multiplication by a constant. McShane showed that normality is in fact superfluous, and also proved a more complicated substitute for the Jacobi condition without normality. Subsequently this proved to be useful in control theory.

In 1923 Wiener opened a whole new field of integration theory; he showed that a mathematical model of the Brownian motion could be constructed by defining a measure in the set of continuous functions of time. Later he defined multiple integrals over that same space, and showed their usefulness in studying nonlinear random processes. McShane extended this last to more general processes. Also he and his students showed that for differential equations whose coefficients are random functions, the solutions depend continuously on the random coefficients, with a suitable ("weak") definition of convergence among random processes.

McShane studied engineering at Tulane, receiving his B.E. in 1925 and his B.S. the same year, with a major in physics. In 1927 he received the M.S. in mathematics from Tulane, and in 1930 the Ph.D. from the University of Chicago. He was a National Research Council fellow from 1930 to 1932, an assistant at the University of Göttingen in 1932–33, taught at Princeton from 1933 to 1935, and at the University of Virginia after 1935. From 1942 to 1945 he worked in exterior ballistics at the Ballistic Research Laboratory of the Aberdeen Proving Ground. He was elected to the National Academy of Sciences in 1948.

McShane wrote *Integration* (1944), *Exterior Ballistics*, with J. L. Kelley and F. V. Reno (1953), *Order-preserving Maps and Integration Processes* (1953), and *Real Analysis*, with T. A. Botts (1959).

For background information *see* CALCULUS, DIFFERENTIAL AND INTEGRAL in the McGraw-Hill Encyclopedia of Science and Technology.   □

★ MEDAWAR, Peter Brian
British biologist and medical scientist
Born Feb. 28, 1915, Petropolis, Rio de Janeiro, Brazil

FOR THE discovery of acquired immunological tolerance, Medawar shared with F. M. Burnet the 1960 Nobel Prize for physiology or medicine.

Medawar started research on factors controlling growth in tissue cultures and on the mathematical description of the changes of shape that occur during an animal's development, but the outbreak of World War II in 1939 directed his research into medical biology. In the course of an investigation on the healing of nerves he devised the first biological "glue" (essentially a strong solution of fibrinogen, the blood-clotting protein, in blood plasma) and used it both experimentally and clinically to reunite severed nerves and to fix nerve grafts into place.

One of the most desperate medical problems of the war was the replacement of skin lost after severe burns. Medawar was urged to study methods of making what little was left of the patient's skin cover the areas from which it had been burned away. He devised the now familiar method of separating the epidermis from the dermis by treatment with trypsin, and attempted to cover the areas with suspensions of living epidermal cells. These and similar methods failed because they did not stop the disabling process of wound contracture. The obvious solution was to use skin grafts from voluntary donors, but these never gave permanent results. Medawar set himself to the task of finding out why skin taken from one human being (or mouse or chicken) would not form a permanent graft on the body of another and how, if at all, the barrier preventing the use of such "homografts" could be broken down.

Experimentation on a massive scale by the standards then prevailing showed that the rejection of skin homografts in rabbits was brought about by an acquired immunological reaction that left its recipient in a specially refractory state, so that a second set of grafts transplanted subsequently from the same donor would be destroyed much more rapidly than the first grafts. This state of heightened resistance was in force throughout the body, that is, the reaction was systemic and not local. Other things being equal, a large graft was rejected more quickly than a small graft. The chief variable controlling the survival time of a skin homograft was, however, the genetic relationship between donor and recipient, and Medawar designed experiments that showed that there must be at least 127 skin-grafting groups in rabbits. Yet although everything pointed to active immunity as the cause of rejection, all attempts to show that antibodies were the effector agent gave negative results.

At the end of the war Medawar was joined by a brilliant graduate student, R. E. Billingham, and after a few years spent in studying the behavior of melanocytes they joined together in a renewed attack on the homograft problem. Invited to devise a foolproof method of distinguishing identical from fraternal twins in cattle, they exchanged skin grafts between twin pairs

and found that even twins of unlike sex (which cannot be identical) would usually accept each other's skin. R. D. Owen's illuminating discovery of the exchange of red-cell precursors in cattle twins before birth made it natural to suppose that exchange of living cells before birth brought about tolerance of grafts exchanged after birth, and so the concept of "actively acquired tolerance" came to be formulated, along lines already theoretically foreseen by F. M. Burnet. It remained now to prove the case experimentally. Joined now by another highly able graduate student, L. Brent, Medawar and Billingham showed that the deliberate inoculation of fetal mice with living cells from a future donor made them tolerant of homografts from those donors in later life. The three workers thereupon proceeded to an exhaustive study of the general physiology of transplantation tolerance. The discovery of acquired tolerance showed that the problem of using homografts was soluble in principle, and this had an inspiriting effect on clinical research in the field of transplantation. More recent work by Medawar's group included the first demonstration that the antigens that excite transplantation immunity could be extracted from cells. With Billingham's departure for America, Brent and Medawar concentrated their attention on the theory of inducing tolerance in adult animals and on the relationship between homograft reactivity and hypersensitivity reactions of the delayed type—work that pointed to the sensitized lymphocyte rather than to the humoral antibody as the agent of the immunological response.

The field of transplantation immunology, at one time the interest of not more than a dozen workers throughout the world, had now become a major branch of experimental and clinical biology, and thousands of workers attend the biennial New York conferences. The clinical problems of, for example, transplanting kidneys, are not yet solved, but they are nearer solution than anyone 20 years ago believed possible.

Medawar was a professional teacher of zoology until 1962, when he became director of the National Institute for Medical Research in London. As undergraduate, graduate student, and fellow of Magdalen College, Medawar was at Oxford University from 1932 until 1947, thereafter becoming successively chairman of the department of zoology in Birmingham University and in University College, London. Medawar's interest in that area of biology where human demography and genetics overlap found expression in his books *The Uniqueness of the Individual* (1956) and *The Future of Man* (1960).

For background information *see* IMMUNOLOGY in the McGraw-Hill Encyclopedia of Science and Technology.   □

★ MELVILLE, Sir Harry (Work)

British chemist
Born Apr. 27, 1908, Edinburgh, Scotland

MELVILLE'S PRINCIPAL scientific achievement was the complete elucidation of the complex mechanism and chemistry of radical chain reactions, particularly those concerned with the formation of polymers. This was done mainly by devising techniques for following nonstationary phases of such reactions and by using various quantitative techniques associated with reactions of this type. For his work in this field Melville received the Davy Medal of the Royal Society of London in 1955.

Between 1932 and 1939, at Edinburgh and subsequently at Cambridge University, Melville followed up the ideas put forward by C. N. Hinshelwood and N. N. Semenov to explain explosion limits in gas reactions. This theory gave an acceptable explanation for these phenomena but was not supported by much direct experimental evidence. By the study of these reactions, both within and outside of the explosion limits, Melville demonstrated that this theory was correct and developed further methods to measure the velocity coefficients of the elementary steps of the process. Then by an extension of the theory he was able actually to measure, for the first time, the branching coefficients of a chain reaction. This gave practically complete basic formulation to the processes leading from stable to explosion combustion.

The development of these ideas and methods then made it practicable to see whether they were applicable to the study of polymerization processes. Melville discovered several suitable systems that permitted the theory to be applied to gas phase polymerization and even enabled measurements to be made of the time required for high polymer molecules to grow to their final size.

Melville's work along this line stopped during World War II but was restarted, particularly on the mechanism of polymerization, in 1945. His basic object was to attempt to specify completely polymerization reactions by measuring the velocity coefficients of all the elementary processes, the concentration of the polymer radicals, and the time of growth of the molecules. This was in fact achieved in 1945 in the case of the vinyl acetate reaction by employing a combination of techniques involving the use of rotating sector for the measurement of lifetime, the measurement of molecular weights by osmotic pressure, and the rate of initiation of reactions by the use of selected inhibitors, so that for the first time a chain reaction was numerically described. Melville applied these methods to many other systems so that some idea of the effect of structure on reactivity could be established. Besides the rotating-sector technique, nonstationary methods were devised that involved measuring the amount of reaction in the very early stages. This led to the construction of specially sensitive physical recording methods for following reactions. These methods were then applied to the reactions in the semisolid state and thus gave information about the behavior of giant radicals in highly viscous media. Further extension was made to the study of polymerization in two- and even three-component systems, which gave further information about polymeric radical behavior and added support to the complete picture.

The study of the breakdown of high-polymer molecules revealed a simple system for suitable investigation by using a powerful combination of methods. The details of the mechanism of the breakdown of high polymers was achieved in a quantitative fashion. This development made possible the calculation of equilibria data from kinetic experiments that were in accord with the direct observations of such equilibria. Radioactive labeling became available at this stage and helped appreciably in Melville's investigation into how branched-chain polymers could be synthesized and characterized. Likewise the synthesis of nonrandom copolymers became possible, and a number of methods were devised to construct molecules with this kind of internal structure. The developments in the understanding of polymer synthesis also applied to the elucidation of oxidation and other radical reactions, thus giving an added dimension to reaction kinetics.

In the same context and over the whole period, Melville did a great deal of work to determine the elementary reactions of radicals in the gas phase. This led to more complete understanding of the elementary photochemical decomposition processes of simple molecules. Further, his devising of special methods of great sensitivity enabled extremely fast chemical reactions to be quantitatively studied. These were concerned with the interactions of hydrogen atoms with hydrocarbon molecules of all kinds.

Melville took his B.Sc. in chemistry in 1930 at the University of Edinburgh, Scotland, and later graduated Ph.D. and D.Sc. in the same university. Going to Cambridge in 1933 with an 1851 Senior Scholarship, he became a fellow of Trinity College in 1935 and assistant director of research of the Colloid Science Laboratory in 1938. The war years were spent in the Ministry of Supply in the chemical warfare department and also in the Radar Research Station. He was appointed professor of chemistry at Aberdeen University in 1940 but did not take up the appointment until 1945. In 1948 he was appointed to the Mason Chair of Chemistry at Birmingham, and in 1956 he became secretary of the department of scientific and industrial research. On the reorganization of civil science in the United Kingdom in 1965 he became chairman of the Science Research Council.

Melville wrote *Experimental Methods in Gas Reactions*, with A. Farkas (1939) and *Big Molecules* (1958).

For background information *see* CHAIN REACTION, CHEMICAL in the McGraw-Hill Encyclopedia of Science and Technology.   □

MERRILL, Paul Willard

American astronomer
Born Aug. 15, 1887, Minneapolis, Minn., U.S.A.
Died July 16, 1961, Los Angeles, Calif., U.S.A.

W HILE STUDYING the spectra of long-period variable stars, Merrill discovered the presence of technetium in stars of spectral type S. Since no stable isotopes of technetium had been found on the Earth, the discovery necessitated the postulation of a nuclear process within S-type stars that would result in the formation of technetium atoms to replenish those lost through radioactive decay.

Technetium, the first of the man-made elements, was identified in 1937 after Emilio Segrè and Carlos Perrier had bombarded molybdenum with deuterons in the 57-in. cyclotron at the University of California. Although technetium has since been isolated from fission products of heavy elements, no completely stable isotope has been found. William F. Meggers and Bourdon F. Scribner at the National Bureau of Standards investigated the spectrum of technetium in 1950.

Their work made it possible to identify the element in the spectra of celestial bodies.

In 1952, while working with the 100-in. telescope at the Mt. Wilson Observatory in California, Merrill prepared the spectrogram of the long-period variable star R Andromedae. The spectrum of R Andromedae, an S-type star, should have been characterized by bands of zirconium oxide and by relatively strong lines of heavy metals, such as zirconium and barium. The spectrogram, however, which had a dispersion of 10 A per millimeter, showed several lines that had never before been observed. Merrill identified these as strong absorption lines of neutral technetium. The strongest of the lines were in the $a^6S - z^6P^0$ multiplet, analogous to the triplet at the wavelength of 4030 A in the spectrum of manganese. Merrill also found the strong absorption lines in the spectra of the other S-type stars, and his discovery was verified by Ira Sprague Bowen using the 200-in. telescope at the Mt. Palomar Observatory.

To explain the presence in S-type stars of an element of which no stable isotopes are known, Merrill offered three alternatives. One, of course, was that a stable isotope of technetium exists, although it is not yet known on the Earth. A second was that S-type stars represent a comparatively transient phase of stellar existence and that what holds true for them need not hold true for earlier-type stars. The third alternative was that S-type stars somehow produce techne-

tium as part of their internal nuclear process. It is this latter alternative that has gained the greatest acceptance.

Merrill was primarily an observational astronomer and he rarely offered detailed theoretical explanations of his findings. He specialized in the study of stars whose spectra deviate from those of normal stars. Merrill was greatly interested in long-period variables, and his spectrographic studies established correlations between stellar brightness, radial velocities of the emission and absorption lines, emission line intensities, and general spectral variations. He also proved that the strong hydrogen emission lines in these variables were produced below the reversing layers of the stars. Merrill also made significant contributions to the study of interstellar matter and did pioneer spectral research in the infrared portion of the spectrum.

The son of a Congregationalist minister, Merrill was educated at Stanford University in Palo Alto, Calif., receiving his A.B. in mathematics, with minors in physics and astronomy, in 1908. After working for the U.S. Coast and Geodetic Survey for a year, he became a graduate student at the University of California at Berkeley and a fellow at the Lick Observatory. Upon receiving his Ph.D. in astronomy in 1913, Merrill became an instructor of astronomy at the University of Michigan. In 1916 he joined the National Bureau of Standards in Washington, D.C., as a physicist, working there for 3 years. He joined the staff at the Mt. Wilson Observatory in 1919, remaining there until his retirement in 1952. He was awarded the Bruce Medal of the Astronomical Society of the Pacific in 1946.

Merrill wrote *Space Chemistry* (1963).

For background information *see* ASTRONOMICAL SPECTROSCOPY in the McGraw-Hill Encyclopedia of Science and Technology. □

★ **MILLER, Neal Elgar**
American psychologist
Born Aug. 3, 1909, Milwaukee, Wis., U.S.A.

A COMBINATION of theory and experiment bridging different disciplines characterized Neal Miller's work, which ranged from the social to the physiological borders of psychology. For this work, which showed how principles of learning and motivation could be applied to the understanding of personality dynamics and social behavior, and which opened up new ways of analyzing the physiological basis of motivation, he was awarded the National Medal of Science for 1964.

Miller's early work at the Yale Institute of Human Relations in collaboration with John Dollard showed how the laws of learning discovered in the laboratory and the social conditions of learning studied by sociologists and cultural anthropologists could explain significant aspects of social learning, imitation, neuroses, and psychotherapy. His interest in the dynamics of behavior observed in the clinic led to a series of experimental studies of fear and conflict. In these studies, he measured gradients of approach and of avoidance, separately in simple situations. From these gradients he predicted the behavior to be expected in more complex situations in which the subject was motivated both to approach and to avoid the same goal. Then he designed experiments to test these predictions. In this way he explained and verified a number of the phenomena of conflict behavior and displacement. For this work the Society of Experimental Psychologists awarded him its Warren Medal in 1954.

The results of this earlier work emphasized the importance of motivation and reward as determinants of behavior. Miller then went on to use a combination of behavioral and physiological techniques to analyze the mechanisms of motivation and reward. He discovered that food injected via a chronic cannula directly into the stomach of a hungry rat could serve as a reward, causing the rat to learn to choose the side of a T-maze in which the food was injected, but that a similar amount of distension produced by inflating a balloon on the end of the cannula served as a punishment to cause the rat to learn to avoid the side where the balloon was inflated. He and his collaborators used a variety of behavioral tests to show that direct electrical stimulation of certain areas of the brain could elicit motivation with all of the functional properties of normal fear and pain. They discovered that trial-and-error learning could be motivated by electrical stimulation of certain areas of the brain and rewarded by escape from such stimulation. In subsequent studies, he and his students showed that electrical stimulation of the lateral hypothalamus, which had been known to elicit eating, did not involve mere reflex gnawing, but instead had many, and perhaps all, of the properties of normal hunger. For the initial stages of this work, the American Association for the Advancement of Science awarded Miller the Newcomb-Cleveland Prize in 1957, which he shared with James Olds.

An interest in probing deeper into the mechanisms of motivation next led Miller and his students to test the behavioral effects of chemically stimulating the brains of animals with substances believed to act as transmitters in the synapses of the peripheral nervous system. Such chemical stimulation was found to be more selective than electrical stimulation, suggesting that different behavioral systems may be chemically coded.

Miller's work led to increased understanding of the physiological mechanisms of motivation and of how motivation and learning affect social behavior. He brought together concepts and techniques from different disciplines to open up new areas of basic research.

The son of Irving E. Miller, an educational psychologist, Miller took a general science major at the University of Washington, where he elected psychology in his senior year and got his B.S. in 1931. He received his M.A. in psychology at Stanford University in 1932 and a Ph.D. at Yale in 1935. After studying psychoanalysis in Vienna as a Social Science Research Council fellow the following year, he was appointed a research assistant in psychology in the Institute of Human Relations at Yale University in 1936. During World War II he became an officer in the Air Corps, doing research on the selection and classification of air crews during the first 2 years and on pilot training during the last 2 years. Returning to Yale in 1946, he became a full professor in 1950 and the James Rowland Angell Professor of Psychology in 1952. He was elected to the National Academy of Sciences in 1958.

Miller wrote *Personality and Psychotherapy*, with J. Dollard (1960).

For background information *see* LEARNING THEORIES; MOTIVATION in the McGraw-Hill Encyclopedia of Science and Technology.   □

stein introduced his special and general theories of relativity. A number of cosmological models, based on the general theory of relativity and therefore called "relativistic models," were developed to explain the expanding universe by such men as the English astronomer and physicist Arthur Stanley Eddington and the Belgian astronomer Abbé Georges Lemaître. In these relativistic models, emphasis is placed upon the geometry of the universe, that is, whether it is open or closed, and upon the accelerated motion of the galaxies.

Although Milne accepted the special theory of relativity, he rejected the general theory. He believed that it was possible to deduce the laws governing the universe from a few self-evident general principles, or axioms, and that the number of general principles required tended to become smaller as science progressed. Therefore, Milne believed, the more advanced the branch of science, the greater its reliance on inference and the less its appeal to the experiences of the scientist.

From 1932 until his death, Milne devoted himself to the development of a metaphysical system of kinematic relativity based on inference. For example, he deduced a law of motion equivalent to Newton's first law by a study of the position and velocity of a free particle relative to an observer situated anywhere in the universe. He then proceeded to deduce the law of gravitation by extending the analysis to the relative motion of two or more free particles. By a series of similar deductions, Milne derived his simplified model of the universe. He pointed out that if the motion of the galaxies were unaccelerated, that is, if the system were such that the galaxies moved uniformly in all directions, then in the course of time the universe would become an expanding system in which the fastest-moving

MILNE, Edward Arthur

English mathematician and astrophysicist
Born Feb. 14, 1896, Hull, England
Died Sept. 21, 1950, Dublin, Ireland

W HILE ENGAGED in the study of cosmic dynamics, Milne developed a metaphysical system, based on atomic time measurement, which he called "kinematic relativity." Through the use of this conceptual framework, he advanced new systems of dynamics and electrodynamics and from these developed a model of the universe that was not based on the general theory of relativity.

During the first quarter of the 20th century, the American astronomer Vesto Melvin Slipher discovered that many of the nearby galaxies are receding from the Milky Way, and Albert Ein-

galaxies would have receded the farthest from the starting point. The respective distances and speeds, Milne reasoned, would tend to obey the law $r = vt$, where r is the distance receded, v is the velocity of recession, and t is the time elapsed. Since all of the galaxies would be receding from a central point, Milne deduced, all of the galaxies must have been compressed into a very small volume a finite number of years ago. The number of years, represented by t in his equation, Milne computed to be 2×10^9 (based on the scale of galactic distances announced by the American astronomer Edwin P. Hubble). Thus, his approach was to base his cosmological model on time measurement rather than on the geometry of space. The deductions of kinematic relativity were not completed at the time of Milne's death. Because of the system's appeal to inference, which is contradictory to the scientific method, it had met considerable opposition from Milne's contemporaries and Milne left no large school of followers. For this reason, little work has been done on it since his death, and Milne's cosmological model has been largely neglected in favor of the "big-bang" and "steady-state" theories.

Milne is also known for his theoretical investigations of stellar atmospheres, performed in collaboration with the English astrophysicist R. H. Fowler. Their work on atomic ionization, which they used to fix a temperature scale for the stellar spectral sequence, advanced the knowledge of the surface conditions of stars to a considerable extent. Milne also contributed to the study of the escape of molecules from planetary atmospheres and to the study of white dwarf stars.

The eldest son of the headmaster of a Church of England school, Milne was educated at Hymers College, Hull, and Trinity College, Cambridge, where he received his M.A. in 1920 and his D.Sc. in 1925. He served as assistant director of the Solar Physics Observatory at Cambridge from 1920 to 1924, as a lecturer in mathematics at Trinity College from 1924 to 1925, and as a university lecturer in astrophysics from 1922 to 1925. Milne became a professor of applied mathematics at the University of Manchester in 1925. In 1928 he left to become a professor of mathematics and a fellow of Wadham College at Oxford University, posts he retained until his death. During World War II he served on the Ordnance Board of the Ministry of Supply. Milne was awarded the Gold Medal of the Royal Astronomical Society in 1935, the Royal Medal of the Royal Society in 1941, and the Bruce Medal of the Astronomical Society of the Pacific in 1945.

Among the books written by Milne are *Relativity, Gravitation, and World-structure* (1935) and *Kinematic Relativity* (1948).

For background information *see* COSMOLOGY in the McGraw-Hill Encyclopedia of Science and Technology. ☐

★ MINNAERT, Marcel Gilles Jozef
Dutch astrophysicist
Born Feb. 12, 1893, Bruges, Belgium

IN THE solar spectrum there are thousands of Fraunhofer lines, much darker than the surrounding continuous spectrum but still possessing a certain amount of light, even in their centers. Minnaert was one of the first to measure the intensity distribution inside Fraunhofer lines. He showed how from such measurements considerable information could be drawn concerning the outer solar layers. For his investigations in solar physics he received the Gold Medal of the Royal Astronomical Society and the Catherine Wolfe Bruce Medal of the Astronomical Society of the Pacific.

W. H. Julius began the study of solar radiation and the Fraunhofer lines at the Utrecht Physical Laboratory in 1901. About 1920 Moll invented his microphotometer with which L. S. Ornstein, H. C. Burger, and P. H. van Cittert made the first spectrophotometric measurements on emission lines in laboratory spectra. This inspired Minnaert to carry out similar measurements on the absorption lines of the Sun.

A number of difficulties had to be overcome. Most Fraunhofer lines are very narrow; one had to be sure that the spectrograph and the microphotometer had a sufficient resolving power. Stray light could easily account for an appreciable part of the intensity within the line. Photographic effects might influence the photographic image of a narrow dark line surrounded by a bright background. The introduction of the concept of "equivalent width" proved to be very useful. The equivalent width is the width of an imaginary line, entirely black and with sharp edges, that would absorb the same amount of light actually absorbed by the Fraunhofer line. Until then, the "strength" of the Fraunhofer lines had been estimated on an arbitrary scale (the Rowland scale). It was now possible to calibrate this scale in units of equivalent width.

In 1928 H. N. Russell had found a relation between the Rowland strength and the number of absorbing atoms (or ions) per unit volume. This relation was translated into equivalent widths and gave the "curve of growth" for Fraunhofer lines, which became an important tool for the analysis of the solar and the stellar atmospheres. The importance of this curve became evident when W. Schütz, working with laboratory emission lines, showed (1930) that its shape was determined by the temperature of the absorbing atoms and by the damping of their radiation. Minnaert and his collaborator, G. F. W. Mulders, applied this interpretation directly to the Fraunhofer lines. From the curve it now proved possible to derive the quantities of the different elements, the temperatures of the solar or stellar surface layers, and the amount of damping. Later O. Struve showed that the turbulent motions in stellar atmospheres were also evidenced in the curve of growth.

Minnaert, together with Mulders and J. Houtgast, then took spectrograms of the whole solar spectrum, recorded these with an apparatus of their own making, and published (1940) their *Photometric Atlas of the Solar Spectrum*, which was widely used. It represented the intensity distribution over the Fraunhofer lines between λ3612 and 8871 A on a scale of 2 cm/A. This atlas became the basis of a photometric catalog of Fraunhofer lines, elaborated by Minnaert and Houtgast; this is now included in *The Solar Spectrum 2935 A to 8770 A: Second Revision of Rowland's Preliminary Table of Solar Spectrum Wavelengths* (1966), published jointly with Charlotte E. Moore.

Minnaert studied many other features of the Sun: the brightness distribution at the solar limb; the intensity of the flash lines (with A. Pannekoek); the radiation of sunspots (with A. J. M. Wanders); the intensity of prominence lines (with C. Slob); and the brightness and polarization of the corona. He worked, too, on the photometry of the Moon.

Minnaert studied botany at the University of Ghent (Ph.D., 1914), then physics at the University of Utrecht (Ph.D., 1925). In 1936 he became a professor of astronomy and director of the Utrecht Observatory "Sonnenborgh." He retired in 1963. A member of numerous academies, he was elected in 1964 a foreign associate of the U.S. National Academy of Sciences.

Besides the *Photometric Atlas of the Solar Spectrum* (1940), Minnaert wrote *De Natuurkunde van 't Vrije Veld* (3 vols., 1937–42; Part I translated as *Light and Color in the Open Air*),

De Sterrekunde en de Mensheid (1947), and *Dichters over Sterren* (1949).

For background information *see* SPECTROSCOPY; SUN in the McGraw-Hill Encyclopedia of Science and Technology. ☐

MONIZ, Antonio Caetano de Abreu Freire Egas

Portuguese neurosurgeon
Born Nov. 29, 1874, Avança, Portugal
Died Dec. 13, 1955, Lisbon, Portugal

B ASED ON earlier work identifying the particular sites in the brain that control higher psychic functions, Moniz developed an operation to relieve severe mental disorders by interrupting the lines of communication between the frontal lobes of the brain (where higher cerebral activity is localized) and the lower centers of the brain. In recognition of this contribution to neurological surgery, Moniz received half of the 1949 Nobel Prize for physiology or medicine.

The event that led, albeit indirectly, to Moniz's development of the prefrontal lobotomy (or leucotomy) occurred in the United States nearly 100 years before. In 1848, an iron rod was accidentally driven through the head of Phineas Gage, a road construction worker. Amazingly, Gage survived. The rod, 4 feet long and over 1 inch thick, had penetrated his left cheek obliquely and emerged from the top of his head. He was stunned, but within an hour walked with assistance to a surgeon. The rod was removed and although a wound infection developed, Gage recovered with significantly few aftereffects. His memory and ability to work were unimpaired, but there was a slight diminution in his intellectual capacities. What had altered significantly, however, was his personality. Of mild and considerate disposition prior to the accident, afterwards he was notably restless, obstinate, profane, lax about work, and inconsiderate of the feelings of others. For the remaining 12 years of his life he traveled about exhibiting his healed wound and the rod that had inflicted it. He died of causes unrelated to the injury in San Francisco. An autopsy performed there showed that the left frontal lobe of his brain was severely damaged and that the right frontal lobe was also injured.

The observations on Gage, plus later observations on symptoms produced by brain tumors and other types of brain damage, indicated that injury to the frontal lobes has no effect on any vital bodily processes. The same observations indicated that personality changes are the most pronounced sequelae to frontal lobe damage.

During the early 1930s American physiologists began experimenting with chimpanzees in order to verify earlier hypotheses on the location of the various areas of the brain that control psychic and bodily functions. It was noted that when one frontal lobe was removed, no observable change occurred in the chimpanzee. When both lobes were removed, however, the animal's ability to perform sequential operations was impaired. An incidental, but extremely enlightening, finding was made on an intact chimpanzee. When this particular animal, who had been quite docile before being subjected to psychological experimentation, made errors in problem solving, she became extremely violent and frustrated, so much so that she was of no use as a psychological subject. It was decided to operate, and both of her frontal lobes were removed. After recovery she was noted to be docile and cooperative, attempting all problem-solving tasks presented to her. What was most remarkable was that although her problem-solving ability was now almost nil and she made innumerable mistakes, she did not seem to care.

In 1935 the chimpanzee studies, which had been performed by the American investigator Carlyle Jacobsen, were reported at the International Neurological Conference in London. It was here that Moniz learned of this work and determined to develop a similar operative procedure to be used in human mental patients. Moniz's rationale for such a procedure was that in certain severe mental diseases (particularly the affective psychoses) there occurred an abnormal stabilization of cellular connections in the frontal lobes, correlated with a fixation of ideas and repetitive behavior. During 1935–36 Moniz operated on 20 mental patients in Lisbon. By removing cores of central white matter in each frontal lobe he transected the fibers connecting the frontal cortices (the outermost, gray layer of the frontal lobes) to the deeper brain structures. Seven of his patients were reported cured, eight improved, and five unchanged. The results observed following these operations were remarkably like those noted by Jacobsen in his chimpanzee studies. The human patients persisted in their abnormal thoughts and actions, but were no longer excessively anxious about them.

As a corollary to Moniz's pioneering work in human psychosurgery, it was later noted that prefrontal lobotomy was effective in controlling intractable pain. Following operation, the perception of pain was not altered but the individual became indifferent to it.

In addition to his introduction of prefrontal lobotomy in human subjects, Moniz is remembered for a highly important contribution to neurological diagnostic technique: the development of cerebral angiography, a method of visualizing the vasculature of the brain through the use of a radio-opaque dye and x-ray examination.

Following early tutoring by his uncle, Moniz joined the faculty of medicine at Coimbra University in Portugal and later studied at medical schools in Bordeaux and Paris. He became professor at Coimbra in 1902 and later (1911) assumed the chair in neurology at Lisbon, holding that position until his death. Concurrent with his academic career, Moniz was active politically, serving as a deputy in the Portuguese parliament from 1903 to 1917. In 1917 he was named ambassador to Spain and in that same year was appointed Minister for Foreign Affairs. At the 1918 Paris Peace Conference he served as president of the delegation from Portugal.

For background information *see* BRAIN; NEUROPHYSIOLOGY in the McGraw-Hill Encyclopedia of Science and Technology.   □

☆ MONOD, Jacques
French biologist
Born 1910, Paris, France

W HILE CONDUCTING a series of physiologico-genetic studies, Monod, in collaboration with the French biologist François Jacob, proposed the concepts of messenger RNA (ribonucleic acid) and of the operon. These concepts helped to provide a unified theory of the molecular mechanisms of the genetic apparatus. In recognition of this work, Monod shared the 1965 Nobel Prize for physiology or medicine with Jacob and the French biologist André Lwoff, who had made important contributions to the study of lysogenic bacteria.

During the mid-1950s, Mahlon B. Hoagland and Paul Zamecnik of Harvard University discovered that the conveyor of the amino acid during polypeptide formation was a variety of RNA that they named soluble, or transfer, RNA. In 1956, Elliot Volkin and L. Astrachan of the Oak Ridge National Laboratories found that a variety of RNA formed after bacteriophage infection mimicked the ratio of the bases in the DNA (deoxyribonucleic acid) of the bacteriophage. They concluded that a "DNA-like RNA" was produced as a result of the infection. Three years later, Sam Weiss of the Argonne National Laboratories produced "DNA-like RNA" in a test tube. However, the role of this substance in protein synthesis remained unknown.

In 1958, while working with François Jacob and a visiting American biologist, Arthur Pardee, at the Pasteur Institute in Paris, Monod participated in what is now known as the "Pa-Ja-Mo experiment." By conjugating female mutant bacteria synthesizing β-galactosidase constitutively with normal male bacteria, which could only synthesize β-galactosidase by exogenous induction, it was demonstrated that inducibility is dominant over constitutivity. This led the experimenters to put forth the concept that enzyme synthesis is initiated when the inducer neutralizes a repressor, which is itself produced by a particular regulatory gene. Monod and Jacob continued to experiment with a variety of regulatory mutant bacteria and in 1961 proposed the concepts of messenger RNA and the operon.

According to their proposal, the first step in protein production is the transcription of the sequence of bases in the DNA helix into a complementary sequence of those bases in RNA. This RNA is the "DNA-like RNA" of Volkin and Astrachan. Monod and Jacob named it messenger RNA, because it was this that carried the genetic message to the ribosomes. The messenger RNA combines with the preexisting transfer-RNA–rich ribosomes and there directs the ordered synthesis of polypeptides.

The operon, they proposed, comprises genes of related functions in contiguous regions of the chromosome and a shared gene of regulation called their operator. When the operator is "open," the genes can synthesize messenger RNA. When the operator is "closed" by a specific repressor substance, itself the product of a regulatory gene, the messenger RNA is not produced. The repressor is activated by its interaction with an effector molecule. The operon

concept not only helped to explain bacterial enzyme synthesis but also gave insight into prophage induction, which had been discovered by André Lwoff of the Pasteur Institute a decade earlier.

Monod's earlier work was primarily concerned with the synthesis of the inducible bacterial enzyme β-galactosidase. In studies begun in 1946, he demonstrated that the induced formation of the enzyme was not the conversion of preexisting proteinaceous material but instead the direct synthesis of protein molecules. He also noted that the inducer does not interact with the enzyme. He later extended the studies, in collaboration with Germaine Cohen-Bazire, to show that mutant bacteria existed in which β-galactosidase synthesis proceeds constitutively, that is, without exogenous induction.

Monod received his B.S. in 1931 and his D.Sc. in 1941. From 1932 to 1934 he did laboratory research on the evolution of organic life. In the latter year he was named assistant professor of zoology in the Faculté des Sciences of the University of Paris. He maintained this position until 1945, when he became laboratory chief at the Pasteur Institute. In 1953 he was appointed head of the Institute's department of cellular biochemistry. Monod was named professor in the Faculté des Sciences of the University of Paris in 1959.

For background information *see* NUCLEIC ACID in the McGraw-Hill Encyclopedia of Science and Technology.   □

★ **MOORE, Raymond Cecil**
American geologist and paleontologist
Born Feb. 20, 1892, Roslyn, Wash., U.S.A.

MOORE'S CHIEF scientific contribution was the elucidation of principles relating to the classification and interpretation of layered sedimentary deposits and their contained organic remains, both as a record of Earth history and as a source of economic resources. Especially he pioneered in the investigation of cyclically arranged strata, widespread in parts of the geologic column of North America and Europe, which furnish a record of repetitive shallow-sea invasions of continental areas; and he specialized in the study of such invertebrate fossil groups as corals, bryozoans, and crinoid echinoderms. For his achievements he received, among other honors, the 1956 Hayden Memorial Geological Award of the Academy of Natural Sciences of Philadelphia and in 1963 the first Paleontological Society Medal.

A very unusual beginning for a career in scientific work was Moore's completion of a dozen years of courses in classic languages (Latin, Greek, and Sanskrit), in addition to French and German, before he came under the spell of an exceptional teacher of geology, Frank Carney of Denison University, Granville, Ohio. Moore's father was a Baptist minister, but the son now abandoned an intent to follow in his footsteps in favor of summers "out West" as a cub member of a U.S. Geological Survey party and winters of full-time graduate studies in geology. After graduating from Denison in 1913, Moore earned a Ph.D. at the University of Chicago in 1916. That year he was appointed assistant professor at the University of Kansas. At the same time he was designated State Geologist of Kansas. An advancement inconceivable in universities of the present day gave Moore the rank of full professor in 1919, and in 1920 he was made chairman of the department of geology.

Meanwhile, Moore retained his connection with the U.S. Geological Survey and in 1923 was selected to be the geologist on a party traveling by boat through the Grand Canyon of the Colorado River for the purpose of studying possible dam sites. This and work in other seasons led to publication of several papers on Colorado Plateau geology and to doctoral studies by Kansas students in the region. An episode of the 1923 survey on the river that gained the attention of the nation's press was the reported drowning of the entire party of 11 men, which enabled Moore to share with Mark Twain the distinction of having a prematurely published obituary.

Moore's detailed stratigraphic and paleontologic investigations, including studies that led to definition of numerous cyclically repeated sequences of sedimentary layers and to interpretations of their significance, were made chiefly in Kansas, Missouri, Nebraska, Oklahoma, Arkansas, and Texas in the 1920s, 1930s, 1940s, and 1950s. In 1930–33 he was one of the leaders in preparing the first Code of Stratigraphic Nomenclature, which became recognized as the authoritative statement of principles and a guide used throughout North America. Later (1946) Moore initiated creation of the American Commission on Stratigraphic Nomenclature, composed of representatives of the national and state surveys and major geological societies of North America, and served as its first chairman. In 1952 he was elected by the International Geological Congress as president of its permanent Commission on Stratigraphy and served in this capacity until his resignation in 1960. This commission coordinated the efforts of stratigraphic geologists in approximately 75 nations. The most important project undertaken by Moore, beginning in 1948, was the organization and direction of a huge collaborative program to produce a 26-volume *Treatise on Invertebrate Paleontology*. By 1965, 16 volumes had been published.

For background information *see* SEDIMENTARY ROCKS; SEDIMENTATION (GEOLOGY) in the McGraw-Hill Encyclopedia of Science and Technology.   □

★ MORDELL, Louis Joel

British mathematician
Born June 28, 1888, Philadelphia, Pa., U.S.A.

MORDELL'S WORK covered a wide range in the theory of numbers and allied subjects. His contributions may be arranged under four headings:

Diophantine equations. These deal with integer and rational solutions of polynomial equations with several variables. Mordell found many new results and new methods. The most important one is the finite basis theorem for the rational points on a cubic curve $f(x,y) = 0$, that is, points whose coordinates x,y are rational numbers. Suppose that a set S of rational points P_1, P_2, . . . , P_n is known. Then the tangent at P_1 meets the curve again in a rational point $P_{1,1}$ in general different from P_1. So the secant P_1,P_2 meets the curve in a point $P_{1,2}$ in general different from P_1 or P_2. By adding the points $P_{1,1}$ and $P_{1,2}$ to the set S and continuing the procedure, we may expect to find an infinity of rational points. Mordell proved the so-called finite basis theorem, namely, that all the rational points on the cubic could be derived in this way from a finite set S. This was a basic result.

He found many results for equations for three variables, and they were the starting points for many investigations on the rational and integer points on a cubic surface by himself and others.

Geometry of numbers. The fundamental problem is to find the minimum value $M(f)$ of a homogeneous function $|f(x,y)|$ for integers $(x,y) \neq (0,0)$. When $f(x,y)$ is a binary quadratic, the best possible results were classical and had been known for many years. Important results had been found by H. Minkowski. Call a point $P(x,y)$ a lattice point when its coordinates are integers. Let K be a bounded convex region in n dimensional space symmetrical about the origin O and of volume V. Then if $V > 2^n$, K contains a lattice point other than O.

For nonconvex regions very little was known. Thus when $f(x,y)$ is a binary cubic, partial results for $M(f)$ had been known from about the middle of the 19th century. Mordell found the best possible result in 1940. His method led also to results for some general nonconvex regions. This was the starting point of researches by himself and others that completely transformed this subject.

Analytic number theory. Let $f(x) = x_1{}^2 + x_2{}^2 + \ldots + x_r{}^2$. The problem of finding the number $N(n)$ of integer solutions of $f(x) = n$ has been one of the most interesting and important problems in number theory. The results for $r \leqq 8$ are classic and were found in most cases by arithmetical processes, and sometimes by the use of elliptic functions. The latter method had been applied in an unsystematic way, no general theory underlying this process. Mordell was the first to show that the use of modular functions led to a direct attack on the problem for all values of r. Then if $|q| < 1$, the theory could be applied to a discussion of the function of q defined by

$$F(q) = \sum_{n=1}^{n} N(n)\, q^n = \left(\sum_{n=-\infty}^{\infty} q^{n^2} \right)^r$$

Gauss' sums play a prominent part in number theory and have been studied for many years. Mordell gave the simplest analytic proof. His studies of the class number of binary quadratic form led him to the evaluation of the definite integer

$$\int_{-\infty}^{\infty} \frac{e^{at^2} + b}{e^{ct} + d}\, dt$$

Quadratic forms. Among Mordell's contributions to this subject were his proof of the formula for the class number of definite ternary quadratic forms given without proof by F. Eisenstein in the middle of the last century; his representations of binary quadratic forms as the sum of the squares of five linear forms; his proof for the class number of quadratic forms in eight variables of determinant one. He also generalized a classical theorem of A. Meyer, which stated that every indefinite quadratic form in five variables represented zero. He proved that, if f and g are indefinite quadratic forms in 13 variables, then subject to some simple and natural conditions, zero can be represented simultaneously by f and g.

Mordell attended the Philadelphia public elementary schools and the Central High School. There he developed an independent interest in mathematics. In 1906, he participated in an entrance scholarship examination at St. John's College, Cambridge, England, in which he was first. He then studied at Cambridge University, taking his B.A. degree in 1910, and spent a further year there in research. After appointments at Birkbeck College, London, and the Manchester College of Technology, he was professor at Manchester from 1923 to 1945. He was then appointed to the Sadleirian Professorship of Pure Mathematics at Cambridge, from which he retired in 1953. Mordell became a British subject in 1929. He was awarded the Sylvester Medal of the Royal Society of London in 1949 and the Larmor Medal and Berwick Prize of the London Math Society.

For background information *see* NUMBER THEORY in the McGraw-Hill Encyclopedia of Science and Technology.   □

★ MORREY, Charles Bradfield, Jr.

American mathematician
Born July 23, 1907, Columbus, Ohio, U.S.A.

THE CALCULUS of variations is concerned with the determination of arcs $y = y(x)$ which minimize an integral of the form

$$\int_a^b f[x, y(x), y'(x)]\, dx \qquad (1)$$

among all arcs joining two given points; here y' denotes the derivative dy/dx. Typical quantities represented by such an integral are the length of the arc and the area of the surface obtained by revolving the arc around the x axis. The functions $f(x,y,y')$ occurring in (1) are given in these cases by

$$\sqrt{1 + (y')^2} \quad \text{and} \quad 2\pi y\, \sqrt{1 + (y')^2}$$

respectively. The minimizing arc is known to satisfy a (generally nonlinear) differential equation of the second order which is known as Euler's differential equation. The well-developed theory of ordinary differential equations was very useful in the development of the theory of integrals of the form (1). Indeed, there was little difficulty in considering such integrals in which y and y' were replaced by $y_1, \ldots, y_n$, and $y'_1, \ldots, y'_n$ as long as there was only one independent variable x.

Early in his career, Morrey became interested in studying integrals of the form

$$\iint_G f[x,y,z(x,y),z_x(x,y),z_y(x,y)]\,dx\,dy \quad (2)$$

which are analogous to (1) but involve two independent variables. The Euler differential equations for such integrals are partial differential equations. Except for the Dirichlet integral

$$\iint_G (z_x{}^2 + z_y{}^2)\,dx\,dy \quad (3)$$

for which the Euler equation is Laplace's equation

$$\frac{\partial^2 z}{\partial x^2} + \frac{\partial^2 z}{\partial y^2} = 0 \quad (4)$$

and other integrals whose corresponding Euler equations are linear or of a related special form, there was essentially no existence theory either for the partial differential equations or for the variational problems.

The problem of finding a surface of least area bounded by a given curve had very recently been solved. By the use of conformal mapping theory, that problem was reduced to minimizing the sum of the Dirichlet integrals (3) for the several unknown functions under a nonlinear boundary condition. L. Tonelli had proved a few existence theorems for a fairly wide class of integrals of the form (2). However, he employed the so-called "direct methods" (which

he had done a great deal to develop) of the calculus of variations which yielded only the information that the solution was "absolutely continuous in the sense of Tonelli"; that is, the solution belonged to a general class of functions in which the first derivatives were merely integrable in the Lebesgue sense, and hence the second derivatives were not known to exist at all. Since the Euler equations are of the second order, it was not at all obvious from Tonelli's results that the solution satisfied Euler's equation.

By employing some still more general "admissible" functions that had been introduced and studied by G. C. Evans in his early (1920) work on potential theory, Morrey found first that he could extend Tonelli's existence results to a very general class of integrals like (2) but which could involve any number of independent and dependent variables. These results still suffered from the defect that the solution was known only to be in some general space of functions. These spaces are now known as Sobolev spaces after the Russian mathematician S. Sobolev.

During the same year (1937–38), while at the Institute for Advanced Study in Princeton, Morrey proved the continuity of the first and second derivatives of the minimizing functions of integrals like (2) with two independent variables but any number of dependent variables, provided that the integrand function f belonged to a certain wide class. In this work, Morrey first noticed that the minimizing (vector) function satisfies the system of Euler equations in a certain "weak" or "distribution" sense. Then, by using an old device known to L. Lichtenstein in 1912, Morrey showed that the difference quotients

$$\frac{z^i(x + h,y) - z^i(x,y)}{h}$$

and

$$\frac{z^i(x,y + h) - z^i(x,y)}{h}$$

$$h \neq 0, \ i = 1, \ldots, n$$

of the unknown functions $z^1, \ldots, z^n$, satisfied certain systems of linear equations of the second order in the same distribution sense. These equations had discontinuous coefficients but were of elliptic type and so the solutions could be shown by methods invented by Morrey to possess a certain type of strong continuity (Holder continuity) on interior regions that was independent of h. Morrey could then let $h \to 0$ and conclude that the first derivatives were Holder continuous and satisfied (in the distribution sense) second order linear equations with

Holder continuous coefficients. Morrey was able to extend known (E. Hopf, 1929) results for single equations of this type to his systems to conclude that those first derivatives had Holder continuous first derivatives which implies that the z^i have continuous second derivatives.

These differentiability results were later extended by Morrey and a student, E. R. Buley, and independently by O. A. Ladyzenskaya and N. Ural'tseva to integrals (2) of a wide class involving any number of independent variables but only one dependent variable. The key to this work was the very difficult extension by E. De Giorgi and J. Nash in 1957–58 of Morrey's results concerning the Holder continuity of the "distribution solutions" of the linear elliptic equations with discontinuous coefficients that were mentioned above.

A professor's son, Morrey majored in mathematics at Ohio State University, where he received his A.B. in 1927 and his M.A. in 1928. He received his Ph.D. from Harvard in 1931 and was a National Research fellow (at Princeton, Chicago, and Rice Institute) from 1931 to 1933. In 1933, he joined the faculty of the University of California, Berkeley. During World War II (1942–45) he was a mathematician at the Ballistic Research Laboratory at Aberdeen Proving Ground, Md., working mainly on fire control problems. He was a member of the Institute for Advanced Study in 1937–38 and 1954–55. In 1962 he was elected to the National Academy of Sciences.

In addition to several textbooks, Morrey wrote *Multiple Integrals in the Calculus of Variations* (1966).

For background information *see* EULER'S EQUATIONS OF MOTION; EULER'S MOMENTUM THEOREM in the McGraw-Hill Encyclopedia of Science and Technology.   □

Morse's first study concerned the "stationary" or "critical" points of a differentiable function $p \longrightarrow f(p)$ defined on a differentiable manifold Σ. A point p is termed "critical" if the differential of the function at p vanishes. Suppose that $u_1, \ldots, u_n$ are local coordinates on Σ near p. A critical point p is termed "N.D." (nondegenerate) if the quadratic terms in the Taylor's representation of f near p, for suitable choice of admissible local coordinates, takes the form

$$-u_1{}^2 - \ldots - u_k{}^2 + u_{k+1}{}^2 + \ldots + u_n{}^2 \quad (1)$$

A function, all of whose critical points are N.D., is itself termed N.D. A first theorem discovered by Morse was that every function that is threefold differentiable is either N.D. or can be approximated arbitrarily closely by an N.D. function.

The integer k in (1) is called the index of the critical point p. If f is a potential k is called the index of instability of k.

The finite theory has applications in physics, geography, economics, and biology. The simplest application is to geography and concerns an island with a single shore line. Let P be a point on a small island whose algebraic height above sea level is denoted by $f(x,y)$, where (x,y) is the vertical projection of P onto a point (x,y) at sea level. For $k = 0$, 1, or 2 let M_k be the number of critical points of f of index k. In geographical terms M_0, M_2, and M_1 are respectively the numbers of pits, peaks, and passes on the island. It is true that

$$M_0 - M_1 + M_2 = 1 \qquad M_2 > 0 \qquad (2)$$

and that any nonnegative integers M_0, M_1, and M_2 which satisfy the relations (2) correspond to some island that can be constructed as a model. For example, there is an island with

★ MORSE, Harold Marston
American mathematician
Born Mar. 24, 1892, Waterville, Maine, U.S.A.

THE PROBLEM of three bodies is related by Henri Poincaré and George Birkhoff to the Jacobi least action integral. While studying this problem, Morse made the initial discoveries that led to a new branch of mathematics called "variational theory in the large." The periodic orbits sought in the problem of three bodies have their finite analogs in the points of equilibrium in a field of forces derived from an electric, magnetic, or gravitational potential. Morse's first results were in this finite case and completed results sought but not obtained by Clerk Maxwell. Morse combined topology and analysis in a new way.

1 pit, 1 pass, and 1 peak, but no island with 2 pits, 2 passes, and 2 peaks.

A small ball, free to move on the surface of

the island, would be in stable equilibrium at each point of index 0, completely unstable at each point of index 2, and 1-way unstable at each point of index 1.

The island can be considered as defined by the altitude function f. One notes that f increases as one enters the island from the shore. A "3-dimensional island" is analogously defined by a function $F(x,y,z)$ on a region R bounded by a surface S which is topologically equivalent to a sphere, provided F is constant on S and increases at a positive rate as one crosses S to enter R.

For $k = 0, 1, 2, 3$, let M_k be the number of critical points of F on R of index k. Then as Morse showed

$$M_3 \geqq 1$$
$$M_3 - M_2 \leqq 1$$
$$M_3 - M_2 - M_1 \geqq 1 \qquad (3)$$
$$M_3 - M_2 + M_1 - M_0 = 1$$

and corresponding to any nonnegative integers that satisfy these relations there can be constructed a model with the corresponding number of critical points.

From these relations a result can be derived completing the study in which Maxwell was interested. Let there be given r small fixed copper balls, each bearing a unit charge of positive electricity, and s small fixed copper balls, each bearing a unit charge of negative electricity. Suppose $r > s$. The potential F due to these charges has a remote equipotential surface S which is approximately spherical, and on which F is increasing as one enters R by crossing S. One can thus regard F as defining a 3-dimensional island with shore S, with $M_3 = r$ infinite peaks and $M_0 = s$ infinite pits. The relations (3) show that the corresponding field of force has at least $(r\text{-}1)$-points of equilibrium with index 2 and s points with index 1.

An n-dimensional island was analogously defined by Morse and the triangle of relations (3) replaced by a similar triangle of $n + 1$ relations. Complete results exist when F is no longer constant on the boundary of its region of definition.

Morse's principal achievement was the extension of the above results concerning functions $F(p)$ to integrals $J(g)$, regarded as functions of curves g. In the simplest example $J(g)$ is the length of a curve g joining two points P and Q on a differentiable manifold Σ. The analog of a critical point p is a geodesic g joining p to Q. The index k of g is the number of points conjugate to P on g. The condition that p be N.D. becomes the condition that Q be not conjugate to P on g. The index k can be any positive integer. The corresponding numbers $M_0, M_1, \ldots$ form an infinite set and the relations (3) are replaced by an infinite set of inequalities.

Morse proved that there is a retrograde periodic orbit for each value of the parameter μ in the Poincaré formulation of the restricted problem of three bodies. Morse believed that a topological theory of quantum mechanics is possible in the sense of his theory.

A farmer's son, Morse graduated from Colby College in 1914. He received his M.A. in 1915 and his Ph.D. in 1917 at Harvard University. After service in the Army during World War I, he taught at Cornell (1920–25), Brown (1925–26), and Harvard (1926–35) before becoming professor of mathematics at the Institute for Advanced Study, Princeton, N.J. He was elected to the National Academy of Sciences in 1932. In 1964 he was awarded the National Medal of Science.

Morse wrote *The Calculus of Variations in the Large* (1934), *Lectures on Analysis in the Large* (1937), *Functional Topology and Abstract Variational Theory* (1939), *Topological Methods in the Theory of Functions of a Complex Variable* (1947), *Introduction to Analysis in the Large* (1947; 3d ed. 1957), and *Differentiable and Combinatorial Manifolds* (1964).

For background information *see* TOPOLOGY in the McGraw-Hill Encyclopedia of Science and Technology. ☐

☆ MÖSSBAUER, Rudolf Ludwig
German physicist
Born Jan. 31, 1929, Munich, Germany

WHILE CONDUCTING research into the emission and absorption of gamma radiation by atomic nuclei, Mössbauer discovered that certain nuclei, bound in solid crystals, can emit and absorb gamma rays without loss of energy through nuclear recoil. When this is the case, even very small motions of the receiver with respect to the source of gamma rays can destroy the resonance absorption of the ray, thus providing a powerful method of measuring minute differences between the states of two systems as well as providing laboratory means of testing some of the predictions of general relativity and solid-state physics. For this discovery Mössbauer shared with Robert Hofstadter the 1961 Nobel Prize in physics.

The basic facts underlying the fluorescence properties of gamma radiation in solids were accumulating since 1927, but no real advances were made until Mössbauer's discovery of recoilless resonance absorption. It was known that a nucleus of a radioactive isotope emitted its excitation in small packets of energy, at a single frequency, in a single unpredictable direction. When projected toward a suitable absorber—a stable nucleus of the same kind as the emitter—the electromagnetic radiation was resonantly absorbed. The resonant frequencies served as a nuclear spectrum providing information concerning nuclear energy levels analogous to optical and x-ray spectra in interpreting atomic resonance phenomena. However, the recoil effects from both emitter and absorber introduced an uncertainty in the determination of an exact evaluation of the nuclear resonant frequency. Since this uncertainty was sufficient to destroy resonance, physicists sought ways to minimize the recoil effects. P. B. Moon had shown in 1951 that this energy loss could be compensated for by the Doppler effect obtained by means of moving the source with respect to the receiver. In 1953 K. G. Malmfors had produced the resonance also by means of broadening the absorption lines through changes in temperature. Mössbauer succeeded in eliminating recoil effects entirely.

Mössbauer began his experiments by using Malmfors's technique to produce resonance and thus to measure the lifetime of the 129,000-electron-volt state of Ir^{191}. Unlike Malmfors he cooled both the source and the receiver and obtained results that were inexplicable. He then repeated the experiment, cooling only the source, and obtained the desired measurement.

In the first experiment Mössbauer had observed a marked increase in absorption where classical theory had predicted a decrease when the source and receiver were cooled. In the attempt to explain this phenomenon he was led to make a complete reevaluation of the classical theory of nuclei bound in crystals using quantum-mechanical methods and adaptations of the theory of neutron capture by atoms bound in crystals, the theory of which had been developed as early as 1939 by W. E. Lamb.

This work led him to realize that it might be possible for an emission of gamma radiation to occur without giving any recoil to the emitting nuclei. Mössbauer attributed the effect to the fact that, in solids, the recoil momentum does not always produce a change in the vibrational state of the crystal lattice. He then came to the conclusion that a certain fraction of the gamma rays emitted by nuclei in solids are emitted without individual nuclear recoil. By utilizing certain experimental conditions, Mössbauer had made possible a vanishingly small recoil energy and in effect produced frequencies that underwent only negligible Doppler shifts, with the result that these spectral lines appear undisplaced at the resonance energy positions. Thus, with the nuclei in natural resonance, any change in the system that changes the frequencies involved— for example, impurities in the crystal lattice— can be investigated by observing the resonance changes. The extreme sensitivity of the resonance conditions makes possible measurements of frequency changes of unparalleled precision.

Mössbauer's work was repeated and extended by physicists at Los Alamos and Argonne. All the experiments performed with Ir^{191}, a platinumlike metal, were complicated by low-temperature requirements and by the smallness of the effect. The use of Fe^{57}—independently discovered at Harvard, Harwell, University of Illinois, and Argonne—made possible the enormous wave of experimentation that followed. Since then over 30 radioactive isotopes have been found that exhibit the Mössbauer effect of gamma-ray emission and absorption. One of the first applications of the Mössbauer effect was a test of Einstein's prediction that gravity distorts light or other electromagnetic radiation by shifting its wavelength. Experiments in the United States and in England reported results indicating that the equivalence principle is correct within 1%.

The most extensive use of the Mössbauer effect appears to be in solid-state physics involving investigations of lattice properties, internal fields, impurities and imperfections in crystals, and low-temperature problems. The usefulness of the Mössbauer effect as an interdisciplinary research tool has been extensive. In chemistry, it is being used to investigate the relationship between nuclear characteristics and valence properties of the atom.

A phototechnician's only son, Mössbauer majored in physics at the Technische Hochschule, Munich, where he received his bachelor's degree in 1953, master's degree in 1955, and Ph.D. in 1958. From 1955 to 1957 he was a research assistant at the Max-Planck Institut, Heidelberg; from 1958 to 1960 he was a research fellow at the Technische Hochschule in Munich. In 1960 he went to the California Institute of Technology as a research fellow, becoming a senior research fellow in 1961 and, in December, 1961, a full professor of physics.

For background information *see* ABSORPTION;

Mössbauer effect; Resonance (molecular structure) in the McGraw-Hill Encyclopedia of Science and Technology. ☐

★ **MOTT, Sir Nevill (Francis)**

British physicist
Born Sept. 30, 1905, Leeds, England

Mott began research in Ernest Rutherford's Cavendish Laboratory at Cambridge in 1927, just after the first formulation of quantum mechanics by Werner Heisenberg and Erwin Schrödinger. Most of his scientific work was based on the application of quantum mechanics to the explanation of physical phenomena. For his discoveries, he was awarded the Royal Society's Hughes Medal in 1941 and its Royal Medal in 1953.

His first work was the application of quantum mechanics to the scattering of alpha particles by an atomic nucleus, and the proof that in general the Rutherford scattering formula, derived from Newtonian mechanics and used by Rutherford in 1905 in his proof of the existence of the nucleus, remained valid when the scattering was deduced from the Schrödinger equation. A year or two later he proved that there was an important exception to this conclusion: if the scattering nucleus was of the same type as the alpha particle, namely, a helium nucleus, the scattering at 45° was twice as intense as the Rutherford formula would predict. This followed from straightforward application of the fact that the wave functions must be symmetrical in the coordinates of the two particles, and in fact the use of symmetrical and antisymmetrical functions in scattering problems had been introduced a year earlier by J. R. Oppenheimer. Mott's predictions were soon verified experimentally by James Chadwick and independently by P. M. S. Blackett. To this period belongs his book with H. S. W. Massey, *The Theory of Atomic Collisions* (1933).

In 1933 Mott became professor of theoretical physics at Bristol. There was already a school of experimental metal physics there, and Mott set about developing it and applying quantum mechanics to the results obtained. With Harry Jones and H. W. B. Skinner he was the first to show why the Fermi limit in an electron gas is not broadened by electron-electron interactions. He also developed the theory of transition metals and their alloys, and was author, with Jones, of a book, *The Theory of the Properties of Metals and Alloys* (1936).

In the period at Bristol immediately before the war Mott started work on the theory of semiconductors, doing a good deal to elicit the nature of the impurity centers and producing independently of W. Schottky the "Mott-Schottky" theory of a rectifying barrier, which is now accepted. Also with R. W. Gurney he produced a theory of the latent image in photographic emulsions, later developed with J. W. Mitchell. His reasoning was as follows: Light is absorbed all over a photographic grain and consequently photoelectrons are ejected into the conduction point of the silver bromide and they are mobile there. On the other hand the photolytic silver, a speck of which probably forms the latent image, is formed at one or at a few places only. It was known at that time that silver bromide is an ionic conductor, interstitial silver ions being produced thermally and being able to move. Mott and R. W. Gurney suggested that the electrons are trapped at silver sulfide specks on the surface of the screen and that the resulting field attracts interstitial silver ions to the speck, enabling it to grow into a submicroscopic crystal of silver. This theory led to a long and fruitful collaboration with the research laboratories in England and the United States of the Kodak Company and to a detailed program of experimental research carried out at Bristol by J. W. Mitchell. This work is described in his book with Gurney, *Electronic Processes in Ionic Crystals* (1940).

Just before the war, in collaboration with F. R. N. Nabarro, and after the war, Mott started to develop G. I. Taylor's theory of dislocations and of work hardening to take account of the observed properties of metals. He published several papers, which, while by no means giving a complete or fully correct picture, were instrumental in stimulating research on the subject, particularly in the Cavendish Laboratory under P. B. Hirsch. He also worked on the formation of protective films on metals and on the contact between a metal and an electrolyte.

At Cambridge, where he was appointed head of the Cavendish Laboratory in 1954, Mott returned to his original interest in metals, stimulated by the work on the Fermi surface under David Shoenberg and A. B. Pippard. He put forward the hypothesis that, whereas a crystalline array of one-electron atoms would normally be a metal, there should be a sharp transition to a nonconducting state as the interatomic distance was increased. He supported this conclusion by quoting much experimental material. Later researches by W. Kohn and J. Hubbard have shown quite clearly that a nonconducting state must exist, but the question of the sharp transition remains controversial.

Both Mott's parents had worked in the Cavendish Laboratory under J. J. Thomson, and he was interested in physics during his schooldays. At Cambridge, however, he studied mathematics, and his career was in theoretical physics. He taught for a year at Manchester under W. L. Bragg and at Cambridge from 1930 to 1933, going to Bristol as professor of theoretical physics in 1933. During the war he worked on operational research. He was appointed Cavendish Professor of Experimental Physics in the Cavendish Laboratory, Cambridge, in 1954. He was knighted in 1962. A fellow of the Royal Society of London, he was elected a foreign associate of the U.S. National Academy of Sciences.

Besides the books mentioned above, Mott wrote *Wave Mechanics and its Application*, with I. N. Snedden (1948), *Elements of Wave Mechanics* (1952), and *Atomic Structure and the Strength of Metals* (1956).

For background information *see* QUANTUM MECHANICS; SEMICONDUCTOR in the McGraw-Hill Encyclopedia of Science and Technology. □

★ **MULLER, Hermann Joseph**
American biologist
Born Dec. 21, 1890, New York, N.Y., U.S.A.

MULLER'S CHIEF scientific contributions were: 1. The proposal and development, from 1921 onward, of the theory that the genetic material of the chromosomes, comprising the genes, formed the starting point and still forms the basis of all life; that it does so by reason of its ability to reproduce itself, or replicate, and to undergo lasting changes, or mutations, that also become reproduced; and that it thereby constitutes a mechanism for all biological evolution by natural selection.

2. The designing and application from 1918 onward, along with E. Altenburg, of quantitative methods of determining, in fruit flies, the frequencies of gene mutations of diverse types occurring under specific conditions; the stipulation and interpretation of the more prevalent kinds of effects exerted by mutations, for example, reduced fitness, reduced gene effectiveness, incomplete recessivity; and the discovery of the principle that lasting changes in chromosome structure occur by the union of chromosome fragments at their breakage points. In the course of these studies Muller found in 1926 that ionizing radiation (x-rays) causes mutations of varied kinds; for this he received the Nobel Prize in physiology or medicine in 1946.

3. The conclusion (1935) that modern conditions result in a reduced elimination of harmful mutations in human populations and thus in their gradual genetic deterioration; the estimation (1950) of the overall frequency of spontaneous and of radiation-induced mutations, and of the amount that fitness is reduced thereby; the proposal, coincidentally (1935) with H. Brewer, that genetic improvement be instituted through the exercise by couples of voluntary germinal choice, in behalf of their children, from among banks of preserved germ cells derived from individuals whose lives had given evidence of their outstanding worth.

The concept that the genetic material constitutes the basis of life and evolution received an enormous impetus with the revolution in molecular biology occasioned by the establishment by J. D. Watson (one of whose professors Muller had been) and F. H. C. Crick, beginning in 1953, of the chemical structure of genetic nucleic acid and of the basic nature of its replication and mutation. The principles put forward by Muller in the fields of gene-character relations, chromosome properties, mutation effects, and mutation frequencies have been increasingly accepted, despite long and often bitter opposition by many medical men and others to his conclusions regarding radiation-induced damage. His ideas regarding human evolution and the means of guiding it are at present gaining increasing numbers both of opponents and of advocates.

Between 1910 and 1915 Muller was a student member of the Columbia University group that demonstrated that in fruit flies the genes are arranged linearly in the chromosomes, in fixed positions disclosed by the amount of linkage between them in inheritance. During this period Muller also devised techniques involving linkage with "marker" genes. This work, done jointly with Altenburg, showed that the individual genes are very stable although their recombination and the varying influences of environment cause quantitative characters to fluctuate. He developed these methods further, along with the theory of balanced lethals, at the Rice Institute in Houston. Again at Columbia (1918–20), and then at the University of Texas (1920–32), he proceeded to the above-mentioned studies on mutation.

Muller spent the next 8 years in Europe: 1932–33 in Berlin, on a Guggenheim Foundation fellowship; 1933–37 as senior geneticist at the Institute of Genetics of the U.S.S.R. Academy of Sciences on the invitation of N. I. Vavilov; and 1937–40 at the Institute of Animal Genetics of Edinburgh University on the invitation of F. A. E. Crew. Thereafter he spent 5 years at Amherst College. In 1945 he was called to Indiana University, where he became Distinguished Service Professor in 1953 and reached emeritus status in 1964. In the following year Muller was a member of The City of Hope Medical Center in Duarte, Calif., and in 1965–66 was visiting professor at the University of Wisconsin. He was elected to the National Academy of Sciences in 1931.

In addition to more than 350 articles on scientific and cultural subjects, including a contribution of 275 pages on radiation genetics to *Radiation Biology*, edited by A. Hollaender and others (1954), Muller was coauthor of *The Mechanism of Mendelian Heredity* (1915; 2d ed. 1923) and *Genetics, Medicine and Man* (1947), and author of *Out of the Night, a Biologist's View of the Future* (1935; 3d ed. 1938) and *Studies in Genetics* (1963), which includes a bibliography of his works to that time.

For background information *see* GENE; LINKAGE, GENETIC in the McGraw-Hill Encyclopedia of Science and Technology.   □

★ MÜLLER, Paul Hermann
Swiss chemist
Born Jan. 12, 1899, Olten, Solothurn, Switzerland
Died Oct. 12, 1965, Basel, Switzerland

WHILE SEARCHING for an insecticide with applications to insects harmful to agriculture, Müller discovered the insecticidal properties of dichlorodiphenyltrichloroethane, commonly abbreviated as DDT. This insecticide had proved especially useful for fighting disease-carrying insects, such as the *Anopheles* mosquito. For his discovery of the strong contact insecticidal action of dichlorodiphenyltrichloroethane, Müller was awarded the Nobel Prize for physiology or medicine in 1948.

While stationed in Cuba in 1900, the American Army surgeon William Crawford Gorgas showed that the *Aedes* mosquito transmitted yellow fever. He realized that the malady could be eliminated if the mosquito were destroyed, and he employed pyrethrum, an insecticide derived from plants, to this end. When he was sent to Panama in 1904, he applied similar techniques during the construction of the Panama Canal. In this way, many thousands of workers were saved from the ravages of yellow fever and malaria, the latter malady being transmitted by the *Anopheles* mosquito. Pyrethrum, however, is not an especially useful insecticide, since it has a very limited application and insufficient permanent action. Still, Gorgas showed that a fight against an illness transmitted through an insect is possible by eliminating the transmitter.

About 1935, while working for J. R. Geigy A.G. in Basel, Müller was commissioned to study the field of insecticides, in particular those insecticides of importance to agriculture. After studying the literature and investigating those agricultural insecticides that had already been patented, he came to the conclusion that a contact, or "touch," insecticide would possess far greater value than an oral poison. He further realized that the insecticide must be chemically stable so that it would achieve a longer-lasting action than the known stomach poisons or the plant-contact poisons pyrethrum and rotenone.

Müller conducted his tests with a large glass chamber of the Peet-Grady type that had a volume of about 1 cubic meter. Into the chamber he placed specimens of the fly species *Caliphora vomitoria*, which he first treated with a fine spray of the substance being investigated. In earlier experiments he had found that compounds containing the groups $>$ CH—CH$_2$Cl, $>$ CH—CHCl$_2$, and —CO—CHCl$_2$ showed a positive action as insecticides. Since chloroform, HCCl$_3$, was a known poison used by many insect collectors, Müller decided to investigate compounds containing the group CH—CCl$_3$. He

Formula I

first tried diphenyl-trichloroethane (Formula I), which demonstrated a weak insecticide activity. As further analogs of the compound were prepared, Müller in 1939 found dichlorodiphenyl-

Formula II

trichloroethane (Formula II), which had originally been prepared as early as 1873 by an Austrian student. The compound demonstrated a definite, strong, lasting insecticide contact activity. Indeed, the chamber became so toxic after a short period that, even after it had been thoroughly cleaned, untreated flies were killed on coming into contact with its walls. Dichlorodiphenyltrichloroethane was soon confirmed as an excellent economical agricultural insecticide. Field trials later showed the compound to be effective against a wide variety of pests, among them the louse and the mosquito, as well as the common housefly.

The son of an official of the Swiss Federal Railway, Müller began working as a laboratory assistant at Dreyfus and Company in 1916, and in the following year became an assistant chemist in the Scientific-Industrial Laboratory of Lonza A.G. In 1918 he returned to school, receiving his diploma a year later. In 1919 he began his studies at the University of Basel, and in 1925 he received his Ph.D., with a major in physical chemistry and a minor in botany. Müller immediately began his long association with J. R. Geigy A.G., becoming deputy director of scientific research on substances for plant protection in 1946.

For background information *see* INSECTICIDE in the McGraw-Hill Encyclopedia of Science and Technology.   □

☆ **MULLIKEN, Robert Sanderson**
American chemist
Born June 7, 1896, Newburyport, Mass., U.S.A.

APPLICATION OF the principles of quantum mechanics to the problems associated with chemical bonding proved extremely fruitful in the hands of Mulliken. His major accomplishments are discussed below:

1. In connection with experimental work on the separation of mercury isotopes, Mulliken in 1922 discussed the theory of isotope separation by various methods and proposed the method of evaporative centrifuging. He then turned to an experimental study of the isotope effect in diatomic spectra. This led him to further experimental work on diatomic spectra, and to an extensive systematization of the theory of such spectra, and thereafter to a consideration of the nature of the electronic states of molecules.

2. Together with F. Hund, he achieved the theoretical systematization of the electronic states of molecules in terms of molecular orbitals. He showed that this description has advantages over the alternative description in which the electronic configuration of an individual atom is retained when that atom enters into chemical combination with other atoms to form a molecule. Mulliken showed that each individual atom in the molecule can lose the original electron configuration and the electrons become associated with the molecule as a whole. The new configuration thus formed was characterized by Mulliken in terms of molecular orbitals, analogous to the atomic orbitals occupied by the electrons about the individual atoms. Mulliken was also able to show the actual shape of the molecular orbitals for a large number of compounds and, using molecular spectra, was able to determine the relative energies of the orbitals.

3. Quantitative determination of the amount

of overlap between the various atomic orbitals in a molecule gave indications of the bond energy of that molecule, and Mulliken obtained widely applicable semiquantitative formulas for estimating heats of atomization. He introduced group theory to deal with electronic states of polyatomic molecules.

4. Another contribution was his work on the estimation of the ionic character of a bond and studies on electronegativity. Electronegativity is a measure of the power of an atom to attract electrons to itself. Mulliken showed that this can be given quantitatively by the expression $\frac{1}{2}(I + E)$ where I is the ionization potential and E the electron affinity of the atom in question. Concurrently he investigated the polarity of orbitals in molecules that have dipole moments and derived significant relations between the forms of the molecular orbitals and the dipole moment of the molecule.

5. Research on the theoretical interpretation of absolute intensities of electronic spectra led to the consideration of conjugated organic molecules, that is, molecules that possess alternating double bonds. On the basis of quantum-mechanical considerations, Mulliken explained the phenomenon of hyperconjugation—similar to conjugation but bringing methyl, methylene, or other attached groups into interaction with the conjugated system—and first pointed out its widespread significance.

6. In 1952 Mulliken developed a quantum-mechanical theory for the interaction of electron donor with electron acceptor molecules, and in particular of the charge-transfer spectra of molecular complexes. This covers a wide variety of interesting cases and has stimulated much work by others.

7. Mulliken considered himself a "middleman between experiment and theory," and while in recent years he did not carry on experimental work himself, he always had experimental spectroscopic work being carried out under his supervision in the Laboratory of Molecular Spectra and Structure, where also his colleague, C. C. J. Roothaan, supervised extensive theoretical computations on atoms and molecules. Mulliken's papers often dealt with problems in the interpretation of specific diatomic and polyatomic spectra as well as with general related theory. In 1964–66 he was especially concerned with the Rydberg states of H_2, He_2, and other molecules, and showed that many of them have rather large maxima in their potential curves.

Mulliken received his B.S. in 1917 at the Massachusetts Institute of Technology, where his father was a professor of chemistry, and his Ph.D. in physical chemistry in 1921 at the University of Chicago. From 1921 to 1925 he was a National Research Council fellow at Chicago

and Harvard. He taught at New York University from 1926 to 1928, then returned to the University of Chicago, where he was associate professor of physics (1928–31), professor of physics (1931–61), and professor of physics and chemistry (1961). From 1956 to 1961 he was the Ernest DeWitt Burton Distinguished Service Professor. Although formally emeritus after 1961, he continued active as Distinguished Service Professor of Physics and Chemistry at Chicago and as Distinguished Research Professor of Chemical Physics at Florida State University, where he spent the winter months. Mulliken was honored by the American Chemical Society with the award of its Gilbert Newton Lewis Medal (1960), Theodore William Richards Medal (1960), Peter Debye Award (1963), John G. Kirkwood Medal (1964), and Willard Gibbs Medal (1965). He was elected to the National Academy of Sciences in 1936.

For background information *see* CHEMICAL BINDING; QUANTUM MECHANICS in the McGraw-Hill Encyclopedia of Science and Technology. □

★ **MURNAGHAN, Francis Dominic**
American mathematician
Born Aug. 4, 1893, Omagh, Co. Tyrone, Ireland

MURNAGHAN'S PRINCIPAL contributions to applied mathematics were in the theory of large deformations of an elastic solid and in group theory. He also wrote books on *Vector Analysis and the Theory of Relativity* (1922), *Theoretical Mechanics*, with J. S. Ames (1929), and *Hydrodynamics*, with H. Bateman and H. L. Dryden (1932).

In the ordinary theory of elasticity, as used in engineering, it is assumed, for reasons of simplicity, that the deformations are small, that the material is initially free from stress, and that the material is elastically isotropic. These assumptions, particularly the second, are not valid for points deep in the Earth, the pressure at the center of the Earth being estimated to be several million atmospheres. In the engineering theory of elasticity, the relation between stress and strain, known as Hooke's Law, is derived from the fact that the stress tensor is the gradient, with respect to the strain tensor, of the energy of deformation. Murnaghan showed that this is not true when the deformation is large and gave the correct formulation of Hooke's Law for large deformations. He also took account of the initial stress of the material and showed that an elastic material whose state of stress is not hydrostatic cannot be isotropic. One consequence of considering the initial stress is that, in the problem of the propagation of waves through an elastic solid, the modulus of rigidity, μ, is lessened by the initial hydrostatic pressure, p. Thus the propagation of shear waves is inhibited, not when $\mu = 0$ but when $\mu = p$. This result has a bearing on speculations as to whether the material near the center of the Earth is liquid or not. A summary of Murnaghan's theory is in his *Finite Deformation of an Elastic Solid* (1951).

In group theory, Murnaghan studied the representations of the symmetric groups and of the general linear group. He gave a formula that simplified the calculation of the characters of the irreducible representations of the symmetric group on any number of symbols and furnished the analysis into its irreducible components of the Kronecker product of irreducible representations of the symmetric group. He also analyzed the Kronecker product of irreducible representations of the general linear group, the n-dimensional rotation group, and the $2n$-dimensional symplectic group. A summary of his work in this field is contained in *The Theory of Group Representations* (1938; reprinted 1963).

Son of an Irish member of the English House of Commons, Murnaghan majored in applied mathematics at University College, Dublin, and received his B.A. and M.A. from the National University of Ireland in 1913 and 1914, respectively. He received his Ph.D. from the Johns Hopkins University in 1916, working under H. Bateman. He was an instructor at the Rice Institute from 1916 to 1918 and taught at the Johns Hopkins University from 1918 to 1948, serving as head of the department of mathematics from 1928 to 1948. From 1949 to 1955 he established the curriculum in mathematics for the newly formed Instituto Technológico Aeronáutica of Brazil. From 1955 to 1963 he served as consultant in applied mathematics to the David Taylor Model Basin, Washington, D.C. He was elected to the National Academy of Sciences in 1942.

For background information *see* GROUP THEORY; HOOKE'S LAW in the McGraw-Hill Encyclopedia of Science and Technology.   □

N-P

★★★

★ **NAMIAS, Jerome**
American meteorologist
Born Mar. 19, 1910, Bridgeport, Conn., U.S.A.

B Y EXTENDING the study of weather phenomena in three dimensions to hemisphere-
wide areas, Namias developed methods of treating interactions between wind and weather systems over vast areas of the Earth and over time
intervals up to a season. These studies led to a
better understanding of short-period climatic
fluctuations and to economically valuable methods of predicting the character of the weather
for periods ranging from 5 days to a month. For
this work he received a Rockefeller Public Service Award, the American Meteorological Society
Award for Extraordinary Scientific Accomplishment, and the Department of Commerce Gold
Medal Award.

In the 1930s, when the great droughts of the
dust bowl area were affecting the agricultural
heartland of the United States, the Bureau of
Agricultural Economics and the U.S. Weather
Bureau sponsored a project under the direction
of C. G. Rossby at the Massachusetts Institute of
Technology. Namias was the junior member of
this team of three principal investigators, the
other member being H. C. Willett. The trio
worked together for 5 years trying to formulate
ideas and develop new methods of long-range
forecasting. The attack was three-pronged: physical, statistical, and synoptic. It soon became
apparent that surface weather maps covering
only the United States or North America were
inadequate for purposes of long-range forecasting, and, more importantly, that atmospheric
conditions aloft (well removed from the complications induced by the Earth's surface) had to
be included. Namias developed methods of improving the analysis of weather both at the
surface and, particularly, aloft, and invented
ways of estimating pressure and wind patterns
over areas where data were sparse. These studies
led him to discover geographical and seasonal
positions and characteristics of jet streams.

When the new maps covering the temperature
latitudes of the hemisphere were prepared, it
became apparent that there were much larger-
scale wind patterns aloft than the conventional
high- and low-pressure areas of the weather map
and that these larger patterns (planetary waves
in the westerlies) strongly influenced the life
histories of cyclones, anticyclones, and air
masses. Rossby developed a theory that explained some of the interactions between planetary waves and thereby established a foundation
upon which a method for predicting evolutions
out to 5 days could be built. This theory held that
redistribution of the vorticity of the upper wind
patterns was the primary reason for the movement and development of the upper waves and
anticyclones. Namias reasoned that the highly
imperfect results obtained by straightforward
use of this theory were due to its failure to
consider important thermodynamic influences
that might be generated by abnormal constraints
imposed by the inhomogenous character of the
Earth's surface, seasonal variations in solar radiation, and even seasonal variations in heat supplied by parts of the oceans and continents.
Accounting for all of these factors by physical
theory was a monumental task. Namias felt that
their cumulative effects might be approximated
by judicious empirical methods. After the transfer of the Extended Forecasting Project to the
U.S. Weather Bureau in 1941, Namias, in view of
the pressing military requirements for long-
range predictions, initiated a program designed
to incorporate implicitly these missing factors.

First, he developed normal pressure and wind
charts for each month for several altitude levels.
Second, he obtained deviations of individual
charts from the normal—that is, anomalies.
Third, he introduced averaging for periods of 5
to 30 days to filter out the day-to-day variations
and bring into focus the slowly evolving patterns
that determine prevailing weather. There were
then two principal parts to the problem: (1) to
predict correctly the average pressure and wind
circulations for the desired period, and (2) to
specify the average or prevailing weather from
average pressure charts and their anomalies.
Phase 2 turned out to be easier than phase 1 and
computer methods were developed for this work.
Phase 1, the prediction of prevailing wind currents, was attacked in a semiempirical fashion
(later also programmed for computer). It was
also found that circulation predictions made for
a month could supply some of the information
about the effects of abnormal surfaces on the
atmosphere (such as those produced by departures from normal of sea-surface temperature), and that these effects could be incorporated into the computerized system for making
5-day forecasts.

An unanticipated bonus arrived in the late 1950s and early 1960s when it was found that wind and weather patterns prevailing for a month or more had a profound effect on sea-surface temperatures and that abnormalities in these, in turn, provided long-lasting heat reservoirs that could affect subsequent large-scale weather patterns. Thus the ocean and atmosphere had to be treated as coupled media for proper forecasting of either. After 1959 Namias devoted much of his research to documenting these interactions and identifying causal factors. He believed that the solutions to the challenging problems of improving forecast accuracy would continue to be found in the combined physical-statistical-synoptic attack, but with increasing emphasis on physical methods.

The son of an optometrist, Namias acquired an avid interest in meteorology while studying high-school physics under a stimulating teacher. After a period of home study and correspondence courses, he attended the Massachusetts Institute of Technology, where he took an M.S. degree (1941). He worked at Blue Hill Observatory during the early 1930s and, beginning in 1936, served as a research associate at MIT for 5 years. In 1941, he was called to Washington to set up the Extended Forecast Section of the U.S. Weather Bureau, and thereafter made extended forecasts for Atlantic convoys, invasions, and other military maneuvers during World War II. He-remained at the U.S. Weather Bureau as head of its Extended Forecast Division and assistant director of its National Meteorological Center at Suitland, Md.

Namias wrote *An Introduction to the Study of Air Mass and Isentropic Analysis* (1936), *Extended Forecasting by Mean Circulation Methods* (1947), and *Thirty-day Forecasting* (1953) as well as many papers for scientific journals.

For background information *see* WEATHER (FORECASTING AND PREDICTION) in the McGraw-Hill Encyclopedia of Science and Technology. □

★ **NATTA, Giulio**
Italian chemist
Born Feb. 26, 1903, Imperia, Italy

WHILE STUDYING petrochemical problems, in particular the use of olefin monomers for the production of high polymers, Natta in 1954 discovered stereospecific polymerization. By its means, linear high polymers having a regular structure, also from the steric point of view, could be obtained from asymmetric olefin monomers (propylene, 1-butene, and so forth).

The first stereoregular polymers were obtained in the presence of the catalysts that Karl Ziegler had already proposed for the polymerization of ethylene. These catalysts, as they were improved by Natta, yielded polymers that exhibited a high steric regularity, a high melting temperature, and a high crystallinity. Thus new classes of macromolecules could be obtained from raw materials of very low cost produced by the petroleum industry. These macromolecules exhibit very good mechanical and thermal properties; hence they are suitable for the production of plastics, films, and synthetic fibers of excellent properties.

Natta also discovered stereospecific processes for the polymerization of diolefins. For example, he obtained different types of stereoregular polymers of butadiene and of its higher homologs having different chemical structure and different physical properties. The elastomeric properties of *cis*-1,4 polymers are higher than those of the other synthetic rubbers previously known. Many stereoregular polymers are produced on a large industrial scale.

The coordinated catalysis was applied by Natta also to the production of amorphous polymers, such as the ethylene-propylene copolymers, and of their terpolymers, with more highly unsaturated monomers. In this way new synthetic rubbers were obtained, the industrial production of which is possible at a lower cost than that of any other rubber, including natural rubber.

For his studies on polymerization, Natta shared with Ziegler the 1963 Nobel Prize for chemistry.

Natta's scientific research began in 1923 when, at the age of 20, he applied x-rays to the study of the lattice structure of organic and inorganic chemical substances and to the solution of

different chemical problems. For instance, he applied x-ray methods to the study of catalysts, isomorphism phenomena, and so on. In 1932 he went to Freiburg, Germany, to learn the new techniques in the study of interferences of electron rays; there he became acquainted with

Hermann Staudinger's work in macromolecular chemistry and started his first research on the crystal structure of high polymers. His studies on catalysis enabled Natta to develop original research on the synthesis of methanol and of the higher alcohols from water gas and to cooperate with important chemical industries in the design of plants for the synthesis of methanol, both in Italy and abroad.

In 1938 the Italian government appointed Natta to direct the organization of research for the production of synthetic rubber in Italy. He then started to study petrochemical problems, such as the production of butadiene and the oxosynthesis starting from low olefin hydrocarbons. Such a background allowed him to study the production of high polymers from petroleum and to rapidly discover and develop the stereospecific polymerization processes.

A judge's son, Natta graduated Doctor in Chemical Engineering in 1924 at the Polytechnic Institute of Milan. In 1933 he was appointed professor and director of the Institute of General Chemistry at the University of Pavia, where he stayed until 1935. From 1935 to 1937, he was professor and director of the Institute of Physical Chemistry at the University of Rome, and from 1937 to 1938 of the Institute of Industrial Chemistry at the Polytechnic Institute of Turin. In 1938 he became professor and director of the Institute of Industrial Chemistry at the Polytechnic Institute of Milan.

For background information *see* POLYMERIZATION; STEREOCHEMISTRY in the McGraw-Hill Encyclopedia of Science and Technology. ☐

structures, he applied basic procedures involving numerical methods of stress analysis and developed design techniques for resistance to bomb blasts and other types of impulsive load that have been in general use since that time. His work naturally extended itself to effects of nuclear bombs and to the development of procedures for effective protection against nuclear blasts and shock forces. In developing the principles governing structural design to resist high-intensity blast forces, he was associated with all the major nuclear weapons effects tests, and he was able to verify the bases of the procedures that he developed by experiments under actual conditions. At the same time he became interested in the problem of developing design procedures to insure earthquake resistance of structures and of dams. In 1949 he was engaged as a consultant on the design of the Latino Americana Tower in Mexico City. This structure successfully resisted several major earthquakes, demonstrating the validity of the principles used in its construction through comparison with predictions and measurements during the earthquakes to which it was subjected.

Newmark's engineering work involved many unusual problems, including: (1) tests of structures to resist wave and wind action in Lake Maracaibo, Venezuela; (2) the design of flexible and rigid pavements for airfields; (3) seismic studies of a number of high rock-fill dams; (4) extensions of runways at LaGuardia Airport, New York, supported on structural framing; (5) seismic design of a proposed 43-story hotel in Montreal; and (6) seismic resistance of the

★ NEWMARK, Nathan Mortimore

American structural engineer
Born Sept. 22, 1910, Plainfield, N.J., U.S.A.

NEWMARK'S PRINCIPAL engineering achievements were associated with structural design to resist dynamic loadings of the type due to earthquakes, nuclear bomb blasts, or wind and wave action. He was also concerned with the simplification of methods of stress analysis and, in particular, the development of numerical methods for rapid computation of stresses and deflections of complex structures under unusual loading conditions. His work in these areas was recognized by numerous honors, including election as a founding member of the National Academy of Engineering.

Just before World War II, Newmark became associated with the work of Division 2 of the National Defense Research Committee and with the Committee on Passive Protection Against Bombing of the National Research Council. In his early studies of the effects of bombs on

tunnels and other parts of the San Francisco Bay Area Rapid Transit System, including the tunnel under Oakland Bay, the longest subaqueous tunnel in the world.

Newmark received his B.S. (1930) at Rutgers University and his M.S. (1932) and Ph.D. (1934) in engineering at the University of Illinois. He remained at Illinois, becoming head of the Structural Research Laboratory there in 1946 and head of the department of civil engineering in 1956. In 1949 he helped to organize the Digital Computer Laboratory at the University, and until September, 1957, was its chairman. He was a founder of the National Academy of Engineering.

For background information *see* STRESS AND STRAIN in the McGraw-Hill Encyclopedia of Science and Technology.   □

★ **NEYMAN, Jerzy**
American statistician
Born Apr. 16, 1894, Bendery, Russia

NEYMAN'S PRINCIPAL achievement was the idea underlying what he called "behavioristic statistics," a methodology of making decisions under uncertainty. More specifically, this methodology applies when decisions must be made using only the results of experiments or observations subject to chance. Roughly, the characteristic features of the methods considered are (1) in any particular case it is impossible to predict whether the method will yield a correct or a wrong decision; (2) the long-run frequency of correct decisions resulting from consistent use of the methods developed is calculable and the calculations may be verified empirically; (3) the theory provides means of determining methods of making decisions that are, in a well-defined sense, optimal. For example, "optimal" may mean minimizing the frequency of errors of a particular kind. One illustrative, even though somewhat artificial, example must suffice. Consider a box containing an unknown number N of marbles. The marbles are numbered 1, 2, . . . , N. Suppose that an important decision depends upon the number N of marbles in the box and that the only way of obtaining information about N is through repeated random extractions of

marbles from the box, with each extracted marble being replaced in the box and the box being well shaken before the next extraction.

Suppose that 10 marbles are to be so extracted and denote by one letter X the numbers, say $X_1, X_2, \ldots, X_{10}$ written on the extracted marbles. Our problem is that of using the numbers X for "estimating" the unknown "parameter" N. Obviously, the observable variables X are subject to chance. In particular, owing to chance, each of the 10 extractions may yield the same marble, perhaps marble No. 1 or marble No. 100. Also, the 10 random extractions may yield $X = (101, 37, 51, 20, 83, 19, 16, 75, 30, 10)$, and so on. One of the possible behavioristic methods of estimating N is to use the observable X in order to calculate two limits, say $N_1(X)$ and $N_2(X)$, supposed to bracket the unknown N so that $N_1(X) \leq N \leq N_2(X)$. These limits, called "confidence limits," are to be so adjusted that the frequency of cases where the true unknown N actually is between $N_1(X)$ and $N_2(X)$ be equal to a number α chosen in advance, perhaps $\alpha = 0.9$ or $\alpha = 0.99$, and so on. Also there is the all-important theoretical problem of determining such pair of confidence limits, say $[N_1{}^*(X), N_2{}^*(X)]$, that is, in a sense, optimal, perhaps such that the difference $N_2{}^*(X) - N_1{}^*(X)$ is most frequently small.

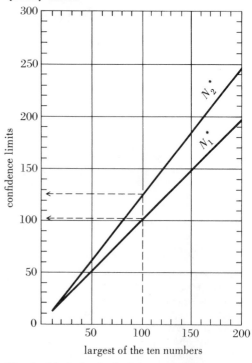

Fig. 1. Method of obtaining approximate optimal confidence limits for N.

Fig. 1 gives an easy method of obtaining approximate optimal confidence limits for N, corresponding to $\alpha = 0.9$. In order to obtain $N_1^*(X)$ and $N_2^*(X)$, all one has to do is to find the largest among the numbers on the 10 extracted marbles and to locate it on the horizontal scale in Fig. 1. Then a vertical is drawn through this point. The intersection of the vertical with the line marked N_1^* determines the lower confidence limit and the intersection with the line marked N_2^* gives the upper confidence limit. In the third hypothetical result of 10 extractions indicated above, the largest number is 101, and Fig. 1 indicates the corresponding optimal confidence limits $101 \leqq N \leqq 126$.

An alternative pair of confidence limits for N may be obtained in a similar fashion from Fig. 2. Here, however, the horizontal scale is that of the average of the numbers on the 10 extracted marbles, not the largest of them. In the third hypothetical result of 10 extractions the average is 43.2 and the indicated confidence limits are 66 and 122.

In order to gain an intuitive feeling for the working of the confidence limits in general and for the meaning of their "optimality," the reader is encouraged to perform a certain number, say 100, of experiments with the box and marbles as described. It is instructive to vary the number N from one experiment to the next, say $N = 20$ in one experiment, $N = 30$ in the second, $N = 100$ in the third, and so on. For each experiment Figs. 1 and 2 will each provide a pair of confidence limits. With reasonable care to replace each extracted marble and to shake the box, the reader will find that the frequency with which either pair of confidence limits brackets the true N is approximately nine out of ten. Also, the reader will find that, very frequently, the optimal confidence limits for N of Fig. 1 are substantially narrower than the alternative limits determined by Fig. 2.

Classical nonbehavioristic methods of treating problems of the kind described are based on variously defined "measures of confidence" in statements like the following: "The unknown N is between 100 and 110." One of the frequently used measures of confidence is the famous Bayes' formula calculated with arbitrarily selected probabilities a priori. Because confidence is subjective and may easily be betrayed by nature, behavioristic statistics renounces all reference to the feelings of confidence or diffidence, and concentrates on methods whose consistent use has demonstrable desirable frequency properties. It is, therefore, somewhat ironical that the term invented to

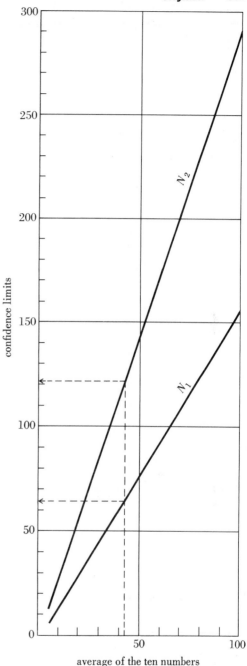

Fig. 2. Method of obtaining an alternative pair of confidence limits for N.

designate the behavioristic method of estimation just described involves the word "confidence."

Since its invention in the 1930s, behavioristic statistics has found application in many domains of scientific research, such as astronomy, physics, biology, and medicine, wherever it is desired to decrease the frequency of errors.

Neyman received his Ph.D. in mathematics from the University of Warsaw, Poland (1923). He taught at the universities of Warsaw and Cracow in Poland (1923–34), University College, London (1934–38), and, after 1938, at the University of California, Berkeley. He was elected to the National Academy of Sciences in 1963.

Neyman wrote *First Course in Probability and Statistics* (1950).

For background information *see* STATISTICS in the McGraw-Hill Encyclopedia of Science and Technology.   □

★ NORRISH, Ronald George Wreyford
British physical chemist
Born Nov. 9, 1897, Cambridge, England

FOR HIS contributions to chemical kinetics, especially to photochemistry, Norrish was awarded the Davy Medal of the Royal Society in 1958, the Lewis Medal of the Combustion Institute in 1964, and the Faraday Medal of the Chemical Society in 1965.

In the 1920s photochemistry and its relation to spectroscopy were beginning to emerge from the empirical stage to become a fundamental branch of science, largely because of the work of James Franck and Victor Henri based on the earlier theoretical work of Albert Einstein and Max Planck. Norrish's interest early took him to the study of the primary photochemical reactions of simple compounds such as nitrogen peroxide, aldehydes, ketones, and analogous compounds such as ketene and diazomethane. With his collaborators he established the mechanism of the photolysis of carbonyl compounds by two routes, giving on the one hand free radicals and on the other stable molecules. All these compounds have since been used as a source for the study of free radicals and for the initiation of chain reactions of combustion and polymerization. As a result of this work, C. H. Bamford and Norrish first demonstrated experimentally the well-known Franck-Rabinowitch effect, in which two free radicals resulting from the photolysis of a solute molecule are confined by a cage of solvent molecules with a very high probability of recombining before they can escape. Such studies as these, with special reference to quantum yield, fluorescence, and spectral type, threw light on the processes of photolysis by ultraviolet and visible light.

In some photochemical processes, such as the reaction between hydrogen and chlorine, the primary dissociation of the photoactive constituent can generate a chain reaction. Thus, for every chlorine molecule dissociated, up to 10^6 molecules of hydrogen chloride are formed. Norrish and M. Ritchie made a comprehensive study of the kinetics of this reaction by a new method and were able to amplify considerably the work of M. Bodenstein, D. L. Chapman, and others. With his colleagues, Norrish later elucidated the mechanism of other chain processes, such as the photolysis of nitrogen trichloride and pure ozone sensitized by chlorine.

In the years between the two wars, the study of the combustion of hydrocarbons was taking shape, especially as a consequence of N. M. Semenov's and C. N. Hinshelwood's conception of the branching-chain kinetics. Norrish and his coworkers early participated in this work. They were the first to elucidate the mechanism of the combustion of methane and ethylene, which depend for their branching-chain mechanisms on the formation of formaldehyde as an intermediate. They were able easily to influence the combustion of these substances by the action of ultraviolet light on the aldehydic intermediates —even to the extent of turning a slow reaction into an explosion. With S. A. Foord and F. S. Dainton, Norrish also studied hydrogen and hydrocarbon oxidation, particularly the effect of nitrogen peroxide and nitrosyl chloride as catalytic agents for initiation and branching of chains under the influence of light.

Much work at this time was also carried out on the mechanism of polymerization of vinyl compounds and other substances. The effects of cross linking by divinyl compounds on the physical properties of the polymer and the kinetics of the chain processes of polymerization and copolymerization were studied in relation to the nature of the solvent medium and other parameters.

After World War II, besides continuing his work on combustion and polymerization, Norrish made a new approach to the study of photochemical and explosive processes. The methods of flash photolysis and kinetic spectroscopy developed by Norrish and G. Porter and their colleagues made possible the study of very fast reactions—reactions measured in microseconds or milliseconds. Their technique depended upon applying to a photochemically active system a flash of such power as "instantly" to dissociate the reactant species into radicals or atoms. Use of a second and weaker flash, triggered electronically at precise intervals of microseconds or milliseconds after the first, enabled Norrish and Porter to record the spectra of the very reactive short-lived transients. By varying the times between the first and second flashes, they could observe the growth and decay of the free radicals and study the kinetics of their reactions.

In gaseous reactants with no inert diluent, very high temperatures can be generated by the absorption of the light energy. Thus an adiabatic shock can be administered which in suitable systems can generate explosive reactions in which the nature and reactions of the transients can be objectively observed. In this way Norrish and his coworkers studied explosive combustion of hydrogen, hydrocarbons, ammonia, phosphine, hydrogen sulfide, and other substances, as well as their pyrolyses. Working in solutions or using sufficient inert diluent made it possible to control temperature so the reactions of atoms and free radicals could be studied under isothermal conditions, as were also the reactions of oxygen atoms derived from ozone, and the relaxation of gaseous molecules in a high state of vibration. Norrish also successfully studied reactions of polymerization and photolysis in solution by the method of kinetic spectroscopy.

Educated at the Perse Grammar School in Cambridge, Norrish obtained a scholarship to Emmanuel College, Cambridge, in 1915. He served in France in World War I as a lieutenant in the Royal Field Artillery. Returning to Cambridge, he graduated in 1921, received his Ph.D. in 1924, and was elected to a fellowship of Emmanuel College. He was appointed university demonstrator in physical chemistry in 1926. His studies for the Ph.D. under E. K. (later Sir Eric) Rideal introduced him to the study of photochemistry and chemical kinetics. In 1930 he was appointed Humphrey Owen Jones Lecturer in Physical Chemistry. He received the degree of Sc.D. and was elected to the Royal Society in 1936. In 1937 he became professor of physical chemistry and director of the department of physical chemistry in the University of Cambridge, from which he retired in 1965.

For background information see PHOTOCHEMISTRY in the McGraw-Hill Encyclopedia of Science and Technology.   □

★ **NORTHROP, John Howard**
American biochemist
Born July 5, 1891, Yonkers, N.Y., U.S.A.

NORTHROP AND his collaborators isolated and crystallized several enzymes and proved them to be proteins. By methods similar to those used for the enzymes, W. M. Stanley isolated and crystallized tobacco mosaic virus, and Northrop isolated a bacterial virus. These viruses, like all subsequently isolated viruses, were nucleoproteins. Thus the chemical nature of enzymes and viruses was established for the first time. In recognition of their achievements, Northrop and Stanley shared half of the Nobel Prize in chemistry in 1946.

One of the most striking attributes of living organisms is the rapidity and precision with which their essential chemical reactions are carried out. During the 18th and 19th centuries, chemists discovered that this remarkable property was due to small amounts of some unknown substances, which have since become known as enzymes. In the 19th century these substances were shown to act as catalysts, but their chemical nature eluded all attempts at identification for over 100 years.

In attempting to unravel the chemistry of cells, Northrop, like all his predecessors, was confronted with the question: "What is an enzyme?" Like many of his predecessors, he attempted first to purify and isolate one of them. While this work was in progress (1926), James B. Sumner described the isolation and crystallization of a protein that he considered to be the enzyme "urease." This conclusion was so startling and so contrary to current theory, which considered enzymes to be a totally unknown class of compounds, that little attention was paid to it.

Northrop, however, considered that this was pretty good evidence of the protein nature of enzymes and planned his work with this point in mind. The usual method of enzyme research up to that time was to keep the enzymatic activity of the various fractions about the same, with the result that a solution was finally obtained that was highly active but gave no test for protein, carbohydrate, or any other known compound. This was poor technique for isolating a protein. Northrop reversed the procedure, keeping the total concentration, instead of the activity, of each succeeding fraction constant, and applied classical methods for purification and isolation of proteins. This procedure required the use and preparation of relatively large quantities of material, and for this reason Northrop chose the enzyme pepsin, which regulates gastric digestion, since partially purified preparations were available commercially in any quantity.

By the use of these methods, Northrop isolated and crystallized pepsin in 1930. In the next five years, he and his collaborators, M. Kunitz, R. M. Herriott, and M. Anson, isolated and crystallized trypsin and its precursor trypsinogen, chymotrypsin and its precursor, carboxypeptidase, ribonuclease, and desoxyribonuclease. All were proteins. The chemical nature of enzymes was thereby established, although it required another 10 years before the conclusion was widely accepted.

In the meantime, Northrop thought that viruses might also be proteins and that the same methods that had been successful in isolating the enzymes might succeed in isolating a virus. In 1936 the method was successfully applied by W. M. Stanley to the isolation and crystallization of tobacco mosaic virus. This proved to be a nucleoprotein. In 1938 Northrop isolated the first bacterial virus. This, too, and all subsequently isolated viruses, were nucleoproteins, although the work of the last decade has shown that the nucleic acid is the essential part of the molecule.

As a result of the work of Northrop and his associates, many enzymes and viruses have been isolated and crystallized so that it has become possible for the first time to study and understand the specific chemical reactions characteristic of living cells. The enzymes, ribonuclease and desoxyribonuclease, isolated by Kunitz, have been indispensable tools in the recent extraordinary advance in knowledge of nucleic acids, the master molecule of the living cell.

Northrop's father, John I. Northrop, was an instructor in zoology at Columbia University and was killed in a laboratory explosion. His mother was a botanist and had been an instructor in botany at Hunter College. Northrop received his B.S. from Columbia in 1912, his M.A.

in 1913, and his Ph.D. in 1915. He was appointed to the staff of the Rockefeller Institute in Jacques Loeb's department in 1916 and was a member of the Institute until his retirement in 1961. During World War I he served as a captain in the Chemical Warfare Service; in World War II he was a consultant to the Office for Scientific Research and Development in connection with chemical warfare problems. He was elected to the National Academy of Sciences in 1934.

Northrop wrote *Crystalline Enzymes* (1939; 2d ed., with M. Kunitz and R. M. Herriott, 1948).

For background information *see* ENZYME; VIRUS in the McGraw-Hill Encyclopedia of Science and Technology.   □

★ **NOYES, William Albert, Jr.**
American chemist
Born Apr. 18, 1898, Terre Haute, Ind., U.S.A.

DURING A study of the fluorescence of acetone vapor at Brown University in 1937–38, one of Noyes's graduate students noticed that the intensity increased with time. This indicated that some molecule was formed by the action of light on acetone that, by some mechanism and even without absorbing light itself, could be made to emit light. Two of the graduate students identified the substance as biacetyl. These observations led to a long series of studies in which light emission was used as a tool to study the details of photochemical processes. Those molecules that emit radiation when exposed to ultraviolet light have proved to be widely useful in initiating chemical effects through the action of light.

Farrington Daniels, at the University of Wisconsin, observed in 1933 that acetone gave out both blue and green light when exposed to ultraviolet light. He also observed that there was no green emission in the presence of oxygen. A careful examination of these phenomena showed that there were two reasons for the lack of green emission. In the first place, the acetone fragments, the acetyl radicals, which might unite to form biacetyl, react instead with oxygen when that substance is present. In the second place, the green emission from biacetyl comes from a state that is itself destroyed by oxygen. G. N. Lewis and his coworkers designated this state as a "triplet" state, one with two unpaired electrons. Over the years the preferential excitation of biacetyl to green emission by other molecules in triplet states proved to be a powerful tool for the identification of certain excited states of molecules. By coupling these studies with the study of reaction products over a range of experimental conditions, Noyes was able to describe in fairly quantitative terms the histories of molecules that absorb light. Also by use of molecules labeled with isotopes, particularly heavy hydrogen, he showed how certain non–free-radical reactions occur. With Davis, Noyes suggested in 1947 that a type of reaction originally found by R. G. W. Norrish to be non–free-radical proceeds by transfer of a hydrogen atom when a six-membered ring is temporarily formed.

Noyes's father was chairman of the department of chemistry at the University of Illinois from 1907 to 1926. Noyes attended Grinnell College and the University of Illinois before his studies were interrupted by service in the Army Signal Corps during World War I. He received his A.B. from Grinnell College in 1919 and his D.-ès-Sc. from the Sorbonne in 1920. After a further year of graduate study at the University of California, Berkeley, he taught there (1921–22), at the University of Chicago (1922–29), at Brown University (1929–38), and at the University of Rochester (1938–63). At Rochester he was chairman of the chemistry department (1939–55), dean of the Graduate School (1952–56), and acting dean of the College of Arts and Sciences (1956–58). In 1963 he became Ashbel Smith Professor of Chemistry at the University of Texas. Noyes received the American Chemical Society's Priestley Medal in 1954 and Willard Gibbs Medal in 1957. He was elected to the National Academy of Sciences in 1943.

Besides some 200 articles in chemistry journals, Noyes wrote *Photochemistry of Gases*, with P. A. Leighton (1941), and edited *Chemistry*, Vol. VI of *Science in World War II* (1948), and *Advances in Photochemistry*, vols. 1–3, with George Hammond and J. N. Pitts (1963–65).

For background information *see* PHOTOCHEMISTRY in the McGraw-Hill Encyclopedia of Science and Technology.   □

☆ **OCHOA, Severo**
American biochemist
Born Sept. 24, 1905, Luarca, Spain

WHILE ENGAGED in studies on oxidative phosphorylation, the main biological mechanism for harnessing the chemical energy of foodstuffs, Ochoa accidentally discovered a bacterial enzyme that synthesizes RNA from nucleoside diphosphates. This marked the first time that a ribonucleic acid, which plays an important role in cell growth, had been synthesized. For this significant achievement, Ochoa shared the 1959 Nobel Prize for physiology or medicine with the American biochemist Arthur Kornberg, who had been the first to synthesize deoxyribonucleic acid, or DNA.

Nucleic acids were discovered by the Swiss biochemist Friedrich Miescher in 1869. A decade later, the German biochemist Albrecht Kossel began the studies that led to his identification of the bases in nucleic acids as purines and pyrimidines—organic nitrogen-containing compounds arranged respectively in one and two rings. The carbohydrate portion of the nucleic acid molecule was identified by the Russian-American chemist P. A. T. Levene, who in 1909 showed that some nucleic acids contain the five-carbon sugar ribose and in 1929 showed that others contain another, related five-carbon sugar, deoxyribose. During the 1940s, the Scottish chemist A. R. Todd described the chemical properties of the nucleic acids, and in 1953 the English biochemist F. H. C. Crick and the American biochemist J. D. Watson announced their discovery of the double-helix structure of DNA. However, despite the progress made by these men, little was known of the mechanism of synthesis of the macromolecules of the nucleic acids.

The four bases of DNA occur in pairs as thymine (T) and adenine (A), cytosine (C) and guanine (G). In the molecule, the pairs form the rungs of a "ladder." The "rungs" are attached at each end to deoxyribose sugars (S). The sugars are attached to phosphate groups (P) and form the "uprights" of the "ladder" thus:

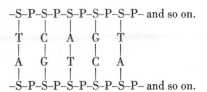

(In replication the split occurs by separating the pairs of bases.)

The RNA molecule differs from the DNA molecule in two main features. Its sugar, ribose, has one more atom of oxygen than does deoxyribose, and uracil (U) takes the place of thymine as one of the four bases. The pairs in RNA are usually U-A and G-C.

When the proper cellular conditions occur, RNA is synthesized according to the sequence in the DNA. For example, if the sequence on one strand of the DNA helix is T A A G C A C G T, and so on, then the sequence of the bases in the synthesized RNA strand is A U U C G U G C A, and so on. Such a synthesis would require catalysis by an enzyme.

Working at New York University in New York City, Ochoa extracted his RNA-synthesizing enzyme from bacteria that are rapidly metabolizing organisms. In 1955, with the assistance of M. Grunberg-Manago, he isolated from the microorganism *Azotobacter vinelandii* an enzyme that promotes a reversible reaction between phosphate and polynucleotides similar to that promoted between phosphate and polysaccharides by phosphorylase. For this reason the enzyme was named polynucleotide phosphorylase. Ochoa found that this enzyme, in the presence of magnesium ions, could catalyze the synthesis of high molecular weight polyribonucleotides from nucleoside diphosphates with the release of orthophosphate in the reversible reaction

$$n \, [\text{X-R-P-P}] \xrightleftharpoons{\text{Mg}^{2+}} (\text{X-R-P})_n + n\text{P}$$

where X represents one or more nitrogenous bases, R represents ribose, P-P represents pyrophosphate, and P represents orthophosphate. For example, when the adenosinediphosphate (ADP) was employed as the substrate, Ochoa synthesized polyadenylic acid, or poly A. By using a mixture of the nucleotides adenosinediphosphate, guanosine diphosphate (GDP), uridinediphosphate (UDP), and cytidine diphosphate (CDP) as the substrate, he was able to prepare synthetic RNA, or poly AGUC.

The molecular weight of the synthetic polyribonucleotide resembled that of natural RNA, as did its nonspecific biological activity. To check the nucleotide composition of the synthesized RNA, Ochoa broke it down with digesting enzymes. The chemical fragments, in solution, were then analyzed by paper chomatography. The patterns produced were identical to those that could be found in the chromatography of natural, digested *Azotobacter* RNA.

Ochoa then began to study the mechanism of action of polynucleotide phosphorylase. The highly purified preparations required were obtained by using chromatography as the final step in the purification. The enzyme, in solution, separated from the contaminants since it moved up the paper at a different rate. At this point the possibility that the enzyme might be a mixture was also tested. Ochoa compared the effect of crude enzyme preparations on individual nucleotides and on combinations of them with the effect of preparations at different degrees of purification. He found that the enzyme's activity in linking the nucleotide bases increased to the same degree as did the purification. Ochoa concluded that only one enzyme was the catalyst for each of the nucleotides and thus that polynucleotide phosphorylase was not a mixture.

The synthesis of RNA opened a vast field of research on the method by which cells synthesize proteins. By 1961, with the use of his synthetic RNA, Ochoa established that different sequences of A, G, U, and C in RNA set the positions, that is, establish the order, for amino acids in protein synthesis. Ochoa discovered a number of different combinations of nucleotides that affected the linking of 20 different amino acids into proteins. Polynucleotide phosphorylase was the key to the deciphering of the genetic code in the laboratories of Ochoa, M. W. Nirenberg, and others.

In addition to his work with RNA, Ochoa discovered two enzymes involved in the Krebs, or citric-acid, cycle, which is the process that supplies energy for life functions. In 1948 Ochoa discovered malic enzyme, which catalyzes the reversible decarboxylation of malic acid to pyruvic acid and carbon dioxide. This supported the view, first advanced by H. G. Wood and C. H. Werkman in 1938, that animals as well as plants can use carbon dioxide and build up carbohydrates. The other enzyme, discovered and crystallized by Ochoa in 1951, is called condensing enzyme. In the Krebs cycle, the condensing enzyme catalyzes the transfer of the acetyl group of acetyl coenzyme A to oxaloacetic acid, with subsequent formation of citric acid and the liberation of coenzyme A. Condensing enzyme was the first enzyme of the Krebs cycle to be crystallized. The methods used by Ochoa for this research exerted added influence in enzymology, for they demonstrated the value of spectrophotometry in biochemical studies. In spectrophotometry, results can be obtained using very small quantities of material, which is all that is usually available when new enzymes are being investigated.

The youngest child of a lawyer, Ochoa was educated at Malaga College, receiving his B.A. in 1921. In 1922 he entered the Medical School at the University of Madrid and received an M.D. (cum laude) in 1929. He then went to Germany to conduct research at the Kaiser Wilhelm Institute in Berlin and later in Heidelberg, leaving in 1931 to accept a position as lecturer in physiology at the University of Madrid. From 1932 to 1934, on a leave of absence from Madrid, he performed research in enzymology at the National Institute for Medical Research, London, England. Ochoa returned to Spain in 1934 and was appointed head of the physiology division of the Institute for Medical Research of Madrid University in 1935. In the following year he returned to the Kaiser Wilhelm Institute. He visited England again in 1937, spending that year at the Marine Biological Laboratory in Plymouth, and from 1938 to 1941 he was a research assistant at Oxford University. In the latter year he left for the United States, where he worked as a research associate in the department of pharmacology at the Washington University School of Medicine, St. Louis, Mo. In 1942 he joined the faculty of the New York University School of Medicine as a research associate in medicine, becoming assistant professor of biochemistry in 1945, professor of pharmacology in 1946, and professor of biochemistry and chairman of the department of biochemistry in 1954. Ochoa became an American citizen in 1956. He was elected to the National Academy of Sciences in 1957.

For background information *see* NUCLEIC ACID in the McGraw-Hill Encyclopedia of Science and Technology.   □

★ **ONSAGER, Lars**
American chemist
Born Nov. 27, 1903, Oslo, Norway

F OR THE foundation of "irreversible thermodynamics" and for his contributions to the theories of dielectrics, electrolytes, and cooperative phenomena, Onsager in 1953 received the Rumford Medal of the American Academy of Arts and Sciences, in 1958 the Lorentz Medal of the Royal Netherlands Academy of Sciences, and in the period 1962–65 several medals of the American Chemical Society, as well as the Peter Debye Award in Physical Chemistry.

In 1887, not long after chemists had started to appreciate the mass-action law and the useful analogy between dilute solutions and gases, Arrhenius's theory of electrolytic dissociation accomplished much more than the solution of a mystery. From then on, charged ions were recognized as valid species in chemical kinetics, and the transport processes of electrical conduction and diffusion were correlated with the thermodynamic properties. Still, the advantages were somewhat impaired by the circumstance that ions in solution exhibit a characteristic behavior different from that of ordinary molecules, so that complete additivity prevails only at very low concentrations.

Such effects might well be attributed to long-range electrostatic interaction; indeed, in 1923 the calculations of P. Debye and E. Hückel fully accounted for the observed linear variation of the several "anomalies" with the square root of the concentration. The coefficients were predictable, too. Debye and Hückel first claimed that much only for the thermodynamic functions, but in the following year Onsager revised their computations and laid the basis for an equally complete theory of conduction and diffusion. The issues involved were subtle: He had to recognize that in the course of its own irregular thermal motion every ion helps to readjust any disturbances of its environment. An apparent ambiguity in the earlier estimate of a hydrodynamic interaction could be eliminated by a more direct approach to the problem. As the conclusions were published in 1926 and 1927, together with a careful critique of the experimental data, the comparison was convincing; before long all the new theoretical results served routinely to sharpen the interpretation and to facilitate the correlation of experimental studies.

Meanwhile Onsager had pondered the fundamental reason why his results were compatible with Helmholtz's theory of diffusion potentials. Like Kelvin's theory of thermoelectric phenomena, this invoked an extraneous hypothesis with the thermodynamic reasoning; while the predictions had been verified whenever feasible, the proper status of such theories had long been in doubt. In wider context, Onsager recognized an analogy with the consequences of microscopic reversibility, as in 1924 he had applied that well-known principle in his analysis of C. N. Riiber's three-way chemical reaction. But in the theory of a transport process, which quantity corresponded to the concentration of a reacting substance? How about a displacement? The thermal motion of the atoms creates departures from the uniform distribution of molecular species and of the energy; the average regression of such fluctuations ought to obey the ordinary laws of transport. The link to thermodynamics was available through the precise cybernetic interpretation of thermodynamic functions according to Boltzmann, Gibbs, and Einstein. On this basis Onsager in 1931 derived a general "principle of the least dissipation" from the hypothesis of symmetry in past and future, with natural modifications for phenomena dependent on magnetic fields or Coriolis forces.

In the following year, when Onsager and Fuoss completed a comprehensive treatment of transport processes in electrolytes, they regarded the Helmholtz relation as one member of a whole set of symmetry conditions, otherwise new, to be imposed on the entire matrix of cross-coefficients for mobility in conduction and diffusion. As a result, the fruit of their arduous effort could be summarized compactly in terms of a dissipation function. From time to time Onsager dealt with other problems in this area; for example, in 1934 he showed that the dissociation equilibrium of a weak electrolyte must be shifted by an electric field. The computed effect accounts for departures from Ohm's law in a great variety of ionic conductors, liquid or solid. Moreover, the effect is exploited in the study of very fast chemical reactions.

The dipole theory of dielectrics, proposed by Debye in 1912, proved very fruitful and stimulated intense experimental activity from 1925 on, as convenient techniques became available. It seemed as if nothing much could be done about the shortcomings of the theory as applied to liquids of high dielectric constant, where the predictions bore but faint resemblance to the observations. This was properly ascribed to the mutual orientation of the molecules, but the word "association" buried that problem. Onsager naively embedded a model molecule in a dielectric continuum and computed the orienting effect of an applied field from the torque—and obtained a result that looked fairly realistic when he consulted the data. He had made a distinction between permanent and induced dipoles; Debye had treated them alike in applying the Clausius-Mosotti formula. Averaging the

torque was right, as long as he could rely on classical mechanics. This question had been under a cloud until the consequences of quantum mechanics were clarified, but in 1927 the clouds were parting. Just in case, he consulted E. Schrödinger. Still, whichever was more accurate, his interpretation of the measurements was not as precise as Debye's, and he did not have the heart to throw cold water on the rising enthusiasm for the study of dipole moments just then. By 1936 the situation had changed. In a desperate search for a reasonable interpretation of his measurements on aqueous solutions of polypeptides, J. Wyman proposed an empirical formula that came very close to Onsager's prediction. When Onsager saw that—at the instigation of J. G. Kirkwood—he realized that he would never have a better opportunity, and he arranged for simultaneous publication. Later developments, including some of Onsager's own work, suggest that although a certain systematic error is inherent in his model, any marked refinement of the theory must depend on more detailed specifications of molecular structure and arrangement. In any event, Wyman's analysis indicated that proton-bonded liquids like water and formic acid are in a class by themselves, and this invited attempts to estimate the effects of chain association. In particular, water might behave like a system of cross-linked chains; the solid seemed a little simpler, and in 1935 L. Pauling had made a start on that.

Onsager soon came to appreciate the depth of the problems involved in the theory of disordered solids. In 1941, M. A. Kramers and G. Wannier located the critical point of the two-dimensional Ising model. With fascination Onsager examined their methods and saw that he could add a trick or two, then followed up one encouraging lead after another until he had computed the partition function, which determines the thermodynamic properties. The result was obtained in 1942; he took time to tidy up various details and published it in 1944. More recent specific heat measurements through the critical range of real three-dimensional systems indicate logarithmic singularities quite similar to those computed for the two-dimensional models, only somewhat less symmetrical.

From about 1940 Onsager was much interested in low-temperature physics. Below 2.16°K helium enters a peculiar superfluid state, where it lacks ordinary heat resistance and cannot rotate without the formation of localized vortices of strength h/m, that is, Planck's constant divided by the mass of a helium atom. Onsager suggested the existence of such vortices in 1949, R. P. Feynman independently a few years later. The most clear-cut proof was obtained by G. W. Rayfield and F. Reif in 1963, when they showed that electrons or positive ions accelerated in helium at temperatures below 0.3°K attach vortex rings;

as the accelerating voltage is increased, the motion of the charges slows down. In 1952 Onsager, this time followed independently by E. Lifshitz, showed how highly significant information about the distribution of electrons among the possible states of motion in a metal could be extracted from studies of the de Haas-van Alphen effect if more powerful experimental methods were developed. Within a few years D. Shoenberg rose to the challenge and applied intense magnetic fields by a pulse technique, then picked up the fine ripples of the magnetic response as the field changed.

In 1951 N. Bjerrum showed that the dielectric relaxation of ice must involve the motion of bonding errors, while the conduction involves in addition intermolecular jumps of protons, whereby an ion exchanges roles with a neighboring molecule. In 1956 M. Eigen and L. DeDaeyer determined the rate of formation of new ion pairs as they extracted the entire saturation current from a thin sheet of ice, and they found a significant increase of this current with the applied field. As interpreted by Onsager's long-known theory, this result implied an attraction between the combining charges about 10 times stronger than that expected from the macroscopic dielectric constant. In 1959 Onsager and M. Dupuis supplied the explanation: Ions and bonding errors must be treated on an equal footing. Each kind carries an effective charge of about half an elementary charge, and the high-frequency dielectric constant of about 3.1 determines their electrostatic interaction. In addition a weak statistical interaction by way of the polarization field differentiates the two species of carriers; the transition from local to macroscopic behavior is mediated by charge clouds of the Debye-Hückel type. In this picture, as in the parallel work by C. Jaccard in 1959, the dielectric constant becomes essentially a kinetic concept. A symmetry relation implicit in the kinetic equations of Onsager and Dupuis was derived independently by Jaccard in 1964 from the principles of irreversible thermodynamics.

Onsager obtained a Ch.E. at the Norwegian Technical Institute, Trondheim, Norway, in 1925. He was a student at the Federal Institute of Technology at Zurich, Switzerland, until 1928, when he went to the United States to work as an associate in chemistry at the Johns Hopkins University. From 1928 to 1933 he was an instructor at Brown University. A Sterling fellow at Yale University (1933–34), he received his Ph.D. there in 1935. In 1934 he was appointed an assistant professor at Yale, becoming J. Willard Gibbs Professor of Theoretical Chemistry in 1945. The same year he became an American citizen. He was elected to the National Academy of Sciences in 1947.

For background information *see* ELECTROLYTIC CONDUCTANCE; OPEN SYSTEMS, THERMODYNAMICS OF (BIOLOGY); THERMODYNAMICS (CHEMICAL) in the McGraw-Hill Encyclopedia of Science and Technology.   □

★ OORT, Jan Hendrik

Dutch astronomer
Born Apr. 28, 1900, Franeker, Netherlands

OORT'S INTEREST in stellar astronomy was aroused by J. C. Kapteyn, a pioneer in the search for the structure of our galaxy. A major part of his subsequent research was devoted to problems concerning the structure and the dynamics of the galactic system.

At the time Oort, as a student, first came into contact with the subject, the Sun was thought to be nearly centrally located in this system. His first investigation was concerned with stars of high velocity; he showed that all stars with velocities in excess of a certain limit (about 65 km/sec) moved toward one hemisphere of the sky, while no such asymmetry was found among slower-moving stars. These facts did not fit in with the symmetrical "Kapteyn system." Later investigations by Bertil Lindblad and Oort showed that this remarkable asymmetry in the high velocities could be explained as a consequence of the rotation of the galactic system around a center at large distance from the Sun. The Kapteyn system proved to be only a small part of a very much larger galaxy, most of which was invisible because of obscuration by interstellar dust clouds The first direct observational evidence for this rotation was discovered by Oort. He showed that the inner parts of our galaxy revolved with shorter periods than the outer parts.

Oort subsequently investigated relations between the velocity distribution of stars and the way the population density of the stars decreases with increasing distance from the galactic center and with increasing distance from the galactic plane. As a direct result of these investigations he determined the total density of matter in the general vicinity of the Sun. The more general aims of these investigations were to determine the gravitational force throughout our galaxy and to obtain a model of the distribution of the mass.

An entirely new impetus toward the solution of this problem was given by the study of interstellar hydrogen through its radiation at a wavelength of 21 cm. Impressed by the new possibilities that seemed to open up through the use of radiation at radio frequencies, as shown by Grote Reber's observations in the United States just before and during World War II, Oort, immediately after the war, helped found a center for radio astronomical research in the Netherlands. With H. C. Van de Hulst, who had suggested the possibility that a hydrogen line at a wavelength of 21 cm might be observable from interstellar space, and with several other Leiden astronomers, a nearly complete map of the distribution of gas in the galactic disk was prepared. As the radiation at radio frequencies passes unhindered through the interstellar dust clouds, the entire galactic system could now for the first time be surveyed. It was shown that the gas clouds in our galaxy were arranged in a spiral pattern like those observed in many other galaxies. Also, the rotation of our galaxy could be studied in regions that had hitherto been invisible, in particular near its nucleus. It was found that there is a very strong concentration of mass toward the galactic center. During a special investigation of the central region, W. Rougoor and Oort found an entirely unexpected phenomenon, namely, that the gas in this region is expanding away from the center, at speeds of the same order as the rotational velocity of our galaxy. The cause of these motions is still unknown.

Besides these problems of the distribution and motion of the gas through the entire galaxy, Oort also investigated the smaller-scale motions in the interstellar medium. As a result of collisions between individual clouds, these tend to lose their random motions and to agglomerate together. Oort and Lyman Spitzer showed how the birth of massive stars within these agglomerations splits them up into smaller parts and restores the random cloud motions. Oort studied too the effects of expanding supernova shells on the surrounding medium. With Van de Hulst, he produced a theory of growth and evaporation of solid particles in interstellar space.

On the subject of the solar system, Oort investigated the origin of comets. He showed that all comets come from a vast swarm around the solar system, extending almost to the nearest stars. By gravitational perturbations from the surrounding stars, comets from this huge reservoir are regularly brought into orbits that take them into the inner parts of the solar system and make them observable. Mainly through the action of the Sun, they then gradually disintegrate but are replenished by new ones coming from the big swarm. The swarm of comets must have been formed soon after the origin of the planetary system, when many of the "stray" bodies moving between the major planets were diffused outward by exactly the same processes by which they are now diffused back into the planetary system.

In 1956 Oort and T. Walraven made the first extensive study of the polarization of the light of the Crab nebula, an expanding mass of gas that resulted from a supernova explosion in the year 1054. They showed that the polarization is exceedingly strong, proving beyond doubt that the continuous radiation emitted by the nebula is of the synchrotron type. While all ordinary light is emitted by electron jumps on an atomic scale, the light of the Crab nebula comes from electrons moving in huge orbits in large-scale magnetic fields. This is called synchrotron radiation. The electrons concerned have energies in the same range as cosmic rays. The total energy contained in these high-energy electrons is extremely large. This same mechanism causes the strong radio-frequency radiation of the Crab nebula and, in fact, of all radio sources.

Oort came from an academic family. His grandfather, professor of Hebrew at the University of Leiden, was one of the principal contributors to the so-called "Leiden translation" of the Bible into Dutch. His father was a medical doctor. After his studies at the University of Groningen, Oort spent 2 years as a research assistant at the Observatory of Yale University. He went to the Leiden Observatory in 1924 and became its director in 1945. He was appointed professor of astronomy at Leiden in 1935. From 1935 to 1948 he was general secretary, and from 1958 to 1961 president, of the International Astronomical Union. Among the honors given Oort in the United States was the 1942 Bruce Medal of the Astronomical Society of the Pacific. He was elected a foreign associate of the U.S. National Academy of Sciences in 1953.

For background information *see* COSMOGONY; COSMOLOGY in the McGraw-Hill Encyclopedia of Science and Technology. □

☆ **OPIE, Eugene Lindsay**
American pathologist
Born July 5, 1873, Staunton, Va., U.S.A.

THROUGH HIS studies on the epidemiology of tuberculosis, Opie was able to demonstrate the value of x-ray examination in diagnosing asymptomatic tubercular lesions and to determine the likelihood of transmission of the dis-

ease within a household by sputum examination. He also developed a method of immunization against tuberculosis, using heat-killed tubercle bacilli. For his contributions to knowledge of the pathogenesis of tuberculosis and his studies on pancreatic function and various aspects of immunity, Opie received, among many other honors, the 1959 Kovalenko Medal of the National Academy of Sciences.

During the last year of World War I Opie directed a clinical and pathological laboratory in a British military hospital at Rouen. Here he found that 25 per cent of young British soldiers had healed or healing tubercular lesions caused by drinking the milk of infected cows. He was a member of an army commission that showed that trench fever, which disabled many soldiers, was caused by vermin. Returning to the United States, he headed a commission for the investigation of the pneumonia that was prevalent in the army. Its report on epidemic respiratory diseases was a detailed study of the disastrous influenza epidemic of 1918.

Opie resumed his work in tuberculosis at the Henry Phipps Institute of the University of Pennsylvania. Since there was a great deal of uncertainty about the manner of transmission of tuberculosis, Opie instituted a large-scale study, which demonstrated that the disease is spread by contact and that it occurs in families, being spread from one member to another and from one generation to the next. He also found that in children who have contracted the disease, spread from the lungs to the regional lymph nodes frequently occurs. In adults, however, a measure of immunity obtained by earlier infection generally limits the disease to the lungs.

In his studies on the epidemiology of tuberculosis Opie found that the tuberculin reaction was an accurate gage of the extent of tuberculosis present in a community. He also verified the reliability of x-ray examination as a means of detecting asymptomatic tuberculosis, and in addition he demonstrated that the sputum test could be used as an index of the probability of tuberculosis transmission within a household.

In a large study of tuberculosis among Jamaican Negroes, Opie concluded that individuals who failed to react to the tuberculin test (which indicated that they had not been exposed to the disease) were especially susceptible to the infection (because they lacked the degree of immunity conferred by prior exposure). Opie also demonstrated that injections of heat-killed tubercle bacilli were effective in preventing infection.

Opie was educated at the Johns Hopkins University, from which he received his A.B. in 1893 and his M.D. in 1897. He was then affiliated with the pathology laboratories at Johns Hopkins. From 1904 to 1910 he was a member of the Rockefeller Institute for Medical Research. In 1910 he was named professor of pathology at Washington University School of Medicine in St. Louis, where he served as dean from 1912 to 1915. In 1923 he was named professor of experimental pathology at the University of Pennsylvania and director of the Henry Phipps Institute for the Study of Tuberculosis. From 1932 to 1941 he was professor of pathology at Cornell University Medical College. Thereafter he pursued research at the Rockefeller Institute. He was elected to the National Academy of Sciences in 1923.

Opie wrote *Diseases of the Pancreas* (1902) and *Epidemic Respiratory Disease* (1921).

For background information *see* TUBERCULOSIS in the McGraw-Hill Encyclopedia of Science and Technology. ☐

★ **PAGE, Irvine Heinly**
American physician
Born Jan. 7, 1901, Indianapolis, Ind., U.S.A.

P AGE WORKED in three major fields: (1) chemistry of the brain; (2) mechanisms and treatment of arteriosclerosis; and (3) mechanisms and treatment of hypertension.

The first of these interests began in 1928, when Page was invited to start a novel division of brain chemistry at the Kaiser Wilhelm Institute in Munich, Germany. This interest helped stimulate the initiation of a new field of research and culminated in the discovery with M. M. Rapport and A. A. Green of serotonin, or 5-hydroxytryptamine. In 1937 he wrote the second book on the chemistry of the brain, the first having been by J. L. W. Thudichum in 1884.

In 1931 Page went to the Rockefeller Institute Hospital in New York and began work on arteriosclerosis and hypertension. At that time there was almost no interest in either subject. Heart

attacks, or myocardial infarction, were given small credence, and hypertension was all too often viewed as a beneficial compensatory mechanism to force blood through thickened blood vessels.

It was first necessary to show that blood pressure could be lowered from high to normal levels without interfering with the blood supply of organs, especially the brain and kidneys. This was the first work of some importance conducted by Page in this new field of research. Experimental hypertension was then elicited in dogs by treating their explanted kidneys with large doses of x-rays. Page also began work on the extraction of renin from the kidneys; in 1939, with D. M. Helmer, he demonstrated that renin is an enzyme and acts on a substrate synthesized by the liver to produce angiotensin, an octapeptide of great potency. This peptide, along with serotonin and noradrenaline, formed an important part of the basis for Page's mosaic concept of control of the circulation. In 1956 angiotensin was synthesized by F. M. Bumpus, H. Schwarz, and Page.

Page and his clinical associates, A. C. Corcoran, R. D. Taylor, and H. P. Dustan, showed, along with others, that several drugs could be used successfully in the treatment of hypertension. They introduced for clinical use such drugs as hydralazine and guanethidine. They showed that the effectiveness of most antihypertensive drugs was greatly enhanced by the diuretic chlorothiazide. After many years this work culminated in the demonstration that in some patients hypertension could be reversed and that drugs were no longer necessary. Further, Page was the first to show that malignant hypertension was reversible. With Dustan and E. F. Poutasse, Page corrected hypertension due to stenosis of the renal arteries following renal angiography. And, with J. W. McCubbin, Page showed that the resetting of the carotid sinus mechanism occurred as an adjustment to experimental hypertension developing from Page's method of cellophane perinephritis.

Page's work on arteriosclerosis began with his discovery of a new steroid in starfish eggs in 1923. In 1931, with W. G. Bernhard, he studied the preventive effects of iodide, using the carbon combustion method for measuring plasma lipids developed with D. D. Van Slyke and E. Kirk. Subsequent work subtended the structure and quantitation of lipoproteins, effects of Triton, and most recently the organization and conduct of the National Diet-Heart Study. From Page's 35-year interest in diseases of the circulation and the normal physiology and chemical control of the heart, blood vessels, and kidneys grew his concept of hypertension and arteriosclerosis as "diseases of regulation."

Page graduated from Shortridge High School in Indianapolis, then studied chemistry, followed by medicine, at Cornell University. After a 2-year internship in New York, he became director of chemical research at the Kaiser Wilhelm Institute in Munich and subsequently became an associate member of the Rockefeller Institute for Medical Research. In 1937 he left to become director of clinical research at the Lilly Laboratories for Clinical Research in Indianapolis and in 1945 moved to the Cleveland Clinic as director of research. Among other honors, Page received the Albert Lasker Award of the American Heart Association in 1958, the John Phillips Memorial Award of the American College of Physicians in 1962, the Gairdner Foundation Award in 1963, and the Distinguished Service Award of the American Medical Association in 1964.

Page wrote *Chemistry of the Brain* (1937), *Neurochemistry* (1955; 2d ed. 1962), *Hypertension, A Manual for Patients* (1943; 2d ed. 1956), *Arterial Hypertension: Its Diagnosis and Treatment*, with A. C. Corcoran (1945; 2d ed. 1949), and *Experimental Renal Hypertension*, with A. C. Corcoran (1948).

For background information *see* HYPERTENSION in the McGraw-Hill Encyclopedia of Science and Technology.   □

PALADE, George Emil
American cytologist
Born Nov. 19, 1912, Jassy, Romania

PALADE ELUCIDATED the ultrastructure of cells, particularly the cytoplasm and its inclusions. For his achievements in this field he received the 1964 Passano Foundation Award.

With the development of the electron microscope and methods of separating cellular components by differential centrifugation, knowledge of the ultrastructure of the cell advanced

rapidly. The morphology of the cytoplasmic bodies, the mitochondria, discovered some 70 years ago by Altmann, was intensively investigated by Palade and his colleagues at the Rockefeller Institute. Although some basic techniques were available, Palade originated some of his own, such as methods of fixation. Palade's observations with the electron microscope of sectioned cells and material obtained from centrifuged fractions revealed that the mitochondria possess a characteristic structure below the limits of resolution of the light microscope. The edge of each organelle, he found, is marked by two generally parallel membranes, each about 50 A thick and separated by a space of 60 to 80 A. The outer membrane is the limiting membrane of the mitochondrion; the inner membrane is characterized by a series of laminated structures called *cristae mitochondriales*. The mitochondrial membranes delimit two chambers: an outer one between the two membranes and an inner one bounded by the inner membrane. The inner is, generally, incompletely partitioned by the cristae. The base of the cristae are attached to the inner mitochondrial membrane, while the opposite ends are free, projecting more or less deeply into the inner chamber. For the most part, the cristae are perpendicular to the longitudinal axis of the organelle, although various other arrangements have been observed. At higher magnifications, each crista shows a composite layered structure consisting of a light central layer, covered on each side by a darker, dense layer. Frequently, at their bases, the dense layers appear to be continuous with the inner mitochondrial membrane while the light layer seems continuous with the outer chamber. The inner chamber is filled with a rather dense, homogeneous material called the mitochondrial matrix where occasionally small granules of a rather high density are found. The material of the outer chamber generally tends to be less dense.

Electron microscopic studies of the ultrastructure of the cytoplasm by Palade and others revealed that the hyaloplasm contains a delicate network, the endoplasmic reticulum, so named by K. R. Porter. Using a variety of techniques and surveying some 40 different avian and mammalian cell types, Palade showed that endoplasmic reticulum is a cytoplasmic constituent of all cells except the mature erythrocyte. His observations indicated that the reticulum consists of a variety of vesicles, tubules, and relatively large, flat sacs he called cisternae. The membranes of the network were either rough or smooth, depending on whether or not small electron-dense particles were attached to the membrane's outer surface. Careful examination showed that the two types of membranes are often interconnected and merely represent local differentiations within a common, continuous system, not two different and unrelated structures. Smooth-surfaced and rough-surfaced elements were found in the reticulum of all animal cells, but the relative amount varied considerably and characteristically with the cell type. In many cells, there were indications that endoplasmic reticulum reached the cell surface where the cell membrane was continuous with the membranes of the network, and cavities of the network appeared to merge with the extracellular environment. In a few cell types, the network also appeared to be connected with the outer surface of the nuclear membranes.

In collaboration with Philip Siekevitz, Palade examined the postmitochondrial fractions, that is, the fractions remaining after the separation of the mitochondria by differential centrifugation of tissue homogenates. Electron micrographs of these cell components revealed that they consist mostly of fragments of rough-surfaced elements of the endoplasmic reticulum. These fragments, called microsomes, consist of small pieces of membranes with the particles still attached. Palade found that the particles possess a definite and more or less characteristic morphology, while chemical analysis revealed that they have a high RNA content. These particles are presently known as ribosomes and are considered to be the site of protein synthesis.

Palade also investigated the nature of other cellular inclusions, such as the Golgi apparatus, chloroplasts, and the centrosphere.

Palade received his M.D. from the University of Bucharest in 1940. He remained there as assistant professor and associate professor of anatomy until 1946, when he went to the United States to join the Rockefeller Institute. In 1958 he became member and professor of cytology there. Palade became a naturalized citizen in 1952. He was elected to the National Academy of Sciences in 1961.

For background information *see* Cell (BIO-

LOGICAL); CYTOLOGY; MITOCHONDRIA in the Mc-Graw-Hill Encyclopedia of Science and Technology. ☐

★ PALMÉN, Erik Herbert

Finnish meteorologist and oceanographer
Born Aug. 31, 1898, Vasa, Finland

WHILE WORKING in oceanography, primarily with problems concerning the interaction between atmosphere and sea, Palmén became interested in the dynamics of the atmosphere and especially in the structure and behavior of the extratropical cyclones. In collaboration with other Scandinavian meteorologists, especially with J. A. B. Bjerknes, he conducted synoptic investigations of selected cyclones during the years before World War II. After the war Palmén was invited to attend a research group under the leadership of C. G. Rossby at the University of Chicago, where fundamental researches were carried out on the general atmospheric circulation. In connection with this work Palmén, in close collaboration with Rossby and other meteorologists, developed the concept of atmospheric jet streams in the upper troposphere. The jet stream was immediately recognized as an important global phenomenon closely associated with the general atmospheric circulation and its disturbances.

Somewhat later Palmén showed that there exist two principal jet streams in the Northern Hemisphere, and obviously also in the Southern Hemisphere. The jet stream at lower latitudes, around 30°N, is called the "subtropical" jet and the more northerly jet stream the "polar-front" jet. The former derives its energy from the tropical mean circulation (Hadley circulation), whereas the polar-front jet is maintained by energy transformations associated with the polar-front disturbances. In the cores of the jet streams, at levels between 30,000 and 40,000 ft,

very high wind velocities of up to 150–250 kt may be observed. Hence the atmospheric jet streams play an important role in the atmospheric dynamics and are, in addition, of great practical importance for the planning of the flight routes of commercial aircraft.

The investigations of the atmospheric jet streams led Palmén to further studies of the energy conversions in the atmosphere. Through synoptic-aerological studies of the three-dimensional air motion in extratropical cyclones, he computed the rate of generation of kinetic energy as a result of the complicated vertical circulations occurring in connection with the polar-front cyclones. He also, partly in collaboration with other meteorologists, computed the mean meridional mass circulation in the tropical and subtropical atmosphere and showed the importance of this circulation for the maintenance of the atmospheric energy budget.

While working on the tropical circulation, Palmén became interested in the problem of tropical cyclones, hurricanes, and typhoons. He showed why tropical hurricanes form in special oceanic regions and only during the so-called hurricane seasons in these regions. An explanation of this characteristic behavior of the hurricanes was found in the thermal structure of the tropical atmosphere and its dependence on the surface temperature of the oceans. He also presented a model of the thermal structure of a mature hurricane and showed how this is related to the thermal structure of the tropical atmosphere and the ocean temperature. In collaboration with American meteorologists, mainly with H. Riehl, he computed the budget of energy and angular momentum in tropical hurricanes. In connection with these investigations the problem of the transformation of tropical hurricanes into extratropical storms was clarified with the aid of some synoptic case studies.

In recent years Palmén returned to the problem of the general atmospheric circulation and tried to work out a satisfactory energy budget for the whole atmosphere by considering radiation, flux of sensible and latent heat from the Earth's surface, and the mean meridional and vertical energy flux in the atmosphere.

The son of a judge, Palmén received his university training at the University of Helsinki, Finland, taking his Ph.D. in 1927. From 1922 to 1946 he worked at the Finnish Institute of Marine Research, from 1939 to 1946 as its director. During most of this time he also taught geophysics at the University of Helsinki. In 1947–48 Palmén was professor of meteorology at the University of Helsinki. In 1948 he received a research professorship at the Academy of Finland. Palmén was awarded the Symons Medal of the Royal Meteorological Society in 1957, the Rossby Medal of the American Meteorological

Society in 1960, and the Buys Ballot Medal of the Royal Academy of Sciences of the Netherlands in 1964.

For background information *see* ATMOSPHERIC LOW; HURRICANE; JET STREAM in the McGraw-Hill Encyclopedia of Science and Technology. □

★ PANOFSKY, Wolfgang Kurt Herman
American physicist
Born Apr. 24, 1919, Berlin, Germany

IN ORDER to determine the properties of the newly discovered pi-mesons (pions), Panofsky in 1950 conceived a method to analyze the γ-ray spectra when negative pions are absorbed in hydrogen. The results determined the "parity" of the pi-mesons, showed that charged pions are heavier than the neutral pions, and determined precise mass values of the pions. In addition various other constants of importance to the understanding of pion-nucleon and nucleon-nucleon forces were determined in the same experiment.

When the pi-mesons were produced artificially in Berkeley in 1948, little was known about their properties and their role in particle interactions. This situation did not improve very rapidly in subsequent years. Most research was devoted to production experiments of mesons in complex nuclei; such reactions involve many nucleons and are too involved to permit simple analysis and thus to shed light on the properties of the pi-mesons. The only interaction experiments studied at that time involved analysis of stopped negative mesons (π^-) in nuclear emulsions; the reaction taking place is

$$\pi^- + p + \text{remainder of nucleus} \rightarrow$$
$$n + \text{excited nucleus} \qquad (1)$$

where p and n stand for proton and neutron respectively. The simpler reaction

$$\pi^- + p \rightarrow n \qquad (2)$$

on free protons (in hydrogen) cannot occur since energy and momentum cannot be balanced.

Panofsky reasoned that since reaction (2) was "forbidden" by the energy and momentum conservation laws, an additional particle of integral spin would have to be emitted when negative pions are stopped in hydrogen. At that time the only particle, other than the pions themselves, fitting that description was the γ-ray. Accordingly, an experiment was set up aimed at analyzing the γ-ray spectrum from the negative pions stopped in hydrogen. At the time of the experiment (1950–51), technology in high-energy–particle physics was considerably more primitive than it is today. There were no "beams" of unstable particles like pi-mesons, nor was there any convenient technology involving liquid hydrogen targets. Accordingly, the experiment was arranged as shown in the accompanying diagram. The production target for pi-mesons, and the absorption target in which the presumed reaction

$$\pi^- + p \rightarrow n + \gamma \qquad (3)$$

could take place, had to be placed inside the vacuum tank of the 184-in. synchrocyclotron at Berkeley. The circulating proton beam would strike the production target; the resulting pions were then to be absorbed in the hydrogen pressure vessel, cooled to liquid-nitrogen temperature in order to increase the density. The resultant γ-rays, presumed from reaction (3) were to be analyzed in a "pair spectrometer." This device analyzes γ-rays by letting them produce electron-positron pairs in a "converter" through the reaction $\gamma \rightarrow e^+ + e^-$ and then determining the energies of each of the pair fragments e^+ and e^- by their curvature in a magnetic field. The sum of the e^+ and e^- energies then measures the γ-ray energy; analysis of the distribution of this sum thus measures the energy spectrum of the γ-rays presumably from reaction (3). According to the mechanical conservation laws, the energy of the γ-ray from this reaction should be unique; that is, a single spectral "line" should be observed.

In 1950 and 1951, Panofsky and his associates Herbert York, Lee Aamodt, and James Hadley carried out a number of runs using the general scheme described. It should be noted that only the final counts in the electron and positron counter were actually observed. That the chain of events on which the experiment was predicated actually took place had to be inferred; this could be ascertained by numerous check runs. Moreover, the counting rates were low—only a few per hour—so that phenomena could not be explored under a wide variety of conditions.

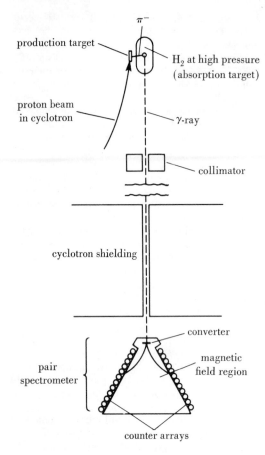

Schematic diagram of apparatus used to measure energy spectrum of photons resulting from the capture of π^- mesons in hydrogen and deuterium.

The observed γ-ray spectra, initially composed of only a hundred events or so, turned out to be surprising. The predicted narrow line corresponding to reaction (3) did indeed appear, but there was also a lower-energy γ-ray group, in a spectrum of substantial width centered at about one-half the energy of reaction (3). The interpretation of this other group is that a reaction

$$\pi^- + p \to n + \pi^0 \tag{4}$$
$$\qquad\qquad \hookrightarrow \gamma + \gamma$$

occurs at a rate competitive to reaction (3). The experiment thus confirmed the suspected existence of a neutral pion and showed that it must be lighter than the charged pions. In addition to this gross result, there are several implications depending on more detailed analysis.

Since the pion is being created or destroyed by the basic reaction

$$\text{nucleon} \rightleftarrows \text{nucleon} + \pi \tag{5}$$

it is relevant to ask: what are the "intrinsic" properties of the pion, or what property does it add or take away from the nucleus as the pion is absorbed or emitted? Analysis of the reaction described by Eq. (4) indicates that the rate of this process can only be competitive with reaction (3) if, whatever else is true, the "intrinsic properties" of the neutral and charged pions were the same; this implies that the three particles π^-, π^0, and π^+ are "triplet" members of the same family. It becomes clear that if deuterium (each nucleus consisting of a neutron and a proton) were substituted for the hydrogen in the pressure vessel, then not only some of the relative but also the absolute intrinsic properties of the pion could be determined. In deuterium three reactions are presumably possible when pions are absorbed:

$$\pi^- + D \to n + n \tag{6}$$
$$\pi^- + D \to n + n + \gamma \tag{7}$$
$$\pi^- + D \to n + n + \pi^0 \tag{8}$$
$$\qquad\qquad \hookrightarrow \gamma + \gamma$$

The main interest is focused on reaction (6): If the pion is a "scalar"—that is, if on absorption neither the parity nor the angular momentum of the nucleon is changed—then this reaction is strictly forbidden. If (6) does occur, then the charged pion is probably "pseudoscalar"—that is, the parity of the nucleon (the symmetry of the nucleon state with its mirror image) must change whenever a meson is absorbed from rest. Note, however, that reaction (6) cannot be observed directly using the methods described, since γ-rays are not emitted.

The experimental results showed that the rate of reaction (8) was negligible, and that reaction (7) did occur but only at a rate about one-third of the one observed for hydrogen. The inference is thus that reaction (6) does occur and that therefore the pions must be "pseudoscalar," that is, have odd "intrinsic parity."

This result appears to be an isolated fact of little interest to other areas. Actually the contrary is true. The result was the first assignment of an "intrinsic property" to an unstable, artificially created particle. With knowledge of such properties, it is possible to determine the "selection rules" governing the reactions among the unstable particles—that is, the rules that govern when reaction can or cannot "go."

In addition to these basic conclusions, studies of these new reactions produced a number of additional results: (*a*) Analysis of the γ-ray spectra gave a new, precise value of the mass of the charged pion. (*b*) Comparison of the two spectra from reactions (3) and (4) gave a quantitative measurement of the mass difference between the charged and neutral pion. (*c*) Analysis of the γ-ray spectrum from reaction

(7) is sensitive to the interaction between the two neutrons. Thus the experiment gave results corresponding to "neutron-neutron scattering" and these answers could be compared to those obtained from "proton-proton scattering," which can be observed directly. The results indicated that two neutrons could not form a stable "dineutron"; there had been speculations that such a nuclear species might exist.

To summarize, studies of the "stopped pion" reactions produced an unexpectedly rich group of results. These reactions are still being studied extensively today in order to improve the quantitative knowledge of the reaction rates involved in such processes and to obtain more accurate masses of the particles involved.

The son of an art historian, Panofsky went to the United States in 1934. He entered Princeton in that year and received his B.A. in physics in 1938. He received his Ph.D. at the California Institute of Technology in 1942. During that year and until 1945 he was involved in military research at Caltech and Los Alamos. From 1945 to 1951 he worked at the Radiation Laboratory of the University of California and taught in the physics department of the University. In 1951 he became a professor at Stanford University. He became director of the High Energy Physics Laboratory of the University in 1952 and director of the Stanford Linear Accelerator Center, which includes the two-mile accelerator as its principal tool, in 1962. He served on the President's Science Advisory Committee from 1960 to 1965. In 1961 Panofsky received the U.S. Atomic Energy Commission's E. O. Lawrence Award, both for the kind of work described here and for work on the detection of nuclear explosions in space. He was elected to the National Academy of Sciences in 1954.

Panofsky wrote, with Melba Phillips, *Classical Electricity and Magnetism* (1955; 2d ed. 1962).

For background information *see* MESON in the McGraw-Hill Encyclopedia of Science and Technology. ☐

★ PANTIN, Carl Frederick Abel

British zoologist
Born Mar. 30, 1899, Blackheath, London, England

FOR HIS contributions to the comparative physiology of the Invertebrata, particularly his work on nerve conduction in Crustacea and Actinozoa, Pantin received the Royal Medal of the Royal Society of London in 1950 and the Gold Medal of the Linnean Society in 1964.

As a result of service in France in 1918 with the Royal Engineers in sound ranging and field survey, Pantin determined to read physics at Cambridge. At Cambridge, however, he was attracted by physiology and zoology, and he began research at the Marine Biological Laboratory, Plymouth, as a comparative physiologist. Influenced by the work of James Gray, G. H. Parker, and H. S. Jennings, he attacked the problem of behavior and movement of *Amoebae*.

In 1929 Pantin moved to the zoological department, Cambridge, where in 1959 he became professor of zoology. The inadequacy of contemporary physicochemical models in explanation of ameboid movement led him to investigate the physiology of the behavior machinery in sea anemones and other marine organisms, particularly at the Stazione Zoologica, Naples. During the 1930s he was able to show that the responses of anemones involved nervous conduction of precisely the same character as that observed in Vertebrata. The quality of the response to a stimulus was governed by the "facilitating" effect of successive all-or-nothing nervous impulses in the transmission of excitation across adjoining elements of the nerve net and also between elements of the nerve net and the responding muscles.

The next phase of this work involved histological identification of the nerve net tracts concerned with the various responses. Thanks to the beautiful histological preparations of his colleague, E. J. Batham, in this part of the work, these identifications met with considerable success. Partly as the result of this histological work Pantin wrote a small textbook, *Notes on Microscopical Technique for Zoologists* (1946).

While this work was in progress, Pantin and Batham noted slow muscular activity, particularly in the anemone *Metridium senile*. This led during the 1940s and 1950s to a series of papers on the hydrostatics of muscular contraction in these and other animals, and also to an analysis of the slow contractile movements. These were found to be based on rhythmic coordinated activity of muscular fields, leading to well-defined feeding, locomotor, and tonic responses, as well as diurnal responses to light. The "purposive" character of such activity is easily seen with lapse-rate cinematography.

Parallel with these analyses of behavior, Pantin from early days attacked the problem of the relation between the organism and the physical environment. This led to work on osmoregulation in worms and to the study of the adaptation of soft-bodied invertebrates to terrestrial conditions. This in turn raised the question of convergent physiological evolution in related species and genera. As a result of these studies, begun when access to the marine animals was difficult during World War II, Pantin launched upon a considerable excursion into taxonomy, which, apart from its intrinsic aim, raised the philosophical question of how we, and other organisms, recognize species. This led in turn to a reconsideration of the nature of the information that a living animal receives and upon which its behavior depends.

Coupled with his physiological and environmental studies and a strong interest in field geology, Pantin undertook the philosophical study of the nature of organisms and the relation between the different sciences. He made an important distinction between the "restricted sciences," in which certain fields of scientific knowledge are deliberately discarded (as nuclear physics discards biological information), and the "unrestricted sciences," as in much of biology and geology, where the investigator can afford to disregard no part of natural knowledge.

For background information *see* NERVOUS SYSTEM (INVERTEBRATE) in the McGraw-Hill Encyclopedia of Science and Technology.   □

★ PATT, Harvey Milton
American physiologist
Born Aug. 2, 1918, Chicago, Ill., U.S.A.

IN THE course of an investigation of physiologic consequences of radiation exposure, Patt in 1949 discovered chemical protection against radiation effects in higher organisms. This finding, by focusing attention on the chemical reactions occurring during the absorption of radiation energy, catalyzed the development of an important area of inquiry, namely, the modification of radiation effects by chemical means. For his achievements in radiobiology, Patt received in 1964 the U.S. Atomic Energy Commission's E. O. Lawrence Award.

Two broad concepts of radiation action were advanced early in the history of radiobiology. It was assumed that some biological effects were direct results of energy absorption in a vital structure, while others were supposed to be indirect results of some sort of chemical intermediation, possibly involving toxic breakdown products of irradiated water. There was circumstantial evidence for both direct and indirect types of action in simple biological systems, and it was inferred that this applied to higher organisms as well. Whatever the initiating mechanism, the biological effects of the high-energy radiations were rather nonspecific. This apparent nonspecificity of action was the point of departure for Patt's studies.

It was known that a variety of stresses elicited a profound response of the adrenal glands that was mediated by another gland, the pituitary. Patt observed a similar phenomenon in the x-irradiated animal; it occurred within a few hours after irradiation and before there were obvious signs of toxicity. In seeking an explanation, he wondered whether chemical events occurring during x-ray exposure might be responsible for triggering the pituitary-adrenal response. If leading chemical reactions occurred during irradiation, their rate should be altered by change in body temperature. To avoid the stress of severe body-temperature change, he turned to the frog, a cold-blooded animal, and learned that temperature shifts of as much as 20°C during x-ray exposure seemingly had no effect. The apparent low-temperature coefficient signified that more or less conventional types of chemical reactions were not particularly important during exposure to radiation. A sustained body-temperature change after irradiation—that

is, one lasting many days or weeks—was of considerable influence, but this was another matter and related to the general phenomenon of the unmasking of damage by activity.

Since the absorption of radiation by water

molecules results in the formation of short-lived free radicals whose reactivity should be relatively independent of temperature, Patt questioned whether such chemical species might perhaps be involved. Only one molecule in about 10,000,000 will be ionized directly by an amount of radiation sufficient to destroy a cell. Since a typical cell contains some 10^{14} molecules, most of which are water, only 10^7 would be ionized directly. Even if each ionization of a water molecule led to the formation of several reactive breakdown products, Patt realized that their demonstration in vivo by the techniques then available would be virtually impossible, which turned out to be the case.

Aware that the predominant free radical reactions in irradiated water were of the oxidative type, Patt reasoned that it should be possible to show indirectly, by appropriate chemical intervention, if such reactions were of biological consequence. Because of the very brief life span of the free radicals, he assumed that a potential neutralizing agent would have to be present during the radiation exposure. He and his associated at Argonne National Laboratory studied in this way series of substances with a proclivity for oxidation. Many proved ineffectual, possibly because of their selective distribution or their very rapid inactivation in the body. Patt found, however, that cysteine, an amino acid that reacts readily with oxygen and oxidizing substances generally, doubled the resistance of mice and rats to the lethal action of x-rays when given just before the irradiation. Subsequent work indicated that cysteine afforded comparable protection against a number of effects, suggesting action at an early and common stage in the development of radiation injury.

The precise mechanism of this protective phenomenon is not yet known, but it is still presumed to be related to the radiochemistry of water. Although it has not yet led to a practical prophylaxis, it has led to a number of studies of chemical protection by others, the results of which are providing a clearer picture of the basic mechanisms of radiation actions.

Patt majored in physiology at the University of Chicago, receiving a B.S. in 1939 and a Ph.D. in 1942. During World War II he worked as a civilian on a chemical toxicity program at the University of Chicago and as a naval officer on applied physiology problems at the Medical Field Research Laboratory, Camp LeJeune, N.C. He was on the staff of Argonne National Laboratory from 1946 to 1964, when he joined the faculty of the University of California, San Francisco, as professor and director of the Laboratory of Radiobiology.

For background information *see* RADIATION MICROBIOLOGY in the McGraw-Hill Encyclopedia of Science and Technology.   □

PAULI, Wolfgang

Swiss physicist
Born Apr. 25, 1900, Vienna, Austria
Died Dec. 15, 1958, Zurich, Switzerland

IN SEEKING to explain a particular facet of atomic spectra known as the anomalous Zeeman effect, Pauli formulated the [Pauli] exclusion principle. This principle, in its simplest form, says that two electrons in an atom can never exist in the same state. The consequences of this statement make it one of the most important concepts of modern physics. For this discovery, Pauli was awarded the 1945 Nobel Prize in physics.

In 1913 Niels Bohr advanced the theory that the hydrogen atom consists of a single electron revolving about the nucleus in any one of a number of specified circular orbits. Later, in 1916, Arnold Sommerfeld extended Bohr's hypothesis to include elliptical orbits, the nucleus being at one focus of the ellipse. The original Bohr theory stated that only those orbits were possible whose angular momenta were integral multiples of a universal physical constant. This postulate implies that an allowed orbit has a unique or "quantized" energy, which can be characterized by a specific integer or quantum number known as the principal quantum number. The theory based on elliptical orbits allowed for another set of quantum numbers associated with each principal quantum number. These are known as azimuthal quantum numbers and may be considered to be associated with different elliptical orbits whose energies are not quite the same as those given by circular orbits. The principal quantum number gives rise to a coarse structure of the optical spectrum associated with electron transitions from one energy level to another; the azimuthal quantum number gives rise to a fine structure of this spectrum. Finally, a third quantum number, the magnetic quantum number, was postulated to account for the allowed orientations of the plane of the electron orbit with respect to an applied magnetic field. This theory, embodying the specification of three quantum numbers, was entirely satisfactory in explaining the spectral lines emitted by hydrogen, in which the single electron in each atom can occupy any one of the possible orbits. Such was not the case for atoms that contained more than one electron.

The Bohr-Sommerfeld theory left unexplained two phenomena associated with spectra: the doublet nature of alkali spectra and the anomalous Zeeman effect. In this effect, a spectral line may be split into many lines in the presence of a weak magnetic field, not into a triplet of lines as in the normal Zeeman effect. Pauli was attempting to explain this effect in 1924, at the University of Hamburg, when he realized that he had to overcome the difficulty of finding a sufficiently precise and yet completely general definition of the concept, "the state of an electron." He solved this problem by concluding that the quantum numbers used at that time were not sufficient and that there must exist another property, that is, another quantum number, a double-valued one, which leads to a doubling of the number of states then known. His fundamental idea can be stated in the following way: At most, only one electron in an atom can occupy a given state that is completely specified by four quantum numbers. This exclusion principle was completely successful in explaining the previously unresolved problems of atomic spectra.

In 1925, G. E. Uhlenbeck and S. A. Goudsmit introduced the hypothesis of electron spin: an electron behaves as though it were rapidly rotating about an axis through its center of gravity. They assigned to this property a spin quantum number with values of either $+\frac{1}{2}$ or $-\frac{1}{2}$, corresponding to counter-clockwise and clockwise rotation respectively. In other words, they provided a physical model in agreement with Pauli's earlier work. At the time, the fundamental relation between spin and the exclusion principle was unknown, but in 1940 Pauli was able to show, under very general assumptions, that all particles with half-integer spin have to obey the exclusion principle. The proof was based on quantum field theory, which he helped to develop, and is one of the most important deductions that can be made by applying relativistic theory to quantum mechanics. Because of the wide application of the exclusion principle it must be characterized as a fundamental law of nature. It is a deciding factor in the structure of matter and, for example, is essential in describing the properties of atomic nuclei as well as in describing the electrical conductivity in metals.

Pauli's important contributions to modern theoretical physics spanned a lifetime. When barely 20 years of age, he wrote a 200-page encyclopedia article, "The Theory of Relativity." Later, in 1926 and in 1933, he wrote lengthy articles for the *Handbuch der Physik* on "Quantum Theory" and "Principles of Wave Mechanics." In each instance, he won acclaim for his lucid and concise formulation. He applied himself in 1931 to the problem of beta decay of nuclei in which the emitted particles have a wide range of energy. He suggested that there existed an electrically neutral particle with small or negligible mass to carry away energy not accounted for. Three years later Enrico Fermi elaborated on these ideas, naming the then undetected neutral particles neutrinos. In 1953 F. Reines and C. L. Cowan carried out a complex experiment that showed evidence of the neutrino's existence. Pauli took an active part in the whole development of the quantum theory, but more importantly he exerted an immeasurable and decisive influence in its evolution through his scientific publications, his extensive personal correspondence, and his discussions.

Son of a professor of physical chemistry, Pauli studied physics under Sommerfeld in Munich, where he received his Ph.D. in 1921. He spent a year as an assistant at the University of Göttingen and another at the University of Copenhagen before becoming a docent at the University of Hamburg, a position he held from 1923 to 1928. In 1928 he was appointed professor of theoretical physics at the Federal Institute of Technology in Zurich.

Pauli's *Collected Scientific Papers* were edited by R. Kronig and V. F. Weisskopf (1964).

For background information *see* EXCLUSION PRINCIPLE; NEUTRINO; QUANTUM MECHANICS in the McGraw-Hill Encyclopedia of Science and Technology.   □

☆ PAULING, Linus Carl

American chemist
Born Feb. 28, 1901, Portland, Ore., U.S.A.

MOLECULAR SPATIAL configurations and their relevance to intermolecular and intramolecular interactions were the basis of the major part of Pauling's work. The methods and results of his research have been of fundamental importance in determining the complex structure of protein molecules. For his research into the nature of the chemical bond and its application to the elucidation of the structure of complex substances, he received the Nobel Prize in chemistry in 1954.

Pauling's early work was concerned with the determination of crystal structure through the analysis of x-ray diffraction patterns. Realizing

that the equations of quantum mechanics constituted a reliable basis for the theory of molecular configurations, he applied the methods of this science to many atomic and subatomic phenomena. These studies led him to consider the nature of the chemical bond, and in a decade of inquiry he discovered several fundamental principles. Included among these are the hybridization of bond orbitals and the theory of directed valence (1928), the relation of hybrid bond orbitals to magnetic properties of substances (1931), the partly ionic character of single bonds and its relation to heats of formation of substances (1932), the resonance of molecules between two or more electronic structures and the determination of the configuration through resonance, as in conjugated systems (1932), and the correlation of interatomic distances and other structural features with electronic structure (1932).

Until 1934 Pauling's investigations were largely confined to physics and physical chemistry. Then, because of his interest in hemoglobin and other proteins, he turned to biochemistry. Working with C. D. Coryell he analyzed the effects of the oxygenation of hemoglobin molecules by measuring their magnetic susceptibility. In 1936, with A. E. Mirsky, he developed a theory of native, denatured, and coagulated proteins. In 1950 he and R. B. Corey described the structure of several types of protein molecules and made the first model of a protein molecule showing the correct three-dimensional configuration.

The decade of study of the nature of the chemical bond is summarized in his book *The Nature of the Chemical Bond* (1939). During the period 1932–57, when Pauling was a professor and also (from 1936) director of the Gates and Crellin Laboratories at the California Institute of Technology, 225 papers on electron diffraction determinations of the structure of molecules were published from that laboratory.

Pauling's personal approach to basic research was stochastic; intuition and intelligent guesses often imparted the initial direction to this research. The following brief descriptions of the development of two of his theories illustrate this approach.

In 1949, in a conversation with W. D. Castle, Pauling learned that the red blood cells in victims of sickle-cell anemia assume their twisted shape only in the venous circulation. Pauling's immediate thought was that sickle-cell anemia must be caused by a genetic defect in the hemoglobin. Three years later he and H. A. Itano were able to announce that their investigation of this hypothesis had led to the discovery that in electrophoresis, at a pH of 6.9, normal hemoglobin moved toward the anode while the hemoglobin of sickle-cell anemia moved toward the cathode. The concept of complementary molecules, previously ascribed by Pauling to antibodies and antigens, was then applied to abnormal hemoglobin to explain why sickling occurred. Combination with oxygen destroys the self-complementariness, and thus sickling is reversed in the arterial circulation. The hereditary character of the disease is evidenced by the finding that the parents of patients have, in the red blood cells, a half-and-half mixture of normal and abnormal hemoglobin, thus making the evidence for genetic linkage complete.

A second example of the stochastic method as used by Pauling is the origin of his theory of the molecular mechanism of general anesthesia. He was led to this theory while reading a paper on the crystalline hydrate structure of an alkylammonium salt. The alkylammonium salt had been found to stabilize cagelike structures of water molecules, converting liquid water into an ice-like framework consisting of twelve-sided chambers. Pauling knew that the melting point of these structures could be raised from 25°C to 37°C if the chambers were not empty but were occupied by molecules small enough to fit into the cages yet large enough almost to fill them. He then observed that these alkylammonium salts resemble the amino acid chains of proteins normally found in the brain. Now, assuming that the structuring of the water molecules around the proteins of the brain might interfere with the motion of ions or electrically charged protein side chains that normally contribute to the electrical oscillations of the brain involved in consciousness, it can be expected that the amplitude of these oscillations might be reduced enough to alter the state of consciousness. If this is the mechanism by which the small, spherical, symmetrical inert gases, such as xenon, and simple molecules without any permanent electric dipole produce narcosis, then the narcotizing potency of an anesthetic must be proportional to the effectiveness with which these anesthetics stabilize the structuring of water molecules into hydrate crystals. This theory, published in 1961, is currently under experimental investigation.

The son of a druggist, Pauling received a B.S. in chemical engineering at Oregon State College in 1922 and a Ph.D. in chemistry at the California Institute of Technology in 1925. He remained at Caltech as research fellow (1925–27), assistant professor of chemistry (1927–29), associate professor (1929–31), and professor (from 1931). From 1936 to 1958 he was director of the Gates and Crellin Laboratories of Chemistry at the California Institute of Technology. He won numerous awards in chemistry, including most of the major awards. For his efforts on behalf of a nuclear test ban treaty he was awarded the Nobel Peace Prize in 1963, thereby becoming the only recipient of two individual Nobel awards. He was elected to the National Academy of Sciences in 1933.

Pauling's books include *The Nature of the Chemical Bond, and the Structure of Molecules and Crystals* (1939; 3d ed. 1960); *General Chemistry* (1947; 2d ed. 1953); and *No More War!* (1958; 3d ed. 1962).

For background information *see* CHEMICAL BINDING in the McGraw-Hill Encyclopedia of Science and Technology.   ☐

★ PENFIELD, Wilder Graves

Canadian neurosurgeon, neurophysiologist, neuropathologist
Born Jan. 26, 1891, Spokane, Wash., U.S.A.

FOR HIS contributions to science and neurosurgery, Penfield received, among other honors, the 1958 Lannelongue Medal (France), the 1961 Lister Medal of the Royal College of Surgeons, and the British Order of Merit.

In the operative treatment of focal epilepsy— by wide exposure of the cerebral cortex under local anesthesia and removal of epileptogenic convolutions—Penfield was able to increase accuracy and improve treatment by gentle electrical stimulation. He mapped out the functional areas of the human cerebral cortex: first, the previously recognized sensory and motor areas; second, new cortical localizations—for example, vocalization control, supplementary motor, supplementary speech, gustatory, and gastrointestinal. A gentle electrical current, he showed, produced aphasia by interference in any one of the three cortical speech areas of the dominant hemisphere—temporal (Wernicke), lower frontal (Broca), and superior frontal (Penfield).

Finally, Penfield discovered that stimulation of the interpretive cortex, in either hemisphere, activated at times the neuronal record of past experience. The patient was suddenly made aware of the detailed unfolding of an experience that had been his in earlier life. The record of memory, which is in a subcortical position, had responded to axonal conduction from the cortex (as in normal perception) while the individual continued to be aware of what was happening in the operating room.

These experiential responses, as Penfield called them, are flashbacks of previous experience that may be auditory (including even orchestral music or talk), visual, or both visual and auditory. The sensations, emotions, and interpretations of which the subject was previously aware are also reproduced. Nothing more is included. There is apparently no record of the sensations originally ignored. When the stimulator is withdrawn, the evoked stream of previous experience stops at once. If the stimulator is reapplied, without too long a wait, the same experience is summoned again and begins at the same moment in time.

To explain the normal selective use of functional areas of cerebral cortex, Penfield maintained, it is necessary to conclude that there is an as yet ill-defined centrencephalic integrating system. It connects the two hemispheres and makes possible the organization and coordination of function within the brain. The fiber circuits and the cell collections that constitute this system are located within the higher brainstem (the diencephalon, including the thalamus). Without normal activity here, voluntary action as well as thought processes and consciousness are impossible.

Penfield's centrencephalic hypothesis includes the assumption that the varied streams of neuronal input flow through the cortical sensory areas and on into the centrencephalic system, or that this input becomes available to it in the thalamus. By means of the centrencephalic system, the various functional mechanisms can be activated selectively—for example, the voluntary motor mechanisms of the cortex and medulla, the speech mechanism of the left hemisphere, and the mechanism of perception that makes use of the interpretive cortex and the record of consciousness.

Finally, Penfield assumed that "conscious control" of attention and behavior is mediated through the centrencephalic system. The action of this system, employing the mechanisms of the hemispheres selectively in an ever-changing pattern, is the physical basis of the mind. It is the means through which thought (apparently) initiates voluntary action, the means through which neuronal activity (apparently) determines the state of conscious awareness.

Penfield studied at Princeton (Litt.B., 1913), Oxford (B.A., 1916; M.A. and B.Sc., 1920; D.Sc., 1935) and Johns Hopkins (M.D., 1918) universities. In Sir Charles Sherrington's laboratory at Oxford he began with nerve cell cytology, but his major research was on the mammalian brainstem. He studied neurology and pathology with Sir Gordon Holmes and Godwin Greenfield in London, cytology with Pio del Rio Hortega in Madrid, epilepsy with Otfried Foerster in Breslau. Appointed neurosurgeon at the Presbyterian Hospital in New York in 1921, he embarked at once on a study of wound healing in the brain. Because of the confusion in the current textbooks, he set himself the task of editing a 3-volume handbook, *The Cytology and Cellular Pathology of the Nervous System* (1932). In 1928 he moved to Montreal to become associate professor of neurosurgery in McGill University and neurosurgeon to the Royal Victoria Hospital and the Montreal General Hospital. In 1934 he became professor and chairman of the newly created department of neurology and neurosurgery at McGill and director of the Montreal Neurological Institute. He retired in 1960. A fellow of the Royal Societies of Canada, London, and Edinburgh, he was elected a foreign member of the national academies of science of the United States and the Soviet Union.

Penfield wrote *Cerebral Cortex of Man*, with Theodore Rasmussen (1950), *Epilepsy and the Functional Anatomy of the Human Brain*, with Herbert Jasper (1954), *Excitable Cortex in Conscious Man* (1958), *Speech and Brain-mechanisms*, with Lamar Roberts (1959), and *The Second Career* (1963). He also wrote two historical novels, *No Other Gods* (1954) and *The Torch* (1960), and a biography of Alan Gregg (1966).

For background information *see* BRAIN; NEUROPHYSIOLOGY in the McGraw-Hill Encyclopedia of Science and Technology.   □

★ PERUTZ, Max Ferdinand

British crystallographer and molecular biologist
Born May 19, 1914, Vienna, Austria

PERUTZ is best known for his work on the structure of hemoglobin and for having introduced the method of isomorphous replacement with heavy atoms into protein crystallography. For this he shared with J. C. Kendrew the 1962 Nobel Prize in chemistry.

Together with J. D. Bernal and I. Fankuchen, Perutz took the first x-ray diffraction pictures of crystals of hemoglobin and chymotrypsin in 1937. At that time it was realized that all chemical reactions in living cells were catalyzed by enzymes and that all enzymes might be proteins, but the catalytic function of enzymes could not be understood without knowing their structure. Enzyme molecules combined a degree of order and complexity transcending that of any other chemical substance handled by scientists at the time. It was clear that a solution of their structure would require a combination of chemical methods to determine the sequence of aminoacid residues along the polypeptide chain and of physical methods to unravel their three-dimensional architecture.

Chemical methods were developed by Frederick Sanger, who later received the Nobel Prize for elucidating the amino-acid sequence of insulin. X-ray crystallography proved the most powerful of the physical tools, and Perutz devoted most of the time between 1937 and 1953 to its development.

Unfortunately, the x-ray diffraction pattern of a crystal provides only the amplitudes of the diffracted rays, while interpretation of the pattern also requires knowledge of their phases. Determination of the phases is never easy but is generally possible in simpler crystals by methods that either are, or were thought to be, inapplicable to substances as complex as proteins. In 1953, Perutz introduced the method of isomorphous replacement with heavy atoms to his study of hemoglobin crystals and showed that it was capable of determining the phases. This discovery opened the way to solving the structure of crystalline proteins by x-ray analysis.

Kendrew and his collaborators applied the method to the muscle protein myoglobin and obtained the first three-dimensional picture of this protein in 1957. Two years later Perutz and his colleagues obtained a three-dimensional picture of hemoglobin. Hemoglobin serves to transport oxygen from the lungs to the tissues and facilitates the transport of bicarbonate and carbon dioxide back to the lungs. It has a molecular weight of 65,000 and consists of four separate polypeptide chains and four heme groups. X-ray analysis showed that each chain had a structure closely resembling that of the single chain of myoglobin and that the four chains together formed a tetrahedral arrangement. The four heme groups lay in separate pockets at the surface of the molecule, each carrying one atom of iron to which a molecule of oxygen could attach itself.

In 1938, F. Haurowitz had found evidence that the reaction with oxygen was accompanied by a change in the structure of the molecule. This was the problem next taken up by Perutz, and in 1962 Hilary Muirhead and he showed that the change of structure consisted in a rearrangement of the four subunits. Discovery of the change of structure had wide implications, as it suggested the way in which certain enzymes might change on combining with their substrates.

Perutz's earlier work was concerned with the general properties of protein crystals. He found that a large part of their volume consisted of liquid of crystallization that was in dynamic equilibrium with their suspension medium, and that hemoglobin molecules in the crystal lattice could undergo all the same reactions with ligands as the molecules in solution. This made it seem likely that the protein molecules in the crystal also had the same structure as in solution.

In 1950, following L. Pauling and H. Itano's discovery of sickle-cell hemoglobin as a distinct chemical species, Perutz discovered that oxygen-free sickle-cell hemoglobin had an abnormally low solubility and that its precipitation, and possibly crystallization, accounted for the change in shape undergone by the venous red cells of patients suffering from sickle-cell anemia.

In 1951, when L. Pauling and R. B. Corey discovered the α-helix, Perutz predicted that, owing to the regular periodicity of amino-acid residues along the helical axis, all substances containing α-helices arranged in parallel would show an x-ray reflection at 1.5 A spacing. He then demonstrated the presence of this reflection in fibers of protein and synthetic polypeptides of the α-type, thereby excluding all alternative models of the polypeptide chain.

As a side line Perutz worked on the flow of glaciers. In 1938, with G. Seligman, he made a crystallographic study of the transformation of snow into glacier ice, which gave interesting information about the microscopic mechanism of flow. Ten years later, together with J. A. F. Gerrard and A. Roch, he measured for the first time the velocity distribution of a glacier as a function of depth, proving that glaciers flow fastest at the surface and slowest near the bed. He also stimulated laboratory research on the plasticity of ice, which did much to explain the mechanism of glacier flow.

Perutz studied chemistry at Vienna from 1932 to 1936. He then migrated to Cambridge, England, where he began research at the Cavendish Laboratory under J. D. Bernal and later continued under W. L. Bragg, with whom he worked until 1953. Together with Kendrew he founded the Medical Research Council Unit for Molecular Biology in 1947, and later became chairman of the laboratory bearing the same name. This unit was the scene of J. D. Watson's and F. H. C. Crick's discovery of the structure of DNA, and later of Crick's and S. Brenner's discovery of the triplet nature of the genetic code. Many other advances in molecular biology originated there.

Perutz wrote *Proteins and Nucleic Acids* (1962).

For background information *see* HEMO-GLOBIN; X-RAY CRYSTALLOGRAPHY in the McGraw-Hill Encyclopedia of Science and Technology.   □

★ PETERS, Sir Rudolph (Albert)

British biochemist
Born Apr. 13, 1889, Kensington, London, England

WHILE ENGAGED in a study of the isolation of thiamine, Peters realized the importance of combining researches in vitro with those in vivo; from this emerged the concept of the biochemical lesion, meaning the first biochemical change in a tissue that precedes recognizable pathological change. His studies were pursued with colleagues, first in vitamin-B_1 deficiency and then in arsenical and mustard-gas poisoning. For his work in these fields he received in 1949 the Royal Medal of the Royal Society of London. Later researches, extending his work on toxic substances, led to a phenomenon called by him

"lethal synthesis," based on observation of the toxic plants containing fluoroacetate (compound 1080). He gave the Croonian Lecture of the Royal Society on this work.

Peters's work was guided, in the first instance, by the practical object of trying to understand the action of toxic war gases used in World War I and trying to produce antidotes to their action. He was also moved by philosophical considerations of the constitution of the living cell, which he published in 1929 and in which he stated the view that there must be an integrating structure in the living cell (since called the "cytoskeleton"). These theoretical views received striking confirmation from the brilliant researches on the endoplasmic reticulum made possible by the electron microscope and the application of the high-speed centrifuge.

The work on the biochemical lesion in thiamine deficiency developed from the original discovery by Christian Eijkman in Java in 1889 that birds fed upon a diet of polished rice developed nervous signs; in pigeons, these showed up as an acute head retraction (opisthononus). By 1920, it was realized that this was due to the deficiency of a water-soluble dietary factor known as vitamin B_1. The physiology and biochemistry of the condition of head retraction, used then as a test for thiamine, intrigued Peters, as it also did others. Peters realized that the biochemical lesion preceding the convulsions must be sought for in the brain, and he studied the biochemistry of this with colleagues. From this study the fact emerged that there was a deficiency of pyruvate oxidation in the tissue, reversible by adding extracts of the vitamin in vitro and correlated with the development of the nervous signs. Pyruvate was important because it was postulated then as a stage in glycolysis according to the Embden-Meyerhof scheme. When it was found in Germany that cocarboxylase, the cofactor in alcoholic fermentation in yeast, was thiamine

pyrophosphate, Peters, Ilona Banga, and Severo Ochoa were able to prove that this was the form of the vitamin in the tissue; even in vitro brain converted thiamine into the pyrophosphate.

During the assignment in World War II to study the biochemical action of the toxic war gases, it turned out that the same pyruvate oxidase system, which failed in thiamine deficiency, was the one that was poisoned in lewisite poisoning. A team of which Peters was the leader succeeded in developing the antidote known as "British antilewisite" (Dimercaprol). This is an outstanding example of an antidote discovered by logical biochemical reasoning; the members of the team especially to be commended were R. H. S. Thompson and L. A. Stocken.

After 1947, Peters and his pupils studied the biochemistry of the toxic cattle poisons containing the carbon-fluorine link; this, strangely enough, led back to the same pyruvate oxidase system, owing to the fact that the system includes the citric acid or tricarboxylic acid cycle. It was found that it was not the fluoroacetate itself that was toxic; instead, it "bluffs" the so-called "condensing enzyme" of the citric acid cycle, so that it becames combined with the C_4 oxaloacetate to form fluorocitrate instead of ordinary citrate (C_6 compound). This leads to severe tetanic convulsions and death owing to the blockage of the enzyme concerned with the further degradation of citrate in the citric acid cycle, together with relatively enormous accumulations of citrate in the tissues, much above the normal. So a new principle came into being—a "lethal systhesis." The idea has been used in cancer research in the attempt to find compounds that are converted to toxic compounds only by the cancer tissues themselves. The scientific work related can be said to justify the thesis that a steady application of research even in a therapeutic field will bring into its orbit valuable contributions to theoretical science, and also lead to logical developments. Fluorocitrate showed in a striking way the reality of the citric acid cycle in vivo.

In his first research (1912), under the direction of the distinguished Cambridge physiologist Joseph Barcroft, Peters proved that the combination of oxygen with the iron in hemoglobin was a chemical one and was not a matter of adsorption. This provided the first instance in which a large colloid protein molecule was shown to react chemically at one part of its molecule.

The son of a medical practitioner, Peters took his Science Tripos at Cambridge, and then his M.D. degree there in 1920 after studying at St. Bartholomew's Hospital, London. He taught at

Cambridge in Gonville and Caius College, in the physiological laboratory, and also in the newly developing department of biochemistry. In 1923 he went to Oxford to be, for 31 years, professor of biochemistry, after which he became the first head of the biochemistry department of the Agricultural Research Council Institute of Animal Physiology at Babraham, Cambridge, for five years.

Peters wrote *Biochemical Lesions and Lethal Synthesis* (1963).

For background information *see* CHEMICAL WARFARE; THIAMINE; TOXICOLOGY in the McGraw-Hill Encyclopedia of Science and Technology.   □

☆ **PICKERING, William Hayward**
American physicist
Born Dec. 24, 1910, Wellington, New Zealand

UNDER PICKERING's leadership, the Jet Propulsion Laboratory of the California Institute of Technology carried out programs that resulted in the first U.S. artificial satellite (*Explorer I*), the first successful U.S. cislunar space probe, the Ranger lunar-impact flights of 1964–65, and the Mariner flights to Venus in 1962 and to Mars in 1964–65.

As a young faculty member at Caltech, Pickering, a cosmic-ray physicist, worked under Robert A. Millikan in a program of world-wide high-altitude research. He developed and built balloon-borne instruments used to detect cosmic rays at altitudes up to 100,000 feet. During World War II, he conducted applied research in electronics at Caltech and other laboratories. In July, 1944, he organized the electronics effort at JPL in support of guided-missile research and development. He developed the telemetry system for a small test vehicle that, later in 1944, made the first U.S. telemetered rocket flight.

The Corporal was the first operational missile resulting from the new effort. It was equipped with a radio-command guidance system and, in the research and development rounds, a telemetry system that returned about 100 measurements to the ground. It is interesting to note that the German V-2 program, lacking a substantial telemetry system, required over 500 research and development firings, while the Corporal needed approximately 40 such launches. Pickering was project manager for Corporal while retaining responsibility for electronics research and development at JPL. He continued to press for advanced development in two fields intimately related in the Corporal: guidance and two-way communications.

Appointed director of JPL in 1954, Pickering was immediately involved in U.S. Army proposals for Earth-satellite launchings in the International Geophysical Year, 1957–58. Although an alternative Earth-satellite development was chosen, portions of the Army Ballistic Missile Agency's system were developed in support of the Jupiter missile program. When a sudden revival of the JPL/ABMA satellite was necessary, the successful launch of *Explorer I* occurred within 90 days of approval to succeed. Subsequently, Pickering had the task of converting JPL from an Army-sponsored guided-missile laboratory to a major contractor of the new National Aeronautics and Space Administration, responsible for unmanned lunar and planetary flight projects.

The Ranger lunar impact flights of 1964–65 returned approximately 17,000 close-up photographs of the lunar surface and culminated, with the final mission, in a flight to within 2.76 miles of the aiming point within the crater Alphonsus. The flight of *Mariner IV* to the vicinity of Mars in 1965 yielded the first close-up photographs ever taken of another planet. The photographs showed the surface of Mars to be pocked with craters; there was no evidence of river valleys or ocean basins, no indication of any water erosion. The flight also revealed that Mars has virtually no magnetic field and no significant radiation belt and that its atmosphere is extremely thin.

Pickering received his early education in Wellington, New Zealand. He emigrated to the United States in 1929 and obtained his B.S. (1932) in electrical engineering and his M.S. (1933) and Ph.D. (1936) in physics at the California Institute of Technology. He joined the Caltech faculty in 1940, in 1946 becoming professor of electrical engineering. Elected to the National Academy of Sciences in 1962, he was a founder of the National Academy of Engineering.

For background information *see* GUIDED MISSILE; SATELLITE, ARTIFICIAL in the McGraw-Hill Encyclopedia of Science and Technology.   □

★ **PIERCE, John Robinson**
American engineer
Born Mar. 27, 1910, Des Moines, Iowa, U.S.A.

Pierce's principal contribution was the application of analytic insight and judgment to a number of important ideas and projects in communication, including the production of high-density electron beams, the traveling-wave tube, the use of communication theory in connection with practical problems, and communication satellites. In recognition of this body of work he was awarded the National Medal of Science in 1963.

In 1936 Pierce joined the Bell Telephone Laboratories and was put to work on vacuum tubes. He devised a new type of electrostatically focused electron multiplier and worked on tubes for broader-band amplification. He devised the Pierce gun for producing high-current electron beams. Work at the Bell Telephone Laboratories taught him the importance of crucial problems and their amenability to mathematical as well as experimental attack. He saw the need for amplifiers with broad band, high frequency of operation, and low noise.

During World War II Pierce worked on microwave tubes. Together with J. O. McNally and W. G. Shepherd he devised low-voltage reflex klystron oscillators that found almost universal application in American microwave radar receivers. He also worked on amplifiers; he was struck by R. Kompfner's traveling-wave tube. Over a decade he made important contributions that were summed up in *Traveling-wave Tubes* (1950). Pierce was also impressed by C. E. Shannon's communication theory, had an early interest in pulse code modulation and related problems, and in 1961 published *Symbols, Signals and Noise*, a semipopular exposition of communication theory. About 1954 Pierce became interested in communication satellites. His work led to the *Echo I* communication satellite program and the later Telstar program, which demonstrated the technical feasibility of satellite communication. Although his work on electron guns, traveling-wave tubes, and communication satellites became most widely known, Pierce published variously on communication, microwaves, psychology and psychoacoustics, and the use of the computer as a musical instrument. He published science fiction under the name of J. J. Coupling.

Pierce's father was in the millinery and ready-to-wear business in Minnesota, Iowa, and California, and Pierce attended public schools in those three states. He received his B.S. (1933), M.S. (1934), and Ph.D. (1936) at the California Institute of Technology. In 1961 he was made executive director, Research, and later headed the Communications Sciences Division of Bell Telephone Laboratories. He was elected to the National Academy of Sciences in 1955.

Pierce wrote six technical books and many technical articles.

For background information *see* Communications, electrical; Traveling-wave tube in the McGraw-Hill Encyclopedia of Science and Technology. ☐

★ **PORTER, Keith Roberts**
American biologist
Born June 11, 1912, Yarmouth, Nova Scotia, Canada

The rapid growth that cell biology has enjoyed over the past 20 years has been generously nourished by the introduction and application of electron microscopy to this field. With this development Porter was closely linked from the beginning, first in the perfection of techniques and instrumentation for the use of this new and powerful microscope on cells and tissues, and subsequently with the definition and interpretation of the structural microcosm and instrument revealed. For his contribution in this area of biology he received (with George Palade) the Passano Foundation Award in 1964 and the annual award of the Gairdner Foundation in the same year.

In the late 1930s, just before World War II, it became apparent that the electron microscope would become a major tool in biological research. The early images of bacterial cells and fragments of other cells were crude, frequently little better than those derived from the light microscope. But from these beginnings the potential was evident, and it remained mostly for biologists to discover ways to make biological units available to this peculiar form of microscope. This presented some problems, for the material, perhaps a cell, had to be dessicated and extremely thin.

Then engaged in the study of tissue cells, mostly for purposes of following in vitro transformations of the normal to the malignant, Porter recognized that many of these units possessed characteristics of thinness required for electron microscopy. He devised techniques of preparation, and with colleagues at the Rockefeller Institute and Interchemical Corporation in New York he succeeded in getting the first useful high-resolution pictures of intact cells of higher organisms. From the study of such preparations there came the first descriptions of a complex system of membrane-limited channels and vesicles, including the nuclear envelope, which exists in the cytoplasm of all cells. This system, not anticipated as a component of cells from earlier light microscopy, has come to be called the "endoplasmic reticulum." Studied extensively by Porter and his colleagues, it has emerged as a system for the segregation and transport of the products of biosynthesis, especially as these are made for export from the cell.

The techniques and instruments developed for these discoveries have been equally valuable in providing new information on the whole microcosm, which is now cell fine structure. Porter's observations and interpretations in this area covered the endoplasmic reticulum in its various forms, the cell surface and its derivations, and the surface and cortex of cells as involved in the organization of collagen-rich extracellular matrices. In the continuing pursuit of an earlier interest in mechanisms by which genetic information is translated into the shapes and forms that cells show, he drew attention to arrays of intracellular microtubules that in their characteristics have the attributes expected of cytoskeletal elements.

Porter received his early education in Yarmouth, Nova Scotia, where he was strongly influenced in his choice of a later career by a high school science teacher, John Oliver. He subsequently majored in biology at Acadia University

and went from there to Harvard for his Ph.D. in 1938. After a year as a National Research fellow at Princeton, he moved to the Rockefeller Institute in New York. There he began adapting tissue cells to electron microscopy, the work for which he became known. He eventually became a member and professor at the institute. In 1961 he moved from the Rockefeller Institute to Harvard University, where he became professor of biology and chairman of the department. Porter was instrumental in starting the commercial production of media for tissue culture, in the initiation of the *Journal of Cell Biology*, and in the organization of the Tissue Culture Association and the American Society for Cell Biology. He was elected to the National Academy of Sciences in 1964.

Besides authoring or coauthoring about 150 scientific papers, Porter wrote *An Introduction to the Fine Structure of Cells and Tissues*, with M. Bonneville (1963; 2d ed. 1964).

For background information *see* CYTOLOGY; MICROSCOPE, ELECTRON in the McGraw-Hill Encyclopedia of Science and Technology.   □

☆ POWELL, Cecil Frank
British physicist
Born Dec. 5, 1903, Tonbridge, England

POWELL MADE practical the use of photographic emulsions in atomic nuclear research and was the first to show their value when systematically employed. The methods he invented opened new vistas, both in cosmic-ray studies and when used in conjunction with artificial particle accelerators in the laboratory. In 1947, with G. P. S. Occhialini and other colleagues, he discovered and investigated the production of π mesons (pions) from cosmic radiation in the Earth's atmosphere. For these achievements he received the Nobel Prize in physics in 1950.

By the early 20th century it was known that photographic emulsions were able to record the passage through them of certain charged particles. In traversing the emulsion, the particle ionized grains of silver iodide lying in its path; when the plate was developed, the grains that had been ionized were seen as more or less continuous dark lines. The faster the particle, the more widely spaced the developed grains, since the faster particles had less power to ionize. The distance between these grains was thus a measure of the particle's speed; and, of necessity, the faster the particle, the more difficult it was to detect and measure it in the emulsion. By the late 1930s, photographic emulsions were still considered to be too unreliable, and insufficiently sensitive, for effective use in nuclear physics.

The Wilson or cloud chamber technique, then much in vogue as the chief tool of atomic nuclear research, had certain drawbacks. For one thing, the chamber was sensitive only for brief periods of time, while a photographic emulsion could record the track of every particle that impinged on it. Feeling that the possibilities of emulsions well merited the effort, Powell embarked on extensive investigations into the technology of the problem.

Between 1939 and 1945, Powell and his colleagues at Bristol University made experiments on the treatment and sensitization of emulsions, development of the necessary photographic techniques, and the interpretation of the tracks left in the emulsion. This led to use of the so-called Ilford "half-tone" emulsion, which, in experiments at high altitudes, proved able to record accurately and consistently the tracks of cosmic-ray "primaries." Powell and his colleagues used the plates to investigate cosmic-ray showers, and a number of significant discoveries were made. The salient advantages of the plates were the simplicity of this method of recording particle tracks, the completeness of the record left (thus making possible the study of whole "showers" of cosmic rays), and, finally, the connection between the length of a track and the speed of the particle that made it.

In 1947, the power of the above methods was increased by the development of the Ilford C2 emulsions, a further improvement over the original variety. A group of them were exposed on the Pic du Midi (in the Pyrenees, 9,000 feet above sea level) in a cosmic-ray experiment designed to detect new nuclear events. At this altitude the fast, heavy atomic nuclei among the incoming primary cosmic-ray particles have already fragmented in collisions with nuclei in the air. But fast protons and α-particles do penetrate to the lower altitude at which the plates were exposed, and it was among these that Powell and his colleagues hoped to detect certain new events, especially related to meson production.

An analysis of "disintegration stars" in the plates indicated that μ mesons (muons) are created when cosmic primaries collide with atmospheric nuclei. Tracks recording the precise mechanism seemed to give evidence for a previously unknown stage in the meson-formation process. The production of muons had been detected in cosmic radiation by C. D. Anderson in 1937, but the complete process was first described by Powell, who discovered that the muons decayed from slightly heavier mesons, which he called pions. He noted that it was just such a particle that Hideki Yukawa, in 1935, had called for as a theoretical necessity. Yukawa had concluded that there should be a particle that functioned as the quantum of the "strong force," and described it as having a rest mass of about 250 electron masses. Yukawa's nuclear quantum must of course interact with nucleons, and the muon, which did not, was thus unsatisfactory for the part. However, the pion suited Yukawa's requirements perfectly, and Powell correctly concluded that it was the long-sought nuclear quantum. Muons were ejected, he found, when pions were brought to rest in the emulsions. In experiments involving other methods of detection, the short-lived pions had decayed in flight and thus had gone unnoticed.

Powell and his colleagues discovered the positive and negative pions, and the modes of decay of the heavier K-mesons. He also gave a detailed explanation of the production of cosmic-ray cascades in the atmosphere, with classification into "soft" (electrons, photons) and "hard" (muons, neutrinos) components.

Powell continued his investigations of the cosmic-ray process using balloons and rockets, and made later discoveries concerning the heavy nuclei encountered above 100,000 feet.

The son of a gunsmith, Powell graduated from Cambridge University in 1925. He worked as a graduate student in the Cavendish Laboratory under C. T. R. Wilson and E. Rutherford until 1927, when he received his Ph.D. He then became research assistant to A. M. Tyndall in the H. H. Wills Physical Laboratory, University of Bristol. He progressed to lecturer, then reader, and in 1948 became Melville Wills Professor of Physics there. He became director of the Laboratory in 1964. He was elected a fellow of the Royal Society in 1949, winning its Hughes Medal in 1949 and its Royal Medal in 1961.

Powell wrote *Nuclear Physics in Photographs*, with G. P. S. Occhialini (1947), and *The Study of Elementary Particles by the Photographic Method*, with P. Fowler and D. Perkins (1959).

For background information *see* COSMIC RAYS; PARTICLE DETECTOR in the McGraw-Hill Encyclopedia of Science and Technology.   □

PROCHOROV, Aleksandr Mikhailovich
Russian physicist
Born 1916

Prochorov and N. G. Basov devised a new method for amplifying electromagnetic radiation. This discovery led to the invention, by other physicists, of the maser and laser. For their fundamental achievements in the area of electromagnetic amplification, Prochorov and Basov received the 1964 Nobel Prize in physics, which they shared with the American physicist C. H. Townes. *See* Basov, Nikolai Gennediyevich; Townes, Charles Hard.

After graduating from Leningrad University in 1939, Prochorov served with the Red Army in World War II. He joined the Lebedev Institute, Moscow, in 1946 as senior associate. In 1954 he became head of the laboratory, where he and Basov developed the molecular amplifier. He was awarded a Lenin Prize for this work in 1959. In 1960 he was elected a corresponding member of the Soviet Academy of Sciences, a title that is a step lower than academician.   □

★ PROUDMAN, Joseph
English applied mathematician and oceanographer
Born Dec. 30, 1888, Unsworth, Lancashire, England

Proudman studied the dynamical equations of the ocean tides, devising methods of solution of the differential equations involved. He also studied the more general questions of dynamical oceanography, and especially the propagation of storm surges. His publications on these subjects were continuous from 1913 to 1959. His work earned him the Agassiz Medal of the U.S. National Academy of Sciences in 1946

and the Hughes Medal of the Royal Society of London in 1957.

While still at Cambridge in 1912, Proudman consulted H. Lamb of Manchester as to a subject for research, and was advised to try to determine the theoretical distribution of the tidal oscillations of a flat sea on a rotating Earth whose coasts had the form of a sector of a circle. (In 1928 Proudman published a solution of this problem in the special case when the sector is a semicircle.) One of his first general results was a transformation of the differential equations into equations of Lagrange's type with an infinite number of coordinates. This was published in 1917, and the chief applications, relating to a hemispherical ocean bounded by a complete meridian, were published by Proudman and A. T. Doodson in 1935 and 1937.

In 1916 the British Association for the Advancement of Science asked Lamb to prepare a report on the state of research on tides, and Lamb asked Proudman to help him. This led to a report on harmonic analysis of tidal observations that was written by Proudman and published by the Association in 1920. While engaged on this work, Proudman conceived the need for an institute devoted to tides, and in 1919 he induced two Liverpool shipowners to found the Tidal Institute in the University of Liverpool. The chief full-time member of the staff of this institute from 1919 to 1960 was A. T. Doodson. One of the first pieces of collaboration between Proudman and Doodson was the application of the dynamical equations of the tides to determine the distribution of the principal constituent of the tides over the North Sea. This was pub-

lished in 1924. About the same time they carried out a theoretical investigation into the "time relations in meteorological effects on the sea," and wrote a paper that has been much quoted in connection with storm surges.

With one of his research students, Edith Mercer, Proudman studied the oscillations of a rotating mechanical system of infinite freedom. They published two papers on this in 1927, and Proudman published applications to the tides in 1928, 1931, and 1932.

As professor of oceanography, Proudman studied the distribution of temperature and salinity in the Irish Sea and began an observational study of turbulence that was continued by his successor, K. F. Bowden.

After the flooding of the east coast of England in 1953, the British government set up a committee under the chairmanship of Lord Waverley to investigate the circumstances of such flooding, and Proudman was made a member. This led him to study the propagation of a combination of tide and storm surge and he published a number of papers on this subject.

The son of a farmer, Proudman took his first degree (B.Sc., 1910) in mathematics and physics at the University of Liverpool. He then entered Trinity College, Cambridge, to study pure and applied mathematics, taking the Mathematical Tripos in 1912 (B.A. 1913, M.A. 1917). In 1913 he was appointed a lecturer in mathematics in the University of Liverpool and in 1916 was awarded the degree of D.Sc. of that University. From 1915 to 1921 he was a Fellow of Trinity College, Cambridge. In 1919 Proudman was made the first professor of applied mathematics in the University of Liverpool and also director of the Tidal Institute there. In 1933 he was transferred from the professorship of applied mathematics to that of oceanography and from 1940 to 1946 he was pro-vice-chancellor of the university. He retired in 1954.

Proudman published *Dynamical Oceanography* (1953).

For background information *see* OCEANOGRAPHY; STORM SURGE in the McGraw-Hill Encyclopedia of Science and Technology.   □

PURCELL, Edward Mills

American physicist
Born Aug. 30, 1912, Taylorville, Ind., U.S.A.

WHILE INVESTIGATING the behavior of atomic particles spinning in magnetic fields, Purcell and his collaborators discovered a way to tune in to the frequencies of such particles using radio and microwave oscillations. His method of nuclear resonance absorption, developed independently by Felix Bloch, provided a refined tool for measuring the magnetic moments of nuclei and molecules, and for detailed investigation of the fine structure of materials. For their simultaneous discovery, Purcell and Boch shared the Nobel Prize in physics in 1952.

In 1924, Wolfgang Pauli described a model of the atom, including characteristics of intrinsic spin (angular momentum) and a magnetic moment. The magnetic moments of nuclei, as distinguished from the much stronger ferromagnetic effects, were presumed to be so weak as to be barely detectable. Information on magnetic moments was of importance in investigating the structure of matter in a variety of ways.

Beginning in the 1930s, I. I. Rabi conducted a series of experiments using the molecular-ray technique of Otto Stern. A narrow beam of molecules of the substance to be measured was sprayed into an evacuated cavity. Two electromagnets, whose fields were at right angles to each other, surrounded the cavity. The first created a powerful, static field in which the molecules passing through precessed, just as a tipped gyroscope's pole describes a circle as it spins in the Earth's magnetic field. The second magnet created a weaker, alternating field perpendicular to the first. The frequency of the radio waves that controlled this magnet could be altered until it matched precisely the rate of precession of the nuclei or molecules in the field. When this happened, the spinning particles would suddenly reverse their direction of spin, and this effect was detectable by the subsequent deflection of the particles. The precession frequency of the nuclear magnets was thus determined, and fairly accurate values for nuclear magnetic moments could be calculated, using a theorem of Larmor.

Rabi's method required that the substance being examined be vaporized. It was, furthermore, only moderately accurate. Searching for a method that would be more accurate and less destructive of the sample, Purcell discovered a way of observing resonance between an oscillat-

ing magnetic field and the precession of nuclei in a small sample of a solid or liquid. He constructed a very large static electromagnet and inserted at right angles between its poles a smaller, weaker magnet activated by a radio-frequency oscillator. The sample was placed within this smaller magnet, and the oscillator was turned on. When the frequency was exactly matched to the rate of precession of the particular atoms being measured, a receiver would register a very sharp dip in the strength of the signal being passed through the sample. Each nucleus, Purcell found, had a unique frequency at which, and only at which, it would exhibit nuclear magnetic resonance (NMR). Further, the point at which the resonance takes place could be much more accurately determined, since its detection did not depend on the observation of the deflection of a particle beam. The precision with which this could be gaged, then, depended only on the accuracy with which a particular magnetic field strength could be measured. Thus, once field strength had been measured in one experiment and the results calibrated, the NMR principle could be embodied in a magnetometer to provide extremely accurate measurements of magnetic fields, using only radio equipment.

Purcell found that, in a given material such as a crystal or liquid, the structure of the material is revealed by the way in which NMR spectra are altered by interference of neighboring nuclei. This so-called "chemical shift" provided a very powerful tool for investigating molecular structures and chemical interactions inside crystalline and organic materials.

In addition to the original purpose of giving accurate values for nuclear magnetic moments, the principle of nuclear magnetic absorption found use in measurement of magnetic fields (the proton vector magnetometer) and provided a means of physical analysis that left the sample unaffected.

After taking a B.S. in electrical engineering at Purdue University in 1933, Purcell traveled to Karlsruhe, Germany, where he was an international exchange student at the Technische Hochschule for a year. He then returned to Harvard University, taking his A.M. in 1935 and his Ph.D. in 1938. Until 1940 he was an instructor in physics there. In 1941 he joined the Fundamental Development Group, Radiation Laboratory, Massachusetts Institute of Technology, serving as group leader until 1945. From 1946 to 1949 he was associate professor of physics at Harvard and professor from 1949 to 1958. After two further years as Donner Professor of Science, Purcell assumed the Gerhard Gade University Professorship in 1960. He was elected to the National Academy of Sciences in 1951.

For background information *see* MAGNETIC MOMENT; MAGNETIC RESONANCE in the McGraw-Hill Encyclopedia of Science and Technology. □

R

★★

★ RABI, Isidor Isaac

American physicist
Born July 29, 1898, Raymanov, Austria

BEGINNING WITH his dissertation "On the Principal Magnetic Susceptibilities of Crystals," Rabi worked chiefly in the area of phenomena connected directly or indirectly with magnetic fields. In his dissertation, he invented a novel and simple method for locating the ellipsoid of induction in monolithic crystals that yielded results of very high accuracy. This method was the foundation of a long series of researches in magnetochemistry by Krishnan and his school in India.

While working in Otto Stern's laboratory in Hamburg on a 1927 Barnard fellowship from Columbia University, Rabi was attracted to the experimental field that utilized molecular and atomic beams for the study of atomic and molecular phenomena. Stern was the originator of the basic technique in this field and in 1922, with Walter Gerlach, had discovered the phenomena of space quantization. Rabi spent a year in this laboratory on an experiment that utilized a novel method of deflection to obtain a higher accuracy for the measurement of atomic magnetic moments. On his return to the United States in 1929 he applied this technique with a view to studying the hyperfine structure of atomic energy levels. With his student Victor Cohen, he demonstrated—by a complicated series of deflections of a selected portion of an atomic beam of sodium in weak magnetic fields —that there were indeed four hyperfine structure levels and, therefore, that the spine of the sodium nucleus was equal to 3/2 in units of $\frac{2\pi}{h}$.

These methods were further extended to the method of zero moments by utilizing the fact that at certain values of the magnetic field the total atomic moment was equal to zero and hence no deflection would be suffered by the atom in these states in the inhomogenous deflecting field. This method permitted the measurement of both spin and the hyperfine structure constant and, therefore, the evaluation of the nuclear magnetic moment.

In 1933 Stern and his coworkers obtained the startling result that the magnetic moment of the proton was about 2½ times larger than expected according to the Dirac theory. This result was obtained with molecular hydrogen. Rabi and his coworkers, using atomic hydrogen and atomic deuterium, confirmed these important results and gave an independent measurement of the magnetic moment of the proton and deuteron. These methods were later extended in the measurement of the sign of the magnetic moment of the proton and deuteron. In the course of this work, Rabi invented a method for the utilization of resonance phenomena to cause transitions between the hyperfine levels, Zeeman levels, or indeed any set of energy levels. Essentially, the method utilized an applied radio frequency to cause transitions between energy levels, either through absorption or through stimulated radiation, for measurement of hyperfine structure. The atomic or molecular beam was passed through a homogenous magnetic field and a weak oscillating magnetic field applied in the direction perpendicular to the static homogenous field. When the frequency of the oscillating field approached the transition frequency by responding to the Bohr relation $\frac{W_1 - W_2}{h} = \nu_{12}$, transitions were induced from state 1 to state 2 and vice versa. These transitions could be made manifest by subsequent deflecting fields through the change in the magnetic moment of the system.

This method has been generalized and has had very wide application, as for example to the atomic clock, nuclear magnetic resonance, and, ultimately, the maser and laser. Perhaps the most significant discoveries that resulted from the application of these methods were the anomalous magnetic moment of the electron, the quadrupole moment of the deuteron, and the Lamb shift associated with the polarizability of the vacuum.

For the method in general, Rabi was awarded the Nobel Prize for physics in 1944. At the same time Otto Stern was awarded the Nobel Prize for physics for 1943.

From 1940 to 1945 Rabi was concerned with military research and development in the field of microwave radar and was associate director of the Radiation Laboratory in Cambridge, Mass. This work grew naturally out of the previous experimental work on molecular beams. In the postwar years he devoted himself to the political and educational problems that arose from the war effort, particularly from the development of atomic weapons and other means of mass destruction. He was for 10 years (1946–56) a member of the General Advisory Committee of the Atomic Energy Commission and for 4 years its chairman. He was a member and chairman for a time of the President's Science Advisory Committee and other government bodies, as well as the United Nations Science Committee. He was active in arranging for the various United Nations Conferences on the Peaceful Uses of Atomic Energy. Through his membership in the United States delegation to UNESCO he originated the movement that resulted in the great international laboratory for high-energy physics in Geneva known as CERN. Rabi was one of the founders of the Brookhaven National Laboratory and its parent organization, Associated Universities, Inc.

Rabi was brought to the United States in early childhood. He was graduated from the New York City public schools and Cornell University, where he received his B.Chem. degree in 1919. He went back to Cornell in 1922 for graduate work in physics, which he completed at Columbia with a Ph.D. in 1927. He spent 2 years in Europe in the principal institutions, chiefly in Germany, Denmark, and Switzerland, with A. Sommerfeld, Niels Bohr, Wolfgang Pauli, Otto Stern, and Werner Heisenberg. Returning to Columbia, he went through the various grades and obtained the rank of full professor in 1937. In 1945, at the close of World War II, he returned to Columbia as executive officer of the physics department and used his influence to put that department in a leading position in the new fields of high-energy physics and applications of microwaves to scientific and practical purposes. In 1964 he became the first University Professor at Columbia, a professorship without departmental ties. He was elected to the National Academy of Sciences in 1940.

Aside from articles on technical subjects published in *The Physical Review*, Rabi contributed to *The Atlantic Monthly* and other periodicals and published a small booklet of two lectures on general topics, *My Life and Times as a Physicist* (1960).

For background information *see* MAGNETIC MOMENT; MAGNETIC RESONANCE; MOLECULAR BEAMS in the McGraw-Hill Encyclopedia of Science and Technology.   □

★ RAINWATER, Leo James
American physicist
Born Dec. 9, 1917, Council, Idaho, U.S.A.

WHILE WORKING on μ-mesonic x-rays at Columbia University's cyclotron laboratory in 1953, Rainwater and Val Fitch established the presently accepted nuclear charge radius. Their result, smaller than that previously accepted, was later confirmed by the electron scattering experiments of Robert Hofstadter and his students at Stanford University. In an improved study in 1960–62, Rainwater and W. Frati obtained precision values for the 2p fine-structure splitting. This work was later extended in a massive collaboration experiment with C. S. Wu, Samuel Devons, and others using high-resolution Li-drifted Ge detectors. The studies of S. Koslov, Fitch, and Rainwater on the 3d–2p μ-mesonic x-ray transition for phosphorus using K absorption edge techniques gave an experimental demonstration of the importance of vacuum polarization effects and a precision measurement of the μ mass. This method was later extended by Devons and others to achieve the present best value of the muon mass.

During 1954–55, Rainwater and L. N. Cooper cooperated on an analysis of experiments that were claimed to demonstrate an anomalous scattering of cosmic-ray muons in matter. They developed a theory of multiple Coulomb scattering by extended nuclei that has since given excellent fit to better experiments. A parallel line of research on the angular distribution for elastic and inelastic scattering of π+ and π− mesons by light nuclei was carried out by Rainwater's graduate students between 1954 and 1961.

Beginning in 1942, a major part of Rainwater's total research effort was his neutron cross section research. This was carried on in collaboration with W. W. Havens, Jr.; over the years many graduate students and short-term research associates were connected with the work. In recent years, Columbia's Nevis synchrocyclotron was used about six weeks per year as a high intensity pulsed source for high resolution neutron resonance spectroscopy. The remaining time was needed to analyze the large amounts of data that were collected.

In the fall of 1949 C. H. Townes gave a colloquium at Columbia on the experimental situation for nuclear electric quadrupole moments and their relation to the shell model. He pointed out the very large values of the observed values relative to expected single-proton values in a spherical nucleus. As he spoke, Rainwater worked out a valid mechanism for producing such a collective distortion. This was contained in his best-known paper, "Energy Level Argument for a Spheroidal Nuclear Model."

The son of a civil engineer, Rainwater majored in physics at the California Institute of Technology, where he received his B.S. in 1939. He received his M.A. in 1941 and his Ph.D. in 1946 at Columbia University. He remained at Columbia as instructor (1946–47), assistant professor (1947–49), associate professor (1949–52), and professor of physics (from 1952). He was director of the cyclotron laboratory at Columbia from 1951 to 1953 and from 1956 to 1961. In 1963 Rainwater received the U.S. Atomic Energy Commission's E. O. Lawrence Memorial Award.

For background information *see* CYCLOTRON in the McGraw-Hill Encyclopedia of Science and Technology.   □

tution of Washington and as an associate at the University of Illinois, Ramsey continued his studies of the forces between elementary particles by measurements on the scattering of neutrons and protons from hydrogen, helium, and other nuclei. These studies were interrupted by the impending involvement of the United States in World War II. In 1940 at the Massachusetts Institute of Technology's Radiation Laboratory he headed the groups that developed the first three-centimeter-wavelength magnetrons and the first radar systems at that wavelength. Later he was appointed expert consultant to the Secretary of War, initially to advise the Air Force on the use of radar and subsequently to assist the Los Alamos Laboratory for atomic weapons. At Los Alamos he was a group leader, associate division chief, and chief scientist for the technical group at Tinian.

At the end of 1945, Ramsey returned to Columbia University as an associate professor. There he studied properties of molecules and nuclei by the molecular-beam resonance method. He was executive secretary of the group that established Brookhaven National Laboratory and served as the first chairman of its physics department before joining the faculty of Harvard University in 1947, first as an associate professor and, after 1950, as professor of physics.

At Harvard, Ramsey continued his studies of elementary particles at high energies and of molecules and atoms at low energies but with high accuracy. He studied the scattering of 150-Mev protons and neutrons by protons and other nuclei. He was chairman of the Scientific Committee for the 6-Mev Cambridge electron accel-

★ RAMSEY, Norman Foster

American physicist
Born Aug. 27, 1915, Washington, D.C., U.S.A.

RAMSEY'S RESEARCH centered on the properties of molecules, atoms, nuclei, and elementary particles. For his achievements in this area he received the U.S. Atomic Energy Commission's E. O. Lawrence Award in 1960.

In his Ph.D. thesis at Columbia with I. I. Rabi, Ramsey made (1940) the first accurate measurements of rotational magnetic moments of molecules and observed for the first time how these magnetic moments depended on the weight of the nuclei. He also participated with Rabi in the discovery that the heavy hydrogen nucleus was football-shaped instead of spherical as previously assumed. This discovery showed the existence of a new variety of force—tensor force—between the neutron and proton.

As a postdoctoral fellow at the Carnegie Insti-

erator during its period of construction. On its completion, this was the world's most energetic electron accelerator, and it produced the fastest artificially accelerated particles of any kind—99.9999996% of the velocity of light. Ramsey, along with R. Wilson and others, used the accelerator to study the scattering of high-energy electrons from protons and deuterons. Their experiments showed that the form factors for both electric and magnetic scattering fell to low values at high energy, corresponding to the distribution of the electric charge and the magnetism being more smoothly distributed throughout the nucleons than had been anticipated.

Shortly after he joined the Harvard faculty, Ramsey invented a new molecular-beam resonance method with two separated oscillatory fields. This gave much more accurate magnetic resonance spectra than was previously possible. With this technique and with an improved electron-bombardment detector, he and his students over a period of years measured a wide variety of molecules including H_2, D_2, HD, Ne^{21}, HF, DF, HCl, F_2, CH_4, LiH, LiF, and CO. These experiments measured both nuclear and molecular properties, including the nuclear magnetic moment, nuclear quadrupole moment (shape of the nuclear electrical charge distribution), magnetic interactions of the nuclei with each other, interaction of the nucleus with the magnetic field due to the rotation of the molecule, dependence of the diamagnetic susceptibility of the molecule on its orientation, rotational magnetic moment of the molecule, shape of the charge distribution of the molecule, and so forth.

To interpret the chemical shifts observed in NMR (nuclear magnetic resonance) experiments that form the basis of the later extensively used NMR techniques of chemical analysis, Ramsey developed the theory of magnetic shielding of nuclei in molecules. He also developed the thermodynamics and statistical mechanics of systems at negative absolute temperatures and showed that some formulations of the second law of thermodynamics had to be rephrased in view of the possibility of nuclear spin systems possessing negative absolute temperatures.

In 1950 Ramsey and E. M. Purcell pointed out that there was little evidence for the generally accepted parity symmetry in nuclear forces and undertook an experiment to find a neutron electric dipole moment, which was thought to be contrary to such symmetry. They found none but set a low upper limit to its value. Subsequently, Ramsey used the techniques developed in this search to measure the magnetic moment of the neutron to high accuracy.

Ramsey, D. Kleppner, and H. M. Goldenberg developed a new device—atomic hydrogen maser —with which measurements of unprecedented accuracy could be made. They and their students used it to measure the hyperfine frequencies of hydrogen, deuterium, and tritium. The ratio of the tritium to the hydrogen hyperfine frequency, for example, was measured to an accuracy of one part in 10^{12}, and for the first time a measurement was made of the small shift of the hydrogen hyperfine frequency by an electric field.

A general's son, Ramsey received his A.B. (1935), M.A. (1939), and Ph.D. (1940) from Columbia University. A Kellett fellowship permitted him to study for 2 years at Cambridge University, where he received B.A. (1937), M.A. (1940), and Sc.D. (1954) degrees. He was elected to the National Academy of Sciences in 1952.

Ramsey was the author or coauthor of *Experimental Nuclear Physics* (1953), *Nuclear Moments* (1953), *Molecular Beams* (1956), *Nuclear Interaction in Molecules* (1963), *Quick Calculus* (1965), and 160 articles in the *Physical Review* and other scientific journals.

For background information *see* MOLECULAR BEAMS in the McGraw-Hill Encyclopedia of Science and Technology.   □

★ **READ, Herbert Harold**
British geologist
Born Dec. 17, 1889, Whitstable, Kent, England

DURING THE last half-century, Read played a major part in the understanding of the metamorphic, migmatitic, and granitic rocks—the rocks of deep-seated origin that he grouped as plutonic. From his lengthy investigations in the old mobile belt of the Caledonides in Scotland and Ireland, he built up a synthesis of the relationship, in space and time, of these three groups of the plutonic rocks.

Read's work (1933–42) in Unst in the Shetland Islands was an early demonstration of the interpretation of a terrain of crystalline schists in terms of their metamorphic and tectonic history. He showed that in this island three successive metamorphisms—controlled by markedly different temperature-pressure conditions and each characterized by different mineral assemblages, textures, and structures—are superimposed. This method of approach has since been found to be very fruitful, and the idea of polymetamorphism, developed as a result of the Unst work, has been successfully applied in many other crystalline complexes. These and related studies enabled Read to formulate ideas on metamorphic correlation, convergence, and differentiation that are now commonplace in the investigation of the metamorphic rocks.

In Aberdeenshire and Banffshire in northeast Scotland, Read determined (1920–56) the stratigraphical order of thick successions of Dalradian (late Precambrian) rocks and was thereby able to propose that the metamorphic rocks over an extensive area were arranged in a gigantic recumbent fold. The rocks of this region are characterized by the development of andalusite and cordierite in pelitic members; his zonation of this Buchan type of regional metamorphism, as he named it, is now recognized as widely developed among the metamorphic rocks of the world.

Read became best known for his proposals concerning the relationships of migmatites and granites, based mainly on his field experience of the plutonic rocks of Sutherland in Scotland and Donegal in Ireland (1925–63). He played a large part in gaining general acceptance of the idea that granitic material could be produced by metamorphic and metasomatic processes within the crust. From the more tentative and restricted notions of others, he developed the concept of the Granite Series. In this, granites were fitted into the framework of the mobile belts of the crust according to their composition, form, and environment. During the lengthy debate on the origin of granite, Read took the stand indicated by his well-known watchword that "there are granites and granites"; modern workers, except extremists on both flanks, have come to take up the same position.

In a different field, Read was largely responsible for the investigation of a well-characterized basic igneous province in northeast Scotland. In this he presented many demonstrations of the effect of the reaction between basic magma and enclosed pelitic xenoliths. The modified rocks he called "contaminated igneous rocks," and the name has been adopted, for general use, for the products of similar processes elsewhere.

Of Kentish farming stock, Read graduated in geology from Imperial College, University of London, B.Sc. 1912, D.Sc. 1924. During World War I he served in the infantry in Egypt, Gallipoli, and France. He was a member of the British Geological Survey in Scotland from 1914 to 1931, resigning to become professor of geology at the University of Liverpool. In 1939 he was appointed professor of geology in the University of London at his old college, Imperial; retiring in 1955, he became senior research fellow there until 1964. He was elected to the Royal Society in 1939 and received the Royal Medal of the Society in 1963.

Read wrote *Geology, An Introduction to Earth-History* (1949), *The Granite Controversy* (1957), and *Introduction to Geology*, Vol. I, *Principles*, with Janet Watson (1962).

For background information *see* GRANITE; MIGMATITE in the McGraw-Hill Encyclopedia of Science and Technology. □

★ REICHSTEIN, Tadeus
Swiss organic chemist
Born July 20, 1897, Wloclawek, Poland

THE HORMONES of the adrenal cortex were first recognized for their role in Addison's disease. Since then they have been found to be of great importance in controlling such functions of the body as the innervation of internal organs like the heart, the metabolism of sugar, sex characters, and others. Of the more than 40 substances produced by the cortex, Reichstein isolated about 30 and produced the first synthesis of many of them. For this and related work describing the structure and properties of these substances, he received, with E. C. Kendall and Philip Hench, the 1950 Nobel Prize in physiology or medicine.

Reichstein began his work on the hormone of the adrenal gland in 1934. A preliminary paper was published in 1935, but the field proved to be so complex that the research lasted until 1956. In the United States Kendall, O. Winterseiner, and later H. L. Mason were working on the same problem. It appeared that the adrenal produced a complicated mixture of related substances. By 1946 the single hormone that Reichstein had originally thought he was working with had been identified as consisting of at least 29 separate steroid derivatives. The steroid nature of these substances was proved by Reichstein, and their structure and composition were considerably clarified by him. Out of the above compounds, corticosterone, 17-hydroxy-corticosterone (hydrocortisone), and aldosterone were later found to be the biologically most important compounds in the adrenal secretions.

Even before these substances had all been isolated and identified, Reichstein had succeeded in producing a partial synthesis of the compound desoxycorticosterone. This substance was found to be very active biologically in the sense that it was effective in prolonging the lives of animals from which the adrenal gland had been removed. It was also found to be the best means, at that time, for treating Addison's disease. For several years this compound remained the only representative of the corticoids that could be mass produced.

Further clarification of the constitution and structure of the adrenal hormones, by Reichstein, was instrumental in the discovery of the first practically feasible partial synthesis of cortisone by L. H. Sarett in the United States. This important adrenal compound is effective in the treatment of rheumatoid arthritis. It was principally for their collaboration in isolating cortisone and discovering its therapeutic value that Reichstein, Kendall, and Hench received the Nobel award.

Previous to the work described above, Reichstein, through work on the aromatic substances of coffee and chicory, had become interested in furan and pyrol derivatives. In the early 1930s the literature of several nations described research and chemical formulas for ascorbic acid (vitamin C) involving derivatives of furan. Although the formulas proved to be false, he succeeded in producing the first synthesis of this substance in 1933. An improved method, discovered by him in the same year, is still the method used for mass production of vitamin C.

In collaboration with J. von Euw, Simpson, Tait, Wettstein, and Neher he isolated and explained (1953–54) the structure of aldosterone, a hormone of the adrenal cortex that had not been isolated before, and one that plays an important part in the supply of salt and water to the body. He also worked on plant glycosides, such as digitalis, which play important roles in regulating the heart.

The son of an engineer, Reichstein became a naturalized Swiss citizen in 1914. He studied chemistry at the Eidgenossische Technische Hochschule in Zurich, from which he received his diploma in 1920 and his Ph.D. under Hermann Staudinger in 1922. After working in industry he returned to that institution as lecturer in organic and physiological chemistry in 1929. In 1934 he was appointed titular professor, in 1937 associate professor, and in 1938 professor in pharmaceutical chemistry and director of the Pharmaceutical Institute in the University of Basel. In 1946 he took over, in addition, the chair of organic chemistry and held both these positions until 1950. In 1952 he moved with his students to the new Institute of Organic Chemistry, the building and equipment of which he had supervised between 1948 and 1952 and of which he became director. He retired as director of the Institute in 1960 but continued to lead a group of research students. Reichstein was elected a foreign associate of the U.S. National Academy of Sciences in 1952.

For background information *see* ADRENAL CORTEX STEROID in the McGraw-Hill Encyclopedia of Science and Technology.   □

★ **REYNOLDS, Doris Livesey**
English geologist
Born July 1, 1899, Manchester, England

FROM COMBINED field, petrological, and chemical evidence, Reynolds investigated the chemical interchanges and migrations that have taken place within various types of rocks during their metasomatic transformation to granite. She made the fundamental discovery that, at subvolcanic levels within the Earth's crust, chemical interchanges and mobility may result in intrusion or extrusion by the operation of a process akin to the industrial method of fluidization by through-flowing gas. For this work she was awarded the Lyell Medal of the Geological Society of London in 1960.

During the early years of this century J. J. Sederholm observed in Finland that transitional rocks with a mixed appearance (migmatites) had been formed between relatively young granites and either older granites or crystalline rocks of sedimentary or volcanic origin. He concluded that migmatites, and ultimately granite itself, were formed progressively from the older rock components by a process of ultrametamorphism culminating in flow and intrusion. Subsequently, Eugène Wegmann discovered from structural evidence that some migmatites, while remaining essentially solid, had flowed bodily upward, like salt domes, and had become intrusive within overlying rocks.

Reynolds tackled the problems of granitization by combining petrological and chemical methods with structural investigations in the field. For chemical analysis she selected in the field sedimentary rocks of various kinds together with their respective granitized counterparts. From the analyses she discovered that during granitization sodium, calcium, and silicon were introduced into pelitic rocks, the first to be granitized, with concomitant expulsion of variable amounts of potassium, aluminum, and cafemic constituents. The materials lost from pelitic rocks during granitization she found to be qualitatively correlatable with those introduced into calcareous rocks and quartzites. Her results revealed that granitization commonly takes place in two stages. During the first stage the rock concerned is chemically desilicated, for example, by feldspathization of quartz-rich rocks or basification of other types. Certain constituents thus become concentrated relative to their abundances in the end members. From the sum total of chemical data she found the chief introduction from an external source to be sodium. By field and petrochemical investigations she confirmed that these chemical migrations and interchanges were intimately associated with shear movements.

At higher—that is, subvolcanic—structural levels, Reynolds found examples showing all stages of transformation from Dalradian quartzite to Caledonian granophyre and syenite, and, even more striking, examples of Caledonian granodiorite pseudomorphed by Tertiary granophyre. Chemical analyses showed that these transformations included introduction of potassium while microscopic examination revealed that the chemical migrations and interchanges took place predominantly along the boundaries of quartz grains. In all these examples of subvolcanic granitization Reynolds observed that the transformed rocks intruded as veins and larger bodies into adjacent rocks, for example, veins of Tertiary microgranite extending from transformed Caledonian granodiorite into Tertiary dolerite. By reference to analogous structural forms provided by intrusive Tertiary tuffs and agglomerates, derived from the Caledonian granodiorite concerned, Reynolds inferred that at subvolcanic levels through-flowing gas was the agent responsible for chemical transformation, disaggregation, and transport. The industrial process of fluidization provided an actualistic basis for these interpretations. In this way she introduced for the first time the concept of fluidization as a geological process of wide application, including the origin of diamond pipes and a great variety of volcanic phenomena.

Daughter of a merchant in the textile trade, Doris Reynolds studied geology at Bedford College, University of London, graduating B.Sc. with first class honors in 1920, and gaining the D.Sc. of London University in 1937 for her researches in petrogenesis. From 1921 to 1943 she taught successively at Queen's University, Belfast; Bedford College and University College, London; and Durham University. From 1943 to 1962 she was an honorary research fellow of the University of Edinburgh. In 1962 she became an honorary research fellow of Bedford College, University of London.

For background information *see* FLUIDIZATION OF SOLIDS; GRANITIZATION in the McGraw-Hill Encyclopedia of Science and Technology.   □

☆ RICHARDS, Dickinson Woodruff
American physician
Born Oct. 30, 1895, Orange, N.J., U.S.A.

DURING INVESTIGATIONS of cardiopulmonary function in human patients, Richards, in collaboration with André Cournand, utilized the technique of cardiac catheterization and proved its value as a diagnostic tool in the study of many cardiac and pulmonary diseases. For his work, Richards received the 1956 Nobel Prize in physiology or medicine, which he shared with Cournand and Werner Forssmann.

The first cardiac catheterization on a human being was performed in 1929, when the German physician Werner Forssmann passed a catheter, inserted into a vein in his own arm, into his right atrium. Later studies, performed by other investigators, showed that such a catheter could be left in place for some time without harming the individual. Thus it was possible to make accurate analyses of blood gases and to measure cardiac output over a period of time.

Richards, in relation to his work on pulmonary disease, was especially eager to find a method whereby pulmonary efficiency could be measured. He showed that cardiac catheterization provided a much needed set of answers, since by this method the state of the blood as it entered the right heart (from the pulmonary circulation) could be assessed with respect to its rate of flow, pressure relations, and gas contents.

In addition to its use in the study of chronic pulmonary disease, cardiac catheterization was later found by Richards and his colleagues to be a valuable tool in the study of traumatic shock and in the diagnosis of heart failure and the identification of congenital heart lesions. Coupled with angiocardiography (x-ray examination of the heart after injection of radio-opaque dyes), cardiac catheterization proved to be of inestimable value to surgeons in assessing the nature and location of cardiac lesions, and postoperatively determining the degree to which normal circulation had been restored.

Richards studied at Yale University, from which he received his A.B. in 1917. After two years in the Army he entered Columbia University, receiving his M.A. in physiology in 1922 and his M.D. in 1923. After spending four years on the staff of Presbyterian Hospital in New York, he worked at the National Institute for Medical Research in London for one year, then returned to Presbyterian Hospital, where he began to study pulmonary and circulatory physiology. His collaboration with Cournand began in 1931, their work being done at Bellevue Hospital in New York. In 1945 Richards became professor of medicine at Columbia University and, in 1947, Lambert Professor of Medicine. He retired in 1961. He was elected to the National Academy of Sciences in 1958.

For background information see CARDIOVASCULAR SYSTEM; HEART in the McGraw-Hill Encyclopedia of Science and Technology.   □

RICKOVER, Hyman George

American naval officer and engineer
Born Jan. 27, 1900, Russia

RICKOVER ACHIEVED national recognition for his leadership in the design, development, construction, and operation of nuclear propulsion systems for submarines and other naval ships. As early as 1946, before the Atomic Energy Commission was established, Rickover was assigned responsibility for investigating the use of nuclear reactors for this purpose. He assembled a team of naval officers and civilians at Oak Ridge, Tenn., and early in 1948 he headed the joint AEC-Navy program to develop the first naval nuclear propulsion system.

Utilizing the fundamental research on reactor materials and conceptual systems developed by the Oak Ridge and the Argonne National Laboratories, Rickover's group made steady progress in compiling the information and perfecting the techniques necessary to build the first nuclear submarine. He made American industry a partner in this effort at the Bettis Atomic Power Laboratory near Pittsburgh, at the Knolls Atomic Power Laboratory near Schenectady, and at the National Reactor Testing Station in Idaho. At these places the development of naval nuclear propulsion systems was carried out. A landmark in this effort was the initial operation on Mar. 31, 1953, of the Submarine Thermal Reactor, Mark I, the land-based prototype of the first nuclear submarine propulsion plant. This prototype plant performed a continuous full-power run of 66 days duration. This was enough time to have carried a ship twice around the world without refueling and contrasts with the 4-hour full-power run that is required for acceptance of new naval ships. This run served to highlight the virtually unlimited cruising range of the *Nautilus*, even at high speed. On June 14, 1952, the keel of the *Nautilus*, the world's first nuclear submarine, was laid by President Truman at Groton, Conn. She was launched by Mrs. Eisenhower on Jan. 21, 1954, and went to sea on Jan. 17, 1955.

This event was the beginning of a revolution in naval strategy and tactics. For the first time a true submarine was possible—one that could steam long distances almost indefinitely at high speeds. In February, 1957, the *Nautilus* completed operation on its first nuclear core, having traveled 62,500 miles in more than 2 years without refueling. The arctic region was accessible to the nuclear submarine, as demonstrated by the voyages of the *Nautilus* and the *Skate* under the north polar icecap. A new record was established in naval history by the *Triton*, the

first submarine to circumnavigate the world underwater, completely independent of the Earth's atmosphere. The impact of the development of nuclear power on the Navy's surface fleet was demonstrated by the round-the-world cruise of the nuclear ships *Enterprise, Long Beach,* and *Bainbridge* without replenishment of supplies or fuel.

In addition to his contributions to the development of the nuclear navy, Rickover also led the scientific, technical, and industrial team that developed and constructed the Shippingport Pressurized Water Reactor (PWR) at Shippingport, Pa. This project has served as the basic laboratory for much of the reactor technology that has gone into the nation's atomic power plants. The Shippingport power station has supplied electricity to the Pittsburgh area since late 1957.

Two of the most important contributions of the Shippingport PWR project have been in the fields of reactor physics and reactor fuel technology. The PWR, with its "seed-and-blanket" design, demonstrated that it is feasible to obtain large amounts of power from a "blanket" of natural uranium surrounding a "seed" of highly enriched uranium core that serves as the driving element in a reactor that is cooled and moderated with ordinary water. While producing power, the seed-and-blanket design has the additional advantage of making possible the breeding of fissionable material from the very abundant element thorium in the blanket.

In the field of fuel metallurgy the Shippingport PWR project team, led by Rickover, was responsible for the development of uranium oxide as a fuel material for large power reactors. Engineering studies of the PWR also produced many design improvements that have extended the life of reactor fuel elements and thus have contributed to the reduction in nuclear power costs. The first PWR core, placed in the reactor in late 1957, operated until February, 1964, more than three times its original design life.

To extend the knowledge of basic technology both in the United States and abroad, Rickover was also instrumental in establishing a school for reactor operators at Shippingport in which personnel from U.S. and foreign utility companies are trained as atomic power plant operators. Rickover also established the Navy's program for the nuclear training of all officers and enlisted personnel involved in the operation of the Navy's nuclear power plants.

In developing components and materials for naval propulsion and civilian power reactor systems, Rickover and those working with him soon discovered that the standards of reliability and safety established for conventional power systems were by no means sufficient for nuclear power plants. The result was the development of technical standards and specifications in the nuclear industry that would have been inconceivable a few years ago, and the formulation of realistic and comprehensive safety standards for propulsion and power reactors. So rigorous have been the standards for fabrication and operation of nuclear systems that they have surpassed conventional equipment in safety and reliability.

Taken to the United States as a child, Rickover was educated in the Chicago public schools and graduated from the U.S. Naval Academy in 1922. Thereafter he served in various seagoing duties, becoming a qualified submariner in 1930. He then requested and was assigned to engineering duty in 1937. He studied electrical engineering at the U.S. Naval Post Graduate School and completed the course at Columbia University, from which he received an M.S. in electrical engineering. During World War II he directed the Electrical Section of the Bureau of Ships and served briefly with the Manhattan District atomic bomb project. After the war he turned his attention to nuclear ship propulsion. In 1946 he was assigned to the Atomic Submarine Project, then under the Manhattan District, as assistant director of operations. From 1947 he worked in a dual capacity as manager, naval reactors, U.S. Atomic Energy Commission and as assistant chief for nuclear propulsion, Bureau of Ships, Department of the Navy. He was promoted to rear admiral in 1953 and to vice admiral in 1958. In addition to numerous other honors, he received the U.S. Atomic Energy Commission's Enrico Fermi Award in 1964 "for engineering and administrative leadership in the development of safe and reliable nuclear power and its successful application to our national security and economic needs."

Rickover wrote three books—*Education and Freedom* (1959), *Swiss Schools and Ours: Why Theirs Are Better* (1962), and *American Education: A National Failure* (1963)—and two reports to the House Appropriations Committee (issued as separate publications)—*Report on Russia* (1959) and *Education for All Children: What We Can Learn from England* (1962).

For background information *see* REACTOR, SHIP PROPULSION; SUBMARINE in the McGraw-Hill Encyclopedia of Science and Technology. □

★ RIDEAL, Sir Eric (Keightley)
British chemist
Born Apr. 11, 1890, London, England

FOR HIS contributions to the subject of surface chemistry, Rideal was awarded the Royal Society's Davy Medal in 1951.

The fundamental link between two large sections of physical chemistry, namely, colloids and heterogeneous catalysis, is that they both involve the properties, physical and chemical, of interfaces. Fifty years ago the purely descriptive

aspects of colloid science alone were available, and there were two diametrically opposing views as to the mechanism of catalytic actions. It was to this field that Rideal devoted his interest.

The mathematical theory of surface tension was by then firmly established by Willard Gibbs, Lord Kelvin, and Lord Rayleigh, but with the exception of G. W. Hardy at Cambridge and H. Devaux in France little work had been done on the nature and properties of the surface phase. Hardy had shown that matter "in the boundary state" differed in properties from the bulk material, and he was advancing the view that the layer was but one or two molecules thick and that these molecules were orientated. This concept was then not generally acceptable and had to wait for the 1917 confirmation by Irving Langmuir and W. D. Harkins in the United States and by A. Marcelin in France. A remark by Hardy to the effect that "at present the colloidal kingdom seems to be an Alsatia wherein difficult states of matter find refuge from too exacting an enquiry" gave Rideal his initial spur.

Toward the end of World War I, submarine warfare compelled England to attempt to develop synthetic ammonia, and Rideal was called back from France for this purpose. He thus had to prepare and use catalysts for the synthesis of hydrogen and ammonia and for the oxidation of the latter. Extended collaboration with Hugh Taylor on hydrogen catalysts brought home to Rideal the realization that knowledge of matter in the boundary state at solid surfaces was in the same state of confusion as that at the liquid surfaces. Paul Sabatier, who coined the term catalysis, believed that the modus operandi was the formation and breakdown of intermediary chemical compounds. This view was opposed to that of Michael Faraday, who had considered condensation and compression the important factors. Faraday's views were receiving strong support at that time from the development in 1904 of E. A. M. Bodenstein's diffusive mecha-

nisms. Again it was Langmuir who in 1917 revived the chemical view and laid the foundations of the mechanisms by which the observed kinetics of catalytic processes could be understood. In *Kapillarchemie* (1909), Herbert Freundlich attempted a systematic treatment of interfaces, but it was not until the book's second edition (1922) that the importance of the work was generally recognized.

In 1920 the International Education Board of the Rockefeller Foundation established a laboratory at Cambridge, under Rideal's direction, devoted to colloid science in which the study of interfacial phenomena was to be the guiding theme. Of the more important investigations on liquid surfaces carried out under Rideal's direction there, and later at the Royal Institution in London, may be mentioned those on phase equilibria and thermodynamics by D. J. Crisp, R. K. Schofield, and C. Kemball, and those on chemical reactions in surface phases by A. E. Alexander, J. T. Davies, Geoffrey Gee, and J. S. Mitchell (these included both surface polymerization and photochemical action). J. H. Schulman commenced a long investigation on surface potentials. L. Tronsted employed elliptically polarized light for structure examination. Other interesting discoveries were the properties of film penetration and the retardation in passage across a film barrier.

At solid surfaces J. K. Roberts employed accommodation coefficients of the rate gases and Pirani gauges to study chemisorption on clean wires, R. C. L. Bosworth used the photoelectric effect for the same purpose, while F. P. Bowden adopted electrometric methods. R. M. Barrer commenced his investigations on molecular sieves, which extended over 30 years. Deuterium was first made electrolytically in England at Cambridge by A. F. Farkas and employed by him, H. W. Melville, and D. D. Eley in the catalytic reactions, while R. G. W. Norrish and Bernard Lewis examined the catalytic behavior of coated glass. The first application of a computer to a catalytic action was made by G. H. Twigg in his study of the oxidation of ethylene. Finally, an alternative mechanism to that proposed by Langmuir for the interaction of two species at a catalytic surface was found to be applicable to a number of reactions.

Rideal obtained his M.A. at Cambridge, a Ph.D. at the University of Bonn, and a D.Sc. at London University. A captain in the Royal Engineers during World War I, he taught at the University of Illinois in 1919–20 before going to Cambridge. From 1930 to 1946 he was professor of colloid science at Cambridge. In 1946 he became Fullerian Professor of Chemistry in the Royal Institution and director of the Davy-Faraday Laboratory there. From 1950 until his retirement in 1955 he continued his work as professor of physical chemistry at King's College, London.

Rideal wrote *Water Supplies* (1914), *Electrochemistry* (1918), *Catalysis in Theory and Practice*, with H. S. Taylor (1919), *Ozone* (1920), *Disinfectants*, with S. Rideal (1921), *Surface Chemistry* (1926), and *Interfacial Phenomena*, with J. T. Davies (1961).

For background information *see* COLLOID; INTERFACE OF PHASES; SURFACE PHENOMENON in the McGraw-Hill Encyclopedia of Science and Technology. □

★ RIGGS, Lorrin Andrews
American psychologist
Born June 11, 1912, Harpoot, Turkey

Riggs DEVELOPED objective methods for the study of human vision and investigated the electroretinogram (ERG) generated by the visual cells of an eye stimulated by light. For his achievements in this field he was awarded the Warren Medal of the Society of Experimental Psychologists in 1957.

Early investigations by E. D. Adrian, H. K. Hartline, C. H. Graham, and R. Granit established the ERG as a useful indicator of visual sensitivity in a variety of experimental animals. No satisfactory method was available, however, for making firm contact with the human eye until 1941, when Riggs devised the first plastic contact lens electrode. This device, coupled with the necessary amplifying and recording equipment, made possible a long series of experimental and clinical studies of human vision. A major feature of this research was to compare the objective, or purely retinal, responses obtained in this way with the subjective, or verbalized, reports obtained in more traditional procedures used with the same human observers. Of special interest was the ease with which ERG responses from the colorless, scotopic mechanisms of peripheral vision were recorded. The ERG has become a diagnostic tool in ophthalmological practice, especially useful because distortions in response due to pathological conditions of the eye are detected with relative ease.

A second line of Riggs's research concerned the role of eye movements in human vision. Again the plastic contact lens came into play, but this time to give firm support to a tiny plane mirror that could reflect a beam of light onto a moving strip of film. The movement of the mirror, and hence of the reflected beam, corresponded to that of the eye. Experiments by Riggs and his coworkers with this technique showed that human eyes are never completely at rest. The eye movement records revealed small, rapid oscillatory motions as well as the well-known saccadic jumps and slower drifts that continue to occur even during attempts to stare fixedly at one point. These findings raised the question of whether the small involuntary motions of the eye sharpen visual acuity or degrade it. The ideal way to answer this question would have been to test a subject's vision with and without eye movements, but human eyes cannot easily be paralyzed or clamped to achieve the no-movement condition.

The solution to the problem of motionless vision was achieved in the early 1950s by Riggs and his colleagues and, independently, by R. W. Ditchburn and D. H. Fender in England. Neither group was able to immobilize the eye; but in each laboratory an optical scheme was worked out to counteract the eye movements so effectively that the optical image at the back of the eye remained motionless with respect to the retinal receptors. Thus for the first time experiments compared normal vision with vision in which the involuntary image motions were eliminated.

The most striking effect that occurs with a motionless visual image is its disappearance. A black line that appears sharp and clear at the outset gradually fades and then disappears completely; even a bright patch of light fades into a homogeneous gray background. This seems to be an example of negative adaptation, like becoming accustomed to a constant odor or the pressure of clothing. It was made evident by these experiments that an important function of eye movements is to prevent the eye from becoming momentarily blind as it continues to stare at an object. With regard to visual acuity, however, it has been found that the first look at a test object is equally good whether or not normal involuntary eye movements are present. These movements are too small to cause any blurring or sharpening effects when one's best vision is tested.

The son of the president of a small American college in Turkey, Riggs received his A.B. in 1933 from Dartmouth College. At Clark University he went on to a doctorate in physiological psychology in 1936, doing his research with C. H. Graham on electrical responses from the eyes of rats, pigeons, and frogs. His career of teaching and research in psychology began after a postdoctoral year with H. K. Hartline in the Johnson Foundation for Medical Physics, University of Pennsylvania. He taught at the University of Vermont in 1937–38 and 1939–41 and at Brown University in 1938–39 and after 1941. He became L. Herbert Ballou University Professor of Psychology at Brown in 1960. In 1961 he was elected to the National Academy of Sciences.

For background information *see* VISION in the McGraw-Hill Encyclopedia of Science and Technology.　□

☆ ROBBINS, Frederick Chapman
American microbiologist
Born Aug. 25, 1916, Auburn, Ala., U.S.A.

ROBBINS SHARED with J. F. Enders and T. H. Weller the 1954 Nobel Prize in physiology or medicine for the discovery that poliomyelitis virus could be grown in test-tube cultures of various human tissues. *See* ENDERS, JOHN FRANKLIN.

Son of a plant physiologist who became director of the New York Botanical Garden, Robbins received his A.B. (1936) and B.S. (1938) from the University of Missouri and his M.D. (1940) from the Harvard Medical School. From 1940 to 1942 he was resident physician in bacteriology and intern in medicine at the Children's Hospital Medical Center in Boston. During the next four years as an Army doctor in the United States, North Africa, and Italy, he investigated infectious hepatitis, typhus fever, and Q fever and supervised a diagnostic virus laboratory. He returned to the Children's Hospital Medical Center in 1946. From 1948 to 1950 he was a National Research Council fellow in virus diseases, work-

ing with Enders at the Research Division of Boston's Children's Medical Center. During this period and until he left Boston, Robbins conducted investigations on the cultivation of polioviruses in tissue culture and the application of these techniques. In 1952 he was appointed professor of pediatrics at Western Reserve University School of Medicine and director of the department of pediatrics at the Cleveland Metropolitan General Hospital.　□

★ ROBERTSON, John Monteath
British chemist
Born July 24, 1900, Auchterarder, Perthshire, Scotland

WHILE STUDYING the structures of certain organic molecules by x-ray crystal analysis, Robertson developed the heavy atom and isomorphous substitution methods of phase determination. These methods have enabled scientists to elucidate the detailed molecular structures of a great variety of important natural products, including terpenoids, alkaloids, antibiotics, and vitamins, many of which are so complex as to have defied the classical methods of organic chemistry. For this achievement, Robertson was awarded the Royal Society of London's Davy Medal in 1960.

The diffraction of x-rays by crystals was discovered by M. T. F. von Laue in 1912. During the next 20 years the science of crystal analysis developed rapidly, and the atomic arrangements in many metals, minerals, inorganic compounds, and a few organic compounds were discovered.

The geometry of the diffraction pattern obtained when a crystal is exposed to x-rays defines the dimensions of the unit cell, the smallest repeating unit of the crystal. To obtain the detailed structure and the positions of all the atoms it is necessary to study the intensities of the diffracted beams as well as their positions. If the atomic positions are known or can be guessed, the intensities are easily calculated. But the converse problem of calculating the atomic positions from the observed intensities is extremely difficult. To solve it completely it is necessary to know not only the intensities, or amplitudes, of the diffracted waves but also their relative phases. Unfortunately, this last piece of information concerning the relative phases is inevitably lost in making the experiment, because successive reflections (or diffractions) occur at different times with the crystal in different positions. If the structure is not too complex, a great deal can be done by trial-and-error calculations, or by various mathematical methods that employ only the intensities. But for complex organic molecules of unknown chemical constitution containing perhaps a hundred or more atoms, there is little hope of a solution by such methods.

The methods developed by Robertson depend upon inserting in the structure at a known or ascertainable position an additional atom or atoms of considerable scattering power. The extra and calculable contribution of these atoms will alter the resultant amplitude of the scattered wave in a way that depends on the unknown phase, and so this phase can often be determined. The solution is seldom complete in one step and generally requires a lot of refinement by iterative processes and a forbidding amount of calculation. This latter obstacle, however, has now been effectively removed by the invention of the electronic digital computer. These powerful methods of phase determination have made possible tremendous progress in crystal analysis during the last 10 years.

Robertson developed these methods during his work on the phthalocyanine structures in 1935 and 1936, and these were the first organic structures to be determined completely without making use of any chemical knowledge, and even without assuming the existence of atoms in the molecule. An earlier and partial observation on isomorphous replacement in the inorganic alum series had been made by J. M. Cork in 1927, but the more general heavy-atom method was first established in the phthalocyanine work. In 1939 Robertson suggested that even protein structures might be solved in this way, if a heavy atom like mercury could be inserted in the molecule.

In addition to his work on many complex natural product structures, Robertson carried out many accurate measurements on simpler aromatic compounds and was the first to establish the existence of definite bond-length variations in condensed-ring hydrocarbons.

A farmer's son, Robertson was educated at Perth Academy and Glasgow University, where he graduated B.Sc. in chemistry, mathematics,

and geology in 1923 and Ph.D. in organic chemistry in 1926. From 1928 to 1930 he studied chemistry and theoretical physics at the University of Michigan, Ann Arbor, and from 1930 to 1939 he was on the staff of the Davy-Faraday Laboratory of the Royal Institution, London, where his phthalocyanine work was done. From 1939 to 1940 he taught physical chemistry at the University of Sheffield, and during World War II (1941–44) was scientific adviser (chemical) to Bomber Command. In 1942 he was appointed professor of chemistry at Glasgow University, and most of his work on organic crystal structure analysis was carried out there.

Robertson wrote *Organic Crystals and Molecules* (1953).

For background information *see* MOLECULAR STRUCTURE AND SPECTRA in the McGraw-Hill Encyclopedia of Science and Technology. □

★ **ROBINSON, Sir Robert**
British chemist
Born Sept. 13, 1886, Chesterfield, Derbyshire, England

R OBINSON RECEIVED the 1947 Nobel Prize in chemistry for his investigations on plant products of biological importance, especially the alkaloids.

Robinson's first interest in Manchester around 1906 was the rich chemistry of brazilin and of haematoxylin. Early results included the establishment of the structures by synthesis of degradation products such as brazilinic acid (with W. H. Perkin, Jr.). The transformations of trimethylbrazilone (and brazilein) were explored and explained. Especially significant was the recognition of so-called isobrazilein salts as brazylium salts containing a pyrylium nucleus.

The first substance (derived from brazilin and containing the intact ring skeleton) to be synthesized was a trimethylbrazylium salt (H. G. Crabtree and Robinson, 1918) at Liverpool.

Later trimethylbrazilone was synthesized (with Perkin and J. N. Rây) in the second Manchester period and the problem of the synthesis of brazilin and haematoxylin was solved in 1950 (F. Morsingh and Robinson).

The work on brazylium salts led to the discovery of a general synthesis of pyrylium salts (simultaneously disclosed by H. Decker and T. von Fellenberg, 1907) and this was later exploited at St. Andrew's, Manchester, University College, and Oxford in a long series of syntheses of anthocyanidins and anthocyanins, the latter identical with widely distributed plant pigments (D. G. Pratt, W. Bradley, A. Robertson, T. R. Seshadri, and A. R. Todd were some collaborators). Incidentally, the discovery of the formation and reactions of diazoketones was made in this connection. A natural side issue was the synthesis by new methods of flavones, flavonols, and isoflavones.

Robinson's brazilin studies involved the use of veratraldehyde and other catechol derivatives. This suggested their use for attempted synthesis in the isoquinoline group of the alkaloids. Papaverine was synthesized, but the work was not published because of anticipation by A. Pictet, and Robinson turned to narcotine and hydrastine with satisfactory outcome. However, the main significance of this work was that it directed attention anew to the reactions of pseudo bases. Their condensations were so facile that it seemed likely that they occurred in the course of biogenesis. At Sydney, Robinson developed a hypothesis of the biogenesis of pseudopelletierine from lysine, methylamine (or ammonia plus methylation), and a reactive acetone derivative. This was recalled at Liverpool and led to his synthesis of tropinone from succindialdehyde, methylamine, and acetonedicarboxylic acid. He immediately developed a more general theory of alkaloid biogenesis (1917) on the basis of this type of reaction. These ideas were later elaborated, and one useful result was the revision of the structures of the morphine-thebaine group of alkaloids. Such speculations are now superseded by experimental studies with radioactive isotope tracers.

Examination of the alkaloids harmine and harmaline, begun at Manchester with Perkin and continued at Liverpool, led to their recognition as indole derivatives related to tryptophan. Later many years were spent in the study of the strychnine group of alkaloids; the Leuchs degradations were explained, and later the structures were established. Study of ajmaline (with collaborators including R. B. Woodward in the last phases) eventually disclosed the structure of this interesting alkaloid.

The last experimental study of an alkaloid was that of akuammicine (with K. Aghoramurthy) and here the correct structure was found and confirmed by M. M. Janot's mass spectrum studies.

Attempts to synthesize the steroid hormones and cholesterol were started in 1933 and successfully completed in 1953 by Robinson and numerous collaborators, of whom J. W. Cornforth made outstanding contributions. This was the first synthesis of the tetracyclic skeleton in correct stereochemical form. In 1939, guided by a structural analogy, the useful synthetic estrogen, stilbestrol, was made (with E. C. Dodds, L. Golberg, and W. Lawson).

Robinson's most important contribution was the adumbration of a qualitative electronic theory in organic chemistry. This is sometimes, but erroneously, attributed to the "English School" and it is true that Arthur Lapworth, a close friend of Robinson at Manchester, made outstanding contributions, especially on the electrochemical aspect. Apart from Lapworth, no other person was involved in the formulation of the main principles of the theory. These ideas have stood the test of time, and it is hardly possible to open a current issue of a journal devoted to organic chemistry without finding applications of the theory.

Robinson's starting point was a modification of F. K. J. Thiele's partial valence such that the part valencies were obtained by division of normal linkages and not merely appendages to unsaturated atoms. This theory was applied to enols and enams, including aromatic amines and phenols, and such heterocycles as pyrrole. Experimentally it led to the C-methylation of enamic substances (1917), which threw light on the reactions of ethyl acetoacetate, and other compounds. Later the part valencies were interpreted electronically (1921–22), and a general scheme of conjugative electron displacement was found to provide a basis for the theory of organic chemical reactions. This was tested in studies of aromatic substitution and a 4 years' controversy with C. K. Ingold and B. Flürschein was virtually settled in favor of the electronic interpretations by the discovery (H. R. Ing and Robinson) that m-nitrobenzyltrimethylammonium nitrate was the sole isolated product of the nitration of benzyltrimethylammonium salts. This was the verification of a prediction based on the anticipated consequence of the distribution of the cationic field over the aromatic nucleus.

Robinson used the nitration of catechol and quinol ethers to study the interaction of conjugative and general electronic displacements. After he published four papers in this field (1925–26) there was no further opposition.

Other domains that Robinson entered were those of intramolecular rearrangements and hybrid molecules. In both cases the ideas were developed in rudimentary form in terms of partial valencies, but the translation into electronic representation threw a flood of light on the subject. Robinson also collaborated with E. B. Chain, E. P. Abraham, and W. Baker in the elucidation of the structure of penicillin. His most recent interests included a theory of the duplex origin of petroleum, biological and abiological.

Robinson's father, William B. Robinson, was a pioneer manufacturer and inventor. William wished Robert to enter the large family business that he had created, and he directed his studies to chemistry on account of the difficulty he experienced in starting up a bleach works with the information gleaned from a well-known encyclopedia. Robert Robinson graduated at Manchester University in 1906 (D.Sc. 1910) and then worked with W. H. Perkin, Jr. In 1912 he became the first professor of organic chemistry at the University of Sydney, N.S.W., and subsequently held university chairs at Liverpool (1915–20), St. Andrew's (1921), Manchester (1922), University College, London (1928), and Oxford (1930–55). Always closely associated with the chemical industry, he became, after leaving Oxford, a director of Shell Chemical Co., Ltd., London, and a consultant. Besides the Nobel Prize, Robinson's numerous scientific honors included the Copley, Davy, and Royal medals of the Royal Society of London. He was knighted in 1939 and received the Order of Merit in 1949. He was president of the Royal Society from 1945 to 1950. In 1934 he was elected a foreign associate of the U.S. National Academy of Sciences.

For background information *see* ALKALOID; ORGANIC CHEMICAL SYNTHESIS in the McGraw-Hill Encyclopedia of Science and Technology. ☐

hood. He was taken to New York for treatment and there visited the American Museum of Natural History, where he was impressed by the displays of fossil vetebrates. In college, he studied mainly the arts, but taking a compulsory science course, he found himself in the presence of a research worker on fossil vertebrates; his boyhood interest in this area was renewed and reinforced, and he resolved to make the evolution of vertebrates his life interest.

W. K. Gregory of Columbia University was the research worker in this area to whom Romer turned for training as a graduate student. Because of duties as a teaching assistant, Romer was unable to take Gregory's course in vertebrate paleontology but was invited to join a special course being organized in myology. He expressed his pleasure at the prospect and then went to consult a dictionary to discover the meaning of this term. He thought it had to do with clams. It proved, however, to pertain to muscles, and the course was aimed at an attempt to ascertain the evolutionary history of muscles as an aid in the evolution of the associated skeletal system. Within a month he produced a novel explanation of the way in which the simple muscles of fish fins had evolved into the complex musculature of tetrapod limbs. This not only developed into a thesis for the doctorate but resulted in much further work on muscle evolution by Romer and his students, particularly when it was found that (contrary to earlier opinions) the study of embryological differentiation could shed much light on the subject.

Although he retained a lively interest in the anatomy of present-day animals, Romer's research in later years lay mainly in their evolutionary history as shown in the fossil record—

★ ROMER, Alfred Sherwood

American zoologist and paleontologist
Born Dec. 28, 1894, White Plains, N.Y., U.S.A.

T HROUGH HIS lifelong interest in the evolutionary history of the vertebrates, with emphasis on comparative anatomy and, especially, paleontology, Romer elucidated many aspects of the life patterns through which their ancestors passed and which left indelible effects on their present-day structures and functions. For his contributions to vertebrate paleontology, Romer received the Thompson and Elliot medals of the National Academy of Sciences (1954 and 1956), the Hayden Memorial Geological Award of the Academy of Natural Sciences of Philadelphia (1962), and the Penrose Medal of the Geological Society of America (1962).

Romer's interests in this area were due in part to a bite by a rabies-infected dog during boy-

particularly the great step made in the development of land vertebrates from fishes, and the radiation of primitive tetrapods into later types of amphibians and varied reptiles, including mammal ancestors. When Romer was appointed to a post in vertebrate paleontology at the University of Chicago, he found there a considerable collection of fossils from the redbeds, notably of Texas, of early Permian age. At that time of the Earth's history, reptiles had developed and begun their radiation, but there were still present amphibians of archaic types and even survivors of the fish group from which they had descended. This seemed a very appropriate field in which to continue work. For the rest of his career Romer spent a fraction of nearly every year exploring and collecting in these Texas beds, and he published numerous works on his finds there. He made a broad review of the pelycosaurs, a group of reptiles of interest as the beginning of the trend toward mammal evolution. There were numerous side products of this work, such as the discovery that aestivation for summer drought, found today in African and South American lungfishes, had already developed in the Permian. He also explained the peculiar "sail" rising above the backs of many Permian pelycosaurs (a primitive thermal regulating device). A major interest, however, was to trace the evolutionary series downward from the primitive reptiles through the complex series of archaic amphibians, toward and to the ancestral fish types. This he did with the purpose not only of obtaining the factual data as to the ancestral series but also of interpreting the underlying evolutionary factors (the effects of seasonal drought appear to have been very important; no recourse to teleology is necessary).

While mainly concerned with early Permian vertebrates, Romer did not confine his interests to animals of this age. For example, the discovery in the late 1920s of a seemingly fresh skull of an American camel, then thought to have been extinct since early Ice Age days, led to a review of the evidence as to the time of extinction of the great animals—elephants, sloths, and so on—native to the United States in the Pleistocene, and the then surprising conclusion that all of them had survived until relatively recent times (a conclusion now substantiated by carbon-14 dating). He also collected mammallike reptiles from late Permian and Triassic deposits in South Africa.

The study of early amphibian history led Romer and his students to explore Carboniferous beds in the Appalachians and the maritime provinces of Canada and to restudy the remains of amphibians of that age found in the Coal Measures. In 1958 Romer took part in a Harvard paleontological expedition to Argentina, in which a Triassic reptile deposit was developed. This led him and his associates to return in 1964 to western Argentina where a rich fauna of early Triassic age was discovered and collected for future study.

Graduating from Amherst College in 1917,

Romer spent 2 years in the American Army in France and then did graduate work at Columbia, gaining his Ph.D. in 1921. He taught anatomy in the New York University Medical School for 2 years, and from 1923 to 1934 served as associate professor and later professor of vertebrate paleontology at the University of Chicago. In 1934 he joined the Harvard staff as professor of zoology—later Alexander Agassiz Professor of Zoology—and curator of vertebrate paleontology, and from 1946 to 1961 was director of the Museum of Comparative Zoology—the "Agassiz Museum." He became professor emeritus in 1965, but continued research in the Harvard Museum. He was elected to the National Academy of Sciences in 1944.

Romer wrote *Vertebrate Paleontology* (1933), *Man and the Vertebrates* (1933), *The Vertebrate Body* (1949), *Osteology of the Reptiles* (1956), and *The Vertebrate Story* (1959).

For background information *see* PALEONTOLOGY in the McGraw-Hill Encyclopedia of Science and Technology.   □

★ **ROSEN, Louis**
American physicist
Born June 10, 1918, New York, N.Y., U.S.A.

ONE OF the forces that govern the structure of nuclei and the course of nuclear reactions is postulated to arise from the interaction of the spin of nucleons with their angular momentum. Rosen and his collaborators devised a method for systematically investigating this force and for employing it as a means for probing atomic nuclei. For this work, and for his work on diagnostics of nuclear weapons, Rosen received the U.S. Atomic Energy Commission's E. O. Lawrence Award in 1963.

Because they appear to behave like tiny gyroscopes, nucleons (neutrons and protons) are said to embody an intrinsic property called "spin." Inside the nucleus, the nucleons are imagined to move in orbits, each nucleon maintaining a constant angular momentum. Maria Mayer and J. Hans D. Jensen, in proposing a model for the structure of nuclei, hypothesized a strong interaction between the spin of each nucleon and its orbital angular momentum. Rosen reasoned that if a spin-orbit force affects the arrangement of nucleons within nuclei, it should also manifest itself in the interaction of medium-energy nucleons with nuclei. A spin-orbit force should therefore influence the scattering probabilities for nucleons; that is, nucleons with spin aligned (polarized) in one direction should scatter differently from nucleons polarized in the opposite direction.

In 1956 Rosen and J. E. Brolley, Jr., and their colleagues at the Los Alamos Scientific Laboratory undertook to prepare an intense, highly polarized beam of 10-Mev protons for use in scattering experiments. From previous experimental and theoretical work on the scattering of protons by He^4 nuclei (alpha particles), it was deduced that 6-Mev protons, back-scattered from He^4, should be almost completely polarized. However, to prepare a beam in this manner was impractical. It occurred to Rosen that the reverse of the above process might yield the desired beam of polarized protons (24-Mev alpha particles interacting with stationary protons is relativistically equivalent to 6-Mev protons interacting with stationary alpha particles). A beam of alpha particles was accelerated in a cyclotron and permitted to impinge upon a hydrogen target. Under these conditions, polarized protons were emitted in the forward, rather than the backward, direction with respect to the velocity of the bombarding particle, thus providing a useful high-intensity beam of polarized protons. Using this beam, a large number of measurements were performed to evaluate the effect of beam polarization on the probability for scattering through a given angle. From these measurements was deduced the polarization that would occur in the scattering of unpolarized protons from the various nuclei studied. The polarizing power for many nuclei was thus determined, and from these results was derived the strength of the spin-orbit force as well as the parameters of a phenomenological model describing nucleon-nucleus interactions.

To determine whether the model derived corresponded to reality, it was used to predict additional observables in nucleon-nucleus interactions. It was found that experimental information on elastic scattering and reaction cross sections for neutrons and protons were well reproduced by the model over a large region of mass and energy.

Polarization experiments have improved the description of the nucleon-nucleus interaction. They have led to more reliable predictions of the properties of proton- and neutron-induced interactions. The latter are of particular value in the practical applications of nuclear science and technology.

Rosen majored in physics and minored in mathematics at the University of Alabama (B.A., 1939; M.S., 1941) and obtained a Ph.D. from Pennsylvania State University in 1944. He taught physics at both institutions. In 1944 he joined the Manhattan Project at Los Alamos, N. Mex., where he participated in the development of the first atomic bomb. Following World War II, Rosen continued at the Los Alamos Scientific Laboratory, dividing his time between basic research in nuclear physics and nuclear weapons diagnostics.

For background information *see* NUCLEON; SCATTERING EXPERIMENTS, NUCLEAR in the McGraw-Hill Encyclopedia of Science and Technology. □

★ **ROSENBLUTH, Marshall Nicholas**
American physicist
Born Feb. 5, 1927, Albany, N.Y., U.S.A.

NUCLEAR ENERGY can be released by utilizing either of two types of nuclear reactions: the fission of certain rare heavy elements (uranium or plutonium) by neutrons, or the fusion of the common light nuclei such as deuterium, the heavy isotope of hydrogen. It is this latter energy source that is utilized by the stars and that holds the ultimately greater promise for mankind because of its cheapness (a gallon of ordinary water has a nuclear-energy content equivalent to the chemical energy of 300 gallons of gasoline) and lack of associated radioactivity. For his role in helping to harness this great source of energy, Rosenbluth received the 1964 E. O. Lawrence Award from the U.S. Atomic Energy Commission.

In the early 1930s, Hans Bethe, George Gamow, and others pointed out that, under the conditions of temperature and pressure present in the center of the Sun, the nuclei of the light elements could react with each other—for example, deuteron + deuteron ⟶ proton + triton—and that this vast source of energy undoubtedly provided us with our solar light and heat. The nuclear-fusion reaction is quite similar in behavior to a chemical reaction, requiring the proper ingredients and sufficiently high temperatures and pressures. The difference is a quantitative one, as the nuclear reaction produces about a million times as much energy per unit weight as a chemical reaction, and also, unfortunately, needs enormous temperatures of about 10^8 °C to overcome the great electrical repulsion between the charged particles. For this reason the fusion reaction is often referred to as a thermonuclear process.

After the development of the atomic bomb it became evident to Edward Teller that the ordinary fission bomb could serve as a trigger to provide the extreme physical conditions necessary for thermonuclear reactions, and that such a hydrogen bomb would be enormously cheaper and more powerful than a fission bomb. Rosenbluth and Conrad Longmire, at the Los Alamos Scientific Laboratory, played the leading roles in doing the theoretical investigations necessary to implement Teller's ideas. This work led on Nov. 1, 1952, to the world's first thermonuclear explosion.

Turning in 1954 to the possible peaceful use of the fusion reaction as an energy source, Rosenbluth joined the small group under James Tuck at the Los Alamos Laboratory that was already at work on the problem, as were several other groups in the United States, the United Kingdom and the Soviet Union. At temperatures of 10^8 °C nuclei move at speeds of about 1,000 miles per second. In a bomb the density is high enough for the nuclear reactions to occur before these speeds lead to disassembly. In a reactor, however, this is impossible, since such densities would imply an enormous pressure and a violent explosion. The basic problem, then (and one that is not yet completely solved), was how to contain such very hot material for a long enough time to permit the reaction to occur at low density in a slow and controlled fashion. As Tuck had noted, hope of doing this was afforded by the fact that at extreme temperatures all matter is in the plasma state—that is, the atoms are broken down into nuclei and electrons, which, being electrically charged, may be manipulated by electromagnetic fields. In particular, it was well known that "magnetic bottles" could be made that would confine individual charged particles for extremely long periods. It soon developed, however, that when one tried to confine macroscopic amounts of hot material, rather than individual energetic par-

ticles, in such a "magnetic bottle," it leaked. The plasma itself produced electric currents that created electromagnetic fields capable of neutralizing the confining fields of the magnetic bottle.

Thus it turned out that a plasma in a magnetic field is an extremely complex thing, capable of many novel types of wave propagation and instability. It became apparent around 1956 that, in order to solve the controlled-fusion problem, a whole new discipline of physics would have to be developed. Rosenbluth has played a leading role in the development of plasma physics, pointing the way, for example, to the cure for the most dangerous class of instabilities—the so-called "hydrodynamic" instabilities, in which the plasma leaves the magnetic bottle in much the same way as water falls out of an inverted glass. These studies in plasma physics proved to have many other applications besides controlled fusion; in particular, they contributed to studies of the ionosphere and of interstellar space, which is itself a vast plasma.

Rosenbluth majored in physics, obtaining a B.S. from Harvard in 1945 and a Ph.D. from the University of Chicago in 1949. From 1949 to 1950 he was an instructor at Stanford University. During this early period of his career he worked primarily in high-energy physics, discovering the so-called "Rosenbluth formula," which pointed the way to experiments with high-energy electrons for exploring the structure of the nucleon. From 1950 to 1956 he was at the Los Alamos Scientific Laboratory, where, in addition to studying fusion, he collaborated with his wife, the former Arianna Wright, in developing the Monte Carlo technique for computer studies of the liquid state. In 1956 Rosenbluth joined the General Atomic Corporation, and after 1960 served jointly as senior research advisor at General Atomic and professor of physics at the University of California, San Diego.

For background information see PLASMA PHYSICS in the McGraw-Hill Encyclopedia of Science and Technology.   □

ROSSBY, Carl-Gustaf Arvid

American meteorologist
Born Dec. 28, 1898, Stockholm, Sweden
Died Aug. 19, 1957, Stockholm, Sweden

R OSSBY'S THEORIES of large-scale air movements, formulated during the 1930s, became the basis of a new system of meteorology. This system views the upper westerly airflow of the middle latitudes as a basic element, thereby supplementing—and in considerable part replacing—the older polar-front concept. In 1952 Rossby received the American Meteorological

Society's Award for Extraordinary Scientific Accomplishment in Meteorology, which was later called, in his honor, the Rossby Award.

In developing techniques for effective long-range weather forecasting, Rossby and his associates at the Massachusetts Institute of Technology deemphasized the lesser and more transitory empirical phenomena. It was apparent to Rossby that a system of slow progressive waves, with linear dimensions of the order of 5,000 km, existed superimposed on the westerly current of the middle latitudes. Invoking the concept of a tendency toward conservation of absolute vorticity (vorticity refers to the rotation of an air particle about a vertical axis), he was able to show how particles moving north or south change in vorticity relative to the Earth and how future distribution and particle motion may then be computed.

In what were perhaps his most important papers, Rossby derived from a series of simplifications and use of a rectangular coordinate system the now universally known Rossby formula relating the speed of propagation of perturbations relative to airflow and the wavelength of the perturbations. Not only is this quantitative tool used in weather forecasting, it also underlies current theory of large-scale circulation in the atmosphere. Indeed, the waves analyzed by Rossby are sometime referred to as "Rossby waves."

Rossby's scientific contributions touched virtually every area of meteorology. The so-called Rossby diagram for plotting air mass properties, devised in 1932, has become a standard tool. Rossby's application of thermodynamics and the latest results of aerodynamics brought new understanding of turbulence and instability in the atmosphere. Isentropic charts became widely employed following Rossby's use of them in studies of lateral mixing. His inquiring mind reached into oceanography, studying ocean circulations and surface boundary phenomena. He looked to joint oceanographic-meteorological projects, reaching toward a general Earth-and-Sun theory for climatic change. Renewed worldwide interest in atmospheric chemistry followed Rossby's description of the atmosphere as a bearer of chemical substances that constantly interact with earth and sea, bringing about a massive geochemical balance.

Rossby's organizing achievements matched in significance his theoretical work. He created the model airway weather service between Los Angeles and San Francisco in 1928. During World War II he helped build an extensive educational program in meteorology for the U.S. Armed Forces, and started an institute of tropical meteorology for study of the special problems of the low latitudes. Rossby himself went on many arduous journeys to the remote fighting fronts, helping to solve operational weather problems. From 1950 until his death he organized and directed the institute of meteorology at the University of Stockholm and reorganized the Swedish government's meteorological research and services programs.

The eldest of five children of a Stockholm engineer, Rossby attended the University of Stockholm, receiving in 1925 the Filosofie Licentiat, a degree somewhat beyond the M.A., in mathematical physics. In 1926 he went to the United States on a fellowship of the American-Scandinavian Foundation for Research at the U.S. Weather Bureau in Washington, D.C. He joined the faculty of the Massachusetts Institute of Technology in 1928, there establishing America's first complete program of meteorological education. He remained at MIT until 1939, when he accepted a post as assistant chief of the Weather Bureau in charge of research and education. From 1941 to 1950 he was associated with the University of Chicago. Although he became an American citizen in 1938, he returned to Stockholm in 1950.

For background information *see* METEOROLOGY in the McGraw-Hill Encyclopedia of Science and Technology.   □

★ ROSSI, Bruno Benedetto

American physicist
Born Apr. 13, 1905, Venice, Italy

Rossi's LIFE history as a scientist closely paralleled the evolution of cosmic-ray physics. His interest in cosmic rays was aroused by the well-known experiment of W. W. Bothe and W. Kolhörster, which challenged the then accepted view identifying cosmic rays with high-energy photons and thus threw open the problem of the nature of cosmic rays. Among the results of his early experiments, two stand out.

The first was the discovery (1931) that cosmic-ray particles (athough electrically charged and, therefore, losing energy at a fast rate in their interactions with atoms) could traverse enormous thicknesses of matter—up to one meter of lead. This meant that their energies were orders of magnitude greater than had previously been assumed. The second was the discovery (1931) that individual cosmic rays, on colliding against atoms, often gave rise to unexpectedly large numbers of secondary particles. These interactions (later to be named "showers" by P. M. S. Blackett and G. Occhialini, who first succeeded in obtaining their picture by means of a cloud chamber) were further evidence of the enormous energies associated with cosmic rays. Moreover, Rossi's findings implied that the cosmic radiation directly observed may not be identical to the radiation entering the atmosphere from outer space but may consist largely of secondary particles produced by collisions of primary cosmic rays in the atmosphere.

As this viewpoint became gradually accepted, physicists found themselves confronted with two different, although interrelated, problems: The first concerned the nature of the primary cosmic radiation, the second concerned the nature of the local cosmic radiation as observed in the atmosphere. Rossi applied himself to both problems. At that time, scientists were divided among those who still thought that primary cosmic rays were photons (γ-rays) and those who thought that they were electrons. Starting from a mathematical theory developed by C. Størmer in his studies of northern lights, Rossi showed (1930) that, if primary cosmic rays were electrons (and, therefore, negatively charged particles), their deflection in the Earth's magnetic field should cause them to arrive more abundantly from the east than from the west. On the other hand, photons, having no electric charge, should not be affected in any way by the Earth's magnetic field. Rossi, working with one of his

students in the mountains of Eritrea, was among the first scientists to detect the "east-west effect," his observations following by a few months those of T. H. Johnson, and of L. W. Alvarez and A. H. Compton in Mexico. However, cosmic rays were found to come with greater intensity from the west rather than from the east. This observation proved that primary cosmic rays were positively charged and led eventually to their identification as protons and nuclei of the heavier elements. (It is because the secondary rays largely preserve the direction of the particles by which they are produced that the local radiation observed in those experiments exhibits the same east-west effect as the primary cosmic radiation.)

Between 1933 and 1943, the detailed study of the local cosmic radiation by an increasing number of scientists led to the discovery of the positive electrons, of the μ-mesons, and of the many peculiar properties of high-energy particles. Rossi's work and that of his collaborators laid the experimental basis for the theoretical interpretation of showers ("Rossi's shower curve") and established the distinction between "shower-producing rays" (later identified as electrons and photons) and "non–shower-producing rays" (later identified as μ-mesons). This work also produced the first unambiguous proof for the radioactive decay of the μ-meson and supplied the first accurate measurement of its mean life. In addition, it showed that the μ-meson mean life increased with increasing speed as predicted by Einstein's relativity theory, thus providing the first experimental test of this prediction.

After an intermission during the war, Rossi resumed his work in cosmic rays in 1946, directing his attention mainly to the nuclear interactions of cosmic rays and to the giant showers produced in the atmosphere by primary particles of highest energies. He and his collaborators were largely responsible for demonstrating the existence in the cosmic radiation of two different groups of particles: those that are and those that are not capable of producing nuclear interactions. They also contributed to the discovery of the neutral π-mesons, to the discovery of the new "strange" particles born in high-energy interactions, and to the study of their properties. Their work on air showers established, among other things, the existence of primary particles with energies up to the incredibly high value of 10^{20} electron volts, whose origin must be sought outside our galaxy.

Rossi's interest in cosmic rays led him naturally into space research as soon as the technical means for placing instruments outside the Earth's atmosphere became available. One of the most important results achieved by him and his coworkers in this field was the experimental proof for the existence of a "plasma wind" originating from the Sun and flowing past the Earth at a speed of several hundred kilometers per second. This work also established experimentally the existence of a "cavity" surrounding the Earth, from which the wind is excluded by the Earth's magnetic field. In addition, Rossi's name appears among those of the scientists who first detected the existence of x-ray sources outside the solar system.

The son of an electrical engineer, Rossi studied physics at the universities of Padova and Bologna, where he received a doctoral degree in 1927. From 1928 to 1932 he was an assistant at the University of Florence, and from 1932 to 1938 he held the chair of physics at the University of Padova. Dismissed by the Fascist regime because of the racial laws, he left Italy and, after short periods spent at the Institute for Theoretical Physics in Copenhagen, at the University of Manchester, and at the University of Chicago, he joined, in 1940, the staff of Cornell University. From 1943 to 1946 he worked at the Los Alamos Laboratory, where, among other things, he planned and directed an experiment for the measurement of the reaction time of the first atom bomb. In 1946 Rossi became a professor of physics at the Massachusetts Institute of Technology. Besides contributing to the advance of scientific knowledge, Rossi was also responsible for the development of new instrumental techniques, of which the best known, perhaps, is the so-called Rossi's coincidence circuit. He was elected to the National Academy of Sciences in 1950.

Rossi wrote *Rayons Cosmiques* (1935); *Ionization Chambers and Counters,* with H. Staub (1949), *High-energy Particles* (1952), *Optics* (1957), and *Cosmic Rays* (1964).

For background information *see* COSMIC RAYS in the McGraw-Hill Encyclopedia of Science and Technology.   □

★ ROUS, Francis Peyton

American physician and virologist
Born Oct. 5, 1879, Baltimore, Md., U.S.A.

IN 1910 Rous was studying tumor phenomena in rodents at the Rockefeller Institute when a breeder of chickens brought him a hen with a growth. He transplanted this to fowls of the same inbred stock, proved it a typical cancer by the accepted criteria, and tried to get a causative agent from it, no tumor having yielded one previously. From its tissue he procured an "agent" that passed through filters retaining tumor cells and on inoculation into normal chickens caused cancers resembling the original tumor. Tests showed the agent to be a virus. He then obtained other "spontaneous" tumors of differing sorts from a chicken market, and he got from each a virus producing tumors of precisely the kind yielding it.

These revolutionary findings were generally disbelieved: Either the growths were not tumors or else the agents were tumor cells that the filters had let through. The work had almost been forgotten when in 1925 W. E. Gye of London enthusiastically called attention to it, stimulating many British scientists to seek its meaning. The first chicken cancer and its virus are still widely studied.

Rous had gone on to reveal the exquisite host-within-a-host relationship existing between a chicken virus, the cells containing it, and the body supporting both. In corollary he devised a method, much utilized now, whereby the living cells of solid tissues can be obtained separately in suspension by exposure to trypsin. He also showed that phagocytic cells that contain bacteria or red corpuscles of a foreign species will, while living, protect these from destructive substances, including antisera, but not when they have died. Long afterward, by using trypsin, he proved that the same holds true of living cells harboring pathogenic viruses. The cells are a main obstacle to combatting these.

Rous and J. B. Murphy early found that grafts of the first chicken cancer grew rapidly in chick embryos, and that the virus flourished in them, causing cancers by itself. Nowadays tumors from many creatures, including man, are maintained for study in embryonated eggs, and these have been much used for the preparation of vaccines against viral diseases.

After fruitless efforts to get causative viruses from mammalian tumors, Rous turned in 1915 to blood problems. He and J. R. Turner sought to preserve human red cells for transfusion, a great need in World War I; by extensive trials they obtained a solution wherein refrigerated cells could be kept for weeks. Another young associate, O. H. Robertson, undertook to test such corpuscles in exsanguinated soldiers, and just behind the British front he built the first blood banks ever made and found the kept cells to be life-saving. After the war transfusions were still infrequent, and not until World War II did blood banks come into their own, and the R-T solution as well. Immense quantities were used in England during the blitz, and it has since been the mainstay of blood banks, except where liquid nitrogen is available to freeze blood.

As a physiological pathologist Rous next studied the events when worn-out red cells are destroyed. He and P. D. McMaster examined the bile in this relation and found a way to intubate dogs' bile ducts, whereby sterile samples of this fluid could be collected over many months. Thus they discovered that the dog's gall bladder concentrates it more than 10 times. This led a surgeon, Evarts Graham, to test for the presence of gallstones by injecting patients intravenously with a harmless dye that became so concentrated in the gall bladder as to cast an x-ray shadow outlining the stones. This is still current surgical practice.

Incidentally Rous showed that the size of the normal liver depends directly on how much it has to do. When a healthy rat is fasted the liver soon becomes much smaller, but if most of it has just been cut away the remainder hypertrophies despite the fasting and soon reaches the size ordinarily attained by atrophy. Also by injecting dyes that diffuse slowly from blood vessels he disclosed the existence of a gradient of vascular permeability in mammals, this being greatest where the blood reaches the tiny venules. Utilizing in the same way other harmless dyes that swiftly stain the entire body of living mice, and roughly indicate acidity or alkalinity by their hue, he found that the reaction of the matrix tissues—cartilage, tendons, bones, aorta, and heart valves—corresponds with that of the blood, whereas the parenchymal tissues maintain their own individual reactions. Any marked functional reduction of the circulation brings on a generalized "outlying acidosis" of the superficial tissues, while the reaction of the blood remains unaltered.

In 1933 Richard Shope of the Rockefeller Institute procured a causative virus from the giant warts of wild "cottontail" rabbits that produced even more vigorous growths in domestic ones. These looked like tumors, and after describing them and the virus, Shope offered this to Rous. Thus he generously gave a friend far more than either knew.

Together with J. W. Beard and J. G. Kidd, Rous showed the warts to be true tumors, benign epidermal papillomas resembling those induced by tarring rabbit skin yet with distinctive morphological traits; and, closely studying their course, he saw cancers originate from their cells, as often happens in tar papillomas and sometimes in benign human tumors. After transfer to newborn rabbits the cancers succeeded in adults, and many have been thus maintained, but the only virus they have yielded is Shope's papilloma virus, and not always that. One notably malignant cancer has now been propagated for 27 years and during the last 19 has yielded not even an immunological trace of the virus. This had merely induced the cancer.

Concurrent tests showed the Shope virus to be capable of infecting tumors actuated in ways unknown, namely, the papillomas and cancers induced by tar or certain polycyclic hydrocarbons. When the cancers were "anaplastic," consisting of cells so degraded as to be incapable of differentiation, the sole effect of the virus was to hasten their growth markedly, whereas when acting on the papillomas it not only had this effect but changed them into mongrel neoplasms consisting of cells expressive of the combined formative influences of their unknown cause and the virus. This latter had acted not only as a synergist but as an alterative of morphology. On further test the virus proved capable of acting in concert with chemical agents to induce cancerous changes in normal epidermal cells. Here were several new roles for a neoplastic virus.

All along Rous had studied tumor phenomena intensively. He showed that the influences changing normal cells into tumor cells differ from those encouraging their growth, and he coined for them the now-familiar terms "initiators" and "promoters." Certain tumor viruses are of the one sort or the other, in distinction from the few capable of actuating the growths they induce. Also he showed that the broadcast application of chemical carcinogens to a multitude of normal cells causes a vastly greater number to become tumor cells than ever manifest themselves ordinarily. Indeed many are so poorly equipped as to multiply only on persistent stimulation, and some of the resulting growths are unique in character.

Rous received his B.A. (1900) and M.D. (1905) at the Johns Hopkins University. After serving as instructor in pathology at the University of Michigan from 1906 to 1908, he joined the staff of the Rockefeller Institute for Medical Research in New York, becoming a member in pathology and bacteriology in 1920. He became a member emeritus in 1945 but continued to work actively. For his contributions to viral oncology, Rous received many honors, including the 1956 Kovalenko Medal of the National Academy of Sciences, the 1958 Lasker Award of the American Public Health Association, and the 1966 National Medal of Science. He was elected to the National Academy of Sciences in 1927.

For background information *see* ONCOLOGY in the McGraw-Hill Encyclopedia of Science and Technology.   □

☆ RUBEY, William Walden

American geologist
Born Dec. 19, 1898, Moberly, Mo., U.S.A.

IN A time of ever-increasing specialization in the Earth sciences, Rubey remained a geological generalist. His publications that received most attention dealt with aspects of the origin of sedimentary rocks, the mechanics of sediment transportation by streams, the tectonic history of folded mountain ranges, and a geochemical and petrological approach to the origin of continents and oceans.

In attempting to explain the origin of certain phosphate rock deposits, Rubey was faced with the unanswered question as to how sea water may have varied in composition throughout geologic time. Pursuit of supporting data led him to the ultimate question as to the origin of the Earth's waters as well as other volatile constituents of the Earth's atmosphere. His conclusions supported the hypothesis that these volatiles—including water—had accumulated gradually by escape from within the Earth itself.

Reasoning that if the Earth had originated as a molten mass all volatiles of similar molecular weight would have behaved similarly, Rubey noted that elements such as neon, argon, krypton, and xenon are much less abundant in the Earth's atmosphere than in the atmospheres of certain stars. However, H_2O, CO_2, Cl, N, and S are in great excess in the Earth's atmosphere. Rubey questioned why these volatiles would not all have been lost by the Earth in similar proportions during its evolution.

Arguing that extreme changes in quantity of the Earth's excess volatiles through time would be evidenced in the geologic record, and noting that such evidence was lacking, Rubey postulated a slow accumulation of these volatiles throughout geologic history. He believed that the excess volatile constituents had derived from intrusive magmatic sources and escaped to the surface through thermal springs. Volcanism and surface flows of lava, he indicated, were only sources of secondary importance. A continuous magmatic source is necessary through time in order to support this hypothesis, and Rubey favored a selective fusion of subcrustal rock matter.

Rubey's broad interests and concern for great detail as well as his habit of bringing together supporting data from other sciences did much to stress the importance of interdisciplinary study in geology. Although primarily a field geologist, his quest for the total picture led him into many related areas. Rubey's work was instrumental in guiding geology from a descriptive science to one in which quantitative aspects gained increasing significance and importance. For example, Rubey was a pioneer in the application of the principles of hydrodynamics to studies of contemporary sedimentary processes to gain greater understanding and insight into the evolution of sedimentary rocks.

Rubey was born in a small town in the Middle West, where he early developed a range of naturalist interests that continued active through later years. As an undergraduate at the University of Missouri, he majored in geology for his A.B. in 1920. He joined the staff of the U.S. Geological Survey later that year and undertook part-time graduate study at the Johns Hopkins University. He was an instructor in geology at Yale University from 1922 to 1924 and then returned to the Geological Survey. During the next 17 years he did geologic field work in areas of the Middle West, the Southwest, the northern Great Plains, and particularly the northern Rocky Mountains. In 1942 to 1945 he supervised surveys for vanadium and uranium ores in the West and elsewhere and served part-time as chairman of the Division of Geology and Geography of the National Research Council. After World War II he continued for several years in administrative work at the Geological Survey and as chairman of the National Research Council. In 1954 he returned to full-time geologic research. In 1960 Rubey was appointed a member of the National Science Board by President Dwight Eisenhower. He also joined the faculty of the University of California at Los Angeles. He was awarded the Penrose Medal of the Geological Society of America in 1963 and the National Medal of Science in 1966. He was elected to the National Academy of Sciences in 1945.

For background information *see* EARTH in the McGraw-Hill Encyclopedia of Science and Technology.   □

S

★★

(continued)

☆ **SABIN, Albert Bruce**
American physician and virologist
Born Aug. 26, 1906, Bialystok, Poland

D URING HIS long and fruitful career, Sabin discovered and investigated B virus, which, although indigenous to monkeys, causes a fatal disease in humans; made many significant researches into the nature of encephalitis and its causative viruses; isolated and elucidated the nature of sandfly fever viruses; isolated and developed a protective vaccine for dengue fever viruses; and made studies on ECHO viruses and their role in human disease. The work for which he became best known, however, were his studies on the nature, mode of transmission, and epidemiology of human poliomyelitis, and his development of an attenuated, orally administered polio virus vaccine. For his many contributions to virology and the study of bacterial and parasitic human disease, Sabin received numerous honors, among them the Bruce Memorial Award of the American College of Physicians in 1961, the Feltrinelli Prize of the Accademia dei Lincei of Rome in 1964, and the Lasker Clinical Science Award in 1965.

Sabin first began his human poliomyelitis research in 1931, at New York University, and continued his studies in 1936 at the Rockefeller Institute for Medical Research, New York. One of his early achievements was the first demonstration of the growth of poliovirus in human nervous tissue outside the body. His experiments on monkeys provided methods by which the portal of entry of the virus in human beings could be studied. His observations refuted the then current concept that the poliovirus entered the human body through the nose; in 1941 he established that human poliomyelitis is primarily an infection of the alimentary tract.

Sabin's poliomyelitis researches were inter-rupted during World War II and for several years thereafter, while he investigated the American and Japanese types of insect-borne encephalitis, sandfly fever, and dengue.

In 1951 he resumed his poliovirus studies, contributing knowledge about their nature and behavior that was fundamental in the development of oral vaccines for the prevention of the disease. The original studies on the selection of the optimum attenuated poliovirus strains and elucidation of their mode of action were carried out between 1954 and 1957 on human volunteers at the Federal Reformatory in Chillicothe, Ohio. During 1957–58 a series of cooperative studies with investigators in the United States, Mexico, Holland, and the Soviet Union—on increasingly large numbers of human beings—set the stage for the first field trials, performed in 1958 on hundreds of thousands of children in Malaya and Czechoslovakia. These preliminary trials led to major field trials, early in 1959, on more than 6×10^6 adults and children in the Soviet Union and on about 200,000 children in Mexico. As a result of these successful tests, the Sabin oral polio vaccine was accepted for use by the Soviet government in late 1959. In August, 1961, it was approved for use in the United States, but more than a year passed before it was manufactured in the United States and licensed for general distribution.

Sabin's researches embraced many areas other than the study of human poliomyelitis. From 1927 to 1931 he investigated pneumococcus infection in experimental animals and human beings. In 1932 he isolated the B virus from a colleague who died after being bitten by a monkey and later, in 1934, demonstrated that the natural habitat of the B virus is in the monkey, and that the virus is closely related to the human herpes simplex virus.

Sabin later studied the mechanism of immunity to viruses, and from 1935 to 1939 carried out basic studies on the behavior of viruses affecting the nervous system, on toxoplasmosis, and on experimental arthritis produced by the filtrable microorganisms of the pleuropneumonia group. Sabin's subsequent discovery of the hemagglutinating properties of the insect-borne viruses became very useful for the laboratory diagnosis of encephalitis and of diseases like dengue and yellow fever. His studies on sandfly fever and dengue established the existence of multiple antigenic types of these viruses and led to the development of attenuated live-virus vaccines.

Sabin's polio virus studies led indirectly to his discovery of many new viruses in the human alimentary tract, viruses later implicated as causative agents of such human diseases as aseptic meningitis, rare types of paralysis and encephalitis, and infantile diarrhea. In 1961

Sabin began studying the role of viruses in cancer, searching especially for indications of latent virus activity in experimentally produced animal cancers, which might provide new approaches to determining the possible role of viruses in human cancer.

After emigrating from Russian Poland to the United States, Sabin studied at New York Univeristy, from which he received his M.D. degree in 1931. From 1932 to 1933 he trained in pathology, surgery, and internal medicine at Bellevue Hospital, New York, and during 1934 he did research at the Lister Institute of Preventive Medicine, London. In 1935 he joined the scientific staff of the Rockefeller Institute for Medical Research, serving as assistant until 1937 and as associate from 1937 to 1939. In 1939 he was appointed associate professor of pediatrics at the University of Cincinnati College of Medicine and chief of the division of infectious diseases at the Children's Hospital Research Foundation there. In 1946 he became professor of research pediatrics and in 1960 was named Distinguished Service Professor of Research Pediatrics. He was elected to the National Academy of Sciences in 1951.

For background information *see* POLIOMYELITIS in the McGraw-Hill Encyclopedia of Science and Technology. □

★ **SALISBURY, Sir Edward (James)**
British botanist
Born Apr. 16, 1886, Harpenden, Hertfordshire, England

S ALISBURY'S INVESTIGATIONS concerned the ecology of British vegetation, with special emphasis on the influence of soil conditions and the biological adaptations of individual species to their environments. For his pioneering work on the reproductive capacity of British species

he received in 1945 the Royal Medal of the Royal Society of London. These studies revealed the importance of seed size in relation to habitat conditions, of seed output as a factor determining frequency rather than a mere insurance against elimination, and of germination behavior as a safeguard to survival.

Salisbury recognized the relation between spatial distribution and temporal sequence often presented by sand-dune and shingle-beach systems as peculiarly favorable for the study of prolonged successional changes. He studied the sequence in dunes from an initially alkaline and highly mobile substrate of low water-retaining capacity occupied by a small number of species shown to exhibit marked biological specialization. These pioneers conferred a diminishing instability and, by their yield of humus, an increasing water retention. Such ameliorating physical conditions were shown to support a continually augmented flora of changing biological aspect until, with the advent of woody perennials, a more restrictive environment is again established with species once more reduced to a tolerant minority. Earlier studies on woodland biology had similarly demonstrated the selective influence of soil conditions and also of artifically induced changes in the light climate.

As a young man Salisbury often found himself addressing well-educated audiences whose horticultural and floristic interests had elicited an unsatisfied curiosity. This caused him to write *The Living Garden* (1935), which presented, for the horticulturist, the scientific background then available. The unprecedented success of this work both in England and abroad and the award of the Veitchian Gold Medal by the Royal Horticultural Society indicated that a real need had been provided for.

At this period Salisbury occupied the Quain Chair of Botany at University College, London. With the advent of World War II, he was drawn into agricultural administration as a member of the Agricultural Research Council and later as chairman of the joint committee of that body and the Agricultural Improvement Council. In 1943 he became director of the Royal Botanic Gardens at Kew, a post he held for thirteen years. He was responsible for the rehabilitation of the gardens after the wartime damage and for considerable expansion of the scientific staff. From 1945 to 1955 he was Biological Secretary of the Royal Society.

Subsequent to his retirement, Salisbury continued his researches on reproduction, especially of those plants which, because of their successful attributes, are termed weeds. Such studies revealed the importance, for species of habitats only intermittently available, of seed outputs large in relation to the size of the species and of germination behavior that is quasi-simultaneous. To Salisbury, the evidence suggested that from the beginnings of man's cultivation of plants he has exercised an unconscious selection of those strains of annual species characterized by a high productivity of seed and marked intermittence of their germination, in contrast to the quasi-simultaneous germination of the more characteristic species of forest clearings and exposed mud.

Salisbury wrote *The East Anglian Flora* (1933), *The Living Garden* (1935), *The Reproductive Capacity of Plants* (1942), *Downs and Dunes* (1952), and *Weeds and Aliens* (1961).

For background information *see* SEED (BOTANY) in the McGraw-Hill Encyclopedia of Science and Technology.   □

★ SALK, Jonas Edward

American physician
Born Oct. 28, 1914, New York, N.Y., U.S.A.

USING EXISTING concepts and techniques of immunology and virology, which he developed further in the course of his work, Salk succeeded in making a killed-virus vaccine that proved to be effective in preventing poliomyelitis. For his efforts, which helped greatly in virtually eliminating polio as a public health threat, Salk was awarded the 1956 Lasker Award of the American Public Health Association and the 1958 Bruce Memorial Award of the American College of Physicians.

Salk's work in virology and immunology was begun in 1938 when, as a senior medical student at New York University, he came into contact with Thomas Francis, Jr., who was conducting a study on methods of killing influenza virus without destroying the virus's capacity to stimulate the production of antibodies. Salk worked with Francis for several months after receiving his medical degree in 1939, then began a 2-year internship. In 1941, Francis became chairman of the department of epidemiology at the University of Michigan; the following year Salk obtained a National Research Council fellowship financed by the National Foundation for Infantile Paralysis and joined Francis's group, which was concerned with the problem of immunization against influenza. In 1943, Francis and Salk field-tested a vaccine effective against influenza A and influenza B as part of a program of the influenza commission of the board for the control of epidemic diseases in the armed forces.

In 1947, Salk went to the University of Pittsburgh School of Medicine to serve as head of the Virus Research Laboratory. There he continued his work on influenza and became involved in studies on polio as well. Asked to participate in a program conducted at four universities to sort and classify into types the various strains of polio virus, Salk concluded this phase of his work in 1951, confirming earlier findings that there were, indeed, only three types of polio virus.

Salk then turned to the actual development of a polio vaccine. Using a strain of each type (I, II, and III) of polio virus, grown in cultures of monkey kidney tissue and killed with formaldehyde, he showed that the vaccine was safe (that is, that it no longer contained live virus) and that it was capable of inducing antibody formation in monkeys. He was then faced with the problem of determining its effects in the human body. In 1952, he tested a type I vaccine on a group of children who had had polio (and would therefore have polio virus antibodies in their blood streams) and found that after inoculation their antibody levels rose significantly. The vaccine tests were then successfully extended to persons who had never had polio, this time using a triple vaccine containing killed virus of all three types.

Salk reported his encouraging findings in the *Journal of the American Medical Association* early in 1953. In May of that year the possibility of a mass field trial of the vaccine was suggested by the National Foundation for Infantile Paralysis, and plans were begun. On Apr. 26, 1954, mass vaccination was begun for a field trial that was conducted and evaluated by Thomas Francis, Jr., of the University of Michigan. When this study was completed, 422,743 children between 6 and 9 years of age had each received three spaced doses of the vaccine. For comparison, a similarly large group had been given placebo inoculations, and another large group was observed but received no injections. By the end of 1954, the results of the trial indicated that the vaccine was safe and effective in reducing the incidence of polio. On Apr. 12, 1955, after careful evaluation of all data, the vaccine was officially announced to be safe, effective, and potent. But only a few weeks later a case of paralytic polio possibly attributable to the vaccine was diagnosed. When several similar cases were discovered and investigated, all the affected children were found to have received vaccine made by a single firm. On May 7, 1955, polio vaccination was temporarily halted by the Surgeon General. Following extensive investigation, it was found that faulty batches of virus culture (containing particles that protected the live virus from the action of formaldehyde) had been used in the manufacture of the vaccine. After steps were taken to see that such a potentially disastrous error would not be repeated, the Salk vaccine was again released for use.

By the summer of 1961 there was a reduction by approximately 96% in the amount of polio in the United States as a whole, as compared to the 5-year period before introduction of vaccination, even though only about 50% of the population had been vaccinated. While it is true that vaccine had been administered to the most susceptible younger age groups, it was found nevertheless that a greater reduction in the amount of polio occurred than could be explained on the basis of the number of persons vaccinated. This observation suggested that the amount of virus in circulation and available for dissemination of disease was reduced by the administration of the killed-virus vaccine, as evidenced by the lower-than-expected amount of polio in the unvaccinated segment of the population at all age levels. Thus polio immunization with a killed-virus vaccine had induced what is known as a "herd effect" in a manner similar to the observed effect in immunization against diphtheria and influenza, for example. It was also found that immunity induced by the killed-virus vaccine was of relatively long duration. Salk developed these observations into a theory of the way in which a killed-virus vaccine works in preventing polio in the population as well as in the individual. The essence of his view was that antibody in the serum, or a prompt antibody response on re-infection, blocks access of virus from the blood stream to the spinal cord and brain and also to the throat. He believed that the virus from the throat is an important mode of spread, especially in societies with good hygienic conditions, while under circumstances of poor hygiene virus is as readily spread by fecal contamination.

The son of a New York garment worker, Salk received his B.S. in 1934 from the City College of New York and his M.D. from New York University in 1939. He was a National Research Council fellow (1942–44), research associate in epidemiology (1944–46), and assistant professor of epidemiology (1946–47) at the University of Michigan's School of Public Health. In 1947 he became associate professor of bacteriology and head of the Virus Research Laboratory at the University of Pittsburgh's School of Medicine. He was promoted to research professor of bacteriology in 1949, and later was named professor of preventive medicine (1954) and then professor of experimental medicine (1957). In 1963, he became director and fellow of the Salk Institute for Biological Studies at San Diego, Calif.

For background information *see* POLIOMYE-LITIS in the McGraw-Hill Encyclopedia of Science and Technology.   □

★ SANDER, Bruno Hermann Max
Austrian geologist
Born Feb. 23, 1884, Innsbruck, Austria

IN 1909 Sander began to develop a purely descriptive terminology for geologic structures to replace the mainly genetic terminology then in use. This made possible a new, unprejudiced discussion of the physical and geological conditions for the genesis of geologic structures. His terminology, which was applied first in petrology, also led to a critical analysis of tectonics.

Sander's investigation and statistical characterization of morphological anisotropy from grain fabric to profile provided the basis for the pointing out and elucidation of anisotropic stress-strain behavior. Moreover, it led to the distinguishing and delineating of domains of different dimensions and their mutual relationships. Sander chose the name *Gefügekunde* ("structural science") for the new terminology because the many details it brought out became organized into a delineated field of research with its own principles and general conclusions—a development still perceptible today.

Sander developed the *Gefügekunde* over many years in the course of investigations as a mapping geologist and a microscopist. He applied it first to deformed geologic structures and later to other fields of geology. Many thousands of measurements on rock patterns revealed the symmetries of the patterns. From these patterns Sander evolved inductively, among other general symmetry considerations, the idea of a worldwide occurrence of mapped symmetries (*Abbildungssymmetrien*). Later this was realized to be the dominant principle of formation for the Earth and other analogous celestial bodies, pertinent to both nonliving and living things. The *Gefügekunde* was brought into contact with material-testing and technological geology as well as with the behavior of nongeological structures. Also generally pertinent was the principle (formulated in 1915) of orientation, under mechanical domain deformation, of heterometric or anisotropic components. Hence the *Gefügekunde* was relevant for minerals and metals. In tectonics a considerably enriched description of tectonic styles was obtained by means of a unique characterization of linear elements and numerous measurements in the field. The wide occurrence of tectonics with steep B-axes expressed in grain fabric or folds was clearly evidenced. Further results of general interest concerned the correlation between grain fabric and tectonics, analysis of axes distribution (AVA) in mapping and microscopic analysis, x-ray analysis of rock patterns, temporal relationship between mechanical deformation and crystallization, a unique determination of tectonic kinematics through grain pattern analysis, the relationship between spatially rhythmic sediments and time rhythms, and so on.

The son of a public prosecutor, Sander received his Ph.D. in 1907 at the University of Innsbruck. Thereafter he was assistant in geology at the Technische Hochschule, Vienna (1908) and the University of Innsbruck (1909), docent in geology at Innsbruck (1912–13) and Vienna (1914–22), and mapping geologist with the Geologische Reichsanstalt, Vienna (1912–22). He worked as a mining geologist in Bulgaria (1917) and Turkey (1918). From 1925 to 1956 he was professor of mineralogy and petrography at the University of Innsbruck, becoming professor emeritus in 1956. In 1957 he was awarded the Penrose Medal of the Geological Society of America.

Sander wrote *Gefügekunde der Gesteine* (1930) and *Einführung in die Gefügekunde der Geologischen Korper* (2 vols., 1948–50).

For background information *see* TECTONIC PATTERNS in the McGraw-Hill Encyclopedia of Science and Technology.   □

☆ **SANGER, Frederick**
English chemist
Born Aug. 13, 1918, Rendcombe, Gloucestershire, England

FOLLOWING THE experimental demonstrations by Emil Fischer and others that all proteins were complex molecules built up from amino acids, Sanger determined the exact order of the amino acids in insulin. Proteins—the chemical substances encompassing enzymes, viruses, antibodies, toxins, and some hormones such as insulin—contain approximately the same 20 amino acids. Therefore a knowledge of their arrangement is indispensable for an understanding of a protein's activity in a life process. Sanger was the first to establish the amino-acid sequence for a protein, and for this achievement he received the 1958 Nobel Prize in chemistry.

By 1943 it was known that the amino acids were bound together by peptide bonds, involving the α-amino groups and the α-carboxyl groups, into polypeptide chains with some cross linking between the chains and between parts of the same chain. These bonds could be cleaved by the action of acids or enzymes to yield peptide fragments of various smaller sizes. If the degradation were carried out under suitable conditions, the protein could be cleaved completely into its constituent amino acids. About this time A. H. Gordon, A. J. P. Martin, and R. L. M. Synge developed a method of separating complex mixtures of amino acids and peptides by silica-gel chromatography. Subsequently, the more satisfactory paper chromatography was used. In 1945 Sanger introduced a reagent for identifying the free α-amino group (N-terminal group) of a peptide chain. This reagent, 2,4 dinitrofluorobenzene (DNFB), formed bonds with the N-terminal group to give an identifiable derivative.

Sanger reasoned that if the molecule were fragmented some of the resulting peptides would contain parts of the same amino-acid sequences. Sanger's approach may be illustrated with the hypothetical separation and identification of the four dipeptides, glycine-glutamine, glutamine-arginine, arginine-arginine, and arginine-cystine. A first guess at their sequence in the original molecule would be glycine-glutamine-arginine-arginine-cystine.

Sanger and his associates in the department of biochemistry, Cambridge University, worked on this problem from 1943 until 1955. They began by reacting the entire molecule of insulin with DNFB reagent. In this way they saw that two N-terminal groups were present and that the best molecule weight for insulin was 6,000. The two end groups indicated that insulin consisted of two chains of 20 and 30 amino acid residues, respectively. The chains were joined together by disulfide bridges. They next attempted to separate the chains by splitting the disulfide bridges by oxidation with performic acid. Work proceeded on the larger chain first, and by 1950 Sanger was able to deduce the whole of the sequence. The shorter chain was more difficult because there were fewer amino acids that occurred only once in the molecule. It was not possible to deduce the complete sequence of either chain simply from the small peptides produced by acid digestion because of two problems: First, the presence of the amino acids tyrosine and leucine resulted in fragments that were technically difficult to separate. Their presence gave rise to a mixture of peptides that moved fast on paper chromatograms and were not well resolved. The second problem was posed by the unstable bonds of the amino groups of serine and threonine during acid hydrolysis. It was never possible to find these groups intact within a peptide fragment and therefore to know the preceding residues. Appropriate proteolytic enzymes for breaking the peptide bonds were used successfully and the structure of the shorter chain was found.

The only remaining difficulty was to find how the disulfide bridges joined the two chains. It was necessary to isolate, from unoxidized insulin, peptide fragments with intact bridges. When oxidized, these would give smaller peptides that could be recognized, since they would be the same as those found in the hydrolysis of the oxidized molecule. Work continued until the positions of the three disulfide links were found and hence the complete structure of insulin was known.

The structure revealed that each position in the two bound chains was occupied by one specific amino-acid residue. Upon this unique structure must depend the important physiological action of the hormone. Sanger proceeded, by the same methods, to determine the structure of insulin from four species other than the original insulin from cattle. All insulins show the same activity and so, if their molecular structures were compared, a particular difference would indicate that this section of the molecule was not important for physiological activity. Differences were found within the three amino acids contained within the disulfide ring of the smaller chain for the species cattle, pig, sheep, and whale. It does not follow that all of the rest of the molecule is essential. Sanger indicated that his type of analysis of protein structure and activity could lead to similar success with other proteins.

A doctor's son, Sanger was educated at St. John's College, Cambridge, where he majored in natural sciences and received a B.A. in 1939. He obtained a Ph.D. in 1943 after investigating the metabolism of the amino acid lysine. From 1944 until 1951 he was a fellow of the Medical Research Council, Cambridge. In 1951 he joined the council's staff, becoming head of the Division of Protein Chemistry in the M.R.C. Laboratory for Molecular Biology at Cambridge. He was elected a fellow of the Royal Society in 1954.

For background information *see* INSULIN in the McGraw-Hill Encyclopedia of Science and Technology.   □

★ **SAX, Karl**
American biologist
Born Nov. 2, 1892, Spokane, Wash., U.S.A.

S AX'S FIELDS of interest covered a wide range—cytology, genetics, horticulture, radiation biology, and demography. While an undergraduate at Washington State College he became interested in wheat breeding and later made a cytogenetic study of the origin and relationships of the species of wheat. He found that the bread-wheat species, which have 21 pairs of chromosomes, were derived from ancestral forms with 7 pairs of chromosomes. Hybridization between the ancestral species was followed by chromosome doubling to produce the 14-chromosome species. This tetraploid species again became hybridized with still another 7-chromosome species, followed by chromosome doubling, to give rise to the 21-chromosome bread wheats. In recent years plant breeders in the United States and Japan have synthesized the bread-wheat types by crossing the 14- and 7-chromosome species, followed by artificial chromosome doubling.

Sax's major contribution to science was not initiated as a preconceived project but was based upon several fortuitous events. Edgar Anderson had assembled at the Bussey Institution greenhouse at Harvard University a collection of *Tradescantia* species, and Sax was making a routine survey of the chromosome numbers in relation to a joint cytotaxonomic survey of the genus. The *Tradescantia* microspores proved to be ideal material for experimental work in cytology, and when one of E. M. East's postdoctoral students wanted to do some work in experimental cytology Sax suggested that he study the effect of x-rays on *Tradescantia* chromosomes. This project led Sax and many of his graduate students to continue work on radiation cytology.

It was found that the types and frequencies of induced chromosome aberrations varied at different stages in the mitotic cycle and that aberrations could be induced by either one of two "hits." The single-hit aberrations were linearly related to dosage, while the two-hit aberrations tended to increase as the square of the dosage. This relationship led Lea to formulate his "target theory" regarding the effects of ionizing radiation. This early work in radiation cytology was a major factor in Sax's election as a member of the National Academy of Sciences in 1941.

Sax made both theoretical and practical contributions to horticulture. As a staff member of the Arnold Arboretum at Harvard, he produced a number of new ornamental trees and shrubs, which are now available from commercial nurserymen. These include the Hally Jolivette (Mrs. Karl Sax) ornamental cherry, the Beatrix Farrand forsythia, the Merrill magnolia, and the Henrietta Crosby and the Blanche Ames ornamental apples. He also developed a method for dwarfing peach and plum trees that is used by commercial nurserymen.

Sax obtained his B.S. in agriculture at Washington State College in 1916. His graduate work (interrupted by military service in 1918–19) was done at the Bussey Institute of Harvard University, where he obtained his Sc.D. degree in 1922. He was a research biologist at the Maine Agricultural Experiment Station from 1920 to 1928 and a member of the Arnold Arboretum staff

from 1928 to 1959. From 1936 to 1959 he was also professor of botany at Harvard University, and from 1947 to 1954 the director of the Arnold Arboretum.

Sax wrote *Standing Room Only* (1955).

For background information *see* RADIATION CYTOLOGY in the McGraw-Hill Encyclopedia of Science and Technology.   □

★ SCATCHARD, George
American chemist
Born Mar. 19, 1892, Oneonta, N.Y., U.S.A.

SCATCHARD DEVOTED most of his research to the physical chemistry of solutions. The importance and interest of this field lie in the fact that nearly every chemical reaction occurs in solution. Scatchard's chief unifying idea was that the resemblances between solutions are more important than the differences. For example, the differences between gaseous, liquid, and crystalline solutions are largely in the different techniques required for their study. The simplest solutions contain only nonpolar components. The addition of a polar, particularly a hydrogen-bonding, nonelectrolyte adds complications, and the addition of an electrolyte adds even more, but none of the interactions of the simpler systems is lost.

Scatchard always tried to keep his descriptions general, as free as possible from assumptions and restrictions to low concentrations or to two component systems. He recognized early that graphical methods were useless for polycomponent systems and that analytical expressions had great advantages for binary systems also.

For his achievements in the physical chemistry of solutions, Scatchard received the American Chemical Society's T. W. Richards Medal in 1954.

Scatchard's first independent papers showed that the vapor pressure of water and the rate of inversion of sucrose by acid in concentrated sucrose solutions can be explained approximately by using mole fractions instead of volume concentrations; they showed that the residual effects are related, and they tried to explain these effects. These papers antedated by a year J. N. Brønsted's publication of his theories of the "critical complex" (now more often called the "activated complex") in reaction rates and of "specific ion interaction," and by 2 years the papers of P. J. W. Debye and E. Hückel on the theory of electrolyte interaction. These theories so revolutionized and speeded up the study of electrolyte solutions that Scatchard spent the next decade largely in confirming, applying, and extending them.

In 1931 Scatchard showed that the total free energy of mixing and the excess free energy of solutions have many advantages over the partial molar free energies and the activity coefficients of the components. This concept was quickly accepted by the workers with nonelectrolytes but is still not appreciated by many students of electrolyte solutions. He also showed that for many cases the volume fraction is a better unit than the mole fraction and that the excess free energy of binary mixtures with nonpolar components may be calculated approximately from the square of the difference in the square roots of the "cohesive energy densities" of the components. (The cohesive energy density is minus the difference between the energy of unit volume and of the same amount of the substance as a perfect gas at the same temperature. Many of these square roots were tabulated by J. H. Hildebrand and R. L. Scott as "solubility parameters.") He immediately applied the relevant parts of these concepts to electrolyte solutions.

A decade of consolidation, both theoretical and experimental, was followed by a swing toward protein and other colloidal systems, with the thesis that the important characteristic of colloids is that more things can happen many more times on a macromolecule than on a small one. A huge macromolecule, like a membrane or an ion exchange bead, may enmesh many thousand small molecules. Such solutions and membranes are the important materials of living beings.

Scatchard received his early education in the Oneonta State Normal School. He received his A.B. from Amherst College in 1913 and his Ph.D. in organic chemistry from Columbia University in 1917. From 1917 to 1919 he was a lieutenant in the Sanitary Corps, U.S. Army, assigned to work on war gases with Victor Grignard in the laboratory of Georges Urbain at the Sorbonne. He was associate professor of chemistry at Amherst College from 1919 to 1923. From 1923 to 1957 he progressed from National Research fellow to emeritus professor of phys-

ical chemistry at the Massachusetts Institute of Technology. During World War II he was "scientific advisor" to Edwin J. Cohn on the fractionation of plasma proteins and to Harold C. Urey on the fractionation of isotopes of hydrogen and of uranium. In 1946 he was director of the Scientific Research Branch, Office of Military Government, and scientific advisor to General Lucius D. Clay. He was elected to the National Academy of Sciences in 1946.

For background information *see* PHYSICAL CHEMISTRY in the McGraw-Hill Encyclopedia of Science and Technology.   □

★ SCHAEFER, Vincent Joseph
American meteorologist and science consultant
Born July 4, 1906, Schenectady, N.Y., U.S.A.

O N A hot humid afternoon during July, 1946, in a desperate attempt to produce colder air in his small experimental cold chamber at the General Electric Research Laboratory in Schenectady, Schaefer placed a block of dry ice on the bottom of the chamber and suddenly discovered the effect he had been seeking for several years. By this serendipitous event he initiated the science of experimental meteorology and weather control.

A study of precipitation static, which started in 1943 at the summit of Mt. Washington, led Schaefer to further field and laboratory research in atmospheric electricity and the related problems of aircraft icing. This latter phenomenon, which occurs when aircraft fly through supercooled clouds, was then a very serious problem related to the flight safety of military aircraft. The studies at Mt. Washington established the relationship of cloud droplet sizes to collection efficiency and the role played by ice nuclei at temperatures colder than 0°C. Observations showed that ice formation on airplanes ended when sufficient numbers of ice particles were in the air to eliminate the supercooled water phase.

Early in 1945, Schaefer started his search for a practical way to produce large numbers of ice nuclei, the search that ended in his laboratory cold chamber on that hot afternoon.

As soon as Schaefer saw the dense cloud of ice crystals that formed instantly as he lowered the dry ice into the cloud in the chamber, he quickly removed it, formed a new supercooled cloud, and excitedly put in a smaller piece of dry ice. Obtaining the same spectacular effect, he quickly determined that only a few tiny fragments, produced by scratching the surface of a chunk of dry ice with a nail, were needed to completely transform a water droplet cloud into a dense mass of ice crystals.

This discovery was the culmination of a series of events that began when Schaefer, as a youngster, wondered as he watched fingers of ragged cloud emerging from a wet forested mountainside. Ten years later he observed the movements of cirrus clouds speeding across the skies of central New York. He was then acting as field assistant to the state archeologist of New York, making an archeological survey of one of the counties of the Finger Lakes region. This experience, while in his teens, led Schaefer to want to become a scientist. When plans to attend college had to be canceled due to sickness in his family, he became a machinist's apprentice and managed to obtain an assignment in the G. E. Research Laboratory. There he became laboratory assistant and instrument maker with Irving Langmuir. In a few years, Schaefer was appointed a research associate in the laboratory, working with Langmuir on studies of surface chemistry from 1931 to 1940. With the threat of World War II, Langmuir became involved in defense preparations. This led to studies of gas mask filters, the production of artificial fogs on a massive scale, submarine detection, and other activities. All of these basic and applied studies involved some relationship to the atmosphere, so that by late 1945 Schaefer was engaged almost full-time in atmospheric research.

A discovery by Schaefer in 1940 of a very simple method of replicating snow crystals played an important role in his subsequent work in the atmospheric sciences. Interestingly, an outgrowth of the replica work led to the first practical method for aluminizing the picture-producing surfaces of television tubes, more than doubling the contrast and brightness of the television image. He also worked out a technique for preparing very thin replicas of metallic surfaces for use in the electron microscope. One of the advantages gained by his early work in surface chemistry turned out to be highly useful. After developing techniques for working with and measuring the dimensions of monomolecular films having thicknesses the order of a ten-millionth of an inch, he found that problems connected with the measurement of atmospheric nuclei and cloud droplets seemed to be relatively simple, since their dimensions were from one to four orders of magnitude larger.

Following his discovery of a practical means for modifying supercooled laboratory clouds, Schaefer showed it was equally feasible to do the same with supercooled clouds in the free atmosphere. On Nov. 13, 1946, with six pounds of dry ice fragments, he converted a large supercooled altocumulus cloud to ice crystals in the sky east of Schenectady. This initial experiment and three others carried out in the fall and early winter of 1946 led to the formation of Project Cirrus, a joint atmospheric research program supported by the U.S. Army, Navy, and Air Force, with technical guidance from Langmuir, Schaefer, and Bernard Vonnegut of the G. E. Research Laboratory. In 1947 Vonnegut discovered the effectiveness of silver iodide as a cloud-seeding material. This was followed the next year by Langmuir's demonstration that plain water could sometimes trigger the precipitation process in warm clouds by developing a sort of chain reaction in droplet growth.

During the 5-year operation of Project Cirrus, nearly 200 research flights were made for evaluating the possibilities and limitations of cloud modification. In 1946 and 1947 spectacular effects were produced in cutting holes in stratus clouds several thousand feet thick and in dissipating supercooled ground fogs. More than 15 years elapsed before such operations were initiated on a routine basis at airports troubled with supercooled fog and low stratus. Modifications of cumulus clouds achieved during Project Cirrus are still questioned by some meteorologists.

In 1954 Schaefer left General Electric to become research director of the Munitalp Foundation. During the next 4 years, he and Vernon Crudge, the Foundation's executive director, developed cooperative research studies of orographic and noctilucent clouds with the International Institute of Rossbys in Stockholm, a world-wide program of time-lapse cloud photography, a lightning research program with the U.S. Forest Service, and a mobile field laboratory for atmospheric research. When a decision was made to move the foundation's headquarters to Nairobi in East Africa, Schaefer resigned. After 1958 he devoted full time to education and research consulting. In 1959 he inaugurated the Atmospheric Sciences Program, a summer institute for outstanding high-school juniors held at the Loomis School in Connecticut and subsequently at the Desert Research Institute of the University of Nevada at Reno. In 1960 he joined the faculty of the State University of New York at Albany, and in 1961 he helped Dean Oscar Lanford form the Atmospheric Sciences Research Center, of which he became director of research. In 1964 he was appointed professor of atmospheric science at Albany.

For background information *see* Cloud in the McGraw-Hill Encyclopedia of Science and Technology.   □

★ SCHAIRER, George Swift

American aeronautical engineer
Born May 19, 1913, Pittsburgh, Pa., U.S.A.

SCHAIRER DIRECTED a Boeing aerodynamic design team in a search for aircraft design arrangements that, in conjunction with modern gas turbine engines, would provide for efficient load carrying over long ranges. They evolved the (now standard) large jet aircraft design arrangement employing highly swept wings. The 707, 880, and DC-8 commercial jet transports that evolved from this work revolutionized passenger transportation throughout the world. For this Schairer received the Sylvanus Albert Reed Award of the Institute of Aerospace Sciences in 1950 and the Spirit of St. Louis Medal of the American Society of Mechanical Engineers in 1959.

Jet engines obtain their thrust by directing a very high-velocity jet of hot air rearward out of aft-facing nozzles. The efficiency of such propulsion is a function of the ratio of forward speed to jet velocity. A forward speed of half the jet velocity gives a propulsive efficiency of 67%, and a forward speed of three-quarters of jet velocity an efficiency of 86%. To make efficient use of jet engines, therefore, it is necessary to use the highest practicable speed of the aircraft. However, the large propellered bombers and transports of the early 1940s, when jet engines were first developed, were limited in forward speed to about 60% of the speed of sound; at this speed jet engines were quite inefficient. This limit was imposed by the drag and buffeting that occurred if these straight-winged aircraft were flown any closer to the speed of sound. As the speed of

sound was approached, the air found it more and more difficult to flow around the body, nacelles, and straight wings of these aircraft. This was due to compressibility effects.

Schairer, at that time chief of Aerodynamics and Power Plants at Boeing, led a concerted effort to find aircraft arrangements that would permit efficient, buffet-free operation at speeds much closer to the speed of sound. At first the attention of the Boeing group, as of other aircraft designers of the world, was directed toward the use of much thinner wings than those then in common use; but this led to severe weight, structural, and stalling problems.

In March 1945, Schairer learned of a study and tests by R. T. Jones of the National Advisory Committee for Aeronautics to defer the onset of compressibility problems by the use of pointed wings such as the now-common delta wing. Discussions of this concept with H. S. Tsein, H. L. Dryden, and Theodore von Karman convinced Schairer that sweeping a wing would also delay the onset of compressibility problems. On VE day, Schairer and Dryden found documents in Germany that confirmed this with theory and very recent experiments. The theory of sweepback at supersonic speeds had been expounded by Adolf Busseman in 1935 and had been overlooked for almost a decade. Schairer sent a brief letter describing the concept of sweepback to the Boeing design team and also brought sweepback to the attention of other aircraft designers in England and the United States for possible use in the continuing war with Japan.

Upon his return to the United States in the summer of 1945, Schairer led the Boeing effort to apply sweepback to the design of large aircraft. Many problems were encountered, but a satisfactory arrangement was found and many hundreds of B-47 jet bombers were built to this arrangement. Further refinement of sweptwing technology resulted in the B-52 jet bomber. The use of pod-mounted engines placed in carefully chosen spots was an important element in achieving both low drag and good stalling in these designs. Both of these designs used wings mounted high on the fuselage and bicycle-type landing gear mounted in the front and rear parts of the fuselage. This arrangement was satisfactory for bombers but undesirable for use on commercial aircraft. In 1949 Schairer made the first sketches of an airplane with a swept wing on the bottom of the body plus a tricycle landing gear retracting into the body. In 1952 the Boeing Company started the construction of an experimental aircraft known as the Dash 80 that used this arrangement and that became the prototype of the 707. This same basic arrangement was used subsequently on the 880 and DC-8 designs. The 707 cruises the airways at 85% of the speed of sound and provides efficient propulsion as well as attractive high-speed passenger transportation.

Son of a lawyer-inventor-engineer and research leader, Schairer majored in general engineering at Swarthmore College, from which he graduated B.S. with highest honors in 1934. He received an M.S. from the Massachusetts Institute of Technology in 1935. He worked for two years at the Bendix Products Corporation in South Bend, Ind., then for two years at Consolidated Aircraft Corporation in San Diego, before joining Boeing in 1939 as head of the Aerodynamics Unit. He rose to staff engineer, Aerodynamics and Power Plant; chief of technical staff; assistant chief engineer; and director of research. In 1959 he became vice-president for research and development. He participated in the aerodynamic design of such Boeing airplanes as the Stratoliner, B-17, B-29, B-50, XPBB-1, C-97, Stratocruiser, B-47, B-52, 707, and the KC-135.

For background information *see* AERODYNAMICS in the McGraw-Hill Encyclopedia of Science and Technology.   □

★ SCHULTZ, Adolph Hans
Swiss anthropologist
Born Nov. 14, 1891, Zurich, Switzerland

TRAINED AS a physical anthropologist, Schultz was deeply interested in the entire mammalian order of Primates. Most of his research attempted to explain man's specializations and their development during the past by means of systematic comparisons with corresponding conditions in as many nonhuman primates as possible. For this work he was awarded the Viking Fund Medal in physical anthropology in 1948.

Schultz's first major investigation after graduation dealt chiefly with the prenatal growth of man; it demonstrated, among other findings, that certain racial differences as well as most individual variations and even asymmetries ap-

pear long before birth. Undertaking similar studies on monkeys and apes, he gradually became able to determine in which respects human changes during growth follow generally valid rules or have become specialized. Such comparative work, however, required intensive collecting of suitable material, which at that time was not yet available in adequate amounts. By long-continued, periodic examinations of living, captive macaques and chimpanzees, Schultz gained the needed information on postnatal growth and on developmental changes at known ages. Preserved specimens of fetuses, infants, and adults of many other nonhuman primates formed a basis for establishing the general trend and rates of growth and the age changes in body proportions as well as in the development of the skeleton, dentition, skin, hair, and so forth, together with the degrees of their variability. All the latter material was obtained in steadily increasing amounts through loans, gifts, purchases, and, especially, Schultz's five collecting expeditions to Nicaragua, Panama, Thailand, and Borneo.

With this successful accumulation of material and data, Schultz demonstrated that the remarkably close similarity of man and apes early in life diminishes with advancing age through differing relative growth rates in the various parts of the body and according to diverging developmental processes. The systematic and detailed recording of these ontogenetic conditions clearly showed also that man is not unique in retaining many infantile features to maturity, as is commonly claimed, but that retardations as well as accelerations appear in the development of man just as in that of many other primates. Furthermore, it became evident that man is not distinguished by being born in an especially immature state, as widely believed, since there exist far more pronounced differences in this respect between the lower and higher primates than between man and the great apes. Man, however, had gained the longest postnatal periods of growth, the latest beginning and end of fertility, and the longest life span, facts that are of continuing and manifold consequence in his evolution. Schultz was impressed by the unexpected prevalence of disease, injuries, and malformations among most species living in a state of nature. Among the skeletons of apes of advanced age, he found healed fractures, arthritic changes, sinus infections, and dental decay more common than in any human race. These comparative studies on large series of primates shed new light on man's early acquisition of the erect posture and on the accompanying adaptations in the detailed construction of his body. The new statistical data on secondary sex differences and on the intraspecific variability in nonhuman primates were bound to revise some older views on these conditions in recent man and to help in the critical interpretation of fossil apes and men.

After 6 years as a student of the natural sciences at the University of Zurich, Schultz obtained his Ph.D. in 1916 and became a research associate in the department of embryology of the Carnegie Institution of Washington, located in Baltimore, where he remained until 1925. From 1925 until 1951 he was associate professor of physical anthropology at Johns Hopkins University. In 1951 he returned to the University of Zurich as professor of anthropology and director of its anthropological institute. He retired in 1962.

For background information *see* ANTHROPOLOGY, PHYSICAL; PRIMATES in the McGraw-Hill Encyclopedia of Science and Technology.   □

SCHWINGER, Julian Seymour
American physicist
Born Feb. 12, 1918, New York, N.Y., U.S.A.

S CHWINGER MADE fundamental contributions to the development of the quantum theory of radiation. He produced a mathematical formalism that has led to a better understanding of the interaction between charged particles and an electromagnetic field and eliminated, by means of a charge and mass renormalization, the problems concerned with the infinite change in energy of an electron due to its interaction with the quantized radiation field. This successful theory of quantum electrodynamics was brought about by the union of relativity and quantum theory. Schwinger's formulation of quantum electrodynamics was consistent and relativistically covariant. In recognition of this work, Schwinger was awarded the National Medal of Science in 1964 and the Nobel Prize for physics in 1965.

The first work in relativistic quantum mechanics was initiated by P. A. M. Dirac in 1927. Dirac was concerned with the quantization of the electromagnetic radiation field that made possible the treatment of processes involving a single photon. During the following 30 years the equations produced by Dirac, and later by Werner Heisenberg and Wolfgang Pauli, were tested and found to explain all phenomena accessible to exact measurement—in particular complicated details of atomic spectra. Although Dirac's relativistic wave equation was a fundamental advance, difficulties with the theory became apparent. One of these was the prediction of negative-energy states, a concept that at that time seemed unphysical but was later accepted on a broader theoretical basis. However, the difficulties encountered in the divergences of the field theories, in infinite electromagnetic self-energy that predicted an electron behaving like a particle in infinite mass, later plagued the theorists. It was realized that when an electromagnetic field is quantized, the average field-strength value will fluctuate. The electromagnetic field fluctuations in empty space cause an isolated electron continuously to emit and absorb radiation. This phenomenon involves the virtual emission and absorption of photons with unlimited energy. The electron carries these virtual quanta around with it as parts of its field, which in turn gives rise to an infinite electromagnetic self-energy. Attempts were made to allow for a belief in the general correctness of quantum electrodynamics and in Newton's law of equality of action and reaction, an effect arising out of the inertia of the electron's self-field. According to one group, the measured reaction force should be zero; that is, they simply deleted the infinite terms from the theory. However, this theory of omission failed in the low- and moderate-energy region. Another group figured the reaction force to be finite but small. This group also failed to justify their ideas. Furthermore, a demonstration of disagreement between theory and experiment was offered in 1947 by W. E. Lamb and R. C. Retherford. They detected a small displacement of the 2S energy level of the hydrogen atom from the position predicted by the Dirac theory. This was followed by further disagreement with Dirac's theory when a precise measurement of the magnetic moment of the electron was made.

In 1947 Schwinger, beginning with an idea by Kramers, built a new mathematical formalism for quantum electrodynamics to overcome the above problems. His idea was that the problematical inertial force experienced by an electron due to an interaction with a quantized external field could not be separated from the effects of the electron's ordinary mechanical inertia. Hence, the only observable inertia is the total inertia, which is the result of its mechanical and electrical effects. Therefore Schwinger did not try to eliminate the infinite terms; rather he analyzed them mathematically. He felt that these infinites contained terms that were of fundamental importance and that were required to insure a completely relativistic covariant theory. Schwinger was able to isolate the infinite electromagnetic self-energy terms from the finite terms. He identified the finite terms to be those that yield radiative correction effects due to the interaction of an electron with an external field. These finite terms predicted the correct level displacement of the hydrogen $2^2S \frac{1}{2}$ and $2^2P \frac{1}{2}$ lines in hydrogen as found by Lamb.

Schwinger identified the infinite electromagnetic self-energy term in the interaction energy as that due to the interaction of the electron with the electromagnetic field vacuum fluctuations. These fluctuations give to the electron an additional electromagnetic mass. The actual observed electron mass—the measured mass—is the sum of the mechanical mass and this new electromagnetic mass. Schwinger showed that the Dirac equation contained the wrong electron mass term—the mechanical mass instead of the total mass. This fact was not revealed until Schwinger analyzed the electromagnetic self-energy infinities in his mathematical formalism of quantum electrodynamics.

Schwinger received his B.A. (1936) and his Ph.D. (1939) in physics from Columbia University. He was at the University of California as a National Research Council fellow in 1939–40 and a research associate in 1940–41. From 1941 to 1943 he was an instructor and later an assistant professor of physics at Purdue University. During 1943–46 he worked at the Radiation Laboratory of the Massachusetts Institute of Technology. After the war he went to Harvard University as an associate professor of physics, becoming full professor in 1947. He was elected to the National Academy of Sciences in 1949.

For background information *see* QUANTUM THEORY, RELATIVISTIC in the McGraw-Hill Encyclopedia of Science and Technology.   □

☆ SEABORG, Glenn Theodore

American chemist
Born Apr. 19, 1912, Ishpeming, Mich., U.S.A.

FOLLOWING E. M. McMillan's discovery, in 1940, of the first transuranium element, neptunium (element 93), Seaborg and his collaborators began a search for element 94. They succeeded in producing, isolating, and identifying this element, which they called plutonium, and went on to synthesize and identify eight additional transuranium elements as well as over 100 isotopes distributed throughout the periodic table. For their discoveries in the chemistry of the transuranium elements, Seaborg and Mc-

Millan shared the 1951 Nobel Prize in chemistry.

In 1934 Enrico Fermi had shown that nuclear transmutations could be brought about by irradiating the very heavy elements with neutrons. This led Otto Hahn and Lise Meitner to consider the possibility of producing transuranium elements by this method, but their efforts to synthesize an element beyond uranium in the periodic table were not successful. In 1940, working at the University of California at Berkeley, McMillan and P. H. Abelson made the first such synthesis of the element with atomic number 93. This was isolated chemically and conclusively identified as a transuranium element and given the name neptunium.

Neptunium was found to be unstable and to be a beta emitter with a half-life of about 2 days. Thus the decay product should be the next element in the transuranium series, element 94. In December, 1940, Seaborg, with his associates, bombarded uranium oxide with 16-Mev deuterons and succeeded in isolating chemically the unstable element-93 fraction of the resulting products, which decayed, according to expectation, by emitting a beta particle to yield element 94, with a mass number of 238. Both elements 93 and 94 were studied by the tracer method, and element 94 was positively identified and given the name plutonium.

Further research with plutonium led to the production of isotope Pu^{239}, which was found to be a potential source of nuclear energy. In the spring of 1942, Seaborg and a number of his colleagues moved to the Metallurgical Laboratory of the University of Chicago to continue research on Pu^{239} and, in particular, to find a way to produce it in usable amounts for the

production of nuclear energy. Microchemical aspects of this work were carried out chiefly by B. B. Cunningham and L. B. Werner under Seaborg's direction.

With the completion of the major part of the work on plutonium, Seaborg again turned to the problem of the production of further transuranium elements. He began with the supposition that the next element should be much like plutonium, in that it should be possible to oxidize it to the VI oxidation state and to use this in chemical isolation procedures. For a long time, work along these lines resulted in failure. Finally, in the summer of 1944, Seaborg recognized that the next elements could be oxidized above the III state only with extreme difficulty, and this fact led to the quick identification of an isotope (Cm^{242}) of element 96. Identification of element 95 came shortly thereafter.

The recognition that the III oxidation state was stable and was the dominant feature of the chemistry of these elements led to the recognition also that these elements, and all other transuranium elements previously discovered, were actually part of an actinide transition series. The chemical properties of these elements corresponded to the filling of the $5f$ electron shell, and they could be expected to resemble each other chemically, analogously to the chemical resemblance of the rare-earth or lanthanide series elements, and they should also bear strong resemblance to the rare-earth elements themselves. This hypothesis of an actinide transition series and strong resemblance to the rare earths proved to be so true, that for a while great difficulties were encountered in separating elements 95 and 96 from each other and from the rare-earth elements. For this reason element 95 was named americium after the Americas by analogy with the naming of its rare-earth homolog europium after Europe. Element 96 was named curium, using a similar analogy with the naming of its rare-earth homolog gadolium.

In 1945 Seaborg returned to Berkeley and, armed with the actinide concept that made possible the prediction of the chemical properties of the yet-unsynthesized transuranium elements, he and his colleagues were able to isolate and identify elements 97, 98, 99, 100, 101, and 102. These were named berkelium, californium, einsteinium, fermium, and mendelevium respectively, with element 102 as yet unnamed.

Seaborg received his A.B. in 1934 at the University of California, Los Angeles, and his Ph.D. in chemistry in 1937 at the University of California, Berkeley. Except for the war years, he was a member of the professorial staff of the university until his elevation to the chancellorship in 1958. He left that post in 1961 upon his appointment by President John F. Kennedy to the chairmanship of the U.S. Atomic Energy Commission. He was elected to the National Academy of Sciences in 1948.

Seaborg wrote *Chemistry of the Actinide Elements* (1957) and *The Transuranium Elements* (1958).

For background information *see* PLUTONIUM; TRANSURANIUM ELEMENTS in the McGraw-Hill Encyclopedia of Science and Technology.   □

☆ SEGRÈ, Emilio Gino
Italian-American physicist
Born Feb. 1, 1905, Tivoli (Rome), Italy

SEGRÈ'S SCIENTIFIC discoveries ranged from early investigations in atomic spectroscopy to the discovery of artificial elements and experiments in particle physics. For his discovery of the antiproton in 1955 with Owen Chamberlain, C. E. Wiegand, and T. J. Ypsilantis, he and Chamberlain were awarded the 1959 Nobel Prize in physics.

From a study of relativity and quantum mechanics, the English theoretical physicist P. A. M. Dirac had concluded in 1928 that electrons had a mirrorlike counterpart, a particle with similar properties except that the electric charge was positive instead of negative. Dirac's theory was substantiated in 1932 with C. D. Anderson's discovery of the positron in cosmic rays. A generalization of the Dirac theory led physicists to believe that the proton should also have a twin of opposite electric charge. Extensive research in cosmic rays never yielded a positive identification of the antiproton. The construction of the Bevatron at the University of California, Berkeley, meant that the particle could be created in the laboratory. Nevertheless, the problem of identifying the antiproton remained.

Segrè and his colleagues set up targets in the Bevatron from which antiprotons emerged together with many more particles of other types. The problem was to single out the antiprotons. This was done by measuring their velocity and momentum. The velocity was measured by using a "time-of-flight" method and a Cerenkov counter. The momentum was measured by deflecting particles in a magnetic field. Only approximately 1 in 100,000 particles satisfied the necessary and sufficient conditions for indentification as an antiproton. Once the existence of antiprotons was established, other antiparticles, such as antineutrons, were discovered. It became apparent that, in principle, worlds of antimatter are possible.

For an inhabitant of it, such an antiworld would be indistinguishable from our usual world. An observer, making an optical astronomical observation, would be unable to distinguish a star of matter from a star of antimatter. However, if the two worlds should come together, they would annihilate each other. The result would be energy moving away from the place of the catastrophe with the velocity of light.

Segrè's versatility in his scientific work was a trait he developed as a student and a member of Enrico Fermi's famous "Roman school" of physics in the late 1920s. The son of an industrialist, Segrè began his university studies in 1922 with the idea of becoming an engineer. In part due to Fermi's influence, he changed his field of study to physics, which had fascinated him since childhood. He took his doctor's degree in 1928 under Fermi.

His earliest experiments were in the field of atomic spectroscopy, in which he studied "forbidden lines," their Zeeman effect, and highly excited atoms. Following a period of military service, he did postgraduate work with Otto Stern in Hamburg and Pieter Zeeman in Amsterdam before returning to the University of Rome as an assistant professor.

Segrè and his colleagues participated in the experiments on neutrons directed by Fermi in 1934. In this work all available elements, including uranium, were bombarded with neutrons and transuranic elements were formed. However, Fermi and his coworkers did not fully grasp the meaning of the uranium work at that time. The significance of the work was clarified 4 years later when Otto Hahn and Fritz Strassmann discovered nuclear fission.

In 1935, the neutron work was crowned by the discovery of slow neutrons. These are neutrons that, through successive collisions with light nuclei, are reduced to velocities comparable to thermal agitation. Slow neutrons acquire peculiar properties that later proved to be very important for the development of nuclear power.

Segrè left Rome in 1936 to accept a position at the University of Palermo. Although his laboratory was not well equipped, by using simple techniques he discovered the first artificial element, technetium (meaning, in Greek, "artificial"), in collaboration with his colleague, C. Perrier, a professor of mineralogy. The material used for this discovery originated with the Berkeley cyclotron. E. O. Lawrence and other physicists at the University of California's Radiation Laboratory had given the material to Se-

grè during a visit the Italian scientist had made to Berkeley.

While visiting California in 1938, Segrè was dismissed from his position at the University of Palermo by the Fascist government. He remained at Berkeley and continued his researches in problems of nuclear chemistry. With D. R. Corson and K. R. McKenzie, he discovered the element astatine, and with J. W. Kennedy, G. T. Seaborg, and A. C. Wahl, he discovered plutonium-239. From 1943 to 1946, he was a group leader at the Los Alamos laboratory. In 1946, he became a professor of physics at the University of California, Berkeley. He was naturalized as an American citizen in 1944. He was elected to the National Academy of Sciences in 1952.

For background information *see* ANTIPROTON; TECHNETIUM in the McGraw-Hill Encyclopedia of Science and Technology.   □

★ **SEMENOV, Nikolai Nikolaevich**
Soviet chemist
Born Apr. 16, 1896, Saratov, U.S.S.R.

S EMENOV'S MAIN activities were directed toward the mechanisms of chemical reactions. A great number of these, such as oxidation, cracking, halogenation, and polymerization, proceed by a chain mechanism, making the investigation of chain chemical reactions very important. For his work in this field, Semenov was awarded the State Prize in 1941 and shared with C. N. Hinshelwood the 1956 Nobel Prize in chemistry.

In 1926 Semenov and his coworkers discovered branched-chain reactions in the oxidation of phosphorus. A sharp change from quiescence to a very violent reaction with changes in the external parameters—such as pressure, density or mass of the reacting compounds, the reactor dimensions, the amount of admixtures terminating the chain, and so on—are characteristic of branched-chain reactions. A critical value (limit) is reached with a change in any of these parameters. Below (above) this value the reaction does not seem to occur at all, and above (below) it the reaction is often completed in fractions of a second (the so-called chain explosion). Chain ignition or explosion is completely independent of heating induced by the prior slow reaction, in contrast to thermal explosion. Chain ignition or explosion may occur under isothermic conditions, often at low temperatures. Similar phenomena were observed for many other chemical reactions.

Semenov explained all these peculiar phenomena on the basis of his theory of branched-chain reactions. He suggested that there is probably more than one active center formation at every step of the main chain involving atoms and radicals. If the number of branchings exceeds that of terminations, the chain reaction rate will increase in avalanche, resulting in ignition of the whole mixture (chain explosion). If there is less than one branching throughout the chain length, the reaction will be stationary, and at a low chain initiation rate it will be negligibly slow. Beyond the limits the reaction does not seem to proceed at all. This is the reason for critical values of external parameters. Semenov proposed a concept of chain termination at the wall and in the gas phase. He also developed a quantitative theory for propagation of a branched-chain reaction within the ignition limits.

In 1931 Semenov discovered a new type of branched-chain reactions, namely, those involving degenerate branching. He suggested that active intermediates were formed in the course of the main chain propagation. With subsequent conversions these would result in the appearance of active centers, atoms, or radicals, that is, in chain branching. All oxidation reactions for both low- and high-molecular compounds belong to this type of reaction.

Along with the above chain ignition reactions there is another and very widespread type of ignition. Many reactions are known to occur with liberation of heat. When the heat emitted by a reaction does not succeed in escaping from the reaction zone to the external medium, the reaction becomes heated. This results in acceleration of the reaction and a consequent increase in heat liberation. Under favorable conditions the supply of heat will exceed its escape, and the reaction rate will attain its explosive value. This is the mechanism of thermal explosion. The first quantitative theory of thermal ignition was given by Semenov in 1928 and then, more explicitly, in 1940. Thus in thermal explosion heat is the reason for—and in chain explosion the consequence of—explosion.

In the monograph *Chain Reactions* (1934; English translation 1935) Semenov generalized the huge amount of experimental data available on the basis of his theory and showed that a considerable number of chemical reactions, including polymerization, develop by a chain (branched or unbranched) mechanism. Thereafter investigations of the mechanisms of chemical reactions rapidly increased. The experimental results accumulated during the next 20 years were extensively analyzed by Semenov from the kinetics standpoint in his monograph *Certain Problems of Chemical Kinetics and Reactivity* (1954; 2d ed., enlarged, 1958). He investigated the chemical mechanism as such for many chemical reactions. The mechanisms of branched oxidation of hydrogen, methane (degenerate branching), decomposition of alkylbromides, alkylchlorides, and so on, were discussed in detail. He treated explicitly the probability of radical and chain reactions competing with molecular ones. Series of the relative activities of radicals were established, and an empiric rule connecting the heat of a radical reaction with its activation energy was given. His theoretical concept of the possible formation of radicals by reaction of two molecules, proposed in this book, obtained experimental confirmation in recent years.

In 1960 Semenov developed a theory of collective interaction providing an explanation for the anomalous rates of low-temperature polymerization and addition reactions in the solid state.

Semenov graduated from the Leningrad University in 1917. He was chief of the Electronic Phenomena Laboratory of the Leningrad Physicotechnical Institute from 1920 to 1931 and director of the Institute of Chemical Physics of the Academy of Sciences of the U.S.S.R. after 1931. From 1920 to 1944 he was lecturer and then professor at the Leningrad Polytechnic Institute. In 1944 he was appointed professor at the Moscow State University. A member of the Academy of Sciences of the U.S.S.R. since 1932, he was elected to academies of science in several other countries, including the Royal Society of London (1958), the Hungarian Academy of Sciences (1961), and the Czechoslovakian Academy of Sciences (1965). In 1963 he was elected a foreign associate of the U.S. National Academy of Sciences.

For background information *see* CHAIN REACTION, CHEMICAL in the McGraw-Hill Encyclopedia of Science and Technology.   □

SHANNON, Claude Elwood
American mathematician
Born Apr. 30, 1916, Gaylord, Mich., U.S.A.

S HANNON HELPED found the modern science of communication theory with his revolutionary mathematical theory of communication, which he developed in response to technical engineering problems. This theory was found to

have applications far beyond the range of thought within which it was originally conceived. As elaborated by Shannon and others, the theory assumed fundamental importance in all disciplines involving problems of meaning, communication, language, and related concepts. For his work, Shannon was awarded the Franklin Institute's Ballantine Medal (1955) and the National Research Corporation Award (1956).

The mathematical theory of communication, first presented in 1948, was the culmination of Shannon's mathematical and engineering investigations at the Bell Telephone Laboratories of the concepts "communication," "information," and "message." In these Shannon considered a simple communication system consisting of: an *information source*, which selected, from an array of possible messages, the message to be sent; a *transmitter*, which encoded the message into a *signal*; a *communication channel*, through which the signal was sent; a *receiver*, which decoded the message; and finally, a *destination*, which was analogous to the source. An inevitable item in any communication system was also *noise* of external origin, consisting of unintentional and undesirable variations in the received signal.

A novel feature of Shannon's theory was the importation of the concept of *entropy* from classical thermodynamics. According to the second law of thermodynamics, as stated in the 19th century, the entropy (degree of randomness) in any system always increased. Shannon seized upon the analogy between entropy and "information." In his definition, "information" refers not to the meaningful content of a particular message but to the degree of freedom with which the information source may choose among elements to compose a given message. The greater the freedom of choice, clearly, the greater the information of a system. Shannon found an exact analogy between entropy (or degree of randomness) and information (or uncertainty, or freedom of choice in selecting ele-

ments for a message). Thus used, the idea of entropy came to have central importance in Shannon's theory.

The theory, as first formulated, dealt with a communication system not subject to noise. Shannon designated the capacity of the information channel as C units per second and the output of the information source as H units per second. He then proposed that there existed an upper limit to the average rate of symbol transmission and that this limit was the ratio C/H, which could be approximated—but never exceeded—by judicious coding.

To generalize this deceptively simple theorem to describe a channel afflicted with noise, Shannon distinguished between that (undesirable) uncertainty caused by errors or extraneous noise and that (desirable) uncertainty which arose in the source and was equated with information. He than described "useful information" as the uncertainty of the source minus the equivocation introduced by noise. Then he restated the original theorem more broadly. By interpreting H generally as the entropy of the source, while C continued to designate the channel capacity, Shannon could now say that, for C greater than or equal to H, errors in transmission could be made vanishingly small; but for C less than H, this was not possible. The undesirable uncertainty of the message must then be equal to, or greater than, $H - C$. Finally, there must be at least one code able to reduce this equivocation to an amount extremely close to $H - C$.

Shannon initially conceived his ideas for limited application in the technical and engineering aspects of communication systems. But it soon became apparent that he had developed a tool of the utmost flexibility and utility for the investigation of communication in its broadest sense. For example, one of the predictions of the theory was that on the basis of probability alone words, letters, or other symbols had a distinct tendency to arrange themselves in meaningful sequences. One could thus say that in any code there existed a portion of a message the disposition of whose symbols was dictated by probability. This percentage Shannon called the "redundancy" of a code. He pointed out the usefulness of redundancy in many situations, and showed that it was not always advantageous to eliminate it entirely, even if possible. For example, the redundancy of the English language is about 50 per cent. A message, "TO ERR IS HUMAN," may well be read intelligibly even if noise has interfered with the transmission—to give, say, "TOO ERR IS FUMAN." But in a message of minimal redundancy, "YANKS BEAT REDS," the introduction of noise, "YANKS BEAT REBS," often proves fatal to comprehension.

Shannon was ultimately able to extend his theory to deal with continuous, as well as discrete, transmission of information. This generalization called for no particular modification of any of the basic premises involved. When applied to a variety of problems, the theory revealed its power by yielding a mass of new data and correlations in semantics; in comparative linguistics (evidence of statistical regularity in language); in cryptography (where the notion of redundancy is of primary importance); in computer design and theory; and in many other disciplines, some of them touching only tangentially on electronics.

Shannon's other work, besides his theory of communication, included the application of the calculus of probability to language. In 1938 he published the classic paper *A Symbolic Analysis of Relay and Switching Circuits,* in which he pointed out the identity between the two "truth values" of symbolic logic and the binary values "1" and "0" of electronic circuits. Shannon showed how a "logic machine" could be built using switching circuits corresponding to the propositions of Boolean algebra. Also at about that time, he coined the term "bit," which gained widespread use to designate a computer quantum of information.

Shannon took his B.S. at the University of Michigan in 1936, and in 1939 became a Bowles fellow at the Massachusetts Institute of Technology. A year later he received his M.S. and Ph.D. in mathematics from that institution. After a year (1940–41) as a National Research Council fellow at Princeton University, Shannon joined the Bell Telephone Laboratories. He remained there as a mathematician until 1958, when he assumed the position of Donner Professor of Science at MIT. He was elected to the National Academy of Sciences in 1956.

Shannon wrote *A Mathematical Theory of Communication,* with Warren Weaver (1949).

For background information *see* INFORMATION THEORY in the McGraw-Hill Encyclopedia of Science and Technology.   □

☆ SHAPLEY, Harlow

American astronomer
Born Nov. 2, 1885, Nashville, Mo., U.S.A.

WHILE STUDYING globular clusters and establishing their distances from the Sun, Shapley determined the size and shape of the Milky Way galaxy and the position of the solar system within it. This marked the beginning of galactic astronomy, for by defining the limits of the Milky Way he made it possible to determine which celestial objects were extragalactic.

The first attempt to determine the limits of the Milky Way by systematic observations was made by the English astronomer William Herschel

about 1784. Herschel counted the stars in different areas of the sky to determine how far they extended in each direction. He concluded that the galaxy was shaped like a convex lens, with the Sun located at the center, and that the ratio of the diameter to the thickness of the galaxy was about 16:3. However, this method yielded no exact dimensions. In 1901, the German astronomer Hugo von Seeliger announced a model of the galaxy, also derived by the star-count method, similar to Herschel's with a diameter of 23,000 light-years and a thickness of 6,000 light-years.

During his study of globular clusters, Shapley was impressed by two findings. One was that globular clusters are found in both the northern and southern celestial hemispheres, although they are concentrated in the southern hemisphere in the direction of Sagittarius. The other was that the distribution of the clusters is symmetric with respect to the plane of the Milky Way. Shapley realized that the first finding would be expected if the globular clusters formed a spherical system of which the Sun were a part but located far from the center. He reasoned that his second finding would be explained if the system of globular clusters and the more flattened system of stars and gaseous nebulae called the Milky Way galaxy were related. By assuming that the system of globular clusters was of the same dimensions as, and concentric with, the stars and nebulae of the Milky Way, Shapley felt he could determine the extent of the galaxy by determining the dimensions of the system of globular clusters. He further assumed that since most of the globular

clusters contain RR Lyrae variable stars, he could calibrate the period-luminosity relation of such stars—discovered by Henrietta Swan Leavitt of the Harvard College Observatory in 1912—to establish the distances of the globular clusters from the Sun.

Using the 60-in. telescope at the Mt. Wilson Observatory in California, Shapley took innumerable photographs of the globular clusters in 1916–17. He measured the apparent and absolute magnitudes of the brightest as well as the variable stars in these clusters and, by calibrating a period-luminosity curve for the variable stars, established their distances. He then proceeded to derive the distances—for the brightest and nearest clusters from the variable stars and for the fainter and more distant ones from their apparent diameter and total magnitude—of the 86 globular clusters then known. In 1917 Shapley announced his conclusions. He envisaged the Milky Way as a convex lens–shaped system 300,000 light-years in diameter and 30,000 light-years thick. He calculated that the center of the galaxy was in the direction of Sagittarius, some 50,000 light-years from the Sun. Because he disregarded the effects of interstellar absorption, his estimates were too high. By 1930, however, when his model became generally accepted, Shapley had revised his estimates to a diameter of 100,000 light-years, with the Sun 25,000 to 30,000 light-years from the center. His 1917 pronouncement was revolutionary, for he not only was the first to remove the Sun from its position of eminence at the galactic center, he also increased the galaxy's size by a factor of 13. Furthermore, by defining the limits of the Milky Way, Shapley established that many nebulae were extragalactic and, even more important, were galactic systems similar to the Milky Way.

In addition to his determination of the size of the galaxy, Shapley developed the pulsation theory of cepheid variables and demonstrated the associated variability of stellar spectra. He also established the color-luminosity relation for the bright stars in globular clusters, discovered the first of the Sculptor-type galaxies, and proved the equal velocity of blue and yellow light with an accuracy of one part in 20×10^9.

Shapley attended the University of Missouri, receiving his A.B. in 1910 and his A.M. in 1911. He then went to Princeton University, where he received his Ph.D. in 1913. In 1914 he became an astronomer at the Mt. Wilson Observatory, leaving in 1921 to become the director of the Harvard College Observatory. He retained this post until 1952, when he became director emeritus of the observatory and Paine Professor of Astronomy at Harvard University. In 1956 he became professor emeritus, but remained active as a lecturer on cosmography at Harvard and other institutions. Among his many awards were the Gold Medal of the Royal Astronomical Society and the Bruce Medal of the Astronomical Society of the Pacific. He was elected to the National Academy of Sciences in 1924.

Shapley wrote *Galaxies* (1943; rev. ed. 1961),

Of Stars and Men (1958; rev. ed. 1964), and *The View from a Distant Star* (1963).

For background information *see* STAR CLUSTERS; VARIABLE STAR in the McGraw-Hill Encyclopedia of Science and Technology.   □

★ SHERWOOD, Thomas Kilgore

American chemical engineer
Born July 25, 1903, Columbus, Ohio, U.S.A.

SEPARATION PROCESSES play key roles in the manufacture of most chemical and petroleum products. Mixtures are separated and products purified by effecting preferential transfer ("mass transfer") of one or more constituents of a mixture from one phase (gas, liquid, or solid) to another and then separating the two phases mechanically. Sherwood was responsible for the development of procedures and data employed by engineers in the design of equipment for separation by gas absorption, solvent extraction, and evaporation. His data and correlations of mass transfer and flooding in packed absorption towers, though developed in the late 1930s, are still used by design engineers.

Recognizing that engineering design data and procedures must be based on a sound knowledge of the basic phenomena, Sherwood undertook studies of the mechanism of mass transfer between two phases. This led to one of the first studies of eddy diffusion in a turbulent gas stream and to the development of the wetted-wall apparatus as a tool for studies of mass transfer in turbulent boundary layers, with and without chemical reaction. These were followed by experimental investigations of mass transfer from a surface to a supersonic gas stream and the sublimation of solids at very low pressures.

These studies provided a basis for the application of mass-transfer theory in various applications, including absorption refrigeration. Sherwood served as a consultant in the development of the first commercial heat-operated refrigeration equipment for air conditioning. This employed water as refrigerant and aqueous lithium bromide as absorbent in a gas-fired device that contained no moving parts. Mass-transfer principles were again found applicable in the design of industrial catalytic processes in which reacting chemicals were required to diffuse in and out of highly porous catalyst pellets in large reactors of the fixed-bed type.

Born in Columbus, Ohio, Sherwood spent his youth in Montreal and graduated from McGill University in 1923. Following graduate study at the Massachusetts Institute of Technology (Sc.D. 1929), he joined the MIT faculty in 1930, becoming professor of chemical engineering in 1941. In Washington from 1940 to 1945 he served the National Defense Research Committee and the Office of Scientific Research and Development in the organization and prosecution of research on new materials and devices needed by the military. These included screening-smoke generators, low-temperature hydraulic fluids, ship-bottom paints, photoflash bombs, aviation oxygen masks, and numerous other items. Following the war he served for 6 years as dean of engineering at MIT. Elected to the National Academy of Sciences in 1958, he was a founder of the National Academy of Engineering.

Sherwood wrote *Absorption and Extraction* (1937), *Applied Mathematics in Chemical Engineering,* with C. E. Reed (1939), and *Physical Properties of Gases and Liquids,* with R. C. Reid (1958).

For background information *see* SEPARATION (CHEMICAL AND PHYSICAL); SEPARATION (MECHANICAL) in the McGraw-Hill Encyclopedia of Science and Technology.   □

cated, filled by successive electrons, also could wander and carry charge ("*p*-type," "positive" or "acceptor" conductivity). Very small amounts of *p*- or *n*-type impurities, introduced into the lattices of artificially grown semiconductor crystals, made one or another region of the crystal exhibit that type of conductivity.

In 1946, Shockley, Bardeen, and Brattain began a fundamental research program on semiconductors at the Bell Telephone Laboratories. They especially sought to develop a semiconductor device for electronic amplification. One of the early approaches, initially unsuccessful, led Shockley to formulate the "field effect" theory. A very thin slab of germanium was made one plate of a parallel-plate condenser. Shockley predicted that voltage applied across the condenser would cause a change of conductance in the slab of germanium. Experiments done with evaporated films of semiconductors, however, gave results much smaller than the predicted effect. To explain the discrepancy, he supposed that the surface of the semiconductor exhibited an effect analogous to rectification in metallic conductors—current was passing freely in one direction only. Further experiment confirmed this hypothesis and showed that samples containing high concentrations of both *n*-type and *p*-type impurities had a particularly large difference in contact potential.

There were indications that effects comparable to those on a surface could be observed in the flow through an inversion layer of opposite conductivity near the surface of a solid semiconductor. On a block of *n*-type germanium were evaporated two gold spots as rectifying contacts. A positive voltage was applied to one spot. Very

SHOCKLEY, William
American physicist
Born Feb. 13, 1910, London, England

IN THE course of a research program in solid-state physics, Shockley and his colleagues discovered the transistor effect for electronic amplification by means of solid-state semiconductors which were smaller, less fragile, and more efficient than conventional vacuum tubes. This work formed the basis for transistor theory and technology. For it, Shockley shared with W. H. Brattain and John Bardeen the 1956 Nobel Prize in physics.

By the 1940s, it was known that semiconductors like silicon or germanium acted in two distinct ways to conduct electricity. In "*n*-type" ("negative" or "donor") conductivity, weakly held outer valence electrons in a crystal were liberated by photoelectric action to drift in an electric current. The valence "hole" thus va-

close to the spot was placed a point contact, biased in the direction opposite to the applied voltage. A very small reverse bias was sufficient to decrease the number of electrons available in the *p*-type inverting layer. This in turn raised the number of holes flowing in the reverse current to the point contact. The net result was amplification of the reverse current.

This first observed instance of the transistor effect was explained in terms of Shockley's initial "field effect" theory; the conductance of the p-type inverting layer, according to this theory, was controllable by the voltage applied across the point contact, in the direction of difficulty of flow. This phenomenon was embodied in the point-contact transistor. To a germanium block were attached two point contacts ("emitter" and "collector") and a large, low-resistance base electrode. Voltage amplification was due to the tendency of holes to drift toward the collector, which, biased in the reverse direction, had high impedance and could be connected to a high impedance load.

Simultaneously with the development of the point-contact transistor, Shockley investigated the phenomenon of "p-n rectification" and from these studies ultimately proposed the radically different junction transistor, in which the transistor effect takes place throughout a semiconductor rather than only at the surface. A current was applied to a single crystal of germanium, divided by controlled introduction of impurities into adjoining regions of p- and n-type conductivity. Holes and electrons began to cross the p-n junction, to recombine on the other side, causing an excess of minority carriers on both sides of the junction. Reversing the bias produced a tendency for both holes and electrons to be repulsed from the p-n junction. Accordingly, applied voltage encountered greater difficulty in this case, and the flow of current in both directions was reduced.

Shockley developed a theory to account for this effect, using the types of imperfection present in the crystal lattice and other known factors. Other experiments confirmed his assertion that the donor and acceptor imperfections carried the charge of an electron.

By placing two p-n junction rectifiers back to back, Shockley produced the junction transistor. The central p-type section (which is extremely thin) was sandwiched between two n-type regions in a single crystal. When a negative voltage was applied to the left-hand region ("emitter"), a flow of minority carriers began across the p-type region. By introducing a reverse bias at the "collector," he caused a drop in potential at the right-hand junction. The result is current amplification: the weak emitter signal controls the high-impedance output at the collector.

Based on these and other early experiments, transistor theory and technology grew rapidly to have great importance in every aspect of electronics, and in fact in every branch of science. The study of the solid-state and semiconductors

also advanced quickly following the impetus given it by these productive experiments.

The son of a mining engineer, Shockley received his B.S. at the California Institute of Technology in 1932, and his Ph.D. in physics at Harvard in 1936. In that year he joined the Bell Telephone Laboratories. Except for absences for war work and two brief visiting lectureships, Shockley remained there until 1955 as head of the transistor physics department. During 1954–55 he was deputy director and research director of the Weapons Systems Evaluation Group for the Defense Department. In 1955 he became head of the Shockley Semiconductor Laboratory of Beckman Instruments, Inc., and in 1963 was appointed first Poniatoff Professor of Engineering Science at Stanford University. He was elected to the National Academy of Sciences in 1951.

Shockley wrote *Electrons and Holes in Semiconductors* (1950).

For background information *see* SEMICONDUCTOR; TRANSISTOR in the McGraw-Hill Encyclopedia of Science and Technology.   □

★ SHULL, Clifford G.

American physicist
Born Sept. 23, 1915, Pittsburgh, Pa., U.S.A.

ONE OF the by-products of scientific research during World War II was the availability of relatively intense beams of slow neutrons from nuclear reactors. Research groups at both the Argonne and Oak Ridge national laboratories realized in 1946 the potential usefulness of slow neutron radiation in studying the structure of solids. Shull's work on a variety of applications of slow neutron radiation led to the development, in the years following 1948, of a magnetic crystallography. For this he was awarded the Buckley Prize of the American Physical Society in 1956.

Neutrons, being uncharged nuclear particles,

interact with the atoms in solids primarily through the nuclear force interaction with the atomic nuclei and are largely unaffected by the nuclear and electronic charge distribution in an atom. Those neutrons that have been moderated in a nuclear reactor to low energy (thermalized) exhibit a DeBroglie wavelength of about 1 angstrom. Since this is comparable to the atom spacing distances in solids, diffraction effects are to be expected. The early work at Oak Ridge by Shull and E. O. Wollan served to place the nuclear scattering in crystals on a quantitative basis and led to a series of diffraction applications wherein crystallographic structure information was obtained beyond that supplied by x-ray and electron diffraction. Most significant among these investigations was the demonstration that hydrogen atom positions in crystals could be determined by this technique. This permitted a more complete understanding of the crystal structure in a large class of organic and inorganic substances.

Following the nuclear scattering studies, Shull searched for the paramagnetic scattering that had been predicted by O. Halpern and M. Johnson in 1939 as arising from an interaction between the magnetic moment carried by the neutron and the atomic magnetic moments present in paramagnetic substances. This was found in the substance MnO, but the room-temperature study showed a short-range-order character to this scattering, immediately suggesting that a more extended ordering should occur at reduced temperature. At the same time a second paramagnetic substance, alpha-Fe_2O_3, was being investigated; this exhibited additional coherent Bragg reflections not permitted by nuclear scattering. The two separate observations were given a common interpretation in terms of a paramagnetic-to-antiferromagnetic transition by studying MnO at low temperature and alpha-Fe_2O_3 at high temperature. This was first reported by Shull and J. S. Smart in 1949, followed by a more complete report (in collaboration with W. Strauser and Wollan) on other antiferromagnetic materials in 1951. Shull later showed that magnetic lattice ordering in ferromagnetic and ferrimagnetic substances could also be studied by neutron diffraction. Subsequently Shull studied the magnetic crystallography of many substances, assaying the relative orientations and strengths of atomic magnetic moments in addition to determining the atomic positions by means of conventional crystallography. Such studies were of interest because of their bearing upon the overlap interaction between electrons of different atoms in the solid structure.

Following these basic studies on the determination of magnetic structures, Shull developed and exploited the use of polarized slow neutron radiation in which the magnetic orientation of the neutron spin was kept under control. This technique proved particularly useful in studying scattering resulting from very weak interactions, in some cases a million times smaller than that normally encountered. With various collaborators, Shull applied the technique to determining the spatial asymmetry of the magnetic electrons in various transition elements, to problems of paramagnetic alignment under external magnetic field application, to exploring a novel neutron spin–neutron orbit interaction, to determining nuclear spin-state scattering amplitudes in nuclear polarization experiments, and to studies of electron spin–pairing in the superconducting state.

Shull did his undergraduate work in physics at the Carnegie Institute of Technology (B.S., 1937); he received his Ph.D. at New York University in 1941. During the war years, he performed physical studies on catalysts used in high-octane fuel production with the Texas Company. He joined the Oak Ridge staff in 1946. Following a period at the Brookhaven National Laboratory in 1955, he was appointed that same year professor of physics at the Massachusetts Institute of Technology.

For background information *see* CRYSTALLOGRAPHY in the McGraw-Hill Encyclopedia of Science and Technology. □

☆ SIKORSKY, Igor Ivanovich

Russian-American aviation pioneer
Born May 25, 1889, Kiev, Russia

SIKORSKY ACHIEVED distinction in three fields of aviation. He created the world's first multiengine airplane in Russia in 1913; he launched a second career in the United States, becoming famous for his flying boats; and he conceived and developed the world's first practical helicopter. For these achievements he received numerous awards, including the Sylvanus

Albert Reed Award (1942) and the Daniel Guggenheim Medal (1951).

Sikorsky built his first experimental helicopter in Russia in 1909. Neither this, nor a second built in 1910, was successful. He then turned to fixed-wing airplanes, and in 1910 he soloed in a plane of his own design and construction. His approach was practical: he made sketches of the plane he wanted to build, built the plane, then trained himself to handle it, correcting his errors as a pilot as he corrected errors in design.

Sikorsky defied the experts of that early period to build the first four-engine airplane, called *The Grand*. Again he served as both designer and test pilot. *The Grand* included such luxuries as an enclosed cabin, a lavatory, upholstered chairs, and an exterior catwalk where passengers could stroll. *The Grand* was followed by a larger aircraft—called *Ilia Mourometz* after a legendary Russian hero of the 10th century—which, in a military version, proved a highly successful bomber in World War I.

After the Russian Revolution, Sikorsky emigrated to the United States, after short stays in England and France. He started the first Sikorsky company in 1923 on a friend's farm on Long Island. The first aircraft built there was the S-29-A (the "A" for "America"), a twin-engine, all-metal transport. A number of aircraft followed, including the S-38 amphibian, with which Pan American Airways blazed new air trails to Central and South America. In 1929 Sikorsky's company became a division of United Aircraft Corporation; from the combination came a series of historic flying boats. The first 40-passenger flying clippers were built in 1931, followed by the first transoceanic flying boats, the S-42 and S-44, which pioneered commercial air transportation across the Pacific and the Atlantic.

By 1938, Sikorsky had returned seriously to the direct-lift field. Through the years he had kept notes on ideas for helicopter designs and had taken out patents on some phases of design. He began his first helicopter, the VS-300, in early 1939 at the Sikorsky plant in Stratford, Conn.; by fall it was completed. Sikorsky was at the controls on Sept. 14, 1939, when the helicopter, simple in design, rose a few feet from the ground.

The VS-300 was powered by a four-cylinder, 75-horsepower, air-cooled engine. There was a three-bladed main rotor, 28 feet in diameter, and a small auxiliary rotor at the rear of the fuselage to counteract torque. It had a welded tubular steel frame, a power transmission combination of v-belts and bevel gears, a two-wheeled landing gear, and a completely open pilot's seat. The VS-300, now exhibited at the Ford Museum in Dearborn, Mich., established a world endurance record by staying aloft 1 hour and 32 minutes on May 6, 1941. Thus, the helicopter fundamentals were established.

Military contracts followed the success of the VS-300, and in 1943 large-scale manufacture of the R-4 made it the world's first production helicopter. Then came the R-5, the R-6, the S-51, the S-55, the S-56, and the S-58, all piston-engine aircraft, all improving and enlarging on preceding designs. The S-51 and S-55 showed the helicopter's usefulness in warfare during the early days of the Korean conflict, serving as rescue and transport vehicles, often behind enemy lines. The S-56, with two piston engines, was considered a giant of its time, being able to carry as many as 40 troops. The 12-passenger S-58 was used as a commercial carrier and construction vehicle as well as a military aircraft.

Practical turbine engines for helicopters became a reality in the 1950s. Sikorsky built the S-62, a single-turbine helicopter with a flying boat hull; the S-61 series, with two turbine engines, used by the Navy for antisubmarine warfare and by helicopter airlines around the world; the S-64, a crane-type helicopter with skeletal fuselage and the ability to lift loads up to 10 tons; and the S-65, a heavy assault transport, built for the Marine Corps, which made its first flight on Oct. 14, 1964.

From his mother, a doctor, and his father, a professor of psychology, Sikorsky acquired an absorbing interest in science, particularly in aviation. He spent 3 years at the Naval College in St. Petersburg, and was still a student at the Mechanical Engineering College of the Polytechnic Institute in Kiev when he determined to build his first helicopter. He traveled to Paris, then the aeronautical center of Europe, where he met such aviation pioneers as Louis Bleriot and Ferdinand Ferber. He returned to Kiev with a 25-horsepower Anzani engine and put together his first helicopter.

Sikorsky's success with fixed-wing aircraft led to a position as head of the aviation subsidiary of the Russian Baltic Railroad Car Works. The Revolution put an end to his career in Russian aviation. In France, he was commissioned to build a bomber for the Allies; the plane was still on the drawing board when the armistice concluding World War I was signed. In the United States, Sikorsky taught and lectured between his arrival in 1919 and the formation in 1923 of the Sikorsky Aero Engineering Corporation. The early Sikorsky company had financial troubles until it joined United Aircraft Corporation. Successive plants were located at Roosevelt Field and College Point on Long Island; Stratford, Conn.; Bridgeport, Conn.; then Stratford again, with completion of the Western Hemisphere's largest helicopter assembly plant in 1955. Sikorsky, president of the company he organized, became engineering manager of Sikorsky Aircraft under United Aircraft Corporation. He retired in 1957.

Sikorsky wrote an autobiography, *The Story of the Winged S* (1938).

For background information *see* HELICOPTER in the McGraw-Hill Encyclopedia of Science and Technology.   □

★ SINNOTT, Edmund Ware

American botanist
Born Feb. 5, 1888, Cambridge, Mass., U.S.A.

SINNOTT'S CHIEF interest was the problem of organic form. This is the simplest expression of the organizing power of living stuff, which pulls together the varied activities of the genes and other protoplasmic agents into the formation of an organism. Sinnott believed that the problem of how this is accomplished—the subject matter of the science of morphogenesis—is the basic one in biology. His scientific work was concerned, in one way or another, with this problem.

He began the study of form as a plant morphologist, concerned especially with the vascular plants. His 1913 paper on the life histories of various members of the Podocarpineae, a little known family of conifers of the Southern Hemisphere, helped determine the position of these plants in classification. He also did much work on the comparative anatomy of vascular plants, using evidence from this source to reconstruct phylogenetic history. He discovered the fact that in the higher plants the anatomy of the node, and particularly the number of bundle gaps in it, has been very slow to change in evolution and is therefore of much value in determining plant relationships. In collaboration with I. W. Bailey he produced a large body of evidence for the conclusion that herbaceous (soft-bodied) plants have evolved from woody forms (trees and shrubs), the body form of the earliest seed plants, presumably in response to the origin of

temperate climates and thus of relatively short growing seasons.

Sinnott also studied the inheritance of form, using the many different fruit shapes in several species of the Cucurbitaceae (the gourds and squashes), and proving that form here is determined by genes in typical mendelian fashion. At that time his was the most extensive genetic analysis of form in a plant organ.

In collaboration with A. F. Blakeslee, Sinnott studied the influence of specific chromosomes in *Datura* on an anatomical character, the structure of the flower stalk. This opened another method of attack on the genetics of form.

Sinnott then began to investigate the cellular basis of these shape differences, using the early developmental stages in the primordia of leaves and fruits and in stem meristems. He showed how the origin of traits of form and size depends on the plane of cell division and the rate and extent of cell enlargement. This work brought together the concepts of plant histology and those of genetics and morphogenesis. The growth of a fruit was found to follow a very precise curve, the character of which was not affected by the method by which growth was accomplished, whether by increase in cell size or in cell number. In some fruits, shape differences are determined in the early meristem, but more commonly they arise from differential, heterogonic growth in the various dimensions. It is this differential growth that genes for shape evidently control. In all this work the relation of cell to organ in plants is of much interest, and here the work of Sinnott and his colleagues and students was of particular importance. Among its results was the first clear description of how cell division is effected in large, vacuolate cells.

A very different problem of form, that of the tree as it is related to the angle and relative size of branches, was found by Sinnott to be determined in many cases by the location and extent of development of "reaction wood," which pulls or pushes the branches upward or downward.

Sinnott presented a discussion of the phenomena of morphogenesis and the main factors determining development in the plant kingdom in *Plant Morphogenesis* (1959). A more philosophical discussion of organic form in general appeared in *The Problem of Organic Form* (1963). He also wrote several textbooks in botany and genetics and about 120 scientific papers.

Sinnott was educated in the public schools of Bridgewater, Mass., and received from Harvard an A.B. in 1908 and a Ph.D. in 1913. He was appointed professor of botany and genetics at the Connecticut Agricultural College (now the University of Connecticut) in 1915, and professor of botany at Barnard College of Columbia University in 1928. In 1940 he went to Yale as Sterling Professor of Botany. He became director of the Sheffield Scientific School at Yale in 1945 and dean of the Graduate School in 1950. He retired from active university work in 1956. He was elected to the National Academy of Sciences in 1936.

For background information *see* PLANT MORPHOGENESIS in the McGraw-Hill Encyclopedia of Science and Technology.   □

★ **SONNEBORN, Tracy Morton**
American geneticist
Born Oct. 19, 1905, Baltimore, Md., U.S.A.

THE FOUNDATIONS of genetics—the chromosome and gene theories—were derived mainly from studies on peas and corn, flies and fowl. Valiant attempts were made to use such organisms to penetrate to the underlying molecular level of genetics and to understand how genes, cytoplasm, and environment acted and interacted in cellular and organismic heredity, differentiation, and evolution. But the results of these attempts were limited and on the whole disappointing. Today microorganisms are the materials of choice for attacking such problems, but they were not the materials of choice until a handful of visionaries made them so not very long ago. The situation with microorganisms was much the same as would have existed for Mendel if peas could have been propagated only by cuttings and by their normal method of self-fertilization; without crossbreeding by experimental transfer of pollen from one type of plant to another, peas would never have taught Mendel the basic principles of genetics. Nothing comparable to crossbreeding was known in viruses, bacteria, protozoa, and many algae and fungi. It was not until the 1930s and 1940s that a few geneticists, who sensed the need and the possibilities, applied themselves successfully to the task in spite of the prevalent opinion that it could not be done. Their success led quickly to the revolutionary genetics we know today.

Sonneborn's part in bringing about this transition was the discovery of how to crossbreed certain unicellular animals, the ciliates, using *Paramecium aurelia* as a model case. This enabled him to lead the way in elucidating the principles of action and interaction of genes, cytoplasm, and environment. For his contributions to genetics, Sonneborn received the Kimber Genetics Award of the National Academy of Sciences in 1959.

When Sonneborn began in 1932 to seek a way to crossbreed *P. aurelia*, it was generally believed that this was impossible. Experiments had already shown that these were exclusively self-fertilizing organisms. When different strains were grown together and both conjugated at the same time, each conjugated only with its own kind. Sonneborn hoped that, by discovering what brought about conjugation, it might be possible to force conjugation between diverse strains. After 5 years of accumulating facts about the conditions for conjugation, he suddenly realized that one of these facts was the key to the problem. One day of feverish experimentation solved it.

The key was the relation of the occurrence of conjugation to the occurrence of autogamy. Conjugation is reciprocal fertilization between two temporarily united cells while autogamy is self-fertilization within an unimpaired cell. The progeny of a cell that has undergone autogamy do not go through autogamy again for some dozens of cell generations. Sonneborn observed that a culture descended from a single cell did not conjugate until after autogamy occurred among the cells of the culture. For some time he accepted this fact to mean that autogamy merely rendered the cells "sticky," for it was commonly believed that conjugation was dependent upon a sticky state that permitted any cell to conjugate with any other sticky cell of the same strain. One day an alternative interpretation occurred to him. Perhaps autogamy differentiated the cells into hereditarily different types and conjugation occurred only between these visibly identical but physiologically diverse types. That same day he mixed together in one container samples of many different nonconjugating pure cultures, each derived from a different autogamous cell in the absence of further autogamy. Before all the samples could be brought together, a startling sight never before seen greeted his eyes. The cells immediately agglutinated in small and then progressively larger clumps and finally broke up into pairs and conjugated. Next he mixed samples of just two cultures. Some pairs of cultures did the same thing; others did not. He then selected two that would react with each other as standards and mixed samples of all of the other cultures with each of them. About half of the cultures reacted with one standard and the rest with the other. Clearly, autogamy had differentiated the cells into two hereditarily different types, which Sonneborn called mating types I and II.

The next step was to find out whether other strains of *P. aurelia* also had the same mating types. If so, the problem of obtaining conjugation between strains was solved and genetic analysis of these organisms would be possible. That could not be discovered the same day; it had to await finding and culturing strains from different natural sources. When this was done, Sonneborn found that every strain had mating types and that some, but not all, of them had mating types I and II. The others contained other pairs of mating types. Some had types called III and IV, others had types V and VI. In other words, he had discovered that the species *P. aurelia* consisted of a number of sexually and genetically isolated varieties, which he called "syngens," a term denoting that each had a potentially common gene pool by reason of being able to interbreed. As the collections accumulated from all over the world, 14 syngens of *P. aurelia* were eventually found. Each consisted of innumerable natural strains and included two mating types. Crossbreeding within a syngen thereby became a routine operation.

With variations in detail only, mating types and syngens were subsequently discovered by Sonneborn and others in many diverse species of ciliates. This opened up the field of the modern genetics of unicellular animals. It led Sonneborn directly and quickly to three important genetic discoveries.

First, he found hereditary strain differences, subjected them to typical Mendelian breeding analysis, and obtained typical Mendelian results. The genetic principles derived from studies of higher plants and animals were thus extended to unicellular animals, showing that the principles were, as expected, of widespread general applicability.

Second, analysis of the determination and inheritance of the mating types revealed new genetic principles. Sonneborn found that the first cell division after autogamy was the critical one: often one daughter cell produced progeny of one mating type and the other daughter cell produced progeny of the other mating type. The explanation of this was traced to nuclear events. After fertilization, the nucleus divides twice; two of the resulting four nuclei grow enormously and develop into highly polyploid macronuclei that control the phenotype, the other two remaining small and diploid micronuclei and serving as a "germ plasm" for participation in the next meiosis and fertilization. Both micronuclei divide at each cell division. The two new macronuclei do not divide at the first cell division, but each passes undivided to one of the first two daughter cells. Thereafter the macronucleus divides at each subsequent division. The segregation of the two new macronuclei to the first two daughter cells paralleled the segregation of mating types. All cells that possessed derivatives of the same original macronucleus also inherited the same mating type. Sonneborn was thus forced to adopt the hypothesis that these developing new macronuclei had somehow become permanently and hereditarily altered so that they determined only one or only the other of the two mating types in spite of possessing genes for both. By chance, sometimes the two new macronuclei were determined to control the same mating type, sometimes different mating types. This new hypothesis of "nuclear differentiation" was tested and confirmed by many experiments. It was subsequently found by others to apply to other protozoa and to the diversification of nuclei in different tissues of the developing amphibian egg.

The third consequence of the discovery of mating types was the discovery of killer paramecia, which led to the first demonstration of cytoplasmic inheritance in any animal. In order to discover and study mating types, Sonneborn broke what was at that time the absolute rule in genetic work with microorganisms: never to mix together different cultures, but to keep cultures "pure." In mixing diverse strains, he observed that certain mixtures always led to the appearance of abnormal cells that were doomed to die. Suspecting that one strain was killing the other, he removed the cells of each strain from fluid in which they had lived and introduced cells of the other strain into that fluid. In one of the combinations of fluid and animals, the cells became abnormal and died; in the reciprocal combination they did not. One strain was a killer and rendered its medium toxic to the other, which was sensitive. Sonneborn found that the two kinds could be crossed; sensitives are resistant during mating. Breeding analysis showed, as with the mating types, that killers and sensitives could have exactly the same homozygous set of genes. Obviously, something else was responsible for this hereditary difference. When killers conjugated with sensitives, the killer mate produced killer progeny and the sensitive mate produced sensitive progeny. These traits seemed to follow the cytoplasm, not the genes, in inheritance. He proved this to be true by learning to make conjugants exchange cytoplasm as well as gamete nuclei. When they did that, both mates produced killer progeny. Sonneborn's quantitative studies indicated that the physical basis of the killer trait was particulate and that cytoplasm of a killer contained a large number of the determining particles, which he called "kappa." He later showed that kappa was infective and that it could survive in paramecia only when the latter possessed gene K, disappearing in the homozygotes, kk. Many different kinds of killers, each dependent upon a different cytoplasmic particle (lambda, mu, and so forth), which in each case required in the paramecia a certain gene (L,M, and so forth) for their persistence, were later found by Sonneborn and others.

The three immediate consequences of the discovery of mating types were but the beginning of a long series of fundamental genetic discoveries in Protozoa by Sonneborn and many others. These included model studies of biochemically linked series of alternative genic repressions and derepressions (in control of surface antigens), age-induced chromosomal and genic mutations, systems of semi-autonomous genetic structures in the cell cortex, and the seeming origin of viruses from genic messenger RNA.

Sonneborn studied at Johns Hopkins University, receiving the B.A. in 1925 and the Ph.D., under H. S. Jennings, in 1928. He stayed on at Johns Hopkins as a postdoctoral fellow of the National Research Council for 2 years, as research assistant to Jennings (1930–31), and as research associate and associate (1931–39). In 1939 he went to Indiana University as associate professor, becoming professor in 1943 and Distinguished Service Professor in 1953. He was elected to the National Academy of Sciences in 1946 and to the Royal Society of London in 1964.

For background information *see* BACTERIAL GENETICS in the McGraw-Hill Encyclopedia of Science and Technology.　□

★ SPENCE, Kenneth Wartinbee

American psychologist
Born May 6, 1907, Chicago, Ill., U.S.A.

SPENCE'S MAJOR contributions were concerned with the nature of basic learning processes in animals and humans. Since the history of science has shown that progress in the development of comprehensive systems of scientific

knowledge is likely to be most rapid when simple phenomena are studied first under carefully controlled conditions, many of Spence's investigations were of classical conditioning, the phenomenon originally discovered by the Russian physiologist Ivan Pavlov in the course of his work with dogs.

In classical conditioning, perhaps the simplest of all forms of learning, an originally neutral stimulus, such as a light or sound, is presented along with an event that regularly elicits an observable response (for example, leg flexion in the dog to an electric shock to the paw, or a reflexive blink to an air puff to the eyeball of humans). With repeated presentations of the paired stimuli, the previously neutral stimulus elicits with increasing frequency the response originally evoked only by the noxious stimulus (learning or conditioning). Spence's research aimed at discovering the basic laws of classical conditioning and at formulating a quantitative theory about conditioning phenomena that could be used as a basis for explaining more complex forms of learning.

This theory, developed in conjunction with Clark Hull of Yale University, specifies certain theoretical variables—for example, the learning or habit factor—that combine multiplicatively with the drive or motivational factor to determine performance. Using this theory, Spence demonstrated, for example, that the probability of appearance of conditioned responses is not only positively related to level of motivation, as determined by such variables as the intensity of the noxious unconditioned stimulus or the degree of emotional responsiveness of the individual subject to the experimental situation, but that the mathematical form of the curves obtained when probability of the conditioned response is plotted against successive presentations of the paired stimuli changes systematically with motivational level.

Deductions from the theoretical structure permitted Spence to predict a number of phenomena in more complex learning situations. For example, the theory specifies that the motivational factor combines with all of the response tendencies elicited by a given stimulus. This assumption, in combination with other assumptions in the theoretical network, led to the prediction, verified in a number of studies of verbal rote learning, that increasing motivational level will facilitate performance on tasks in which the habit strength of the correct, to-be-learned response is stronger than those of other response tendencies elicited by a stimulus but will deter performance on tasks in which the habit strength of the correct response is initially weaker than those of competing response tendencies.

Although born in the United States, Spence,

the son of an electrical engineer, was reared in Montreal, Canada, and received his B.A. in psychology from McGill University in 1929 and his M.A. in 1930. He was granted a Ph.D. in psychology at Yale University in 1933. After serving on the faculties of Yale and the University of Virginia, he went to the State University of Iowa in 1938, where he was head of the department of psychology from 1942 to 1964. In 1964 he became a professor of psychology at the University of Texas. He received the Warren Medal of the Society of Experimental Psychologists in 1953 and the Distinguished Scientific Contribution Award of the American Psychological Association in 1956. In 1955 he was elected to the National Academy of Sciences.

Spence wrote *Behavior Theory and Conditioning* (1956) and *Behavior Theory and Learning* (1960).

For background information *see* LEARNING THEORIES in the McGraw-Hill Encyclopedia of Science and Technology. □

★ **SPENCER, Donald Clayton**
American mathematician
Born Apr. 25, 1912, Boulder, Colo., U.S.A.

D EFORMATION OF the complex structure of a compact (closed) Riemann surface (1-dimensional complex manifold) is an idea dating back to B. Riemann, who, in his famous memoir on abelian functions published in 1857, calculated the number of independent parameters on which the deformation of the structure of a compact Riemann surface depends and called it the "number of moduli." The problems centering around the deformation of the complex structure of a Riemann surface have never lost their interest. The theory of quadratic differentials and extremal quasi-conformal maps was developed by O. Teichmüller in the years 1938–

44 in order to give a systematic theory of the deformation of Riemann surfaces. Teichmüller's methods were perfected during the following years by L. Ahlfors, L. Bers, E. Rauch, A. Weil, and others. The deformation of higher-dimensional complex manifolds, or of algebraic surfaces at least, was first considered by M. Noether in 1888. However, in sharp contrast with the case of complex dimension 1 (Riemann surfaces), the deformation of the structure of higher-dimensional complex manifolds was neglected for nearly 70 years following Noether's work until the subject was taken up by A. Frölicher and A. Nijenhuis and by K. Kodaira and D. C. Spencer.

Kodaira and Spencer developed a systematic theory of deformation of the complex structure of higher-dimensional, compact (closed), complex analytic manifolds. They defined a differentiable family of compact complex manifolds as a fiber space $\mathcal{V}$ over a connected differentiable manifold B whose fiber M_t over the point t of M has a complex structure depending differentiably on the point t. Assume, for simplicity, that B is one-dimensional and let V be a sufficiently small interval containing the point $t = 0$ in its interior. Then there is a covering $\{U_a\}$ of the portion of $\mathcal{V}$ over V by open sets U_a where U_a is covered by the coordinates $(z_a, t) = (z_a{}^1, \ldots, z_a{}^k, \ldots, z_a{}^n, t)$ and $z_a{}^k$ is complex. Denote by $z_a = h_{a\beta}(z_\beta, t)$ the biholomorphic coordinate transformations which determine the complex structure of M_t [that is, $z_a{}^k = h_{a\beta}{}^k(z_\beta, t)$ where k ranges from 1 to n]. Letting
$$\theta_{a\beta}(t) = (\theta_{a\beta}{}^1(t), \ldots, \theta_{a\beta}{}^k(t), \ldots, \theta_{a\beta}{}^n(t)),$$
where $\theta_{a\beta}{}^k(t) = \theta_{a\beta}{}^k(z_a, t) = \partial h_{a\beta}{}^k(z_\beta, t)/\partial t$, we obtain a 1-cocycle $\{\theta_{a\beta}(t)\}$ which defines a cohomology class $\theta(t)$ of the 1-dimensional cohomology $H^1(M_t, \Theta_t)$ of M_t with values (coefficients) in the sheaf Θ_t over M_t of holomorphic vector fields. The class $\theta(t)$, called the "infinitesimal deformation" of M_t, measures the dependence of the complex structure of M_t on the parameter t. In the case where the fibers M_t are compact Riemann surfaces, $H^1(M_t, \Theta_t)$ is isomorphic to the vector space of quadratic differentials of the surface, in the sense of Teichmüller. Proceeding in this fashion, a generalization of Riemann's concept of "number of moduli" was obtained. However, in contrast to the case of Riemann surfaces, this number is not defined for all compact complex manifolds. Particular examples of complex manifolds M_0, of complex dimension exceeding 2, show that not all cohomology classes of $H^1(M_0, \Theta_0)$ are the infinitesimal deformations of actual deformations of the structure of M_0. In fact, some classes of $H^1(M_0, \Theta_0)$ may be "obstructed," the

obstructions occurring as classes in $H^2(M_0,\Theta_0)$. If $H^2(M_0,\Theta_0) = 0$, then any class of $H^1(M_0,\Theta_0)$ is the infinitesimal deformation corresponding to a deformation of finite magnitude.

Kodaira generalized the theory to structures defined by a special (and important) class of complex transitive, continuous pseudogroups, and Spencer later generalized the theory of deformation to structures on (compact) manifolds defined by arbitrary transitive, continuous pseudogroups (in the sense of E. Cartan). In the deformation of a pseudogroup structure, it is necessary to find a fine resolution of the sheaf of germs of infinitesimal transformations of the pseudogroup where the infinitesimal transformations are defined by a system of linear partial differential equations. Spencer found a procedure for defining the resolution in terms of sheaves of germs of (differentiable) sections of jet bundles canonically associated with the system of partial differential equations. This procedure is independent of the notion of pseudogroup and is applicable to an arbitrary homogeneous system of linear partial differential equations on a manifold that has constant rank and possesses formal solutions. Thus Spencer was led to associate, to an arbitrary (homogeneous) system of linear partial differential equations satisfying the above conditions, a resolution of its sheaf of germs of solutions defined in a canonical manner, and the maps connecting the terms of the resolution are defined by means of a linear differential operator of order 1.

In the case of the trivial system of equations $df = 0$, where f is a real-valued function (or, in terms of coordinates, $\partial f / \partial x^k = 0$, $k = 1$, 2, $\ldots$, n), the only solutions are the real numbers (constants), and Spencer's resolution reduces to the classical resolution of G. de Rham. The resolution is known to be exact in the analytic case and in the case of constant coefficients and therefore provides in these cases a generalization of de Rham's theorem. It is highly probable that it is also exact in the elliptic case and provides a generalization, to arbitrary elliptic systems of equations (satisfying the above conditions), a generalization of W. V. D. Hodge's theory of harmonic integrals (harmonic differential forms). In any case the exactness of the resolution at degree 1 is equivalent, as D. G. Quillen has pointed out, to the local solvability of the corresponding nonhomogeneous system of equations under the appropriate compatibility conditions (if the system is overdetermined).

A physician's son, Spencer majored in physics and premedicine at the University of Colorado, where he received his B.A. in 1934. Admitted to the Harvard Medical School, he changed to engineering and received his B.Sc. degree in 1936 from the Massachusetts Institute of Technology. He spent the following 3 years at the University of Cambridge (England) and received his Ph.D. there in 1939. During the latter part of World War II, he worked in the Applied Mathematics Group (NDRC), New York University, on the calculation of impact forces on objects striking water surfaces. Spencer was professor of mathematics at Stanford University from 1946 to 1950, at Princeton University from 1950 to 1963, and he rejoined the faculty of Stanford University in 1963. He was elected to the National Academy of Sciences in 1961.

Spencer wrote *Coefficient Regions for Schlicht Functions*, with A. C. Schaeffer (1950) and *Functionals of Finite Riemann Surfaces*, with M. Schiffer (1954).

For background information *see* GROUP THEORY in the McGraw-Hill Encyclopedia of Science and Technology.   □

★ **SPITZER, Lyman, Jr.**
American astrophysicist
Born June 26, 1914, Toledo, Ohio, U.S.A.

OUR UNDERSTANDING of planets, stars, nebulae and galaxies is largely based on the natural laws that form part of basic physics. Trained as a theoretical physicist, Spitzer analyzed the processes that are important in a variety of astronomical fields, including the atmospheres of the Earth and the stars, stellar motions, and the formation of stars and planets. His best-known work in theoretical astrophysics was concerned with physical processes in interstellar space and the role played by interstellar material in star formation. In addition, he pioneered both in research on controlled nuclear fusion and in the use of artificial satellites for astronomical telescopes.

In 1941 it was apparent that star formation must be taking place in spiral galaxies, where the very luminous, hot stars radiated energy so fast that their nuclear fuel would be exhausted in a few million years. Such systems are also characterized by clouds of interstellar gas and dust (in contrast to elliptical galaxies, with no supergiant stars, in which little gas or dust is observed).

In an attempt to explain these observed differences in terms of star formation in flattened stellar systems, Spitzer undertook a series of interrelated investigations, analyzing the physical processes in the interstellar medium, contrasting the equilibrium of gas in flattened and elliptical systems of stars, and tracing out the different evolutionary stages in a gas cloud that is contracting to form new stars. One of the principal results of this investigation was a theoretical prediction of a large temperature difference between regions of ionized hydrogen surrounding hot, young stars, where the gas temperature is about 10,000°K, and the surrounding regions of neutral hydrogen, where a temperature of 100°K or less may be expected. This predicted temperature difference, which has now been fully verified by observation, may provide the driving force for the observed high velocities of the interstellar gas clouds. These studies have substantially increased our understanding of the conditions under which stars can form from interstellar matter.

Through his interest in ionized gases in the weak interstellar magnetic field, Spitzer became actively involved in research on plasma physics, the study of the basic properties of an ionized gas in a magnetic field. His theoretical research on the electrical resistivity and thermal conductivity of a fully ionized gas was one of the basic early contributions to this subject. He was one of the first to point out specifically how a magnetic field might be used to contain a hot deuterium-tritium plasma at a temperature of 100,000,000°K, which could then be used as a controlled source of thermonuclear power. His brief monograph, *Physics of Fully Ionized Gases* (1956; rev. 1962), is one of the most widely quoted references in the field of plasma physics, and the Princeton University Plasma Physics Laboratory, which he began and for many years directed, is a leading center for research on controlled fusion and basic plasma physics.

In addition, Spitzer was an early advocate of astronomical space research, in 1947 predicting the use of artificial satellites for making astronomical observations above the Earth's atmosphere. Under his directorship, the Princeton University Observatory played a leading role in a program of space astronomy, designed to obtain high-resolution photographs and ultraviolet stellar spectra from balloons, rockets, and satellites.

Spitzer was educated at Phillips Academy, Andover, Mass., and at Yale University, where he received his B.A. in 1935, majoring in physics. After a year in Cambridge, England, as a Henry fellow, working with Sir Arthur Eddington, he returned to Princeton University to study under Henry Norris Russell, receiving his Ph.D. there in 1958. He was awarded a National Research Council fellowship to study for a year at Harvard, after which he returned to Yale as an instructor, first in physics and later in both physics and astronomy. During World War II he participated in undersea warfare research; from 1942 through 1946 he took an active part in the coordination of U.S. oceanographic and underwater sound transmission studies and in the military application of the information obtained. After the war he returned to Yale for a year and a half, and in 1947 went to Princeton as chairman of the astronomy department and professor of astronomy. In 1951 he was appointed Charles A. Young Professor. Spitzer was elected to the National Academy of Sciences in 1952.

For background information *see* ASTROPHYSICS; INTERSTELLAR MATTER; PLASMA PHYSICS in the McGraw-Hill Encyclopedia of Science and Technology.   □

☆ STANLEY, Wendell Meredith
American biochemist
Born Aug. 16, 1904, Ridgeville, Ind., U.S.A.

WHILE TRYING to determine the chemical nature of viruses, Stanley found that a virus is a protein and that, like many other proteins, it can be crystallized even though it is a living entity. In recognition of his work, Stanley shared the 1946 Nobel Prize in chemistry with the American biochemists James Batcheller

Sumner and John Howard Northrup, who had shown enzymes to be crystallizable proteins.

For many years after the French chemist Anselme Payen discovered the first enzyme, diastase, in 1833, it was believed that enzymes were proteinaceous materials. This view was disputed by the German chemist Richard Willstätter, who about 1920 produced evidence that enzymes were nonproteinaceous in nature. However, in 1926 Sumner succeeded in obtaining crystals of the enzyme urease and demonstrated that the crystals were proteins. Although his work was not immediately accepted, the proteinaceous nature of enzymes was established when Northrup succeeded in crystallizing pepsin (1930), trypsin (1932), and chymotrypsin (1935) and proved them to be proteins. Viruses, on the other hand, which had been discovered by the Dutch botanist Martinus Willem Beijerinck in 1898, were a complete mystery. Because viruses can reproduce and mutate, they were accepted as living entities. However, it was not known whether they were hydrocarbon, carbohydrate, lipid, protein, inorganic, or organismal in nature.

In 1932, while working at the Rockefeller Institute for Medical Research in Princeton, N.J., Stanley began his study of the tobacco mosaic virus. He chose this particular virus for three reasons: (1) it was known to be unusually stable; (2) large amounts of highly infectious starting material could be easily obtained; and (3) it was possible to titrate the virus in a solution with a high degree of accuracy. Among the chemical studies performed by Stanley were the effect of the enzymes trypsin and pepsin, the rate of inactivation of the virus at various hydrogen ion concentrations, and the effect of over 100 chemical reagents on the infectivity of the virus.

By 1934 Stanley had concluded that the tobacco mosaic virus was a proteinaceous material. He then began to try to concentrate and purify the virus by methods similar to those that had been used by Sumner and Northrup for the concentration and purification of enzymes, and he achieved success in 1935. He inoculated Turkish tobacco plants with a gauze pad moistened with a virus preparation. After a few weeks, the plants were cut, frozen, and passed through a meat grinder. The pulp was then allowed to thaw to a temperature of 4°C (a temperature at which all the subsequent steps were also carried out) and the juice pressed out. The juice was then adjusted to a pH of 7.2, after which it was recombined with the press cake, well mixed, pressed out a second time (the pH was then about 6.7), and filtered. The globulin fraction was then precipitated with ammonium sulfate, removed by filtration, dissolved in a 0.01 molar phosphate buffer at a pH of 7, and precipitated with ammonium sulfate a number of times until the filtrate was practically colorless. The precipitate was then dissolved in water and the pH adjusted to about 4, which caused the protein to precipitate. The protein was removed by filtration, suspended in water, and the pH adjusted to about 7. At this point the solution contained approximately 80 per cent of the virus that had been in the starting material. The protein was crystallized by slowly adding a saturated solution of sodium sulfate until a cloudiness appeared, and then adding a solution of 10 per cent glacial acetic acid in one-half saturated ammonium sulfate until a pH of 5 was attained. Small needlelike crystals were thus obtained and isolated. Subsequent experimentation showed that the virus activity was a specific property of the crystalline material and, hence, that the material was in actuality the tobacco mosaic virus itself.

Stanley continued his experimentation with the tobacco mosaic virus and in December, 1936, isolated nucleic acid from the crystalline material. By 1937 it had been demonstrated that the nucleic acid was responsible for the virus activity and that the tobacco mosaic virus was therefore a nucleoprotein. Stanley subsequently worked on the amino-acid composition of the protein and the optical and physicochemical properties of solutions of the virus nucleoprotein. He later worked on the preparation and investigation of other viruses, such as the one responsible for influenza. He also developed centrifuge-type influenza vaccine.

Stanley was educated at Earlham College in Richmond, Ind., receiving his B.S. in 1926. He performed his graduate work at the University of Illinois, receiving his M.S. in 1927 and his Ph.D. in chemistry in 1929. He was a research associate and then lecturer at the University from 1929 to 1930, leaving to do research in Germany at the University of Munich as a National Research Council fellow. He returned to the United States in 1931 to become an assistant at the Rockefeller Institute for Medical Research in New York City. In 1932 he transferred to the Rockefeller Institute facility at Princeton, N.J., becoming an associate in 1935, an associate member in 1937, and a member in 1940. In 1948 Stanley left to accept the posts of professor of biochemistry and director of the Virus Laboratory at the University of California at Berkeley. From 1948 to 1953 he served as chairman of the department of biochemistry, and in 1958 he was appointed professor of virology and chairman of the virology department at the University. He was elected to the National Academy of Sciences in 1941.

For background information *see* VIRUS in the McGraw-Hill Encyclopedia of Science and Technology.   □

☆ STARR, Chauncey

American physicist, electrical engineer, corporate executive
Born Apr. 14, 1912, Newark, N.J., U.S.A.

O N APR. 3, 1965, an Atlas-Agena launch vehicle bearing a pioneering nuclear power plant rocketed into orbit from California's Vandenberg Air Force Base. Twelve hours later, the SNAP-10A system was at full power. The world's first nuclear reactor in space was a success and assured the nation's space program a power source capable of meeting the growing electrical requirements of space exploration and utilization.

The historic flight of SNAP-10A represented the culmination of one of the most complex tasks ever undertaken by the atomic energy industry. From its inception, the program was directed for the Atomic Energy Commission by Chauncey Starr, vice-president of North American Aviation, Inc., and president of its Atomics International division.

Starr was one of the first to recognize the potential of atomic energy for space application. In 1946, he brought together at North American Aviation a small group of scientists and engineers to explore the new field of peaceful application of atomic energy. One of the team's first efforts was the completion of an Air Force study on the technical feasibility of nuclear rockets and ramjets. This work accurately identified problem areas in nuclear propulsion, singled out materials problems, and recommended solutions.

By 1951, the group had turned its attention to power supplies for satellites and spacecraft, particularly the possibility of a nuclear reactor. The difficulties inherent in such a concept were tremendous. Reactors of the day were huge structures weighing thousands of tons. A space reactor had to be limited to a few hundred pounds.

Starr and his associates found the key to the necessary compactness and light weight by devising a combined fuel moderator consisting of a homogeneous mixture of uranium suspended in zirconium hydride. Development of a fabrication method for the material as well as a ceramic barrier to prevent hydrogen escape from the fuel-moderator container were in themselves major break-throughs. Once developed, they opened the way for design, construction, and successful operation of test reactors. Still to be solved was a myriad of engineering problems: development of a reliable lightweight system for conversion of reactor heat to electricity; of a suitable lightweight shield to protect the space vehicle payload from radiation; of control mechanisms, wiring, insulation, and electronic instrumentation that would operate reliably in the harsh environment of vacuum and radiation. Finally, a system had to be designed that would stand the shock and vibration of launch, start in orbit by remote command, operate reliably for 1 year, and, upon reentry into the Earth's atmosphere, break up and disperse throughout the upper atmosphere. All this had to be accomplished with the safety of the public and of launch personnel as a prime consideration.

Beginning in 1956, Atomics International's work on the zirconium-hydride reactor received significant support from the U.S. Atomic Energy Commission. It was soon incorporated in the AEC's program designated "SNAP," for Systems for Nuclear Auxiliary Power. Under Starr's direction, this major program constructed highly specialized facilities for development, reactor operation, and testing. Of prime importance were environmental facilities in which SNAP components and systems could be subjected to conditions approaching as closely as possible the environment of space.

The SNAP-10A system that evolved from these efforts weighed only 970 pounds, the reactor only 250 pounds. The system produced over 500 watts of electric power. The 43-day operation of the power plant in space in 1965 confirmed the success of the program and opened the door to the nuclear space age.

Under Starr's direction, Atomics International also pioneered the development of two major nuclear reactor concepts—the sodium-cooled reactor and the organic-cooled reactor. The former is the forerunner of tomorrow's fast-breeder power reactor. Much of the technology developed in the organic program is being utilized in the development of the Heavy Water Organic Cooled Reactor (HWOCR), the leading candidate for large-scale dual-purpose plants for production of electrical power and desalted water.

Starr received a bachelor's degree in electrical engineering in 1932 and a Ph.D. in physics in 1935 from Rensselaer Polytechnic Institute. His doctoral research involved the new field of semiconductor rectifiers. He received a Coffin fellowship for postdoctorate research at Harvard, where he investigated electrical and thermal properties of metals at very high pressures. As a research associate at the Massachusetts Institute of Technology from 1938 to 1941 he designed, operated, and built some of the early cryogenic equipment for use in high-magnetic fields and also performed the nation's first experimental work on the phenomena of paramagnetic dispersion at low temperatures in crystalline compounds of the iron group.

During 1941–42 he directed research work for the Navy's Bureau of Ships on electronic devices for study of transients in ship structures. With the Manhattan District from 1942 through 1946, he helped develop the electromagnetic process for uranium separation, serving as technical director of the Oak Ridge, Tenn., pilot plant where the process was developed and improved. He joined North American Aviation in 1946.

In addition to many research publications and articles on the economics and social impact of nuclear power, Starr wrote, with R. W. Dickinson, *Sodium-graphite Reactors* (1958).

For background information *see* REACTOR, NUCLEAR; REACTOR, NUCLEAR (CLASSIFICATION) in the McGraw-Hill Encyclopedia of Science and Technology. □

★ **STAUDINGER, Hermann**
German chemist
Born Mar. 23 1881, Worms, Germany
Died Sept. 9, 1965, Freiberg, Germany

W HILE STUDYING high-molecular compounds, Staudinger conceived and elaborated the explanation of the phenomenon of polymerization. He thus provided the basic framework for the development of many of the processes that are used in the manufacture of plastics and other high-polymer synthetics. In recognition of his contributions to the study of high-molecular compounds, or macromolecules, Staudinger was awarded the 1953 Nobel Prize in chemistry.

In 1859 the German chemist Friedrich August Kekule proposed a principle by which organic structures can be explained. This led to an understanding of the bonds between the atoms in a molecule and permitted great advances in the synthesis of low-molecular compounds. However, although some of the most important natural substances—such as proteins, enzymes, and polysaccharides—are macromolecules, Kekule's principle failed to elucidate the structure of high-molecular compounds. When the first of all-synthetic plastics, the phenolics, were accidentally discovered in 1906, a large number of researchers began to search for the structural principles behind the macromolecular natural substances and plastics.

About 1920 Staudinger discovered that isoprene, the building block of natural rubber, could be easily prepared through the pyrogenic cleavage of limonene. He then found that he could polymerize the isoprene to obtain a synthetic rubber by using benzoyl peroxide as a catalyst. Staudinger then began a series of experiments by which he hoped to explain the constitution of rubber by preparing hydrates of it. Although it had been predicted by others that a low-molecular distillable hydrocarbon would result, the hydration product was found to have rubberlike properties. This led Staudinger to assign a macromolecular structure to rubber, a premise that had first been advanced by G. Bouchardat in 1879.

About 1922 Staudinger, working at the Federal Technical Institute in Zurich, Switzerland, began to investigate the polymerization of styrene, whose colloidal properties change according to the polymerization temperature. He was struck by the similarity of the behavior of the styrene to that of the homologous series of paraffin waxes, which have the general formula C_nH_{2n+2} and whose physical properties in both the solid and dissolved state vary with the length of the chain. This led Staudinger to propose that there was no one unique product of a polymerization reaction but rather one member of a homologous polymer series built of long chains of repeated identical groups. Although the end product of any given polymerization, he continued, would have a characteristic average length, the length of any particular chain would depend upon a number of arbitrary factors, such as temperature. An excellent indicator of chain length, Staudinger recognized, was the viscosity of the solution, which increases proportionately or approximately proportionate with the chain length. Since this relation holds for all linear molecular material, viscosity measurements played a large role in further investigations, such as the determination of the polymerization rate, of high-molecular compounds. This technique is now in general use to determine chain lengths of linear macromolecular materials.

Staudinger also also showed that the colloidal particles in a dilute solution were macromolecular, which was contrary to the then prevalent theory that attributed a micelle structure to colloids. This discovery led to analogous polymer reactions, in which the initial macromolecular product was maintained in equilibrium with its derivatives. Staudinger was particularly involved in such analogous polymer conversions with the cellulose series, and his work fundamentally altered the earlier conceptions about the structure of cellulose. By means of x-ray analyses of polyoxymethylene, a crystalline macromolecular product, he extended these concepts to the study of synthetic polymers.

The rapid development of macromolecular chemistry can be attributed to the fact that an entire series of natural and synthetic products was studied quite early. The synthetics served as models of the natural materials, and this permitted the detailed addition studies that proved that the physical properties of high-molecular compounds are determined by the shape of the molecules. Furthermore, these addition reactions demonstrated the existence of branched and spherical macromolecules.

In addition to his work with high-molecular compounds, Staudinger contributed to the chemistry of low-molecular compounds. He discovered ketene, H_2CCO; an organic phosphorus compound; and the chemical composition of the effective ingredient of insect powder.

The son of a professor, Staudinger studied at the universities of Halle, Darmstadt, and Munich, obtaining his Ph.D. from Halle in 1903. After further study at the University of Strasbourg, he became an academic lecturer there in 1907. Later that year he accepted a post as assistant professor of organic chemistry at the Chemical Institute of the Technical College of Karlsruhe. In 1912 Staudinger left to become a professor of chemistry at the Federal Technical Institute in Zurich, Switzerland. He was appointed director of the Chemical Institute of the University of Freiberg in 1926, serving in that capacity until becoming emeritus in April, 1951.

Staudinger wrote a number of books, among them *The High-molecular Organic Compounds, Rubber and Cellulose* (new ed. 1961), *Macromolecular Chemistry and Biology* (1947), and *Working Memoirs* (1961).

For background information *see* POLYMER in the McGraw-Hill Encyclopedia of Science and Technology.   □

STEINMAN, David Barnard
American engineer
Born June 11, 1886, New York, N.Y., U.S.A.
Died Aug. 21, 1960, New York, N.Y., U.S.A.

IN HIS long career, Steinman designed over 400 bridges, including the Straits of Mackinac Bridge in Michigan, the Triborough and Henry Hudson bridges in New York City, and the Sydney Harbor Bridge in Australia. Eight of his structures won awards for their beauty. In 1953 Steinman received the William Proctor Prize of the Scientific Research Society of America.

A major scientific problem solved by Steinman concerned aerodynamics and suspension bridges. On Nov. 7, 1940, the Tacoma Narrows Bridge, a $6,400,000 structure opened only 4 months before, shook itself to pieces in a 42-mile-an-hour gale and crashed into Puget Sound. The Tacoma bridge was the third longest suspension bridge in the world and was an extreme example of the trend toward slender flexible construction of suspension bridges. It was strong enough to support its own dead weight and the weight of traffic and it was safe against temperature changes. But the aerodynamic effects of wind on such complex structures as bridges were not well understood and so were unaccounted for in the design. Other suspension bridges, such as the Bronx-Whitestone Bridge and the Golden Gate Bridge, were also aerodynamically unstable as designed and required costly reconstruction to make them safe.

In 1938 Steinman had begun a theoretical and experimental study of the general theory of aerodynamic effects on bridges with the goal of developing formulas to predict the stability of a design and to specify the amount of stiffening required by a suspension bridge. He started with airflow experiments on simple models, such as half-round shapes mounted between a pair of light springs. When the flat surface was exposed to a horizontal wind and was displaced slightly up or down from its equilibrium position, the resulting small vibration quickly built up into a large and violent oscillation. When the round surface faced into the wind, any oscillation that was started quickly dampened. These observations followed the same principles as those that explain lift in an airplane.

Steinman extended this investigation to a wide structure and reasoned that the oscillation is not uniform across the width of a bridge. It takes time for the wind flow to traverse the width and as a result there is a progressive difference of phase of the structure's nature period of vibration as the wind passes across. The differences include differences in velocity and even in direction of motion. Thus the resultant motion is modified by the relative velocity of the wind. In addition, the wind builds up twisting oscillations within the structure if it is torsionally unstable. Because of this phase-difference factor, the stability of a section depends not only upon the shape and proportions of the section but also upon the wind velocity. Steinman investigated the critical values of this velocity function with wind tunnel tests of models of bridge sections, measuring the pressure distributions across the width of such sections. These studies yielded simple working formulas for predicting all critical wind velocities for vertical and torsional oscillations, rates of amplification, limiting amplitudes, and amplitude responses at all velocities. As a result of Steinman's work, it is now possible to apply aerodynamic principles to design bridge cross sections that are fundamentally stable.

The son of an immigrant factory worker, Steinman was raised in a lower East Side tenement in New York City and played in the shadow of the Brooklyn Bridge, which provided his first inspiration and which he always considered the most esthetic of bridges. He graduated from City College of New York, and received his civil engineering degree in 1909 and his Ph.D. in 1911 from Columbia University. His Ph.D. thesis was entitled *The Design of the Henry Hudson Memorial Bridge as a Steel Arch*; more than 20 years later he won the contract to design the real Henry Hudson Bridge over the Harlem River.

In 1917 he joined Holton B. Robinson, builder of the Manhattan and Williamsburg bridges in New York City, in designing the Florianopolis bridge in Brazil. With a main span of 1,114 feet, it was the largest bridge in South America and the longest eyebar suspension bridge in the world. Important innovations developed by Robinson and Steinman and used for the first time on this bridge were a new form of stiffening truss and a new type of cable construction.

In 1923 Steinman founded a consulting engineering firm in which he remained active until 3 months before his death at 73. Bridges he designed but did not live to see built include the bridge across the Tagus River at Lisbon, the Straits of Messina Bridge that will link Sicily with the rest of Italy, and a bridge that will link Asia and Europe across the Bosporus at Istanbul.

Books written by Steinman include *Suspension Bridges: The Aerodynamic Problem and Its Solution* (1954), *Miracle Bridge at Mackinac* (1957), and *Bridges and Their Builders* (rev. ed. 1957).

For background information *see* BRIDGE; BRIDGE VIBRATION in the McGraw-Hill Encyclopedia of Science and Technology.   □

★ STERN, Curt
American geneticist
Born Aug. 30, 1902, Hamburg, Germany

For his contributions in a variety of areas of general and human genetics, Stern received the 1963 Kimber Genetics Award of the National Academy of Sciences.

In the general area, Stern showed that recombination of genes linked together on the same chromosome pair is the result of chromosome exchanges. In 1909 the Belgian F. A. Janssens published a description of chromosome behavior during meiosis and proposed that homologous chromosomes break at corresponding points and rejoin crosswise to form exchange chromosomes. Two years later, Thomas Hunt Morgan, at Columbia University, applied this hypothesis to his discoveries in the genetics of the fruit fly, *Drosophila*. He had found that a female that had received the two genes A and B together in one chromosome from one parent, and the two corresponding genes A^1 and B^1 together in a chromosome from the other parent, would itself form four kinds of eggs, each with a different chromosome. Two of these would contain the original combinations of genes AB and A^1B^1, but the other two would represent recombinations of genes, AB^1 and A^1B. Morgan explained the origin of these recombinations as due to breakage and crosswise reunion of chromosomes, "crossing over."

It had not been possible to study chromosome behavior in living cells, and no direct proof of Morgan's theory had been obtainable. Homologous chromosomes are usually indistinguishable from one another, and crossing over, if it occurred, would again result in chromosomes indistinguishable from the original chromosomes. Stern reasoned that if two homologous chromosomes were visibly different at each end, crossing over should result in visibly new types of chromosomes.

Stern learned *Drosophila* genetics in the famous "fly room" at Columbia University, returning later to the Kaiser Wilhelm Institut für Biologie in Berlin-Dahlem, Germany. The plan for his experiment was conceived in 1925, after he discovered a chromosome with a long translocated chromosome piece attached to its proximal end. The execution of the experiment was delayed until 1931, when H. J. Muller made available a chromosome produced by x-irradiation that was deficient for a large part of its distal end.

Flies were obtained that had one each of these cytologically marked "double heteromorphic" chromosomes. The two chromosomes may be called (1) long-long and (2) short-short. Genetically and invisibly, the first chromosome carried two genes, A and B. The second chromosome carried genes A^1 and B^1 located close to the two ends of the chromosome section held in common by the two chromosomes.

The offspring of these flies consisted of the two genetic nonrecombination classes AB and A^1B^1 and the recombination classes AB^1 and A^1B. Cytological study showed that AB and A^1B^1 offspring carried long-long and short-short noncrossover chromosomes respectively, while AB^1 and A^1B carried long-short and short-long "new" crossover chromosomes. This represented cytological proof for Morgan's theory of crossing over. Simultaneously with these *Drosophila* experiments, Harriett Creighton and Barbara McClintock furnished equivalent proof by work with corn plants (*Zea mays*). The molecular mechanism by which such new chromosomes are formed in recombination is still subject to investigation.

Crossing over was known to occur only in germ cells. However, Stern's analysis (1936) of *Drosophila* individuals, which are mosaics of genetically different cells, showed that crossing over may also occur in somatic cells. This finding added to the knowledge of chromosome behavior and served as a tool in developmental genetics in which the effect on differentiation of two genotypes within the same individual is studied.

As a teacher Stern early felt the need to dwell on human implications of genetics. In 1943, he began giving a course on the principles of human genetics and in 1949 published a book under the same title. This book played a role in making human genetics an important part of research and training in medical schools.

Stern obtained a Ph.D. in zoology at the University of Berlin in 1923. He was a postdoctoral Rockefeller Foundation fellow at Columbia University, being among the first Europeans who reversed the trend of one-sided advanced studies of Americans in Europe. After a period of research in Germany, Stern taught at the University of Rochester from 1933 to 1947. In 1947 he became a professor at the University of California, Berkeley. He was elected to the National Academy of Sciences in 1948.

Stern wrote *Principles of Human Genetics* (1949; 2d ed. 1960).

For background information *see* GENETICS in the McGraw-Hill Encyclopedia of Science and Technology.   □

STERN, Otto
American physicist
Born Feb. 17, 1888, Sorau, Upper Silesia, Germany

STERN'S DEVELOPMENT of the molecular-beam method provided an important tool in the study of the magnetic properties of atoms and of atomic nuclei. He used this method to prove directly the existence of the magnetic moment of atoms and nuclei, and to measure their magnitudes. For these achievements, he was awarded the 1943 Nobel Prize in physics.

Early 20th-century quantum theory pictured the atom as being an electrically charged system in rotation. As such, an atom would have magnetic properties similar to those of a small current-carrying loop of wire. The strength of an atom's magnetic property is designated as the magnetic moment. The direction of the magnetic moment, which may be considered as a minute bar magnet, is perpendicular to the plane of the atom's rotation. There is, however, a considerable difference between the behavior of an ordinary bar magnet and an atomic magnetic moment when an external magnetic field is applied. A bar magnet would simply align itself in the direction of this applied field. An atomic magnet, by virtue of its mechanical angular momentum, would tend to oppose alignment parallel to the applied field. As a result, the axis of the atomic magnet describes a cone about the field direction, with a fixed angle of inclination and a fixed frequency of precession known as the Larmor frequency.

In studying the effect of an external magnetic field on the motion of a beam of silver atoms, Stern made use of the fact that a nonuniform magnetic field would produce a net force on a magnetic dipole of any kind. Thus, by subjecting a beam of atoms to an inhomogeneous magnetic field, one would expect to see a deviation from the beam's straight line motion. Such behavior would prove conclusively the existence of the magnetic moment of the atom. Furthermore, the nature of the deviation, should it exist, would resolve the question of whether the classical or quantum theory provided the correct explanation. According to classical theory, an atomic magnet can precess at any angle to the direction of the applied magnetic field, and one would expect to see a uniform spreading of the beam about its initial direction. The quantum theory predicts that an atomic magnet can precess at only a small number of fixed angles with respect to the applied field. In the case of silver atoms, for example, only two angles (corresponding to parallel and antiparallel alignment with the field) are allowed. This situation would produce a splitting of the beam into two distinct lines, one on either side of the original direction of motion.

Stern first began work on the molecular-beam (or molecular-ray) method at Frankfurt in 1920. The arrangement was as follows: Vapor flowed through a tiny hole bored into an electrically heated furnace and entered a high-vacuum region. This geometry produced a thin beam of vapor that was further narrowed by another slit placed in the path of the escaping particles. Stern's most important use of molecular beams came in the application of this method to the effect of a magnetic field on the motion of atoms and molecules. Working with Walter Gerlach at Rostock in 1922, he sent a ribbon-shaped beam of silver atoms between two irregularly shaped magnet poles, one in the form of a knife edge, the other grooved to produce a U-shape. The beam passed broadside-on very close to the knife edge and emerged from the pole region resolved into two lines as predicted by the quantum theory. A measurement of the separation of the two lines enabled Stern and Gerlach to obtain a quantitative result for the atomic magnetic moment. This, too, was in general agreement with the predictions of the quantum theory. Later these experiments were repeated using hydrogen atoms with no essential difference in the results. The great importance of all this work lay in the fact that a direct method had been found that not only proved the existence of an atomic magnetic moment and measured its magnitude, but that provided unambiguous evidence of spatial quantization for the first time.

Continuing to perfect the molecular-beam method in subsequent years, Stern applied it successfully to problems of both classical and modern physics. Most importantly, he was able to apply his method to the measurement of the magnetic moments of atomic nuclei. In 1933 at Hamburg, he measured the magnetic moment of the proton and found this value to be about $2\frac{1}{2}$ times greater than that theoretically predicted. This result was explained years later when it was known that the proton moments in the hydrogen molecules used were effectively parallel and that, in addition, there was a molecular rotation.

In 1931, 4 years after the electron diffraction experiments by C. J. Davisson and L. H. Germer and by G. P. Thomson that verified the wave nature of electrons, Stern, in collaboration with O. R. Frisch and Estermann, directed beams of helium atoms and hydrogen molecules at a cleaved surface of a lithium fluoride crystal. Diffraction of the beams was observed as expected. Furthermore, measuring the velocity of the helium atoms in a direct, primitive way with a toothed wheel and using the known atomic spacing of the diffracting crystal, he determined the wavelength of the atoms and found that it agreed (within an experimental error of 2%) with the de Broglie formula for the wavelength of moving particles.

Stern spent many years applying molecular beams to the study of kinetic theory. The velocities and velocity distribution of molecules were measured directly in these experiments. The results showed complete agreement with prediction and thus tended to reinforce the fundamentals of the kinetic theory and of the Maxwell velocity distribution law.

Stern attended high school in Breslau, where his parents had moved in 1892. He entered the University of Breslau in 1906, receiving a Ph.D. in physical chemistry 6 years later. He joined Einstein at the University of Prague and later in 1913 followed him to Zurich, becoming privatdocent of physical chemistry at the Technical

High School. In 1914 he became privatdocent of theoretical physics at the University of Frankfurt, remaining there, except for a period of military service, until 1921. He spent 1 year as associate professor of theoretical physics at Rostock before being appointed professor of physical chemistry at the University of Hamburg in 1923. Compelled to leave Germany in 1933, Stern went to the United States as research professor of physics at the Carnegie Institute of Technology. He remained there until 1945 when he retired and took up residence at Berkeley, Calif. He was elected to the National Academy of Sciences in 1945.

For background information *see* MAGNETIC MOMENT; MOLECULAR BEAMS in the McGraw-Hill Encyclopedia of Science and Technology. □

★ **STEVENS, Stanley Smith**
American psychophysicist
Born Nov. 4, 1906, Ogden, Utah, U.S.A.

IN EACH sensory system—such as vision, hearing, taste, and smell—the strength of the sensation grows as the stimulus intensity raised to a power. Each sense has its own exponent, ranging from 0.33 for the visual sense of brightness to about 3.5 for the apparent intensity of an electric current passed through the fingers. The exploration of the many different senses was begun by Stevens in 1953. His experiments led to a general law, often called "Stevens' law," which says that the sensed magnitude ψ grows with the stimulus magnitude ϕ according to the equation

$$\psi = k\phi^\beta$$

The constant k depends on the units of measurement, and the exponent β depends on the sense modality and the parameters of experiment. For example, when the eyes are adapted to the dark, the exponent β has the value 0.33, but this value increases to about 0.44 when the eyes are adapted to a strong light.

In 1860 G. T. Fechner proposed that the "psychophysical law," the function relating psychological magnitude to physical magnitude, is a logarithmic function. The sensory intensity, said Fechner, grows as the logarithm of the stimulus intensity. The logarithmic form of the sensory input-output function was based on a novel but indirect approach to the problem. Fechner reasoned that each time a stimulus is increased by a just noticeable amount, its subjective intensity moves upward by a step of a constant size. It was while lying abed on the morning of Oct. 22, 1850, that the idea came to him. He could measure mental intensity, he thought, by counting off the number of just noticeable differences, starting at the threshold. Since, according to Weber's law, a just noticeable difference tends to be a constant percentage of the stimulus, Fechner was led to suppose that equal stimulus ratios correspond to equal sensation differences. This relation entails the logarithmic function. By contrast, the power law developed by Stevens implies that equal stimulus ratios produce equal sensation ratios.

Both the power function and the logarithmic function had been proposed from time to time in the past. Gabriel Cramer suggested in 1728 that the subjective value of money increases as a power (0.5) of the amount of money. Ten years later Daniel Bernoulli suggested quite independently that the subjective value of money, sometimes called "utility," grows as the logarithm of the amount. Both the square-root function of Cramer and the logarithmic function of Bernoulli accord with the obvious fact that a single added dollar has less value if a man already has a thousand dollars than if he has only one or two.

The century-long conflict between the two laws, power and logarithmic, began to be resolved only when the indirect approach used by Fechner came to be replaced by more direct procedures. In the 1930s, for example, listeners were asked to adjust one sound to make it seem half as loud as some given sound. Experiments using this method of "fractionation," as Stevens called it, were undertaken to solve a practical problem faced by the acoustical engineers who had begun to measure sound in decibels, which are logarithmic units. Simple listening made it obvious that a sound of 50 decibels was not half as loud as a sound of 100 decibels. Fechner's law appeared to be wrong, therefore, and experiments were begun to create a loudness scale that would agree better with people's estimates of loudness. The unit of the loudness scale was named a "sone" by Stevens.

The early form of the loudness scale was neither a logarithmic function nor a very good power function. But as better procedures were developed in the 1950s, it became clear that the loudness of a 1000-cps tone grows as the 0.6 power of its sound pressure. This function has been recommended by the International Standards Organization to be used for engineering purposes.

Of the many procedures now used to scale sensory intensity, two are of special interest. Perhaps the simplest procedure is magnitude estimation. Stimulus intensities are produced in irregular order, and a person is asked to assign numbers proportional to the apparent strength of the sensations produced. The geometric means of the estimates of a group of a dozen persons have been found to give stable values.

The method of cross-modality matching dispenses with estimation and allows a person to adjust the intensity of one stimulus to match that of another. Thus he may adjust a sound to make it appear as strong as a given vibration applied to his finger, or to a brightness applied to his eye. In principle, any sensory system can be matched to any other.

The important question is whether the outcome of the estimation procedure predicts the results of the cross-modality procedure. To a good approximation the results of the two procedures have been found to agree with each other and to confirm the Stevens power law.

Stevens attended Mormon schools in Salt Lake City and spent three years working for the Mormon Church in Belgium and Switzerland. Thereafter he attended Stanford (A.B., 1931) and Harvard (Ph.D., 1933). After a postdoctoral National Research Council fellowship in physiology at the Harvard Medical School and a research fellowship in physics, he became an instructor in experimental psychology at Harvard. During World War II he founded the Psychoacoustic Laboratory, which did research on noise and communication. As the laboratory work began to involve the whole range of sensory phenomena its name was changed to Laboratory of Psychophysics, and in 1962 Stevens became Harvard's first professor of psychophysics. Stevens received the Warren Medal of the Society of Experimental Psychologists in 1943 and the Science Award of the American Psychological Association in 1960. He was elected to the National Academy of Sciences in 1946.

Stevens wrote *Hearing: Its Psychology and Physiology*, with Hallowell Davis (1938); *The Varieties of Human Physique*, with W. H. Sheldon and W. B. Tucker (1940); and *The Varieties of Temperament*, with W. H. Sheldon (1942). He edited the *Handbook of Experimental Psychology* (1951).

For background information *see* BEHAVORIAL PSYCHOPHYSICS; PSYCHOPHYSICAL METHODS in the McGraw-Hill Encyclopedia of Science and Technology. □

★ **STEVER, Horton Guyford**
American physicist and engineer
Born Oct. 24, 1916, Corning, N.Y., U.S.A.

STEVER CONTRIBUTED to the development of flight from the manned subsonic aircraft of the early 1940s to the guided missiles and spacecraft of the 1960s. During these two decades, developments in propulsion, aerodynamics, and structures enabled flight speeds to advance from subsonic—a few hundred miles per hour—through transonic and supersonic to the hypersonic speeds being experimented with today and the orbital speeds of spacecraft. Electronic and inertial sensing and automatic guidance and control enable both pilotless and piloted aircraft, missiles, and spacecraft to navigate over the surface of the Earth and into the near regions of space. Stever's research impinged on several aspects of these.

In 1949, there was need for ground instrumentation and wind tunnels to test the hypersonic aerodynamic properties of unmanned missiles. At the Massachusetts Institute of Technology Stever constructed a small hypersonic (Mach 5 to 7) wind tunnel. A principal problem was to prevent or to interpret the deleterious effects of oxygen and nitrogen condensation as the air was expanded through the wind tunnel nozzle. The straightforward method of getting higher and higher Mach numbers involved simply raising the pressure and temperature of the air before flowing it through the convergent divergent nozzles, but this had practical limitations. This led Stever to a study of the condensation nucleation process to discover how much supersaturation of N_2 and O_2 occurred before nucleation occurred and the single hypersonic flow was changed by a condensation shock wave. It was discovered that, if the air was extremely dry and free of any foreign nuclei, condensation was delayed, enabling somewhat higher Mach numbers to be obtained.

Another example of the application of science to aeronautical development was the use of the shock tube in aerodynamics. Together with colleagues in the Aeroelastic and Structures Laboratory at MIT, Stever designed, built, and used a relatively large ($100 \times 2 \times 1$ ft) shock tube for the study of shock-wave loading of various aerodynamic shapes and aircraft structures. The flow behind the shock wave that progresses down a tube after the bursting of a frangible diaphragm separating a region of high-pressure gas from a low-pressure gas simulates the shock wave from an explosion or the one created by a plane in transonic or supersonic flight. The transient pressure loading of pertinent structures and the build-up of boundary layers on walls and models were studied. This particular shock tube was used as a short-duration wind tunnel also, for it had sufficiently long-duration flow behind the shock for all transient flow conditions to settle down. Effectively steady flow over models was established and pressure distributions were measured.

Still another example of the application of new sciences to flight was the work done by Stever and colleagues in the Transonic Aircraft Control Project at MIT. In the early 1950s, practical manned flight in the transonic speed region was being explored. Aerodynamic problems arose when the flow was mixed subsonic and supersonic. The new aerodynamic designs and the transonic flow created special problems of stability and control. A number of aerodynamic and control studies were made. A principal one had to do with the inertial cross coupling between pitch, yaw, and roll that resulted in serious instabilities in flight, and actual loss of some aircraft. This is now well understood as a result of these and other studies.

A merchant's son, Stever obtained an A.B. in physics at Colgate University in 1938 and a Ph.D. in physics at the California Institute of Technology in 1941. During World War II he was involved in radar development, teaching, and liaison work at MIT's Radiation Laboratory and with the Office for Scientific Research and Development's London Mission. From 1945 to 1965 he was on the faculty of MIT, serving variously as professor of aeronautics and astronautics, associate dean of engineering, and head of the departments of mechanical engineering and naval architecture/marine engineering. In 1965 he became president of Carnegie Institute of Technology. Chief Scientist of the U.S. Air Force in 1955–56, Stever was elected to the National Academy of Engineering at its first election.

For background information *see* AERONAUTICAL ENGINEERING; SHOCK WAVE; WIND TUNNEL in the McGraw-Hill Encyclopedia of Science and Technology.   □

★ **STRAUS, William Levi, Jr.**
American anatomist and physical anthropologist
Born Oct. 29, 1900, Baltimore, Md., U.S.A.

MOST OF Straus's research dealt with the comparative anatomy of the order Primates, both living and fossil. In the extant primates he especially investigated the skeleton and musculature, but he also devoted considerable study to the thoracic and abdominal viscera and other soft parts and to various aspects of the development of the individual. While investigating the morphology of living primates, Straus was impressed by the many characters in which man is more primitive, more generalized, than the anthropoid apes—characters in which man approximates or agrees with the so-called lower primates, notably the Old World monkeys. Especially notable is the absence in man of adaptations to brachiation, or mode of locomotion through the trees via the arms—the type of locomotion common to the anthropoid apes. This caused Straus to challenge the orthodox view that man evolved from an arm-swinging ape. Rather, according to his interpretation, the human stock evolved from essentially generalized, monkeylike quadrupeds. This view was expressed by him in a paper, "The Riddle of Man's Ancestry" (1949), and was further elaborated and supported by his subsequent studies of both living and fossil primates.

The orthodox theory deriving man from a brachiating anthropoid ape had its inception with T. H. Huxley and subsequently was especially developed, particularly in regard to its brachiating aspects, by Sir Arthur Keith and W. K. Gregory. This remains, perhaps, the most generally accepted concept of man's origin at the present time. However, the nonbrachiating theory, most vigorously propounded in recent years by Straus, has gained an increasing number of adherents, particularly since the more recently discovered fossil evidence, especially that of the Australopithecines, lends it plausibility. This theory may be said to have had its inception with Marcellin Boule (1911–13), and was later espoused by H. F. Osborn (1927) and Robert Broom (1946). Straus, however, marshaled the greatest amount of evidence in its support.

Numerous characters of the teeth, skull, trunk, pelvis, and limbs of man can only be regarded as more primitive, more generalized, than the similar characters found in the anthropoid apes. In many of these features, the apes exhibit definite specializations for brachiation not found in man. The structures considered involve not only the skeleton but also the musculature and other soft parts. The evidence suggests that the common ancestors of man and the anthropoid apes were essentially generalized, monkeylike quadrupeds lacking the major adaptations to brachiation. The more recent fossil evidence, in particular that of the Australopithecines, supports this concept of a nonbrachiating, nonanthropoid-ape origin for man.

Straus attended Harvard and Johns Hopkins universities. He received both his A.B. (1920) and his Ph.D. (1926) in zoology from Johns Hopkins. He was a National Research Council fellow at Western Reserve University in 1926–27 and a Guggenheim fellow at the universities of London and Cambridge in 1937–38. In 1927 he joined the faculty of Johns Hopkins. Straus was awarded the Wenner-Gren Foundation's Viking Medal in physical anthropology for 1952. He was elected to the National Academy of Sciences in 1962.

Author of over 70 publications in scientific journals, Straus was also coeditor of *Anatomy of the Rhesus Monkey* (1933; reprinted 1961) and *Forerunners of Darwin 1745–1859* (1959).

For background information *see* PRIMATES in the McGraw-Hill Encyclopedia of Science and Technology.   □

STRÖMGREN, Bengt Georg Daniel
American astronomer
Born Jan. 21, 1908, Göteborg, Sweden

FROM HIS studies of gaseous nebulae—interstellar, sometimes luminous clouds occurring throughout the galaxy—Strömgren concluded that the luminous regions must consist of hydrogen, ionized by radiation from hot stars embedded in the clouds. His theory of "Strömgren spheres" accounted for observed characteristics of many nebulae and provided an accurate means of evaluating the physical processes involved.

Since the 18th century it had been supposed that the masses of luminous gas found in interstellar space must be excited into radiation by nearby stars, though the mechanism of this excitation was not known. Studying the gaseous nebulae found in the vicinity of very hot stars (classes O and B), Strömgren discovered that in many cases the luminous region seemed to be composed of hydrogen gas ionized by radiation from the nearby star, surrounded by a larger region of neutral, nonionized, nonluminous hydrogen and sharply distinct from it. In 1939, and later in 1948, Strömgren conducted work to develop a theory accounting for the observed sizes, shapes (in some cases extremely complex), luminosities, and internal characteristics of some planetary and diffuse nebulae.

Strömgren's theory assumed that a uniformly dense cloud of hydrogen was exposed to radiation from a very hot star (about 30,000°C surface temperature). His approximate first computations showed that the region of gas completely ionized by the stellar radiation should be sharply bounded from the nonionized region, the ionized (H-II) region being bounded by a narrow zone in which recombination of protons and electrons into hydrogen atoms has set in. Thus the star involved would ionize a well-defined H-II region, or "Strömgren sphere," in the galactic drift of gas and dust in which it was embedded. The radius of the H-II region could be calculated, using Strömgren's equations, directly from the temperature of the exciting star and the density of the gas. The surrounding H-I nonluminous region would act as an opaque, obscuring factor in the visible wavelengths, while continuing to radiate in other regions of the

spectrum, particularly the 21-cm radio band of interstellar hydrogen.

For convenience, Strömgren's original equations were approximate. He omitted (1) reemitted diffuse radiation resulting from recaptures of electrons in higher layers of the H-II region. Unlike light radiating from the central star, this diffuse radiation tends to be emitted in random directions. He also ignored (2) the variations in temperature and electron density within the gaseous shell, and (3) changes in the internal radiative process itself. Nevertheless, later workers showed that the Strömgren equations applied accurately to actual nebular regions of varying density and complexity of structure and accounted for the sharply defined H-II regions observed in such clouds. In a model interstellar gas of density 1 atom of H per cm³, a star of class O (about 30,000°C surface temperature) should ionize an H-II region of about 500 light-years diameter; a star of fainter, cooler class A (about 10,000°C at surface) could account for an ionized region of only about 1.5 light-years. These predictions agree with observed luminosities of stars embedded in the bright diffuse nebulae and the smaller, less bright planetary nebulae.

Strömgren's theory provided a means of analyzing the often extremely complex structures of overlapping interstellar gas clouds in the galaxy by regarding them as H-II regions, each excited by one or more central stars (some diffuse nebulae surround entire open clusters). Further, his theory was useful in estimating size, distance, and luminosity of nebular matter in the Magellanic Clouds and other "external" galaxies. His theories were applied to ionized He clouds as well as H, though they are probably not applicable to the ionization process of interstellar oxygen.

Strömgren also conducted research into the internal constitution of stars, spectral classification, stellar pulsation, and ionization of stellar material. He initiated a detailed and complete survey of all diffuse interstellar nebulae in the galaxy.

The son of the astronomer Elis Strömgren, B. G. D. Strömgren received his M.S. in 1927 and Ph.D. in 1929 at the University of Copenhagen. After a time as lecturer in astronomy there, he was assistant, then associate professor at the University of Chicago from 1936 to 1938. Returning to Copenhagen, he succeeded his father as director of the university observatory in 1940. Following a variety of visiting professorships from 1946 to 1950, Strömgren in 1951 became director of both the Yerkes and McDonald observatories, Williams Bay, Wisconsin. In 1952 he also took the related post of Sewell Avery Distinguished Service Professor, University of Chicago. In 1957 he accepted a membership at the Institute for Advanced Study, Princeton, N.J. Strömgren was awarded the Bruce Medal of the Astronomical Society of the Pacific in 1959.

For background information *see* NEBULA, GASEOUS in the McGraw-Hill Encyclopedia of Science and Technology.   ☐

STRUVE, Otto

American astronomer
Born Aug. 12, 1897, Kharkov, Russia
Died Apr. 6, 1963, Berkeley, Calif., U.S.A.

WHILE INVESTIGATING the nature of interstellar matter, Struve demonstrated that vast clouds of gas were found between the stars. He showed that the intensity of interstellar absorption lines is strengthened with increasing distance from the Sun, and he discovered the existence of interstellar hydrogen. These findings have been of great importance in the theory of stellar evolution.

In 1904 the German astronomer Johann Franz Hartmann found that, unlike the other absorption lines in the spectrum of the close double star Delta Orionis, the K-line of calcium failed to oscillate about a mean position in the course of the binary period. In addition, the K-line of calcium was sharp and narrow, while the others were wide and poorly defined. Hartmann referred to the line as the "stationary" calcium line and concluded that it resulted from absorption by a cloud of calcium vapor between Delta Orionis and the Sun. The stationary lines of calcium, and those of other elements, were soon identified in the spectra of a number of stars. In 1924 the Canadian astronomer John Stanley Plaskett suggested that a widely distributed cloud of tenuous gas enveloped the stars. He further suggested that the cloud's calcium ions would be ionized in the vicinity of the hottest stars.

In 1925, working at the Yerkes Observatory in Williams Bay, Wis., Struve attributed the stationary calcium lines to vast clouds that showed a strong concentration in the plane of the Milky Way. He maintained that stars moved in all directions through these clouds, but that only the hot stars of spectral type B3 or earlier were capable of exciting and ionizing the calcium within the clouds at a distance. Struve demonstrated that the clouds were scarcer in high galactic latitudes and maintained that it was probable that no such clouds lay in the line of sight in some directions. He also demonstrated that in low galactic latitudes the average intensity of the absorption lines is proportional to the star's distance up to at least 1,500 light-years from the Sun. The sharpness and narrowness of the lines, Struve proposed, resulted from the extreme rarefaction and low temperatures of the interstellar material.

At about this time, H. Zanstra proposed a mechanism for the production of nebular emission lines. He suggested that the ultraviolet radiation from spectral type O and B stars could ionize interstellar hydrogen atoms, that is, could separate each of them into one free proton and one free electron, so that they could no longer absorb radiation. However, he continued, when the free electrons recombined with the free protons, emission lines covering the entire hydrogen spectrum would be produced.

Beginning in 1936, working in collaboration with Christian Thomas Elvey at the Yerkes Observatory and at the McDonald Observatory on Mount Locke in Texas, Struve tried to determine whether interstellar space was filled with hydrogen. To this end he used the nebular spectrograph, devised at Yerkes and McDonald in 1937–38. In these spectrographs the collimator was eliminated and the slit placed at a great distance from the dispersing unit. Although the light reaching the prism was almost parallel, a camera was required to produce adequate resolution. Using panchromatic emulsions in order to record the hydrogen alpha-line, Struve succeeded in photographing the emission spectrum of hydrogen in various regions of the Milky Way. Photographs were also taken of regions outside the galaxy, but essentially no hydrogen emission lines were detected. Struve concluded that interstellar hydrogen gas was concentrated in and near the plane of the Milky Way. The importance of this finding was not fully appreciated until the later discovery of the importance of the 21-centimeter hydrogen emission to radio astronomy.

In addition to his work on interstellar matter, which also included an analysis of its chemical composition, Struve was active in virtually every area of modern astronomy. He was one of the pioneers in the study of stellar rotation, and he was the first to demonstrate that stars of high temperature, such as blue giants, rotate rapidly on their axes. Struve was a specialist in stellar spectroscopy and made many valuable contributions, especially with regard to the Stark effect and the Zeeman effect. He also advanced a theory of the origin of the solar system, based on his studies of eclipsing binary systems, and contributed to the theory of stellar evolution.

Struve was the fourth in a dynasty of notable astronomers: his great-grandfather, Friedrich Georg Wilhelm von Struve (1793–1864), his grandfather, Otto Wilhelm von Struve (1819–1905), and his father, Gustav Wilhelm Ludwig von Struve (1858–1920), all served as director of the Imperial Observatory at Pulkovo, Russia. Otto Struve was educated at the University of Kharkov, where he specialized in astronomy. He served as a lieutenant of field artillery in the Imperial Russian Army from 1916 to 1918, returning to Kharkov to receive his diploma in 1919. Struve was a lieutenant in the White Russian Army from 1919 to 1921, emigrating to the United States in the latter year to become an assistant at the Yerkes Observatory of the University of Chicago. He received his Ph.D. from the University of Chicago in 1923 and accepted an instructorship there in 1924. In 1927 Struve became a U.S. citizen, and in that same year he became an assistant professor. He was appointed associate professor in 1930 and professor of astrophysics in 1932, a post he retained until 1947. He was named assistant director of the Yerkes Observatory in 1931 and director in 1932. He retained this position until 1947, and then served as chairman and honorary director until 1950. During the period 1932–1947 he was also director of the McDonald Observatory of the University of Texas. In 1950 he became professor of astrophysics, chairman of the department, and director of the Leuschner Observatory at the University of California, Berkeley. In 1959 Struve left to become director of the National Radio Astronomy Observatory at Green Bank, W.Va., holding that post until his death. He was the recipient of a number of awards, among them the Gold Medal of the Royal Astronomical Society of Great Britain in 1944 and the Bruce Medal of the Astronomical Society of the Pacific in 1948.

Struve wrote several books, including *Stellar Evolution* (1950), *The Universe* (1962), and, with Velta Zebergs, *Astronomy of the 20th Century* (1962).

For background information *see* INTERSTELLAR MATTER in the McGraw-Hill Encyclopedia of Science and Technology.   □

☆ STURTEVANT, Alfred Henry

American geneticist
Born Nov. 21, 1891, Jacksonville, Ill., U.S.A.

STURTEVANT BECAME best known for his investigations of the genetics of *Drosophila*, the fruit fly. In recognition of this work, the National Academy of Sciences awarded him its Kimber Genetics Medal in 1957 and John J. Carty Medal in 1965.

Sturtevant's association with genetics began in the famed "fly room" at Columbia University,

when he was a student of Thomas Hunt Morgan. One of his earliest contributions was his demonstration that genes are arranged in a linear order and that this linear array or "linkage" group corresponds to a particular chromosome. Analyzing linkage groups, he devised a method whereby the position and linear order of a gene could be determined with reference to two other genes on the same chromosome. Since three genes were used, the test became known as the three-point cross. The methodology employed by Sturtevant is still basic to chromosome mapping.

Current understanding of gene action owes much to Sturtevant's discovery of the phenomenon of position effect. Utilizing the gene for bar eye, he demonstrated that the effect of a gene may depend upon its position in relation to its neighbors.

An important tool of modern genetic analysis is chromosomal rearrangement. One of the most extensively used types of rearrangement for investigating genetic and evolutionary problems is chromosome inversion, that is, reversal of a portion of the gene sequence. The history of the employment of this chromosomal aberration began with Sturtevant's discovery of crossover suppressors. He hypothesized and later proved that chromosomal inversion could explain the effect of several crossover inhibitors ("C" factor) in *Drosophila*. In collaboration with C. R. Plunkett, he demonstrated that two related species, *D. melanogaster* and *D. simulans*, differed by a major inversion in the third chromosome. This was the first analysis of karyotype (basic chromosome set of a species) differences between related species of the genus, and it was done by showing the different linkage associations of allelic genes in the two species. Later, working with G. W. Beadle, he analyzed and interpreted many of the unusual aspects of the transmission of inversions through the female germ line.

Sturtevant contributed much to understanding of the basic mechanism of sex determination. He discovered and investigated specific genes that cause intersexuality. He also studied mosaics and the maternal effects on sex determination in hybrids.

Comparative studies of specific gene mutations and their significance in the speciation of *Drosophila* were investigated by Sturtevant. His interest in evolution and knowledge of taxonomy enabled him to speculate on various evolutionary mechanisms dealing with the occurrence of lethal genes in wild populations, with the effect of selection on genes affecting the mutation rate, with problems of selection in social insects, and with the origin of sterility in hybrids. Besides his studies of the genetics of *Drosophila*, Sturtevant made major contributions to the systematics of the genus. He also studied various behavioral patterns of *Drosophila*, such as those involved in feeding and mating.

Sturtevant received his A.B. in 1912 and his Ph.D. in 1914 from Columbia University. In 1915 he was employed by the Carnegie Institution of Washington and stationed at Columbia with T. H. Morgan. In 1928 he was appointed professor of genetics at the California Institute of Technology, where from 1947 to 1962 he was Thomas Hunt Morgan Professor of Biology. He became professor emeritus in 1962. He was elected to the National Academy of Sciences in 1930.

Sturtevant wrote *The Mechanism of Mendelian Heredity*, with T. H. Morgan, H. J. Muller, and C. B. Bridges (1915; rev. ed. 1923) and *An Introduction to Genetics*, with G. W. Beadle (1939).

For background information *see* CHROMOSOME ABERRATION; CHROMOSOME THEORY OF HEREDITY; GENETICS; LINKAGE, GENETIC; MUTATION; RECOMBINATION, GENETIC; SEX DETERMINATION in the McGraw-Hill Encyclopedia of Science and Technology.   □

☆ SUITS, Chauncey Guy

American physicist and research director
Born Mar. 12, 1905, Oshkosh, Wis., U.S.A.

BY MEANS of an intensive study of arc phenomena, especially in gases at high pressure, Suits added greatly to man's knowledge of what takes place within an electric arc. This knowledge proved vital in applications where an arc was a necessary evil to be extinguished quickly (as in high-voltage switchgear), those where an arc was produced intentionally (as in electric welding), and in a great variety of gaseous-discharge lighting devices. For this research, he received in 1937 the Eta Kappa Nu Award as America's outstanding young electrical engineer.

When Suits joined the staff of the General

Electric Research Laboratory as a young man, he identified electric-arc phenomena as a basic technology of the electrical industry that seemed to present the greatest mystery and hence challenge. He observed that "much electrical machinery consists of copper, iron, insulation—and arcs; and the part we know the least about is the arc." Thus he began an investigation of arcs, and his initial project was to measure the temperature and other properties of the discharge. He immediately encountered a major obstacle —the arc was so hot that it would vaporize a thermocouple or any other measuring device inserted into its flames.

Suits solved the temperature measurement problem in an ingenious fashion. Knowing that sound passes through gases with a velocity that depends upon temperature, he decided to use a sound wave as a temperature "probe." He therefore produced a sound wave by means of an electric spark and sent it through the arc. The sound wave became visible as a wave of luminosity that could be recorded optically by high-speed photography. From measurements of the velocity of the sound wave, he could then calculate the temperature of the arc itself.

With this new technique, Suits began to investigate arcs in a variety of gases under pressures ranging as high as 50,000 pounds per square inch. In the course of these studies, he became the first man to produce arc temperatures of 18,000°F (nearly twice the temperature of the Sun's surface). In general, these experiments showed that the electrical properties of the arc underwent profound changes as the result of pressure. For example, a 10-ampere arc—which had a diameter of about one-half inch in air—contracted to a tiny thread at pressures of several tons per square inch. At the same time, the voltage drop necessary to drive the current through the arc column increased sharply.

One particularly interesting experiment involved the behavior of an electric arc in an atmosphere of hydrogen gas. Even at atmospheric pressure, Suits found, this arc had an extremely small cross section. It was, in fact, no larger than an arc in a nitrogen atmosphere subjected to pressures greater than 1500 pounds per square inch. Furthermore, when the pressure of the hydrogen atmosphere was increased above 300 pounds per square inch, the stability of the arc was destroyed completely, and it could not be operated at all. From measurements with sound waves, Suits found that when an arc was discharged through an atmosphere of hydrogen, the gas next to the arc reached temperatures between 11,000 and 12,500°F. This heated gas expanded, became very buoyant, and created convection currents around the arc. As the pressure went up, so did the velocity of the convection currents. This terrific "gas blast" cooled the arc and ultimately extinguished it.

Suits's experiments and measurements laid the foundation for the understanding of arc behavior and generally established the basic relationships between the electrical properties of the discharge and the thermal environment by which it lost most of its energy.

The son of a pharmacist, Suits majored in physics and mathematics at the University of Wisconsin, where he received his B.A. in 1927. Awarded an exchange fellowship at the Swiss Federal Institute of Technology, Zurich, Switzerland, he was granted the Sc.D. degree there in 1929. The following year he became a research physicist on the staff of the General Electric Research Laboratory in Schenectady, N.Y. He was made assistant to the director of the laboratory in 1940. During World War II, as chief of Division 15 of the National Defense Research Committee, Suits guided the activities of more than 1,000 scientists and engineers employed on the task of wrecking the German and Japanese radar systems. This was the principal Allied radio and radar countermeasures effort, and late in the war—as elaborate postwar investigations in Germany showed—the Nazi radar system was jammed out of usefulness.

In 1945, Suits was elected vice-president and director of research for the General Electric Company. The following year, he became responsible additionally for the General Electric Company's extensive work for the U.S. Atomic Energy Commission, including the development of nuclear power plants for the production of useful power. For the research and development work of this project he organized, staffed, and operated the Knolls Atomic Power Laboratory near Schenectady. It has since grown to become a separate operating component of the company. Under Suits's direction, hundreds of successful research projects were carried out at the General Electric Research Laboratory, including the development of Man-Made diamonds, light-amplifying phosphors, ceramic vacuum tubes and high-temperature electronics, borazon, high-temperature wire enamels, high-temperature alloys for jet engines, improved soft magnetic materials, "perfect" metal whiskers with extraordinary strengths, improved light sources, fuel cells, thermionic converters, new polymers, lubricants for metals with acute lubrication problems, and a new technique for dating geological specimens. For his direction of this research, Suits was awarded the William Proctor Prize of the Scientific Research Society of America in 1958 and the Industrial Research Institute Medal in 1962. He retired from the General Electric Company in 1965. Elected to the National Academy of Sciences in 1946, Suits was a founder of the National Academy of Engineering.

For background information *see* ARC DISCHARGE; ARC HEATING; ARC LAMP in the McGraw-Hill Encyclopedia of Science and Technology.   □

SUMNER, James Batcheller
American biochemist
Born Nov. 19, 1887, Canton, Mass., U.S.A.
Died Aug. 12, 1955, Buffalo, N.Y., U.S.A.

WHILE WORKING with the enzyme urease, Sumner succeeded for the first time in isolating an enzyme in pure, crystalline form and in characterizing it as a protein. By perfecting a means for concentrating and purifying enzymes and identifying them as proteins, Sumner made it possible to accelerate studies of biocatalysis. For this achievement, Sumner shared the 1946 Nobel Prize in chemistry with the American biochemists John Howard Northrup, who had extended Sumner's work with enzymes, and Wendell Meredith Stanley, who had shown that, like an enzyme, a virus is a crystallizable protein.

After the first enzyme to be discovered, diastase, was isolated by the French chemist Anselme Payen in 1833, the suspicion grew that enzymes were proteinaceous materials. However, about 1920 the German chemist Richard Willstätter produced negative evidence to the effect that enzymes were neither carbohydrates, lipids, nor proteins.

Thus, when Sumner began his studies of urease in the fall of 1917, the chemical nature of enzymes was a complete mystery. He chose this particular enzyme for a number of reasons, among them that he had some familiarity with it, having used urease in earlier analytical work, and that this enzyme could be estimated quantitatively very accurately. In addition, a rich source of urease, the jack bean, *Canavalia ensiformis*, was readily available. Sumner began by trying to isolate and characterize the chemical components of the jack bean, and he found various carbohydrates, extractives, enzymes, lipids, minerals, pigments, and proteins to be present. Among the proteins he paid special attention to the globulins (suspecting urease of being one), and detected three, naming them concanavalin A, concanavalin B, and canavalin. In his attempts to concentrate and purify urease, Sumner employed fractional crystallization with water, with alcohol, glycerol, and other organic solvents, and with ammonium sulfate, magnesium sulfate, and other neutral salts. Of all of these solvents, only the alcohol, the use of which had been suggested by Otto Folin of the Harvard Medical School, intimated eventual success. When kept at low temperatures to prevent inactivation of the enzyme, 30 per cent alcoholic extracts of jack bean meal formed precipitates containing practically all of the urease, concanavalin A, concanavalin B, and other proteins.

In 1926 Sumner, working at the Cornell Medical School in Ithaca, N.Y., decided to use dilute acetone instead of 30 per cent alcohol to concentrate the urease. After extracting the finely powdered jack bean meal with 31.6 per cent acetone and filtering it by gravity, he refrigerated the clear filtrate at about 2°C overnight. Upon examining the filtrate on the following day, Sumner found it differed from the alcoholic filtrates in that it had no noticeable precipitate. However, he further found that the filtrate contained a large number of well-defined, octahedral, colorless crystals. Sumner centrifuged off some of the crystals, redissolved them in water, and tested the solution, which gave a positive reaction for protein and possessed a very high urease activity. Subsequent experiments showed that crystallization increased the purity of the urease 700–1,400 times, that recrystallization increased the purity still further, and that the introduction of traces of poison to the jack bean meal not only inactivated the urease but also prevented the appearance of the crystals. In addition, further analyses confirmed that urease is a protein, both because of its positive reaction to a number of chemical tests and because of its physical characteristics. However, his suspicion that urease was a globulin proved to have been an error.

Sumner's work was not immediately accepted, meeting with great opposition from Willstätter and a number of others. However, the view that enzymes were proteinaceous steadily gained adherents. It finally achieved universal acceptance when Northrup, working at the Rockefeller Institute for Medical Research in New York, extended Sumner's work to crystallize pepsin (1930), trypsin (1932), and chymotrypsin (1935) and demonstrated their proteinaceous nature. The immediate result of Sumner's effort was the encouragement of further research, especially in the related field of viruses and viral diseases, such as influenza and poliomyelitis. His further work with enzymes other than urease, such as those aiding the digestive process, laid the foundation for new research in nutrition.

Sumner was educated at Harvard College, receiving his B.A. in chemistry in 1910. After a brief period of working in a family-owned cotton mill, he began teaching at Mt. Allison College, Sackville, New Brunswick. In 1911 he accepted an assistantship in chemistry at the Worcester Polytechnic Institute, leaving in 1912 to study biochemistry at the Harvard Medical School. Although he was warned that he could not succeed as a chemist with only one arm, having lost the other in a hunting accident in 1904, Sumner persevered and received his M.A. in 1913 and his Ph.D. in biochemistry in 1914. He then accepted a position as assistant professor of biochemistry at the Cornell Medical School. In 1929 he was appointed professor of biochemistry, serving in that capacity until his retirement on July 1, 1955. During his tenure at Cornell, Sumner traveled to Sweden to work on enzymes with Hans von Euler-Chelpin at the University of Stockholm and The Svedberg at the University of Uppsala.

For background information *see* ENZYME in the McGraw-Hill Encyclopedia of Science and Technology. □

SVERDRUP, Harald Ulrik
Norwegian oceanographer
Born Nov. 15, 1888, Sogndal, Norway
Died Aug. 21, 1957, Oslo, Norway

SVERDRUP'S PRINCIPAL contribution to oceanography was the composition of one of the most important modern texts in that field, *The Oceans: Their Physics, Chemistry, and General Biology* (1942), written while he was director of the Scripps Institution of Oceanography. He was

assisted in this project by Martin W. Johnson and Richard H. Fleming.

Oceanography, a comparatively new science, has made tremendous progress in this century. The first systematic collection of data about the sea had begun in the last century aboard merchant vessels, but the formal beginning of the science dates from the deep-sea expedition of the *Challenger* (1872–76). Led by C. Wyville Thomsen, a professor of natural history at the University of Edinburgh, this Royal Society–sponsored undertaking produced the basic data upon which modern oceanographers still draw. The *Challenger* reports (50 vols., 1876–95) permitted scientists to chart the main contours of the ocean deeps, outlined the physical characteristics of the previously unknown deep water of the world's oceans, and identified over 4,000 new marine life forms. The first major voyage to survey systematically an entire ocean did not take place until the German South Atlantic *Meteor* voyage (1925–27). However, many smaller expeditions preceded and followed the *Meteor*'s, and such voyages were increasingly productive in the two decades after 1920. Such gains were made possible by the application of much theoretical research to physical phenomena and by the improvement of techniques for collecting data, such as the sonic depth-finders in use in 1920. The rapid growth of information finally made older general texts in the field obsolete. Prior to Sverdrup's *The Oceans*, the standard reference was Otto Krümmel's *Handbook of Oceanography* (1907).

Sverdrup planned *The Oceans* to present an integrated and comprehensive modern survey of the state of oceanography. The findings of many

separate modern voyages that had concentrated on particular problems in various oceans needed to be brought together in one text. This data included, for instance, water temperatures and salinity at various depths, the patterns of ocean currents, core samples from the bottom, and observations about ocean waves and their causes. Because of Sverdrup's participation in various voyages of deep-sea exploration and his many investigations in the field, he was uniquely qualified to render a balanced account. He had contributed numerous papers from his own observations as the director of the scientific work on the Norwegian north polar expedition of the *Maud* (1918–25) and the Wilkins-Ellsworth submarine arctic expedition on board the *Nautilus* (1931). He had also been the director of the Scripps Institution since 1936. During these years he had evolved the now generally accepted theory explaining the source of salinity in the Pacific Ocean, which he said resulted from antarctic circumpolar currents from the Indian Ocean. He was also one of the main contributors to the theory that accounts for the equatorial countercurrent. After the publication of *The Oceans*, it was not until 1961 that a comparable oceanographic text was published. This was Albert Defant's *Physical Oceanography* (1961), which, however, excluded the subject of marine biology. *The Oceans* appeared at a crucial moment in the history of this science. Naval and military operations of World War II were to stimulate a previously inconceivable growth of knowledge about the oceans of the world. Sverdrup's book provided a substantial and timely foundation for this growth.

Sverdrup also made an important contribution to the success of amphibious landings in World War II. In the first year of the war, the success of these operations was endangered by inability to forecast the state of the sea, especially the surf on a beach. This problem was assigned to Sverdrup and W. H. Munk in 1942. Drawing upon a vast experience in basic ocean research and in the application of mathematical concepts to ocean phenomena, the two scientists produced a workable system. Used in the North African landings with great success, the system became a part of all subsequent amphibious assault planning.

Sverdrup was a research associate in oceanography and meteorology at Oslo and Leipzig from 1911 until 1917, when he received his Ph.D. from the University of Oslo. After his work on the *Maud* expedition, he was a professor of meteorology at the Geophysical Institute in Bergen for two years. Then came the *Nautilus* expedition, followed by four years as a research professor at the Christian Michelsen Institute in Bergen. Appointed director of the Scripps Institution in 1936, he was later professor of geophysics and director of the Norwegian Polar Institute in Oslo, continuing there until his death. Among other honors, Sverdrup received the Agassiz

Medal of the U.S. National Academy of Sciences in 1938 and the Bowie Medal of the American Geophysical Union in 1951.

Besides *The Oceans*, Sverdrup wrote *Breakers and Surf; Principles in Forecasting*, with W. H. Munk (1944), and *Oceanography for Meteorologists* (1945).

For background information *see* OCEANOGRAPHY in the McGraw-Hill Encyclopedia of Science and Technology.   □

☆ SYNGE, Richard Laurence Millington
English chemist
Born Oct. 28, 1914, Liverpool, England

FOR THEIR development of partition chromatography in 1941 Synge and A. J. P. Martin received the 1952 Nobel Prize in chemistry. *See* MARTIN, ARCHER JOHN PORTER.

While working on the separation of acetylated amino acids, Synge was advised to contact Martin, who had used a bizarre-looking countercurrent apparatus in his work on vitamin E. Their collaboration at Cambridge and later at the laboratories of the Wool Industries Research Association at Leeds led to the development of partition chromatography. Using this method, Synge determined the structure of the antibiotic gramicidin-S. An analysis of the amino acid sequence showed it to be a cyclic decapeptide. After 1945 Synge became interested mainly in analytical problems related to amino acids and peptides.

The son of a stockbroker, Synge obtained his Ph.D. at Cambridge in 1941. From 1941 to 1943 he was on the staff of the Wool Industries Research Association. In 1943 he joined the Lister Institute in London. In 1948 he became head of the department of protein chemistry at the Rowett Research Institute, Bucksburn, Aberdeen. There he was concerned with the digestion of proteins by ruminant animals and its associated microorganisms, and with the physicochemical methods of identification and purification of intermediates in protein metabolism, particularly in plants.   □

SZILARD, Leo

American physicist
Born Feb. 11, 1898, Budapest, Hungary
Died May 30, 1964, La Jolla, Calif., U.S.A.

IN 1905 Einstein's special theory of relativity predicted that mass could be converted into energy according to the now famous equation $E = mc^2$, where E is the energy released, m the mass converted, and c the speed of light in vacuo—all three quantities in appropriate units. Although the release of energy through the destruction of mass was possible in theory, many physicists were doubtful that it could be realized in the laboratory. In 1939 Leo Szilard and Walter Zinn, at Columbia University, confirmed that when U^{235} nuclei were bombarded with slow neutrons the nuclei underwent fission with the release of energy according to the Einstein formula and also of one or more neutrons capable of causing further fissions. Self-sustaining nuclear-fission reactions were thus shown to be a practical reality.

Although the history of energy-mass conversion goes back to Einstein's special theory of relativity, the possibility of obtaining large quantities of energy in this way was not seriously considered until the late 1930s. In the early 1930s Enrico Fermi had bombarded uranium nuclei with slow neutrons in the hope of producing transuranium elements by the capture of the neutrons by U^{235} nuclei. His analysis of the products involved showed that there were particles produced that underwent beta decay with at least three distinct half-lives present and possibly as many as two others. Fermi did not know at the time that these were the products of the fission of the uranium nuclei and that there were also neutrons released in the reaction. This was first realized by Otto Hahn and Fritz Strassman in Germany in 1938. It was rediscovered by Szilard and Zinn in 1939.

The importance of the discovery lay in the realization that if a sufficiently rich supply of uranium atoms could be arranged in such a way that the neutrons emitted during fission did not escape, but collided with other uranium nuclei and caused them to undergo fission also, then the reaction could be made self-sustaining and an enormous release of energy obtained. These results were communicated to Fermi, and, working together, Szilard and Fermi determined the necessary masses of uranium, the configuration that would minimize neutron escape, and the means to control the reaction. This enabled them to produce, in a squash court at the University of Chicago, man's first self-sustaining nuclear chain reaction. Out of this came the atomic bomb and the nuclear era.

The son of an engineer, Szilard received his Ph.D. in nuclear physics from the University of Berlin in 1922. He performed research both there and in England before going to the United States, where he became a citizen in 1943. He worked at Columbia University until 1942, when he joined the staff at the University of Chicago, becoming professor of biophysics there in 1946. Shortly before his death in 1956 he joined the Salk Institute of Biological Studies. An ardent pacifist, but aware that Hahn and Strassman had discovered the possibility of nuclear chain reactions in Germany, Szilard was the key figure in convincing Einstein to write his famous letter to President Franklin D. Roosevelt urging him to begin work on an atomic bomb. The Manhattan Project resulted. In 1960 Szilard was awarded the Ford Motor Company's Atoms for Peace Award.

For background information *see* ATOMIC BOMB; CHAIN REACTION, NUCLEAR in the McGraw-Hill Encyclopedia of Science and Technology. □

T-V

****

☆ **TAMM, Igor Yevgenevich**
Russian physicist
Born July 8, 1895, Vladivostok, U.S.S.R.

BETWEEN 1934 and 1936, the Russian physicist P. A. Cerenkov determined the properties of the so-called Cerenkov radiation, the pale-blue light produced in a (usually liquid) medium when gamma radiation passed through it. Tamm and the Russian physicist I. M. Frank formulated a rigorous mathematical theory that explained the physical origin of the radiation and described its various properties. For this work, Tamm was awarded the 1958 Nobel Prize in physics, which he shared with Frank and Cerenkov.

In a classic series of experiments, Cerenkov had outlined the properties of the radiation. It was produced by the secondary electrons discharged in the medium as the result of the passage of incoming gamma rays. The radiation was shown to be neither a fluorescence nor a luminescence phenomenon, and it could be produced in any refractive medium. It was, furthermore, peculiar in that it was generated only in a forward direction with respect to the path of the incoming radiation.

Tamm and Frank began their efforts to provide a theoretical explanation for this set of characteristics by an examination of fundamentals concerning radiation in a medium. In thinking about the subject, they happened to consider the case of a particle moving faster than the speed of light within the medium. This (the "phase velocity") equalled $\frac{c}{N}$, c being the velocity of light in vacuo and N the refractive index of the medium. Tamm and Frank realized that for light frequencies or media in which N exceeded 1, the velocity of a particle could be

greater than $\frac{c}{N}$. They accordingly investigated a system in which a charged particle moved uniformly through a medium with velocity $v(> \frac{c}{N})$. Such a particle, they found, was able to excite wavefronts in the medium. For the sake of simplicity, they considered only a single frequency of the radiation emitted (and later showed that the same conclusions held true for a continuous spectrum of frequencies). Tamm and Frank found a simple interrelationship between θ (the angle of propagation of the emitted radiation with respect to the incoming radiation), N, and a quantity B equal to $\frac{v}{c}$. This they formulated as

$$\cos \theta = \frac{1}{BN}$$

The equation of Tamm and Frank was soon seen to describe one of the most puzzling features of the Cerenkov radiation, namely, its peculiar polarization. In the system they had described it could easily be shown that all secondary radiation other than that emitted in the direction of the angle θ would be extinguished by interference. This correspondence of theory and observation was so striking that Tamm, Frank, and Cerenkov embarked on a series of experiments to test other consequences of the superlight theory.

One of the predictions tested was that the radiation should appear only when the incoming gamma radiation reached a certain threshold of energy, and that it could be produced only when the velocity of the particle exceeded the "phase velocity" of light in the medium. An experiment showed this to be the case with the Cerenkov radiation.

Another prediction of the theory was that the critical "threshold energy" should depend upon the refractive index N of the medium. A series of experiments demonstrated the correctness of this prediction also. Yet another experiment showed that the emergent radiation, in accordance with the theory of Frank and Tamm, was generated in the shape of a hollow cone with its point trailing, expanding in a forward direction surrounding the path of the stimulating radiation.

This theory, then, proved successful in describing and explaining Cerenkov's initial experimental results; further, it was able to predict future results. Tamm and Frank stressed that their theory in no way violated the theory of relativity, though at first glance this seemed to be the case. While the relativity theory did assert that nothing could travel faster than the speed of light in vacuo, the particles responsible for the Cerenkov radiation were in fact only traveling faster than the "phase velocity" $\frac{c}{N}$, which in refractive media where $N>1$, could be considerably less than c. The Cerenkov radiation was the first observed instance of this phenomenon.

The strangest feature of the radiation, and of the theory which explained it, was that light was emitted by a charged particle in uniform motion. Up until the discoveries of Cerenkov, Tamm, and Frank, all known mechanisms of producing radiation were connected with nonuniform motion (oscillation of electrons within atoms, and so on). For some time this fact hindered many physicists from correctly understanding the Cerenkov radiation. It later became clear that the theory of radiation by a charged particle moving at superlight velocity constituted an important chapter in the classical theory of radiation.

Use was made of the Tamm-Frank formulation in the exquisitely sensitive Cerenkov counter developed in the 1950s, a particle detector of unparalleled utility. At the same time, their theory developed into the large theoretical domain of superlight optics, with growing numbers of practical applications in fields such as plasma physics.

Tamm made further contributions to physics in the study of elementary particles, nuclear forces, and the theory of nuclear synthesis. He formulated the so-called β-theory of nuclear forces in 1934. According to this theory, the β-decay of nucleons led to the appearance of forces of a special kind between any two nucleons. Tamm showed that although these forces existed, they were too weak to account for the binding of nucleons within atomic nuclei. The 1935 meson hypothesis of H. Yukawa, which afterwards received brilliant experimental confirmation, proceeded along the same lines as Tamm's theory. Tamm was also responsible for the theoretical prediction (in 1933) of the existence of special bound states of electrons on crystal surfaces (so-called "Tamm's levels"), a hypothesis with implications essential to semiconductor and transistor physics.

The son of an engineer, Tamm studied physics at the Moscow State University, graduating in 1918. From 1919 to 1922 he taught physics at several universities and technical institutions, and in 1924 he became an instructor at Moscow State University. There, he rose to the position of professor in 1927 and occupied the chair of theoretical physics from 1930 to 1941. He received the degree of doctor of physicomathematical sciences in 1933, and the next year he took charge of the Lebedyev Physical Institute

of the U.S.S.R. Academy of Sciences. He became an academician in 1953.

Tamm wrote *Relativistic Interaction of Elementary Particles* (1945) and *On the Magnetic Moment of the Neutrino* (1934). He was author of a university textbook on *Electrodynamics*, published in many languages and editions.

For background information *see* CERENKOV RADIATION in the McGraw-Hill Encyclopedia of Science and Technology. ☐

★ **TATUM, Edward Lawrie**
American biochemist and geneticist
Born Dec. 14, 1909, Boulder, Colo., U.S.A.

TATUM'S RESEARCHES were concerned primarily with the biochemistry and genetics of bacteria, yeasts, and molds. His particular interest was the relation of genes to biochemical reactions in cells of these microorganisms. With G. W. Beadle he found (1941) that gene mutations in the mold *Neurospora crassa* led to failure of synthesis of essential molecules such as amino acids, vitamins, and other growth factors. Tatum then showed (1945) that analogous mutations could be produced in the common bacterium *Escherichia coli*. Using these mutant strains, with J. S. Lederberg he discovered (1947) the phenomenon of genetic recombination in this bacterium. Tatum shared, with Beadle and Lederberg, the 1958 Nobel Prize for medicine or physiology.

The work with nutritionally deficient mutants of *Neurospora* and *E. coli*, showing a direct and specific correlation between genes and biochemical reactions, led to a resurgent general interest in biochemical genetics. The finding of genetic recombination in *E. coli* was soon extended to other bacteria and led to the discovery of other new types of genetic recombination, such as transduction in *Salmonella* (Zinder and Lederberg, 1952), and greatly stimulated the use of bacteria in genetic studies. The use of microorganisms in combined biochemical and genetic studies essentially initiated the present productive, sophisticated, and exponentially growing field of molecular genetics.

Prior to 1930, studies on gene action (biochemical or physiological genetics) had dealt with visible, relatively superficial, characters such as pigmentation in plants, animals, and insects, and had led to the concept that genes controlled the biochemical reactions concerned. The corollary to this, that genes control all enzymes concerned in biochemical reactions, invisible as well as visible, in all living cells, was not generally recognized by biologists or biochemists. Similarly, neither geneticists nor microbiologists thought of microbes as suitable for genetic research.

Studies in the early 1930s on the nutrition of bacteria and other microorganisms led to the recognition of the great diversity and variability in the requirements of different strains for essential "growth factors." It also became clear that the requirement for a specific growth factor represented the failure of a particular strain to synthesize a substance needed by all living cells. Beadle and Tatum reasoned that all biochemical reactions in microorganisms should be under gene control, including the syntheses of essential nutrient molecules such as growth factors. According to their hypothesis, gene mutation in a microorganism should then result in the loss of particular synthetic reactions and hence to the requirement for growth of particular substances such as vitamins or amino acids.

To test this hypothesis, the mold *Neurospora* was selected because of its rapid growth in simple medium and because its genetic system permitted easy genetic analysis of any mutants obtained. Using x-rays to produce mutations, a number of pure lines were isolated on complex media and then tested for their growth on a simple medium. A large number of deficient strains were readily obtained. Each was found to require a different amino acid or vitamin for growth, and on genetic analysis each requirement could be shown to be due to the mutation of a different gene. This work, done at Stanford University in 1940–41, thus substantiated the hypothesis that genes control biochemical reactions in cells.

At Stanford Tatum extended this approach to the bacterium *E. coli* (1944–45), and at Yale University to yeast (1948), with the production and isolation of nutritional or "biochemical" mutants. It was later shown by workers throughout the world that essentially any desired biochemical (enzymatic) reaction in almost any microorganism can be altered by mutation.

The discovery of genetic recombination in *E. coli* strain K-12 (Tatum and Lederberg, 1947)

was made at Yale University, by showing that gene recombination took place when cultures of two different double biochemical mutants were mixed.

Biochemical mutants have been fruitfully used in bioassay for vitamins, amino acids, and so forth, in detailed investigations of biochemical pathways of biosynthesis of these substances, as markers for studying life cycles and genetic systems in various microorganisms, and most recently in studies on the regulation of gene activity and on the mechanism of transfer of information from the gene to the enzyme protein.

In recent years, Tatum concentrated on the genetics and biochemistry of morphology in *Neurospora*, and with his associates he studied problems such as cytoplasmic inheritance in *Neurospora*, the action and biosynthesis of certain antibiotics, and nucleic acid metabolism in mammalian cells in culture.

The son of a professor of pharmacology, Tatum was educated at the universities of Chicago and Wisconsin. At Wisconsin he received his A.B. in chemistry in 1931, his M.S. in microbiology in 1932, and his Ph.D. in biochemistry in 1934. He held faculty positions in biology, botany, microbiology, and biochemistry at Stanford University (1937–45), at Yale University (1945–48), again at Stanford (1948–57), and at the Rockefeller Institute after 1957. He was elected to the National Academy of Sciences in 1952.

For background information *see* BACTERIAL GENETICS; GENE in the McGraw-Hill Encyclopedia of Science and Technology.   □

★ **TAUB, James Monroe**
American metallurgist
Born July 26, 1918, Cleveland, Ohio, U.S.A.

THE ADVENT of nuclear energy introduced many new materials to scientists and engineers. Intensive investigation of plutonium and uranium metals and alloys (the fissionable materials essential for nuclear reactions in both weapons and reactors) was necessary in order to develop methods of preparing the metallic material and to devise techniques for fabricating the radioactive metals into the desired components. Taub entered this new field at the very beginning, and for his contribution to the development of processing techniques for the new materials he received the E. O. Lawrence Award of the U.S. Atomic Energy Commission in 1963.

The development of the first atomic weapon required the fabrication of normal uranium and uranium enriched in the isotope U^{235}. Uranium was not an available metal prior to this requirement, so that a background of ex-

perience and technical data did not exist. In fact, so little was known about the melting point of the metal that it was off by several hundred degrees centigrade in the handbooks.

Utilizing normal uranium as the stand-in material for the U^{235}, Taub and his associates at the Los Alamos Scientific Laboratory developed methods of handling and processing the radioactive metal. Uranium is an alpha emitter as well as a heavy metal so that precautions had to be built into the operating procedures to protect personnel from the radiation as well as from absorption into the body, which could result in heavy-metal poisoning. The material is also very reactive and cannot be heated in air without excessive oxidation and flaking taking place.

Vacuum melting furnaces were designed to melt and cast the metal in the absence of air. At the same time it was necessary to develop melting crucibles of high-purity ceramics that would be compatible with molten uranium and that would not contaminate the metal with impurities. High-purity fused magnesium oxide was the material finally selected, and the powder was fabricated into liners for reduction bombs and into melting crucibles. The uranium metal so obtained was of very high purity.

The development of suitable melting and casting procedures for uranium resulted in metal being available for the development of other fabrication techniques. Over a period of time, Taub and his group carried out successful development programs that made it possible to roll, forge, deep draw, extrude, and weld uranium—to perform, in fact, practically any operation that could be performed with other metals. This information was fed into the Atomic Energy Commission's production plants.

In addition to the specific activities on uranium, Taub developed an integrated Materials Technology Group that worked with all metals as well as with ceramics and plastics. Electrochemical and powder metallurgy operations were

established, as well as a physical metallurgy section, which assisted in all of the development programs. Programs involving alloy formation, high-temperature oxides and carbides of fissionable and other metals, tungsten carbides and tungsten alloys, cermets of refractory metals and oxides or carbides, general refractory metal development including intensive work on tantalum and tungsten alloys, vapor deposition of tungsten, and flame and plasma spraying of high-temperature materials are only a part of the great variety of materials development work undertaken within the group. Reactors utilizing uranium-loaded graphitic fuel elements for high-temperature operation entered the picture, and Taub and his group developed new techniques for incorporating uranium into graphite and for fabricating complex shapes of high strength and density for these reactor applications.

Taub received his B.S. in metallurgical engineering at Case Institute of Technology, Cleveland, Ohio, in 1940. He worked in various phases of steel-making operations at the Republic Steel Corporation for two years, then returned to Case Institute as a research assistant to work on the development of steel cartridge cases for Frankford Arsenal. During the period 1940–44 Taub attended night school, receiving his M.S. in metallurgical engineering in 1944. In late 1944 Taub was recruited for metallurgical development work at Los Alamos in conjunction with the first atomic bomb. He remained with the Los Alamos Scientific Laboratory after the end of the war to direct the activities of the Materials Technology Group.

For background information *see* METAL FORMING; PLUTONIUM; URANIUM in the McGraw-Hill Encyclopedia of Science and Technology.   ☐

★ TAUBE, Henry
American chemist
Born Nov. 30, 1915, Saskatchewan, Canada

TAUBE'S PRINCIPAL contributions were in the area of inorganic reactions in solution. Specifically, he advanced the understanding of solvation of ions, of the mechanisms of substitutional changes at metal ion centers, and of the mechanisms of oxidation-reduction reactions. In 1955 Taube received the American Chemical Society's Award for Nuclear Applications in Chemistry.

Inorganic reactions have played an important role in developing the basic principles of chemical kinetics. Interest in the descriptive aspect of the rates and mechanisms of inorganic reactions as a subject in its own right, however, long lagged behind corresponding development in the field of organic reactions. Despite the contribu-

tions of research workers such as N. Bjerrum, W. C. Bray, and A. B. Lamb, it was not until after World War II that the field began to flourish. Between 1940 and 1950 two factors stimulated development of the subject: radioactive elements, artificially produced, became available in great variety, which led to experimentation with a wide range of inorganic substances; and chemists trained in a variety of disciplines came into contact with inorganic reactions as part of wartime research efforts.

At the University of Chicago in the late 1940s, Taube began an attack on some of the basic problems of inorganic solution chemistry. One of these concerned the interaction of ions in solution with molecules of the solvent. Using an isotopic dilution technique, Taube and J. P. Hunt showed that chromic ion in water can indeed be represented by the formula $Cr(H_2O)_6^{3+}$ and measured the rate of exchange of the bound water with the solvent. Theirs was the first proof of formula for a solvated cation in solution that had been offered. Since then the subject has progressed far as other methods have been introduced, among them those based on nuclear magnetic resonance effects for O^{17} and H, which Taube had a share in developing.

A striking feature of inorganic complexes is the enormous range of substitution labilities they display. Thus, the half-time for the exchange with solvent of water in $Cr(H_2O)_6^{3+}$ is $\sim 10^5$ sec, while for $Cr(H_2O)_6^{2+}$ it is less than 10^{-9} sec. In 1952 Taube presented a correlation of the rates of substitution in inorganic complexes with electronic structure that, in important features at least, still seems to be valid. It was especially useful as a basis for planning experiments exploiting the differences in substitution labilities. One such application was the demonstration by Taube, H. Myers, and R. L. Rich that some inorganic oxidation-reduction reactions involving metal complexes in solution take place by a so-called "bridged" or "inner-

sphere" activated complex. To be specific, it was observed that when $(NH_3)_5CoCl^{2+}$ reacts with Cr^{2+}, $CrCl^{2+}$ is formed; when free radioactive Cl^- is present in solution, virtually none is incorporated into the $Cr(III)$ product. The experiment showed that there is direct contact between the metal reducing agent and the chlorine on the oxidizing agent in the oxidation-reduction reaction, and that, concomitant with the redox process, the chlorine group leaves the coordination sphere of the oxidizing agent to enter that of the reducing agent. The success of the experiment depended on the fact that $(NH_3)_5CoCl^{2+}$ is very slow to undergo substitution, while the product Co^{2+}, formed when $Co(III)$ is reduced, is very labile in this regard. The complementary situation obtains at the chromium center, Cr^{2+} undergoing substitution readily so that $[(NH_3)_5CoClCr(H_2O)_5]^{4+}$ can form. Once Cr^{3+} is formed by electron transfer it undergoes substitution slowly, thus retaining the chromium-chlorine bond that was formed while chromium was in the 2+ oxidation state. In another class of oxidation-reduction reactions ("outer-sphere") there is no interpenetration of coordination spheres, and in these reactions the electrons pass though the intact coordination shells of both partners. One of the current problems in the study of oxidation-reduction reactions is to learn what the mechanism is in a particular case with respect to the important difference in geometry represented by the two kinds of activated complex.

Taube considerably extended the area of the inner-sphere reactions by finding more examples, and also by introducing other basic issues. Groups such as $-O_2CR$, he found, can be transferred; in some cases he observed evidence for attack by the reducing agent at a position on the bridging group remote from that which binds the oxidizing agent. These experiments raised questions about the mechanism of electron transport through the bridging molecules. Thereafter Taube actively pursued this aspect, as well as the question of how the behavior of the different systems can be understood in terms of the electronic structures of the components of the electron transfer system, namely, of the metal ions, the bridging ligands, and the nonbridging ligands.

Taube attended the University of Saskatchewan as an undergraduate and continued there for his M.S., which was granted in 1937. His Ph.D. work was done with W. C. Bray at the University of California, Berkeley. After receiving the Ph.D. in 1940, he served as instructor in chemistry at Berkeley for one year. Thereafter he taught at Cornell University (1941–46), the University of Chicago (1946–62), and Stanford University (from 1962). He was elected to the National Academy of Sciences in 1959.

For background information *see* KINETICS, CHEMICAL; OXIDATION-REDUCTION; SOLUTION in the McGraw-Hill Encyclopedia of Science and Technology.   ☐

★ TAUSSIG, Helen Brooke

American physician, pediatrician, and cardiologist
Born May 24, 1898, Cambridge, Mass., U.S.A.

HELEN TAUSSIG conceived the idea that many cyanotic infants and children could be helped by increasing the circulation to the lungs. Together with surgeon Alfred Blalock, she devised the operation by which it was possible to change the cyanotic infant's color from blue to pink and enable the child to live a nearly normal life. This operation gave a tremendous stimulus to the surgical correction of congenital malformations of the heart. For their achievement, she and Blalock received many honors, including the Passano Foundation Award in 1948, the Lasker Award of the American Public Health Association in 1954, and the Award of Merit of the Gairdner Foundation in 1959.

Taussig's studies at the Johns Hopkins University School of Medicine and the Harriet Lane Home for Invalid Children in Baltimore were based on the careful clinical observation of cyanotic infants throughout their lives. She recognized that a large number of infants died of anoxemia, not of cardiac failure, and furthermore that a number of infants became worse as the ductus arteriosus closed. These observations led her to consider how to keep that pathway open. While she pondered this problem, Robert Gross operated on a child with a persistent patency of the ductus arteriosus and ligated the vessel. Taussig immediately realized that if one could ligate a vessel in a child with too much blood going to the lungs, one should be able to insert a vessel in a child suffering from insufficient pulmonary blood flow.

When Blalock came to Baltimore in 1941 he was already interested in thoracic surgery and had operated on three children with persistent patency of the ductus arteriosus. Taussig immediately interested him in the problem presented by cyanotic infants with decreased pulmonary blood flow and suggested an end-to-side anastomosis between the subclavian artery and the pulmonary artery. Blalock performed numerous experiments on dogs, first to establish the validity of the idea and then to develop the technique of the operation. The result was the Blalock-Taussig operation. When they observed a child turn from blue to pink in the operating room, the validity of the operation was immediately established. The operation was dramatic and aroused the interest of the medical profession both in the diagnosis and also in the surgical treatment of malformations of the heart.

Blalock and Taussig worked together for 20 years. She was the clinician who made the diagnosis and selected the patients suitable for operation, and Blalock performed the operations. Taussig trained many physicians in the clinical diagnosis of congenital malformations; Blalock trained many young doctors to be cardiovascular surgeons.

Taussig made important contributions in other areas. In the field of rheumatic fever, she showed that cardiac enlargement occurred during periods of active infection as well as from strain on the myocardium caused by valvular damage. When the strain from infection or valvular damage was relieved, the heart ceased to enlarge. The child could outgrow the cardiac enlargement.

In the field of congenital malformations of the heart, Taussig was the first to show that by the use of fluoroscopy and x-rays one could detect changes in the size and shape of the heart and gross alteration in the vascularity of the lung fields. She showed that by careful clinical examination and simple laboratory tests, most malformations could be diagnosed on a broad functional basis. Her book, *Congenital Malformations of the Heart* (2 vols., 1947; 2d ed. 1960–61), gave the first systematic correlation of clinical, x-ray, fluoroscopic, and electrocardiographic findings in specific malformations with the findings observed at autopsy.

In 1962, when she heard that there was an outbreak of an unusual malformation in Germany and that a sleeping tablet (Contergan) was suspected to be the cause, Taussig immediately flew to Germany to investigate the situation. Upon her return she alerted American physicians to the danger of thalidomide and the inherent dangers that might lurk in other drugs. Her experience with thalidomide intensified her interest in the etiology of malformations.

The daughter of Frank William Taussig, a

professor of economics at Harvard University, Helen Taussig attended Radcliffe College for two years and then transferred to the University of California, where she obtained her B.A. in 1921. In the fall of 1921 she took histology at Harvard. The following year she attended Boston University in order to study anatomy. It was there that her interest in cardiology started when Alexander Begg gave her a calf heart to study the muscle bundles of the heart. In 1923 she transferred to the Johns Hopkins University School of Medicine, where she obtained her M.D. in 1927.

In 1930 E. A. Park, physician-in-chief of the Harriet Lane Home for Invalid Children, created special clinics to study various diseases and put Taussig in charge of the cardiac clinic. She headed the clinic from 1930 until her retirement in 1963. During the first 15 years the main emphasis of the clinic was on acute rheumatic fever; subsequently the emphasis shifted to the diagnosis and treatment of infants and children with congenital malformations of the heart. During this time she rose from instructor to become, in 1959, the first woman appointed a full professor in the Johns Hopkins Medical School. When she retired in 1963 she was granted the first Thomas Rivers Distinguished Fellowship, a five-year fellowship given by the National Foundation with complete freedom to carry on any desired line of work.

For background information *see* HEART; HEART DISORDERS in the McGraw-Hill Encyclopedia of Science and Technology. □

★ TAYLOR, Sir Hugh (Stott)

British chemist
Born Feb. 6, 1890, St. Helens, Lancashire, England

FOLLOWING EXPERIENCE obtained in England during World War I, when he investigated the catalytic synthesis of ammonia from nitrogen and hydrogen, Taylor worked at Princeton University from 1919 to 1958 on the characteristics of solid catalytic surfaces producing gaseous chemical reactions. The work, involving studies of adsorption of gases, led to considerable expansion in knowledge of the properties of the surfaces; the specificity of adsorption by catalysts; the dual nature of these adsorptions, physical and chemical; and the concept of slow sorption processes requiring activation energies. For his achievements in this area, Taylor was awarded the Franklin Medal of the Franklin Institute of the State of Pennsylvania in 1957 and the Proctor Prize of the Scientific Research Society of America in 1964.

Classical work on the adsorption of gases was carried out on inert porous materials such as charcoal, kieselguhr, and silica gel. On such surfaces there was a parallelism between extent of adsorption and ease of liquefaction. Indeed, van der Waals forces were involved in each case.

Extension of the measurements to catalytic hydrogenating metals, notably nickel, cobalt, iron, copper, and the platinum metals, showed that these adsorptions were highly specific, in no way parallel to ease of liquefaction of the gas. On such surfaces, hydrogen was more strongly held than carbon dioxide. Measurements of the heats of adsorption of hydrogen on copper and nickel indicated molar heats of adsorption of the order of 10-15 kcal in marked excess of the heat of liquefaction, $\sim$1 kcal.

A study of the influence of heat treatment, sintering, and poisoning of catalysts' surfaces led Taylor, in 1925, to a concept of a heterogeneous surface with a whole spectrum of activities, the most active of which he termed "active centers." He extended his work on these centers to oxides that functioned as hydrogenation catalysts—for example, in methanol synthesis—on such oxides as zinc and chromium oxide or their mixtures. Here again, he demonstrated strong specific adsorption of hydrogen. He showed both physical and chemical adsorption of hydrogen on the same catalyst surface, the former at lower temperatures, the latter in a higher temperature range with an intermediate region of miminal adsorption. This led, in 1930, to his formulation of chemisorption requiring an activation energy

of adsorption. Subsequent researches indicated that the activation energy required was a function of the cleanliness of the surface. Hydrogen chemisorbs on clean metal surfaces with negligible activation energies. On incompletely reduced hydrogenating metal surfaces, measurable activation energies are demonstrable.

Stephen Brunauer and Paul Emmett showed that the adsorption of nitrogen on catalytic iron surfaces is a typical case of chemisorption requiring an activation energy. This energy decreases with more thorough reduction of the oxide from which it is obtained. The strong susceptibility of iron surfaces to poisoning by oxygen-containing substances provides additional proof of the heterogeneity of the surface, the existence of "active centers."

Over the years, auxiliary researches supplemented the studies of surfaces, principally in the area of photochemistry. The mercury-sensitized dissociation of hydrogen molecules to atoms, using the resonance radiation $\lambda = 2536$ A, permitted a comparison of the reactivities of gaseous hydrogen atoms with those of adsorbed hydrogen. The reactions of addition of hydrogen atoms to unsaturated hydrocarbons and the cracking of saturated hydrocarbons by hydrogen atoms, the photosensitized decomposition of organic compounds and hydrazine, were among those studied. In 1926, Taylor showed that the metal alkyls, by thermal decomposition, released free radicals that could induce the polymerization of ethylene, a chain reaction that foreshadowed the industrial production of polyethylenes.

In the 1930s Taylor employed isotopic exchange reactions on catalyst surfaces involving hydrogen and deuterium, heavy and light nitrogen, ammonia and deuteroammonias, hydrocarbons and deuterium to supplement the proof of the concepts developed in his earlier work. Out of his work with hydrocarbons came a practical industrial application with John Turkevich: the conversion of n-heptane to toluene over catalysts of the type of chromium oxide gel that dehydrogenate and cyclize the hydrocarbon with minimal breakage of carbon-carbon bonds. This became an important industrial process during World War II with close cuts of gasoline on a variety of dehydrogenation-cyclization catalysts to yield aromatic hydrocarbons. The program was extended to surfaces of ruthenium, rhodium, and platinum, and to the catalytic properties of films of arsenic, antimony, and germanium deposited by decomposition of their hydrides.

The son of a chemist in a glass factory in St. Helens, Taylor majored in chemistry at the University of Liverpool (1906–12), at the Nobel Institute for Physical Chemistry in Stockholm (1912–13), and in the laboratory of Max Bodenstein in Hanover, Germany (1913–14), where he investigated the first chemical chain reaction initiated by alpha particles. His association with Princeton University began in 1914. For 25 years, from 1926 to 1951, he was chairman of the chemistry department there and from 1945 to 1958 was dean of the Graduate School. During World War II he worked in the Manhattan Project on the production of heavy water and the development of the barrier for the separation of U^{235} by diffusion methods. In 1958 he became president of the Woodrow Wilson National Fellowship Foundation.

Taylor wrote *Catalysis in Theory and Practice*, with E. K. Rideal (1919; 2d. ed. 1924), *Fuel Production and Utilization* (1920), and *Industrial Hydrogen* (1921). He edited *Treatise of Physical Chemistry* (1924; 3d ed. 1951) and *Elementary Physical Chemistry*, with H. A. Taylor (1927; 3d ed. 1942).

For background information *see* ADSORPTION; ANTIOXIDANT in the McGraw-Hill Encyclopedia of Science and Technology.   □

★ TAYLOR, Theodore Brewster
American physicist
Born July 11, 1925, Mexico City, Mexico

THE FIRST nuclear fission weapons developed by the United States were large, heavy, and expensive and therefore not adaptable to a wide variety of military uses. The first nuclear fission reactors were also very expensive and required several highly trained specialists to operate them, to a large extent because of the ever-present danger of an accidental excursion of the reactor. For his work on the military uses of nuclear energy, leading to much smaller, lighter, and cheaper nuclear weapons, and for his work on the peaceful uses of nuclear energy, leading to the development of the inherently safe and highly versatile TRIGA reactor, Taylor received the U.S. Atomic Energy Commission's E. O. Lawrence Memorial Award in 1965.

During the late 1940s and early 1950s many physicists, including some who had worked at Los Alamos on the first fission bombs, argued that basic physical principles limited further development of fission explosives to minor increases in efficiency or decreases in weight. During this same period physicists gave considerable attention to the problem of learning how to make thermonuclear explosives, and in 1950

President Truman ordered an intensive effort to develop a hydrogen bomb. In spite of this technical pessimism about future fission explosive developments and the spectacular results expected from thermonuclear explosives, a relatively small but intensive effort on improved fission explosives continued. This effort, in which Taylor was involved at Los Alamos, led to sharp reductions in the weight and cost of fission explosives and increased considerably the practical applications of nuclear explosives. These developments were made possible by concentrating on the details of the hydrodynamics, neutron diffusion and multiplication, and energy transport inside nuclear explosives, and by trying to enhance those effects that made for greater efficiency in the use of all the components of the explosives.

In the summer of 1956, the newly formed General Atomic Division of General Dynamics Corporation assembled a group of scientists and engineers in San Diego, Calif., to study new classes of peaceful applications of nuclear energy. One of these studies was called the "Safe Reactor Project." Its purpose was to develop a research reactor so inherently safe that it could be put in a heavily populated area without expensive safety provisions. As members of this group, Freeman Dyson, Andrew McReynolds, and Taylor proposed that complete safety of a nuclear reactor could be best achieved by designing it to have a prompt, large, negative temperature coefficient, which would insure safety without any mechanical or electronic safety devices. If too much reactivity were inadvertently put into the reactor, the power-level increase would lead to a temperature rise in the core. This would lower the excess reactivity, finally leading to stable operation of the reactor at a higher but not dangerous power level.

Two kinds of effects contributed to the large negative temperature coefficient that became the key to the safety of the TRIGA research reactor. One was the broadening with temperature of the capture resonances in U^{238} mixed with the reactor fuel and neutron moderator, which resulted in an increase in internal "poisoning" of the reactor with increasing temperature. The other is called the "warm neutron" effect. If the fissionable fuel and the neutron moderator are homogeneously mixed, the average energy of the thermal neutrons increases as the temperature of the mixture increases. Since the fission cross section of U^{235} decreases with increasing neutron energy at low energies, the number of neutrons that leak out of the reactor will increase as it gets hotter. In the TRIGA reactor, the situation is somewhat more complicated than this. Most of the moderator is zirconium hydride, mixed uniformly with U^{235} and U^{238} to form cylindrical fuel elements. These are cooled by

water that flows convectively between them. The successful development of the reactor thus required the detailed understanding of the process of energy exchange between neutrons and hydrogen atoms strongly bound to a crystal lattice. Marshall Rosenbluth proposed a theoretical model for this energy exchange based on the existence of so-called "Einstein levels" in such a crystal lattice. McReynolds and others exhibited the details of this model experimentally at Brookhaven National Laboratory. Thus it was that the successful completion of a practical project required the assembly of some fundamental new information concerning the properties of matter and led in turn to several new discoveries.

In October 1957, after *Sputnik I* was put in orbit, Taylor turned to the problem of propulsion in space. He tried methodically to pick out from known energy sources any that showed promise of being suitable for propulsion of very large spacecraft to and from the planets in reasonably short times. A number of years previously, Stanislaw Ulam, at Los Alamos, had suggested that a series of small nuclear explosions could be used to propel objects to Earth-escape velocity. Since nuclear explosions are the most compact form of energy available, Taylor concentrated on extensions of this idea, and in a few weeks he found that it appeared particularly well suited for propelling very large space ships, weighing thousands of tons or more. With Marshall Rosenbluth, Freeman Dyson, and others, he proposed that a project, which he called Orion, be undertaken to find out in detail if this means for propulsion could be used for space exploration on a large scale. The Department of Defense supported the Orion Project at General Atomic until the spring of 1965. Work by a dedicated group of people, over a period of 6 years, showed that the idea had considerably more promise than it appeared to have in 1957. The government terminated support of the project, however, because of a lack of either a clear military need for such a propulsion system or sufficient interest by the National Aeronautics and Space Administration in pursuing it further.

The son of a YMCA secretary in Mexico, Taylor attended Phillips Exeter Academy in New Hampshire and received his B.S. in physics at the California Institute of Technology in 1945. From 1946 to 1949 he was a graduate student in physics at the University of California at Berkeley, working on problems in high-energy physics at the Radiation Laboratory. From 1949 to 1956 he was on the staff of the Theoretical Division of the Los Alamos Scientific Laboratory. In 1956 Taylor joined the General Atomic Division of General Dynamics Corporation, where he became a senior research advisor and chairman of the high-energy fluid dynamics department. In October 1964, he was appointed deputy director (scientific) of the Defense Atomic Support Agency of the Department of Defense.

For background information *see* FISSION, NUCLEAR; NUCLEAR POWER in the McGraw-Hill Encyclopedia of Science and Technology.   □

★ TERMAN, Frederick Emmons

American engineer and educator
Born June 7, 1900, English, Ind., U.S.A.

TERMAN IS known for a variety of contributions to electronics and to education. In the period 1925–41 he built up a program of research and instruction in electronics at Stanford University that was distinctive for its output of ideas, people, and books. It was primarily concerned with research on the properties of circuits, vacuum tubes, and systems involving combinations of tubes and circuits, and with instrumentation. His own books reflected his interest in the systematic organization of knowledge and ideas, and his desire to find simple quantitative ways to treat each topic.

Shortly after Pearl Harbor, Terman was asked to organize and direct a war-research laboratory for countermeasures against enemy radar. This was located at Harvard University, and became known as the Radio Research Laboratory. It devised jammers for use against enemy radar, developed the techniques for manufacturing and using aluminum strips (often called chaff), and designed tunable receivers for detecting and analyzing enemy radar signals. In spite of the fact that this laboratory did not come into existence until February, 1942, by the end of that year its reconnaissance equipment was being used in the principal theaters of the war, and by late 1943 every four-engine bomber in the European and Mediterranean theaters carried both jammers and chaff, a combination that turned out to be very effective in reducing bomber losses from antiaircraft fire. The ships of the Normandy invasion fleet carried several hundred jammers designed by RRL. At its peak, the organization included over 850 employees, of whom about 225 had degrees in engineering or science.

As the end of the war approached, Terman saw clearly that the military services would be supporting postwar research in universities. He was to return to Stanford as dean of engineering, and even before leaving Harvard had developed plans for carrying on such research at Stanford in a way that would enhance rather than compete with academic values. In essence, this involved the recruitment of faculty members who combined high research competence with interest in teaching, building the sponsored research program around the interests and abilities of these faculty members, and carrying out the research largely with faculty and graduate students rather than with full-time research workers. Stanford's leading position today in graduate training and research in engineering attests to the soundness of this approach and to the effectiveness with which it was carried out.

In spite of a life spent primarily on university campuses, Terman was always interested in the practical world of engineering. He recognized that the postwar support of engineering research in universities on a large scale would make universities important factors in regional economic growth, provided an appropriate coupling was developed between the academic and the related industrial activities, and he was one of the first in the country to preach this doctrine. As a result, he became identified with the emergence of the San Francisco Peninsula as an important center of research-oriented industry. Stanford, through its policies and attitudes, made a substantial contribution to this regional development and in turn benefited as this industrial complex developed.

In 1955, Terman was made provost at Stanford, holding this post until his retirement in 1965. His regime as provost is best known within the university for his concern with quality in the faculty, including particularly emphasis on the vigorous recruiting of new faculty members and on high standards in judging those on its staff. Concurrently, he stood for generous salaries for those who met these standards. This program contributed to the rising academic reputation of Stanford during recent years.

Terman's father was the psychologist Lewis Terman, famous for his I.Q. tests and studies of gifted children. Under his influence, the son acquired a deep interest in the abilities of people and in the evaluation of their future potential. Terman graduated from Stanford in 1920 and, after master's-degree-level work under Harris J. Ryan, moved on to the Massachusetts

Institute of Technology. There he received his doctor's degree in electrical engineering in 1924, with Vannevar Bush as his thesis supervisor. After a year lost because of a serious illness, he joined the Stanford faculty in 1925. During and after the war, he served on numerous government advisory committees. In 1950 he was awarded the Medal of Honor of the Institute of Electrical and Electronic Engineers. Elected a member of the National Academy of Sciences in 1946, he was also a founding member of the National Academy of Engineering.

Terman wrote, among other books, *Radio Engineers' Handbook* (1943), *Electronic and Radio Engineering* (4th ed. 1955), and *Electronic Measurements*, with J. M. Pettit (2d ed. 1952).

For background information *see* ELECTRICAL ENGINEERING in the McGraw-Hill Encyclopedia of Science and Technology.   □

☆ **THEILER, Max**
South African physician and virologist
Born Jan. 30, 1899, Pretoria, South Africa

A FTER DISCOVERING in 1930 that yellow fever could be transmitted to mice and later demonstrating that mice given serum from humans or monkeys who had had yellow fever were protected from subsequent infection, Theiler developed a vaccine that prevented human yellow-fever infection. For his contributions to the eradication of this once-dread disease, Theiler received the 1951 Nobel Prize in medicine or physiology.

Since at least 1648, when the first identified epidemic of yellow fever occurred in Mexico, this disease has been an economically and socially devastating plague in certain tropical and subtropical regions of the world. Although the cause and mode of transmission of yellow fever were not determined until the early 20th century, it had been observed during the 18th century that mosquitoes were abundant wherever

the disease occurred. In 1881 a Cuban physician, Carlos Finlay, wrote a treatise in which he implicated mosquitoes as the vector of yellow fever, but this assertion was largely ignored. Finally, after yellow fever had ravaged American troops in Cuba during the Spanish-American War, an army surgeon, Walter Reed, was appointed in 1900 to head a yellow-fever study group.

Reed's group discovered that yellow fever occurred in those who had been bitten by mosquitoes and that the mosquitoes (which were identified as *Aedes aegypti*) had previously fed on the blood of human yellow-fever sufferers. Since the mosquito was found to live in stagnant water in or near human dwellings, it became possible to control yellow fever by killing the mosquitoes and isolating yellow-fever patients in mosquito-free areas. These relatively simple measures enabled the Panama Canal to be constructed, for until yellow fever had been eliminated, many workers had died from the disease.

Another discovery made by the Reed group was that the actual causative organism of yellow fever was a virus. This was the first time that a virus had been implicated as a cause of disease in man.

With the successful work of the Reed commission, it was thought that yellow fever would no longer be a problem, but in 1911 the disease was discovered by South American physicians in persons working in virgin jungles far from human dwellings. Much later, monkeys were found to be capable of transmitting yellow fever to man; and in 1928, with the discovery that the rhesus monkey was susceptible to the disease, a laboratory animal for use in yellow-fever experimentation became available. The strain of virus with which the monkeys were infected was called the Asibi strain, after the patient from whom it had been isolated.

Theiler began his work in yellow fever by discovering that the mouse could be used far more conveniently than the monkey as an experimental subject. The strain of virus used, the French strain, had been isolated by investigators in French West Africa in 1928. When the virus was injected intracerebrally, the mice developed a form of encephalomyelitis unlike the typical human and monkey yellow fever in which the liver, kidneys, and heart are affected. By performing serial passage of the virus from mouse to mouse, Theiler progressively shortened the incubation period of the disease, eventually arriving at a constant period. Serial passage also increased the virulence of the induced disease in mice (injected parenterally). This latter fact suggested to Theiler that it might be possible to develop an attenuated active yellow-fever vaccine for human use.

Two routes were followed in developing human vaccination methods from Theiler's mouse-adapted virus: French investigators used only virus extract; American and English workers injected virus and human-immune serum simultaneously. The results of the French investigations, first reported in 1932, were not entirely satisfactory; although a good immunity was produced, serious complications in the central nervous system were sometimes encountered. Later, this method was modified with mouse yellow-fever virus and vaccinia virus, a method that proved effective and produced relatively few side reactions.

The experimental vaccinations using mouse-adapted virus and human-immune serum were based on the observation that active immunity in monkeys could be produced by this technique. Although the early trials of this method in human subjects were successful, large-scale vaccination was impossible because of the difficulty of obtaining human-immune serum. In an attempt to find a substitute, Theiler experimented with horse-, rabbit-, goat-, and monkey-immune sera, showing that high-titer sera from these animals could replace human-immune serum. This method, however, was still too cumbersome for large-scale application, and Theiler began experimenting with tissue-culture methods to produce attenuated yellow-fever virus suitable for vaccination.

Cultivation of the Asibi yellow-fever virus strain on minced mouse embryo tissue in a fluid medium proved to be highly successful. When the resulting attenuated virus was injected parenterally into monkeys, they remained well and did not develop central nervous system complications. This virus, however (the 17E strain) was not sufficiently attenuated to be used for human vaccination without the concurrent use of human-immune serum.

Theiler continued his tissue-culture experiments and eventually succeeded in producing a highly satisfactory attenuated virus, the 17D strain, utilizing chick embryo tissue containing minimal amounts of nervous tissue. This strain was not only minimally viscerotropic for monkeys but also demonstrated loss of neurotropism in mice and monkeys. When injected intracerebrally into monkeys, it produced only a mild encephalitis. Theiler continued his work on the 17D strain, using it for inoculation into humans without simultaneous use of human-immune serum. Preliminary results and later vaccination of millions of persons proved that this was a successful and safe method for immunization against yellow fever.

Theiler received his early education at Rhodes University College, Grahamstown, South Africa, and the University of Capetown Medical School. He received his medical degree in 1922 after studying in England at St. Thomas's Hospital and the London School of Tropical Medicine. In that same year he became an assistant, and later instructor, in the department of tropical medicine at Harvard Medical School, Boston, Mass. He joined the staff of the International Health Division of the Rockefeller Foundation in 1930; at his retirement from the Foundation in 1964 he was associate director for medical and natural sciences of the Rockefeller Foundation and director of the Rockefeller Foundation Virus Laboratories. In 1964 he became professor of epidemiology and microbiology at Yale University.

For background information *see* YELLOW FEVER in the McGraw-Hill Encyclopedia of Science and Technology.   □

★ THEORELL, Axel Hugo Teodor
Swedish biochemist
Born July 6, 1903, Linkoping, Sweden

FROM 1930 on, Theorell worked exclusively on the enzymes of cell respiration. For his discoveries concerning the nature and mode of action of oxidative enzymes, he received the 1955 Nobel Prize in physiology or medicine.

From the early work of C. A. MacMunn, and in particular from the work of Otto Warburg and David Keilin, it was known that iron-porphyrin-protein compounds (hemoproteins) played a decisive role in "activating" oxygen to take part in physiological combustion. The hemoproteins are, in fact, part of the "oxygen end" of an enzymatic chain that begins with a "hydrogen end." Hydrogen is liberated from various substrates—sugars, amino acids, fats—by the action of enzymes of another kind, "dehydrogenases." The last step in the series of reactions is the combustion of oxygen and hydrogen to form water with the liberation of energy.

Theorell was the first (1932) to crystallize myoglobin, the hemoprotein responsible for the red color in many muscles, and he described some of its main properties, including molecular weight (by ultracentrifugation), adsorption spectrum, magnetic properties, and reactions with oxygen and carbon monoxide. Myoglobin crystals later became uniquely useful in the hands of J. C. Kendrew, who, using x-ray crystallography, for the first time determined the total three-dimensional structure of a protein molecule. Other hemoproteins, like cytochrome *c*, horse radish peroxidase, and lactoperoxidase, were also purified, crystallized, and studied by Theorell, using refined physical and chemical methods.

A decisive step forward in our understanding of the working mechanism of dehydrogenases was taken with Theorell's work on the "yellow enzyme" in Otto Warburg's institute in 1934–35. The yellow dye "lumiflavin" of this "chromoprotein" could, as Warburg showed, be oxidized and reduced, and was thus recognized as the site of activity of the enzyme: hydrogen could be taken up and given off reversibly. Theorell purified the whole enzyme by the aid of electrophoretic methods, new at that time (1934), and cyrstallized it. He succeeded in splitting the enzyme into two parts, a colorless protein and a yellow, low molecular part. The latter was, after purification, analyzed and found to be a monophosphate ester of riboflavin (vitamin B_2). It is now called "FMN," flavin-mono-nucleotide, and was the first representative of the coenzymes to be clearly defined.

FMN and the colorless protein were inactive in the enzymatic test system when separated. The activity, however, appeared when they were reassociated. The conclusion of this "reversible-splitting" experiment turned out to be of general importance: coenzymes and enzymes become active by forming compounds with one another. The same pattern of B-vitamins in the form of phosphate esters, more or less nucleotidelike compounds, was soon found to obtain for nicotinic acid amide, thiamine, and pyridoxin. Spectrophotofluorimetric studies on the kinetics of the reversible splitting of the yellow enzyme led to some elucidation of the chemical groups involved in the reaction.

After 1950, Theorell's main interest was the mode of action and chemical composition of alcohol dehydrogenases. The "ADH" from horse liver was crystallized in 1948 by Theorell's collaborators R. Bonnichsen and A. Wassén. The reactions between the enzyme, its coenzyme, nicotinic acid adenine dinucleotide ("DPN" or "NAD"), and its substrates or inhibitors were probably more thoroughly investigated than any other enzyme system. The light absorption and fluorescence changes accompanying the reactions in these systems made them particularly suitable objects for experimentation. Furthermore, not only the free enzyme, but also its complexes with coenzyme, or coenzyme +

suitable inhibitors, were recently crystallized in Stockholm and studied by the aid of x-ray crystallography in the hope of determining the three-dimensional structure of the molecule.

A son of a medical doctor, Theorell studied medicine at the Karolinska Institutet in Stockholm and was graduated M.D. there in 1930. He was early attracted to biochemistry, and as a young pupil of E. Hammarsten he happened to discover and describe the lipoproteins in blood plasma (1926), the importance of which, however, was not realized until much later. After a short time (1932–33) as assistant professor of biochemistry at Uppsala, where he did ultracentrifugation studies with The Svedberg, he spent one and a half years with Otto Warburg in Berlin-Dahlem. In 1937 he became director of a research institute at the Karolinska Institutet established for him by the Nobel Foundation. He was elected a foreign associate of the U.S. National Academy of Sciences in 1957.

For background information *see* ENZYME in the McGraw-Hill Encyclopedia of Science and Technology.   □

★ **THIMANN, Kenneth Vivian**
American botanist
Born Aug. 5, 1904, Ashford, Kent, England

T HIMANN ISOLATED and purified auxin, the universal growth hormone of plants, and worked out its principal functions: the control of cell elongation (with James Bonner), of the formation of roots (with Frits Went), and of the growth of buds (with Folke Skoog). Later he showed that this third function involves a balance between auxin and another growth substance, isolated by Skoog and his associates and called kinetin. He also studied the formation of the red and purple pigments of plants, the anthocyanins, and proved that this process is controlled by a nucleic acid.

Beginning with the work of Charles Darwin in

1880, evidence had gradually accumulated that the growth of plants and their responses to light and gravity were controlled by a special diffusible "growth substance." In 1928 Frits Went at Utrecht University showed how to measure this by letting it diffuse out of seedlings into tiny blocks of agar and applying these to one side of growing seedlings to cause that side to grow more than the other, so that the plants curved. Went had shown that curvature of plants toward the light had the same ultimate basis—the light causing the growth substance to accumulate on one side. His fellow student at Utrecht, Herman Dolk, had shown that gravity has a comparable effect, auxin accumulating on the lower side of plants and causing upward curvature.

When Thimann, from London, and Dolk, from Utrecht, went to the California Institute of Technology at about the same time, they decided to join forces and to try to isolate the growth substance. For this they used a culture of one of the many fungi that had been found to produce the growth substance in good amounts. In 1933, when the work was well along, Dolk died and Thimann continued alone, obtaining the pure auxin, indole-3-acetic acid, in 1934. When Went came to the Institute in 1933 he had been working on the evidence that root formation was also under the control of a special substance, and soon Thimann showed that Went's proposed root-forming hormone was identical with auxin. Synthetic indole-3-acetic acid produced abundant roots on responsive plants. An opposite case was provided by the development of buds, which he found to be inhibited by young leaves. Very soon Thimann and Skoog showed that when synthetic auxin, in amounts similar to those formed by the leaves, was applied to cut stems the buds (which would otherwise have grown out) were completely inhibited. Thus the "growth" substance auxin was also both an organ-forming substance and an inhibiting substance—in other words, an influence that integrated the structure and functions of the whole plant.

Later A. H. Gustafson found that the setting of fruit was also under the control of auxin. When it became clear that in some plants the growth of buds was only weakly inhibited by auxin, Thimann and his colleagues showed that in reality what was involved was a balance between the inhibiting action of auxin and the stimulating action of kinetin; the growth of buds that were under natural inhibition (by auxin coming from leaves or from the plant apex) could be started up by applying kinetin. Thimann also showed that certain synthetic substances could act as auxins, and this discovery was taken up by synthetic chemists to produce the well-known 2,4-D and other auxins of agricultural importance.

Cuttings of stems of many plants can now be stimulated to form roots by treatment with synthetic auxins. The premature falling of fruits, especially apples, is now usually delayed by spraying the trees with auxins a few weeks before harvest. Horticulturists also use auxins to promote the joining of grafts. Most important, auxins in high concentration are toxic to plants, and hence if plants are sprayed with auxin at 100 or 1,000 times the concentration normally occurring in them they are killed. Thus auxins are used as weed killers in thousands of tons a year. The work on anthocyanins has not yet led to any applications.

Son of a Congregational minister, Thimann went to Caterham School, Surrey, and to Imperial College, London, where he majored in chemistry; he received the B.Sc. in 1924 and the Ph.D. (in biochemistry) in 1928. After teaching in London and studying microchemistry at Graz, Austria, he went to the California Institute of Technology in 1930, moving to Harvard University in 1935. During World War II he worked first on camouflage for the U.S. Army Engineers and then from 1942 until late 1945 on antisubmarine warfare for the U.S. Navy. He returned to Harvard as associate professor and was made full professor in 1948. In 1965 he went to the University of California at Santa Cruz as provost of one of the new residential colleges there. He was elected to the National Academy of Sciences in 1948.

Thimann wrote *Phytohormones*, with F. W. Went (1937), *Les Auxines* (1955), and *The Life of Bacteria* (1955; 2d ed. 1964).

For background information *see* AUXIN in the McGraw-Hill Encyclopedia of Science and Technology. ☐

★ THOMAS, Tracy Yerkes
American mathematician
Born Jan. 8, 1899, Alton, Ill., U.S.A.

THOMAS DEVELOPED an extension of the usual theory of the compatibility conditions for discontinuities over moving surfaces in the mechanics of continuous media. This extended theory permits a determination of the variation of the strength of the discontinuity during its propagation and, when combined with the principle that infinite discontinuities cannot occur in nature, leads to various important physical results. Thus it can be shown that the strength of a weak wave or sonic discontinuity in a gas will either be damped out in the course of its propagation or will become indefinitely large, depending on the geometry of the moving surfaces $\Sigma(t)$ bearing the discontinuity. In the latter case a shock, or strong but finite discontinuity,

will be produced in the gas as a means of preventing the occurrence of the infinite discontinuities; this phenomenon has been verified observationally in a shock tube.

Possible surfaces of fracture in solids subject to high stress can be viewed, on the basis of these concepts, as surfaces of instability over which an initial discontinuity of the nature of a slip of the material particles will tend to become infinite (strong instability) or will merely fail to be damped out (weak instability) as a consequence of the equations governing the behavior of the medium and the pertinent symmetry and boundary conditions. Fracture surfaces have been determined for flat plates and round bars under tension, for round bars under pure torsion, and for circular cylinders subjected to both tension and internal pressure. In all cases good qualitative agreement has been found between the observed and predicted surfaces of fracture.

Gravitational waves or discontinuities propagated in the free space of the general theory of relativity can be treated in a similar manner to obtain the result that the strength of the discontinuities in question must become indefinitely large, under certain conditions, at points of the space-time continuum. Invoking the principle that infinite discontinuities cannot be realized, it follows that abrupt changes in the metric structure of the nature of local explosions must occur in order to prevent these infinite discontinuities. If one assumes, for simplicity, a material energy tensor T whose components are given by

$$T_{AB} = \rho W_A W_B - p h_{AB}$$

where ρ, p, W_A and h_{AB} are the density, pressure, velocity components, and components of the metric tensor, respectively, it is easily shown that

$$\rho = \pm \frac{\sqrt{4C - B^2}}{\sqrt{3}\ \kappa}\ ;\ p = \frac{1}{4\kappa}\left(B \pm \frac{\sqrt{4C - B^2}}{\sqrt{3}}\right)$$

in which κ is the universal constant in the field equations and the quantities B and C are second-order scalar differential invariants of the space. The metric changes or local explosions must therefore, in general, give rise to nonvanishing pressure p and density ρ, including the possibility of the creation of matter of both positive and negative mass in accordance with the foregoing equations.

The above tensor T is obviously too restricted to meet all requirements since it makes no provision for the existence of charged bodies or electric and magnetic fields. Assuming the usual modification of this tensor by which it is possible to account for these electromagnetic effects, we are justified in considering that the local metric explosions will result in the creation of charged as well as uncharged particles and in the creation of electric and magnetic fields. Similar effects must occur as a means of avoiding the infinite discontinuities which would otherwise arise as the result of the collapse of a purely material body beyond the Schwarzschild limit. The extreme state of collapse of a body will therefore lead to the creation of magnetic fields and charged particles which will be ejected, along with matter, from the sides of the body. Such effects, by which one can readily account for the high energy output of the quasi-stellar radio sources, have been observed by astronomers and are evidently responsible for the pair of radio sources which are sometimes found and which are located symmetrically on opposite sides of the plane of a galaxy.

The basic features of the above theory of the creation of matter and the various forms of energy within the framework of the general theory of relativity were used by Thomas in his formulation of the epochal cosmology for the explanation of the discretized cosmological relationships that were recently discovered by A. G. Wilson at the Rand Corporation.

Thomas majored in mathematics and physics at Rice Institute in Houston, Tex., receiving his A.B. in 1921. After obtaining his Ph.D. in mathematics from Princeton University in 1923, he continued his studies as a National Research fellow at the universities of Chicago, Zurich, Harvard, and Princeton from 1923 to 1926. He was an assistant professor and later an associate professor of mathematics at Princeton University from 1926 to 1938, when he left Princeton to accept an appointment as professor of mathematics at the University of California at Los Angeles. In 1944 he became the chairman of the mathematics department at Indiana University, where he organized and was made director of the Graduate Institute for Mathematics and Mechanics. In 1956 he was appointed Distinguished Service Professor of Mathematics at Indiana

University. He was elected to the National Academy of Sciences in 1941.

Thomas wrote *The Elementary Theory of Tensors* (1931), *The Differential Invariants of Generalized Spaces* (1934), *Concepts from Tensor Analysis and Differential Geometry* (1961; 2d ed. 1965), and *Plastic Flow and Fracture in Solids* (1961).

For background information *see* COSMOLOGY in the McGraw-Hill Encyclopedia of Science and Technology.   □

★ **THOMPSON, Stanley Gerald**
American nuclear chemist
Born Mar. 9, 1912, Los Angeles, Calif., U.S.A.

THOMPSON RECEIVED the American Chemical Society's Award for Nuclear Applications in Chemistry in 1965 "for his conception and crucial contributions to the radiochemical process for the first industrial-scale separation and isolation of plutonium; his participation in the discovery of the elements with atomic numbers 97 to 101, inclusive; and his imaginative and effective studies on the nuclear fission process."

Thompson's first important contribution came during 1942–44 in connection with wartime requirements for the development of a chemical process for the extraction of plutonium from uranium and fission products. Enrico Fermi and his coworkers were engaged in the production of Pu^{239} using the chain-reacting pile (nuclear reactor); the first pile was successfully operated in December, 1942. In the reaction, relatively small amounts of plutonium are produced along with a large variety of unstable radioactive isotopes of the medium-weight elements called fission products, which result from the splitting of uranium in the fission reaction. The problem was to find an efficient way of separating plutonium from uranium and the fission products. Thompson was primarily responsible for the conception and early development of the bis-

muth-phosphate process for this purpose. This process was in plant-scale operation within 13 months of its original conception; it played an important role in the termination of the war and was used at Hanford until 1951, when it was replaced by a more economical process.

In 1945 Thompson became interested in the possibility of producing and studying new transuranium elements. Since these elements are unstable and do not exist on the Earth, it was necessary to prepare them by means of nuclear reactions. This meant developing many new techniques involving target preparation and systems for bombardment, especially with reference to handling high levels of radioactivity and making rapid chemical separations. Thompson initiated a program for the production of heavy elements by long-term irradiations with neutrons in nuclear reactors, following which chemical processing separated the various elements. Because of high levels of radioactivity, methods were developed for separating the elements by remote control using heavy shielding.

The search for new elements and isotopes was greatly aided by Thompson's studies of energy relations and masses of the isotopes. These systematics made it possible to predict the decay modes and the half-lives of the heavy isotopes. Thompson also played a major role in working out the chemistry of seven of the actinide elements on the tracer scale (nos. 95 to 101). These results showed that the new elements are very similar to the rare earths and constitute a series in which the $5f$ electron shell is being filled. Much of the information was obtained through the development and improvement of certain ion-exchange methods and techniques.

Thompson and his coworkers also studied nuclear reactions in order to determine the best methods and conditions for making the new elements and their isotopes. This work involved measuring cross sections and excitation functions for the reaction of many heavy nuclei with neutrons and charged particles (H^2, He^4, Li^7, Be^9, C^{12}, N^{13}, and O^{16} ions). The culmination of these efforts was their discovery of five new elements [Bk (no. 97), Cf (no. 98), Es (no. 99), Fm (no. 100), and Mv (no. 101)]. During the same period they discovered about 40 isotopes and measured their decay properties (alpha, beta, electron capture, spontaneous fission, energies, and half-lives). They were also able to observe a subshell (especially stable configuration) at neutron number 152. Two of the new elements (nos. 99 and 100) and many of the isotopes were discovered in the debris of the first thermonuclear device "Mike" in 1952.

Thompson contributed much to knowledge of the nuclear spectroscopy of heavy isotopes, with special reference to alpha decay. In 1955 he and B. B. Cunningham made the first measurements of the macroscopic properties of berkelium and californium using ultramicrochemical methods. These measurements involved determinations of magnetic susceptibilities on less than one microgram of the new elements.

The third phase of Thompson's career was concerned with the study of fission, especially spontaneous fission. In much of his work he took advantage of the fact that many of the heavy isotopes undergo fission spontaneously and that these isotopes were available as a result of the production program he initiated and carried out as a side line for many years. As a result of Thompson's efforts, hundreds of Cf^{252} fission sources are being used in more than 20 laboratories throughout the world. These sources have played a major role in obtaining much new knowledge concerning the fission process and in the development of new types of counters and instruments.

In studying spontaneous fission, Thompson and his coworkers applied the methods of time-of-flight and precise energy determination to the fission fragments and other particles emitted in fission in order to learn much concerning the energy relations in fission and the properties of the neutrons, gamma rays, conversion electrons, and x-rays that are emitted. They obtained accurate data on the neutron-to-proton ratios of the primary fragments, for example. The data on neutron emission gave information on the time of emission of the neutrons; the data on gamma rays, and conversion electrons gave important information concerning the final stages in the deexcitation of the fragments.

They made extensive investigations of the tripartition process involving fission into three fragments of roughly comparable masses and of the long-range alpha particles. They measured the mass and energy distributions in the fission of many elements below radium and found that the results were in agreement with the predictions of a new liquid drop theory developed by Nix and Swiatecki that applies only to the region of elements below radium. By developing some sensitive new methods, they were able to measure fission cross sections for a number of lighter elements over a wide range of excitation energies and were able to determine values for the fission barriers (activation energies) of these elements. The results of this work gave data on some important fundamental constants related to the theory of fission and to the structure of nuclear matter.

Thompson received his A.B. in chemistry at the University of California, Los Angeles, in 1934 and his Ph.D. in chemistry at the University of California, Berkeley, in 1948. He became a senior staff member at the Lawrence Radiation Laboratory in Berkeley.

For background information *see* FISSION, NU-CLEAR; ISOTOPE; TRANSURANIUM ELEMENTS in the McGraw-Hill Encyclopedia of Science and Technology. □

★ **THOMSON, Sir George (Paget)**
British physicist
Born May 3, 1892, Cambridge, England

THOMSON PROVED experimentally by a direct method that free electrons possess wave properties in addition to their well-known behavior as particles. For this he shared the Nobel Prize for physics in 1937 with C. J. Davisson of Bell Telephone Laboratories, who had established the same conclusion independently by a similar method but using a different technique.

In the early 1920s physicists were perturbed by the inconsistent behavior of "light," including in this word a wide spectrum ranging from x-rays to infrared radiation. For some purposes it behaved as waves, for others as particles which Einstein had named "quanta."

In 1925 Louis de Broglie put forward the startling idea that any particle of small momentum would automatically possess a wave structure intimately associated with it. In other words, de Broglie suggested that the abnormal behavior of the quanta of radioaction was really not abnormal at all but bound up with the true conception of a particle. De Broglie's arguments, deduced from the theory of relativity, were difficult to apply to particular problems. Erwin Schrödinger succeeded in adapting them to the behavior of an electron bound in a hydrogen atom and showed that the theory agreed with experiment.

Physicists informally discussed these matters at the meeting of the British Association for the Advancement of Science held at Oxford in 1926, which both Thomson and Davisson attended, although they did not meet. After the meeting, Thomson had the idea that the wave properties of electrons could be tested by just the same kind of experiments as had been used three years before to prove the wave character of x-rays. If de Broglie was right, both electrons and the quanta of x-rays were particles automatically associated with waves. The fact that electrons but not quanta are electrified introduced some experimental difficulties but did not affect the analogy in principle. The experiments on x-rays depended on using the atoms in a crystal as a three-dimensional analog of the ruled gratings employed in optical spectroscopy. Light reflected from or passing through such a grating is thereby analyzed into its component waves, and this analysis is one of the most convincing proofs of the wave character of light. Could something similar be done with electrons?

Thomson and some of his pupils had been working at the University of Aberdeen for two or three years on the scattering of protons produced in a gaseous discharge at low pressure. It hardly required more than the reversal of the electric polarity of the discharge to do the same with "cathode rays" from the discharge; these so-called rays are, of course, electrons. The one serious difficulty was to find a suitable material to act as "diffraction grating." Unlike x-rays, cathode rays have poor penetration and are readily scattered. Excessive scattering would mask the desired effects, just as ground glass prevents one seeing clearly through a window. The thinnest solid readily obtainable was cellulose acetate, thin films of which can easily be made by letting drops of a solution of it spread over water in a bowl. One of Thomson's pupils, A. Reid, tried the experiment with encouraging results. Cathode rays that had passed through such a film and fell on a photographic plate

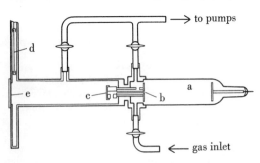

Fig. 1. Cathode rays (a) go through the tube (b) and the specimen (c). They make a fluorescent pattern on the screen (e) which can be recorded by lowering the photographic plate (d).

some distance behind (Fig. 1) produced, on development, patterns that recalled certain experiments with waves of light.

Unfortunately, to make a proper comparison between experiments and the predictions of de

Broglie's theory it is necessary to know the arrangement of the atoms in the film, and it is desirable that it should be crystalline. The cellulose acetate films did not fulfill these requirements. The atomic structure of metals was well known by this time from x-rays, but metals are strong scatterers of electrons.

With the help of C. G. Fraser, chief mechanic of the Aberdeen laboratory, very thin ($\sim$3 $\times$ 10^{-6} cm) films of gold, platinum, and aluminum were obtained by etching down the thinnest films commercially obtainable. Cathode rays going through these films produced patterns on the photographic plates identical, except for scale, with those that x-rays would produce (Fig. 2).

spark gap 20.7 mm   10.7 mm

Fig. 2. The first electron diffraction patterns from gold foil showing change of wavelength (size) with change in the energy of the cathode rays measured by the equivalent spark gap.

On the suppositions that each atom scatters the de Broglie wave of an electron, and that the scattered wavelets have the power of interference, theory permits a precise calculation of the pattern to be expected for electrons of given energy with no adjustable constant.

In all cases the patterns obtained agreed with the theory to within the limits of the measurement of the energy of the rays. Further, the patterns could be deflected by a magnet to just the extent that the original electrons would have been, disposing of the idea that the patterns might be caused by some novel kinds of secondary x-rays. Later, when Nevill Mott produced a theory of the variation of the scattering of the electronic waves with angle, this also was confirmed. In brief, the experiments fully confirmed de Broglie's theory that free electrons, like quanta, have both wave and particle properties.

Once it was established that electrons are diffracted by crystalline matter like x-rays, they could be used like x-rays to investigate the arrangements of the atoms in the specimen. It now becomes an advantage that they are much less penetrating than x-rays, for they will be affected only by surface layers. They are, therefore, well suited to study the peculiarities of surfaces. Thin films can be made much more easily by evaporation or by cathodic sputtering than by etching, but they are fragile and cannot be processed easily. Accordingly, an apparatus was produced at Aberdeen that permitted solid specimens to be used, the electrons being reflected from the surface, which acts like a reflection grating in optical spectroscopy. This has proved to be an important tool in the study of solid surfaces.

Thomson's father was J. J. Thomson, Nobel Prize winner in physics, best known for the discovery of electrons. Thomson was educated at day schools in Cambridge and at Trinity College, Cambridge, qualifying for a degree in mathematics before he took physics. He graduated in 1913 and started research under his father. During World War I, after a short period as an infantry officer in France, he worked at Farnborough on aerodynamical research, mostly in flight. In 1917–18 he visited the United States as a member of the British War Mission and worked for a time under Robert Millikan. After the war he continued research at Cambridge, including work on isotopes, and held a teaching fellowship at Corpus Christi College until appointed professor at the University of Aberdeen in 1922. In 1930 he moved to a professorship at Imperial College, University of London.

At the outbreak of World War II, Thomson returned to work at Farnborough. While there he was appointed chairman of the first British committee on atomic energy, known as the MAUD Committee. In August, 1941, he delivered to Vannevar Bush in the United States copies of the report by that committee that established the feasibility of an atomic bomb. Returning to Britain in August, 1942, he was appointed a vice-chairman of the Radio Board and later scientific adviser to the Air Ministry. In 1946 he became interested in the problem of controlled thermonuclear reactions, experiments on which were studied at first by a group at Imperial College. Later, for security reasons, the work was moved to the Associated Electrical Industries Laboratory. Thomson was a consultant there and at Harwell, the main research laboratory of the British Atomic Energy Authority.

In 1952 Thomson was elected Master of Corpus Christi College, Cambridge, a post he held till his retirement in 1962.

Thomson wrote *Applied Aerodynamics* (1919), *Conduction of Electricity through Gases,* with W. Cochrane (2 vols., 1928–33), *Wave Mechanics of the Free Electron* (1930), *Theory and Practice of Electron Diffraction* (1939), *The Atom* (1930; 6th ed. 1962), *The Forseeable Future* (1955), *The Inspiration of Science* (1961), and *J. J. Thomson and the Cavendish Laboratory* (1964).

For background information *see* ELECTRON; QUANTUM CHEMISTRY; QUANTUM MECHANICS in the McGraw-Hill Encyclopedia of Science and Technology.   □

★ TISELIUS, Arne Wilhelm Kaurin
Swedish biochemist
Born Aug. 10, 1902, Stockholm, Sweden

FOR HIS research on electrophoresis and adsorption analysis, especially for his discoveries concerning the complex nature of the serum proteins, Tiselius received the 1948 Nobel Prize in chemistry.

Tiselius studied chemistry, physics, and mathematics at the University of Uppsala, where he had the good fortune of being appointed (1925) research assistant to The Svedberg, the famous physical chemist. This was the time when Svedberg developed his well-known ultracentrifuge, for which he received the Nobel Prize in chemistry in 1926. New frontiers of research were opening in his laboratory, especially in the field of proteins. Tiselius had developed an intense interest in biochemical problems and now became aware of the importance of particularly gentle methods in studying biological systems. In the ultracentrifuge, molecules of different sizes move at different rates and thus separate, without any of the interference of the more drastic methods (precipitation, and so on) earlier used for their isolation and known often to damage or to destroy many substances essential to life. Other, equally gentle separation methods, based upon a similar "differential migration," appeared worth trying. Migration in an electric field, "electrophoresis," proved to be a method of choice, being highly specific and lending itself more easily to separation of larger quantities of material in preparative work. Tiselius's dissertation (1930) demonstrated the usefulness of such an approach, although he was somewhat disappointed that some results (particularly with such important and complex systems as blood serum) were only indications of something very interesting that the method was not powerful enough to demonstrate clearly.

For a while Tiselius's interests turned in other directions. A professorship of inorganic chemistry was to be vacant, and since there was at that time no chair of biochemistry in the Swedish faculties of science Tiselius decided to try his luck as an inorganic chemist. He took up a study of exchange and diffusion of molecules in certain crystals (zeolites), which he collected on the Faroe Islands. He did not get the chair, but he gained some experience in exchange phenomena that later was to prove useful in his studies on chromatographic methods.

During a visit to the United States in 1934–35 as a Rockefeller Foundation fellow Tiselius was inspired to take up electrophoresis experiments anew. After returning home he made a systematic study of the method and constructed a radically improved apparatus (1937). The test runs, made with blood serum, demonstrated conclusively what could only be guessed at in the earlier experiments, namely, the existence of four distinct main groups of proteins, which were named albumins and α-, β-, and γ-globulins. The new method rapidly came into general use and found applications in various fields of biochemistry for separation and characterization of complex mixtures of proteins and many other substances occurring in nature.

In 1938 a special research chair was established for Tiselius at Uppsala University, and an increasing number of pupils, both Swedish and foreign, came to work in his laboratory. The electrophoresis method was further developed with several collaborators (for example, H. Svensson, J. Porath, S. Hjertén) and is still one of the main items on the research program at the institute. Other methods were also studied, particularly chromatography (from 1940) and partition and gel filtration (from the late 1950s). In 1952 a new building was erected for the institute; this became internationally known as a center for the development of methods for biochemical analysis. Tiselius was elected a foreign associate of the U.S. National Academy of Sciences in 1949.

Tiselius always emphasized that such methods are of importance not only for the isolation and definition of pure substances but also as a tool in the determination of structures, both chemical and biological. Thus in the latter case, isolation of subcellular particles and other structural elements may give very useful information, and Tiselius and his group paid much attention to gentle methods suitable for such materials. Most of the work on methods in Tiselius's laboratory was done in connection with applications to important biochemical problems in the fields of enzymes, hormones, and antibodies, and a mutual stimulation was established, thus avoiding the risk of "gadgeteering" that is sometimes faced in purely methodological work.

For background information *see* ELECTROPHORESIS in the McGraw-Hill Encyclopedia of Science and Technology.   □

★ TODD OF TRUMPINGTON, Baron (Alexander Robertus Todd)

British chemist
Born Oct. 2, 1907, Glasgow, Scotland

TODD'S RESEARCHES covered a wide field of organic chemistry, mainly in relation to biology. His major achievement, for which he received the 1957 Nobel Prize in chemistry, was his work on the structure and synthesis of the nucleosides, nucleotides, and nucleotide coenzymes and on the related problem of phosphorylation. This work led him to the establishment of the general chemical structure of the nucleic acids, a structure that provided the basis for the subsequent development of knowledge on the physical structure and biological function of nucleic acids.

Earlier, Todd worked on the structure and synthesis of vitamins B_1 and E, elucidated the structure of vitamin B_{12} (in collaboration with D. C. Hodgkin), and did extensive researches on the coloring matters of plants and insects. From his work in the vitamin field arose his interest in the function of vitamins. This led him to commence, at Manchester University, a large program of work aimed at the structural elucidation and synthesis of coenzymes. These investigations, which he and his collaborators successfully developed on a large scale after he went to Cambridge University, formed the basis of his Nobel award.

Todd took his B.Sc. at the University of Glasgow and studied subsequently with W. Borsche at the University of Frankfurt (where he took his doctorate in 1931) and with Robert Robinson at the University of Oxford. In 1934 he went to Edinburgh University, where he began his researches on vitamin B_1; these he completed on joining the staff of the Lister Institute of Preventive Medicine in London in 1936. Appointed professor of chemistry and head of the department of chemistry at Manchester University in 1938, he completed his work on vitamin E and on the constituents of hashish there. He was named professor of organic chemistry at Cambridge University in 1944 and in 1963 became master of Christ's College. During World War II Todd worked on a number of government projects and from 1952 to 1964 was chairman of the British government's Advisory Council on Scientific Policy. He was knighted in 1954 and created a baron in 1962. In 1955 he was elected a foreign associate of the U.S. National Academy of Sciences.

For background information *see* NUCLEIC ACID in the McGraw-Hill Encyclopedia of Science and Technology.　□

☆ **TOMONAGA, Sin-itiro**
Japanese physicist
Born Mar. 31, 1906, Tokyo, Japan

WHILE INVESTIGATING inconsistencies in the predictions of quantum electrodynamics, Tomonaga evolved a modern theory of quantum electrodynamics that was quantitatively consistent with observed physical phenomena. In recognition of this achievement, Tomonaga shared the 1965 Nobel Prize for physics with the American physicists Richard Phillips Feynman and Julian Seymour Schwinger, who independently of Tomonaga and of each other had made similar discoveries at a slightly later date.

After the quantum theory had been initiated by the German physicist Max Planck about 1900, it was developed to the point where it was generally recognized that the motions of electrons and other subatomic particles must follow laws that are different from those of classical mechanics. This led to the development of quantum mechanics. Similarly, the classical theory of elec-

tricity and magnetism that had been developed by the Scottish physicist James Clerk Maxwell and others was evolved into quantum electrodynamics by such men as the British physicist Paul A. M. Dirac during the late 1920s. Although the principles of quantum electrodynamics permitted a qualitative study of the effects of light and x-rays on electrons, experiments conducted at Columbia University about 1930 showed a quantitative discrepancy between the predictions of the theory and the observed phenomena. As a result, the 1930s and early 1940s were a period marked by the efforts of physicists to radically alter the principles of quantum electrodynamics in an effort to eliminate the discrepancies.

In 1941, while working at the Tokyo University of Science and Literature, Tomonaga began his researches into the problems of quantum electrodynamics. His approach was on the basis of theoretical considerations only, for his chief concern was with the basic physical principles involved. Working in complete isolation from the scientific communities of the Occident because of the conditions imposed by World War II, he nevertheless had the benefit of an atmosphere of advanced theoretical physics that had been Japan's legacy from the prewar years, and in 1943 he published in Japanese the fundamental paper on his researches. His work came to the attention of Western scientists in *Progress in Theoretical Physics*, published by Hideki Yukawa after the war had ended. At this time, Feynman and Schwinger also published the results of their researches, and it was found that each of the three had independently achieved an essentially identical insight into the problem, even though each had approached it from a different aspect. Their work made the equations of quantum electrodynamics fully consistent with the special theory of relativity and solved the quantitative differences that had threatened to wreck it. Thus Tomonaga, along with Feynman and Schwinger, had reconciled the predictions of the theory with observable phenomena by mathematical revision without drastically altering the basic principles of quantum electrodynamics as proposed by Dirac and others.

Tomonaga also worked in several other areas of theoretical physics. Among his most notable contributions were his work in quantum dynamics, his paper on the theory of neutrons, and his research, in collaboration with Masao Kotani, in electromagnetics.

The eldest son of a philosopher and university professor, Tomonaga was educated at Kyoto University, receiving his degree in atomic physics in 1929. He remained at Kyoto for 3 years, working with Hideki Yukawa as an assistant in the research laboratory of Kajuro Tomaki. In 1932 Tomonaga transferred to the Science Research Institute in Tokyo, where he worked under

Yoshio Nishina. During a visit to Germany, he studied under Werner Karl Heisenberg. Tomonaga was appointed a professor at the Tokyo University of Science and Literature, now the Tokyo University of Education, in 1941, and from 1956 to 1962 he was president of the university. In 1963 he was named chairman of the Japan Science Council.

For background information *see* QUANTUM ELECTRODYNAMICS in the McGraw-Hill Encyclopedia of Science and Technology.   □

★ **TOUSEY, Richard**
American physicist
Born May 18, 1908, Somerville, Mass., U.S.A.

SPACE RESEARCH was born in 1946, when captured V-2 rockets were brought from Germany to the United States. Making use of these vehicles, Tousey pioneered the field of solar extreme ultraviolet spectroscopy. He was the first to fly a spectrograph on a rocket and to discover the ultraviolet spectrum of the Sun. For this, and his continuing researches in rocket spectroscopy, he received, among other honors, the Draper Medal of the National Academy of Sciences in 1963.

Spectra of light sources have been studied in the laboratory for more than a century, with observations extending over an ever-widening range, until no gap remains from the infrared, through the visible, ultraviolet, and extreme ultraviolet, to x-rays and gamma rays. Astronomers, however, have always suffered a great handicap: from stars, and even from the Sun, they could detect radiation only in a narrow range of wavelengths from the near infrared to about 3000 A in the ultraviolet. From even the highest mountains, or with equipment lifted into the stratosphere with balloons, they could see scarcely more than from sea level. Early in this century it was shown that a layer of ozone, extending high into the atmosphere, together with the oxygen and nitrogen of the air itself, absorbed completely all short-wavelength radiation at altitudes too high to reach except with rockets. The Sun was believed to emit these highly energetic radiations, because they were required to account for the production of the ozone layer as well as the ionosphere.

Tousey was well aware of this situation, since his doctoral research concerned extreme ultraviolet radiation. He conducted this research at Harvard University in the laboratory of Theodore Lyman, discoverer of the Lyman series of hydrogen, who himself, from high on Mt. Whitney, had searched in vain for a short-wavelength component of the Sun's radiation. When offered the use of V-2 rockets, Tousey and his colleagues at the U.S. Naval Research Laboratory in Washington, D.C., immediately started to develop a spectrograph to record the long-sought-for ultraviolet spectrum of the Sun, hoping to show that Lyman-alpha, the first line of the Lyman series of hydrogen, would be its strongest emission.

Many difficulties were encountered. First was the problem of recovering the photographic film after crash of the rocket. The second attempt, Oct. 10, 1946, less than a year after conception of the project, was successful. Although Lyman-alpha itself was not detected until later, the solar spectrum was observed from far above the ozone layer and was recorded to much shorter ultraviolet wavelengths than had ever before been seen.

A problem much more serious than recovery concerned the shortness of time available for exposures from a rocket, coupled with the effect of the gyrations of the rocket, which made it difficult to keep instruments pointed at the Sun. In the 20 years after the first experiments, automatic devices were constructed to maintain solar pointing during flight. Only small spectrographs, however, could be carried. Through clever design, Tousey and his colleagues flew small but powerful instruments. Gradually, more and more of the solar spectrum was recorded, until there remained but a few gaps from 3000 A all the way to 33.7 A in soft x-rays.

If one solar emission line were singled out as most important, this would certainly be Lyman-alpha of hydrogen, 1216 A. This was, indeed, found to be the strongest emission line, and also the most interesting. A photograph of the Sun's disk, made from a rocket in 1959 and using only the light of the Lyman-alpha line, showed that the regions of solar activity appear different and are much brighter in this radiation from hydrogen than in visible-light spectroheliograms photographed from the ground. Very high-resolution spectrum profiles of the Lyman-alpha line, made by Tousey and J. D. Purcell in the same year, showed a narrow absorption core at the center of the line. From its strength they derived the amount of hydrogen between the Sun and the rocket, a fundamental fact about the composition of the Earth's outermost atmosphere.

A second important line—the x-ray line at 33.7 A discovered in 1963—marks the short-wavelength limit of the solar spectrum reached up to now by photography. This is the Lyman-alpha line of C VI, that is, carbon with five electrons removed and only one remaining, thus structurally like hydrogen. It is a line coming from the Sun's corona, where the 1,000,000° K+ temperature is sufficient to strip off these outer electrons, leaving only a hydrogenic core.

Tousey received his A.B. degree in physics and mathematics from Tufts College in 1928. After receiving his Ph.D. at Harvard in 1933, he joined the faculty to teach and continue research for 3 years. He then went to Tufts as research instructor in physics, a position he held until 1941, when wartime optical research called him to the Naval Research Laboratory. Remaining at NRL, he became the leader in rocket spectroscopy and allied fields of optical research. He was elected to the National Academy of Sciences in 1960.

For background information *see* SPECTROSCOPY in the McGraw-Hill Encyclopedia of Science and Technology. □

★ **TOWNES, Charles Hard**
American physicist
Born July 28, 1915, Greenville, S.C., U.S.A.

D URING AN extended program of research on the interaction between electromagnetic waves and molecules, Townes invented the maser (acronym for molecular amplification by stimulated emission of radiation). Masers use molecules and atoms to amplify electromagnetic waves or to produce electromagnetic oscillators. They yield the most sensitive amplifiers available, the most constant oscillators or clocks, and because this type of amplification works successfully for very short wavelengths, masers produce light of remarkable intensity and monochromaticity. Pioneering work on infrared, optical, or ultraviolet masers (or lasers for light amplification by stimulated emission of radiation) was done jointly by Townes and A. L. Schawlow. These devices provide scientific and technological tools for applications as widely varied as high-resolution spectroscopy, length standards, surgery, welding, radar, and communications. For his fundamental work in quantum electronics leading to amplifiers and oscillators of the maser or laser type, Townes was corecipient of the 1964 Nobel Prize in physics. He received the basic patent on masers, and he and Schawlow were granted the patent on improvements that are basic to the optical maser or laser.

World War II development of radar stimulated many important applications of electronics to scientific problems. Not the least was the application of microwaves to study of the basic structure of matter. Radar technology had developed electronic oscillators that produced coherent microwave radiation at wavelengths as short as a few millimeters. Townes did wartime work on radar and computing devices, and after the war he was one of three physicists who independently opened up high-resolution spectroscopy of gases in the microwave region. This work used microwave oscillators to probe molecules, atoms, and nuclei—the branch of physics known as microwave spectroscopy.

By the late 1940s, it was clear that the usual types of oscillators could never be built to produce radiation much shorter than about one millimeter in wavelength. Inevitably, some part had to be machined to a dimension as small as the wavelength of the radiation to be generated. Yet coherent oscillators at shorter wavelengths were highly desirable for further high-resolution spectroscopy as well as for some technological uses. Stimulated emission by atoms and molecules had been known to physicists since Einstein proved its existence in 1917 and was increasingly discussed by physicists engaged in microwave spectroscopy during the late 1940s. In 1951, recognizing that amplification of very short wavelengths would probably require molecular action, Townes conceived a system of molecules that could amplify and produce a self-excited coherent oscillator. This idea involved production of a collection of molecules that were predominantly in an excited state and their interaction with electromagnetic waves in a resonator that would provide positive feedback. The waves stimulated the molecules to release their excess energy, thus building up the electromagnetic energy exponentially, provided certain threshold requirements on the number of molecules and quality of the resonator were met.

At Columbia University, where Townes was then a physics professor, he and his associates,

H. J. Zeiger and J. P. Gordon, built the first maser using ammonia gas (NH_3). A beam of ammonia molecules, with the normal thermodynamic distribution of molecules in a high-energy state and in the ground state, was sent through a cylindrical "focuser," which set up an electric field across the beam path. Molecules in the high-energy state tended to remain in the beam and those in the ground state to be drawn away. The beam, now containing predominantly molecules in the high-energy state, was guided into a resonant cavity, where, in response to an electrical field, the molecules gave effective amplification through stimulated emission and produced a microwave output corresponding to the resonance frequency (23,870 mc/sec) of ammonia. Townes and his associates first produced amplification by stimulated emission of radiation in 1954.

In 1956, Townes and his colleagues at the University of Paris, where he was then visiting, showed that the threshold condition required for population inversion and maser action could be achieved in certain solid paramagnetic crystals containing traces of impurities. An improved system of this general type, the three-level solid-state maser invented by N. Bloembergen, is now the most common maser amplifier for microwaves. In 1958, Townes and Schawlow described the conditions required to make masers operate at frequencies in the infrared, optical, and ultraviolet regions, thus laying the theoretical groundwork for the optical maser. The first operating system of this type was made in 1960 by T. H. Maiman.

Maser development in the decade that followed Townes's original ammonia device was explosive. An early application was in radio astronomy. Ruby masers were used to great advantage in amplifying extremely weak radiation from distant radio sources that were otherwise not detectable because of background noise. Because their beams can be made to deliver intense power at tiny spots, lasers became useful in microwelding of materials and in medicine, and for selective microsurgery under experimental conditions. But the maser has also found wide use in the physics laboratory. It has given new impetus to optics and to spectroscopy, and is largely responsible for development of a rather broad field called nonlinear optics. Optical gas masers have allowed new precision in the measurement of length and in spectroscopic experiments. Townes himself used masers to check various aspects of relativity with unprecedented accuracy. In other experiments, he showed that masers can be used to stimulate acoustic maser action and thus produce extremely intense ultra-high-frequency sound, strong enough to break the glass or the quartz crystals in which they are produced.

The son of an attorney, Townes studied modern languages and physics at Furman University, Greenville, S.C., where he received both B.A. and B.S. degrees in 1935. He originally contemplated a career in some field of biological science but was attracted to physics in his sophomore year at Furman. He did 1 year of graduate work at Duke University, where he received an M.A. in physics. This was followed by further graduate work at the California Institute of Technology, where he received the Ph.D. in physics in 1939. He was a physicist at the Bell Telephone Laboratories from 1939 to 1947. During the war years, he worked on radar bombing systems design, although this period included also some early work on radio astronomy. Immediately after the war, he helped open up high-resolution spectroscopy of gases in the microwave region and was concerned with molecular and nuclear structure. This work continued to occupy him after he joined the faculty at Columbia University in 1948. From 1950 to 1952, Townes was director of the Columbia Radiation Laboratory and, from 1952 to 1955, chairman of Columbia University's physics department. On leave of absence from Columbia University from 1959 to 1961, Townes served as vice-president and director of research of the Institute for Defense Analyses in Washington, D.C., where he was concerned with problems of national defense and foreign policy. In 1961, he became provost and professor of physics at the Massachusetts Institute of Technology. He was elected to the National Academy of Sciences in 1956.

In addition to writing the monograph *Microwave Spectroscopy* with A. L. Schawlow (1955), Townes edited *Quantum Electronics* (1960) and *Quantum Electronics and Coherent Light* (1965).

For background information *see* MASER in the McGraw-Hill Encyclopedia of Science and Technology.   ☐

★ **TROTTER, Mildred**
American anatomist
Born Feb. 3, 1899, Monaca, Pa., U.S.A.

To a considerable extent the study of biology has been, and will no doubt continue to be, concerned with the enormous range of variation found in living things. Much of this study has of necessity been purely descriptive, but increasingly biologists have come to appreciate the need for the precise quantitation of the range of variation, not only to correct misleading general impressions but, more significantly, to provide a secure basis for further work. Perhaps nowhere is this more important than in the study of human variation, where vague impressions

that some "races" have more of "this" and bigger "that" than others, have confused true understanding of the role played by genetic, environmental, and cultural factors in determining biological differences of the various ethnic groups. In many ways the population of the United States is an ideal one for this type of investigation, consisting as it does of at least two major racial groups (whites and Negroes) living under similar, if not exactly comparable, environmental conditions; thanks to the farsightedness of earlier scientists, data and material are available covering several generations.

Taking advantage of this situation, Mildred Trotter spent the greater part of her scientific life in quantifying the range of variation in a number of anatomical features between American whites and Negroes, between the two sexes, and, within each group, the changes that have occurred with age and in successive generations.

Her earlier work, in association with C. H. Danforth and others, was concerned mainly with variations in the quantity and distribution of hair. These studies, which were prompted in the first instance by a generous donation to Washington University School of Medicine for the study of facial hypertrichosis, helped to clarify a number of misconceptions (for example, that men have more hairs on their faces than women, that Negroes have fewer facial hairs than whites, that repeated shaving acts as a stimulus to hair growth, and so forth) and at the same time provided statistical data for the use of hair form, size, and color in anthropological studies. Concomitant with these investigations she carried on a longitudinal study of the age changes in head hair from birth through puberty.

The extensive skeletal collection at Washington University, begun by R. J. Terry and subsequently maintained by Trotter, provided a wealth of material for studies of the range of variation in the human skeleton. Among her earlier studies of this material was a comparative investigation of the sacrum of white and Negro Americans, which proved to be of practical significance in caudal analgesia.

Because of this background and interest, shortly after World War II Trotter was appointed anthropologist to the Department of the Army, concerned with the identification of unknown war casualties. The remains were brought from temporary burials scattered throughout the Pacific zone, the climate of the region and the lapse of time since death having skeletonized them. Her task was to determine from the skeletal remains the race, age, and stature of each individual and, in the case of multiple burials, to segregate the commingled bones. The findings on each skeleton were reported to the office of the Quartermaster General and checked against the data recorded for the supposed individual at the time of his induction into military service.

Total stature was estimated from measurements made on individual bones. The best available equations for this estimation had been derived from data accumulated in the last century from a limited number of French cadavers. As it became apparent that the direct application of these equations to the American skeletons introduced errors into the stature estimations, Trotter and her colleagues went on to derive a new set of regression equations that provided estimates of stature of considerably greater accuracy for both white and Negro males. This work served as a basis for several other studies and was extended after the Korean War when she was asked to analyze data from a very large number of war casualties of the period 1950–53. Since this material included remains of Mexican, Mongoloid, and Puerto Rican males, the opportunity was taken to examine in more detail the interracial variation in the relation between the length of individual bones and total stature. Thus Trotter showed, to mention only one example, that the relation between length of long bones of the limbs and stature differs sufficiently among American whites, Negroes, Mexicans, and Mongoloids as to require different equations from which to estimate the stature of each with precision.

More recently, Trotter was interested in the effects of race, sex, and age upon the weight of the skeleton and in some factor that might be combined with these three to allow an estimate to be made of the weight of the total skeletal mass in the living subject. The area of compact substance in a roentgenogram of the shaft of the femur, the largest and heaviest bone, was found to be a critical factor in whites of both sexes and in Negro females, but in Negro males the area of the shaft was a more significant variable. The next step was the comparison of weight-volume ratios (densities) of whole bones of the four sex-race groups. The densities were found to be higher in males than in females, higher in Negroes than in whites, and higher in the long bones of the limbs than in the vertebral column. Decrease in density was found to be related to increase in age and to occur at a uniform rate in bones of the axial as well as of the appendicular skeleton. These findings have been supported and refined by others by measuring the amount of compact substance on successive roentgenograms of living individuals.

The daughter of a Pennsylvania farmer, Mildred Trotter majored in zoology at Mount Holyoke College, from which she received her A.B. in 1920. Immediately after graduating she took up a research assistantship at Washington University School of Medicine, St. Louis,. where she held successive academic appointments, becoming professor in 1946. Her early studies on hair growth, under C. H. Danforth, led to the Sc.M. in 1921 and subsequently to a Ph.D. in 1924. In 1956 she received the Viking Fund Medal and Award in Physical Anthropology.

For background information *see* ANTHROPOMETRY; BIOMETRICS in the McGraw-Hill Encyclopedia of Science and Technology.   □

☆ **TUVE, Merle Antony**
American physicist
Born June 27, 1901, Canton, S.Dak., U.S.A.

TUVE'S RESEARCH career might be characterized by his skill in applying electronics to almost any given problem. Observations he made while a graduate student at the Johns Hopkins University of the very short radio pulses bounced off the ionized regions of the ionosphere were a model for much of the later development of radar techniques. This radiopulse transmission method, devised by Tuve with Gregory Breit, is still widely used for studies of the winds, meteors, and solar effects. As a staff member of the Carnegie Institution's department of terrestrial magnetism, he turned his attention

to the production of very-high-energy particles for studies of the atomic nucleus. As early as 1929 he had developed apparatus for producing potentials as high as 5×10^6 volts. Tuve, L. R. Hafstad, and O. Dahl shared the 1931 American Association for the Advancement of Science Prize for their work in producing beta and gamma rays and high-velocity protons above 10^6 volts. He and his associates made early measurements on nuclear fission, and their work was carried forward to the measurement of the forces inside the atomic nucleus through experiments on "billiard-ball scattering," or simple collisions of high-energy nuclei in hydrogen gas. This important experiment was proposed by Tuve in 1927 and carried out some years later.

As creator and director of the Johns Hopkins University Applied Physics Laboratory during World War II, Tuve directed the development of the proximity fuze that stopped the "buzz bomb" attacks on the British Isles and Antwerp and that is credited with turning the tide in the Battle of the Bulge. Ramjets and guided missiles were among the other devices he worked on in the war years.

In 1946 Tuve returned to the Carnegie Institution as director of the department of terrestrial magnetism. In that position, his geophysical activities included (1) field measurements of the Earth's crust in various parts of the United States by seismic refraction methods; (2) studies of the geophysical properties of the altiplano of Bolivia, Chile, and Peru through analysis of seismic data from stations operated cooperatively by the Carnegie Institution and South American scientists (the establishment of this network was the outgrowth of the 1957 Carnegie-IGY expedition to the Andes led by Tuve and Howard Tatel); (3) the development of image tubes for large telescopes; and (4) studies of the extensive hydrogen gas clouds in our galaxy and in the nearby extragalactic nebulae by radio astronomy techniques using large parabolic reflectors. In recent years Tuve was involved in setting up near La Plata, Argentina, a parabolic antenna of 30-meters diameter with a multichannel hydrogen-line receiver. Sponsored by the Carnegie Institution and the National Science Foundation, the radiotelescope is operated jointly with South American scientists for studies of the southern sky.

Tuve received his B.S. in 1922 and his A.M. in 1923 from the University of Minnesota and his Ph.D. in 1926 from the Johns Hopkins University. He taught at Minnesota (1922–23), Princeton (1923–24), and Johns Hopkins (1924–26) before joining the staff of the Carnegie Institution's department of terrestrial magnetism in 1926. He became its director in 1946. Among his numerous scientific honors were the Research Corporation Award (1947), the Comstock Prize

(1948) and Barnard Medal (1955) of the National Academy of Sciences, and the Bowie Medal of the American Geophysical Union (1963). He was elected to the National Academy of Sciences in 1946.

For background information *see* RADAR in the McGraw-Hill Encyclopedia of Science and Technology.   □

★ **UNSÖLD, Albrecht Otto Johannes**
German astrophysicist
Born Apr. 20, 1905, Bolheim, Württemberg, Germany

FROM A theoretical analysis of the mechanisms that determine the structure and the radiation of stellar atmospheres, Unsöld developed methods for the quantitative analysis of solar and stellar spectra. Using high-dispersion spectra, obtained with the Coudé spectrographs of large telescopes, he determined the effective temperature (T_{eff}) and the surface gravitation (g) as well as the quantitative chemical composition of stellar atmospheres.

In 1905 and 1914 Karl Schwarzschild proposed the theory of radiative equilibrium in the solar atmosphere. He realized that this theory ought to be connected with an atomistic theory describing the interaction of matter and radiation. But in 1916, only three years after Niels Bohr's epoch-making paper, "Atomic Structure and Spectral Lines," Schwarzschild died. So the connection between Bohr's work and the theory of radiative equilibrium was established first in A. S. Eddington's book, *The Internal Constitution of the Stars* (1926). The theory of thermal ionization and excitation developed by M. N. Saha and J. Eggert also formed an important step in the same direction.

The new quantum mechanics (~1925) opened the way also for a quantitative study of solar and stellar atmospheres and their spectra. In 1927, having published several papers on

quantum mechanics as a student of A. Sommerfeld, Unsöld began by measuring and analyzing theoretically the profiles (microphotometer tracings) of the Fraunhofer lines of Na, Al, Ca I and II, Sr I and II, and Ba II in the solar spectrum. The values derived for the average electron pressure in the solar atmosphere as well as for the abundances of these elements agreed quite well with those obtained somewhat later by H. N. Russell using rather different methods.

In the following years line broadening by radiation damping, collisions with electrons and hydrogen atoms (van der Waals forces), Doppler effect and Stark effect (hydrogen and helium lines), as well as the "curves of growth" were investigated by M. Minnaert, O. Struve, Unsöld, and others. The mathematical methods of radiative transfer were improved, Unsöld's contribution being the theory of weight functions describing the contribution of different layers of an atmosphere toward the production of a Fraunhofer line. The temperature distribution for "nongrey" atmospheres in radiative equilibrium was calculated, taking into account the dependence of the absorption coefficients upon wavelength by means of the Λ- and flux-iteration procedures and combinations thereof.

Unsöld's theoretical work was always closely connected with his observational work in solar and stellar spectrophotometry at the Einstein Tower in Potsdam and the Mt. Wilson, McDonald, and other observatories in the United States. Spectra of the B0 V star Tau Scorpii, taken at McDonald Observatory with O. Struve in 1939, resulted in the first complete analysis of a stellar spectrum.

The thermodynamic mechanism of convection in the solar atmosphere was first explained in 1930 by Unsöld's theory of the hydrogen convection zone. In that zone of a stellar atmosphere, a rising volume element (consisting mainly of hydrogen) gains heat by recombination of protons and free electrons and thus continues to move upward like a hot-air balloon, while a downstreaming element loses the energy needed for the ionization of hydrogen and continues to move downward. Convection is still enhanced by an inverse change in the radiative temperature gradient caused by the temperature dependence of the continuous absorption coefficient. The hydrogen convection zone of the Sun—occupying about 10% of its radius—acts as a heat engine driving the solar granulation as well as the 11-year cycle of solar activity and the superthermal radio-frequency and cosmic radiation connected with it. Recent work by N. Baker, R. Kippenhahn, and others has shown that the maintenance of cepheid pulsation is due to a related mechanism.

The son of a Protestant clergyman, Unsöld studied theoretical physics at the universities of

Tübingen and Munich, where he received his Dr. phil. under A. Sommerfeld in 1927. Having been privatdocent in Munich (1929–30) and Hamburg (1930–32), he became professor at the University of Kiel, where he was director of the institute for theoretical physics and the observatory. In recognition of his scientific work he received the Copernicus Prize in 1943, the Bruce Medal of the Astronomical Society of the Pacific in 1956, and the Gold Medal of the Royal Astronomical Society, London, in 1957.

Unsöld wrote *Physik der Sternatmosphären* (1938; 2d ed. 1955).

For background information *see* SOLAR CONSTANT; SOLAR ENERGY; SPECTROSCOPY in the McGraw-Hill Encyclopedia of Science and Technology.   □

effect in question, with the conditions of irradiation, and with the constitution of the individual irradiated. In the induction of leukemia in the mouse, he implicated the action of a leukemia virus that may be acquired before birth and remain latent until activated by irradiation.

A manufacturer's son, Upton received his B.A. in 1944 and his M.D. in 1946 at the University of Michigan. After a rotating internship and a residency in pathology at the University Hospital in Ann Arbor, he served as an instructor in pathology at the University of Michigan during 1950–51. He joined the Biology Division of the Oak Ridge National Laboratory in 1951 as a pathologist and became chief of the pathology-physiology section there in 1954.

For background information *see* RADIATION INJURY (BIOLOGY) in the McGraw-Hill Encyclopedia of Science and Technology.   □

★ UPTON, Arthur Canfield
American pathologist
Born Feb. 27, 1923, Ann Arbor, Mich., U.S.A.

THROUGH STUDY of the action of ionizing radiation on laboratory animals, Upton contributed to understanding of the mechanisms of radiation-induced cancer and other long-term radiation effects. For these studies, he received the U.S. Atomic Energy Commission's E. O. Lawrence Award in 1965.

Although it has been known for decades that overexposure to radiation may increase the risk of certain types of cancer and cause shortening of the life span with signs suggestive of premature aging, the mechanisms of these effects and the quantitative relation between the effects and the amount of radiation exposure remain poorly understood.

Working in the Biology Division of the Oak Ridge National Laboratory, Upton utilized radiation sources of various kinds to study the effects of different types of ionizing radiations on experimental animals. He showed that the dose-effect relation varies markedly with the type of

★ UREY, Harold Clayton
American chemist
Born Apr. 29, 1893, Walkerton, Ind., U.S.A.

IN 1931, with the help of his research assistant, George Murphy, and his friend, Ferdinand Brickwedde, Urey discovered the isotope of heavy hydrogen known as "deuterium." On the theoretical side, deuterium is useful to chemists as a chemical tracer; to physicists it is interesting as the next simplest nucleus after hydrogen, since it consists of one proton and one neutron. On the practical side, deuterium has proved to be the principal source of power for the hydrogen bomb and also a means of securing power from uranium fission. For his discovery Urey received the Nobel Prize in chemistry in 1934.

In the 1920s F. W. Aston determined the atomic weight of hydrogen relative to oxygen. In this he compared the oxygen isotope 16 and the hydrogen isotope of mass 1. Chemists had determined the atomic weight of hydrogen relative to oxygen and secured the same value. Subsequent to this, W. F. Giauque in Berkeley discovered the oxygen isotopes, and it became immediately obvious that the standards for the physical and chemical measurements were not the same. R. T. Birge and Donald Menzel pointed out that if heavy isotopes of oxygen existed, a heavy isotope of hydrogen should also exist. They estimated that the abundance of heavy hydrogen should be about 1 in 5,000. Following this, Urey and his coworkers, after showing theoretically that there should be differences in the vapor pressures of hydrogen and deuterium molecules, concentrated deuterium in a sample of hydrogen by the distillation of liquid hydrogen and proved the presence of deuterium by its emission spectrum.

The interesting sequel to this was that Aston had made a mistake; also, the chemical atomic weight proved to be incorrect. The two mistakes canceled each other and made a correct prediction possible.

The method of concentration of deuterium used in its discovery immediately brought forward again the probability of differences in chemical properties of isotopes, a point that had been discussed by F. A. Lindemann. Urey and his coworkers, during the years after the discovery, investigated the differences in the chemical properties of light and heavy hydrogen and also differences in the chemical properties of the isotopes of other elements. These studies indicated that it should be possible to separate isotopes by chemical methods, and such methods were used during the war for the separation of the boron isotopes and the concentration of heavy hydrogen. In the years since the war these methods have been used for the large-scale production of heavy hydrogen. The production of heavy hydrogen or heavy water, D_2O, is now a commercial process; its cost has been lowered to approximately $20 per pound, and there are indications that it can be lowered still further.

The differences in chemical properties of isotopes led Urey to propose a method for calculating the temperatures in the ancient oceans, the so-called paleotemperatures. The heavier isotopes of oxygen are more concentrated in calcium carbonate shells than in the water from which the shells are deposited, and the lower the temperature the larger the separation. By carefully calibrating the difference in abundance of oxygen-18 in unknown samples against an arbitrary sample, Urey showed it was possible to correlate the abundance of oxygen-18 in carbonate shells with the temperature at which they were laid down. Extensive studies of this kind have been made for the temperatures of oceans back to the Jurassic or thereabouts. It is probably the one quantitative method for attacking the problem of past climates.

His study on paleotemperatures led Urey to the study of geochemistry, particularly with respect to isotopic and elementary abundances. In the early 1950s, he published papers on the abundances of the elements. This was followed by an extensive study in cooperation with Hans Suess resulting in the preparation of abundance tables that are substantially accepted at the present time, with some modifications by these authors as well as by others. This study furnished the observational basis for studies of the origin of the elements by physicists, and today scientists believe they have fairly accurate notions of the origin of the elements and the characteristic abundances of elements in the Sun and the stars.

During these studies in geochemistry, it became obvious that the early history of the Earth must have been a highly reducing one, and Urey published a paper arguing that life originated under reducing conditions on the Earth. This was followed by a brilliant study by his student, Stanley Miller, in which it was shown that under reducing conditions many of the chemical compounds characteristic of living organisms could be produced by inorganic processes. This study has been continued by many people, and today scientists believe they understand a small part of the great problem of the origin of life on Earth.

The problem of the origin of the solar system is a very ancient one and has intrigued scientific men throughout all ages. The origin of the solar system must have been exceedingly complicated. Urey suggested that during the early history of the solar system a gaseous disk rotating in the plane of the ecliptic about the Sun broke up into objects approximately the size of our Moon together with the gases that are associated with the so-called nonvolatile fraction of matter present in the Sun. He emphasized certain problems that needed to be met in connection with this—the melting of the . meteorites, the differing abundances of the elements in the meteorites and in the Sun and planets, mechanisms by which differences in abundances could come about, and, finally, processes by which the planets could accumulate. At the present time this is a very active subject of study. It bears upon many problems of space research, such as the origin of the Moon and the meteorites, the possible structure of the surface of the Moon, and the structure of the planets.

Urey's father was a schoolteacher and a lay minister. Urey received his B.S. with a major in zoology from the University of Montana in 1917, and his Ph.D. in chemistry from the University of California in 1923. He was a fellow at Niels Bohr's Institute of Theoretical Physics in Copenhagen in 1923–24. He was an instructor at the University of Montana (1919–21), associate in chemistry at Johns Hopkins University (1924–29), associate professor and professor at Columbia University (1929–45), and Distinguished Service Professor and Martin A. Ryerson Distinguished Service Professor at the University of Chicago (1945–58). In 1958 he became Professor of Chemistry at Large of the University of California. During World War II he was director of the SAM Laboratories at Columbia University, charged with the problem of separating the isotopes of uranium, hydrogen, and boron for the atomic bomb project. He was elected to the National Academy of Sciences in 1935.

Urey wrote *Atoms, Molecules, and Quanta,* with A. E. Ruark (1930; rev. ed. 1964) and *The Planets* (1952).

For background information *see* DEUTERIUM; HEAVY WATER in the McGraw-Hill Encyclopedia of Science and Technology.   □

★ VALLOIS, Henri Victor

French anthropologist and paleontologist
Born Apr. 11, 1889, Nancy, France

VALLOIS'S RESEARCHES were concerned with the problem of the origin of man, the problem of fossil men and the first human developments, and questions concerning human races. For his contributions in these areas he received, among other honors, the Viking Fund Medal for physical anthropology in 1958.

Vallois's approach to the problem of the human origin was to compare the anatomies of man and of nonhuman primates, studying skeletons, articulations and muscles of lower limbs, spines and spinal muscles, and scapula. All these researches proved a very close morphological resemblance between man and the three Pongidae. So striking in every detail of organization were these resemblances, Vallois concluded that they could not be regarded as the results of an evolutive convergence; they showed a true phyletic affinity. Vallois further pointed out the importance of functional factors in the arrangement of bones, articulations, and muscles of

Primates. Primate walkers, jumpers, or climbers have special characteristics. Man, considered as the only bipedal primate, has some too, but they obviously derive from dispositions special to Pongidae "brachiators." Thus Vallois's work ratified W. K. Gregory's theory.

These researches induced Vallois to study the problem of polyphyletism in human races, that is, the question whether the various races derived from different groups of primates. He proved that this thesis was not reliable.

In his work on fossil men, Vallois studied the mechanism of the internal development of the human phylum. Concerning the remains of Fontéchevade, he proved that this development had not been linear but had been formed according to the "bushing" type of development observed among the various mammals. Born from one stock, the human trunk, according to Vallois, has ramified several times and only some branches now remain. Many branches died out during their development. Such was the case of the Neanderthal men of Europe, whose special differences from *Homo sapiens* were proved by Vallois.

Vallois especially studied some of these human branches. In western Europe, he proved that the mandible of Montmaurin represented the hitherto unknown transition between Heidelberg man and Neanderthal man. The study of numerous mesolithic remains (Teviec, Hoëdic, Gramat, Mugem) proved that only during this period, and in Germany, did the first brachycephales appear. In North Africa, he proved that the two epipaleolithic cultures, Ibero-Maurusian and Capsian, corresponded to two very different human groups. The first was perhaps related to neanderthaloid or preneanderthaloid forms, such as the men of Jebel Irhoud, Temara, and Rabat, which would show that there had been, in this region, a long evolution separated from that of Europe or Western Asia.

Vallois also studied some aspects of the social life of the fossil men. He was the first to prove that their lives had been remarkably short—20 to 40 years at most.

In several works, Vallois clarified the notion of race and studied the meaning of its characteristics. He gave numerous morphological arguments against the racist theory. His researches on special races concerned three regions: France, the Near East, and Africa. In France, he discovered six anthropological regions, defined by the different proportions of four main original types. He designed the first map of distribution of blood group ABO in France. He formed a group of collaborators who undertook to study various parts of France: Corse, Bretagne, Pays Basque, Savoie. In the Near East, Vallois studied some historical and living populations of Iran, Syria, Lebanon, and Palestine. He proved that, in the Plateau of Iran, at least, the Aryan civilization had been brought by brachycephalic and not dolichocephalic peoples. This was an important argument against the racist theory, according to which the diffusion of this civilization is tied to the coming of the Nordic race. In Africa, during the course of several scientific missions, Vallois described with precision the different physical types of the western Negroes. He studied the Pygmies of the western part of the equatorial forest and verified that, far from being a disappearing group, they were still very numerous and remained almost entirely pure, as they do not mix with the Negroes. Their physical type and their way of living are different from those of the eastern Pygmies; they form a special human type. Vallois proved also that study of the habits of this hunting people could shed light on hunters of the Upper Paleolithic.

Vallois studied medicine and natural sciences at the University of Montpellier, receiving his D.M. there in 1914; he earned his D.Sc. at the University of Paris in 1920. He was appointed professor of anatomy on the faculty of medicine, Toulouse, in 1922; director of the anthropological laboratory at the Ecole pratique des Hautes Etudes, Paris, in 1937; professor of the Musée national d'Histoire naturelle and director of the Institut de Paléontologie humaine, Paris, in 1941; and director of the Musée de l'Homme, in 1950. From 1930 he was editor of *L'Anthropologie* and of the *Bulletins et mémoires de la Société d'Anthropologie de Paris*.

Vallois wrote *Traité d'arthrologie* (1926), *Anthropologie de la population française* (1943), *Les races humaines* (1944; 6th ed. 1962), *Les Hommes fossiles, éléments de paléontologie humaine*, with M. Boule (1946; 4th ed. 1962), and *L'ordre des Primates* (1955).

For background information *see* FOSSIL MAN in the McGraw-Hill Encyclopedia of Science and Technology.   □

☆ VAN ALLEN, James Alfred

American physicist
Born Sept. 7, 1914, Mt. Pleasant, Iowa, U.S.A.

EXAMINING DATA broadcast by the first artificial satellites, Van Allen discovered that the Earth is circled by two belts of high-energy radiation, toroidal in shape and extending many thousands of miles from the Earth's surface. These regions, later named the Van Allen belts, were found to consist of electrically charged particles trapped in the terrestrial magnetic field. The discovery of the belts, and later that of the magnetosphere, extending out a possible 100,000 miles, resulted in major revisions in concepts of the Earth's atmosphere and mag-

netic field. They also pointed to a possible radiation danger to astronauts.

Explorer I, launched in 1958 as part of the International Geophysical Year satellite program, carried a simple Geiger counter to measure cosmic rays in the upper atmosphere. Since this radiation is mostly absorbed by air, Van Allen and his associates in the physics department at the University of Iowa (who designed this satellite and its equipment as well as later ones) expected that the satellite would register a steady increase of radiation as its eccentric orbit carried it farther from the Earth. Instead, however, there came reports of a decrease in radiation beyond 500 miles, the count at times dropping to zero over the Equator. Suspecting instrument failure, Van Allen equipped the next satellite, *Explorer III*, with identical apparatus; he obtained the identical puzzling results.

He then reasoned that zero reading could indicate not a drop in radiation but a sharp increase; a very high level of radiation would swamp the counters, jamming them to zero. Accordingly, the next few satellites carried better-shielded, more discriminating counters. They also covered a larger area of the terrestrial surface. Reports indicated the same unexpectedly high intensity levels, apparently active in a toroidal zone girdling the planet above 500 miles. The radiation seemed to conform to the Earth's magnetic field and seemed to be absent near the poles.

Van Allen suspected that these regions must consist of electrically charged particles; however, current ideas about the upper atmosphere were unable to account for a large, continuous flux of high-energy radiation.

In 1907, C. Störmer had suggested that high-speed charged particles could be trapped in the Earth's magnetic field. In such a case, Van Allen reasoned, the particle would describe a helical path centered along one of the magnetic lines of force that connect the northern and southern hemispheres. Approaching one of the hemispheres, the particle would spiral more and more tightly. Eventually its path would become perpendicular to the line of force, at which point the particle would "mirror," that is, would be reflected back along a similar path in obedience to the Lorentz force. Further, the differences in strength of the magnetic field would cause particles to drift in longitude—electrons to the east, protons to the west. The net effect of both effects might account for the observed shape and characteristics of the zone of radiation.

More refined detectors aboard the next few satellites confirmed these theories and established that there were, in fact, two belts. The nearer, "inner" belt peaked at about 2,000 miles from the Earth's surface. The "outer" belt peaked at about 10,000 miles. Adopting in part a suggestion of Christofilos, Van Allen and his colleagues advanced the idea that the two belts had different origins. The inner belt, seemingly composed of high-energy (protons 20–40 Mev) protons and electrons, might be produced by cosmic rays. The rays, colliding with neutrons in the upper atmosphere (which, being uncharged, wander freely through the Earth's magnetic field), would decay, producing electrons and protons. These would be trapped and remain in the field. The outer belt was found to consist of a very large flux of low-energy protons and electrons whose origin was attributed to the "solar wind."

Van Allen's discovery of the belts, and theoretical formulation of their origin, provided a new basis for investigation of upper-atmosphere phenomena. In particular, he led the way to subsequent exploration of the magnetosphere, a tenuous envelope of low-energy charged particles extending inside the high-energy Van Allen belts and out to a possible 100,000 miles. He contributed to knowledge of the mechanisms that generate aurorae and, of course, to further detailed investigation of the belts themselves.

An attorney's son, Van Allen received his B.S. in physics from Iowa Wesleyan College in 1935. In 1936 he took his M.S. at the University of Iowa, and his Ph.D. there in 1939. He then became a research fellow of the department of terrestrial magnetism, Carnegie Institution. From 1942 to 1946 he served as an officer in the U.S. Navy, contributing to the development of the radio proximity fuze. In 1946 he took charge of a research group at the Applied Physics Laboratory, Johns Hopkins University, and in 1951 he was appointed professor of physics and chairman of the department of physics at the University of Iowa. Beginning in 1946 he organized and led many scientific expeditions to study cosmic-ray phenomena, using V-2 and Aerobee rockets and rocket-balloons ("rock-

oons") systematically. In 1956 he assumed responsibility for the internal instrumentation of U.S. IGY satellites and subsequently conducted extensive research utilizing satellites and rockets. For his contributions to space research, Van Allen received the Louis W. Hill Space Transportation Award of the Institute of the Aerospace Sciences in 1959. Also in 1959 he was elected to the National Academy of Sciences.

For background information *see* VAN ALLEN RADIATION in the McGraw-Hill Encyclopedia of Science and Technology.   □

★ VAN HOVE, Leon Charles Prudent
Belgian theoretical physicist
Born Feb. 10, 1924, Brussels, Belgium

VAN HOVE started his research activity in 1945 in mathematics, mainly in calculus of variations and the theory of functional spaces. Around 1948 he turned to theoretical physics, where he contributed to questions in statistical mechanics, solid-state physics, quantum theory of fields, and elementary-particle physics. Up until about 1952, his main interest was oriented toward mathematical aspects of physical theories. Later his attention turned more and more toward the phenomenological contents of physical problems. For his contributions to statistical mechanics and field theory, he received the American Physical Society's Heineman Prize in 1962.

Van Hove's main contribution to mathematics concerns the calculus of variations for integrals containing several functions of several independent variables. Hadamard had proved in 1902 a necessary condition for the positiveness of the second variation. Van Hove established in 1946 that this condition was also sufficient. The method used, based on a simple Fourier transformation, was suggested to him by the properties of the momentum operator in quantum mechanics, a circumstance that strongly oriented him toward mathematical problems occurring in theoretical physics.

Van Hove's main interest from 1948 until about 1952 was to resolve mathematically current problems in theoretical physics. Thus, studying theories of gas-to-liquid condensation, he proved in statistical mechanics that the pressure of a classical system of particles, when calculated exactly from the partition function, can never decrease for increasing density (1949). Dealing with harmonic vibrations of crystals, he used M. Morse's theorems on the minimum number of saddle points of functions defined on topological manifolds to establish that certain singularities of a well-defined type are always present in the frequency distribution of harmonic crystals (1953). In quantum field theory, analyzing the mathematical properties of the Hamiltonian operator for interacting fields, he showed that it is not defined for the state vectors of the free fields. This work, and an independent investigation by K. Friedrichs, gave the first proof that inequivalent representations of the canonical commutation rules exist in field theory (1952), a feature that gave rise to much later theoretical work.

After 1950 Van Hove became increasingly interested in the main task of theoretical physics, which is to contribute to the interpretation and prediction of physical phenomena by whatever mathematical means appear to be most appropriate, without particular regard for the mathematical interest and rigor of the methods used. He also began at that time to have regular contacts with experimental physicists. He nevertheless remained strongly influenced by his previous mathematical inclination in the sense that he often regarded his investigations as attempts to exploit the surprisingly remarkable power of mathematics to elucidate natural phenomena.

In 1950, G. Placzek introduced Van Hove to the theory of thermal neutron scattering in solids, liquids, and gases, a subject that had become of great interest because of the extensive experimental programs under way at several nuclear-reactor laboratories. Van Hove demonstrated in 1953 that, just as x-ray scattering is determined by the correlations between the positions of different atoms at the same instant, neutron scattering is determined by the correlations between atomic positions at different times. This opened up the possibility of measuring such correlations experimentally.

By 1954, various difficulties encountered in extending the theory of neutron scattering from harmonic to anharmonic crystals had convinced Van Hove that a better understanding of dissipative effects in many-particle systems was needed. He started investigations in this field, ranging from ergodicity in quantum systems (where he gave a novel approach to the derivation of

transport equations) to the dynamics of anharmonic crystals and interacting Fermi gases. Thus he contributed, with his students at Utrecht University, to the development of the theory of many-particle systems that took place after 1955.

Beginning in 1960, Van Hove turned toward elementary-particle physics, contributing to the phenomenological theory of high-energy collisions.

Son of a civil servant and of a schoolteacher, Van Hove graduated in mathematics in 1946 at Brussels University. After working there as an assistant for some time, he was for 3 years a member of the Institute for Advanced Study at Princeton. In 1954 he was appointed professor of theoretical physics at the University of Utrecht. In 1960 he joined the European Organization for Nuclear Research (CERN) in Geneva as director of the Theoretical Study Division.

For background information *see* CALCULUS OF VARIATIONS; STATISTICAL MECHANICS in the McGraw-Hill Encyclopedia of Science and Technology. □

★ VAN SLYKE, Donald Dexter
American chemist and physiologist
Born Mar. 29, 1883, Pike, N.Y., U.S.A.

V AN SLYKE's researches included the chemistry and physiology of proteins and amino acids, renal physiology and pathology, and analytical chemistry of biological and radioactive material. Perhaps his principal achievement was his study of the gases and electrolytes of blood, their variations in physiological and pathological conditions, and the laws of physical chemistry that govern their distribution between blood cells and plasma, and between plasma and extravascular fluids. For his contributions to chemistry and medicine, Van Slyke received the 1936 Charles Mickle Fellowship of the University of Toronto, awarded "to the member of the medical profession who has done most during the preceding 10 years to advance sound knowledge of a practical kind in medical art or science"; the 1939 Willard Gibbs Medal of the American Chemical Society; the 1942 Kober Medal of the American Association of Physicians; the 1953 Fisher Award in Analytical Chemistry of the American Chemical Society; the 1954 Phillips Memorial Award of the American College of Physicians; the 1962 Scientific Achievement Award of the American Medical Association; the 1965 Elliott Cresson Award of the Franklin Institute of the State of Pennsylvania; and the 1966 National Medal of Science.

Van Slyke's work in the blood gases and electrolytes had its origin in studies of diabetes begun in the Hospital of the Rockefeller Institute in 1914. A grave condition that occurs in this disease is acid intoxication, caused by formation of hydroxybutyric and acetoacetic acids; the condition may develop suddenly and be fatal. A method was required to detect the acidosis in its early stages. For this purpose measurement of the bicarbonate concentration in the blood proved best, because bicarbonate is the form taken by the body's reserve of alkali in excess of acids other than carbonic.

Van Slyke developed a quick procedure that depended on extraction of the bicarbonate CO_2 from the acidified blood plasma in a vacuum chamber, followed by measurement of the volume of the extracted gas. Extraction in vacuo required only a minute. The procedure was later refined by attaching a manometer to the extracting chamber so that results of a high degree of accuracy could be obtained with minute amounts of gases. The procedure ultimately developed into one for precise general determination of gases dissolved in solutions or formed by reactions in solutions. In blood studies the gases were carbon dioxide, oxygen, nitrogen, carbon monoxide, and the gases used in anesthesia.

His study of acidosis in diabetes led Van Slyke to investigate the entire mechanism by which the acid-base balance of the body is maintained. The conditions of balance he defined as "metabolic" acidosis or alkalosis, caused by loss or gain of the body's buffer alkali, and as "respiratory" acidosis or alkalosis, caused by pulmonary retention or excessive secretion of carbon dioxide by the lungs. These terms have been incorporated into medical terminology, and the techniques developed for diagnosis of the different conditions have been incorporated into diagnostic medicine.

From studies of the acid-base balance Van Slyke turned to a study of the mechanisms by which the electrolytes are distributed between the blood cells, the blood plasma, and the extravascular fluids. He showed that the distribution of electrolyte ions occurs in accordance with the laws of thermodynamics developed by Willard Gibbs and F. G. Donnan, that the chief supply of buffer alkali available for neutralizing acids in the blood is in the alkali hemoglobinate and the bicarbonate, and that the bicarbonate and chloride anions are distributed between blood cells and plasma in such a way that the buffer effect of the hemoglobin is exerted in the plasma as well as in the cells.

Utilization of the blood oxygen method by Van Slyke's associates in the Rockefeller Hospital for studies of cardiac and pulmonary conditions led to the development of the oxygen chamber for treatment of such conditions.

Van Slyke's father was L. L. Van Slyke, who was for 39 years chemist of the New York Agricultural Experiment Station in Geneva, N.Y., and with whom D. D. Van Slyke published in 1907 his first paper. Van Slyke took his Ph.D. in 1907 in organic chemistry under Moses Gomberg, creator of the field of free radicals, at the University of Michigan. For the next 7 years he worked at the Rockefeller Institute in New York on the chemistry of proteins and amino acids under P. A. Levene. He then became chemist of the Hospital of the Rockefeller Institute and held that position until 1949. In 1949 he went to the Brookhaven National Laboratory as assistant director in charge of the departments of biology and medicine and assisted in their organization. In 1951 he became research chemist in the medical department of Brookhaven National Laboratory. He was elected to the National Academy of Sciences in 1921.

Van Slyke wrote *Cyanosia*, with C. Lundsgaard (1923), *Factors Affecting the Distribution of Electrolytes, Water and Gases in the Animal Body* (1926), *Quantitative Clinical Chemistry*, with J. P. Peters (Vol. I, 1931; rev. ed. 1946; Vol. II, 1932; rev. ed. 1943), and *Micromanometric Analyses*, with J. Plazin (1961).

For background information *see* BLOOD in the McGraw-Hill Encyclopedia of Science and Technology.   □

★ VENING MEINESZ, Felix Andries
Dutch geophysicist and geodesist
Born July 30, 1887, The Hague, Netherlands

VENING MEINESZ invented the pendulum method for determining gravity at sea and constructed apparatus for applying this method (1923–28). For his contributions to geodesy and geophysics, made possible by this invention, he received numerous awards, among them the 1962 Vetlesen Prize.

From 1913 to 1919, while making a gravity survey of Holland with a pendulum apparatus, Vening Meinesz had to eliminate the disturbances

strong uniaxial compression in the crust, could be considered as the origin of a well-known geologic structure, namely, a geosyncline.

The further interpretation of the gravity results found in the Indonesian Archipelago led to the hypothesis that the field of strong uniaxial compression causing the crustal deformations was brought about by a great current in the mantle of the Earth. This current could no doubt be considered as a convection current caused by the cooling of the Earth at its surface.

For the study of these convection currents Vening Meinesz found it useful to develop the Earth's topography in spherical harmonics (1951–61). At first a development by A. Prey (1922) was used; later, a new development was made, providing much greater detail.

The interpretation of this development led Vening Meinesz to a hypothesis of the Earth's history, starting with the formation of an urcontinent. In a later stage this urcontinent was drawn apart by mantle currents. In this way the present continents were formed, the currents first forming the shields and, in a still later stage when the mantle had crystallized, the geosynclines.

The son of a burgomaster of Amsterdam, Vening Meinesz studied civil engineering at the Technical University at Delft (1904–10). He began his career as a geodesist with the Netherlands Geodetic Service by making a gravity survey of the Netherlands, which led to the work at sea already mentioned. In 1927 he was named professor of cartography at the University of Utrecht, and in 1935 was made professor of geophysics. In 1938 he became professor of physical geodesy at the Technical University at Delft, retaining his position in Utrecht. From 1945 to 1951 he was director of the Royal Meteorological and Geophysical Institute at De Bilt; in 1951 he became president-curator of that institute. He was elected a foreign associate of the U.S. National Academy of Sciences in 1939.

For background information *see* GRAVITATION; PENDULUM in the McGraw-Hill Encyclopedia of Science and Technology.   □

caused by ground movements. This led to the elaboration of a method by which, swinging several pendulums at the same time on the same apparatus in different phase, this elimination could be achieved. Further elaboration of this method led to the possibility of making precise gravity observations at sea on condition that the ship's movements could be reduced. This became possible by making the observations in a submarine: many expeditions aboard submarines of the Dutch and U.S. navies followed during 1923–37.

The results obtained by Vening Meinesz proved significant for geodesy. By means of Stokes' theorem, the figure of the Earth can be derived from gravity. Stokes' theorem could not be applied, however, until Vening Meinesz succeeded in measuring gravity at sea. From the results of his first two expeditions (1923 and 1926–27), it followed that the supposition that the Earth had a flattening in the equatorial plane was not true. Vening Meinesz showed that the Earth deviates from the equilibrium figure (which is very near to a rotation ellipsoid) by irregularly distributed bulges and depressions of which the height or depth does not exceed 40 km.

From Stokes' theorem Vening Meinesz derived, in 1928, formulas expressing the two components of the deflection of the vertical in the gravity anomalies. They were used for several geodetic problems, for example, to form a world geodetic system joining together geodetic nets in continents separated by oceans.

The results of the gravity expeditions at sea were also applicable to geophysical problems. An important instance of this was shown by the results found in the Indonesian Archipelago (1923–30). A belt of strong negative gravitational anomalies was revealed, running through the whole archipelago, which could be interpreted as a belt where the rigid crust had buckled downward. This phenomenon, caused by

★ VIRTANEN, Artturi Ilmari

Finnish biochemist
Born Jan. 15, 1895, Helsinki, Finland

VIRTANEN'S MANY-SIDED research work in the field of biochemistry was especially concentrated on problems associated with human nutrition and agriculture. For his achievements in these areas he received the 1945 Nobel Prize for chemistry.

In the early 1920s Virtanen studied the mecha-

nism of different bacterial fermentations (lactic acid, propionic acid, and coli bacteria) and factors influencing these processes. In 1924 he discovered the phosphorylation of glucose and the necessity of "cozymase" in all bacterial fermentations studied, which gave evidence of the similarity of the first stages of different fermentations.

The investigations of the influence of the acidity (pH) on different fermentations, on decomposition of proteins by bacteria, and on the respiration of plant cells led to particularly significant practical applications. A pH of 4 proved to be decisive for the successful preservation of fresh fodder plants, because all the harmful decomposition processes were prevented when the pH of the pressed fodder mass was lowered to 4 or below. A theoretical basis was thus laid for silage making. Another of Virtanen's important discoveries based on the regulation of pH was preventing the development of oily and fishy taste during the storage of butter. He found that these faulty flavors, caused by chemical reactions, could be prevented when the pH in the water drops of butter was increased to 6.5–7.0.

Virtanen's research and educational work up to 1931 was carried out in the small laboratory of Valio, the central organization of cooperative dairies of Finland. The economically important achievements described above made possible a considerable extension of Virtanen's research work. In 1931 the Biochemical Research Institute was built, consisting of the laboratories of Valio and of the newly established Foundation for Chemical Research. As the head of this institute and at the same time as professor of biochemistry at the Finland Institute of Technology (1931–39), at the University of Helsinki (1939–48), and as a member of the State Academy of Finland (1948–65), Virtanen expanded knowledge in the field of enzymes, biological nitrogen fixation, nitrogen metabolism in green plants, plant chemistry, and the nutrition of man and animals. In his studies on the formation of enzymes, begun in 1928, he emphasized especially the importance of the work of his collaborator H. Karström on the adaptive formation of enzymes in lactic acid bacteria (1930). In later studies, Virtanen illustrated the effect of the nitrogen content of cells on the adaptive formation of enzymes. He also called attention, in 1942, to the fact that the proteins in young, rapidly dividing cells consisted almost solely of enzyme proteins.

In 1925 Virtanen began investigating biological nitrogen fixation in leguminous root nodules. In 1945 he demonstrated the development of symbiosis between nodule bacteria and the host plant and showed that this was a prerequisite for the formation of effective nodules. This symbiosis consisted of the synthesis of a red pigment, leghemoglobin, and a simultaneous transformation of bacteria to bacteroids, which seemed to be the active nitrogen fixers. In ineffective nodules, neither leghemoglobin nor bacteroids were found.

In connection with their studies of nitrogen fixation, Virtanen and von Hausen found, in 1933, that leguminous plants take from the medium and utilize amino dicarboxylic acids as effectively as nitrate. Thus it was possible to prove that the whole amino acid molecule was utilized. The uptake of many other organic compounds in smaller amounts was also demonstrated. Because some amino acids and their decomposition products induced morphologic changes in the plants, organic compounds in soil may in some cases effect the growth and form of the plants under natural conditions.

For many years Virtanen studied low-molecular organic nitrogen compounds in green plants. He and his collaborators isolated and characterized dozens of new amino acids and γ-glutamylpeptides from different plants and demonstrated the presence of a number of the corresponding γ-keto acids in the same plants. Transamination was thus shown probable as one of the principal regulating systems of the nitrogen metabolism in plants.

Virtanen isolated new cysteine derivatives, including the lachrymatory factor and γ-glutamylpeptides, from onion and related species; with Gmelin he also isolated indole mustard oil glucosides from cabbage. The enzymic decomposition of these glucosides unraveled the problems of the "bound ascorbic acid," "bound growth substance," and the formation of thiocyanate (antithyroid effect).

Beginning in 1958 Virtanen investigated milk production without protein, using urea and ammonium salts as the sole sources of nitrogen for milking cows. In 1958 also he proved that after the administration of $(N^{15}H_4)_2SO_4$ to a milking cow receiving normal feed, all amino acids of milk protein were labeled, but some of them, especially histidine, more weakly than others. On the basis of these results he considered it possible to develop in ruminant animals, by adaptation, a microbial flora more capable of using ammonium nitrogen for protein synthesis than the flora contained on normal feeding. The feeding experiments with purified carbohydrates as the source of energy, and urea and ammonium salt as the source of nitrogen, were begun in 1961. A milk production up to 4000 kg per year has been achieved so far on this feeding. No differences between the proteins of the test milk and of normal milk could be found. The flavors of both milks were also very similar.

After attending the Classical Lyceum in Viipuri, Virtanen studied chemistry, biology, and physics at the University of Helsinki, graduating Ph.D. in 1919. Further studies in Zurich and Stockholm laid the basis for his biochemical studies. In 1919 he was appointed chemist of the laboratory of Valio; he became its director in 1921, and the director of the Biochemical Research Institute (comprising the laboratories of Valio and of the Foundation for Chemical Research), Helsinki, in 1931. He was also docent in chemistry at the University of Helsinki (1924–39); professor of biochemistry at the Finland Institute of Technology, Helsinki (1931–39); and professor of biochemistry at the University of Helsinki (1939–48). From 1948 to 1963 he was president of the State Academy of Science and Arts in Finland.

For background information *see* PLANT FERMENTATION in the McGraw-Hill Encyclopedia of Science and Technology.   ☐

rocket as its first stage. Beginning in 1960 von Braun, as director of NASA's George C. Marshall Space Flight Center, supervised the development of the family of Saturn liquid-fueled rockets for Program Apollo, designed to provide a broad national manned-space-flight capability and to land two Americans on the Moon. For his contributions to space technology, von Braun received the American Institute of Aeronautics and Astronautics' Louis W. Hill Space Transportation Award in 1965.

In 1903, the Russian schoolteacher Konstantin Tsiolkovsky published his book, *The Investigation of Outer Space by Means of Reaction Devices*, wherein he described, in rough outline, a rocket propelled with liquid fuel and capable of leaving the gravitational field of the Earth. In 1918, the American physics professor Robert Hutchins Goddard published a paper entitled "A method of reaching extreme altitudes," wherein he described the principle of multistage rockets. In 1926 Goddard launched the world's first liquid-fueled rocket on a farm near Auburn, Mass. Later he launched liquid-fueled rockets of ever increasing complexity and sophistication at a desert site near Roswell, N.Mex. In 1923, the German physics teacher Hermann Oberth published *The Rocket to Interplanetary Space*. It described in great detail the principle of a two-stage liquid-fueled rocket capable of leaving the Earth's gravitational field. In 1930 Oberth tested a small liquid-fuel rocket engine of about 15 lb of thrust. One of his assistants in these tests was von Braun, then an engineering student of 18.

Von Braun's dedication to rockets originated with his boyhood interest in astronomy, awakened by his scientific-minded mother and

★ VON BRAUN, Wernher

American rocket engineer
Born Mar. 23, 1912, Wirsitz, Germany

As a result of his preceding experimental work with liquid-fueled rockets, von Braun, in 1937, became the technical director of the German Army Rocket Center, Peenemuende, on the Baltic Sea. Under his technical direction the world's first operational guided ballistic missile, the V-2, and the world's first guided antiaircraft missile, the Wasserfall, were developed. Between 1950 and 1955 he directed the development of the first operational ballistic missile in the United States—the Redstone. Using a modified Redstone as first stage, von Braun and his team, in January 1958, were instrumental in placing America's first artificial satellite, *Explorer I*, in orbit around the Earth. In 1959 the same team placed *Pioneer IV*, America's first interplanetary probe, in orbit around the Sun, using a Jupiter

fostered by his boarding school, which permitted him to build a school observatory. After graduation from secondary school in 1930, he enrolled at the Berlin Institute of Technology and in his spare time assisted Hermann Oberth in his experiments with small liquid–fueled rocket engines. His involvement with this program continued after Oberth returned to his teaching post in Romania and the German Society for Space Travel took over sponsorship.

In the fall of 1932, von Braun, after obtaining his bachelor's degree in mechanical engineering, accepted a research grant from the German Ordnance Department that enabled him to develop and conduct scientific investigations on a 300-lb- and a 660-lb-thrust liquid-fueled rocket engine. In 1934 he received his Ph.D. in physics from the University of Berlin. For reasons of military security his thesis bore the nondescript title "About combustion tests," but it contained a complete theoretical investigation, underpinned by experiments, of the injection, combustion, equilibrium, and expansion phenomena involved in a 1933-model liquid-fueled rocket engine.

This work led to von Braun's permanent employment, in 1934, as a rocket development engineer by the German Ordnance Department. By 1937 his experimental station had grown to about 80 people. In December 1934, the group performed two successful launches of liquid-fueled rockets to an altitude of about two miles. In 1937 the group was busy developing a fully inertial-guided rocket designed to climb with about 100-lb pay load to an altitude of 15 miles. During the same year, the first successful experimental flights with a liquid-fueled rocket engine installed in a propeller-driven, single-engine fighter plane were performed.

This busy program led to the establishment of the Rocket Center at Peenemuende, a joint enterprise of the German Army and Air Force. In 1937, von Braun became the technical director of the Army portion of this establishment. It was here that the V-2 long-range and the Wasserfall guided antiaircraft missiles were developed.

In 1945 von Braun and 120 of his associates went to the United States under contract to the U.S. Army Ordnance Department. After five years at Fort Bliss, Tex., and White Sands, N. Mex., where the group assisted in high-altitude research launchings with captured V-2 rockets, von Braun and his men became the nucleus of the newly founded U.S. Army Ordnance Guided Missile Division, Redstone Arsenal, Huntsville, Ala. Between 1950 and 1955 the Redstone ballistic missile was developed there. In 1956 the activities were vastly expanded under the newly formed Army Ballistic Missile Agency, where, under von Braun's technical direction, the Jupiter intermediate range ballistic missile was developed. The fact that both the Redstone and the Jupiter served as first stages of a number of highly successful Explorer and Pioneer launchings led in 1960 to the transfer of the group to the National Aeronautics and Space Administration (NASA), where it became the hard core of the George C. Marshall Space Flight Center. Since 1961 the main task of this Center has been to provide, with the help of a large number of industrial contractors, the Saturn launch vehicles for the Apollo lunar landing program.

Von Braun wrote *Across the Space Frontier* (1952), *The Mars Project* (1953), *Conquest of the Moon* (1953), *The Exploration of Mars* (1956), and *First Men to the Moon* (1960).

For background information *see* ROCKET ENGINE in the McGraw-Hill Encyclopedia of Science and Technology.   □

VON NEUMANN, John
American mathematician
Born Dec. 28, 1903, Budapest, Hungary
Died Feb. 7, 1957, Washington, D.C., U.S.A.

IN 1928, von Neumann founded a new branch of science: the theory of games. The conceptual center of the new discipline was the proof, which von Neumann first advanced, that for all games of strategy there existed at least one optimum line of play that would, in the long run, guarantee the greatest possible minimization of loss. As presented and codified by von Neumann, the theory of games found rapid acceptance and use in economics, warfare, and many branches of the social sciences.

Von Neumann's first presentation of the new doctrine was in a paper entitled *Zur Theorie der Gesellschaftspiele*, read in 1928 at Göttingen. In it he considered, not specific games of cards or chance, but rather a mathematical generalization of the concept of "games"; this he regarded as a set of rules describing the possible behavior (moves) of the participants (players) and the consequences of each move (gains or losses). Von Neumann realized that such a theory must furnish a player with a maximally advantageous strategy, taking into account (1) all the moves that could possibly be made by the other player(s) and (2) any knowledge the player(s) might have of each other's plans.

Von Neumann began with a consideration of "strictly determined" games, in which foreknowledge of one's opponent's plans cannot have any effect on one's own strategy (examples: ticktacktoe and chess. While chess is strictly determined, it is still exciting; the possible moves available to each player are astronomically huge, and the computation of them is possible only in theory). He considered such games as were played according to "pure" (that is, consistent, predictable) strategies. The diagram shows how a table of strategies for such a game between two players A and B would look. A-1, A-2, A-3 are possible strategies for A, and likewise for B. The numbers in the boxes are "values" assigned to all the possible permutations of the strategies played one at a time. In

A \ B	B—1	B—2	B—3
A—1	2	1	4
A—2	2	3	2
A—3	2	—1	1

Table of strategies for a "strictly determined" game between players A and B.

any such table there must clearly exist a strategy that guarantees A the smallest possible loss. Here, it is A-2. This is called A's minimax strategy. B must also have just one, which is B-1 in this instance. The intersection of row A-2 and column B-1 is called the "saddle point" for this game. (The term derives from a comparison with a saddle-shaped structure, made by the intersection of two curves in perpendicular planes, which meet in a single point.) Clearly, for all strictly determined games there existed a saddle point.

Von Neumann now turned to games that were not strictly determined, games in which the outcome depends on how well each player can guess his opponents' intentions. In such games (bridge, poker, and so on) the players' ignorance of each others' strategies is quite important. In theory, each one knows all the relevant possibilities, but his optimal strategy hinges on the plans of the other players, which in turn depend on his, and so on. Thus it would seem impossible in such games to determine a single optimal line of play for each player, regardless of the others' intentions. Von Neumann found his way out of the logical bog by generalizing the minimax concept to apply to such games. To do this, he had to introduce the notion of a "mixed strategy." This he defined as a decision to use a given number of "pure" strategies in a

certain overall proportion, without specifying the choice of a pure strategy for any particular move (in the original presentation, the pure strategy for a given move was to be determined by the throw of one die).

Von Neumann dealt with a very simply non-strictly-determined game called Matching Pennies. Two players each put down a penny and bet as to whether the coins will show the same or different sides. If they show the same side, whether heads or tails, A wins; if they show different sides, B wins. The winning player collects the opponent's coin. Obviously, if A knows B's strategy (or vice versa) A can always win. Any pure strategy employed by either players must then fail (such as always playing heads, or heads and tails alternately, and so forth). Therefore the game is "indeterminate," and "mixed" strategies come into play.

Von Neumann was now able to show that A's best hope lay in changing his strategies at random, preserving, however, the overall proportion of $\frac{1}{2}:\frac{1}{2}$. In this way, his losses would ultimately equal his gains. For the other player the same obviously held true. Such a balance Von Neumann termed a solution to the game; clearly, in Matching Pennies a solution is only possible when mixed strategies are employed. While the individual moves were still indeterminate, the use of mixed strategies gave a statistical determinacy to the game. Referring to the diagram given in connection with strictly determined games, Von Neumann noted that the value of 2 was the largest of the minima for A, while the same number 2 was the smallest of the maxima for B. The former he called "maximin," the latter "minimax." He now showed that the maximin of all possible strategies for A was always equal to the minimax of all possible strategies for B. This was equivalent to proving that for non-strictly-determined games, there always existed at least one mixed strategy leading to a stable solution (equivalent to a saddle point in strictly determined games). He referred to this statement as the main theorem; to prove it he made rigorous use of Brouwer's fixed-point theorem.

Von Neumann treated games involving more than two persons as though they were composed of "coalitions" and were ultimately reducible to two-person games. In these cases also he was able to show that a saddle point must always exist.

In *The Theory of Games and Economic Behavior* (1944), Von Neumann (in collaboration with Oskar Morgenstern) developed the analogy between games of strategy and various situations in economics and sought to demonstrate their substantial identity. He defined "rational" economic behavior by equating it with the pursuit of a minimax strategy. With a quantitative definition of "rationality" at hand, von Neumann was able to construct a mathematical formulation at once more rigorous and more flexible than that offered by "classical" economic theory. The advantages of such a theoretical tool became quickly apparent, and the theory of games found a wide range of applications in a broad spectrum of social sciences.

Much of von Neumann's early scientific work was in quantum theory. His purely mathematical activities involved a variety of disciplines— mathematical logic, set theory, operator theory, and theory of continuous groups. His contributions to the study of almost periodic functions, the ergodic theorem, and the algebra of bounded operators are regarded as classic. Von Neumann was a pioneer in the field of computer theory and design, and he played a major part in the development of the logical theory of automata. A significant advance in electronic computers was the MANIAC I. This, the first computer able to use a flexible stored program, was designed and built by von Neumann and his colleagues at the Institute for Advanced Study in 1952. Von Neumann also explored the analogy between computers and neurological networks, and he evolved one of the first theories of a "self-reproducing" machine.

The son of a banker, von Neumann studied at the University of Berlin and the Zurich Institute of Technology, where in 1925 he received a degree in chemical engineering. In 1926 the University of Budapest granted him a Ph.D. in mathematics. After a brief stint of teaching at the University of Hamburg he went to the United States, where from 1930 to 1933 he was a visiting professor at Princeton University. In 1933 he became professor of mathematics at the Institute for Advanced Study at Princeton, a position he retained until his death. From 1943 until 1955 he was associated with the Los Alamos Scientific Laboratory; from 1949 until 1954, with the Oak Ridge Scientific Laboratory. He was appointed a U.S. Atomic Energy Commissioner in 1954. In 1957 he received the Enrico Fermi Award of the Atomic Energy Commission.

For background information *see* GAME THEORY in the McGraw-Hill Encyclopedia of Science and Technology.   □

W

★★★

☆ **WAKSMAN, Selman Abraham**

American bacteriologist
Born July 22, 1888, Priluka, Russia

IN 1943 Waksman and a team of associates isolated streptomycin, a substance highly effective in combatting many bacteria responsible for human disease. The most dramatic immediate example of streptomycin's effectiveness was in curing tuberculosis, a malady for which there had previously been no chemical remedy. Streptomycin was the first useful antibiotic (a term coined by Waksman) to be isolated from soil microbes and the second important antibiotic to be discovered (penicillin was the first). For his achievement Waksman received the Nobel Prize for physiology or medicine in 1952.

In 1921, Lieske had shown that the class of soil microorganisms called actinomycetes could produce substances harmful to bacteria and fungi. The process is selective. Some strains of microorganisms excreted chemical substances deleterious to a variety of bacteria.

Waksman had been studying actinomycetes for decades, and in 1939 was prompted to begin a broad and intensive search for antibiotic substances produced by them. The development and exploitation of penicillin, which flowered enormously between 1941 and 1943, lent great impetus to the Waksman program. Waksman and his team in the agriculture department at Rutgers University had accumulated a great body of knowledge concerning actinomycete abundance, distribution, taxonomy, behavior in the soil, and effect on bacteria and fungi. Nevertheless, at the outset they knew of only two antibiotic-type preparations that had any effect on pathogenic bacteria.

Waksman and his team examined approximately 10,000 soil microbes for antibiotic activity prior to the isolation of streptomycin. On the way, the first antibiotic produced by an actinomycete, actinomycin, was discovered in 1940. This substance proved to be too toxic for use as a therapeutic agent in vivo. A similar problem impaired the usefulness of streptothricin, the next antibiotic Waksman and his team found (1942). This substance, despite its inutility in fighting human disease bacteria within the body, was most promising; it had a broad spectrum of activity and was later found to be effective against the tubercle bacillus (a microbe resistant to penicillin).

In the course of these researches, Waksman and his team developed specialized techniques of microbe culture and isolation and purification of active antibiotics. This was valuable in the next phase, following the discovery of streptothricin, which had given focus to the team's activities. They now began to look for specific kinds of antinomycetes that would produce substances similar to streptothricin in antibacterial action, only less (one hoped) toxic.

In early 1943, less than 6 months after the isolation of streptothricin, Waksman and one of his assistants, Albert Schatz, found two strains of actinomycetes that, curiously enough, were almost identical with a variety (*Actinomyces griseus*) first described by Waksman himself in 1916. The newly discovered strains, however, differed from the old in having definite antibacterial properties, something like streptothricin. Waksman decided to name the new strains *Streptomyces griseus*.

The laboratory techniques that had been evolved now proved crucial in determining the properties of the new, promising antibiotic. *S. griseus* was grown in submerged cultures; the antibiotic (named streptomycin by Waksman) was isolated by adsorption on charcoal and removal with dilute acid; and it was then concentrated, purified, dried, and crystallized. Its antibacterial properties were evaluated in tests, developed in the laboratory, upon standard strains of bacteria.

Waksman and his team found streptomycin to have a broad spectrum of effective activity, particularly upon the tubercle bacillus. The early results were so promising that tests on laboratory animals were begun within a few months. These experiments, conducted at the Mayo Clinic by W. Feldman and H. C. Hinshaw, were most hopeful. They led in turn to the testing of streptomycin on human TB patients. It was found to be highly effective. Surprisingly, two of the most severe forms of TB (miliary TB and tubercular meningitis) responded especially well to treatment with streptomycin. Other cases also improved greatly.

While these tests were going on, Waksman and his colleagues had continued their researches, and had discovered that not all strains of *S. griseus* could produce large quantities of streptomycin. They proceeded to develop such strains that could produce commercially useful amounts. (One of these 1943 strains later became the standard one for world-wide commercial production.) Waksman and his group performed the first work to determine the chemical structure of streptomycin, a task completed by other workers not long after its discovery.

With unusual rapidity, streptomycin proved itself the most effective known antituberculosis remedy, and one, moreover, with only mildly toxic side effects. It accordingly revolutionized the treatment of TB and saved thousands of lives. Besides this, streptomycin was shown to be effective in the treatment of a great variety of diseases: tularemia, bacterial meningitis, endocarditis, pulmonary and urinary tract infections, and, to a somewhat lesser extent, leprosy, typhoid fever, brucellosis, bacillary dysentery, cholera, and bubonic plague. The first and still one of the most valuable of the antibiotics, streptomycin was soon recognized as a breakthrough in chemotherapy, and its advent was regarded as a major landmark in medicine.

Following the discovery of streptomycin, Waksman and his colleagues continued to prosecute their search for antibiotics, turning up many new ones, including neomycin and candicidin.

Waksman emigrated from Russia to the United States as a young man and obtained his B.S. from Rutgers University in 1915. He received his M.S. there the next year, then went to the University of California as a research fellow and took his Ph.D. in biochemistry there in 1918. In that year he was appointed a microbiologist at the New Jersey Agricultural Experimental Station, where he continued to work until 1954. Meanwhile, he had also become a lecturer in soil microbiology at Rutgers (1918), advancing to associate professor in 1925, professor in 1930, and head of the department of microbiology in 1940. From 1949 to 1958 he directed the Rutgers Institute of Microbiology. In 1958 he became emeritus professor of microbiology. He also served as marine bacteriologist at the Oceanographic Institute at Woods Hole from 1931 to 1942. He was elected to the National Academy of Sciences in 1942.

Waksman's books include *Streptomycin, Its Nature and Applications* (1949), *Soil Microbiology* (1952), and *The Actinomycetes* (3 vols., 1959–62).

For background information *see* ANTIBIOTIC in the McGraw-Hill Encyclopedia of Science and Technology.   □

☆ **WALD, George**
American biologist and biochemist
Born Nov. 8, 1906, New York, N.Y., U.S.A.

FOR HIS work on the chemistry of vision, particularly for his discovery that all organisms having well-formed, image-receiving eyes utilize comparable light-sensitive pigments in vision, all made by joining vitamin A aldehyde to specific retinal proteins, Wald received the Lasker Award of the American Public Health Association in 1953 and the Rumford Medal of the American Academy of Arts and Sciences in 1959.

Ever since the discovery of vitamin A, it had been known that lack of this vitamin is accompanied by eye infections and night blindness. While working in Berlin on a National Research Council fellowship in 1932–33, Wald discovered vitamin A in the retina of the eye. He soon established its role in vision and in subsequent years elucidated the complex chemical reactions through which light stimulates vision.

Vitamin A ($C_{20}H_{29}OH$) has the structure of half a beta-carotene molecule ($C_{40}H_{56}$) with a hydrogen and a hydroxyl group added at the broken double bond where the carotene molecule has been split in half. The pigment in the retina that is stimulated by light is actually retinene, the aldehyde of vitamin A. In the visual pigments the retinene molecule is joined to specific retinal proteins called opsins. When light falls upon such pigments, a series of changes is initiated, ending in the cleavage of retinene from opsin. Then the retinene is reduced by the enzyme alcohol dehydrogenase to vitamin A.

Having worked out the pattern of such changes in mammals, frogs, and marine fishes, Wald found an exactly parallel series of pigments and transformations in the eyes of fresh-water fishes, based upon vitamin A_2 and retinene$_2$. These molecules differ from ordinary vitamin A and retinene by possessing one more double bond. Fishes that migrate back and forth between the sea and fresh water, such as the salmon and eel, use mixtures of vitamin A and A_2 in vision. Land vertebrates that originate in fresh water, such as the frog, may have an A_2 visual pigment as tadpoles, and change over to an A_1 visual pigment at metamorphosis to the land-living adult form.

The amount of light required for this disruption is exceedingly small. If a human eye is kept in complete darkness for some time, it becomes dark-adapted and is then in the most sensitive condition for detecting light. A rod, the structure in the retina chiefly responsible for night vision, will respond to the absorption of a single quantum of visible light. Five such rods must be stimulated within a small area of the retina before the perception of light reaches the conscious portion of the brain.

Chemically, Wald discovered, light stimulates the rod by changing the *cis* isomer of retinene to the *trans* form. *Cis-trans* isomerism involves the two ways of attaching other groups to two carbon atoms joined by a double bond. In the *cis* arrangement they are attached on the same side of the double bond; in the *trans* arrangement, on opposite sides. Carotenoids possess long straight chains of double bonds alternating with single bonds. No other natural pigments approach them in the number of possibilities of *cis-trans* isomers. Before the absorption of light the retinene molecule is bent and twisted, owing to a sterically hindered *cis* linkage. When light is absorbed the *cis*-isomer is changed to the *trans*-isomer, straightening the retinene molecule and eventually severing its attachment to the opsin molecule. It is this process that is triggered by the light. The role of the light is not to supply energy but to activate the change; apparently, the energy required for the change is furnished by internal chemical reactions. The actual severance of the connection to the opsin is not responsible for the sensory response, for it is much too slow. It is some process associated with the *cis-trans* isomerization that excites vision. Wald suggested that phototropic excitation in plants may also be based on this *cis-trans* isomerization of carotenoid pigments.

Wald received his B.S. in 1927 at New York University and his M.A. in 1928 and Ph.D. (1932) at Columbia University, where he worked under Selig Hecht. During 1932–34 he was a National Research Council fellow at the Kaiser Wilhelm Institute in Berlin, Heidelberg University, the University of Zurich, and the University of Chicago. He joined the Harvard University faculty in 1934, becoming professor of biology in 1948. He was elected to the National Academy of Sciences in 1950.

For background information *see* Vision in the McGraw-Hill Encyclopedia of Science and Technology. □

☆ **WALKER, Edmund Murton**
Canadian zoologist
Born Oct. 5, 1877, Windsor, Ont., Canada

Although involved with most groups of invertebrate animals in one way or another as naturalist, biologist, and zoology professor, Walker studied two insect groups in particular depth and in these made his most significant contribution to entomology in North America: the dragonflies (Odonata) and the relict orthopteroid order Grylloblattodea.

His work on dragonflies was largely concentrated on the 200 or so species native to Canada. Before he began, it was not known what species were represented in Canada nor what their overall distribution was. Accurate identification of most species in their larval stages was impossible, and consequently even the precise habitat and general life histories for these species were unknown. An appreciation of the subtle adaptations by which certain species could live in habitats with which others could not contend, the regulation of the life cycle in certain species by such external influences as daylight and temperature—insight into these and many other aspects of the biology of dragonflies was denied to biologists so long as the basic systematic data were lacking.

The significance of Walker's work on dragonflies was that he built up the body of knowledge that now provides this necessary basic information. This he did by conducting field studies over much of Canada, collecting specimens and building up a large study collection, seeking out unknown life history stages of particular species, and making observations on the behavior and other characteristics of the living insects under natural conditions. These studies he continued for nearly 60 years, recording the significant discoveries in some 60 papers, including large monographs on the North American species in two genera. To conclude this lifelong study, he wrote *The Odonata of Canada and Alaska,* of which the first two volumes were published in 1953 and 1958.

As a result of this work the dragonflies have now become one of the best-known groups of invertebrate animals in Canada. Identification of all species native to Canada can now be made in both adult and larval stages; the general distribution of each species is summarized; the habitat for each species is described in some detail; and extensive observations are provided on the life history and behavior of the species. Subsequent workers are now able to begin their studies on other aspects of the biology of dragonflies from this firm foundation of knowledge.

Walker's discovery on Sulphur Mountain, Banff, Alberta, in 1913 of specimens of *Grylloblatta* brought to light the first evidence for the continued existence of an exceedingly ancient line of insects, regarded as the only living representatives of a primitive stock from which the cockroaches and mantids and the grasshoppers and crickets originally diverged and evolved. Several other species have been discovered since that time in western North America, Japan, and the Soviet Union, and these together now comprise the insect order Grylloblattodea. Along with the *Ginkgo* tree, the coelacanth fish *Latimeria, Sphenodon* and the horseshoe crab *Limulus,* the Grylloblattodea are ranked as "living fossils," representatives of very ancient evolutionary lines that have persisted for several hundred million years with only minor changes. Walker's papers on the morphology and phylogenetic relationships of the group demonstrated the unusual significance of the Grylloblattodea in the evolutionary history of the insects.

Walker's contributions to North American entomology began with a series of studies on the taxonomy and distribution of the grasshoppers and crickets (Orthoptera), and he also wrote extensively on the comparative morphology of the orthopteroid insects. He did other work on the occurrence of certain types of dipterous larvae as human parasites, and more recently on the changing limits of northern and southern distributions shown by particular species of insects.

Walker graduated in natural science in 1900 and in medicine in 1903 from the University of Toronto. After completing a year of internship, he chose to follow a deep interest in biology. Following a period of special study in invertebrate zoology at the University of Berlin, he was appointed a lecturer in invertebrate zoology in the department of biology at the University of Toronto in 1906. There he remained for the whole of his academic career, serving as head of the department of zoology from 1934 until his retirement in 1948. In addition to lecturing and his own research, Walker was also involved in the University's Royal Ontario Museum, serving as assistant director of the zoology division from 1918 until 1931, and after 1931 as honorary curator of entomology. In 1960 he was awarded the Flavelle Medal of the Royal Society of Canada.

For background information *see* DRAGONFLY; ODONATA in the McGraw-Hill Encyclopedia of Science and Technology.   □

★ **WALSH, Joseph Leonard**
American mathematician
Born Sept. 21, 1895, Washington, D.C., U.S.A.

WALSH'S MOST important scientific work was in the field of interpolation and approximation to functions of a complex variable. For instance, if a function defined on a given point set can be approximated there by a polynomial as closely as desired, there are certain properties of the function with reference to continuity, integration and differentiation, location of singularities, analytic continuation, and so forth, that follow immediately. In addition, the function is in a sense analyzed by the process into simpler functions whose fundamental properties are well known; this analysis itself implies certain properties of the original function. Moreover, for computational purposes, a given complicated function may often be replaced in a limited area by a far simpler function, for use in hand or machine computation.

Walsh published an important paper on this topic in 1924, concerning polynomial approximation in a region bounded by an analytic simple closed curve; this paper concerned a then-well-recognized open problem. He surmised that for further progress modern results on conformal mapping would be useful, and therefore spent the year 1925–26 with C. Carathéodory in Munich. Carathéodory was thoroughly familiar with conformal mapping and had contributed to the field in a masterly manner. He generously provided Walsh with references to the literature, which eventually led to important results (1926 and later) concerning approximation in a region bounded by an arbitrary simple closed curve, with various applications.

The notion of degree of approximation for a function of a real variable had made gigantic strides by 1911, thanks to S. Bernstein, D. Jackson, and C. J. de la Vallée Poussin. Other writers, notably G. Faber and G. Szegö, had commenced to observe certain properties of degree of approximation by polynomials in the complex variable (Bernstein exhibited a striking example), but without definite results. Walsh developed this field, and rapidly proved deep important results on degree of convergence of polynomials of best approximation as measured in numerous ways, thereby unifying a large number of previous theorems already in the literature.

Walsh then continued to organize a well-rounded theory (1935) of approximation by polynomials and rational functions. The new theory dominated classical results on orthogonal polynomials and orthogonal rational functions, and included deep results (following L. Fejér, L. Kalmar, and M. Fekete) on uniform distribution of poles and points of interpolation.

His later work on approximation was concerned especially with interpolation and approximation by bounded analytic functions (1938 and later), discovery of a new and useful canonical map for multiply connected regions (1954), and approximation by rational functions with some free poles (1963). Walsh collaborated with numerous others in pursuing these topics, and in considering the relation of degree of approximation to boundary properties of the function approximated.

The field of approximation by harmonic polynomials is analogous to that of approximation by polynomials in the complex variable, and Walsh devoted a number of papers also to that topic (1929, 1954, 1960).

Another important field cultivated by Walsh over an extended period of years is the geometric theory of the zeros of various kinds of polynomials. This work began in 1918, and continued intermittently through 1964. Originally, it involved the position of the zeros of two polynomials related algebraically, and continued in the study of polynomials having extremal properties, such as best approximation to a given function according to any one of several interpretations. Some of this work (commencing 1951) was done jointly with T. S. Motzkin, M. Zedek, M. Fekete, and O. Shisha.

In still another field, Walsh exhibited (1922) a closed set of normal orthogonal functions, composed of square waves and with expansion properties similar to those of trigonometric functions. These orthogonal functions have aroused wide interest.

The son of a Methodist minister, Walsh lived in various parts of Maryland as a youth and attended the public schools there. He graduated from Baltimore Polytechnic Institute in 1912, and after a year at Columbia University went to Harvard University for the rest of his undergraduate work. There he was greatly influenced by W. F. Osgood, M. Bôcher, and G. D. Birkhoff. He joined the U.S. Navy in World War I, and after the war returned to Harvard, where he received his Ph.D. in 1920. The next year he studied in Paris, where he was especially influenced by P. Montel, then returned to Harvard to join the faculty. He served again in the U.S. Navy during World War II. In 1946 he became Perkins Professor of Mathematics at Harvard. He was elected to the National Academy of Sciences in 1936.

Books by Walsh are *Approximation by Polynomials* (1935), *Interpolation and Approximation* (1935; 3d ed. 1960), *Location of Critical Points* (1950), and *Approximation by Bounded Analytic Functions* (1960).

For background information *see* COMPLEX NUMBERS AND COMPLEX VARIABLES in the McGraw-Hill Encyclopedia of Science and Technology.   □

★ WALTON, Ernest Thomas Sinton
Irish physicist
Born Oct. 6, 1903, Dungarvan, Co. Waterford, Ireland

WHILE AT the Cavendish Laboratory, Cambridge, during Sir Ernest Rutherford's tenure of the directorship, Walton worked jointly with J. D. Cockcroft on the development of a high-voltage apparatus capable of producing fast atomic particles with energies up to 700,000 electron volts. They showed that these were capable of disintegrating many of the light elements, the disintegrations being of types not known previously. For this work they shared the Nobel Prize in physics for 1951.

Previous to this work the only method known for transmuting one element into another was the method used by Rutherford of bombarding elements with the alpha particles spontaneously emitted by radioactive substances. There was

thus a severe restriction on the nature, numbers, and energies of the bombarding particles available for such experiments. There appeared, however, to be no theoretical reason why fast atomic particles such as protons and alpha particles should not be produced in vastly greater numbers than those of the alpha particles emitted from any practicable radioactive source. Energies higher than that possessed by the natural alpha particles would be an added advantage, while accelerating voltages of less than several million volts were believed to be of but little use. The known difficulties of using such voltages and of applying them to vacuum tubes discouraged attempts. Hence attention was given to indirect methods that did not require the use of high voltages for the production of fast particles. During 1928 Walton tried two methods that were later developed and became known as the betatron and the linear accelerator. Both attempts failed because the necessary high-frequency sources were not available at the time and because almost nothing was known about the conditions necessary for the focusing of particles in an accelerator.

The situation changed radically as a result of calculations made independently by George Gamow and by E. U. Condon and R. W. Gurney. On the basis of the new wave mechanics, they showed that particles had a small chance of moving from one region to another even when these regions were separated by a potential barrier impervious to a particle obeying the Newtonian laws of mechanics. This gave for the first time a satisfactory explanation of the relation between the half-life of a radioactive substance and the energy of the emitted alpha particle. In reverse, it showed that particles of quite low energies could sometimes get into a nucleus across barriers of considerable height. It appeared that disintegrations might be produced by bombarding elements with particles, especially protons, of quite low energies provided that a sufficient number of particles was used. In practice, this meant using streams of particles of energies that might not be very difficult to produce.

Cockcroft brought these results to the attention of Rutherford, and it was decided to develop methods of producing streams of fast protons of energies of some hundreds of thousands of electron volts. Fortunately, some experience of high-voltage work was available in the laboratory. T. E. Allibone had built an electron accelerator powered by a Tesla transformer capable of giving over 500,000 volts. Cockcroft and Walton developed further the techniques of applying high voltages to vacuum tubes. By the use of a suitable voltage-multiplying circuit it became possible to produce and utilize high steady voltages. This is the ideal type of accelerating voltage, as it gives particles of uniform energy and there is no reverse voltage to give troublesome x-rays at the target. Their apparatus produced about 100 microamperes of protons accelerated by voltages of up to about 700,000 volts.

When lithium was bombarded by the proton beam, they found that a copious emission of alpha particles ensued. The reaction was shown to be $_3Li^7 + _1H^1 \longrightarrow _2He^4 + _2He^4$. Various other similar transmutations of the light elements involving alpha-particle emission were found. Later, when heavy hydrogen became available, they showed that fast deuterons could disintegrate elements, giving both proton and alpha-particle emission. After the discovery of artificial radioactivity by the Curie-Joliots, they, along with C. W. Gilbert, were able to produce radioactive nitrogen-13 by bombarding carbon with either protons or deuterons.

These experiments were the first in which nuclear disintegrations were produced without the use of radioactive material. Thus everything was under control, and the way was opened for producing transmutations of matter on a much larger scale than was possible when natural alpha particles had to be used.

The son of a clergyman, Walton studied physics and mathematics at the University of Dublin, Ireland. After graduation he remained there for a year to do experimental and theoretical work on vortex motion in liquids. In 1927 he was awarded a scholarship by the Royal Commissioners for the Exhibition of 1851 and with it he went to work at the Cavendish Laboratory, Cambridge. In 1934 he returned to Dublin, where in 1947 he was elected professor and head of the department of physics.

For background information see NUCLEAR RE-ACTION; PARTICLE ACCELERATOR in the McGraw-Hill Encyclopedia of Science and Technology. □

★ **WANGENSTEEN, Owen Harding**
American surgeon
Born Sept. 21, 1898, Lake Park, Minn., U.S.A.

THE ALIMENTARY canal was the area of most of Wangensteen's work. In the mid-1920s, he began experiments to assess the thesis that mechanical factors contributed to the high mortality of acute intestinal obstruction. The existing belief had been that death from such obstruction was essentially toxic in nature. J. L. Gamble indicated (1925) that early demise of experimental animals from duodenal or high jejunal obstruction was owing in large part to the loss of fluid and electrolytes by vomiting. This lent considerable encouragement to Wangensteen's thesis. By dividing the cervical esophagus of the dog, inverting the distal end of the divided esophagus, and dividing the terminal ileum, Wangensteen and his associate, C. E. Rea, were able to keep dogs alive by daily intravenous injections of glucose and other electrolytes for relatively long periods, despite complete obstruction, by exclusion of swallowed air. On sacrifice, little or no gas was found in the intestine. In the absence of swallowed air, the alimentary tract frequently absorbed all the fluids dumped into it at its upper gateway.

Wangensteen and J. R. Paine began (1931) attempts to relieve the distention of some varieties of acute intestinal obstruction by applying suction to an inlying gastroduodenal tube, a therapeutic device, still in current use, that served to focus notice on the importance of early decompression. H. G. Scott and Wangensteen were able to show (1930) that the "toxic factor" in early strangulating obstruction came primarily from loss of blood (shock) because venous return from the strangulated segment was impaired. Whereas it was then generally held that feculent vomiting was an attendant phenomenon of obstruction of the colon, critical observation established that obstruction of the colon was frequently unaccompanied by any vomiting and that copious and feculent vomiting occurred only in acute obstructions of the small intestine. First evidences of a continuing decline in the mortality of acute intestinal obstruction became obvious with clearer characterization of the clinical features of obstruction of bowel at various levels, together with emphasis upon early intestinal decompression without bacterial contamination. With the help of colleagues G. A. Smith and A. S. Leonard, Wangensteen developed (1955–65) important improvements in techniques of intestinal decompression. The prevailing 40–60% hospital mortality of acute intestinal obstruction of the late 1920s has gradually declined to less than 10% today. In many clinics giving special attention to bowel obstruction, the hospital mortality of nonstrangulating obstructions has been reduced to 2% for the small bowel and 5% for the large bowel. Further improvement awaits reliable objective techniques in the early detection of strangulating obstructions.

With associates C. Dennis and R. E. Buirge, Wangensteen showed (1937–39) that perforation or gangrene of the appendix in man was owing to obstruction rather than to a bacterial source, the then prevailing belief. The great German pathologist, Ludwig Aschoff, had indeed indicated that appendicitis was a disease as specific as a Neisserian infection. Proper selection of animals, Wangensteen felt, could be of the greatest importance in exploration of a thesis. Among 26 species of animals, Dennis and Wangensteen found that only the appendix of rabbit and chimpanzee had, like man's, a secretory capacity outweighing that of absorption. The secretory pressure of the appendix in man, like that of the rabbit and chimpanzee, approximates systolic blood pressure. It is understandable, therefore, that when the appendix is obstructed, usually by a fecolith in its lumen, perforation or gangrene will ensue unless the appendix is excised.

Much of Wangensteen's work over the past 25 years was concerned with the peptic ulcer diathesis. In 1958, with colleagues H. D. Root and P. A. Salmon, he showed that massive gastric hemorrhage could often be arrested by reducing the temperature in the gastric wall to 10–15°C. This was done by circulating a cold fluid through a balloon introduced into the stomach via the esophagus. The cessation of hemorrhage was found to be owing to (1) a 70% reduction of arterial inflow attending cooling temperatures and (2) inhibition of gastric secretion. Attempts were then undertaken to freeze the gastric mucosa and thus impair the secretory capacity of the parietal and chief cells, as well as damage the vagal neural terminals in the gastric wall. Elective gastric freezing has still to find acceptance among clinicians in the same measure as has gastric cooling for massive gastric hemorrhage. The special virtue of gastric freezing lies in its ability to provide almost uniform immediate relief from pain to ulcer sufferers. Its chief failing is that such relief in many instances is only of a few months' duration. However, a number of patients who were candidates for surgery continue asymptomatic more than three years later.

For many years, Wangensteen was a student of alimentary tract cancer. With a colleague, S. R. Friesen, he was able to show (1947) that the asymptomatic interval, when histologic gastric cancer was present, is in the order of two years, a circumstance that points to the necessity of scrutiny of patients who may harbor asymptomatic cancers. Studies prosecuted (1960–65) in the University of Minnesota surgery department's Cancer Detection Center, with colleagues D. B. Shahon and V. A. Gilbertsen, suggest that cancer of the rectum may be a preventable disease and that an annual physical examination will detect breast cancer early; 90% of the Detection Center's patients found to have breast cancer are alive and well more than five years after surgery. Wangensteen suggested (1946) that for certain cancers, notably colon, ovary, and retroperitoneal sarcomas having involvement of regional lymph nodes, reoperation be done at intervals of six months to a year, in the asymptomatic interval, a program that came to be known as the "Second Look." The five-year survival rate with freedom from cancer in these patients, known to have residual cancer on the occasion of the first Second Look, was a modest, though not negligible, 10–15%.

Born of Norwegian-American parents on a farm in western Minnesota, young Wangensteen's sole ambition was to become a farmer. However, his interest in sick farm animals persuaded his father that this son should be a doctor, a suggestion that Wangensteen ultimately accepted with some reluctance. He received his college and medical-school training at the University of Minnesota, and acquired a Ph.D. in surgery there in 1925. He spent 1924 at the Mayo Foundation and 1927–28 in European surgical clinics. In 1930 Wangensteen was appointed chairman of the department of surgery, University of Minnesota. In 1960 he was named Distinguished Professor of Surgery. He received the Passano Foundation Award in 1961.

Besides many articles in surgical literature, Wangensteen wrote *Acute Intestinal Obstruction and Its Management* (1937; 3d ed. 1955) and *Cancer of the Esophagus and Stomach* (1951; 2d ed. 1956).

For background information *see* INTESTINE; INTESTINE, DISORDERS OF in the McGraw-Hill Encyclopedia of Science and Technology.   ☐

★ WARREN, Shields

American pathologist
Born Feb. 26, 1898, Cambridge, Mass., U.S.A.

A PATHOLOGIST and long-time student of the effects of ionizing radiation on man, particularly at Hiroshima and Nagasaki, Warren contributed to the understanding of pathologic effects of ionizing radiation on man. For this he received the 1962 Albert Einstein Medal and Award.

Early in this century the deleterious effects of ionizing radiation on living organisms were recognized but were not intensively studied. In the 1920s about a dozen research workers, of whom Warren was one, were interested in the changes induced in animals and man by ionizing radiation. By the time atomic energy became a practical reality, Warren's work and that of others had demonstrated that overdoses of radiation produced injury and death. As a result of studies of the survivors of the atomic bombings of Japan and of other persons receiving whole-body doses of radiation, it was determined that there was a characteristic acute radiation syndrome. The effects of injury to bone marrow, lymphoid tissue, and gastrointestinal tissue predominated, but such later effects were apparent as complete or partial sterility, genetic damage, and induction of cancer, including leukemia in some cases. Warren and many other workers in the field assumed that the cells of the body varied in sensitivity to radiation in relation to their frequency of reproduction and that the pathologic effects of radiation could be determined as related to diminution of certain cells, permanent modification of some surviving cells and their progeny, persisting damage to intercellular supporting tissue, and damage to blood vessels supplying the irradiated tissue.

Warren's studies—begun in 1925 at Harvard Medical School and continued through the 1930s in close association with Olive Gates and later with Nathan Friedman and Hermann Lisco—were not restricted to human tissue; considerable experiment was devoted to the effects of radiation on carcinogenesis in animals and more recently to the effects on parabiosed rodents, which permitted the exaggeration of the effects by the combination of hormonal and immunologic abnormalities with those induced by radiation. His observations and those of other workers in the field of pathology led to a better understanding of the hazards of ionizing radiation and contributed to the establishment of sound permissible dose levels of radiation for workers in the field of atomic energy and radiology. His experience with pathological effects of radiation enabled him to outline for the U.S. Atomic Energy Commission its initial program in biology and medicine.

A professor's son, Warren majored in biology at Boston University, where he received his A.B. in 1918. He received his M.D. from the Harvard Medical School in 1923. After 1925 he taught at the Harvard Medical School. He became pathologist to the New England Deaconess Hospital in 1927. During World War II and the subsequent period of rapid application of atomic energy, he served in the Naval Reserve. In 1947 he became the first director of the Division of Biology and Medicine, serving until 1952. From 1955 to 1963 he served as the U.S. representative on the United Nations Scientific Committee on the Effects of Atomic Radiation. He was elected to the National Academy of Sciences in 1962.

Warren wrote *The Pathology of Diabetes Mellitus*, with P. M. LeCompte (3d ed. 1952), *A Handbook for the Diagnosis of Cancer of the Uterus*, with O. Gates (1949), *Introduction to Neuropathology*, with S. P. Hicks (1950), *The Medical Effects of the Atomic Bomb in Japan*, with A. W. Oughterson (1956), and *The Pathology of Ionizing Radiation* (1961).

For background information *see* RADIATION INJURY (BIOLOGY) in the McGraw-Hill Encyclopedia of Science and Technology.   ☐

☆ WATSON, James Dewey

American biochemist
Born Apr. 6, 1928, Chicago, Ill., U.S.A.

FOR HIS part in the determination of the three-dimensional structure of deoxyribonucleic acid (DNA), the molecular carrier of heredity, Watson shared the 1962 Nobel Prize for physiology or medicine with F. H. C. Crick and M. H. F. Wilkins. *See* CRICK, FRANCIS HARRY COMPTON; WILKINS, MAURICE HUGH FREDERICK.

Watson received a B.S. in zoology at the University of Chicago in 1947 and a Ph.D., also in zoology, at Indiana University in 1950. At Indiana he was deeply influenced by the geneticists H. J. Muller and T. M. Sonneborn and by the microbiologist S. E. Luria. His thesis, directed by Luria, was a study of the effect of hard x-rays on bacteriophage multiplication. In 1950–51 he was a National Research Council fellow in Copenhagen, where he worked with bacterial viruses under the biochemist Herman Kalckar and the microbiologist Ole Maaløe.

In the spring of 1951, in Naples, he met Wilkins and saw for the first time the x-ray diffraction pattern of crystalline DNA. This stimulated him to change the direction of his research toward the structural chemistry of nucleic acids and proteins. At Cambridge, where he went in October, 1951, he met Crick, who shared his interest in solving the DNA structure. The two investigators thought it would be possible to correctly guess its structure, given Wilkins's experimental evidence plus careful examination of the possible stereochemical configurations of polynucleotide chains. Their first serious effort, in the late fall of 1951, was unsatisfactory. Their second effort, based upon more experimental evidence and better appreciation of the nucleic acid literature, resulted, early in March, 1953, in the proposal of the complementary double helical configuration.

From 1953 to 1955 Watson was a senior research fellow in biology at the California Institute of Technology. During 1955–56 he worked with Crick again at the Cavendish Laboratory at Cambridge. In the fall of 1956 Watson joined the Harvard University faculty as an assistant professor of biology; he became an associate professor in 1958 and a professor in 1961. His major interest in those years was the role of RNA in protein synthesis. He was elected to the National Academy of Sciences in 1962.

For background information *see* DEOXYRIBO-NUCLEIC ACID; NUCLEIC ACID in the McGraw-Hill Encyclopedia of Science and Technology.   ☐

★ WEBER, Ernst
American engineer
Born Sept. 6, 1901, Vienna, Austria

At the beginning of World War II, microwave theory and techniques, particularly in the field of measurements, were in their infancy. Investigators at the Polytechnic Institute of Brooklyn had done some work with ultrahigh frequencies in the range down to 50-cm wavelength. When the Radiation Laboratory at the Massachusetts Institute of Technology was organized and the Office of Scientific Research and Development under Vannevar Bush initiated contracts with universities for research and development, Weber visited MIT's early radar system and selected as the most challenging field measurements at microwave frequencies. Commercial equipment was not available and power sources like the McNally tube could be acquired only under the strictly regulated priority system administered by the Radiation Laboratory.

The first task Weber and his coworkers conceived was the precision measurement of attenuation. W. W. Hansen at Sperry Gyroscope Company produced his own version, glass tubes with Aquadag, which was hydroscopic and often flaked. It occurred to Weber that the only stable material should be metal films—of course, noble metals. Reminded of the art of decorating chinaware with gold and silver, he obtained the metallic solutions from the Hanovia company and acquired the art of painting glass tubes and rods as inner conductors in coaxial systems and of baking them appropriately. Electromagnetic theory told him of the skin effect. To be able to predict the resistance at the frequencies of 3,000 and 10,000 megacycles, it was necessary to have film thicknesses that guaranteed the resistivity of the bulk metal, and yet high resistance was also necessary to obtain appropriate power absorption.

It then occurred to Weber that certain noble-metal alloys had been reported to possess higher resistivity than the component metals. He urged Hanovia to produce metal solutions of mixtures of platinum and palladium, and when glass tubes were painted with these solutions the metal film turned out to be the desired alloy of higher resistivity. He and his associates thus moved into production on the one hand while perfecting measurement techniques on the other hand. From this activity came a rugged design of precision coaxial attenuators that proved to be very useful for field tests of radars. The rapidly increasing demand led by the end of 1953 to the setting up of a company, PIB Products Company.

Corning Glass Works then entered the picture, because the special pyrex glass had to be produced in special production runs. The demand for quantity production of attenuator insert rods led to the establishment of a separate division of Corning Glass Works, later shifted to Bradley, Pa., which worked under subcontracts from PIB Products.

When emphasis shifted to the 3-cm microwave region, wave-guide attenuators had to be conceived. The painting of the metal solutions on glass plates as insert in the wave guide could not be done uniformly enough except with lower resistivity. A different technique was needed. Weber had known about evaporation, so he and his colleagues set up a simple homemade bell with measurement devices to permit controlled evaporations. One of the first materials they checked was nichrome wire produced by Driver Harris Company. They quickly learned that only one variety could be evaporated and deposited on glass plates with the desired resistivity corresponding to the bulk-metal values. The development of techniques combined correct preheating of the glass plates, proper vacuum pressures, and distancing and heating of the crucible, and it required considerable time and effort. Again, when the needed cleanliness and care had been achieved, Corning Glass Works was called upon for the production of the pyrex plates of various shapes and sizes.

In all this art and technology of metallized glass elements, electromagnetic considerations had to run parallel. The discontinuity presented by replacing a solid-metal conductor of high conductivity by a glass rod with a thin high-resistance film required matching sections that could be predetermined from transmission line theory for the coaxial systems. In the wave guides, the shaping of the glass plate as well as a series arrangement of different resistance sections had to be resorted to.

In such a combination of art and science, numerous patentable ideas occurred, many of which in fact were basic. As a result, the PIB

Products Company had assets after the war that its original investors, all trustees of the Polytechnic Institute of Brooklyn, partly donated and partly sold to Polytechnic at their original value. Polytechnic continued to operate the company, changed its name to Polytechnic Research and Development Company, Inc., and made it at that time the leading microwave component and instrument firm. During the war, most of the men employed in the company were Weber's former or concurrent students, who quickly contributed to the art and theory in their own right. After the war the company secured a few men from the MIT Radiation Laboratory for the management and applications engineering aspects. Weber served as president from 1952 until the business was sold to Harris-Intertype Corporation in December, 1959, when it had reached a volume of over $5,000,000.

Weber graduated as an electrical engineer from the Technical University, Vienna, in 1924; he received a Ph.D. from the University of Vienna in 1926 and a Sc.D. from the Technical University in 1927. From 1924 to 1930 he worked as a research engineer in Vienna and Berlin. He went to the United States in 1930 as visiting professor of electrical engineering at the Polytechnic Institute of Brooklyn, staying on as research professor (1931–41), professor of graduate electrical engineering and head of graduate study and research (1942–45), head of the department of electrical engineering and director of the Microwave Research Institute (1945–57), vice-president for research (1957), and president (from 1957). Elected to the National Academy of Science in 1965, he was a founder of the National Academy of Engineering.

Weber wrote *Electromagnetic Fields: Theory and Applications*, Vol. I, *Mapping of Fields* (1950) and *Linear Transient Analysis* (2 vols., 1954–56).

For background information *see* MICROWAVE in the McGraw-Hill Encyclopedia of Science and Technology. □

★ WEINBERG, Alvin Martin

American physicist
Born Apr. 20, 1915, Chicago, Ill., U.S.A.

F OR HIS contributions to the theory and development of fission reactors, Weinberg in 1960 received both the Atoms for Peace Award and the U.S. Atomic Energy Commission's E. O. Lawrence Memorial Award.

Weinberg was a member of the wartime team of theoretical physicists, headed by E. P. Wigner, that designed the first large nuclear power reactors. When the first plutonium-producing reactors were designed, the theory of the nuclear chain reaction was in rudimentary form. The basic problem was to predict—from knowledge of the nuclear properties of uranium, graphite, and water—the distribution in time, space, and energy of the neutron population in a chain reactor as well as the critical mass of the reactor. The neutron distribution determines the heat production distribution in the reactor. Consequently, the engineering design of every power reactor must begin with estimates of the neutron distribution. These "reactor calculations," as they are now called, require a rather sophisticated application of the mathematical theory of diffusion. Although methods for making such calculations were invented independently in several places, the mode of analysis devised originally by Wigner, and to which Weinberg and the other members of Wigner's group contributed, remain the standard today. This work was summarized by Weinberg and Wigner in *The Physical Theory of Neutron Chain Reactors* (1958).

Following the war, Weinberg pursued the development of nuclear reactors for power and research. He had early become interested in the possibility of using water under pressure as both the moderator and coolant of a chain reactor, and he was one of the proponents of this "pressurized-water" reactor system. This reactor is now the fundamental system used in all reactors for naval propulsion, and is also the main line of U.S. development for reactors for civilian power. A forerunner of the pressurized-water reactor was the first really high-powered research reactor, the so-called materials testing reactor (MTR), which, with a neutron flux of 2×10^{14} neutrons/cm^2/sec, was for many years the world's most intense neutron source. The water-moderated core of the MTR was designed at the

Oak Ridge National Laboratory; the reactor was built at the National Reactor Test Station in Idaho.

Weinberg was also an advocate of the so-called fluid-fuel reactor—one in which the uranium or plutonium fuel, instead of being arranged in a lattice of solid fuel elements, is dissolved in a liquid. Fluid-fuel reactors eliminate the necessity of refabricating spent solid-fuel elements. Such reactors lend themselves particularly well to so-called breeders, in which more nuclear fuel is produced (from thorium or U^{238}) than is consumed. The Oak Ridge National Laboratory built four fluid-fuel reactors: two using solutions of uranyl sulfate in water, and two using solutions of uranium-fluoride in molten mixtures of alkali fluorides. The most recent such reactor, the molten salt reactor experiment, operates at 1200°F and is designed to produce 10,000 kw of heat.

As director of the Oak Ridge National Laboratory, Weinberg wrote extensively on some of the difficult problems of public policy posed by the growth of modern science. He coined the phrase "big science" to describe the new kind of large-scale scientific enterprise exemplified by ORNL. He also discussed the criteria for scientific choice, that is, the criteria for deciding which fields of science deserve the most public support in a situation where public support is limited. Weinberg's main criterion was that of "imbeddedness," that is, that scientific discipline has the highest scientific merit that bears most strongly on, and illuminates most brightly, its neighboring scientific discipline. This criterion has been used extensively in present-day debate on the problem of allocation of support among competing scientific fields.

Weinberg received his B.S., M.S., and Ph.D. (1939) at the University of Chicago. He began his research career as a mathematical biophysicist, but the war cut this career short in 1942, when he began work in nuclear energy. He joined the Oak Ridge National Laboratory in 1945 and was designated research director in 1948 and director in 1955. He was elected to the National Academy of Sciences in 1961.

For background information *see* REACTOR, NUCLEAR in the McGraw-Hill Encyclopedia of Science and Technology.   □

★ WELLER, Thomas Huckle
American virologist and parasitologist
Born June 15, 1915, Ann Arbor, Mich., U.S.A.

A PEDIATRICIAN, specializing in infectious diseases and tropical medicine, Weller applied the techniques of tissue culture to the study of viral and parasitic diseases of man. Using cultures of human cells, he isolated the virus of chicken pox (varicella) and of shingles (herpes zoster) and proved the common etiology of these two clinically different diseases. With the same methodology he recovered new viruses, termed the cytomegaloviruses, from infants with cytomegalic inclusion disease. In collaboration with F. A. Neva, the virus of German measles (rubella) was propagated for the first time. Weller also carried out pioneering studies on the growth in culture of two helminths parasitic in man, the nematode, *Trichinella spiralis*, and the trematode, *Schistosoma mansoni*. However, Weller became best known for the observation that the poliomyelitis viruses would grow in cultures of nonnervous human tissues, a finding that initiated a 3-year collaborative study with John F. Enders and Frederick C. Robbins. For this work the group received the Nobel Prize in physiology or medicine for 1954.

The cultivation of poliomyelitis viruses in effect substituted the test tube for the monkey, the only experimental animal susceptible to all types of poliomyelitis virus. As a consequence, tissue cultures could be used for the isolation and identification of poliomyelitis viruses, for assaying the status of immunity in man or in experimental animals, and for the growth in volume of virus. Thus, the groundwork was laid for the several types of poliomyelitis vaccines. Of equal or greater import was the fact that the demonstrated usefulness in the poliomyelitis studies of tissue culture procedures stimulated comparable investigations on other disease entities with the resultant recognition of dozens of new viruses.

Viruses multiply only in the presence of living cells, which are experimentally provided by the inoculated animal or the embryonated hen's egg, or, in the instance of a tissue culture, by cells or tissue fragments nourished in a container in the presence of a suitable nutrient solution. While

the pioneering report of F. Parker and R. N. Nye in 1925 on the growth of vaccinia virus in vitro established the tissue culture as a virologic tool, technical problems precluded widespread acceptance of the methodology. The avoidance of bacterial contamination required meticulous and often cumbersome technical procedures. With the advent of antibiotics, penicillin and streptomycin could be incorporated in the nutrient fluid of the tissue culture and the problem of bacterial contamination was thereby minimized. The demonstration of viral multiplication in vitro presented another problem: virologists, lacking a visual indicator of the presence of virus, were compelled to inoculate culture fluids into a susceptible animal in order to establish the presence of infectious material. Further, in investigating certain diseases of man considered to be of viral etiology, such as chicken pox (varicella), no susceptible laboratory animal could be found, indicating that the responsible virus might be highly host-specific.

These considerations suggested that the virus of varicella might be isolated in cultures of human skin and that its presence might be detected by the microscopic demonstration of changes in infected cells, similar to those occurring in the skin lesions of chicken pox. In March 1948, small flask cultures of human embryonic skin and muscle tissue were prepared with antibiotics in the nutrient. Some were inoculated with varicella material and the remainder with a rodent-adapted strain of poliomyelitis virus that was available in the laboratory. The multiplication of poliomyelitis virus in the cultures was demonstrated by inoculation of mice. It was soon apparent that animal subinoculation was not necessary for the demonstration of the growth of poliomyelitis virus in tissue cultures, for the virus damaged the cultured cells, a phenomenon termed the "cytopathogenic effect." The successful findings on poliomyelitis virus temporarily interrupted work on chicken pox. Evidence that varicella virus had been isolated was obtained in 1949, and serial propagation with overt cytopathic changes was first achieved in 1952.

Weller's later studies with the cytomegaloviruses and rubella virus revealed a previously unrecognized mechanism for the dissemination of human viruses. Congenital infection, that is, infection acquired in utero, may occur as a consequence of a maternal infection with either type of virus. After birth, the congenitally infected infant has the unique capacity to excrete infectious virus for long periods, and thus poses a potential source of infection of epidemiologic significance.

Weller grew up in the academic environment of the University of Michigan, which he attended and where his father was professor of pathology. There he developed an interest in parasitology, which continued at the Harvard Medical School, where he graduated in 1940. In the summer of 1938, he studied malaria in Florida under a Rockefeller Foundation fellowship. As a senior medical student he elected tutorial work under John F. Enders, desiring to learn tissue-culture procedures so as to apply the methodology to the cultivation of the helminth parasites of man. This experience introduced virology as a new area of interest. To acquire clinical training with experience in infectious and parasitic diseases, he sought an appointment at the Children's Hospital, Boston. There, before and after World War II, he completed the requirements for specialty boards in pediatrics. From 1942 to 1945, Weller served in the Army Medical Corps, stationed for the most part in San Juan, Puerto Rico, where he conducted research on schistosomiasis and primary atypical pneumonia.

In 1947, Weller joined Enders in organizing new laboratories, termed the Research Division of Infectious Diseases, at the Children's Medical Center, Boston, and from 1949 to 1954 served as assistant director. Concurrently, he held teaching appointments in tropical medicine or tropical public health at Harvard at the levels of instructor to associate professor. In July, 1954, he was appointed Richard Pearson Strong Professor of Tropical Public Health and chairman of the department at Harvard, at which time he moved his laboratories from the Children's Hospital to the Harvard Medical School. He was elected to the National Academy of Sciences in 1964.

For background information *see* IMMUNITY; VIRUS in the McGraw-Hill Encyclopedia of Science and Technology.   □

★ **WENT, Frits Warmolt**
American botanist
Born May 18, 1903, Utrecht, Netherlands

DURING THE first decade of his research career, Went worked on the internal control of growth in plants, developing methods to study plant hormones. The next two decades were spent in the study of the external control of plant growth, assessing the role of climate, individually and communally, on plants. After a short excursion into public relations as director of the Missouri Botanical Gardens, he returned again to research, concentrating on the effects of plants on their environment.

As a student in his father's laboratory (F. A. F. C. Went was professor of botany and director of the Botanical Laboratory of the State University of Utrecht, Netherlands), Went became interested in the problems of phototropism, the response of plants to unidirectional light. Seedlings and plant stems usually bend toward a source of light. This they do by differential growth of the two sides of the stem, the side facing the light growing more slowly than the one opposite. To analyze the mechanism of this phototropic curvature, it was necessary to study normal growth and the effects of light on it.

In the course of this study Went succeeded in diffusing the plant growth hormone (which is formed in the tip of the plant) into agar or gelatin, and thus was able to handle this growth hormone or auxin outside the plant. Using oat seedlings as test material to determine this auxin quantitatively, he established a number of properties of auxin, even though the hormone was present in extreme dilution. Most importantly, he found that this auxin is both light- and heat-stable, and that therefore a phototropic curvature cannot be explained by destruction of auxin at the lighted side of the stem. Further analysis showed that in a phototropically bending stem, the auxin, which is normally produced in the extreme stem tip and which flows symmetrically down the stem, becomes redistributed under the influence of the unilateral light, resulting in a lower concentration of auxin at the light side and a higher concentration on the dark. This produces differential growth; it also explains the gradual migration of the phototropic curvature toward the lower end of the stem. Whereas Went had succeeded in measuring this light-directed auxin movement experimentally, a Russian investigator, N. Cholodny, had reached the same conclusion theoretically, and ever since then the phototropic theory, explaining light curvatures by lateral auxin movement, has been known as the Cholodny-Went theory.

In succeeding years, Went, working at the California Institute of Technology, demonstrated the role of hormones in the production of roots on plant stems and in time established the role of auxins and other plant hormones in plant development. This exploratory phase of the work on auxins was essentially terminated by the writing of a book by Went and K. V. Thimann, *Phytohormones* (1937).

Between 1939 and 1949, Went built a number of air-conditioned greenhouses at Caltech. This so-called phytotron made it possible to study the effects of climate in general on plants. By differentiating weather into its individual components of temperature, light, wind, humidity, etc., it proved possible to establish which one of the weather factors dominated in the development of different plants, and it became clear that practically every plant responded in a different way to the weather factors. Among the results obtained was that plants are thermoperiodic—that is to say, most plants grow at their optimal rate when the temperature during day is higher than during night. This daily thermoperiodicity is a counterpart of the seasonal thermoperiodicity essential for the development of many plants from temperate regions. He also found that the thermoperiodicity has much deeper roots in the autonomous Circadian rhythm, which pervades practically all plant and animal development. Research in the phytotron made it possible also to establish that the normal climatic cycles that a plant goes through in nature belong to the major factors controlling the distribution of plants. Thus an important step was made toward the development of experimental ecology.

It has now become practically axiomatic that research with plants should be carried out under rigidly controlled environmental conditions. This has led to the construction of phytotrons modeled after the Caltech one in plant research centers in many different countries.

At the Missouri Botanical Gardens the knowledge obtained in the construction of the first air-conditioned greenhouses was utilized in building a large display greenhouse, in which in one enclosure several different tropical climates can be maintained through the interplay of two separate air conditioning systems.

In recent years Went turned his attention to the volatile materials that are produced by plants and that seem to disappear into the atmosphere. He established that terpenes and other plant emanations, after diffusing into the air, are photochemically transformed and result in submicroscopic particles that produce the blue heat or summer haze and that can be measured as so-called condensation nuclei. Their role in meteorological phenomena and their fate in the atmosphere are now under investigation. There is a possibility that these materials end up ultimately in the form of asphaltic materials, giving rise to petroleum formation.

Went received his M.A. and Ph.D. at the University of Utrecht, where from 1923 to 1927 he was an assistant in botany. In 1928 he became botanist at the Botanical Gardens in Java, and in 1930 was appointed director of the Foreigners Laboratory there. He joined the faculty of the California Institute of Technology in 1933, serving as professor of botany from 1935 to 1958. For the next six years he was director of the Missouri Botanical Gardens in St. Louis. In 1964 he became a member of the Desert Research Institute of the University of Nevada in Reno. He was elected to the National Academy of Sciences in 1947.

Besides the volume with K. V. Thimann, Went wrote *Experimental Control of Plant Growth* (1957).

For background information *see* AUXIN in the McGraw-Hill Encyclopedia of Science and Technology. ☐

★ **WETMORE, Ralph Hartley**
American botanist
Born Apr. 27, 1892, Yarmouth, N.S., Canada

WETMORE CENTERED his biological studies on the manifestations of evolutionary survival in plants. He insisted that environment plays a significant part in the determination of the particular expressions that the hereditary patterns assume—that genes alone do not determine morphological and therefore physiological pattern. He emphasized also that the presence of the same organs and often even the same cell types or tissues in phylogenetically unrelated groups of plants must have a natural explanation. For example, what is advantageous or at least not disadvantageous in producing leaves in definite patterns with buds in their axils? What makes such an arrangement the characteristic pattern of organization for most groups of vascular plants even though these plants represent numerous and little-related phyletic lines? Again, his curiosity was piqued by the existence of the embryo sac as a female reproductive device in all groups of seed plants. By contrast, all spore-producing vascular plants—also of numerous evolutionary lines, none being seed producers—possess archegonia. These sex organs are very different from embryo sacs, different structurally and in their associations with developing embryos.

In early investigations, as part of a program with I. W. Bailey at Harvard University, Wet-

more and his students became actively involved in a series of fundamental studies on the significance of diverse patterns in the differentiation of secondary xylem of angiosperms. These patterns served as diagnostic criteria, employed in the taxonomy and putative evolutionary relationships of families of flowering plants. Clearly, heredity must work biochemically in the differentiation of vascular tissues, thereby giving expression locally to the characteristic genetic structural pattern that permits adequate transport and storage to occur for overall vegetative and reproductive survival. Results in these studies, however, were largely statistical correlations rather than biological interpretations.

Efforts to interpret diversity in differentiation as expressed in hereditary patterns of secondary xylem required step-by-step studies during development. Because vascular tissues are located inside the body of the plant, it was necessary to discover new techniques in order to explore these developments. Wetmore turned then to the formative apical regions of plants as more favorable regions for study, especially in faster-growing herbaceous plants, than was the cambial region with its derivative secondary xylem. Comparative studies on species representing all groups of living vascular plants proved to be an aid in securing knowledge of diverse patterns of organization. They showed, however, that adequate knowledge of developmental patterns could not be obtained from descriptive studies alone, nor from the study of angiosperms alone.

By 1945, Wetmore had turned to experimental approaches. At the same time, C. W. Wardlaw in England was independently invoking surgical techniques for studying the effects of excision of actual and ultimately potential leaf and bud primordia with a view to modifying developmental patterns. Wetmore's laboratory supplemented these studies and also invoked the then new results of Ernest Ball (1946), who had successfully grown whole plants in sterile nutrient agar culture from very small pieces of the apices.

Wetmore extended the nutrient culture studies to other groups of vascular plants. As a premise, he accepted the concept that any living plant cell endowed with its nucleus and normal organelles was potentially capable of producing a whole plant if stimulated to divide and adequately nourished. Such potentiality is not that of the fertilized egg alone. The concept proved of profound importance in his subsequent research and became established in the researches of, among others, F. C. Steward et al. (1963, 1964); Walter Halperin and D. F. Wetherell (1963); H. Kato and M. Takeuchi (1963); and Elizabeth D. Earle (1963).

Recently, Wetmore's studies became purely morphogenetic. Expressions of different plant forms from the same genome challenged his interest. For example, the thin, flat, prostrate, unvascularized fern prothallus is in striking contrast to the erect, sturdy, sporophytic fern plant. He became convinced by accumulating evidence that haploidy was not necessary for development of a prothallus, for he succeeded in growing diploid and tetraploid prothalli as well. Nor was diploidy a prerequisite for sporophyte expression, for he produced tetraploid and octoploid fern plants. Chromosome number did not seem basic to the expression of the genome. Recent studies by him and his collaborators suggested that the disposition of the initial fern cell, whether generative or vegetative, is more important than the number of genomes. Free cells, such as spores, excised young zygotes, physiologically isolated leaf cells—all such free cells in sterile culture habitually give prothalli. By contrast, such cells as fertilized eggs developing in situ in the prothallial-contained archegonium, or cells in the thicker part of the prothallus, give sporophytic fern plants. Wetmore suggested that the pattern of a plant that can develop under genetic control may be very different under one set of environmental influences than that which is ordinarily produced under the usual set of conditions.

Having taught in secondary schools, then having served in the Canadian Army during World War I, Wetmore did not receive his bachelor's degree until 1921—from Acadia University, with honors in biology. He obtained his Ph.D. in biology from Harvard University in 1924. After a postdoctoral year as a National Research fellow at Harvard and another year as assistant professor of biology at Acadia University, he returned to Harvard, where he was in turn assistant professor, associate professor, and professor until 1962, when he became professor of botany emeritus. He served as director of the Biological Laboratories and chairman of the department of biology. He was elected to the National Academy of Sciences in 1954.

For background information see PLANT EVOLUTION in the McGraw-Hill Encyclopedia of Science and Technology.   □

WEXLER, Harry

American meteorologist
Born Mar. 15, 1911, Fall River, Mass., U.S.A.
Died Aug. 11, 1962, Falls Church, Va., U.S.A.

To EXPLAIN unexpectedly high concentrations of ozone in the Antarctic atmosphere found by the U.S. International Geophysical Year expedition, Wexler proposed a theory of ozone circulation consistent with information on Antarctic winds, gathered also during the IGY. His theory threw light on the mechanism of Antarctic air circulation and demonstrated the usefulness of ozone as a "trace" element.

The IGY produced the first measurements of the ozone content of the Antarctic atmosphere made over an extended period of time in a variety of locations. Ozone was known to be formed in the stratosphere by the action of far-ultraviolet radiation breaking up oxygen molecules (O_2) into their constituent atoms (O), which then recombined with other oxygen atoms to form ozone (O_3). Measurements made at different points on the Antarctic continent indicated a fairly uniform layer of stratospheric ozone spread over the continent and concentrated in the region from about 15 to 20 kilometers above ground. In this respect the Antarctic ozone layer resembled that of other parts of the globe, although its lesser concentration than the corresponding layer in the Arctic was thought to indicate a weaker meridional flow in the Southern Hemisphere, bringing less warm air from lower latitudes.

Data on ozone in the lower atmosphere, however, indicated considerable variation, difficult to reconcile with the fairly even stratospheric ozone distribution. Ozone near the surface reached a maximum during the Antarctic winter, with highest concentration along the coast of the continent. For example, at the South Pole, the annual average surface ozone was about half that at the Little America station on the coast; the latter might vary from a monthly average of 15 micrograms per cubic meter of air in summer, to about 60 mcg in the winter.

To account for this, Wexler suggested that stratospheric air from equatorial regions, rich in

ozone, might be reaching the Antarctic surface via a discontinuity in the tropopause, the boundary between the troposphere and stratosphere. This discontinuity, called the mid-latitude tropopause break, would permit air of high ozone content to reach the Antarctic surface without affecting stratospheric ozone content. The mid-latitude jet stream, with which the tropopause break is associated, would then transport air from lower latitudes across the Southern Ocean, aided by frequent winter storms in high latitudes. As the ozone-bearing masses of air arrived at Antarctic latitudes, they would become cooled and descend to levels near the surface. Finally, the ozone region would be carried off the continent in a thin layer just above the ground.

This hypothesis helped explain the observed variations of ozone content. It further provided an example of the usefulness of ozone as a "trace" element in demonstrating the exchange of air across the mid-latitude tropopause break.

Besides his work on ozone, Wexler studied volcanic dust and its effect on world climate, propagation of storms in the upper atmosphere, the varied uses of weather satellites, and the formation of the Antarctic polar icecap.

After taking a B.S. in mathematics at Harvard in 1932, Wexler went to the Massachusetts Institute of Technology, where he was granted a Sc.D. in meteorology in 1939. Meanwhile, he had joined the U.S. Weather Bureau as a meteorologist in 1934. Following a year spent in teaching at the University of Chicago, and a position in training and research for the Weather Service of the Air Force during World War II, Wexler became chief of the Scientific Services Division of the Weather Bureau in 1946. From 1955 until his death in 1962, he was the Bureau's Director of Meteorological Research. He also served as chief scientist of the U.S. IGY Antarctic expedition, 1955–58. He was awarded the Rossby Medal of the American Meteorological Society posthumously in 1963.

For background information *see* METEOROLOGY in the McGraw-Hill Encyclopedia of Science and Technology.   □

★ WHEELER, Harold Alden

American radio engineer
Born May 10, 1903, Saint Paul, Minn., U.S.A.

IN THE early days of radio broadcasting, the development of home receivers reached the point where the loudness was a nuisance and needed to be brought under control. The manual "volume control" was an unnecessary burden to the listener, especially when both hands were required for tuning from one station to another. As a solution to this problem, Wheeler originated a particular kind of "automatic volume control" (AVC) that came into universal use and is still relied on in AM broadcast receivers using electron tubes.

Just after graduation from George Washington University in 1925, Wheeler worked during the summer at the Hazeltine Corporation laboratory in Hoboken. There, a few engineers had developed a radio broadcast receiver having plenty of amplification and requiring only two tuning dials for station selection. Wheeler revolted at the need for a third dial, the volume control, which had to be adjusted continually to hear every station while avoiding excessive loudness and distortion.

Over the next 6 months, including the fall when he pursued postgraduate studies at the Johns Hopkins University, Wheeler filled a notebook with various proposals for a circuit to accomplish AVC. During weekends, in the basement of his home in Washington, D.C., he collected the materials for building a superheterodyne receiver with AVC. This set was completed during the Christmas holidays, but he had trouble with the rather complicated AVC circuit he had selected. Finally he reverted to the simplest possible circuit, using a single triode electron tube connected as a diode for detecting the signal and developing the bias voltage needed for controlling the amplification. This was demonstrated to fellow students on Jan. 2, 1926. During the notorious fading of signals from station KDKA in Pittsburgh, the loudness was leveled so that the fluctuation of signal strength could be observed only on a meter in the control circuit.

The functions of the detector were: (1) to rectify the modulated-carrier signal; (2) to separate the ac modulation component for further amplification at audio frequency; and (3) to separate the dc rectified-carrier component for use as a bias voltage in controlling the preceding radio-frequency amplification. The diode circuit performed the first function with both high efficiency and linearity (freedom from distor-

tion), neither of which was common in the detectors then in use. By virtue of the linearity, the dc component was dependent only on the steady carrier and not on the fluctuating modulation, a result not obtained in earlier proposals for AVC.

In later years, Wheeler learned that more senior inventors in prominent laboratories had devised all of the complicated circuits, with their deficiencies, but had failed to take the last step as soon as he had. Also he came to appreciate the greater refinement of performance that was realized in the simple diode circuit. Hazeltine Corporation applied for patents on Wheeler's invention, known as "diode AVC," the first of which was issued on Sept. 27, 1932. Wheeler presented the subject late in 1927 in a brief talk before the Institute of Radio Engineers in New York. It was published in the IRE journal in 1928, sandwiched between major articles by Armstrong and Marconi. It excited little interest in the profession, and some prominent engineers even doubted that it would work.

The first real opportunity came when Philco, in its second season of manufacturing broadcast receivers, had the courage to order AVC in one of the two designs being developed for them by the Hazeltine staff. By that time, in 1929, Wheeler was working full-time in the Hazeltine New York laboratory, where he designed the Philco 95 receiver to introduce diode AVC to the market. Public acceptance was immediate; by the time the patents started to issue 3 years later, use of the circuit was universal.

From 1932 through 1941, the diode AVC patents were the keystone of the Hazeltine patent situation. The royalties from their patents were the entire support of the Hazeltine laboratories, enabling them to continue a healthy level of activity through the depression of the 1930s. Some of the prominent manufacturers, such as Philco and Stromberg-Carlson, were already Hazeltine licensees. Others proceeded to use the diode AVC without a license and were sued for royalties. The patent litigation came to a climax in 1936 in the Wilmington trial against the Radio Corporation of America, which entered into a license agreement without waiting for a court decision. The principal patent was validated in another trial, against Detrola in Detroit. This decision was upheld in the Sixth Circuit Court of Appeals in Cincinnati but ultimately reversed by the U.S. Supreme Court. The damage to Hazeltine resulting from the Supreme Court's adverse decision was overshadowed by U.S. involvement in World War II. This halted the manufacture of broadcast receivers, and the Hazeltine staff was selected for Navy radar activities of the utmost importance. After the war, all AM broadcast receivers using electron tubes continued to rely on diode AVC.

Wheeler received his B.S. in physics at George Washington University in 1925. In 1924, while still in college, he became one of the original employees of Hazeltine Corporation, engaged in the engineering of radio broadcast receivers for various manufacturers licensed under the Hazeltine patents. This activity expanded into the new fields of FM and TV. During World War II, Wheeler was chief consulting engineer in the Navy's IFF radar program at Hazeltine. After the war, he left Hazeltine to form Wheeler Laboratories, Inc., specializing in the design of microwave circuits and tracking radar antennas for guided missile systems. In 1959, Wheeler Laboratories became a subsidiary of Hazeltine Corporation, and Wheeler became also a director and vice-president of the parent company. He became chairman of the board of Hazeltine Corporation in 1965. In 1964 he was awarded the Medal of Honor of the Institute of Electrical and Electronic Engineers.

For background information *see* AUTOMATIC GAIN CONTROL in the McGraw-Hill Encyclopedia of Science and Technology.   □

★ WHIPPLE, Fred Lawrence

American astronomer
Born Nov. 5, 1906, Red Oak, Iowa, U.S.A.

AFTER MANY years of research on comets, meteors, and the interplanetary medium, including the discovery of six new comets, Whipple conceived and developed an answer to the age-old question: What is a comet? On his theory, a comet consists basically of a nucleus, a few kilometers in diameter, composed of various ices such as water, methane, and ammonia mixed with a large array of earthy materials, all of which presumably froze out of a condensing solar-type gas at temperatures of a few degrees absolute. The dirty-snowbank-comet model has now become almost axiomatic in the field of cometary research.

Some comets have long been known to produce streams of particles in space that become meteors or shooting stars in our atmosphere when the Earth crosses the streams. For the precision study of meteors or shooting stars, Whipple developed the two-station photographic method of observation, in which cameras with rotating shutters measure not only a meteor's trajectory through the atmosphere but also its velocity, atmospheric drag, and orbit about the Sun. This program, over some 15 years at Harvard, led Whipple and his associates to conclude that practically all visual meteors arise from pieces of cometary debris and are neither interstellar visitors nor dense irons or stones like the meteorites found on the surface of the Earth. Physical studies of photographic meteors, which earlier led to improved knowledge of the density of the high atmosphere, also showed that the meteor body is oftentimes of very low density and fragile in character. Their spectra, however, show the presence of iron, silicon, and other common earthy materials.

With this background of research on meteors, Whipple based his concept of the icy comet on the fact that certain comets do not exactly obey Newton's law of gravity but tend to change their orbital periods about the Sun. This requires a force acting on the comet normal to the line joining it to the Sun. Whipple argued that an icy comet nucleus would surely be rotating, and the solar heating of a dirty snowbank would leave a thin outer insulating layer of dirt. Thus the solar heat would be delayed in reaching the highly volatile ices within the nucleus, and some of the gases would be ejected on the "evening" side of the comet. The delayed jet action would produce a force component either fore or aft with respect to the comet's motion about the Sun to decrease or increase its orbital period.

Calculations based upon this theory proved to be consistent with other knowledge that had accumulated concerning the nuclei of comets. The known input of solar heat with its resultant production of vapor from ices led to forces of the right size. Since the jet action of gas from the sunny face of a comet should also produce a force generally away from the Sun, Whipple and S. Hamid studied the orbits of some 60 comets. They found a slight systematic reduction in the Sun's effective gravitational attraction for these comets, consistent with the numerical expectations from the icy-comet model. The icy-comet model, furthermore, answers a number of outstanding questions about comets. (1) Some have been observed to survive a passage through the outer solar atmosphere without destruction; for this a solid nucleus is needed. (2) Copious quantities of gas are emitted by comets. Solid surfaces could not absorb enough gas, nor could they replenish the gas in space; an icy reservoir is needed. (3) The gases observed in comets are peculiar fragmentary molecules of radicals, such as CN, CO, CH, NH, OH, and other pieces of larger stable molecules. The evaporation of a complex snowbank by solar heat will produce the parent molecules, and the nucleus might originally have contained some of the radicals. Solar ultraviolet light can break up the parent molecules. (4) The rate at which meteoritic particles should be carried away from cometary nuclei by the outflowing gas, with a velocity of a few meters per second, is consistent generally with the observations of meteor streams about cometary orbits. (5) The icy model also explains why comets have short lives in orbit near the Sun.

Almost simultaneously with Whipple's publication of the icy-comet model, Jan Oort of Leiden presented his theory for the replenishment of the cometary supply from a large reservoir of extremely eccentric cometary orbits extending out almost to the distance of the nearest stars, perhaps 100,000 times the Earth's distance from the Sun. On Oort's theory, the gravitational attraction of passing stars disturbs these long orbits and continually brings comets into orbits close to the Sun to maintain the supply. Hence, the Oort hypothesis provides the deep freeze of outer space to preserve the icy nuclei for huge periods of time, possibly for the 4.5×10^9 years since the solar system developed.

Having spent his first 15 years on a farm in Iowa, Whipple was taken by his parents to California, where he completed his high school work and majored in mathematics at the University of California at Los Angeles. At Berkeley and the Lick Observatory he completed his graduate studies in astronomy in 1931. He immediately accepted an invitation to the Harvard College Observatory; in 1950 he became professor of astronomy at Harvard. For nearly 3 years (1943–45) during World War II, at the Office of Scientific Research and Development at the Harvard Radio Research Laboratories, he headed a project for the research, development, production, and field use of confusion reflectors, small strips of aluminum foil tuned for German radar and dropped from Allied planes to simulate aircraft on the scopes of German radar. In 1955 Whipple accepted the directorship of the Smithsonian Institution Astrophysical Observatory in Cambridge. He was elected to the National Academy of Sciences in 1959.

For his work on meteors, Whipple received the J. Lawrence Smith Medal of the National Academy of Sciences in 1949. In 1960 he was awarded a medal for astronomical research by the University of Liège. He received the American Astronautical Society's Space Flight Award in 1961 for his tracking of artificial Earth satellites at the Astrophysical Observatory.

Whipple wrote *Earth, Moon, and Planets* (1942; rev. ed. 1963).

For background information *see* COMET in the McGraw-Hill Encyclopedia of Science and Technology.   □

★ WHITTLE, Sir Frank
British engineer
Born June 1, 1907, Coventry, England

WHITTLE PIONEERED in the development of the aircraft gas turbine, mainly in its turbojet form but including turbofan and aftfan variants. For this work he was knighted (1948) and awarded £100,000 by the British government. Among numerous scientific awards, he received the Rumford Medal of the Royal Society (1950) and the Franklin Medal of the Franklin Institute of the State of Pennsylvania (1956).

The seeds of Whittle's work were sown at the Royal Air Force College, Cranwell, where, as a flight cadet, he started to seek means of taking advantage of the low resistance to high-speed flight at high altitudes. For this purpose he studied rocket theory and also the problem of the gas turbine; he did not, however, combine the two ideas at that time (1928). Toward the end of 1929, when as a pilot officer in the Royal Air Force he was training as a flying instructor, it occurred to him to use the gas turbine for jet propulsion; he applied for a patent in January, 1930. He failed, however, to arouse the interest of either the British Air Ministry of any of several industrial firms he approached. There were no further developments until 1935, at which time, now a flight lieutenant, he was taking the mechanical sciences tripos at Cambridge University. In that year, with the aid of friends, he succeeded in enlisting the interest of a firm of City bankers, O. T. Falk and Partners. As a result, a company to pioneer the jet engine, Power Jets Limited, was formed, and an order was placed with the British Thomson-Houston

Company, Rugby, England, to build an experimental engine.

The target in mind was a small mail plane capable of crossing the Atlantic at a speed of 500 mph at a height of nearly 70,000 ft, where the atmospheric density was only $\frac{1}{16}$ that at sea level. Whittle was well aware of numerous earlier and unsuccessful attempts to develop gas turbines for power production, but he believed that many of the difficulties that had stood in the way of earlier workers in this field could be overcome by the achievement of much higher efficiencies of the turbine and compressor components through applying the best available aerodynamic knowledge. His view was that the main route to high efficiency for compressor and turbines was to give them as high a throughput as possible in proportion to their size. Thus the rotor of his first centrifugal compressor was only 19 in. in diameter but was designed to deal with 450 cu ft of air per second; it was double-sided. This meant that a single-stage turbine of about $16\frac{1}{2}$ in. in diameter directly coupled to the compressor had to develop a shaft power of over 3,000 hp at sea level. The main problem was to achieve satisfactory combustion, because the combustion intensity aimed at was more than twenty times as great as had ever previously been achieved.

The first experimental engine was completed in the spring of 1937 and made its first run on April 12 of that year in the turbine factory of the British Thomson-Houston Company. Though these initial runs demonstrated that the unit was self-driving and capable of producing a propelling jet, the compressor efficiency was much lower than had been allowed for in design, and the single spiral combustion chamber used proved to be very unsatisfactory. Testing of the engine in its original form was discontinued in July, 1937, and a major reconstruction was carried out. Once again, a single combustion chamber was used, this time axially disposed aft of the turbine. This first reconstruction was completed in the spring of 1938 but suffered considerable damage as a result of turbine blade failure in May of that year. It was then decided to embark on a second reconstruction, in which for the first time multiple combustion chambers were used. These were of the counterflow type and were 10 in number. The second reconstruction was completed in October, 1938, but it was several months before the engine could be made to run up to near design speed, mainly owing to combustion problems. However, in June, 1939, it was running sufficiently well to convince the director of scientific research of the Air Ministry that it could be developed into a practical aeroengine. As a result, the Ministry placed with Power Jets an order for a flight engine (which became known as W.1.) and with the Gloster

Aircraft Company an order for an experimental airplane (which became known as the Gloster/ Whittle E.28/39) to be powered by the engine.

A test bench version of the W.1. flight engine, the W.1.X., was constructed from spares for the first experimental engine and parts rejected from the W.1., and was first bench tested in December, 1940. It was later used for the taxiing trials of the E.28/39, and did, in fact, lift the airplane off the ground for short distances. (This engine is now in the Smithsonian Institution, Washington, D.C.) The W.1. was first run on April 12, 1941; after completing a 25-hour special category test on the bench, it was installed in the E.28/39, which then completed 10 hours of flight trials without incident, beginning on May 15, 1941. These trials showed that the aircraft performance was somewhat better than had been forecast.

The success of the E.28/39 resulted in a great increase in effort in Great Britain on the development and production of the turbojet engine, and also led to the beginning of close collaboration between Britain and the United States. This was initiated by the sending of the W.1.X., a complete set of drawings of the W.2.B., and a small engineering team to the General Electric Company at Lynn, Mass.

Shortly after the outbreak of World War II, it had been decided to prepare for the production of a twin-engined fighter, the Gloster Meteor, to be powered by an engine of improved design, the Power Jets W.2.B., which later became the Rolls-Royce Welland. Work on the W.2.B. and the Meteor, which had been going ahead, was temporarily cut back in 1942 owing to a series of development troubles, such as turbine blade failures, compressor surging difficulties, and combustion chamber unreliability. The program was reinstated early in 1943, when Rolls-Royce, which had then become responsible for production, succeeded in completing a 100-hour test at the design thrust of 1,600 lb. The Meteor went into service in August, 1944, and was used initially to shoot down V-1 flying bombs.

Meanwhile, Power Jets continued its development work under the technical direction of Whittle, who was responsible for the design of the W.1.A., W2/500, and W2/700 engines, in addition to the continuing development of the W.2.B. Many of the design features of the W2/500 and W2/700 were incorporated in such successful engines as the Rolls-Royce Derwent V (which powered the Meteor IV) and Nene.

At the same time, but at a somewhat slower tempo, development work was proceeding on various forms of the bypass type of engine. From the earliest days of his aircraft gas turbine work, Whittle had realized that the principal defect of

the simple turbojet engine was excessive fuel consumption under low speed conditions such as taxiing, takeoff, climb, descent, and standoff; the bypass form of the jet engine promised to ameliorate this problem. Power Jets did pioneer work on both types of the bypass engine used today— the turbofan and the aftfan. Attention was first concentrated on the aftfan type because of its apparent simplicity, and an aftfan engine known as the No. 3 augmentor was constructed and bench-tested. A later and improved version, the No. 4 augmentor, was intended to be combined with the W2/700 engine and, with afterburning, to power the Miles M.52 supersonic airplane. However, because of the cancellation of this project and the nationalization of Power Jets in 1944, the No. 4 augmentor was never completed. The same fate befell the turbofan engine known as the L.R.1.

In 1946 most of the personnel and plant of Power Jets (Research and Development) Limited, the government-owned successor to Whittle's company, were transferred to the newly formed National Gas Turbine Establishment. This resulted in the breakup of the pioneer team and the end of Whittle's direct connection with jet engine development. He then served as technical adviser, with the rank of acting air commodore, to the Ministry of Supply. In 1948 he retired from the R.A.F.

Whittle was the son of a Coventry mechanic. He received his first education at elementary schools in Coventry and Leamington Spa. He won a scholarship to Leamington College (a secondary school). In 1923 he joined the Royal Air Force as an aircraft apprentice and was trained as a metal rigger. In 1926 he was selected for a cadetship at the R.A.F. College. He graduated in 1928 as a pilot officer and was assigned to No. 111 Fighter Squadron. At the end of 1929 he qualified as a flying instructor and was assigned to No. 2 Flying Training School at Digby. He and a partner gave an exhibition of stunt flying at the R.A.F. display at Hendon in 1930. In 1931 he was assigned to the Marine Aircraft Experimental Establishment as a floatplane test pilot; during this period an important part of his duties was the testing of experimental catapults. In 1932 he was posted to the Officers' Engineering Course. Then he was sent to Cambridge University, from which he graduated with first class honors in the mechanical sciences tripos. During a postgraduate year at Cambridge, he worked on jet engine design and did aerodynamic research under Melvill Jones.

After his retirement from the R.A.F. in 1948, Whittle spent four years as technical adviser to the British Overseas Airways Corporation. Then he joined the Royal Dutch Shell Group as mechanical engineering specialist to Bataafsche Petroleum Maatschappij, one of the companies in the Shell Group. After leaving the Shell Group in 1957 he became consulting engineer to Bristol Siddeley Engines. For both Shell and Bristol Siddeley he worked on the design and development of a turbodrill project for oil well drilling.

Whittle wrote *Jet, The Story of a Pioneer* (1953).

For background information *see* JET PROPULSION in the McGraw-Hill Encyclopedia of Science and Technology.   □

★ WHYBURN, Gordon Thomas

American mathematician
Born Jan. 7, 1904, Lewisville, Tex., U.S.A.

NEW RESULTS discovered by Whyburn have influenced and stimulated effective development primarily in the areas of mathematical thought concerned with static-structure theory for continua in geometric topology, dynamic-structure evolution as a set undergoes a continuous deformation or transformation, and topological methods in classical function theory.

Influenced by the work of R. L. Moore and others characterizing the plane and sphere topologically, and of H. Hahn, S. Mazurkiewicz, and W. Sierpinski identifying and characterizing topologically those sets (locally connected continua) that are representable by continuous functions on an interval, Whyburn was led to consider structure-type problems relating to closed, bounded, connected sets, now called "continua." He found that basic structure properties of a continuum are revealed by its cut points and local cut points. Any interior point on an interval cuts the interval—the crossing point of a figure 8 cuts the figure but no other one does; any point on a circle is a local cut point, but not a cut point, of the circle. Whyburn proved that with, at most, a countable number of exceptions, all cut points and all local cut points of a continuum are of order 2 in the sense

that each has an arbitrarily small neighborhood, which is severed from the rest of the continuum by the removal of two points.

This led him to the discovery that the cut points of a continuum, and especially of a locally connected continuum, effect a partitioning of the continuum into cyclic elements so constituted that, when viewed as units of a superset, the structure assumes the simple form of a dendrite —that is, a continuum containing no closed circuit or curve. Whole classes of structure problems immediately become solvable simply by finding answers to the two (frequently easy) questions: (1) Does each cyclic element of the continuum have the required property? (2) Does every dendrite have the property? Also additivity theorems on cyclic elements established by Whyburn and others brought within range of easy answers many basic questions and calculations concerned with connectivity numbers of graphs and higher-dimensional sets, areas of surfaces, independent circuits on a network, imbedding and classifications of graphs, and the like. In many cases it is only necessary to determine the numbers in question for the individual cyclic elements and then add these together.

Attracted by the dynamic phase of topology, Whyburn studied structure invariance and evolution when a set undergoes a light open mapping, that is, a mapping in which open sets map into open sets and sets of constancy are totally disconnected. Whyburn proved that a 2-dimension manifold can only map onto a 2-dimension manifold, though possibly a different one, when it undergoes such a mapping. Further, he fully established the fact that such a mapping on a 2-manifold must behave locally exactly like a power mapping on the unit disk, a result formulated but not satisfactorily proven by S. Stoïlow. He discovered and established the simple numerical relation $kC_2 - C_1 = kr - n$ connecting the degree k of the mapping, the Euler characteristics C_1 and C_2 of the original and image manifolds, and the number n and r of singular points of the mapping on these.

Interest in lightness and openness as the basic topological properties of mappings generated by analytic functions of a complex variable led Whyburn to seek to establish these and other topological and analytical properties of such functions directly by topological methods. Existence, but not continuity, of the first derivative of such a function is assumed. Success in this direction came about largely through the use of the circulation or topological index and lent strong support to the hope of solving by this means the classical Cauchy-Goursat problem of obtaining the infinite differentiability of a function of a complex variable by topological and differential calculus methods. This goal has now been fully attained through the work of Whyburn and his students and associates, and results may be found in the revised edition of the book *Topological Analysis*, listed below. The key step in the solution is his theorem giving the following form of the Maximum Principle: Let the function $w = f(z)$ be continuous on a rectangle C plus its interior R and differentiable on all save a finite number of points of R. Then the image of $R + C$ consists of the image $f(C)$ of C together with certain whole bounded components of the complement of $f(C)$ in the w-plane.

Whyburn studied at the University of Texas, majoring in chemistry for his B.A. (1925) and M.A. (1926), and in mathematics for the Ph.D. (1927). A Guggenheim Fellowship supported his research at the University of Vienna in 1929–30. He taught at the University of Texas and at Johns Hopkins University until 1934, when he became professor of mathematics and chairman of the department at the University of Virginia. He was elected to the National Academy of Sciences in 1951.

Whyburn wrote *Analytic Topology* (1942; 4th ed. 1964), *Topological Analysis* (1958; 2d ed. 1964), and approximately 130 research articles in mathematics.

For background information *see* TOPOLOGY in the McGraw-Hill Encyclopedia of Science and Technology.   □

★ **WIENER, Alexander Solomon**

American physician, immunohematologist
Born Mar. 16, 1907, Brooklyn, N.Y., U.S.A.

INVESTIGATING INDIVIDUAL differences in human blood, Wiener (with Karl Landsteiner) tested the sera of rabbits immunized with rhesus monkey blood cells and found that such sera clumped the red cells of approximately 85% of Caucasians (Rh positive) but did not clump red cells of the remainder (Rh negative). Sensitization of Rh-negative persons to Rh-positive blood was shown by Wiener to be the chief cause of hitherto puzzling intragroup hemolytic transfusion reactions. Moreover, sensitization of Rh-negative expectant mothers was shown by Philip Levine to be the chief cause of erythroblastosis fetalis. For his role in the discovery of the Rh factor, Wiener received the American Public Health Association's Lasker Award in 1947 and the Passano Foundation Award in 1951.

In 1937, with Karl Landsteiner, Wiener had studied the evolution of the agglutinogen M in apes and monkeys. He had shown that different anti-M sera differed in specificity, judging from their reactions with nonhuman primate red cells, and that more than five distinct M blood factors could be distinguished in this way. Moreover, by immunizing rabbits with red cells of rhesus monkeys, he had produced reagents with M-like specificity. Further study of these rhesus antisera led to the discovery of the Rh factor of human blood.

Since rabbit immune sera for rhesus red cells had M specificity, and since it had previously been shown (by F. Schiff and L. Adelsberger) that immune sera for sheep red cells had A specificity, Landsteiner and Wiener reasoned that further study of antisera for nonhuman primate blood might disclose "new" blood groups in man. Indeed antirhesus sera did detect a blood factor, Rh, different from any previously described. In his study of sera from Rh-negative patients who had had hemolytic transfusion reactions, as well as sera from Rh-negative mothers of erythroblastotic babies, Wiener found, using the then available technique, that the expected Rh antibodies were often not demonstrable in the patients' sera. He then reasoned that there must be at least two major forms of Rh antibodies (and other antibodies as well), one demonstrable with the classic saline agglutination method (termed by Wiener "bivalent" antibodies), and the other capable of coating red cells but not clumping them in saline media (called "univalent" or "blocking" antibodies by Wiener). In 1944, he developed his blocking test for the hitherto elusive univalent antibodies, and in 1945, following work by L. K. Diamond, he developed his conglutination test. Other sensitive techniques were proposed by other workers for detecting the same antibodies, notably the antiglobulin test (by R. R. A. Coombs et al.) and the proteolytic enzyme test (by M. M. Pickles et al.).

Wiener reasoned that Rh antibodies in particular, and all antibodies in general, defined serological specificities that are extrinsic attributes of antigenic substances. Moreover, he pointed out that there is not a one-to-one correspondence between antigens and antibodies, and that each antigenic substance is characterized not by one but by multiple serological specificities, theoretically unlimited in number. Wiener emphasized that the main limitations to the number of serological specificities (blood factors) characterizing the Rh agglutinogen were the ingenuity and enterprise of the scientist in searching for and producing new antisera. Thus, applying the newer techniques for blood typing, Wiener (with E. B. Gordon) soon described two additional blood factors, rh' (70% in whites) and rh" (30% in whites), related to the original rhesus factor or Rh_0 (85% in whites). Eight types of blood were defined by these three Rh factors, which Wiener showed were inherited by multiple allelic genes.

Wiener's ideas were confirmed by the discovery of additional blood factors related to the rhesus factor of Landsteiner and Wiener, as well as by the discoveries regarding other blood group systems in man and observations on blood groups in nonhuman primates and lower animals. In the case of the Rh system of man (now known as the Rh-Hr blood types), Wiener and other workers established the existence of as many as 25 different blood factors (serological specificities), defining a vast number of different Rh-Hr blood types. These findings have proved to be important, not only in clinical medicine for the prevention of hemolytic transfusion reactions and in the diagnosis of erythroblastosis fetalis (for which Wiener devised a treatment by exchange transfusion in 1944), but also in forensic medicine (in cases of disputed parentage), physical anthropology, and animal husbandry.

An attorney's son, Wiener majored in biology at Cornell University, where he received his A.B. in 1926. He studied medicine at L.I.C.H. Medical School (later called SUNY College of Medicine) in Brooklyn, New York, receiving his M.D. in 1930. He made a hobby of mathematics, which he later applied in his genetic studies on the blood groups of man and nonhuman primates. In 1932 he began to practice medicine in Brooklyn, specializing in immunohematology. In 1936 he was appointed attending immunohematologist at the Jewish Hospital of Brooklyn, where his clinical studies were done. In 1938 he became also serologist to the Office of the Chief Medical Examiner of New York City, in whose laboratories his blood group investigations were done. He joined the department of forensic medicine of the New York University Medical School in 1945, becoming associate professor in 1958.

Wiener published more than 500 articles on blood grouping and blood transfusion, and the books *Blood Groups and Transfusion* (3d ed. 1943), *Rh-Hr Blood Types* (1954), *Heredity of the Blood Groups* (1958), *Advances in Blood Grouping* (1961), and *Rh-Hr Syllabus* (2d ed. 1963).

For background information *see* SEROLOGY in the McGraw-Hill Encyclopedia of Science and Technology.   □

WIENER, Norbert
American mathematician
Born Nov. 26, 1894, Columbia, Mo., U.S.A.
Died Mar. 18, 1964, Stockholm, Sweden

WIENER WAS a pioneer in the development of mathematical methods for the so-called "semiprecise" sciences. His work culminated in an imaginative and highly fruitful development of the science of communication and control in both mechanical devices and living organisms. This science, which Wiener called "cybernetics" after the Greek word for "helmsman," has had a profound effect on modern science and technology. It provided the theoretical background for the move to automation that has so greatly changed the aspect of the modern world. Toward the end of his life, Wiener became increasingly interested in the cybernetic aspects of living organisms and especially in the functioning of the human brain. He wrote extensively on the biological, sociological, and philosophical aspects of his work.

Wiener's great discoveries were forecast almost from the start by the mathematical topics that aroused his greatest interest. He made a study at an early age of the Lebesgue integral, which directed the methods of calculus toward more general functions than those representable by a continuous graph. Such functions, in which the domain of the independent variable may consist of much more complex sets of points than simple intervals, are of great importance in modern physical studies of discontinuous phenomena. Examples occur in wave mechanics and also in phenomena in which knowledge is of a probabilistic or statistical nature.

In 1920 Wiener formulated a mathematical

theory of Brownian movement, a phenomenon in which the individually random action of molecules in a liquid impart jagged motions to small, suspended particles. Later he turned to the theory of harmonic analysis and, by 1925, had made a number of far-reaching discoveries about the flow of information along a wave. These were accompanied by parallel discoveries in vector and differential spaces and by his placing on a sound mathematical basis the operational calculus of Oliver Heaviside.

Wiener's methods were founded on the use of stochastic—that is, probabilistic and statistical—methods in the analysis of continuous data. Classical Newtonian physics presupposes a set of precise data leading to precise conclusions; for example, the motions of the solar system are used to make accurate predictions of eclipses. An error in the final prediction would usually lead to a reexamination of the analysis leading to it, along with possible corrections and additions. For instance, errors in the predictions of the eclipses of Jupiter's moons led Olaus Roemer to investigate and ultimately determine the speed of light. Newtonian methods are not suited to data that incorporate a degree of randomness. Wiener's greatest discoveries were of methods characterized by a "built-in" assumption of variability of conditions and by continual feedback of results in the pursuit of further analysis. An example of a type of problem that yields to such methods can be found in Wiener's work for the U.S. Air Force during World War II. He aided in the design of antiaircraft fire-control apparatus that took into account evasive action on the part of a human pilot, the most probable motion of the airplane after any given moment, and continual amendment by feeding back the observed motion of the target between firings.

In 1932 Wiener collaborated with the Mexican physiologist A. Rosenblueth in research on mathematical physiology. This played a great part in his developing ideas on cybernetics, and he returned to physiology from time to time throughout his life. Wiener felt strongly that significant mathematical discoveries were more likely to occur in the investigation of the physical and natural sciences than in the purely abstract play of mathematical ideas.

During World War II Wiener aided the military effort not only in the design of apparatus but also by exploring methods of coding and decoding messages. It was at this time that his interest was aroused in automatic computing, and he was one of the early pioneers in this field, along with John von Neumann, Vannevar Bush, J. W. Mauchly, C. E. Shannon, and others. This interest led to a deeper investigation of feedback theory and from it to the statistical analysis of the flow of communication.

His book *Cybernetics* (1948; rev. ed. 1961) gave an extensive mathematical analysis of the new science, and also went on to predict its effect on human affairs. It was here that the educated public first met a serious and quantitative treatment of such concepts as the automatic factory, the robot worker, the assembly line controlled by a digital computer, and other concepts that have since become commonplace in our world. The book projected Wiener into a fame that extended far beyond that of the mathematical and scientific world.

In addition to his scientific genius Wiener had a deep sense of involvement in human affairs. During the remainder of his life he continued to do fruitful scientific research, and he mingled with it efforts to acquaint industrial, labor, and government leaders with the implications of cybernetics for production, employment, and laws. He wrote many articles and several books dealing with the social and religious aspects of his new science.

Wiener's father was professor of Slavic languages at Harvard University. Wiener received his B.A. at Tufts University at 14 and his Ph.D. in philosophy at Harvard at 18, then studied at Cambridge and Göttingen. He taught at Harvard and the University of Maine before joining the faculty of the Massachusetts Institute of Technology in 1919. He retired in 1960. In 1963 he was awarded the National Medal of Science.

Besides his technical books, Wiener wrote *The Human Use of Human Beings* (1950) and the autobiographical *Ex-Prodigy* (1953) and *I Am a Mathematician* (1956).

For background information *see* CYBERNETICS in the McGraw-Hill Encyclopedia of Science and Technology. ☐

★ WIGGLESWORTH, Sir Vincent (Brian)
English biologist
Born Apr. 17, 1899, Kirkham, Lancashire, England

O^{N HIS} appointment at the London School of Hygiene and Tropical Medicine in 1926, Patrick Buxton, believing that the development of applied entomology was being impeded by lack of knowledge of the physiology of insects, invited Wigglesworth to try to build up the science of insect physiology. That became Wigglesworth's life work; for his contributions to this field, he was awarded the Royal Society of London's Royal Medal in 1955.

Wigglesworth used many kinds of insects, but his name is associated particularly with the bloodsucking bug *Rhodnius prolixus*, which had been brought from South America by E. Brumpt

and which proved a splendid experimental animal.

The section of his work that became most widely known concerns the nature of insect metamorphosis. He noted, as S. Kopeč had done in 1917, that the brain was necessary for the secretion of a hormone that caused growth and molting (decapitated insects lived but did not molt). By implanting different parts of the brain into headless *Rhodnius*, Wigglesworth showed that the hormone was produced only in the region containing the neurosecretory cells. This was the first experimental demonstration of a function for the neurosecretory cells of any animal.

Wigglesworth also noted that decapitation of a young insect at the time when molting was just beginning would cause it to undergo a precocious metamorphosis: The head was clearly the source of a hormone that prevented the development of adult characters until the larva was fully grown. Further experiments, such as joining insects together in "parabiosis" and implantation of different organs, proved that this hormone was secreted by the endocrine gland known as the corpus allatum.

By means of this hormone, termed the "juvenile hormone," insects could be caused to continue growing in size but to retain their larval form. Adult insects exposed to the molting hormone molted again; and if exposed also to the juvenile hormone some, at least, of their organs showed a partial return to larval characters. On the basis of these results, Wigglesworth built up a theory of metamorphosis, according to which those components of the gene system that are needed for the production of larval characters are maintained in action by the juvenile hormone; metamorphosis is closely analogous in this respect with cellular differentiation and with environmentally determined polymorphism among the individuals of a species. The juvenile hormone was also found to be necessary for normal reproduction in many insects.

This work on insect growth was just one line among researches that ranged widely over most of the systems of the insect body: the properties of insect enzymes; the nature and formation of the peritrophic membrane in the digestive tract; the mechanisms of hatching from the egg; the mode of action of adhesive organs in walking; the physiology of the insect cuticle and the role of waxes in preventing water loss; the physiology of the Malpighian tubules, rectal glands, and anal papillae in excretion and osmotic regulation; the control of the spiracles in respiration; the properties of the tracheal endings or tracheoles; the respiration of insect eggs; the histology and the nutrition of the central nervous system; the origin of sensory neurones; the role of symbiotic microorganisms as a source of vitamins in insects that subsist only on blood; insect sense organs and their use in orientation; the function of insect blood cells, oenocytes, pericardial cells, and fat body; the storage of reserves; the healing of wounds and the differentiation of pattern; the action of hormones at the cellular level, and much else.

Some of this work was in the main stream of research in insect physiology; much, although original at the time it was done, has been extensively developed by others, with the result that most is now a part of the texture of insect physiology. This diversity of interests and the wide reading and varied observation that it entailed, put Wigglesworth in an exceptionally favorable position for integrating in his books both the whole subject of insect physiology and the more specialized topic of insect growth.

The son of a medical doctor in general practice, Wigglesworth was an officer in the Royal Field Artillery in 1917–18 and served in France. He then graduated in physiology and biochemistry in the University of Cambridge and did two years' research under Gowland Hopkins (some of it in collaboration with J. B. S. Haldane) before qualifying as M.D. at St. Thomas's Hospital, London. From 1926 to 1945 he taught medical entomology in the London School of Hygiene and Tropical Medicine, becoming director of the Agricultural Research Council Unit of Insect Physiology in 1943. In 1945 he returned to Cambridge as head of the subdepartment of entomology and director of the A.R.C. Unit. He became Quick Professor of Biology in 1952. He was knighted in 1964.

Wigglesworth wrote *Insect Physiology* (1934; 6th ed. 1966), *The Principles of Insect Physiology* (1939; 6th ed. 1965), *Physiology of Insect Metamorphosis* (1954), *The Control of Growth and Form* (1959), and *The Life of Insects* (1964).

For background information *see* INSECT PHYSIOLOGY; INSECTA in the McGraw-Hill Encyclopedia of Science and Technology.   □

☆ **WIGNER, Eugene Paul**
American mathematical physicist
Born Nov. 17, 1902, Budapest, Hungary

WIGNER HAS been called one of the great physicists of the 20th century. He contributed to many fields of physics, and in each instance his influence was profound. In 1963 he was awarded the Nobel Prize in physics, and the extent of his work was indicated by the purposely vague Nobel citation "for systematically improving and extending the methods of quantum mechanics and applying them widely." He shared the award with M. G. Mayer and J. H. D. Jensen.

Wigner's early work was concerned with symmetry principles and particularly with the explanation of the regularities found in atomic and molecular spectra as consequences of these principles. His book on group theory, which he wrote as a result of research on this question, has taught many generations of physicists.

The study of nuclear binding energies in the 1930s revealed two separate regularities. One is that nuclei with even numbers of protons and neutrons are generally more strongly bound than those with odd numbers of neutrons or protons or both. This fact was called the short periodicity of binding energies. In addition, there are longer periods of binding energies similar to the periodic system of chemical properties of the elements. These longer periods show particularly strong binding when the number of neutrons or protons, or both, is 2, 8, 20, 28, 40, 50, 82, or 126.

The long periods were attributed to a shell structure of the nucleus similar to the electron shells that surround the nucleus, and it was Wigner who, with Feenberg, wrote one of the first papers on the spectroscopic levels to be expected from this model. At the time only nuclei up to O^{16} could be successfully discussed

on the basis of this model, but even this represented a significant extension of the theory.

In a major work on the short periodicity, the even-odd alternation, Wigner applied mathematical group theory to the energy levels of nuclei up to atomic weight about 50 and was able to account amazingly well for the observed regularities. His work included a quantitative determination of binding energies and excited states; among other things, he predicted the existence of S^{36}, which was subsequently found. His treatment in these papers of the symmetry energy of nuclei is still unsurpassed.

The theory of beta decay provided an application for the work on the symmetry of nuclear wave functions. Wigner pointed out that even if a beta transition is possible the lifetime of the nucleus should depend upon whether the wave functions of the parent and daughter nuclei have the same or different symmetries. This distinction between favored and unfavored transitions has proved to be very useful in work on beta-decaying nuclei.

In 1933, the year after the discovery of the neutron, Wigner wrote a fundamental paper in which he demonstrated that the forces between protons and neutrons must be of very short range in order to explain the large binding energy of the alpha particle as compared with the relatively small binding energy of the deuteron. Experiments had also shown that slow neutrons suffered surprisingly large deflections when they passed close to a proton. Since the neutron has no charge, there was no explanation for this behavior until Wigner postulated the existence of an energy state of the deuteron different from the ground state that had been observed. He did not find this idea worth publishing at the time, but it has been the basis of countless papers since.

Many of Wigner's researches were concerned with the theory of relativistic wave equations and in particular their group theoretic properties. He was one of the first to recognize the role of symmetry principles in predicting invariants of physical processes and was the formulator of many of these principles. Out of this came the first rigorous treatment of parity conservation and time reversal, which provided a basis for increased understanding of these phenomena and a basis for experimental researches for many years.

In 1938 he turned to the problem of obtaining energy from nuclear fission. He developed many of the theoretical techniques of reactor calculations, some of which formed the basis for the first controlled chain reaction produced by Enrico Fermi. In addition to being a theoretician, Wigner was in command of a vast knowledge of technical details of reactor design and mechanical engineering.

Wigner received his early schooling in Hungary, attending the same high school as John von Neumann. He received his Ph.D. in chemical engineering from the Technische Hochschule in Berlin in 1925. He was an assistant in the physics department there from 1926 to 1927 and held a similar position at Göttingen from 1927 to 1928. In 1928 he returned to the Technische Hochschule as privatdocent. In 1930 he went to the United States as lecturer in mathematical physics at Princeton, where he became part-time professor from 1931 to 1937 and professor of mathematical physics in 1938. During World War II he worked at the Metallurgical Laboratory at the University of Chicago and served as director of research and development at the Clinton Laboratories at Oak Ridge from 1946 to 1947. He received the U.S. Atomic Energy Commission's Enrico Fermi Prize in 1958 and the Atoms for Peace Award in 1960. He was elected to the National Academy of Sciences in 1945.

For background information *see* NUCLEAR STRUCTURE; QUANTUM MECHANICS in the McGraw-Hill Encyclopedia of Science and Technology.   □

★ WILDER, Raymond Louis
American mathematician
Born Nov. 3, 1896, Palmer, Mass., U.S.A.

THE CLASSICAL Jordan curve theorem states: "If, in the euclidean plane, J is a topological image of a circle, then the complement of J is exactly two disjoint connected sets whose common boundary is J."

That this theorem, at first considered intuitively obvious, required proof was recognized as early as 1865, but the first proof was attempted by C. Jordan in 1887. Since then, the record of proofs offered for this theorem constitutes one of the longest bibliographies of any theorem in mathematical history. The first to give special

attention to the theorem after Jordan was A. Schoenflies, whose first proof was published in 1896. Of special interest, however, is the fact that Schoenflies posed the problem of finding a converse for the theorem; that is, of finding conditions on the complement of a point set J in the plane that would ensure that J be the topological image of a circle (that is, a simple closed curve).

Since not every common boundary of two domains in the plane is a simple closed curve, the direct converse does not hold. Schoenflies found, however, that the conclusion of the theorem could be strengthened by the addition of the words "and J is arcwise accessible from each of these sets"; and in this form, the converse does hold. One then has: "A necessary and sufficient condition that a bounded subset J of the euclidean plane should be a simple closed curve is that J be a common boundary of two disjoint domains from each of which J is arcwise accessible."

The analog of the Jordan curve theorem for higher dimensions, which concerns the topological image of the $(n-1)$-sphere in n-dimensional euclidean space E^n, or, more generally, the closed $(n-1)$-manifold in E^n, was given by L. E. J. Brouwer in 1912. Brouwer showed that the arcwise accessibility also held in the higher-dimensional case, but noted that this was insufficient for a converse theorem even in E^3. Consequently the problem was posed: Find conditions that the closed $(n-1)$-manifold satisfies in E^n, and that are sufficient to give a converse.

In 1928, by combining the (at that time separated) set-theoretic and algebraic aspects of topology, Wilder solved this problem for the 2-sphere in E^3 as follows: "A necessary and sufficient condition that a bounded subset of E^3 be the topological image of a 2-sphere is that it be the common boundary of two uniformly locally connected domains whose 1-dimensional homology is trivial." At the same time he showed that if M is a closed $(n-1)$-manifold in E^n, then the domains complementary to M are r-ulc (that is, uniformly locally connected in dimension r) for all dimensions r.

In 1932, Wilder devoted the annual Symposium Lecture of the Chicago section of the American Mathematical Society to an exposition of the state of both set-theoretic and algebraic topology, arguing for unification of the two fields. This lecture (published in the bulletin of the Society that same year) evidently exerted considerable influence on the direction subsequently taken by topology. The next year, 1933, in a paper on the boundaries of domains in n-space, E^n, Wilder extended the 1928 theorem quoted above to include the general closed 2-manifold in E^3; the only change needed is to replace the triviality of the 1-dimensional homology by the finiteness of the homology dimension. More precisely, it is sufficient that the 1-dimensional connectivity number of one of the (uniformly locally connected) complementary domains be a finite number k; in which case the configuration forming the common boundary will be a closed 2-manifold of genus k.

In 1934, he extended these findings to the n-dimensional case, finding it necessary, however, to substitute for the configuration forming the boundaries a new concept, that of n-dimensional generalized closed manifold (abbreviated n-gcm). For $n = 2$, the n-gcm coincides with the classical manifolds, but not for $n > 2$. Later, he used the n-gcm itself as imbedding space instead of euclidean space, obtaining results that were incorporated in his 1942 Colloquium Lectures before the American Mathematical Society and published in *Topology of Manifolds* (1949). This book in addition treated many more general problems, such as characterizing various other types of configurations in n-space—general "positional" problems.

In 1952, Wilder published *Introduction to the Foundations of Mathematics*, based on a course in modern mathematical concepts and methods that he had devised as a broadening influence for mathematics majors. This led to an interest in the manner in which mathematical concepts evolve, and resulted in a number of papers treating mathematics as a part of man's culture and especially its interplay with other aspects of culture.

A printer's son, Wilder majored in mathematics at Brown University, where he enrolled in 1914. After spending 1917–18 in the Navy during World War I, he returned to Brown and received the Ph.B. and M.S. in 1920 and 1921, respectively. He received the Ph.D. in 1923 from the University of Texas, where he had gone to work in actuarial mathematics but became converted to research by the famous teacher, R. L. Moore. He taught at Brown (1920–21), Texas (1921–24), Ohio State (1924–26), and after 1926 at the University of Michigan. He was elected to the National Academy of Sciences in 1963.

For background information *see* TOPOLOGY in the McGraw-Hill Encyclopedia of Science and Technology. ☐

☆ WILKINS, Maurice Hugh Frederick

English biophysicist
Born Dec. 15, 1916, Pongaroa, New Zealand

FOR HIS x-ray diffraction studies that contributed so much to the structure determination of deoxyribonucleic acid (DNA), M. H. F. Wilkins shared with J. D. Watson and F. H. C. Crick the 1962 Nobel Prize in physiology or

medicine. It can be said that Wilkins's studies provided the initial impetus for the structure determination, served as a guide to the development of the structure, and, finally, provided proof that the structure proposed by Watson and Crick was essentially correct.

In 1946 scientists knew that nucleic acids were important in protein synthesis, but data published in 1944 that strongly suggested that DNA actually carried the genetic code was still ignored. At the time, Wilkins was interested in DNA because it was a macromolecule that could be isolated and subjected to ultraviolet dichroism studies. A chance observation led to his x-ray diffraction studies of DNA. While examining DNA gels prepared for his dichroism work, Wilkins observed, through a microscope, that each time he touched the gel with a glass rod and then removed the rod a thin fiber of DNA was drawn out. The uniformity of the fibers suggested that the molecules in them might be regularly arranged and that they might be suitable for analysis by x-ray diffraction. This powerful tool, which involves analyzing diffraction patterns obtained on exposing crystalline or near crystalline materials to x-rays, had been successfully employed by J. D. Bernal in the structural analysis of proteins. The problems posed by the proteins were similar to those faced by Wilkins with DNA.

The initial diffraction patterns obtained with makeshift equipment were very encouraging. Before long, much sharper diffraction photographs of DNA were obtained and definite statements could be made concerning its structure. The sharpness of the diffraction patterns showed the DNA molecules to be highly regular; moreover, there were clear indications that they were heli-

cal. Through further analysis of the diffraction photographs, Wilkins found the diameter of the helix to be approximately 20 A and the repeat distance, the length of one turn of the helix, approximately 34 A. It was known that DNA was a long polymer of alternating phosphate and sugar groups with a nitrogenous base attached as a side chain to each of the sugar units. Determination of the helix diameter and the repeat distance, along with some chemical evidence, permitted the conclusion that the phosphate groups were on the outside of the structural unit. This was opposite to the conclusion drawn by L. C. Pauling and R. B. Corey only 2 years before. At this stage in the work the contributions of Wilkins's colleague, Rosalind Franklin, were particularly important.

Density measurements indicated that there were two or three coaxial molecules in the helix. Wilkins and his coworkers thought there were two coaxial molecules and later proved that this was the case. Finally, the x-ray patterns suggested that the nitrogenous bases were stacked like a pile of pennies in the central regions of the helical system. It remained for Wilkins to demonstrate that the structure of DNA was not merely an artifact resulting from isolation. X-ray diffraction photographs taken of intact biological systems bore a close resemblance to those obtained from purified DNA, thus proving that DNA was the same highly structured molecule before and after isolation.

While Wilkins was obtaining his x-ray data, Watson and Crick were building molecular models based on their own calculations and conclusions. The structure suggested by the x-ray work coincided remarkably with the model constructed by Watson and Crick. After the initial publications by the two groups in 1953, Wilkins continued his x-ray studies to demonstrate the unique character of the Watson-Crick model, that is, to show that no alternate model would give the same diffraction patterns. This work also permitted Wilkins to readjust and refine the original model.

The son of a doctor, Wilkins was taken to England at the age of 6. He studied physics at St. John's College, Cambridge, taking his degree in 1938. He received a Ph.D. in physics in 1940 from Birmingham University, where with J. T. Randall he developed, in terms of electron traps, the theory of phosphoresence and thermoluminescence. During World War II he worked on the improvement of cathode-ray tube screens for radar, then on mass spectrograph separation of uranium isotopes for use in the atomic bomb. In 1945 he took a position with a biophysics project at St. Andrew's University, Scotland. The project was under the direction of J. T. Randall. Wilkins and Randall moved to King's College, London, in 1946. Wilkins became a member of the staff of the Medical Research Council Biophysics Research Unit, serving as assistant director after 1950 and deputy director after 1955. He first investigated the genetic effects of ultrasonics, but after a few years he turned to microscopic

and spectrophotometric studies of nucleic acids and tobacco mosaic virus. He then began his x-ray diffraction studies of DNA. In recent years he applied x-ray techniques to the structure determination of RNA. Because transfer RNA is a much smaller molecule than DNA, there is a distinct possibility that the base sequence, the genetic code, may be determined directly by x-ray diffraction analysis.

For background information *see* NUCLEIC ACID; X-RAY DIFFRACTION in the McGraw-Hill Encyclopedia of Science and Technology.   □

★ **WILLARD, John Ela**
American chemist
Born Oct. 31, 1908, Oak Park, Ill., U.S.A.

WILLARD AND his coworkers at the University of Wisconsin contributed to an understanding of the mechanisms of chemical reactions of highly energetic atoms such as are produced by neutron capture and other nuclear processes. In related studies they investigated reactions initiated by gamma rays and light. Radioactive tracers were used extensively in the investigations.

In 1934 L. Szilard and T. A. Chalmers predicted that if compounds such as ethyl iodide (C_2H_5I) were irradiated with neutrons, the iodine atoms that captured neutrons would acquire enough energy to break the chemical bond holding the iodine to the carbon. They proved in the laboratory that this actually occurs. Iodine atoms of mass 127 (I^{127}), which occur in nature, can capture neutrons to form I^{128}, which is radioactive and decays with a 25-minute half-life. The neutron-capture process, which releases energy in the form of a gamma ray, is represented by the notation I^{127} (n,γ) I^{128} (25 min). It is typical of similar processes that occur in many elements. The energy of recoil from the emitted gamma ray is many times greater than chemical-bond energies. Many of the atoms also acquire a high positive charge as a result of their utilization of some of the nuclear energy to eject orbital electrons. Because of their high recoil energy and charge, such atoms are often called "hot atoms," and a study of their reactions is referred to as "hot-atom chemistry."

The earliest theory of the mechanism of the reaction of such atoms was the "billiard ball theory" suggested by W. F. Libby. It assumed that, in order to form new molecules, the recoil atoms must hit other atoms of the same mass in head-on collisions, knocking them on and remaining in their places. New experimental evidence brought this theory into question. This included the "scavenger effect" of low concentrations of added iodine discovered by Willard and his coworkers, and their observations that I^{128} activated by the I^{127} (n,γ) I^{128} process in gaseous methane (CH_4) can replace H to form CH_3I in a large fraction (50%) of the events; chlorine atoms activated by the Cl^{37} $(n,\gamma)Cl^{38}$ process in gaseous propyl chloride (C_3H_7Cl) can replace any atom or group in the molecule to form a multiplicity (over 15) of different compounds containing Cl^{38}; Br^{80} activated by the Br^{80m} (4.4 hr) $\longrightarrow$ Br^{80} (18 min) isomeric transition nuclear process, which produces high positive charge but relatively little recoil energy, gives nearly the same yields of products as the Br^{79} (n,γ) Br^{80} process. These and other findings demonstrated that the hot atoms reenter combination in part by combining with free radicals formed as a result of the energy released by the nuclear process and in part by a unique type of displacement reaction. Willard proposed mechanisms for these chemical effects of nuclear transformation in his "random fragmentation" and "autoradiation" hypotheses. A technique of great value in these studies, pioneered in his laboratories, was the use of gas chromatography in the analysis of trace amounts of radioactive materials.

In solid-state studies, Willard's group investigated the interaction between defects produced in organic crystals by gamma rays and "trapped" metastable recoil atoms formed by the neutron capture process, demonstrating long-range interactions sensitive to time and temperature of annealing. Related studies showed that the yields and chemical reactions of trapped free radicals produced by the gamma irradiation of organic iodides are dramatically different for the glassy state than for the crystalline state at the same temperature. The radicals are detected by the electron spin resonance technique.

By means of the "flash photolysis" technique, the group measured the effectiveness of solvent "cages" in preventing molecular fragments from escaping from each other after the molecule had absorbed sufficient energy to break the chemical bond. In experiments designed to obtain hot atoms by other than nuclear means, hydrogen atoms of well-defined high energy were produced and studied by irradiating HBr with monochromatic ultraviolet light of energy greatly in excess of the energy of the hydrogen–bromine bond.

Willard attended high school in Beloit, Wis., did his freshman year of college work at Pomona College, his sophomore year at Carleton College, and his junior and senior years at Harvard College, where he received the S.B. degree in 1930. He then taught chemistry and physics for two years at Avon Old Farms School, Avon, Conn., before continuing work for the Ph.D., which he received from the University of Wisconsin in 1935. He taught at Haverford College from 1935 to 1937, when he returned to Wisconsin. From 1942 to 1946 he worked with the Manhattan Project at the University of Chicago and the Hanford Engineer Works, Hanford, Wash., on chemical processes for separating the new fissionable element plutonium. From 1958 to 1963 he served as dean of the Graduate School at the University of Wisconsin. In 1958 he received the American Chemical Society's Award for Nuclear Applications in Chemistry.

For background information *see* NEUTRON; RADIATION DENSITY in the McGraw-Hill Encyclopedia of Science and Technology. ☐

★ **WILLETT, Hurd Curtis**
American meteorologist
Born Jan. 1, 1903, Providence, R.I., U.S.A.

FOR HIS contributions to the better understanding of the physical basis of the atmospheric changes that are the primary concern of the weather forecaster, particularly for the longer-range forecast, Willett in 1951 received the Rossby Medal of the American Meterological Society.

In 1928 C. G. Rossby established at the Massachusetts Institute of Technology the first school of modern meteorology in the Western Hemisphere, the school with which Willett was associated almost from its inception. Among the more important contributions made by Rossby and his group during the next 20 years were the extensive incorporation of aerological data to complete the third dimension of the Norwegian polar front and air mass analysis procedures, and the introduction of vertical and lateral mixing, together with vorticity concepts, to the explanation of atmospheric and oceanic circulations and to the prediction of the ever-changing basic flow pattern of the upper atmosphere.

When it became apparent that not even the vertical extension of the Norwegian analytical concepts was extending the time range of reasonably accurate prediction of the clearly observed longer-range weather trends appreciably beyond the day or two previously achieved by more empirical techniques, Willett recognized the necessity of looking further for the basic controls of these extended weather developments. In agreement with the thinking of the MIT group, he hoped to find these controls primarily in the quasi-inertial hydrodynamics of the general or planetary circulation of the atmosphere. When this concept failed of statistical verification, he perforce turned his attention to possible significantly variable thermal sources of control. In this area primarily two possibilities suggested themselves: (1) the large-scale fluctuations of sea-surface temperature as important heat sources or sinks; and (2) the variable insolational energy incident in the upper atmosphere as a result of variable solar activity indicated by sunspot cycles and certain geophysical data.

Preliminary investigations by earlier investigators in these two areas had convinced Willett that variable solar activity was more probably the primary control factor. Accordingly he spent much of the two decades after 1945 attempting to establish the specific pattern of this control.

Part of this effort he directed toward the study of climatic fluctuations during historical and during geological time (glacial-interglacial epochs), comparing the past behavior of terrestrial climate with that during recent observational time in order to identify primary factors of climatic control. His analysis of contemporary climatic fluctuations implicated atmospheric ozone as a possible physical link in solar-climatic relationships, and accordingly he made this the target of further special investigation. Since the role played by sea-surface conditions in long-term anomalous fluctuations of the general circulation recently has been judged by several investigators, but not yet proved, to be the predominant factor of control, Willett extended his investigation to include an analysis of sea-surface conditions relative to atmospheric conditions during a selected period of years.

Except for brief periods of consultation, Willett's entire work was performed as a member of the meteorological group at the Massachusetts Institute of Technology. His long-range forecast studies were initiated in 1936, the study of solar activity and past climates about 1945, that of atmospheric ozone in 1961, and of atmosphere–sea surface interactions in 1962.

Willett's method was primarily inductive rather than deductive, starting with the observed facts or data and reasoning from synoptic and statistical analysis to hypothetical interpretation and explanation of observed relationships. Whether dealing with weather and climatic data, solar data, ozone data, or oceanographic data, he always proceeded from the observed broad-scale distribution and fluctuations of each of these elements singly to the statistical analysis and, whenever possible, the physical interpretation of any interrelationships discovered between their respective behavior patterns.

The results of Willett's studies can be stated only in broad generalizations that will require years of application and verification before their validity can be accepted as noncontroversial and their practical prognostic significance evaluated. These broad generalizations are essentially the following:

1. The internal mechanics or hydrodynamics of the general circulation are inadequate to explain subsequent developments even as little as 5 to 10 days in the future.

2. Climatic fluctuations both in recent observational time and in the more distant past are similar in pattern and apparently more definitely related to a number of cycles of variable solar activity than to any other obvious control factor.

3. The geographical pattern of this relationship is both zonally hemispheric and cellularly continent-ocean in orientation. Clearest relationships are observed in continental interiors in lower latitudes during the summer season.

4. Whereas the hemispheric zonally oriented relationships apparently reflect variations of effective output of solar energy, the continental-oceanic cellularly oriented relationships more probably reflect variations of atmospheric transparency to short- and long-wave radiation, possibly caused by variations of atmospheric ozone with solar activity.

5. Very preliminary results suggest that sea-surface changes are primarily a result of preceding, rather than an important feedback cause of subsequent, climatic fluctuations.

The son of a professor of economics at Carnegie Institute of Technology, Willett grew up in a farming community north of Pittsburgh, where he was known from his early boyhood as a weather forecaster and amateur meteorologist. He planned his education to become a meteorologist, taking his B.S. in math and science at Princeton University in 1924, and his Ph.D. in meteorology—under W. J. Humphreys of the U.S. Weather Bureau—at George Washington University in 1929. During his years of graduate study, he worked in the Forecast Division of the Weather Bureau and spent a year in Europe on a Daniel Guggenheim Foundation scholarship studying the Norwegian polar front theory and the organization of European airways forecasting. On his return from Europe he accepted in 1929 an appointment at the Massachusetts Institute of Technology, where he later became professor of meteorology. During World War II he worked as an expert consultant for the Air Force.

Willett wrote *Descriptive Meteorology* (1944; 2d ed., with Sanders, 1959).

For background information *see* WEATHER (FORECASTING AND PREDICTION) in the McGraw-Hill Encyclopedia of Science and Technology. □

★ **WILLIAMS, Robert R.**
American chemist
Born Feb. 16, 1886, Nellore, India
Died Oct. 2, 1965, Summit, N.J., U.S.A.

WILLIAMS'S PRINCIPAL scientific achievement was the isolation, the structural determination, and the synthesis of thiamine, or vitamin B_1, the antiberiberi vitamin. He began working on the subject of beriberi in the Philippines in 1910 and concluded the research on the synthesis of vitamin B_1 in 1936. Thus the study occupied the greater part of his active life.

Beriberi is an important disease that has been known to Western medicine for more than 200 years. About 100,000 deaths from the disease have been recorded in the literature of many countries of the Orient. In fact, it was prevalent throughout all rice-eating areas of the world and also in Labrador and Newfoundland, where it was due to white flour rather than to white rice.

It has been known in every continent, and especially on ships, where it was called ship's beriberi. Through the work of Williams and others, beriberi was the first disease to be recognized as being due to a deficiency in the diet. Williams's achievement was the identification of what was lacking. Now that this substance—vitamin B_1—is manufactured by the ton, the disease can be eradicated anywhere if people will undertake the necessary measures to combat it. The cost of combatting beriberi is very small.

The son of a Baptist missionary, Williams spent the first 10 years of his life in India. He received his B.S. in 1907 and his M.S. in 1908 at the University of Chicago. Immediately thereafter he went to the Philippines to work as a teacher and later in the Bureau of Science in Manila, where he became acquainted with beriberi. Much of his work on vitamin B_1 was done in his spare time because of the necessity to support himself and his family by other work. From 1919 to 1946 he was employed by the Bell System, for the last 20 years of this period as chemical director of the Bell Telephone Laboratories, where he worked on submarine insulation, textile insulation, and many other projects. During World War II he conducted the research program on the quality of synthetic rubber.

After he retired from Bell, Williams joined the Research Corporation and devoted his energies to programs of cereal enrichment throughout the world. He had already taken a leading part in the introduction of cereal enrichment in the United States, especially the enrichment of bread and flour, which became generally effective in 1942. In 1948, in preparation for an attack on the incidence of beriberi in Asian countries, he inaugurated, through Juan Salcedo, a study of beriberi in Bataan in the Philippines. This study led to the elimination of all beriberi from Bataan for a period of 7 months in 1951 by the addition of vitamin B_1 to the population's rice supply. However, the extension of this rice-enrichment project to all the Philippines has not yet come about. While associated with the Research Corporation, Williams founded the Williams Waterman Fund for the Combat of Dietary Diseases. Consisting of royalties from the manufacture of thiamine, this fund has distributed several hundred thousand dollars for research in nutrition throughout the world. Williams received eight honorary degrees and numerous scientific awards, including the Willard Gibbs Medal of the American Chemical Society in 1938 and the William Proctor Prize of the Scientific Research Society of America in 1955. He was elected to the National Academy of Sciences in 1945.

For background information *see* BERIBERI; VITAMIN in the McGraw-Hill Encyclopedia of Science and Technology. □

WILSON, Morley Evans
Canadian geologist
Born Feb. 8, 1882, Bright, Ont., Canada

AFTER FIVE years of painstaking field work in Quebec, Wilson, a geologist employed by the Geological Survey of Canada, emerged with a report in the late 1930s that detailed the geologic history of some of the oldest rocks on Earth—the Archean. Leading geologists had claimed that the complex history of these rocks, dating back 2×10^9 years, would never be unraveled.

Much of Canada is covered by ancient rocks known to geologists as Precambrian. Among these, the Archean are the oldest. They represent the "stumps" or "roots" of incredibly old mountains that long ago were worn away by the relentless forces of erosion. From the time of their formation, these rocks have been repeatedly folded, faulted, or otherwise altered. The result of this deformation has been the creation of amazingly complex rocks that had long baffled geologists.

In 1932 Wilson, mindful that many of the problems in geology require meticulous care and attention to detail, began field investigations in a 45-square-mile area north of Noranda, Quebec. The rocks there consisted of an uninterrupted succession of stratified lavas and other volcanics aggregating 25,000 feet in thickness. Wilson's basic problem was to determine the structural attitude of these rocks and, by so doing, to clarify the sequence of events to which the rocks had been subject.

Geologists who had examined these volcanic beds knew that many of the beds had been turned upside down, or inverted, during the process of folding. It was clear that the structural history could not be reconstructed unless some method were found to differentiate the topside of a lava flow from the base.

In the course of his investigations Wilson discovered that, despite the antiquity of the lavas, several features within individual lava flows were still preserved. Furthermore, these features provided the answer as to whether the lava flow was undisturbed or overturned. For instance, the tops of lava flows often contained a thin layer of breccia (broken, angular fragments). The breccia did not occur at the base. Also, peculiar pillowlike or bunlike masses were frequently encountered in flows. The arched or rounded part of the "pillows" pointed to the top of the flow. Although the exact origin of these pillow lavas is not completely understood, it seems that they result from submarine eruptions.

Wilson utilized these and other "top indicators" to systematically reconstruct the original attitude of thousands of feet of volcanic beds. He was able to conclude that the lavas north of Noranda had been folded into four major anticlines (upfolds) with intervening synclines (downfolds), and later were displaced by numerous east and northeast trending faults.

As a result of Wilson's work, the rich gold and copper ores of the district, whose occurrence is largely controlled by these structures, could be sought with greater understanding and success. Also, many field geologists working in other parts of Canada were able to apply Wilson's techniques with good results.

Wilson received his bachelor's degree from the University of Toronto in 1907 and then did graduate work at the universities of Wisconsin and Chicago before taking his Ph.D. at Yale in 1912. From 1907 to 1947 he was connected with the Geological Survey of Canada. In 1945 Wilson received the Willet G. Miller Medal of the Royal Society of Canada and in 1950 the Penrose Medal of the Geological Society of America.

For background information *see* GEOLOGY; PETROLOGY in the McGraw-Hill Encyclopedia of Science and Technology. □

★ WOODRING, Wendell Phillips
American geologist and paleontologist
Born June 13, 1891, Reading, Pa., U.S.A.

WOODRING'S WORK centered on Cenozoic molluscan faunas from the Caribbean region and California. Inasmuch as paleontologists have a better understanding of their fossils if they know the field relations of the fossil-bearing rocks they are dealing with, he also undertook geological mapping, chiefly in California.

His most widely used publication describes and analyzes a Miocene fauna of some 600 species found at Bowden, Jamaica. This fauna is a death assemblage representing diverse habitats: leaf litter on the forest floor, brackish-water

streams and mangrove swamps, beach vegetation, coastal sand flats, and inner and outer shelf to a depth greater than 200 meters, possibly as great as 500 meters.

In 1947 he undertook an extended study of the geology of the Canal Zone and adjoining parts of Panama. The emergence of the Panama land bridge, which began in late Miocene time and was completed in late Pliocene time, disrupted a Tertiary marine faunal province that embraced both western Atlantic and eastern Pacific waters.

The son of a clergyman, Woodring received his A.B. in 1910 at Albright College, a small liberal arts college of which his father was president. After teaching 2 years in high school, he majored in geology at the Johns Hopkins University, receiving his Ph.D. in 1916. With the exception of 3 years of teaching at the California Institute of Technology (1927–30), he was on the staff of the U.S. Geological Survey until his retirement in 1961. Thereafter he was a research associate of the Smithsonian Institution. In 1949 Woodring was awarded the Penrose Medal of the Geological Society of America. He was elected to the National Academy of Sciences in 1946.

For background information *see* PALEONTOLOGY in the McGraw-Hill Encyclopedia of Science and Technology. □

☆ WOODWARD, Robert Burns
American chemist
Born Apr. 10, 1917, Boston, Mass., U.S.A.

WOODWARD BECAME known in organic chemistry primarily for his successful development of the total synthesis of very complex natural products. His success in opening up this area of study derived from his intense application of modern instrumental as well as physical organic tools and a detailed and rigorous intel-

lectual logic involving the entire synthetic route seen as a whole. The same approach was responsible for his successful structure determination of several complex natural molecules, some of which he later confirmed by total synthesis. For his contributions to organic chemistry, he received many scientific honors, including the National Medal of Science in 1964 and the Nobel Prize in chemistry in 1965.

Woodward's interest in physical methods was evident in his 1940–41 publication of the useful correlations of ultraviolet spectra with structure, long known as "Woodward's rules." His first major synthesis was that of quinine with W. von E. Doering in 1944, but he was also active during the World War II period in the international effort to ascertain the structure of penicillin. The correct structure for penicillin was first successfully defended by Woodward. The late 1940s also saw his syntheses of sempervirine and patulin and a conclusive structure proof of strychnine, one of the oldest and most active structure problems in the organic literature.

In 1951 Woodward and his associates at Harvard University announced a total synthesis of a fully saturated steroid. Since many steroids, including cortisone and cholesterol, had previously been interconverted, this constituted a synthesis of most of the known steroids and was especially adaptable in that the direct product of the synthesis, methyl 3,11-diketoetiocholanate, contained the difficultly accessible functionality at the 11-position. The synthesis was also noteworthy in that considerable attention to stereochemistry was required, there being in the product 7 centers of asymmetry or 64 possible racemic isomers.

Syntheses in 1954 of strychnine, with a group at Harvard, and of lysergic acid, with a group at Eli Lilly Company, followed the steroid achievement with alkaloids of similar complexity. In 1956 Woodward and four collaborators succeeded in completing in a single year a masterful synthesis of the potent alkaloid, reserpine. This synthesis of only 11 steps, which provided the reserpine molecule with complete stereoselectivity at all six of its asymmetric centers and in high yield, is probably the most elegant synthesis of a natural product to date.

Concomitantly, Woodward was active in structure determinations of two active antibiotics, terramycin (oxytetracycline) and magnamycin. His structure determination of the first was especially noteworthy for the extensive use of acidity measurements and spectrophotometric determinations to guide a very involved logical development of the structure. In collaboration with a group at Chas. Pfizer & Company, he subsequently synthesized the tetracyclines as well.

The next higher level of molecular complexity is represented in chlorophyll, the universal green pigment of plant cells active in photosynthesis. The subject of much degradative study, this substance was finally elucidated by Hans Fischer in the 1930s. The porphyrinlike skeleton is composed of four different pyrrolic rings, themselves joined in a ring about a magnesium atom. In order to avoid the random mixing of these four units characteristic of Fischer's earlier porphyrin syntheses from pyrrol derivatives, Woodward developed a synthetic route in which two units of two different pyrrols each are first constructed and then joined unambiguously "head to tail" to close the large ring. The successful completion of the synthesis of chlorophyll in 1960 marked the first synthesis of a molecule of this complexity. Thereafter extensive efforts were made to complete a synthesis of vitamin B_{12}, an even more complex porphyrinlike molecule with a cobalt atom at the center. In the meanwhile, however, a very important theoretical concept for organic chemistry, the conservation of orbital symmetry, had developed out of certain aspects of these synthetic studies and was published in 1965 by Woodward and Hoffmann.

In addition to these major synthetic studies, Woodward also collaborated in the development of the octant rule, which allows determination of the absolute configuration of cyclic ketones from measurements of optical rotatory dispersion. He also developed several new synthetic procedures, including several new peptide-forming reagents, and published on the mechanism of the Diels-Alder reaction. The unique π-electron sandwich structure of ferrocene was first announced and confirmed by Woodward and his coworkers; an entire new branch of organic research developed from this formulation. In the field of natural products, Woodward also synthesized lanosterol, ellipticine, and colchicine and elucidated the structures of calycanthine, gliotoxin, santonic acid, parasantonide, and tetrodotoxin. In all of these achievements Woodward's intensely rigorous, critical, and logical mode of thinking was clearly evident, and his impact in teaching this to a great many younger chemists has often been termed his most important contribution to chemistry.

Woodward received his B.S. (1936) and Ph.D. (1937) at the Massachusetts Institute of Technology. In 1937–38 he was a postdoctoral fellow at Harvard, remaining there as a member of the faculty and becoming Morris Loeb Professor of Chemistry in 1953 and Donner Professor of Science in 1960. He was elected to the National Academy of Sciences in 1953.

For background information see ALKALOID; ASYMMETRIC SYNTHESIS; ORGANIC CHEMICAL SYNTHESIS; STEREOCHEMISTRY in the McGraw-Hill Encyclopedia of Science and Technology.   □

★ **WRIGHT, Sewall**
American geneticist
Born Dec. 21, 1889, Melrose, Mass., U.S.A.

THROUGHOUT HIS career, Wright conducted research in two apparently diverse fields: experimental physiological genetics of the guinea pig; and studies, partly experimental but largely mathematical, of the consequences of mendelian heredity in populations.

Wright's research on the physiological genetics of the guinea pig began in 1914 with his discovery of a series of four (later five) alleles in the guinea pig with effects on various coat and eye colors that were not parallel. A program was started and continued to 1960 of studying quantitatively the effects, in many hundreds of combinations, of the available factors affecting quality, intensity, and pattern of pigmentation. The 16 mutant genes ranged from those major in effect to those isolated only with difficulty, and there remained some nine multifactorial systems, unanalyzable because of serious nongenetic complications but capable of yielding wide differences under selection.

Wright assumed from the first that the primary effects of genes were simple, each determining the specificity or inactivation of an enzyme, but it was evident that these led to the characters actually observed through branching chains of interacting processes. The effect of any given gene replacement varied greatly in different genetic backgrounds. It might be large, small, absent, or reversed. The simplest adequate pattern of interactions was deduced.

Wright carried out similar studies on morphological characters of diverse sorts: growth patterns in the skin, reflected in epidermal ridges and hair direction; occurrence of little toe, thumb, and big toe, digits normally absent in the Caviidae; and gross abnormalities, such as otocephaly. Again he found complicated interaction patterns. Such characters as birth weight and later growth, frequency and size of litters, prenatal and postnatal mortality were not analyzable genetically except for pleiotropic effects of genes with effects on the preceding characters, but a pattern of interactions was worked out from studies of correlations.

Wright's studies of population genetics began in 1915, when he took charge of a project of the U.S. Department of Agriculture in which 23 lines of brother-sister matings had been started with guinea pigs. These lines came to differ profoundly in all characters studied. All suffered deterioration but in different ways, in spite of the correlations among the characters. Vigor was fully restored by crossbreeding.

The mathematical theory of the inbreeding effect, under mendelian heredity, had previously been worked out only for lines of one or two individuals. Wright now arrived at a theory applicable to any system of mating. The most important parameter, the coefficient of inbreeding, gave the relative decrease in heterozygosis. He also developed a theory of how best to combine inbreeding, crossbreeding, and selection in the improvement of livestock. This was later applied to evolution in nature.

Wright accepted change of gene frequency as the elementary evolutionary process and derived formulas for the "pressures" of recurrent mutation, immigration, and selection on gene frequencies in interaction systems. These might lead to losses of genes, but usually led to a set of equilibrium values about which the gene frequencies varied in a multidimensional probability distribution, because of random processes (sampling, fluctuations in the pressures).

In a random-breeding population, selection operates wholly according to the *net* effect of each gene, and it was generally accepted that evolution must depend on occasional replacement of an established gene by a more favorable mutation. Rate is severely limited by the very rare occurrence of such mutations. Wright saw, however, that there would be no such limitation if somehow there could be selection among the indefinitely large numbers of recombinant types provided by even a rather small number of mutations, largely unfavorable at first but maintained by balancing of opposed pressures. He showed that this is possible if the species includes many small local populations, sufficiently isolated to permit differentiation but not so isolated as to prevent spreading of the more successful interaction systems throughout the species.

The situation found by Wright to be most favorable involved five phases: (1) mutation; (2) storage of variability by balancing opposed pressures, especially that between selection and immigration separately in each locality; (3) random processes that permit occasional crossing, locally, of a "saddle" leading to a superior interaction system; (4) local mass selection toward establishment of this system; and (5) interlocality selection, consisting of excess local population growth where the more successful systems have become established and spreading by excess emigration. These two kinds of selection differ somewhat in that (4) relates wholly to individual advantage while (5) relates to group advantage.

Wright was educated at Lombard College, Galesburg, Ill. (B.S. 1911), where his father taught economics and mathematics. He received his M.S. (zoology) in 1912 at the University of Illinois and his Sc.D. (zoology) at Harvard in 1915 under W. E. Castle. He was in charge of animal-breeding investigations in the U.S. Department of Agriculture (1915–24) and was a member of the zoology department of the University of Chicago (1925–54) and the genetics department of the University of Wisconsin (1955–60). He became emeritus in 1960. Wright was elected to the National Academy of Sciences in 1934. Among other scientific honors, he received the Academy's 1945 Elliot Medal and the 1952 Kimber Genetics Award. He was president of the X International Congress of Genetics in 1958, and in 1963 he was elected a foreign member of the Royal Society of London.

For background information *see* GENETICS; MENDELISM in the McGraw-Hill Encyclopedia of Science and Technology.   □

★ WU, Chien-Shiung

American physicist
Born May 31, 1912, Shanghai, China

FOR HER contributions to the understanding of beta decay and the weak interactions, and especially for the first clear experimental demonstration, through beta decay of oriented

nuclei, of the violation of parity conservation and charge conjugation invariance, C. S. Wu received the 1958 Research Corporation Award and the 1964 Comstock Award of the National Academy of Sciences.

In 1956, in a classic paper, T. D. Lee of Columbia and C. N. Yang of the Institute for Advanced Study questioned the long-accepted principle that nature did not distinguish between right and left in the nuclear phenomena known as weak interactions. The processes involved the radioactive decay of matter. They pointed out that there had been no experiment thus far to prove or disprove the validity of the parity law for this class of physical interactions, and suggested a number of possible tests.

Prior to 1956, C. S. Wu had been well known for her precise and extensive experimental work in nuclear beta decay. She had demonstrated the source effects on the shape of the beta spectrum, thus clarifying some misinterpretation of beta theory. She had also made a systematic study on all orders of unique forbidden transitions and thus had further strengthened belief in the forbidden theory of beta decay. When the question of parity conservation came up in beta decay, she was well prepared to take up such crucial experiments in beta decay.

In collaboration with scientists at the National Bureau of Standards, C. S. Wu announced early in 1957 the results of the first experiment that established beyond a doubt that parity was, in fact, violated in weak interactions. This demonstration involved the beta decay of radioactive cobalt-60. The essence of the experiment was to line up the spins of the Co^{60} nuclei along the same axis and then to determine whether the beta particles were emitted preferentially in one direction or the other along the axis. In order to reduce the thermal agitation, which tends to disrupt the orderly orientation, the crystal was cooled down to a temperature of 0.01°C above absolute zero. The results showed that the elec-

trons were emitted preferentially in the direction opposite to that of nuclear spin and therefore conclusively proved that the beta decay of Co^{60} behaved like a left-handed screw. Left could be distinguished from right; parity was not conserved.

Within a few weeks, the nonconservation of parity first observed for beta decay had been shown in work at Columbia and the University of Chicago to exist in many other weak interactions as well. The discovery resulted in a sudden liberation of thinking about the basic structure of the physical world, and spurred an unprecedented advance in both experimental and theoretical study of the weak interactions.

In 1963, in collaboration with Columbia research physicists Y. K. Lee and L. W. Mo, C. S. Wu again reported clear experimental confirmation of a new fundamental theory in nuclear physics, the theory of conservation of vector current in nuclear beta decay. This important theory was originally proposed in 1958 by R. P. Feynman and Murray Gell-Mann of the California Institute of Technology to explain the mysterious, almost equal interaction strength of beta decay and muon decay. One of the possible experimental tests of this theory suggested by Gell-Mann was to measure precisely and accurately the shapes of the beta spectra of B^{12} and N^{12} and compare them with predicted spectrum shapes based on the conserved-current hypothesis.

Experimental results of Wu and her collaborators on B^{12} and N^{12} showed clearly the nearly equal but opposite effect of the conservation term on the electron and the position spectra as predicted. Confirmation of the theory had important consequences for other parts of nuclear theory. It put the universal Fermi interaction on a much firmer foundation, since the lack of renormalization of the vector current in beta decay could now be rationally understood.

C. S. Wu received her B.S. degree from the National Central University in China. She went to the United States in 1936 for graduate studies at the University of California under the late E. O. Lawrence, and received her Ph.D. from that institution in 1940. After teaching at Smith College and Princeton University, she joined the scientific staff of the Division of War Research at Columbia University in 1944. She was appointed to the physics faculty of Columbia in 1952. In 1958 she was elected to the National Academy of Sciences.

C. S. Wu wrote *Beta Decay*, with S. Moszkowski (1965) and edited *Methods of Experimental Physics: Nuclear Physics*, with L. C. L. Yuan (1961).

For background information *see* PARITY (QUANTUM MECHANICS) in the McGraw-Hill Encyclopedia of Science and Technology. □

Y-Z

★★★

☆ **YANG, Chen Ning**
American physicist
Born Sept. 22, 1922, Hofei, China

Ｉｎ 1956, Yang and his colleague T. D. Lee predicted that the "law of conservation of parity" would break down in the case of "weak interactions" such as beta decay. To test their hypothesis, they proposed a series of experiments that would both confirm it and add further information about the nonconservation of parity in weak interactions. Their discovery led to extensive revision of basic theory in atomic and subatomic physics. For this accomplishment, Yang and Lee were awarded the Nobel Prize in physics in 1957.

In physics, laws of symmetry, which govern invariance of physical relationships under various transformations of coordinates, have among their corollaries the isotropy (that is, lack of distortion due to direction) of physical space. Another special case of the symmetry laws states that physical events show no preference with respect to right and left. With the rise of quantum mechanics, the symmetry laws assumed great importance; P. A. M. Dirac, for example, was able to predict the existence of antiparticles from the symmetry principle under Lorentz transformation.

In 1924, Laporte, working with atomic spectra, found an empirical "law of conservation of parity." Parity is a quantized property associated with every elementary particle and nucleus; it describes the symmetry of a wave function under simultaneous inversion of all spatial coordinates. The parity of a particle or system may have only the two quantized values +1 (called "even parity") or −1 ("odd parity"). Laporte's formula stated that in electromagnetic interactions (involving emission of photons, which have odd parity) the parity of

the initial state and the total parity of the final state are equal. "Total parity" was defined as the product of the parity of the final state and that of the photon(s) emitted.

Shortly thereafter E. P. Wigner deduced the law of conservation of parity from the right-left symmetry of electromagnetic forces. It appeared natural to assume that this "parity conservation," so elegant and intuitively "obvious," would apply to all the interactions. Together with the laws of conservation of energy, momentum, angular momentum, and charge, the law of conservation of parity seemed one of the basic laws of modern physics.

In the early 1950s the weak interactions, which included almost all elementary-particle decays, received much attention. It was noticed that the so-called tau and theta mesons had identical masses and lifetimes and, in fact, seemed to be two modes of the same particle (later identified as the K meson). According to the law of parity conservation, the same initial state could not lead to final states of opposite parities. Nevertheless, the tau meson decayed to three pi mesons (total parity odd) while the theta meson decayed to two pi mesons (total

The seeming paradox attracted the attention of Yang and Lee who, in 1956, evaluated the problem and came to the tentative conclusion that possibly the conservation of parity was violated in the above decay and, further, that it might also be violated in such another weak interaction as beta decay. Noting that previous experiments (a) had been so arranged that parity conservation or nonconservation would not affect the results, (b) had simply assumed conservation of parity, or (c) had been inadequate to confirm or disprove conservation during the entire decay process, they were also aware that at least one conservation law (that of isotopic spin) was approximate rather than exact: it held for the "strong" interactions but not for weaker ones. There was, therefore, at least some ground to suppose that parity conservation, although fairly well substantiated for strong and electromagnetic interactions, might be violated in weak interactions.

They then proposed a number of experiments that would, they believed, provide the first specific and unequivocal test of parity conservation in weak-interaction decay. The initial experiment was performed by C. S. Wu and her collaborators at the National Bureau of Standards. Co^{60} (which decays to Ni^{60} + e^- + neutrino) was cooled to within a fraction of a degree of 0°K. Equal quantities were then placed in two identical systems, each consisting of a magnetic coil (solenoid) and a counter to measure the beta radiation. The two systems were mirror images of each other; if parity were not conserved, the radioactive cobalt, polarized by the magnetic fields, should show asymmetrical decay emission. The two counters did in fact show large discrepancies, and it was established that decay electrons were emitted preferentially in a direction opposite to the direction of spin of the Co^{60} atoms.

There followed a series of experiments suggested by Yang and Lee and performed by numerous workers in different localities. Each experimental set-up consisted, as did the first, of two identical parts, mirror images of each other. In each case, differences in the two readouts led to the conclusion that parity was not conserved. The decay of pi mesons into mu mesons plus neutrinoes, and the decay in turn of mu mesons into electrons and neutrinoes, led to the measurement of two distinct and separate preferential emissions in the same experiment; in neither was parity conserved. The decay of K mesons and lambda particles led to much the same results.

These experiments and many subsequent ones established conclusively the nonconservation of parity in weak interactions (of which nearly 20 were then known). Also, it showed that the invariance of these interactions was violated under the charge conjugation operation (reversal of a particle's charge, keeping its spatial and spin wave functions the same). The violation of these two symmetry laws (and possibly a third, called time reversal invariance) led to numerous conclusions concerning behavior of elementary particles. Experimental evidence of parity nonconservation lent weight to the two-component neutrino theory and led to the conclusion that the neutrino has mass zero. There also followed the law of conservation of leptons (light particles with half-integral spin), closely paralleling the already-current law of conservation of baryons.

Apart from the philosophical ramification of the violation of parity, weak interactions seemed to belong together in a group, since they all violated parity conservation and all showed a remarkable similarity of "dimensionless" coupling constants. Indeed, Yang and Lee reasoned, weak interactions might provide the key to an "absolute" definition of left or right, providing that one described what was meant by "matter" or "antimatter." This followed from the suggestion that if, in the beta-decay experiment for example, the cobalt and all the rest of the apparatus (magnet, counters, etc.) were replaced by antimatter, the decay "positrons" would be preferentially emitted in the opposite direction. There was good indirect evidence for this supposition, although it was nearly impossible to confirm experimentally.

Son of a mathematics professor, Yang received his B.Sc. from the National Southwest Associated University at Kunming, China, in 1942. After taking an M.Sc. at Tsinghua University, also at Kunming, Yang traveled to America on a Tsinghua University fellowship. At the University of Chicago he worked under Enrico Fermi and Edward Teller, receiving his Ph.D. in 1948. After a year as an instructor in physics at the University of Chicago, he became associated in 1949 with the Institute for Advanced Study at Princeton, N.J. He became a professor of physics there in 1955. In 1965 he was appointed to the Albert Einstein Chair in Science at the Stony Brook campus of the State University of New York. Yang was elected to the National Academy of Sciences in 1965.

For background information *see* PARITY (QUANTUM MECHANICS) in the McGraw-Hill Encyclopedia of Science and Technology.   □

★ **YORK, Herbert Frank**
American physicist
Born Nov. 24, 1921, Rochester, N.Y., U.S.A.

YORK'S SCIENTIFIC career began at the University of California's Radiation Laboratory shortly after World War II. E. O. Lawrence's 184-in. synchrocyclotron had just been completed, and was providing particles at energies that were almost an order of magnitude higher than those that had been available previously (for example, protons of 350 Mev). Using this machine, and in collaboration with Emilio Segrè, Owen Chamberlain, and others, York measured the differential neutron-proton–scattering cross section at 90 Mev; in collaboration with B. J. Moyer and others, he made the first observations and studies of π^0 mesons (through the gamma rays produced in their decay); and in collaboration with J. W. Hadley, he made the first observations and studies of the loosely bound light nuclei (including deuterons and tritons) that came out of other nuclei when bombarded with neutrons having energies much higher than the binding energy (specifically 90 Mev).

In 1950 York turned to problems of applied nuclear science directly related to the national security. (In 1949, the Soviet Union had exploded its first nuclear weapon, and shortly thereafter President Truman had determined that the United States should proceed with the development of thermonuclear weapons.) In 1951, during Operation Greenhouse at Eniwetok, H. Bradner and York directed a team that made fundamental observations of certain phenomena involved in thermonuclear reactions. The following year, under the general direction of Ernest Lawrence, and in collaboration with Edward Teller, Harold Brown, John Foster, and many others, York established and directed the Livermore Laboratory, now known officially as the University of California Lawrence Radiation Laboratory, Livermore. During his tenure as director, the Livermore Laboratory developed nuclear and thermonuclear weapons of new types, began an attack on the problem of controlled thermonuclear energy (primarily focused on the "mirror" geometry), and initiated a program for the development of reactors for propulsion, particularly for use in a ramjet (the Pluto reactor).

From 1957 to 1961, York held several posts in the Federal government, all having to do with the administration and direction of "research and development." These included membership in the President's Science Advisory Committee (1957–58), chief scientist for the Advanced Research Projects Agency (1958), and director of Defense Research and Engineering (1958–61). In 1961 he returned to the University of California to be chancellor at San Diego, a post he held through 1964. During the period of his chancellorship, the first nonscience departments were established, and the first undergraduates were admitted. In 1964 he became a professor of physics at the University of California, San Diego. He continued his government activities as a member of the President's Science Advisory Committee, the General Advisory Committee of the U.S. Arms Control and Disarmament Agency, and other advising bodies.

A railway expressman's son, York majored in physics at the University of Rochester, where he received an A.B. (1942) and an M.S. (1943), and at the University of California, Berkeley, where he received a Ph.D. (1949). In 1962 he received the U.S. Atomic Energy Commission's E. O. Lawrence Award.

For background information *see* NUCLEAR EXPLOSION in the McGraw-Hill Encyclopedia of Science and Technology. □

☆ **YUKAWA, Hideki**
Japanese physicist
Born Jan. 23, 1907, Tokyo, Japan

IN 1935, while investigating the "strong" interactions within the atomic nucleus, Yukawa postulated the existence of a new fundamental particle to act as quantum for these forces. He predicted that this particle (later called the "meson") would be intermediate in mass between the electron and proton, and he correctly designated high-energy cosmic-ray collisions as the most likely source of such particles. Following the discovery of mu mesons in cosmic radiation in 1937, meson theory developed rapidly into an area of basic importance for nuclear physics. For his accomplishment Yukawa received the Nobel Prize in physics for 1949.

By the 1930s, scientists knew of three main types of forces at work within the atom. The first, electromagnetic force, was involved in interactions of charged particles. The next, the so-called "weak interactions," had been accounted for by Enrico Fermi in the case of beta decay and generalized to include most of the decay processes of fundamental particles. The last, the strong interaction, was known to be the binding force of the atomic nucleus. The nature of this force was not known, but some of its characteristics had been observed. It was more powerful than the electromagnetic or weak forces and worked over a very short range, about the order of magnitude of atomic nuclei.

To develop a theory that would account for the observed nature of the nuclear binding force, Yukawa began with an analogy. The electromagnetic field, he reasoned, according to quantum mechanics might be interpreted also as quanta that act as carriers of energy and momentum of finite amount between particles. These quanta (photons) interacted with charged particles and could be emitted or absorbed by them. Now the electromagnetic "fine structure constant" that described the strength of the force was nearly 1/137; the range of the electromagnetic field was infinite. In contrast, the coupling constant for nuclear forces was shown to be much larger than 1/137, while its range was less than 10^{-12} cm. Nevertheless, Yukawa thought it might be possible to modify the electromagnetic field so as to yield a description for the quantum of nuclear force, whose existence he set out to determine.

Yukawa noted that there was a simple relation between the range of a field of force and the mass of the quanta composing that field. Assuming a field with range about 5×10^{-12} cm, Yukawa arrived at the value of about 200 electron masses (m_e) for a quantum of nuclear force. To account for nuclear interactions, he assumed that it coupled strongly with nucleons and could carry either positive or negative charge. Thus, emission/absorption of nuclear quanta (later called "mesons") would be the "quantized" aspect of nuclear force. Mesons, intermediate between electrons $(m_e = 1)$ and nucleons $(m_e = 1800+)$ in mass, would have lifetimes of about 10^{-8} sec, decaying spontaneously into electrons (positrons) and neutrinos. Further, on the basis of scattering experiments Yukawa predicted the existence of uncharged mesons of mass similar to the charged ones.

In 1937, C. D. Anderson discovered particles of intermediate mass (about 200 m_e) in hard cosmic radiation. These particles, later called "mu mesons" or "muons," had the mass required for nuclear quanta; they also exhibited the type of decay mode indicated by his theory. However, muons turned out to be coupled only weakly with nucleons. Also, their observed lifetime of 10^{-6} sec was a hundred times longer than the predicted 10^{-8} sec.

To explain these discrepancies, it was proposed by S. Sakata and Y. Tanikawa that there were actually two sorts of mesons. One sort, muons, did not interact strongly with nucleons. The other, pi mesons or pions, coupled strongly with nucleons, had a lifetime in agreement with theory and decayed into muons. One could then view muons in cosmic radiation at sea level as decay products from pions created in the upper atmosphere. This would account for the discrepancy between the predicted and observed lifetimes.

In 1947, the heavier (about 270 m_e) pions were discovered in cosmic rays by C. Powell. As anticipated, pions decayed into muons, which in turn decayed into electrons. The pions interacted strongly with nucleons and were regarded as the mesons predicted by Yukawa as quanta of nuclear force.

In 1949, experiments in artificial meson production with particle accelerators indicated the existence of Yukawa's "neutral pion" with the mass nearly equal to the charged pion. It had a lifetime of less than 10^{-16} sec, decaying into two photons. Thus within 15 years of the initial hypothesis, experimental confirmation was found for almost every tenet of the original meson theory proposed by Yukawa.

Son of a professor of geology at Kyoto University, Yukawa received his B.S. there in 1929. After lecturing there, he became lecturer and in 1936 assistant professor of physics at Osaka University. In 1938 he obtained a D.Sc. from Osaka University and in 1939 assumed the post of professor of theoretical physics at Kyoto University. Following two visiting professorships, at the Institute for Advanced Study (1948) and Columbia University (1949–53), Yukawa returned to Kyoto, where he became director of the Research Institute for Fundamental Physics. He was elected a foreign associate of the U.S. National Academy of Sciences in 1949.

For background information *see* MESON in the McGraw-Hill Encyclopedia of Science and Technology.   □

ZERNIKE, Frits
Dutch physicist
Born July 16, 1888, Amsterdam, Netherlands
Died Mar. 10, 1966, Naarden, Netherlands

Z ERNIKE DISCOVERED the phase-contrast effect in the "ghost" images produced by diffraction gratings and conceived the idea of making use of it in a microscope. The phase-contrast microscope that he developed made possible for the first time the microscopic examination of the internal structure of living cells. For this he won the Nobel Prize in physics for 1953.

Zernike's discovery stemmed from an investigation of diffraction gratings. In these mirrors, ruled with many minute, equidistant grooves, engineering error sometimes resulted in an aberration such that, instead of reflecting a central spectral line alone, the grating also produced a number of flanking, equidistant "ghost" lines. Zernike viewed one such flawed grating from its focal point. Instead of the usual evenly illuminated surface, the grating seemed brightly striped. When a small telescope was focused on the grating, the stripes vanished completely.

To account for these phenomena, Zernike supposed that the spurious images were a half-wavelength out of phase with the central line. If this were so, then the focusing of all the images on a concave surface (for example, the rear of the eyeball) should reinforce the phase contrast, while focusing in a plane (for example, the telescope objective) should result in cancellation of all images from interference—for all the light was of the same amplitude. Zernike then proceeded to make "phase strips"—glass plates with minute etched grooves. When these were placed in the focal plane of the telescope so that the main spectral line fell on the groove, the interference phenomenon could once more be observed. The groove brought the direct and diffracted images back into phase, and the stripes appeared in the telescope.

Zernike recalled the theory of image formation proposed by the microscopist Ernst Abbe, which stated that diffraction gratings and transparent objects behaved similarly when viewed through a microscope. He knew that conventional microscopy was unable to reveal internal structure of transparent objects such as most biological and medical specimens. Dark-field illumination was often misleading; staining specimens invariably killed them.

According to Abbe, the magnified image seen through the ocular was actually the result of interference between the direct and diffracted images brought together in the back focal plane of the objective. In the case of transparent objects, would not a phase strip, inserted into the focal plane, have the same reinforcing effect observed with the gratings? Zernike tested this idea and found it correct. A modified annular phase strip, centered so that the direct beam fell on the groove and was brought into phase with the diffracted beam, produced an image that gave the effect of staining so as to bring out minute details. Phase contrast actually revealed, he found, not only variations in opacity, like conventional microscopic techniques, but also variations in thickness of transparent objects. This resulted from the variations in phase caused by different thicknesses of the refractive medium, which differences were usually invisible unless brought to view by phase contrast. Zernike also found that modifications of his method could be made to reveal extremely minute variations and defects in reflecting surfaces and that it could

be used to study the surface of nontransparent objects.

Phase-contrast techniques greatly advanced microbiology by making possible examination of living tissues in detail. They also found ready use in the field of optics.

Zernike, both of whose parents taught mathematics, took his B.S. at the University of Amsterdam, and obtained an assistant's post at the astronomy laboratory, University of Groningen, in 1913. There, in 1915, he received his Ph.D. and in the same year became a lecturer in theoretical physics. From 1920 until 1958, he served at Groningen as professor of theoretical and technical physics and theoretical mechanics. In 1948 he was briefly a visiting professor at Johns Hopkins University, Baltimore, Md. He retired in 1958.

For background information *see* MICROSCOPE, PHASE CONTRAST in the McGraw-Hill Encyclopedia of Science and Technology.   □

☆ **ZIEGLER, Karl**
German organic chemist
Born Nov. 26, 1898, Helsa, Germany

W HILE INVESTIGATING the preparation of aluminum alkyls, Ziegler devised a low-pressure process for the production of polyethylene, which previously had been synthesized only at high pressures. This process, known as the Ziegler process, results in a straight-chain polymer rather than in a branched-chain polymer, thus producing a polyethylene with improved strength and temperature properties. In recognition of this achievement, Ziegler shared the 1963 Nobel Prize in chemistry with the Italian chemist Giulio Natta, who had devised a method for producing isotactic polymers.

The first plastic, celluloid, was developed in 1869 by the American inventor John Wesley Hyatt. More than a quarter of a century later, during the first decade of the 20th century, the

Belgian-American chemist Leo Hendrik Baeke-land developed the first completely synthetic plastic, bakelite. This marked the beginning of the plastics industry, and a great deal of research was conducted by a large number of chemists throughout the world in an effort to develop better plastics. However, despite the progress in the understanding of polymerization through the work of such men as the German chemist Hermann Staudinger, no means of orienting the molecules in the polymer was developed; that is, there was no way to eliminate unwanted branching within the chain.

After World War II, working at the Max Planck Institute for Coal Research at Mül-heim-Ruhr, Ziegler conducted research on organic aluminum compounds. In 1953, with the assistance of E. Holzcamp, he obtained a complete conversion of the ethylene monomer to the ethylene dimer, 1-butene, by heating ethylene with aluminum triethyl. Ziegler found that the presence of trace quantities of colloidal nickel, which had accidentally been introduced into the autoclave, were responsible for this catalytic effect. Based on this finding, Ziegler began a systematic investigation of these "nickel effects." This led to his discovery of organometallic mixed catalysts. He found that a mixture of triethyl aluminum, $Al(C_2H_5)_3$ and titanium tetrachloride, $TiCl_4$, resulted in the production of a linear polyethylene of high molecular weight. In addition, the process could be carried out at relatively low temperatures and pressures (50–150° C and 5–200 psi), while conventional processes, which produced branched-chain polymers, required high temperatures and pressures (150–250° C and 20,000–35,000 psi). The combination of $Al(C_2H_5)_3$ and $TiCl_4$, known as a Ziegler-type stereospecific catalyst results in polymers in which the molecular units have a particular orientation. The linear polymer, Ziegler found, was commercially desirable, for the more ordered arrangement resulted in a plastic that was tougher and had a higher melting point than the branched-chain product.

Ziegler-type catalysts have proved to be valuable in the synthesis of other plastics, such as polypropylene, man-made fibers, and synthetic rubbers. Among the multitude of reactions promoted by such organometallic mixed catalysts are (1) yields from the other diolefins as well as the α-olefins, (2) synthesis of 1,4-cis-polyisoprene, which is identical with natural rubber, (3) production of oligomers, as well as polymers, of α-olefins and 1,3-diolefins, and (4) the cyclic trimerization of butadiene forming cyclododecatriene-(1,5,9). In addition, the investigation of these catalysts led to the discovery of new organometallic compounds of the transition metals.

Ziegler also made a contribution to the synthesis of many-membered ring structures. In 1912 Paul Ruggli had suggested that such syntheses might be performed at high dilution. Ziegler approached this problem in 1933 and, through the use of what is now known as the "Ruggli-Ziegler dilution principle," succeeded in synthesizing a high-ring ketone from α,ω-dinitriles. An immediate result of the new cyclic ring method was the synthesis of perfumes from racemic muscones that had the aroma of animal musk. Continuing to work in this field, Ziegler succeeded in accomplishing the thermal dimerization of butadiene to form cyclooctadiene-(1,5).

Another area of Ziegler's research was alkaline organic compounds. In 1928 he began to study the sodium-catalyzed polymerization of butadiene in the production of buna rubbers, and he was the first to explain the polymerization mechanism involved. His second major contribution to the chemistry of alkaline organic compounds was the discovery of a single manufacturing process for the production of lithium alkyls from lithium metal and alkyl halides. The lithium alkyls promote the same reactions as do the Grignard reagents, discovered by the French chemist François Auguste Victor Grignard in 1900, but are more reactive.

Also of fundamental importance was Ziegler's discovery of addition through the bonding of metal hydrides to a carbon-carbon double bond. This led to the preparation of lithium-aluminum-tetraalkyls from lithium-aluminum hydride.

The work for which Ziegler was awarded the Nobel Prize was an outgrowth of his earlier efforts with organometallic compounds. He discovered that metallic aluminum, hydrogen, and an olefin reacted strongly to form an aluminum trialkyl. This gave him the opportunity, which he had previously had with lithium, to study the synthesis of a metallo-organic "building up" reaction for aluminum systems. From this work, several important results were achieved: (1) the manufacture of unbranched α-olefins from ethylene, (2) the catalytic dimerization of α-olefins to form uniformly higher α-olefins, (3) the synthesis of higher primary alcohols, which are now important ingredients in detergents and of importance in biology, from ethylene, (4) the synthesis of terpene alcohols from olefins, (5) the production of alkyls of other metals from aluminum alkyls via a chemical or electrochemical path, and (6) the use of alkyl-aluminum hydrides and aluminum trialkyls as reducing agents for functional groups of organic compounds.

The son of a protestant clergyman, Ziegler was educated at the University of Marburg, receiving his Ph.D. in chemistry in 1920. He remained at Marburg as a lecturer until 1925, when he accepted a position at the University of Frankfurt. In 1926 he moved to the University of Heidelberg, becoming a professor of chemistry in 1927. In 1936 he left Heidelberg to become professor of chemistry and director of the Chemical Institute at the University of Halle-Saale. He served in this capacity for 7 years, leaving in 1943 to become the director of the Kaiser Wilhelm Institute for Coal Research, later renamed the Max Planck Institute for Coal Research, Mülheim-Ruhr. Beginning in 1947, he simultaneously served as honorary professor at the Technical High School in Aachen.

For background information, see POLYOLEFIN RESINS; TITANIUM in the McGraw-Hill Encyclopedia of Science and Technology. ☐

☆ ZWORYKIN, Vladimir Kosma

American physicist
Born July 30, 1889, Mourom, Russia

W HILE CONDUCTING research on the radio transmission of visual images, Zworykin invented the iconoscope, or television pickup tube, and developed the kinescope, or television receiving tube. These resulted in the first all-electronic television system and made possible the growth of television to its present stature as an entertainment medium and commercial and industrial tool.

The first practical television system was patented by Paul Gottfried Nipkow in Germany in 1884. This system was electromechanical in nature, for at its heart was a rapidly rotating metallic disk called a scanning disk. The disk was perforated with a number of small apertures, arranged in a spiral, which dissected the light image into a number of parallel lines. A photoelectric device behind the disk produced electrical impulses corresponding to the variation of light at each point of the image. Although the system worked, it did not transmit images in sufficient detail. In 1907, the Russian physicist Boris Rosing proposed picture reconstruction by an electromagnetic scanning device

based on the cathode-ray tube, which had been devised by the German physicist Karl Ferdinand Braun in 1897. In 1908, the English physicist A. A. Campbell-Swinton independently published a note suggesting the use of electron scanning in both signal generation and picture reconstruction. Although Campbell-Swinton developed his ideas in more detail in a later article, in 1911, there is no evidence of any attempt to translate them into practice.

Zworykin, who had studied under Rosing, decided to find a parallel in nature and follow it in devising a completely electronic television system. To Zworykin, the obvious natural design to emulate was the human eye. In general terms, light enters the eye through the iris and passes through a lens, which focuses an image of the object from which the light emanates on the retina. The retina is comprised of millions of rods and cones, which are connected to the brain by optic nerves, and in the brain the image is registered and seen. As Zworykin visualized his electronic analogy to the eye, the television lens corresponded to the lens behind the iris, a series of photosensitive elements corresponded to the rods and cones of the retina, an electron beam corresponded to the optic nerves, and the television receiver corresponded to the brain. In particular, the "electric eye" devised by Zworykin was to have in common with the human eye the important property of "storage." Just as in the human eye all of the light falling on the retina within a period of the order of the persistence of vision is integrated to produce the sense impression, so, in Zworykin's pickup device, all of the light falling on the photosensitive elements in the time required for the transmission of a single picture (e.g., 1/30 second) was to be utilized for generating the corresponding picture signal. This feature led to an enormous gain in sensitivity over all television pickup devices constructed or proposed before then and is incorporated in all modern general-purpose television cameras.

In 1923 Zworykin and his associates at the Westinghouse Electric and Manufacturing Company in Pittsburgh, Pa., constructed the first iconoscope, an electronic television pickup tube. In the iconoscope, an ordinary lens was used to focus an image on a screen comprised of microscopic photoelectric cells, each separated from the others by mica insulation backed by a metal plate. Since the screen was insulated from the plate by the mica, each cell formed a capacitor with the plate. The current produced in every photoelectric element varied with the light falling on it, causing an overall charge pattern corresponding to the image to develop on the plate. An electron gun at the other end of the tube produced an electron beam that scanned the photosensitive screen in successive parallel lines from the top to the bottom. This discharged the individual capacitors, whose charge was collected and amplified, forming the transmitted picture signal. The basic patent application for this device was filed by Zworykin in 1923 and the patent issued in 1938. It is interesting to note that a patent for a completely electronic color television system, based on an application filed in 1925, was issued to Zworykin in 1928.

Along with the iconoscope, Zworykin developed the kinescope, for the reconstruction of the image. The kinescope is a cathode-ray tube in which the electron beam is focused sharply by means of electric or magnetic fields and is modulated in intensity by the picture signal, applied to a grid electrode. In the all-electronic television system developed by Zworykin the beam in the kinescope, tracing out the reconstructed picture on a fluorescent screen, is synchronized with the scanning beam in the iconoscope transmitting the picture.

Late in 1923 Zworykin demonstrated a rudimentary form of such an all-electronic television system, transmitting a crossmark, to Westinghouse officials, but his superiors were unimpressed. In 1929, however, after refining the iconoscope and the kinescope, Zworykin demonstrated the first practical all-electronic television system at a meeting of the Institute of Radio Engineers at Rochester, N.Y. This achievement impressed David Sarnoff of the Radio Corporation of America with the future of television, and he invited Zworykin to join R.C.A. and continue the commercial development of his invention. This association led to the perfection of the iconoscope, which not only became the primary television pickup tube until it was superseded by the image orthicon but also was the basis of important later developments in the field. Television thus rose from a laboratory curiosity to a giant commercial property that has shown its value in the arts, in crime detection and prevention, and in education.

Zworykin also made a number of other contributions to electron optics. It was under his direction that James Hillier and his associates developed the electron microscope, which enabled man to see objects as small as viruses and protein chains. The sniperscope and snooperscope of World War II were outgrowths of Zworykin's development of the electron image tube. Zworykin's secondary-emission multipliers find application in the scintillation counter, the most sensitive tool for the measurement of radioactivity. In 1957 Zworykin introduced the ultra-violet, color-translating television microscope, operating on the principle of selective absorption, which provides an instantaneous color representation of specimens examined in the ultraviolet range of the electromagnetic spectrum.

The son of a river-boat merchant, Zworykin attended the Petrograd Institute of Technology, receiving his degree in electrical engineering in 1912. He immediately went to Paris to begin his graduate work at the College de France, where he did x-ray research under Paul Langevin. At the outbreak of World War I, Zworykin returned to Russia to serve as an officer in the radio corps from 1914 to 1917. He went to the United States in 1919 and, after working as a bookkeeper to learn English, joined the staff of the Westinghouse Electric Corporation in 1920. While at Westinghouse Zworykin enrolled at the University of Pittsburgh in 1923 to continue his graduate work, receiving his Ph.D. in physics in 1926, 2 years after he had become an American citizen. In 1929 Zworykin left Westinghouse to become director of electronic research of the R.C.A. Manufacturing Company. From 1942 to 1945 he served as associate research director of the R.C.A. Laboratories, becoming director of electronic research in 1946. Beginning in 1947, he simultaneously served as vice president and technical consultant of the Radio Corporation of America, R.C.A. Laboratories Division. In 1954 he retired from both of these positions to become an honorary vice-president and technical consultant of the Radio Corporation of America. Thereafter his work was primarily concerned with the medical aspects and applications of electronics. Among other honors, Zworykin received the Rumford Medal of the American Academy of Arts and Sciences in 1941, the Medal of Honor of the Institute of Electrical and Electronic Engineers in 1951, the Edison Medal of the American Institute of Electrical Engineers in 1953, and the Faraday Medal of the British Institution of Electrical Engineers in 1965. In 1943 he was elected to the National Academy of Sciences, and in 1965 to the newly founded National Academy of Engineering.

Zworykin was coauthor of a number of books, among them *Television: The Electronics of Image Transmission* (1940; 2d ed. 1954), *Electron Optics and the Electron Microscope* (1945), *Photoelectricity and Its Applications* (1949), and *Television in Science and Industry* (1958).

For background information *see* TELEVISION CAMERA TUBE in the McGraw-Hill Encyclopedia of Science and Technology. ☐

Indexes

McGRAW-HILL MODERN MEN OF SCIENCE

Preface to the Indexes

Two indexes, an analytical and a classified, are offered here to facilitate use of this volume.

The first, the analytical index, provides a guide to persons, subjects, books, institutions, and so forth mentioned in the text. The general arrangement is alphabetical, word by word. For a main entry the spelled-out form rather than an abbreviation is used; that is, "Deoxyribonucleic acid" is to be consulted rather than "DNA." Hyphenated words are treated as single words. Numbers are ignored in alphabetizing such terms as "A4D Skyhawk."

As in most indexes, it is advisable to look first under the most specific heading. For example, the reader interested in penicillin should look first under "Penicillin," not "Antibiotics." Some topics are listed only on the specific level. Others are listed under more general headings as well, but the information is more complete under the specific heading. Names of universities and institutions are followed by references to the biographees who have been as-sociated with them. United States government agencies are listed under "U.S." (alphabetized as "United States").

It should be remembered that this is an index to a volume of scientific biographies, not to a scientific encyclopedia. Scientific concepts can be looked up in order to connect them with particular scientists. If an *explanation* of the concept is desired, the reader should consult the index to the *McGraw-Hill Encyclopedia of Science and Technology*.

The second index, the classified, lists major scientific fields followed by the names of the biographees closely associated with them. It will serve the reader interested in making comparisons among the careers of scientists in the same discipline, or in selecting one or more scientists in a particular field for further study.

Index design was by Dr. Theodore C. Hines. The chief indexer was Alan Greengrass, and the classified index was largely compiled by Mrs. Janet Kozera.

Classified Index

BIOLOGY—cont.
Walker, E. M.
Weller, T. H.
Went, F. W.
Wetmore, R. H.
Wigglesworth, Sir V.
Wilkins, M. H. F.
Wright, S.

BIOPHYSICS
Békésy, G. von
Chance, B.
Crick, F. H. C.
Hodgkin, A. L.
Huxley, A. F.
Kendrew, J. C.
Pauling, L. C.
Perutz, M. F.
Tiselius, A. W. K.
Watson, J. D.
Wilkins, M. H. F.

BOTANY
Anderson, E. S.
Bonner, J. F.
Braun, A. C. J.
Chaney, R. W.
Clausen, J. C.
Cleland, R. E.
Darlington, C. D.
Esau, K.
Hendricks, S. B.
Kramer, P. J.
Mangelsdorf, P. C.
Salisbury, Sir E.
Sax, K.
Sinnott, E. W.
Thimann, K. V.
Went, F. W.
Wetmore, R. H.

CHEMICAL ENGINEERING
Natta, G.
Sherwood, T. K.

CHEMISTRY
Adams, L. H.
Adams, R.
Alder, K.
Bailar, J. C., Jr.
Bartlett, P. D.
Barton, D. H. R.
Bigeleisen, J.
Bolton, E. K.
Bowen, E. J.
Boyd, W. C.
Brewer, L.
Brown, H. C.
Calvin, M.
Carter, H. E.
Chain, E. B.
Chance, B.
Clark, W. M.
Cowan, G. A.
Dam, H.
Daniels, F.
Debye, P. J. W.
Diels, O. P. H.
Doisy, E. A.
Du Vigneaud, V.

CHEMISTRY—cont.
Emeléus, H. J.
Eyring, H.
Folkers, K. A.
Fraenkel-Conrat, H. L.
Giauque, W. F.
Hahn, O.
Hammett, L. P.
Hastings, A. B.
Hendricks, S. B.
Hevesy, G. de
Heyrovský, J.
Hildebrand, J. H.
Hinshelwood, Sir C.
Hirst, Sir E.
Hodgkin, D. C.
Ingold, Sir C.
Katz, J. J.
Kolthoff, I. M.
Libby, W. F.
Lipmann, F. A.
Lonsdale, Dame K.
Mark, H. F.
Martin, A. J. P.
Marvel, C. S.
Mayer, J. E.
Melville, Sir H.
Müller, P. H.
Mulliken, R. S.
Natta, G.
Norrish, R. G. W.
Northrop, J. H.
Noyes, W. A., Jr.
Onsager, L.
Pauling, L. C.
Peters, Sir R.
Reichstein, T.
Rideal, Sir E.
Robertson, J. M.
Robinson, Sir R.
Sanger, F.
Scatchard, G.
Seaborg, G. T.
Segrè, E. G.
Semenov, N. N.
Sherwood, T. K.
Stanley, W. M.
Staudinger, H.
Sumner, J. B.
Synge, R. L. M.
Taube, H.
Taylor, Sir H.
Theorell, A. H. T.
Thimann, K. V.
Thompson, S. G.
Tiselius, A. W. K.
Todd of Trumpington,
  Baron
Urey, H. C.
Virtanen, A. I.
Watson, J. D.
Willard, J. E.
Williams, R. R.
Woodward, R. B.
Ziegler, K.

CIVIL ENGINEERING
Ammann, O. H.
Newmark, N. M.
Steinman, D. B.

CRYSTALLOGRAPHY
Bragg, Sir L.
Hodgkin, D. C.
Kendrew, J. C.
Lonsdale, Dame K.
Pauling, L. C.
Perutz, M. F.
Shull, C. G.

ELECTRICAL AND ELECTRONIC
  ENGINEERING
Bardeen, J.
Black, H. S.
Brown, G. H.
Forrester, J. W.
Kouwenhoven, W. B.
Pickering, W. H.
Starr, C.
Suits, C. G.
Terman, F. E.
Weber, E.
Wheeler, H. A.
Zworykin, V. K.

ENGINEERING
Ammann, O. H.
Bardeen, J.
Benedict, M.
Black, H. S.
Brown, G. H.
Chadwick, W. L.
Collins, S. C.
Douglas, D. W.
Draper, C. S.
Forrester, J. W.
Gibbs, W. F.
Heinemann, E. H.
Hinton of Bankside,
  Baron
Hoffman, S. K.
Hunsaker, J. C.
Kouwenhoven, W. B.
Natta, G.
Newmark, N. M.
Pickering, W. H.
Pierce, J. R.
Rickover, H. G.
Schairer, G. S.
Sherwood, T. K.
Sikorsky, I. I.
Starr, C.
Steinman, D. B.
Stever, H. G.
Suits, C. G.
Taub, J. M.
Terman, F. E.
Von Braun, W.
Weber, E.
Wheeler, H. A.
Whittle, Sir F.
Zworykin, V. K.

EXPERIMENTAL PSYCHOLOGY
Beach, F. A.
Békésy, G. von
Graham, C. H.
Harlow, H. F.
Hilgard, E. R.
Köhler, W.
Miller, N. E.

EXPERIMENTAL PSY-
  CHOLOGY—cont.
Riggs, L. A.
Spence, K. W.
Stevens, S. S.

GENETICS
Anderson, E. S.
Beadle, G. W.
Clausen, J. C.
Cleland, R. E.
Darlington, C. D.
De Beer, Sir G.
Delbrück, M.
Demerec, M.
Dobzhansky, T.
Fisher, Sir R.
Ford, E. B.
Haldane, J. B. S.
Hershey, A. D.
Jacob, F.
Lederberg, J.
Luria, S. E.
Monod, J.
Muller, H. J.
Sonneborn, T. M.
Stern, C.
Sturtevant, A. H.
Tatum, E. L.
Wright, S.

GEOLOGY
Adams, L. H.
Benioff, H.
Bucher, W. H.
Buddington, A. F.
Chaney, R. W.
Cloos, H.
Dunbar, C. O.
Ewing, W. M.
Gilluly, J.
Hewett, D. F.
Holmes, A.
Kuenen, P. H.
Moore, R. C.
Read, H. H.
Reynolds, D. L.
Rubey, W. W.
Sander, B. H. M.
Wilson, M. E.
Woodring, W. P.

GEOPHYSICS AND
  GEOCHEMISTRY
Adams, L. H.
Bartels, J.
Benioff, H.
Bucher, W. H.
Bullard, Sir E.
Bullen, K. E.
Chapman, S.
Elsasser, W. M.
Ewing, W. M.
Heiskanen, W. A.
Jeffreys, Sir H.
Sverdrup, H. U.
Tuve, M. A.
Urey, H. C.
Vening Meinesz, F. A.

ORGANIC CHEMISTRY—*cont.*
Robinson, Sir R.
Staudinger, H.
Todd of Trumpington,
  Baron
Williams, R. R.
Woodward, R. B.
Ziegler, K.

PALEONTOLOGY AND
  PALEOBOTANY

Chaney, R. W.
Dart, R. A.
Dunbar, C. O.
Moore, R. C.
Romer, A. S.
Vallois, H. V.
Woodring, W. P.

PARASITOLOGY

Cameron, T. W. M.
Weller, T. H.

PHARMACOLOGY

Bovet, D.
Houssay, B. A.

PHYSICAL ANTHROPOLOGY

Coon, C. S.
Dart, R. A.
Howells, W. W.
Schultz, A. H.
Straus, W. L., Jr.
Trotter, M.
Vallois, H. V.

PHYSICAL CHEMISTRY

Adams, L. H.
Bowen, E. J.
Brewer, L.
Chance, B.
Daniels, F.
Debye, P. J. W.
Eyring, H.
Giauque, W. F.
Hahn, O.
Hammett, L. P.
Hendricks, S. B.
Hevesy, G. de
Heyrovský, J.
Hildebrand, J. H.
Hodgkin, D. C.
Kolthhoff, I. M.
Libby, W. F.
Lonsdale, Dame K.
Mark, H. F.
Mayer, J. E.
Melville, Sir H.
Mulliken, R. S.
Natta, G.
Norrish, R. G. W.
Noyes, W. A., Jr.
Onsager, L.

PHYSICAL CHEMISTRY—*cont.*
Pauling, L. C.
Rideal, Sir E.
Robertson, J. M.
Scatchard, G.
Seaborg, G. T.
Semenov, N. M.
Taylor, Sir H.
Urey, H. C.
Willard, J. E.

PHYSICS

Alvarez, L. W.
Anderson, P. W.
Apker, L.
Appleton, Sir E.
Bardeen, J.
Basov, N. G.
Békésy, G. von
Bethe, H. A.
Blackett, P. M. S.
Bloch, F.
Bloembergen, N.
Bohr, N. H. D.
Born, M.
Bothe, W.
Bragg, Sir L.
Brattain, W. H.
Bridgman, P. W.
Brueckner, K. A.
Burch, C. R.
Cerenkov, P. A.
Chadwick, Sir J.
Chamberlain, O.
Cockcroft, Sir J.
Dirac, P. A. M.
Edlund, M. C.
Esaki, L.
Fermi, E.
Feynman, R. P.
Foster, J. S., Jr.
Frank, I. M.
Friedman, H.
Gamow, G.
Gaydon, A. G.
Gell-Mann, M.
Giaever, I.
Glaser, D. A.
Goldberger, M. L.
Goudsmit, S. A.
Greenstein, J. L.
Hafstad, L. R.
Harrison, G. R.
Herring, W. C.
Hofstadter, R.
Hurwitz, H., Jr.
Jensen, J. H. D.
Kittel, C.
Kohn, W.
Kouts, H. J. C.
Kusch, P.
Lamb, W. E., Jr.
Land, E. H.

PHYSICS—*cont.*
Landau, L. D.
Lawrence, E. O.
Lax, B.
Lee, T. D.
Lighthill, M. J.
Matthias, B. T.
Mayer, M. G.
McMillan, E. M.
Mössbauer, R. L.
Mott, Sir N.
Mulliken, R. S.
Panofsky, W. K. H.
Pauli, W.
Pickering, W. H.
Powell, C. F.
Prochorov, A. M.
Purcell, E. M.
Rabi, I. I.
Rainwater, L. J.
Ramsey, N. F.
Rosen, L.
Rosenbluth, M. N.
Rossi, B. B.
Schwinger, J. S.
Segrè, E. G.
Shockley, W.
Shull, C. G.
Starr, C.
Stern, O.
Stever, H. G.
Suits, C. G.
Szilard, L.
Tamm, I. Y.
Taylor, T. B.
Thomson, Sir G.
Tomonaga, S. I.
Tousey, R.
Townes, C. H.
Tuve, M. A.
Unsöld, A. O. J.
Van Allen, J. A.
Van Hove, L. C. P.
Walton, E. T. S.
Weinberg, A. M.
Wigner, E. P.
Wilkins, M. H. F.
Wu, C. S.
Yang, C. N.
York, H. F.
Yukawa, H.
Zernike, F.
Zworykin, V. K.

PHYSIOLOGY

Best, C. H.
Cournand, A. F.
Doisy, E. A.
Eccles, Sir J.
Elvehjem, C. A.
Erlanger, J.
Gasser, H. S.
Hess, W. R.
Hoar, W. S.

PHYSIOLOGY—*cont.*
Hodgkin, A. L.
Houssay, B. A.
Huggins, C. B.
Huxley, A. F.
Patt, H. M.
Richards, D. W.
Van Slyke, D. D.

PSYCHOLOGY

See Experimental
  Psychology.

SOLID-STATE PHYSICS

Anderson, P. W.
Apker, L.
Bardeen, J.
Bloembergen, N.
Brattain, W. H.
Esaki, L.
Giaever, I.
Herring, W. C.
Kittel, C.
Kohn, W.
Lax, B.
Matthias, B. T.
Mott, Sir N.
Shockley, W.
Starr, C.

STATISTICS

Fisher, Sir R.
Neyman, J.

VIROLOGY

Burnet, Sir M.
Delbrück, M.
Enders, J. F.
Fraenkel-Conrat, H. L.
Francis, T., Jr.
Goodpasture, E. W.
Hershey, A. D.
Luria, S. E.
Rous, F. P.
Sabin, A. B.
Salk, J. E.
Stanley, W. M.
Theiler, M.
Weller, T. H.

ZOOLOGY

Brambell, F. W. R.
De Beer, Sir G.
Frisch, K. von
Hoar, W. S.
Huntsman, A. G.
Johnson, M. W.
Medawar, P. B.
Pantin, C. F. A.
Romer, A. S.
Stern, C.
Walker, E. M.
Wigglesworth, Sir V.